BIOGRAPHICAL DICTIONARY
OF
MATHEMATICIANS

BIOGRAPHICAL DICTIONARY OF MATHEMATICIANS

REFERENCE BIOGRAPHIES FROM THE
Dictionary of Scientific Biography

Volume 3

THOMAS KIRKMAN – ISAAC NEWTON

CHARLES SCRIBNER'S SONS
MACMILLAN LIBRARY REFERENCE USA
Simon & Schuster Macmillan
NEW YORK

Simon & Schuster and Prentice Hall International
LONDON · MEXICO CITY · NEW DELHI · SINGAPORE · SYDNEY · TORONTO

Copyright © 1970, 1971, 1972, 1973, 1974, 1975, 1976, 1978, 1980, 1990, 1991
American Council of Learned Societies.

Library of Congress Cataloging-in-Publication Data

Biographical Dictionary of Mathematicians: reference biographies from
the Dictionary of scientific biography.
   p.cm.
   "Published under the auspices of the American Council of Learned
Societies."
   Includes bibliographical references and index.
   ISBN 0-684-19282-9. – ISBN 0-684-19290-X (v. 3)
   1. Mathematicians–Biography–Dictionaries. I. American Council
of Learned Societies. II. Dictionary of scientific biography.
QA28.B534   1991
510'.92'2—dc20   90-52920
[B]   CIP

Charles Scribner's Sons
An Imprint of Simon & Schuster Macmillan
1633 Broadway
New York, NY 10019-6785

3   5   7   9   11   13   15   17   19   20   18   16   14   12   10   8   6   4

Printed in the United States of America.

BIOGRAPHICAL DICTIONARY
OF
MATHEMATICIANS

BIOGRAPHICAL DICTIONARY
OF MATHEMATICIANS

KIRKMAN, THOMAS PENYNGTON (*b*. Bolton, England, 31 March 1806; *d*. Croft, near Warrington, England, 3 February 1895)

Raised in an unscholastic mercantile family, Kirkman had to struggle for a decent education, and even so he received no instruction in mathematics at any level. He earned an arts degree at Dublin University in 1833 (M.A., 1850), and was ordained into the Church of England, becoming rector at Croft, Lancashire. Nominally, this was his life's work, for there the Reverend Mr. Kirkman tended his parish and defended his creed by sermon and pamphlet for more than fifty years. But he also taught himself mathematics with a thoroughness and insight that propelled him swiftly to the frontiers of current research and earned him the admiration and friendship of Cayley, De Morgan, and William Rowan Hamilton. He was elected to the Royal Society in 1857. Kirkman was a good linguist and an individualistic writer, if perhaps overly fond of neologisms and stylistic gimmickry. He delighted in versifying problems and in devising mnemonics for troublesome formulas—in fact he wrote a whole book on this topic.

Kirkman's interests extended to the controversies of the times, and he was fierce in his opposition to the new materialistic trends. Herbert Spencer's philosophy aroused his especial contumely, and his satiric paraphrase of Spencer's definition of evolution is a notable example of a Kirkmannerism. Spencer, he wrote, was really defining the concept as "a change from a nohowish untalkaboutable all-likeness, to a somehowish and in-general-talkaboutable not-all-likeness, by continuous somethingelseifications and sticktogetherations."

His mathematical work contributed to five topics then in infancy: topology, group theory, hypercomplex numbers, combinatorics, and knots. He also wrote lengthily on a very old topic: polyhedra (or, as he insisted, on calling them, *polyedra*). Hamilton's discovery of quaternions stimulated Kirkman to one of the earliest attempts to extend the notion further, and he named his new numbers *pluquaternions*. It is, however, in combinatorics that Kirkman's name is now best known, and his Fifteen Schoolgirls Problem and its variations became and remained famous. (Essentially, it concerns ways of rearranging a sevenfold 5×3 array of distinct objects, with the restriction that the triples are individually unique and collectively comprehensive.) Many other problems of this nature were first enunciated and solved by Kirkman.

BIBLIOGRAPHY

Fifty-nine of Kirkman's chief papers are listed in the Royal Society *Catalogue of Scientific Papers*. Three of note are "On Pluquaternions and Homoid Products of n Squares," in *Philosophical Magazine*, **33** (1848), 447–459, 494–509; "Application of the Theory of Polyedra to the Enumeration and Registration of Results," in *Proceedings of the Royal Society*, **12** (1862–1863), 341–380; and "The Complete Theory of Groups, Being the Solution of the Mathematical Prize Question of the French Academy for 1860," in *Memoirs and Proceedings of the Manchester Literary and Philosophical Society*, **4** (1865), 171–172.

His Fifteen Schoolgirls Problem was first posed in the *Lady's and Gentleman's Diary* (1850), p. 48, and it is thoroughly discussed in W. W. R. Ball, *Mathematical Recreations and Essays*, revised by H. S. M. Coxeter, 11th ed. (London, 1939).

Only recently has the generalized problem (for $6n + 3$ girls) been solved: "Solution of Kirkman's Schoolgirl Problem," in D. K. Ray-Chaudhuri and R. M. Wilson, *Combinatorics*, Vol. XIX of *Proceedings of Symposia in Pure Mathematics* (Providence, R. I., 1971).

Some miscellaneous publications of Kirkman's are cited in *Memoirs and Proceedings of the Literary and Philosophical Society*, **9** (1894–1895), 241–243, preceded by a short memoir on the author. A fuller account of the man and his work is Alexander Macfarlane, *Lectures on Ten British Mathematicians of the Nineteenth Century* (New York, 1916), pp. 122–133.

NORMAN T. GRIDGEMAN

KLEIN, CHRISTIAN FELIX (*b.* Düsseldorf, Germany, 25 April 1849; *d.* Göttingen, Germany, 22 June 1925)

Klein graduated from the Gymnasium in Düsseldorf. Beginning in the winter semester of 1865–1866 he studied mathematics and physics at the University of Bonn, where he received his doctorate in December 1868. In order to further his education he went at the start of 1869 to Göttingen, Berlin, and Paris, spending several months in each city. The Franco-Prussian War forced him to leave Paris in 1870. After a short period of military service as a medical orderly, Klein qualified as a lecturer at Göttingen at the beginning of 1871. In the following year he was appointed a full professor of mathematics at Erlangen, where he taught until 1875. From 1875 to 1880 he was professor at the Technische Hochschule in Munich, and from 1880 to 1886 at the University of Leipzig. From 1886 until his death he was a professor at the University of Göttingen. He retired in 1913 because of poor health. During World War I and for a time thereafter he gave lectures in his home. In August 1875 Klein married Anne Hegel, a granddaughter of the philosopher; they had one son and three daughters.

One of the leading mathematicians of his age, Klein made many stimulating and fruitful contributions to almost all branches of mathematics, including applied mathematics and mathematical physics. Moreover, his extensive activity contributed greatly to making Göttingen the chief center of the exact sciences in Germany. An opponent of one-sided approaches, he possessed an extraordinary ability to discover quickly relationships between different areas of research and to exploit them fruitfully.

On the other hand, he was less interested in work requiring subtle and detailed calculations, which he gladly left to his students. In his later years Klein's great organizational skill came to the fore, enabling him to initiate and supervise large-scale encyclopedic works devoted to many areas of mathematics, to their applications, and to their teaching. In addition Klein became widely known through his many books based on his lectures dealing with almost all areas of mathematics and with their historical development in the nineteenth century.

Klein's extraordinarily rapid development as a mathematician was characteristic. At first he wanted to be a physicist, and while still a student he assisted J. Plücker in his physics lectures at Bonn. At that time Plücker, who had returned to mathematics after a long period devoted to physics, was working on a book entitled *Neue Geometrie des Raumes, gegründet auf der geraden Linie als Raumelement*. His sudden death in 1868 prevented him from completing it, and the young Klein took over this task. Klein's dissertation and his first subsequent works also dealt with topics in line geometry. The new aspects of his efforts were that he worked with homogeneous coordinates, which Plücker did only occasionally; that he understood how to apply the theory of elementary divisors, developed by Weierstrass a short time before, to the classification of quadratic straight line complexes (in his dissertation); and that he early viewed the line geometry of P_3 as point geometry on a quadric of P_5, which was a completely new conception.

In 1870 Klein and S. Lie (see *Werke*, I, 90–98) discovered the fundamental properties of the asymptotic lines of the famous Kummer surface, which, as the surface of singularity of a general quadratic straight-line complex, occupied a place in algebraic line geometry. Here and in his simultaneous investigations of cubic surfaces (*Werke*, II, 11–63) there is evidence of Klein's special concern for geometric intuition, whether regarding the forms of plane curves or the models of spatial constructions. A further result of his collaboration with Lie was the investigation, in a joint work, of the so-called W-curves (*Werke*, I, 424–460). These are curves that admit a group of projective transformations into themselves.

Klein's most important achievements in geometry, however, were the projective foundation of the non-Euclidean geometries and the creation of the "Erlanger Programm." Both of these were accomplished during his enormously productive youth.

Hyperbolic geometry, it is true, had already been discovered by Lobachevsky (1829) and J. Bolyai (1832); and in 1868, shortly before Klein, E. Beltrami had recognized that it was valid on surfaces of constant negative curvature. Nevertheless, the non-Euclidean geometries had not yet become common knowledge among mathematicians when, in 1871 and 1873, Klein published two works entitled *Über die sogenannte nicht-euklidische Geometrie* (*Werke*, I, 254–351). His essential contribution here was to furnish so-called projective models for three types of geometry: hyperbolic, stemming from Bolyai and Lobachevsky; elliptic, valid on a sphere on which antipodal points have been taken as identical; and Euclidean. Klein based his work on the projective geometry that C. Staudt had earlier established without the use of the metric concepts of distance and angle, merely adding a continuity postulate to Staudt's construction. Then he explained, for example, plane hyperbolic geometry as a geometry valid in the interior of a real conic section and reduced the lines and angles to cross ratios. This had already been done for the Euclidean angle by Laguerre in 1853 and, more generally, by A. Cayley in 1860; but Klein was the first to recognize clearly that in this way the geometries in question can be constructed purely projectively. Thus one speaks of Klein models with Cayley-Klein metric.

The conceptions grouped together under the name "Erlanger Programm" were presented in 1872 in "Vergleichende Betrachtungen über neuere geometrische Forschungen" (*Werke*, I, 460–498). This work reveals the early familiarity with the concept of group that Klein acquired chiefly through his contact with Lie and from C. Jordan. The essence of the "Erlanger Programm" is that every geometry known so far is based on a certain group, and the task of the geometry in question consists in setting up the invariants of this group. The geometry with the most general group, which was already known, was topology; it is the geometry of the invariants of the group of all continuous transformations—for example, of the plane. Klein then successively distinguished the projective, the affine, and the equiaffine or principal group of the particular dimension; in certain cases the succeeding group is a subgroup of the previous one. To these groups belong the projective, affine, and equiaffine geometries with their invariants, whereby the equiaffine geometry is the same as the Euclidean elementary geometry.

The non-Euclidean geometries accounted for with the aid of the Cayley-Klein models, as well as the various types of circular and spherical geometries devised by Moebius, Laguerre, and Lie, could likewise be viewed as the invariant theories of certain subgroups of the projective groups. In his later years Klein returned to the "Erlanger Programm" and, in a series of works (*Werke*, I, 503–612), showed how theoretical physics, and especially the theory of relativity, which had emerged in the meantime, can be understood on the basis of the ideas presented there. The "Programm" was translated into six languages and guided much work undertaken in the following years: for example, the analytic geometry of Lothar Heffter, school instruction, and the lifelong efforts of W. Blaschke in differential geometry. Only later in the twentieth century was it superseded.

Klein considered his work in function theory to be the summit of his work in mathematics. He owed some of his greatest successes to his development of Riemann's ideas and to the intimate alliance he forged between the latter and the conceptions of invariant theory, of number theory and algebra, of group theory, and of multidimensional geometry and the theory of differential equations, especially in his own fields, elliptic modular functions and automorphic functions.

For Klein the Riemann surface is no longer necessarily a multisheeted covering surface with isolated branch points on a plane, which is how Riemann presented it in his own publications. Rather, according to Klein, it loses its relationships to the complex plane and then, generally, to three-dimensional space. It is through Klein that the Riemann surface is regarded as an indispensable component of function theory and not only as a valuable means of representing multivalued functions.

Klein provided a comprehensive account of his conception of the Riemann surface in 1882 in *Riemanns Theorie der algebraischen Funktionen und ihre Integrale*. In this book he treated function theory as geometric function theory in connection with potential theory and conformal mapping—as Riemann had done. Moreover, in his efforts to grasp the actual relationships and to generate new results, Klein deliberately worked with spatial intuition and with concepts that were borrowed from physics, especially from fluid dynamics. He repeatedly stressed that he was much concerned about the deficiencies of this method of demonstration and that he expected them to be eliminated in the future. A portion of the existence theorems employed by Klein had already been proved, before the appearance of the book by Klein, by H. A. Schwarz and C. Neumann. Klein did not incorporate their results in his own work: He opposed the spirit of the reigning school of Berlin mathematicians led by Weierstrass, with its abstract-critical, arithmetizing tendency; Riemann's approach, which inclined more toward geometry and spatial representation, he considered more fruitful. The rigorous foundation of his own theorems and the fusion of Riemann's and Weierstrass' concepts that Klein hoped for and expected found its expression—still valid today—in 1913 in H. Weyl's *Die Idee der Riemannschen Fläche*.

A problem that greatly interested Klein was the solution of fifth-degree equations, for its treatment involved the simultaneous consideration of algebraic equations, group theory, geometry, differential equations, and function theory. Hermite, Kronecker, and Brioschi had already employed transcendental methods in the solution of the general algebraic equation of the fifth degree. Klein succeeded in deriving the complete theory of this equation from a consideration of the icosahedron, one of the regular polyhedra known since antiquity. These bodies sometimes can be transformed into themselves through a finite group of rotations. The icosahedron in particular allows sixty such rotations into itself. If one circumscribes a sphere about a regular polyhedron and maps it onto a plane by stereographic projection, then to the group of rotations of the polyhedron into itself there corresponds a group of linear transformations of the plane into itself. Klein demonstrated that in this way all finite groups of linear transformations are obtained, if the so-called dihedral group is added. By a dihedron Klein meant a regular polygon with n sides, considered as a rigid body of null volume.

Through the relationships of the fifth-degree equations to linear transformations and through the joining of his investigations with H. A. Schwarz's theory of triangular functions, Klein was led to the elliptic modular functions, which owe their name to their occurrence in elliptic functions. He dedicated a long series of basic works to them and, with R. Fricke, presented the complete theory of these functions in two extensive volumes that are still indispensable for research. Individual aspects of the theory were known earlier. It was a question here of holomorphic functions in the upper half-plane $\mathscr{H}$ with a pole at infinity, which remain invariant under the transformations of the modular group Γ:

$$ z \to \frac{az + b}{cz + d} \,;\ a,\, b,\, c,\, d \text{ integers}\,;\ ad - bc = 1. $$

If one sets $z = x + iy$, then the set F of points z, with

$$ -\tfrac{1}{2} \leqslant x < \tfrac{1}{2},\ x^2 + y^2 \geqslant 1,\ y > 0; $$

and additionally, $x \leqslant 0$ if $x^2 + y^2 = 1$, has at every point in $\mathscr{H}$ exactly one point equivalent to that point under Γ. F is a fundamental domain for Γ relative to $\mathscr{H}$. It had already been recognized as such by Gauss. In 1877, somewhat later than Dedekind and independently of him, Klein discovered the fundamental invariant $J(\tau)$, which assumes each value in F exactly once and by means of which all modular functions are representable as rational functions.

Klein next investigated the subgroups Γ_1 of Γ with finite index, their fundamental domains, and the related functions. He thus arrived at algebraic function fields, which he investigated with the concepts and methods of Riemann's function theory. The Abelian integrals and differentials, and thereby the modular forms, as a generalization of the modular functions, lead to the modular functions on Γ_1. We also owe to Klein the congruence groups. These are subgroups Γ_1 of Γ that contain the group of all transformations

$$ z \to \frac{az - b}{cz + d} \,;\ a \equiv d \equiv \pm 1,\ b \equiv c \equiv 0 \bmod m $$

for fixed natural number m. The least possible m for a group Γ_1 Klein designated as the level of the group. The congruence groups are intimately related to basic theorems of number theory. The theory of modular functions was further developed by direct students of Klein, such as A. Hurwitz and R. Fricke, and most notably by Erich Hecke; its application to several variables was due especially to David Hilbert and Carl Ludwig Siegel.

From the modular functions Klein arrived at the automorphic functions, which, along with the former, include the singly and doubly periodic functions. Automorphic functions are based upon arbitrary groups Γ of linear transformations that operate on the Riemann sphere or on a subset thereof; they have interior points in their domain of definition that have neighborhoods in which no two points are equivalent under Γ. They also possess a fundamental domain F. Klein studied the various types of networks produced from F by the action of Γ. A primary role is played by the *Grenzkreisgruppen*, by means of which the net fills the interior of a circle that goes into itself under Γ; and under them there are again finitely many generators. The groups lead to algebraic function fields, and thus Klein could apply the ideas of Riemann that he had further developed. At the same time as Klein and in competition with him, Poincaré developed a theory of automorphic functions. In opposition to Klein, however, he established his theory in terms of analytic expressions—called, accordingly, Poincaré series. The correspondence between the two mathematicians during 1881 and 1882, which was beneficial to both of them, can be found in volume III of Klein's *Gesammelte mathematische Abhandlungen*.

The path from automorphic functions to algebraic functions may be traveled in both directions—that is the essence of the statements that Klein termed the "fundamental theorems," which were set forth by both himself and Poincaré in reciprocally influential works. Among the fundamental theorems, for example, is the following portion of the *Grenzkreistheorem*: Let $f(w, z)$ be an irreducible polynomial in w and z in the field of the complex numbers. Then one obtains all solution pairs of the equation $f(w, z) = 0$ in the form $w = g_1(t)$, $z = g_2(t)$, where $g_1(t)$ and $g_2(t)$ are rational functions in t, or doubly periodic functions, or automorphic functions under a *Grenzkreis* group, according to whether the Riemann surface corresponding to $f(w, z) = 0$ is of genus 0, 1, or higher than 1. The variable t is said to be *Grenzkreis* uniformizing; it is well defined up to a linear transformation. Klein, like Poincaré, worked with the fundamental theorems without being able to prove them fully. This was first accomplished at the beginning of the twentieth century by Paul Koebe. The progress made in the theory of automorphic functions since the 1930's is due primarily to W. H. H. Petersson (*b*. 1902).

In the 1890's Klein was especially interested in mathematical physics and engineering. One of the first results of this shift in interest was the textbook he composed with A. Sommerfeld on the theory of the gyroscope. It is still the standard work in this field of mechanics.

Klein was not pleased with the increasingly abstract nature of contemporary mathematics. His long-standing concern with applications was further strengthened by the impressions he received during two visits to the United States. He sought, on the one hand, to awaken a greater feeling for applications among pure mathematicians and, on the other, to lead engineers to a greater appreciation of mathematics as a fundamental science. The first goal was advanced by the founding, largely through Klein's initiative, of the Göttingen Institute for Aeronautical and Hydrodynamical Research; at that time such institutions were still uncommon in university towns. Moreover, at the turn of the century he took an active part in the major publishing project *Encyklopädie der mathematischen Wissenschaften mit Einschluss ihrer Anwendungen*. He himself was editor, along with Konrad Müller, of the four-volume section on mechanics.

What a fruitful and stimulating teacher Klein was can be seen from the number—forty-eight—of dissertations prepared under his supervision. Starting in 1900 he began to take a lively interest in mathematical instruction below the university level while continuing to pursue his academic functions. An advocate of modernizing mathematics instruction in Germany, in 1905 he played a decisive role in formulating the "Meraner Lehrplanentwürfe." The essential change recommended was the introduction in secondary schools of the rudiments of differential and integral calculus and of the function concept. In 1908 at the International Congress of Mathematicians in Rome, Klein was elected chairman of the International Commission on Mathematical Instruction. Before World War I, the German branch of the commission published a multivolume work containing a detailed report on the teaching of mathematics in all types of educational institutions in the German empire.

BIBLIOGRAPHY

I. ORIGINAL WORKS. Klein's papers were brought together in *Gesammelte mathematische Abhandlungen*, 3 vols. (Berlin, 1921–1923). His books include *Über Riemanns Theorie der algebraischen Funktionen und ihrer Integrale* (Leipzig, 1882); *Vorlesungen über das Ikosaeder und die Auflösung der Gleichungen vom 5. Grade* (Leipzig, 1884); *Vorlesungen über die Theorie der elliptischen Modulfunktionen*, 2 vols. (Leipzig, 1890–1892), written with R. Fricke; *Über die Theorie des Kreisels*, 4 vols. (Leipzig, 1897–1910), written with A. Sommerfeld; *Vorlesungen über die Theorie der automorphen Funktionen*, 2 vols. (Leipzig, 1897–1912), written with R. Fricke; *Elementarmathematik vom höheren Standpunkt aus*, 3 vols. (Berlin, 1924–1928); *Die Entwicklung der Mathematik im 19. Jahrhundert*, 2 vols. (Berlin, 1926); *Vorlesungen über höhere Geometrie* (Berlin, 1926); *Vorlesungen über nicht-euklidische Geometrie* (Berlin, 1928); and *Vorlesungen über die hypergeometrische Funktion* (Berlin, 1933).

II. SECONDARY LITERATURE. See Richard Courant, "Felix Klein," in *Jahresberichte der Deutschen Mathematikervereinigung*, **34** (1925), 197–213; the collection of articles by R. Fricke, A. Voss, A. Schönflies, C. Carathéodory, A. Sommerfeld, and L. Prandtl, "Felix Klein zur Feier seines 70. Geburtstages," which is *Naturwissenschaften*, **7**, no. 17 (1919); G. Hamel, "F. Klein als Mathematiker," in *Sitzungsberichte der Berliner mathematischen Gesellschaft*, **25** (1926), 69–80; W. Lorey, "Kleins Persönlichkeit und seine Verdienste um die höhere Schule," *ibid.*, 54–68; and L. Prandtl, "Kleins Verdienste im die angewandte Mathematik," *ibid.*, 81–87.

WERNER BURAU
BRUNO SCHOENEBERG

KLÜGEL, GEORG SIMON (*b*. Hamburg, Germany, 19 August 1739; *d*. Halle, Germany, 4 August 1812)

Klügel was the first son of a businessman and received a solid mathematical education at the Hamburg Gymnasium Academicum, which he attended after completing the local Johanneum. In 1760 he entered the University of Göttingen to study theology; but he soon came under the influence of A. G. Kaestner, who interested him in mathematics and induced him to devote himself exclusively to that science. At Kaestner's suggestion Klügel took as the subject of his thesis, which he defended on 20 August 1763 (*Conatuum praecipuorum theoriam parallelarum demonstrandi recensio*), a critical analysis of the experiments made thus far to prove the parallel postulate. His criticism of the errors provided a new incentive to investigate this problem. (For instance, Lambert, one of the outstanding forerunners of non-Euclidean geometry, expressly referred to Klügel, who is also cited by most later critics of the problem of parallel lines.)

After five years at Göttingen, Klügel went in 1765 to Hannover, where he edited the scientific contributions to the *Intelligenzblatt*; two years later he was appointed professor of mathematics at Helmstedt. His extensive work in mathematics and physics began then and increased after his transfer to the chair of mathematics and physics at the University of Halle. His work included papers, textbooks, and handbooks on various branches of mathematics.

Despite the generally encyclopedic character of his works, in some respects Klügel put forward new ideas. His most important contribution was in trigonometry. His *Analytische Trigonometrie* analytically unified the hitherto separate trigonometric formulas and introduced the concept of trigonometric function, which in a coherent manner defines the relations of the sides in a right triangle. He showed that the theorems on the sum of the sines and cosines already "contain all the theorems on the composition of angles" and extended the validity of six basic formulas for a right spherical triangle. Not even Euler, who returned to the problem of extending Euclid's trigonometry nine years after Klügel, was able to achieve Klügel's results in certain respects. Klügel's trigonometry was very modern for its time and was exceptional among the contemporary textbooks. Other work in advance of its time concerned stereographic projection, where the properties of this transformation of a spherical surface onto a plane were geometrically derived and the ideas were also applied to spherical trigonometry and gnomonics.

In 1795 in the small publication *Über die Lehre von den entgegengesetzten Grössen,* Klügel dealt with questions of formal algebra and tried to define formal algebraic laws. His most popular and useful work was his mathematical dictionary, *Mathematisches Wörterbuch oder Erklärung der Begriffe, Lehrsätze, Aufgaben und Methoden der Mathematik,* to which three volumes by Mollweide and Grunert were added in 1823–1836; it was used throughout much of the nineteenth century.

While at Halle, Klügel was elected member of the Berlin Academy on 27 January 1803. In 1808 he became seriously ill, and he died four years later.

BIBLIOGRAPHY

I. ORIGINAL WORKS. A complete list of Klügel's works can be found in *Hamburger Schriftstellerlexikon* (see below). They include *Conatuum praecipuorum theoriam parallelarum demonstrandi recensio . . .* (Göttingen, 1763); *Analytische Trigonometrie* (Brunswick, 1770); *Von den besten Einrichtung der Feuerspritzen* (Berlin, 1774); *Geschichte und gegenwärtiger Zustand der Optik nach der Englischen Priestleys bearbeitet* (Leipzig, 1776); *Analytische Dioptrik,* 2 vols. (Leipzig, 1778); *Enzyklopädie oder zusammenhängender Vortrag der gemeinnützigsten Kennt-*

nisse, 3 pts. (Berlin–Strettin, 1782–1784, 2nd ed. in 7 pts., 1792 1817); "Über die Lehre von den entgegengesetzten Grössen," in Hindenburg's *Archiv der reinen und angewandten Mathematik,* **3** (1795); and *Mathematisches Wörterbuch oder Erklärung der Begriffe, Lehrsätze, Aufgaben und Methoden der Mathematik,* 3 vols. (Leipzig, 1803–1808).

II. SECONDARY LITERATURE. On Klügel or his work, see M. Cantor, *Vorlesungen über Geschichte der Mathematik,* IV (Leipzig, 1908), especially pp. 27, 88, 389, 406, 412 ff., 424 ff., 616, which evaluates Klügel's mathematical work; *Lexikon der hamburgischen Schriftsteller . . .,* IV (Hamburg, 1858), 65–73, which includes a complete list of Klügel's writings; and A. H. Niemeyer, obituary, in *Hallisches patriotisches Wochenblatt* (5 September 1812), 561–569.

JAROSLAV FOLTA

KNESER, ADOLF (*b.* Grüssow, Germany, 19 March 1862; *d.* Breslau, Germany [now Wrocław, Poland], 24 January 1930)

One of the most distinguished German mathematicians of the years around 1900, Kneser was the son of a Protestant clergyman who died when the boy was one year old. His mother moved to Rostock in order to educate her four sons. There Kneser completed his secondary schooling and studied for a year at the university. As early as this (1880) he published his first paper, on the refraction of sound waves. He then went to Berlin. Of the great Berlin mathematicians Kronecker was above all his teacher, but certainly Kneser was also influenced by Weierstrass. In 1884 he received his doctorate and began his teaching activity. In 1889 he became associate professor, and in 1890 full professor, at Dorpat. In 1900 he went to the Bergakademie at Berlin; and in 1905 he received a professorship at the University of Breslau which he held for the rest of his life. Kneser was "Dr. e. h." (honorary doctor in engineering) of the Technische Hochschule at Breslau and a corresponding member of the Prussian and Russian Academies of Sciences. In 1894 he married Laura Booth; they had four children. Their son Helmuth was professor at the University of Tübingen, and Helmuth's son Martin became professor at the University of Göttingen. So Kneser may be considered as the founder of a mathematical dynasty.

Although Kneser appears in the history of mathematics primarily as a master of analysis, he was, at first, more concerned with algebra. His dissertation and some subsequent papers are dedicated to algebraic functions and algebraic equations. He next turned to geometry, with a series of interesting works on space curves (1888–1894). Much later Kneser made another important discovery in the theory of curves: the so-called four-vertex theorem (1912). In 1888 he had begun his analytical investigations, the first of which involved elliptic functions, a subject still of interest to him in later years. Soon, however, he turned his attention to one of the two main subjects of his lifework: linear differential equations, and especially the group of ideas associated with the so-called Sturm-Liouville problem (from 1896). Since 1906, integral equations were added, after Fredholm's fundamental works had appeared, the two subjects being closely connected. Kneser's decisive achievement was to bring the theory of developing arbitrary functions into series with respect to the eigenfunctions of a Sturm-Liouville differential equation to the same level of generality that Dirichlet had achieved in the special case of Fourier series. Kneser's treatment of all this, which found final expression in his book on integral equations (1911), is characterized by a very intensive consideration of the theory's applications to mathematical physics, the theory of heat conduction, for instance.

The calculus of variations, the other main subject of Kneser's research (from 1897)—in fact the most important—is also of value to physics. His engagement in this classical topic was not the direct result of his studies with the field's great master, Weierstrass, but, rather, of his teaching experience at Dorpat. Kneser brought the theory of the so-called second variation to a certain conclusion. Especially, he favored one of its geometric aspects, the theory of families of resolution curves and their envelopes, closely connected with the Jacobian theory of conjugate points. But above all, the decisive advances toward the solution of the so-called Mayer Problem, recently introduced to the calculus of variations, are due to Kneser. His textbook on the calculus of variations (1900) had an enduring influence on later research. Many of the technical terms nowadays usual in calculus of variations were created by Kneser, e. g. "extremal" (for a resolution curve), "field" (for a family of extremals), "transversal," and "strong" and "weak" extremum.

An example of Kneser's interest in the history of mathematics is his booklet *Das Prinzip der kleinsten Wirkung von Leibniz bis zur Gegenwart* (1928).

BIBLIOGRAPHY

I. ORIGINAL WORKS. A bibliography of Kneser's works can be found in Koschmieder (see below). They include *Lehrbuch der Variationsrechnung* (Brunswick, 1900; 2nd ed., 1925); "Variationsrechnung," in *Encyklopädie der mathematischen Wissenschaften*, II, pt. 1 (1904), 571–625; *Die Integralgleichungen und ihre Anwendungen in der mathe-matischen Physik* (Brunswick, 1911; 2nd ed., 1922); and *Das Prinzip der kleinsten Wirkung von Leibniz bis zur Gegenwart* (Leipzig, 1928).

II. SECONDARY LITERATURE. See *Zur Erinnerung an Adolf Kneser* (Brunswick, 1930), reprint of the commemorative addresses delivered at Breslau in Feb. 1930; and L. Koschmieder, "Adolf Kneser," in *Sitzungsberichte der Berliner mathematischen Gesellschaft*, **29** (1930), 78–102, which includes a bibliography of 81 items; and "El profesor Adolfo Kneser," in *Revista matemática hispano–americana*, 2nd ser., **5** (1930), 281–288.

HERMANN BOERNER

KNOPP, KONRAD (*b*. Berlin, Germany, 22 July 1882; *d*. Annecy, France, 20 April 1957)

After one semester at the University of Lausanne in 1901, Knopp returned to Berlin to study at its university. He passed the teacher's examination in 1906 and received the Ph.D. in 1907. In the spring of 1908 he went to Nagasaki to teach at the Commercial Academy; he also traveled in China and India. In the spring of 1910 he returned to Germany, where he married the painter Gertrud Kressner. They moved to Tsingtao, where Knopp taught at the German-Chinese Academy. Back in Germany in 1911, he received his *habilitation* at Berlin University while teaching at the Military Technical Academy and at the Military Academy. An officer in the German army, he was injured early in World War I. In the fall of 1914 Knopp resumed teaching at Berlin University, in 1915 he became extraordinary professor at Königsberg University and in 1919 ordinary professor. In 1926 he was appointed to Tübingen University, where he remained until retiring in 1950.

Knopp was a specialist in generalized limits. He not only contributed many details but also clarified the general concept and the aims of the theory of generalized limits. He is well known for his extremely popular books on complex functions, which have often been republished and translated. He was responsible for the sixth through tenth editions of H. von Mangoldt's popular *Einführung in die höhere Mathematik*. He was a cofounder of *Mathematische Zeitschrift* in 1918 and from 1934 to 1952 was its editor.

BIBLIOGRAPHY

Knopp's writings include *Grenzwerte von Reihen bei der Annäherung an die Konvergenzgrenze* (Berlin, 1907), his diss.; "Neuere Untersuchungen in der Theorie der divergenten Reihen," in *Jahresbericht der Deutschen Mathematiker-Vereinigung*, **32** (1923), 43–67; "Zur Theorie der Limitierungsverfahren I. II," in *Mathematische Zeitschrift*,

31 (1929), 97–127, 276–305; *Theorie und Anwendung der unendlichen Reihen*, which is Grundlehren der mathematischen Wissenschaften, II, 4th ed. (Berlin, 1947); *Funktionentheorie*, 2 vols., which is Sammlung Göschen, nos. 668 and 703, 9th ed. (Berlin, 1957); *Aufgabensammlung zur Funktionentheorie*, 2 vols., which is Sammlung Göschen, nos. 877 and 878, 5th ed. (Berlin 1957–1959); and *Elemente der Funktionentheorie*, which is Sammlung Göschen, no. 1109, 7th ed. (Berlin, 1966).

An obituary is E. Kamke and K. Zeller, "Konrad Knopp †," in *Jahresbericht der Deutschen Mathematiker-Vereinigung*, **60** (1958), 44–49.

HANS FREUDENTHAL

KÖBEL (or **KOBEL** or **KOBILIN** or **KIBLIN** or **CABALLINUS**), **JACOB** (*b*. Heidelberg, Germany, 1460/1465; *d*. Oppenheim, Germany, 31 January 1533)

Köbel was the son of Klaus Köbel, a goldsmith. He began his studies at the University of Heidelberg on 20 February 1480[1] and earned his bachelor's degree from the Faculty of Arts in July 1481. Concerning the following years it is known only that "Jacobus Kiblin" was active in the book trade in 1487. Simultaneously he studied law, receiving the bachelor's degree on 16 May 1491. He appears to have gone then to Cracow, where he studied mathematics, a subject then flourishing at the Jagiellonian University. He is also reported to have been a fellow student of Copernicus, who had enrolled there in 1491 under the rectorship of Mathias de Cobilyno (perhaps a relative of Köbel).[2] In 1494 Köbel was in Oppenheim, where on 8 May 1494 he married Elisabeth von Gelthus, the daughter of an alderman. They are known to have had one son and two daughters. Köbel worked as town clerk and official surveyor, as well as manager of the municipal wine tavern. A scholar of manifold interests, he wrote extensively and was also a printer and publisher. As a member of the Sodalitas Litteraria Rhenana he was friendly with many humanists.[3] In the religious conflicts he stood with the Catholic reformers. He died after suffering greatly in his last years from gout and was buried in Oppenheim, in the Church of St. Katherine. A portrait of him can be found in his 1532 essay on the sundial.[4]

Between 1499 and 1532 Köbel published ninety-six works, at first those of others and then his own. Among the authors whose writings he published were Albertus Magnus, Virdung, and especially his friend Johann Stöffler.[5] Köbel's publishing activity decreased markedly after 1525, no doubt as a result of his poor health.

Köbel wrote three arithmetic books of varied content, all of which were well received. They appeared during the period in which the algorithm, with new numerals and methods—propagated especially through the writings of Sacrobosco—was gradually supplanting the traditional computation with the abacus and with Roman numerals (which Köbel called "German" numerals). Köbel's first book was *Rechenbüchlein vf den Linien mit Rechenpfenigen* because such a book was the easiest sort for beginners, who had to know only the corresponding Roman letters. The book was widely read and went through many editions, most of them under altered titles, and was continually revised and enlarged. In it Köbel treated the manipulation of the abacus, computational operations (with duplication, mediation, and progression but without the roots, since they are "unsuitable for domestic use"), the rule of three, fractions (also with Roman numerals), and a few problems of recreational mathematics.

The next to appear was *Eyn new geordent Vysirbuch* (1515), which dealt with the calculation of the capacity of barrels. Köbel presented the new methods of calculation with Arabic numerals in *Mit der Kryden oder Schreibfedern durch die Zeiferzal zu rechnen* (1520).

Köbel's writings were most widely disseminated in a collection that he himself had prepared, *Zwey Rechenbüchlin: uff der Linien und Zipher. Mit eym angehenckten Visirbuch* (1537). It contained almost verbatim the line arithmetic book of 1525 (now without Roman numerals), as well as the *Vysirbuch* and *Mit der Kryden oder Schreibfedern*. In the editions after 1544 a chapter was added on the commercially important measures and coins of many foreign lands.

A *Geometrei* appeared posthumously (1535) and was in print until 1616. This work consisted of three papers by Köbel: "Von vrsprung der Teilung ..." (1522), which contained formulas for the surveyor;[6] an essay on the Jacob's staff, written in February and May 1531,[7] and "Feldmessung durch Spiegel," which was first published in the *Geometrei*.

As an astronomer Köbel was concerned with the astrolabe and with the publication of numerous popular calendars. His *Astrolabii declaratio* (1532) went through several editions. He also published a treatise entitled *Eyn künstliche sonn-Uhr inn eynes yeden menschen Lincken handt gleicht wie in eynem Compass zu erlernen ...* (1532), which later appeared under the titles *Bauren Compas* and *LeyenCompas*.[8]

Besides informative handbooks and many poems, Köbel wrote works on law—for example, on inheritance cases and rules of the court. He also wrote on imperial history and continued the chronicle of Steinhöwel from the time of Frederick III to his own day.

The high esteem accorded to Köbel's writings is reflected in the numerous editions that appeared until the beginning of the seventeenth century. Today his importance lies principally in his dissemination of mathematical knowledge, especially of the new Hindu numerals and methods, among broad segments of the population. He accomplished this through the use of German in his work, a practice he was the first to adopt since the publication of the arithmetic books of Bamberg (1482, 1483) and Widmann (1489)—which, moreover, were basically collections of problems. Adam Ries, who replaced Köbel as teacher of the nation, used his books, having become acquainted with them while in Erfurt (1518–1522) through the humanist Georg Sturtz.[9]

NOTES

1. The printed register of Heidelberg University, I, 367, gives the name Johannes Köbel; the original has the correct form.
2. Starowolsky, *Scriptorum Polonicorum* . . ., p. 88; in it Köbel is cited as Cobilinius in *Catalogus illustrium Poloniae scriptorum* (p. 133). Benzing, in *Jakob Köbel zu Oppenheim, 1494–1533*, p. 8, remarks that we have no proof that Köbel studied at Cracow.
3. Vigilius, who was a guest of Köbel (Caballinus), reports in a letter to Conradus Celtis (Heidelberg, 19 Apr. 1496) that Köbel was estranged from Johann von Dalberg because Köbel had, without permission, given Celtis a book he had borrowed from Dalberg. See Rupprich, *Der Briefwechsel des Konrad Celtis*, pp. 178–227 ff.; and Morneweg, *Johann von Dalberg*, pp. 196 ff.
4. The portrait can be found in Benzing, *op. cit.*, p. 6.
5. For example, Stöffler's *Calendarium Romanorum magnum* (1518); *Der newe grosz Römisch Calender* (1522); and *Elucidatio fabricae ususque astrolabii* (1513).
6. With regard to the errors criticized by Kaestner (*Geschichte der Mathematik*, 1 [1796], 655), it should be said that Köbel intended to provide the surveyor only with formulas, such as the ancient Egyptian approximation formula for quadrangles.
7. Köbel explained this work by stating that he himself was now obliged to use a staff.
8. See Benzing, *op. cit.*, pp. 79 ff.
9. Köbel never realized his intention to write on algebra. See Unger, *Die Methodik der praktischen Arithmetik*, p. 45.

BIBLIOGRAPHY

I. ORIGINAL WORKS. A list of all of Köbel's writings, with full titles, subsequent eds., and present locations, is in Joseph Benzing, *Jakob Köbel zu Oppenheim, 1494–1533. Bibliographie seiner Drucke und Schriften* (Wiesbaden, 1962). Most of his works were published "under such varied titles and in such different combinations with his other books, that it is difficult to say whether a given edition is a new work or merely a revision" (Smith, *Rara Arithmetica*, p. 102). Among them are *Rechenbüchlein vf den Linien mit Rechenpfenigen* (Oppenheim–Augsburg, 1514; 2nd ed., 1517; 3rd ed., 1518); *Eyn new geordent Vysirbuch* (1515; 1527), later issued with line arithmetic book (also with square and cube roots) (1531; 1532); *Über die Pestilenz* (1519); *Was Tugend und Geschicklichkeit ein Oberster regirer an ynn haben soll* (1519), an exhortation to Charles V; *Mit der Kryden oder Schreibfedern durch die Zeiferzal zu rechnen* (1520); the line arithmetic book, *Eyn new Rechenbüchlin Jacob Köbels Stadtschreiber zu Oppenheym auff den Linien vnd Spacien gantz leichtlich zu lernen mit Vyelen zusetzen* (Oppenheim, 1525); *Astrolabii declaratio* (1532), also published with Stöffler's *Elucidatio* and later trans. into German as *Von gerechter Zubereitung des Astrolabiums . . .* (1536); *Eyn künstliche sonnUhr inn eynes yeden menschen Lincken handt gleich wie in eynem Compass zu erlernen . . .* (1532); *Geometrei* (1535; 1550; 1570; 1584; 1598; 1616), with a treatise on the quadrant by Johann Dryander, who also published a work on the *Nachtuhr* begun by Köbel (1535); and *Zwey Rechenbüchlin: Uff der Linien und Zipher. Mit eym angehenckten Visirbuch* (1537; 1543; 1564; 1584).

II. SECONDARY LITERATURE. On Köbel or his work, see *Allgemeine deutsche Biographie*, XVI, 345–349, and XIX, 1827; M. Cantor, *Vorlesungen über Geschichte der Mathematik*, 2nd ed., II (Leipzig, 1913), 419 f.; S. Günther, *Geschichte des mathematischen Unterrichts im deutschen Mittelalter bis zum Jahre 1525* (Berlin, 1887), p. 386; K. Haas, "Der Rechenmeister Jakob Köbel," in *Festschrift zum 125-jährigen Jubiläum des Helmholtz-Gymnasiums in Heidelberg* (Heidelberg, 1960), pp. 151–155; K. Morneweg, *Johann von Dalberg* (Heidelberg, 1887); F. W. E. Roth, "Jakob Köbel, Verleger zu Heidelberg, Buchdrucker und Stadtschreiber zu Oppenheim am Rhein 1489–1533," in *Neues Archiv zur Geschichte der Stadt Heidelberg*, 4 (1901), 147–179; H. Rupprich, *Der Briefwechsel des Konrad Celtis* (Munich, 1934); D. E. Smith, *Rara arithmetica* (Boston–London, 1908), pp. 100–114; Szymon Starowolsky, *Scriptorum Polonicorum ʹΕΚΑΤΟΝΤᾺΣ* (Frankfurt, 1625); and F. Unger, *Die Methodik der praktischen Arithmetik* (Leipzig, 1888), pp. 44–46.

KURT VOGEL

KOCH, HELGE VON (*b.* Stockholm, Sweden, 25 January 1870; *d.* Stockholm[?], 11 March 1924)

Von Koch is known principally for his work in the theory of infinitely many linear equations and the study of the matrices derived from such infinite systems. He also did work in differential equations and in the theory of numbers.

The history of infinitely many equations in infinitely many unknowns is long; special cases of infinite systems were studied by Fourier, who used them naïvely in his celebrated *Théorie analytique de la chaleur;* and there are even earlier examples. Yet despite the many applications in differential equation theory and in geometry, the rigorous study of infinite systems began only in 1884–1885 with the publication by Henri Poincaré of a few special results.

Von Koch's interest in infinite matrices came from his investigations in 1891 into Fuchs's equation:

$$D^n + P_2(x) D^{n-1} + \cdots + P_n(x) y = 0,$$

where

$$D^r = \frac{d^r y}{dx^r} \text{ and } P_r(x) = \sum_{k=-\infty}^{\infty} a_{rk} x^k,$$

all of which converge in some annulus A with center at the origin. It was known that there existed a solution

$$y = \sum_{k=-\infty}^{\infty} b_k x^{k+\rho}$$

which also converged in A; but in order explicitly to calculate the coefficient b_k and the exponent ρ, von Koch was led to an infinite system of linear equations. Here he used Poincaré's theory, which forced him to assume some unnaturally restrictive conditions on the original equation.

To remove the restrictions, von Koch published another paper in 1892 which was concerned primarily with infinite matrix theory. He considered the infinite array or matrix

$$A = \{A_{ik} : i, k = \cdots, -2, -1, 0, 1, 2, \cdots\}$$

and set

$$D_m = \det\{A_{ik} : i, k = -m, \cdots, m\}.$$

The determinant D of A was defined to be $\lim_{m \to \infty} D_m$ if this limit existed. He then noted that the same array could give rise to denumerably many different matrices—by the use of different systems of enumeration—each with a different main diagonal. He was, however, able to prove that if $\prod_{i=-\infty}^{\infty} A_{ii}$ converged absolutely and $\sum_{i,k=-\infty; i \neq k}^{\infty} A_{ik}$ also converged absolutely, then D existed and was independent of the enumeration of A. A matrix which satisfied the above hypotheses was said to be in normal form.

Various methods to evaluate D were then given by von Koch, all of them analogous to the evaluation of finite determinants. Minors of finite and infinite order were defined, and it was proved that D could be evaluated by the method of expansion by minors in a direct generalization to infinite matrices of the Laplace expansion. Finally, he showed that

$$D = 1 + \sum_{p=-\infty}^{\infty} a_{pp} + \sum_{p<q} \det \begin{pmatrix} a_{pp} & a_{pq} \\ a_{qp} & a_{qq} \end{pmatrix}$$
$$+ \sum_{p<q<r} \det \begin{pmatrix} a_{pp} & a_{pq} & a_{pr} \\ a_{qp} & a_{qq} & a_{qr} \\ a_{rp} & a_{rq} & a_{rr} \end{pmatrix} + \cdots.$$

Here, $a_{pq} = A_{pq} - \delta_{pq}(\delta_{jk} = 1$ if $j = k$, $\delta_{jk} = 0$ if $j \neq k$); the largest summation index in each term is to range over all integers; and the others are to range over all integers as indicated. This is particularly interesting because it was the form used by Fredholm in 1903 to solve the integral equation

$$\phi(x) + \int_0^1 f(x, y) \phi(y) \, dy = \psi(x)$$

for the unknown function ϕ, the other functions being supposed known.

Von Koch then went on to prove that if A and B are in normal form, then the usual product matrix $C = A'B$ can be formed. The matrix C will also be in normal form and $\det C = (\det A)(\det B)$. He also was able to show that the property of being in normal form is not a necessary condition for D to exist and indicated how his theory could be extended to matrices whose entries are functions all analytic in the same disk.

Finally, von Koch applied his results to systems of infinitely many linear equations in infinitely many unknowns. Although he claimed a certain amount of generality, he actually considered only the homogeneous case

$$\sum_{k=-\infty}^{\infty} A_{ik} x_k = 0 \qquad (i = -\infty, \cdots, \infty).$$

Here the matrix $\{A_{ik}\}$ was supposed to be in normal form, and the only solutions sought were those for which $|x_k| \leq M$ for $k = -\infty, \cdots, \infty$. He then established that if $\det\{A_{ik}\}$ is different from zero, then the only such solution for the above equation is $x_k = 0$ for $k = -\infty, \cdots, \infty$. He then showed that if $D = 0$ but $A_{ik} \neq 0$, there will always exist a minor of smallest order m which is not zero. Then if the nonvanishing minor is obtained from $\{A_{ik}\}$ by deleting columns $k_1, k_2, \cdots, k_m$, a solution $\{x_k\}$ can be obtained by assigning arbitrary values to $x_{k_1}, x_{k_2} \cdots, x_{k_m}$ and expressing each of the remaining x_k's as a linear combination of $x_{k_1}, x_{k_2} \cdots, x_{k_m}$. This is similar to the finite case. Von Koch then asserted that analogous results could be obtained for unhomogeneous systems, which is now known to be false unless further restrictions are placed on $\{A_{ik}\}$.

Von Koch's work cannot be called pioneering. His results were all fairly readily accessible, although many of the calculations are lengthy. He was aware, through a knowledge of Poincaré's work, of the possibility of obtaining pathological results but did little to explore them. Yet this work can be said to be the first step on the long road which eventually led to functional analysis, since it provided Fredholm with the key for the solution of his integral equation.

BIBLIOGRAPHY

A complete bibliography of von Koch's papers is in *Acta mathematica*, **45** (1925), 345–348. Of particular interest is "Sur les déterminants infinis et les équations différentielles linéaires," in *Acta mathematica*, **16** (1892–1893), 217–295.

A secondary source is Ernst Hellinger and Otto Toepletz, "Integralgleichungen und Gleichungen mit unendlichenvielen Unbekannten," in *Encyklopädie der mathematischen Wissenschaften*, II, pt. C (Leipzig, 1923–1927), 1335–1602, also published separately.

MICHAEL BERNKOPF

KOCHIN, NIKOLAI YEVGRAFOVICH (*b.* St. Petersburg, Russia [now Leningrad, U.S.S.R.], 1901; *d.* Moscow, U.S.S.R., 31 December 1944)

Kochin's father was a clerk in a dry goods store. After graduating from Petrograd University in 1923, Kochin gave courses in mechanics and mathematics there from 1924 to 1934 and then at Moscow University until 1944. From 1932 to 1939 he worked in the Mathematics Institute of the Soviet Academy of Sciences, and from 1939 to 1944 he was head of the mechanics section of the Mechanics Institute of the Academy.

Kochin's work covered a wide range of scientific problems. At the beginning of his career he published a number of very important works in meteorology. He made significant contributions in the development of gas dynamics. His research on shock waves in compressed liquids was of great importance in the development of this area of science. In hydrodynamics he was responsible for a number of classical investigations. His "K teorii voln Koshi-Puassona" ("Towards a Theory of Cauchy-Poisson Waves," 1935) gives the solution of the problem of small-amplitude free waves on the surface of an uncompressed liquid. In 1937 Kochin published "O volnovom soprotivlenii i podyomnoy sile pogruzhennykh v zhidkosty tel" ("On the Wave Resistance and Lifting Strength of Bodies Submerged in Liquid"), in which he proposed a general method of solving the two-dimensional problem of an underwater fin, the formulas for the resistance of a body (a ship), forms of a wave surface, and lifting force. Using this method, Kochin in 1938 solved the two-dimensional problem of the hydroplaning of a slightly curved contour on the surface of a heavy uncompressed liquid. "Teoria voln, vynuzhdaemykh kolebaniami tela pod svobodnoy poverkhnostyu tyazheloy neszhimaemoy zhidkosti" ("Theory of Waves Created by the Vibration of a Body Under a Free Surface of Heavy Uncompressed Liquid,"

1940) provided a basis for a new theory of the pitch and roll of a ship, taking into account the mutual influence of the hull of the ship and the water.

In aerodynamics Kochin was the first (1941–1944) to give strict solutions for the wing of finite span; he introduced formulas for aerodynamic force and for the distribution of pressure.

Kochin also produced important works on mathematics and theoretical mechanics. He wrote textbooks on hydromechanics and vector analysis, was coauthor and editor of a two-volume monograph on dynamic meteorology, and was the editor of the posthumous edition of the works of A. M. Lyapunov.

BIBLIOGRAPHY

Kochin's works were brought together as *Sobranie sochineny* ("Collected Works"), 2 vols. (Moscow–Leningrad, 1949). There is also a bibliography: *Nikolai Yevgrafovich Kochin. Bibliografia sost. N. I. Akinfievoy* ("Bibliography Compiled by N. I. Akinfieva"; Moscow–Leningrad, 1948).

See also P. I. Polubarinova-Kochina, *Zhizn i deyatelnost N. Ye. Kochina* ("Life and Work of N. Y. Kochin"; Leningrad, 1950).

A. T. GRIGORIAN

KOEBE, PAUL (*b.* Luckenwalde, Germany, 15 February 1882; *d.* Leipzig, Germany, 6 August 1945)

The son of Hermann Koebe, a factory owner, and Emma (née Kramer) Koebe, Paul Koebe attended a Realgymnasium in Berlin. He started university studies in 1900 in Kiel, which he continued at Berlin University (1900–1905) and Charlottenburg Technische Hochschule (1904–1905). He was a student of H. A. Schwarz; the other referee of his thesis was F. H. Schottky. His habilitation as a *Privatdozent* at Göttingen University took place in 1907. He was appointed a professor extraordinary at Leipzig University in 1910, a professor ordinary at Jena University in 1914, and again at Leipzig in 1926. His numerous papers are all concerned with one chapter of the theory of complex functions, which is best characterized by the headings "conformal mapping" and "uniformization." In fact, in 1907, simultaneously with and independently of H. Poincaré, he accomplished the long-desired uniformization of Riemann surfaces.

The strange story of uniformization has still to be written. Its origin is the parametrization of the algebraic curves (z, w) with $w^2 = (z - a_1)(z - a_2)(z - a_3)(z - a_4)$ by means of elliptic functions, achieved by Abel and Jacobi. The attempt to use abelian integrals for general algebraic curves of genus p in the same way as elliptic ones had been used in the case of genus one led Jacobi to reformulate the problem: parametrization of the p-th power of the Riemann surface by means of a p-tuple of functions of p variables—the Jacobi inversion problem, which was solved by B. Riemann. By Poincaré's intervention in 1881 and 1882, history took a quite unexpected turn. When studying differential equations, Poincaré discovered automorphic functions, which F. Klein was investigating at the same time. If in C the group G is generated by rotations with centers $a_1, a_2, \ldots, a_{n+1}$ and corresponding rotation angles $2\pi/k_i$ (integral k_i, $i = 1, \ldots, n$), an automorphic function F of G is easily constructed by Poincaré series. Such an F maps its domain conformally on a Riemann surface branched at the $F(a_i)$ with degrees k_i. Its inverse achieves the "uniformization" of that Riemann surface. Counting parameters and applying "continuity" arguments, Klein (1882) and Poincaré (1884) stated that the scope of this method included Riemann surfaces of all algebraic functions, although their proofs were unsatisfactory. It was not until 1913 that the "continuity method" of proof was salvaged by L. E. J. Brouwer.

At present, if a Riemann surface is to be uniformized, it is wrapped up with, rather than cut up into, a simply connected surface, which is then conformally mapped upon a standard domain (circular disk, plane, or plane closed at infinity), and in this framework automorphic functions are an a posteriori bonus. The idea of uniformizing the universal wrapping rather than the Riemann surface itself goes back to Schwarz. As early as the 1880's various methods were available to solve the boundary value problem of potential theory for simply connected (even finitely branched) domains, or, equivalently, to map them conformally upon the standard domain, as long as the boundary was supposed smooth, say piecewise analytic; and as early as 1886 Harnack's theorem had made convergence proofs for sequences of harmonic functions easy. Using these tools, uniformization could have been achieved in the 1880's were it not for the blockage of this access by automorphic functions.

In 1907 the lock was opened. Koebe and Poincaré simultaneously noticed that if an arbitrary simply connected domain (the universal wrapping of the Riemann surface) has conformally to be mapped on the standard domain, it suffices to exhaust it by an increasing sequence of smoothly bounded ones. As a matter of fact, because of Harnack's theorem, it was preferable to use Green's functions of the ap-

proximating domains, with the $\log \frac{1}{r}$ – singularity at P, which form an increasing sequence u_n. If the $u_n - \log \frac{1}{r}$ are bounded at P, it converges toward Green's function u for the prescribed domain, which together with its conjugate v solves the mapping problem by $\exp [-(u + iv)]$. If not (the case of mapping upon the whole plane) the goal is attained by noticing that all *schlicht* images of the unit circle by f with $f(0) = 0$, $f'(0) = 1$ contain a circle with center $f(0)$ and a radius independent of f (this "Koebe constant" has been proved to be 1/4). The latter remark is a weak form of Koebe's distortion theorem, which for *schlicht* mappings f of the unit circle states for $|z| < r$ an inequality of the form

$$Q(r) \leq |f'(z_1)/f'(z_2)| \leq Q(r) \quad ^1$$

with $Q(r)$ independent of f.

Koebe's most influential contribution to conformal mapping on the unit circle was his 1912 proof by *Schmiegung*, which has become so common that textbooks are silent about its authorship. It rests on the remark that $z \to z^2$ for $|z| < 1$ increases the distances from the boundary, and consequently the square root reduces them. To use the square root univalently the given domain D is transformed by linear fractions such as to lie on one sheet of the square root surface, with the branching outside D. Then the square root operation brings the boundary of D nearer to that of the unit circle. This process is repeated with suitable branching points such as to deliver a sequence of mappings converging to that of the unit circle. This square root trick goes back to Koebe's 1907 paper; it seems that Carathéodory suggested it be applied that fundamentally.

Koebe's mathematical style is prolix, pompous, and chaotic. He tended to deal broadly with special cases of a general theory by a variety of methods so that it is difficult to give a representative selective bibliography. Koebe's life-style was the same; Koebe anecdotes were widespread in interbellum Germany. He never married.

BIBLIOGRAPHY

I. ORIGINAL WORKS. See Poggendorff. The following papers by Koebe are particularly important: "Über die Uniformisierung beliebiger analytischer Kurven," in *Nachrichten von der Königlichen Gesellschaft der Wissenschaften zu Göttingen, Math.-Phys. Kl.* (1907), 191–210, 633–669; "Über eine neue Methode der konformen Abbildung und Uniformisierung," *ibid.* (1912), 844–848; "Über die Uniformisierung der algebraischen Kurven,

I.," in *Mathematische Annalen*, **67** (1909), 145–224; "Allgemeine Theorie der Riemannschen Mannigfaltigkeiten," in *Acta Mathematica*, **50** (1927), 27–157.

II. SECONDARY LITERATURE. Ludwig Bieberbach, "Das Werk Paul Koebe," and H. Cremer, "Erinnerungen an Paul Koebe," in *Jahresbericht der Deutschen Mathematiker-Vereinigung*, **70** (1968), 148–158, 158–161; L. E. J. Brouwer, *Collected Works*, H. Freudenthal, ed., II (Amsterdam, 1976), 572–576, 583, 585–586; H. Freudenthal, "Poincaré et les fonctions automorphes," in *Le livre du centenaire de la naissance de Henri Poincaré* (Paris, 1955), 212–219, and "A Bit of Gossip: Koebe," in *Mathematical Intelligencer*, **6**, no. 2 (1984), 77; Reiner Kühnau, "Paul Koebe und die Funktionentheorie," in Herbert Beckert and Horst Schuman, eds., *100. Jahre Mathematisches Seminar der Karl-Marx-Universität* (Leipzig, 1981), 183–194; Otto Volk, "Paul Koebe," in *Neue Deutsche Biographie*, XII (1980).

HANS FREUDENTHAL

KOENIG (KÖNIG), JOHANN SAMUEL (*b*. Büdingen, Germany, July 1712; *d*. Zuilenstein, near Amerongen, Netherlands, 21 August 1757)

Koenig was the son of the theologian, philologist, and mathematician Samuel Koenig (1671–1750), who after a very active existence spent his last twenty years as a professor of Oriental studies in his native city of Bern. Koenig received his first instruction in science from his father, whose enthusiasm he shared. After studying for a short time in Bern, in 1729 he attended the lectures of Frédéric de Treytorrens in Lausanne. In 1730 he left for Basel to study under Johann I Bernoulli and, beginning in 1733, under the latter's son Daniel as well—thus receiving the best mathematical training possible. During his stay of more than four years in Basel, Koenig, along with Clairaut and Maupertuis, studied the whole of mathematics, particularly Newton's *Principia mathematica*. Koenig was introduced to Leibniz' philosophical system by Jakob Hermann, who returned from St. Petersburg in 1731. He was so impressed by it that in 1735 he went to Marburg to further his knowledge of philosophy and law under the guidance of Leibniz' disciple Christian von Wolff.

Koenig's first mathematical publications appeared in 1735. In 1737 he returned to Bern to compete for the chair at Lausanne left vacant by the death of Treytorrens (the position went to Crousaz). Koenig then began to practice law in Bern and was so successful that he seriously intended to give up mathematics, which he had found something less than lucrative. First, however, he wanted to write on dynamics; two articles appeared in 1738. Before the start of the new

year Koenig was in Paris, where in March 1739 Maupertuis introduced him to the marquise du Châtelet, Voltaire's learned friend. During the following months Koenig instructed the marquise du Châtelet in mathematics and Leibnizian philosophy. He also went to Charenton with Voltaire and the marquise to visit Réaumur, who inspired Koenig to write his paper on the structure of honeycombs. On the basis of this work Koenig was named a corresponding member of the Paris Academy of Sciences. Following the break with the marquise—the result, according to René Taton, of a disagreement about money—Koenig remained in Paris for a year and a half and then settled in Bern. By this time, after repeated unsuccessful attempts, he had given up hope of obtaining a chair in Lausanne. Besides conducting his legal practice, he studied the works of Clairaut and Maupertuis, whose influence is evident in his book on the shape of the earth (1747, 1761).

In 1744 Koenig was exiled from Bern for ten years for having signed a political petition that was considered too liberal, although it was in fact very courteously written. Through the intervention of Albrecht von Haller, Koenig finally obtained a suitable position as professor of philosophy and mathematics at the University of Franeker, in the Netherlands, and had considerable success there. Under the patronage of Prince William IV of Orange he moved to The Hague in 1749 as privy councillor and librarian. He became a member of the Prussian Academy on Maupertuis's nomination.

While still in Franeker, Koenig wrote the draft of his important essay on the principle of least action, which was directed against Maupertuis. The controversy touched off by this work, which was published in March 1751, resulted in perhaps the ugliest of all the famous scientific disputes.[1] Its principal figures were Koenig, Maupertuis, Euler, Frederick II, and Voltaire; and, as is well known, it left an unseemly stain on Euler's otherwise untarnished escutcheon. The quarrel occupied Koenig's last years almost completely; moreover, he had been ill for several years before it started. Koenig emerged the moral victor from this affair, in which all the great scientists of Europe—except Maupertuis and Euler—were on his side. The later finding of Kabitz[2] testifies to Koenig's irreproachable character.

Koenig never married. A candid and amiable man, he was distinguished by erudition of unusual breadth even for his time. He was a member of the Paris Academy of Sciences, the Royal Prussian Academy, the Royal Society, and the Royal British Society of Sciences in Göttingen. The opinion is occasionally voiced that were it not for the controversy over the principle of least action, Koenig would be completely forgotten in the history of science. His formulation of the law (named for him) of the kinetic energy of the motion of a mass point system relative to its center of gravity[3] is sufficient in itself to refute this view. According to Charles Hutton, Koenig "had the character of being one of the best mathematicians of the age." It is most regrettable that Koenig never accomplished his favorite project, publication of the correspondence between Leibniz and Johann Bernoulli.

NOTES

1. See *Dictionary of Scientific Biography*, IV, 471.
2. Willy Kabitz, "Ueber eine in Gotha aufgefundene Abschrift des von S. Koenig in seinem Streite mit Maupertuis und der Akademie veröffentlichten, seiner Zeit für unecht erklärten Leibnizbriefes," in *Sitzungsberichte der K. Preussischen Akademie der Wissenschaften zu Berlin*, **2** (1913), 632–638.
3. The law states that the kinetic energy of a system of mass points is equal to the sum of the kinetic energy of the motion of the system relative to the center of gravity and of the kinetic energy of the total mass of the system considered as a whole, which moves as the center of gravity of the system; therefore

$$\Sigma m_i v_i^2 = M V^2 + \Sigma m_i v_i'^2.$$

See A. Masotti, "Sul teorema di Koenig," in *Atti dell' Accademia pontificia dei Nuovi Lincei*, **85** (1932), 37–42. Koenig's original formulation of the law can be found in "De universali principio aequilibrii et motus . . . .."

BIBLIOGRAPHY

I. ORIGINAL WORKS. Koenig's writings include *Animadversionem rhetoricarum specimen subitum quod cessante professoris rhetorices honore Academico d. 17. Nov. 1733 propon. Ant. Birrius respondente lectissimo juvene J. Sam. Koenigio, J. Sam. Bernate, philos. imprimisque mathesi sublimiori studioso* (Basel, 1733); "Epistola ad geometras," in *Nova acta eruditorum* (Aug. 1735), 369–373; "De nova quadam facili delineatu trajectoria, et de methodis, huc spectantibus, dissertatiuncula," *ibid.* (Sept. 1735), 400–411; "De centro inertiae atque gravitatis meditatiuncula prima," *ibid.* (Jan. 1738), 34–48; "Demonstratio brevis theorematis Cartesiani," *ibid.*, p. 33; "Lettre de Monsieur Koenig à Monsieur A. B., écrite de Paris à Berne le 29 novembre 1739 sur la construction des alvéoles des abeilles, avec quelques particularités littéraires," in *Journal helvétique* (Apr. 1740), 353–363; and *Figur der Erden bestimmt durch die Beobachtungen des Herrn von Maupertuis . . .* (Zurich, 1741; 2nd ed., 1761).

Subsequent works are *De optimis Wolfianae et Newtonianae philosophiae methodis earumque consensu* (Franeker, 1749; Zurich, 1752); the MS of the 2nd pt. of this history of philosophy must have been in existence at Koenig's death but appears to have been lost; "Mémoire sur la véritable raison du défaut de la règle de Cardan dans le cas irréducible des équations du troisième degré et de sa bonté dans les autres," in *Histoire de l'Académie Royale de Berlin* (1749), pp. 180–192, on which see M. Cantor, *Geschichte der Mathematik*, 2nd ed. (Leipzig, 1901), III, 599 ff.; "De universali principio aequilibrii et motus, in vi viva reperto, deque nexu inter vim vivam et actionem, utriusque minimo dissertatio," in *Nova acta eruditorum* (Mar. 1751), 125–135, 162–176; *Appel au publique du jugement de l'Académie royale de Berlin sur un fragment de lettre de Monsieur de Leibnitz cité par Monsieur Koenig* (Leiden, 1752); *Défense de l'Appel au publique* (Leiden, 1752); *Recueil d'écrits sur la question de la moindre action* (Leiden, 1752); *Maupertuisiana* (Hamburg, 1753), published anonymously (see *Mitteilungen der Naturforschenden Gesellschaft in Bern* [1850], 138); and *Élémens de géométrie contenant les six premiers livres d'Euclide mis dans un nouvel ordre et à la portée de la jeunesse sous les directions de M. le prof. Koenig et revus par M. A. Kuypers* (The Hague, 1758).

Miscellaneous mathematical works can be found in *Feriis Groningianis*. Correspondence with Haller was published by R. Wolf in *Mitteilungen der Naturforschenden Gesellschaft in Bern*, nos. 14, 20, 21, 23, 29, 34, and 44 (1843–1853). A portrait of Koenig by Robert Gardelle (1742) is in the possession of Dr. Emil Koenig, Reinach, Switzerland; it is reproduced in the works by E. Koenig and I. Szabó (see below). MSS and unpublished letters are scattered in the libraries of Basel, Bern, Franeker, The Hague, Leiden, Paris, and Zurich. Two unpublished MSS, "Demonstrationes novae nonnullarum propositionum principiorum philosophiae naturalis Isaaci Newtoni" and "De moribus gysatoriis," appear to have been lost.

II. SECONDARY LITERATURE. See *Frieslands Hoogeschool und das Rijksathenaem zu Franeker*, II, 487–491; J. H. Graf, *Geschichte der Mathematik und der Naturwissenschaften in Bernischen Landen*, no. 3, pt. 1 (Bern–Basel, 1889), pp. 23–62; E. Koenig, *400 Jahre Bernburgerfamilie Koenig* (Bern, 1968), pp. 31–35, and *Gestalten und Geschichten der Bernburger Koenig* (Bern, 1972), pp. 6–8; O. Spiess, *Leonhard Euler* (Frauenfeld–Leipzig, 1929), pp. 126 ff.; and R. Wolf, *Biographien zur Kulturgeschichte der Schweiz*, II (Zurich, 1858–1862), pp. 147–182.

On the principle of least action, see P. Brunet, *Étude historique sur le principe de la moindre action*, Actualités Scientifiques, no. 693 (Paris, 1938), with bibliography; *Leonhardi Euleri opera omnia*, J. O. Fleckenstein, ed., 2nd ser., V, intro. (Zurich, 1957), pp. vii–xlvi, including a bibliography by P. Brunet; and I. Szabó, "Prioritätsstreit um das Prinzip der kleinsten Aktion an der Berliner Akademie im XVIII. Jahrhundert," in *Humanismus und Technik*, **12**, no. 3 (Oct. 1968), 115–134.

E. A. FELLMANN

KOENIG, JULIUS (*b.* Györ, Hungary, 16 December 1849; *d.* Budapest, Hungary, 8 April 1914)

Koenig studied at Vienna and Heidelberg, where he

earned his Ph.D. in 1870. He qualified as a lecturer at Budapest in 1872 and became a full professor only two years later at the city's technical university. He remained in Hungary; and during his last years he was involved, as a senior civil servant in the Ministry of Education, with the improvement of training in mathematics and physics. He was also a secretary of the Royal Hungarian Academy of Sciences in Budapest.

Koenig's two years at Heidelberg (1868–1870) were of decisive importance for his scientific development. Helmholtz was still active there, and under his influence Koenig began working on the theory of the electrical stimulation of the nerves. But the mathematician Leo Königsberger, who was very well known at that time, soon persuaded Koenig to devote himself to mathematics; Koenig therefore wrote his dissertation on the theory of elliptic functions.

In Hungary, Koenig progressed very rapidly in his academic career. He was also productive in various fields of mathematics, chiefly analysis and algebra. Some of his works appeared simultaneously in German and Hungarian; others published only in Hungarian were naturally less influential. Among Koenig's writings is the prize essay for the Royal Hungarian Academy of Sciences, which was published in German in *Matematische Annalen* under the title "Theorie der partiellen Differentialgleichungen Ordnung mit 2 unabhängigen Veränderlichen." In it Koenig specified when the integration of a second-order differential equation can be reduced to the integration of a system of total differential equations, for which there already existed the integration methods devised by Jacobi and Clebsch.

Koenig's most important work is the voluminous *Einleitung in die allgemeine Theorie der algebraischen Grössen*, published in German and Hungarian in 1903. This book draws heavily on a fundamental study by Kronecker, *Grundzüge einer arithmetischen Theorie der algebraischen Grössen* (1892), although Koenig had had very little personal contact with Kronecker. In his work Kronecker had set forth the principles of the part of algebra later called the theory of polynomial ideals. Koenig developed Kronecker's results and presented many of his own results concerning discriminants of forms, elimination theory, and Diophantine problems. He also employed Kronecker's notation and added some of his own terms, but these did not gain general acceptance. The theory of polynomial ideals later proved to be a highly important topic in modern algebra and algebraic geometry. To be sure, many of Kronecker's and Koenig's contributions were simplified by later writers, notably Hilbert, Lasker, Macaulay, E. Noether, B. L. van der Waerden, and Gröbner; and their terminology was modified extensively. Hence, despite its great value, Koenig's book is now of only historical importance.

In the last eight years of his life Koenig took great interest in Cantor's set theory and the discussion that it provoked concerning the foundations of mathematics. The result of his investigations was the posthumous *Neue Grundlagen der Logik, Arithmetik und Mengenlehre* (1914) published by his son Dénes. The title originally planned was *Synthetische Logik;* and in it Koenig intended to reduce mathematics to a solidly established logic, hoping in this way to avoid the many difficulties generated by the antinomies of set theory. Dénes Koenig (*b.* 1884) also has become known in the literature of mathematics through his *Theorie der endlichen und unendlichen Graphen* (Leipzig, 1936).

BIBLIOGRAPHY

Koenig's writings include *Zur Theorie der Modulargleichungen der elliptischen Funktionen* (Heidelberg, 1870); "Theorie der partiellen Differentialgleichungen 2. Ordnung mit 2 unabhängigen Veränderlichen," in *Matematische Annalen*, **24** (1883), 465–536; *Einleitung in die allgemeine Theorie der algebraischen Grössen* (Leipzig, 1903); and *Neue Grundlagen der Logik, Arithmetik und Mengenlehre* (Leipzig, 1914), with a portrait of Koenig.

WERNER BURAU

KOENIGS, GABRIEL (*b.* Toulouse, France, 17 January 1858; *d.* Paris, France, 29 October 1931)

After achieving a brilliant scholarly record, first at Toulouse and then in Paris at the École Normale Supérieure, which he entered in 1879, Koenigs passed the examination for the *agrégation* in 1882 and in the same year defended his doctoral thesis, "Les propriétés infinitésimales de l'espace réglé." After a year as *agrégé répétiteur* at the École Normale he was appointed a deputy lecturer in mechanics at the Faculty of Sciences of Besançon (1883–1885) and then of mathematical analysis at the University of Toulouse. In 1886 he was named lecturer in mathematics at the École Normale and deputy lecturer at the Sorbonne, which post he held until 1895. In addition he taught analytical mechanics on a substitute basis at the Collège de France.

Appointed assistant professor (1895) and professor (1897) of physical and experimental mechanics at the Sorbonne, Koenigs henceforth devoted himself to the elaboration of a method of teaching mechanics based on integrating theoretical studies and experimental research with industrial applications. He created a laboratory of theoretical physical and experimental mechanics designed especially for the experimental study of various types of heat engines and for perfecting different testing procedures. This laboratory, which began operations in new quarters in 1914, played a very important role during World War I. Koenigs won several prizes from the Académie des Sciences and was elected to that organization, in the mechanics section, on 18 March 1918.

A disciple of Darboux, Koenigs directed his first investigations toward questions in infinitesimal geometry, especially, following Plücker and F. Klein, toward the study of the different configurations formed by straight lines: rules surfaces and straight-line congruences and complexes. In analysis he was one of the first to take an interest in iteration theory, conceived locally; and in analytic mechanics he applied Poincaré's theory of integral invariants to various problems and advanced the study of tautochrones.

His *Leçons de cinématique* (1895–1897) enjoyed considerable success. They were characterized by numerous original features, including a definite effort to apply recent progress in various branches of geometry to kinematics. This work also contains a thorough investigation of articulated systems, an area in which Koenigs made several distinctive contributions. He demonstrated, in particular, that every algebraic surface can be described by an articulated system, and he produced various devices for use in investigating gyrations. His interest in the study of mechanisms is also reflected in his important memoir on certain types of associated curves, called conjugates.

Starting about 1910, however, Koenigs, working in his laboratory of physical and experimental physics, increasingly concentrated on research in applied thermodynamics and on the development of more precise test methods. Despite his successes in these areas it is perhaps regrettable that this disciple of Darboux thus abandoned his initial approach, the originality of which appeared potentially more fruitful.

BIBLIOGRAPHY

I. ORIGINAL WORKS. Koenigs' books are *Sur les propriétés infinitésimales de l'espace réglé* (Paris, 1882), his dissertation; *Leçons de l'agrégation classique de mathématiques* (Paris, 1892); *La géométrie réglée et ses applications. Coordonnées, systèmes linéaires, propriétés infinitésimales du premier ordre* (Paris, 1895); *Leçons de cinématique . . .* (Paris, 1895); *Leçons de cinématique . . . Cinématique théorique* (Paris, 1897), with notes by G. Darboux and E. Cosserat; *Introduction à une théorie nouvelle des méca-nismes* (Paris, 1905); and *Mémoire sur les courbes conjuguées dans le mouvement relatif le plus général de deux corps solides* (Paris, 1910).

Koenigs published some 60 papers, most of which are listed in Poggendorff, IV, 778–779; V, 652–653; and VI, 1354; and in the Royal Society *Catalogue of Scientific Papers*, X, 429; and XVI, 376–377.

Koenigs analyzed the main points of his work in his *Notice sur les travaux scientifiques de Gabriel Koenigs* (Tours, 1897; new ed., Paris, 1910).

II. SECONDARY LITERATURE. Besides the bibliographies and his *Notice* (see above), Koenigs' life and work have been treated in only a few brief articles: A. Buhl, in *Enseignement mathématique*, **30** (1931), 286–287; L. de Launay, in *Comptes rendus hebdomadaires des séances de l'Académie des sciences*, **193** (1931), 755–756; M. d'Ocagne, in *Histoire abrégée des sciences mathématiques* (Paris, 1955), pp. 338–339; and P. Sergescu, in *Tableau du XXe siècle (1900–1933)*, II, *Les sciences* (Paris, 1933), pp. 67–68, 98, 117, 177.

RENÉ TATON

KOLOSOV, GURY VASILIEVICH (*b.* Ust, Novgorod guberniya, Russia, 25 August 1867; *d.* Leningrad, U.S.S.R., 7 November 1936)

Kolosov graduated from the Gymnasium in St. Petersburg with a gold medal in 1885 and in that year joined the faculty of physics and mathematics of St. Petersburg (now Leningrad) University. He graduated from the university in 1889 and remained there to prepare for a teaching career.

In 1893 Kolosov passed his master's examination and was named director of the mechanics laboratory of the university and teacher of theoretical mechanics at the St. Petersburg Institute of Communications Engineers. From 1902 to 1913 he worked at Yurev (now Tartu) University, as privatdocent and then as professor. In 1913 he returned to St. Petersburg, where he became head of the department of theoretical mechanics at the Electrotechnical Institute; in 1916 he also became head of the department of theoretical mechanics at the university. Kolosov worked in these two institutions until the end of his life. In 1931 he was elected a corresponding member of the Academy of Sciences of the U.S.S.R.

Kolosov's scientific work was devoted largely to two important areas of theoretical mechanics: the mechanics of solid bodies, with which he began his career; and the theory of elasticity, on which he worked almost exclusively from 1908.

Kolosov's first important achievement in the mechanics of solid bodies was his discovery of a new "integrated" case of motion for a top on a smooth surface, related to the turning of a solid body about a fixed point. This result was published by Kolosov in 1898 in "Ob odnom sluchae dvizhenia tyazhelogo tverdogo tela, . . ." ("On One Case of the Motion of a Heavy Solid Body Supported by a Point on a Smooth Surface"). His basic results in the mechanics of solid bodies are discussed in his master's dissertation, "O nekotorykh vidoizmeneniakh nachala Gamiltona . . ." ("On Certain Modifications of Hamilton's Principle in its Application to the Solution of Problems of Mechanics of Solid Bodies" [1903]).

Kolosov's main results in the theory of elasticity are contained in his classic work *Ob odnom prilozhenii teorii funktsy kompleksnogo peremennogo . . .* ("On One Application of the Theory of Functions of Complex Variables to the Plane Problem of the Mathematical Theory of Elasticity," 1909). Kolosov's most important achievement was his establishment of formulas expressing the components of the tensor of stress and of the vector of displacement through two functions of a complex variable, analytical in the area occupied by the elastic medium. In 1916 Kolosov's method was applied to heat stress in the plane problem of the theory of elasticity by his student N. I. Muskhelishvili. Specialists in the theory of elasticity still use Kolosov's formulas.

Many of Kolosov's more than sixty works in mechanics and mathematics were published in major German, English, French, and Italian scientific journals.

BIBLIOGRAPHY

I. ORIGINAL WORKS. Kolosov's most important works are "Ob odnom sluchae dvizhenia tyazhelogo tverdogo tela, opirayushchegosya ostriem na gladkuyu ploskost" ("On One Case of the Motion of a Heavy Solid Body Supported by a Point on a Smooth Surface"), in *Trudy Obshchestva lyubiteley estestvoznania,* Otd. fiz. nauk, **9** (1898), 11–12; *O nekotorykh vidoizmeneniakh nachala Gamiltona v primenenii k resheniyu voprosov mekhaniki tverdogo tela* ("On Certain Modifications of Hamilton's Principle in Its Application to the Solution of Problems of Mechanics of Solid Bodies"; St. Petersburg, 1903); *Ob odnom prilozhenii teorii funktsy kompleksnogo peremennogo k ploskoy zadache matematicheskoy teorii uprugosti* ("On One Application of the Theory of Functions of Complex Variables to the Plane Problem of the Mathematical Theory of Elasticity"; Yurev [Tartu], 1909); and *Primenenie kompleksnoy peremennoy k teorii uprugosti* ("Application of the Complex Variable to the Theory of Elasticity"; Moscow–Leningrad, 1935).

II. SECONDARY LITERATURE. See N. I. Muskhelishvili, "Gury Vasilievich Kolosov," in *Uspekhi matematicheskikh nauk,* no. 4 (1938), 279–281; and G. Ryago, "Gury Vasilievich Kolosov," in *Uchenye zapiski Tartuskogo gosudarstvennogo universiteta,* no. 37 (1955), 96–103.

A. T. GRIGORIAN

KÖNIGSBERGER, LEO (*b.* Posen, Germany [now Poznań, Poland], 15 October 1837; *d.* Heidelberg, Germany, 15 December 1921)

The son of a wealthy merchant, Königsberger began to study mathematics and physics at the University of Berlin in 1857. After graduating in 1860, he taught mathematics and physics to the Berlin cadet corps from 1861 to 1864. In the latter year his academic career commenced at the University of Greifswald, as an associate professor; in 1869 he became a full professor at Heidelberg. After teaching at the Technische Hochschule in Dresden (1875–1877) and at the University of Vienna (1877–1884), he returned in 1884 to Heidelberg, where he remained until his death. He retired in 1914.

Königsberger was one of the most famous mathematicians of his time, member of many academies, and universally respected. He contributed to several fields of mathematics, most notably to analysis and analytical mechanics.

Königsberger's mathematical work was early influenced by his teacher Weierstrass. In 1917 he published a historically important account of Weierstrass' first lecture on elliptic functions, which he had heard in 1857, during his first semester at Berlin. Königsberger also was extremely skillful in treating material from the Riemannian point of view, as can be seen from his textbooks on elliptic functions (1874) and hyperelliptic integrals (1878). In addition he worked intensively on the theory of differential equations. This subject, which grew out of function theory, is associated especially with Lazarus Fuchs, with whom Königsberger was friendly during his youth. Königsberger was the first to treat not merely one differential equation, but an entire system of such equations in complex variables.

In Heidelberg, Königsberger maintained close friendships with the chemist Bunsen and the physicists Kirchhoff and Helmholtz. These contacts undoubtedly provided the stimulation both for his series of works on the differential equations of analytical mechanics and his biography of Helmholtz (1902). The latter and the biographical *Festschrift* for C. G. J. Jacobi (1904) have proved to be his best-known works, despite his many other publications.

BIBLIOGRAPHY

Königsberger's writings include *Vorlesungen über elliptische Funktionen* (Leipzig, 1874); *Vorlesungen über die Theorie der hyperelliptischen Integrale* (Leipzig, 1878); *Lehrbuch der Theorie der Differentialgleichungen mit einer unabhängigen Veränderlichen* (Leipzig, 1889); *H. v. Helmholtz*, 2 vols. (Brunswick, 1902); *C. G. J. Jacobi, Festschrift zur 100. Wiederkehr seines Geburtstages* (Leipzig, 1904); "Weierstrass' erste Vorlesung aus der Theorie der elliptischen Funktionen," in *Jahresberichte der Deutschen Mathematikervereinigung*, **25** (1917), 393–424; and *Mein Leben* (Heidelberg, 1919).

WERNER BURAU

KORTEWEG, DIEDERIK JOHANNES (*b.* 's Hertogenbosch, Netherlands, 31 March 1848; *d.* Amsterdam, Netherlands, 10 May 1941)

Korteweg studied at the Polytechnical School of Delft, but before graduation as an engineer he turned to mathematics. After teaching in secondary schools at Tilburg and Breda, he entered the University of Amsterdam, where he received his doctorate in 1878. From 1881 until his retirement in 1918 he was professor of mathematics at the same university, where, with P. H. Schoute at Groningen and J. C. Kluyver at Leiden, he did much to raise mathematics in the Netherlands to the modern level.

The subject of Korteweg's dissertation was the velocity of wave propagation in elastic tubes. His sponsor was the physicist J. D. van der Waals, with whom Korteweg subsequently worked on several papers dealing with electricity, statistical mechanics, and thermodynamics. His main scientific work was thus in applied mathematics, including rational mechanics and hydrodynamics; but through his work on Huygens he also contributed greatly to the history of seventeenth-century mathematics. Korteweg established a criterion for stability of orbits of particles moving under a central force (1886), investigated so-called folding points on van der Waals's thermodynamic ψ-surface (1889), and discovered a type of stationary wave advancing in a rectangular canal given by $y = h \operatorname{cn}^2 (ax)$, the "cnodoil wave" (1895).

From 1911 to 1927 Korteweg edited the *Oeuvres* of Christiaan Huygens, especially volumes XI–XV. He was an editor of the *Revue semestrielle des publications mathématiques* (1892–1938) and of the *Nieuw archief voor wiskunde* (1897–1941).

BIBLIOGRAPHY

I. ORIGINAL WORKS. Most of Korteweg's papers appeared in *Verhandelingen* and *Mededelingen der K. nederland-* sche akademie van wetenschappen (Amsterdam) and in *Archives néerlandaises des sciences exactes et naturelles* between 1876 and 1907, the latter often publishing French translations of the Dutch papers appearing in the former. Other papers include "Über Stabilität periodischer ebener Bahnen," in *Sitzungsberichte der K. Akademie der Wissenschaften in Wien*, Math.-naturwiss. Kl., **93**, sec. 2 (1886), 995–1040; "Ueber Faltenpunkte," *ibid.*, **98** (1889), 1154–1191; *Het bloeitydperk der wiskundige wetenschappen in Nederland* (Amsterdam, 1894); and "On the Change of Form of Long Waves Advancing in a Rectangular Canal, and on a New Type of Stationary Waves," in *Philosophical Magazine*, 5th ser., **39** (1895), 422–443, written with G. de Vries.

II. SECONDARY LITERATURE. For biographies see H. J. E. Beth and W. van der Woude, "Levensbericht van D. J. Korteweg," in *Jaarboek der koninklyke nederlandsche akademie van wetenschappen 1945–1946* (Amsterdam, 1946), pp. 194–208; and L. E. J. Brouwer in *Euclides* (Groningen), **17** (1941), 266–267. Appreciations of his work are by H. A. Lorentz in *Algemeen Handelsblad* (Amsterdam), *Avondblad* (12 July 1918); and an unsigned article, *ibid.* (30 March 1928), p. 13, on the occasion of Korteweg's eightieth birthday.

D. J. STRUIK

KOTELNIKOV, ALEKSANDR PETROVICH (*b.* Kazan, Russia, 20 October 1865; *d.* Moscow, U.S.S.R., 6 March 1944)

Kotelnikov was the son of P. I. Kotelnikov, a colleague of Lobachevsky, and the only one to publicly praise Lobachevsky's discoveries in geometry during the latter's lifetime. In 1884, upon graduation from Kazan University, Kotelnikov taught mathematics at a Gymnasium in Kazan. Later he was accepted by the department of mechanics of Kazan University in order to prepare for the teaching profession. He began his teaching career at the university in 1893, and in 1896 he defended his master's dissertation, "Vintovoe ischislenie i nekotorie primenenia ego k geometrii i mekhanike" ("The Cross-Product Calculus and Certain of Its Applications in Geometry and Mechanics"). Kotelnikov's calculus is a generalization of the vector calculus, describing force moments in statics and torques in kinematics. In his many years of teaching theoretical mechanics, Kotelnikov was an advocate of vector methods.

In 1899 Kotelnikov defended his doctoral dissertation, "Proektivnaya teoria vektorov" ("The Projective Theory of Vectors"), for which he simultaneously received the doctorate in pure mathematics and the doctorate in applied mathematics. Kotelnikov's projective theory of vectors is a further generalization of the vector calculus to the non-Euclidean spaces of Lobachevsky and Riemann and the application of this calculus to mechanics in non-Euclidean spaces.

Kotelnikov served as professor and head of the department of pure mathematics at both Kiev (1899–1904) and Kazan (1904–1914). He headed the department of theoretical mechanics at Kiev Polytechnical Institute (1914–1924) and at the Bauman Technical College in Moscow (1924–1944).

Among his many works, special mention must be made of his paper "Printsip otnositelnosti i geometria Lobachevskogo" ("The Principle of Relativity and Lobachevsky's Geometry"), on the relationship between physics and geometry, and "Teoria vektorov i kompleksnie chisla" ("The Theory of Vectors and Complex Numbers"), in which generalizations of the vector calculus and questions of non-Euclidean mechanics are again examined.

His papers on the theory of quaternions and complex numbers in application to geometry and mechanics are of considerable significance.

Kotelnikov edited and annotated the complete works of both Zhukovsky and Lobachevsky.

In 1934 Kotelnikov was named an Honored Scientist and Technologist of the R.S.F.S.R. In 1943 he was awarded the State Prize of the U.S.S.R.

BIBLIOGRAPHY

I. ORIGINAL WORKS. Among Kotelnikov's papers are *Vintovoe ischislenie i nekotorie primenenia ego k geometrii i mekhanike* ("The Cross-Product Calculus and Certain of its Applications in Geometry and Mechanics"; Kazan, 1885); *Proektivnaya teoria vektorov* ("The Projective Theory of Vectors"; Kazan, 1899); *Vvedenie v teoreticheskuyu mekhaniku* ("Introduction to Theoretical Mechanics"; Moscow–Leningrad, 1925); "Printsip otnositelnosti i geometria Lobachevskogo" ("The Principle of Relativity and Lobachevsky's Geometry"), in *In Memoriam N. I. Lobatschevskii*, II (Kazan, 1927); and "Teoria vektorov i kompleksnie chisla" ("The Theory of Vectors and Complex Numbers"), in *Nekotorie primenenia geometrii Lobachevskogo k mekhanike i fizike* ("Certain Applications of Lobachevsky's Geometry to Mechanics and Physics"; Moscow–Leningrad, 1950).

II. SECONDARY LITERATURE. See A. T. Grigorian, *Ocherki istorii mekhaniki v Rossi* ("Essays on the History of Mechanics in Russia"; Moscow, 1961); and B. A. Rosenfeld, "Aleksandr Petrovich Kotelnikov," in *Istoriko-matematicheskie issledovania*, IX (Moscow, 1956).

A. T. GRIGORIAN

KOVALEVSKY, SONYA (or **Kovalevskaya, Sofya Vasilyevna**) (*b.* Moscow, Russia, 15 January 1850; *d.* Stockholm, Sweden, 10 February 1891)

Sonya Kovalevsky was the greatest woman mathematician prior to the twentieth century. She was the daughter of Vasily Korvin-Krukovsky, an artillery general, and Yelizaveta Shubert, both well-educated members of the Russian nobility. The general was said to have been a direct descendant of Mathias Korvin, king of Hungary; Soviet writers believe that Krukovsky's immediate background was Ukrainian and that his family coat of arms resembled the emblem of the Polish Korwin-Krukowskis.

In *Recollections of Childhood* (and the fictionalized version, *The Sisters Rajevsky*), Sonya Kovalevsky vividly described her early life: her education by a governess of English extraction; the life at Palabino (the Krukovsky country estate); the subsequent move to St. Petersburg; the family social circle, which included Dostoevsky; and the general's dissatisfaction with the "new" ideas of his daughters. The story ends with her fourteenth year. At that time the temporary wallpaper in one of the children's rooms at Palabino consisted of the pages of a text from her father's schooldays, namely, Ostrogradsky's lithographed lecture notes on differential and integral calculus. Study of that novel wall-covering provided Sonya with her introduction to the calculus. In 1867 she took a more rigorous course under the tutelage of Aleksandr N. Strannolyubsky, mathematics professor at the naval academy in St. Petersburg, who immediately recognized her great potential as a mathematician.

Sonya and her sister Anyuta were part of a young people's movement to promote the emancipation of women in Russia. A favorite method of escaping from bondage was to arrange a marriage of convenience which would make it possible to study at a foreign university. Thus, at age eighteen, Sonya contracted such a nominal marriage with Vladimir Kovalevsky, a young paleontologist, whose brother Aleksandr was already a renowned zoologist at the University of Odessa. In 1869 the couple went to Heidelberg, where Vladimir studied geology and Sonya took courses with Kirchhoff, Helmholtz, Koenigsberger, and du Bois-Reymond. In 1871 she left for Berlin, where she studied with Weierstrass, and Vladimir went to Jena to obtain his doctorate. As a woman, she could not be admitted to university lectures; consequently Weierstrass tutored her privately during the next four years. By 1874 she had completed three research papers on partial differential equations, Abelian integrals, and Saturn's rings. The first of these was a remarkable contribution, and all three qualified her for the doctorate *in absentia* from the University of Göttingen.

In spite of Kovalevsky's doctorate and strong letters of recommendation from Weierstrass, she was unable to obtain an academic position anywhere in Europe. Hence she returned to Russia where she was reunited with her husband. The couple's only child, a daughter, "Foufie," was born in 1878. When Vladimir's lectureship at Moscow University failed to materialize, he and Sonya worked at odd jobs, then engaged in business and real estate ventures. An unscrupulous company involved Vladimir in shady speculations that led to his disgrace and suicide in 1883. His widow turned to Weierstrass for assistance and, through the efforts of the Swedish analyst Gösta Mittag-Leffler, one of Weierstrass' most distinguished disciples, Sonya Kovalevsky was appointed to a lectureship in mathematics at the University of Stockholm. In 1889 Mittag-Leffler secured a life professorship for her.

During Kovalevsky's years at Stockholm she carried on her most important research and taught courses (in the spirit of Weierstrass) on the newest and most advanced topics in analysis. She completed research already begun on the subject of the propagation of light in a crystalline medium. Her memoir, *On the Rotation of a Solid Body About a Fixed Point* (1888), won the Prix Bordin of the French Academy of Sciences. The judges considered the paper so exceptional that they raised the prize from 3,000 to 5,000 francs. Her subsequent research on the same subject won the prize from the Swedish Academy of Sciences in 1889. At the end of that year she was elected to membership in the Russian Academy of Sciences. Less than two years later, at the height of her career, she died of influenza complicated by pneumonia.

In mathematics her name is mentioned most frequently in connection with the Cauchy-Kovalevsky theorem, which is basic in the theory of partial differential equations. Cauchy had examined a fundamental issue in connection with the existence of solutions, but Sonya Kovalevsky pointed to cases that neither he nor anyone else had considered. Thus she was able to give his results a more polished and general form. In short, Cauchy, and later Kovalevsky, sought necessary and sufficient conditions for the solution of a partial differential equation to exist and to be unique. In the case of an ordinary differential equation the general solution contains arbitrary constants and therefore yields an infinity of formulas (curves); in the general solution of a partial differential equation, arbitrary functions occur and the plethora of formulas (surfaces or hypersurfaces) is even greater than in the ordinary case. Hence additional data in the form of "initial" or "boundary" conditions are needed if a unique particular solution is required.

The simplest form of the Cauchy-Kovalevsky theorem states that any equation of the form

$$p = f(x, y, z, q)$$

where $p = \partial z/\partial x$, $q = \partial z/\partial y$, and the function f is analytic (has convergent power series development) in its arguments for values near (x_0, y_0, z_0, q_0), possesses one and only one solution $z(x, y)$ which is analytic near (x_0, y_0) and for which

$$z(x_0, y) = g(y)$$

where $g(y)$ is analytic at y_0 with

$$g(y_0) = z_0 \quad \text{and} \quad g'(y_0) = q_0$$

In the general theorem, the simple case illustrated is generalized to functions of more than two independent variables, to derivatives of order higher than the first, and to systems of equations.

To place Sonya Kovalevsky's second doctoral paper and some of her later research in a proper setting, one must examine analytic concepts developed gradually in the work of Legendre, Abel, Jacobi, and Weierstrass. It is a familiar fact of elementary calculus that the integral,

$$\int f(x, y)\, dx,$$

can be expressed in terms of elementary functions (algebraic, trigonometric, inverse trigonometric, exponential, logarithmic) if y^2 is a polynomial of degree 1 or 2 in x, and $f(x, y)$ is a rational function of x and y. If the degree of the polynomial for y^2 is greater than 2, elementary expression is not generally possible. If the degree is 3 or 4, the integral is described as *elliptic* because a special case of such an integral occurs in the problem of finding the length of an arc of an ellipse. If the degree is greater than 4, the integral is called *hyperelliptic*. Finally, one comes to the general type that includes the others as special cases. If y is an algebraic function of x, that is, if y is a root of $P(x, y) = 0$, where P is a polynomial in x and y, the above integral is described as *Abelian*, after Abel, who carried out the first important research with such integrals. Abel's brilliant inspiration also clarified and simplified the theory of elliptic integrals (just after Legendre had given some forty years to investigating their properties).

If the integral

$$u = \int_0^x \frac{dt}{\sqrt{1 - t^2}} = \sin^{-1} x$$

is "inverted," one obtains $x = \sin u$, which elementary trigonometry indicates to be easier to manipulate than its inverse, $u = \sin^{-1} x$. Therefore it occurred to Abel (and subsequently to Jacobi) that the inverses of elliptic integrals might have a simpler theory than that of the integrals themselves. The conjecture proved to be correct, for the inverses, namely the *elliptic functions*, lend themselves to a sort of higher trigonometry of doubly periodic functions. For example, while the period of sin x is 2π, the corresponding elliptic function, sn z, has two periods whose ratio is a complex number, a fact indicating that the theory of elliptic functions belongs to complex (rather than real) analysis. Inversion of Abelian integrals leads to *Abelian functions* which, in the first generalization beyond the elliptic functions, have two independent complex variables and four periods.

Abel died within a year of the research he started in that area, and there was left to Weierstrass and his pupils the stupendous task of developing the theory of general Abelian functions having k complex variables and $2k$ periods and of considering the implications for the inverses, the corresponding Abelian integrals. Kovalevsky's doctoral research contributed to that theory by showing how to express a certain species of Abelian integral in terms of the relatively simpler elliptic integrals.

Complex analysis and nonelementary integrals were also a feature of the Kovalevsky paper which won the Bordin Prize. In her paper she generalized work of Euler, Poisson, and Lagrange, who had considered two elementary cases of the rotation of a rigid body about a fixed point. Her predecessors had treated two symmetric forms of the top or the gyroscope, whereas she solved the problem for an asymmetric body. This case is an exceedingly difficult one and she was able to solve the differential equations of motion by the use of hyperelliptic integrals. Her solution was so general that no new case of rotatory motion about a fixed point has been researched to date.

In her study of the form of Saturn's rings, as in her other research, she had great predecessors—Laplace, in particular, whose work she generalized. Whereas, for example, he thought certain cross sections to be elliptical, she proved that they were merely egg-shaped ovals symmetric with respect to a single axis. Although Maxwell had proved that Saturn's rings could not possibly be continuous bodies—either solid or molten—and hence must be composed of a myriad of discrete particles, Kovalevsky considered the general problem of the stability of motion of liquid ring-shaped bodies; that is, the question of whether such bodies tend to revert to their primary motion after disturbance by external forces or whether deviation from that motion increases with time. Other researchers completed her task by establishing the instability of such motion.

Her concern for Saturn's rings caused the British algebraist Sylvester to write a sonnet (1886) in which he named her the "Muse of the Heavens." Later, Fritz Leffler, the mathematician's brother, stated in a poetic obituary,

> While Saturn's rings still shine,
> While mortals breathe,
> The world will ever remember your name.

She was remembered by the eminent Russian historian Maxim Kovalevsky (who was unrelated to her husband) who dedicated several works to her. She had met him when he came to lecture at Stockholm University in 1888 after he had been discharged from Moscow University for criticizing Russian constitutional law. It was believed that they were engaged to be married but that she hesitated because his new permanent position was in Paris, and joining him there would have meant sacrificing the life professorship for which she had worked so long and hard.

She was remembered, too, by her daughter who, at the age of seventy-two, was guest speaker when the centenary of her mother's birth was celebrated in the Soviet Union. After her mother's death, Foufie had returned to Russia to live at the estate of her godmother Julia Lermontov, a research chemist and agronomist, and a good friend from Sonya's Heidelberg days. Foufie studied medicine and translated major foreign literary works into Russian.

An unusual aspect of Sonya Kovalevsky's life was that, along with her scientific work, she attempted a simultaneous career in literature. The titles of some of her novels are indicative of their subject matter: *The University Lecturer*, *The Nihilist* (unfinished), *The Woman Nihilist*, and, finally, *A Story of the Riviera*. In 1887 she collaborated with her good friend and biographer, Mittag-Leffler's sister, Anne Charlotte Leffler-Edgren (later Duchess of Cajanello), in writing a drama, *The Struggle for Happiness*, which was favorably received when it was produced at the Korsh Theater in Moscow. She also wrote a critical commentary on George Eliot, whom she and her husband had visited on a holiday trip to England in 1869.

BIBLIOGRAPHY

I. ORIGINAL WORKS. Among Kovalevsky's papers are "Zur Theorie der partiellen Differential-gleichungen," in *Journal für die reine und angewandte Mathematik*, **80** (1875), 1–32; "Zusätze und Bemerkungen zu Laplaces Untersuchungen über die Gestalt der Saturnsringe," in *Astronomische Nachrichten*, **3** (1883), 37–48; "Über die Reduction einer bestimmten Klasse Abelscher Integrale dritten

Ranges auf elliptische Integrale," in *Acta Mathematica*, **4** (1884), 393–414; and "Sur le problème de la rotation d'un corps solide autour d'un point fixe," in *Acta Mathematica*, **12** (1889), 177–232.

II. SECONDARY LITERATURE. See E. T. Bell, *Men of Mathematics* (New York, 1937), 423–429; J. L. Geronimus, *Sofja Wasilyevna Kowalewskaja—Mathematische Berechnung der Kreiselbewegung* (Berlin, 1954); E. E. Kramer, *The Main Stream of Mathematics* (New York, 1951), 189–196, and *The Nature and Growth of Modern Mathematics* (New York, 1970), 547–549; A. C. Leffler-Edgren, duchessa di Cajanello, *Sonia Kovalevsky, Biography and Autobiography*, English trans., L. von Cossel (New York, 1895); O. Manville, "Sophie Kovalevsky," in *Mélanges scientifiques offerts à M. Luc Picart* (Bordeaux, 1938); G. Mittag-Leffler, "Sophie Kovalevsky, notice biographique," in *Acta Mathematica*, **16** (1893), 385–390; and P. Polubarinova-Kochina, *Sophia Vasilyevna Kovalevskaya, Her Life and Work*, English trans., P. Ludwick (Moscow, 1957).

EDNA E. KRAMER

KRAFT, JENS (*b.* Fredrikstad, Norway, 2 October 1720; *d.* Sorø, Denmark, 18 March 1765)

Kraft's mother, Severine Ehrensfryd Scolt, died when he was only two, and his father, Anders Kraft, a senior lieutenant in the Norwegian army, died when he was five years old. He was privately educated in Denmark at the manor of his uncle, Major Jens Kraft, and took the master's degree in Copenhagen in 1742. Kraft was married twice, to Bodil Cathrine Evertsen, who died in 1758, and to Sophie Magdalene Langhorn, who survived him.

A traveling grant enabled him to study philosophy with Christian Wolff in Germany, and mathematics and physics in France. Later he often expressed his admiration for Wolff, Daniel Bernouilli, Clairaut, and d'Alembert, whose works changed his general scientific outlook. On his return in 1746, he was admitted as a fellow of the Royal Danish Academy of Science and Letters. The following year he became the first professor of mathematics and philosophy in the reestablished academy for the nobility at Sorø, where he remained until his death. An eminent teacher, Kraft's lectures and private colloquia helped to diminish the prevailing influence of Cartesianism, and to bring Danish science back into the mainstream of the eighteenth century.

Kraft's best-known work is a textbook on theoretical and technical mechanics (1763–1764). The book, written in an easy and fluent style, contains a series of lectures based on Newtonian principles. Each lecture is provided with a supplement giving a more advanced mathematical exposition of the subject matter. In Denmark this work gave theoretical physics a firm basis as an academic subject, while its large section on machines stimulated the expansion of industry. The book was favorably received abroad and was translated into Latin and German.

Kraft's broad cultural interests were also reflected in a book on the life and manners of primitive peoples which is regarded as a pioneer work in social anthropology. It was written in the belief that a study of savage cultures would reveal the general origin of human institutions and beliefs.

His first paper, presented to the Royal Danish Academy of Science and Letters in 1746, was a clear exposition of the systems of Descartes and Newton. In opposition to his admired teacher, Christian Wolff, Kraft sided with Newton by showing that the Cartesian vortex theory was incompatible with accepted mechanical principles. Kraft did write several textbooks, nevertheless, on logic, ontology, cosmology, and psychology, inspired primarily by Wolffian philosophy.

Mathematics was one of Kraft's major areas of interest. Two early theses (written in 1741 and 1742) present no really new contributions to mathematics, but they show Kraft to have been a skilled and well-read mathematician. For example, the theses contain discussions of equations which are solved by means of Descartes's method of cuts between parabolas and circles. In 1748–1750 Kraft published two mathematical treatises. In the first he proved that if

$$y = \sum_{i=0}^{n} \beta_i x^i$$

has two equal roots α, then α is also a root in dy/dx. In the second paper Kraft discusses the following problem: Given an equation

$$A = \alpha x^r y^f + \beta x^m y^t + \gamma x^p y^l + \delta x^q y^h + \cdots$$

with rational exponents, y can be found as a series

$$y = Bx^n + Cx^{n+k} + Dx^{n+2k} + \cdots$$

with rational exponents. In his introduction, Kraft mentioned Newton, Leibniz, Maclaurin, Sterling, and 's Gravesande as examples of mathematicians who had treated this problem before, and Kraft's own method is a refinement of that of 's Gravesande.

Furthermore, in two small treatises from 1751–1754 Kraft argued that the concepts of infinitely large and infinitely small do not exist in an absolute sense in mathematics and physics, and that they must be conceived as relative quantities.

BIBLIOGRAPHY

I. ORIGINAL WORKS. Kraft's textbook on mechanics was published in two volumes. The first, *Forelæsninger over mekanik med hosføiede tillæg* (Sorø, 1763) was translated into Latin, *Mechanica Latine* (Wismar, 1773), and into German, *Mechanik, aus Lateinischen mit Zusätzen vermehrten Uebersetzung Tetens ins Deutsche übersetzt und hin und wieder verbessert von Joh. Chr. Aug. Steingrüber* (Dresden, 1787); the other appeared as *Forelæsninger over statik og hydrodynamik med Maskin-Væsenets theorier* (Sorø, 1764).

His book on ethnology, *Kort fortælning af de vilde folks fornemmeste indretninger, skikke og meninger, til oplysning af det menneskeliges oprindelse og fremgang i almindelighed* (Sorø, 1760), was translated into German, *Die Sitten der Wilden zur Aufklärung des Ursprungs und Aufnahme der Menschheit* (Copenhagen, 1766), and Dutch, *Verhandeling over de zeden en gewoontens der oude en hedendaagsche wilde volker* (Utrecht, 1779).

Kraft's paper on the systems of Descartes and Newton, "Betænkning over Neutons og Cartesii systemer med nye Anmærkninger over Lyset," was published in *Det Kiøbenhavnske Selskabs Skrifter*, **3** (1747), 213–296. Kraft's mathematical papers include *Explicationum in Is. Neutoni Arithmeticam universalem particulam primum* (Copenhagen, 1741); *Theoria generalis succincta construendi aequationes analyticas* (Copenhagen, 1742); "Anmerkning over de Liigheder, i hvilke af flere Værdier af den ubekiendte Størrelse er lige store" in *Det Kiøbenhavnske Selskabs Skrifter*, **5** (1750), 303–309; and "Metode at bevise, hvorledes man i alle Tilfælde kand bestemme den ene Ubekiendte ved en u-endelig Følge af Terminis, som gives ved den anden, i de algebraiske Liigheder, som indeholde to Ubekiendte," *ibid.*, 324–354.

His most important philosophical papers are *Systema mundi deductum ex principiis monadis, Dissertation, qui a remporté le prix proposé par l'Académie des sciences et belles lettres sur le système des monades avec les pièces, qui ont concouru* (Berlin, 1748); and "Afhandling om en Deel Contradictioner, som findes i det sædvanlige Systema over Materien og de sammensatte Ting," in *Det Kiøbenhavnske Selskabs Skrifter*, **6** (1754), 189–216.

II. SECONDARY LITERATURE. See *Dansk Biografisk Leksikon*. An account of Kraft's contribution to ethnology is given by Kaj Birket-Smith, "Jens Kraft, A Pioneer of Ethnology in Denmark" in *Folk, Dansk etnografisk tidsskrift*, **2** (Copenhagen, 1960), 5–12.

KURT MØLLER PEDERSEN

KRAMP, CHRÉTIEN *or* **CHRISTIAN** (*b.* Strasbourg, France, 8 July 1760, *d.* Strasbourg, 13 May 1826)

Kramp's father, Jean-Michel, was a teacher (*professeur régent*) at the Gymnasium in Strasbourg. Brought up speaking French and German, Kramp studied medicine and practiced in several Rhineland cities that were contained in the region annexed to France in 1795. Turning to education, Kramp taught mathematics, chemistry, and experimental physics at the École Centrale of the department of the Ruhr in Cologne. Following Napoleon's reorganization of the educational system, whereby the Écoles Centrales were replaced by lycées and faculties of law, letters, medicine, and science were created, Kramp, around 1809, became professor of mathematics and dean of the Faculty of Science of Strasbourg. A corresponding member of the Berlin Academy since 1812, he was elected a corresponding member of the geometry section of the Academy of Sciences of Paris at the end of 1817.

In 1783, the year the Montgolfier brothers made the first balloon ascension, Kramp published in Strasbourg an account of aerostatics in which he treated the subject historically, physically, and mathematically. He wrote a supplement to this work in 1786. In 1793 he published a study on crystallography (in collaboration with Bekkerhin) and, in Strasbourg, a memoir on double refraction.

Kramp published a medical work in Latin in 1786 and another, a treatise on fevers, in German in 1794. His critique of practical medicine appeared in Leipzig in 1795. Moreover, in 1812 he published a rather mediocre study on the application of algebraic analysis to the phenomenon of the circulation of the blood. He corresponded with Bessel on astronomy and made several calculations of eclipses and occultations in the years before 1820; his most important astronomical work, however, is the *Analyse des réfractions astronomiques et terrestres* (1798), which was very favorably received by the Institut de France. He wrote several elementary treatises in pure mathematics, as well as numerous memoirs, and the *Éléments d'arithmétique universelle* (1808). A disciple of the German philosopher and mathematician K. F. Hindenburg, Kramp also contributed to the various journals that Hindenburg edited. He may thus be considered to be one of the representatives of the combinatorial school, which played an important role in German mathematics.

In the *Analyse des réfractions astronomiques* Kramp attempted to solve the problem of refraction by the simplifying assumption that the elasticity of air is proportional to its density. He also presented a rather extensive numerical table of the transcendental function

$$\varphi(x) = \int_0^x e^{-t^2}\, dt,$$

which is so important in the calculus of probabilities, and which sometimes is called Kramp's transcendental. In this same work he considered products of which the factors are in arithmetic progression. He indicated the products by $a^{n|d}$; hence

$$a(a + d)(a + 2d) \cdots [a + (n - 1)\, d] = a^{n|d}.$$

He called these products "facultés analytiques," but he ultimately adopted the designation "factorials," proposed by his fellow countryman Arbogast.

Although Kramp was not aware of it, his ideas were in agreement with those of Stirling (1730) and especially those of Vandermond. The notation $n!$ for the product of the first n numbers, however, was his own. Like Bessel, Legendre, and Gauss, Kramp extended the notion of factorial to non-whole number arguments, and in 1812 he published a numerical table that he sent to Bessel. In his *Arithmétique universelle* Kramp developed a method that synthesizes the fundamental principles of the calculus of variations as stated by Arbogast with the basic procedures of combinatorial analysis. He thus strove to create an intimate union of differential calculus and ordinary algebra, as had Lagrange in his last works.

BIBLIOGRAPHY

I. Original Works. Kramp's writings include *Geschichte der Aërostatik, historisch, physisch und mathematisch ausgefuehrt*, 2 vols. (Strasbourg, 1783); *Anhang zu der Geschichte der Aërostatik* (Strasbourg, 1786); *De vi vitali Arteriarum diatribe. Addita nova de Febrium indole generali Conjectura* (Strasbourg, 1786); *Krystallographie des Mineralreichs* (Vienna, 1794), written with Bekkerhin; *Fieberlehre, nach mecanischen Grundsaetzen* (Heidelberg, 1794); *Kritik der praktischen Arzneykunde, mit Ruecksicht auf die Geschichte derselben und ihre neuern Lehrgebaeude* (Leipzig, 1795); *Analyse des réfractions astronomiques et terrestres* (Strasbourg–Leipzig, 1798); *Éléments d'arithmétique* (Cologne–Paris, 1801); *Éléments de géométrie* (Cologne, 1806); and *Éléments d'arithmétique universelle* (Cologne, 1808). He also translated into German Lancombe's *Art des Accouchements* (Mannheim, 1796) and contributed to Hindenburg's *Sammlung combinatorisch-analytischer Abhandlungen* and *Archiv der reinen und angewandte Mathematik* (1796); the *Nova Acta* of the Bayerische Akademie der Wissenschaften (1799); and Gergonne's *Annales des mathématiques pures et appliquées* (from 1810 to 1821).

II. Secondary Literature. Poggendorff, I, col. 1313 contains a partial list of Kramp's work. See also Gunther, in *Allgemeine deutsche Biographie*, XVII (Leipzig, 1883), 31–32; L. Louvet, in Hoefer, *Nouvelle Biographie générale*, XXVIII (Paris, 1861), 191–192; Niels-Nielsen, *Géomètres français sous la Révolution* (Copenhagen, 1929), pp. 128–134; and Royal Society of London, *Catalogue of Scientific Papers*, III (1869), 743–744, which lists 32 memoirs published after 1799.

Jean Itard

KRASOVSKY, THEODOSY NICOLAEVICH (*b.* Galich, Kostroma guberniya, Russia, 26 September 1878; *d.* Moscow, U.S.S.R., 1 October 1948)

Krasovsky graduated from the Moscow Geodetic Institute in 1900. Until 1903 he studied physics and mathematics at Moscow University and astronomy at the Pulkovo observatory. An instructor at the Geodetic Institute from 1902, he became professor in 1916 and chairman of higher geodesy in 1921. He was also a corresponding member of the Academy of Sciences of the U.S.S.R., an Honored Scientist and Technologist of the R.S.F.S.R., and in the mid-1930's, vice-president of the Baltic Geodetic Commission.

Krasovsky contributed considerably to the study of the geometry of the figure of the earth—the "spheroid." He devised an efficient method of adjusting primary triangulation, deduced the parameters of the earth's spheroid, and drew up scientific specifications for triangulation and subsequent geodetic work for the U.S.S.R. subcontinental territory. With M. S. Molodenski, Krasovsky was a pioneer in his emphasis on geodetic gravimetry rather than isostatic theory.

He reorganized the institutions of higher geodetic study in the U.S.S.R., and his pupils were future Soviet specialists. In his last years Krasovsky studied the earth's interior by combining geodetic and other geophysical as well as geological data. The figure of the earth now generally accepted differs only slightly from the "Krasovsky spheroid."

BIBLIOGRAPHY

I. Original Works. The most important of Krasovsky's more than 120 published works are in *Izbrannye sochinenia* ("Selected Works"), 4 vols. (Moscow, 1953–1956). Vol. I is devoted to the figure of the earth and to the adjustment of primary triangulation, and contains an essay on Krasovsky's life and works; vol. II to various branches of geodesy, field astronomy, and map projections; vol. III to geodetic control; and vol. IV to the geometry of the spheroid. A few of Krasovsky's papers and reports were published in German in *Comptes rendus de la Commission géodésique baltique*, sessions 5, 6, 7, 8, and 9 (Helsinki, 1931–1937).

II. Secondary Literature. The most comprehensive source is G. V. Bagratuni, *T. N. Krasovsky* (Moscow, 1959), which includes a bibliography. There is a short obituary by V. V. Danilov and M. S. Molodenski in *Izvestiya Akademii nauk SSSR*, Geograf.-geofiz. ser., **13**, no. 1 (1949), 3–4; and brief information on Krasovsky is in *Bolshaya sovetskaya entsiklopedia* ("Greater Soviet Encyclopedia"), XXIII (1953), 281, with portrait.

O. B. Sheynin

KRONECKER, LEOPOLD (*b*. Liegnitz, Germany [now Legnica, Poland], 7 December 1823; *d*. Berlin, Germany, 29 December 1891)

Kronecker's parents were Isidor Kronecker, a businessman, and his wife, Johanna Prausnitzer. They were wealthy and provided private tutoring at home for their son until he entered the Liegnitz Gymnasium. At the Gymnasium, Kronecker's mathematics teacher was E. E. Kummer, who early recognized the boy's ability and encouraged him to do independent research. He also received Evangelical religious instruction, although he was Jewish; he formally converted to Christianity in the last year of his life.

Kronecker matriculated at the University of Berlin in 1841. He attended lectures in mathematics given by Dirichlet and Steiner; in astronomy, by Encke; in meteorology by Dove; and in chemistry, by Mitscherlich. Like Gauss and Jacobi, he was interested in classical philology, and heard lectures on this subject. He also attended Schelling's philosophy lectures; he was later to make a thorough study of the works of Descartes, Spinoza, Leibniz, Kant, and Hegel, as well as those of Schopenhauer, whose ideas he rejected.

Kronecker spent the summer semester of 1843 at the University of Bonn, having been attracted there by Argelander's astronomy lectures. He also became acquainted with such democrats as Eduard Kinkel, and was active in founding a *Burschenschaft*, a student association. Kronecker's career might thus have been endangered by his political associations. The following autumn he went to Breslau (now Wrocław, Poland) because Kummer had been appointed professor there. He remained for two semesters, returning to Berlin in the winter semester of 1844-1845 to take the doctorate.

In his dissertation, "On Complex Units," submitted to the Faculty of Philosophy on 30 July 1845, Kronecker dealt with the particular complex units that appear in cyclotomy. He thereby arrived at results and methods closely related to the theory of "ideal numbers" that Kummer was to propound a short time later. (In 1893 Frobenius, in a memorial address on Kronecker, compared this dissertation to a work of "chemistry without the atomic hypothesis.") In evaluating the dissertation, Dirichlet said that in it Kronecker demonstrated "unusual penetration, great assiduity, and an exact knowledge of the present state of higher mathematics."

Kronecker took his oral examination on 14 August 1845. Encke questioned him on the application of the calculus of probabilities to observations and to the method of least squares; Dirichlet, on definite integrals, series, and differential equations; August Boeckh, on Greek; and Adolf Trendelenburg, on the history of legal philosophy. He was awarded the doctorate on 10 September.

Dirichlet, his professor and examiner, was to remain one of Kronecker's closest friends, as was Kummer, his first mathematics teacher. (On the occasion of the fiftieth anniversary of the latter's doctorate, in 1881, Kronecker said that Kummer had provided him with the "most essential portion" of his "intellectual life.") In the meantime, in Berlin, Kronecker was also becoming better acquainted with Eisenstein and with Jacobi, who had recently returned from Königsberg (now Kaliningrad, U.S.S.R.) for reasons of health. During the same period Dirichlet introduced him to Alexander von Humboldt and to the composer Felix Mendelssohn, who was both Dirichlet's brother-in-law and the cousin of Kummer's wife.

Family business then called Kronecker from Berlin. In its interest he was required to spend a few years managing an estate near Liegnitz, as well as to dissolve the banking business of an uncle. In 1848 he married the latter's daughter, his cousin Fanny Prausnitzer; they had six children. Having temporarily renounced an academic career, Kronecker continued to do mathematics as a recreation. He both carried on independent research and engaged in a lively mathematical correspondence with Kummer; he was not ambitious for fame, and was able to enjoy mathematics as a true amateur. By 1855, however, Kronecker's circumstances had changed enough to allow him to return to the academic life in Berlin as a financially independent private scholar.

This was a momentous time for mathematics in Germany. In 1855 Dirichlet left Berlin to go to Göttingen as successor to Gauss; Kummer succeeded Dirichlet in Berlin; and Carl Wilhelm Borchardt became editor of the *Journal für die reine und angewandte Mathematik*, following the death of its founder Crelle. In 1856 Weierstrass was called to Berlin and Kronecker and Kummer soon became friends with Borchardt and Weierstrass.

Although Kronecker had published some scientific articles before he returned to Berlin, he soon brought out a large number of mathematical tracts in rapid succession. Among other subjects he wrote on number theory (one of his earliest interests, instilled in him by Kummer), the theory of elliptical functions, algebra, and, particularly, on the interdependence of these mathematical disciplines. In 1860 Kummer, seconded by Borchardt and Weierstrass, nominated Kronecker to the Berlin Academy, of which he became full member on 23 January 1861.

In the winter semester of the following year Kronecker, at Kummer's suggestion, made use of a statutory right held by all members of the Academy to deliver a series of lectures at the University of Berlin. His principal topics were the theory of algebraic equations, the theory of numbers, the theory of determinants, and the theory of simple and multiple integrals. He attempted to simplify and refine existing theories and to present them from new perspectives. His teaching and his research were closely linked and, like Weierstrass, he was most concerned with ideas that were still in the process of development. Unlike Weierstrass—and for that matter, Kummer—Kronecker did not attract great numbers of students. Only a few of his auditors were able to follow the flights of his thought, and only a few persevered until the end of the semester. To those students who could understand him, however, Kronecker communicated something of his joy in mathematical discusssion. The new ideas that he offered his colleagues and students often received their final formulation in the course of such scholarly exchanges. He was allowed a considerable degree of autonomy in his teaching at Berlin, so much so that when in 1868 he was offered the chair at Göttingen that had been held successively by Gauss, Dirichlet, and Riemann, he refused it.

Kronecker was increasingly active and influential in the affairs of the Academy, particularly in recruiting the most important German and foreign mathematicians for it. Between 1863 and 1886 he personally helped fifteen mathematicians in becoming full, corresponding, or honorary members, or in obtaining a higher degree of membership. The names of these men constitute a formidable catalog; they were, in the order in which Kronecker assisted them, Heine, Riemann, Sylvester, Clebsch, E. Schering, H. J. Stephen Smith, Dedekind, Betti, Brioschi, Beltrami, C. J. Malmsten, Hermite, Fuchs, F. Carorati, and L. Cremona. The formal nominations that Kronecker made during this period are of great interest, not least because of their subjectivity Thus, to give one example, in his otherwise comprehensive evaluation of Dedekind's work (1880), Kronecker, who was then seeking to reduce all mathematical operations to those dealing in positive whole numbers, ignored Dedekind's *Stetigkeit und irrationale Zahlen* of 1872.

Kronecker's influence outside Germany also increased. He was a member of many learned societies, among them the Paris Academy, of which he was elected a corresponding member in 1868, and the Royal Society of London, of which he became a foreign associate in 1884. He established other contacts with foreign scientists in his numerous travels abroad and in extending to them the hospitality of his Berlin home. For this reason his advice was often solicited in regard to filling mathematical professorships both in Germany and elsewhere; his recommendations were probably as significant as those of his erstwhile friend Weierstrass.

Kronecker's relations with Weierstrass had been disintegrating since the middle of the 1870's. They continued to work together, however; in 1880, following Borchardt's death, Kronecker took over the editorship of the *Journal für die reine und angewandte Mathematik*, in which Weierstrass for a time assisted him. In 1883 Kummer retired from the chair of mathematics, and Kronecker was chosen to succeed him, thereby becoming the first person to hold the post at Berlin who had also earned the doctorate there. He was simultaneously named codirector of the mathematics seminar that Kummer and Weierstrass had founded in 1861. Kronecker continued to lecture, as he had done for twenty years, but now, as a member of the faculty, was able to assume all the rights thereof, including participation in the granting of degrees, the nomination of professors, and the qualifying examinations for university lecturers. He was enabled, too, to sponsor his own students for the doctorate; among his candidates were Adolf Kneser, Paul Stäckel, and Kurt Hensel, who was to edit his works and some of his lectures.

The cause of the growing estrangement between Kronecker and Weierstrass was the following. The very different temperaments of the two men must have played a large part in it, and their professional and scientific differences could only have reinforced their personal difficulties. Since they had long maintained the same circle of friends, their friends, too, became involved on both levels. A characteristic incident occurred at the new year of 1884-1885, when H. A. Schwarz, who was both Weierstrass' student and Kummer's son-in-law, sent Kronecker a greeting that included the phrase: "He who does not honor the Smaller [Kronecker], is not worthy of the Greater [Weierstrass]." Kronecker read this aliusion to physical size—he was a small man, and increasingly self-conscious with age—as a slur on his intellectual powers and broke with Schwarz completely. (Other scholars, among them Hofmann and Helmholtz, maintained lasting good relations with Kronecker by displaying more tact toward his special sensitivities.)

At any rate, personal quarrel became scholarly polemic. Weierstrass, for example, believed (perhaps rightly) that Kronecker's opposition to Cantor's views on "transfinite numbers" reflected opposition to his own work.

The basis of Kronecker's objection to Weierstrass' methods of analysis is revealed in his well-known dictum that "God Himself made the whole numbers— everything else is the work of men." Kronecker believed that all arithmetic could be based upon whole numbers, and whole numbers only; he further classified all mathematical disciplines except geometry and mechanics as arithmetical, a category that specifically included algebra and analysis. He never actually stated his intention of recasting analysis without irrational numbers, however, and it is possible that he did not take his radical notions altogether seriously himself. Weierstrass could not afford to regard Kronecker's demands as merely whimsical; in 1885 he claimed indignantly that for Kronecker it was an axiom that equations could exist only between whole numbers, while he, Weierstrass, granted irrational numbers the same validity as any other concepts.

Kronecker's remarks that arithmetic could put analysis on a more rigorous basis, and that those who came after him would recognize this and thereby demonstrate the falseness of so-called analysis, angered and embittered Weierstrass. He saw in these words an attempt by Kronecker not only to invalidate his whole life's work, but also to seduce the younger generation of mathematicians to an entirely new theory. The two men were further at odds over a Swedish mathematics prize contest and over the editing of Borchardt's works. By 1888, Weierstrass had confided to a few close friends that his break with Kronecker was complete, Kronecker, for his part, apparently did not realize how gravely his opinions and activities had wounded Weierstrass, since on several later occasions he still referred to himself as being his friend.

Weierstrass at this time even considered leaving Germany for Switzerland to avoid the constant conflict with Kronecker, but one consideration kept him in Berlin. Kronecker had remained on good terms with Kummer and with Kummer's successor, Fuchs; it was therefore likely that Kronecker would have considerable influence in the choice of Weierstrass' own successor. Weierstrass believed that all his work would be undone by a successor acceptable to Kronecker; for this reason he stayed where he was. In the meantime, new sources of antagonism arose, among them Weierstrass' scruple about the qualifications as a lecturer of Kronecker's protégé Hensel and Kronecker's stated objection to granting an assistant professorship to Weierstrass' pupil Johannes Knoblach. These new difficulties never reached a crucial point, however, since Kronecker's wife died on 23 August 1891, and he survived her by only a few months.

Kronecker's greatest mathematical achievements lie in his efforts to unify arithmetic, algebra, and analysis, and most particularly in his work on ellip-tical functions. His boundary formulas are particularly noteworthy in this regard, since they laid bare the deepest relationships between arithmetic and elliptical functions and provided the basis for Erich Hecke's later analytic-arithmetical investigations. Kronecker also introduced a number of formal refinements in algebra and in the theory of numbers, and many new theorems and concepts. Among the latter, special mention should be made of his theorem in regard to the cyclotomic theory, according to which all algebraic numbers with Abelian and Galois groups (over the rational number field) are rational combinations of roots of unity. His theorem on the convergence of infinite series is also significant.

The most important aspects of Kronecker's work were manifest as early as his dissertation of 1845. In his treatment of complex units, Kronecker sought to present a theory of units in an algebraic number field, and, indeed, to present a whole system of units as a group. Twenty-five years later he succeeded in constructing an implicit system of axioms to rule finite Abelian groups, although he did not at that time apply it explicitly to such groups. His work thus lay clearly in the line of development of modern algebra.

For this reason it might be useful to assess Kronecker's position with respect to other mathematicians. One criterion that suggests itself is the application of the algorithm, and while few mathematicians have held unalloyed opinions on this matter, two sharply differentiated positions may be distinguished. One group of mathematicians then—of whom Gauss, Dirichlet, and Dedekind are representative—found the algorithm to be most useful as a concept, rather than a symbol; their work centered on ideas, not calculations. The other group, which includes Leibniz, Euler, Jacobi, and—as Kneser demonstrated—Kronecker, stressed the technical use of the algorithm, employing it as a means to an end. Kronecker's goal was the perfection of the technique of calculation and he employed symbols to avoid the repetition of syllogisms and for clarity. He termed Gauss's contrasting method of presenting mathematics "dogmatic," although he retained a great respect for Gauss and for his work.

Kronecker's mathematics lacked a systematic theoretical basis, however, and for this reason Frobenius asserted that he was not the equal of the greatest mathematicians in the individual fields that he pursued. Thus, Frobenius considered Kronecker to be inferior to Cauchy and Jacobi in analysis; to Riemann and Weierstrass in function theory; to Kummer and Dirichlet in arithmetic; and to Abel and Galois in algebra.

Kronecker was nevertheless preeminent in uniting the separate mathematical disciplines. Moreover, in certain ways—his refusal to recognize an actual infinity, his insistence that a mathematical concept must be defined in a finite number of steps, and his opposition to the work of Cantor and Dedekind—his approach may be compared to that of intuitionists in the twentieth century. Kronecker's mathematics thus remains influential.

BIBLIOGRAPHY

I. ORIGINAL WORKS. Kronecker's writings, including collected editions, are listed in Poggendorff, I, 1321, 1579; III, 752–753; IV, 807–808; and VI, 1412. See also Ernst Schering, "Briefwechsel zwischen G. Lejeune Dirichlet und Leopold Kronecker," in various issues of *Nachrichten der Königlichen Gesellschaft der Wissenschaften zu Göttingen* beginning with that of 4 July 1885; Emil Lampe, "Schriften von L. Kronecker," in *Jahresbericht der Deutschen Mathematiker-vereinigung*, **2** (1893), 23–31; and "Brief Leopold Kroneckers an Ernst Eduard Kummer vom 9. September 1881," in *Abhandlungen der Geschichte der mathematischen Wissenschaften*, **29** (1910), 102–103. Additional material may be found in the archives of the Deutschen Akademie der Wissenschaften of Berlin and Humboldt University, Berlin.

Kronecker also edited the first vol. of Dirichlet, *Werke* (Berlin, 1889).

II. SECONDARY LITERATURE. On Kronecker and his work see Kurt-R. Biermann, "Vorschläge zur Wahl von Mathematikern in die Berliner Akademie," in *Abhandlungen der Deutschen Akademie der Wissenschaften zu Berlin*, Klasse für Mathematik, Physik und Technik, no. 3 (1960), 29–34; "Karl Weierstrass," in *Journal für die reine und angewandte Mathematik*, **223** (1966), 191–220; "Die Mathematik und ihre Dozenten an der Berliner Universität 1910–1920" (MS, Berlin, 1966); "Richard Dedekind im Urteil der Berliner Akademie," in *Forschungen und Fortschritte*, **40** (1966), 301–302, which contains a reprint of Kronecker's memorial address for Dedekind; Georg Frobenius, "Gedächtnisrede auf Leopold Kronecker," in *Abhandlungen der Königlich Preussischen Akademie der Wissenschaften zu Berlin* (1893); Lotte Kellner, "The Role of Amateurs in the Development of Mathematics," in *Scientia*, **60** (1966), 1–5 (see especially p. 4); Adolf Kneser, "Leopold Kronecker," in *Jahresbericht der Deutschen Mathematiker-vereinigung*, **33** (1925), 210–228; Emil Lampe, "Leopold Kronecker," in *Annalen der Physik und Chemie*, **45** (1892), 595–601; Heinrich Weber, "Leopold Kronecker," in *Jahresbericht der Deutschen Mathematiker-vereinigung*, **2** (1893), 5–23; and Hans Wussing, "Zur Entstehungsgeschichte der abstrakten Gruppentheorie," in '*NTM*,' *Schriftenreihe für Geschichte der Naturwissenschaften, Technik und Medizin*, **2**, no. 5 (1965), 1–16, esp. pp. 7–9.

KURT-R. BIERMANN

KRULL, WOLFGANG (*b*. Baden-Baden, Germany, 26 August 1899; *d*. Bonn, Federal Republic of Germany, 12 April 1971)

Krull was the son of Helmuth Krull, a dentist in Baden-Baden, and Adele Siefert Krull. After graduating from high school in 1919, he studied at the University of Freiburg and the University of Rostock. In 1920 and 1921 he studied at Göttingen, where he became acquainted with Felix Klein, whom he greatly admired. It was Emmy Noether, however, who awakened in Krull an enthusiasm for modern algebra, which at that time was making rapid advances. On his return to Freiburg in 1921, Krull earned his doctor's degree with a dissertation on the theory of elementary divisors.

On 1 October 1922 Krull became an instructor at Freiburg, and in 1926 he was appointed unsalaried associate professor. In 1928 he went to Erlangen as full professor. His early publications were about the theory of rings and the theory of algebraic extensions of fields. In 1925 he had proved a theorem concerning the decomposition of an abelian group of operators as the direct sum of indecomposable groups, the Krull-Schmidt theorem. In a paper published in 1928 Krull applied the fundamental ideas of the Galois theory, at first valid only for finite extensions, to infinite normal separable extensions. In this way the Galois group becomes a topological group with Krull topology (a linear topology), and the classical theorems of Galois theory carry over verbatim to the general case provided we replace the term "subgroup" by "closed subgroup." Later Krull again examined the topological groups he had introduced, especially the compact abelian groups with linear topology and countable bases. The same fundamental thought (introduction of a "natural" topological structure in algebraic systems) is to be found again in a paper published in 1955 with applications to the arithmetic of infinite algebraic number fields and the construction of a generalized multiplicative ideal theory. The theory of groups with subgroup topology, published in 1965, belongs to the same sphere of work.

The years Krull spent as full professor in Erlangen were the high point of his creative life. About thirty-five publications of fundamental importance for the development of commutative algebra and algebraic geometry date from this period. In 1921 Emmy Noether had recognized the importance of rings in which the maximal condition for ideals is satisfied, rings that are now termed Noetherian.

In 1928 Krull introduced the important concept of the Krull dimension of a commutative Noetherian ring. Krull's basic results on dimension (*e.g.*, Krull's principal ideal theorem) mark a turning point in the development of the general theory of Noetherian rings. Previously a Noetherian ring had been a kind of pale shadow of a polynomial ring, but after the publication of Krull's results (1928–1929) the way was open for the introduction of a surprising amount of interesting detail, as shown in the work of D. G. Northcott.

In 1932 Krull introduced the theory of additive valuations. The ideas of this theory are used in the theory of integrally closed rings and in algebraic geometry. Krull also defined rings that today are called Krull rings. The importance of Krull rings lies in the fact that the integral closure of a Noetherian integral domain is not necessarily a Noetherian ring, but it is always a Krull ring. In 1937 Krull proved the main part of the Krull-Akizuki theorem, and in 1938 the Krull-Amazuya lemma, a classical line of reasoning in algebra.

Let p be a proper prime ideal of a Noetherian ring R and put $S = R - p$; then we can form the ring $R_p \subset R$ of quotients of R with respect to S, and R_p has precisely one maximal prime ideal: R_p is a local ring. The name "local ring" has been given to these rings because they are used to study the local properties of algebraic varieties. The German name is *Stellenring*, and the algebraic study of local rings began with Krull's famous investigation of *Stellenringe* (1938). Let R be a Noetherian local ring with maximal ideal m; then $\cap_{n \geq 1} (m)^n = (0)$.

This is Krull's intersection theorem (1938), the basis of the Krull topology of the ring R in which R is a metric space. The Cauchy completion $\overline{R}$ of R is a Noetherian local ring and dim $\overline{R}$ = dim R (1938). Krull posed the problem of determining the structure of all complete local rings, which I. S. Cohen solved in 1946.

While at Erlangen, Krull became chairman of the Faculty of Science. In 1929 he married Gret Meyer; they had two daughters. In 1939 he accepted an appointment to the University of Bonn. During the war he was called up into the naval meteorological service. In 1946 he resumed his work in Bonn. From this time until his death over fifty further publications appeared. These were in part a continuation of his earlier studies, but they also dealt with other fields of mathematics: group theory, calculus of variations, differential equations, Hilbert spaces.

As a mathematician of high international standing he received many invitations and honors. In 1962 the University of Erlangen conferred on him the degree of honorary doctor; he was the only math-ematician given this honor. Krull had close professional and human contact with his many students. He directed thirty-five doctoral theses.

Krull described his attitude toward mathematics as that of an aesthete: "For the mathematician it is not merely a matter of finding theorems and proving them. He wants to arrange and group these theorems together in such a way that they appear not only as correct but also as imperative and self-evident. To my mind such an aspiration is an aesthetic one and not one based on theoretical cognition." Krull ascribed great importance to the mathematical imagination of the mathematician and said that it is the possession of this imagination that distinguishes the great scientist from gifted average people.

BIBLIOGRAPHY

I. Original Works. Important works include "Über verallgemeinerte endliche abelsche Gruppen," in *Mathematische Zeitschrift*, **23** (1925), 161–196; "Galois'sche Theorie der unendlichen algebraischen Erweiterungen," in *Mathematische Annalen*, **100** (1928), 687–698; "Primidealketten in allgemeinen Ringbereichen," in *Sitzungs berichte der Heidelberger Akademie der Wissenschaften, Mathematische-Naturwissenschaftliche Klasse* (1928); "Über einen Hauptsatz der allgemeinen Idealtheorie," ibid., (1929); "Über die ästhetische Betrachtungsweise in der Mathematik," in *Semesterberichte Erlangen*, **61** (1930), 207–220; "Allgemeine Bewertungstheorie," in *Journal für die reine und angewandte Mathematik*, **167** (1932), 160–196; "Galoissche Theorie der ganz abgeschlossenen Stellenringe," in *Semesterberichte Erlangen*, **67/68** (1937), 324–328; "Beiträge zur Arithmetik kommutativer Integritätsbereiche, III, Zum Dimensionsbegriff der Idealtheorie," in *Mathematische Zeitschrift*, **42** (1937), 745–766.

"Dimensionstheorie in Stellenringen," in *Journal für die reine und angewandte Mathematik*, **179** (1938), 204–226; "Allgemeine Modul-, Ring- und Idealtheorie," in *Enzyklopädie der Mathematischen Wissenschaften*, 2nd ed., I (Leipzig, 1939); "Beiträge zur Arithmetik kommutativer Integritätsbereiche, VI, Der allgemeine Diskriminantensatz: Unverzweigte Ringerweiterungen," in *Mathematische Zeitschrift*, **45** (1939), 1–19; "Über separable, insbesondere kompakte separable Gruppen," in *Journal für die reine und angewandte Mathematik*, **184** (1942), 19–48; "Jacobsonsche Ringe, Hilbertscher Nullstellensatz, Dimensionstheorie," in *Mathematische Zeitschrift*, **54** (1951), 354–387; "Jacobsonsche Radikal und Hilbertscher Nullstellensatz," in *Proceedings of the International Congress of Mathematicians, 1950*, II (Cambridge, Mass., 1952); "Charakterentopologie, Isomorphismentopologie, Bewertungstopologie," *Memorias de matematica del Instituto Jorge Juan* (Spain), no. 16 (1955); "Zur Theorie der Gruppen mit Untergruppentopologie," in *Abhandlungen aus dem Mathematischen Seminar Universität Hamburg*, **28** (1965), 50–97; *Idealtheorie* (New York, 1968).

II. Secondary Literature. H. J. Nastold, "Wolfgang Krull's Arbeiten zur kommutativen Algebra und ihre Bedeutung für die algebraische Geometrie," in *Jahresberichte der Deutschen Mathematiker-Vereinigung*, **82** (1980), 63–76; H. Schoeneborn, "In Memoriam Wolfgang Krull," *ibid.*, 51–62, and complete bibliography of Krull's works, *ibid.*, 77–80; D. G. Northcott, *Ideal Theory* (Cambridge, England, 1953).

Heinz Schoeneborn

KRYLOV, ALEKSEI NIKOLAEVICH (*b.* Visyaga, Simbirskoy province [now Ulyanovskaya oblast], Russia, 15 August 1863; *d.* Leningrad, U.S.S.R., 26 October 1945)

Krylov was born on the estate of his father, Nikolai Aleksandrovich Krylov, a former artillery officer. In 1878 he entered the Maritime High School in St. Petersburg. When he left in 1884 he was appointed to the compass unit of the Main Hydrographic Administration, where he began research on a theory of compass deviation, a problem to which he often returned. In 1888 Krylov joined the department of ship construction of the Petersburg Maritime Academy where he received a thorough mathematical grounding under the guidance of A. N. Korkin, a distinguished disciple of Chebyshev. In 1890 Krylov graduated first in his class from the Maritime Academy and at Korkin's suggestion remained there to teach mathematics. He taught various theoretical and engineering sciences for almost fifty years at this military-maritime institute, creating from among his students a large school of shipbuilders who were both engineers and scientists. From 1900 to 1908, he directed the experimental basin, where he engaged in extensive research and tested models of various vessels. Krylov's work covered an unusually wide spectrum of the problems of what Euler referred to as naval science: theories of buoyancy, stability, rolling and pitching, vibration, and performance, and compass theories. His investigations always led to a numerical answer. He proposed new and easier methods of calculating the structural elements of a ship, and his tables of seaworthiness quickly received worldwide acceptance. From 1908 to 1910 Krylov, who had attained the rank of general, served as chief inspector for shipbuilding and was a president of the Maritime Engineering Committee. His courage and integrity led to conflicts with officials of the Maritime Ministry and to his refusal to do further work for them.

In 1914, Moscow University awarded Krylov the degree of doctor of applied mathematics, *honoris causa*, and the Russian Academy of Sciences elected him a corresponding member. He was elected to full membership in 1916.

After the October Revolution, Krylov sided with the Soviet government. During this period he continued to be both active and productive. From 1927 to 1932 he was director of the Physics and Mathematics Institute of the Soviet Academy of Sciences. He also played an important role in the organization, in 1929, of the division of engineering sciences of the Soviet Academy. The title of honored scientist and engineer of the Russian Soviet Federated Socialist Republic was conferred upon Krylov in 1939, and in 1943 he was awarded the state prize (for his work in compass theory) and the title of hero of socialist labor.

While using mathematics and mechanics to work out his theory of ships, Krylov simultaneously improved the methods of both disciplines, especially that in the theory of vibrations and that of approximate calculations. In a paper on forced vibrations of fixed-section pivots (1905), he presented an original development of Fourier's method for solving boundary value problems, pointing out its applicability to a series of important questions: for example, the theory of steam-driven machine indicators, the measurement of gas pressure in the conduit of an instrument, and the twisting vibrations of a roller with a flywheel on its end. Closely related to this group of problems was his ingenious and practical method for increasing the speed of convergence in Fourier and related series (1912). He also derived a new method for solving the secular equation that serves to determine the frequency of small vibrations in mechanical systems (1931). This method is simpler than those of Lagrange, Laplace, Jacobi, and Leverrier. In addition, Krylov perfected several methods for the approximate solution of ordinary differential equations (1917).

In his mathematical education and his general view of mathematics, Krylov belonged to the Petersburg school of Chebyshev. Most representatives of this school, using concrete problems as their point of departure, developed primarily in a purely theoretical direction. Krylov, however, proceeded from theoretical foundations to the effective solution of practical engineering problems.

Krylov's practical interests were combined with a deep understanding of the ideas and methods of classical mathematics and mechanics of the seventeenth, eighteenth, and nineteenth centuries; and in the works of Newton, Euler, and Gauss he found forgotten methods that were applicable to the solution of contemporary problems.

BIBLIOGRAPHY

I. ORIGINAL WORKS. Krylov's works are collected in *Sobranie trudov* ("Complete Works"), 11 vols. (Moscow–Leningrad, 1936–1951). His original development of Fourier's method appears in the article "Über die erzwungenen Schwingungen von gleichförmigen elastischen Stähen," in *Mathematische Annalen,* **61** (1905), 211–234; further work on Fourier and related series is found in *O nekotorykh differentsialnykh uravneniakh matematicheskoy fiziki, imeyushchikh prilozhenie v tekhnicheskikh voprosakh* ("On Several Differential Equations of Mathematical Physics Which Have Application in Engineering Problems"; St. Petersburg, 1912). For his work on the secular equation see "O chislennom reshenii uravnenia, kotorym v tekhnicheskikh voprosakh opredelaitsia chastoty malykh kolebanii materialnykh system" ("On the Numerical Solution of Equation by Which are Determined in Technical Problems the Frequencies of Small Vibrations of Material Systems"), in *Izvestiya Akademii nauk S.S.S.R.,* Otd. mat. nauk (1931), 491–539; see also *ibid.* (1933), 1–44.

Among his numerous works in the history of science, his Russian translation of Newton's *Principia* (*Matematicheskie nachala naturalnoy philosophii;* St. Petersburg, 1915) is especially noteworthy for its lucidity and for the depth of its scientific commentary.

II. SECONDARY LITERATURE. A list of Krylov's works appears in N. A. Kryzhanovskaya, *Akademik A. N. Krylov, bibliografichesky ukazatel* ("Academician A. N. Krylov, Bibliographical Guide"; Leningrad, 1952). For a study of Krylov's life, see S. Y. Shtraykh, *Aleksei Nikolaevich Krylov, ego zhizn i deyatelnost* ("Aleksei Nikolaevich Krylov, His Life and Work"; Moscow Leningrad, 1950).

A. T. GRIGORIAN

KRYLOV, NIKOLAI MITROFANOVICH (*b.* St. Petersburg, Russia, 29 November 1879; *d.* Moscow, U.S.S.R., 11 May 1955)

N. M. Krylov graduated from the St. Petersburg Institute of Mines in 1902. From 1912 to 1917 he was a professor there, and then from 1917 to 1922 he was a professor at Crimea University. In 1922 he was chosen a member of the Academy of Sciences of the Ukrainian S.S.R., and was appointed chairman of the mathematical physics department. In 1928 Krylov was elected an associate member of the Academy of Sciences of the U.S.S.R.; a year later he became a member. The rank of honored scientist of the Ukrainian S.S.R. was conferred on him in 1939.

Krylov's works relate mainly to problems of the theory of interpolation, of approximate integration of differential equations (applicable in mathematical physics), and of nonlinear mechanics. In his study on approximate integration, Krylov obtained extremely effective formulas for the evaluation of error in a field in which, prior to this work, one was limited either to proofs of existence or, at best, to proofs of the convergence of the method of approximation. Using the proof of Ritz's method of convergence, Krylov was the first to study—with the aid of the theory of infinite-order determinants—the general case of an arbitrary quadratic form standing under the variable integral sign. By using Ritz's method itself, he investigated the creation of more general methods which would be applicable to both the proof of the existence of a solution and the actual construction of the solution.

In 1932 Krylov began a study of actual problems of nonlinear oscillatory processes; in this work he succeeded in laying the foundation of nonlinear mechanics.

Krylov's work received wide application in many fields of science and technology. He published some 200 papers in mathematical analysis and mathematical physics.

BIBLIOGRAPHY

I. ORIGINAL WORKS. A compilation is N. M. Krylov, *Izbrannye trudy* ("Selected Works"), 3 vols. (Kiev, 1961).

II. SECONDARY LITERATURE. N. N. Bogolyubov, "Nikolai Mitrofanovich Krylov (k 70-letiyu so dnya rozhdenia)" ("Nikolai Mitrofanovich Krylov" [on his Seventieth Birthday]") in *Uspekhi matematicheskikh nauk,* **5,** no. 1 (1950); and O. V. Isakova, *Nikolai Mitrofanovich Krylov* (Moscow, 1945), includes material for bibliographical works of Soviet scientists.

A. T. GRIGORIAN

KUMMER, ERNST EDUARD (*b.* Sorau, Germany [now Zary, Poland], 29 January 1810; *d.* Berlin, Germany, 14 May 1893)

After the early death in 1813 of Kummer's father, the physician Carl Gotthelf Kummer, Ernst and his older brother Karl were brought up by their mother, the former Friederike Sophie Rothe. Following private instruction Kummer entered the Gymnasium in Sorau in 1819 and the University of Halle in 1828. He soon gave up his original study, Protestant theology, under the influence of the mathematics professor Heinrich Ferdinand Scherk and applied himself to mathematics, which he considered a kind of "preparatory science" for philosophy. (Kummer maintained a strong bent for philosophy throughout his life.) In 1831 he received a prize for his essay on the question posed by Scherk: "De cosinuum et sinuum potestatibus secundum cosinus et sinus arcuum multiplicium evolvendis."

In the same year Kummer passed the examination for Gymnasium teaching and on 10 September 1831 was granted a doctorate for his prize essay. After a year of probation at the Gymnasium in Sorau he taught from 1832 until 1842 at the Gymnasium in Liegnitz (now Legnica, Poland), mainly mathematics and physics. His students during this period included Leopold Kronecker and Ferdinand Joachimsthal, both of whom became interested in mathematics through Kummer's encouragement and stimulation. Kummer inspired his students to carry out independent scientific work, and his outstanding teaching talent soon became apparent. Later, together with his research work, it established the basis of his fame. His period of Gymnasium teaching coincided with his creative period in function theory, which began with the above-mentioned prize work. Its most important fruit was the paper on the hypergeometric series.[1] While doing his military service Kummer sent this paper to Jacobi. This led to his scientific connection with the latter and with Dirichlet, as well as to a corresponding membership, through Dirichlet's proposal, in the Berlin Academy of Sciences in 1839. After Kummer had thus earned a name for himself in the mathematical world, Jacobi sought to obtain a university professorship for him, in which endeavor he was supported by Alexander von Humboldt.

In 1840 Kummer married Ottilie Mendelssohn, a cousin of Dirichlet's wife. On the recommendation of Dirichlet and Jacobi, he was appointed full professor at the University of Breslau (now Wrocław, Poland) in 1842. In this position, which he held until 1855, he further developed his teaching abilities and was responsible for all mathematical lectures, beginning with the elementary introduction. During this period an honorary doctorate was bestowed on Ferdinand Gotthold Eisenstein; it had been proposed by Jacobi (probably on Humboldt's suggestion) and was carried out by Kummer despite considerable opposition. The second period of Kummer's research began about the time of his move to Breslau; it was dominated especially by number theory and lasted approximately twenty years. Not long after the death of his first wife in 1848, Kummer married Bertha Cauer.

When Dirichlet left Berlin in 1855 to succeed Gauss at Göttingen, he proposed Kummer as first choice for his Berlin professorship and Kummer was appointed. Kummer arranged for his former student Joachimsthal to become his successor at Breslau and hindered the chances of success for Weierstrass' application for the Breslau position, for he wanted the latter to be at the University of Berlin. This plan succeeded; Weierstrass was called to Berlin in 1856 as assistant professor. When Kronecker, with whom Kummer carried on an exchange of scientific views, also moved to Berlin in 1855, that city began to experience a new flowering of mathematics.

In 1861 Germany's first seminar in pure mathematics was established at Berlin on the recommendation of Kummer and Weierstrass; it soon attracted gifted young mathematicians from throughout the world, including many graduate students. It is permissible to suppose that in founding the seminar Kummer was guided by his experiences in Halle as a student in Scherk's Mathematischer Verein. Kummer's Berlin lectures, always carefully prepared, covered analytic geometry, mechanics, the theory of surfaces, and number theory. The clarity and vividness of his presentation brought him great numbers of students— as many as 250 were counted at his lectures. While Weierstrass and Kronecker offered the most recent results of their research in their lectures, Kummer in his restricted himself, after instituting the seminar, to laying firm foundations. In the seminar, on the other hand, he discussed his own research in order to encourage the participants to undertake independent investigations.

Kummer succeeded Dirichlet as mathematics teacher at the Kriegsschule. What would have been for most a heavy burden was a pleasure for Kummer, who had a marked inclination to every form of teaching activity. He did not withdraw from this additional post until 1874. From 1863 to 1878 he was perpetual secretary of the physics-mathematics section of the Berlin Academy, of which—on Dirichlet's recommendation —he had been a full member since 1855. He was also dean (1857–1858 and 1865–1866) and rector (1868–1869) of the University of Berlin. Kummer did not require leisure for creative achievements but was able to regenerate his powers through additional work.

In his third period, devoted to geometry, Kummer applied himself with unbroken productivity to ray systems and also considered ballistic problems. He retired at his own request in 1883 and was succeeded by Lazarus Fuchs, who had received his doctorate under him in 1858. Kummer spent the last years of his life in quiet retirement; his second wife and nine children survived him.

Kummer was first *Gutachter* for thirty-nine dissertations at Berlin. Of his doctoral students, seventeen later became university teachers, several of them famous mathematicians: Paul du Bois-Reymond, Paul Gordan, Paul Bachmann, H. A. Schwarz (his son-in-law), Georg Cantor, and Arthur Schoenflies. Kummer was also second *Gutachter* for thirty dissertations at Berlin. In addition, he was first referee when Alfred Clebsch, E. B. Christoffel, and L. Fuchs qualified for lectureships; and he acted as second referee at four other qualifying examinations. Kummer's popularity as a professor was based not only on the clarity of his lectures but on his charm and sense of humor as well. Moreover, he was concerned for the well-being of his students and willingly aided them when material difficulties arose; hence their devotion sometimes approached enthusiasm.

On Kummer's nomination Kronecker became a member of the Berlin Academy and Louis Poinsot, George Salmon, and Ludwig von Seidel became corresponding members. He himself became a correspondent of the Paris Academy of Sciences in 1860 and a foreign associate in 1868. This Academy had already awarded him its Grand Prix des Sciences Mathématiques in 1857 for his "Theorie der idealen Primfaktoren." Of his other memberships in scientific societies, that in the Royal Society as foreign member (1863) should be mentioned.

Kummer's official records reflect his characteristic strict objectivity, hardheaded straightforwardness, and conservative attitude. Thus it seems in keeping that during the revolutionary events of 1848, in which almost every important German mathematician except Gauss took an active role, Kummer was in the right wing of the movement, while Jacobi, for example, belonged to the progressive left. Kummer advocated a constitutional monarchy, not a republic. When, on the other hand, Jacobi, with his penchant for slight overstatement, declared that the glory of science consists in its having no use, Kummer agreed. He too considered the goal of mathematical research as the enrichment of knowledge without regard to applications; he believed that mathematics could attain the highest development only if it were pursued as an end in itself, independent of the external reality of nature. It is in this context that his rejection of multidimensional geometries should be mentioned.

Kummer's greatness and his limits lay in a certain self-restraint, manifested—among other ways—in his never publishing a textbook, but only articles and lectures. Weierstrass was led to state that, to some extent in his arithmetical period and more fully later, Kummer no longer concerned himself with

> ... what was happening in mathematics. If you say to him, Euclidean geometry is based on an unproved axiom, he grants you this; but proceeding from this

insight, the question now is phrased: How then does geometry look without this axiom? That goes against his nature; the efforts directed toward this question and the consequent general considerations, which free themselves from the empirically given or the presupposed, are to him idle speculations or simply a monstrosity.[2]

To be sure, the time at which this criticism was made must be considered: after Kummer, Kronecker, and Weierstrass had worked for twenty years in friendly, harmonious agreement and close scientific contact, an estrangement between Weierstrass and Kronecker took place in the mid-1870's which led to an almost complete break. Kummer's continuing friendship with Kronecker was not without its repercussions on Weierstrass' attitude toward Kummer. If, therefore, Weierstrass' evaluation of Kummer is to be taken with a grain of salt, it is nevertheless essentially correct.

Kummer's sudden decision to retire was another example of his inflexible principles. On 23 February 1882 he surprised the faculty by declaring that he had noticed a weakening of his memory and of the requisite ability to develop his thoughts freely in logical, coherent, and abstract arguments. On these grounds he requested retirement. No one else had detected such impairments, but Kummer could not be dissuaded and compelled the faculty to arrange for a successor.

Gauss and Dirichlet exerted the most lasting influence on Kummer. Each of Kummer's three creative periods began with a paper directly concerning Gauss, and his reverence for Dirichlet was movingly expressed in a commemorative speech on 5 July 1860 to the Berlin Academy.[3] Although he never attended a lecture by Dirichlet, he considered the latter to have been his real teacher. Kummer in turn had the strongest influence on Kronecker, who thanked him in a letter of 9 September 1881 for "my mathematical, indeed altogether the most essential portion of my intellectual life."

Today, Kummer's name is associated primarily with three achievements, one from each of his creative periods. From the function-theory period date his investigations, surpassing those of Gauss, of hypergeometric series, in which, in particular, he was the first to compute the substitutions of the monodromic groups of these series. The arithmetical period witnessed the introduction of "ideal numbers" in an attempt to demonstrate through multiplicative treatment the so-called great theorem of Fermat. After Dirichlet had pointed out to Kummer that the unambiguous prime factorization into number fields did not seem to have general validity, and after he had convinced himself of this fact, between 1845 and 1847, he formulated his theory of ideal prime factors.[4] It permitted unambiguous decomposition into general number fields and with its help Kummer was able to demonstrate Fermat's theorem in a number of cases.[5] It is again characteristic that Kummer elaborated his theory only to the extent required by those problems which interested him—the proof of Fermat's theorem and of the general law of reciprocity. Kummer's works were developed in the investigations of Richard Dedekind and Kronecker, thus contributing significantly to the arithmetization of mathematics.

The third result dates from Kummer's geometric period, in which he devoted himself principally to the theory of general ray systems, following Sir William Rowan Hamilton but treating them purely algebraically: the discovery of the fourth-order surface, named for Kummer, with sixteen isolated conical double points and sixteen singular tangent planes.[6] The number of other concepts connected with Kummer's name indicates that he was one of the creative pioneers of nineteenth-century mathematics.

NOTES

1. "Über die hypergeometrische Reihe . . .," in *Journal für die reine und angewandte Mathematik*, **15** (1836), 39–83, 127–172.
2. Gösta Mittag-Leffler, "Une page de la vie de Weierstrass," in *Comptes rendus du 2ᵉ Congrès international des mathématiciens* (Paris, 1902), pp. 131–153, see pp. 148–149, letter to Sonya Kovalevsky, 27 Aug. 1883.
3. "Gedächtnisrede auf G. P. L. Dirichlet," in *Abhandlungen der K. Preussischen Akademie der Wissenschaften* (1860), 1–36.
4. See "Über die Zerlegung der aus Wurzeln der Einheit gebildeten complexen zahlen in ihre Primfactoren," in *Journal für die reine und angewandte Mathematik*, **35** (1847), 327–367.
5. "Beweis des Fermatschen Satzes der Unmöglichkeit von $x^\lambda - y^\lambda = z^\lambda$ für eine unendliche Anzahl Primzahlen λ," in *Monatsberichte der K. Preussischen Akademie der Wissenschaften* (1847), 132–141, 305–319.
6. "Über die Flächen vierten Grades, auf welchen Schaaren von Kegelschnitten liegen," *ibid.* (1863), 324–338; "Über die Flächen vierten Grades mit sechzehn singulären Punkten," *ibid.* (1864), 246–260; "Über die Strahlensysteme, deren Brennflächen Flächen vierten Grades mit sechzehn singulären Punkten sind," *ibid.*, 495–499.

BIBLIOGRAPHY

I. ORIGINAL WORKS. Kummer published no books, nor has an edition of his works been published. His major writings appeared in *Journal für die reine und angewandte Mathematik*, **12–100** (1834–1886) and in *Monatsberichte der Königlichen Preussischen Akademie der Wissenschaften zu Berlin* (1846–1880).

Bibliographies of his writings may be found in Poggendorff, I, 1329–1330; III, 757; IV, 817; the Royal Society *Catalogue of Scientific Papers*, III, 770–772; VIII, 134–135; X, 475; XVI, 510; *Jahresbericht der Deutschen Mathematiker-vereinigung*, **3** (1894), 21–28; and Adolf Harnack, *Geschichte der Königlich Preussischen Akademie der Wis-senschaften zu Berlin*, III (Berlin, 1900), 160–161.

Some of his correspondence appears in "Briefe Ernst Eduard Kummers an seine Mutter und an Leopold Kronecker," in Kurt Hensel, *Festschrift* ...(see below), 39–103.

MS material is in the archives of the Deutsche Akademie der Wissenschaften zu Berlin (D.D.R.) and of Humboldt University, Berlin (D.D.R.), and in the Deutsches Zentralarchiv, Merseburg (D.D.R.).

II. SECONDARY LITERATURE. For a bibliography of secondary literature, see Poggendorff, VIIa Suppl., 343–344. See also the following, listed chronologically: O. N.-H., "Eduard Kummer," in *Münchener allgemeine Zeitung*, no. 139 (20 May 1893); Emil Lampe, "Nachruf für Ernst Eduard Kummer," in *Jahresbericht der Deutschen Mathemátiker-vereinigung*, **3** (1894), 13–21; Leo Koenigsberger, *Carl Gustav Jacob Jacobi* (Leipzig, 1904); Wilhelm Ahrens, *Briefwechsel zwischen C. G. J. Jacobi und M. H. Jacobi* (Leipzig, 1907); Kurt Hensel, *Festschrift zur Feier des 100. Geburtstages Eduard Kummers* (Leipzig–Berlin, 1910), 1–37; Wilhelm Lorey, *Das Studium der Mathematik an den deutschen Universitäten seit Anfang des 19. Jahrhunderts* (Leipzig–Berlin, 1916); Leo Koenigsberger, *Mein Leben* (Heidelberg, 1919), 21, 24, 25, 27, 28, 31, 53, 114; Felix Klein, *Vorlesungen über die Entwicklung der Mathematik im 19. Jahrhundert*, I (Berlin, 1926), 167, 172, 199, 269, 282, 321–322; Kurt-R. Biermann, "Zur Geschichte der Ehrenpromotion Gotthold Eisensteins," in *Forschungen und Fortschritte*, **32** (1958), 332–335; Kurt-R. Biermann, "Über die Förderung deutscher Mathematiker durch Alexander von Humboldt," in *Alexander von Humboldt. Gedenkschrift zur 100. Wiederkehr seines Todestages* (Berlin, 1959), pp. 83–159; "J. P. G. Lejeune Dirichlet," in *Abhandlungen der Deutschen Akademie der Wissenschaften zu Berlin*, Kl. für Math., Phys. und Tech. (1959), no. 2; "Vorschläge zur Wahl von Mathematikern in die Berliner Akademie," *ibid.* (1960), no. 3; and "Die Mathematik und ihre Dozenten an der Berliner Universität 1810–1920" (Berlin, 1966), MS; and Hans Wussing, *Die Genesis des abstrakten Gruppenbegriffes* (Berlin, 1969).

Information on Kummer is also contained in Weierstrass' letters and in the secondary literature on him and on Leopold Kronecker.

KURT-R. BIERMANN

KURATOWSKI, KAZIMIERZ (*b*. Warsaw, Poland, 2 February 1896; *d*. Warsaw, 18 June 1980)

Kuratowski's father was a well-known Warsaw lawyer. After completing his secondary education in Poland, Kuratowski enrolled as an engineering student at the University of Glasgow in 1913. He was spending his summer vacation of 1914 at home when war broke out, so he had to remain in Poland. In 1915 he began to study mathematics at the University of Warsaw, which had reopened after almost half a century of inactivity. He was a student of Stefan Mazurkiewicz and Zygmunt Janiszewski in the Seminar on Topology (initiated in 1916), and of the philosopher and logician Jan Łukasiewicz. Kuratowski graduated from the university in 1919. He obtained his doctorate in 1921 under the supervision of Wacław Sierpiński, with a dissertation on fundamental questions in set theory that contributed to international recognition of the embryonic Polish school of mathematics.

In 1927 Kuratowski was named to the chair of mathematics at Lwów Technical University. In 1933 he became professor at Warsaw University, where he was in charge of a wide range of academic and administrative functions inside and outside of Poland. He was secretary of the Mathematical Commission of the Council of Exact and Natural Sciences, which formulated the organizational plan of the Polish school of mathematics from 1936 to 1939. The outbreak of the war and the dramatic events of the following years did not put an end to mathematical education, which the scientific elite carried out through the clandestine university network. Kuratowski was active in the restructuring of mathematics in Poland after the liberation in February 1945.

Kuratowski is prominent in the history of mathematics in Poland as a result of his original contributions and his intense activity in mathematical education. A member of the editorial board of *Fundamenta mathematicae* from 1928, Kuratowski replaced Sierpiński as its editor in chief (1952) and held the post until his death. He was one of the founders and editor of the series Monografie Matematyczne (1932), which published the works of well-known Polish mathematicians. Kuratowski was vice president of the Polish Academy of Sciences and founded and directed its Institute of Mathematics. He was also vice president of the International Mathematical Union and a foreign member of the Academy of Sciences of the U.S.S.R., of the Royal Society of Edinburgh, of the Accademia Nazionale dei Lincei, and of the academies of Palermo, Hungary, Austria, the German Democratic Republic, and Argentina.

Kuratowski's mathematical activity focused on the properties and applications of topological spaces. His first contribution to general topology was the axiomatization of the closure operator (1922). He used Boolean algebra to characterize the topology of an abstract space independently of the notion of points. Subsequent research showed that, together with Felix Hausdorff's definition of a topological space in terms of neighborhoods, the closure operator yielded more fertile results than the axiomatic theories based on Maurice Fréchet's convergence (1906)

and Frigyes Riesz's points of accumulation (1907).

Another field that interested Kuratowski was compactness, which, along with the metrization of topological spaces, was a pillar of mathematics in the 1920's. Prior to the appearance of the pioneering work of Pavel Aleksandrov and Pavel Urysohn (1923), many workers in this field used the properties of Émile Borel and Henri Lebesgue, of Bernard Bolzano and Karl Weierstrass, and of Georg Cantor, with little discretion. Kuratowski and Sierpiński were the first to publish a comprehensive study of the Borel-Lebesgue property (1921). In this context they made a remarkable presentation of Lindelöf spaces. Kuratowski and his colleagues in the Seminar of Mathematics at Warsaw made important contributions in the field of metric spaces, the spaces of greatest interest in that period. The first volume of his *Topologie* (1933) was the first complete work on metric spaces to appear in several decades.

In the theory of connectedness, the efforts of Bronisław Knaster and Kuratowski to organize the ideas of contemporary mathematicians culminated in an important contribution (1921) that revealed the conditions for connectedness of a subspace and the union of a family of subspaces of a topological space. However, the most remarkable feature of this work was the ingenious construction of a set known as the Knaster-Kuratowski fan, a subspace of the plane, obtained from the Cantor set by the category method, that has a central point that, if removed, causes the fan to become completely disconnected. The appearance of the Knaster-Kuratowski fan and its singular characteristics gave a new impulse to the research in connectedness and dimension.

The topology of the continuum was one of the original areas of activity of the Polish mathematicians. Kuratowski, who made significant contributions in this field, dealt with the problem of the indecomposable continuum and the common frontier. He showed that such a frontier is itself an indecomposable continuum or the union of two indecomposable continua (1924). Knaster proved the second of these propositions (1925). The implicit use of minimal principles in the study of irreducible continua and the need for a theory to deduce a method to eliminate the transfinite ordinals from the topological demonstrations led Kuratowski to formulate the Kuratowski-Zorn lemma, one of the fundamental notions in set theory. Before Max Zorn formulated this lemma (1935), Kuratowski used the axiom of choice to establish a minimal principle in a paper that proposed to generalize certain results of Janiszewski (1910) and L. E. J. Brouwer (1911) with regard to an irreducible continuum containing two given points (1922). The appearance of such a general method represented a historic moment of reaction to the generalized and even artificial use of the well-ordered sets and the transfinites of Cantor. From this time on, it became customary to use the transfinites only when it was absolutely necessary. A detailed account of Kuratowski's impact in this area is in Kuratowski and Andrzej Mostowski's *Set Theory* (1968).

Another concern of the Polish school of mathematics was measure theory. Are there nonmeasurable sets in the theory of a completely additive measure? The study of this question led to the Banach-Tarski paradox (1929). Stefan Banach and Kuratowski (1929) answered in the affirmative, provided the continuum hypothesis is assumed. In his general formulation of the problem, Banach raised questions about the cardinality of a set on which a measure was desired (1930). Stimulated by Kuratowski, his student Stanisław Ulam provided the solution in the same year. This was a beautiful example of scientific collaboration and understanding, and of the ability to organize and encourage creative activity at its height.

Even though at first the theory of dimension was considered to be a part of point-set topology, the situation changed radically after the publication of the work of Aleksandrov (1926), in which the dimension of a metric space was characterized in terms of the dimension of its polyhedra. The work of Kuratowski in this field reveals his talent and his ability to adapt to new theories. Extending the principal results of Aleksandrov, Kuratowski (1933) devised a method to characterize the dimension of a metric space by means of barycentric mapping into the nerve of an arbitrary finite cover. The generality of this method permitted the extension of various spaces to normal spaces. In addition to the generalization of the theorem of Georg Nöbeling and Lev S. Pontriagin, Kuratowski, working alone or with Karl Menger and Edward Otto, among others, derived many additional results in the theory of dimension.

Mention also should be made of the theory of projective sets and analytic sets, in which Kuratowski extended the results in Euclidean spaces to Polish spaces (complete and separable); the theory of graphs, in which he obtained a rather difficult characterization of planar graphs; and the structure and classification of linear spaces from the point of view of topological range or type of dimension.

BIBLIOGRAPHY

I. ORIGINAL WORKS. Most of Kuratowski's papers were written in French and appeared mainly in *Fundamenta mathematicae*. They include "Le théorème de Borel-Lebesgue dans la théorie des ensembles abstraits," in *Fundamenta mathematicae*, **2** (1921), 172–178, with Wacław Sierpiński; "Sur les ensembles connexes," *ibid.*, 206–255, with B. Knaster; "Une méthode d'élimination des nombres transfinis des raisonnements mathématiques," *ibid.*, **3** (1922), 76–108; "Sur l'opération Ã de l'analysis situs," *ibid.*, 182–199; "Sur les coupures irréductibles du plan," *ibid.*, **6** (1924), 130–145; "Sur une généralisation du problème de la mesure," *ibid.*, **14** (1929), 127–131, with Stefan Banach; and "Sur un théorème fondamental concernant le nerf d'un système d'ensembles," *ibid.*, **20** (1933), 191–196. His books include *Topology*, 2 vols., I translated by J. Jaworski and II translated by A. Krikor (New York, 1966–1968), which also appeared in French, Russian, and Polish; and *Set Theory* (Amsterdam and New York, 1968; 2nd. rev. ed., 1976), with Andrzej Mostowski. See also his autobiography, "Zapsiki do autobiografii," in *Kwartalnik historii nauk i techniki*, **24**, no. 2 (1979), 243–289; and *A Half Century of Polish Mathematics: Remembrances and Reflections*, Andrzej Krikor, trans. (Oxford and New York, 1980).

II. SECONDARY LITERATURE. P. S. Aleksandrov, "In Memory of C. Kuratowski," A. Lofthouse, trans., in *Russian Mathematical Surveys*, **36** (1981), 215–216; J. Krasinkiewicz, "A Note on the Work and Life of Kazimierz Kuratowski," in *Journal of Graph Theory*, **5** (1981), 221–223; and Mary Grace Kusawa, *Modern Mathematics: The Genesis of a School in Poland* (New Haven, 1968).

LUIS CARLOS ARBOLEDA

KÜRSCHÁK, JÓZSEF (*b.* Buda, Hungary, 14 March 1864; *d.* Budapest, Hungary, 26 March 1933)

Kürschák's father, András Kürschák, an artisan, died when his son was six; the boy was very carefully brought up by his mother, the former Jozefa Teller. Kürschák's mathematical talent appeared in secondary school, after which he attended the Technical University in Budapest (1881–1886), which, although a technical school, also trained teachers of mathematics and physics. After graduating Kürschák taught for two years at Rozsnyó, Slovakia. In 1888 he moved to Budapest, where he worked toward the Ph.D., which he received in 1890. The following year he was appointed to teach at the Technical University, where he served successively as lecturer, assistant professor, and professor (1900) until his death. In 1897 he was elected a corresponding, and in 1914 an ordinary, member of the Hungarian Academy of Sciences.

Kürschák's mathematical interests were wide, and

he had the ability to deal with various kinds of problems. His first paper (1887) concerned the extremal properties of polygons inscribed in and circumscribed about a circle and proved the existence of the extremum. Another paper (1902) showed, in connection with Hilbert's *Grundlagen der Geometrie*, the sufficiency of the ruler and of a fixed distance for all discrete constructions. Meanwhile, in extending a result of Julius Vályi's, Kürschák had turned to the investigation of the differential equations of the calculus of variations (1889, 1894, 1896), proved their invariance under contact (Legendre) transformations (1903), and gave the necessary and sufficient conditions —thereby generalizing a result of A. Hirsch's—for second-order differential expressions to provide the equation belonging to the variation of a multiple integral (1905). These investigations also furthered his interest in linear algebra, aroused by Eugen von Hunyady, an early exponent of algebraic geometry in Hungary, and led to a series of papers on determinants and matrices.

Kürschák's main achievement, however, is the founding of the theory of valuations (1912). Inspired by the algebraic studies of Julius König and by the fundamental work of E. Steinitz on abstract fields, as well as by K. Hensel's theory of *p*-adic numbers, Kürschák succeeded in generalizing the concept of absolute value by employing a "valuation," which made possible the introduction of such notions as convergence, fundamental sequence, distance function, and limits into the theory of abstract fields. He proved that any field with a valuation on it can be extended by the adjunction of new elements to a "perfect" (i.e., closed and dense in itself) field which is at the same time algebraically closed. Kürschák's valuation and his method were later developed, mainly by Alexander Ostrowski, into a consistent and highly important arithmetical theory of fields.

Above all, Kürschák was a versatile and thought-provoking teacher. One of the main organizers of mathematical competitions, he contributed greatly to the selection and education of many brilliant students and certainly had a role in the fact that—to use the words of S. Ulam—"Budapest, in the period of the two decades around the First World War, proved to be an exceptionally fertile breeding ground for scientific talent" (*Bulletin of the American Mathematical Society*, **64**, no. 3, pt. 2 [1958], 1). Among Kürschák's pupils were mathematicians and physicists of the first rank, the most brilliant being John von Neumann.

BIBLIOGRAPHY

I. Original Works. Kürschák's longer works include "Propriétés générales des corps et des variétés algébriques," in *Encyclopédie des sciences mathématiques pures et appliquées*, I, pt. 2 (Paris–Leipzig, 1910), 233–385, French version of C. Landsberg's German article, written with J. Hadamard; *Analizis és analitikus geometria* (Budapest, 1920); and *Matematikai versenytételek* (Szeged, 1929), trans. into English by Elvira Rapaport as *Hungarian Problem Book*, 2 vols. (New York, 1963).

Articles are "Ueber dem Kreise ein- und umgeschriebene Vielecke," in *Mathematische Annalen*, **30** (1887), 578–581; "Über die partiellen Differentialgleichungen zweiter Ordnung bei der Variation der doppelter Integrale," in *Mathematische und naturwissenschaftliche Berichte aus Ungarn*, **7** (1889), 263–275; "Ueber die partielle Differentialgleichung des Problems $\delta \iint V(p, q)\, dx\, dy = 0$," in *Mathematische Annalen*, **44** (1894), 9–16; "Über eine Classe der partiellen Differentialgleichungen zweiter Ordnung," in *Mathematische und naturwissenschaftliche Berichte aus Ungarn*, **14** (1896), 285–318; "Das Streckenabtragen," in *Mathematische Annalen*, **55** (1902), 597–598; "Ueber die Transformation der partiellen Differentialgleichungen der Variationsrechnung," *ibid.*, **56** (1903), 155–164; "Über symmetrische Matrices," *ibid.*, **58** (1904), 380–384; "Über eine characteristische Eigenschaft der Differentialgleichungen der Variationsrechnung," *ibid.*, **60** (1905), 157–165; "Die Existenzbedingungen des verallgemeinerten kinetischen Potentials," *ibid.*, **62** (1906), 148–155; "Über Limesbildung und allgemeine Körpertheorie," in *Journal für die reine und angewandte Mathematik*, **142** (1913), 211–253, presented at the International Congress of Mathematicians (1912); "Ein Irreduzibilitätssatz in der Theorie der symmetrischen Matrizen," in *Mathematische Zeitschrift*, **9** (1921), 191–195; "On Matrices Connected With Sylvester's Dialytic Eliminant," in *Transactions of the Royal Society of South Africa*, **11** (1924), 257–260; and "Die Irreduzibilität einer Determinante der analytischen Geometrie," in *Acta mathematica Szeged*, **6** (1932–1933), 21–26.

II. Secondary Literature. See G. Rados, "Kürschák József emlékezete," in *Magyar tudományos akadémia Elhunyt tagjai fölött tartott emlékbeszédek*, **22**, no. 7 (1934), 1–18; L. Stachó, "Kürschák József," in *Müszaki Nagyjaink*, III (Budapest, 1967), 241–282, with complete bibliography; T. Stachó, "Kürschák József 1864–1933," in *Matematikai és physikai lapok*, **43** (1936), 1–13; and S. Ulam, "John von Neumann, 1903–1957," in *Bulletin of the American Mathematical Society*, **64**, no. 3, pt. 2 (1958), 1–49.

L. VEKERDI

KUSHYĀR IBN LABBĀN IBN BĀSHAHRĪ, ABU-'L-ḤASAN, AL-JĪLĪ (*fl. ca.* 1000)

Little is known about Kushyār's life. The word "al-Jīlī" added to his name refers to Jīlān, a region of northern Iran south of the Caspian Sea.

The earliest Arabic biographer to write about Kushyār is al-Bayhaqī (*d.* 1065), who states that

Kushyār lived in Baghdad and died about A.H. 350 (A.D. 961). Later biographers copy al-Bayhaqī and add several attributes to Kushyār's name, including the title "al-kiya," which seems to mean "master." But ʿAlī ibn Aḥmad al-Nasawī, an arithmetician who flourished after 1029, is said to have been a student of Kushyār's. This makes 961 too early; and accordingly, Schoy, Suter, and Brockelmann state that Kushyār must have flourished between 971 and 1029. It may be pointed out, however, that Ibn al-Nadīm does not mention Kushyār. Ibn al-Nadīm completed the main bulk of his *Fihrist* about 987 but continued to make additions to it until about 995. It would be rather strange if *al-kiya* Kushyār, the prolific writer, had lived in the same city at the same time and remained unnoticed by Ibn al-Nadīm. In his study of Kushyār's *zījes*, Kennedy points out that most of them were probably written after 1000. Accordingly, until further evidence appears, it will be safe to state only that Kushyār ibn Labbān flourished around A.D. 1000.

The works attributed to Kushyār have survived, but of these only three have received scholarly attention, two *zījes* and an arithmetic. The two *zījes* are *al-Jāmiʿ*, "The Comprehensive," and *al-Bāligh*, "The Far-reaching." Each is in four sections: introductory notes, tables, explanations, and proofs. Of the *al-Bāligh* only the first two sections are extant in the Berlin manuscript. In his "Survey of Islamic Astronomical Tables," E. S. Kennedy refers to the doubts whether Kushyār actually wrote two distinct *zījes* and gives the impression that *al-Bāligh* is an abbreviated copy of *al-Jāmiʿ*.

Kushyār's arithmetic is *Uṣūl Ḥisāb al-Hind*, "Elements of Hindu Reckoning." There is a Hebrew commentary to this work written by ʿAnābī in the fifteenth century.

Kushyār also wrote *al-Lāmiʿ fī amthilat al-zīj al-Jāmiʿ*, "The Brilliant [Work] on the Examples Pertaining to *al-Jāmiʿ zīj*"; *Kitāb al-Asṭurlāb wa kayfiyyat ʿamalihi wa iʿtibārihi*, . . ., "A Book on the Astrolabe and How to Prepare It and Test It . . .""; *Tajrīd Uṣūl Tarkīb al-Juyūb*, "Extracts of the Principles of Building up Sine Tables"; *al-Madkhal* [or *al-Mujmal*] *fī ṣināʿat ahkām al-Nujūm*, "An Introduction [or Summary] of the Rules of Astrology [and Astronomy]"; and *Risāla fī al-Abʿād wa al-Ajrām*, "A Treatise on Distances and Sizes," i.e., mensuration.

It is believed that Kushyār did not make any astronomical observations of his own; his *zījes* are classified with a few others called "al-Battānī's group." These take their elements from Muḥammad ibn Jābir ibn Sinān al-Battānī's *al-Zīj al-Ṣābiʾ*.

Kushyār is, however, credited with having developed the study of trigonometric functions started by Abu'l-Wafāʾ and al-Battānī. Abu'l-Wafāʾ gives sine tables, and al-Battānī gives sines and cotangents; but Kushyār's *zījes* contain sines, cotangents, tangents, and versed sines, together with tables of differences. In most of these tables the functions are calculated to three sexagesimal places and the angles increase in steps of one degree.

Kushyār's unique position in the development of Hindu arithmetic is not yet well understood. The Muslims inherited two arithmetical systems: the sexagesimal system, used mainly by astronomers, and finger reckoning, used by all. Finger reckoning contained no numeration. Numbers were stated in words, and calculations were done mentally. To remember intermediary results, calculators bent their fingers in distinct conventional ways; hence the name finger reckoning. Scribes were able to denote manually numbers from 1 to 9,999, one at a time.

The sexagesimal system used letters of the Arabic alphabet for numeration. Its fractions were always in the scale of sixty, but integers could be in the scale of sixty or of ten. We have arithmetic books that explain the concepts and practices of finger reckoning —the most important being the arithmetic written by Abu'l-Wafāʾ for state officials—but we do not have books that show how astronomers performed their calculations in the scale of sixty before the Indian methods began to exert their influence.

Almost every *zīj* starts by giving arithmetical rules stated rhetorically. Mainly these comprise rules of multiplication and division that may be expressed as

$$60^m \cdot 60^n = 60^{m+n}$$
$$60^m \div 60^n = 60^{m-n}$$

In books on finger reckoning and on Hindu arithmetic we find statements describing sexagesimal algorisms; these seem to bear Hindu influence. One is thus left with the impression that before they learned Hindu arithmetic, astronomers, like finger reckoners, made their calculations mentally, probably depending on finger reckoning as well as sexagesimal calculation. It should be stressed, however, that in Islam the system of finger reckoning used fractions to the scale of sixty and was very rich: it comprised algebra, mensuration, and the elements of trigonometry. It must therefore have been elaborated by the more gifted mathematicians. But whatever the case may be, there remains the question of whether there were any special manipulational methods devised for astronomical calculations.

Abu'l-Wafāʾ was more of an astronomer than an arithmetician; but since his arithmetic was expressly written for state officials, he may have deliberately avoided bothering his readers with material that he considered too advanced for them.

The importance of Kushyār's *Uṣūl Ḥisāb al-Hind* lies in his having written it to introduce the Hindu methods into astronomical calculations. Abū Ḥanīfa al-Dīnawarī, a lawyer, wrote on arithmetic to introduce these methods into business. 'Alī ibn Aḥmad al-Nasawī, known to have been Kushyār's student, commented sarcastically on these two works because Abū Ḥanīfa's was lengthy and Kushyār's was compact; he said that the former proved to be for astronomers and the latter for businessmen. But al-Nasawī copied Kushyār freely in his work and showed no better understanding of the Hindu system.

Kushyār's *Uṣūl* is in two sections supplemented by a chapter on the cube root. The first section gives the bare rudiments of Hindu numeration and algorisms on the dust board, and in at least one place we find that Kushyār was not well informed on the new practice. Wishing to solve 5625 — 839, like any other computer he puts the array

5625
839

on the dust board.

Other Arabic writers on Hindu artihmetic (excluding al-Nasawī) would start by subtracting 8 from 6; as this was not possible, they "borrowed" 1 from the 5, broke it down to 10, and thus subtracted 8 from 16. This process of borrowing and breaking down was not known to Kushyār (and his student). He subtracted 8 from 56 complete, obtaining 48. His next step was to subtract 3 from 82.

The second section of Kushyār's *Uṣūl* presents calculations in the scale of sixty, using Hindu numerals and the dust board. Here it seems, although it cannot always be proved decisively, that the author is dealing with concepts and manipulational schemes alien to both the Hindu system and what is found in books on finger reckoning. These must be schemes in the scale of sixty practiced by astronomers.

Briefly Kushyār states that the scale of sixty is indispensable because it is precise. In the absence of decimal fractions, which were added to the Hindu system by Muslim arithmeticians, Kushyār's statement is true. He then shows how to convert decimal integers to this scale; this is necessary for the methods he presents. His multiplication, division, and extraction of roots require the use of a multiplication table extending from 1×1 to 60×60, expressed in alphabetic numeration and in the sexagesimal scale. With this background he presents homogeneous methods of addition, subtraction, multiplication, division, and extraction of the square root (and, in the supplementary section, the cube root).

Kushyār certainly worked on the dust board and resorts to erasure and shifting of numbers from place to place; these were the distinguishing feature of the Hindu methods as they came to the Arabic world. But apart from these, he worked out $49°36' \div 12°25'$ as an endless operation of division in decimal fractions would be worked out. He obtained the answer $3°59'$ and had $8'25''$ left as a remainder. He added that the division could be continued if more precise results are desired.

The same applied to roots. Kushyār found the square root of $45°36'$, obtaining the result $6°45'9''59'''$, with a remainder. He added that the process could be continued to find the answer to higher degrees of precision.

From this treatment there is only one step to decimal fractions. Al-Uqlīdisī made that step in the tenth century, and al-Kāshī made it again in the fifteenth; but it was left to Stevin to establish it in his *La Disme* (1585).

BIBLIOGRAPHY

I. ORIGINAL WORKS. Kushyār's writings are *al-Bāligh* (Berlin 5751); *al-Jāmi'* (Leiden, Or. 1054), sec. 1 also available as Cairo MS 213; *Uṣūl Ḥisāb al-Hind* (Aya Sofya 4857), in M. Levey and M. Petruck, *Principles of Hindu Reckoning* (Madison, Wis., 1965), pp. 55–83, also edited with ample comparative notes in Arabic by A. S. Saidan in *Majallat Ma'had al-Makhṭūṭāt* (Cairo, 1967); *al-Lāmi' fī amthilat al-zīj al-Jāmi'* (Fātiḥ 3418); *Kitāb al-Asṭurlāb wa kayfiyyat 'amalihī wa i'tibārihī* (Paris, BN 3487; Cairo, MS 138); *Tajrīd Uṣūl Tarkīb al-Juyūb* (Jarullah 1499/3); *al-Madkhal* or *al-Mujmal fī ṣinā'at ahkām al-Nujūm* (Berlin 5885; Escorial 972; British Museum 415); and *Risāla fī al-ab'ād wa al-Ajrām* (Patna).

II. SECONDARY LITERATURE. See C. Brockelmann, *Geschichte der arabischen Literatur* (Leiden, 1943); E. S. Kennedy, "A Survey of Islamic Astronomical Tables," in *Transactions of the American Philosophical Society*, n.s. **46**, pt. 2 (1966); M. Krause, "Stambuler Handschriften islamischer Mathematiker," in *Quellen und Studien zur Geschichte der Mathematik, Astronomie und Physik*, Abt. B, Studien, **3** (1936). 472–473; C. A. Nallino, *Al-Battani sive Albattanii opus astronomicum*, 3 vols. (Milan, 1899-1907); C. Schoy, "Beiträge zur arabischen Trigonometrie," in *Isis*, **5** (1923), 364–399; and H. Suter, "Die Mathematiker und Astronomen der Araber und ihre Werke," in *Abhandlungen zur Geschichte der Mathematik*, **10** (1900); and "Nachträge und Berichtigungen zu 'Die Mathematiker und Astronomen ...,'" *ibid.*, **14**, no. 2 (1902).

A. S. SAIDAN

LA CONDAMINE, CHARLES-MARIE DE (*b.* Paris, France, 27 January 1701; *d.* Paris, 4 February 1774)

La Condamine came from an established, wealthy, and well-connected noble family. His father, district tax collector of the Bourbonnais, married in 1700, at the age of sixty. His mother, the former Marguerite-Louise de Chourses, daughter of a president of the Cours des Comptes of Montpellier, was about half his age. They had two children: Charles-Marie, the elder, and a daughter.

La Condamine completed his studies, with no marked enthusiasm, under the direction of the Jesuit fathers of the Collège Louis-le-Grand in Paris. There he had several remarkable teachers: the famous Père Poree, for the humanities; Père Brisson, in philosophy; and Père Castel, in mathematics. Lacking a pronounced vocation, La Condamine took up a military career when he left the *collège.* War broke out against Spain, and he joined the army of Roussillon commanded by the Maréchal de Berwick. Present at the siege of Rosas (1719), he distinguished himself by his contempt for danger. He soon found life in the army unsuited to his taste, however. La Condamine thereupon established contact with scientific circles in Paris, which were better able to satisfy his unquenchable curiosity, sometimes carried to the point of recklessness.

Through his new relations, La Condamine entered the Académie Royale des Sciences, as *adjoint-chimiste,* on 12 December 1730. But the Academy was no more able than the army to hold his interest for long, and in May 1731 he sailed on a naval ship for the commercial parts of the Levant, under the command of Duguay-Trouin. He thus came to Algiers, Alexandria, the coast of Palestine, Cyprus, and Smyrna, disembarking at Constantinople (October 1731), where he spent five months. After about a year, La Condamine returned to Paris and presented to the Academy, on 12 November 1732, his "Observations mathématiques et physiques faites dans un voyage de Levant en 1731 et 1732." Although the memoir did not consist entirely of new results, it was sufficient to earn him the reputation of a competent mathematician, an observant traveler, and a good storyteller. It is thus not astonishing that, a few months later, the Academy chose him to participate in the mission known as the *Académiciens du Pérou.*

The expedition to Peru, encouraged by the minister Maurepas, had as its goal the verification of Newton's hypothesis on the flattening of the terrestrial globe in the polar regions and, thereby, the resolution of the controversy regarding the form of the earth that was then dividing French scientists. Maupertuis, Clairaut, and Le Monnier went to Lapland to measure several degrees of meridian at the arctic circle, while Godin, Bouguer, and La Condamine were sent to Peru, territory belonging to Philip V of Spain, in order to make the same measurement in the vicinity of the equator. La Condamine left Paris on 14 April 1735 for La Rochelle, where he embarked with his two companions and the naturalist Joseph de Jussieu. They set sail for America on 16 May and made stops at Martinique (22 June to 1 July), Santo Domingo (11 July to 31 October), and Carthagena (16 November to 24 November). On 29 November they dropped anchor at Portobelo, Panama, arriving at the city of Panama a month later (29 December), after having traversed the isthmus. They set sail again on 22 February 1736; and on 10 March the mission finally disembarked at Manta, the port of the province of Quito. In order to reach the city of Quito, Godin and Bouguer sailed to Guayaquil. La Condamine went overland and did not rejoin the others in Quito until 4 June.

The arc of meridian that had been selected passes through a high valley nearly perpendicular to the equator, extending from Quito in the north to Cuenca in the south. Work had scarcely begun when tension arose between Louis Godin, the head of the mission, and Pierre Bouguer. From 3 October to 3 November, however, the team conducted the measurements of the base for the triangulation operations in the Yaruqui plain. This task completed, the members returned to Quito at the beginning of December. In the meantime, the financial aid expected from Paris had not arrived, and money was beginning to run short. La Condamine, who upon leaving France had provided himself with letters of credit addressed to banks in Lima, offered his assistance. He left Quito on 19 January 1737, in the midst of the rainy season and traveled the long and difficult journey to Lima, which he reached on 28 February. He extended his journey in order to observe, near Loja, the cinchona tree, which was still not well-known to Europeans. Having concluded his business with some trouble, at the offices of the Lima bankers, he headed back to Quito, arriving on 20 June, just in time to observe the solstice there.

By this time, Godin was working alone and refused to communicate any of his results to his colleagues. Consequently, La Condamine began to collaborate with Bouguer; and after two years of work that was often interrupted, the geometric measurement of the arc of the meridian, undertaken in a mountainous and difficult country, was completed in August 1739. It remained to make the astronomical measurement of the same arc by determining exactly the latitude of its two extremities. In the meantime, the misunderstanding between the scientists steadily worsened. Godin broke definitively with his colleagues and continued to work by himself. In December 1741, while verifying observations made jointly with La Condamine, Bouguer discovered a small error, which he corrected but which gave rise to a long dispute. La Condamine wished to recheck the observations that they had made together, but Bouguer refused. Henceforth each man pursued his measurements and observations independently. The work was finally completed in 1743. Leaving behind them a commemorative plaque on the wall of the Jesuit church in Quito (preserved at the Quito observatory) and two pyramids at the extremities of the base in the Yaruqui plain (soon destroyed by the Spaniards but reconstructed in 1836), the three scientists left for home, traveling separately.

La Condamine chose the longest and most dangerous route, the Amazon. Heading south from Tarqui, near Cuenca, on 11 May 1743 he reached the village of Jaen, having passed through Loja, Valladolid, and Loyola. On 4 July he set off from Jaen in a canoe and, descending the Chuchungas River, reached its confluence with the Rio Marañón, which is a source of the Amazon. Traveling down the Amazon took him more than two months. Although concerned primarily with astronomical observations and topographical details, La Condamine also observed the use of rubber by several tribes. His remarks on this subject, however, are far less interesting than his observations concerning the cinchona. On 19 September 1743 he reached the Atlantic at Pará. He left that city on 29 December and sailed to Cayenne, French Guiana, where he landed on 25 February 1744.

Unable to find a ship leaving for France, La Condamine spent five months in Cayenne. There he repeated Richer's experiments on the variation of weight at different latitudes (see Jean Richer, "Observations astronomiques et physiques faites en l'isle de Caïenne" [1679]) and made many observations on physics, natural history, and ethnology. He met the physician and naturalist Jacques-François Artur and the royal engineer François Fresneau. Later he presented the results of Fresneau's research to the Académie des Sciences in his memoir "Sur une résine élastique . . . nou-

vellement découvert à Cayenne" (26 February 1751). La Condamine finally left Cayenne on 22 August 1744, going first to Paramaribo, capital of Surinam. He embarked from there on 3 September for Amsterdam, where he arrived on 30 November. On 23 February 1745 he was back in Paris, after an absence of ten years, bringing with him copious notes and a collection of more than two hundred natural history specimens and various works of art, which he soon gave to Buffon for the royal Cabinet d'Histoire Naturelle. La Condamine's health had not been weakened to any serious degree, but he did suffer from a deafness that later worsened and from a growing lack of sensitivity in the extremities, especially his feet, no doubt caused by the rigors of the Andean climate.

The scientific result of the expedition was clear: the earth is indeed a spheroid flattened at the poles, as Newton had maintained. Bouguer and La Condamine were unable, however, to agree on the joint publication of their works. Their long quarrel continued through a series of memoirs that were essentially mutual refutations of no scientific value; it ceased only with the death of Bouguer in 1758. (Godin died in 1760.) The last survivor of the expedition, La Condamine, who was a less gifted astronomer than Godin and a less reliable mathematician than Bouguer, often received the major part of the credit, probably because of his amiable nature and his talent as a writer.

La Condamine returned from Peru with a project for a universal measurement of length, the unit of which would be the length of a pendulum beating once a second at the equator. Although Huygens had already suggested the idea in his *Horologium oscillatorium* (1673), La Condamine explained it more clearly in a memoir presented to the Academy in November 1747, which was read at a public meeting the following April. His proposal was not acted upon, but the idea remained under consideration and was taken up again by Turgot and, before the Constituent Assembly in 1790, by Talleyrand.

In his youth La Condamine had contracted smallpox, which perhaps led him to take such a resolute stand in the debate over inoculation. His role in this matter was that of a popularizer, and he played it with considerable talent. The clarity and grace of his style served him well, as did his good nature. Even in his polemical writings, whether in prose or in verse (see, for example, his *Mémoire pour servir à l'histoire des révolutions du pain mollet* [1768]), his tone remained measured and courteous. His other works on inoculation include three memoirs read before the Academy (in 1754,

1758, and 1765), as well as his *Lettres . . . à M. le Dr Maty sur l'état présent de l'inoculation en France* (1764) and a two-volume *Histoire de l'inoculation de la petite vérole* (1773). By the end of his life, the "Don Quixote of inoculation," as Louis Petit de Bachaumont called him, had seen the triumph of the ideas he had defended with such passion.

La Condamine's poems, although skillfully fashioned, do not merit special attention, nor does his *Lettre critique sur l'éducation,* published anonymously in 1751. The *Lettre* contains some valid ideas, such as the utility of modern foreign languages and of the exact sciences (in the front rank of which the author places geometry); but they are joined with reflections characteristic of the period and that prefigure Rousseau's *Émile* (1762). For example, he writes: "That the child becomes virtuous by becoming reasonable; that to the degree that his ideas develop, he learns that virtue is only the perfection of reason, while waiting to be shown that religion is the perfection of virtue."

A member of the Académie Royale des Sciences since 1730, as well as foreign member of the academies of London, Berlin, St. Petersburg, and Bologna, La Condamine was elected to the Académie Française on 29 November 1760. Piron greeted his election with a biting epigram:

> La Condamine est aujourd'hui
> reçu dans la troupe immortelle.
> il est bien sourd, tant mieux pour lui:
> mais non muet, tant pis pour elle.

The admission ceremony took place on 12 January 1761. The new member's speech was well regarded and the short reply by Buffon, who welcomed him in the name of the members, was magnificently eloquent.

To the end of his life La Condamine displayed the traits that had characterized him since his youth. He was inquisitive, restless, jealous of his reputation, gay, loyal, and at once malicious and credulous—in sum, very charming. A lively pastel portrait of him by Maurice Quentin de la Tour appeared in the Salon of 1753. During his trip to Italy, La Condamine obtained from Pope Benedict XIV a dispensation that allowed him to marry his niece, Charlotte Bouzier d'Estouilly, in August 1756. He was then fifty-five, and she twenty-five. Their marriage was a happy one. La Condamine had many friends, the closest of whom was certainly the impetuous and anxious Maupertuis, who bequeathed him all his papers. La Condamine died of the effects of a hazardous hernia operation, which, in a final bout of curiosity, he decided to undergo despite the risk involved.

BIBLIOGRAPHY

I. ORIGINAL WORKS. La Condamine's principal books are *Relation abrégée d'un voyage fait dans l'intérieur de l'Amérique méridionale . . .* (Paris, 1745)—the text differs from that printed in the *Mémoires de l'Académie des sciences* in having a preface and many variations in wording—also published as *Nouvelle édition augmentée de la Relation de l'émeute de Cuenca au Pérou et d'une lettre de M. Godin des Odonais contenant la relation du voyage de Madame Godin, son épouse . . .* (Maastricht, 1778); *Lettre à Mme *** sur l'émeute populaire excitée en la ville de Cuenca . . . contre les académiciens des sciences envoyés pour la mesure de la terre,* 2 pts. (Paris, 1745–1746), most of which is concerned with judicial proceedings following the death of the surgeon Seniergues; *Journal du voyage fait par ordre du roi à l'équateur, servant d'introduction historique à la mesure des trois premiers degrés du méridien* (Paris, 1751); *Lettre critique sur l'éducation* (Paris, 1751), published anonymously; and *Mesure des trois premiers degrés du méridien dans l'hémisphère austral . . .* (Paris, 1751).

Also see *Supplément au Journal historique ou Voyage à l'équateur et au livre de la mesure des trois premiers degrés du méridien, servant de réponse à quelques objections* (Paris, 1752), of which there was also a *Seconde partie . . .* (Paris, 1754); *Lettre de M.D.L.C.* [de La Condamine] *à M *** sur le sort des astronomes qui ont eu part aux dernières mesures de la terre, depuis 1735 . . . 20 octobre 1773* (n.p., n.d.); *Lettres de M. de La Condamine à M. le Dr Maty sur l'état présent de l'inoculation en France . . .* (Paris, 1764); and *Histoire de l'inoculation de la petite vérole . . .* (Amsterdam, 1773).

La Condamine published many articles in the "Mémoires" of the *Histoire de l'Académie royale des sciences.* Earlier ones include "Sur une nouvelle espèce de végétation métallique," 1731 (Paris, 1733), 466–482 and pls. 28–29; "Observations mathématiques et physiques faites dans un voyage de Levant . . . ," 1732 (Paris, 1735), 295–322 and pls. 16–18; "Description d'un instrument qui peut servir à déterminer, sur la surface de la terre, tous les points, d'un cercle parallèle à l'équateur," 1733 (Paris, 1735), 294–301 and pls. 22–23; "Nouvelle manière d'observer en mer la déclinaison de l'aiguille aimantée," *ibid.,* 446–456 and pl. 26; "Recherches sur le tour. Premier mémoire . . . . Description et usage d'une machine qui imite les mouvements du tour," 1734 (Paris, 1736), 216–258 and pls. 13–19; "Recherches sur le tour. Second mémoire. . . . Examen de la nature des courbes qui peuvent se tracer par les mouvements du tour," *ibid.,* 295–340 and pls. 20–25; and "Addition au memoire . . . 'Nouvelle manière d'observer en mer la déclinaison de l'aiguille aimantée' . . . ," *ibid.,* 597–599.

Further articles are "Manière de déterminer astronomiquement la différence en longitude de deux lieux eu éloignés l'un de l'autre," 1735 (Paris, 1738), 1–11; "De la mesure du pendule à Saint-Domingue," *ibid.*, 529–544 and pl. 17; "Observations des degrés de hauteur du thermomètre, faites en 1736 . . . ," 1736 (Paris, 1739), 500–502; "Sur l'arbre du quinquina," 1738 (Paris, 1740), 226–243 and pls. 5–6; "Relation abrégée d'un voyage fait dans l'intérieur de l'Amérique méridionale . . . ," 1745 (Paris, 1749), 391–492 and pl. 8; "Extrait des opérations trigonométriques, et des observations astronomiques, faites pour la mesure des degrés du méridien aux environs de l'équateur," 1746 (Paris, 1751), 618–688 and pls. 43–44; "Nouveau projet d'une mesure invariable propre à servir de mesure commune à toutes les nations," 1747 (Paris, 1752), 489–514; "Mémoire sur une résine élastique, nouvellement découverte à Cayenne par M. Fresneau; et sur l'usage de divers sucs laiteux d'arbres de la Guiane ou France équinoctiale," 1751 (Paris, 1755), 319–333 and pls. 18–20; "Mémoire sur l'inoculation de la petite vérole," 1754 (Paris, 1759), 615–670; "Extrait d'un journal de voyage en Italie," 1757 (Paris, 1762), 336–410; "Second mémoire sur l'inoculation de la petite vérole . . . ," 1758 (Paris, 1763), 439–482; and "Suite de l'histoire de l'inoculation de la petite vérole. . . . Troisième mémoire," 1765 (Paris, 1768), 505–532.

La Condamine's papers and correspondence, formerly preserved at the chateau of Estouilly, near Ham (Somme), have been scattered. His dossier at the archives of the Academy of Sciences contains letters, notes concerning the mission to Peru (particularly on his quarrels with Bouguer), and statements favoring inoculation against smallpox. Many of the items are addressed to Grandjean de Fouchy, the perpetual secretary of the Academy since 1743. Other documents are at the Bibliothèque Nationale, MS department: Fr 11333; Fr 12222; Fr 22133; Fr 22135; NA Fr 3543, fol. 231; NA Fr 6197, fols. 9, 14, 22; NA Fr 3531, fol. 174; NA Fr 21015.

II. SECONDARY LITERATURE. See "Bicentenaire de la découverte du caoutchouc par La Condamine, 1736–1936," *Revue générale du caoutchouc*, **13**, no. 125 (Oct. 1936); Pierre Bouguer, *La figure de la terre, déterminée par les observations des Messieurs Bouguer & de La Condamine . . .* (Paris, 1749); M. J. Condorcet, "Éloge de M. de La Condamine," in *Histoire de l'Académie royale des sciences*, 1774 (Paris, 1778), 85–121; *Discours prononcés dans l'Académie françoise, le lundi 11 juillet 1774 à la réception de M. l'abbé Delille* (Paris, 1774), a eulogy of La Condamine; Victor Wolfgang von Hagen, *South America Called Them . . .* (New York, 1945), 3–85, translated as *Le continent vert des naturalistes* (Paris, 1948); Abbé Achille Le Sueur, *La Condamine, d'après ses papiers inédits . . .* (Paris, 1911); and M. C. Wolf. "Recherches historiques sur les étalons de l'observatoire," in *Annales de chimie et de physique*, 5th ser., **25** (1882), 5–112.

YVES LAISSUS

LACROIX, SYLVESTRE FRANÇOIS (*b.* Paris, France, 28 April 1765; *d.* Paris, 24 May 1843)

Lacroix, who came from a modest background, studied at the Collège des Quatre Nations in Paris, where he was taught mathematics by the Abbé Joseph François Marie. He became ardently interested in the exact sciences at a very young age; as early as 1779 he carried out long calculations on the motions of the planets, and 1780 he attended the free courses given by Gaspard Monge, who became his patron. The friendship between the two remained constant throughout the sometimes dramatic events of their lives. Monge, who was an examiner of students for the navy, in 1782 secured for Lacroix a position as professor of mathematics at the École des Gardes de la Marine at Rochefort. Following Monge's advice, Lacroix then began to concern himself with partial differential equations and with the calculus of variations. In 1785 Lacroix sent a memoir on partial differences to Monge which he reported on to the Académie des Sciences. In that same year Lacroix also sent new solar tables to the Academy.

Lacroix returned to Paris to substitute for Condorcet in his mathematics course at the Lycée, a newly founded free institution whose lectures attracted many members of the nobility and of the upper bourgeoisie. The course in pure mathematics had few auditors and was soon discontinued. Lacroix then taught astronomy and the theory of probability. He also shared a 1787 Academy prize (which they never received) with C. F. Bicquilley for a work on the theory of marine insurance. In the meantime he had married. Lacroix also succeeded d'Agelet first in the duties and eventually in the title to the chair of mathematics at the École Militaire in Paris, and began to gather material for his *Traité du calcul différentiel et du calcul intégral* (1797–1798).

Because the chair at the Lycée was abolished and the École Militaire closed in 1788, Lacroix once again left Paris; he took up a post as professor of mathematics, physics, and chemistry at the École Royale d'Artillerie in Besançon. In 1789 the Academy chose him to be Condorcet's correspondent, and in 1793 he succeeded Laplace as examiner of candidates and students for the artillery corps. In 1794 he became *chef de bureau* of the Commission Exécutive de l'Instruction Publique. He and Hachette later assisted Monge in the practical work connected with his course in descriptive geometry at the École Normale de l'An III. About this time Lacroix published his *Eléments de géométrie descriptive*, the materials for which had been assembled several years previously. The printing of his great *Traité* began during this period. Until 1791 Lacroix was a member of the admissions committee of the École Polytechnique.

Upon the creation of the Écoles Centrales, schools for intermediate education that were the forerunners of the modern lycée, Lacroix became professor of mathematics at the École Centrale des Quatres Nations. He then undertook to publish numerous textbooks, which further contributed to his fame. In 1799 he was elected a member of the Institute. He also succeeded to Lagrange's chair at the École Polytechnique, a position he held until 1809, when he became a permanent examiner.

The first volume of Lacroix's treatise on the calculus, in which he "united all the scattered methods, harmonized them, developed them, and joined his own ideas to them," appeared in 1797. It was followed by a second volume in 1798, and a third appeared in 1800 under the title *Traité des différences et des séries* (a second edition appeared in three volumes [1810, 1814, 1819]). This monumental work constituted a clear picture of mathematical analysis, documented and completely up to date. While Lacroix followed Euler on many points, he incorporated the various advances made since the middle of the eighteenth century. The treatise is a very successful synthesis of the works of Euler, Lagrange, Laplace, Monge, Legendre, Poisson, Gauss, and Cauchy, whose writings are followed up to the year 1819.

In his teaching, particularly at the École Polytechnique, Lacroix utilized his *Traité élémentaire du calcul différentiel et du calcul intégral*, which appeared in 1802. A work of enduring popularity, it was translated into English and German. From 1805 to 1815 Lacroix taught transcendental mathematics at the Lycée Bonaparte and, with the creation of the Facultés, he became dean of the Faculté des Sciences of Paris and professor of differential and integral calculus.

When Lacroix succeeded to the duties of Antoine Rémi Mauduit in 1812 at the Collège de France, he arranged for Paul Rémi Binet to succeed to his post at the Lycée Bonaparte. Upon Mauduit's death, Lacroix was appointed to the chair of mathematics at the Collège de France; he then definitively ended his connection with the Lycée Bonaparte, which in the meantime had become the Collège Bourbon.

Lacroix retired from his post as dean of the Faculté des Sciences in 1821 and a few years later from that of professor as well. In 1828 Louis Benjamin Francoeur succeeded to Lacroix's duties at the Collège de France, and beginning in 1836, Libri succeeded to these duties.

At the time of his visit to Paris in 1826, Abel found Lacroix "frightfully bald and remarkably old." Although he was only sixty-one, his astonishing activity since adolescence had affected his health.

Lacroix's mathematical work contained little that was absolutely new and original. His writings on analytic geometry, which refined ideas he derived from Lagrange and above all from Monge, served as models for later didactic works. It was he who actually proposed the term "analytic geometry": "There exists a manner of viewing geometry that could be called *géométrie analytique*, and which would consist in deducing the properties of extension from the least possible number of principles, and by truly analytic methods" (*Traité du calcul différentiel et du calcul intégral*, I [Paris, 1797] p. xxv).

A disciple of Condillac in philosophy, Lacroix brought to all his didactic works a liberal spirit, open to the most advanced ideas. He was particularly inspired by the pedagogical conceptions of Clairaut and, in addition, by those of the masters of Port-Royal and Pascal and Descartes. In this regard, the contrast is quite striking between Lacroix's *Éléments de géométrie* and the similar contemporary work by Legendre, which is a great deal more dogmatic.

Lacroix's sense of history is evident in all his writings. The preface to the first volume of the second edition of the great *Traité* (1810) is a model of the genre. He also wrote excellent studies, in particular those on Borda and Condorcet, for Michaud's *Biographie universelle*. In addition he participated in the editing of volume III of Montucla's *Histoire des mathématiques*, composed the section on mathematics for Delambre's report on the state of science in 1808, and prepared an essay on the history of mathematics, which unfortunately remained in manuscript form and now appears to have been lost.

His *Essais sur l'enseignement* (1805), a pedagogical classic, display his acute psychological penetration, rich erudition, liberal cast of mind, and broad conception of education.

For more than half a century, through his writings and lectures, Lacroix thus contributed to an era of renewal and expansion in the exact sciences and to the training of numerous nineteenth-century mathematicians. The young English school of mathematics, formed by Babbage, Peacock, and Herschel, wished to breathe a new spirit into the nation's science, and one of its first acts was to translate the *Traité élémentaire du calcul différentiel et du calcul intégral*.

BIBLIOGRAPHY

I. ORIGINAL WORKS. Lacroix's writings are *Essai de géométrie sur les plans et les surfaces* (Paris, 1795; 7th ed., 1840), also in Dutch trans. by I. R. Schmidt (1821); *Traité élémentaire d'arithmétique* (Paris, 1797; 20th ed., 1848), also in English trans. by John Farrar (Boston, 1818) and

Italian trans. by Santi Fabri (Bologna, 1822); *Traité élémentaire de trigonométrie rectiligne et sphérique et d'application de l'algèbre à la géométrie* (Paris, 1798; 11th ed., 1863), also in English trans. by John Farrar (Cambridge, Mass., 1820) and German trans. by E. M. Hahn (Berlin, 1805); *Élémens de géométrie* (Paris, 1799; 19th ed., 1874); and *Complément des élémens d'algèbre* (Paris, 1800; 7th ed., 1863).

Subsequent works are *Traité du calcul différentiel et du calcul intégral*, 2 vols. (Paris, 1797–1798); 2nd ed., 3 vols. (Paris, 1810–1819); *Traité des différences et des séries* (Paris, 1800); *Traité élémentaire du calcul différentiel et du calcul intégral* (Paris, 1802; 9th ed., 1881), also in English trans. by C. Babbage, John F. W. Herschel, and G. Peacock (Cambridge, 1816) and German trans. (Berlin, 1830–1831); *Essais sur l'enseignement en général, et sur celui des mathématiques en particulier, ou manière d'étudier et d'enseigner les mathématiques* (Paris, 1805; 4th ed., 1838); *Introduction à la géographie mathématique et physique* (Paris, 1811); *Traité élémentaire du calcul des probabilités* (Paris, 1816); and *Introduction à la connaissance de la sphère* (Paris, 1828).

Works to which Lacroix was a contributor are *Lettres de M. Euler a une princesse d'Allemagne . . . avec des additions par M.M. le marquis de Condorcet et de la Croix*, new ed., 3 vols. (Paris, 1787–1789); *Élémens d'algèbre par Clairaut*, 5th ed. (Paris, 1797), with notes and additions drawn in part from the lectures given at the École Normale by Lagrange and Laplace and preceded by *Traité élémentaire d'arithmétique*, 2 vols. (Paris, 1797)—the notes, additions, and treatise are by Lacroix; J. F. Montucla, *Histoire des mathématiques*, 2nd ed., III (Paris, 1802), in which Lacroix revised ch. 33, pp. 342–352, on partial differential equations; *Rapport historique sur les progrès des sciences mathématiques depuis 1789 et sur leur état actuel, redigé par M. Delambre* (Paris, 1810)—in this report, presented in 1808, "everything concerning pure mathematics and transcendental analysis is drawn from a work of M. Lacroix, who submitted it to the assembled mathematics sections" (Delambre); and J. F. Montucla, *Histoire des recherches sur la quadrature du cercle*, 2nd ed. (Paris, 1831), which was prepared for publication by Lacroix.

II. SECONDARY LITERATURE. On Lacroix and his work, see Carl Boyer, "Cartesian Geometry from Fermat to Lacroix," in *Scripta mathematica*, **13** (1947), 133–153; "Mathematicians of the French Revolution," *ibid.*, **25** (1960), 26–27; and *A History of Mathematics* (New York, 1968); Gino Loria, *Storia delle matematiche*, 2nd ed. (Milan, 1950), 771–772; Niels Nielsen, *Géomètres français sous la révolution* (Copenhagen, 1929), 134–136; Leo G. Simons, "The Influence of French Mathematicians at the End of the Eighteenth Century Upon the Teaching of Mathematics in American Colleges," in *Isis*, **15** (1931), 104–123; and René Taton, *L'oeuvre scientifique de Monge* (Paris, 1951), *passim;* "Sylvestre François Lacroix (1765–1843): Mathématicien, professeur et historien des sciences," in *Actes du septième congrès international d'histoire des sciences* (Paris, 1953), 588–593; "Laplace et Sylvestre Lacroix," in *Revue d'histoire des sciences*, **6** (1953), 350–

360; "Une correspondance inédite: S. F. Lacroix–Quetelet," in *Actes du congrès 1953 de l'Association française pour l'avancement des sciences* (Paris, 1954), 595–606; "Une lettre inédite de Dirichlet," in *Revue d'histoire des sciences*, **7** (1954), 172–174; and "Condorcet et Sylvestre François Lacroix," *ibid.*, **12** (1959), 127–158, 243–262.

JEAN ITARD

LA FAILLE, CHARLES DE (*b.* Antwerp, Belgium, 1 March 1597; *d.* Barcelona, Spain, 4 November 1652)

The son of Jean Charles de La Faille, seigneur de Rymenam, and Marie van de Wouwere, Charles de La Faille received his early schooling at the Jesuit College of his native city. On 12 September 1613 he became a novitiate of the Jesuit order at Malines for two years. Afterward he was sent to Antwerp where he met Gregory of St. Vincent, who was renowned for his work on quadrature of the circle. La Faille was counted among Gregory's disciples, and in 1620 he was sent to France to follow a course of theology at Dôle, and to teach mathematics. After his return to Belgium in 1626, he taught mathematics at the Jesuit College of Louvain for the next two years. In 1629 he was appointed professor at the Imperial College in Madrid; he departed for Spain 23 March 1629. In 1644 Philip IV appointed him preceptor to his son Don Juan of Austria, whom he also accompanied on his expeditions to Naples, Sicily, and Catalonia. He died in Barcelona in 1652, a month after the capture of the town by Don Juan.

La Faille owed his fame as a scholar to his tract *Theoremata de centro gravitatis partium circuli et ellipsis*, published at Antwerp in 1632. In it the center of gravity of a sector of a circle is determined for the first time. In the first nine propositions each is established step by step. His procedure can be rendered as follows: If α is the angle of a given sector of a circle with radius R, and β is a sufficiently small angle of the same sector, the length

$$\frac{R\alpha^2}{\sin^2 \alpha}\left(1 - \frac{\sin \beta}{\beta}\right)$$

can be made arbitrarily small. For his proof, La Faille supposed that there can be constructed on one of the radii a triangle the area of which is equal to that of the sector. Of the next five propositions the first is especially interesting: If there are three lines AB, AC, and AD, and the straight line BCD cuts the lines given in such a way that $BD : BC =$ angle $BAD :$ angle CAD, then $AD < AC < AB$, if $BAD < CAD$. The proof is based on the theorem which La Faille found in Clavius (*De sinibus*, prop. 10); it is also to be found in the first book of the *Almagest*.

In the next eight propositions the author proved that the centers of gravity of a sector of a circle, of a regular figure inscribed in it, of a segment of a circle, or of an ellipse lie on the diameter of the figure. These theorems are founded on a postulate from Luca Valerio's *De centro gravitatis solidorum* (1604). In his proofs, La Faille referred to Archimedes' *On the Equilibrium of Planes or Centers of Gravity of Planes* (book I). Propositions 23–31 lead to the proof that the distance between the center of gravity of a sector of a circle and the center of the circle is less than $\frac{2}{3} R$, but the difference between this distance and $\frac{2}{3} R$ can be made arbitrarily small by making the angle of the sector sufficiently small. Proposition 32, the main one of the work, can be rendered as follows: If A is the angle of a sector of a circle with radius R, the center of gravity lies on the bisector, and the distance d to the vertex of the angle of the sector is given by

$$d = \frac{2}{3} R \frac{\text{chord } A}{\text{arc } A}$$

Propositions 33–37 are consequences of 32, and 38–45 are an extension of the results on a sector and segment of an ellipse. La Faille ended his work with four corollaries which revealed his ultimate goal: an examination of the quadrature of the circle.

BIBLIOGRAPHY

According to C. Sommervogel, *Bibliothèque de la Compagnie de Jésus*, III (Brussels–Paris, 1897), cols. 529–530, there are some more works of La Faille in Spanish, but all of them are manuscripts and nothing is known about their contents. Moreover, there exists the correspondence of La Faille with the astronomer M. van Langren covering the period 20 Apr. 1634–25 Sept. 1645.

A very extensive biography was written by H. P. van der Speeten, "Le R.P. Jean Charles della Faille, de la Compagnie de Jésus, Précepteur de Don Juan d'Autriche," in *Collection de Précis Historiques*, 3 (1874), 77–83, 111–117, 132–142, 191–201, 213–219, and 241–246. Some information on his life and work can be found in A. G. Kästner, "Geschichte der Mathematik," 2 (Göttingen, 1797), 211–215; H. G. Zeuthen, "Geschichte der Mathematik im 16. und 17. Jahrhundert" (Leipzig, 1903), pp. 238–240.

See also H. Bosmans, "Deux lettres inédites de Grégoire de Saint-Vincent publiées avec des notes bibliographiques sur les oeuvres de Grégoire de Saint-Vincent et les manuscrits de della Faille," in *Annales de la Société Scientifique de Bruxelles*, 26 (1901–1902), 22–40; H. Bosmans, "Le traité 'De centro gravitatis' de Jean-Charles della Faille," *ibid.*, 38 (1913–1914), 255–317; H. Bosmans, "Le mathématicien anversois Jean-Charles della Faille de la Compagnie de Jésus," in *Mathésis*, 41 (1927), 5–11; and J. Pelseneer, "Jean Charles de la Faille (Anvers 1597–Barcelona 1652)," in *Isis*, 37 (1947), 73–74.

H. L. L. Busard

LAGNY, THOMAS FANTET DE (*b.* Lyons, France, 7 November 1660; *d.* Paris, France, 11 April 1734)

There are certain obscurities in our knowledge of Lagny's life, talented calculator though he was. Fantet was the name of his father, a royal official in Grenoble. It appears that Lagny studied with the Jesuits in Lyons and then at the Faculty of Law in Toulouse. In 1686 he appeared in Paris under the name of Lagny. He was a tutor in the Noailles family and the author of a study on coinage. His collaboration with L'Hospital and his first publications concerning the approximate calculation of irrationals (1690–1691) show that he was a good mathematician. He was living in Lyons when he was named an associate of the Académie Royale des Sciences on 11 December 1695. He stayed in Paris in 1696 and then, in 1697, through the Abbé Jean-Paul Bignon, obtained an appointment as professor of hydrography at Rochefort. This position assured him a salary but in a distant residence which allowed him only written contact with the Academy. His former pupil, the Maréchal Duc de Noailles, president of the Conseil des Finances of the regency, called upon him in 1716 to assume the deputy directorship of the Banque Générale founded by John Law. He resigned this job in 1718, at the time of the institution's transformation into the Banque Royale, and was not involved in the bankruptcy that shook the French state.

A *pensionnaire* of the Academy from 7 July 1719, Lagny finally earned his living from science, as he wished to do, but he was growing weaker and could barely revise his old manuscripts. His declining powers obliged him to retire in 1733, and the Academy completed the book that he planned to crown his work.

Lagny's work belonged to a type of computational mathematics at once outmoded and unappreciated. He lived during the creation of integral calculus without being affected by it. While the idea of the function was gaining dominance, he continued to approach mathematical problems—both ancient problems such as the solution of equations and new ones such as integration—with the aid of numerical tables. Employing with great skill the property possessed by algebraic forms of corresponding to tables in which the differences of a determined order are constant, he recognized the existence of transcendental numbers in the calculation of series.

Lagny made pertinent observations on convergence,

in connection with the series that he utilized to calculate the first 120 decimal places in the value of π. He attempted to establish trigonometric tables through the use of transcription into binary arithmetic, which he termed "natural logarithm" and the properties of which he discovered independently of Leibniz.

In this regard his meeting with the inventor of the differential and integral calculus is interesting, but it was only the momentary crossing of very different paths. Lagny generally confined himself to numerical computation and practical solutions, notably the goniometry necessary for navigators. Nevertheless, his works retain a certain didactic value.

BIBLIOGRAPHY

I. ORIGINAL WORKS. Lagny's writings include "Dissertation sur l'or de Toulouse," in *Annales de la ville de Toulouse* (Toulouse, 1687), I, 329–344; *Méthode nouvelle infiniment générale et infiniment abrégée pour l'extraction des racines quarrées, cubiques . . .* (Paris, 1691); *Méthodes nouvelles et abrégées pour l'extraction et l'approximation des racines* (Paris, 1692); *Nouveaux élémens d'arithmétique et d'algèbre ou introduction aux mathématiques* (Paris, 1697); *Trigonométrie française ou reformée* (Rochefort, 1703), on binary arithmetic; *De la cubature de la sphère où l'on démontre une infinité de portions de sphères égales à des pyramides rectilignes* (La Rochelle, 1705); and *Analyse générale ou Méthodes nouvelles pour résoudre les problèmes de tous les genres et de tous les degrés à l'infini*, M. Richer, ed. (Paris, 1733).

Lagny addressed many memoirs to the Academy, and most of them were published. Perhaps the most important is "Quadrature du cercle," in *Histoire et Mémoires de l'Académie . . . pour 1719* (Amsterdam, 1723), pp. 176–189.

There is a portrait of Lagny in the Lyons municipal library, no. 13896.

II. SECONDARY LITERATURE. See Jean-Baptiste Duhamel, *Regiae scientiarum academiae historia* (Paris, 1698), pp. 430–432; and B. de Fontenelle, "Éloge de M. de Lagny," in *Histoire et Mémoires de l'Académie . . . pour 1734* (Amsterdam, 1738), 146–155.

PIERRE COSTABEL

LAGRANGE, JOSEPH LOUIS (*b.* Turin, Italy, 25 January 1736; *d.* Paris, France, 10 April 1813)

Lagrange's life divides very naturally into three periods. The first comprises the years spent in his native Turin (1736–1766). The second is that of his work at the Berlin Academy, between 1766 and 1787. The third finds him in Paris, from 1787 until his death in 1813.

The first two periods were the most fruitful in terms of scientific activity, which began as early as 1754 with the discovery of the calculus of variations and continued with the application of the latter to mechanics in 1756. He also worked in celestial mechanics in this first period, stimulated by the competitions held by the Paris Academy of Sciences in 1764 and 1766.

The Berlin period was productive in mechanics as well as in differential and integral calculus. Yet during that time Lagrange distinguished himself primarily in the numerical and algebraic solution of equations, and even more in the theory of numbers.

Lagrange's years in Paris were dedicated to didactic writings and to the composition of the great treatises summarizing his mathematical conceptions. These treatises, while closing the age of eighteenth-century mathematics, prepared and in certain respects opened that of the nineteenth century.

Lagrange's birth and baptismal records give his name as Lagrangia, Giuseppe Lodovico, and declare him to be the legitimate son of Giuseppe Francesco Lodovico Lagrangia and Teresa Grosso. But from his youth he signed himself Lodovico LaGrange or Luigi Lagrange, adopting the French spelling of the patronymic. His first published work, dated 23 July 1754, is entitled "Lettera di Luigi De la Grange Tournier." Until 1792 he and his correspondents frequently employed the particle, very common in France but quite rare in Italy, and named him in three words: de la Grange. The contract prepared for his second marriage (1792) is in the name of Monsieur Joseph-Louis La Grange, without the particle. In 1814 the *éloge* written for him by Delambre, the permanent secretary of the mathematics section of the Institut de France, was entitled "Notice sur la vie et les ouvrages de M. le Comte J. L. Lagrange"; and his death certificate designated him Monsieur Joseph Louis Lagrange, sénateur. As for the surname Tournier, he used it for only a few years, perhaps to distinguish himself from his father, who held office in Turin.

His family was, through the male members, of French origin, as stated in the marriage contract of 1792. His great-grandfather, a cavalry captain, had passed from the service of France to that of Charles Emmanuel II, duke of Savoy, and had married a Conti, from a Roman family whose members included Pope Innocent XIII.

His grandfather—who married Countess Bormiolo—was Treasurer of the Office of Public Works and Fortifications at Turin. His father and later one of his brothers held this office, which remained in the family until its suppression in 1800. Lagrange's mother, Teresa Gros, or Grosso, was the only daughter of a physician in Cambiano, a small town near Turin. Lagrange was the eldest of eleven children, most of whom did not reach adulthood.

Despite the official position held by the father—who had engaged in some unsuccessful financial speculations—the family lived very modestly. Lagrange himself declared that if he had had money, he probably would not have made mathematics his vocation. He remained with his family until his departure for Berlin in 1766.

Lagrange's father destined him for the law—a profession that one of his brothers later pursued—and Lagrange offered no objections. But having begun the study of physics under the direction of Beccaria and of geometry under Filippo Antonio Revelli, he quickly became aware of his talents and henceforth devoted himself to the exact sciences. Attracted first by geometry, at the age of seventeen he turned to analysis, then a rapidly developing field.

In 1754 Lagrange had a short essay printed in the form of a letter written in Italian and addressed to the geometer Giulio da Fagnano. In it he developed a formal calculus based on the analogy between Newton's binomial theorem and the successive differentiations of the product of two functions. He also communicated this discovery to Euler in a letter written in Latin slightly before the Italian publication. But in August 1754, while glancing through the scientific correspondence between Leibniz and Johann Bernoulli, Lagrange observed that his "discovery" was in fact their property and feared appearing to be a plagiarist and impostor.

This unfortunate start did not discourage Lagrange. He wrote to Fagnano on 30 October 1754 that he had been working on the tautochrone. This first essay is lost, but we know of two later memoirs on the same subject. The first was communicated to the Berlin Academy on 4 March 1767.[1] Criticized by the French Academician Alexis Fontaine des Bertins, Lagrange responded in "Nouvelles réflexions sur les tautochrones."[2]

At the end of December 1755, in a letter to Fagnano alluding to correspondence exchanged before the end of 1754, Lagrange speaks of Euler's *Methodus inveniendi lineas curvas maximi minimive proprietate gaudentes, sive solutio problematis isoperimetrici latissimo sensu accepti*, published at Lausanne and Geneva in 1744. The same letter shows that as early as the end of 1754 Lagrange had found interesting results in this area, which was to become the calculus of variations (a term coined by Euler in 1766).

On 12 August 1755 Lagrange sent Euler a summary, written in Latin, of the purely analytical method that he used for this type of problem. It consisted, he wrote in 1806, in varying the y's in the integral formula in x and y, which should be a maximum or a minimum by ordinary differentiations, but relative to another characteristic δ, different from the ordinary characteristic d. It was further dependent on determining the differential value of the formula with respect to this new characteristic by transposing the sign δ after the signs d and $\int$ when it is placed before. The differentials of δy under the $\int$ signs are then eliminated through integration by parts.

In a letter to d'Alembert of 2 November 1769 Lagrange confirmed that this method of maxima and minima was the first fruit of his studies—he was only nineteen when he devised it —and that he regarded it as his best work in mathematics.

Euler replied to Lagrange on 6 September 1755 that he was very interested in the technique. Lagrange's merit was likewise recognized in Turin; and he was named, by a royal decree of 28 September 1755, professor at the Royal Artillery School with an annual salary of 250 crowns—a sum never increased in all the years he remained in his native country.

In 1756, in a letter to Euler that has been lost, Lagrange applied the calculus of variations to mechanics. Euler had demonstrated, at the end of his *Methodus*, that the trajectory described by a material point subject to the influence of central forces is the same as that obtained by supposing that the integral of the velocity multiplied by the element of the curve is either a maximum or a minimum. Lagrange extended "this beautiful theorem" to an arbitrary system of bodies and derived from it a procedure for solving all the problems of dynamics.

Euler sent these works of Lagrange to his official superior Maupertuis, then president of the Berlin Academy. Finding in Lagrange an unexpected defender of his principle of least action, Maupertuis arranged for him to be offered, at the earliest opportunity, a chair of mathematics in Prussia, a more advantageous position than the one he held in Turin. This proposition, transmitted through Euler, was rejected by Lagrange out of shyness; and nothing ever came of it. At the same time he was offered a corresponding membership in the Berlin Academy, and on 2 September 1756 he was elected an associate foreign member.

In 1757 some young Turin scientists, among them Lagrange, Count Saluzzo (Giuseppe Angelo Saluzzo di Menusiglio), and the physician Giovanni Cigna, founded a scientific society that was the origin of the Royal Academy of Sciences of Turin. One of the main goals of this society was the publication of a miscellany in French and Latin, *Miscellanea Taurinensia ou Mélanges de Turin*, to which Lagrange contributed fundamentally. The first three volumes appeared at the beginning of the summers of 1759 and 1762 and in the summer of 1766, during which time Lagrange was in Turin. The fourth volume, for the years 1766–1769, published in 1773, included four of his memoirs, written in 1767, 1768, and 1770 and sent from Berlin.

The first three volumes contained almost all the works Lagrange published while in Turin, with the following exceptions: the courses he gave at the Artillery School on mechanics and differential and integral calculus, which remained in manuscript and now appear to have been lost; the two memoirs for the competitions set by the Paris Academy of Sciences in 1764 and 1766; and his contribution to Louis Dutens's edition of Leibniz' works.

In volume 1 of the *Mélanges de Turin* are Lagrange's "Recherches sur la Méthode de maximis et minimis,"[3] really an introduction to the memoir in volume 2 on the calculus of variations (dating, as noted above, from the end of 1754).

Another short memoir, "Sur l'intégration d'une équation différentielle à différences finies, qui contient la théorie des suites récurrentes,"[4] was cited by Lagrange in 1776 as an introduction to investigations on the calculus of probabilities that he was unable to develop for lack of time. There is also his unfinished and unpublished translation of Abraham de Moivre's *The Doctrine of Chances*, the third edition of which appeared in 1756. Lagrange mentioned this translation —which seems to have been lost—in a letter to Laplace of 30 December 1776.[5]

Recherches sur la nature et la propagation du son[6] constitutes a thorough and extensive study of a question much discussed at the time. In it Lagrange displays an astonishing erudition. He had read and pondered the writings of Newton, Daniel Bernoulli, Taylor, Euler, and d'Alembert; and his own contribution to the problem of vibrating strings makes him the equal of his predecessors.

Work of the same order is presented in "Nouvelles recherches sur la nature et la propagation du son"[7] and "Additions aux premières recherches,"[8] both published in volume 2 of the *Mélanges*. His most important contribution to this volume, though, is "Essai d'une nouvelle méthode pour déterminer les maxima et les minima des formules intégrales indéfinies,"[9] a rather brief memoir in which Lagrange published his analytic techniques of the calculus of variations. Here he developed the insights contained in his Latin letter to Euler of 1755 and added two appendixes, one dealing with minimal surfaces and the other with polygons of maximal area. Although published in 1762, the memoir and its first appendix were written before the end of 1759.

"Application de la méthode précédente à la solution de différens problèmes de dynamique"[10] made the principle of least action, joined with the theorem of *forces vives* (or *vis viva*), the very foundation of dynamics. Rather curiously, Lagrange no longer used the expression "least action," which he had employed until then, a minor failing due, perhaps, to the death of Maupertuis. This memoir heralded the *Mécanique analytique* of 1788 in its style and in the breadth of the author's views.

Volume 3 of the *Mélanges de Turin* contains "Solution de différens problèmes de calcul intégral."[11] An early section treats the integration of a general affine equation of arbitrary order. Lagrange here employed his favorite tool, integration by parts. He reduced the solution of the equation with second member to that of the equation without second member. This discovery dates—as we know from the correspondence with d'Alembert[12]—from about the end of 1764.

Lagrange's research also encompassed Riccati's equations and a functional equation, which he treated in a very offhand manner. Examining some problems on fluid motion, he outlined a study of the function later called Laplacian. He was following Euler, but with the originality that marked his entire career.

The consideration of the movement of a system of material points making only infinitely small oscillations around their equilibrium position led Lagrange to a system of linear differential equations. In integrating it he presented for the first time—explicitly—the notion of the characteristic value of a linear substitution.

Lagrange finally arrived at applications to the theory of Jupiter and Saturn. In September 1765 he wrote on this subject that, due to lack of time, he was contenting himself with applying the formulas he had just discovered to the variations in the eccentricity and position of the aphelia of the two planets and to those in the inclination and in the position of the nodes of their orbits. These were inequalities that "no one until now has undertaken to determine with all the exactitude" demanded.

Investigations of this kind were related to the prize questions proposed by the Paris Academy of Sciences. In 1762 it established a competition, for 1764, based on the question "Whether it can be explained by any physical reason why the moon always presents almost the same face to us; and how, by observations and by theory, it can be determined whether the axis of this planet is subject to some proper movement similar to that which the axis of the earth is known to perform, producing precession and nutation."

In 1763 Lagrange sent to Paris "Recherches sur la

libration de la lune dans lesquelles on tâche de résoudre la question proposée par l'Académie royale des sciences pour le prix de l'année 1764."[13] In this work he provided a satisfactory explanation of the equality of the mean motion of translation and rotation but was less successful in accounting for the equality of the movement of the nodes of the lunar equator and that of the nodes of the moon's orbit on the ecliptic.

Lagrange also fruitfully applied the principle of virtual velocities, which is intimately and necessarily linked with his techniques in the calculus of variations. He also made it the basis of his *Mécanique analytique* of 1788. This principle has the advantage, over that of least action, of including the latter principle as well as the principle of *forces vives* and thus of giving mechanics a unified foundation. He had not yet achieved a unified point of view in the memoir published in 1762. Arriving at three differential equations, he demonstrated that they are identical to those relating to the precession of the equinoxes and the nutation of the earth's axis that d'Alembert presented in the *Mémoires* of the Paris Academy for 1754. Lagrange returned to this question and gave a more complete solution of it in "Théorie de la libration de la lune et des autres phénomènes qui dépendent de la figure non sphérique de cette planète," included in the *Mémoires* of the Berlin Academy for 1780 (published in 1782).[14] Laplace wrote to him on this subject on 10 February 1783: "The elegance and the generality of your analysis, the fortunate choice of your coordinates, and the manner in which you treat your differential equations, especially those of the movement of the equinoctial points and of the inclination of the lunar equator; all that, and the sublimity of your results, has filled me with admiration."

In 1763 d'Alembert, then on his way to Berlin, was not a member of the jury that judged Lagrange's entry. He had already been in correspondence with Lagrange but did not know him personally. Nevertheless, he had been able to judge of his ability through the *Mélanges de Turin*. In the meantime the Marquis Caraccioli, ambassador from the kingdom of Naples to the court of Turin, was transferred by his government to London. He took along the young Lagrange, who until then seems never to have left the immediate vicinity of Turin.

Lagrange departed his native city at the beginning of November 1763 and was warmly received in Paris, where he had been preceded by his memoir on lunar libration. He may perhaps have been treated too well in the Paris scientific community, where austerity was not a leading virtue. Being of a delicate constitution, Lagrange fell ill and had to interrupt his trip. His mediocre situation in Turin aroused the concern of

d'Alembert, who had just returned from Prussia. D'Alembert asked Mme. Geoffrin to intercede with the ambassador of Sardinia at the court of Turin:

> Monsieur de la Grange, a young geometer from Turin, has been here for six weeks. He has become quite seriously ill and he needs, not financial aid, for M^r le marquis de Caraccioli directed upon leaving for England that he should not lack for anything, but rather some signs of interest on the part of his native country. . . . In him Turin possesses a treasure whose worth it perhaps does not know.

In the spring of 1765 Lagrange returned to Turin by way of Geneva and, without attempting to visit Basel to see Daniel Bernoulli, went on d'Alembert's advice to call on Voltaire, who extended him a cordial welcome. Lagrange reported: "He was in a humorous mood that day and his jokes, as usual, were at the expense of religion, which greatly amused the gathering. He is, in truth, a character worth seeing."

D'Alembert's intervention had had some success in Turin, where the king and the ministers held out great hopes to Lagrange—in which he placed little trust.

Meanwhile the Paris Academy of Sciences had proposed for the prize of 1766 the question "What are the inequalities that should be observed in the movement of the four satellites of Jupiter as a result of their mutual attractions . . . ." D'Alembert publicly objected to this subject, which he considered very poorly worded and incorrect, since the actions of the sun on these satellites were completely ignored. His stand on this matter led to a very sharp correspondence between him and Clairaut.

In August 1765 Lagrange sent to the Academy of Sciences "Recherches sur les inégalités des satellites de Jupiter . . . ,"[15] which won the prize. He wrote to d'Alembert on 9 September 1765: "What I said there concerning the equation of the center and the latitude of the satellites appears to me entirely new and of very great importance in the theory of the planets, and I am now prepared to apply it to Saturn and Jupiter." He was alluding to the works published in volume 3 of the *Mélanges de Turin*.

The fine promises of the court of Turin had still not been fulfilled. In the autumn of 1765 d'Alembert, who was on excellent terms with Frederick II of Prussia, suggested to Lagrange that he accept a position in Berlin. He replied, "It seems to me that Berlin would not be at all suitable for me while Mr Euler is there." On 4 March 1766 d'Alembert notified him that Euler was going to leave Berlin and asked him to accept the latter's post. It seems quite likely that Lagrange would gladly have remained in Turin had the king been willing to improve his material and scientific situation. On 26 April, d'Alembert transmitted to Lagrange the very precise and advantageous propositions of the king of Prussia; and on 3 May, Euler, announcing his departure for St. Petersburg, offered him a place in Russia. Lagrange accepted the proposals of the Prussian king and, not without difficulties, obtained his leave at the beginning of July through the intercession of Frederick II with the king of Sardinia.

Lagrange left for Berlin on 21 August 1766, traveling first to Paris and London. After staying for two weeks with d'Alembert, on 20 September he arrived in the English capital, summoned there by Caraccioli. He then embarked for Hamburg and finally reached Berlin on 27 October. On 6 November he was named director of the mathematics section of the Berlin Academy. He quickly became friendly with Lambert and Johann III Bernoulli; but he immediately encountered the silent hostility of the undistinguished Johann Castillon, who stood sullenly aloof from the Academy when it passed him over for a colleague young enough "to be his son."

Lagrange's duties consisted of the monthly reading of a memoir, which was sometimes published in the Academy's *Mémoires* (sixty-three such memoirs were published there), and supervising the Academy's mathematical activities. He had no teaching duties of the sort he had had in Turin and would have again, although more episodically, in Paris. His financial compensation was excellent, and he never sought to improve on it during the twenty years he was there.

In September 1767, eleven months after his arrival, Lagrange married his cousin Vittoria Conti. "My wife," he wrote to d'Alembert in July 1769, "who is one of my cousins and who even lived for a long time with my family, is a very good housewife and has no pretensions at all." He also declared in this letter that he had no children and, moreover, did not want any. He wrote to his father in 1778 or 1779 that his wife's health had been poor for several years. She died in 1783 after a long illness.

The Paris Academy of Sciences had become accustomed to including Lagrange among the competitors for its biennial prizes, and d'Alembert constantly importuned him to participate. The question for 1768, like the one for 1764, concerned the theory of the moon. D'Alembert wrote to him: "This, it seems to me, is a subject truly worthy of your efforts." But Lagrange replied on 23 February 1767: "The king would like me to compete for your prize, because he thinks that Euler is working on it; that, it seems to me, is one more reason for me not to

work on it."

The prize was postponed until 1770. Lagrange excused himself on 2 June 1769: "The illness that I have had these past days, and from which I am still very weakened, has completely upset my work schedule, so that I doubt whether I shall be able to compete for the prize concerning the moon as I had planned."

Lagrange did, however, participate in the competition of 1772 with his "Essai sur le problème des trois corps."[16] The subject was still the theory of the moon. In 1770 half the prize had been awarded to a work composed jointly by Euler and his son Johann Albrecht. The question was proposed again for 1772, and the prize was shared by Lagrange and Euler. On 4 April 1771 Lagrange wrote to d'Alembert: "I intend to send you something for the prize. I have considered the three-body problem in a new and general manner, not that I believe it is better than the one previously employed, but only to approach it *alio modo;* I have applied it to the moon, but I doubt very much that I shall have the time to complete the arithmetical calculations."

On 25 March 1772 d'Alembert announced to Lagrange: "You are sharing with Mr Euler the double prize of 5,000 livres, ... by the unanimous decision of the five judges MM de Condorcet, Bossut, Cassini, Le Monnier, and myself. We believe we owe this recognition to the beautiful analysis of the three-body problem contained in your piece." In a note on this memoir J. A. Serret wrote:

> The first chapter deserves to be counted among Lagrange's most important works. The differential equations of the three-body problem . . . constitute a system of the twelfth order, and the complete solution required twelve integrations. The only knowns were those of the *force vive* and three from the principle of areas. Eight remained to be discovered. In reducing this number to seven Lagrange made a considerable contribution to the question, one not surpassed until 1873. . . .[17]

For the prize of 1774, the Academy asked whether it were possible to explain the secular equation of the moon by the attraction of all the celestial bodies, or by the effect of the nonsphericity of the earth and of the moon. Lagrange, who was equal to the scope of the subject, felt very stale and at the end of August 1773 withdrew from the contest. At d'Alembert's request Condorcet persuaded him to persevere. He was granted an extension and thanked the jury for this favor in February 1774. He took the prize with "Sur l'équation séculaire de la lune."[18]

The topic proposed for 1776 was the theory of the perturbations that comets might undergo through the action of the planets. Lagrange found the subject unpromising, withdrew, and wrote to d'Alembert on 29 May 1775: "I am now ready to give a complete theory of the variations of the elements of the planets resulting from their mutual action." These personal investigations resulted in three studies. One was presented in the *Mémoires* of the Paris Academy: "Recherches sur les équations séculaires des mouvements des noeuds et des inclinaisons des orbites des planètes."[19] Another appeared in the *Mémoires* of the Berlin Academy: "Sur le mouvement des noeuds des orbites planétaires."[20] The third was published in the Berlin *Ephemerides* for 1782: "Sur la diminution de l'obliquité de l'écliptique."[21]

It is understandable that Lagrange, having set out on his own path and being occupied with many other investigations, neglected to enter the competition on the comets. He excused himself by referring to his bad health and the inadequacy of the time allowed, and he pointed out to d'Alembert: "You now have young men in France who could do this work."

Only one entry, from St. Petersburg, was submitted, and the contest was adjourned until 1778. Lagrange "solemnly" promised to compete this time but sent nothing, and the prize was given to Nicolaus Fuss. The same subject was proposed for 1780, and in the summer of 1779 Lagrange submitted "Recherches sur la théorie des perturbations que les comètes peuvent éprouver par l'action des planètes,"[22] which won the double prize of 4,000 livres. This was the last time that he participated in the competitions of the Paris Academy.

Lagrange's activity in celestial mechanics was not confined solely to these competitions: in Turin it had often taken an independent direction. In 1782 he wrote to d'Alembert and Laplace that he was working "a little and slowly" on the theory of the secular variations of the aphelia and of the eccentricities of all the planets. This research led to the *Théorie des variations séculaires des éléments des planètes*[23] and the memoir "Sur les variations séculaires des mouvements moyens des planètes," the latter published in 1785.[24] A work on a related subject is "Théorie des variations périodiques des mouvements des planètes," the first part of which, containing the general formulas, appeared in 1785.[25] The second, concerning the six principal planets, was published in 1786.[26]

Lagrange's work in Berlin far surpassed this classical aspect of celestial mechanics. Soon after his arrival he presented "Mémoire sur le passage de Vénus du 3 Juin 1769,"[27] an occasional work that disconcerted the professional astronomers and contained the first somewhat extended example of an elementary astronomical problem solved by the method of three rectangular coordinates. He later returned sporadically to questions of pure astronomy, as in the two-part memoir "Sur le problème de la détermination des comètes d'après trois observations,"[28] published in 1780 and 1785, and in some articles for the Berlin *Ephemerides*. Furthermore, in 1767 he wrote "Recherches sur le mouvement d'un corps qui est attiré vers deux centres fixes,"[29] which generalized research analogous to that of Euler.

In October 1773 Lagrange composed *Nouvelle solution du problème du mouvement de rotation d'un corps de figure quelconque qui n'est animé par aucune force accélératrice*.[30] "It is," he wrote Condorcet, "a problem already solved by Euler and by d'Alembert . . . . My method is completely different from theirs. . . . It is, moreover, based on formulas that can be useful in other cases and that are quite remarkable in themselves." His method was constructed, in fact, on a purely algebraic lemma. The formulas he provided—with no proof—in this lemma pertain today to the multiplication of determinants.

A by-product of this study of dynamics was Lagrange's famous *Solutions analytiques de quelques problèmes sur les pyramides triangulaires*.[31] Starting from the same formulas as those of the lemma mentioned above, again asserted without proof, he expressed the surface, the volume, and the radii of circumscribed, inscribed, and escribed spheres and located the center of gravity of every triangular pyramid as a function of the lengths of the six edges. Published in May 1775, this memoir must have been written shortly after the preceding one, perhaps in the fall of 1773. It displays a real duality. Today it would be classed in the field of pure algebra, since it employs what are now called determinants, the square of a determinant, an inverse matrix, an orthogonal matrix, and so on.

From about the same period and in the same vein is "Sur l'attraction des sphéroïdes elliptiques,"[32] in which, after praising the solutions obtained by Maclaurin and d'Alembert with "the geometric method of the ancients that is commonly, although very improperly, called synthesis," Lagrange presented a purely analytic solution.

Lagrange had devoted several of his Turin memoirs to fluid mechanics. Among them are those on the propagation of sound. The study of the principle of least action, which appeared in volume 2 of the *Mélanges de Turin*, contained about thirty pages dealing with this topic; and "Solution de différens problèmes de calcul intégral" included another sixteen. He returned to this subject toward the end of his stay in Berlin with "Mémoire sur la théorie du mouvement des fluides,"[33] read on 22 November 1781 but not published until 1783. Laplace, before undertaking a criticism of this work, wrote to him on 11 February 1784: "Nothing could be added to the elegance and generality of your analysis."

Lagrange submitted to the *Mémoires de Turin* for 1784–1785 "Percussion des fluides."[34] In 1788 he published in the Berlin Academy's *Mémoires* "Sur la manière de rectifier deux endroits des principes de Newton relatifs à la propagation du son et au mouvement des ondes."[35] These works are contemporary with or later than the composition of his *Mécanique analytique*.

Lagrange began works of a very different sort as soon as he arrived in Berlin. They were inspired by Euler, whom he always read with the greatest attention.

First Lagrange presented in the *Mémoires* of the Berlin Academy for 1767 (published in 1769) "Sur la solution des problèmes indéterminés du second degré,"[36] in which he copiously cited his predecessor at the Academy and utilized the "Euler criterion." On 20 September 1768 he sent "Solution d'un problème d'arithmétique"[37] to the *Mélanges de Turin* for inclusion in volume 4. Through a series of unfortunate circumstances this second memoir was not published until October 1773. In it Lagrange alluded to the preceding memoir, and through a judicious and skillful use of the algorithm of continued fractions he demonstrated that Fermat's equation $x^2 - ay^2 = 1$ can be solved in all cases where x, y, and a are positive integers, a not being a perfect square and y being different from zero. This is the first known solution of this celebrated problem. The last part of this memoir was developed in "Nouvelle méthode pour résoudre les problèmes indéterminés en nombres entiers,"[38] presented in the Berlin *Mémoires* for 1768 but not completed until February 1769 and published in 1770.

On 26 August 1770 Lagrange reported to d'Alembert the publication of the German edition of Euler's *Algebra* (St. Petersburg, 1770): "It contains nothing of interest except for a treatise on the Diophantine equations, which is, in truth, excellent. ... If you have the time you could wait for the French translation that they hope to bring out, and to which I shall be able to add some brief notes." The translation was done by Johann III Bernoulli and sent, with Lagrange's additions,[39] to Lyons for publication around May 1771. The entire work appeared in the summer of 1773.

In his additions Lagrange paid tribute to the works of Bachet de Méziriac on indeterminate first-degree equations and again considered the topics discussed in the memoirs cited above, at the same time simplify-

ing the demonstrations. In particular he elaborated a great deal on continued fractions.

Meanwhile, in the Berlin *Mémoires* for 1770 (published 1772) he presented "Démonstration d'un théorème d'arithmétique."[40] On the basis of Euler's unsuccessful but nevertheless fruitful attempts, he set forth the first demonstration that every natural integer is the sum of at most four perfect squares.

On 13 June 1771 Lagrange read before the Berlin Academy "Démonstration d'un théorème nouveau concernant les nombres premiers."[41] The theorem in question was one developed by Wilson that had simply been stated in Edward Waring's *Meditationes algebraicae* (2nd ed., Cambridge, 1770). Lagrange was the first to prove it, along with the reciprocal proposition: "For n to be a prime number it is necessary and sufficient that $1 \cdot 2 \cdot 3 \cdots (n-1) + 1$ be divisible by n."

A fundamental memoir on the arithmetic theory of quadratic forms, modestly entitled "Recherches d'arithmétique,"[42] led the way for Gauss and Legendre. It appeared in two parts, the first in May 1775 in the Berlin *Mémoires* for 1773 and the second in June 1777, in the same periodical's volume for 1775.

Always timid before d'Alembert, whom he knew to be totally alien to this kind of investigation, Lagrange wrote to him regarding his memoirs recently published in Berlin: "The 'Recherches d'arithmétique' are the ones that caused me the most difficulty and are perhaps worth the least. I believe you never wished to find out very much about this material, and I don't think you are wrong. ...." The encouragement that he vainly sought from his old friend was perhaps given him by Laplace, to whom he declared, when sending him the second part of his memoir on 1 September 1777: "I hastened to have it published only because you have encouraged me by your approval."

In any case, Lagrange was well aware of the value of his investigations—and posterity has agreed with his judgment. In the first part of the paper he stated: "No one I know of has yet treated this material in a direct and general manner, nor provided rules for finding a priori the principal properties of numbers that can be related to arbitrarily given formulas. As this subject is one of the most curious in arithmetic and particularly merits the attention of geometers because of the great difficulties it contains, I shall attempt to treat it more thoroughly than has previously been done." It may be said that Lagrange, who in many of his works is the last great mathematician of the eighteenth century, here opens up magnificently the route to the abstract mathematics of the nineteenth century.

On 20 March 1777 Lagrange read another paper before the Academy: "Sur quelques problèmes de l'analyse de Diophante."[43] It includes an exposition of "infinite descent" inspired by Fermat's comment on that topic, but this designation does not appear, since Fermat used it only in manuscripts that were unknown at the time. Lagrange writes: "The principle of Fermat's demonstration is one of the most fruitful in the entire theory of numbers and above all in that of the whole numbers. Mr Euler has further developed this principle." This memoir also contains solutions to several difficult problems in indeterminate analysis.

Lagrange's known arithmetical works end at this point, while he was still in Berlin. Yet "Essai d'analyse numérique sur la transformation des fractions,"[44] published at Paris in the *Journal de l'École polytechnique* (1797–1798), shows that Lagrange did not lose interest in problems of this type. But the main portion of his work in this area is concentrated in the first ten years of his stay in Berlin (1767–1777). The fatigue mentioned in the letter of 6 July 1775 (cited above) was probably real, for this pioneering work was obviously exhausting.

During these ten years Lagrange also tackled algebraic analysis—or, more precisely, the solution of both numerical and literal equations. On 29 October 1767 he read "Sur l'élimination des inconnues dans les équations"[45] (published in 1771), in which he employed Cramer's method of symmetric functions but sought to make it more rapid by use of the series development of log $(1 + u)$. Nothing seems to remain of this "improvement" of Cramer's method.

Two important memoirs appeared in 1769 and 1770, respectively: "Sur la résolution des équations numérique" and "Addition au mémoire sur la résolution des équations numériques."[47] In them Lagrange utilized the algorithm of continued fractions, and in the "Addition" he showed that the quadratic irrationals are the only ones that can be expressed as periodic continued fractions. He returned to the question in the additions to Euler's *Algebra*. The two memoirs later formed the framework of the *Traité de la résolution des équations numériques de tous les degrés*,[48] the first edition of which dates from 1798.

On 18 January and 5 April 1770 Lagrange read before the Academy his "Nouvelle méthode pour résoudre les équations littérales par le moyen des séries."[49] The method was probably suggested to him by a verbal communication from Lambert. The latter had presented, in the *Acta helvetica* for 1758, related formulas for trinomial equations but had not demonstrated them. Lagrange's formula was destined to make a great impact. He stated it in a letter to d'Alembert of 26 August 1770, as follows: "Given

the equation $\alpha - x + \varphi(x) = 0$, $\varphi(x)$ denoting an arbitrary function of x, of which p is one of the roots; I say that one will have $\psi(p)$ denoting an arbitrary function of p,

$$\psi(p) = \psi(x) + \varphi(x)\,\psi'(x) + \frac{d[\varphi(x)^2\,\psi'(x)]}{2dx}$$
$$+ \frac{d^2[\varphi(x)^3\,\psi'(x)]}{2\cdot 3 dx^2} + \cdots +,$$

where

$$\psi'(x) = \frac{d\psi(x)}{dx},$$

provided that in this series one replaces x by α, after having carried out the differentiations indicated, taking dx as a constant."

Euler, his disciple Anders Lexell, d'Alembert, and Condorcet all became extremely interested in this discovery as soon as they learned of it. The "demonstrations" of it that Lagrange and his emulators produced were hardly founded on anything more than induction. Laplace later presented a better proof. Lagrange's formula occupied numerous other mathematicians, including Arbogast, Parseval, Servois, Hindenburg, and Bürmann. Cauchy closely examined the conditions of convergence, which had been completely ignored by the inventor; and virtually every analyst of the nineteenth century considered the problem.

On 1 November 1770 Lagrange communicated to the Academy the application of his series to "Kepler's problem."[50] But the culmination of his research in the theory of equations was a memoir read in 1771: "Réflexions sur la résolution algébrique des équations."[51] In November 1770 Vandermonde read before the Paris Academy an analogous but independent and perhaps more subtle study, published in 1774. These two memoirs constituted the source of all the subsequent works on the algebraic solution of equations. Lagrange publicly acknowledged the originality and depth of Vandermonde's research. As early as 24 February 1774 he wrote to Condorcet: "Monsieur de Vandermonde seems to me a very great analyst and I was very delighted with his work on equations."

Whereas Lagrange started from a discriminating critical-historical study of the writings of his predecessors—particularly Tschirnhausen, Euler, and Bezout—Vandermonde based his work directly on the principle that the analytic expression of the roots should be a function of these roots that can be determined from the coefficients alone. Yet each of these two memoirs reveals the appearance of the concept of the permutation group (without the term, which was coined by Galois), a concept which later played a fundamental role.

Two other memoirs on this subject should be mentioned. "Sur la forme des racines imaginaires des équations,"[52] ready for printing in October 1773, evoked the following response from d'Alembert: "Your demonstration on imaginary roots seems to me to leave nothing to be desired, and I am very much obliged to you for the justice you have rendered to mine, which, in fact, has the minor fault (perhaps more apparent than real) of not being direct, but which is quite simple and easy." D'Alembert was alluding to his *Cause des vents* (1747). According to the extremely precise testimony of Delambre in his biographical notice, the demonstration by François Daviet de Foncenex that appeared in the first volume of *Mélanges de Turin* was very probably at least inspired by Lagrange. It is known that in 1799 Gauss subjected these various attempts to fierce criticism.

The last memoir in this area that should be cited appeared in 1779: "Recherches sur la détermination du nombre des racines imaginaires dans les équations littérales."[53]

Lagrange's works in infinitesimal analysis are for the most part later than those concerned with number theory and algebra and were composed at intervals from about 1768 to 1787. More in agreement with prevailing tastes, they assured Lagrange a European reputation during his lifetime.

Returning, without citing it, to his letter to Fagnano of 1754, Lagrange presented in the Berlin *Mémoires* for 1772 (published in the spring of 1774) "Sur une nouvelle espèce de calcul relatif à la différentiation et à l'intégration des quantités variables."[54] This work, which is in fact an outline of his *Théorie des fonctions* (1797), greatly impressed Lacroix, Condorcet, and Laplace. Based on the analogy between powers of binomials and differentials, it is one of the sources of the symbolic calculuses of the nineteenth century. A typical example of Lagrange's thinking as an analyst is this sentence taken from the memoir: "Although the principle of this analogy [between powers and differentials] is not self-evident, nevertheless, since the conclusions drawn from it are not thereby less exact, I shall make use of it to discover various theorems. . . ."

On 20 September 1768 he sent to the *Mélanges de Turin*, along with "Mémoire d'analyse indéterminée," the essay "Sur l'intégration de quelques équations différentielles dont les indéterminées sont séparées, mais dont chaque membre en particulier n'est point intégrable."[55] In it Lagrange drew inspiration from some of Euler's works; and the latter wrote to him on 23 March 1775, when the essay finally came to his attention: "I was not sufficiently able to admire the skill and facility with which you treat so many thorny

matters that have cost me much effort . . . in particular the integration of this differential equation:

$$\frac{m \, dx}{\sqrt{A + Bx + Cx^2 + Dx^3 + Ex^4}}$$

$$= \frac{n \, dy}{\sqrt{A + By + Cy^2 + Dy^3 + Ey^4}}$$

in all cases where the two numbers m and n are rational."

With this essay, as with certain works of Jakob Bernoulli, Fagnano, Euler, Landen, and others, we are in the prehistory of the theory of elliptic functions, to which period belongs one other memoir by Lagrange. Included in volume 2 of the miscellany of the Academy of Turin for 1784–1785—this academy was founded in 1783 and Lagrange was its honorary president—it was entitled "Sur une nouvelle méthode de calcul intégral pour les différentielles affectées d'un radical carré sous lequel la variable ne passe pas le quatrième degré."[56] Lagrange here proposed to find convergent series for the integrals of this type of differential, which is frequent in mechanics. To this purpose he transformed these differentials in such a way that the fourth-degree polynomial placed under the radical separated into the factors $1 + px^2$ and $1 + qx^2$, the coefficients p and q being either very unequal or almost equal. Lagrange also utilized in this work the "arithmetico-geometric mean" and reduced the integration of the series

$$(A + A'U + A''U^2 + A'''U^3 + \cdots) \, V \, dx$$

to that of the differential $V dx/(1 - aU)$. This memoir, which is difficult to date precisely, was written in the last years of his stay in Berlin, after the death of his wife.

We shall now consider some earlier works on differential and partial differential equations. About March 1773 Lagrange read before the Berlin Academy his study "Sur l'intégration des équations aux différences partielles du premier ordre."[57] The Berlin *Mémoires* for 1774 (published in 1776) contained the essay "Sur les intégrales particulières des équations différentielles."[58] In these two works he considered singular integrals of differential and partial differential equations. This problem had only been lightly touched on by Clairaut, Euler, d'Alembert, and Condorcet. Lagrange wrote: "Finally I have just read a memoir that Mr de Laplace presented recently. . . . This reading awakened old ideas that I had on the same subject and resulted in the following investigations . . . [which constitute] a new and complete theory." Laplace wrote on 3 February 1778 that he considered Lagrange's essay "a masterpiece of analysis, by the importance of the subject, by the beauty of the method, and by the elegant manner in which it is presented."

The Berlin *Mémoires* for 1776 (published 1778) included the brief study "Sur l'usage des fractions continues dans le calcul intégral."[59] The algorithm Lagrange proposed in it had, according to him, the advantage over series of giving, when it exists, the finite integral of a differential equation, while the other method can yield only approximations.

The memoir "Sur différentes questions d'analyse relatives à la théorie des intégrales particulières"[60] may have been written about 1780. In it Lagrange extended and deepened his studies of particular integrals. He demonstrated the equivalence of the integrations of the equation

$$\xi_1 \frac{\partial f}{\partial x_1} + \xi_2 \frac{\partial f}{\partial x_2} + \cdots + \xi_n \frac{\partial f}{\partial x_n} = 0$$

and the system

$$\frac{dx_1}{\xi_1} = \frac{dx_2}{\xi_2} = \cdots = \frac{dx_n}{\xi_n}.$$

Finally, just as he was leaving Prussia, Lagrange presented in the Berlin *Mémoires* for 1785 (published in 1787) "Méthode générale pour intégrer les équations partielles du premier ordre lorsque ces différences ne sont que linéaires."[61] This "general method" completed the preceding memoir.

Lagrange's contribution to the calculus of probabilities, while not inconsiderable, is limited to a few memoirs. We have cited one of them written before 1759 and mentioned his translation of de Moivre. Two others are "Mémoire sur l'utilité de la méthode de prendre le milieu entre les résultats de plusieurs observations . . .,"[62] composed before 1774, and "Recherches sur les suites récurrentes dont les termes varient de plusieurs manières différentes . . .,"[63] read before the Berlin Academy in May 1776. The latter memoir was inspired by two essays of Laplace, the reading of which recalled to Lagrange his first writing on the question, which predated 1759. He proposed to add to this early work and to Laplace's essays, and to treat the same subject in a manner at once simpler, more direct, and above all more general. Last we may mention, from the Paris period, "Essai d'arithmétique politique sur les premiers besoins de l'intérieur de la République,"[64] written in *an* IV (1795–1796).

The considerable place that mechanics, and more particularly celestial mechanics, occupied in Lagrange's works resulted in contributions that were scattered among numerous memoirs. Thinking it proper to present his ideas in a single comprehensive work, on 15 September 1782 Lagrange wrote to Laplace: "I have almost completed a *Traité de mécanique analytique,*

based uniquely on [the principle of virtual velocities]; but, as I do not yet know when or where I shall be able to have it printed, I am not rushing to put the finishing touches on it."

The work was published at Paris. A. M. Legendre had assumed the heavy burden of correcting the proofs; and his former teacher, the Abbé Joseph-François Marie, was entrusted with the arrangements with the publishers, agreeing to buy up all the unsold copies. By the time the book appeared, at the beginning of 1788, Lagrange had settled in Paris.

About 1774 there was already talk of Lagrange's returning to Turin. In 1781, through the mediation of his old friend Caraccioli, then viceroy of Sicily, the court of Naples offered him the post of director of the philosophy section of the academy recently established in that city. Lagrange, however, rejected the proposal. He was happy with his situation in Berlin and wished only to work there in peace. But the death of his wife in August 1783 left him very distressed, and with the death of Frederick II in August 1786 he lost his strongest support in Berlin. Advised of the situation, the princes of Italy zealously competed in attracting him to their courts.

In the meantime Mirabeau, entrusted with a semiofficial diplomatic mission to the court of Prussia, asked the French government to bring Lagrange to Paris through an advantageous offer. Of all the candidates, Paris was victorious. France's written agreement with Lagrange was scrupulously respected by the public authorities through all the changes of regime. In addition, Prussia accorded him a generous pension that he was still drawing in 1792.

Lagrange left Berlin on 18 May 1787. On 29 July he became *pensionnaire vétéran* of the Paris Academy of Sciences, of which he had been a foreign associate member since 22 May 1772. Warmly welcomed in Paris, he experienced a certain lassitude and did not immediately resume his research. Yet he astonished those around him by his extensive knowledge of metaphysics, history, religion, linguistics, medicine, and botany. He had long before formulated a prudent rule of conduct: "I believe that, in general, one of the first principles of every wise man is to conform strictly to the laws of the country in which he is living, even when they are unreasonable." In this frame of mind he experienced the sudden changes of the Revolution, which he observed with interest and sometimes with sympathy but without the passion of his friends and colleagues Condorcet, Laplace, Monge, and Carnot.

In 1792 Lagrange married Renée-Françoise-Adélaïde Le Monnier, the daughter of his colleague at the Academy, the astronomer Pierre Charles Le

Monnier. This was a troubled period, about a year after the flight of the king and his arrest at Varennes. Nevertheless, on 3 June the royal family signed the marriage contract "as a sign of its agreement to the union." Lagrange had no children from this second marriage, which, like the first, was a happy one.

Meanwhile, on 8 May 1790 the Constituent Assembly had decreed the standardization of weights and measures and given the Academy of Sciences the task of establishing a system founded on fixed bases and capable of universal adoption. Lagrange was naturally a member of the commission entrusted with this work.

When the academies were suppressed on 8 August 1793 this commission was retained. Three months later Lavoisier, Borda, Laplace, Coulomb, Brisson, and Delambre were purged from its membership; but Lagrange remained as its chairman. In September of the same year the authorities ordered the arrest of all foreigners born within the borders of the enemy powers and the confiscation of their property. Lavoisier intervened with Joseph Lakanal to obtain an exception for Lagrange, and it was granted.

The Bureau des Longitudes was established by the National Convention on 25 June 1795, and Lagrange was a member of it from the beginning. In this capacity he returned to concerns that had been familiar to him since his participation, with Johann Karl Schulze and J. E. Bode, among others, in the editing of the Berlin *Ephemerides.*

A decree of 30 October established an *école normale,* designed to train teachers and to standardize education. This creation of the Convention was short-lived. Generally known as the École Normale de l'An III, it lasted only three months and eleven days. Lagrange, with Laplace as his assistant, taught elementary mathematics there.

Founded on 11 March 1794 at the instigation of Monge, the École Centrale des Travaux Publics, which soon took the name École Polytechnique, still exists. Lagrange taught analysis there until 1799 and was succeeded by Sylvestre Lacroix.

The constitution of *an* III replaced the suppressed academies with the Institut National. On 27 December 1795 Lagrange was elected chairman of the provisional committee of the first section, reserved for the physical and mathematical sciences.

By the coup d'état of 18–19 Brumaire, *an* VIII (9–10 November 1799) Bonaparte replaced the Directory with the Consulate. A Sénat Conservateur, which continued to exist under the Empire, was established and included among its members Lagrange, Monge, Berthollet, Carnot, and other scientists. In addition Lagrange, like Monge, became a grand

officer of the newly founded Legion of Honor. In 1808 he was made count of the Empire by a law covering all the senators, ministers, state councillors, archbishops, and the president of the legislature. He was named *grand croix* of the Ordre Impérial de la Réunion—created by Napoleon in 1811—at the same time as Monge, on 3 April 1813.

Lagrange was by now seriously ill. He died on the morning of 11 April 1813, and three days later his body was carried to the Panthéon. The funeral oration was given by Laplace in the name of the Senate and by Lacépède in the name of the Institute. Similar ceremonies were held in various universities of the kingdom of Italy; but nothing was done in Berlin, for Prussia had joined the coalition against France. Napoleon ordered the acquisition of Lagrange's papers, and they were turned over to the Institute.

With the appearance of the *Mécanique analytique* in 1788, Lagrange proposed to reduce the theory of mechanics and the art of solving problems in that field to general formulas, the mere development of which would yield all the equations necessary for the solution of every problem.

The *Traité* united and presented from a single point of view the various principles of mechanics, demonstrated their connection and mutual dependence, and made it possible to judge their validity and scope. It is divided into two parts, statics and dynamics, each of which treats solid bodies and fluids separately. There are no diagrams. The methods presented require only analytic operations, subordinated to a regular and uniform development. Each of the four sections begins with a historical account which is a model of the kind.

Lagrange decided, however, that the work should have a second edition incorporating certain advances. In the *Mémoires de l'Institut* he had earlier published some essays that represented a last, brilliant contribution to the development of celestial mechanics. Among them were "Mémoire sur la théorie générale de la variation des constantes arbitraires dans tous les problèmes de la mécanique,"[65] read on 13 March 1809, and "Second mémoire sur la théorie de la variation des constantes arbitraires dans les problèmes de mécanique dans lequel on simplifie l'application des formules générales à ces problèmes,"[66] read on 19 February 1810. Arthur Cayley later deemed this theory "perfectly complete in itself."

It was necessary to incorporate the theory and certain of its applications to celestial mechanics into the work of 1788. The first volume of the second edition appeared in 1811.[67] Lagrange died while working on the second volume, which was not published until 1816.[68] Even so, a large portion of it only repeated the first edition verbatim.

"Les leçons élémentaires sur les mathématiques données à l'École normale" (1795)[69] appeared first in the *Séances des Écoles normales recueillies par les sténographes et revues par les professeurs*, distributed to the students to accompany the class exercises and published in *an* IV (1795–1796). These lectures, which are very interesting from several points of view, included Lagrange's interpolation: If y takes the values P, Q, R, S, when $x = p$, q, r, s, then $y = AP + BQ + CR + DS$, with

$$A = \frac{(x - q)(x - r)(x - s)}{(p - q)(p - r)(p - s)}, \text{ and so on.}$$

(This interpolation had already been outlined by Waring in 1779.) The text of the "Leçons" as given in the *Oeuvres* is a much enlarged reissue that appeared in the *Journal de l'École polytechnique* in 1812.

Traité de la résolution des équations numériques de tous les degrés[70] was published in 1798. It is a reissue of memoirs originally published on the same subject in 1769 and 1770, preceded by a fine historical introduction and followed by numerous notes. Several of the latter consider points discussed in other memoirs whether in summary or in a developed form. In this work, which was republished in 1808, Lagrange paid tribute to the works of Vandermonde and Gauss.

Théorie des fonctions analytiques contenant les principes de calcul différentiel, dégagés de toute considération d'infiniment petits, d'évanouissants, de limites et de fluxions et réduits à l'analyse algébrique des quantités finies[71] indicates by its title the author's rather utopian program. First published in 1797 (a second edition appeared in 1813), it returned to themes already considered in 1772. In it Lagrange intended to show that power series expansions are sufficient to provide differential calculus with a solid foundation. Today mathematicians are partially returning to this conception in treating the formal calculus of series. As early as 1812, however, J. M. H. Wronski objected to Lagrange's claims. The subsequent opposition of Cauchy was more effective. Nevertheless, Lagrange's point of view could not be totally neglected. Completed by convergence considerations, it dominated the study of the functions of a complex variable throughout the nineteenth century.

Many passages of the *Théorie*, as of the "Leçons" (discussed below), were wholly incorporated into the later didactic works. This is true, for example, of the study of the tangents to curves and surfaces and of "Lagrange's remainder" in the expansion of functions by the Taylor series.

The "Leçons sur le calcul des fonctions,"[72] designed to be both a commentary on and a supplement to the preceding work, appeared in 1801 in the *Journal de l'École polytechnique* as the twelfth part of the "Leçons de l'École normale." A separate edition of 1806 contained two complementary lectures on the calculus of variations, and the *Théorie des fonctions* also devoted a chapter to this subject. In dealing with it and with all other subjects in these two works, Lagrange abandoned the differential notation and introduced a new vocabulary and a new symbolism: first derivative function f'; second derivative function, f''; and so on. To a certain extent this symbolism and vocabulary have prevailed.

Without having enumerated all of Lagrange's writings, this study has sought to make known their different aspects and to place them in approximately chronological order. This attempt will, it is hoped, be of assistance in comprehending the evolution of his thought.

Lagrange was always well informed about his contemporaries and predecessors and often enriched his thinking by a critical reading of their works. His close friendship with d'Alembert should not obscure the frequently striking divergence in their ideas. D'Alembert's mathematical production was characterized by a realism that links him with Newton and Cauchy. Lagrange, on the contrary, displayed in his youth, and sometimes in his later years, a poetic sense that recalls the creative audacity of Leibniz.

Although Lagrange was always very reserved toward Euler, whom he never met, it was the latter, among the older mathematicians, who most influenced him. That is why any study of his work must be preceded or accompanied by an examination of the work of Euler. Yet even in the face of this great model he preserved an originality that allowed him to criticize but above all to generalize, to systematize, and to deepen the ideas of his predecessors.

At his death Lagrange left examples to follow, new problems to solve, and techniques to develop in all branches of mathematics. His analytic mind was very different from the more intuitive one of his friend Monge. The two mathematicians in fact complemented each other very well, and together they were the masters of the following generations of French mathematicians, of whom many were trained at the École Polytechnique, where Lagrange and Monge were the two most famous teachers.

NOTES

All references are to volume and pages of Lagrange's *Oeuvres* cited in the bibliography.
1. II, 318–332.
2. III, 157–186.

3. I, 3–20.
4. I, 23–36.
5. XIV, 66.
6. I, 39–148.
7. I, 151–316.
8. I, 319–332.
9. I, 334–362.
10. I, 365–468.
11. I, 471–668.
12. XIII, 30.
13. VI, 5–61.
14. V, 5–123.
15. VI, 67–225.
16. VI, 229–324.
17. VI, 324.
18. VI, 335–399.
19. VI, 635–709.
20. IV, 111–148.
21. VII, 517–532.
22. VII, 403–503.
23. V, 125–207, pt. 1, published in 1783; V, 211–344, pt. 2, published in 1784.
24. V, 382–414.
25. V, 348–377.
26. V, 418–488.
27. II, 335–374.
28. IV, 439–532.
29. II, 67–121.
30. III, 581–616.
31. III, 661–692.
32. III, 619–649.
33. IV, 695–748.
34. II, 237–249.
35. V, 592–609.
36. II, 377–535.
37. I, 671–731.
38. II, 655–726.
39. VII, 5–180.
40. III, 189–201.
41. III, 425–438.
42. III, 695–795.
43. IV, 377–398.
44. VII, 291–313.
45. III, 141–154.
46. II, 539–578.
47. II, 581–652.
48. VIII, 13–367.
49. III, 5–73.
50. III, 113–138.
51. III, 205–421.
52. III, 479–516.
53. IV, 343–374.
54. III, 441–476.
55. II, 5–33.
56. II, 253–312.
57. III, 549–575.
58. IV, 5–108.
59. IV, 301–332.
60. IV, 585–635.
61. V, 544–562.
62. II, 173–234.
63. IV, 151–251.
64. VII, 573–579.
65. VI, 771–804.
66. VI, 809–816.
67. XI, 1–444.
68. XII, 1–340.
69. VII, 183–287.
70. VIII, 13–367.
71. IX, 15–413.
72. X, 1–451.

BIBLIOGRAPHY

I. ORIGINAL WORKS. *Oeuvres de Lagrange*, J. A. Serret, ed., 14 vols. (Paris, 1867–1892), consists of the following:

Vol. I (1867) contains the biographical notice written by Delambre and the articles from vols. 1–4 of *Mélanges de Turin*.

Vol. II (1868) presents articles originally published in vols. 4 and 5 of *Mélanges de Turin* and vols. 1 and 2 of *Mémoires de l'Académie des sciences de Turin*, and in the *Mémoires de l'Académie royale des sciences et belles lettres de Berlin* for 1765–1768. It should be noted that the Berlin *Mémoires* generally appeared two years after the date indicated.

Vol. III (1869) contains papers from the Berlin *Mémoires* for 1768 and 1769 and from the *Nouveaux mémoires de l'Académie de Berlin* for 1770–1773 (inclusive) and 1775.

Vol. IV (1869) reprints articles from the *Nouveaux mémoires de Berlin* for 1774–1779 (inclusive), 1781, and 1783.

Vol. V (1870) contains articles from the *Nouveaux mémoires de Berlin* for 1780–1783, 1785, 1786, 1792, 1793, and 1803.

Vol. VI (1873) consists of articles extracted from publications of the Paris Academy of Sciences and of the Class of Mathematical and Physical Sciences of the Institute.

Vol. VII (1877) contains various works that did not appear in the academic publications—in particular, the lectures given at the École Normale.

Vol. VIII (1879) is *Traité de la résolution des équations numériques de tous les degrés, avec des notes sur plusieurs points de la théorie des équations algébriques*. This ed. is based on that of 1808.

Vol. IX (1881) is *Théorie des fonctions analytiques, contenant les principes du calcul différentiel dégagés de toute considération d'infiniment petits, d'évanouissants, de limites et de fluxions, et réduits à l'analyse algébrique des quantités finies*, based on the ed. of 1813.

Vol. X (1884) is *Leçons sur le calcul des fonctions*, based on the 1806 ed.

Vol. XI (1888) is *Mécanique analytique*, vol. I. This ed. is based on that of 1811, with notes by J. Bertrand and G. Darboux.

Vol. XII (1889) is vol. II of *Mécanique analytique*. Based on the ed. of 1816, it too has notes by Bertrand and Darboux. These two vols. have been reprinted (Paris, 1965).

Vol. XIII (1882) contains correspondence with d'Alembert, annotated by Ludovic Lalanne.

Vol. XIV (1892) contains correspondence with Condorcet, Laplace, Euler, and others, annotated by Lalanne.

Vol. XV, in preparation, will include some MSS that had been set aside by the commission of the Institute entrusted with publication of the collected works. This vol. will also present correspondence discovered since 1892 that has been published in various places or was until now unpublished—particularly the correspondence with Fagnano. It will also provide indexes and chronological tables to facilitate the study of Lagrange's works.

Opere matematiche del Marchese Giulio Carlo de Toschi di Fagnano, III (Milan–Rome–Naples, 1912), contains the correspondence between Lagrange and Fagnano: nineteen letters dated 1754–1756 and two from 1759.

There is also *G. G. Leibnitti opera omnia*, Dutens, ed., 6 vols. (Geneva, 1768).

II. SECONDARY LITERATURE.

1. Sylvestre François Lacroix, "Liste des ouvrages de M. Lagrange," supp. to *Mécanique analytique* (Paris, 1816), pp. 372–378; and (Paris, 1855), pp. 383–389.

2. *Catalogue des livres de la bibliothèque du Comte Lagrange* (Paris, 1815).

3. Gino Loria, "Essai d'une bibliographie de Lagrange," in *Isis*, **40** (1949), 112–117, which is very complete.

4. Adolph von Harnack, *Geschichte der Königlich Preussischen Akademie der Wissenschaften*, 3 vols. in 4 pts. (Berlin, 1900), which includes (III, pt. 2, 163–165) the list of the memoirs Lagrange published in the *Mémoires* and *Nouveaux mémoires de Berlin* and (II, 314–321) the correspondence between the minister Hertzberg, Frederick William II of Prussia, and Lagrange on the subject of the latter's departure from Prussia and settling in Paris.

5. Honoré Gabriel Riquetti, comte de Mirabeau, *Histoire secrette de la cour de Berlin, ou correspondance d'un voyageur françois depuis le cinq juillet 1786 jusqu'au dix-neuf janvier 1787*, 2 vols. (Paris, 1789).

6. Jean-Baptiste Biot, "Notice historique sur M. Lagrange," in *Journal de l'empire* (28 Apr. 1813), repr. in Biot's *Mélanges scientifiques et littéraires*, III (Paris, 1859), 117–124.

7. Carlo Denina, *La Prusse littéraire sous Frédéric II*, II (Berlin, 1790), 140–147.

8. Pietro Cossali, *Elogio di L. Lagrange* (Padua, 1813).

9. Jean Baptiste Joseph Delambre, "Notice sur la vie et les ouvrages de M. le Comte J. L. Lagrange," in *Mémoires de la classe des sciences mathématiques de l'Institut* for 1812 (Paris, 1816), repr. in *Oeuvres de Lagrange*, I, ix–li.

10. Frédéric Maurice, "Directions pour l'étude approfondie des mathématiques recueillies des entretiens de Lagrange," in *Le moniteur universel* (Paris) (26 Feb. 1814).

11. Frédéric Maurice, "Lagrange," in Michaud's *Biographie universelle*, XXIII (Paris, 1819), 157–175.

12. Dieudonné Thiebault, *Mes souvenirs de vingt ans de séjour à Berlin*, 5 vols. (Paris, 1804).

13. Julien Joseph Viery and [Dr.] Potel, *Précis historique sur la vie et la mort de Lagrange* (Paris, 1813).

14. Poggendorff, I, 1343–1346.

15. J. M. Quérard, "Lagrange, Joseph Louis de," in *La France littéraire*, IV (Paris, 1830), 429–432.

16. A. Korn, "Joseph Louis Lagrange," in *Mathematische Geschichte Sitzungsberichte*, **12** (1913), 90–94.

17. *Annali di matematica* (Milan), 3rd ser., **20** (Apr. 1913) and **21** (Oct. 1913), both published for the centenary of Lagrange's death.

18. Gino Loria, "G. L. Lagrange nella vita e nelle opere," *ibid.*, **20** (Apr. 1913), ix–lii, repr. in Loria's *Scritti, conferenze, discorsi* (Padua, 1937), pp. 293–333.

19. Gino Loria, *Storia delle matematiche*, 2nd ed. (Milan, 1950), pp. 747–760.

20. Soviet Academy of Sciences, *J. L. Lagrange. Sbornik statey k 200-letiyu so dnya rozhdenia* (Moscow, 1937), a collection of articles in Russian to celebrate the second centenary of Lagrange's birth. Contents given in *Isis*, **28** (1938), 199.

21. George Sarton, "Lagrange's Personality (1736–1813)," in *Proceedings of the American Philosophical Society*, **88** (1944), 457–496.

22. G. Sarton, R. Taton, and G. Beaujouan, "Documents nouveaux concernant Lagrange," in *Revue d'histoire des sciences*, **3** (1950), 110–132.

23. J. F. Montucla, *Histoire des mathématiques*, 2nd ed., IV (Paris, *an* X [1802]; repr. 1960). Despite some confusion the passages written by J. Lalande on Lagrange are interesting, especially those concerning celestial mechanics.

24. Charles Bossut, *Histoire générale des mathématiques*, II (Paris, 1810). Provides an accurate and quite complete description of Lagrange's *oeuvre*, particularly in celestial mechanics. The author was a colleague of Lagrange's at the Institute and had previously been one of his judges at the time of the competitions organized by the Academy of Sciences.

25. Moritz Cantor, ed., *Vorlesungen über Geschichte der Mathematik*, IV (Leipzig, 1908), *passim*. Very useful for situating Lagrange's work within that of his contemporaries.

26. Heinrich Wieleitner, *Geschichte der Mathematik*, II, *Von Cartesius bis zur Wende des 18 Jahrhunderts*, pt. 1, *Arithmetik, Algebra, Analysis*, prepared by Anton von Braunmühl (Leipzig, 1911), *passim*. Renders the same service as the preceding work.

27. Niels Nielsen, *Géomètres français sous la Révolution* (Copenhagen, 1929), pp. 136–152.

28. Maximilien Marie, *Histoire des sciences mathématiques et physiques*, IX (Paris, 1886), 76–234.

29. Nicolas Bourbaki, *Éléments d'histoire des mathématiques*, 2nd ed. (Paris, 1969). A study of the history of mathematics, including the work of Lagrange, from a very modern point of view.

30. Carl B. Boyer, *A History of Mathematics* (New York, 1968), pp. 510–543.

31. René Taton *et al.*, *Histoire générale des sciences*, II, *La science moderne*, and III, *La science contemporaine*, pt. 1, *Le XIXème siècle* (Paris, 1958–1961). Numerous citations from the work of Lagrange, which is considered in all its aspects.

32. Carl Ohrtmann, *Das Problem der Tautochronen. Ein historischer Versuch*; also trans. into French by Clément Dusausoy (Rome, 1875).

33. Robert Woodhouse, *A History of the Calculus of Variations in the Eighteenth Century* (Cambridge, 1810; repr. New York, 1965), pp. 80–109.

34. Isaac Todhunter, *A History of the Calculus of Variations in the Nineteenth Century* (Cambridge, 1861; repr. New York, n.d.), pp. 1–10.

35. C. Carathéodory, "The Beginning of Research in the Calculus of Variations," in *Osiris*, **3** (1938), 224–240.

36. Isaac Todhunter, *A History of the Mathematical Theory of Probability* (Cambridge, 1865; repr. New York, 1965), pp. 301–320.

37. René Dugas, *Histoire de la mécanique* (Neuchâtel–Paris, 1950), pp. 318–332. Includes an important study of the *Mécanique analytique* based on the 2nd ed. The development of Lagrange's thinking in mechanics is not considered; but his influence on his successors, such as Poisson, Hamilton, and Jacobi is well brought out.

38. Ernst Mach, *Die Mechanik in ihrer Entwicklung* (Leipzig, 1883), *passim*. Mach states that he found the original inspiration for his book in Lagrange's historical introductions to the various chapters of the *Mécanique analytique*. See especially ch. 4, "Die formelle Entwicklung der Mechanik."

39. Clifford Ambrose Truesdell, *Essays in the History of Mechanics* (Berlin–Heidelberg–New York, 1968), 93, 132–135, 173, 245–248. The author, who is more concerned with the origin and evolution of concepts than with personalities, nevertheless has a tendency to diminish the role of Lagrange in favor of Euler.

40. Julian Lowell Coolidge, *A History of Geometrical Methods* (Oxford, 1940; repr. New York, 1963). Provides several insights into Lagrange's work in geometry, in particular on minimal surfaces.

41. Gaston Darboux, *Leçons sur la théorie générale des surfaces*, I (Paris, 1887), 267–268, on minimal surfaces.

42. A. Aubry, "Sur les travaux arithmétiques de Lagrange, de Legendre et de Gauss," in *L'enseignement mathématique*, XI (Geneva, 1909), 430–450.

43. F. Cajori, *A History of the Arithmetical Methods of Approximation to the Roots of Numerical Equations of One Unknown Quantity*, Colorado College Publications, General Series, nos. 51 and 52 (Colorado Springs, Colo., 1910).

44. Leonard Eugene Dickson, *History of the Theory of Numbers*, 3 vols. (Washington, 1919–1923; repr. New York, 1952). Contains numerous citations from Lagrange throughout. Several of his memoirs are summarized.

45. Hans Wussing, *Die Genesis des Abstrakten Gruppenbegriffes* (Berlin, 1969). The author closely analyzes the 1771 memoir on the resolution of equations and describes Lagrange's role in the birth of the group concept.

JEAN ITARD

LAGUERRE, EDMOND NICOLAS (*b.* Bar-le-Duc, France, 9 April 1834; *d.* Bar-le-Duc, 14 August 1886)

Laguerre was in his own lifetime considered to be a geometer of brilliance, but his major influence has been in analysis. Of his more than 140 published papers, over half are in geometry; in length his geometrical work represents more than two-thirds of his total output. He was also a member of the geometry section of the Academy of Sciences in Paris.

There was no facet of geometry which did not engage Laguerre's interest. Among his works are papers on foci of algebraic curves, on geometric interpretation of homogeneous forms and their invariants, on anallagmatic curves and surfaces (that is, curves and surfaces which are transformed into themselves by inversions), on fourth-order curves, and on differential geometry, particularly studies of curvature and geodesics. He was one of the first to investigate the complex projective plane.

Laguerre also published in other areas. Geometry led him naturally to linear algebra. In addition, he discovered a generalization of the Descartes rule of signs, worked in algebraic continued fractions, and toward the end of his life produced memoirs on differential equation and elliptical function theory.

The young Laguerre attended several public schools as he moved from place to place for his health. His education was completed at the École Polytechnique in Paris, where he excelled in modern languages and mathematics. His overall showing, however, was relatively poor: he ranked forty-sixth in his class. Nevertheless, he published his celebrated "On the Theory of Foci" when he was only nineteen.

In 1854 Laguerre left school and accepted a commission as an artillery officer. For ten years, while in the army, he published nothing. Evidently he kept on with his studies, however, for in 1864 he resigned his commission and returned to Paris to take up duties as a tutor at the École Polytechnique. He remained there for the rest of his life and in 1874 was appointed *examinateur*. In 1883 Laguerre accepted, concurrently, the chair of mathematical physics at the Collège de France. At the end of February 1886 his continually poor health broke down completely; he returned to Bar-le-Duc, where he died in August. Laguerre was pictured by his contemporaries as a quiet, gentle man who was passionately devoted to his research, his teaching, and the education of his two daughters.

Although his efforts in geometry were striking, all Laguerre's geometrical production—with but one exception—is now unknown except to a few specialists. Unfortunately for Laguerre's place in history, this part of his output has been largely absorbed by later theories or has passed into the general body of geometry without acknowledgment. For example, his work on differential invariants is included in the more comprehensive Lie group theory. Laguerre's one theorem of geometry which is still cited with frequency is the discovery—made in 1853 in "On the Theory of Foci"—that in the complex projective plane the angle between the lines a and b which intersect at the point O is given by the formula

$$\angle(ab) = \frac{R(a, b, OI, OJ)}{2i} \pmod{\pi}, \qquad (1)$$

where the numerator is the cross ratio of a, b and lines joining O to the circular points at infinity: $I = (i, 1, 0)$ and $J = (-i, 1, 0)$.

Actually, Laguerre proved more. He showed that if a system of angles $A, B, C, \cdots$ in a plane is related by a function $F(A, B, C, \cdots) = 0$, and if the system is transformed into another, $A', B', C', \cdots$, by a homographic (cross ratio-preserving) mapping, then $A', B', C', \cdots$, satisfies the relation

$$F \left(\frac{\log \alpha}{2i}, \frac{\log \beta}{2i}, \frac{\log \gamma}{2i}, \cdots \right) = 0,$$

where $\alpha, \beta, \gamma, \cdots$ are cross ratios, as in expression (1).

This theorem is commonly cited as being an inspiration for Arthur Cayley when he introduced a metric into the projective plane in 1859 and for Felix Klein when he improved and extended Cayley's work in 1871.[1] These assertions appear to be false. There is no mention of Laguerre in Cayley, and Cayley was meticulous to the point of fussiness in the assigning of proper credit. Klein is specific; he states that Laguerre's work was not known to him when he wrote his 1871 paper on non-Euclidean geometry.[2] Presumably the Laguerre piece was brought to Klein's attention after his own publication.

Nevertheless, Laguerre's current reputation rests on a very solid foundation: his discovery of the set of differential equations (Laguerre's equations)

$$xy'' + (1 + x) y' - ny = 0, (n = 0, 1, 2, \cdots) \quad (2)$$

and their polynomial solutions (Laguerre's polynomials)

$$\sum_{k=0}^{n} \frac{n^2 (n - 1)^2 \cdots (n - k + 1)^2}{k!} x^{n-k}. \quad (3)$$

These ideas have been enlarged so that today generalized Laguerre equations are usually considered. They have the form

$$xy'' + (s + 1 - x) y' + ny = 0, (n = 0, 1, 2, \cdots) \quad (4)$$

and have as their solutions the generalized Laguerre polynomials,

$$L_n^s(x) = \sum_{k=0}^{n} \frac{(-1)^k n!}{k! (n - k)!} \left(\prod_{j=0}^{k-1} (n + s - j) \right) x^{n-k}, \quad (5)$$

which also are frequently written as

$$L_n^s(x) = (-1)^n x^{-s} e^x \frac{d^n}{dx^n} (x^{s+n} e^{-x}).$$

The alternating sign of (5) not present in (3) is due to the change of signs of the coefficients of the y and y' terms in (4). The Laguerre functions are defined from the polynomials by setting

$$\underline{\psi}_n^s(x) = e^{-x/2} x^{s/2} L_n^s(x).$$

If $s = 0$, the notations $L_n(x)$ and $\underline{\psi}_n(x)$ are often used. These functions and polynomials have wide uses in mathematical physics and applied mathematics—for example, in the solution of the Schrödinger equations for hydrogen-like atoms and in the study of electrical networks and dynamical systems.[3]

Laguerre studied the Laguerre equation in connection with his investigations of the integral

$$\int_x^\infty \frac{e^{-x}}{x} dx \quad (6)$$

and published the results in 1879.

He started by setting

$$F(x) = \sum_{k=0}^{n-1} (-1)^k k! \frac{1}{x^{k+1}}, \quad (7)$$

from which the relation

$$\int_x^\infty \frac{e^{-x}}{x} dx = e^{-x} F(x) + (-1)^n n! \int_x^\infty \frac{e^{-x}}{x^{n+1}} dx \quad (8)$$

was obtained by integration by parts. Observe that as n increases beyond bound in (7), the infinite series obtained diverges for every x, since the nth term fails to go to zero. Nevertheless, for large-value x the first few terms can be utilized in (8) to give a good approximation to the integral (6).

Next, Laguerre set

$$F(x) = \frac{\varphi(x)}{f(x)} + \left\{ \frac{1}{x^{2m+1}} \right\}, \quad (9)$$

where f is a polynomial, to be determined, of degree m, which is at most $n/2$; φ is another unknown polynomial; and $\{1/(x^{2m+1})\}$ is a power series in $1/x$ whose first term is $1/x^{2m+1}$. He then showed that f and $\varphi(x)$ satisfy

$$x[\varphi'(x) f(x) - f'(x) \varphi(x) - \varphi(x) f(x)] + f^2(x) = A,$$

where A is a constant. This was used to show that f is a solution of the second-order differential equation

$$xy'' + (x + 1) y' - my = 0. \quad (10)$$

Another solution, linearly independent of f, is

$$u(x) = \varphi(x) e^{-x} - f(x) \int_x^\infty \frac{e^{-x}}{x} dx. \quad (11)$$

Substitution of f back into (10) shows, by comparison of coefficients, that it must satisfy (Laguerre's polynomial)

$$f(x) = x^m + m^2 x^{m-1} + \frac{m^2(m - 1)^2}{2!} x^{m-2} + \cdots + m!.$$

These results were combined by Laguerre to obtain the continued fraction representation for (6)

$$\int_x^\infty \frac{e^{-x}}{x}\,dx = \cfrac{e^{-x}}{x+1-\cfrac{1}{x+3-\cfrac{1}{\cfrac{x+5}{4}-\cfrac{1/4}{\cfrac{x+7}{9}-\cfrac{1/9}{\cfrac{x+9}{16}-\cfrac{1}{\cfrac{16}{x+\cdot}}}}}}} \quad (12)$$

$$\cdots$$

Then Laguerre proved that the mth approximate of the fraction could be written as $e^{-x}[\varphi_m(x)/f_m(x)]$, where $f_m(x)$ is the Laguerre polynomial of degree m and φ_m is the associated numerator in expression (9). From this the convergence of the fraction in (12) was established.

Finally, Laguerre displayed several properties of the set of polynomials. He proved that the roots of $f_m(x)$ are all real and unequal, and that a quasi-orthogonality condition is satisfied, that is,

$$\int_{-\infty}^0 e^x f_n(x) f_m(x)\,dx = \delta_{mn}(n!)^2, \quad (13)$$

where $\delta_{mn} \neq 0$ if $m \# n$, 1 if $m = n$. Furthermore, from (13) he proved that if $\Phi(x)$ is "any" function, then Φ has an expansion as a series in Laguerre polynomials,

$$\Phi(x) = \sum_{n=0}^\infty A_n f_n(x). \quad (14)$$

The coefficients, A_n, are given by the formula

$$A_n = \frac{1}{(n!)^2} \int_{-\infty}^0 e^x \Phi(x) f_n(x)\,dx, \ n = 0, 1, 2, \cdots. \quad (15)$$

In particular,

$$x^m = (-1)^m\, m! \left[f_0(x) + \sum_{k=1}^m \frac{(-1)^k\, m(m-1)\cdots(m-k+1)}{(k!)^2} f_k(x), \right]$$

which led Laguerre to the following inversion: if (14) is symbolically written as $\Phi(x) = \theta(f)$, then $\theta(-x) = \Phi(-f)$.

This memoir of Laguerre's is significant not only because of the discovery of the Laguerre equations and polynomials and their properties, but also because it contains one of the earliest infinite continued fractions which was known to be convergent. That it was developed from a divergent series is especially remarkable.

What, then, can be said to evaluate Laguerre's work? That he was brilliant and innovative is beyond question. In his short working life, actually less than twenty-two years, he produced a quantity of first-class papers. Why, then, is his name so little known and his work so seldom cited? Because as brilliant as Laguerre was, he worked only on details—significant details, yet nevertheless details. Not once did he step back to draw together various pieces and put them into a single theory. The result is that his work has mostly come down as various interesting special cases of more general theories discovered by others.

NOTES

1. Arthur Cayley, "Sixth Memoir on Quantics" (1859), in *Collected Works*, 11 (Cambridge, 1898), 561–592; Felix Klein, "Uber die sogenannte nicht-Euklidische Geometrie," in *Mathematische Annalen*, **4** (1871), 573–625, also in his *Gesammelte mathematische Abhandlungen*, 1 (Berlin, 1921), 244–305.
2. Klein, *Gesammelte mathematische Abhandlungen*, I, 242.
3. V. S. Aizenshtadt, *et al.*, *Tables of Laguerre Polynomials and Functions*, translated by Prasenjit Basu (Oxford, 1966); J. W. Head and W. P. Wilson, *Laguerre Functions. Tables and Properties*, ITS Monograph 183 R (London, 1961).

BIBLIOGRAPHY

Laguerre's works were brought together in his *Oeuvres*, 2 vols. (Paris, 1898), with an obituary by Henri Poincaré. This ed. teems with errors and misprints.

See also Arthur Erdelyi, *et al.*, *Higher Transcendental Functions* (New York, 1953).

MICHAEL BERNKOPF

LA HIRE, PHILIPPE DE (*b.* Paris, France, 18 March 1640; *d.* Paris, 21 April 1718)

La Hire was the eldest son of the painter Laurent de La Hire (or La Hyre) and Marguerite Cocquin. His father was a founder of and a professor at the Académie Royale de Peinture et de Sculpture and one of the first disciples of the geometer G. Desargues. Philippe de La Hire was educated among artists and technicians who were eager to learn more of the theoretical foundations of their trades. At a very early age he became interested in perspective, practical mechanics, drawing, and painting. Throughout his life La Hire preserved this unusual taste for the parallel study of art, science, and technology, which he undoubtedly derived from the profound influence of the conceptions of Desargues.

Following the death of his father, La Hire suffered, according to the testimony of Fontenelle, "very violent palpitations of the heart" and left for Italy in 1660, hoping that the trip would be as salutary for his health as for his art. During his four years' stay in Venice, he developed his artistic talent and also studied classical geometry, particularly the theory of the conics of Apollonius. For several years after his return to France, he was active primarily as an artist, and he formed a friendship with Desargues's last disciple, Abraham Bosse. In order to solve, at the latter's request, a difficult problem of stonecutting, he developed, in 1672, a method of constructing conic sections, which revealed both his thorough knowledge of classical and modern geometry and his interest in practical questions.

His *Nouvelle méthode en géométrie pour les sections des superficies coniques, et cylindriques* (1673) is a comprehensive study of conic sections by means of the projective approach, based on a homology which permits the deduction of the conic section under examination from a particular circle. This treatise was completed shortly afterward by a supplement entitled *Les planiconiques*, which presented this method in a more direct fashion. The *Nouvelle méthode* clearly displayed Desargues's influence, even though La Hire, in a note written in 1679 and attached to a manuscipt copy of the *Brouillon projet* on Desargues's conics, affirmed that he did not become aware of the latter's work until after the publication of his own. Yet what we know about La Hire's training seems to contradict this assertion. Furthermore, the resemblance of their projective descriptions is too obvious for La Hire's not to appear to have been an adaptation of Desargues's. Nevertheless, La Hire's presentation, which was in classical language and in terms of both space and the plane, was much simpler and clearer. Thus La Hire deserves to be considered, after Pascal, a direct disciple of Desargues in projective geometry.

In 1685 La Hire published, in Latin, a much more extensive general treatise on conic sections, *Sectiones conicae in novem libros distributatae*. It was also inspired, but much less obviously, by the projective point of view, because of the preliminary study of the properties of harmonic division. It is primarily through this treatise that certain of Desargues's projective ideas became known. Meanwhile, in 1679, in his *Nouveaux élémens des sections coniques, les lieux géométriques*, La Hire provided an exposition of the properties of conic sections. He began with their focal definitions and applied Cartesian analytic geometry to the study of equations and the solution of indeterminate problems; he also displayed the Cartesian method of solving several types of equations by intersections of curves. Although not a work of great originality, it summarized the progress achieved in analytic geometry during half a century and contributed some interesting ideas, among them the possible extension of space to more than three dimensions. His virtuosity in this area appears further in the memoirs that he devoted to the cycloid, epicycloid, conchoid, and quadratures. This ingenuity in employing Cartesian methods was certainly what accounts for his hostility toward infinitesimal calculus in the discussions of its value raised in the Academy of Sciences starting in 1701. While he did not persist in ignoring the new methods, he nonetheless used them only with reservations. Having actively participated in the saving and partial publication of the mathematical manuscripts of Roberval and Frénicle de Bessy, La Hire was also interested in the theory of numbers, particularly magic squares.

Mathematics was only one aspect of La Hire's scientific activity, which soon included astronomy, physics, and applied mathematics. His nomination to the Academy of Sciences as *astronome pensionnaire* (26 January 1678) led him to undertake regular astronomical observations, a task which he pursued until two days before his death. In 1682 he moved into the Paris observatory where he was able to use rather highly developed equipment, in particular the large quadrant of a meridian circle that was installed in 1683. If the bulk of his observations have remained unpublished, at least he extracted from them numerous specific observations: conjunctions, eclipses, passages of comets, sunspots, etc. In 1687 and 1702, La Hire published astronomical tables containing his observations of the movements of the sun, the moon, and the planets; they were severely criticized by Delambre for their purely empirical inspiration. Furthermore, he studied instrumental technique and particular problems of observation and basic astronomy. As a result of his wide-ranging interests, he produced a body of work that was important and varied but that lacked great originality.

During these years La Hire also took part in many geodesic projects conducted by groups from the Paris observatory. From 1679 to 1682, sometimes in collaboration with Picard, he determined the coordinates of different points along the French coastlines in the hope of establishing a new map of France. In 1683 he began mapping the extension of the meridian of Paris toward the north. In 1684–1685 he directed the surveying operations designed to provide a water supply for the palace of Versailles. La Hire devoted several works to the methods and instruments of surveying, land measurement, and gnomonics. During his journeys, he made observations in the natural sciences, meteorology, and physics. In addition, he played an increasingly active role in the various regular observations pursued at the Paris observatory: terrestrial magnetism, pluviometry, and finally thermometry and barometry.

Appointed on 14 December 1682 to the chair of mathematics at the Collège Royal, which had been vacant since Roberval's death, La Hire gave courses in those branches of science and technology in which mathematics was becoming decisive—astronomy, mechanics, hydrostatics, dioptrics, and navigation. Although his lectures were not published, numerous memoirs presented to the Academy of Sciences preserve their outline. In the area of experimental science La Hire's efforts are attested by the description of various experiments—falling bodies, done with Mariotte in 1683, magnetism, electrostatics, heat reflected by the moon, the effects of cold, the physical properties of water, and the transmission of sound. He also studied the barometer, thermometer, clinometer, clocks, wind instruments, electrostatic machines, and magnets.

La Hire's work extended to descriptive zoology, the study of respiration, and physiological optics. The latter attracted him both by its role in astronomical observation and by its relationship to artistic technique, especially to the art of painting which La Hire continued to practice at the same time that he sought to grasp its basic principles.

La Hire was appointed, on 7 January 1687, professor at the Académie Royale d'Architecture, replacing F. Blondel. The weekly lectures that he gave until the end of 1717 dealt with the theory of architecture and such associated techniques as stonecutting. In the *Procès-verbaux de l'Académie royale d'architecture* there are many references to La Hire. In this regard he again appeared as a disciple of Desargues. Desargues's influence is confirmed by the manuscript of La Hire's course on "La pratique du trait dans la coupe des pierres pour en former des voûtes," which displays a generous use of the new graphic methods introduced by Desargues.

The important *Traité de mécanique* that La Hire published in 1695 represents a synthesis of his diverse theoretical and practical preoccupations. Although passed over by the majority of the historians of mechanics, this work marks a significant step toward the elaboration of a modern manual of practical mechanics, suitable for engineers of various disciplines. La Hire thus partially answered the wish expressed by Colbert in 1675 of seeing the Academy produce an exact description of all the machines useful in the arts

and trades. On the theoretical plane, La Hire's treatise was already out of date at the time of its appearance because it ignored Newton's laws of dynamics and the indispensable infinitesimal methods. On the other hand, while La Hire did not tackle the problem of energy, he furnished useful descriptions and put forth the suggestion (already made in his *Traité des épicycloides* ... [1694]) following Desargues, of adopting an epicycloidal profile for gear wheels.

Associated with the leading scientists of the age, La Hire was, for nearly half a century, one of the principal animators of scientific life in France. Not satisfied with publishing a multitude of books and memoirs, he also edited various writings of Picard, Mariotte, Roberval, and Frénicle, as well as several ancient texts.

His family life was simple and circumspect. From his marriage with Catherine Lesage (*d. ca.* 1681), he had three daughters and two sons, one of whom, Gabriel-Philippe, continued his father's work in various fields. From a second marriage, with Catherine Nouet, he had two daughters and two sons; one of the latter, Jean-Nicolas, a physician and botanist, was elected an associate member of the Academy of Sciences.

It is difficult to make an overall judgment on a body of work as varied as La Hire's. A precise and regular observer, he contributed to the smooth running of the Paris observatory and to the success of different geodesic undertakings. Yet he was not responsible for any important innovation. His diverse observations in physics, meteorology, and the natural sciences simply attest to the high level of his intellectual curiosity. Although his rejection of infinitesimal calculus may have rendered a part of his mathematical work sterile, his early works in projective, analytic, and applied geometry place him among the best of the followers of Desargues and Descartes. Finally, his diverse knowledge and artistic, technical, and scientific experience were factors in the growth of technological thought, the advance of practical mechanics, and the perfecting of graphic techniques.

BIBLIOGRAPHY

I. ORIGINAL WORKS. An exhaustive list of La Hire's numerous memoirs inserted in the annual volumes of the *Histoire de l'Académie royale des sciences* from the year 1699 to the year 1717 and, for the earlier period, in vols. **9** and **10** of the *Mémoires de l'Académie royale des sciences depuis 1666 jusqu'en 1699* is given in vols. I-III of M. Godin, *Table alphabétique des matières contenues dans l'histoire et les mémoires de l'Académie royale des sciences*; see vol. I, *1666–1698* (1734), 157–164; vol. II, *1699–1710* (1729), 306–

317; vol. III, *1711–1720* (1731), 166–169 (cf. also J. M. Quérard, *La France littéraire*, IV [Paris, 1830], 445–447).

His principal works published separately are, in chronological order: *Observations sur les points d'attouchement de trois lignes droites qui touchent la section d'un cone . . .* (Paris, 1672); *Nouvelle méthode en géométrie pour les sections des superficies coniques et cylindriques* (Paris, 1673); *Nouveaux élémens des sections coniques, les lieux géométriques, la construction ou effection des équations* (Paris, 1679; English trans., London, 1704); *La gnomonique . . .* (Paris, 1682; 2nd ed., 1698; English trans., 1685); *Sectiones conicae in novem libros distributae . . .* (Paris, 1685); *Tabularum astronomicarum . . .* (Paris, 1687); *L'école des arpenteurs . . .* (Paris, 1689; 4th ed., 1732); *Traité de mécanique* (Paris, 1695); *Tabulae astronomicae . . .* (Paris, 1702; 2nd ed., 1727; French ed., by Godin, 1735; German trans., 1735).

In addition, La Hire edited several works: J. Picard, *Traité du nivellement* (Paris, 1684); Mariotte, *Traité du mouvement des eaux . . .* (Paris, 1686); *Veterum mathematicorum Athenaei, Apollodori, Philonis, Bitonis, Heronis et aliorum opera*, with Sédillot and Pothenot (Paris, 1693). He also participated in the editing of the *Mémoires de mathématiques et de physique . . .*, published by the Académie des Sciences in 1692 and 1693.

Some of La Hire's manuscripts are preserved in the Archives of the Académie des Sciences de Paris and in the Library of the Institut de France (copy of the *Brouillon projet* of Desargues, "La pratique du trait dans la coupe des pierres").

II. SECONDARY LITERATURE. The basic biographical notice is the one by B. Fontenelle in *Histoire de l'Académie royale des sciences pour l'année 1718*, *éloge* read on 12 Nov. 1718 (Paris, 1719), pp. 76–89. Other more recent ones are by E. Merlieux, in Michaud, *Biographie universelle*, XXIII (Paris, 1819), 196–198, new ed., XXII (Paris, 1861), 552–553; and F. Hoefer, *Nouvelle biographie générale*, XXVIII (Paris, 1861), cols. 901–904.

Complementary details are given by L. A. Sédillot, "Les professeurs de mathématiques et de physique générale au Collège de France," in *Bullettino di bibliografia e di storia delle scienze matematiche e fisiche*, **2** (1869), 498; A. Jal, *Dictionnaire critique de biographie et d'histoire*, 2nd ed. (Paris, 1872), pp. 730–731; J. Guiffrey, *Comptes des bâtiments du roi sous le règne de Louis XIV*, 5 vols. (Paris, 1881–1901)—see index; and H. Lemonnier, ed., *Procès-verbaux de l'Académie royale d'architecture, 1682–1726*, II–IV (Paris, 1911–1915)—see index in vol. X (1929).

La Hire's mathematical work is analyzed by J. F. Montucla, *Histoire des mathématiques*, 2nd ed., II (Paris, 1799), 169, 641–642; M. Chasles, *Aperçu historique . . .* (Brussels, 1837)—see index; R. Lehmann, "De La Hire und seine Sectiones conicae," in *Jahresberichte des königlichen Gymnasiums zu Leipzig* (1887–1888), pp. 1–28; N. Nielsen, *Géomètres français du XVIIIe siècle* (Copenhagen–Paris, 1935), pp. 248–261; J. L. Coolidge, *History of the Conic Sections and Quadric Surfaces* (Oxford, 1945), pp. 40–44; R. Taton, "La première oeuvre géométrique de Philippe de La Hire," in *Revue d'histoire des sciences*, **6** (1953), 93–

111; and C. B. Boyer, *A History of Analytic Geometry* (New York, 1956)—see index.

The astronomical work is studied by J. B. Delambre, *Histoire de l'astronomie moderne*, II (Paris 1821), 661–685; C. Wolf, *Histoire de l'Observatoire de Paris . . .* (Paris, 1902)—see index; and F. Bouquet, *Histoire de l'astronomie* (Paris, 1925), pp. 381–383. On the technical work see M. Daumas, ed., *Histoire générale des techniques*, II (Paris, 1964), 285–286, 540–541.

RENÉ TATON

LALOUVÈRE, ANTOINE DE (*b.* Rieux, Haute-Garonne, France, 24 August 1600; *d.* Toulouse, France, 2 September 1664)

Lalouvère is often referred to by the Latin form of his name, Antonius Lalovera. Such a use avoids the problem of known variants; for example, Fermat wrote to Carcavi, on 16 February 1659, that the mathematician had a nephew who called himself Simon de La Loubère. Whatever the spelling, the family was presumably noble, since a château near Rieux bears their name.

Lalouvère himself became a Jesuit, entering the order on 9 July 1620, at Toulouse, where he was later to be professor of humanities, rhetoric, Hebrew, theology, and mathematics. The general of the order was at that time Guldin, a mathematician who may be considered, along with Cavalieri, Fermat, Vincentio, Kepler, Torricelli, Valerio—and indeed, Lalouvère—one of the precursors of modern integral calculus. That Lalouvère was on friendly terms with Fermat is evident in a series of letters; he further maintained a close relationship with Pardies in France and Wallis in England. His mathematics was essentially conservative; while modern analysis was alien to him, he was expert in the work of the Greeks, the Aristotelian-Scholastic tradition, and the commentators of antiquity. He depended strongly upon Archimedes.

Lalouvère's chief book is the *Quadratura circuli*, published in 1651, in which he drew upon the work of Charles de La Faille, Guldin, and Vincentio. His method of attack was an Archimedean summation of areas; he found the volumes and centers of gravity of bodies of rotation, cylindrical ungulae, and curvilinearly defined wedges by indirect proofs. He was then able to proceed by inverting Guldin's rule whereby the volume of a body of rotation is equal to the product of the generating figure and the path of its center of gravity. Thus, Lalouvère established the volume of the body of rotation and the center of gravity of its cross section; then by simple division he found the volume of the cross section.

By the time he published this work, Lalouvère was teaching Scholastic theology rather than mathematics, and believed that he had reached his goals as a mathematician. Indeed, he stated that he preferred to go on to easier tasks, more suited "to my advanced age." Nonetheless, he was drawn into the dispute with Pascal for which his name is best known.

In June 1658, Pascal made his conclusions on cycloids the subject of an open competition. The prize was to be sixty Spanish gold doubloons, and solutions to the problems he set were to be submitted by the following 1 October. Lalouvère's interest was attracted by the nature of the problems, rather than by the prize, and Fermat transmitted them to him on 11 July. Lalouvère returned his solutions to Pascal's first two problems only ten days later, having reached them by simple proportions rather than by calculation. The calculation of the volumes and centers of gravity of certain parts of cycloids and of the masses formed by their rotation around an axis was central to Pascal's problems, however; he did not accept Lalouvère's solutions, and Lalouvère himself later discovered and corrected an error in computation (although another remained undetected). The matter might have ended there had not Pascal, in his *Histoire de la roulette*, accused Lalouvère (without naming him) of plagiarizing his solutions from Roberval. Pascal's allegations were without foundation; Lalouvère asserted that he had reached all his conclusions independently, and became embittered, while Fermat, who might have helped to resolve the quarrel, chose instead to remain neutral. A second, incomplete solution to Pascal's problems was submitted by Wallis, and on 25 November 1658 the prize committee decided not to give the award to anyone.

Having returned to mathematics, Lalouvère went on to deal with bodies in free fall and the inaccuracies of Gassendi's observations in *Propositiones geometricae sex* (1658). He returned to problems concerning cycloids—including those posed by Pascal—in 1660, in *Veterum geometria promota in septem de cycloide libris*. In addition to these publications, Lalouvère maintained an active correspondence on mathematical subjects, several of his letters to Pascal being extant. Two of his letters to D. Petau may be found in the latter's *Petavii orationes*; the same work contains Petau's refutation of Lalouvère's views on the astronomical questions of the horizon and calculation of the calendar.

Lalouvère's work, rooted firmly in that of the ancients, was not innovative; nevertheless, he showed himself to be a man of substantial knowledge and clear judgment. He was a tenacious worker with a great command of detail. Montucla thought his style sufficient to keep "the most intrepid reader from straying."

BIBLIOGRAPHY

I. ORIGINAL WORKS. Lalouvère's writings are *Quadratura circuli et hyperbolae segmentorum ex dato eorum centro gravitatis* ... (Toulouse, 1651); *Propositiones geometricae sex quibus ostenditur ex carraeciana hypothesi circa proportionem, qua gravia decidentia accelerantur* ... (Toulouse, 1658); *Propositio 36ª excerpta ex quarto libro de cycloide nondum edito* (Toulouse, 1659); *Veterum geometria promota in septem de cycloide libris* (Toulouse, 1660), which has as an appendix Fermat's "De linearum curvarum cum lineis rectis comparatione dissertatio geometrica"; and *De cycloide Galilei et Torricelli propositiones viginti* (n.p., n.d.).

Works apparently lost are "Tractatus de principiis librae" and "De communi sectione plani et turbinatae superficiei ex puncto quiescente a linea recta per ellipsim ...," both mentioned by Lalouvère in his works; and "Opusculum de materia probabile" and "Explicatio vocum geometricarum ...," mentioned by Collins in a letter to Gregory of 24 Mar. 1671 (or 1672).

A reference to seven letters to D. Petau (1631–1644) at Tournon and Toulouse may be found in Poggendorff, II, col. 412.

Two letters from Petau to Lalouvère are in *Dionysii Petavii, Aurelian Society of Jesus Orations* (Paris, 1653).

II. SECONDARY LITERATURE. On Lalouvère or his work, see A. de Backer and C. Sommervogel, eds., *Bibliothèque de la Compagnie de Jesus*, V (Brussels–Paris, 1894), cols. 32–33; Henry Bosmans, in *Archives internationales d'histoire des sciences*, 3 (1950), 619–656; Pierre Costabel, in *Revue d'histoire des sciences et de leurs applications*, 15 (1962), 321–350, 367–369; James Gregory, *Tercentenary Memorial Volume*, Herbert Turnbull, ed. (London, 1839), p. 225; Gerhard Kropp, *De quadratura circuli et hyperbolae segmentorum des Antonii de Lalouvère*, thesis (Berlin, 1944), contains a long list of secondary literature; J. E. Montucla, *Histoire des mathématiques*, II (Paris, 1758), 56–57; and P. Tannery, "Pascal et Lalouvère," in *Mémoires de la Société des sciences physiques et naturelles de Bordeaux*, 3rd ser., 5 (1890), 55–84.

HERBERT OETTEL

LAMB, HORACE (*b*. Stockport, England, 29 November 1849; *d*. Manchester, England, 4 December 1934)

Lamb's father, John, was a foreman in a cotton mill who had a flair for inventing. Horace was quite young when his father died, and he was brought up by his mother's sister in a kindly but severely puritan manner.

At the age of seventeen he qualified for admission to Queen's College, Cambridge, with a scholarship in classics but proceeded to a mathematical career. He gained major prizes in mathematics and astronomy and became second wrangler in 1872, when he was elected a fellow and lecturer of Trinity College. After three further years in Cambridge, he went to Australia as the first professor of mathematics at the University of Adelaide. He returned to England in 1885 as professor of pure mathematics (later pure and applied mathematics) at Owens College, Manchester, and held this post until his retirement in 1920. He married Elizabeth Foot; they had seven children.

Lamb was one of the world's greatest applied mathematicians. He was distinguished not only as a contributor to knowledge but also as a teacher who inspired a generation of applied mathematicians, both through personal teaching and through superbly written books. As a young man he was noted as a hard worker, shy and reticent; in later life he played a prominent part in academic councils. He also possessed considerable literary and general ability and enjoyed reading in French, German, and Italian. He liked walking and climbing and was one of the early climbers of the Matterhorn.

Like his teachers, Sir George Stokes and James Clerk Maxwell, Lamb saw from the outset of his career that success in applied mathematics demands both thorough knowledge of the context of application and mathematical skill. The fields in which he made his mark cover a wide range—electricity and magnetism, fluid mechanics, elasticity, acoustics, vibrations and wave motion, statics and dynamics, seismology, theory of tides, and terrestrial magnetism. Sections of his investigations in different fields are, however, closely linked by a common underlying mathematics. It was part of Lamb's genius that he could see how to apply the formal solution of a problem in one field to make profound contributions in another.

To the scientific world in general, Lamb is probably most widely known for his work in fluid mechanics, embodied in his book *Hydrodynamics*, which appeared first in 1879 as *A Treatise on the Motion of Fluids*, the title being changed to *Hydrodynamics* in the second, much enlarged, edition of 1895. Successive editions, to the sixth and last in 1932, showed a nice assimilation and condensation of new developments and increasingly included Lamb's own important contributions. The book is one of the most beautifully arranged and stimulating treatises ever written in a branch of applied mathematics—a model which modern scientific writers are often adjured to emulate.

In addition to solving numerous problems of direct hydrodynamical interest, as well as others of direct interest to electromagnetism and elasticity theory, Lamb applied many of the solutions with conspicuous success in geophysics. His much-quoted paper of 1904 gave an analytical account of the propagation, over the surface of an elastic solid, of waves generated by various assigned initial disturbances. The cases he studied bear intimately on earthquake wave transmission, and this paper is regarded today as one of the fundamental contributions to theoretical seismology. Modern attempts to interpret the finer details of earthquake records rest heavily on it. Another famous paper, published in 1882, analyzed the modes of oscillation of an elastic sphere. This paper is a classic in its completeness, and it recently rose to new prominence when free earth oscillations of the type Lamb had described were detected for the first time on records of the great Chilean earthquake of 1960. In 1903 he gave an analysis of two-dimensional wave motion which showed why the record of an earthquake usually has a prolonged tail.

Lamb's contributions to geophysics were by no means confined to seismology but extended to the theory of tides and terrestrial magnetism. In 1863 Lord Kelvin, using theory on fortnightly tides, came to the historic conclusion that the average rigidity of the earth exceeds the rigidity of ordinary steel. A significant point in Kelvin's theory, not well evidenced at the time, later came to be questioned. In 1895 Lamb gave an argument which placed the theory on a new basis and made Kelvin's conclusion inescapable. In 1915, in collaboration with Lorna Swain, he gave the first satisfactory account of the marked phase differences of tides observed in different parts of the oceans and seas, thereby settling a question which had been controversial since the time of Newton. In 1917 he worked out the deflection of the vertical caused by the tidal loading of the earth's surface.

In 1889 Arthur Schuster raised the question of the causes of diurnal variation of terrestrial magnetism. Lamb thereupon showed that the answer was immediately derivable from results he had published in 1883—that the variation is caused by influences outside the solid earth. He showed further that the magnitude of the variation is reduced by an increase in electrical conductivity below the earth's surface.

In addition to *Hydrodynamics* and numerous research papers, Lamb wrote texts, some of them still used today, on infinitesimal calculus, statics, dynamics, higher mechanics, and the dynamical theory of sound. His polished expositions led to his sometimes being called "the great artist" of applied mathematics.

Lamb continued to be active after his retirement; he was, for example, a key member from 1921 to 1927 of the Aeronautical Research Committee of Great Britain. He was elected a fellow of the Royal Society in 1884 and later received its Royal and Copley medals. He received many honors from overseas universities and academies and was knighted in 1931.

BIBLIOGRAPHY

Lamb wrote the following books: *A Treatise on the Motion of Fluids* (Cambridge, 1879)—the 2nd (1895) through 6th (1932) eds., greatly enl., are entitled *Hydrodynamics; Infinitesimal Calculus* (1897), *Statics* (1912), *Dynamics* (1914), *Higher Mechanics* (1920), all published by the Cambridge University Press, with several editions; and *The Dynamical Theory of Sound* (London, 1910). He contributed the article "Analytical Dynamics," in the *Encyclopaedia Britannica* supplement (London, 1902) and the article "Schwingungen elastischer Systeme, insbesondere Akustik," in *Encyclopädie der mathematischen Wissenschaften* (Leipzig, 1906).

Lamb's great contributions in the field of hydrodynamics are incorporated in his book bearing that title. His most important papers in other fields are: "On the Vibrations of an Elastic Sphere," in *Proceedings of the London Mathematical Society*, **13** (1882), 189–212; "On Electrical Motions in a Spherical Conductor," in *Philosophical Transactions of the Royal Society*, **174** (1883), 519–549; "On Wave-Propagation in Two Dimensions," in *Proceedings of the London Mathematical Society*, **35** (1903), 141–161; "On the Propagation of Tremors over the Surface of an Elastic Solid," in *Philosophical Transactions of the Royal Society*, **203** (1904), 1–42; "On a Tidal Problem" (with Lorna Swain), in *Philosophical Magazine*, **29** (1915), 737–744; "On the Deflection of the Vertical by Tidal Loading of the Earth's Surface," in *Proceedings of the Royal Society*, **93A** (1917), 293–312.

References to several further papers of Lamb and further details of his life and career may be found in *Obituary Notices of Fellows of the Royal Society*, **1** (1935), 375–392.

K. E. BULLEN

LAMBERT, JOHANN HEINRICH (*b*. Mulhouse, Alsace, 26 [?] August 1728; *d*. Berlin, Germany, 25 September 1777)

The Lambert family had come to Mulhouse from Lorraine as Calvinist refugees in 1635. Lambert's father and grandfather were tailors. His father, Lukas Lambert, married Elisabeth Schmerber in 1724. At his death in 1747, he left his widow with five boys and two girls.

Growing up in impoverished circumstances, Johann Heinrich had to leave school at the age of twelve in order to assist his father. But the elementary instruction he had received together with some training in French and Latin were sufficient to enable him to continue his studies without a teacher. He acquired all his scientific training and substantial scholarship by self-instruction—at night, when the tailoring in his father's shop was finished, or during any spare time left after his work as a clerk or private teacher.

Because of his excellent handwriting, Lambert was appointed clerk at the ironworks at Seppois at the age of fifteen. Two years later he became secretary to Johann Rudolf Iselin, editor of the *Basler Zeitung* and later professor of law at Basel University. There he had occasion to continue his private studies in the humanities, philosophy, and the sciences.

In addition to astronomy and mathematics, Lambert began to take a special interest in the theory of recognition. In a letter he reported:

> I bought some books in order to learn the first principles of philosophy. The first object of my endeavors was the means to become perfect and happy. I understood that the will could not be improved before the mind had been enlightened. I studied: [Christian] Wolf[f] "Of the powers of the human mind"; [Nicholas] Malebranche "Of the investigation of the truth"; [John] Locke "Thoughts of the human mind." [Lambert probably refers to the *Essay Concerning Human Understanding*.] The mathematical sciences, in particular algebra and mechanics, provided me with clear and profound examples to confirm the rules I had learned. Thereby I was enabled to penetrate into other sciences more easily and more profoundly, and to explain them to others, too. It is true that I was well aware of the lack of oral instruction, but I tried to replace this by even more assiduity, and I have now thanks to divine assistance reached the point where I can put forth to my lord and lady what I have learned.

In 1748 Lambert became tutor at Chur, in the home of the Reichsgraf Peter von Salis, who had been ambassador to the English court and was married to an Englishwoman. Lambert's pupils were von Salis' grandson, eleven-year-old Anton; Anton's cousin Baptista, also eleven; and a somewhat younger relative, Johann Ulrich von Salis-Seewis, seven years old. Lambert remained as tutor for ten years, a decisive period for his intellectual development. He was able to study intensively in the family library and to pursue his own critical reflections. He also met many of the friends and visitors of this noble Swiss family. Although Lambert became more refined in this cultivated atmosphere, he remained an original character who did not conform to many bourgeois conventions.

Lambert instructed his young charges in languages, mathematics, geography, history, and the catechism.

The Salis family was very pious, and Lambert himself preserved his naturally devout attitude throughout his life. Later, when he lived in Berlin, this caused some embarrassment.

During the years at Chur, Lambert laid the foundation of his scientific work. His *Monatsbuch*, a journal begun in 1752 and continued until his death, lists his main occupations month by month. Besides theoretical investigations, Lambert carried out astronomical observations and constructed instruments for scientific experiments. Later, when he had access to improved instruments, he preferred to employ his simple homemade ones.

Lambert's spirit of inquiry did not remain unnoticed. He was made a member of the Literary Society of Chur and of the Swiss Scientific Society at Basel. On request of the latter he made regular meteorological observations, which he reported in 1755. His first of several publications in *Acta Helvetica* appeared in the same year in volume 2 and dealt with the measurement of caloric heat.

In 1756 Lambert embarked with Anton and Baptista on a *Bildungsreise*, or educational journey, through Europe. Their first stop was at Göttingen, where Lambert attended lectures in the faculty of law and studied works by the Bernoullis and Euler. He talked with Kaestner, with whom he continued to exchange books and letters until his death, and with the astronomer Tobias Mayer. He also participated in the meetings of the Learned Society at Göttingen and was elected corresponding member when he left the city after the French occupation in July 1757 during the Seven Years' War.

The greater part of the following two years was spent at Utrecht, with visits to all the important Dutch cities. Lambert visited the renowned physicist Pieter van Musschenbroek in The Hague, where his first book, on the path of light in air and various media, was published in 1758. Late in 1758 Lambert returned with his pupils to Chur via Paris (where he met d'Alembert), Marseilles, Nice, Turin, and Milan. A few months later he parted from the Salis family.

Seeking a permanent scientific position, Lambert at first hoped for a chair at the University of Göttingen. When this hope came to nothing, he went to Zurich, where he made astronomical observations with Gessner, was elected a member of the city's Physical Society, and published *Die freye Perspektive*. (It is also reported that the Zurich streetboys mocked him for his strange dress.) Lambert then spent some months with his family at Mulhouse.

During the following five years Lambert led a restless, peripatetic life. At Augsburg in 1759 he met the famous instrument maker Georg Friedrich Brander. (Their twelve-year correspondence is available in *Lamberts deutscher gelehrter Briefwechsel*, vol. III.) Lambert also found a publisher for his *Photometria* and his *Cosmologische Briefe*.

Meanwhile plans had been made for a Bavarian academy of sciences, based on the plan of the Prussian Academy at Berlin. Lambert was chosen a salaried member and was asked to organize this academy at Munich. But differences arose, and in 1762 he withdrew from the young academy. Returning to Switzerland, he participated as geometer in a resurvey of the frontier between Milan and Chur. He visited Leipzig in order to find a publisher for his *Neues Organon*, published in two parts in 1764.

In the meantime Lambert had been offered a position at the St. Petersburg Academy. Yet he hoped for a position at the Prussian Academy of Sciences in Berlin, of which he had been proposed as a member in 1761. He arrived in the Prussian capital in January 1764. Lambert was welcomed by the Swiss group of scientists, among them Euler and Johann Georg Sulzer, the director of the class of philosophy, but his strange appearance and behavior delayed his appointment until 10 January 1765. Frederick the Great is said to have exclaimed, after having seen Lambert for the first time, that the greatest blockhead had been suggested to him for the Academy, and at first he refused to instate him. Frederick changed his mind later and praised Lambert's "immeasurableness of insight." He raised his salary and made him a member of a new economic commission of the Academy, together with Euler, Sulzer, and Hans Bernard Merian. Lambert also was appointed to the committee for improving land surveying and building administration, and in 1770 he received the title *Oberbaurat*.

As a member of the physical class for twelve years, until his death at the age of forty-nine, Lambert produced more than 150 works for publication. He was the only member of the Academy to exercise regularly the right to read papers not only in his own class, but in any other class as well.

Of Lambert's philosophical writings only his principle works, *Neues Organon* and *Anlage zur Architectonic*, as well as three papers published in *Nova acta eruditorum*, appeared during his lifetime. Although the composition of the main books and papers was done during the period of his appointment to the Berlin Academy in the winter of 1764–1765, Lambert was occupied with philosophical questions at least as early as 1752, as his *Monatsbuch* testifies. During the last ten years of his life his interest centered on problems in mathematics and physics.

Lambert's philosophical position has been described

in the most contradictory terms. R. Zimmermann in *Lambert, der Vorgänger Kants* (Vienna, 1879) tried to demonstrate the germs of Kant's philosophy everywhere in Lambert's writings. Two years later J. Lepsius' *J. H. Lambert* and *Das neue Organon und die Architektonik Lamberts* appeared in Munich. Although more reserved they still interpreted Lambert in terms of Kant. Otto Baentsch arrived at the opposite conclusion in his *Lamberts Philosophie und seine Stellung zu Kant* (Tübingen-Leipzig, 1902); he believed that Lambert might without harm be omitted from the history of critical philosophy. Kant himself recognized in Lambert a philosopher of the highest qualities; and he expected much from his critical attitude. He had drafted a dedication of the *Critique of Pure Reason* to Lambert, but Lambert's untimely death prevented its inclusion.

Lambert's place in the history of philosophy, however, should not be seen only in its relation to Kant. The genesis of his philosophical ideas dates from a time when Kant's major works had yet to be conceived. It was the philosophical doctrines of Leibniz, Christian Wolff, and Locke that exerted the more important influence—insofar as one can speak of influence in connection with a self-taught and wayward man such as Lambert. The Pietist philosophers Adolf Friedrich Hoffmann and Christian August Crusius, antagonists of the Wolffian philosophy, through their logical treatises also had some effect on his thinking.

The two main aspects of Lambert's philosophy, the analytic and the constructive, were both strongly shaped by mathematical notions; hence logic played an important part in his philosophical writing. Following Leibniz' ideas, Lambert early tried to create an *ars characteristica combinatoria*, or a logical or conceptual calculus. He investigated the conditions to which scientific knowledge must be subjected if it is to enjoy the same degree of exactness and evidence as mathematical knowledge. This interest was expressed in two smaller treatises, *Criterium veritatis* and *Über die Methode, die Metaphysik, Theologie und Moral richtiger zu beweisen*, published from manuscript in 1915 and 1918, respectively, by Karl Bopp (*Kantstudien*, supp. nos. 36 and 42). The second of these papers was composed with regard to the prize question posed for 1761 by the Berlin Academy:

What is to be asked is whether metaphysical truths in general, and the first principle of natural theology and morality in particular are subject to the same evidence as mathematical truth; and in case they are not, what then is the nature of their certainty, how complete is it, and is it sufficient to carry conviction?

Lambert's paper, although fragmentary, firmly claimed that theorems and proofs in metaphysics can be given with the same evidence as mathematical ones.

In *Neues Organon, oder Gedanken über die Erforschung und Bezeichnung des Wahren und dessen Unterscheidung vom Irrthum und Schein* (Leipzig, 1764) these ideas are further developed. Lambert first dealt with the logical form of knowledge, the laws of thought, and method of scientific proof; he then exhibited the basic elements and studied the systematic character of a theory; he next developed (in the section headed "Semiotik") the idea of a characteristic language of symbols to avoid ambiguities of everyday language; and finally, in the most original part of his work called "Phänomenologie," he discussed appearance and gave rules for distinguishing false (or subjective) appearance from a true (or objective) one that is not susceptible to sensory illusions.

In his second large philosophical work, *Anlage zur Architectonic, oder Theorie des Einfachen und des Ersten in der philosophischen und mathematischen Erkenntnis* (Riga, 1771), Lambert proposed a far-reaching reform of metaphysics, stemming from discontent with the Wolffian system. Starting from a certain set of concepts which he analyzed, he turned to their a priori construction. Modeled on mathematical procedures, the body of general sciences so constructed was to be true both logically and metaphysically. Its propositions would be applied to experience. Each of the particular sciences would be founded on observations and experiments; the rules thereby abstracted would have to be joined with the propositions to give a foundation for truth. Leibniz' concept of a prestabilized harmony underlay Lambert's ideas, and Lambert followed Leibniz' belief in the best of all possible worlds. But Lambert's subtle discussions of basic notions, axioms, and elementary interrelations heralded the critical period in philosophy; and his logical analysis of a combinatorial calculus is particularly interesting in the development of mathematical logic.

Lambert's work in physics and astronomy must be seen in relation to his general philosophical outlook and his attempts to introduce mathematical exactness and certitude into the sciences. His interest in the paths of comets was stimulated by the appearance of a comet in 1744. While studying the properties of such paths, he discovered interesting geometrical theorems, one of which carries his name. It was later proven analytically by Olbers, Laplace, and Lagrange. In 1770 Lambert suggested an easy method of determining whether the distance between the earth and the sun is greater than the distance from the earth to a given comet.

Lambert's efforts to improve communication and collaboration in astronomy were noteworthy. He promoted the publication of astronomical journals and founded the *Berliner astronomisches Jahrbuch oder Ephemeriden.* Many of the articles that he contributed to it were not published until after his death. Lambert also suggested the publication of specialized trigonometrical and astronomical tables in order to reduce laborious routine work. Moreover, he proposed to divide the composition of such tables among several collaborating observatories. He also favored the founding of the Berlin observatory. These suggestions, in line with Leibniz' far-reaching plans for international cooperation of scientific societies, inaugurated a new period of scientific teamwork.

Of special interest among Lambert's astronomical writings—apart from applications of his physical doctrines (see below)—are his famous *Cosmologische Briefe über die Einrichtung des Weltbaues* (Augsburg, 1761). Not familiar with the similar ideas of Thomas Wright (published in 1750) and with Kant's *Allgemeine Naturgeschichte und Theorie des Himmels* (1755), Lambert had the idea (in 1749) that what appears as the Milky Way might be the visual effect of a lens-shaped universe. On this basis he elaborated a theory according to which the thousands of stars surrounding the sun constituted a system. Moreover, he considered the Milky Way as a large number of such systems, that is, a system of higher order. Certain difficulties and interpretations concerning the motions of Jupiter and Saturn had led him to conclude that a force must exist outside our planetary system, which must be but a small part of another, much larger system of higher order. These bold speculations, born of the Leibnizian belief in the most perfect of all possible worlds, far transcended astronomy. The whole universe, Lambert postulated, had to be inhabited by creatures like human beings. Hence collisions of heavenly bodies are not to be expected, and the widespread fear that comets (which Lambert also supposed to be inhabited) might destroy the earth was unfounded; the *Cosmologische Briefe* was a great sensation and was translated into French, Russian, and English. Only when William Herschel systematically examined the heavens telescopically and discovered numerous nebulae and "telescopic milky-ways" did it become obvious that Lambert's description was not mere science fiction but to a large extent a bold vision of the basic features of the universe.

Lambert's numerous contributions to physics center on photometry, hygrometry, and pyrometry. Many marked advances in these subjects are traceable to him. In Lambert's fundamental work in the sciences, he (1) searched for a basic system of clearly defined concepts, (2) looked for exact measurements (and often collected them himself), and (3) after establishing them tried to develop a mathematical theory that would comprise these foundations and would result in quantitative laws.

In his famous *Photometria sive de mensura et gradibus luminis, colorum et umbrae* (Augsburg, 1760), Lambert laid the foundation for this branch of physics independently of Bouguer, whose writings on the subject were unknown to him. Lambert carried out his experiments with few and primitive instruments, but his conclusions resulted in laws that bear his name. The exponential decrease of the light in a beam passing through an absorbing medium of uniform transparency is often named Lambert's law of absorption, although Bouguer discovered it earlier. Lambert's cosine law states that the brightness of a diffusely radiating plane surface is proportional to the cosine of the angle formed by the line of sight and the normal to the surface. Such a diffusely radiating surface does therefore appear equally bright when observed at different angles, since the apparent size of the surface also is proportional to the cosine of the said angle.

Lambert's *Hygrometrie* (Augsburg, 1774–1775) was first published in two parts in French as articles entitled *Essai d'hygrométrie.* A result of his meteorological studies, this work is mostly concerned with the reliable measurement of the humidity of the atmosphere. The instrument maker G. F. Brander constructed a hygrometer according to Lambert's description. Another product of Lambert's research in meteorology was his wind formula. Now discarded, it attempted to determine the average wind direction on the basis of observations made over a given period.

The *Pyrometrie oder vom Maasse des Feuers und der Wärme* (Berlin, 1779) was Lambert's last book, completed only a few months before his death; his first publication had also dealt with the question of measuring heat. It is characteristic of him that he dealt not only with radiation but also with reflection of heat, although the latter could not yet be demonstrated, and his results could only have been preliminary in nature. Lambert also took into consideration the sensory effect of heat on the human body and tried to give a mathematical formulation for it. Similarly, his work in acoustics, on speaking tubes, touched on the physical as well as on the psycho-physical aspects of the problems.

In mathematics Lambert's largest publication was the *Beyträge zum Gebrauch der Mathematik und deren*

Anwendung (3 pts. 4 vols., Berlin, 1765–1772). This is not at all a systematic work but rather a collection of papers and notes on a variety of many topics in pure and applied mathematics.

One of Lambert's most famous results is the proof of the irrationality of π and e. It was based on continued fractions, and two such fractions still bear his name. Of importance also is Lambert's series in which the coefficient 2 occurs only when the exponent is a prime number. Although it was expected that it might be useful in analytic number theory, it was not until 1928 that Norbert Wiener was able to give a proof of the prime number theorem employing this type of series. Lambert himself was interested in number theory and developed a method of determining the prime factors of a given (large) number and suggested a simplified arrangement for factor tables.

Many of Lambert's investigations were concerned with trigonometry and goniometry. He studied the hyperbolic functions and introduced them in order to reduce the amount of computation in trigonometric problems. He solved goniometric equations by infinite series, and he worked out a tetragonometry—a doctrine of plane quadrangles—corresponding to the common trigonometry. That he also discovered a number of theorems in the geometry of conic sections has already been mentioned in connection with his astronomical work.

Lambert's second book, *Die freye Perspektive, oder Anweisung, jeden perspektivischen Aufriss von freyen Stücken und ohne Grundriss zu verfertigen* (Zurich, 1759; 2nd ed. 1774), was also published in French (Zurich, 1759). Intended for the artist wishing to give a perspective drawing without first having to construct a ground plan, it is nevertheless a masterpiece in descriptive geometry, containing a wealth of geometrical discoveries. In this work Lambert proved himself a geometer of great intuitive powers. In the generality of his outlook, as in certain specific aspects, his work resembles that of Monge later on, usually considered the founder of descriptive geometry as a distinct branch of mathematics. Lambert's investigations of possible constructions by the use of a simple ruler, for example, constructing an ellipse from five given points, was similar in spirit to the program of Poncelet and J. Steiner two generations later.

Lambert contributed significantly to the theory of map construction. For the first time the mathematical conditions for map projections (to preserve angles and area) were stated, although analytically superior formulations were later given by Lagrange, Legendre, and Gauss. More important, Lambert made practical suggestions on how, for different purposes, either one of these contradicting conditions could best be satisfied. He also described constructions to determine the true distance between two places on a map drawn according to one of his projections. Lambert's map projections are still basic for the modern theory in this field.

One of Lambert's most important contributions to geometry was his posthumously published *Theorie der Parallel-Linien*. Here he returned to the famous question that had baffled mathematicians since Euclid: Is it not possible to give a proof for Euclid's axiom of parallels? As a starting point Lambert chose a quadrangle having three right angles, and assumed in turn the fourth angle to be a right angle, an obtuse angle, or an acute angle. He showed that the first assumption is equivalent to Euclid's postulate, and that the second leads to a contradiction (assuming each straight line to possess an infinite length). Having attempted to display a contradiction in case of the third assumption using the same line of argument unsuccessfully, he tried a different mode of attack but overlooked that his "proof" implicitly contained an assumption equivalent to his hypothesis. Obviously not satisfied with his investigations, Lambert did not publish them; yet he had already arrived at remarkable results. He had discovered that under the second and third assumption an absolute measure of length must exist and that the area of a triangle in these cases must be proportional to the divergence of its angle sum from two right angles. He noticed that the second assumption would correspond to the geometry of the sphere; and he speculated that the third assumption might be realizable on an imaginary sphere. An example for this last case was not given until the latter half of the nineteenth century by Beltrami, after this non-Euclidean geometry had been studied in particular by Lobachevsky. The quadrangle used as starting point by Lambert is called Saccheri's quadrangle. Whether Lambert was directly familiar with the investigations of this Italian mathematician is not known.

Lambert's work in non-Euclidean geometry had been overlooked until it was republished by F. Engel and Stäckel in their *Theorie der Parallellinien von Euklid bis auf Gauss* (Leipzig, 1895).

BIBLIOGRAPHY

I. Original Works. Since there exists a carefully prepared bibliography by M. Steck (see below), only some recent republications are mentioned here. Material for a scientific biography may be found in Max Steck, ed., *Johann Heinrich Lambert: Schriften zur Perspektive* (Berlin, 1943), which contains also a *Bibliographia Lambertiana*.

Johannis Henrici Lamberti opera mathematica, Andreas Speiser, ed., 2 vols. (Zurich, 1946–1948), contains papers in analysis, algebra, and number theory. Further volumes did not appear. *Johann Heinrich Lambert: Gesammelte philosophische Werke,* H. W. Arndt, ed. (Hildesheim, 1967–   ), will comprise 10 vols.

II. SECONDARY LITERATURE. Most important is Max Steck, *Bibliographia Lambertiana* (Berlin, 1943). An enl. 2nd ed. ("Neudruck") was issued shortly before the author's death (Hildesheim, 1970). It contaïns, apart from G. C. Lichtenberg's biography of Lambert, chronological bibliographies of all of Lambert's publications, including posthumous editions, translations, a survey of Lambert's scientific estate (formerly at Gotha, since 1938 in the university library at Basel), an incomplete chronological list of secondary literature, and reprints of two articles by Steck on Lambert's scientific estate and on his scientific correspondence. Steck also left in manuscript an index of Lambert's scientific manuscripts and correspondence.

The standard bibliography is still *Johann Heinrich Lambert nach seinem Leben und Wirken . . . in drei Abhandlungen dargestellt,* Daniel Huber, ed. (Basel, 1829). *Johann Heinrich Lambert—Leistung und Leben,* Friedrich Löwenhaupt, ed. (Mulhouse, 1943), is a collection of articles on various aspects of Lambert's life and work; its appendix contains a selection from the *Cosmologische Briefe.* About 90 references to Lambert are to be found in Clémence Seither, "Essai de bibliographie de la ville de Mulhouse des origines à 1798," in *Supplément au bulletin du Musée historique de Mulhouse,* **74** (1966), esp. 211–214, 250–253.

Some recent articles about Lambert which (with the exception of Berger) are not listed in the second edition of Steck's *Bibliographia* are (in chronological order): Peter Berger, "Johann Heinrich Lamberts Bedeutung in der Naturwissenschaft des 18. Jahrhunderts," in *Centaurus,* **6** (1959), 157–254; Wilhelm S. Peters, "Lamberts Konzeption einer Geometrie auf einer imaginären Kugel," in *Kantstudien,* **53** (1961–1962), 51–67 (short version of a dissertation [Bonn, 1961], 87 pp.); Roger Jaquel, "Vers les oeuvres complètes du savant et philosophe J.-H. Lambert (1728 à 1777): Velléités et réalisations depuis deux siècles," in *Revue d'histoire des sciences et de leurs applications,* **22** (1969), 285–302; Roger Jaquel, "Jean Henri Lambert (1728–1777) et l'astronomie cométaire au XVIIIe siècle," in *Comptes rendus du 92e Congrès national des Sociétés savantes (Strasbourg, 1967), Section des sciences,* **1** (Paris, 1969), 27–56; Roger Jaquel, "Le savant et philosophe mulhousien J. H. Lambert vu de l'étranger. Essai historiographique sur la façon dont les encyclopédies générales présentent le Mulhousien Lambert," in *Bulletin du Musée historique de Mulhouse,* **78** (1970), 95–130; Karin Figala and Joachim Fleckenstein, "Chemische Jugendschriften des Mathematikers J. H. Lambert (1728–1777)," in *Verhandlungen der Naturforschenden Gesellschaft Basel,* **81** (1971), 40–54; O. B. Sheynin, "J. H. Lambert's Work on Probability," in *Archive for History of Exact Sciences,* **7** (1971), 244–256.

CHRISTOPH J. SCRIBA

LAMÉ, GABRIEL (*b.* Tours, France, 22 July 1795; *d.* Paris, France, 1 May 1870)

Like most French mathematicians of his time, Lamé attended the École Polytechnique. He entered in 1813 and was graduated in 1817. He then continued at the École des Mines, from which he was graduated in 1820.

His interest in geometry showed itself in his first article, "Mémoire sur les intersections des lignes et des surfaces" (1816–1817). His next work, *Examen des différentes méthodes employées pour résoudre les problèmes de géométrie* (1818), contained a new method for calculating the angles between faces and edges of crystals.

In 1820 Lamé accompanied Clapeyron to Russia. He was appointed director of the School of Highways and Transportation in St. Petersburg, where he taught analysis, physics, mechanics, and chemistry. He was also busy planning roads, highways, and bridges that were built in and around that city. He also collaborated with Pierre Dominique Bazaine on the text *Traité élémentaire du calcul intégral,* published in St. Petersburg in 1825. In 1832 he returned to Paris, where he spent the rest of his career and life.

For a few months after his return to Paris, Lamé joined with Clapeyron and the brothers Flachat to form an engineering firm. However, he left the firm in 1832 to accept the chair of physics at the École Polytechnique. He remained there until 1844.

Lamé always combined his teaching positions with work as a consulting engineer. In 1836, he was appointed chief engineer of mines. He also helped plan and build the first two railroads from Paris to Versailles and to St.-Germain.

In 1843 the Paris Academy of Sciences accepted him to replace Puissant in its geometry section. In 1844 he became graduate examiner for the University of Paris in mathematical physics and probability. He became professor of mathematical physics and probability at the university in 1851. In 1862, he went deaf, and resigned his positions. He was in retirement until his death in 1870. In spite of the unsettled and often troubled political climate, Lamé managed to lead a serene and quiet academic life. His sole and quite tenuous connection with politics was his *Esquisse d'un traité de la république* (1848).

Although Lamé did original work in such diverse areas as number theory, thermodynamics, and applied mechanics, his greatest contribution to mathematics was the introduction of curvilinear coordinates and their use in pure and applied mathematics. These coordinates were conceived as intersections of confocal quadric surfaces. By their means, he was able to transform Laplace's equation $\nabla^2 V = 0$ into ellipsoidal coordinates in a form where the variables were separable, and solve the resulting form of the generalized Laplace equation.

In 1836, Lamé had written a textbook in physics for the École Polytechnique, *Cours de physique de l'Ecole polytechnique*. In 1852 he published his text *Leçons sur la théorie mathématique de l'élasticité des corps solides*, in which he used curvilinear coordinates. This work resulted from his investigation into the conditions for equilibrium of a spherical elastic envelope subject to a given distribution of loads on the bounding spherical surfaces. He succeeded in the derivation and transformation of the general elastic surfaces.

As early as 1828, Lamé had shown an interest in thermodynamics in an article "Propagation de la chaleur dans les polyèdres," written in Russia. In 1837 his "Mémoire sur les surfaces isothermes dans les corps solides homogènes en équilibre de température" appeared in Liouville's *Journal*. In these articles Lamé used curvilinear coordinates and his elliptic functions, which were a generalization of the spherical harmonic functions of Laplace, in a consideration of temperatures in the interior of an ellipsoid. *Leçons sur les fonctions inverses des transcendentes et les surfaces isothermes* appeared in 1857, and *Leçons sur la théorie analytique de la chaleur* followed in 1861.

In *Leçons sur les coordonnés curvilignes et leurs diverses applications* Lamé extended his work in thermodynamics to the solution of various problems of a physical nature involving general ellipsoids, such as double refraction in the theory of propagation of light in crystals.

Lamé's investigations in curvilinear coordinates led him even into the field of number theory. He had begun with a study of the curves

$$\left(\frac{x_1}{a_1}\right)^n + \left(\frac{x_2}{a_2}\right)^n + \left(\frac{x_3}{a_3}\right)^n = 0,$$

which are symmetric with respect to a triangle (as well as the space analogs symmetrical with respect to a tetrahedron). When these equations are written in nonhomogeneous form, they appear as

$$\frac{x^n}{a^n} + \frac{y^n}{b^n} = 1;$$

and, when $a = b$, as $x^n + y^n = a^n$. This naturally led Lamé to study Fermat's last theorem.

In 1840 he was able to present a proof of the impossibility of a solution of the equation $x^7 + y^7 = z^7$ in integers (except for the trivial cases where $z = x$ or y, and the remaining variable is zero). In 1847 he developed a solution, in complex numbers, of the form $A^5 + B^5 + C^5 = 0$, and in 1851 a complete solution, in complex numbers, of the form $A^n + B^n + C^n = 0$.

Another result in number theory having nothing to do with Lamé's main interests and endeavors was the theorem: The number of divisions required to find the greatest common divisor of two numbers is never greater than five times the number of digits in the smaller of the numbers. This theorem is yet another example of the attraction that number theory has always seemed to have for mathematicians. This result and the "*Esquisse*" previously mentioned are the only examples of Lamé's work that were not devoted entirely to his main purposes.

Lamé was considered an excellent engineer. While in Russia, he wrote a number of articles that appeared in Gergonne's *Journal*, "Sur la stabilité des voûtes," on arches and mine tunnels (1822); "Sur les engrenages," on gears (1824); and studies on the properties of steel bridges. His work on the scientific design of built-up artillery was considered a standard reference and was much used by gun designers. His final text, *Cours de physique mathématique rationnelle* (1865), was a composite of practice and theory. All of his researches were undertaken with practical application in mind.

It is difficult to characterize Lamé and his work. Gauss considered Lamé the foremost French mathematician of his generation. In the opinion of Bertrand, who presented a eulogy of Lamé on the occasion of his demise, Lamé had a great capacity as an engineer. French mathematicians considered him too practical, and French scientists too theoretical.

Lamé himself once stated that he considered his development of curvilinear coordinates his greatest contribution to mathematical physics. True, his applications were all to physics—to the theory of elasticity, the thermodynamics of ellipsoids and other solids, ellipsoidal harmonics, among others. In his opinion, just as rectangular coordinates made algebra possible, and spherical coordinates made celestial mechanics possible, so general curvilinear coordinates would make possible the solution of more general questions of physics. Yet the work he began was generalized almost as soon as it appeared by such mathematicians as Klein, Bôcher, and Hermite. It now has a strictly mathematical format, being used in the study of ordinary and partial differential equations. We can conclude that Lamé's major work was in the field of differential geometry.

BIBLIOGRAPHY

A bibliography of Lamé's writings is in Poggendorff, I, pt. 1, 1359–1360; and in Royal Society *Catalogue of Scientific Papers*, III, 814–816; VIII, 152; and X, 501.

Works mentioned in the text are "Mémoire sur les intersections des lignes et des surfaces," in *Annales de mathéma-*

tiques pures et appliquées, **7** (1816–1817), 229–240; *Examen des différentes méthodes employées pour résoudre les problèmes de géométrie* (Paris, 1818); "Mémoire sur la stabilité des voûtes," in *Annales des mines*, **8** (1823), 789–836, written with Clapeyron; "Mémoire sur les engrenages," *ibid.*, **9** (1824), 601–624, written with Clapeyron; *Traité élémentaire du calcul intégral* (St. Petersburg, 1825); "Mémoire sur la propagation de la chaleur dans les polyèdres," in *Journal de l'École polytechnique*, cahier 22 (1833), 194–251; "Mémoire sur les surfaces isothermes dans les corps solides homogènes en équilibre de température," in *Journal de mathématiques pures et appliquées*, **2** (1837), 147–188; *Cours de physique de l'École polytechnique*, 2 vols. (Paris, 1836–1837); *Esquisse d'un traité de la république* (Paris, 1848); *Leçons sur la théorie mathématique de l'élasticité des corps* (Paris, 1852); *Leçons sur les fonctions inverses des transcendentes et les surfaces isothermes* (Paris, 1857); *Leçons sur les coordonnés curvilignes et leurs diverses applications* (Paris, 1859); *Leçons sur la théorie analytique de la chaleur* (Paris, 1861); and *Cours de physique mathématique rationnelle* (Paris, 1865).

SAMUEL L. GREITZER

LAMY, BERNARD (*b.* Le Mans, France, June 1640; *d.* Rouen, France, 29 January 1715)

Lamy found his vocation at the Oratorian *collège* in Le Mans, where his parents, Alain Lamy and Marie Masnier, had sent him. As soon as his "Rhétorique" ended, he entered as a novice at the Maison d'Institution in Paris on 6 October 1658.

Lamy was both a product and a master of Oratorian pedagogy. In his principal work, *Entretiens sur les sciences*, the first edition of which appeared in 1683, he proposes an art of learning and teaching all the secular and religious disciplines. This book, admired later by Rousseau, is simultaneously an educational treatise, a discourse on method, and a guide to reading.

During his career Lamy taught almost all subjects. Following his novitiate (1658–1659) and two years of philosophical studies at the *collège* of Saumur, he became professor of classics at Vendôme (1661–1663) and at Juilly (1663–1668). In 1675, drawing on his knowledge of belles lettres, he composed *De l'art de parler*, which in 1688, became *La rhétorique ou l'art de parler*.

Ordained a priest in 1667, Lamy in 1669 finished his training at the École de Théologie de Notre-Dame des Ardilliers, at Saumur. There his teacher was Père André Martin, who found in Descartes support for his Augustinianism. Lamy's admiration for and attachment to Descartes were unwavering. When he became a professor of philosophy, it was Cartesianism that he taught, first at the *collège* of Saumur, and then, beginning in 1673, at the *collège* of Angers, which

bore the title Faculté des Arts. This instruction was the cause of his misfortunes. Attacked and denounced for Augustinianism, Cartesianism, and antimonarchical opinions, Lamy was exiled by order of the king in Dauphiné at the beginning of 1676.

At first Lamy lived in a "solitude" at Saint-Martin de Miséré, but soon, thanks to the support of the bishop, Le Camus, he moved into the seminary in Grenoble, where he was again able to teach. During this period he published his principal scientific works: *Traitez de méchanique*, *Traité de la grandeur en général*, and *Les élémens de géométrie*.

These works were still those of a good teacher and not of a researcher; Lamy was more concerned with diffusion than with discovery. Connected with the small Oratorian group of mathematicians that his very good friend Malebranche inspired and animated, he asked of it more than he brought to it. He himself acknowledged his debt to his colleague Jean Prestet. Even when in 1687, in an appendix to the second edition of his *Traitez de méchanique*, Lamy stated, at the same time as Varignon, the rule of the parallelogram of forces, he did not see all of its implications and consequences. Despite Duhem's opinion, Varignon must be conceded the greater originality and awareness of novelty.

In 1686 Lamy obtained permission to live in Paris, but a work on the concordance of the evangelists provoked sharp polemics and his superior general judged it best to send him away again. Beginning in 1690 he lived in Rouen, where he remained until his death, occupied with historical and scriptural studies.

BIBLIOGRAPHY

I. ORIGINAL WORKS. Lamy's writings include *Traitez de méchanique, de l'équilibre des solides et des liqueurs* (Paris, 1679); *Traitez de méchanique . . . Nouvelle Édition où l'on ajoute une nouvelle manière de démontrer les principaux théorèmes de cette science* (Paris, 1687); *Traité de la grandeur en général* (Paris, 1680); *Entretiens sur les sciences* (Grenoble, 1683), also in critical ed. by François Girbal and Pierre Clair (Paris, 1966); *Les élémens de géométrie* (Paris, 1685); and *Traité de perspective* (Paris, 1701).

II. SECONDARY LITERATURE. See Pierre Costabel, "Varignon, Lamy et le parallélogramme des forces," in *Archives internationales d'histoire des sciences*, no. 74–75 (Jan.–June 1966), 103–124; Pierre Duhem, *Les origines de la statique* (Paris, 1906), II, 251–259; and François Girbal, *Bernard Lamy. Étude biographique et bibliographique* (Paris, 1964).

JOSEPH BEAUDE

LANCRET, MICHEL ANGE (*b.* Paris, France, 15 December 1774; *d.* Paris, 17 December 1807)

Son of the architect François Nicolas Lancret—who was the son of an engraver and nephew of the painter Nicolas Lancret—and Germaine Marguerite Vinache de Montblain, the daughter of a sculptor, Michel Ange Lancret was initiated into the plastic arts and architecture at a very early age. He entered the École des Ponts et Chaussées in 1793 and was sent as a student to the port of Dunkerque. Admitted on 21 November 1794 to the first graduating class of the École Polytechnique (at that time the École Centrale des Travaux Publics), he studied there for three years and, along with twenty-four of his fellow students—including J. B. Biot and E.-L. Malus—he served as monitor. After several months of specialization Lancret was named engineer of bridges and highways in April 1798, and in this capacity he was made a member of the Commission of Arts and Sciences attached to the Egyptian expedition. He reached Egypt on 1 July 1798 and was entrusted with important topographical operations, irrigation projects, and canal maintenance, as well as with archaeological studies, the description of the ancient monuments of the Upper Kingdom, and entomological studies.

On 4 July 1799 Lancret was named a member of the mathematics section of the Institut d'Égypte, where he presented several memoirs on his topographical work and communications from others, including one on the discovery of the Rosetta stone (19 July 1799) and Malus's first memoir on light (November 1800). Sent home at the end of 1801, he was soon appointed secretary of the commission responsible for the *Description de l'Egypte*, eventually succeeding Nicolas Conté as the official representative of the government in December 1805. The author of several memoirs on topography, architecture, and political economy, and of numerous drawings of monuments, he devoted himself passionately to this editorial assignment while continuing to do research in infinitesimal geometry.

In his first memoir on the theory of space curves, presented in April 1802, Lancret cites an unpublished theorem of Fourier's on the relationships between the curvature and torsion of a curve and the corresponding elements of the cuspidal edge of its polar curve. In addition he studied the properties of the rectifying surface of a curve and integrated the differential equations of its evolutes. In a second memoir (December 1806) he developed the theory of "développoïdes," cuspidal edges of developable surfaces which pass through a given curve and whose generating lines make a constant angle with this curve.

Although limited in extent, this work places Lancret among the most direct disciples of Monge in infinitesimal geometry.

BIBLIOGRAPHY

I. ORIGINAL WORKS. Lancret's writings on Egypt appeared in the collection *Description de l'Égypte:* "Description de l'Ile de Philae," in no. 1, *Antiquité. Descriptions,* I (Paris, 1809), 1–60; "Mémoire sur le système d'imposition territoriale et sur l'administration des provinces de l'Égypte dans les dernières années du gouvernement des Mamlouks," in no. 71, *État moderne,* I (Paris, 1809), 233–260; "Notice sur la branche Canoptique," in no. 46, *Antiquité. Mémoires,* I (Paris, 1809), 251–254; "Mémoire sur le canal d'Alexandrie," in no. 90, *État moderne,* II (Paris, 1812), 185–194, written with G.-J. C. de Chabrol, previously pub. in *La décade égyptienne,* II (Cairo, 1799–1800), pp. 233–251; "Notice topographique sur la partie de l'Égypte comprise entre Rahmânich et Alexandrie et sur les environs du lac Maréotis," in no. 100, *État moderne,* II (Paris, 1812), 483–490, written with Chabrol; and "Description d'Héliopolis," in no. 28, *Antiquité. Descriptions,* II (Paris, 1818), 1–18, written with J. M. J. Dubois-Aymé. Architectural illustrations are in *Antiquité. Descriptions,* I, II, III, and V.

His mathematical writings include "Mémoire sur les courbes à double courbure," in *Mémoires présentés par divers savants . . . ,* 2nd ser., 1 (1806), 416–454, an extract of which had appeared in *Correspondance sur l'École polytechnique,* 1, no. 3 (Jan.–Feb. 1805), 51–52; and "Mémoire sur les développoïdes des courbes à double courbure et des surfaces développables," *ibid.,* 2 (1811), 1–79, extracts in *Nouveau Bulletin des Sciences par la Société philomatique de Paris,* 2nd series, 1 (1807), issues 56 and 57, and in *Correspondance sur l'École polytechnique,* 3, no. 2 (May 1815), 146–149.

II. SECONDARY LITERATURE. There are only a few brief and incomplete accounts of Lancret's life: G. Guémard, in *Bulletin de l'Institut d'Égypte,* 7 (1925), 89–90; J. P. N. Hachette, in *Correspondance sur l'École polytechnique,* 1, no. 9 (Jan. 1808), 374; A. Jal, in *Dictionnaire critique de biographie et d'histoire* (Paris, 1872), pp. 734–735; A. de Lapparent, in *École polytechnique, livre du centenaire,* I (Paris, 1895), 91–92; A. Maury, in Michaud's *Biographie universelle,* new ed., XXIII (Paris, n.d.), 137–138; and F. P. H. Tarbé de Saint-Hardouin, in *Notices biographiques sur les ingénieurs des Ponts et Chaussées . . .* (Paris, 1884), pp. 123–124.

His mathematical work, on the other hand, has been analyzed quite thoroughly by M. Chasles, *Rapport sur les progrès de la géométrie* (Paris, 1870), pp. 10–13; J. L. Coolidge, *A History of Geometrical Methods* (Oxford, 1940), p. 323; N. Nielsen, *Géomètres français sous la Révolution* (Copenhagen, 1929), pp. 155–157; M. d'Ocagne, *Histoire abrégée des sciences mathématiques* (Paris, 1955), 199; and R. Taton, *L'oeuvre scientifique de Gaspard Monge* (Paris, 1951), see index.

RENÉ TATON

LANDAU, EDMUND (*b*. Berlin, Germany, 14 February 1877; *d*. Berlin, 19 February 1938)

Landau was the son of the gynecologist Leopold Landau and the former Johanna Jacoby. He attended the "Französische Gymnasium" in Berlin and then studied mathematics, primarily also in Berlin. He worked mostly with Georg Frobenius and received his doctorate in 1899. Two years later he obtained the *venia legendi*, entitling him to lecture. He taught at the University of Berlin until 1909 and then became full professor at the University of Göttingen, suceeding Hermann Minkowski. David Hilbert and Felix Klein were his colleagues. Landau was active in Göttingen until forced to stop teaching by the National Socialist regime. After his return to Berlin he lectured only outside of Germany, for example, in Cambridge in 1935 and in Brussels in 1937, shortly before his sudden death.

Landau was a member of several German academies, of the academies of St. Petersburg (now Leningrad) and Rome, and an honorary member of the London Mathematical Society. In 1905 he married Marianne Ehrlich, daughter of Paul Ehrlich; they had two daughters and one son.

Landau's principal field of endeavor was analytic number theory and, in particular, the distribution of prime numbers. In 1796 Gauss had conjectured the prime number theorem: If $\pi(x)$ designates the number of prime numbers below x, then $\pi(x)$ is asymptotically equal to $x/\log x$, i.e., as $x \to \infty$, the quotient of $\pi(x)$ and $x/\log x$ approaches 1. This theorem was demonstrated in 1896 by Hadamard and de la Vallée-Poussin, working independently of each other. In 1903 Landau presented a new, fundamentally simpler proof, which, moreover, allowed the prime number theorem and a refinement made by de la Vallée-Poussin to be applied to the distribution of ideal primes in algebraic number fields. In his two-volume *Handbuch der Lehre von der Verteilung der Primzahlen* (1909), Landau gave the first systematic presentation of analytic number theory. For decades it was indispensable in research and teaching and remains an important historical document. His three-volume *Vorlesungen über Zahlentheorie* (1927) provided an extremely comprehensive presentation of the various branches of number theory from its elements to the contemporary state of research.

Besides two further books on number theory, Landau was author of *Darstellung und Begründung einiger neuerer Ergebnisse der Funktionentheorie*, which contains a collection of interesting and elegant theorems of the theory of analytic functions of a single variable. Landau himself discovered some of the theorems and demonstrated others in a new and simpler fashion. In *Grundlagen der Analysis* he established arithmetic with whole, rational, irrational, and complex numbers, starting from Peano's axioms for natural numbers. Also important is *Einführung in die Differentialrechnung und Integralrechnung*.

Written with the greatest care, Landau's books are characterized by argumentation which is complete, and as simple as possible. The necessary prerequisite knowledge is provided, and the reader is led securely, step by step, to the goal. The idea of the proof and the general relationships are, to be sure, not always clearly apparent, especially in his later works, which are written in an extremely terse manner—the so-called Landau style. Through his books and his more than 250 papers Landau exercised a great influence on the whole development of number theory in his time. He was an enthusiastic teacher and sought contact with fellow scientists. Harald Bohr and G. H. Hardy were often his guests in Göttingen.

BIBLIOGRAPHY

I. ORIGINAL WORKS. Landau was the author of more than 250 papers published in various journals. His books are *Handbuch der Lehre von der Verteilung der Primzahlen*, 2 vols. (Leipzig–Berlin, 1909); *Darstellung und Begründung einiger neuerer Ergebnisse der Funktionentheorie* (Berlin, 1916; 2nd ed., 1929); *Einführung in die elementare und analytische Theorie der algebraischen Zahlen und Ideale* (Leipzig–Berlin, 1918; 2nd ed., 1927); *Vorlesungen über Zahlentheorie*, 3 vols. (Leipzig, 1927); *Grundlagen der Analysis* (Leipzig, 1930); *Einführung in die Differentialrechnung und Integralrechnung* (Groningen, 1934); *Über einige Fortschritte der additiven Zahlentheorie* (Cambridge, 1937).

II. SECONDARY LITERATURE. A biography with portrait is in *Reichshandbuch der deutschen Gesellschaft*, II (Berlin, 1931), 1060; see also the obituaries in *Nachrichten von der Gesellschaft der Wissenschaften zu Göttingen* for 1937–1938, 10; by J. H. Hardy and Heilbronn in *Journal of the London Mathematical Society*, **13** (1938), 302–310; and by Konrad Knopp in *Jahresberichte der Deutschen Mathematiker-vereinigung*, **54** (1951), 55–62.

BRUNO SCHOENEBERG

LANDEN, JOHN (*b*. Peakirk, near Peterborough, England, 23 January 1719; *d*. Milton, near Peterborough, 15 January 1790)

Landen was trained as a surveyor and from 1762 to 1788 was land agent to William Wentworth, second Earl Fitzwilliam. He lived a quiet rural life with mathematics as the occupation of his leisure, taking up those topics which caught his fancy. He contributed to the *Ladies' Diary* from 1744 and to the *Philosophical Transactions of the Royal Society*; he published his *Mathematical Lucubrations* in 1755 and the two-volume *Mathematical Memoirs* in 1780 and 1790; the latter volume was placed in his hands from the press the day before he died. He was elected a fellow of the Royal Society in 1766.

Landen wrote on dynamics, in which he had the temerity to differ with Euler and d'Alembert, and on the summation of series. He also tried to settle the arguments about the validity of limit processes used as a basis for the calculus by substituting a purely algebraic foundation.

Landen's name is perpetuated by his work on elliptic arcs (*Philosophical Transactions*, 1775). Giulio Carlo Fagnano dei Toschi had obtained elegant theorems about arcs of lemniscates and ellipses. Landen's development expressed the length of a hyperbolic arc in terms of lengths of arcs in two ellipses. The connection in size between these ellipses permits Landen's work to be seen as a relation between two elliptic integrals. In Legendre's notation, if

$$F(\phi, k) = \int_0^\psi \sqrt{(1 - k^2 \sin^2 \phi)} \, d\phi,$$

then in Landen's transformation

$$F(\phi, k) - \tfrac{1}{2}(1 + k_1) F(\phi_1, k_1),$$

where, writing $k' = \sqrt{(1 - k^2)}$ as usual, the new parameters ϕ_1, k_1 are expressed in terms of ϕ, k by the relations

$$\sqrt{(1 - k^2 \sin^2 \phi)} \cdot \sin \phi_1 = (1 + k') \sin \phi \cos \phi,$$

$$k_1 = (1 - k')/(1 + k').$$

By considering an iterated chain of such transformations, Legendre obtained a method for the rapid computation of elliptic integrals, of which Gauss's method of the arithmetico-geometric mean is another form. The Landen transformation can also be shown as a relation between elliptic functions; in the Jacobian notation,

$$\mathrm{sn}\{(1 + k') u, k_1\} = (1 + k') \,\mathrm{sn}(u, k) \,\mathrm{cd}(u, k).$$

An interest in integration, or "fluents," led Landen to discuss (*Philosophical Transactions*, 1760, and later) the dilogarithm

$$Li_2(z) = -\int_0^z \frac{\log(1 - z) \, dz}{z}$$

(the notation is modern). He obtained several formulas and numerical values that were found at almost the same time by Euler. In the first volume of the *Memoirs*

he initiated discussion of the function (now sometimes called the trilogarithm)

$$Li_3(z) = \int_0^z \frac{Li_2(z) \, dz}{z},$$

deriving functional relations and certain numerical results, work followed up by Spence (1809) and Kummer (1840).

BIBLIOGRAPHY

I. ORIGINAL WORKS. Landen's books are *Mathematical Lucubrations* (London, 1755); and *Mathematical Memoirs*, 2 vols. (London, 1780–1790). Articles are "A New Method of Computing the Sums of Certain Series," in *Philosophical Transactions of the Royal Society*, **51**, pt. 2 (1760), 553–565, and "An Investigation of a General Theorem for Finding the Length of Any Conic Hyperbola . . .," *ibid.*, **65**, pt. 2 (1775), 283–289.

II. SECONDARY LITERATURE. A short biography is C. Hutton, "John Landen," in *A Mathematical and Philosophical Dictionary*, II (London, 1795), 7–9. For the life and work of Fagnano and of Landen, see G. N. Watson, "The Marquis and the Land-Agent," in *Mathematical Gazette*, **17** (Feb. 1933). Landen's transformation is discussed in any standard text on elliptic functions. For the dilogarithm and its generalizations, see L. Lewin, *Dilogarithms and Associated Functions* (London, 1958).

T. A. A. BROADBENT

LANDSBERG, GEORG (*b.* Breslau, Germany [now Wrocław, Poland], 30 January 1865; *d.* Kiel, Germany, 14 September 1912)

Landsberg spent his youth in Breslau. He studied at the universities of Breslau and Leipzig from 1883 to 1889, receiving his doctorate in mathematics from the former in 1890. He then went to the University of Heidelberg, where he became a privatdocent in mathematics in 1893 and extraordinary professor in 1897. He returned to Breslau in this capacity in 1904, but in 1906 he accepted an offer from the University of Kiel, where he was appointed professor ordinarius in 1911. He remained at Kiel until his death.

Landsberg investigated the theory of algebraic functions of two variables, which was then a hardly accessible subject that did not attain its major successes until much later. He also considered the theory of curves in higher dimensional manifolds and its connection with the calculus of variations and the mechanics of rigid bodies. In addition he studied theta functions and Gaussian sums. In this work he touched on the ideas of Weierstrass, Riemann, and Weber.

Landsberg's most important achievement lay in his contributions to the development of the theory of algebraic functions of one variable. In this field arithmetic, algebra, function theory, and geometry are most intimately related. In addition to Riemann's function-theoretical approach and the geometric approach favored by Italian mathematicians as an especially easy and sure access, there existed the arithmetical approach from Weierstrass. Landsberg's most important work in this area was his algebraic investigations of the Riemann-Roch theorem, which had been stated by Riemann in the context of his theory of algebraic functions and greatly extended by Roch. Landsberg provided a foundation for it within arithmetic theory, which then finally led to the modern abstract theory of algebraic functions.

BIBLIOGRAPHY

Landsberg's *Theorie der algebraischen Funktionen einer Variablen und ihre Anwendungen auf algebraische Kurven und abelsche Integrale* (Leipzig, 1902), written with Kurt Hensel, was a standard text for decades. A complete listing of Landsberg's articles can be found in Poggendorff, IV, 835; V, 706.

BRUNO SCHOENEBERG

LANSBERGE, PHILIP VAN (*b.* Ghent, Belgium, 25 August 1561; *d.* Middelburg, Netherlands, 8 December 1632)

On account of the religious troubles of those days his parents Daniel van Lansberge, lord of Meulebeke, and Pauline van den Honingh found themselves obliged to go to France in 1566 and afterward to England, where Philip studied mathematics and theology. He was already back in Belgium in 1579, where he received a call to be a Protestant minister in Antwerp in 1580. After the conquest of Antwerp by Spain on 16 August 1585, Philip left Belgium definitively to establish himself in the Netherlands. He went to Leiden, where he enrolled as a theological student. From 1586 to 1613 he was a Protestant minister at Goes in Zeeland, after which he went to Middelburg, where he died in 1632.

The Danish mathematician Thomas Finck had published an important work, the *Geometriae rotundi,* in Basel in 1583. It is this work that Van Lansberge seems to have followed very closely in his first mathematical study, *Triangulorum geometriae libri IV* of 1591. The first book is devoted to the definitions of the trigonometric functions. Van Lansberge, following Maurice Bressieu, used the term "radius" instead of "sinus totus." The second book contains the method of constructing the tables of sines, tangents, and secants, largely derived from those of Viète and Finck, and the tables themselves, which were used by Kepler in his calculations. The third book is devoted to the solution of plane triangles and is accompanied by numerical illustrations. Van Lansberge's statement and proof of the sine law differs very little from that given by Regiomontanus. The fourth book deals with spherical trigonometry; the first eleven items concern spherical geometry. In the solution of spherical triangles Van Lansberge employs a device similar to that of Bressieu in his *Metrices astronomicae* (Paris, 1581), the marking of the given parts of a triangle by two strokes. Van Lansberge's new proof for the cosine theorem for sides (Book IV, item 17) marks the first time that the theorem appeared in print for angles as well as sides. But although Van Lansberge may lay claim to the discovery of the theorem for angles, sufficient evidence indicates that this theorem was known to Viète and to Tycho Brahe. On the whole Van Lansberge shows little originality in the content of his trigonometry, but his arrangement of definitions and propositions is less complicated and more systematic than that of Viète and Clavius.

In 1616 Van Lansberge published his *Cyclometriae novae libri II,* which was attacked the same year by Alexander Anderson in his *Vindiciae Archimedis, sive elenchus cyclometriae novae a Philippo Lansbergio nuper editae.* In this book Van Lansberge occupied himself with approximating the ratio between the circumference (Book I), the area (Book II), and the diameter of the circle. He carried the value of π to 28 decimal places by means of a method in which he seems to have joined the quadratrix of the ancients to trigonometric considerations. He thought that he had found a better approximation than that of Ludolf van Ceulen, who had used the Archimedean method of inscribed and circumscribed polygons and had carried the value of π to thirty-five decimal places in 1615. In his *Progymnasmatum astronomiae restitutae de motu solis* (Middelburg, 1619) Van Lansberge taught the probability of the earth's motion according to the Copernican doctrine; the same is true of *Bedenckingen op den dagelyckschen, ende jaerlyckschen loop van den aerdt-kloot* (Middelburg, 1629), translated into Latin by M. Hortensius as *Commentationes in motum terrae diurnum, et annuum* (Middelburg, 1630).

Both works were attacked for their Copernican ideas by Morin in his *Famosi et antiqui problematis de telluris motu vel...* (Paris, 1631), and by Libert Froidmond in his *Anti-Aristarchus; sive orbis-terrae immobilis; liber I* (Antwerp, 1631). Although a follower of Copernicus, Van Lansberge did not accept the planetary theories of Kepler altogether. His *Tabulae motuum coelestium perpetuae* (Middelburg, 1632), founded on an epicyclic theory, were much used among astronomers, although they were very inferior to Kepler's Rudolphine tables.

BIBLIOGRAPHY

I. ORIGINAL WORKS. Van Lansberge's works were published as *Philippi Lansbergii Astronomi Celebrium Opera Omnia* (Middelburg, 1663).

II. SECONDARY LITERATURE. A very good biography is by C. de Waard in *Nieuw Nederlandsch biografisch woordenboek* (Leiden, 1912), cols. 775–782. See also the following (listed chronologically): J. E. Montucla, *Histoire des mathématiques*, II (Paris, 1799), 334; D. Bierens de Haan, "Notice sur quelques quadrateurs du cercle dans les Pays-Bas," in *Bullettino di bibliografia e di storia della scienze matematiche e fisiche*, **7** (1874), 120, 121; A. J. van der Aa, *Biographisch woordenboek der Nederlanden*, XI (Haarlem, 1876), 154–157; D. Bierens de Haan, "Bibliographie néerlandaise," in *Bullettino di bibliografia e di storia della scienze matematiche e fisiche*, **15** (1882), 229–231; A. Von Braunmühl, *Vorlesungen über Geschichte der Trigonometrie*, I (Leipzig, 1900), 175, 176, 192; C. de Waard, "Nog twee brieven van Philips Lansbergen," in *Archief vroegere en latere mededelingen ... in Middelburg* (1915), 93–99; H. Bosmans, "Philippe van Lansberge, de Gand, 1561–1632," in *Mathésis; recueil mathématique*, **42** (1928), 5–10; C. de Waard, ed., *Correspondance du M. Mersenne*, II (Paris, 1937), 36, 511–513; and M. C. Zeller, *The Development of Trigonometry From Regiomontanus to Pitiscus* (Ann Arbor., Mich., 1946), 87, 94–97.

H. L. L. BUSARD

LAPLACE, PIERRE-SIMON, MARQUIS DE (*b.* Beaumont-en-Auge, Normandy, France, 23 March 1749; *d.* Paris, France, 5 March 1827)

Laplace was among the most influential scientists in all history. His career was important for his technical contributions to exact science, for the philosophical point of view he developed in the presentation of his work, and for the part he took in forming the modern scientific disciplines. The main institutions in which he participated were the Académie Royale des Sciences, until its suppression in the Revolution, and then its replacement, the scientific division of the Institut de France, together with two other Republican foundations, the École Polytechnique and the Bureau des Longitudes. It will be convenient to consider the scientific life that he led therein as having transpired in four stages, the first two in the context of the old regime and the latter two in that of the French Revolution, the Napoleonic regime, and the Restoration.

The boundaries must not be taken more categorically than biography allows, but in the first stage, 1768–1778, we may see Laplace rising on the horizon, composing memoirs on problems of the integral calculus, mathematical astronomy, cosmology, theory of games of chance, and causality, pretty much in that order. During this formative period, he established his style, reputation, philosophical position, certain mathematical techniques, and a program of research in two areas, probability and celestial mechanics, in which he worked mathematically for the rest of his life.

In the second stage, 1778–1789, he moved into the ascendant, reaching in both those areas many of the major results for which he is famous and which he later incorporated into the great treatises *Mécanique céleste* (1799–1825) and *Théorie analytique des probabilités* (1812). They were informed in large part by the mathematical techniques that he introduced and developed, then or earlier, most notably generating functions, the transform since called by his name, the expansion also named for him in the theory of determinants, the variation of constants to achieve approximate solutions in the integration of astronomical expressions, and the generalized gravitational function that, through the intermediary of Poisson, later became the potential function of nineteenth-century electricity and magnetism. It was also during this period that Laplace entered on the third area of his mature interests, physics, in his collaboration with Lavoisier on the theory of heat, and that he became, partly in consequence of this association, one of the inner circle of influential members of the scientific community. In the 1780's he began serving on commissions important to the government and affecting the lives of others.

In the third stage, 1789–1805, the Revolutionary period and especially that of the Directory brought him to his zenith. The early 1790's saw the completion of the great series of memoirs on planetary astronomy and involved him centrally in the preparation of the metric system. More important, in the decade from 1795 to 1805 his influence was paramount for the exact sciences in the newly founded Institut de France; and his was a powerful position in the counsels of the École Polytechnique, which was training the first generation of mathematical physicists. The educational mission attributed to all science in that period of intense civic consciousness changed the mode of scientific publication from academic memoir to general treatise. The first four volumes of *Mécanique céleste* (Laplace himself coined the term), generalizing the laws of mechanics for their application to the motions and figures of the heavenly bodies, appeared from 1799 through 1805. The last parts of the fourth volume and the fifth volume, really a separate work that appeared in installments from 1823 to 1825, contain important material (on physics) not already included in the sequence of Laplace's original memoirs published previously by the old Academy.

Laplace accompanied both *Mécanique céleste* and *Théorie analytique des probabilités* by verbal paraphrases addressed to the intelligent public in the French tradition of *haute vulgarisation*. The *Exposition du système du monde* preceded the *Mécanique céleste* and appeared in 1796. The *Essai philosophique sur les probabilités*, published in 1814 as an introduction to the second edition of *Théorie analytique* and printed separately earlier in the same year, originated in a course of lectures at the École Normale in 1795.

The work of the fourth stage, occupying the period from 1805 until 1827, exhibits elements of culmination and of decline. It was then that the mature—perhaps the aging—Laplace, in company with Berthollet, formed a school, surrounding himself with disciples in the informal Société d'Arcueil. But the science that he set out to shape was not astronomy. The center of their interest, following Volume IV of *Mécanique céleste*, was in physics—capillary action, the theory of heat, corpuscular optics, and the speed of sound. The Laplacian school of physics has had a bad scholarly press since its identity was established, excessively so perhaps. But whatever else may be said about it,

there can be no doubt about the encouragement that it gave to the mathematization of the science.

Beginning in 1810, Laplace turned his attention to probability again, moving back by way of error theory into the subject as a whole. Mathematically speaking, the *Théorie analytique des probabilités* (1812) may be said to belong to the previous phase of drawing together and generalizing the researches on special topics of his younger years. There were important novelties in the application, however, notably in the treatment of least squares, in the extension of probability in later editions to analysis of the credibility of witnesses and the procedures of judicial panels and electoral bodies, and in the increasing sophistication of the statistical treatment of geodesic and meteorological data.

A further preliminary word is in order about the circumstances of this article, for it is the work of many hands. Two successive agreements with individual contributors broke down, failure to honor the first having been responsible for the absence of an article from Volume VIII and similar failure in the case of the second for much delay in publication of the present volume. In what was becoming an extremity, there seemed no alternative but for the editor to enlist the collaboration of colleagues qualified in the several branches of science and to seek to combine their contributions into a coherent whole. Accordingly, Dr. Brian G. Marsden undertook to give an account of the *Mécanique céleste*, Dr. C. A. Whitney of the *Exposition du système du monde*, Dr. Ivo Schneider of the *Théorie analytique des probabilités*, and Dr. Robert Fox of Laplacian physics. All four have kindly and generously done so.

When I began writing the background, however, the account assumed a scale different from what we had imagined. At that stage, I also benefited from the investigations of members of my seminar at Princeton University, which was devoted in 1976–1977 to the career of Laplace. Papers by Messrs. George Anastaplo, Robert Bernstein, Chikara Sazaki, and Sherwin Singer were especially illuminating. Further, I have had invaluable guidance and criticism from two other colleagues, Dr. Stephen M. Stigler on the earliest memoirs and on statistical aspects in general, and Dr. Ivor Grattan-Guinness on mathematics, bibliography, style, organization—indeed, on everything. In the end, I have written Parts I, II, and III, together with Sections 25, 26, and 28 in Part IV. In composing the accounts of the respective treatises I have profited from the essays of Drs. Marsden, Whitney, and Schneider. Responsibility for errors or other shortcomings is, of course, not to be laid at their door. I have also compiled the Bibliography, with the able assistance of Mr. Joel Honig, whose editorial collaboration has been invaluable throughout. Dr. Robert Fox has written Sections 22, 23, 24, and 27 in Part IV, dealing with the Laplacian school of physics. Those four parts correspond to the stages of Laplace's career outlined above. In addition, Dr. Grattan-Guinness has written Part V (Section 29), on the history of the Laplace transform.

Before proceeding further, the reader would do well to turn to the Bibliography and familiarize himself with its several categories. The citations throughout have reference to titles that will be found in appropriate sections of the Bibliography as indicated; and its central section [I] constitutes a dual chronology of Laplace's work, by order of composition and by order of publication. References to the former sequence (Section I, Part 1) are given in italic: (23). References to the latter sequence (Section I, Part 2) are given by bracketing the italicized date. The several memoirs published in any given year are distinguished by letters of the alphabet, thus: [1777a]. Inevitably, the organization of the Bibliography reflects the complexity of that work, but I venture to hope that it may be a first approximation to that which does not yet exist, a complete bibliography of Laplace.

CHARLES COULSTON GILLISPIE

PART I: EARLY CAREER, 1768–1778

1. Youth and Education
2. Election to the Academy
3. Finite Differences, Recurrent Series, and Theory of Chance
4. Probability of Events and of Their Causes
5. Universal Gravitation
6. Cometary Distribution
7. Partial Differential Equations, Determinants, and Variation of Constants
8. The Figure of the Earth and the Motion of the Seas

PART II: LAPLACE IN HIS PRIME, 1778–1789

9. Influence and Reputation
10. Variation of Constants; Differential Operators
11. Probability Matured
12. Generating Functions and Definite Integrals
13. Population
14. Determination of the Orbits of Comets
15. Lavoisier and Laplace: Chemical Physics of Heat
16. Attraction of Spheroids

17. Secular Inequalities: Jupiter and Saturn; the Moons of Jupiter; Lunar Theory

PART III: SYNTHESIS AND SCIENTIFIC STATESMANSHIP

18. The Revolution and the Metric System
19. Scientific Work in the Early Revolution
20. *Exposition du système du monde*
21. *Mécanique céleste*

PART IV: LAPLACIAN PHYSICS AND PROBABILITY

22. The Velocity of Sound ⎫
23. Short-range Forces ⎬ (Robert Fox)
24. The Laplacian School ⎭
25. Theory of Error
26. Probability: *Théorie analytique* and *Essai philosophique*
27. Loss of Influence (Robert Fox)
28. The Last Analysis

PART V: THE LAPLACE TRANSFORM

29. Laplace's Integral Solutions to Partial Differential Equations (Ivor Grattan-Guinness)

BIBLIOGRAPHY

PART I: EARLY CAREER, 1768–1778

1. Youth and Education. Genealogical records of the Laplace family in lower Normandy go back to the middle of the seventeenth century (J: Boncompagni, Simon). Laplace's father, Pierre, was a syndic of the parish, probably in the cider business and certainly in comfortable circumstances. The family of his mother, Marie-Anne Sochon, were well-to-do farmers of Tourgéville. He had one elder sister, also called Marie-Anne, born in 1745. There is no record of intellectual distinction in the family beyond what was to be expected of the cultivated provincial bourgeoisie and the minor gentry. One paternal uncle, Louis, an abbé although not ordained, is said to have been a mathematician and was probably a teacher at the *collège* (secondary school) kept at Beaumont-en-Auge by the Benedictines. He died in 1759, when his nephew was ten. Laplace was enrolled there as a day student from the age of seven to sixteen. Pupils usually proceeded to the church or the army; Laplace's father intended him for an ecclesiastical vocation.

In 1766 he went up to the University of Caen and matriculated in the Faculty of Arts, still formally a cleric. During his two years there he must have discovered his mathematical gifts, for instead of continuing in the Faculty of Theology, he departed for Paris in 1768. Apparently, he never took his M.A., although he may briefly have been a tutor in the family of the marquis d'Héricy and may also have taught at his former *collège*. The members of the faculty at Caen who opened his eyes to mathematics and their own to his talent were Christophe Gadbled and Pierre Le Canu. All that we know about them is that they were points of light in the philosophic and scientific microcosm of Caen, professors with the sense to recognize and encourage a gifted pupil.

On Laplace's departure for Paris at the age of nineteen, Le Canu gave him a letter of recommendation to d'Alembert, who immediately set him a problem and told him to come back in a week. Tradition has it that Laplace solved it overnight. Thereupon d'Alembert proposed another, knottier puzzle—which Laplace resolved just as quickly (J: Bigourdan, 381). The story may be apocryphal, but there is no doubt that d'Alembert was somehow impressed and took Laplace up, as he had other young men in the evening of his own career, although none of comparable merit mathematically. The next question was a livelihood, and d'Alembert himself answered to that necessity, securing his new protégé the appointment of professor of mathematics at the École Militaire. Imparting geometry, trigonometry, elementary analysis, and statics to adolescent cadets of good family, average attainment, and no commitment to the subjects afforded little stimulus, but the post did permit Laplace to stay in Paris.

2. Election to the Academy. It was expected of Laplace that he should concentrate his energies on making a mathematical reputation, and he won election to the Academy of Sciences on 31 March 1773, after five years in Paris. Condorcet had become acting permanent secretary earlier that month. Never, he wrote in the preface to the volume in which the first memoirs that Laplace published in Paris were printed (*SE*, 6 [1774], "Histoire," p. 19), had the Academy received from so young a candidate in so short a time as many important papers on such varied and difficult topics. On two previous occasions his candidacy had been passed over: in 1771, in favor of Alexandre Vandermonde, fourteen years his senior, and the fol-

lowing year in favor of Jacques-Antoine-Joseph Cousin, ten years older and a professor at the Collège Royal de France. Evidently, Laplace felt slighted, despite his youth. On 1 January 1773 d'Alembert wrote to Lagrange asking whether there was a possibility of obtaining a place in the Prussian Academy and a post at Berlin, since the Paris Academy had just preferred a person of markedly inferior ability (*Oeuvres de Lagrange*, XIII [1882], 254–256). The approach lapsed three months later when Laplace was chosen an adjunct member in Paris. Bigourdan's statement that he was admitted directly to the second rank of *associé* is incorrect (J: 384).

If the records are complete, the papers to which Condorcet was alluding numbered thirteen (*1–13*), presented in just under three years, beginning on 28 March 1770. The topics were extreme-value problems; adaptation of the integral calculus to the solution of difference equations; expansion of difference equations in a single variable in recurrent series and in more than one variable in recurro-recurrent series; application of these techniques to theory of games of chance; singular solutions for differential equations; and problems of mathematical astronomy, notably the variation of the inclination of the ecliptic and of planetary orbits, the lunar orbit, perturbations produced in the motion of the planets by the action of their satellites, and "the Newtonian theory of the motion of the planets" (*9*). Of these papers, four were published (*1, 5, 8, 13*). Laplace translated the first two into Latin and placed them in the *Nova acta eruditorum*, where the second ([*1771a*]) was printed before the first ([*1774a*]).

Perhaps it will be appropriate to call this pair of memoirs Laplace's juvenilia. The earlier, the first paper that he read before the Academy, was presented on 28 March 1770, five days after his twenty-first birthday, and was entitled "Recherches sur les maxima et minima des lignes courbes" (*1*). After a review of extreme-value problems, he proposed several improvements in the development that Lagrange had given to Euler's *Methodus inveniendi lineas curvas maximi minimive proprietate gaudentes . . .* (1744). One modification concerned Lagrange's finding, in a paper published in the *Mélanges . . . de la Société royale de Turin* (**2** [1760–1761]; *Oeuvres de Lagrange*, **1**, 335–362), that there was no need to follow Euler in assuming a constant difference. If the assumption was justified, the number of equations might be reduced by at least one, and otherwise the problem was unsolvable. Laplace found the same result by a method that his commissioners called "less direct, less rigorous in appearance, but simpler and fairly elegant" (*1*). In cases where a difference is not constant, the difficulty was shown to arise from a faulty statement of the problem. A variable was concealed that should have appeared in the function, and when it was identified the equations became determinate. If the solutions yield maximum values, the equations involve double curvature. Laplace further gave a general analytic criterion for distinguishing a true maximum or minimum from instances in which two successive values happen to be equal, and he appeared to have regarded this as his chief contribution.

It was, however, with the other Leipzig paper, "Disquisitiones de calculo integrale" ([*1771a*]), that Laplace made his debut in print. The subject is a particular solution for one class of differential equations. The method that he developed subsequently led to enunciation of a theorem, the statement of which he annexed without proof to his first memoir on probability ([*1774c*]; *OC*, VIII, 62–63), although it has nothing to do with that subject (see Section 7, Equation 23 below). Reworking this material in later years ([*1777a*]), Laplace repudiated this earliest publication, or very nearly so, apologizing for grave faults that he blamed on the printer ([*1774c*]; *OC*, VIII, 83). That was the only reference that he ever made to either of these youthful ventures into Latin.

3. Finite Differences, Recurrent Series, and Theory of Chance. Among his early interests, it turned out to be a memoir on the solution of difference equations that marks the beginning of one of the main sequences of his lifework. We may reasonably surmise that the applicability of such equations to problems of games of chance, and not any *a priori* penchant for that subject matter, was mainly responsible for the appearance given by the published record that probability attracted him more strongly than did celestial mechanics in this opening phase of his career. The appearance is misleading, or at least ironic. For chance was never mentioned in the titles of any of his investigations until February 1772, when the applicability had made itself evident (*10*). In 1771, at the outset of "Recherches sur le calcul intégral aux différences infiniment petites, et aux différences finies," he observed that the equations that he was studying turn up more frequently than any other type in applications of the calculus to nature. A general method for integrating them would be correspondingly advantageous to mechanics, and especially to "physical astronomy" ([*1771b*], p. 273). That sci-

ence looms largest in the unpublished record (*1–13*); and judging from a report in the archives of the Academy, a paper (*9*) of 27 November 1771 may even have been the germ of *Mécanique céleste*.

Earlier in the same year Laplace had published "Recherches sur le calcul intégral aux différences infiniment petites, et aux différences finies," and since he was still only knocking at the door of the Academy, he sent it to the Royal Society of Turin for its *Mélanges*. It was almost surely the expansion of a paper on difference equations alone that he had read on 18 July 1770 in his second appearance before the Academy (*2*). He now reserved that topic for the second half of the memoir, where he proposed to adapt to the solution—or as he said in the looser terminology of the time, the "integration"—of difference equations a method that he was developing for infinitesimal expressions in the earlier version. He began by confirming in his own manner a theorem that Lagrange had recently proved concerning integration of equations of the following form ([*1771b*], p. 173):

$$X = y + H\frac{dy}{dx} + H'\frac{d^2y}{dx^2} + H''\frac{d^3y}{dx^3} + \cdots$$
$$+ H^{n-1}\frac{d(d^n y)}{dx^n}, \quad (1)$$

where X, H, H', H'', $\cdots$, are any function of x. Lagrange had shown that such equations can always be integrated if integration is possible in the homogeneous case when $X = 0$. His proof was of a type classical in analysis. It involved introducing a new independent variable, z; multiplying both sides of the equation by $z\,dt$; supposing integration of the resulting adjoint equation accomplished; and examining the steps needed to reduce the order one degree at a time until a solvable form should be reached. The proof worked for solving differential equations; but the procedure presupposed the validity of infinitesimal methods in analysis, and the operations were not applicable to the solution of difference equations.

Laplace's approach appears to be more cumbersome and turns out to be more general. Instead of introducing a multiplying factor and supposing the subsequent integration accomplished, which step restricted the method to the infinitesimal calculus, Laplace employed integrating factors obtained by substituting

$$\omega\frac{dy}{dx} + y = T, \quad (2)$$

where T and ω are functions of x. He then differentiated that expression successively n times. Of the resulting equations, he multiplied the first by ω', the second by ω'', the third by ω''', and so on; added the products to (1); and grouped the terms of the enormous resulting expression by orders of y. Manipulation then allowed for the determination of ω', ω'', ω''', $\cdots$, in terms of ω and H', H'', H''', $\cdots$. Thus, he could write equations equivalent to (1) in either finite or infinitesimal differences and evaluate them generally. Since his purpose was to extend a method from infinitesimal to finite analysis, his operations all conform to the rules of algebra, except that at the point where they involved differentiation, he justified the analogous step for finite differences.

The episode is largely typical of the relation of Laplace's point of departure to the work of elders and near contemporaries. There is the not quite ritual obeisance to a principle or practice, in this case the formulation of problems in terms of differential equations in general, attributed to d'Alembert, the patron. There is the tactful nod to a result found quite differently by Condorcet, the well-placed official. There is the pioneer analytical breakthrough achieved by Euler, although in restricted form. There is the formal mathematical theorem stated by Lagrange, emphasizing analyticity. There is, finally, the adaptation imagined and executed by Laplace, his motivation being the widest applicability to problems in the real world.

Although the memoir had opened with mention of mechanics and astronomy, Laplace introduced its raison d'être, the solution of difference equations, with a reminder that their calculus was the foundation of the entire theory of series ([1771b], p. 299). Coherently enough, therefore, he continued the discussion with a determination of the general term of series of the important class (op. cit., p. 330)

$$y^x = A\phi^x y^{x-1} + {}'A\phi^x\phi^{x-1}y^{x-2} + {}''A\phi^x\phi^{x-1}\phi^{x-2}y^{x-3} + \cdots \quad (3)$$

wherein ϕ is a function of x. (In his early notation, the superscripts are often, as here, indices, not exponents.) In the simplest case, in which $\phi = 1$, Equation (3) reduces to the recurrent form,

$$y^x = Ay^{x-1} + {}'Ay^{x-2} + {}''Ay^{x-3} + \cdots. \quad (4)$$

The memoir ends with an application of the calculus of finite differences to a solution of this equation, and Laplace gives a method for determining the constants.

This finding that equations of the form (3) are always integrable became the starting point for the next memoir, dealing with what Laplace called "recurro-recurrent" series and their application to the theory of chance. Still not a member of the Academy, he submitted it for their judgment on 5 February 1772 and placed it in the Savants étrangers series ([1774b]). Recurrent series of the familiar form (3) were restricted to a single variable index, the definition being that "every term is equal to any number of preceding terms, each multiplied by a function of x taken at will" ([1774b]; OC, VIII, 5). While investigating certain problems in the theory of chance, so Laplace said a little later ([1776a, 1°]; OC, VIII, 71), he came upon equations in finite differences of another, novel type. They were the analogues in finite analysis of partial differential equations and gave rise to a complex set of series, the general term of which has two or more variable indices. In such series as (4), if ϕ is a function of x and n rather than of x alone, and if the integers $1, 2, 3, \cdots$, are substituted for x and n, then for each value of n, a series results in which ${}^n y^x$ designates the term corresponding to the number x and n. The definition of a recurro-recurrent series is that ${}^n y^x$ is equal to any number of preceding terms, taken in rank or in order, in any number of such series, each multiplied by a function of x. Here is the example that Laplace displayed:

$$\begin{aligned}
&{}^1 y^x + A' y^{x-1} + B' y^{x-2} + \cdots + N = 0 \\
&{}^2 y^x + A'' {}^2 y^{x-1} + B'' {}^2 y^{x-2} + \cdots + N'' \\
&\quad = H'' {}^1 y^x + M'' {}^1 y^{x-1} + P'' {}^1 y^{x-2} + \cdots \\
&\cdots\cdots\cdots\cdots\cdots\cdots\cdots\cdots\cdots\cdots\cdots \quad (5) \\
&{}^n y^x + A^n {}^n y^{x-1} + B^n {}^n y^{x-2} + \cdots + N^n \\
&\quad = H^n {}^{n-1} y^x + M^n {}^{n-1} y^{x-1} + \cdots.
\end{aligned}$$

The value of ${}^n y^x$ must be determined, when A^n, B^n, $\cdots$, N^n, H^n, $\cdots$ are any functions of n; when also A'', B'', $\cdots$ $'''A$, $'''B$, $\cdots$ are what those functions become on substituting $1, 2, 3, \cdots$ for n; and when, finally, $A, B, \cdots, N$ are any constants.

The solution consists in showing that Equation (5) can always be transformed as follows (OC, VIII, 7):

$$^n y^x = a^n {}^n y^{x-1} + b^n {}^n y^{x-2} + c^n {}^n y^{x-3} + \cdots + u^n, \quad (6)$$

where a^n, b^n, $\cdots$, u^n are functions of n and of constants that can be determined. This equation (6), in turn, is an expression for a recurrent series precisely of the type (3) that he had shown to be integrable in [1771b], his Turin memoir. A further problem of a third-degree equation in finite differences is then shown to be reducible successively to the forms (5) and (6), and Laplace went on to propose a general procedure for reducing an equation of any degree r to a lower degree, the requirement being that by the assumption made for the value of n, the equation of degree r become one of degree $r - 1$.

A passage included many years later in the *Essai philosophique sur les probabilités* (*OC*, VII, xxvi–xxvii) makes clearer to the noninitiate how he was visualizing these series. A recurrent series is the expression of a difference equation with a single variable index. Its degree is the difference in rank between its two extreme terms. The terms may be determined by means of the equation, provided the number of known terms equals its degree. These terms are in effect the arbitrary constants of the expression for the general term or (which comes to the same thing) of the solution of the difference equation. The reader is next to imagine a second series of terms arranged horizontally above the terms of the first series, a third series above the second, and so on to infinity. It is supposed that there is a general equation between the terms that are consecutive both horizontally and vertically and the numbers that indicate their rank in both directions. This will be an equation in finite partial differences, or recurro-recurrent. The reader is finally to imagine that on top of the plane containing this pattern of series there is another containing a similar pattern, and so on to infinity, and that a general equation relates the terms that are consecutive in the three dimensions with the numbers indicating their rank. That would be an equation in finite partial differences with three indices. Generally, and independently of the spatial model, such equations may govern a system of magnitudes with any number of indices. Some eight years later, Laplace replaced the use of recurro-recurrent series with the more efficient tools of generating functions ([*1782a*], see Section 12) for solving problems in finite differences, which he encountered mainly in the calculus of probability.

It is important biographically to notice his passing remark that investigations in the theory of chance had led him to the formulation of recurro-recurrent series. The latter part of the memoir illustrates how they might be applied to the solution of several problems concerning games of chance. In the first such example, two contestants, A and B, play a game in which the loser at each turn forfeits a crown to his opponent. Their relative skills are as a to b. At the outset A has m crowns, and B has n. What is the probability that the game will not end with x or fewer turns? Laplace found it by substituting values given by the conditions of the problem in a series of equations of the form (5), first for the case in which $a = b$, $m = n$, and n is even, and then for all possible suppositions about the parameters. This problem, like many others that Laplace adduced, appears in De Moivre, who seems to have furnished his first reading in the subject, but whose solutions were less direct (*Doctrine of Chances*, 3rd ed. [London, 1756], Problem LVIII, p. 191). A further example was suggested to Laplace by a bet made on a lottery at the École Militaire. What is the probability that all the numbers 1, 2, 3, · · ·, n will be taken after x draws? That, too, he found by formulating the problem in a recurro-recurrent series in two variable indices, observing that the approach could clearly have wide applicability in the theory of chance, where the most difficult problems often concern the duration of events.

Laplace chose precisely this juncture for defining probability. The statement occurs immediately after his development of the method of recurro-recurrent series and just before its application to the foregoing examples ([*1774b*]; *OC*, VIII, 10–11):

> The probability of an event is equal to the sum of each favorable case multiplied by its probability, divided by the sum of the products of each possible case multiplied by its probability, and if each case is equally probable, the probability of the event is equal to the number of favorable cases divided by the number of all possible cases.

The definition is noteworthy not for its content, which was standard, but for its location in the development of his work and for its phrasing. The wording should serve to temper the criticism often made of Laplace, particularly in respect to inverse probability (which, to be sure, he had not yet started), that he gratuitously assumed equal *a priori* probabilities or possibilities. It is true that he often did—although not, as will appear, when he had anything to go on. It is also interesting that in the passage immediately preceding the definition, Laplace should have written "duration of events" rather than "duration of play." For this was the first remark that he ever printed about the subject as a whole.

4. Probability of Events and of Their Causes. Historically and biographically, the instinctive choice of words is often more indicative than the deliberate. There is much anachronism in the literature, and it may be well, therefore, to take this, the juncture at which Laplace was entering upon one of the central preoccupations of his life, as the occasion to venture an observation about the early history of probability. For more substance has sometimes been attributed to it than the actual content warrants. It is true that adepts of the subject were much given to celebrating its applicability, but prior to Laplace what they were praising was a prospect rather than actual accomplishment—except in the theory of games of chance. Even there, most of the experiments were thought experiments. Jakob Bernoulli's *Ars conjectandi* (1713) is justly famous mathematically, although it is seldom mentioned that Part IV, headed "Usum et applicationem praecedentis doctrinae in civilibus, moralibus, & oeconomicis," contained simply the law of large numbers and otherwise remained uncompleted. As for the Dutch and English insurance industry in the eighteenth century, and the sale of annuities practiced by governing agencies, the tables on which actuarial transactions depended were numerically insecure. Risks were estimated empirically rather than calculated analytically.

The statement that games of chance provided the principal subject matter in which theorems could be demonstrated and problems solved mathematically will be confirmed by close attention to contemporary usage, which refers to *théorie des hasards*, or "theory of chance." The word "probability" was not used to designate the subject. That word appears in two ways, one more restricted and the other vaguer than in the post-Laplacian science. In the mathematical "theory of chance," probability was a quantity, its basic quantity, that which Laplace defines above. *Calcul des probabilités* refers to calculation of its amount for certain outcomes in given situations. The phrase *théorie des probabilités* rarely, if ever, occurs. The word "probability" had its second and larger sense, one that would have befitted a theory if any had existed, rather in the philosophic tradition started by Pascal's wager on the existence of God (for which see Hacking [L: 1975]). The changes rung on that idea belong to theology, epistemology, and moral philosophy, some pertaining to what is now called decision-making and others to political economy. Such is the discourse in Diderot's article "Probabilité" in the *Encyclopédie*. It was largely skepticism about the mathematical prospects for that sort of thing that inspired d'Alembert's overly deprecated hostility to the subject, and optimism about it that inspired Condorcet's overly celebrated enthusiasm. Laplace himself was clear about the difference, although in other terms. Indeed, he insisted

upon it in the distinction between mathematical and moral expectation in one of the pair of papers to be discussed next, which between them did begin to join mathematical theory of games with philosophic probability and scientific methodology.

The bibliographical circumstances need to be discussed before the significance of these two papers can be fully appreciated. Both were composed before Laplace became a member of the Academy and were printed in successive volumes of the *Savants étrangers* series. The more famous was entitled "Mémoire sur la probabilité des causes par les événements" ([*1774c*]). The second, and lengthier, was delayed for two years and was then combined with an astronomical memoir under the title, "Recherches, 1°, sur l'intégration des équations différentielles aux différences finies, et sur leur usage dans la théorie des hasards. 2°, sur le principe de la gravitation universelle, et sur les inégalités séculaires des planètes qui en dépendent" ([*1776a*], 1° and 2°). As we shall see, this early coupling of probability with astronomy was no mere marriage of convenience; Laplace spent his entire professional life faithful to the pattern that it started. Before discussing that, however, we shall need to consider the way in which the aleatory part of the dual memoir completed his earlier application of recurro-recurrent series to solving problems in the theory of chance and at the same time complemented his new departure into the determination of cause. He submitted this resumption of his work on difference equations to the Academy on 10 March 1773 (*13*)—a marginal note dating it 10 February is in error.

The preamble of the paper on cause declares, and cross-references in both essays confirm, that they were conceived as companion pieces on the subject that Laplace was now beginning to call probability, the one breaking new ground in what was later called its inverse aspect, the other extending and systematizing a direct approach. It was, indeed, in these two writings that probability began to be broadened from the mathematics of actual games and hypothetical urns into the basis for statistical inference, philosophic causality, estimation of scientific error, and quantification of the credibility of evidence, to use terms not then coined. In preferring the word "probability" to suggest the wider scope that he was giving the subject itself as a branch of mathematics, Laplace may well have been following the precept of Condorcet, newly the acting permanent secretary of the Academy, who, in prefatory remarks to the volume in which the "Causes" paper appeared, praised it for its approach to predicting the probability of future events. "It is obvious," he wrote, "that this question comprises all the applications that can be made of the doctrine of chance to the uses of ordinary life, and of that whole science; it is the only useful part, the only one worthy of the serious attention of philosophers" (*SE*, 6 [1774], "Histoire," p. 18).

The memoir on cause opens with a preamble most of which might more appropriately have belonged to the concurrent piece on the solution of difference equations. Laplace referred readers to the latter memoir after reviewing what De Moivre and Lagrange had contributed to these problems and the way in which they had then involved him in the theory of chance. The present memoir had a different object, the determination of the probability of cause, given knowledge of events. Uncertainty, we are told, concerns both events and their causes (notice that at the outset Laplace took probability to be an instrument for repairing defects in knowledge). When it is given that an urn contains a set number of black and white slips in some definite ratio, and the probability is required of drawing a white one, then we know the cause and are uncertain about the event. But if the ratio is not given, and after a white slip is drawn the probability is required that it be as *p* is to *q*, then we know the event and are uncertain about the cause. All problems of theory of chance could be reduced to one of these two classes, and Laplace here proceeded to investigate problems of the second type. He began on the basis of a theorem that, like the definition of probability in the previous memoir, he enunciated verbally:

> If an event can be produced by a number *n* of different causes, the probabilities of the existence of these causes, reckoned from the event, are to each other as the probabilities of the event, reckoned from the causes; and the probability of each cause is equal to the probability of the event, reckoned from that cause, divided by the sum of all the probabilities of the event, reckoned from each of the causes ([*1774c*]; *OC*, VIII, 29).

In substance, this theorem is the same as that published in 1763, eleven years previously, by Thomas Bayes. Not only is it now named "Bayes's theorem" or "Bayes's rule," but the entire approach to probability and statistics depending on it is generally called Bayesian, at least in the literature influenced by the British tradition in analysis and philosophy of science since the early nineteenth century. That usage derives from the vindi-

cation by Augustus De Morgan and Boole of their obscure countryman's priority. Laplace did not mention Bayes in this memoir. Later he did refer to him in one sentence in the *Essai philosophique sur les probabilités* (*OC*, VII, cxlviii). It seems likely that in 1774 he had not read Bayes's paper in the *Philosophical Transactions of the Royal Society of London*; at this period leading Continental mathematicians seldom read or referred to their British contemporaries, and the statement and context of the relation in Bayes's piece are very different. On the other hand, he may have heard of it. Richard Price was known on the Continent, and especially among political theorists, including Condorcet. Moreover, in introducing the analysis of cause Laplace did not claim that it was an altogether new subject. He said it was novel "in many respects" and chimed in with Condorcet's prefatory remarks to the effect that the approach "the more merits being developed in that it is mainly from that point of view that the science of chance can be useful in civil life." It must also be said (once equity is served) that in the sequel the analysis of inverse probability derived from Laplace's memoir and further work and that Bayes remains one of those pioneers remembered only after the subject they intrinsically might have started had long been flourishing, in spite of their having been little noticed and thanks to work of others that did have consequence.

However that may be, Laplace proceeded from the statement of the theorem to an example. From an urn containing an infinite number of white and black slips in unknown ratio, *p* + *q* slips are drawn, of which *p* are white and *q* black. What is the probability that the next slip will be white? The above theorem gives the following formula for the probability that *x* is the true ratio (*OC*, VIII, 30):

$$\frac{x^p (1-x)^q \, dx}{\int x^p (1-x)^q \, dx}, \tag{7}$$

where the integral is taken from $x = 0$ to $x = 1$; and Laplace calculated that the required probability of drawing a white slip on the next try is

$$\frac{p+1}{p+q+2}. \tag{8}$$

A second example from the same urn leads to the application that was the point of this analysis. What is the probability after pulling *p* white and *q* black slips in *p* + *q* draws of then taking *m* white and *n* black slips in the next *m* + *n* draws? For that probability, Laplace obtained the expression

$$\frac{\int x^{p+m}\,(1-x)^{q+n}\,dx}{\int x^{p}\,(1-x)^{q}\,dx}, \qquad (9)$$

where the limits are again 0 to 1, and went on to ask the more significant question: how large would $(p + q)$ need to be, and how small would $(m + n)$ need to remain, in order to calculate the probability of the ratio of m to n on the basis of p and q? Clearly, the solution of that problem would give a basis for calculating the probability of a future event from past experience or for statistical inference (although Laplace never used that phrase). He did not try to solve the problem in general, pleading the lengthiness of the calculation. Instead, he proceeded to the demonstration of a limit theorem, which is nothing other than Bernoulli's law of large numbers, although Laplace did not call it that. In effect, he showed, in what he called a "curious proof," that the numbers $p + q$ can be supposed so large as to bring as close as you please to certainty the probability that the ratio of white slips to the total lies between $\dfrac{p}{p+q} + \omega$ and $\dfrac{p}{p+q} - \omega$, ω being less than any given magnitude.

Laplace had two changes to ring on one of the classic problems, the division of stakes in an interrupted game. First, he referred the reader to the companion memoir for deduction by the method of recurro-recurrent series of the canonical solution for the standard case, in which the relative skills of two players are given; and he also promised a general solution in the case of three or any number of players. So far as he knew, that problem had never been solved. (Laplace was not reticent about claiming credit when he believed himself to have done something altogether new, although Todhunter points out (L: [1865], 468) that this time he was wrong, for De Moivre had solved the problem.) Second, the case in which the relative skill of the players is unknown pertained to the probability of future events, and Laplace solved it for a two-man game, without attempting the generality of three or more players in this inverse example.

Altogether more significant is the next topic, first for its subject, which was the determination of the mean value among a series of observations; second for the area from which Laplace took it, which was astronomy; and third for the application, which was to the minimization of observational and instrumental error. In view of the whole development of Laplace's later career, this may well appear to be a highly indicative article, not least in his manner of introducing it. Two years previously, he said, he had worked out a solution

for taking the mean value among several observations of the same phenomenon. Thinking it would be of little use, however, he decided to delete it from the memoir on recurro-recurrent series ([1774b]), where he had originally intended it as a postscript. He had since learned from the *Journal astronomique* that Daniel Bernoulli and Lagrange had both investigated the same problem ([1774c]; OC, VIII, 41–42). Their memoirs remained unpublished and he had never seen them. This announcement, together with what he now calls the utility of the matter, had led him to set out his own ideas. It would appear that he must have given them some further development, for the approach turned on treating the true value as the unknown cause of three observed values, taken for effects. Afterward, the mean value giving the minimum probability of error would be determined. It is evident from the outset that the observations Laplace had in mind were astronomical, for the point to be fixed was the time at which the event occurred.

Laplace now constructed a graph and a probability curve. In Figure 1, the line AB represents time; the points a, b, and c, the three successive observations of the phenomenon; and the point V its true instant. In Figure 2, the probability that an observation differs from the truth by the amounts Vp and Vp' is represented by the ordinates of the curve RMM'. The probability decreases with time according to an unknown law, which is expressed in the equation for the curve, $y = \omega(x)$.

Now then, either of two things may be intended in speaking of the mean to be taken among several such observations. One is the instant at which it is equally probable that the true time of the phenomenon occurs before or after it. That may be

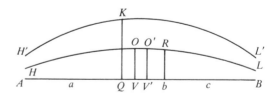

FIGURE 1

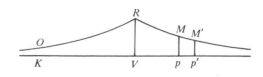

FIGURE 2

called the "probabilistic mean." The other is the instant at which the sum of errors to be incurred ("feared" in Laplace's terminology) multiplied by their probability is a minimum. That value may be called the "mean of error" or "astronomical mean," the latter because it is the term that astronomers ought to prefer. A lengthy calculation now shows that in fact the probabilistic and astronomical means come to the same value. Its determination in this memoir becomes too complicated to follow in detail. To find it, Laplace needed to identify the nature of the function $\phi(x)$. It is reasonable to suppose that the ratio of two consecutive infinitesimal differences is the same as that of the two corresponding ordinates, so that $d\phi/\phi$ is constant. Then the equation relating the ordinates to their infinitesimal differences is (*ibid.*; *OC*, VIII, 46):

$$\frac{d\phi(x+dx)}{d\phi(x)} = \frac{\phi(x+dx)}{\phi(x)}, \qquad (10)$$

whence

$$\frac{d\phi(x)}{dx} = -m\phi(x), \text{ and } \phi(x) = \beta e^{-mx}; \qquad (11)$$

m being constant, $\beta = m/2$ by symmetry, and

$$\phi(x) = \frac{m}{2} e^{-mx}. \qquad (12)$$

Thus Laplace did not here arrive at the famous least-square rule. His stated purpose was to convince astronomers that their normal practice of taking an arithmetical average was erroneous, although he had to acknowledge that his method was difficult to use. A further application of the principle of inverse probability calculates the probabilities that the different values of m are to each other as the probabilities that the values when obtained will be in the proportion of their respective distances. That calculation yielded a fifteen-degree equation. Resorting to approximation, therefore, Laplace gave a table for the correction that he advised applying to whichever of the two extreme observations was further from the middle one.

The final topic in the probability of cause may be thought equally significant in view of the importance that the finding assumed in its later application—and, indeed, in the philosophy of probability. It concerns the effect of inequalities in the prior probabilities that are unknown to the players (the examples come from theory of chance), or more largely to persons involved in the outcome of quantifiable events in the civic realm. In the normal theory, the assumption is that the various cases capable of producing an event are equally probable or, if not, that their relative probabilities are known. In physical fact, of course, everyone recognizes that there is no such thing as perfectly balanced coins or ideally symmetrical dice; but it was further assumed that the game is nevertheless fair, provided that both players are ignorant of the actual inequalities. On the contrary, Laplace found—and claimed to be the first to have noticed and demonstrated the fallacy ([*1774c*]; *OC*, VIII, 62)—that the latter assumption is valid only for situations involving simple probabilities. For example, if B should agree to give two crowns to A if A tosses heads on the first flip of a coin, then before the game begins, a fair division of the stakes would be 50–50 even if the coin is weighted, since neither knows which side is heavier. The assumption ceases to be valid, however, as soon as the game continues under the same rules, according to which B will then give A four crowns if a head turns up only at the second turn, six crowns at the third turn, and so on to x turns. Laplace pursued the matter in the case of a game of dice. A and B play, the rule being that if A throws a given side in n tosses of one dice, B pays him the sum a. What, then, should A forfeit to B if he fails? By the classical theory of chance, the amount equals the expectation of A, which is $a - (5^n a/6^n)$. In fact, however, given any asymmetry at all, A's expectation will be less than that, for B has the advantage as the game continues. Determining the correct value gave Laplace a very lengthy calculation, issuing in a complicated function of the degree of asymmetry.

Laplace accompanied this discussion with a warning against excessively literal applications of mathematical theory to the actual world, physical or civic. In a somewhat unconvincing passage he claimed to have made experiments with English dice, the most regular he could obtain, only to find that they never fall true to theory in long runs. It is more interesting that this analysis contains the germs of two of the most characteristic techniques that Laplace employed in later work. Both pertain to inverse probability and the study of causes. First, the occurrence of seemingly aberrant patterns invites investigation of the source of departures from the results that equipossibility would entail. Second, the multiplication of observations provides the basis for calculating from experience the value of the prior probabilities when they are not equal. By the law of large numbers it can then be determined how large the sample must be in order to reduce the probability of error within prescribed limits.

There are textual grounds for thinking that the implications of asymmetries were an important factor in opening Laplace's eyes to the wider prospects for probability. He enlarged on them in a philosophical, or methodological, article ([*1776a*, 1°], no. XXV; *OC*, VIII, 144–153) strategically situated in the midst of the companion memoir on difference equations and theory of chance, to which we now turn, deferring for a moment the question of its combination with the first gravitational memoir. The *analyse des hasards* is there said to have objects of two kinds: first, the probability of happenings about which we are uncertain, whether in their occurrence or in their cause (it is worth noting that in the way he puts it here probability is still subsidiary to theory of chance); and second, the hopes that attach to their eventuality. Laplace acknowledged that questions could legitimately be raised about the very enterprise of applying mathematical analysis to situations of both sorts. In concerns of the former type, he attributed the difficulty to the mode of application, not to the definition. There is no ambiguity about the definition of probability itself, and no legitimate objections could be lodged against its calculus unless equal prior probabilities were to be assigned to cases that are not in fact equally probable. He had to admit that, unfortunately, all applications yet attempted to problems of civil life entailed precisely that fallacy. Laplace proceeded to illustrate it by a simplified repetition of the demonstration that the false supposition of symmetry in coins or dice is unfair to one of two players in any game involving compound probabilities.

The question of equipossibility was also involved in exposing the error committed by commentators who argued that a run of heads or tails is less likely than any alternation in a sequence of the same number of tosses of a coin. Proceeding from a mistaken notion of common sense, they supposed that each time a head turns up, the odds increase against another. In effect, they were saying that past events influence future ones. Laplace characterized that idea as "inadmissible" and proceeded to refute it in a general statement, his earliest, on the relation between regularity, chance, and causality. Why does so-called common sense give us to suppose that a sequence of twenty heads is not due to chance, whereas we would think nothing of any equally possible mixture of heads and tails in a total of twenty? The reason is that wherever we encounter symmetry, we intuitively take it for the effect of a cause acting in an orderly manner. If we were to come upon letters from a printer's font lying in the order I N F I N I T E S I M A L on some composing table, we should be disin-

clined to think the arrangement random, although if that were not a word in some known language, we should pay it no heed. Laplace even made a little calculation to show how our intuition that order bespeaks causality is itself conformable to probability. A symmetrical event has to be the result either of cause or of chance. Let $1/m$ be its probability in case it is due to chance, and $1/n$ its probability in case it is due to a regular cause. By his basic theorem (i.e., Bayes's rule) the probability of the cause will then be $\dfrac{1/n}{1/m + 1/n}$ or $\dfrac{1}{1 + n/m}$. The greater m in relation to n, the greater the probability that a symmetrical event is due to a regular cause.

In retrospect, it seems clear that an element of wanting it both ways was always lurking at the bottom of Laplace's outlook. On the one hand, the regularity of the universe as a whole bespeaks the rule of natural law. Order governs amid the infinity of its combinations. On the other hand, where there do appear to be disturbing factors, such as in the results of real games with imperfect dice or (to anticipate for a moment) in anomalies of planetary motion, indeterminacies in the shape of the earth, widely varying inclinations among the planes of cometary orbits, and inequality in the partition of births between boys and girls, such data call for identification of a particular cause. We do not seek out one that will be an exception to the larger realm of causality but, rather, one that, if properly calculated, will vindicate it. Thus, both apparent symmetry and exceptions to it bespeak causality, general or particular as the case may be, and the goal of analysis is to make the two cases one. Everything that a modern student wants to read into Laplace's outlook says that he should have attributed the larger regularity to randomness, and many things that he actually said point toward that anachronism. He did not, however. The notion of an order of chance would have been a contradiction in terms to Laplace ([*1776a*]; *OC*, VIII, 145):

Before going further, it is important to pin down the sense of the words *chance* and *probability*. We look upon a thing as the effect of chance when we see nothing regular in it, nothing that manifests design, and when furthermore we are ignorant of the causes that brought it about. Thus, chance has no reality in itself. It is nothing but a term for expressing our ignorance of the way in which the various aspects of a phenomenon are interconnected and related to the rest of nature.

In regard to the second set of objections to

probability as a branch of analysis, namely that hopes, fears, and states of mind cannot be quantified, Laplace considered that reservations of this sort arose from a fundamental misunderstanding and not from a mere fallacy in the procedures. They could, therefore, be obviated by making clear distinctions in the definition of terms. Such had been the root of d'Alembert's resistance to the calculus of probability. In the future, practitioners of the science would feel obligated to him for having forced upon it clarification of its principles and recognition of its proper limitations. Laplace took the limits of probability to be identical with those of all the "physicomathematical sciences. In all our research, it is the physical cause of our sensations that is the object of analysis, and not the sensations themselves" (*ibid.*; *OC*, VIII, 147). It is obvious that out of estimates of the likelihood of future happenings come hopes and fears, and that the prospect for calculating probability was the reason that the science of chance had long been heralded for its potential utility in civil life. Taking advantage of that opportunity in the measure possible depended, however, upon seizing the distinction between *espérance morale* and *espérance mathématique*, between aspiration and expectation. (The French makes the contrast rhetorically more effective, but perhaps the English makes the difference more inescapable.) In the theory of chance, expectation is simply the product of the amount to be gained by the probability of winning it. It is a number, like probability itself—nothing more. No doubt something similar might be said about aspiration in the ordinary concerns of life, but only in a qualitative way; for that always depended on such indefinable factors that it was illusory ever to think of calculating it. Even Daniel Bernoulli's suggestion for measuring personal gain by the quotient of the value of the winnings (or other profit) divided by the total worth of the winner, although an ingenious idea, was one incapable of generalized mathematical application.

The article that makes this apology for probability in general opens with language famous from its reemployment almost verbatim nearly forty years later in the *Essai philosophique sur les probabilités* (*OC*, VII, vi). We give these thoughts of his youth as he set them down when he was twenty-six ([*1776a*]; *OC*, VIII, 144–145):

> The present state of the system of nature is evidently a consequence of what it was in the preceding moment, and if we conceive of an intelligence which at a given instant comprehends all the relations of the entities of this universe, it could state the respective position, motions, and general affects of all these entities at any time in the past or future.

> Physical astronomy, the branch of knowledge which does the greatest honor to the human mind, gives us an idea, albeit imperfect, of what such an intelligence would be. The simplicity of the law by which the celestial bodies move, and the relations of their masses and distances, permit analysis to follow their motions up to a certain point; and in order to determine the state of the system of these great bodies in past or future centuries, it suffices for the mathematician that their position and their velocity be given by observation for any moment in time. Man owes that advantage to the power of the instrument he employs, and to the small number of relations that it embraces in its calculations. But ignorance of the different causes involved in the production of events, as well as their complexity, taken together with the imperfection of analysis, prevents our reaching the same certainty about the vast majority of phenomena. Thus there are things that are uncertain for us, things more or less probable, and we seek to compensate for the impossibility of knowing them by determining their different degrees of likelihood. So it is that we owe to the weakness of the human mind one of the most delicate and ingenious of mathematical theories, the science of chance or probability.

Long afterward, Laplace observed, also in the *Essai philosophique* (*OC*, VII, lxv), that his early investigations of probability were what had led him to the solution of problems of celestial mechanics in the first place. The historian is bound to temper respect for creative people with skepticism about their reminiscences of how they came to do their work. Nevertheless, it is at least interesting that Laplace's first general statement about nature and knowledge should have been consistent with the entire configuration of his *oeuvre*. That configuration had its origin in the relation of the two parts of the dual memoir under discussion. The structure of the first part is clear. It consists of thirty-five articles. Articles I–XXIV develop the integration of equations in finite differences by means of recurro-recurrent series. They constitute a comprehensive résumé of what Laplace and others had already done, incorporating many improvements. Article XXV then treats probability in general, opening with the sentences just quoted and concluding with a repetition of the exordium about the two classes of problems in probability from the companion "Mémoire sur la probabilité des causes par les événements" ([*1774c*]). The reader is directed there for inverse probability, while Laplace goes on in Articles XXVI–XXXV to apply the methods developed in the first twenty-four articles to the solution of problems of direct probability in the theory of games of chance.

Article XXXVI, although it continues the numbering, is subheaded "Sur le principe de la gravitation universelle, et sur les inégalités séculaires des planètes qui en dépendent." Matters of mathematical astronomy are treated throughout this second half of the dual memoir in a sequence of twenty-nine further articles, which we shall discuss in the next section. We do not know precisely when Laplace wrote them, but they must have been completed in the early months of 1774, for on 27 April he submitted another investigation of secular inequalities in planetary motion ([1775a]), which is described as a sequel (15), although it was printed earlier because of accidents in the academic publishing schedule. Almost certainly, therefore, he must have turned to Part 2° of the dual memoir immediately after completing the paper on the probability of causes ([1774c]) and the concurrent revision of Part 1°, which had occupied him between March and December 1773 (13). It also seems likely that the methodological Article XXV, with its philosophic propositions about the relation between probability and astronomy, would have been interpolated in the midst of the aleatory Part 1° during the time when Laplace was composing the astronomical Part 2°. As we shall see, passages introducing the latter are as prophetic, or rather programmatic, of his celestial mechanics as the paragraphs quoted above are of his epistemology. It would appear, therefore, that Laplace framed the main questions that his enormous lifework refined, extended, and largely answered, during a crucial period of about a year following his election to the Academy in March 1773.

5. Universal Gravitation. These questions were slightly but significantly different from what they are sometimes said to have been. A close reading of the astronomical part of the dual memoir, Laplace's first comprehensive piece on the mechanics of the solar system, serves to temper the conventional image of a vindicator of Newton's law of gravity against the evidence for decay of motion in the planets. Nothing is said about apparent anomalies gathering toward a cosmic catastrophe; on the contrary, the state of the universe is assumed to be steady. The problem is not whether the phenomena can be deduced from the law of universal gravity, but how to do it. Since that appeared to be impossible on a strict Newtonian construction of the evidence, Laplace proposed modifying the law

of gravity slightly. He proceeded to try out the notion that gravity is a force propagated in time instead of instantaneously. Its quantity at a given point would then depend on the velocity of bodies as well as on their mass and distance. Even more interesting, the reasoning in this argument was not that of normal mathematical astronomy but was of the type that he brought to physics in other, much later writings. Lastly, in a problem that he did handle in the tradition of theoretical astronomy, namely the secular variations in the mean motions of Jupiter and Saturn, the conclusion is that the mutual attraction of the planets cannot account for them, contrary to what we expect from *Mécanique céleste*. Let us, therefore, examine these matters more fully.

As in other early papers, Laplace's point of departure was an analysis by Lagrange. In a memoir (*Oeuvres de Lagrange*, VI, 335–399) that had won the prize set by the Paris Academy for 1774, Lagrange had argued that it was impossible to derive from the theory of gravity an equation for the acceleration of the mean motion of the moon giving values large enough to agree with observation. Lagrange then wondered whether resistance of the ether might be slowing the rotation of the earth enough to resolve the apparent discrepancy. Laplace for his part took the question to be one involving the sufficiency of the law of gravity with implications for all of cosmology. (Even so he had expanded the significance of problems in the theory of chance and discussed probability in relation to all of knowledge.)

Announcing at the outset his intention of doing a series of memoirs on physical astronomy, he began by deriving general equations of motion for extended bodies referred to polar coordinates in a form especially adapted to analyzing problems of secular inequalities. Thereupon, he turned to the "principle of universal gravitation" in general, which he called the most incontestable truth in all of physical science. It rested, in his view, upon four distinct assumptions generally accepted among *géomètres*, or persons doing exact science. Given their importance in marking out the main lines along which Laplace developed his celestial mechanics, we shall state them in the form of a close paraphrase ([1776a, 2°]; *OC*, VIII, 212–213):

1. the force of attraction is directly proportional to mass and inversely proportional to the square of the distance;

2. the attractive force of a body is the resultant of the attraction of each of the parts that composes it;

3. the force of gravity is propagated instantaneously;

4. it acts in the same manner on bodies at rest and in motion.

The plan was to examine the respective physical consequences of these assumptions. Since Laplace continued that examination throughout his life, the tactics of this memoir in effect became the strategy of much of his subsequent research. We need to note, therefore, what he believed it was that followed physically from each of those four propositions.

The inverse-square law came first. Laplace asserted roundly that it was no longer permissible to doubt its applicability to the solar system. It is obvious to the modern reader that this law was the one ultimately served by his resolution of apparent irregularities in planetary motion. Only later, however, in a series of memoirs composed from 1785 through 1787, did he succeed in bringing off those investigations (see Section 17). Here at the outset, deductions from the inverse-square law engaged his interest in a different order of effects. In a speculative vein, he took issue with philosophers who doubted whether it holds for forces acting at very short ranges. Even though the radius of the earth was the smallest distance over which its validity had been confirmed by observation, analogy and canons of simplicity still gave reasonable grounds for supposing that the gravitational-force law obtains universally. If it be asked why gravity should diminish with the square of the distance rather than in some other ratio, Laplace—after duly objecting that such questions make mathematicians uncomfortable—would consent to say only that it is pleasing to think that the laws of nature are such that the system of the world would be the same whatever its size, provided the dimensions are increased or decreased proportionally.

It is perhaps somewhat surprising to find that in the first stage of Laplace's astronomical work, his analysis of the consequences following from the second of these assumptions, the principal of universal attraction, took precedence over the theory of planetary motion. Although a less famous topic, it may have been an even more fruitful preoccupation, if not necessarily for astronomy itself, then certainly for mathematical science in general; since the problem of the attraction of a spheroid was the source of the potential function (see Section 16). It may also be surprising to learn that in the later eighteenth century, skepticism persisted about whether the force of attraction really operates between all the particles of matter individually or only between centers of mass of macrocosmic bodies of which the shape and internal structure are governed by other, unknown laws. Again, Laplace saw no reason to suppose that there exists some least measure of distance below which analogy becomes an unconvincing mode of argument. For the present purpose, that did not matter, however, since this second assumption, unlike the inverse-square law of the intensity of short-range forces, could be subjected to analysis and the results submitted to the test of observation on the scale of terrestrial physics. D'Alembert had already derived the precession of the equinoxes and the nutation of the axis of the earth from the principle of universal attraction among all the particles of the globe, and he found the prediction confirmed by data. The tides were too complicated a phenomenon to tackle yet—although Laplace attacked them soon afterward in a major calculation (see Section 8).

There remained the shape of the earth. By Newtonian theory, it should be an ellipsoid with the polar and equatorial axes in a ratio of 229/230. Two sets of independently measured values existed. The first derived from geodesic surveys of the length of meridional arcs in Lapland by the Maupertuis expedition in 1735–1736, at the equator in Peru by the Bouguer-La Condamine expedition in 1736–1737, in France itself on the meridian of Paris by Lacaille in 1741–1742, and at the Cape of Good Hope again by Lacaille in 1751–1752. The other set of values derived from determinations of the length of the seconds pendulum at various latitudes during those expeditions and on other occasions. The geodesic data gave a flattening greater than an axial ratio of 229/230 would produce, and the pendulum yielded a smaller departure from the spherical than Newton required. Laplace considered it likely that simplifications introduced into the calculation were at fault rather than the theory itself. The most serious were the assumption of uniform density and the neglect of irregularities of the surface. However that might be, the failure of the earth's longitudinal profile to fit an elliptical curve would not disprove the mutual attraction of all its particles, unless it were shown that an ellipsoid was the only solid that could satisfy the equilibrium conditions for such a force, or else that every theoretically possible figure had been tried without satisfying the observations. Since neither of those propositions had ever been demonstrated, the principle of universal interparticle attraction held its ground. Thus, because of the relevance to that principle of the shape of celestial bodies considered as solids of revolution, Laplace entered upon this, another of his continuing preoccupations.

So much for the long-range importance of the first two gravitational assumptions in Laplace's work; the latter two, on the other hand, are interesting mainly for the discussion of them that he gave in the ensuing articles of the present memoir, and it was there that he least resembled the celestial dogmatist for which he has sometimes been taken. The third and fourth assumptions have a different standing from the inverse-square law and the principle of attraction. Anyone doing planetary astronomy would have thought it necessary to write down those first two principles in the axiomatic structure of a treatise. To most of Laplace's colleagues, on the other hand, the instantaneous propagation of gravity and its indifference to motion would have seemed prior, self-evident truths, like the rectilinear transmission of light or the three-dimensionality of space, something not usually needing statement. Not so the young Laplace, who stated these assumptions for the sake of taking issue with them. It is unreasonable, he observed immediately, to suppose that the power of attraction or any other force acting at a distance should be propagated instantaneously. Our sense is rather that it should correspond in its passage to all the intervening points of space successively. Even if communication should appear instantaneous, what really happens in nature may well be different, "for it is infinitely far from an unobservable time of propagation to one that is absolutely nil" (*ibid.*; *OC*, VIII, 220). (It later became a distinctive characteristic of Laplace's physics that the phenomena he analyzed should occur in the realm of the unobservable.) Thus, he would try what followed from the supposition that gravitation does take place in time. On the amount of time, however, he would disagree with Daniel Bernoulli, who in a piece on tidal motion had advanced the proposition that the action of the moon takes a day or two to reach the earth.

Broaching the matter in a more abstract manner, Laplace posited a corpuscle to be the bearer of gravitational force. In his analysis, the effect of weight in a particle of matter is produced by the impulse of such a gravitational corpuscle, infinitely smaller than the particle, moving toward the earth at some undetermined velocity. Given this model, the received hypothesis, according to which gravity has an identical effect whether bodies are at rest or in motion, is equivalent to supposing that velocity infinite. Laplace supposed it indefinite and determinable by observations, and his reasoning was similar to that employed to account for the aberration of light. Let us see how he set up the problem.

The calculation analyzes the motion of an infinitely small body p describing any orbit around S in the plane pSM. $Sp = r$; $\angle pSM = \phi$; and N is the corpuscle causing p to gravitate toward S.

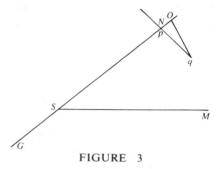

FIGURE 3

Resolving the forces and motions along the radius vector Sp and the perpendicular direction pq, Laplace introduced the expression θ/α for the measure of the distance described by the corpuscle N in time T. T and α are constants, α being an extremely small numerical coefficient and αe the ratio of the original eccentricity to the mean distance; t is time, and θ varies according to any function of the distance Sp. Calculation yields as equations of motion,

$$r = a\left(1 + \alpha e \cos nt - 2\frac{a\alpha}{\theta} Tn^2 t\right) \qquad (13)$$

and

$$\phi = nt - 2\alpha e \sin nt + \frac{3}{2}\frac{a\alpha}{\theta} Tn^3 t^2, \qquad (14)$$

where a and n are terms introduced in the change of variables

$$r = a(1 + \alpha y) \quad \text{and} \quad \phi = nt + \alpha x, \qquad (15)$$

which refers the equations to rectangular coordinates for manipulation (*OC*, VIII, 224).

From the above equations, it appears that the mean motion of p is governed by a secular equation proportional to the square of the time. In the normal assumption of instantaneous gravitation, $a\alpha/\theta$ is infinitely small, and the secular equation vanishes. If that term were not zero, however, its effect would appear in the mean motion of planets and satellites. At this point, therefore, Laplace turned to the observations and particularly to the lunar tables, knowing that ancient and modern records of eclipses showed that the earth's satellite has been increasing its mean speed of revolution.

Laplace placed more confidence in Tobias Mayer than in any other practical astronomer. In his view, the acceleration of the mean lunar motion had amounted to one degree in 2,000 years. D'Alembert had shown that the acceleration could not be explained within the ordinary theory by any calculation involving the sun, earth, and moon alone. Lagrange had then shown that the nonsphericity of earth and moon, taken together with the influence of other planets, failed to account for the acceleration ("Sur l'équation séculaire de la lune" [1776], *Oeuvres de Lagrange*, VI, 335–399). It might be worthwhile, therefore, to try out the notion that gravitation takes time, which is to say that the term $a\alpha/\theta$ is not nil. To recall the conditions of the problem, θ/α is the space traversed by the gravitational corpuscle that is impelling the moon toward the earth during one revolution of the moon in its orbit. The velocity then is $\theta/\alpha T$. Substituting Mayer's values for the acceleration of the mean motion in these expressions, Laplace found that the velocity of the gravitational corpuscle is 7,680,000 times as great as the velocity of light. Since Mayer's values were thought to be off by 12' in 2,000 years, the correct velocity was 6,400,000 times that of light.

Discussing this, which he admitted to be a conjecture, Laplace acknowledged that the Abbé Bossut's postulate of a very subtle fluid in space also permitted a calculation agreeing closely with the secular equation of the mean motion of the moon. What could that fluid be, however, unless it were light itself, emanating from the sun? If so, the consequences could be computed, for the orbit of the earth would have expanded and its mean motion would have been retarded. Unfortunately for Bossut's scheme, that has not happened. Its advocates might still say that sunlight has dilated the terrestrial atmosphere so as to produce the trade winds and has thus retarded the earth's rotation in another manner. Such a mechanism would indeed explain the apparent acceleration of the moon, but Laplace had also found, by a method that he promised to give elsewhere ([*1779b*]; see Section 8), that the earth's rotation cannot be detectably retarded by the friction of those winds. Thus, we are left with the force of gravity, "astonishing" in its activity but finite in velocity.

Following this analytic flight of fancy, Laplace "returned" to the normal assumptions about gravity and attacked traditional problems of mathematical astronomy concerning inequalities or variations in the elements of planetary motion. He thought of them in four main classes: positions of nodes and apsidal lines, eccentricities, inclinations of the orbital planes, and mean motions. The last were the most significant, and even they were less well-determined than Laplace could desire. On so signal a matter as the irregularities of the mean motions of Jupiter and Saturn, Euler and Lagrange disagreed, Euler having found them to be about equal and Lagrange very different (*Oeuvres de Lagrange*, I, 667). Laplace was worried about the applicability even of Lagrange's differential equations, for terms involving sines and cosines of very small angles with very small coefficients were dropped. Since the coefficients became large on integration, he feared lest the resulting formulas for determining the true movement of the planets would hold good for limited periods only. In his own calculation, Laplace took account of those terms and obtained formulas agreeing with Lagrange's in the values for apsides, eccentricities, and inclinations but differing drastically for the mean motions. Although his equations did contain terms proportional to the time and the square of the time, he would not claim that they succeeded in representing the true motions rigorously (*ibid.*; *OC*, VIII, 241). That question was interesting only mathematically and of no practical importance for astronomy over the historic span of recorded observations. More important were the results he obtained for Jupiter and Saturn.

Over the centuries most astronomers had come to consider that the observations show an acceleration for Jupiter and a much larger deceleration for Saturn. But when Laplace substituted values from Halley's tables in the expression that he had just derived for the secular equation of the mean motion of a planet, it reduced approximately to zero, leaving him to conclude that if an alteration existed in the mean motion of Saturn, it could not be caused by the influence of Jupiter (*ibid.*; *OC*, VIII, 252).

In Article LVIII (*OC*, VIII, 254–258), he applied d'Arcy's principle of areas to the same problem and obtained the same null results. It seemed unreasonable to suppose that so nearly complete a canceling out of positive and negative terms could be due to particular circumstances, and Laplace concluded that mutual gravitation between any two planets and the sun failed mathematically to account for any inequalities in their mean movements and that some other cause must be responsible for the observed anomalies. As candidate for the disturbing factor, he suggested—again by way of conjecture—the action of the comets.

He recognized that the conclusion was "contrary to what all mathematicians who have worked at the subject have hitherto supposed" (*ibid.*; *OC*,

VIII, 258). This statement will be equally surprising to students of the *Mécanique céleste*, still more so to those who know only the *Système du monde*, and most of all to those who are told in many textbooks that Laplace rescued the Newtonian planetary system from increasing instability by proving that precisely such mutual interactions do resolve the apparent inequalities that are actually periodic. That this finding, which he emphasized for its importance, should seem contrary to what he is most famous for, is explicable largely in consequence of the mathematics. He had not yet developed perturbation functions, and there was no provision in his expressions for long-term periodicity. Moreover, he nowhere worried about instability, unless that was what he had in mind in a passing remark that his conclusion would be less convincing if the secular inequalities increased proportionally to the square of the time, for that would mean that a continuously acting force was at work—and none other than universal gravitation was known.

The remaining articles of this, the first memoir on gravitation, will be somewhat anticlimactic to the modern reader, although there is no indication that Laplace thought them so. He considered that Euler in treating the secular inequalities in the motion of the earth had neglected significant terms and thus had given an incomplete analysis, particularly with respect to the eccentricity and apogee of the sun. The latter value, determined with precision from Halley's tables, could serve to establish the mass of Venus with sufficient accuracy for Laplace to calculate the share in the decrease of the obliquity of the ecliptic due to the action of the planets. In the brief Articles LXII and LXIII, he gave a method for determining that variation in general by means of analytic geometry (*ibid.*; *OC*, VIII, 268–272). They may possibly represent the memoir on that problem which Laplace had read before the Academy in November 1770, one of his earliest (*3*). In principle the method could have been applied to calculating the position of the equinoxes and hence the degree of that inclination at any time past or future, but the ancient observations were too imprecise to render the exercise worthwhile. Another conjecture about cometary influence speculates that it may be a factor offsetting the attraction of the planets in their influence on the decreasing inclination of the ecliptic. Finally, a postscript reviews the calculations of Lagrange that had left their author uncertain about the acceleration of the moon (*Oeuvres de Lagrange*, VI, 335–399).

Laplace found, on the contrary, that they strengthen the case for it.

6. Cometary Distribution. In the same volume with the dual memoir on probability and gravitation discussed in the preceding two sections, Laplace published the tripartite "Mémoire sur l'inclinaison moyenne des orbites des comètes, sur la figure de la terre, et sur les fonctions" ([*1776b*]), the last work that he published in the *Savants étrangers* series. The three parts are entirely independent, and we shall discuss only the first here, deferring the others for consideration in connection with the further development that he gave to those respective topics (see Sections 8 and 10). Occupying over two-thirds of the entire memoir, it consists in an actual application of his work in probability to a study of the distribution of the orbital planes of comets in space.

Let us begin by recalling Laplace's remark about having been led into astronomy through probability (see Section 4). In construing what he meant, it will be helpful to distinguish between weak and strong interactions in the evolution of his interests. To the weak, or philosophical, sort belong the regulative remarks about order, causality, and knowledge; to the strong, or technical, belong the probabilistic analysis of the phenomena themselves and also of distributions and errors in the data, and more rarely the application of mathematical techniques conceived for one set of problems to another. The memoir on comets illustrates both aspects. Its motivation pertained to the weaker, philosophical or cosmological, aspect of probability and its execution, to the stronger.

Uncertainty still bedeviled the status of comets in the solar system. Did they fully belong to it or not? Like many others, Laplace was undecided. We have just seen, in Section 5, how at this early stage he invoked their action as a possible *deus ex machina* to explain the secular inequalities of the mean motions of Jupiter and Saturn, which appeared inexplicable on the basis of forces operating within the system. He opened the present memoir by pointing to the anomaly that their motions constitute if they do belong to the system of the world. All the planets and their satellites, some sixteen bodies in all, revolve in the same direction and almost in the same plane. The probability that a common cause lies behind the arrangement could be calculated and was approximately equal to certainty (although to the further question of what that cause might be, Laplace confessed that he had never found a convincing answer). The comets are quite another matter: they move in any direction in very eccentric orbits inclined at all angles to the plane of the ecliptic. Laplace's senior colleague, Dionis du Séjour, one of the few aristocratic amateurs who actually contributed to astronomy, had analyzed the problem of whether the cause of planetary motion—whatever it might be—had also produced the phenomena of comets. He calculated the mean inclination of the sixty-three known orbits and found it to be 46°16'. The departure from 45° was clearly insignificant. Moreover, the ratio of forward to retrograde motions was five to four, or nearly one to one. Dionis du Séjour had concluded, therefore, that the comets serve a principle of indifference characteristic of the universe at large, within which the causal system of the planets constitutes a distinctive ordering.

The conclusion was reasonable enough in Laplace's view, but a further calculation was needed to establish the degree of certainty that it held. Supposing the comets randomly projected into space, what are the probabilities that the mean inclination of their orbits, and also the ratio of clockwise to counterclockwise revolutions, will be contained within given limits? For if the value of the mean inclinations were $45° + \alpha$ and if there were very large odds (say a million to one), to bet that it should be less, it could plausibly be concluded that some particular cause does account for their moving in one plane rather than another. The same logic could be applied to the ratio of forward to retrograde motions; there the calculation is easy, involving only two possibilities. Not so the problem of the orbits. Perhaps the mention of a bet hints that he was thinking of it in terms that antedate the analysis of causes from events that he might have been expected to apply. At any rate, he went on to qualify the problem as one of the most complicated in the entire analysis of *hasards*, especially so since the goal was a general formula applicable to any number of comets.

The problem then posits an indefinite number of bodies randomly projected into space and revolving around the sun, and the probability is required that the mean inclination of the orbits with respect to a given plane lies between two limits. Laplace approached it by constructing probability curves for the simple cases, much as he had done in discussing the mean value of a series of astronomical observations in the memoir on probability of causes. Here, however, the mean is the arithmetical average, and the probability sought is direct, not inverse. The first case is that of two bodies

only, and the probabilities are represented in Figure 4.

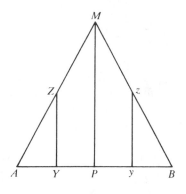

FIGURE 4

The line AB represents an inclination of 90°, and the ordinates determining the slope of the line $AZMzB$ are proportional to the probability that the corresponding abscissa measured along AB represents the mean inclination. Thus the probability that the mean inclination is AY, equal to x, is given by YZ; and Laplace set out the elementary reasoning to show that the required probability that the mean inclination lies between the limits Y and y will be equal to the area $YZMzy$ divided by the whole area AMB.

Laplace then turned to the case of three bodies (or comets) for which the curve is as shown in Figure 5:

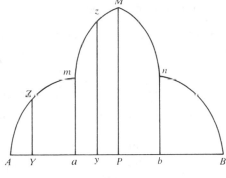

FIGURE 5

where $Aa = ab = bB$. Drawing on the above results for two bodies, he obtained the equations

$$ay = \frac{9}{2}x^2 \quad \text{and} \quad ay = \frac{1}{2}a^2 + 3az - 9z^2 \quad (16)$$

for the curves AZm and mMn respectively. Again the required probability that the mean inclination falls between certain limits is given by the quotient of the area between those limits divided by the entire area under the curve AMB.

In a figure corresponding to a system of four comets, the equations for *am* and *mM*, obtained from the results for three comets, are respectively

$$a^2 y = \frac{32}{3} x^3 \text{ and } a^2 y = \frac{1}{6} a^3 + 2a^2 z + 8az^2 - 32z^3. \quad (17)$$

It would have been possible to continue inductively, dividing *AB* into five or more equal parts and obtaining the equations of the curves corresponding to *n* bodies from the results for $(n - 1)$. To that end Laplace supposed the line *AB* of Figure 5 divided into *n* equal parts and sought an expression for the curve relative to the *r*th part, as shown in Figure 6:

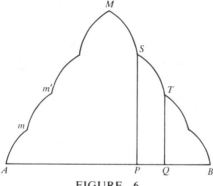

FIGURE 6

In finding it, he let $\dfrac{r-1}{n} a + z$ be the distance of one of its ordinates from *A* (*z* being less than *a/n*), and represented by $_r y_{n,z}$ the number of cases in which the mean inclination of *n* bodies is $\dfrac{r-1}{n} a + z$. That general expression could be given a value in the form

$$_r y_{n,z} = {_r}A_n z^{n-1} + {_r}B_n z^{n-2} + {_r}C_n z^{n-3}$$
$$+ \cdots + {_r}G_n z + {_r}H_n, \quad (18)$$

where $_r A_n, {_r}B_n, \cdots$, etc., are functions of *r* and *n* to be determined. Now it becomes evident what Laplace had been up to all the time. He could determine the value and solve the problem by a method that he had published in Article XII of the double memoir on difference equations and gravitation ([*1776a*, 1°]; *OC*, VIII, 97–102). Essentially, the problem was to find the general expression for quantities subject to a law governing their formation. In this instance, when $AB = a = 90°$, and *AB* is divided into *n* equal parts, the method gives the equation for the curve corresponding to the *r*th part ([*1776b*]; *OC*, VIII, 299),

$$a^{n-2} y = {_r}y_{n,z}. \quad (19)$$

The probability that the mean inclination of *n* orbits lies between any two points *P* and *Q* is then given by the quotient of the area *AMB* divided into the area *STQP*. In a complete application of the theory, the value for *n* would be 63, that being the number of comets for which astronomers had calculated the orbits. Leaving that computation to whoever wished to undertake it, Laplace calculated the probability that the mean inclination of twelve comets lies between 37-1/2° and 52-1/2° (for which case he divided the line *AB* into twelve equal parts of 7-1/2°). The resulting value is 0.339. Thus, the odds that the mean inclination is greater than 37-1/2° or less than 52-1/2° are 839 to 161, and the odds that it falls within those limits are 678 to 322. Referring to data, Laplace found that the mean inclination of the twelve most recently observed comets was 42°31'. There could be no reason to assign a cause tending to make these comets move in the plane of the ecliptic unless the contrary assumption of random projection resulted in enormous odds that the mean inclination should exceed 42°31'. In fact, the odds are less than six to one that it would exceed 37-1/2° and are very much smaller that it would exceed 42°31'. Hence, no such cause can be supposed to exist.

The important element here is not the support that this heaviest of probabilistic artillery brings to the position that Dionis du Séjour had already occupied in a comparatively straightforward and lightweight analysis. (Nor is it germane that no one had yet appreciated that the probability of an orbit is as the sine of the inclination, so that the mean should have been 60° rather than 45°.) What is interesting is Laplace's virtuosity in applying to the distribution of the comets a method for formulating in a general manner a problem encountered in the theory of chance.

7. Partial Differential Equations, Determinants, and Variation of Constants. The remaining mathematical investigations in Laplace's early period involved techniques of analysis developed in a group of three memoirs, two of them concerned also with astronomical problems. It will be convenient to begin with the piece that had no special astronomical relevance, "Recherches sur le calcul intégral aux différences partielles" ([*1777a*]), which, although published later than the other two, was started earlier. Laplace read a version in 1773 but did not submit it for publication until December 1776 (*19*). It consists of a reworking of his youthful *Acta eruditorum* paper ([*1771a*]), for which he had already apologized (see Section 2) in the paper on probability of causes ([*1774c*]). He had there appended a preliminary statement of the main theorem that he was now demonstrating. The long delay suggests that he may have had trouble with it. In any case, he had arrived at a general method (since called the cascade method) for solving linear partial differential equations by an approach that yielded the complete integral when it could be obtained and further served to identify equations that are insoluble. As originally printed, the memoir employs Euler's bracket notation, in which a general second-order linear partial differential equation is ([*1777a*]; *OC*, IX, 21)

$$0 = \left(\frac{ddz}{dx^2}\right) + \alpha\left(\frac{ddz}{dxdy}\right) + \beta\left(\frac{ddz}{dy^2}\right) + \gamma\left(\frac{dz}{dx}\right)$$
$$+ \delta\left(\frac{dz}{dy}\right) + \lambda z + T, \tag{20}$$

α, β, γ, δ, λ and T being functions of x and y. Laplace then simplified the form by changing the variables x and y into others, ω and θ, which are functions of x and y, and by regarding z as a function of these new variables. He could thereby obtain the equation in a new form (*OC*, VIII, 22):

$$0 = M\left(\frac{\partial^2 z}{\partial \omega \cdot \partial \theta}\right) + N\left(\frac{\partial z}{\partial \omega}\right) + L\left(\frac{\partial z}{\partial \theta}\right) + Rz + T'. \tag{21}$$

It followed that any second-order linear partial differential equation is reducible to the simple form

$$0 = \left(\frac{\partial^2 z}{\partial \omega \cdot \partial \theta}\right) + m\frac{\partial z}{\partial \omega} + n\left(\frac{\partial z}{\partial \theta}\right) + lz + T. \tag{22}$$

Since m, n, and l are functions of ω and θ, ω and θ can be determined and substituted in (21), thus transforming it into (22), which in turn has all the generality of (20) but is simpler and easier to investigate. Laplace was now in a position to restate the theorem that is the heart of the matter. In cases where the complete integration of (22) is possible in finite terms (and those cases could always be identified), one of the two integral signs affecting the arbitrary functions $\phi(\omega)$ or $\psi(\theta)$ can be eliminated and the remaining integration performed. Moreover, the cases wherein such a solution is possible include almost all the problems encountered in mathematical physics. For that was the field in which Laplace expected the method to be applicable. Among the many uses of linear partial differential equations, he singled out for special mention the determination, whatever the state of a system, of infinitesimal oscillations among an infinite number of corpuscles interacting in any manner whatsoever ([*1777a*]; *OC*, IX, 7).

A paper started at about the same time, "Mémoire sur les solutions particulières des équations différentielles et sur les inégalités séculaires

des planètes" ([*1775a*]), begins with the demonstration of a second theorem that Laplace had stated without proof in an appendix to the paper on probability of causes ([*1774c*]; *OC*, VIII, 64; cf. Section 2). It concerns Euler's discovery of singular solutions, which then appeared to be an anomaly in the theory of differential equations. Certain functions can satisfy a differential equation and still not be contained in its general integral, and the consequence is that integration of an expression is not necessarily tantamount to the complete solution of a problem. All the singular solutions also have to be determined, and the method that Euler gave was restricted to first-degree equations. Laplace went on to find further methods of determining special solutions. For example, given the differential equation $dy = p\ dx$, if $\mu = 0$ is a particular solution, then μ is a factor common to the expressions (*OC*, VIII, 339),

$$p + \frac{\dfrac{\partial^2 p}{\partial x\ \partial y}}{\dfrac{\partial^2 p}{\partial y^2}} \quad \text{and} \quad \frac{1}{\dfrac{\partial p}{\partial y}}, \tag{23}$$

and, reciprocally, any factor common to both expressions is a particular solution to the equation when it can be set equal to zero. He also obtained results for equations of higher degree.

In the case of this memoir, Condorcet observed (*HARS* [1772, part 1/1775], 70) that the two topics in the title are entirely distinct and have totally different objects. Formally, that is no doubt true; and indeed the mathematical part was submitted in July 1773 and the astronomical in December 1774 (*14* and *17*). More significant, however, is the evidence that throughout these years Laplace's mind was moving back and forth between problems of analysis and astronomy, and that the relation of emulation and competition with Lagrange embraced both domains. The astronomical section resumes his discussion (see Section 5) of the long-term invariance of the mean motions and hence the mean distances of the planets in respect to any gravitational interaction. (Although written earlier, this piece [*1776a*, 2°] was printed later.) Receipt of a manuscript memoir from Lagrange dealing with secular inequalities in the motions of the nodes and also in variations of orbital inclinations stimulated him to return to the subject after laying it aside in some frustration. By means of a transformation that Laplace greatly admired, Lagrange succeeded in reducing the problem to the integration of as many linear differential equations as there were unknowns and then to the determination of the constants, whatever the number of planets. Hastening to apply the transformation to his own formulas for secular inequalities of mean motion, Laplace succeeded in deriving the same equations. With considerable enthusiasm, he also tried whether he could determine the secular inequalities of the eccentricities and motions of aphelion by an analogous method—and happily he could. He apologized ([*1775a*]; *OC*, VIII, 355–356 n.) for rushing into print before Lagrange himself could publish. Between them, however, they had the makings of a complete and rigorous theory of all the secular inequalities, and Laplace for his part now proposed to draw together just such a general theory in a further study. Notice that this is the second intimation of the famous astronomical program eventually realized in the late 1780's (see Section 17) and first announced in the astronomical part of the dual probability-gravitation memoir ([*1776a*, 2°]) discussed above (see Section 5).

In the meantime, he had imagined a new method for approximating the solutions of differential equations in which problems of planetary motion were formulated. He gave a very summary idea of the technique in a hastily printed "Addition" ([*1775b*]; *OC*, VIII, 361–366) to the memoir ([*1775a*]) on singular solutions and secular inequalities, reserving its development in detail for the next volume of *Mémoires*. The essay "Recherches sur le calcul intégral et sur le système du monde" ([*1776c*]) constitutes the third item in this mainly mathematical series. Perhaps it was the most important, for the approach became a mainstay of Laplace's later work in planetary theory and thereby of positional astronomy in general. For readers unfamiliar with that calculus, Laplace explained how the complexity of planetary motions rules out all hope of achieving rigorous solutions to the problems they present. Called for instead were simple and convergent methods for integrating the differential equations by approximation. The most widely practiced technique, which Laplace attributed to d'Alembert, consisted in an adaptation of Newton's method for approximating the roots of polynomials. Since the values were known with only a small degree of uncertainty, accurate quantities could be substituted in their place and a very small indeterminate term added. Then the squares and higher powers of this new indeterminate might be neglected and the problem reduced to the integration of as many linear differential equations as there were variables.

All available methods for that, however, entailed one or both of two drawbacks. They were inapplicable to planets with more than one satellite and to the motion of two or more planets around the sun. Moreover, in some cases, notably that of the moon, the second approximation in the process of integration introduced secular terms with no physical meaning—then called "arcs of circles"—which spoiled the convergence. The method that he had just imagined avoided these inconveniences. It was specifically applicable to expressions in which the variables are functions of periodic quantities and also of other quantities that increase very slowly. That is precisely the situation in physical astronomy. The trick consisted in varying the arbitrary constants in the approximate integrals and then determining their values for a given time by integration. In the preface Condorcet despaired of conveying an idea of it verbally (*HARS* [1772, pt. 2/1776], 87–89). Agreeing that examples would convey a better notion than any generalities, Laplace produced a large number in a memoir of some 100 pages followed by several additions.

Andoyer does attempt a summary account, which may be of interest (J:[1922], pp. 54–55). Given a differential equation

$$\frac{d^2x}{dt^2} = P, \tag{24}$$

in which P, a function of x and of dx/dt, is periodic with respect to appropriate linear arguments in t, it is supposed that its general integral is obtained and that it takes the form

$$x = X + tY + t^2Z + \cdots. \tag{25}$$

The functions X, Y, Z, $\cdots$, depend on two arbitrary constants C_1 and C_2 and are periodic in t, as well as in any other arguments introduced by integration. Here Laplace restricted the conditions so that a function can be developed consistently with the above equation for x in only one way. The expression

$$x' = X' + (t - \theta) Y' + (t - \theta)^2 Z' + \cdots \tag{26}$$

will then satisfy the equation, where θ is any arbitrary quantity and X', Y', Z', $\cdots$ are the forms taken by X, Y, Z, $\cdots$ when the constants C_1 and C_2 are replaced by similar variants, C'_1 and C'_2.

If C'_1 and C'_2 are now properly determined as functions of C_1, C_2, and θ, the expressions for x and x' become identical. Since x' will then be independent of θ, any value can be assigned to θ at will; and if θ is set equal to t, the expression for x reduces to

$$x = X', \qquad (27)$$

when C'_1 and C'_2 are assigned corresponding values. If those are periodic, the manipulation will have eliminated the secular terms from the initial expression for x. In order to determine those values, it can be asserted that the value of x' becomes independent of θ, in such a way that

$$\frac{dx'}{dC'_1}\frac{dC'_1}{d\theta} + \frac{dx'}{dC'_2}\frac{dC'_2}{d\theta} + \frac{dx'}{d\theta} = 0. \qquad (28)$$

That equation permits the determination of C'_1 and C'_2, given the further condition that for $\theta = 0$, these quantities reduce to C_1 and C_2.

Among his examples, Laplace applied the method to the determination of inequalities in eccentricities and the inclinations of the orbit; he derived anew his theorem from the probabilistic-astronomical memoir concerning the long-term invariance of the mean motions with respect to gravitational interactions ([1776a, 2°], Article LIX; OC, VIII, 258–263); and he tried out an analysis of a new sort of problem, the secular inequalities that a planet would exhibit if it moved in a resisting medium. His examples amount to the elements of just such a theory as he had promised in the previous memoir, and it was certainly the astronomical possibilities opened to him by the variation of constants that motivated the present paper. The reader who wishes an abbreviated recapitulation by Laplace himself may turn to Articles XVI–XIX of the great memoir on the "Théorie de Jupiter et de Saturne" ([1788a]; OC, XI, 131–140; see Section 17 below). Yet it is characteristic of Laplace that along the way he should have developed a method for solving problems capable of much more general applicability. Early in the course of the analysis ([1776c], Article IV; OC, VIII, 395–406), Laplace found himself confronting a set of linear equations from which n quantities had to be eliminated. The technique he there introduced involved an expansion since called by his name in the theory of determinants. Muir (N: [1906], I, 25–33) gives a summary of its importance in the development of that branch of mathematics.

8. The Figure of the Earth and the Motion of the Seas. Geophysical topics occupied Laplace in the final investigation that we wish to assign to his early period. The attribution is somewhat arbitrary, perhaps, since in *Mécanique céleste* (Volume II, Book IV) he did employ much the same method for the analysis of the tides. He there improved the calculations enough to make the difference a substantial one, however. At all events,

in the program of the probability-gravitation memoir ([1776a, 2°], see Section 5) measurements of the figure of the earth constituted the one set of data by which the principle of universal interparticle attraction might be tested. Laplace first took up the matter in a single article of the tripartite memoir that opened with his analysis of the distribution of cometary orbits ([1776b], Article X; OC, VIII, 362–313). He conceived the problem to be one of determining the equilibrium conditions governing the form of planets considered as spheroids of revolution. Appropriately enough, the table of contents classifies the discussion under "Hydrostatics" rather than geodesy (SE [1773/1776], xv), for Laplace analyzed the same model that Newton had, a homogeneous fluid mass spinning on its axis with all the particles serving the inverse-square law of attraction among themselves. He considered Newton's assertion that such a body would be an ellipsoid to be very shaky, however. Although it was easy to show that an ellipsoid, or indeed some other solid of revolution, satisfied the conditions *a posteriori*, it was enormously difficult to determine *a priori* what those conditions must be.

Laplace undertook that task in a further brief analysis ([1776d]; OC, VIII, 481–501) tacked on to the memoir ([1776c]) on variation of constants in the integration of astronomical expressions. Although he failed to determine the equation for the curve described by a meridian, he did there discover the law of gravity in a generalized homogenous spheroid: on the surface of any such body in a state of internal gravitational equilibrium, the variation of gravity from the equator to the poles follows the same law as in an ellipsoid. Its force at any point on the surface is given by ([1776d]; OC, VIII, 493)

$$P = P'\left(1 + \frac{5}{4}\,\alpha m\cos^2\theta\right), \qquad (29)$$

where P' is the value at the equator, αm is the ratio of centrifugal to gravitational force (α being infinitesimally small), and θ is the complement of the latitude.

Those two small pieces were forerunners of the "Recherches sur plusieurs points du système du monde" ([1778a], [1779a], [1779b]), which Laplace submitted to the Academy in three installments in 1777 and 1778 and which, taken together, comprise a treatise of over 200 pages in its *Mémoires*. The investigation had three objects: (1) the law of gravitational force on the surface of homogeneous spheroids in equilibrium; (2) the motion of the tides, together with the precession of the equinoxes and the nutation of the earth's axis; and (3) the oscillations of the atmosphere caused by the gravitational action of the sun and the moon. The first section is entirely formal and quite in the d'Alembert tradition, except that Laplace dispensed with the stipulation that the solid be generated by the revolution of a curve. He set up the problem by means of a diagram in which an element of surface fluid in the form of an infinitesimal parallelogram exerts a force upon the center of mass, and after eight pages of analysis he obtained the equation ([1778a]; OC, IX, 85)

$$P = P' + \frac{5}{4} \alpha f \cos^2 \theta - \frac{1}{2} \alpha V + \alpha R, \qquad (30)$$

where again θ is the complement of latitude, P' is a constant of integration, R is a centrally directed force at a point on the surface and hence a function of latitude and longitude, V is a term expressing the departure (assumed to be small) of the spheroid from the spherical, and αf is the centrifugal force at the equator. None of this would be very interesting, perhaps, except for what emerges as the motivation. Only at the end does it become evident why Laplace had reversed directions and determined the attraction of a surface element for the center. For he there adduced a special case in which the forces are produced by the attraction of any number of bodies near to or far from the spheroid and subject to the conditions that they change its form negligibly and that they either participate in its rotation or are infinite in number and disposed in a uniform ring. Laplace frequently indulged in the practice of specifying some peculiarity of the world in highly abstract terms in order to make it appear to follow from a general analysis. This example is an instance, for the case is that of Saturn's rings. The conditions give a series expression for the last two terms in (30)

$$\sum \left(\frac{S}{2rs} - \frac{3}{2} Sb - \frac{3}{r^2 s} \frac{dr}{ds} \right), \qquad (31)$$

where S is the mass of a discrete body in an assembly constituting a ring, r its distance from the point M on the surface of the planet, and s the radius of the point M. If the shape and density of the ring, and its position relative to the axis of rotation of Saturn, were known, and also if the planet were supposed to be uniform in density, the law of gravity at the surface could be determined. For S would then be infinitesimal, and summing the series would become a simple exercise in integration. Laplace attempted no numerical solution, however, and the general significance of the analysis is

its applicability to systems of particles external to the surface of an attracting spheroid.

It is the second topic in this series of memoirs that is the most interesting, as much for its subject matter as for the example it affords of Laplace's mode of thinking. The phenomenon analyzed is the tidal ebb and flow of the seas. In the program of the dual probability-gravitation memoir ([1776a, 1°], see Section 5) he had put that problem aside as too complicated for calculation. Now that he felt ready to take it on, the question (as always) was not whether the motion of the tides is subject to gravitational forces, which fact no one doubted, but how the law could be derived. He started with the assumption classically brought to the problem in the study it had received from Newton through Daniel Bernoulli and Maclaurin to d'Alembert, namely that the spheroid covered by a fluid should differ very little from a sphere; that the axis of rotation should be invariant; that the centrifugal force of the fluid particles and other forces, such as attraction of the stars, should be small compared to self-gravity; and that the sidereal motion should be slow compared to the speed of rotation of the sphere. To these a priori conditions, Laplace added two others that emerged in the course of his analysis and that are very interesting for the question they raise about what his sense actually was of the relation between the operations of analysis and physical facts.

The new conditions emerging from the analysis were that the seas be approximately uniform in depth and that the depth be about four leagues (twelve miles). If one were to read no further in Laplace than this lengthy memoir, one would be bound to suppose that he took these assertions to be statements about the way the world is made emerging from a mathematical analysis of tidal action under gravitational force. He acknowledged that if the case were different, his expressions would have been unmanageable. He repeatedly referred to it as "the case in nature," however, and nowhere stipulated that it was a simplification introduced in order to make the analysis possible at all. On the contrary, he took his predecessors to task for having simplified matters in a manner that was unfaithful to the facts. Beginning with Newton, the form they had investigated was that which would be assumed on a stationary planet by a thin covering of fluid in equilibrium under the gravitational pull of a stationary star. They then assumed that if the star were given a real or apparent motion around the planet, it would simply drag the bulge around without changing the form.

Laplace, for his part, would now give the problem a realistic analysis. The most obvious discrepancy with fact in the classical picture arose from the consequence it entailed that the two full tides occurring in a single day should differ markedly in height and most notably when the declination between the sun and moon was greatest. Actually, however, it was common knowledge at any seaside that consecutive high tides differ very little in level. A second difficulty was formal. The traditional analysis overlooked the variation of "the angular motion of rotation" ([*1778a*]; *OC*, IX, 90) of molecules of seawater with latitude, which would produce longitudinal displacements of the same order as those induced by the direct gravitational action of the sun and moon. From the frequency with which Laplace recurred to the former anomaly, it would appear to have been that which had fixed his attention on the problem at just this juncture. A letter of 25 February 1778 to Lagrange confirms that the lack of conformity between theory and observation over the inversion of the tides had struck him very forcibly (*Oeuvres de Lagrange*, XIV, 78–81). In his own analysis Laplace formed expressions containing terms for the actual momentum of fluid elements at all latitudes on a rotating globe. When he developed them, he was pleased to be able to argue that the theory yielded a convincing explanation for the near equality of consecutive high tides. Indeed, he said, it exhibited any number of reasons for it. What those expressions were like, we shall show in a moment.

Meanwhile, his analysis had led him to notice another deficiency in existing theory, this one affecting the precession of the equinoxes and the more recently discovered motion of nutation. Heretofore, calculations of these variations in the direction of the earth's axis had presupposed the action of the sun and moon on a solid globe. To be fully accurate, however, account would also need to be taken of the gravitational interaction of both bodies with the seas. If the sun and the moon were in the plane of the equator, the pull on the waters in the northern and southern hemispheres would be symmetrical and no problem would arise. In actuality, the inclination of the plane of the ecliptic is bound to result in uneven tidal distributions, and there can therefore be no warrant *a priori* for supposing that the unequal reaction of the waters in the two hemispheres will fail to produce disturbances in the direction of the polar axis. Quite the contrary.

As it happened, Laplace's calculations showed (he did not say to his surprise) that introducing these considerations produced no changes in the overall laws of precession and nutation. It turned out that only the ratio of the quantity of the nutation to that of precession is influenced by including terms for tidal asymmetry between the hemispheres. That composite effect is very small, moreover, when calculated on the basis of reasonable hypotheses concerning the depth and density of the seas. Nor was Laplace disappointed, for its amount came out to be proportional to the very small difference between consecutive high tides. Thus, the validity of the four-league uniform depth of the sea, which had been introduced to facilitate calculation of the tides, was confirmed by its applicability to the interrelation between the tides and the variations in direction of the earth's axis.

This piece of research makes a very nice example of the juncture at which Laplace came into the history of astronomical and geodesic problems, and equally of the approach that he brought to them. The first stage, the discovery of the laws themselves, had pertained to Newton for the most part; and the second, their analytic formulation, to the Bernoullis, Euler, Clairaut, and d'Alembert. Laplace's was a third stage, that of deriving interactions and interrelations and reducing or extending the scale between macrocosmic and microcosmic levels. Even so, the dynamical explanation of the tides belonged to Newton and its subsequent expression in terms of analytical mechanics to Laplace's predecessors. He cut into the theory by attacking the anomaly of the near equality of consecutive high tides and proceeded to derive from its resolution a relation to precession and nutation. When he corrected predecessors, it was seldom if ever over physical data: it was because their analyses did not account for the data. Thus, the existing theory of precession and nutation did not give the wrong result. But it ought to have done so, and discovering why it did not led Laplace to an unsuspected and higher-order relation between the two axial oscillations.

Here, as throughout, his own analyses bespeak an enormous fund of physical knowledge and acuteness of insight into the body of existing theory. He saw into the physical situation for consequences—for example, the asymmetrical gravitational pull on the seas in the two hemispheres—that others had either not noticed or had not been able to calculate. Then he would calculate them, in memoirs that run, like this one, into hundreds of pages of differentiation, integration, and approximation. Did he see how to make an analysis come out before deciding which phenomena to handle—

or the other way about? That question cannot be answered in the present state of scholarship, and probably the alternatives are two sides of the same coin. However that may have worked, one remark may be ventured with a certain confidence. His instinct for what was true and interesting in a set of physical relations was prompted by its accessibility to the kind of analysis in which he was a virtuoso. His knowledge of physics itself, however, was that of an omnivorous reader, an *érudit*, rather than an inquirer or discoverer.

A further feature of Laplace's mature technique first became fully apparent in these "Recherches," and that is the ingenuity with which he formulated expressions to contain terms representing the separate elements of a composite cycle of physical events. In this instance, the several cycles of oscillation—annual, diurnal, and semidiurnal—that when taken together produce the gross ebb and flow of the tides, are handled serially. Laplace himself did not use the term harmonic theory that has since been applied to the type of tidal analysis that he started here. The phrase is apt, however. In effect, he did treat the determination of the location of a molecule of seawater relative to its equilibrium position like that of the displacement of a point on a string vibrating so as to produce a beat of tones and overtones. The actual position at any moment is the linear resultant of the respective displacements suffered in consequence of oscillations of several frequencies. The technique appears to good advantage in the second installment of this series, submitted to the Academy on 7 October 1778, almost a year after the first. There Laplace went over the same material just summarized, cleaning up and ordering the analysis that he had spun out more or less as it came to him the first time around. Perhaps it will be useful to single out the salient features as they pertain to the elements of tidal oscillation. The problem is set up to consider the displacements of a fluid molecule, M, on the surface of the sea. The following are the parameters at the outset ([*1779a*]; *OC*, IX, 187–188):

θ complement of the latitude; and

ω longitude in relation to a meridian fixed in space

(after time t, θ becomes $\theta + \alpha u$; and ω becomes $\omega + nt + \alpha v$, where nt represents the rotational motion of the earth, and α is a very small coefficient);

αy elevation of M above the surface in the equilibrium state it would have

reached without the action of the sun and moon;

$\alpha \delta B$,   components of the attraction for M of
$\alpha \delta C$ an aqueous spheroid of radius $(1 + \alpha y)$, decomposed perpendicularly to the radius in the planes of the meridian and the parallel of latitude;

δ density of seawater;

s mass of the attracting star;

ν complement of its declination;

ϕ longitude reckoned on the equator from the fixed meridian;

h distance from the center of the earth, the minor semiaxis of which is taken for unity, and we let $\dfrac{3s}{2h^3} = \alpha K$;

g gravitational constant; and

$l\gamma$ depth of the sea, l being very small and γ being any function of θ.

With these quantities, Laplace restated in terms of polar coordinates three equations that he had formulated in his initial analysis governing the motions of M, thus obtaining (*ibid.*; *OC*, IX, 188):

$$y = -\frac{l}{\sin\theta}\frac{\partial\,(\mu y \sin\theta)}{\partial\theta} - l\gamma\frac{\partial v}{\partial\omega} \tag{32}$$

$$\frac{d^2u}{dt^2} - 2n\frac{dv}{dt}\sin\theta\cos\theta = -g\frac{\partial y}{\partial\theta} + \delta B + \frac{\partial R}{\partial\theta} \tag{33}$$

$$\frac{d^2v}{dt^2}\sin^2\theta + 2n\frac{du}{dt}\sin\theta\cos\theta$$
$$= -g\frac{\partial y}{\partial\omega} + \delta C\sin\theta + \frac{\partial R}{\partial\omega} \tag{34}$$

where

$$R = K\,[\cos\theta\cos\nu + \sin\theta\sin\nu\cos\,(\phi - nt - \omega)]^2. \tag{35}$$

(In these papers, R represents a force acting in a given direction to disturb the equilibrium of the particle M. Its derivatives are taken with respect to θ and ω; the terms K, ν, and ϕ are given by the law of motion of the attracting star as functions of time t [*ibid.*, nos. III, XXII, XXIV; *OC*, IX, 95, 187–189, 198–199; cf. *Mécanique céleste*, Book IV, nos. 1, 4; *OC*, II, 184, 195]). Equations 33, 34, and 35 were then combined and transformed by various manipulations into a single equation in rectangular coordinates, setting

$$\begin{aligned} y &= a\cos\,(it + s\omega + A) \\ y' &= a'\cos\,(it + s\omega + A) \\ u' &= b\cos\,(it + s\omega + A) \\ v &= c\sin\,(it + s\omega + A), \end{aligned} \tag{36}$$

where i and s are any constant coefficients, and a, a', b, and c are functions of θ. Then, when $\sin\theta = x$, the following equation comprises the entire theory of the tides:

$$ix^3 a\,(i^2 - 4n^2 + 4n^2 x^2)^2$$

$$= -lgzix^2\,(1-x^2)\,(i^2 - 4n^2 + 4n^2 x^2)\frac{\partial^2 a'}{\partial x^2}$$

$$+ lgzix^3\frac{\partial a'}{\partial x}\,(i^2 + 4n^2 - 4n^2 x^2)$$

$$+ lgsza'\,[\,(is+2n)\,(i^2 - 4n^2 + 4n^2 x^2)$$

$$+ 16n^3 x^2\,(1-x^2)\,] \qquad (37)$$

$$- lg\frac{\partial z}{\partial x}x\,(1-x^2)\,(i^2 - 4n^2 + 4n^2 x^2)$$

$$\left(ix\frac{\partial a'}{\partial x} + 2nsa'\right).$$

Fortunately, it did not have to be solved; it needed only to be satisfied, and that could be done piecemeal, introducing simplifications by dint of reasonable suppositions about the physical factors at work — as to equilibrium, fluid friction, resistance, and so on — and determining the coefficients i and s, and the function a' in terms of a.

To accomplish this task, Laplace grouped the different terms of the expression for R (35) according to the cycle that they represent in the total tidal flow. Thus:

$$R = K[\cos\theta\cos\nu + \sin\theta\sin\nu\cos(\phi - nt - \omega)]^2$$

$$= K\cos^2\nu + \frac{1}{2}K\sin^2\theta\,(\sin^2\nu - 2\cos^2\nu)$$

$$\qquad\qquad\qquad\qquad\qquad\qquad (38)$$

$$+ 2K\sin\theta\cos\theta\sin\nu\cos\nu\cos(nt + \omega - \phi)$$

$$+ \frac{1}{2}K\sin^2\theta\sin^2\nu\cos(2nt + 2\omega - 2\phi).$$

Developing the values for R, Laplace obtained, in place of the three ranks of terms above, three series of the respective forms

(1°) $K' + K''\sin^2\theta\cos(it + A)$,
(2°) $K'\sin\theta\cos\theta\cos(it + \omega + A)$,   (39)
(3°) $K'\sin^2\theta\cos(it + 2\omega + A)$,

where K', K'', and A are any constant coefficients. These three classes of the expressions for R, and consequently for y, group terms in the following manner:

(1°) includes terms that are independent of ω. Their period is thus proportional to the time of

revolution of the star in its orbit — annual in the case of the sun;

(2°) includes terms of which the period is approximately one day;

(3°) includes terms of which the period is half a day.

(By the conditions of the problem, i was small compared to n in terms of the first form; and if the orbit is assumed circular, $i = 0$ or $2m$, m being the mean motion; in terms of the second form, i differs very little from n, and this difference is 0 or $2m$ if the orbit is circular. In terms of the third form, i is very little different from $2n$, which difference is again 0 or $2m$ in the case of circular orbits.)

Examining now the terms of the first class (1° of Equation 39), which has the form

$$K' + K''\sin^2\theta\cos(it + A), \qquad (40)$$

the condition that they govern the annual revolution gives values for the coefficients that need to be determined in order to satisfy (37), such that, for this part of the oscillation,

$$y = \frac{K\left(\cos^2\nu - \dfrac{1}{2}\sin^2\nu\right)}{6g\left(1 - \dfrac{3\delta}{5\delta'}\right)}(1 + 3\cos 2\theta), \quad (41)$$

where δ' is the mean density of the earth, and $g = (4/3)\pi\delta'$. The expression is exact for the action of the sun, although less so for the moon, since the waters have less time to return to equilibrium in a month than in a year. But any errors are of little importance in the theory of the tides, since they affect only the absolute heights relative to the phases of the moon, and not the difference between high and low tide.

The depth of the sea figures in this analysis, its expression being $(1 + q^2\sin\theta)$ in polar coordinates. Since $\gamma = 1 + (q/l)\sin^2\theta$, then $z = x + (q/l)x^3$ in rectangular coordinates, q being a very small constant coefficient of the order of l. This value is important for two reasons. Physically, the equilibrium considerations require that the mass of the seawater remain constant. Analytically — and this is more important, although it comes in rather unobtrusively — the determination of the values of a and a' to be substituted in (37) depended on assuming that q is approximately zero, and that the depth of the sea is constant. "This method," Laplace observed, "can thus serve to find the approximate values of a, given this hypothesis concerning the depth [of the sea], which we shall see in the following article is approximately that of nature" ([1779a]; OC, IX, 202).

It is the terms of the second class (2° of Equation 39) that are the most important for the inversion of the tides, their form being

$$K' \sin \theta \cos \theta \cos (it + \omega + A) , \qquad (42)$$

and their period approximately a single day. Here the conditions are such that analysis yields the expression for the part of y corresponding to these terms

$$\frac{2q}{2qg\left(1 - \frac{3\delta}{5\delta'}\right) - n^2} K' \sin \theta \cos \theta \cos (it + \omega + A) . \qquad (43)$$

And now we begin to see the reason for all this. Laplace next sums all terms of this second form given by the development of R and designates by Y the corresponding expression for y:

$$Y = \frac{4Kq \sin \nu \cos \nu \sin \theta \cos \theta}{2qg\left(1 - \frac{3\delta}{5\delta'}\right) - n^2} \cos (nt + \omega - \phi) . \qquad (44)$$

The value of Y will be a maximum when $nt + \omega - \phi = 0$ or π, which is to say, when the star that is the origin of the attracting force passes the meridian. The expression has a negative value when $nt + \omega - \phi = \pi$; and the difference between the maximum positive and negative values, which equals twice the former, will measure the difference between the two full tides of the same day. That difference will be proportional to the unwieldy coefficient of cos $(nt + \omega - \phi)$ in (44). Since observation shows this difference to be extremely small, the value of q must be nil or almost nil. And finally, since the depth of the sea is $l + q \sin^2 \theta$, it follows that "in order to satisfy the phenomena of ebb and flow of the tides, this depth must be approximately constant" (ibid., MARS [1776/1779], 199–200). That is, it must be l, which result agrees with what he had already found. Thus, he could conclude— "without fear of observable error" (ibid., 200)— that $Y = 0$ and determine the values needed to satisfy (37).

Laplace went on to set out verbally what he had in mind as a physical picture. For this purpose, he designated by u and U the parts of u and v that correspond to the terms of the second class for the expression of R. It will be recalled that u and v are the variations respectively of θ, the complement of latitude, and of ω, the longitude. Thus defined,

$$\mathbf{u} = \frac{2K}{n^2} \sin \nu \cos \nu \cos (nt + \omega - \phi) , \qquad (45)$$

and

$$\mathbf{U} = -\frac{2K}{n^2} \sin \nu \cos \nu \frac{\cos \theta}{\sin \theta} \sin (nt + \omega - \phi) . \qquad (46)$$

Confining attention now to expressions of the form

$$2K \sin \nu \cos \nu \sin \theta \cos \theta (nt + \omega - \phi) , \qquad (47)$$

and to the force they represent, it is (Laplace says) "easy to see" (ibid., 200–202) that the molecules will slide over each other as if isolated, with no detectable loss from internal collisions in the system. We are to imagine a slice of this fluidity contained between two meridians and two parallels infinitely close together. Since the value of u is constant for all molecules located under the same meridian, the length of the slice remains constant in that direction. To the extent that the fluid flows toward the equator, however, the space enclosed between the two meridians increases. Since the slice thus widens along the parallels, the surface of the water would tend to descend if it were not for the latitudinal component of the velocity of the molecules, which tends to squeeze the two meridians together and correspondingly diminish the width. Again "it is easy," we are assured, to conclude that this diminution, resulting from the value for U, is compensated by the motion of the slice toward the equator. Therefore, the width actually remains constant along the parallels, and the height of the slice is not affected detectably by the motion of the fluid. That is the reason for which in a sea of uniform depth (such as would be constituted by the sum of all such slices taken side by side), the difference between consecutive high tides is almost undetectable. (It is essential to refer to the original printing for this passage, since OC, IX, 212, mixes up the notation.)

Now then, whatever may be thought of this argument, it can have referred only to the notion that Laplace had actually formed of physical reality. He was thus enlarging on the phenomenon, he said, because it was very important for the understanding of the tides and entirely contrary to received theory. He went on to illustrate the argument by data drawn from observations made at Brest and turned it against Daniel Bernoulli's idea that the earth rotates too rapidly for the tides to differ conformably with the results of theory. He himself had just shown that whatever the speed of rotation, consecutive high tides would be very unequal if the sea were not everywhere of approximately the same depth. "It seems to me," he concluded, "to result from these considerations that only an explanation founded on a rigorous calculation like this one . . . is capable of meeting all the objections that can be lodged against the principle of universal gravitation on this score" (*ibid.*; *OC*, IX, 214).

Terms of the form $K' \sin^2 \theta$ (cos $it + 2 \omega + A$) constitute the third class (3° of Equation 39) produced by the development of R. Their period is half a day, or that of a single tidal cycle. Examining these terms, Laplace substituted values for the observed tidal range, or difference between low and high tides, in various localities and determined that deriving the law of gravity from the data required assigning the figure of four leagues to the mean depth of the sea "on which only vague and uncertain conjectures have been formed until now" (*ibid.*; *OC*, IX, 216). We shall not excerpt that analysis, which is of the same type as the foregoing, nor summarize the calculation that exhibits the proportionality of the slight difference between daily high tides to the influence of the tides on the ratio of nutation to precession. We shall also pass over the third installment of this memoir, in which Laplace calculated much more succinctly that the gravitational effect of the sun and moon on the atmosphere is bound to cause oscillations comparable to tides but too slight to detect (see Section 28). More important, he redeemed the promise of an earlier memoir ([*1776a*, 2°]; see Section 5) and showed that these effects cannot be the source of the trade winds, recognizing that oversimplified assumptions, most notably that of constant temperature, reduced his results to a qualitative significance.

Instead, let us conclude this discussion of Laplace's youthful period with a further memoir, "Sur la précession des équinoxes" ([*1780c*]), which he read before the Academy on 18 August 1779. It opens with a simplified derivation of the results of his previous research on the relation of tidal action to precession and nutation, the consequence of which is now stated as a theorem (*ibid.*; *OC*, IX, 341–342):

> If the earth be supposed an ellipsoid of revolution covered by the sea, the fluidity of the water in no way interferes with the attraction of the sun and the moon on precession and nutation, so that this effect is just the same as if the sea formed a solid mass with the earth.

This theorem might well have been thought to hold true for any spheroid, observed Laplace, although he had been unable to demonstrate its generality by his previous analysis. The expressions that he formed there to represent the influence of the oscillations of the sea on precession could not be integrated generally. In the meanwhile, he had found a much simpler method, which formed the subject of the present memoir and which met this difficulty. Essentially it consisted of nothing other than the application to the problem of d'Arcy's principle of areas. Unlike the other basic principles, particularly vis viva conservation or least action, which are limited to gradual and continuous changes of motion, d'Arcy's principle holds good in cases of shock or turbulence, such as friction with the bed of the sea and resistance from the coasts in tidal movements. We shall not follow the analysis, except to note its crux, which was that the expression of the variation of the overall motion of the fluids covering a globe contains no terms dependent on the secular passage of time. Thus, both for mechanical and formal reasons, the new method might be extended to what Laplace now, not even a year later, called the case in nature, "in which the figure of the earth and the depth of the sea are very irregular, and the oscillations of the water are modified by a vast number of obstacles" (*ibid.*; *OC*, IX, 342).

Now that the seabed had suddenly—and one is tempted to say analytically—become very irregular instead of uniform, Laplace was led to speculate that the spinning earth may not be perfectly symmetrical. In that event, the resulting irregularities in angular momentum, added to the direct gravitational effects of the sun and the moon and the reaction of the seas to their tidal pull, might change the axis of rotation over very long periods. The poles would then migrate into other regions in the course of time—but this he would leave as a conjecture, worthy of the attention of mathematicians because of its difficulty and importance.

PART II: LAPLACE IN HIS PRIME, 1778–1789

9. Influence and Reputation. By the late 1770's Laplace had begun to win a reputation extending beyond the small circle of mathematicians who could understand his work, and by the late 1780's he was recognized as one of the leading figures of the Academy. On 15 May 1788 he was married to Marie-Charlotte de Courty de Romanges, of a Besançon family (J: Marmottan [1897], 7). She was twenty years younger than he, and they had two children. Laplace's son, Charles-Émile, born in 1789, followed a military career, became a general, and died without issue in 1874. The daughter,

Sophie-Suzanne, married the marquis de Portes and died in childbirth in 1813. Her child, a girl, survived and married the comte de Colbert-Chabannais. The living descendants derive from that marriage, having taken the name Colbert-Laplace.

We know practically nothing of Laplace's personal life in the years before his marriage, but there are a few indications of his effect on others. Not a single testimonial bespeaking congeniality survives. There are hints that the aged d'Alembert began to resent the regularity with which his recent protégé was relegating his own work to the history of rational mechanics. Overly elaborate tributes by Condorcet and Laplace himself bear the scent of mollification, notably in the prefaces to the "Recherches sur plusieurs points du système du monde," which we have just discussed. Anders Johan Lexell, a Swedish astronomer who spent part of the winter of 1780–1781 in Paris, wrote in a gossipy account of the Academy that Laplace let it be known that he considered himself the best mathematician in France. He also had extensive knowledge in other sciences, reported Lexell, but presumed too far upon it, "for in the Academy he wanted to pronounce on everything" (*Revue d'histoire des sciences*, **10** [1957], 148–166).

At about the same time, Laplace fell into a heated dispute with Jacques-Pierre Brissot, the future Girondist leader and a rising scribbler, over the optical experiments of Jean-Paul Marat, who was then seeking scientific recognition and entry to the Academy. In Brissot's dialogue on "academic prejudice" Laplace is the original of the Newtonian idolater, arrogant in his *fauteuil* and contemptuously spurning the aspiring "physicist" from the impregnable—and irrelevant—plane of mathematics (Brissot, *De la vérité* [Neuchâtel, 1782], 335).

In 1784 the government appointed Laplace to succeed Bezout as examiner of cadets for the Royal Artillery (J: Duveen and Hahn [1957]). The candidates had generally completed secondary school and a year or two of special preparatory school before going on to La Fère or one of the other artillery schools, or in some cases to Mézières for engineering. The responsibility was more serious than might at first glance be supposed. An individual report had to be written on each cadet, all of whom were of good family. The annual scrutiny brought Laplace, as it did Monge, the newly appointed examiner for naval cadets, into regular contact with ministers and high officers; and it introduced them to the practice of recruiting an elite by competitive examination that was later greatly expanded in scale and intensified in mathematical content by the procedures for selecting students to enter the École Polytechnique. (For Laplace's reports, see Bibliography, Section A). The government also named him to the most famous of the blue-ribbon commissions through which the Academy investigated and made recommendations on matters of civic concern in the last years of the old regime. Laplace was a member of the commission headed by Bailly to investigate the Hôtel Dieu, the major hospital in Paris, as well as hospital care in general. Calculations on the relative probabilities of emerging alive from its wards, and comparisons of the mortality there to other hospitals in France and abroad, must almost certainly have been his contribution to its report (*HARS* [1785/1788], 44–50).

Laplace was promoted to the senior rank of pensioner in the Academy in April 1785 in the vacancy created by the death of Le Roy. In this, technically the most proficient and productive period of his life, he pressed forward with all the topics that he had begun investigating in his youth, added physics to them, and achieved many of the results for which he is famous. From the published record, it appears that in the early 1780's his emphasis shifted from the problems of attraction, which were occupying him in 1777 and 1778 (*24, 26, 28*), to probability again, both in its calculus and now in its application to demography, and equally to the experimental and mathematical physics of heat. In the mid-1780's his interest again centered on attraction and the figure of the earth, and in the latter half of the decade it turned to planetary motions. It will be best to discuss these subjects in that sequence, beginning with a pair of relatively brief but important mathematical memoirs and continuing into probability. These dictates of convenience, however, must not obscure the evidence that, to an extraordinary degree, Laplace was able to hold and mature all these matters in his mind concurrently, readily turning from one to another. For even while occupied with probability about 1780, and with the Lavoisier collaboration simultaneously underway, he did the paper on precession already noticed and in 1781 drafted another, very important, memoir on the determination of cometary orbits, to be discussed in Section 14.

10. Variation of Constants; Differential Operators. The earlier of the two mathematical papers that preceded his resumption of probability pertained to astronomy and was entitled "Mémoire sur l'intégration des équations différentielles par approximation" ([*1780a*]). Laplace there simplified the technique of varying arbitrary constants in approximate solutions to differential equations of planetary motion in order to eliminate the troublesome secular terms that crept in and destroyed convergence. Having brought out the method by means of numerous examples in a very lengthy memoir ([1776c]; see Section 7), he now gave rules for applying it generally in problems of theoretical astronomy. Laplace's technical innovations were often thus introduced discursively and then shortened and pointed for restatement.

The latter paper, "Mémoire sur l'usage du calcul aux différences partielles dans la théorie des suites" ([1780b]), was the more important mathematically. It belongs to the nascent stages of the calculus of operations, as it was called in the nineteenth century, or, more recently, the calculus of differential operators. Laplace submitted it to the Academy on 16 June 1779 (29). Three years previously he had appended Articles XI and XII, "Sur les fonctions," to his memoir on the mean inclination of the comets ([1776b]) and there gave what he considered a general demonstration of a theorem that Lagrange had obtained by induction ("Sur une nouvelle espèce de calcul," Oeuvres de Lagrange, III, 441–476). Lagrange had developed the analogy between positive exponents and indices of differentiation, and reciprocally between negative exponents and indices of integration, and stated the following theorem. We give it in the notation of Laplace, who unlike Lagrange considered only a single variable:

$$\Delta^n u = \left(e^{\alpha \frac{du}{dx}} - 1 \right)^n \quad \text{and} \quad \Sigma^n u = \frac{1}{\left(e^{\alpha \frac{du}{dx}} - 1 \right)^n}. \quad (48)$$

Laplace's 1776 proof depends on showing that in the expression for the developments

$$\alpha^n \frac{d^n u}{dx^n} = \Delta^n u + s \Delta^{n+1} u + s' \Delta^{n+2} u + \cdots \quad (49)$$

and

$$\frac{1}{\alpha^n} \int^n u \, dx^n = \Sigma^n u + f \Sigma^{n-1} u + f' \Sigma^{n-2} u + \cdots \quad (50)$$

the coefficients $s, s', \cdots, f, f', \cdots$ are constant and independent of α, thus depending only on n (ibid.; OC, VIII, 314–319). Lagrange's expressions are obtained if $u = e^x$, and the coefficients can thus be determined by the choice of the funtion u. Now, in the fullness of an entire memoir ([1780b]), Laplace dealt more generally with the possibility of moving back and forth between powers and indices of differentiation and integration, giving several alternative demonstrations of the Lagrange theorems and drawing out corollaries.

According to his own testimony, this research was one of the factors leading to the development of his theory of generating functions ([1782a]; OC, X, 2), which followed immediately after the memoir on probability ([1781a]) that he submitted to the Academy on 31 May 1780 (33). The draft was entitled "Mémoire sur le calcul aux suites appliqué aux probabilités," but as will appear in the next section, the treatment is far more comprehensive than that phrase would imply. For with principles or motifs, Laplace's pattern contrasts with that just noticed in the development that he often gave his technical innovations. Whereas the latter were abbreviated and focused after a lengthy initial statement, whole topics such as universal gravitation or inverse probability were first mentioned almost in passing and then, as the ideas continued germinating in his mind, were broadened to embrace entire domains of science and knowledge.

11. Probability Matured. The "Mémoire sur les probabilités" ([1781a])—the change of title epitomizes the process outlined above—gives the appearance of a finished piece of work. In a letter to Lagrange of 11 August 1780 he said that the principal object is the "method of going behind events to causes" (Oeuvres de Lagrange, XIV, 95). The preamble is more general. It reviews the entire status of inverse probability, pertaining as it does to a "very delicate metaphysics," the use of which is indispensable if the theory of probability is to be applied to life in society. The subject has two main aspects, closely related. In the first, the task is to calculate the probability of complex events compounded of elementary events of which the respective possibilities are unknown. In the second, the problem is to determine numerically the influence exerted by past events on the probability of future ones or, as we would say, to draw statistical inferences. In Laplace's view, the goal was to uncover the law that reveals the causes.

Before discussing problems of the former class, Laplace refined his epistemology slightly while distinguishing his procedure from previous practice in the theory of chance. In the traditional approach, the respective possibilities of simple events—that is, heads or tails in the tossing of a coin—had been determined in one of three ways: (1) a priori, by the assumption of equal possibility; (2) a posteriori, by repeated experiment; and (3) by whatever reasons we may have to judge the likely occurrence of the event. As to the last, if there is no reason to suppose player A more skillful than his opponent B, the probability assigned to his chance of winning is 1/2. The first approach gives the absolute possibility of events; the second—as he will show later—the approximate possibility; and the third, only their possibility relative to our information.

Since every event is actually determined by the general laws of the universe and is probable only relative to our knowledge, these distinctions may appear unreal. Still, they have their uses, and Laplace went on to consider a little more fully what they involve. Amid all the factors that produce some event, some are different every time, such as the precise movements of the hand in throwing dice. It is the overall effect of these factors that we call chance. Other factors are constant, such as the relative skill of the players or the weighting of the dice. Taken together, these are what constitute the "absolute possibility" (to which he intended to assimilate the approximate, although he did not say that at the outset). It is our greater or lesser knowledge of constant factors that constitutes their "relative possibility." These invariant factors do not suffice to produce the event. They must be joined to the operation of the chance or variable factors first mentioned and only increase the probability of events without determining their occurrence. Thus (if we have construed this passage correctly) Laplace considered at this juncture that the state of knowledge enters into the determination of probability at two levels: in what we know (relative possibility) of the absolute possibility (invariant factors) in events, and in our ignorance of the laws that will always appear to produce chance events. In this class of problems, then, the calculation of the probability of complex events, Laplace drew (as he had previously) upon models offered by games of chance and generalized the treatment that he had already given to estimating the influence of such unknown factors as slight asymmetries in coins or dice and differing habits or skills in players.

The development that he gave to the second topic, the estimation of causes from effects, broke new ground in the field of application. Indeed, it could be argued that social statistics as a mathematical subject had its beginning in this memoir. Laplace began the discussion by addressing himself to the first of two difficulties that impeded the application of Bayes's theorem to problems in the real world. (It is interesting that, although Laplace himself still ignored Bayes, whether in the French or English sense of the verb, Condorcet mentioned Bayes and Price in the summary of Laplace's memoir in his historical preface to the volume in which it appears [*HARS* (1778/1781), 43]. They are said to have stated the principle for determining causes from effects, but without any calculations.) The first impediment that Laplace identified was practical: experience was virtually never sufficiently extensive or controlled to yield reliable values for the *a priori* probabilities. The second impediment was analytical: in order to achieve numerical solutions, it was often necessary to integrate differential equations containing terms raised to very high powers. Laplace touched on that problem in the present memoir but reserved its full resolution for an even more technical companion paper that he appears to have been evolving concurrently.

To overcome the former, experiential difficulty, Laplace turned to the one subject on which statistically significant information had already been assembled—population. Population studies as a science owe much substance to the growing professionalism of eighteenth-century public administration. French parish registers in principle contained records of all births, marriages, and deaths. In 1771 the controller general of finance, the Abbé Terray, instructed all intendants in the provinces to have the figures for their generalities compiled annually and to report the results regularly to Paris in order that the government might have accurate information on the entire population. Turgot, a statesman close to the scientists in spirit and in program, was appointed controller general in August 1774. Through his influence, the Academy of Sciences became interested and published a summary of the figures for the city of Paris and the faubourgs covering the years 1709 through 1770. The record showed that in the last twenty-five years of that period, 251,527 boys and 241,945 girls had been born; and the ratio of approximately 105 to 101 remained virtually constant year by year. Figures also existed for London, and there too, more boys than girls had been born, although in the slightly greater ratio of 19 to 18.

Unlike imaginary black and white balls drawn from a hypothetical urn, the births of real children afforded a genuine numerical example, and Laplace seized on the opportunity to try out his technique for determining the limits of probability of future events based on past experience. Given p male and q female babies, the probability of the birth of a boy is $p/(p + q)$. Laplace next reiterated the theorem identical with Bernoulli's law of large numbers—again without mentioning Bernoulli (see Section 4)—to the effect that if P designates the probability that the chance of the birth of a boy

1366

is contained within the limits $p/(p + q) + \theta$ and $p/(p + q) - \theta$, where θ is a very small quantity, the difference between P and unity would vary inversely as the value of p and q. The latter quantity could be increased so that the difference between P and unity would be less than any given magnitude. To that end, he represented the definite integral for P by a highly convergent series, which on evaluation reduced to unity when p and q became infinite.

Readers may be interested in a précis of the calculation on which the above results depend ([1781a], no. XVIII; OC, IX, 422–429). What follows is a very close paraphrase in Laplace's notation. If x is the probability of the birth of a boy, and $(1 - x)$ that of a girl, then to determine the probability that x will fall within arbitrary limits became a problem of evaluating between those limits the definite integral

$$\int x^p (1-x)^q \, dx \qquad (51)$$

taken from $x = 0$ to $x = 1$, where p and q are very large numbers. Now, letting

$$y = x^p (1-x)^q, \qquad (52)$$

it followed that

$$y \, dx = \frac{x(1-x)}{p-(p+q)x} \, dy. \qquad (53)$$

If we set

$$p = 1/\alpha \quad \text{and} \quad q = \mu/\alpha, \qquad (54)$$

α being a very small fraction since p and q are very large, then (53) becomes

$$y \, dx = \alpha z \, dy, \qquad (55)$$

where

$$z = \frac{x(1-x)}{1-(1+\mu)\,x}. \qquad (56)$$

Thus, whatever the value of z,

$$\int y\,dx = C + \alpha yz\left\{1 - \alpha\frac{dz}{dx} + \alpha^2\frac{d(z\,dz)}{dx^2}\right.$$
$$\left. - \alpha^3\frac{d[z\,d(z\,dz)]}{dx^3} + \cdots\right\}, \qquad (57)$$

where C is an arbitrary constant depending on the initial value of $\int y\,dx$.

The series (57) would no longer be convergent if the denominator of z in (56) were of the same order of magnitude as α, which would be the case when x only differed from $1/(1 + \mu)$ by a quantity of that order. The series was to be employed, there-

fore, only when that difference was very large with respect to α. But even that did not suffice. Since each differentiation increased the powers of the denominators of z and its derivatives by one, the term of which the coefficient was α^i had for denominator the term in z raised to the power z^{i-1}.

Thus, for the series to be convergent, α had to be not only much less than the denominator of z, but even much less than the square of the denominator. Under those conditions, the series (57) by very rapid approximations would give the value of the integral $\int y\,dx$ between the limits $x = 0$ and $x = 1/(1 + \mu) - \theta$ provided that α was much less than θ^2. If $x = 0$, then $y = 0$ and $z = 0$, and in that case (57) becomes

$$\int y\,dx = \frac{\alpha\mu^{q+1}[1-(1+\mu)\,\theta]^{p+1}\left(1+\dfrac{1+\mu}{\mu}\theta\right)^{q+1}}{\theta\,(1+\mu)^{p+q+3}}$$
$$\times\left\{1 - \frac{\alpha[\mu+(1+\mu)^2\theta^2]}{\theta^2(1+\mu)^3} + \cdots\right\}. \qquad (58)$$

That series gave the limits between which the value of $\int y\,dx$ was contained, a value less than the first term in the curled brackets and greater than the sum of the first two terms (OC, IX, 425).

A similar demonstration shows that the series (57) also gave values of $\int y\,dx$ from $x = 1/(1 + \mu) + \theta$ to $x = 1$. In showing that such was the case, Laplace proved that the more p and q were increased, the more α was diminished, and that the difference between P and unity was proportional to α, so that by increasing p and q, and thus diminishing α, the difference could be reduced below any given magnitude.

It remained to draw upon the data. Calculating the probability that the possibility of a male birth in Paris was greater than 0.5, he found it to be less than unity by the fraction 1.1521×10^{-13}. He further calculated that the probability that in any year baby boys would fail to exceed baby girls in number was 1/259 in Paris, whereas in London it was 1/12,416. Although the ratio of male to female births was only slightly higher in London, the probability of male preponderance approached certainty at a drastically increasing rate as the proportion grew. It would have been reasonable to bet that boys would outnumber girls in any of the next 179 years in Paris and in any of the next 8,605 in London. Here, then, Laplace had worked out a method for finding numerical solutions to a type of problem the analytical solutions of which contained terms raised to such high powers that the expressions became impracticable when the numbers were substituted in the formulas. Moreover, his method was applicable to practical calculation of future events given the experience of the past. In short, not only did he have a method for statistical inference in hypothetical circumstances, but he actually drew inferences in the area of population.

12. Generating Functions and Definite Integrals. Of the next two memoirs to be discussed, the first, "Mémoire sur les suites" ([*1782a*]), was entirely mathematical. The second, "Mémoire sur les approximations des formules qui sont fonctions de très grands nombres" ([*1785a*]), was largely so. Both were motivated mainly, though not exclusively, by probabilistic concerns. The former, which introduced the theory of generating functions, was particularly important to Laplace. Years later, when composing the *Théorie analytique des probabilités*, he subordinated all of the analytical part to the theory of generating functions and represented the whole subject as their field of application; the first part of Book I is in the main a reprinting of this memoir, incorporating clarifications and simplifications in detail and several important additions. He defined generating functions in much the same words in the opening pages of the *Théorie analytique* and of the "Mémoire sur les suites" (*OC*, VII, 7; *OC*, X, 5):

> Let y_x be any function of x. If there be formed the infinite series, $y_0 + y_1 t^1 + y_2 t^2 + y_3 t^3 + \cdots + y_x t^x + y_{x+1} t^{x+1} + \cdots + y_\infty t^\infty$, and u be designated the sum of that series, or (which comes to the same thing) the function of which the development forms the series, this function will be what I call the *generating function* of the variable y_x.

Thus, he explained, the generating function of a variable y_x is a function of t that, developed in powers of t, has that variable for the coefficient of t^x. Reciprocally, the corresponding variable of a generating function is the coefficient of t^x in the development of the function in powers of t. The exponent expressing the power of t then indicates the place that the variable y_x occupies in the series, which may also be extended indefinitely to the left according to negative powers of t.

Laplace regarded generating functions as something of a panacea for problems involving the development of functions in series and evaluation of the sums. Those procedures embraced nothing less than most of the possible applications of mathematics to nature. His memoir consists in showing how to apply the device to problems of interpolation both in convergent and recurrent series. As a corollary to the latter, he gave a method for solving the linear finite difference equations that express the relation between terms. From finite analysis he proceeded to the comparable infinitesimal expressions and from there to series involving two variables, recurro-recurrent as well as convergent in nature, observing by the way that he himself had initiated the theory of recurro-recurrent series. In the course of considering the solution of linear partial difference equations on which recurro-recurrent series depended, he had reduced the problem to one of infinitesimal differences by means of definite integrals involving a new variable. In effect, the technique results in finding discontinuous solutions to differential equations, the existence of which had emerged historically in the analysis of sound waves. Laplace reminded the reader that the integral of second-order partial differential equations contains two arbitrary functions in the form of differentials. Euler and Lagrange had been the ones to discover these mathematical objects in analyzing acoustical problems in which the movements of the air in transmitting sound were considered three-dimensionally. (This occasion was Laplace's first mention of the theory of sound.) It had been left to him, however, to find a general method for integrating second-order linear partial differential equations in the cases where that was possible and for identifying those cases in which it was not ([*1777a*]; see Section 7). Now he had found a method for integrating many such expressions by means of these definite integrals involving a new variable. The technique was further applicable to problems of vibrating cords, which in turn led to consideration of the employment of discontinuous functions in problems involving partial differences.

Thus, many of Laplace's existing analytical and probabilistic interests merged with certain of his future physical concerns in this memoir. What led him to the idea of generating functions may well have been further reflection on the calculus of differential operators (see Section 10). He mentioned at the outset how the relation between a generating function and its independent variable leads directly to the analogy between positive powers and derivatives and between negative powers and integrals. Lagrange had formulated that relation in a theorem that Laplace himself had demonstrated in a general manner. His calculus of generating functions is, in a sense, a calculus of exponents and characteristics (or operators) as well as of coefficients and variable quantities, and indeed he devoted Article X to deriving a theorem of Lagrange (*Oeuvres de Lagrange*, III, 450; cf. Section 10) in the form

$$'\Delta y_x = e^{\alpha \frac{dy_x}{dx}} - 1 \qquad (59)$$

by means of generating functions; the symbol $'\Delta y_x$ meaning that x varies by the quantity i.

An example will illustrate the method. Laplace analyzed the series formed by multiplying the terms of a convergent series by the terms of a geometric progression. The general term of the series produced would be $h^x y_x$ (y_x being the general term of the convergent series). Then u would be the sum of the infinite series

$$y_0 + y_1 ht + y_2 h^2 t^2 + y_3 h^3 t^3 + \cdots + y_x h^x t^x. \qquad (60)$$

It followed from the general analysis that he had already given of the relation between the coefficients of t and the corresponding powers of the variable that, in this example,

$$u\left(\frac{1}{t^i} - 1\right)^n = n\left[h^i\left(1 + \frac{1}{ht} - 1\right)^i - 1\right]^n. \qquad (61)$$

The coefficient of t^x on the left of that equation is the nth finite difference of $h^x y_x$, where x varies by the quantity i. Moreover, if the right-hand side of (61) is developed in powers of $\frac{1}{ht} - 1$, the coefficient of t^x in $u\left(\frac{1}{ht} - 1\right)^r$ will be $h^x \Delta^r y_x$, whatever the value of r. If the exponent n is negative instead of positive, the analysis will relate to integration instead of differentiation.

We do not know when Laplace resumed work upon the matter that had concerned him in a special case at the conclusion of the "Mémoire sur les probabilités" ([*1781a*]; see Section 11), namely numerical approximation of formulas that are functions of very large numbers; but four years had elapsed before he published his comprehensive treatment of the analytical aspects of the topic ([*1785a*]). It was chiefly, although not exclusively, in the theory of chance that analysis would often result in formulas impossible to use when large numbers were substituted in them. Only in two special cases, the product of the natural numbers 1, 2, 3, 4, $\cdots$, and determination of the middle term of a binomial raised to a high power, did techniques exist for readily achieving numerical solutions.

In the latter case, if the power were supposed even and equal to $2s$, that term would be, as everyone knew,

$$\frac{2s(2s-1)\,(2s-2)\,(2s-3)\cdots(s+1)}{1.2.3.4\cdots s}.$$

Even there, formulating the expression in numbers became difficult once s grew large. James Stirling, whose work Laplace consistently admired, had seen how to transform it into a series the sum of which was equivalent to $\sqrt{\pi}/2$ and which converged more rapidly as s grew larger. The transformation was remarkable in that it introduced a transcendent quantity into the investigation of purely algebraic quantities. It was still applicable only to special cases, however. Laplace himself had given a method in [*1781a*] for converting integrals of differential functions containing factors raised to very high powers into rapidly converging series. But he was busy with other matters, and only since then had further reflection shown him the way to extend the method generally to any functions involving very large numbers, thus reducing them to series that, even like the series of Stirling's theorem, become more convergent as the numbers increase.

Since the central difficulty lay in finding numerical solutions for complicated expressions containing many terms, the strategy had to be to transform such formulas into series that converged rapidly enough so that only the first few terms had to be considered. If each of them contained only a few factors, then it would not matter if they were raised to high powers, and resort to logarithms would yield solutions. On the face of it, there seemed no natural way to transform such complicated functions into convergent series. Reflecting, however, that differential expressions simple in form often yield just such functions on integration if the terms have large exponents, Laplace considered that complicated functions of any sort ought to be reducible to integrals of that type, which could then be transformed into convergent series. The problem had two aspects: on the one hand, to integrate by approximation differential equations involving functions that contain very large factors; and on the other, to convert the functions for which approximate values are required into integrals of this type.

Laplace expected that a solution to the former aspect would prove particularly valuable in estimating the probability of causes. The approximation involved series that complement each other: one type was to be employed for points far from the maximum value of the differential function, and the other was to be used for points close to it. The latter contained transcendent quantities, usually reducing to the form

$$\int e^{-t^2}\,dt. \qquad (62)$$

Since that integral, evaluated from $t = 0$ to $t = \infty$, equals $\sqrt{\pi}/2$, Stirling's theorem came out as a particular case of the general analysis.

As for transforming the approximate evaluation into the integration of differential expressions multiplied by factors raised to a high power, Laplace outlined a more indirect approach. The method consisted of representing complicated functions of s (where s is a large integer) by y_s, y'_s, y''_s, $\cdots$. These functions are to be supposed given by linear differential or difference equations of which the coefficients are rational functions of s. The equations are then manipulated so that

$$y_s = \int x^s \phi \, dx; \, y'_s = \int x^s \phi' \, dx; \cdots; \qquad (63)$$

and also so that they can be separated after integration by parts, one part coming under the integral sign and the other outside it. Equating the parts under the integral sign to zero then yields as many linear differential equations as there are variables ϕ, ϕ', ϕ'', $\cdots$, which can thereby be determined as functions of x. Turning to the parts outside the integral sign, they also may be equated to zero. When the arbitrary constants of integration in the values for ϕ, ϕ', ϕ'', $\cdots$, are eliminated, a definitive equation in x results. The roots of this equation then determine the limits between which the integrals $\int x^s \phi \, dx$, $\int x^s \phi' \, dx$, $\cdots$, are to be taken. It is very important to notice that the series obtained for y_s, y'_s, $\cdots$, hold good generally when the constants they contain change sign, because this circumstance greatly extends the applicability of the method, although as a result of such change of sign, the definitive equation in x, which gives the limits of the integrals, no longer has several real roots. The most serious difficulty to be overcome in applying this analysis arises from the nature of the differential equations in ϕ, ϕ', ϕ'', $\cdots$, which often cannot be integrated. That obstacle might normally be surmounted through representing the functions y_s, y'_s, $\cdots$, in terms of multiple integrals such as $\int x^s x'^s \phi \, dx \, dx'$, $\int x^s x'^s \phi' \, dx \, dx'$, $\cdots$. The variables ϕ, ϕ', $\cdots$ might then be determined by equations of a lower order that could be integrated. All these possibilities being considered, Laplace claimed that the analysis might be employed generally for very complicated functions represented by ordinary or partial difference or differential equations—or for all the normal uses of analysis ([1785a]; OC, X, 213: cf. Section 29).

He reserved his own application for a sequel ([1786b]) to this memoir, which had grown very lengthy. Reading the continuation before the

Académie des Sciences on 25 and 28 June 1785 (49), Laplace again reviewed the epistemological status of probability. It was there that he first employed phrasing of which the second sentence is famous from the Essai philosophique thirty years later (OC, X, 296; VII, viii):

> The word "chance" then expresses only our ignorance of the causes of the phenomena that we observe to occur and to succeed one another in no apparent order.
> Probability is relative in part to that ignorance and in part to our knowledge.

For the first sentence, however, Laplace substituted the following in the Essai philosophique: "The curve described by a simple molecule of air or of vapor is regulated in as certain a manner as the planetary orbits; there is no difference between them except that which our ignorance creates there" (cf. [1810d], p. 100).

We come now to the final technical factor that drew Laplace to the study of population statistics. In order to appreciate its role in his mathematical development, let us take stock of how far he had prevailed against difficulties still thwarting probabilistic analysis as he had outlined them at the beginning of the "Mémoire sur les probabilités" ([1781a]). He had there found in birth data a basis for determining the law according to which a succession of events gives access to knowledge of causes in a real case. In the intervening two memoirs he had developed generating functions and the technique for numerical evaluation of integrals of differential equations containing terms with very large exponents. It remained to put on a footing more realistic than the hypothetical case of lightly loaded dice the class of problems calling for the probability of complex events compounded from simple ones the respective possibilities of which are unknown quantities, and reciprocally for estimating the number of observations necessary in order that a predicted result might have a specified probability. It was in furnishing data for these calculations that the record of births, with its slight but known disproportion between male and female, proved to be such a valuable resource. Laplace devoted the remainder of the memoir to resolving from this point of view, and with the use of his improved techniques, the population problems that he had already handled ([1781a]; see Section 11), arriving in most instances at identical values.

13. Population. In 1786 Laplace finally addressed himself directly to demography, not merely as a convenient repository of problems and examples but as a subject in its own right. He then published a study of the vital statistics of Paris from 1771 to 1784, together with an estimate of the total population of France over a two-year period ([1786c]). As yet there was no actual census, which did not begin until 1801 under Napoleonic administration. Late eighteenth-century demography proposed to reach estimates of the population through determining the factor by which the average number of annual births was to be multiplied in order to approximate the total. Laplace's memoir consists of an application of the rule for predicting future events from the observation of those past. As always, direct numerical calculation was impractical. The problem was precisely the sort, however, that could be managed by the technique of predicting probable error and computing how far observations would need to be extended in order to reduce its range to specified limits. Samplings showed the number 26 to be the multiplier to be applied to the figure for annual births in order to give the population at any given time. Applying it to the average annual birth figure for the years 1781 and 1782 gave 25,299,417 for the population of France. In order to reduce to 1,000 to 1 the odds against making an error no greater than half a million in the estimate, the sampling that had established the factor of 26 would have needed to consist of 771,469 inhabitants. If the multiplier had been taken to be 26-1/2, then the figure for the population would have come to 25,785,944, and the sampling would have needed to be 817,219 in order to maintain the same odds against the same error. Faced with those results, Laplace recommended that the count be carried to 1,000,000 or even 1,200,000 in order to assure a degree of accuracy compatible with the importance of the information.

For the information was indeed important. Population, Laplace observed, is an index to national prosperity. A comparison of its variations in the light of antecedent events would serve as the most accurate measure of the effect of physical or moral agencies upon human welfare. Aware of the guidance that such information might provide to those responsible for public policy, the Academy had decided (Laplace noted) to insert each year in its published memoirs the summary of births, marriages, and deaths throughout the kingdom. In consequence of this decision, the Academy's last volumes of memoirs in the old regime contain annual installments of an "Essai pour connaître la population du royaume" (*MARS* [1783/1786], 703–718; [1784/1787], 577–592; [1785/1788], 661–689;

[1786/1788], 703–717; [1787/1789], 601–610; [1788/1791], 755–767). Its purpose was to estimate the populations of municipalities and regions marked out on the Cassini map of France through multiplying the average number of annual births in each locality by a factor of 26. Citations to this compilation usually attribute it to the joint authorship of Condorcet, Laplace, and Dionis du Séjour, following therein the table of contents of the volumes themselves. That attribution is in error. Those three served merely as a commission to receive and communicate to the Academy the work of La Michodière, a magistrate who at the behest of the government was continuing research that he had undertaken at his own initiative some thirty years earlier in Auvergne and the Lyonnais, where he was then intendant.

There is no evidence that Laplace wrote further on probability prior to his series of lectures at the abortive École Normale in 1795 (see Section 20), one of which was the nucleus of the *Essai philosophique*, and (although there are probabilistic considerations in *Mécanique céleste*, notably in Book X) there is no evidence of his resuming sustained work until twenty-five years later, when he published a memoir ([1810b]) that derived the central-limit theorem for the reduction of error from his method for approximating the evaluation of formulas containing terms raised to very high powers (see Section 25). Let us turn back, therefore, to two sets of interests that occupied him concurrently with probability and with each other, cometary theory and his collaboration with Lavoisier in the chemical physics of heat.

14. Determination of the Orbits of Comets. Laplace's interest in the problem of the curves described by comets antedated the only publication he had yet devoted to these bodies, namely his probabilistic calculation that the cause behind the configuration of the planetary system fails to account for the distribution of the inclinations of the planes of cometary orbits ([1776d]; see Section 6). Earlier in 1776 he had involved himself in a controversy that became very acrimonious with Rudjer Boscović, then resident in Paris. In 1771 Boscović had presented to the Académie des Sciences a refinement of the method for determining cometary orbits that he had first advanced in 1746 and had advocated ever since ("De orbitis cometarum determinandis," *SE*, 6 [1774], 198–215).

In the case of comets, uncertainty about the nature of the conic sections they describe, combined with the irregularity of opportunities for observation, left a much wider gap between theoretical and practical astronomy than in the case of planets. In practice, the trajectories of the known comets had been mapped empirically, by fitting the curves to as many observations as could be recorded in the periods of visibility. Theoretically, on the supposition started by Newton (and widely adopted afterward) that the observable trajectory is a parabola approximately coinciding with a highly eccentric ellipse, three observations should suffice to determine the curve. The problem was how to arrive at it mathematically. At the very end of *De systemate mundi*, Newton gave an approximate solution that depended on considering a very short element of the trajectory as if it were a straight line that the comet traverses at constant velocity (*Principia mathematica*, Florian Cajori, ed., II [Berkeley, Calif., 1962], 619–626).

Bošcović's memoir consists in an analytical development of this, the standard approach, issuing in an elaborate sixth-degree equation of motion. According to Laplace's own account ([*1784b*]; *OC*, X, 93), it was on reading this memoir, published in 1774 in volume **6** of the *Savants étrangers* series — along with two of his own early papers ([*1774b*] and [*1774c*]) — that he realized that the entire method involved a fatal fallacy. Treating the interval between the first and third observations as a first-order infinitesimal entailed neglecting second-order quantities that depend on the curvature of the orbit and on changes in velocity of the comet. At the same time, the position of the (supposedly) rectilinear fragment of trajectory that the comet is observed to describe has to be determined by second derivatives of its geocentric latitude and longitude. Thus, second-order quantities were both neglected and employed.

From the floor of the Academy, Laplace apparently read out a criticism of the Bošcović memoir, castigating all such procedures as "faulty, illusory, and erroneous." We do not know the precise date of his attack, which Bošcović took as a derogation of Newton and an insult to himself, demanding the appointment of a commission to adjudicate the dispute and the exchange with Laplace that ensued. The report of that commission, consisting of Vandermonde, d'Arcy, Bezout, Bossut, and Dionis du Séjour, is recorded in the minute book of the Academy (*PV* [5 June 1776], fols. 172–177). The members acknowledged that Laplace was right analytically, while deploring the abrasive manner in which he had couched his criticism and regretting that Bošcović had taken it personally. Both parties were counseled to bring their findings before the public rather than to quarrel in camera.

Evidently, however, Laplace could not let the matter drop. On 19 June he read a further set of remarks (*ibid.*, fol. 191). We do not know what they contained, except that now he also had Lalande in his sights, and another commission was appointed to resolve the affair. Its report has not survived. Years later, in the opening paragraph of the "Mémoire sur la détermination des orbites des comètes" ([*1784b*]; *OC*, X, 93–94) Laplace recalled how he had proved that the method he was criticizing was so bad that it was capable, in an extreme instance, of reversing the apparent direction of a comet's motion from retrograde to direct.

Having refrained from pressing the investigation at that time, he now resumed it, stimulated by the recent work of Lagrange and Dionis du Séjour. As it was analytically impossible to operate with three widely separated observations, the standard method necessarily depended on three observations of positions that were fairly close together. Inevitably, therefore, small errors of observation would affect the results very considerably. Compensation of errors was then attempted, not by multiplying observations but by increasing the number of terms in the series that expressed the result, in order that it might approximate more closely to the truth. The technique was mathematically laborious and of little practical use. Seeking a simpler way to correct for observational error, Laplace saw that closely contiguous observations could serve that purpose if their number were increased. Standard methods of interpolation could then be applied to determine the observational data needed for a solution. The choice of parameters being arbitrary, he preferred to work with the geocentric longitude and latitude of the comet at a given moment and with the first and second derivatives of these quantities with respect to time. These data were the easiest to manipulate analytically, and he could obtain simple formulas that became more precise the larger the number and the greater the accuracy of the observations.

This approach to the determination of cometary orbits had the further advantage that observations separated by as much as 30° or 40° might be employed. In contrast to the established procedure, in which the analysis was an approximation and the observations had to be supposed perfectly exact, Laplace characterized his method as one in which the analysis is rigorous and the observations are acknowledged to be approximations. The second-order differential equations of motion of a comet around the sun at the focus of a conic section yielded directly a seventh-degree equation determining the distance of the comet from the earth (*ibid.; OC*, X, 110):

$$[\rho^2 + 2R\rho \cos \theta \cos (A - \alpha) + R^2]^3 \times (\mu R^2 \rho + 1)^2 = R^6 \qquad (64)$$

where ρ is the comet-earth distance, α the geocentric longitude, θ the latitude, R the radius vector of the earth, r the radius vector of the comet, A the heliocentric longitude of the earth, and where $\mu\rho = d\rho/dt$. Since the theory holds for any conic section, the supposition that the orbit is a parabola and the major axis infinite yields a new sixth-degree equation for determining the distance of the comet from the earth (*ibid.; OC*, X, 121):

$$[\rho^2 + 2R\rho \cos \theta \cos (A - \alpha) + R^2] \times \left(m\rho^2 + n\rho + \frac{1}{R^2} \right)^2 - 4 = 0 \qquad (65)$$

where, besides the above, m and n are abbreviations representing respectively

$$u^2 + \left(\frac{d\theta}{dt}\right)^2 + \left(\frac{d\alpha}{dt}\right)^2 \cos^2\theta$$

and

$$\left(2u \cos \theta - 2\frac{d\theta}{dt} \sin \theta\right)$$
$$\times \left[(R' - 1) \cos (A - \alpha) - \frac{\sin (A - \alpha)}{R} \right]$$
$$+ 2\frac{d\alpha}{dt} \cos \theta \left[(R' - 1) \sin (A - \alpha) + \frac{\cos (A - \alpha)}{R} \right],$$

and R' is the radius vector of the earth at longitude $90° + A$. It was possible to combine (64) and (65) and to obtain a linear equation for the distance and an equation of the conditions that the data must satisfy in the case of a parabolic orbit. But the calculation was difficult, and it was more direct to satisfy (64) or (65) by making trials with the data.

Since the problem of determining parabolic cometary orbits could be formulated in a system of equations exceeding the number of unknowns by one, there was a choice of ways to determine the distance of the comet from the earth. The important tactic was to select a method that would minimize the effect of observational error. The second derivatives of the geocentric latitude and longitude $(d^2\theta/dt^2)$ and $(d^2\alpha/dt^2)$ were the quantities most affected. Either but not both might be eliminated, and Laplace formulated two further sets of equa-

tions to be used alternatively, according to whether the second derivative of longitude or of latitude was the greater. The former ratio obtained in the case of comets of which the orbital plane was close to the ecliptic, and Laplace was pleased to discover that his first set of equations was nothing other than a translation into the language of analysis of what Newton had demonstrated synthetically in the *Principia mathematica*, Book III, Proposition XLI.

Although Laplace's method of determining cometary orbits was largely superseded by those of Olbers in the 1790's and of Gauss after 1801, its formulation marks an important stage in his career. It was the first piece of work that brought him into immediate contact with workaday observational astronomers. Following the analytical part of the memoir, the eighth article (*ibid.; OC*, X, 127–141) contains instructions for applying the method to comets themselves and even gives numerical examples. Prior to publication, Laplace sent a copy to the Abbé Pingré (*34*), who immediately applied it to computations in his monumental *Cométographie* (1783–1784). The memoir closes with a contribution by Méchain further illustrating the technique in the determination of a comet, the second that he discovered in the year 1781 (*ibid.; OC*, X, 141–146).

Laplace must have requested that computation from Méchain shortly after reading the draft of the analytical parts of the memoir before the Academy on 21 March 1781 (*34*). An entry in the *procès-verbaux* of 2 May (*35*) probably refers to that. Over three years elapsed before the memoir was published, after a delay rather longer than would be expected from the normal academic lag. The explanation may well be that Laplace became involved with William Herschel's discovery of an object that turned out to be the planet Uranus, initially taken for a comet. Herschel made the observation in Bath on 13 March 1781, and Laplace could scarcely have heard of it—and certainly cannot have been influenced in his treatment even if he had—when he delivered his paper eight days later. On 13 June, however, he read a note (*36*) to the Academy reporting that he had tried his general method on the new comet but found that neither it nor that of Lagrange—nor any other that he knew—was applicable to the present object, of which the apparent motion in latitude was almost indetectable relative to the motion in longitude (even so the notion of there being an unknown planet did not then occur to Laplace). He had been trying to find a new method by combining his equations in a different manner and believed that he had succeeded. He planned to read his investigations shortly but needed time to complete the calculations before the comet emerged from the sun, where it was presently hidden. On 28 July (*37*) he reported those calculations, still taking the object for a comet. Not until a year and a half later, on 22 January 1783 (*40*), did he make written reference to "Herschel's planet," the ephemerides of which he had been calculating in collaboration with Méchain. Their results showed it to be identical with the supposed star that Mayer had recorded in 1756 and that had mysteriously disappeared (*42*).

In the meantime, Laplace had become increasingly drawn into another aspect of empirical science, one involving hand as well as eye, and had entered into problems of physics in collaboration with Lavoisier.

15. Lavoisier and Laplace: Chemical Physics of Heat. Henry Guerlac has published a monograph (M:[1976]) on the investigations that Lavoisier carried out jointly with Laplace, beginning with phenomena of vaporization and evaporative cooling. The earliest record of Laplace's interest in the problem, or indeed in any physical experiment, is an entry (*22*) in the *procès-verbaux* of the Académie des Sciences. On 9 April 1777 at the Easter meeting, an occasion always open to the public, Laplace read a paper on "the nature of the fluid that remains in the receiver of the pneumatic machine." No trace of the text remains, but it is evident from the Lavoisier materials that the experiments pertained to determinations by the two colleagues of the effects of varying degrees of temperature and pressure on the vaporization of water, ether, and alcohol. Guerlac considers it virtually certain that Lavoisier instigated the trials.

Lavoisier and Laplace never published the memoir that they intended. They probably never wrote it, but their procedures and conclusion are evident from Lavoisier's other writings (M: Guerlac [1976], 198–199). The experiments gave Lavoisier the physical framework that he needed to come forward in November 1777 with a much rumored criticism of the phlogiston theory coupled with a statement of his own hypothesis on combustion and calcination. In a preface drafted in 1778 for a projected but phantom second volume of his *Opuscules* of 1774, Lavoisier wrote of his intention to practice so far as possible "la méthode des géomètres" (*ibid.*, 215–216).

As for Laplace, apart from the intrinsic interest of the work itself, collaboration with Lavoisier, almost six years his senior, offered him the chance to be more than a mathematician. It associated him with the one person who was clearly emerging as the scientific leader of the Academy in their generation, the newly appointed administrator of the Arsenal and reformer of the munitions industry, with influential connections in the worlds of government and finance.

That much transpired in 1777, and although Laplace and Lavoisier served together on occasional committees of the Academy and must have been in each other's company at its semiweekly meetings, they seem to have suspended active collaboration and to have resumed it only in 1781. During that summer they worked together to verify a design for fabricating a barometer with a flat meniscus imagined by Dom Casbois, a Benedictine in Metz (*ibid.*, 224). The occasion was Laplace's first recorded scrutiny of the problem of capillary action. Much more immediately, the barometric question led them during the winter of 1781–1782 to determinations of the thermal expansibility of glass as well as mercury and other metals (*38*). The motivation was both instrumental and theoretical. The experience stood them in good stead in the early 1790's, when both were serving on the commission charged with fabricating the standard weights and measures for the revolutionary metric system (see Section 18). Already, in their registers they were using decimal subdivisions of linear and gravimetric units. Along with these practical questions of measurement, the investigation set them both to thinking on heat capacities in general.

Their physical interests transcended heat. Electricity offered the companion example of a subtle fluid for which bodies have characteristic capacities. It was natural for Lavoisier and Laplace to explore the analogy between heat and electricity when Volta came to Paris early in 1782 for an extended visit. He brought with him an electroscope for detecting weak charges and was then harboring the theory that electrical charges in the atmosphere might be produced by vaporization. Lavoisier designed and had constructed a condenser with a marble plate to detect such charges, and Volta tried it in the company of Laplace. Conditions were bad and the experiment failed. Laplace and Lavoisier then tried it again on their own (*39*) and published a brief note on what they construed as positive effects ([*1784c*]).

Even then, they were planning the campaign of their experiments on heat, and Lavoisier must have commissioned construction of the famous ice calorimeters at much the same time. The *Mémoire sur la chaleur* first appeared in a separate printing ([*1783a*]). Laplace's influence was clearly paramount in its theoretical aspect, extending to the idea for measuring a quantity of heat by the amount of ice that it would melt and also to the choice of many experiments. The memoir consists of four articles. The first discusses the nature of heat and its quantification; the second, the determination of specific heats of selected substances and also certain heats of reaction; the third, theoretical consequences and a program for a chemical physics; and the fourth, the application of the techniques to the study of combustion and respiration.

Article I opens with a frequently paraphrased contrast between the fluid (soon called the "caloric") and the mechanical theories of heat, which hypotheses are said to be the only conceivable alternatives. It has generally been supposed that the contrast here was also between the opinions of the two authors, and there is no doubt that Lavoisier preferred the former. Moreover, Laplace would certainly have been the one to compose the passage elaborating the kinetic theory. According to that school, the quantity of heat in bodies is measured by the sum of the vis viva (mv^2) of the vibratory motions of their particles, and the conservation of heat in transfers is a form of the conservation of vis viva in gradual changes of motion. Robert Fox, however, has recently raised the question whether Laplace ever did adopt that position for himself (M: Fox [1971], 30). If that was his view at the time, he certainly changed it for the physics of his later years, when he consistently preferred the caloric model for analysis. In this connection, it is to be remarked that conservation of vis viva did not play an important part in his mechanics, any more than it had for Newton; and the body of the memoir consistently and naturally employs the vocabulary of the fluid theory. The contrast concludes with the authors' abstention from choosing between the alternatives. "Perhaps," it is said, "they both obtain at the same time" ([1783a]; OC, X, 153), an aside about which it may be worth remarking that in Laplace's final view caloric like other subtle fluids is itself particulate. In any case, the only admissible propositions are those that save the phenomena under both theories.

Foremost among those principles are conservation and reversibility in exchanges of heat within a system of bodies. Definitions are needed. *Chaleur libre*, or free heat, is that portion of the total heat contained in a body that may pass to another. Since different quantities of heat are required to raise the temperature of the same mass of different bodies equally, some unit must be designated with which to quantify these comparisons. The heat absorbed in raising one pound of water one degree makes a convenient amount, in terms of which the "specific heats" of other bodies may be expressed. Although probably not invariant with temperature, specific heats may be taken as nearly constant for the range between the freezing and boiling points of water ($0° - 80°$ on the Réaumur scale).

It is to be noticed that the notion of specific heat is not quite the modern way of putting it, although it comes to the same thing when reduced to unit mass and referred to the amount for water as unit heat. A more serious reservation must be entered, however, lest this lead to anachronism. The free heat of a body is only that portion of its absolute quantity which may be exchanged with other bodies in consequence of differences of temperature, change of state, or chemical reaction. It is also the only manifestation of heat that is accessible to measurement, which, moreover, is in degrees of the thermometer. Here the reader must be especially careful to avoid thinking of the absolute quantity in terms of a hypothetical scale of absolute temperature, for there is no anticipation of Kelvin. The conception is that of the eighteenth-century theory of matter, which distinguishes between the electricity, heat, ether, or whatever, that is "fixed" in bodies, and the portion that may be disengaged in natural phenomena or in experiments.

These presuppositions in no way vitiated the design or execution of the experimental program. The problem of measuring specific heats in the simplest case of mixing two miscible substances was formulated algebraically, no doubt by Laplace. He let m and m' be the respective masses, a and a' the initial temperatures, and b the temperature resulting from mixture. Then the ratio of specific heats, q and q' is given by

$$\frac{q}{q'} = \frac{m'(b-a')}{m(a-b)}. \tag{66}$$

So straightforward an approach was inapplicable, however, to determinations of heat effects involving chemical combination, combustion and respiration, or change of state, the three most important and interesting processes. Faced with this limitation, the authors imagined a method of general applicability. The amount of ice melted in any process involving the evolution of heat could serve to measure the quantity. The notion is introduced by means of an image that bespeaks Laplace and mathematical modeling more obviously than does the elementary algebraic formulation for specific heats in mixture. We are to imagine a hollow sphere of ice with a shell thick enough to insulate the inner surface from the heat of the surroundings. Suppose a warm body were to be introduced in principle into the cavity. Its heat would melt away a portion of the inner surface until it had cooled to zero, and the weight of water would be proportional to the heat required to accomplish that effect.

Lavoisier commissioned the instruments and later named them calorimeters; two were made, each about three feet high. Air could be admitted into one for respiration experiments. A concentric nest of containers like an ice-cream freezer was packed with ice around a central receptacle. A basket could be suspended inside to hold the objects under study. Ice lining the inner shell served for the melting layer of the model. The water was run off through a petcock and weighed. The authors established first that the heat needed to melt a pound of ice will raise the temperature of a pound of water from 0° to 60° R. Here again, it must be emphasized that the concepts of intensity and quantity of heat were not yet differentiated. Ice, as they put it, "absorbs 60 degrees of heat in melting" (*ibid.; OC*, X, 167). Thereupon the remainder of their second, entirely experimental article reports the determination of certain specific heats, heats of reaction, and animal heats.

The third article is pure Laplace and exhibits both his capacity to analyze a set of physical phenomena in a highly abstract manner and also the limitations inherent in even the most sophisticated notion of a general theory of heat in the absence of any notion of thermodynamics. Not that Laplace fancied himself in a position to attain such a theory, although what he thought he needed was to know (1) whether specific heat increases with temperature at a uniform rate for all substances; (2) the absolute quantity of heat contained in bodies at given temperatures; and (3) the quantities of free heat given off or absorbed in chemical reactions. Lacking such data, which only a very elaborate program of investigation could work up, he would simply examine a few problems raised by experiments that the two authors had performed, beginning with the second topic just mentioned, the absolute or total quantity of heat in bodies.

Clearly, its amount is considerable, even at 0° on the thermometer. We wish to know that amount in degrees of the thermometer, but experiments such as those just tried on specific heat could form no basis for calculation, unless it was legitimate to suppose that the specific heats of bodies are proportional to their total heats. That would be a very risky relation to assume without examination.

Moreover, there was unfortunately no way to get at it from the values determined by simple mixtures of substances at different temperatures; all that happens there is the exchange of heat. The case is comparable to local exchanges of motion, which tell the investigator nothing of the absolute motion of the earth through space.

There might be a deeper way, however, leading through chemistry. Since the heat of reaction is not the consequence of mere inequality of temperature, it might furnish a basis for relating change of temperature to absolute heat. As usual, Laplace's approach was analytic. He let x be the ratio of the absolute heat contained in water at 0° to the amount that can raise its temperature by 1° (note that he was not yet sufficiently prepared with his own definitions to call the latter "specific heat" and designate it unity). Then, the total heat contained in a pound of water at 0° would melt $x/60$ pounds of ice. Consider any two substances at 0°, m and n being their respective weights, and a and b the ratio of the heat contained in each to the heat contained in a pound of water. They react chemically, and the heat produced when the products are cooled down to 0° melts g pounds of ice. The heat of reaction alone is sufficient to melt y pounds (y being negative if the reaction is endothermic). Finally, c is the ratio of the heat contained in the mingled products of reaction to that in a pound of water. With these parameters, Laplace formulated and equated two expressions for the quantity of ice that would be melted by the residual free heat:

$$\frac{(ma+nb)x}{60}+y = \frac{(m+n)\,cx}{60}+g, \qquad (67)$$

whence

$$x = \frac{60(g-y)}{m(a-c)+n(b-c)}. \qquad (68)$$

Here x represents the number of degrees of heat contained by water at 0°. But how are numbers to be substituted for a, b, c, and y? Two hypotheses made evaluation possible. The first, conservation of free heat in chemical combinations, was generally admitted. The second, that the specific heats of substances are proportional to their absolute heat content, was precisely the risky assumption that could be tested from data tabulated in the preceding article. If it were correct, then $y = 0$, and

$$x = \frac{60g}{m(a-c)+n(b-c)}. \qquad (69)$$

Those data contain values for the specific heats,

a, *b*, and *c*, in a few selected instances; and if the proportionality of specific heat to total heat was a justifiable hypothesis, all of the different cases ought to give the same value for *x*. Alas, they did not.

It is true—Laplace immediately went on (*ibid.; OC*, X, 178)—that a very small correction in each, no more than 1/40, would make them all satisfy the relation. Such a correction would be less than the margin of experimental error. Other considerations made such an exercise in curve-fitting unpromising, however. Endothermic reactions could not at all be accommodated, and neither could the phenomenon of the dilation of solids on heating. It was very probable that heat is fixed thereby, even as in change of state, although gradually and undetectably; and this reflection gave another reason to surmise that specific heats do increase with temperature but at a different rate for each substance.

Finally, Laplace turned to change of state itself, in order to consider what such episodes can reveal about equilibrium conditions in heat. Again, it was the analogy that is mechanical, rather than the theory of heat itself. Just as there are several positions of equilibrium for (say) a rectangular parallelepiped (resting on its side, balanced on one end, and so on), there may be several conditions around a change of state in which heat is in equilibrium, each involving different physical arrangements of the molecules and different distributions between the portions of the heat that are going into cooling and into freezing. As usual, Laplace formulated analytical expressions. He then adduced the example of super-cooling followed by a sudden crystallization creating a new equilibrium. We need not follow the algebra. The interesting feature is the glimpse that the discussion gives into Laplace's preoccupation with forces and structures at the molecular level. The mutual affinity of molecules of water draws them together on freezing and frees the heat that is keeping them apart. Thus, it seemed probable that their arrangement when frozen is that in which the force of affinity is at its most effective. Hence, it is natural that the surest means of inducing a supercooled sample to freeze is to introduce a bit of ice. The same holds true in all crystallizations.

More generally, and here Laplace laid down a program for research, study of the equilibrium between heat, which tends to separate molecules, and affinity, which draws them together, might well offer a method for comparing the intensities of these forces of affinity. For example, a certain mass of ice plunged into an acid would be melted to the point at which the acid was sufficiently weakened so that its attraction for the molecules of ice would be balanced by their mutual forces of adherence. That point would depend also on the temperature. The further below zero it fell, the higher would be the concentration at which the acid ceases to melt ice. It would thus be possible to construct a statical scale expressing the force of the affinity of the acid for water in terms of degrees of the thermometer. If this procedure were to be followed with solutions of every sort, the relative mutual affinities of all bodies could be stated numerically. But, our author breaks off, this is a major subject; another memoir would be devoted to it.

We shall not consider the final article, in which Lavoisier drew the threads together for the theory of combustion and respiration. Guerlac's monograph shows how it prepared the ground for the "Réflexions sur le phlogistique" (1786) and how, more generally, the further collaboration with Laplace styled the aspiration to make of chemistry in its revolution a mathematical science. Our concern is with Laplace. There are indications that just before undertaking this research, he had been somewhat on-again, off-again in his commitment. In a letter of 7 March 1782 he asked Lavoisier to release him from their agreement to work together (M: Guerlac, 240). On 21 August 1783 a covering letter to Lagrange (*Oeuvres de Lagrange*, XIV, 123–124), enclosing a finished copy of the memoir, was defensive about the time that he had invested in *physique*. Nevertheless, the passages on heat and affinity just discussed are evidence that the work had finally gripped his interest and carried him into the first stages of his physics of interparticulate forces. Only with Laplace, indeed, did chemical affinities begin to be seriously considered as physical forces of attraction. In the preface to the work to be discussed next, *Théorie du mouvement et de la figure elliptique des planètes* ([*1784a*]), Laplace referred to the experiments with Lavoisier and repeated the reflection that equilibrium between the attractive force of affinity and the repulsive force of heat might one day furnish analysis with the handle on chemistry that the discovery of gravitation had afforded to the mathematicians who had perfected astronomy since Newton. It also remained to determine the laws of force responsible for the physical effects of solidity in bodies, of crystallization, of the refraction and diffraction of light, and of capillary action.

Laplace continued working with Lavoisier into 1784, when the treatise just mentioned was published. They then began the program of research that he had imagined on affinity. They repeated, largely at his insistence, measurements of the heat generated by the combustion of charcoal, phosphorus, and other substances. The joint paper reporting those experiments was not written until 1793 and appeared after Lavoisier's execution ([*1793d*]). Laplace also worked with Lavoisier on the closely related combustion of hydrogen to produce water. He strengthened Lavoisier's hand in the battle against the phlogistonists by setting him straight on the source of hydrogen when acids act on metals. The gas comes from the acid and is not to be taken for phlogiston escaping from the metal (M: Guerlac, 265). Thereafter, however, his own affinities seem to have drawn him rather toward Berthollet in his chemical interests. But we must turn outward now, from particles to stars, from physics and chemistry to astronomy again.

16. Attraction of Spheroids. It is significant that the paragraph just discussed on physical and chemical forces should have figured in the opening of the *Théorie du mouvement et de la figure elliptique des planètes* ([*1784a*]), for that work is very revealing in other important ways of the continuity and persistence of Laplace's interests. It was his first separate publication, and the preface was his first writing suited to the comprehension of laymen. It consists of a summary view of the world in nontechnical language and might easily be taken for a prospectus of the *Exposition du système du monde*. He began by explaining how he came to write the book at the behest of an honorary member of the Academy, Jean-Baptiste-Gaspard Bochart de Saron, a magistrate of the Parlement of Paris and (although Laplace did not put it this way) one of several patrons of science who also contributed to its content. That Bochart de Saron should have commissioned the work and personally subsidized publication is the clearest evidence that Laplace's qualities had come to be recognized in high places. Long ago, he said, he had conceived the notion of drawing into a single work an exposition of the way in which planetary paths and figures follow mathematically from the law of gravity. It seems probable that he was referring here to one of the papers of his youth, "Une théorie générale du mouvement des planètes" (*9*), which he had submitted to the Academy in November 1771. But he would never have composed the treatise had Bochart de Saron not encouraged him on several occasions to show how the general properties of elliptical and parabolic motion may be derived from the second-order differential equations that determine the motion of celestial bodies.

That exposition occupies Part I of the treatise

and, unlike the preface, is addressed to mathematically — and not merely verbally — literate readers. It has the quality of a textbook in the rational mechanics of the solar system limited to the principal motions of the celestial bodies and might appear to consist of a sketch for Books I and II of the *Mécanique céleste*. Besides that, Laplace explained certain of the techniques that he had imagined for achieving approximate solutions to equations that defied rigorous integration, and he also included a set of calculations to determine the orbit of Uranus. This topic bulks rather larger than its importance in the solar system would have warranted. It would appear that Laplace took the occasion to publish an analysis that he had submitted to the Academy on 22 January 1783 (*40*), in which he recognized that the object discovered by William Herschel in March 1781 was a planet and not a comet, as was first thought. Beyond that, he reprinted much of his memoir ([*1784b*]; see Section 14) on the determination of cometary orbits — or rather, preprinted it, since the memoir, although composed in 1781, came out some months later than the treatise. There is no other novelty in this first part, and Laplace simply hoped that the treatment would be pleasing to mathematicians and astronomers.

Part II, subtitled "De la figure des planètes" and addressed "uniquely to mathematicians" ([*1784a*], p. xxi), is quite another matter. Laplace there resumed investigating the laws of gravitational attraction of spheroids in a far more abstract manner than he had in his earlier pieces on the figure of the earth and on the oscillations of the tides ([*1778a*], [*1779a*], [*1779b*]); see Section 8). At the same time, the mathematical problems are of a more specific nature, and it is clear that he had matured his approach since the memoir on the precession of the equinoxes ([*1780c*]). In retrospect, the most interesting feature of the entire treatise is bound to be the emergence of the concept of what is now called potential, although that name was not given to the sum or integral of the action of the elements of an attracting body upon an external point until 1828, when George Green adopted Poisson's application of the expression for it to electrostatic and magnetic effects. There is no reason to suppose that here, at the outset, Laplace thought the notion more signal than other main aspects of his treatise.

In all these researches on attraction, Laplace played leapfrog with Legendre in a manner very like his relation of collaboration and competition with Lagrange over the integral calculus of planetary theory. In the present treatise, he referred ([*1784a*], pp. 96–97) to a formulation by Legendre that he had seen in the latter's "Attraction des sphéroïdes homogènes," which memoir was not published until 1785 (*SE*, **10** [1785], 411–434). Legendre for his part there attributed to a communication from Laplace in 1783 the notion that he developed, by way of generating functions, into the polynomials later named for Legendre; on this topic, see (N: Burckhardt [1908], pt. 5, 367–397). Legendre was not yet a member of the Academy, and the exchange must have occurred in connection with Laplace's preparation of a report on the memoir on behalf of Bezout, d'Alembert, and himself, who constituted the committee to which it was referred (*41*). Whatever these priorities may have been, Laplace in the treatise under discussion took as his point of departure the equation for a second-order surface where the origin of coordinates is the center of the spheroid,

$$x^2 + my^2 + nz^2 = k^2, \qquad (70)$$

m, *n*, and *k* being any constants. For the attraction that the enclosed solid exerts on an external point, he then formulated the integral (*ibid.*, 69)

$$V = \int \frac{dM}{(a-x')^2 + (b-y')^2 + (c-z')^2}, \qquad (71)$$

where *dM* is the mass of a particle of the solid with coordinates *x'*, *y'*, and *z'*, and *a*, *b*, and *c* are the coordinates of the external point. Then, when the attraction is decomposed along the three principal coordinates,

$$A = -\frac{\partial V}{\partial a}; \quad B = -\frac{\partial V}{\partial b}; \quad \text{and } C = -\frac{\partial V}{\partial c}. \quad (72)$$

Applying the analysis, Laplace began by looking backward to Newton's *Principia* rather than forward and by showing that the value of *V* is the same as if all the mass of the spheroid were concentrated at the center of gravity. In seeking to determine that value in a general manner capable of giving numerical solutions, Laplace turned to polar coordinates and expanded the transformed expression into an infinite series that could be evaluated by approximation. Wishing to achieve a rigorous solution, he in effect reverted to a strategy that he had employed in a fragmentary analysis of 1778, wherein he first investigated the attraction between a spheroid and an external point. At that time he had the rings of Saturn in mind and inverted the problem to consider the attraction of the point for the spheroid ([*1778a*]; *OC*, IX, 71–87; see Section 8). In the same manner, he now inverted the conditions and made the externally attracted

point the origin of polar coordinates. Manipulating the resulting expressions yielded a theorem often called by his name: all ellipsoids with the same foci for their principal sections attract a given external point with a force proportional to their masses. The finding generalized a result already won by Maclaurin for the restricted case of particles located on the extension of the major axis. In modern terms, Laplace's theorem is said to assert that the potentials of confocal ellipsoids at a given point are proportional to their volumes. For the gravitational case, this would presuppose homogeneous density. His having conceived the theorem in terms of mass was not intended to obviate that restriction, however, since he did not then envisage any other application. It was simply consistent with his initial motivation, which was to give an up-to-date demonstration of the point-mass gravitational theorem. More significant, for the appreciation of Laplace himself, is to notice that his interest was first mathematical and second physical. His solution compared the attraction of the original ellipsoid to that of a new, confocal ellipsoid containing the attracted point in its surface. That is how he made the problem solvable, for rigorous integration was possible when a point lies on the surface of a figure. Physically, the procedure presented the further advantage of opening the possibility of distinguishing more directly between central attractions and perturbing forces in the motion of planets and their satellites.

Thereupon, Laplace turned to internal particles and found another theorem that surprised him more than anything so far: the attractive force exerted at any point within a homogeneous ellipsoidal shell is equal in all directions. For the component of such an attractive force parallel to the major axis, Laplace obtained the important definite integral (*ibid.*, 89),

$$A = \frac{2a\pi}{\sqrt{mn}} \int_0^1 \frac{x^2\, dx}{\sqrt{\left(1 + \frac{1-m}{m}x^2\right) + \left(1 + \frac{1-n}{n}x^2\right)}}, \quad (73)$$

m and *n* (Equation 70) being positive for finite surfaces.

The rest of the treatise consists of similar mathematical investigations of particular problems concerning the equilibrium conditions and shape of rotating fluid masses. An important application to the moon shows that the difference in length between the earth-directed axis and the diameter of a spherical body of identical mass is four times the comparable elongation of the orthogonal axis in the orbital plane (*ibid.*, 116). The coincidence of the moon's periods of revolution and rotation is then deduced from that relation. The dependence of angular velocity on ellipticity forms another topic, and its application to the earth gives limits for the polar flattening. From his earlier essays, Laplace reiterated in simplified language the finding that, although it can be determined whether any given form for a solid (or, rather, a fluid) of revolution satisfies specified forces, it is impossible to determine in a general manner all the forms that do so. All these results appear in appropriate passages of Book III of *Mécanique céleste*, although he did not incorporate whole articles or sections from this treatise in his synthesis.

On 11 August 1784, less than a year after finishing the treatise just discussed (*47*), Laplace read the draft of a further memoir (*48*), most of which is reproduced with little change in *Mécanique céleste*, Book III, chs. 1–4. Entitled "Théorie des attractions des sphéroïdes et de la figure des planètes" ([*1785b*]), it contains the basic mathematical theory, which for Laplace meant formulation, of the subject. The entire memoir is an exercise in partial differential equations, manipulation of which enabled Laplace to solve problems by differentiation, series expansion, and analysis of coefficients when integration was impossible, as it normally was. The first of the memoir's five parts contains the simpler and more direct derivations that this method permitted for the main results of Part II of the immediately preceding *Théorie du mouvement et de la figure elliptique des planètes* ([*1784a*]). The rapid sequence fits the pattern in which Laplace often acted. Dissatisfied with his initial treatment of a subject as soon as he saw it in print, he would immediately set to work simplifying the analysis and generalizing the treatment.

That process marks a further stage in the development of what became the concept of potential. At the outset of his second section, Laplace gave it a formulation that provided him with a basic equation from which he could derive the whole theory of spheroidal attraction. The form will not be immediately recognizable to the modern reader, however, since the expression is in polar coordinates. He began by referring to an elementary observation of his earlier treatise, namely that if $V = \int dM/r$, differentiating V along a direction will give the attraction of a spheroid in that direction. In the equilibrium case, the attraction exerted on the particles of a planet takes that form, and Laplace proceeded to investigate V. With the origin of coordinates inside the spheroid,

a, b, c, are the coordinates of the point where the attraction is exerted;

x, y, z, the coordinates of a particle of the spheroid;

$r = \sqrt{a^2 + b^2 + c^2}$ the distance to the origin of the point attracted;

θ the angle that the radius r makes with the x-axis;

ω the angle formed by the intersection of the invariant plane in which the x-axis and y-axis lie with the plane that passes through the x-axis and the attracted point.

Designating by R the distance $\sqrt{x^2 + y^2 + z^2}$ from the origin to the attracting particle, and by θ' and ω' the values of θ and ω at the point occupied by that particle, Laplace obtained the following expression for V ([*1785b*]; *OC*, X, 362):

$$\int \frac{R^2\, dR\, d\omega'\, d\theta'\, \sin\theta'}{\sqrt{r^2 - 2rR[\cos\theta\cos\theta' + \sin\theta\sin\theta'\cos(\omega - \omega')] + R^2}}$$

(74)

in which the integral relative to R is taken from $R = 0$ to the value of R at the surface of the spheroid; that relative to ω' from 0 to 2π, and that relative to θ' from 0 to π.

Laplace's general mathematical virtuosity is nowhere more impressive than in this memoir, which also offers a particularly explicit example of the specific advantage that he could draw from his own mathematical innovations. At this point (and this may have been the breakthrough that made the approach possible at all), he applied an important finding of the memoir on generating functions ([*1782a*], Section XVIII; *OC*, X, 54–60, referring back to [*1777a*], Section V; *OC*, IX, 21–24). He had there shown that integrating second-order linear partial differential equations was often possible by means of—and only by means of—definite integrals of a form similar to the expression just given for V. In this instance, he found it easy to show that if $\cos\theta = \mu$, then differentiation produces the following partial differential equation (*ibid.; OC*, X, 362):

$$0 = \frac{\partial\left[\,1 - \mu^2\,\right] \dfrac{\partial V}{\partial\mu}}{\partial\mu} + \frac{\dfrac{\partial^2 V}{\partial\omega^2}}{1 - \mu^2} + r\frac{\partial^2(rV)}{\partial r^2}. \quad (75)$$

That equation is in fact equivalent to the modern expression for potential, $\Delta^2 V = 0$. Laplace never transformed it from spherical polar coordinates into Cartesian form in this memoir, however. Rather, he substituted for V in (74), so that he could write Legendre's equation (*ibid.; OC*, X, 375):

$$0 = \left\{ \frac{\partial\left[\left(1-\mu^2\right)\dfrac{\partial U^i}{\partial\mu}\right]}{\partial\mu} \right\} + \frac{\dfrac{\partial^2 U^i}{\partial\omega^2}}{1-\mu^2} + i(i+1)\, U^i, \quad (76)$$

where U^i is a polynomial function of μ, $\sqrt{1-\mu^2}\sin\omega$, and $\sqrt{1-\mu^2}\cos\omega$. In determining that function, and investigating the dependence of the variables on the angles ω and θ, sometimes called Laplace's angles, Laplace arrived at a formula for evaluating auxiliary factors ([*1785b*], 141)

$$\nu\lambda = 2\,\frac{1\cdot3\cdot5\cdots\cdots(2i-1)}{2\cdot4\cdot6\cdots\cdots(i+n)\ 2\cdot4\cdot6\cdots\cdots(i-n)}. \quad (77)$$

(An error arising from the assumption that $(i + n)$ is always even was corrected in *Mécanique céleste*, Book III, no. 15; *OC*, II, 42–43; cf. K: Todhunter, II, 57.) When the attracted point is internal, the expression for V has to be developed in a series of terms of ascending powers of r; and the analysis compounds the attraction of the sphere, on the surface of which the point lies, with that of the shell constituting the remainder of the spheroid.

Simplifying the problem to the case of almost spherical spheroids, Laplace in a third section achieved a general solution even on the supposition of heterogeneous density. Again he recurred to results he had won in an earlier piece ([*1776d*]), namely the equation for the attraction at the surface of a spheroid ([*1785b*]; *OC*, X, 372),

$$-a\frac{\partial V}{\partial r} = \frac{2}{3}\pi a^2 + \frac{1}{2}\,V, \quad (78)$$

where a represents half the common diameter of the spheroid and the inscribed sphere, and r is the distance of the attracted point from the center of mass. Laplace reiterated that equation in *Mécanique céleste* (Book III, no. 10; *OC*, II, 30) and always accorded it great importance. The further analysis was now fairly simple. Again, he decomposed the attraction V into two components, the force exerted at the surface of a sphere and that exerted by a further shell of which the outer surface bounds the spheroid. According to the conditions of the problem,

$$r = a(1 + \alpha y) \quad (79)$$

at the surface of the spheroid. Substitution in the basic expansion,

$$V = \frac{U^0}{r} + \frac{U^1}{r^2} + \frac{U^2}{r^3} + \frac{U^3}{r^4} + \cdots, \quad (80)$$

and in (78) yielded the equation

$$4\alpha\pi a^2 y = \frac{U'^{(0)}}{a} + \frac{3U^{(1)}}{a^2} + \frac{5U^{(2)}}{a^3} + \cdots. \quad (81)$$

Since y is also a polynomial function of μ, $\sqrt{1-\mu^2}\cos\omega$, and $\sqrt{1-\mu^2}\sin\omega$, then it could be thought of as a series of functions,

$$y = Y^0 + Y^1 + Y^2 + Y^3 + \cdots, \quad (82)$$

where Y^0, Y^1, Y^2, Y^3, $\cdots$ like U'^0, U^1, U^2, U^3, $\cdots$, serve the partial differential equation,

$$0 = \frac{\partial\left[1-\mu^2\,\dfrac{\partial Y^i}{\partial\mu}\right]}{\partial\mu} + \frac{\dfrac{\partial^2 Y^i}{\partial\omega^2}}{1-\mu^2} + i(i+1)\,Y^i. \quad (83)$$

The functions Y and U are similar in form, and

$$U^i = \frac{4\alpha\pi}{2i+1}\,a^{(i+3)}Y^i. \quad (84)$$

Hence

$$V = \frac{4}{3}\pi\frac{a^3}{r} + 4\alpha\pi\frac{a^3}{r}\left[Y^0 + \frac{a}{3r}Y^1 + \frac{a^2}{5r^2}Y^2 + \frac{a^3}{7r^3}Y^3 + \cdots\right]. \quad (85)$$

It thus proved possible to determine V by expanding y in a series of functions $Y^0 + Y^1 + Y^2 + Y^3 + \cdots$. Laplace then gave a method for evaluating V by analysis of the coefficients in the case of a spheroid the equation of whose surface, referred to Cartesian coordinates, is a polynomial function of the coordinates (*ibid.; OC*, X, 371–374).

Turning to the figure of the planets, Laplace treated the problem as a corollary of the foregoing analysis. In the simplified assumption that these bodies are homogeneous spheroids of revolution, he was finally able to demonstrate the long-sought theorem that, under the law of gravity, they can only be ellipsoids flattened at the poles. Proving that theorem enabled him to derive the law of attraction at the surface by an analysis *a priori*, which fully confirmed the validity of the above method of expansion of the function V into a series of what have been called Laplace's functions. The form in which he obtained it permitted comparison of the force of gravity, determined by means of the pendulum, with the value calculated for any point where the radius had been determined by geodesic measurements along the meridian. (It should be emphasized that this possibility helps to explain Laplace's strong preference in 1790 for basing the metric system on such a survey, instead of on a standard seconds pendulum [see Section 18]). Although existing data were less exact than he could have desired, they nevertheless permitted calculating that the figures assumed by the planets in the course of their rotations, even like their motions in orbit around the sun, confirm the principle of gravity with an overwhelming degree of probability. He had long since calculated ([1779a]; OC, IX, 269) that if the law of gravity were to satisfy the phenomena, the ellipticity of the earth had to be between the values 0.001730 and 0.005135. Since observation of the pendulum gives 0.0031171, it is well within the limits.

In the course of this analysis, Laplace demonstrated in passing a theorem, which assumed increasing importance in his later work, with respect to two functions of different orders of the type that he was here employing. If Y^i and $U^{i'}$ are polynomial functions of μ, $\sqrt{1 - \mu^2} \sin \omega$, and $\sqrt{1 - \mu^2} \cos \omega$, and if both satisfy partial differential equations of the form (83), then they have the property of orthogonality, namely that

$$\int_{-1}^{1} \int_{0}^{2\pi} Y^i \, U^{i'} \, d\mu \, d\omega = 0 \qquad (86)$$

([1785b]; OC, X, 389), if i and i' are different positive integers. Todhunter points out (K: [1873], II, no. 857, pp. 61–62) that although Laplace did not here consider the case in which i and i' are identical, there is an important equation in *Mécanique céleste* (Book III, no. 17; OC, II, 47) that does express all that this entails, namely

$$\int \int Y'^{(i)} \, d\mu' \, d\omega' \, Q^i = \frac{4\pi \, Y^i}{2i + 1}, \qquad (87)$$

where Q^i is a known function of μ and $\sqrt{1 - \mu^2} \cos (\omega' - \omega)$, by means of which U^i may be calculated (*ibid.*, no. 9; OC, II, 26–27). Laplace did not write that equation down in his memoir; but he might well have done so, for it is implicit throughout the discussion of the figure of the planets.

Armed now with a general theory of the attraction of spheroids, which was precisely what he had lacked in his earlier investigation of tidal oscillations ([1779a]), Laplace returned to that subject and demonstrated conclusively that the equilibrium conditions entail periodicity and that the equilibrium will be stable only if the density of a layer of fluid is less than that of the spheroid it covers. There was nothing new in this, but it served to complete his theoretical investigation of the phenomena of spheroids of revolution serving the law of gravity.

Two short memoirs, on the shape of the earth ([1786a]) and the rings of Saturn ([1789a]), apply the theory of gravitational potential, or the attraction of a spheroid as Laplace always called it, to their respective topics. Like the problem of tidal oscillations, both represent earlier interests that Laplace had been unable to resolve in a conclusive manner for lack of an adequate theory. And although both pertain, again like the tides, to application rather than to innovation, both also contain—perhaps for that very reason—important clarifications and simplifications of the mathematical formalism. Thus, in the paper on the figure of the earth, he gave much greater prominence to (86), making it the basis of the analysis ([1789a]; OC, XI, 12).

That paper offers a particularly good example of Laplace's tendency to be preoccupied in the first instance with the analytical representation of the facts and only secondarily with the facts themselves, with how something could be the case, given what the case was. For he was not indifferent to the latter. In navigational and astronomical tables the apparent motions of the sun and moon are referred to the center of gravity of the earth; and it was incumbent, therefore, to know its precise location relative to the point of observation, particularly for the theory of the moon. If the flattening at the poles were 1/178, the lunar parallax would amount to 20″ at certain localities. Thus, it is again clear—to anticipate for a moment—that all these uncertainties about geodesic data were bound to reinforce the motivation to base the metric system on yet another survey of the meridian when the opportunity arose in the Revolution (see Section 18).

For the moment, however, the empirical state of the question was what it had been when Laplace in his initial programmatic dual memoir on probability and universal gravitation ([1776a]; see Section 5) first confronted the discrepancy between the shape of the earth calculated from measurements of the length of a seconds pendulum at different latitudes and that given by the classic surveys of the lengths of the arc in Lapland, Peru, the Cape of Good Hope, and France. From the former data, the ratio of minor to major axis came out to be 320:321; from the latter, 249:250. A brief calculation based on data from these surveys (apparently Laplace's first application of error theory to instrumental data) finds the probability negligible that the departure from the elliptical had resulted from observational error. The survey data also yielded a finite probability that the northern and southern hemispheres are not symmetrical, as well as a possibility that the earth might not be a solid of revolution at all.

As for the lengths of the radii determined by measurements of the seconds pendulum, they too failed to satisfy an ellipsoidal figure. That would have been troublesome to theory only if the earth were assumed to be of homogeneous density, for the differences did follow a regular pattern; and, most important, values for the force of gravity calculated from the length of the seconds pendulum approximated very closely to the law that its variation is proportional to the square of the sine of the latitude. This relation being of the utmost significance for the theory of the earth, Laplace proposed to combine it with the equilibrium conditions for the oscillations of the seas in order to draw from the combination the law of the variation of the radius of the earth.

He had already shown how the expression for the radius of any nearly spherical spheroid may take the form

$$1 + \alpha (Y^0 + Y^2 + Y^3 + Y^4 \cdots). \qquad (88)$$

(In the case of the earth, the equilibrium conditions for the seas require that $Y^1 = 0$ and αY^0 be a constant (*ibid.; OC*, XI, 13). If the equilibrium is to be stable, it is a further condition that the axis of rotation be one of the principal axes of the earth. That requirement entailed the following form for Y^2:

$$H\left(\mu^2 - \frac{1}{3}\right) + H^{IV} (1 - \mu^2) \cos 2\omega, \qquad (89)$$

where the constants H and H^{II}, depending on the physical constitution of the earth, are to be determined by observation (*ibid.; OC*, XI, 16).

These are equilibrium conditions that would hold for any celestial body covered by a fluid. In the case of the earth, measurements of the length of the seconds pendulum make it possible to calculate the values numerically. The constant H comes out approximately equal to 0.003111; H^{II} is negligible relative to H; the quantity $Y^3 + Y^4 + \cdots$ is very small by comparison to Y^2, and so also is its first derivative by comparison to the first derivative of Y^2. Thus there would be no detectable error in calculating values for the radius of the earth, and also for its first derivative, from the formula

$$1 - 0.003111\left(\mu^2 - \frac{1}{3}\right). \qquad (90)$$

What the surveys of the meridian show is that the same approximation is invalid for the second derivatives of the terrestrial radius. The reason for the discrepancy between the results of the two methods for calculating the length of the radius is that the function $Y^3 + Y^4 + \cdots$ becomes significant on a second differentiation. The expression for the radius of the earth has the form

$$1 + \alpha H\left(\mu^2 - \frac{1}{3}\right) + \alpha Y^i, \qquad (91)$$

where αY^i is the term representing the variation between the calculated value and the value that satisfies the law of the variation of gravity with the square of the sine of the latitude. Given this expression, the formula for the length of the seconds pendulum is (*ibid.; OC*, XI, 18):

$$l = L\left[1 + \alpha\left(H + \frac{5}{2}\phi\right)\left(\mu^2 - \frac{1}{3}\right) + (i - 1)\,\alpha Y^i\right], \qquad (92)$$

where l and L are the lengths of the seconds pendulum corresponding to the force of gravity at two different latitudes. The formula for the degree of the meridian is

$$c + \frac{2}{3}\alpha c H - 3\alpha c H\left(\mu^2 - \frac{1}{3}\right) - i(i+1)\,\alpha c Y^i$$

$$+ \alpha c\,\frac{\partial(\mu Y^i)}{\partial \mu} - \alpha c\,\frac{\dfrac{\partial^2 Y^i}{\partial \omega^2}}{1 - \mu^2}. \qquad (93)$$

We need not follow the calculation in detail in order to seize Laplace's explanation, which is that the term Y^i, representing the variation of the value for the radius calculated from observation from the value that satisfies the law of the square of the sine of the latitude, is differentiated once for the pendulum method and twice for the geodesic method. It becomes detectable only in the latter case. (On the significance of this paper in the history of error theory, see a remark in L: Plackett [1972], p. 239.)

The paper on the rings of Saturn was a much more provisional exercise. An "essay for a theory" Laplace called it, pending the development of telescopes powerful enough to reveal the correct number and dimensions of the rings. Like Galileo, Huygens, and many others, Laplace quite evidently found the phenomenon one of the most tantalizing in the whole field of astronomy. In his hands, of course, it was bound to take the form of a gravitational problem. He had first alluded to it in print in a special case discussed at the end of the opening section of his earliest major memoir on spheroid attraction ([*1778a*]; *OC*, IX, 86–87). There the rings are mentioned as the phenomenon instan-

1383

tiating the problem of the (reversed) attraction of an external point for a spheroid. The manuscript draft of that section, which he read on 22 January 1777 (20), closes with an undertaking to devote a future memoir to the problem of the figure of Saturn and the influence on it of the attraction of the rings. That was omitted in the printed text. Now that Laplace was finally redeeming the promise twelve years later, the problem was rather the figure of the rings themselves. There is still some appearance of hesitation. Laplace did not publish the memoir until 1789, five years after submitting the basic theory of spheroidal attraction ([1785b]) to the Academy (48).

Given the paucity of data, the discussion offers a particularly transparent example of recourse to a mathematical model. Instead of seeking the stability of the ring in any sort of mechanical connection between the particles, Laplace imagined its surface covered with an infinitely thin layer of a fluid in equilibrium under the influence of the forces at work. The shape of the ring would then be determined by the equilibrium conditions of the fluid. The most notable single feature of the memoir is the statement at the outset of the basic equation of spheroidal attraction theory, here referred to the rectangular coordinates that make it immediately recognizable for the first time as the potential function of later physics ([1789a]; OC, XI, 278):

$$0 = \frac{\partial^2 V}{\partial x^2} + \frac{\partial^2 V}{\partial y^2} + \frac{\partial^2 V}{\partial z^2}. \tag{94}$$

In the case of a spheroid of revolution, the equation becomes

$$0 = \frac{1}{r}\frac{\partial V}{\partial r} + \frac{\partial^2 V}{\partial r^2} + \frac{\partial^2 V}{\partial z^2}, \tag{95}$$

where $r^2 = x^2 + y^2$. If the body is a solid sphere, or a hollow sphere with a homogeneous shell, the equation becomes

$$0 = \frac{2}{r'}\frac{\partial V}{\partial r'} + \frac{\partial^2 V}{\partial r'^2}, \tag{96}$$

where $r' = \sqrt{(r^2 + z^2)}$.

Investigating the continuity of the ring, Laplace calculated that since the mass of Saturn must be much greater than that of the ring, and since a sphere exerts a much greater force on a particle at its surface than a flattened body of the same mass would do, the relation between the forces of attraction at a point on its inner circumference, its outer circumference, and the surface of Saturn are such that the ring must in fact be a series of concentric

rings. He claimed to have been able to predict the discontinuity between the rings from the theory of gravity alone. He then showed how such a ring may be generated mathematically by a very flat ellipse of which the prolongation of the major axis passes through the center of Saturn and which revolves about that center in a plane perpendicular to its own. There is no point in following the formalism. Todhunter (L: [1865], II, 65–73) reproduced it more fully than was his wont, and Laplace himself omitted the derivations depending on the most questionable hypotheses from Mécanique céleste, where the topic occupies Book III, chapter 6 (OC, II, 166–177). It involves the analytic necessity of constructing another ellipse with an infinite major axis on the same equator as the generating ellipse. The two must exert an identical attraction at every point. The ring might then be invested with unequal dimensions in its different parts—and even with double curvature. It had to be so, for if it were circular and concentric with Saturn it would collapse into the planet. The most important findings are that the conditions for stability require that it revolve in the equatorial plane of Saturn, along with the four inner satellites, and that the center of gravity not coincide with the center of rotation. Abstract though the analysis was, Laplace pictured the rings physically as solid bodies, oscillating stably in asymmetrical rotation around the planet in such a way that their centers of gravity described elliptical orbits about the center of gravity of the planet even like normal satellites. With the delay in publication until 1789, the paper on Saturn's rings comes as an afterthought on the theory of attraction in the midst of the series of memoirs on planetary motion.

17. Secular Inequalities: Jupiter and Saturn; the Moons of Jupiter; Lunar Theory. Only in that series does vindication of the stability of the solar system, which became the central feature of the Laplace stereotype through its celebration in the nineteenth century, finally appear to be the central motivation. Laplace himself began insisting upon it in a sequence of five memoirs imparting his main discoveries in planetary theory. He composed them between November 1785 and April 1788 (50, 52, 53, 55, 56). Scientifically, however, they inaugurated an even lengthier preoccupation, for from then on his attention remained focused on problems of positional astronomy, practical as well as theoretical, for the next twenty years, through the completion of Volume IV of Mécanique céleste in 1805. A near coincidence marks the start of that orientation. He read the first of these pieces, "Un mémoire sur les inégalités séculaires des planètes" ([1787a]), on 23 November 1785 and one week later (51) read the last of his demographic papers ([1786c]; see Section 13).

The paper on the secular inequalities of the planets ([1787a]), a relatively brief piece by Laplace's standards, must be considered, together perhaps with "Théorie des attractions des sphéroïdes et de la figure des planètes" ([1785b]) and "Sur la probabilité des causes par les événements" ([1774c]), one of the really signal memoirs in his *oeuvre*. It opens with a serene and comprehensive survey of the history and state of the question of apparently cumulative discrepancies between the theoretical and observed positions of celestial bodies, and largely resolves them with a statement of two of his most famous determinations, the interdependence of the apparent acceleration of Jupiter's mean motion with the deceleration of Saturn's, and the rigorous necessity for the mathematical games played by the Jovian planets, the three inner satellites of Jupiter, in the figure dance of their revolutions around their parent. The second two memoirs in the sequence, actually a single enormous memoir with a sequel, on the theory of Jupiter and Saturn ([1788a] and [1788b]), contain calculations in detail. Only the further argument, that the apparent acceleration of the mean motion of our own moon over time depends upon the action of the sun compounded by variation of the eccentricity of the earth's orbit, would appear to have come to him after writing the covering paper on secular inequalities; for he announced it in the preamble to the Jupiter and Saturn memoir, which was presented on 6 May 1786 (52), reserving its development for a further memoir on lunar theory, the fourth of the series ([1788c]), submitted on 19 December 1787 (55).

Laplace began by explaining the distinction that astronomers habitually made between periodic and secular inequalities in the ellipticity of planetary orbits. The former depend on the positions of the planets in orbit, relative to each other and to their aphelions, and compensate for themselves in a few years time. They are to be considered as very small oscillations on either side of a point in motion on an ellipse described in consequence of the attractive force exerted by the sun alone. Secular inequalities are those that modify the elements of the orbits themselves—their inclinations, eccentricities, and longitudes—so slowly as to be undetectable in the course of a single revolution but

that finally change the nature and position of the orbits (*ibid.; OC*, XI, 49). Their effects on the shape and position of the orbits become manifest only over centuries, hence the term "secular." The terminology may have become a touch inappropriate, since what Laplace was setting out to demonstrate precisely was that secular inequalities are themselves periodic, the periods occupying centuries. It is true that the term "secular" did not necessarily imply that very gradual inequalities need to be indefinitely cumulative, but such was certainly the apprehension. He himself spoke of them, perhaps inadvertently, as "accumulating ceaselessly" (*ibid.; OC*, XI, 49). Also, he was slightly less than candid—or at any rate clear—about the background of his own views on the matter. The most important secular inequalities would be those (if any such there were) that might change the mean motion of a planet and with it, by Kepler's third law, the mean distance from the sun; and practical astronomers were constrained to include a correction factor proportional to the square of the time in their expressions for the mean motions of Jupiter and Saturn. In writing now about his own early investigation of this problem ([1776a, 2°]; see Section 5), he claimed to have found that theory admitted no secular inequality in the mean motions or mean distances and to have concluded that such an inequality had been nonexistent or at least unobservable throughout the recorded history of astronomy. What he had actually said was not quite that. Rather, it was that theory proves the nonexistence of secular inequalities due to the interaction of any two mutually gravitating planets in historic time. He recalled that he had once thought to invoke the action of the comets to explain the undeniable speeding of Jupiter and slowing of Saturn. The analysis did not preclude that, although the physics did when he came to consider how slight the masses of the comets are. Moreover, whether the comets or some other agents were at work, Laplace had not at this early stage discussed or even mentioned the possibility of a long-term periodicity in these greater inequalities.

That opportunity to save the system was opened by the work of Lagrange. In a crucial memoir of 1783, "Sur les variations séculaires des mouvements moyens des planètes" (*Oeuvres de Lagrange*, V, 381–414), Lagrange investigated the question whether, even allowing unlimited time, the perturbing forces of other planets, themselves subject to variations in the elements of their orbits, could progressively alter the mean motions and mean distances of a planet and thus disturb its service to Kepler's third law. His analysis was more abstract than Laplace's had been, and he extended it to investigating the terms involving the squares of the eccentricities. There he did find a secular equation; but its maximum value was one-thousandth of a second, and its effect was negligible over all time, even in the case of the largest observed inequalities, those of Jupiter and Saturn. The question, therefore, was not whether those inequalities were to be explained by expressions involving lengthy periodicity, but how to do it. It was unthinkable that they should be random. This was ever the sort of problem at which Laplace excelled, and he set himself to examining the figures.

The first hope was that the mutual gravitation of the two planets might suffice to reveal periodicity. In planetary interaction over long periods, the sum of the masses of each planet divided by the major axis of the respective orbits is approximately constant. Thus, given Kepler's third law, if Saturn is slowed by Jupiter, Jupiter should be accelerated by Saturn. Their masses are respectively 1/1067.195 and 1/3358.40 that of the sun. It followed that the ratio of Jupiter's acceleration to Saturn's deceleration should have been approximately 7:3. Halley assumed 9°16' for the deceleration of Saturn in two millennia. If that were correct, Jupiter's acceleration should have been 3°58' — which differed from the tables by only 9 arc minutes. Thus, near equality made it probable that their theory did indeed contain an inequality of very long term depending on their configuration and not on their positions individually. The problem was to find it.

That their mean motions were nearly commensurate was well known. Five times the mean motion of Saturn almost equals twice the mean motion of Jupiter. It was characteristic of Laplace that he saw how to exploit this fact. He suspected that the variations in inclination and eccentricity of the orbits were responsible for the changes in speed. Might not the differential equations of motion contain terms with an argument of $5n' - 2n$ (to use his designation for the two mean motions) that would become detectable on integration, even though they were involved with the cubes and third-order products of the eccentricities and inclinations? For the motions were not quite commensurate; actually $5n' - 2n$ came to about 1/74 of the mean motion of Jupiter. The differential equations for the longitude worked out so that on two integrations, the square of this quantity appeared in the divisors. Such terms were normally very minute, the order of magnitude being that also of cubes of eccentricities and inclination. In the

case of Jupiter and Saturn, however, the smallness of the divisors rendered the terms detectable on the second integration. By a fortunate coincidence, the necessity to introduce the inequalities depending on the third and higher powers of eccentricities and inclinations also permitted neglecting the quantities that would have made their determination impossible. So theory could be compared to observation. The expressions for Saturn yielded a secular equation of approximately 46'50" with a period of approximately 817 years; the theory of Jupiter contained an equation of 20' with opposite sign and identical period. The ratio is about 3:7 ([1787a]; OC, XI, 49–56). Recalculating in the full Jupiter-Saturn memoir ([1788a]), Laplace found 48'44" for Saturn and 20'49" for Jupiter with a period of 929 years.

With these figures, and designating by nt and $n't$ the sidereal motions of Jupiter and Saturn respectively since the epoch of 1700, the longitudes will be given by the following formulas. For Jupiter:

$$nt + \epsilon + 20' \sin (5n't - 2nt + 49°8'40'') ; \quad (97)$$

and for Saturn,

$$n't + \epsilon' - 46' 50'' \sin (5n't - 2nt + 49° 8' 40''), \quad (98)$$

where ϵ and ϵ' are constants that depend on the longitudes of the two planets on 1 January 1700. In order to evaluate the acceleration and deceleration empirically, the mean motions determined over a very long period could be compared to the values obtained from recent data. The time elapsed between the opposition of Saturn recorded for 228 B.C. and that for 1714 should give the "true" mean motion.

If the deceleration given by the above theory was correct, the value computed for the mean motion between observations of 1595 and 1715 should be too small by 16.8". In fact, the deceleration was 16" — and the fit between observation and theory was as good as the imprecision of sixteenth-century observation could allow. Agreement with Halley's tables was equally good for the acceleration of Jupiter, which comes out in the ratio of 7:3 to be approximately 7". The changes of speed were at their maximum around A.D. 1580. Since then Saturn's deceleration and Jupiter's acceleration have been diminishing and the apparent mean motions coming closer to the "true" values taken over all time (ibid.; OC, X, 53–54). Laplace also showed his calculation to be conformable to a set of corrections to be applied over short periods that Lambert had published as "Résultat des recherches sur les irrégularités du mouvement de Saturne et de Jupiter" in the *Nouveaux mémoires de l'Académie royale de Berlin* ([1773/1775], 216–221). His object had been an empirical determination of *la loi des erreurs* in Halley's tables, and it may be worth mentioning because it seems to be the first time that Laplace used the phrase "law of error."

Also contributing to determination of the inequalities of Jupiter and Saturn are terms due to the ellipticity of the orbits on the assumption that $5n' = 2n$ exactly, and others expressing perturbations due to variations in eccentricity of the orbits. Other mathematicians had calculated these effects, but with such discordant results that the whole procedure needed to be verified. That task Laplace deferred to a further memoir containing the calculations — here he gave only the results — in which all ancient and modern oppositions of both planets would be accommodated, and certain strange aberrations of Saturn explained. Centuries would have been required to accomplish that empirically: "Thus, on this point, the theory of gravity has moved ahead of observation" (*op. cit.; OC*, IX, 56).

The present memoir had two other objects, for which it does contain the analysis. They were equally integral to the system of the world. The first still concerned the uniformity of mean motion of celestial bodies, in the case of satellites rather than the primary planets, however, and specifically that of the moons of Jupiter. At issue was the invariance of their mean distances from a principal center of force. The second concerned the other variations of celestial orbits. The methods for determining the inclinations and eccentricities were very simple. But were these elements oscillating within certain, presumably narrow limits, or did permanent changes occur?

The motions of Jupiter's moons were a well-studied set of phenomena when Laplace took up the question of their stability over the span of astronomical time. They were most famous for the observations that had enabled Römer in 1676 to measure the velocity of light by recording the dependence of variations in the apparent time of Io's eclipses on the distance of Jupiter from the earth. More immediately, they were the main resort for navigators in determining longitude before the availability of reliable chronometers. The Swedish astronomer Pehr Wargentin had devoted much of his life to perfecting the tables, first published in 1746, which he revised constantly in correspondence with Lalande. In the theory of these bodies, the most important item by far was a memoir by Lagrange (*Oeuvres de Lagrange*, VI, 67–225), which had won the prize for 1766 set by the Acadé-

mie des Sciences for a study of their inequalities. Lagrange calculated the effects on each of the four satellites of the oblateness of Jupiter, the action of the sun, and the action of the other three. He did not investigate the relation of the inequalities in longitude to the variations of eccentricity and inclination; and his results, however impressive analytically, were of no help in improving the tables. Moreover, he made a mistake. He assumed that the angle between the planes of Jupiter's equator and orbit was negligible.

Such, in summary, was the state of knowledge when Laplace took the problem in hand. The mean motion of the first satellite is about twice that of the second, which is about twice that of the third. Curiously enough, however, the difference between the mean motions of the first and second was incomparably closer to being precisely twice that between the mean motions of the second and third, than was the near doubling of mean motions in successive pairs. (The fourth was the odd moon out, its motions being incommensurable with the inner three; and Laplace neglected its influence here, as well as that of the sun.) If the tripartite relation were to prove really exact, so that

$$n + 2n'' = 3n', \qquad (99)$$

it would follow from this simple equation that the three moons could never be in simultaneous eclipse. In point of predictable fact, the data from Wargentin's tables show that such an eventuality could not occur in the next 1,317,900 years, and it would be entirely precluded by a modification in the annual motion of the second smaller than the margin of error in the tables. "Now," Laplace observed, "it may be laid down as a general rule that, if the result of a long series of precise observations approximates a simple relation so closely that the remaining difference is undetectable by observation and may be attributed to the errors to which they are liable, then this relation is probably that of nature" (*ibid.; OC*, XI, 57).

The remark offers an especially strategic example of the role of probability, causality, and error theory in his planning of an investigation. The equation (99) of the mean motions of Jupiter's moons could scarcely be thought the effect of chance; yet it was improbable that those bodies had originally been placed at just the distances from Jupiter that it requires. It was natural, therefore, to try out the hypothesis that their mutual attraction is the true cause. Thus, Laplace observed, in anticipation of a later investigation ([*1788c*]), the action of the earth on the moon had brought about the equality between its periods of revolution and rotation, which might have been very different at the beginning.

The object of the research, therefore, was to determine whether the mean motions of Jupiter's first three satellites became and remain stable by virtue of the law of universal gravitation. Laplace based the analysis on the motion of the second satellite. He set up general equations of motion of a system of mutually attracting bodies and applied them to the motions of all three satellites, showing how the principal inequalities of the second depend on the influence of the first and third. In his expressions,

t designates the time;

n, n' and n'', the mean motions of the first three satellites;

s, the quantity $n - 3n' + 2n''$;

$nt + \epsilon$, $n't + \epsilon'$, $n''t + \epsilon''$, the projections onto the same plane of the mean longitudes taken from the x-axis; and

V, the angle $(2n'' - 3n' + n) t + 2\epsilon'' - 3\epsilon' + \epsilon$, the mean longitudes being taken from a fixed point in Jupiter's orbit.

The tables call for s and V to be approximately constant in value, but Laplace could find no reflection of that fact in any terms that depended on the first powers of the perturbing masses. Accordingly, he proceeded to an examination of terms that depended on the squares and products of the masses. Multiplication of the expressions by the masses of the satellites, taken two at a time, did introduce into the values of s and V quantities proportional to time, giving for the variation of s,

$$\delta s = \alpha n^2 t \sin V, \tag{100}$$

where α stands for an immensely complicated function multiplied by $n^2 t \sin V$ in the equation ([1787a]; OC, XI, 77)

$$2\delta n'' - 3\delta n' + \delta n = \frac{3}{2} \alpha n^2 t \sin V \alpha. \tag{101}$$

Laplace then eliminated from (100) the quantities that increase with time, using his method of varying the constants of integration (see Sections 7 and 10). He thus obtained two first-order differential equations among s, V, and t:

$$\frac{ds}{dt} = \alpha n^2 \sin V \tag{102}$$

and

$$dV = dt\, (2n'' - 3n' + n) = s dt, \tag{103}$$

whence

$$\frac{d^2 V}{dt^2} = \alpha n^2 \sin V. \tag{104}$$

Multiplying by dV and integrating gives

$$\frac{\pm dV}{\sqrt{\lambda - 2\alpha n^2 \cos V}} = dt, \tag{105}$$

where λ is an arbitrary constant. Of the three possibilities, first that λ is positive and $> \pm 2\alpha n^2$, second that α is positive and $\lambda < 2\alpha n^2$, and third that α is negative and $\lambda < -2\alpha n^2$, the second case entailed a periodic value for V oscillating around a mean of 180°; and the data showed this to be the case in nature, with the oscillations of very small amplitude.

Laplace drew four consequences from the analysis pushed thus far. The first was practical. Since both s and V are periodic, the relation (99), $n + 2n'' = 3n'$, is rigorously exact, and Wargentin's tables needed only slight corrections. The second was historical. It was not a necessary condition that the three satellites should originally have been placed at distances from Jupiter's center of mass that by Kepler's laws would result in mean motions satisfying (99). If they had merely been close to those distances (and Laplace calculated what the limits were), then their mutual attractions would bring them into that relation with each other. The third consequence concerned the stability of the system. There was no need to fear that the tables for the principal equation of the second satellite would be off, even after the lapse of many centuries. The fourth, and in Laplace's eyes the most important, raised problems for the future. Consideration of the angle V created a second condition that the tables had to satisfy, namely that

$$nt + 3n't - 2n''t = 180°, \tag{106}$$

where nt, $n't$, and $n''t$ are the respective mean longitudes.

The angle V is subject to a periodic inequality that Laplace likened to the oscillations of a pendulum, and that inequality affects the motions of the three satellites in varying degrees, according to the ratio of their respective masses and distances from the center of Jupiter. The mass of the second is adequately determined by the inequalities that it produces in the motions of the first—that is why Laplace could make its motion the basis of reference. The masses of the first and third were still unknown, however. All that could be said was that a relation exists that accounts for the inequalities of the second. That was how he was able to determine that the libration of V is contained within limits of 4-1/8 and 11-1/3 years. Both its zero point and amplitude are quantities to be determined by observation. To consider only the action of Jupiter's first three satellites on each other, their motion depends on no less than nine second-degree differential equations, the integrals of which contain eighteen arbitrary constants. The eccentricities, orbital inclinations, and positions of nodes and aphelia determine twelve of those constants. The mean motions and their epochs would give six others, without the two conditions to which these six arbitrary quantities are subject. That reduces them to four. To answer to that, the expression for V contains two arbitrary quantities. Since the tables do work well without regard to the periodic inequality of V, its amount must be small. But the uncertainties still prevailing over most of the elements of the theory of Jupiter's satellites made the determination very difficult, and Laplace left that question to the astronomers to resolve. He had shown them the two conditions that the tables must satisfy, namely (99) and (106). Concluding this discussion, he again recurred to the analogy with our own moon. Those conditions would still obtain if, like the moon, Jupiter's satellites showed an acceleration in the mean motions such that the mean distances progressively decreased. Even as the satellites drew in on Jupiter, the same relations would be preserved (*ibid.; OC*, XI, 60–61).

Thus, Laplace showed that the mean motions of Jupiter's moons are subject only to periodic inequalities, and he felt justified in drawing conclusions for the whole planetary system from this test case. Considering only the laws of universal gravity, the mean distances of celestial bodies from their principal centers of force are immutable. It by no means followed that the same is true of the other orbital elements, namely eccentricities, inclinations, and the positions of nodes and aphelia, all of which undergo continual change. Good methods for determining these quantities existed, subject to the hypothesis that the orbits differ little from the circular and that their planes are only slightly inclined to that of the ecliptic. Laplace himself had long since shown ([*1776c*]) that the eccentricities and inclinations of the orbits are bound to remain small under the operation of gravity, provided that only two planets are considered; and in 1782 Lagrange had further shown (*Oeuvres de Lagrange*, V, 211–345) that the same is true generally of the location of nodes and aphelia, given plausible hypotheses about the masses (over several of which some uncertainty did linger). But before the entire system of the world could be deduced from the law

of gravity, it remained to demonstrate that the eccentricities and inclinations of any number of planets are contained within narrow limits. That was the final object of the present memoir. Analytically, what was required was to prove that the expressions for the secular inequalities of eccentricities and inclinations contain neither secular terms nor exponential terms. The analysis is uncharacteristically brief and occupies the final two chapters (*ibid.; OC*, XI, 88–92).

In those expressions,

$m, m', m'', \cdots$, designate the relative masses of the planets, referred to the sun as unity;

$a, a', a'', \cdots$, the semimajor axis;

$ea, e'a', e''a'', \cdots$, orbital eccentricity;

$V, V', V'', \cdots$, longitude of aphelion;

$\theta, \theta', \theta'', \cdots$, tangent of orbital inclination referred to a fixed plane; and

$I, I', I'', \cdots$, longitude of ascending node.

The quantities $e \sin V$, $e \cos V$, $e' \sin V'$, $e' \cos V', \cdots$, $\theta \sin I$, $\theta' \sin I'$, $\theta \cos I$, $\theta' \cos I', \cdots$, could then be given by linear differential equations with constant coefficients. Since the eccentricities and inclinations are very small, the system of equations for the eccentricities is independent of the system for the inclinations. The former system is the same as if the orbits were coplanar, and the latter is the same as if they were circular.

When the former system is integrated, each of the quantities $e \sin V$, $e \cos V$, $e' \sin V'$, $e' \cos V'$, $\cdots$ is given by the sum of a finite number of sines and cosines of angles proportional to time t. The numbers by which the times are to be multiplied to give the angles are the roots of an algebraic equation of a degree equal to the number of planets. Laplace calls that equation k. The same is true for the quantities of the second system, although the equation on which the angles depend is not the same. He calls that equation k', referring the reader to his discussion in [*1776c*] (*OC*, VIII, 406) and to Lagrange's "Théorie des variations séculaires des éléments des planètes" (1782) (*Oeuvres de Lagrange*, V, 211–344, esp. 249, 325).

If all the roots of k and k' are real and unequal, the values of the preceding quantities contain neither secular terms nor exponentials and thus remain within narrow limits. It is otherwise if some of the roots are imaginary, for then the sines and cosines change into secular terms or exponentials. But, in any event, the values of $e \sin V$, $e \cos V$, e' $\sin V'$, and $e' \cos V'$, $\cdots$ would always take the form shown in the four expressions

$$e \sin V = \alpha f^{it} + \beta f^{i't} + \cdots + \gamma t^r + \lambda t^{r-1} + \cdots + h$$
$$e \cos V = \mu f^{it} + \epsilon f^{i't} + \cdots + \phi t^r + \psi t^{r-1} + \cdots + l$$
$$e' \sin V' = \alpha' f^{it} + \beta' f^{i't} + \cdots + \gamma' t^r + \lambda' t^{r-1} + \cdots + h'$$
$$e' \cos V' = \mu' f^{it} + \epsilon' f^{i't} + \cdots + \phi' t^r + \psi' t^{r-1} + \cdots + l'.$$
$$(107)$$

(It should be explained that f stands for the e of later notation — that is the base of the natural system of logarithms — but i is not $\sqrt{-1}$.) In these expressions, the coefficients α, β, μ, ϵ, $\cdots$, α', β', μ', ϵ', of the exponential terms are real quantities not subject to exponentials. They may, however, become functions of the arc t and of sines and cosines of angles proportional to that arc. As for the quantities γ, λ, ϕ, ψ, $\cdots$, h, l, γ', λ', ϕ', ψ', $\cdots$, h', l', $\cdots$, they are real, containing no exponentials or secular terms, and hence are either constant or periodic.

Laplace then supposes that, without regard to signs, $i > i'$, $i' > i''$, $\cdots$, when $e = (e \sin V)^2 + (e \cos V)^2$. It would then follow that

$$e^2 = (\alpha^2 + \mu^2)\, f^{2it} + \cdots$$
$$+ (\gamma^2 + \phi^2)\, t^{2r} + \cdots + h^2 + l^2. \qquad (108)$$

Similarly,

$$e'^2 = (\alpha'^2 + \mu'^2)\, f^{2it} + \cdots$$
$$+ (\gamma'^2 + \phi'^2)\, t^{2r} + \cdots + h'^2 + l'^2, \qquad (109)$$

and so on. These expressions give the values of the eccentricities, which hold good, however, only for a limited period of time. The precondition that they remain small, varying within narrow limits, is valid if — and only if — all the roots of the equation k are in fact real and unequal. It is very difficult to show this directly, and Laplace goes back to an expression for the eccentricities that he had obtained in discussing the general equations of motion of a system of mutually attracting bodies under the law of gravity (ibid.; OC, XI, 69):

$$c = m\sqrt{\frac{a\,(1-e^2)}{1+\theta^2}} + m'\sqrt{\frac{a'\,(1-e'^2)}{1+\theta'^2}}$$
$$+ m''\sqrt{\frac{a''\,(1-e''^2)}{1+\theta''^2}} + \cdots, \qquad (110)$$

neglecting constant and periodic quantities of the degree m^2, where a, a', a'', $\cdots$ are the semimajor axes of the orbits of bodies m, m', m''; ea, $e'a'$, $e''a''$, $\cdots$ are the eccentricities; and θ, θ', θ'', $\cdots$ are the tangents of the inclinations; and c is an arbitrary constant.

If quantities of the degree e^4, $e^2\theta^2$, and θ^4 are ignored, then (110) becomes

$$c = m\sqrt{a} + m'\sqrt{a'} + \cdots - \frac{1}{2} m\,(e^2 + \theta^2)\sqrt{a}$$
$$- \frac{1}{2} m'\,(e'^2 + \theta'^2)\sqrt{a} - \cdots. \qquad (111)$$

Furthermore, since the mean distances of the planets from the sun are unaffected by their interactions,

$$m(e^2 + \theta^2)\sqrt{a} + m'\,(e'^2 + \theta'^2)\sqrt{a'} + \cdots = \text{constant}. \qquad (112)$$

It had already been pointed out that the values of e, e', e'', $\cdots$ are independent of those for θ, θ', θ'', $\cdots$, so that they will be the same as if the latter were null. Thus (112) reduces to

$$me^2\sqrt{a} + m'e'^2\sqrt{a'} + \cdots = \text{constant}, \qquad (113)$$

which is the equation that must be satisfied by the values of e, e', e'', $\cdots$, after the lapse of any amount of time.

Substituting the general expression of those quantities as given in (107) into (113) gives

$$[m\sqrt{a}\,(\alpha^2 + \mu^2) + m'\sqrt{a'}\,(\alpha'^2 + \mu'^2) + \cdots]f^{2it} + \cdots$$
$$+ [m\sqrt{a}\,(\gamma^2 + \phi^2) + m'\sqrt{a'}\,(\gamma'^2 + \phi'^2) + \cdots]\,t^{2r} + \cdots$$
$$+ m\sqrt{a}\,(h^2 + l^2) + m'\sqrt{a'}\,(h'^2 + l'^2) + \cdots$$
$$= \text{constant} \qquad (114)$$

This equation must hold whatever the value of t, and it is therefore essential to eliminate exponential powers of t and secular terms. To that end, the coefficient f^{2it} is equated to zero, so that

$$0 = m\sqrt{a}\,(\alpha^2 + \mu^2) + m'\sqrt{a'}\,(\alpha'^2 + \mu'^2) + \cdots. (115)$$

Since $m\sqrt{a}$, $m'\sqrt{a'}$, $\cdots$ are positive quantities, and since α, μ, α', μ', $\cdots$ are real quantities, (115) will hold only on the supposition that $\alpha = 0$, $\mu = 0$, $\alpha' = 0$, $\mu' = 0$, $\cdots$. It follows that there are no exponential terms in the values of e, e', e'', $\cdots$.

Returning now to (114) and equating the coefficient t^{2r} to zero gives

$$0 = m\sqrt{a}\,(\gamma^2 + \phi^2) + m'\sqrt{a'}\,(\gamma'^2 + \phi'^2) + \cdots, (116)$$

whence $\gamma = 0$, $\phi = 0$, $\gamma' = 0$, $\phi' = 0$, $\cdots$. Thus, neither do the values for e, e', $\cdots$, contain secular terms. They reduce, therefore, to periodic quantities of the form $\sqrt{h^2 + l^2}$, $\sqrt{h'^2 + l'^2}$, $\cdots$, and we know from (114) that these quantities serve the equation

$$\text{constant} = m\sqrt{a}\,(h^2 + l^2) + m'\sqrt{a'}\,(h'^2 + l'^2) + \cdots. \qquad (117)$$

When the right-hand side of that equation is expanded in a series of sines and cosines, the coefficients of each sine and cosine vanish automatically.

As for the inclinations, the same reasoning may

1390

be applied to the expressions for θ, θ', θ'', $\cdots$. Laplace thus satisfied himself analytically of the periodicity of variations in the orbital eccentricities and inclinations, thereby completing the mathematical demonstration that ". . . the system of the planets is contained within invariant limits, at least with respect to their action on each other" (*ibid.*; *OC*, XI, 92).

The calculations justifying the long-term interdependence of the inequalities of Jupiter and Saturn are enormously lengthier. Laplace deferred their publication to the "Théorie de Jupiter et de Saturne" ([*1788a*] and [*1788b*]), presented in two installments. Unlike the above, which was mainly a mathematical exercise, they involved him in detailed reference to the corpus of recorded astronomical observation and also in arriving at numerical solutions to his equations. He had tried, he said, to give his results a simple and convenient form. At the same time, he thought to improve on the existing practice of mathematicians, who limited themselves to the first powers of the eccentricities and inclinations in their calculations. He had come to recognize that the resulting approximations were insufficiently exact, and in working out the analytical theory of the mutual perturbations he took into account the inequalities that depend on the squares and higher powers of these variations, carrying the approximation up to the fourth power of the eccentricities.

The necessity to recur to the most ancient as well as the most recent data led Laplace into the way of certain historical reflections. It was a curious chance that the maximum acceleration of Jupiter and deceleration of Saturn, *ca.* 1560, should have largely coincided with the revival of astronomy in the generations of Copernicus and after. Since that time, the apparent values were approaching the true values of the mean motions. If astronomy had been reborn three centuries sooner, its practitioners would have observed the contrary phenomena. The motions that a culture attributes to the two planets might thus serve as an index of the period in which it was founded or at least sufficiently developed to support astronomical observation. Laplace would judge by data from Hindu astronomy that in India the mean motions had been determined at a time when Saturn appeared to be at its slowest and Jupiter at its fastest. Two of the principal Hindu astronomical eras appeared to fulfill these conditions, one centering around 3103 B.C. and the other around A.D. 1491 (*ibid.*; *OC*, XI, 178–179). For Laplace was as credulous in accepting historical fact as he was critical of astronomical information. He probably had the former from Bailly's *Traité de l'astronomie indienne et orientale* (1787).

Saturn being the more recalcitrant and less-studied planet, Laplace devoted the first installment of the memoir to calculating its theory in detail. The general strategy for finding its inequalities was to substitute its elements, together with those of Jupiter, into the formulas. Before that could be done, another inequality besides the long inequality deriving from the action of Jupiter had to be noticed. It was responsible for the slight discrepancy in what was only a near equality between twice the mean motion of Jupiter and five times that of Saturn, and its amount was about 10 arc minutes. If that equality had been exact, it would have coincided with the inequality due to the ellipticity of the orbit. A complete theory of Saturn had to provide for all these inequalities. Working out the mathematical basis in the first section of the memoir required varying the constants to eliminate terms introduced in successive integrations that increased with time and that would have precluded stability for the system if they referred to something real. Laplace included a more succinct account of the variation of constants than he had yet given (*ibid.*; *OC*, XI, 131–140).

Before Laplace could give his formulas numerical values, which task was carried out in the second section, he had to know what the arbitrary constants represented. In the expressions for the elliptical motion of the planets, these constants are the mean distance, inclination, the mean longitude at a given moment, the eccentricity, and the positions of aphelion and nodes. They come from the data of observation, which need to be corrected both for inaccuracies and for the effect of the perturbations to which the bodies are subject. The latter effects have to be known in advance from theory. For that purpose, the masses had to be known, taken relative to the sun as unity. In the cases of Jupiter and Saturn, the determination of their inequalities and of the elements of the orbits depend the one on the other in a reciprocal manner. The determination could therefore be accomplished by successive approximations. Halley's tables were the main source of data for Saturn. Dating back to 1719, they needed systematic correction, and Laplace had first of all to arrive at a formula, or "law of errors" (*ibid.*; *OC*, XI, 190), to be applied in using them. He then perfected the law by trying it on numerous oppositions of the planet. Jupiter presented less of a problem: Wargentin's tables were more up-to-date for that planet, and their author had allowed for the inequalities that were independent of eccentricity and also for those depending on the first power of that element. He had not known about the effect of the long inequality on the mean motion, eccentricity, and position of aphelion, and had bundled those effects into his terms for ellipticity, from which they could simply be subtracted in correcting the several elements. Laplace referred his numerical calculations to the beginning of the year 1750, mean time of Paris, choosing that date because it was in the midst of the period of good modern astronomical observations. Perhaps it will help the non-astronomer to visualize what he was about, if some numbers for Saturn are reproduced:

Mean longitude ϵ'	$7^s21°17'20''$
Mean longitude of aphelion ω'	$8^s28°7'24''$
Eccentricity e'	0.056263
Mean longitude of ascending node	$3^s21°31'17''$
Inclination of orbit to ecliptic ($\tan\theta'$)	$2°30'20''$
Sidereal motion during 365-day common year, n	$12°12'46.5'' = 43966''.5$
Mean distance to sun (earth-sun = 1)	9.54007.

$$(118)$$

The mean sidereal motion of Jupiter (n') was $30°19'42''$, or $109,182''$. The problem was then to determine numerically the secular inequalities affecting the orbits of both planets, beginning with those dependent on the angle $5n't - 2nt + 5\epsilon' - 2\epsilon$. Calculation from the theory yielded the amount by which to correct the observed value for this class of inequality. Next came the periodic inequalities that are independent of eccentricities and inclinations, followed by those that derive from the eccentricity, and finally, those depending on the squares and higher powers of inequalities and inclinations. When the conversion from mean to true anomaly was included, Laplace could find the formula for determining the heliocentric longitude of Saturn in its orbit at any instant past or future.

These measures presupposed, however, that the above elements for Saturn in 1750 were exactly correct, together with the theory by which the inequalities were determined. No doubt the approximation was very close, but the values needed to be checked against the entire body of modern observations. To that end Laplace designated by $\delta\epsilon$, $\delta n'$, $\delta e'$, and $\delta\omega'$ the corrections that would need to be applied to the 1750 values for mean longitude, annual mean motion, eccentricity, and position of aphelion, respectively. To determine those quantities empirically, he drew on twenty-four opposi-

tions of Saturn, choosing instances that were well distributed in time from 1591 to 1785 and that his prior investigation of the law of errors in Halley's tables had shown to be tolerably precise. Not that these could be supposed to represent the "true" longitudes – Halley's calculations on the basis of Flamsteed's observations had been executed in ignorance of the phenomena of aberration and nutation and of modern data on the location of certain reference stars. It would be well to recalculate them all. Pending that immense task, however, Laplace proposed to compensate for the lack of precision of the individual observations by increasing the number of them that he employed.

That procedure meant minimizing the error, and to that end Laplace wrote twenty-four linear equations of condition for the theory of the motion of Saturn. Here, for example, is the equation for the opposition observed on 25 December 1679 at 22h 39m Paris time, when the longitude was $3^s4°54'0''$:

$$0 = 3'9''.9 + \delta\epsilon' - 70.01\,\delta n' + 2\delta e'\,0.12591$$
$$- 2e'\,(\delta\omega' - \delta\epsilon')\,0.99204. \qquad (119)$$

In an interesting article (L: [1975]) Stephen Stigler has recently characterized Laplace's solution of his system of twenty-four equations as an early example of a multiple linear regression. For Laplace combined them into a set of four equations by (1) summing all twenty-four; (2) subtracting the sum of the second twelve from the sum of the first twelve; (3) combining one set of twelve in the order: $-1 + 3 + 4 - 7 + 10 + 11 - 14 + 17 + 18 - 20 + 23 + 24$; and (4) combining the remaining twelve in the order: $+2 - 5 - 6 + 8 + 9 - 12 - 13 + 15 + 16 - 19 + 21 + 22$. He then solved these four equations to get

$$\delta\epsilon' = 3'23''.544$$
$$\delta\omega' = 5'45''$$
$$2\delta e' = 30''.094 \qquad (120)$$
$$\delta n' = 0''.11793.$$

Applied to the elements for 1750, these corrections gave

$$\epsilon' = 7^s21°20'44''$$
$$\omega' = 8^s28°13'19'' \qquad (121)$$
$$e' = 0.056336,$$

and the value of $\delta n'$ showed that the mean sidereal motion of Saturn had to be increased by 1/9 second.

Armed with these corrections, Laplace gave simple formulas for finding the location of Saturn at any instant, having now brought theory and practice into conformity. Thus, the mean longitude

$n't + \epsilon'$ is given by taking the corrected mean longitude for 1 January 1750, $7^{\mathrm{s}}21°20'44''$ (121), and adding to it the angular distance traversed in the mean sidereal motion at a rate of 43966''.6 per year of 365 days for the number of days elapsed, instead of 43966''.5, as supposed in (118). A similar procedure was employed with the other elements of the orbit, and Laplace constructed a table not only of the twenty-four oppositions used in refining the data but of some forty-three extending from 1582 to 1786. In it he gave observed heliocentric longitudes together with the excess or residual differences between the observed value, the value that Halley had calculated in 1719, and the value that he had just calculated. Stigler points out that Laplace's solution—for the twenty-four equations that he linearized—had a residual sum of squares only 11 percent greater than a least-squares solution would have yielded and that the residual sum of squares from Halley's calculation was eighty times greater. The increase of Laplace's powers is no less striking in the contrast between this memoir and his early essays in error theory (see Section 4) than it is in astronomy itself. He concluded this part with an application of his formulas to the Ptolemaic data, the most ancient observation being that reported from the Babylonian legacy for 1 March 228 B.C.

The memoir had grown so lengthy that Laplace postponed Jupiter to the sequel. There he again turned the crank to accomplish the mutual reconciliation of the observations with the theory of the largest planet, in its interaction with Saturn as in its lesser inequalities ([1788b]; OC, XI, 226–239). More interesting for the history of his career is the evidence of his involvement in the activities of routine instrumental and positional astronomy. That had already begun, to be sure, in 1781 with the memoir on determination of cometary orbits and the discussion that followed Herschel's discovery of Uranus (see Section 14). With the Saturn memoir ([1788a]) the association became systematic. He read the first installment to the Academy on 10 May and the second on 15 July 1786 (52, 53). In the preamble to the second, he recognized that the theory of Saturn still contained three very small though detectable inequalities. Their sum came to less than one arc second, but they would need to be taken into account in the most exact and rigorous possible calculation. What was needed was that an astronomer familiar with such computations should rework all the oppositions of Jupiter and Saturn in the seventeenth and eighteenth centuries, calculating them directly from the perfected theory

in each instance. Jean-Baptiste Delambre had come forward and volunteered to undertake that task—a *délicate et pénible* discussion, Laplace called it (*ibid.; OC*, XI, 211). The word drudgery might occur to others. For his part, he made the small corrections just mentioned in the theory, and Delambre proceeded to compare the formulas to a very large number of observations and to compile the results. His *Tables de Jupiter et de Saturne* were published in 1789, having been presented to the Academy on 26 April (57). Laplace called them the first tables ever to be based "on the law of gravity alone," since they depended on observation only for the data needed to determine the arbitrary constants introduced by the integration of the differential equations of planetary motion. One particular advantage of that austerity was the possibility that they afforded of deciding whether causes of any sort external to the solar system could disturb its motions. More mundanely, wrote Laplace of Delambre, "I acknowledge with pleasure that, if my research is useful to astronomers, the merit is owing principally to him" (*ibid.; OC*, XI, 211–212). From then on, Laplace in his astronomy was never without a calculator at his beck and call.

There remained the moon, the last member of the solar family whose apparent behavior failed to conform in all respects to the rule of universal gravity. Halley had discovered the acceleration of its mean motion, and since then astronomers had tried correcting for it by adding to the mean longitude a quantity proportional to the number of centuries elapsed since 1700. There was some disagreement among them on the exact rate of the increase in particular centuries, but none on its overall effect. Delambre had just confirmed that the secular motion was three or four minutes greater than in Babylonian times. As to the cause, the Academy had offered several prizes, but no one had been able to identify anything in the configuration or the motion of the earth or its satellite that would explain these variations in the lunar mean motion in a manner conformable to the law of gravity. Various ad hoc hypotheses had been invoked—resistance of the ether, the action of comets, the transmission of gravity with finite velocity. It seemed a pity to Laplace that the moon should still be a renegade, and he had decided to investigate the phenomenon, failing in his first few attempts and telling of his eventual success in "Sur l'équation séculaire de la lune" ([1788c]), the final substantive memoir in the seminal series on planetary motion. He had been led to his formula for the moon—so he recalled in later years—by the application that he had been able to make of his theory of Jupiter and Saturn to the problem of the moons of Jupiter ([1799a]; OC, XII, 193).

The cause, in a word, lies in the action of the sun combined with variations in the eccentricity of the earth's orbit owing to the action of the planets. The action of the sun—to take that first in a qualitative summary of the finding—tends to diminish the gravitational attraction of the earth for the moon and thus to expand its orbit. In itself that effect would slow the angular velocity and appear as a deceleration in the lunar mean motion. The solar action is strongest when the sun is in perigee, and the lunar orbit is then at its maximum, decreasing as the sun moves toward apogee. Thus, in the motion of the moon there is an annual equation that is identical in period with that of the apparent motion of the center of the sun, though opposite in sign. But the gravitational force exerted by the sun on the moon also varies with the changes in the terrestrial orbit that are caused by the resultant of the influence of the other planets. Over the long term, the major axis is fixed and the other elements—eccentricity, inclination, position of nodes and aphelion— change incessantly. The mean force exerted by the sun on the moon varies as the square of the eccentricity of the terrestrial orbit. This effect produces contrary variations in the motion of the moon, the periods of which are enormously longer, extending over centuries. Presently the eccentricity of the earth's orbit is decreasing, and the consequence is an acceleration of the moon. The motions of the lunar nodes and apogee are also subject to secular equations of a sign opposite to that of the equation of the mean motion: for the nodes the ratio to the equation of mean motion is $1:4$ and for the apogee, $7:4$.

It might also have been expected that variations in the position of the ecliptic would influence the action of the sun on the moon by changing the angle between the lunar orbit and the ecliptic. The sun keeps the angle between the lunar and terrestrial orbits constant, however, so that the declinations of sun and moon serve the same periodic law. Finally, Laplace calculated that neither the direct influence of planets on the moon, nor consequences arising from its figure, had any detectable effect on the mean motion. To Laplace, the most surprising finding was that the decrease in the eccentricity of the earth should have had an effect so much more evident in the motion of the moon than in the solar theory itself. The decrease in eccentricity of the earth's orbit came to less than 4 minutes since

ancient times, while the mean motion of the moon had increased by more than $1\text{-}1/2°$. The influences causing these variations clearly affect the lunar motion of revolution differently from the motion of rotation, and it might have been expected that they would disturb the identity of period between the two so that in time the moon would show the earth its other hemisphere. In fact, however—and this effect was the subject of Laplace's final calculation— the period of the moon's secular variation in mean motion of revolution was so long, and the earth's gravity by comparison so powerful a force, that the major axis of the lunar equator is always drawn toward the center of the earth, subject only to the slight libration that shows a tiny rim of the hidden hemisphere, now on one side and now on the other. The period of the moon's long inequality was the greatest that Laplace had yet studied, amounting to millions of years. Yet there could be no doubt of its existence, and he could assure his readers that the acceleration would be reversed one day, also by the force of gravity, and that the moon would retreat from the earth on its next beat. It would never come crashing down upon us, therefore, as it surely would do if ether resistance or a temporal transmission of gravity were the cause of its present approach. Acknowledging that his numerical results in these calculations were much less secure than in the theory of Jupiter and Saturn, he left it to posterity to perfect them. Posterity has obliged. In 1853 John Couch Adams estimated that barely half of the lunar acceleration can be explained by decrease in the earth's orbital eccentricity, and in 1865 Charles Delaunay attributed the remaining increase to slowing of the earth's rotation by tidal friction.

Laplace himself returned to the theory of the moon on several occasions prior to the publication of *Mécanique céleste* ([1798c], [1799a]; see Section 21). He there modified this analysis and its application more fully than he needed to do for his treatment of the other topics in what he had already developed into a body of celestial mechanics, dispersed amid these memoirs and lacking only the name. Since the last, and briefest, in the series, "Mémoire sur les variations séculaires des orbites des planètes" ([1789b]), merely gives a more general proof of the final item that he had demonstrated in the first ([1787a]), namely the periodicity of the variation of orbital eccentricities and inclinations, perhaps it will be fitting to conclude this account of the work that Laplace accomplished at the height of his powers with the peroration to the lunar memoir, presented in April 1788 (56), just one year prior to the onset of the French Revolution (*ibid.; OC*, XI, 248–249):

> Thus the system of the world only oscillates around a mean state from which it never departs except by a very small quantity. By virtue of its constitution and the law of gravity, it enjoys a stability that can be destroyed only by foreign causes, and we are certain that their action is undetectable from the time of the most ancient observations until our own day. This stability in the system of the world, which assures its duration, is one of the most notable among all phenomena, in that it exhibits in the heavens the same intention to maintain order in the universe that nature has so admirably observed on earth for the sake of preserving individuals and perpetuating species.

PART III: SYNTHESIS AND SCIENTIFIC STATESMANSHIP

18. The Revolution and the Metric System. There is no more instructive example of the effect that institutional developments may have, even in the most mathematical reaches of science, even upon the most insensitive of political temperaments, than the modification in the pattern of Laplace's career in consequence of the events following the French Revolution. The earliest recorded expression of his initiative in a reform was a proposal that he advanced—"anew," according to the minutes of the Academy—on 4 July 1789. It went dead against the current, not to say the torrent, of the times. Laplace wished the Academy to require an elementary knowledge of mathematics and physics of artisans qualified for a *brevet* in its licensed corps (*PV*, **108** [4 July 1789], fol. 184). A discussion was postponed to the next session, when his colleagues voted by a large majority to "require" nothing and resolved only that they would "prefer" to license those who knew these subjects (*ibid.* [8 July 1789], fols. 190–191). On 18 July, four days after the fall of the Bastille, Laplace read a paper on the inclination of the ecliptic (58). That autumn the Academy began considering a liberalization of its own structure and procedures to bring its regime into congruence with the emerging constitutional order. Laplace was appointed to a committee to review suggestions along these lines advanced by the duc de la Rochefoucauld (*ibid.* [23 Nov. 1789]), and he joined with Condorcet, Borda, Bossut, and Tillet in composing a memoir on the subject submitted on 1 March 1790 (*ibid.*, **109** [1790–1793], fol. 75). There is no evidence that

he took further part in the reformation or political defense of the Academy, however, the leadership of which was left largely to Lavoisier, whose efforts proved increasingly forlorn as the extremists gained in power.

In the early years of the Revolution, the Academy was inundated with proposals for inventions and technical schemes of many sorts, and Laplace's committee work, like that of all his colleagues, became much more demanding. On 2 November 1791 he was elected to the panel of fifteen academicians who, together with a like number of representatives of inventors' societies, constituted a new Bureau de Consultation des Arts et Métiers intended to relieve the Academy itself of responsibility for advising government agencies on patents and technological policy in general. Prior to that, Laplace had taken one other initiative, together with Condorcet and Dionis du Séjour. Jointly, they framed a petition, subscribed to by others of their colleagues, and addressed it to the National Assembly, urging that body to instruct departmental authorities under the new system of local government to continue the population inquest begun by provincial intendants and published by the Academy (*ibid.*, **109** [11 Dec. 1790], fol. 257; see Section 13). The one revolutionary enterprise that consistently engaged Laplace's interest, however, was the preparation of the metric system, and there his part in the design was more decisive than has been appreciated.

Like other aspects of modern polity, the standardization of weights and measures in France had been urged in the programs of the Turgot ministry (1774–1776) and then frustrated until the Revolution made reform not only possible but imperative. It was also the sector in which science and civil life overlapped most extensively. We have seen the interest that Laplace was already taking in units during his collaboration with Lavoisier on the measurement of heat (see Section 15) and in geodesic surveying during his analysis of the figures of the planets (see Section 16). In the matter of the metric system, the scientists moved before the politicians did. On 27 June 1789 the Academy appointed a commission "for a piece of work on weights and measures"; the members were Lavoisier, Laplace, Brisson, Tillet, and Le Roy (*ibid.*, **108** [1789], fol. 170). No record remains of their deliberations or of a memoir of 14 April 1790 drawn up by Brisson on the relation of linear units to units of capacity and weight (*ibid.*, **109** [1790–1793], fol. 83). It is probable, however, that these early proposals revived a suggestion advanced by La Condamine on returning from the 1735–1736 expedition to Peru. His thought had been to take the length of the seconds pendulum at 45° latitude for the basic linear unit and to decimalize subdivisions. A pamphlet by one recalcitrant commissioner, Tillet, written together with a certain Louis-Paul Abeille on behalf of the Society of Agriculture, attacked precisely such a scheme (*Observations . . . sur l'uniformité des poids et mesures* [1790]). The authors urged limiting the reform to the standardization of existing units, pointing out that with a duodecimal basis the shopkeeper and engineer can manage quarters, thirds, and halves, and warning against sacrificing the daily convenience of farmer, merchant, and builder to the exigencies of a perfectionist science.

It may reasonably be surmised that the scientists, alarmed, felt the need for a spokesman skilled in the ways of the political world. The proposal that formed the basis of the initial metric law was adopted by the Constituent Assembly on 8 May 1790 (*Archives parlementaires*, 1st ser., 15 [1790], 438–443). Written by Talleyrand, it overwhelmed petty anxieties about habit with the grandeur of a universal reform drawing its units from nature (*Proposition . . . sur les poids et mesures* [1790]). The seconds pendulum was to be the linear basis, and gravimetric units were to be related to linear through the volume occupied by a unit weight of water at a given temperature. The last value had just been determined by Lavoisier, who almost surely had coached Talleyrand on these matters.

Thereupon, the Academy appointed a new commission on weights and measures consisting now of Laplace, Lagrange, Monge, Borda, and Condorcet. Less than a year later, on 25 March 1791, they made a different recommendation, which was enacted into law the very next day (*HARS* [1788/1791], 7–16). It provided for a new geodesic survey of the meridian of Paris, to be measured from Dunkerque to Barcelona, and for defining the still unnamed meter as the ten-millionth part of the quadrant. Its subdivisions and multiples would be decimal, and its length would be close to that of the seconds pendulum. The reason given for the change was that the length of the seconds pendulum depended upon a parameter in time, which was arbitrary, and upon the force of gravity at the surface of the earth, which was extraneous to the determination of a truly natural unit. In the words of Condorcet, who drafted the report:

If it is possible to have a linear unit that depends on no other quantity, it would seem natural to prefer it. Moreover, a mensural unit taken from the earth itself offers another advantage, that of being perfectly analogous to all the real measurements that in ordinary usage are also made upon the earth, such as the distance between two places or the area of some tract, for example. It is far more natural in practice to refer geographical distances to a quadrant of a great circle than to the length of a pendulum . . . (*ibid.*, 9–10).

It has become conventional wisdom to dismiss this reasoning as a piece of grantsmanship (A. Favre, *Les origines du système métrique* [1931], 121–130). The argument is that eminent mathematicians and engineers must surely have understood that there is no such thing as a naturalistic metric and that any unit is based on a mere convention, the true meter being an agreed-upon stick. Their real motivation, it is said, was to mount another elaborate and costly scientific traverse at the expense of the state, with the immediate purpose of establishing the reputation of a new surveying instrument, an ingenious repeating circle, invented by one of their number, Borda. These dark thoughts were also noised at the time and were probably unfair, then as now. It seems likely that Laplace would have been instrumental in changing the commission's recommendation. He and Borda were the only members with any background in geodesy — Borda as a navigator and engineer, and Laplace as a theorist analyzing the figure of the earth. The law of 8 May 1790 had been passed in haste to forestall Tillet and the defenders of routine. The draft left it to the Academy to recommend an appropriate scale of subdivision. The importance of that was further emphasized in a companion decree passed the same day (*Archives parlementaires*, 1st ser., 15 [1790], 443), also calling for recommendations from the Academy for a new monetary system.

Evidently the vision of a universal decimal system, embracing not only ordinary weights and measures but also money, navigation, cartography, and land registry, unfolded before the commissioners as they explored the prospect in the summer and autumn of 1790. In such a system, it would be possible to move from the angular observations of astronomy to linear measurements of the earth's surface by a simple interchange of units involving no numerical conversions; from these linear units to units of area and capacity by squaring or cubing; from these to units of weight by taking advantage of the principle of specific gravity; and finally from weight to price by virtue of the value of gold and silver in alloys held invariant in composition through a rigorous fiscal policy. The seconds pendulum could never anchor that. The earth is round, and we fix our position by astronomical observation. The crux, therefore, was that linear units should be convertible to angular. At ordinary dimensions the curvature of the earth's surface would introduce no detectable error. In April 1795 Laplace put the point very simply in a lecture (see Section 20) before the École Normale:

> It is natural for man to relate the units of distance by which he travels to the dimensions of the globe that he inhabits. Thus, in moving about the earth, he may know by the simple denomination of distance its proportion to the whole circuit of the earth. This has the further advantage of making nautical and celestial measurements correspond. The navigator often needs to determine, one from the other, the distance he has traversed from the celestial arc lying between the zeniths at his point of departure and at his destination. It is important, therefore, that one of these magnitudes should be the expression of the other, with no difference except in the units. But to that end, the fundamental linear unit must be an aliquot part of the terrestrial meridian. . . . Thus, the choice of the meter was reduced to that of the unity of angles (*OC*, XIV, 141).

Laplace went on to justify taking decimal parts of the quadrant rather than of the whole circumference by reason of the role of the right angle in trigonometry. All the rhetoric about the universality of units taken from the earth itself thus turns out to have a perfectly sensible foundation. (The substance of the lecture was incorporated into the *Système du monde*, Book I, chapter 14; *OC*, VI, 64–86.) That only Laplace should have explained it clearly—then or now—gives further reason (in addition to the inherent probability, judging from the personalities involved) for thinking that he must have been the moving spirit in the design. Delambre confirmed the cogency of the reasoning in his authoritative account of the origins of the metric system (*Base du système métrique décimal*, 3 vols. [Paris, 1806–1810], III, 304). It is certainly indicative, moreover, that when the two surveying teams took the field in the summer of 1792, one for the southern and the other for the northern sector of the meridian, those chosen to head them should have been Laplace's first two calculators, Méchain, for cometary data (see Section 14), and

Delambre, for the tables of Jupiter and Saturn (see Section 17).

A related project needs to be mentioned. The abolition of feudal landholding and the reorganization of local government made it essential to create a new land registry, or *cadastre*, for determinations of title and assessments of tax. The engineer in charge, Gaspard de Prony, was mandated by law to base the task upon the Cassini map of France, which was also the point of reference for the metric survey. He proposed to concert his efforts with those of the metric commission, construct his instruments on a decimal scale, and convert his units to the new basis as soon as it might be accurately known. His "Instruction" was submitted to the Academy and was largely approved in two reports, both drafted by Laplace. The first, which concerned methods, was also signed by Borda, Lagrange, and Delambre (*PV* [12 May 1792], fols. 147–151). In the second, Laplace took up units and proposed the names meter, decimeter, centimeter, and millimeter. The square on 100 meters was to have been an "are," divided into deciare, centiare, and milliare (*ibid.* [11 July 1792], fols. 205–207; the Bibliothèque Nationale has a *Recueil des documents . . . concernant le cadastre* [Lf^{158}.**236**]).

Laplace had an uncomfortable moment in connection with the design of the Revolutionary calendar, represented by its sponsors as an extension of the metric system to the realm of history and the arts (*Procès-verbaux du Comité d'instruction publique*, II [1894], 440–450, report of Romme, 20 Sept. 1793). Together with Lagrange and Lalande, he was consulted by the enthusiast who conceived it, Gilbert Romme. Lalande's notes of the encounter are in the archives of the Paris Observatory. According to him, Laplace refrained from bringing home to the zealots the incompatibility between their desire for a calendar that would embed the civil year in nature and the incommensurability between the day and the year entailing an unavoidable irregularity in the number of leap years per hundred years in centuries to come (Bibliothèque de l'Observatoire de Paris, B-5, 7). One of Laplace's political detractors (J: Merlieux) later called it apostasy in an astronomer that Laplace should have consented to draft the recommendation ([*P1805*]) on the strength of which Napoleon restored the Gregorian calendar effective 1 January 1806. In fact, astronomers require not a natural but an arbitrary and universal system of intercalation, and the Republican calendar conjured up instead the confusion of ancient Greek chronology, when particular cities intercalated a day or month named after some hero or victory. It may be true, however, that Laplace lacked the temerity to voice this sentiment in what was soon to be called the Year II.

As for the metric system itself, there is no doubt about his fidelity. Subsequent writings made a point of expressing angles in the form of decimal subdivisions of a right angle. After 1795 the metric system, the Observatory of Paris, and indeed all matters pertaining to navigation and official astronomy were placed under the administration of the new Bureau des Longitudes, organized under a law of 25 June 1795 (*Procès-verbaux du Comité d'instruction publique*, VI [1907], 321–327). Laplace served regularly as a member, often chose it as the forum to present appropriate papers, and published frequently in its journal, the *Connaissance des temps*. It is perhaps significant that his son in later years should have made himself something of a watchdog of the integrity of the metric system, as he did of the form of his father's work in general ("Notice sur le Général Marquis de Laplace," *OC*, I, v–viii).

Laplace took no other part in the affairs of the Revolution during the phase of radical republicanism. He had been among the scientists vilified by Marat in the diatribe *Les charlatans modernes* (1791), although not as virulently as Lavoisier. As power shifted to the left in the spring and summer of 1793, the Academy came under increasing pressure from the radicals, and it was suppressed by a decree of the National Convention on 8 August. Laplace appears to have withdrawn from participation as its political vulnerability increased. His attendance became increasingly infrequent in the latter part of 1792, and he was present for the last time on 21 December (*PV* [21 Dec. 1792], fol. 325). A provisional commission was left in charge of the metric system after the abolition of the Academy. On 23 December 1793 Laplace was purged from its membership, along with Lavoisier, Borda, Brisson, Coulomb, and Delambre, on the grounds that such responsibilities were to be entrusted only to those worthy of confidence "by their Republican virtues and hatred of kings" (*Procès-verbaux du Comité d'instruction publique*, III [1897], 239). By then the Terror was approaching its climax. Some time previously (we do not know precisely when) Laplace had decided to remove from Paris. He had then been married for five years, and his two children were infants. He and his wife took a lodging in Melun, thirty miles southeast of Paris, and remained there until he was recalled to Paris

to participate in the reorganization of science that followed the fall of Robespierre and the Jacobin dictatorship in July 1794 (see Section 20).

19. Scientific Work in the Early Revolution. It is sometimes said that Laplace began writing the *Exposition du système du monde* and *Mécanique céleste* during this retreat at Melun. It may be so; there is no way of knowing. We do know that he had presented three further memoirs to the Academy before its situation deteriorated to the point that such works could scarcely have been received, even if they could have been composed. In July 1789 he communicated a memoir on the obliquity of the ecliptic (*58*), later combined with a miscellany of other topics ([*1793a*]); in April 1790 a further memoir on the satellites of Jupiter (*59*), to be followed by a sequel ([*1791a*] and [*1793b*]); and in December 1790 a study of tidal phenomena (*60*), largely in the port of Brest ([*1797a*]). The disparity of publication dates bespeaks the confusion of the circumstances.

All three memoirs exhibit the pattern of the investigations that Laplace put in hand during this second half of his career, alongside the magisterial treatises that remain its monument. On the whole the topics were not new to him, except for those in addition to heat that he took up in physics (see Sections 22–24, 27); neither, with the same exceptions, were the results. They contain no great surprises, nothing like the period of the long inequality of Jupiter and Saturn or the potential function. Instead, he returned to phenomena that he had already dealt with, usually with one or both of two purposes in mind: to give them a more detailed and general analysis and, where possible, to give the analysis numerical expression in actual instances. There was precedent, of course. The theory of Jupiter and Saturn had already issued in Delambre's tables (see Section 17), the cometary theory in the Abbé Pingré's *Cométographie* (see Section 14), and the probability of cause in population studies (see Section 13). It would therefore be difficult to say to what extent external pressure and opportunity favored the shift in emphasis that was occurring anyway in the natural evolution of his lifework. There can be no doubt about the pressures or the opportunities, however, and no reason to question their efficacy in this, as in any evolutionary process. Laplace was forty years old in 1789. Henceforth, his special investigations were conducted in regular and continuing interaction with practical astronomers, physicists, geodesists, meteorologists, and civil officials. The great treatises, on the other hand, owed much to the educational context, which is another, related story (see Section 20).

In the opening sentence of the voluminous "Théorie des satellites de Jupiter," Laplace took upon himself the challenge that he had posed to astronomers four years previously in concluding his discussion ([1787a]; see Section 17) of the pendulumlike libration of the three inner moons. He now intended to give "a complete theory of the perturbations that the satellites experience and to place before astronomers the resources that analysis can provide to perfect the tables of these stars" ([1791a]; OC, XI, 309). The earlier analysis had been cosmologically motivated. The moons of Jupiter were a test case for the stability of the planetary system, and the proof was limited to a relatively brief demonstration that, for the inner three, the two relations, $n - 3n' + 2n'' = 0$ and $nt - 3n't + 2n''t = 180°$, are rigorously exact. A more complete demonstration confirming those theorems occupies Articles XIII–XIV of the present memoir (ibid.; OC, XI, 369–387) concerning inequalities that depend on the squares and products of the perturbing forces. For the rest, he no longer restricted the problem to the three inner satellites, nearly coplanar and concentric with Jupiter and bound in their triune libration. He now included the outer moon, the orbit of which is more eccentric and a bit more inclined to the plane of Jupiter's equator. The calculations involve the interactions of all four together with the effects exerted by two other perturbing forces, those due to Jupiter's own oblateness and to the gravity of the sun, which is affected in its incidence by the angle between Jupiter's orbit and equator. The latter two factors made themselves felt mainly in the inequalities of motion of the fourth satellite.

Handling these complications one after another, Laplace drew successively on each of the main investigations that he had completed in planetary astronomy. The memoir amounts to a reprise of the entire subject put directly into practice within the compass of the Jovian system. In the overall strategy, he followed the model of the Jupiter-Saturn memoir ([1788a] and [1788b]). After first setting up general equations of motion for satellites, he then went through the calculation of the effect of each class of inequalities to which they are subject: those independent of eccentricity and inclination, those depending on eccentricity of orbit, those depending on the action of the sun, those appearing in the squares and products of expressions for the perturbing forces, and those depending on motion in latitude, where the angle of the planes of

Jupiter's orbit and equator is significant. For the theory of the figure of Jupiter ([1791a]; OC, XI, 317) he drew on his work on the attraction of spheroids of revolution ([1785b]) and on its application to the figure of the earth ([1786a]). For the determination of inequalities independent of eccentricity and inclination ([1791a]; OC, XI, 329) he drew on the formula of the comparable section of the Jupiter-Saturn memoir ([1788a]). For the action of the sun on the motion of the satellites ([1791a]; OC, XI, 346) he drew on his discovery of the effect of variations in the eccentricity of the earth's orbit on the motions of our moon ([1788c]). In an interesting aside he explained how the data for Jupiter's moons were calculated from observation of the times and duration of eclipses ([1791a]); OC, XI, 361–369). The first three satellites disappear behind Jupiter on every revolution, and the fourth intermittently. All that the observer needs to report are the instants of disappearance and reappearance, and the information thus obtained is far more accurate than could be yielded by tracking the actual motions. The further possibility of multiplying observations indefinitely reduces the already small risk of instrumental error to zero.

Armed with this information from the Wargentin tables (see Section 17), Laplace could compute provisional numerical values for the mean motions and the mean distances from the center of Jupiter. For the distances, the most accurate method consisted in deriving the values for the three inner satellites from observed positions of the fourth, by means of Kepler's laws. With these quantities, he could calculate the flattening of Jupiter and the masses of the four satellites. Theoretically, determining those unknowns was the main object of the investigation. Practically, its purpose was to permit Delambre to construct tables for the satellites which, like his tables for Jupiter and Saturn, would be derived theoretically from the law of gravity. Observation would confirm the values and not be their source, as in the older tables. Laplace himself published a sample in the *Connaissance des temps* ([1790a]), the first of a series of contributions to practical astronomy in that journal. Delambre incorporated a more fully developed set, drawing on an enormous body of observations, in the third (1792) edition of Lalande's *Astronomie*.

Solving for the unknowns required manipulating a formidable array of equations. The three differential equations obtained at the outset govern the motion of each satellite; for four satellites there are twelve equations. Integration introduced twenty-four arbitrary constants, to be determined by deriving the elements of the orbits from observations of the eclipses. (Actually, the two relations of longitudes and mean motions among the inner three reduced the number of arbitrary constants to twenty-two, but the need to include terms for their libration added two others.) The indeterminate quantities—that is, the flattening of Jupiter and the masses of the four satellites—raised the number to twenty-nine. Five further items of observational data were required to make their determination possible: the principal inequality of the first satellite, the principal inequality of the second, the annual and sidereal motion of the apside of the fourth, the equation of the center of the third relative to the apside of the fourth, and finally the annual and sidereal motion of the orbital node of the second. It is a measure of Laplace's insight into the conditions of the problem that he could seize on these pieces of information as practically obtainable and analytically sufficient for a solution. Substituting those values in the analysis, he fixed the masses at 0.184113, 0.258325, 0.865185, and 0.5590808, each multiplied by 10^{-4}, the mass of Jupiter being taken for unity. As for the figure of Jupiter itself, the ratio of the minor to major axis came out to be 67:72 ([1793b]; OC, XI, 421). Formulas to compute the motion of each satellite in orbit then follow readily.

The first time that Laplace had run through these calculations, which appeared in a sequel ([1793b]) to the parent memoir, it had been with reference to a relatively small body of data, and he regarded his results as a first approximation to be corrected by a process of successive approximations that he set forth at the same time. All this was handed along to Delambre, and the original plan was that he would set to work preparing yet a further stage in the evolution of the tables toward perfection ([1793a]; OC, XI, 477–481). The preemption of Delambre's services by the survey of the meridian prevented that, and Laplace took back the material himself, substituting in the analysis the more exact and fuller data from the tables just mentioned in the Lalande compilation, which although still imperfect were far fuller than his own sketchy figures ([1793b]; OC, XI, 415–416). Delambre began work on the metric system in May 1792, and readying the calculations for publication must therefore have been occupying Laplace in the latter part of that year and perhaps into 1793.

The reflections with which he concluded the investigation are predictable in one respect. He held that the magnitude of the effect that the flattening of Jupiter has upon the inequalities of mo-

tion in its satellites proves that the attraction is compounded of the gravitational force exerted by every particle of the planet, that hypothesis having been assumed in the formulation of the equations of motion. A second rumination may be no more surprising in itself. It concerns the velocity of light, for which topic the moons of Jupiter had been instrumental long before Laplace's interest in them. He had Delambre calculate a value for aberration from figures for the eclipses of the first satellite. The results exactly confirmed Bradley's value drawn from the well-known method of direct observation of the fixed stars. That it should be so confirmed the uniformity of the velocity of light, at least within the dimensions of the diameter of the earth's orbit. Considering the configuration of his career, the conclusion that Laplace drew from this assertion is significant in a way different from the remark on gravity. Rather than celebrating a victory, it anticipates a battle that he would lose (ibid.; OC, XI, 473):

That uniformity is a new reason for thinking that the light of the sun is an emanation from that body; for, if it were produced by the vibrations of an elastic fluid, there would be every reason to think that this fluid would be more elastic and denser on approaching closer to the sun, and that the velocity of its vibrations would thus not be uniform.

One further paper—or, more accurately, collection of short papers—appeared in the volume that the Academy managed to get printed in 1793 prior to its demise. "Sur quelques points du système du monde" ([1793a]) obviously consists of odds and ends from Laplace's worktable. The opening article, which concerns the investigation just discussed, was evidently written after completion of the analytical part ([1791a]) and before Laplace had decided to publish the numerical application himself ([1793b]). Thereafter, the two topics discussed most extensively are the variation in the obliquity of the ecliptic and geodesic data bearing on the figure of the earth.

Laplace had read a draft on the former topic in July 1789 (58). He reminds readers that the decrease in obliquity of the ecliptic was one of the best-studied celestial phenomena, that it occurs in consequence of the action of the other planets on the earth, and that in overall rate and period it is independent of the shape of the earth. Nevertheless, flattening at the poles and bulging at the equator do affect the action on the earth of the sun and moon, and the present analysis investigates the magnitude of these secondary effects in the variation of the plane of the ecliptic. They will appear in the rate of precession of the equinoxes and in the length of the year, and the chief purpose of the discussion was to correct the equations that astronomers employed for precession.

Two main points are to be noted. First of all, the results formed part of a work that he intended to publish on what he still called *astronomie physique* (*ibid.; OC*, XI, 483). This is the first indication since the general treatise on planetary motion ([*1784a*]; see Section 16) that *Mécanique céleste* was in gestation. Second, the mode of analysis recalls a technique that he had introduced in deriving general equations of motion of a system of mutually attracting bodies in the covering memoir on secular inequalities ([*1787a*], Article II; *OC*, XI, 69–70; see Section 17) and that he employed again in considering the motions of Jupiter's moons in latitude ([*1791a*], Article X; *OC*, XI, 347–361). He projected the orbits of planetary bodies onto a fixed plane, passing through the center of the sun, which served as the basis of a coordinate system for calculating angular momentum. Calculations of planetary motion in times past or future could always be reduced to such a plane invariant in space. It seems possible and even probable that this approach derives from his early enthusiasm for the application of d'Arcy's principle of areas to problems of planetary motion (see Sections 5 and 8). At any rate, Articles XXI–XXII ([*1793a*]; *OC*, XI, 547–553) develop it preparatory to a much more extensive use in *Mécanique céleste* (Book I, chapter 5; Book II, chapter 7; *OC*, I, 57–73, 309–345).

Laplace goes on to inquire whether the results of many meridional surveys, and also of determinations of the length of the seconds pendulum at various latitudes, could "without doing too much violence to the observations" ([*1793a*]; *OC*, XI, 493) be reconciled with the hypothesis that the earth is an ellipsoid. The method was simply to compare the data in the literature with the ellipsoidal requirement that the force of gravity at the surface vary with the square of the sine of the latitude. The answer in both cases was negative, although the data from measurements of the pendulum were about eight times closer to satisfying an ellipsoidal figure than were those from meridional surveying. It cannot be said that this finding carried Laplace much farther than his full-scale memoir on the figure of the earth ([*1786a*]; see Section 16), and perhaps the chief interest that it affords for the development of his work is the evidence that error theory was occupying a growing place in his think-

ing about physical problems. The form of the question was whether the discrepancies between the observed and calculated values exceeded what might be attributed to observational error. Calculating those limits represented another step in error theory itself ([*1793a*], Article XI; *OC*, XI, 506–509). It is worth mentioning that the degree measured by Mason and Dixon in Pennsylvania figures in these data.

For the rest, the memoir is a grab bag. One article points out that the earth cannot have taken form in the fluid state, since if it had, it could have assumed only an ellipsoidal figure under gravity. Another observes that the stability of the seas tolerates disturbances sufficiently great so that occasionally the highest mountains are submerged, a consideration that explains certain curious facts of natural history. There is new proof from the conservation of vis viva that the long-term equilibrium of the sea is stable, whatever its depth and whatever the law of rotation of the earth. Laplace gives yet another simplified and generalized demonstration of the variation of constants to eliminate secular terms introduced into the solution of integrals by the standard methods of approximation. Finally, there is a new and purely analytic formulation of the laws of motion of a system of any number of bodies attracting each other by any law whatever. Like the material on the variation of the ecliptic, much of this found its way into appropriate passages of *Mécanique céleste*.

Laplace returned to the problem of the tides in a memoir ([*1797a*]) first read in December 1790 (*60*). After remaining in manuscript for seven years, it was finally published together with other *Nachlässe* from the Academy in its posthumous volume. He may probably have touched it up during that long interval, for although none of the data refers to observations more recent than 1790, in recurring at the outset to the difficulty of the problem, he called it "the thorniest in all of celestial mechanics" (*ibid.; OC*, XII,·4). Thus, he casually launched that phrase in print two years before the appearance of the first two volumes that bear it for their title. The memoir has a very different quality from the enormous and intricate mathematical model that he had constructed some twenty years previously ([*1778a*], [*1779a*], [*1779b*]; see Section 8), which smells of the lamp and not of the brine. In the meantime, he had fixed his attention on the most considerable existing body of data, a corpus of tidal observations in the port of Brest dating from the early eighteenth century, which Jean-Dominique Cassini had found at the Paris Observatory among the papers of his grandfather, Jacques, intendants of that establishment each in his turn. In 1771 Lalande published this find in the second edition of his *Astronomie.* Jacques Cassini himself had drawn on the data for memoirs of no lasting value. Laplace took the occasion to remark how important it was in serious research on such topics to publish the original observations. The whole mass needed to be available before patterns could be discerned, trivial or accidental effects distinguished from fundamental rhythms, and causes assigned to the latter. When he examined the tables, he found one essential item of information missing; the collection contained no observations on the rate of the rise and fall of the tides at Brest. He therefore requested that detailed observations be made, evidently in the year 1790. He does not say who had carried out that commission; presumably, the naval authorities would have been responsible. It was a stroke of good fortune that Cassini had fixed on Brest; for Brittany juts into the sea, and the harbor itself had a long, narrow entrance to a large protected basin so that wave action and other irregular oscillations were damped. Few other locations could have been equally advantageous.

This memoir reads differently, somehow, from any of Laplace's previous works. It would abstract the discussion too far from his own career to say that he did not need to be the mathematician he was in order to compose it, but it can be said that the formulas were not beyond the grasp of anyone capable of doing astronomy or geodesy. It is tempting to infer that so direct a contact with the facts about something as tangible as the tides, all laden with seaweed washing in and out of a working harbor, had a chastening effect at least upon the writing. Whatever the truth may be, however, it is more enigmatic than that. For Laplace did mention, although in a somewhat subdued manner, that his earlier theory had predicted certain of the phenomena and that it had been deepened by others that he had thought irreconcilable on first learning of them ([*1797a*]; *OC*, XII, 21). The difficulty is that when the two memoirs are compared, the theory—unless Laplace meant the theory of gravity, a claim so broad as to be empty—appears to have been changed in certain respects that appear significant to the outside observer two centuries later.

It is natural simply to suppose that by 1790 he had learned to be clear about a physical picture that had been obscured in a thicket of calculation the first time around. Certainly his verbal account of the conclusions could hardly be clearer. Even

now, it would be difficult to think of a better place to send a reader for a qualitative explanation of how the sun and moon contribute to the motions of the tides and of how the magnitude and incidence vary with the seasons and relative positions of those bodies and of the spinning earth. Why does the tide never fall to the lowest point called for in gravitational theory? Why does it always take a little less time to rise than to fall? Why is the magnitude of tidal effects greater the shallower and more extensive the oceanic area? How may local circumstances affect height and times? Why do tides as a rule run most swiftly in shallow bays and narrow passages? The reasons for these and many other effects are expounded with admirable lucidity.

Once again, as in the youthful analysis, there are three systems of tidal oscillation affecting the seas concurrently and superimposing their effects on the motions of individual particles of water. There, however, the identity of the two accounts ceases and merges into a resemblance wherein differences are at least as striking as similarities. In the earlier paper, the three cycles were accorded equal attention and were discussed in the order of the length of their annual, daily, and semidiurnal period. Now the order is reversed. The emphasis is also different, and—what is more surprising—so are important effects attributed to each system. In 1777, an account of the near equality of successive high tides (*23*), which the canonical Newtonian approach failed to give, was the starting point, if not quite the motivation, of the entire investigation. Moreover, Laplace then discussed it by means of a mathematical analysis of the terms in his expressions governing the middle set of oscillations, the period of which is one day. Physically, that analysis presupposed a uniform depth of the sea, and its success was said to confirm that hypothesis. Now, in 1790, nothing is said of the latter argument. Even more curious, the near equality of consecutive high tides is attributed to the physical conditions governing the first cycle discussed, the semidiurnal oscillation. What is attributed to the daily cycle is the small difference, rather than the near equality, between the two tides of the same day in times of syzygy.

Neither of these effects is now deduced in the first instance from the mathematics. The return of consecutive high tides to almost the same level is explained in terms of the equilibrium conditions affecting a single particle of seawater. Suppose the sun (or moon) is acting in the plane of the equator. The gravitational force that it exerts on a particle of water directly underneath will be slightly stronger than the force exerted on the center of the earth. Hence, the action of the sun will tend to separate the particle from the center of the earth. Twelve hours later, the particle is in opposition and the sun attracts the center of the earth more strongly than it does the particle. It will then tend to separate the center of the earth from the particle. Since the radius of the orbit is enormously greater than that of the earth, the two effects are virtually identical in magnitude. Thus it happens, generalizing over the whole ocean, that the seas return to the same state every twelve hours.

Oscillations of the second sort, with a period of one day, are also given a physical explanation. They arise because the attracting body does not normally act in the plane of the equator, and their amplitude is proportional to the product of the sine and cosine of the declination. This daily variation is now held responsible for the small difference in consecutive high tides. At Brest, the tide in the morning was about seven inches higher than in the evening during syzygies at the winter solstice. The magnitude was small in European latitudes. There might be places, however, where geographic conditions would be such that, in the semidiurnal cycle, a tidal crest coming from one direction would coincide with a trough coming from the other, so that the normal tides would annul each other. In such localities, the second system would produce the only tidal motion, and there would be one tide a day. Laplace understood the port of "Batsha" [Ba-dong?]in Tonkin (Vietnam) to be such an instance (*ibid.; OC*, XII, 20).

Finally, Laplace discussed very briefly a system of oscillations like those that he had treated first, and at equal length with the others, in the early memoirs. They are no longer given the period of a year, however, but are simply said to be independent of the rotation of the earth and to result from the sharing of the seas in its other motions. Hence their period is very long though still finite, and their amplitude at Brest very small though still detectable. Centuries of observation would be needed to determine them precisely, after which time the values could be relied on to afford a valuable means of calculating the ratio of the mean density of the earth to that of the seas.

To what extent the theory that Laplace confirmed by the tidal data from Brest remained the theory that he had conceived in his youth is problematic, therefore. Fortunately the point is not one that needs to be settled. The burden of the new exercise would appear to have been descriptive rather than theoretical anyway. It culminates in a formula for finding the level of the tides at Brest at any instant by means of astronomical data (*ibid.; OC*, XII, 112), and the table with which it concludes was of a type that could have served the operations of any enlightened harbor master.

20. Exposition du système du monde. From the fall of Robespierre and the Jacobin regime on 27 July 1794 (9 thermidor an II) until 26 October 1795, France was governed by the Revolutionary Convention, purged of its radical elements and often said to have been reactionary. From then until the coup d'etat of 9 November 1799 (18 brumaire an VIII) that brought Napoleon Bonaparte to power, executive authority was vested in the collective hands of a Directory that never achieved stability, confronted by the survival of Jacobinism on the left and the revival of royalism on the right. Many judgments, mostly adverse, have been passed on the political tone of the period, but there is general agreement among historians about its importance in the institutionalization of modern French society. For science, the most signal instances are the first École Normale, which held classes for three months beginning on 21 January 1795; the École Polytechnique, which was given that name on 1 September 1795, having started classes on 21 December 1794 as the École Centrale des Travaux Publics; and the Institut de France, the scientific division of which began regular meetings on 27 December 1795. They were intended to be the apex of a system of primary and secondary education, trade schools, and medical schools in which science and systematic knowledge would largely replace the classics as the staple subject matter.

Conceptually, the dominant influence was the school of *idéologie*, certain of whose adepts had become administrators of science and culture in the government and who thought to implement a philosophy of science deriving from the Enlightenment. In their outlook the moral and civic function of science is to educate citizens in the order of nature and, by extension, of society. In practice, the Institute never became the quasi-ministry of education originally imagined. The planning for the École Normale was inadequate and it closed after three months, not to reopen until 1812. Napoleon dispersed the *idéologues*, and positivism predominated at the École Polytechnique after 1800. The practical effects were nonetheless decisive in the long run — and even in the short. The center of activity in science moved from academies, its home since the seventeenth century, to institutions of higher education, where it instilled the spirit of research. Scientists—Laplace among them—became educators and professors (cf. J: Lacroix [1828]).

There is no evidence that he was among the organizers or promoters of these enterprises but every indication that when called on to participate, he did so with alacrity and enthusiasm, naturally assuming a leading role. The first, or scientific, class of the Institute amounted to a reincarnation of the Academy decked out in national and republican garb, elitist rather than privileged, civic rather than royal. It so commanded attention in the world of learning that reference to the Institute brings to mind its doings rather than those of its fellow divisions concerned with social science and humanistic culture. At the organizational meeting on 27 December 1795, Laplace was elected vice-president and, on 26 April 1796, president. The office was mainly honorific, and more significant was his presence from the outset on a host of committees where policies were formulated and decisions preempted. To name only the most influential, he was a member of the committees that dealt with bylaws, with weights and measures, with finances, and with the specification of prize contests in physics as well as mathematics (*PVIF*, I [1910], 1, 30, 46, 410). At the end of the Institute's first year, Laplace was chosen to present before the joint meeting of the two legislative councils a formal address and résumé of the work accomplished ([*P1796*]). He took the occasion to exhort the legislators to support the implementation of the metric system.

Laplace's activities at the Institute were a case of new or increased prominence in a set of revised procedures, whereas his involvement with the École Polytechnique marked a new departure, for him and for scientific education at large. There, physics first came to be taught systematically as a mathematical subject to well-qualified and highly selected students. True, the graduates were intended to be engineers, but it cannot have been an accident that the most famous of them in the early nineteenth century were engaged in what is now called physics—Ampère, Sadi Carnot, Fresnel, Malus, and Poisson, to name only the best known. Laplace did not give a course before the Napoleonic period. The technique of teaching was more affected by Monge, the prime mover in the first foundation. Monge built upon the experience of the former Royal Engineering School at Mézières, where he had established his career. Laplace's post from 1795 to 1799 was examiner. It gave him power over content as well as standards. From 1797 until the end of 1799, Monge and Berthollet were largely absent with Napoleon, first in the Italian campaign and then in Egypt. In the interval Laplace became the predominant personality in the affairs of Polytechnique, and the experience that he gained there pertained to the professionalization of science.

The experience gained at the Ecole Normale, on the other hand, pertained rather to popularization. In addition to Laplace, the professors of exact science were Lagrange, Monge, Haüy, and Berthollet. Together with colleagues expounding natural history, geography, and political economy, they lectured in the auditorium of the Jardin des Plantes before audiences of more than 1,200 pupils. The students had been assembled in haste from all parts of the country with the notion that they would return to their own localities to impart what they had learned in a system of secondary schools through which science and learning would radiate. They ranged in age from extreme youth to near senility, and in ability from virtual illiteracy to the talent of the young Fourier, who moved to the staff of Polytechnique in 1795 as assistant lecturer. Laplace was named to a committee to select teachers for the Paris region (*Procès-verbaux du Comité d'instruction publique*, V [1904], 546), and he gave a course of ten lectures that was subsequently published ([*1800d*]). The first eight deal with elementary mathematics—arithmetic, algebra, plane geometry, trigonometry, and the simplest aspects of analytic geometry. The ninth describes the metric system. The tenth introduces probability, summarizing in nontechnical language the highlights of his earlier work in that field; he later enlarged and deepened it into the *Essai philosophique sur les probabilités*. In the opening sentences he explained that he was skipping to this because of its intrinsic interest and its relevance to many matters of great social utility. The program announced for his course had committed him to treat also of the differential and integral calculus, mechanics, and astronomy. Time did not permit, and he would simply refer his auditors to a book that he had in preparation, to be entitled *Description du système du monde*, in which he would give a nonmathematical account of all that had been discovered in these subjects (*ibid.*; *OC*, XIV, 146).

Whatever the comprehension of his lectures on the overcrowded benches of a noisy auditorium, the promised book proved to be one of the most successful popularizations of science ever composed. The impression it made is conveyed by an autograph on the flyleaf of a copy of the first edition presented by a graduate of the College of New Jersey to what is now the library of Princeton University:

> This treatise, considering its object and extent, unites (in a much higher degree than any other work on the same subject that we ever saw) clearness, order and accuracy. It is familiar without being vague; it is precise but not abstruse; its matter seems drawn from a vast stock deposited in the mind of the author; and this matter is impregnated with the true spirit of philosophy.

The *Système du monde* appeared in 1796; the two-volume work consists of five books. Book I begins with what any attentive observer may see if he will open his eyes to the spectacle of the heavens on a clear night with a view of the whole horizon. Book II, which is considerably shorter, sets out the "real" motions of planets, satellites, and comets and gives the dimensions of the solar system. Book III is a verbal précis of the laws of motion as understood in eighteenth-century rational mechanics, with special reference to astronomy and hydrostatics. In Book IV, Laplace in effect summarized his own work in gravitational mechanics. Much of it consists of simplification of the prefatory sections to the published memoirs. The topics are perturbations in planetary motions, the shape of the earth, the attraction of spheroids and the rings of Saturn, motions of the tides and atmosphere, the moons of Jupiter, precession, and lunar motions. Only Book V contains material that Laplace had not written up in technical form or presupposed. It gives an overview of the history of astronomy and concludes with the speculation since called the nebular hypothesis and another on the nature of the universe in outer space.

Laplace kept his book alive and abreast of his thinking and work throughout his life. A second edition was published in 1799 simultaneously with the first two volumes of *Mécanique céleste* (67), as a companion volume to that work and in identical format. The third edition appeared in 1808. For the commentary on the Republican calendar (Book I, chapter 3) it substitutes an explanation of why the Gregorian was more practical after all, despite its imperfections (*OC*, VI, 21–22). Laplace was by then deeply involved with the Arcueil group in problems of physics, most notably sound, capillary action, and refraction of light (see Sections 22 and 23). The fourth edition (1813) preceded by a few months the first printing (1814) of *Essai philosophique sur les probabilités* ([E]), which complemented it in giving intelligent laymen access to that

subject. The fifth edition (1824) announced Laplace's intention to make molecular forces the basis of a theory of heat and gases (see Section 27), a project that he had apparently modified before preparing the sixth edition for a publication that was delayed until 1835, eight years after his death ([H]). We do not know what more he had in mind.

The work itself being a summary of the astronomical investigations that we have been discussing, it hardly seems practical or necessary to attempt a further epitome, the less so since it is readily available in one or another of the above editions and in translations in many libraries. It well repays perusal. Indeed, it may serve a purpose for modern students not unlike that which Laplace had in mind in writing for contemporaries, except that no one will need to feel edified and that by now it may be equally useful in a retrospective way to the scientifically initiated. It is a handbook of what was known of cosmology at the end of the eighteenth century. Perhaps it will be helpful to those who are not experts in the sciences concerned if the present author, who, although incapable of specializing in mechanics or its history, has had occasion to explore certain topics, singles out passages that he has found especially suggestive or illuminating. The discussion of the motion of a material point is a reminder that throughout the eighteenth century, force was taken to be proportional not to acceleration but to velocity, and that when Laplace and others spoke of the "force of a body" they meant the quantity of motion, mass times velocity, later called momentum (Book III, chapters 2, 3; *OC*, VI, 155–161, 173). For the equivalent of the quantity mass times acceleration, the more restricted term accelerative force was used. The importance to Laplace of d'Arcy's principle of areas and its equivalence to conservation of angular momentum emerges very explicitly in Book III, chapter 5 (*OC*, VI, 195–196). An especially felicitous analogy between the secondary and tertiary oscillations of a pendulum and the perturbations experienced by the planets makes it easier to see how he was envisioning and formulating problems of the latter sort (Book III, chapter 5; *OC*, VI, 190–193).

A chapter of "Reflections" on the law of gravity (Book IV, chapter 17) recapitulates the basic assumptions about the operation of this force that Laplace had stated as his point of departure in the dual probability-gravitation memoir ([*1776a*, 2°]; see Section 5). Now they are five instead of four, since the supposition that gravity is indifferent to the state of motion or rest of bodies, and that it acts instantaneously, has become two principles.

An interesting passage explains how his analysis of the secular inequalities of the moon had led him to change his mind on the latter point (*OC*, VI, 346). Finally, a passing observation is reminiscent of a saying of Einstein, to the effect that it is the laws of nature that are simple, not nature itself, which on the contrary is very complicated:

> The simplicity of nature is not to be measured by that of our conceptions. Infinitely varied in its effects, nature is simple only in its causes, and its economy consists in producing a great number of phenomena, often very complicated, by means of a small number of general laws (Book I, chapter 14; *OC*, VI, 65).

The remark is a reminder that Laplace, too, was a thinker about the world and not merely an indefatigable calculator or an overbearing dogmatist, although in the mix that made his personality those aspects may also have been combined.

Only in Book V did Laplace deal with matters on which he had not already published mathematical investigations. It consists of six chapters, the first five on the history of astronomy. He must have taken his history seriously, for he included it in all editions and published a revision separately ([*1821e*]). Laplace, however, was not the scholar that Delambre was, whose histories of ancient and modern astronomy continue to be valuable. Laplace's remarks on the great discoveries of the past are further evidence—if any is needed—that inventiveness in one discipline can accompany banality in another; and his treatment of the place of astronomy in the growth of knowledge is not so much warmed-over as it is cooled-down Condorcet, whose *Esquisse d'un tableau historique des progrès de l'esprit humain* had been posthumously published the previous year.

In the sixth, and last, chapter of Book V, Laplace introduced a speculation on the origin of the solar system and another on the nature of the universe beyond its confines. These concluding nineteen pages written for a popular audience have sustained a more continuing, although not a better-informed, commentary than all of Laplace's other pages put together. The former speculation, which has quite generally come to be misnamed the nebular hypothesis, was presented with the "misgivings" [*défiance*] that anything should arouse that is in no way the product of observation or calculation (B: [1796], II, 303). Perhaps it will not strain analogy (one of Laplace's favorite modes) too far to liken it to the Queries at the end of Newton's *Opticks*. It makes a curious commentary upon the history of science that the indulgence of exact minds

in such flights of fancy should excite so much more interest—to be sure, it is a human interest—even among scientists in later times, than does the content, let alone the detail, of the work that gives them a claim on our attention in the first place. Laplace revised this concluding chapter for each edition of the *Système du monde*, as indeed he did other passages throughout the work, in the light of further reflection and of continuing astronomical discovery. S. L. Jaki has recently reviewed the successive modifications of his cosmogony (K: [1976]). We shall confine our attention to the first rendition and attempt to situate it in the context of Laplace's own thought.

In the century or more since the emergence of evolutionary modes of analysis and explanation, the Laplacian cosmogony along with the Kantian—it is very unlikely that Laplace knew of Kant in 1796—has conventionally been cited as an early instance, perhaps as marking the introduction, of a historical dimension into physical science. That attribution, indeed, has been its chief attraction. Unfortunately, however, it is also quite anachronistic. If the text itself is allowed to speak for Laplace, it will be altogether evident that evolutionary considerations in the nineteenth-century sense formed no part of his mentality. The conclusions that he had reached concerned stability; the evidence for that he had calculated, many and many a time. Although that was not the main burden of these passages, he again referred to it as a warranty for the care that nature has taken to ensure the duration of the physical universe, just as it has the conservation of organic species (for he did allude to them, in terms like Cuvier's). Clearly, it was not about the development of the solar system that he was thinking. It was about the birth.

If we were to find a phrase that would characterize what Laplace had in mind about that event, it would not be "nebular hypothesis." It would be "atmospheric hypothesis." And if, further, we were to identify the context in which he raised the question at all, it would not be the evolution or history of nature. It would be the probability of cause. The motifs are altogether familiar to the student of Laplace's own development. The reader is summoned to contemplate the whole disposition of the solar system. At the center spins the sun, turning on its axis every twenty-five and a half days. Its surface is covered by an "ocean" of luminous matter spotted with dark patches, some of which are the size of the earth. Above that zone is a vast atmosphere; how far it extends into space cannot be told. Beyond it turn the planets, seven of them, in almost circular orbits, with fourteen known satellites among them, all revolving almost in the same plane and in the same direction. Those whose rotation is observable—the sun, moon, five planets, and the rings and outer satellites of Saturn—also turn west to east on their respective axes. The question is, can such an arrangement be the effect of chance, or is the existence of a cause to be inferred? There are twenty-nine discrete movements in addition to the revolution of the earth around the sun. The earth's orbital plane serves as reference for determining whether the motion of other bodies is direct or retrograde. If any of the orbits fell outside a quadrant centered on the earth's orbital plane, the motions would appear retrograde. Now then, if the arrangement of the solar system were due to chance, the probability that at least one such inclination would exceed the quadrant is $1 - \frac{1}{2^{29}}$. Since that value amounts to virtual certainty, and since in fact no orbit does fall outside the quadrant, the arrangement cannot be the result of chance and must therefore bespeak a cause. Other appearances are no less remarkable, notably the very slight eccentricity of the orbits of all planets and satellites. Comets, on the other hand, are highly eccentric. They travel into regions still of the sun's dominion but far beyond the planetary sphere, in orbits inclined at all angles to the plane of the ecliptic.

What, then, can the cause be? It would need to explain five distinct sets of phenomena: (1) motion of the planets in the same direction; (2) motion of satellites in the same direction; (3) motion of rotation in the same direction; (4) small eccentricity of orbits for all the above; and (5) extreme eccentricity of cometary orbits.

The only modern writer Laplace had read who had tried to think seriously about the origin of the planets and satellites was Buffon. In his scheme, a comet had struck the sun and released incandescent matter that cooled and coalesced to become the planetary system. That hypothesis satisfied only the first among the above sets of phenomena. Laplace proposed to rise above that to the "true cause."

Whatever it was, it had to have included all the bodies. It had, therefore, to have been originally in the fluid state in order to have been expansible to the dimensions of the planetary system. It must, in a word, have surrounded the sun like an atmosphere. Might it not, indeed, have been the atmosphere of the sun, which in the course of contracting formed the planets by condensations in the plane of the solar equator at the successive limits

of its extension? Similar processes centered on the planets could equally have produced the satellites. Such a mechanism would also account for the cometary appearances. The clue was in the absence of gradation between the near circularity of planetary and the extreme elongation of cometary orbits. The less eccentric comets, which would exhibit such a progression, had been drawn into the sun with the contracting atmosphere, leaving behind those describing the extreme trajectories. Hence, the appearance of chance in the distribution of their inclinations. Contraction of the solar atmosphere did not explain it—which was not to say that there was no other cause. It is often said that Laplace was mistaken in ruling the comets out of the solar system; only in respect to causality did he really do so, not physically.

So much for the origins of the solar system. It is true that Laplace mentioned nebulae in this chapter, but he did so in the course of the second speculation about the immensity of the universe beyond the solar system, and not in connection with contraction of the sun's atmosphere to form the latter. Large telescopes reveal great patches of undifferentiated light in the heavens. It is plausible to suppose that these *nébuleuses* without stars are really groups of very distant stars. This passage contains another conjecture that has recently been picked up in the light (or, perhaps, the dark) of black holes, rather than of evolution. The gravitational attraction of a star with a diameter 250 times that of the sun, if any such exists, would be so great that theoretically no light would escape from its surface, and it would be invisible by reason of its very magnitude ([*1799d*]).

The first edition of *Exposition du système du monde* (11, 312) closes with a panegyric of astronomy—and a political statement. The great merit of the science is that it

> . . . dissipates errors born of ignorance about our true relations with nature, errors the more damaging in that the social order should rest only on those relations. TRUTH! JUSTICE! Those are the immutable laws. Let us banish the dangerous maxim that it is sometimes useful to depart from them and to deceive or to enslave mankind to assure its happiness.

21. Mécanique céleste. Publication of the *Traité de mécanique céleste* was not only coincidentally but also circumstantially associated with the beginning of the Napoleonic regime. Laplace had first encountered the young Bonaparte at the École Militaire in Paris in September 1785 among the artillery cadets whom he examined that year in mathematics. On 25 December 1797 the Institute elected General Bonaparte, fresh from his victories in Italy, to the vacancy in the section of mechanics created by the exile of Lazare Carnot following the coup d'etat of fructidor (*PVIF* [21 brumaire an VI], I, 296). Laplace accompanied Berthollet in the ceremony of escorting the young general to take his seat. In October 1799, three weeks before the coup d'etat of 18 brumaire (9 November) that brought Napoleon to power as first consul, Laplace presented him with copies of the first two volumes of *Mécanique céleste*. The acknowledgement is famous. Bonaparte promised to read them "in the first six months I have free" and invited Laplace and his wife to dine the next day, "if you have nothing better to do" (*Correspondance de Napoléon Ier*, 27 vendémiaire an VIII [19 October 1799], no. 4384; VI [1861], 1). Laplace and Bonaparte were then serving on a commission together with Lacroix to report on an early mathematical memoir of Biot (69). Bonaparte never made the personal favorite of Laplace that he did of Monge and Berthollet, but in 1807 and 1808 his sister, Elisa, having been elevated to the rank of princess, took up Madame de Laplace and attached her as lady-in-waiting to her court in Lucca. Their correspondence offers a glimpse into the Napoleonic world of fashion (J: Marmottan [1897]).

On seizing power, Napoleon named Laplace minister of the interior. That ministry had responsibility for most aspects of domestic administration other than finance and police. Laplace lasted six weeks in the government, to be replaced by Napoleon's brother, Lucien. Napoleon's reminiscence at St. Helena is also famous. Laplace, he said, could never "get a grasp on any question in its true significance; he sought 'everywhere for subtleties, had only problematic ideas, and in short carried the spirit of the infinitesimal into administration" (*Correspondance de Napoleon Ier*, XXX [1870], 330). Thereupon, Napoleon saw value in Laplace as an ornament, though not as an instrument, of state. He appointed him to the senate and made him chancellor of that body in 1803, an office that Laplace enjoyed throughout the Consulate and Empire at an annual income of 72,000 francs. With other emoluments and honors, he "touched" (as the French has it) well over 100,000 francs a year and became a rich man. In 1805 Napoleon further named Laplace to the Legion of Honor, ennobled him the following year with the title of count of the empire, and in 1813 conferred on him the Order of La Réunion.

Laplace in return dedicated the third volume of *Mécanique céleste* (1802) and *Théorie analytique des probabilités* (1812) to Napoleon. The dedication in the latter is adulatory, even by sycophantic standards, and is not reproduced in the *Oeuvres complètes*, where the third edition occupies Volume VII. These apostrophes to power have incurred Laplace much odium since 1815 and have been taken by his detractors to epitomize a willingness to serve every set of masters in the state quite without regard to principle. It may have been so; his voice was rarely if ever raised in opposition to any action of any government in power. Fairness, however, requires the observation that his political conduct was no different from that of the scientific community as a whole. His eminence there exposed him to closer and more jealous scrutiny than has been directed at his colleagues, and his personality and influence may also have aroused greater hostility than was provoked by others. Fairness also requires recalling that the government of the restored monarchy showed no scruple in associating his reputation with its own, anticlimactic attempt at prestige.

In 1816 he was elected to the Académie Française, and in 1817 Louis XVIII elevated him in the peerage to the dignity of marquis. The reason for that was obvious, however, whereas the relation between Napoleon and the scientific community presents a problem that calls for further study and deeper insight. It was more than a straightforward matter of patronage, important though that was. Some special affinity was involved, comparable perhaps to the interdependence between artist and despot discerned by Jakob Burckhardt in *The Civilization of the Renaissance in Italy*. With all due allowances for differences in century and locus of talent, when this new cultural pact, which recruited scientists as courtiers, finds its analyst, he too may discover a clue to motivations in the illegitimacy of both parties with regard to traditional sources respectively of authority and of knowledge. The key to institutionalization, on the other hand, was the systematic need that authority, in the form of the modern state, and knowledge, in the form of science, were just then beginning to develop for each other in practical fact.

Reorganization of the École Polytechnique was the one important accomplishment that marked Laplace's tenure of the ministry of the interior. A law promulgated on 25 frimaire an VIII (16 December 1799) established a Conseil de Perfectionnement to oversee the curriculum and standards. The course was cut from three to two years and was made preparatory to the specialist schools, the École des Ponts et Chaussées, École des Mines, and École d'Artillerie, which became essentially professional schools at what would now be called the graduate level. Napoleon, well-disposed at first toward Polytechnique, was persuaded to provide adequate financing. Three members of the council were to be delegated from the Institute. Laplace, Berthollet, and Monge were chosen and reelected annually until Lagrange replaced Monge in October 1805 (*PVIF* [15 vendémiaire an XIV], III, 261). Laplace and Berthollet continued to serve throughout the Napoleonic regime, and, indeed, Laplace was commissioned by the government of the restored monarchy to oversee a further reorganization in 1816. His report at the end of the first year of the council's responsibility (24 December 1800) amounts to a catalog of courses and requirements and a prospectus of services to be expected of science by the state ([*P1800*]).

From this, the period of Laplace's greatest prominence, testimony remains of friendships no less than of enmities. They clustered around his work, naturally enough, and if the element of discipleship was predominant, that is not unusual in the lives of scientists. The most sympathetic personal recollection comes from Biot, who made it the subject of a reminiscence half a century later before the Académie Française. Biot had graduated from Polytechnique with the first class in 1797 and had received a post teaching mathematics at the École Centrale in Beauvais. It was common knowledge in scientific circles that Laplace was preparing *Mécanique céleste* for publication. Wishing to study the great work in advance, Biot offered to read proof. When he returned the sheets, he would often ask Laplace to explain some of the many steps that had been skipped over with the famous phrase, "It is easy to see." Sometimes, Biot said, Laplace himself would not remember how he had worked something out and would have difficulty reconstructing it. He was always patient in going back over these deductions and equally so with Biot's own early efforts. He encouraged him to present before the Institute the memoir (*69*) on the general method that Biot had conceived, in the isolation of Beauvais, for solving difference-differential equations. Only some time afterward did Laplace show Biot a paper he had put away in a drawer, a paper in which Laplace had himself arrived at much the same method years before.

Biot would often stay to lunch along with others of his age. After a morning of work, Laplace liked to relax in the company of students and young men at the beginning of their careers. In their mature years, they remained an entourage grouped around him like—Biot's phrase may be more revealing than he intended—"so many adopted children of his thought" (J: Biot [1850], 68). Madame de Laplace, still young and beautiful, treated them like a mother who could have been a sister. Lunch was frugality itself—milk, coffee, fruit. They would talk science for hours on end. Laplace would often ask them about their own studies and research, and tell them what he would like to see them undertake. He was equally concerned with practicalities of their future prospects and would point out opportunities. "He looked after us so actively," said Biot, "that we did not have to think of it ourselves" (*ibid.*, 69; cf. J: Lacroix [1828], *passim*). In 1800 Biot himself was appointed to the chair of mathematics at the Collège de France.

Among contemporaries, the friendship with Berthollet was the closest and most enduring of which record remains. They had begun to draw together in the mid-1780's, attracted to each other scientifically at least by their mutual interest in the physics of chemical forces. Both enjoyed greater prestige and influence at the Institute than either had achieved in the last years of the Academy, where Lavoisier had predominated. They were also close scientifically, at least after Berthollet's return from Egypt with Napoleon in 1799. Laplace contributed two notes on pressure-temperature relations in an enclosed gas to Berthollet's master treatise *Essai de statique chimique* ([*1803c*]). Berthollet then had a country house in the village of Arcueil, five miles south of Paris. He installed a chemical laboratory there and also a physical laboratory, and gathered around his work a younger group, the most notable among them being Gay-Lussac and Thenard. In 1806 Laplace bought the neighboring property. The transfer of his salon there, and their collaboration with Berthollet and his group, created a circle of mathematically and experimentally capable people under strong leadership who soon began informally calling themselves the Société d'Arcueil; its institutional history has been written by Maurice Crosland (J: [1967]). Laplace's part in the work of the group, which also included Bérard, Descotils, Biot, Arago, Malus, and Poisson on the side of physical sciences, occupies Sections 22–24 of the present article. One chronological fact is important to emphasize here. The activities of the Arcueil group clearly postdated Laplace's completion of his astronomical system with the publication of Volume IV of *Mécanique céleste* in 1805 (*83*). As will appear, he did do further astronomical work, but it was of an occasional nature, and Volume V comprises a series of addenda.

Before we proceed to a discussion of that treatise, two further memoirs on particular topics need to be noticed briefly. In January 1796 Laplace read before the Institute the draft of "Un mémoire sur les mouvements des corps célestes autour de leurs centres de gravité" ([*1798a*]) and had it revised and ready for publication less than a year later (*61*). His summary reflections on gravity in the *Système du monde* grouped the problems that the law presented into three categories—the motion of centers of gravity of celestial bodies about centers of force, the figures of the planets and the oscillations of the fluids that cover them, and the motion of bodies about their own centers of gravity (Book IV, chapter 17; *OC*, VI, 341). He did not say so, but his own work clearly had been addressed largely to problems of the first two types, and he had dealt with rotation only incidentally to analysis of precession, tidal motion, and the coincidence between the lunar periods of revolution and rotation. Now he proposed to give a complete analysis of motions of the last type.

In fact, the memoir is both more and less than that. The most important example, he says, is the earth. Precession of the equinoxes is produced by one of its motions, and we tell time by its rotation. First, however, he digressed to give an application that he had just developed of the generalized gravitational function (see Section 16, Equation 94) to the theory of perturbations in planetary motion. The approach came out of his studies of the moon. In analyzing its motion around the earth, he now treated its mass as infinitesimal and attributed to the earth a mass equal to the sum of the two masses. The new, and Laplace thought quite remarkable, equation of condition ([*1798a*]; *OC*, XII, 136) that permitted this gave a direct relation between parallactic inequality and inequalities of lunar motion in longitude and latitude. Moreover, it was easy to verify the theoretical values by observation, since the constants were given by the mean longitudes of the moon and of its perigee and nodes at a given time. More generally, the same equation was applicable to verifying the calculation of the perturbing influence exerted on one planet by another, whose own perturbation is ignored, which procedure was standard in astronomical practice. Laplace promised to develop this first-order theory further and kept his word in *Mécanique céleste* (Book II, nos. 14–15; *OC*, I, 163–170).

Coming back to the theory of rotation about centers of gravity, Laplace considered that the equations Euler had formulated in his *Mechanica* were the simplest and most convenient that he could use. In order to integrate them, terms needed to be expanded in series, and the whole art consisted in identifying those that on integration produced detectable quantities. The finding for the earth was that the only periodic variation in the position of the axis that needed to be considered was the so-called nutation, which depends on the longitude of the nodes of the lunar orbit. Two other axial wobbles, one much smaller and the other of much longer period, might be disregarded. Motions of the axis (and they are the main subject of this memoir) depend upon the shape of the earth, and the analysis led Laplace back to a review of his general memoir on attraction and the shape of spheroids ([*1785b*]; see Section 16).

He now found that the phenomena of nutation and also of precession confirmed the figure for the flattening, namely 1/320, given by the measurements of the length of the seconds pendulum at different latitudes. These results were in agreement and were much closer to satisfying an ellipsoidal figure than the curve constructed by the various surveys of arcs of the meridian. As was often the case when Laplace was changing his mind, he did not actually say that this was what he was doing. He said only that it had to be supposed that terms for the radius of the earth derived from geodesic surveys have less influence than those obtained from a seconds pendulum and that an ellipsoid is to be preferred for calculations of parallax, a figure flattened in the above degree and derived from measurements of the seconds pendulum and analysis of axial variation (*ibid.; OC*, XII, 131). He further gave a direct proof of the theorem that he had long since found indirectly ([*1780c*]; see Section 8), that precession and nutation have the same quantity as if the seas and the earth formed a solid mass. In the preliminary remarks, Laplace said that he was also extending the analysis to the variations in the direction of the lunar axis and in the inclination of the rings of Saturn. In fact, however, the memoir breaks off with an apology for its length and refers the reader to a further volume of the *Mémoires de l'Institut* for a continuation. That second installment never appeared, although what must probably have been the same thing was incorporated in appropriate passages of *Mécanique céleste*, Book V, chapters 2 and 3 (*OC*, II, 375–402). One other feature of this memoir is noteworthy. Laplace was now being assisted in his research by Alexis Bouvard, who had succeeded Delambre in the role of calculator and who performed all the work of calculation for *Mécanique céleste*.

Bouvard also made the calculations for a further investigation of lunar variations, the results of which Laplace read before the Institute on 20 April 1797 (*63*). The seminal series on planetary motions in the 1780's (see Section 17) had culminated in a paper on the secular inequalities of the moon ([*1788c*]), which Laplace had arrived at through the application to the moons of Jupiter of his approach to the theory of Jupiter and Saturn. He had there given a formula for determining the variations in mean motion, having found them to depend on variations of opposite sign in the eccentricity of the earth's orbit. The motions of nodes and apogee of the lunar orbit also exhibit secular inequalities. Laplace had then restricted his determination of those values to terms given by the first power of the perturbing force, although well aware that this was only half the story for the motion of the lunar apogee. The other half was expressed in terms dependent on the square of the perturbing force. Clairaut had discovered that this part was the resultant of the two large inequalities called variation and evection. The secular equation Laplace found for the motion of apogee, added to that for mean motion, gave a secular equation of the anomaly equal to 4.3 times that for mean motion. In like fashion, when he included terms depending on the square of the perturbing force in the secular equation of the nodes, he found its value to be 0.7 that of the mean motion, which amount was to be added to their mean longitudes. Thus, the motions of nodes and apogee decelerated when the mean motion of the moon accelerated, and the secular equations of the three effects were in the ratio 7·33·10 (*OC*, XII, 193 – 194).

These were large inequalities. One day they would produce changes in the secular motion of the moon equal to 1/40 of the circumference and up to 1/12 of the circumference in the secular motion of the apogee. Like the variations of the eccentricity of the earth's orbit, on which they depended, they were periodic; but the periods, which were enormously longer than any others that Laplace had yet identified, occupied millions of years. Slow though the changes were, they were sufficiently important to be incorporated in the tables and to appear in the comparison of ancient to modern observations. Laplace had Bouvard compare some twenty-seven eclipses recorded in antiquity, by Ptolemy and by the Arabs, to the figures in the tables, and he made no doubt of the importance of the acceleration of the motion of the lunar anomaly. He took the occasion to review the ancient corpus of lunar data as calculated by Ptolemy on the basis of the observations of Hipparchus and corrected by the further observations of al-Battānī.

Laplace's presentation of this research differed from his previous practice. He published the results in a brief paper in the *Connaissance des temps* ([*1798b*]), the almanac for practical astronomy and navigation, roundly recommending that astronomers increase the motion of the lunar anomaly by 8′30″ per century and apply a correction to its secular equation equal to 4.3 times the mean motion (*ibid.*; *OC*, XIII, 11). The details of the analysis he kept for publication in the *Mémoires* of the Institute ([*1799a*]). There he chided mathematicians for having been insufficiently scrupulous in examining which of the terms they might legitimately neglect in the successive integration of astronomical expressions (*ibid.*; *OC*, XII, 191 – 192). In this investigation, he found it best to follow d'Alembert's example and express the lunar coordinates in series of sines and cosines of angles depending on the true motion. In those expressions, he made the true longitude the independent variable, rather than the time, as he always did in his planetary theory. There would be an advantage, he thought, in constructing tables that would give time as a function of the true motion of the moon, since terrestrial longitudes were determined in practice on the basis of the time at which the moon was observed to be at some certain position in its motion in longitude.

The papers of this period are indicative of the pattern of Laplace's later work. Henceforth, he tended to divide his efforts between short communications giving the results or applications of his current investigations and the great treatises still to be compiled and issued. These brief reports appeared in the *Connaissance des temps* when they were astronomical; otherwise they were published in one of the other journals started in the 1790's concomitantly with the movement toward specialization in the sciences. Often, as will appear in the Bibliography, he published the same paper in several journals, sometimes with slight modifications. The day of the communication of scientific investigations through the medium of monographic research memoirs was, in any case, almost over. Those that Laplace had yet to publish show the tendency, already evident in the 1790's, to explore ever finer points of his earlier investigations. The first two volumes of *Mécanique céleste* were published in the same year, 1799, as the lunar analysis just discussed. In thus drawing together his science into the form of a treatise. Laplace like many of his colleagues was answering to another aspect of the evolution of science, the creation, actual or potential, by the new system of higher education of a truly scientific public within the larger audience that could be expected for his *Exposition du système du monde.*

Traité de mécanique céleste is a composite work. It has the aspects of a textbook, a collection of research papers, a reference book, and an almanac, and contains both theoretical and applied science. The first two volumes form a largely theoretical unit. Methodologically, their purpose is to reduce astronomy to a problem in mechanics, in which the elements of planetary motions become the arbitrary quantities. Phenomenologically, the purpose is to derive all the observed data from the law of gravity. The textbook character of the work is most apparent in Book I and, to a lesser degree, in Book II, which occupy the first volume.

Book I is a mathematical exposition of the laws of statics and dynamics in a development adapted to the formulation of astronomical problems. Laplace's normal practice in those investigations had been to open each memoir with a derivation of the laws of motion in a form suited to the particular set of problems. Here he arranged the same material systematically. The sequence was canonical: first the statics and dynamics of mass points, second of systems of bodies, and third of fluids; the point of view is d'Alembert's. Dynamical laws are derived from equilibrium conditions. Apart from the motivation, only two features appear to be distinctively Laplacian. In chapter 5, which is concerned with the general principles of mechanics, Laplace incorporated his concept of an invariant plane into the discussion of the principle of conservation of areas. His introduction of that idea ([*1793a*]; *OC,* XI, 547–553; see Section 19) had been the first published statement that a general work on physical astronomy was in preparation. He there emphasized the utility of such a plane in providing a frame of reference, fixed in space, to which calculations of planetary motion could be reduced in centuries to come. In the *Système du monde,* he had specified that a plane "that would always be parallel to itself" would pass through the center of the sun perpendicularly to the plane in which the sum of projected angular momentums of the bodies in the solar system is a maximum (Book III, chapter 5; Book IV, chapter 2; *OC,* VI, 198–199, 218–219). In later terminology, the reference plane is perpendicular to the total angular momentum vector of the system. Laplace had given the

mathematical rule for finding it in the *Journal de l'École polytechnique* ([*1798c*]). Now, in *Mécanique céleste,* he moved the origin of coordinates from the sun to the center of the earth (Book I, no. 21; *OC,* I, 63–69), no doubt because in practice astronomers refer their observations of the motion of celestial bodies to the plane of the earth's orbit (cf. Book I, no. 60; *OC,* I, 337–338).

The second feature that one would not expect to find in a textbook of rational mechanics is the discussion in chapter 6 of the laws of motion of a system of bodies given any mathematically possible hypothesis concerning the relation of force to velocity (K: Vuillemin [1958]). In that apparent digression, Laplace may have been following Newton's example in certain propositions of Book II of the *Principia mathematica.* A completely abstract and general system of dynamics might be imagined in which the number of such relations involving no contradiction would be infinite. There are two laws of nature, however, that hold good as principles of dynamics only in the simplest case, that of force directly proportional to velocity. The first is the principle of rectilinear inertia; the second is the conservation of areas in angular motion. It is in this discussion that it becomes clearest how, in the astronomical application, Kepler's law of equal times in equal areas had become for Laplace a special case of the principle of conservation of areas, or of angular momentum. He was usually careful to point out, however, that an accurate determination of the masses of all the planets had yet to be achieved.

Taken in isolation, Book II might also appear to have been conceived as a manual in which the mathematically qualified student learns the analysis required for theoretical astronomy. In it the laws of motion are applied to deriving the law of gravity from phenomena and to calculating the displacements of celestial bodies. Here also Laplace is more concerned to impart techniques than results. As he moved beyond the differential equations of gravitational attraction (chapter 2) and of elliptical motion (chapter 3), however, the techniques became increasingly his own. Chapter 6, for example, on perturbation theory, generalizes the combination of perturbations in coordinates and in the orbital elements that he had evidently begun working out in the first gravitational memoir ([*1776a*, 2°], Article LXIII; *OC,* VIII, 241–246). Two bodies are assumed to move in coplanar, circular orbits with radii equal to the semimajor axis of the planetary orbits. A disturbing function is developed in sine and cosine series of the longitudinal difference between the bodies in orbit. The coefficients of the series are functions of the ratio of the semimajor axes, and Laplace established the analytical relationships among them and among their derivatives with respect to that ratio, finding expressions for which he could later give numerical values for all possible pairs of planets. The sequence of topics is also distinctively Laplacian; indeed, it is identical to that in the *Système du monde*. At the outset of Book II, Laplace says that he intends to give the mathematization of the phenomena that he had there described in detail. Even in this book, however, the treatment grows more specialized as he continues, and already he was incorporating blocs of material from earlier researches in the exposition. Passages from the memoir on cometary orbits ([*1784b*]), for example, reappear in chapter 4, on motion in very eccentric and parabolic orbits. Similarly, the reciprocity of the acceleration of Jupiter and deceleration of Saturn, and also the libration of the inner three satellites of Jupiter, are introduced to illustrate methodological points. The Jupiter-Saturn relation (chapter 8, no. 65) exemplifies the method of approximating periodic inequalities that appear in elliptical motion when it is legitimate to neglect terms involving squares or products of perturbing forces; the libration of the Jovian moons (chapter 8, no. 66) depends on inequalities that appear only in terms of the order of the squares of the perturbing masses.

Volume II continues and completes the mathematical analysis of the three main categories of phenomena outlined in the *Système du monde*. Having handled the motion of celestial bodies in translation in Book II, Laplace turned to the figure of the planets in Book III, to the motions of the seas and atmosphere in Book IV, and to rotational motion in Book V. Book III, nos. 8–15, on the attraction of spheroids, is a systematic reprinting, with some simplification of the mathematical development, of the material from his memoirs on the subject ([*1785b*], [*1786a*], [*1793a*]). He had promoted the statement of the most important equation, which gives the potential function (see Section 16, Equation 94), to the passage developing the basic differential equations governing the motions of mutually attracting bodies in Book II, no. 11 (*OC*, I, 153). For the rest, he repeated his discussion of the attraction exerted by spheroids of revolution on internal and external points, restated his theorem on the attractions of confocal ellipsoids, showed how to expand the expressions in series, and considered the cases of homogeneous and variable density (see Section 17). The third chapter

brings in the demonstration that a liquid mass rotating under the influence of gravitational force will satisfy an ellipsoidal figure and that its axis of rotation will be in the direction that at the outset would have given it the maximum angular momentum (cf. [*1785b*]; [*1793a*], Article XV). The fourth chapter considers the spheroid covered with a layer of fluid and analyzes the equilibrium conditions (cf. [*1779a*], Article XXVIII; [*1785b*], Article XV); and the sixth and seventh discuss respectively the shape of the rings of Saturn (cf. [*1789a*]) and an equation governing the atmospheres of celestial bodies applied to the sun (cf. *Système du monde*, Book V, chapter 6; see Section 20).

The main novelty is the comparison (chapter 5) of spheroidal attraction theory with the results of geodesic surveys of meridional arcs. Laplace had introduced that topic in the miscellany published and largely lost to view in the waning days of the Academy ([*1793a*], no. 9; see Section 19). In *Mécanique céleste* he could draw on the data, not previously analyzed, from the Delambre-Méchain survey of the meridian from Dunkerque to Barcelona, on which the metric system was to have been based (see Section 18). He also, and perhaps more importantly, went further than he had previously done in applying error theory to the investigation of physical phenomena. An initial theoretical article (Book III, no. 38) develops the analytic geometry of geodesic lines and results in the following expressions applicable to the case of the earth. For the radius vector of an osculatory ellipsoid,

$$1 - \alpha \sin^2 \psi \left\{ 1 + h \cos 2 \left(\phi + \beta \right) \right\}; \quad (122)$$

for the length of a meridional arc,

$$\epsilon - \frac{\alpha\epsilon}{2} \left\{ 1 + h \cos 2 \left(\phi + \beta \right) \right\}$$

$$\left\{ 1 + 3 \cos 2\psi - 3\epsilon \sin 2\psi \right\}; \quad (123)$$

and for the degree measured orthogonally to the meridian,

$$1° + 1° \alpha \left\{ 1 + h \cos 2 \left(\phi + \beta \right) \right\} \sin^2\psi$$

$$+ 4° \alpha h \tan^2 \psi \cos 2 \left(\phi + \beta \right); \quad (124)$$

where ψ is latitude, ϕ is the angle formed by intersection of the plane xz with the plane that includes the radius vector and the z axis, and β is a correction for the deviation of the true figure of the earth from an ellipsoid (*OC*, II, 133–134). Bowditch had to point out that Laplace erred in the calculation, and that his numerical application suffered from this as well as from several arithmetical mistakes (F: [1829–1839], II, 394, 412–416, 447, 459, 471).

Nevertheless, it was in the derivation of these expressions that spheroidal analysis was brought to bear on actual geodesic measurement. The science of geodesy was thereby moved a significant distance along the scale from the observational to the mathematical.

The method itself is more interesting than the results. It had two stages. The first (Book III, no. 39) involved estimates of observational error. The quantities $a^{(1)}$, $a^{(2)}$, $a^{(3)}$, $\cdots$, represent the lengths measured for a degree of the meridian in different latitudes; and $p^{(1)}$, $p^{(2)}$, $p^{(3)}$, $\cdots$, are the squares of the sines of the respective latitudes. On the supposition that the meridian describes an ellipse, the formula for a degree will be $z + py$. Designating the observational errors $x^{(1)}$, $x^{(2)}$, $x^{(3)}$, $\cdots$, Laplace wrote the following series of equations (OC, II, 135):

$$
\begin{aligned}
a^{(1)} - z - p^{(1)}y &= x^{(1)}, \\
a^{(2)} - z - p^{(2)}y &= x^{(2)}, \\
a^{(3)} - z - p^{(3)}y &= x^{(3)}, \\
&\cdots\cdots\cdots\cdots\cdots, \\
a^{(n)} - z - p^{(n)}y &= x^{(n)},
\end{aligned}
\qquad (125)
$$

where n is the number of meridional degrees measured. The purpose is to determine y and z by the condition that the greatest of the quantities $x^{(1)}$, $x^{(2)}$, $x^{(3)}$, $\cdots$, $x^{(n)}$, shall have the least possible value. Laplace gave solutions for the cases of two, three, or any number of such equations of condition, pointing out that the method was applicable to any problem of the same type. He mentioned specifically the example of n observations of a comet, from which it would be required to determine (1) the parabolic orbit for which the largest error is smaller than in any parabola, and (2) whether the hypothesis of a parabolic trajectory can be reconciled with the observations in question. In the present, geodesic case the problem is to determine the ellipse for which the greatest deviation from measured values is a minimum.

The solution would reveal whether the hypothesis of an elliptical figure was contained within the limits of observational error. It would not, however, give the ellipse that the measured values themselves showed to be the most probable—the most probable ellipse, Laplace called it. Determining that figure was the object of the second stage of the analysis (ibid., no. 40). Two conditions had to be satisfied, first that the sum of all the errors made in the surveys of entire arcs should be zero, and second that the sum of all the errors taken positively should be a minimum. In the preliminary version of this analysis ([1793a]) Laplace had at-

tributed the idea for this approach to Boškovíc (K: Todhunter [1873], no. 962, II, 134), of whom he made no mention in Mécanique céleste. Having developed it, he proceeded to numerical calculations of the ellipticity of the earth, concluding from the data of the metric survey that it cannot be an ellipsoid and that the ratio of flattening of an osculatory ellipsoid is 1/250. The remainder of chapter 5 consists of calculations of the probable degree of error in the results of other surveys (Lapland, Peru, Cape of Good Hope, Pennsylvania), of the flattening of Jupiter, and of the length of the seconds pendulum at various latitudes.

A propos of the last topic, it is perhaps worth noting that as Laplace came to consider that measurements of the length of the seconds pendulum might be reconciled with an ellipsoidal figure ([1798a]; OC, XII, 131), his interest in them appears to have slackened. Instead, he increasingly turned his attention to the data from direct geodesic surveys, determining how much of the deviation of that figure was owing to observational error and how much of it to nature. For what the second stage in this investigation finds him estimating is how far nature itself departed from theoretically determined forms. In other words, Laplace was now applying error theory to an investigation of phenomena and not merely to the probability of cause. He had not yet arrived at the least-square rule, and Quetelet's notion that errors of observation and errors of nature may follow an identical distribution would have been foreign to Laplace (L: Gillispie [1963], 449). Both lay not far in the future along the same path, however.

Book IV, on the oscillations of the sea and the atmosphere (the last four of the 144 pages concern the atmosphere), contains less novelty in principle. Here, too, he first develops theory, which occupies three chapters, and compares it to the observations in a fourth. In his memoir on the tides at Brest ([1797a]) he had already revised the approach of his youthful investigations of the ebb and flow of the tides ([1778a], [1779a], [1779b]). The first chapter now gives the mathematical treatment which that revision had summarized. The second restates his two theorems, to the effect that the seas are in stable equilibrium if their density is less than the mean density of the earth, and conversely. The last chapters are largely a repetition of the Brest memoir on the influence of local conditions, illustrated by the same early eighteeenth-century data, the use of which is now tempered by incidental consideration of probable error in the observations. The second volume ends with Book V, on the rotation of celestial bodies. It is one of the shorter books of *Mécanique céleste*; and, like the memoir ([*1798a*]) hurried into print before publication of the work, has the appearance of an afterthought included for completeness.

Laplace had Volume III ready to present to the Institute in December 1802 (*80*). Three years of the Napoleonic consulate had elapsed since the publication of the first two volumes, which he had designated as Part I. The main purpose of Part II, he announced in the preface, was to improve the precision of astronomical tables. That motivation is consistent with the overall configuration of his career, at least in astronomy and probability. In both, the emphasis shifts to application, and only in physics did new theoretical problems engage his interest. The tendency was already evident in the internal sequence of particular investigations, and it would not force matters unduly to describe the first two volumes as representing largely the work of the early Laplace, and the second two that of the later Laplace. The transition occurred somewhere in the interval between 1790 and 1795, the years of the revolutionary liquidation of the old Academy and the quasi-technocratic reorganization of science at the Institute and related bodies. Nothing more than the kind of environmental conditioning that accompanies change of circumstance can be claimed for the coincidence, but influence is nonetheless important for being felt pervasively.

The third volume is entirely occupied by the theory of the planets in Book VI and of the moon in Book VII. In developing the general formulas and methods for planetary astronomy in Book II, Laplace had limited himself to expressions for inequalities in the motions that are independent of orbital eccentricities and inclinations or that depend only on the first power of those quantities. The precision was insufficient for accurate positional astronomy, however, and Book VI applied to all the planets the method employed for the theory of Saturn in the great Jupiter-Saturn memoir ([*1788a*]). Approximations were carried to the terms involving the squares and higher powers of these quantities and also to those depending on the squares of perturbing forces. Laplace then had Bouvard substitute the numerical values for each planet in these formulas, combined with the general formulas from Book II. The successive chapters then give numerical expressions for the radius vector and for its motion in longitude and latitude. It is in this book, and later in Book VIII (Volume IV) on the moons of Jupiter, that *Mécanique céleste* could serve the practical navigator and

observer as the basis for an astronomical almanac. Bouvard was responsible for the enormous labor of numerical computation, for comparing the results with the findings of other astronomers, and for pinpointing the sources of disagreement. There might still be errors, Laplace acknowledged, but he was confident that they were too inconsiderable to vitiate the tables that might now be compiled.

Laplace himself had not previously worked on theories for Mercury, Venus, the earth, and Mars, for all of which the periodic inequalities are small and are now precisely given. Chapters 12 and 13, on Jupiter and Saturn, mainly repeat his classic work on their long periodic inequality. Although he had investigated the motion of Uranus as early as January 1783 (*40*), Chapter 14 is his first theoretical account of its motion. Chapter 15 formulates equations of condition for long-term periodic inequalities produced by the mutual perturbations of pairs of planets other than Jupiter and Saturn — earth-Venus, Mars-earth, Uranus-Saturn, Jupiter-earth — and shows how they corroborate the respective planetary theories. Finally, the masses of the planets and of the moon are calculated relative to the sun, the values for Saturn and Uranus still needing considerable refinement. In the preface, he mentioned the discovery of Ceres on the first day (Gregorian style) of the new century, followed by that of Pallas, but gave no detail.

Book VII is devoted to lunar theory. Its object is to exhibit in numerical detail the finding of the initial memoir on the moon ([*1788c*]) that all the inequalities of lunar motion, namely variation, evection, and the annual equation, result from the operation of universal gravity, and then to deduce from that law further explanations concerning finer points of the motion, and also of the parallax of the sun and moon and of the flattening of the earth. Laplace followed the practice of his second memoir ([*1799a*]) in taking true longitude rather than time for the independent variable in his differential equations of motion, which he had taken the precaution of adapting for the purpose in Book II (no. 15, Equation K). It will be recalled that he had published this paper only a few weeks before the first two volumes of *Mécanique céleste* itself, having worked out the analysis early in 1797 (*63*). In the meantime, the Austrian astronomer Johann Tobias Bürg had been investigating what appeared to be a periodic inequality in the motion of the lunar nodes with an interval of about seventeen years between the maximum positive values and about nineteen years between the maximum negative values. In 1800 the Institute awarded Bürg a prize for this research (*PVIF* [11 germinal an VIII], II, 129). He had already asked Laplace to investigate what the cause of these effects might be. Employing the appropriate equations from *Mécanique céleste* (Book II, no. 14; Book III, no. 35), Laplace analyzed the data in a memoir ([*1801b*]) read before the Institute in June 1800 (*71*). The episode illustrates that from the outset, *Mécanique céleste* was furnishing the apparatus for further research and calculation in both practical and theoretical astronomy. Laplace found that the effects result from a nutation in the lunar axis created by a variation in the inclination of the lunar orbit to the plane of the ecliptic. Its inclination is constant with respect to another plane passing through the equinoxes between the equator and the ecliptic. That angle would amount to 6.5″ on the assumption that the flattening of the earth is 1/334. Further comparison by Bouvard of Bürg's observations with those of Maskelyne indicated rather a figure of 1/314. In any case, the value was far from the fraction of 1/230 that spheroidal theory predicted for an earth of homogeneous density. Laplace was delighted that so minuscule an anomaly in the position of lunar nodes could thus confirm the direct measurements of geodesy on the shape of the earth and on conclusions to be drawn concerning its internal constitution. He incorporated the material in Book VII of *Mécanique céleste*, where it formed the major novelty, the bulk of the discussion being a recapitulation of his earlier research fortified by Bouvard's indefatigable calculation of numerical values for the formulas to serve in compiling precise tables.

For Volume IV, presented to the Institute in May 1805, over two years after Volume III, there remained the practical theory of the satellites of the outer planets, and also of the comets. Book VIII is almost entirely devoted to the moons of Jupiter. It consists of a revision of the calculations of the memoirs of the early 1790's ([*1791a*], [*1793b*]; see Section 19), which had issued in values for the masses of the four satellites relative to that of Jupiter and for the flattening of the latter. Laplace now gives greater numerical detail on the inequalities of the three inner satellites, concealed in the invariance of the libration that he had discovered in his first memoir on these bodies ([*1787a*]). He likens their lockstep to the observable libration of our own moon and compares other particularities of the motion of the Jovian satellites to the lunar evection, annual equation, and variation in latitude discussed in Book VII. (It is interesting that, having been led to his explanation of the apparent lunar acceleration by his first work on the moons of Jupiter, he was now illuminating finer points in their theory by analogy to the moon.) Chapter 7, giving numerical values for the various inequalities, is new. In deriving his formulas for the variations in radius vectors and longitudes, Laplace made several errors that were detected by Airy and corrected by Bowditch (F: Book VIII, no. 21, Vol. IV, 176–185). In all these formulas, Bouvard calculated the numerical values of the coefficients, although the tables to which Laplace refers navigators continue to be Delambre's (*OC*, IV, x – xi). The entire topic is presented as the confirmation by another method of the purely analytic demonstration in Book II, chapter 8 (*OC*, I, 346–395) of the theorems on the libration of the three inner moons. The difference in method consisted in the substitution of synodic for sidereal mean motions and longitudes, and of a moving for a stationary axis of rotation (*OC*, IV, viii). In general, Laplace made more than he had previously done of the spectacle offered by the Jovian satellites of a gravitational system in miniature, its elements oscillating about mean values at a higher rate than those of the whole slow-motion solar system.

The two brief chapters on the satellites of Saturn and Uranus that complete Book VIII are essentially a reprinting of a paper published in the *Mémoires de l'Institut* ([*1801a*]). The outermost satellite of Saturn and all six Uranian satellites that Herschel thought to have observed appeared to be inclined to the plane of the ecliptic at a much greater angle than other planetary bodies. Laplace's analysis demonstrates how that can follow from the weakening of the force of gravity given the distances and ratios of the masses. He acknowledged the data to be very uncertain, however, and indeed it has since been learned that the fifth and sixth moons of Uranus do not exist.

In Book IX, the shortest in the four main volumes, Laplace developed formulas for calculating cometary perturbations from the general equations of motion set forth in Book II, chapter 4 (*OC*, I, 210–254). The planetary formulas were inapplicable to orbits involving large eccentricities and inclinations. For comets, different formulas had to be applied to different parts of the same orbit. Laplace showed how to obtain numerical values for perturbations in orbital elements by means of generating functions. He would have liked to illustrate his techniques by calculating the elements of the curve to be described in the impending return of the comet last seen in 1759. Unfortunately, he was too busy and left the formulas to whoever wished to substitute the numerical data. He did complete two other examples. A chapter on the perturbation of comets that pass very close to a planet concludes that the gravity of Jupiter had drawn the perihelion of a previously invisible comet within range of sight in 1770 and then reversed the effect in 1779, after which year it never reappeared. A second calculation shows that the same comet produced no detectable change in the length of the sidereal year in 1770 despite its proximity to the earth. Laplace felt safe in concluding that the mass of comets is so small that they can have no influence on the stability of the solar system or on the reliability of astronomical tables.

Book X, subtitled "On Different Points Concerning the System of the World," contains largely new material and marks the shifting of Laplace's interest, as he was completing the fourth volume, to problems involving physics. Analysis of the effects of atmospheric refraction upon astronomical observation is the first topic. Laplace had already committed himself to a corpuscular emission theory of light in the remarks on aberration with which he concluded his numerical memoir on the moons of Jupiter ([1793b]; see Section 19). Now his derivation of the phenomena of atmospheric refraction presupposed that model, as did the investigations of 1808 in optics proper, discussed below in Section 24. The first problem in Book X is to find the law governing the dependence of refrangibility on the variation of atmospheric density with altitude and temperature. An elaborate analysis of the passage of light through a refracting medium yielded a formula (OC, IV, 269) that Laplace reckoned to be applicable when a star had risen to an elevation of 12° above the horizon. At angles greater than that, only the atmospheric pressure and temperature in the vicinity of the observer significantly affected the refraction, and these values could be read directly from the barometer and the thermometer.

In order to evaluate his expression numerically, Laplace needed to know the index of refraction of atmospheric air at a given temperature and pressure and the variation of its density respectively with pressure and with temperature. Delambre had determined the index of refraction for apparent elevations of 45° by observations of the least and greatest elevations of certain circumpolar stars at 0° with the barometer at 76 centimeters of mercury. As for the pressure-volume relations of atmospheric air, physicists were all agreed on the direct proportionality of density to pressure at constant temperature (Laplace did not call the law by the name of either Boyle or Mariotte). Despite many attempts at measurement, however, there was still no agreement about temperature-volume relations in gases, and Laplace engaged Gay-Lussac's assistance in examining the matter. For that purpose, Gay-Lussac calibrated a mercury thermometer against an air thermometer, took extraordinary precautions to dry the air and tubes composing the latter (for humidity was the main source of error), and found that at constant pressure of 76 centimeters of mercury, a unit volume of air at 0° expanded to a volume of 1.375 at 100°. Comparison of the two thermometers at intermediate temperatures argued for a linear expansion within that range. The final value represented the mean of twenty-five determinations, although Laplace did not say how the mean was calculated.

All this discussion, which somehow conveys a greater sense of enthusiasm than the preceding books of recapitulation and tabulation, bespeaks Laplace's growing interest in instrumentation, measurement, and the minimization of observational error. No one, he observed, had yet thought how to compensate for variations in humidity in measurements of atmospheric refraction. Small though he calculated the effect to be, he gave a correction table compiled on the reasonable hypothesis that the indices of refraction of air and water vapor are proportional to their densities. In a like, almost offhand manner he reported Gay-Lussac's ascension in a balloon to an altitude of over 6,500 meters, where the proportions of oxygen and nitrogen in the atmosphere turned out to be about the same as at the surface. As Laplace drew toward the intended conclusion of his treatise, the topics grew more recondite and more fanciful in the object — the effect of extreme atmospheric conditions on astronomical observations, the influence of differences in latitude on barometric measurements of altitude, the absorption of light by the atmospheres of earth and sun, and the influence of the earth's rotation on the trajectories of projectiles and on free fall from great heights (cf. [1803b]).

Before writing Book X, Laplace evidently intended to end it with calculations, which occupy chapter 7, contrasting consequences to be deduced from the wave theory and from the corpuscular theory of light. He there purported to show how the resistance of any ethereal medium supporting luminous oscillations would have entailed deceleration of planetary motion. The continuous impact of light corpuscles would, on the other hand, accelerate the planets, except that the effect is exactly compensated by the weakening of the sun's gravitational force through loss of mass. None of this disturbs stability, however. Since the mean motion of the earth shows no change over a 2,000-year span, Laplace calculated that the sun had not lost a two-millionth part of its substance in recorded history and that the effect of the impact of light particles on the secular equation of the moon is undetectable. In a way, it would have been fitting had this chapter been the last, for Laplace applied the calculation that he had just made to the gravitational force considered as the effect of a streaming of particles through space. Thus he would have emerged full circle from his celestial mechanics, coming out just where he went in with the first calculation of the youthful probability-gravitation memoir ([1776a, 2°]; see Section 5), except that now gravity is given a velocity of 1×10^9 times the speed of light, which is to say infinite.

That chance for symmetry (if such it may be called) disappeared with the publication of two further memoirs on the theory and tables of Jupiter and Saturn ([1804a] and [1804b]). Laplace immediately grafted them on to Book X, where they form the basis of chapters 8 and 9. The return to planetary astronomy was unconformable with the overall plan of the treatise, although it will already have been noticed that throughout its composition Laplace found ways to interpolate pieces of continuing research. He called chapter 8 "Supplément aux théories des planètes et des satellites," which may be bibliographically confusing since these chapters did appear in the first edition, unlike the true supplements to be mentioned in a moment. At any rate, in the interval since the publication of Book VI (Volume III, 1802), Bouvard had scrutinized all the oppositions of both planets observed at Greenwich and Paris since Bradley's time, and Laplace himself had reviewed the theory. The result was several new inequalities, and by taking them into account the agreement between his formulas and the observations was improved. The most signal advantage of the new data was that they permitted the first precise calculation of the mass of Saturn, hitherto known only roughly through the elongations of its satellites.

"Nothing more remains for me," wrote Laplace in the concluding sentence to the preface to Volume IV, "in order to fulfill the engagement that I undertook at the beginning of this work, but to give a historical notice of the works of mathematicians and astronomers on the system of the world: that will be the object of the eleventh and last book" (OC, IV, xxv). In fact, quite a lot remained, beginning with the studies of capillary action presented to the Institute on 28 April and 29 Septem-

ber 1806 (86, 87) and separately printed as Supplements I and II to Book X. The years from 1806 through 1809 were evidently occupied with the further work in physics proper discussed in Sections 22–24 below, and those from 1810 through 1814 largely with probability (see Sections 25 and 26). Indeed, prior to 1819, by which time Laplace was seventy years old, he published only occasionally on problems of celestial mechanics, and these papers were on minor points. His only major addition in all that fifteen-year interval was a mathematical improvement in the method of calculating planetary perturbations, presented to the Bureau des Longitudes in August 1808 (90) as a supplement to Volume III of Mécanique céleste.

PART IV: LAPLACIAN PHYSICS AND PROBABILITY

22. The Velocity of Sound. Laplace apparently gained his first experience in physics in the experiments conducted jointly with Lavoisier (see Section 15). It will be recalled that in 1777 they investigated evaporation and vaporization, in 1781–1782 dilation of glass and metals when heated, and in 1782–1783 specific heats, heats of reaction, and animal heats. Apart from occasional collaboration with Lavoisier in the later 1780's, Laplace took little active interest in physics between 1784 and 1801. In the latter year he published a brief piece ([1801d]), which applies spheroidal attraction theory to analysis of the forces exerted by an infinitely thin layer of electrical fluid spread upon such a surface, and which may, therefore, have been a noteworthy link between gravitational theory and potential theory.

In 1802 Laplace made one of his enduring contributions to the science, in a paper that was written not by himself but by his young protégé Biot ("Sur la théorie du son," in Journal de physique, **55** [1802], 173–182). Using a knowledge of adiabatic phenomena, which had only recently become available in France (even though the heating and cooling associated with the rapid compression and expansion of a gas had been quite well known among British, Swiss, and German scientists since the 1770's), Laplace had suggested to Biot how the notorious discrepancy of nearly 10 percent between the experimental value for the velocity of sound in air and the calculated value using Newton's expression, $v = \sqrt{P/\rho}$, might be removed. According to Laplace, the discrepancy arose from Newton's neglect of the changes in temperature that occur in the regions of compression and rarefaction composing the sound wave. Hence Newton's assumption that $P \propto \rho$, which holds good only if isothermal conditions are maintained, was invalid.

Biot expressed the density of air at any point in a sound wave as $\rho' = \rho(1 + s)$, where ρ is the density of the undisturbed air and s the fractional change in density, taken as positive for compression. Where isothermal conditions were maintained, it followed simply that the pressure of the air could be similarly expressed as $P' = P(1 + s)$, where P is the pressure of the undisturbed air. However, if, as Biot supposed, heating and cooling occurred, respectively in the regions of compression and rarefaction, this equation could not hold. Making the reasonable but unproven assumption that the change in temperature was proportional to s, Biot arrived at the expression $P' = P(1 + s)(1 + ks)$, where k is a constant. Hence, assuming that s is small and neglecting the terms in s^2, Biot could show that the velocity of sound in air is

$$v = \sqrt{\frac{P}{\rho}(1 + k)}.$$

The expression reduces to the more familiar

$$v = \sqrt{\gamma \frac{P}{\rho}}$$

if we substitute the modern term γ for Biot's constant $(1 + k)$.

Although Laplace's explanation of the discrepancy, as expounded by Biot, won immediate acceptance, replacing a variety of unsubstantiated proposals made during the eighteenth century by Lambert and Lagrange among others, the experimental evidence necessary for a rigorous proof became available only over the next twenty years. By 1807, however, Biot had made the important observation that sound waves could be transmitted through a saturated vapor ("Expériences sur la production du son dans les vapeurs," in *Mémoires de physique et de chimie de la Société d'Arcueil*, **2** [1809], 94–103). Thus he confirmed that some heating and cooling must occur, for if this were not so, condensation would take place in the regions of compression and the sound would not pass. Another major step forward came in 1816, when Laplace showed that Biot's constant $(1 + k)$ was equal to the ratio between the specific heat at constant pressure (c_p) and the specific heat at constant volume (c_v)—the ratio we now express as γ. Finally, in 1822, experiments by Gay-Lussac and J. J. Welter, for which Laplace was clearly the inspiration, yielded the first reliable, independently derived values for γ ("Sur la dilatation de l'air," in *Annales de chimie et de physique*, **19** [1822], 436–

437). By observing the changes in temperature that occurred when air was suddenly allowed to enter a partially evacuated receiver (a method pioneered some years before by Clément and Desormes), Gay-Lussac and Welter arrived at a figure of 1.3748 for γ. This brought the theoretical value of v (337.14 meters per second) into good agreement with the currently accepted experimental figure.

How Laplace derived the correction factor of $\sqrt{\gamma}$ in Newton's expression for v was left unclear in the paper on the subject that he published as [*1816c*], but a reconstruction resting partly on [*1822a*] suggests that he began by showing that v must be equal to $\sqrt{dP/d\rho}$. In demonstrating that this quantity is in turn equal to $\sqrt{\gamma P/\rho}$, he assumed not only that the difference between c_p and c_v represents the heat required solely to bring about expansion in a gas expanding at constant pressure, but also that it is this same heat that causes heating when the gas is rapidly compressed. By this argument, a decrease in the volume of a unit mass of the gas from V_0 to $(V_0 - \Delta V)$ would release an amount of heat $(\Delta V/\alpha V_0)(c_p - c_v)$ which, in adiabatic conditions, would go to raise the temperature of the gas by $\Delta V/\alpha V_0 \{(c_p - c_v)/c_v\}$, where α is the temperature coefficient of expansion. The effect of this rise in temperature would be to increase the pressure of the compressed gas by $P_0(\Delta V/V_0) \{(c_p - c_v)/c_v\}$, in addition to the increment in pressure that would be expected for an isothermal compression. Hence the total increase in pressure is given by

$$\left(\frac{\Delta P}{\Delta V}\right)_a = \frac{P_0}{V_0} + \frac{P_0}{V_0}\left\{\frac{c_p}{c_v} - 1\right\} = \frac{c_p}{c_v}\left(\frac{\Delta P}{\Delta V}\right)_i,$$

where $\left(\dfrac{\Delta P}{\Delta V}\right)_i$ represents the pressure increment that

would have been obtained under isothermal conditions. It followed simply that, when conditions were adiabatic, $\sqrt{dP/d\rho}$ – Laplace's expression for the velocity of sound – was equal to

$$\sqrt{\frac{c_p}{c_v} \cdot \frac{P}{\rho}}.$$

It now remained to calculate a numerical value for c_p/c_v. At a time when no experimental data for c_v existed, this was no easy task, and in [*1816c*] Laplace was vague about the method that he had used. However, two attempts at a reconstruction (M: Finn [1964], 15; Fox [1971], 162–165), although differing on matters of detail, reveal quite clearly not only the unsatisfactory nature of the argument but also the importance for Laplace of the erroneous data concerning the specific heats of gases that had been published by Delaroche and Bérard in 1813. In particular, Laplace's argument rested squarely on their false observation that the specific heat of air decreases as it is compressed. Hence the similarity between Laplace's own figure for γ (1.5) and the figure of 1.43, required in order to secure exact agreement between prediction and observation, was quite fortuitous. Nevertheless, the plausibility of Laplace's treatment appears to have gone unquestioned, and the measurements of γ by Gay-Lussac and Welter in 1822 only confirmed a result that had already won general acceptance.

23. Short-range Forces. Nearly all of Laplace's work in physics from 1802 was characterized by an interest in what he saw as the outstanding problems of the Newtonian tradition; in this respect the attempt to correct Newton's expression for the velocity of sound was typical. From 1805, however, his interest in Newtonian problems assumed a more mathematical character. As we shall see, much of this later work was severely criticized. But, whatever its shortcomings—and it did little to enhance Laplace's reputation in his later life—it contained many results of enduring value, most notably perhaps in the theory of capillary action; and, even more important, it served to tighten the bond between mathematics and physics. This is not to imply that Laplace was in any sense the founder of mathematical physics—there were too many precursors in the eighteenth century for that claim to be sustained—but he did make a major contribution to the mathematization of a subject that had hitherto been predominantly experimental.

The increasingly mathematical thrust of Laplace's work in physics is very apparent in the studies of molecular physics that he pursued, and encouraged others to pursue, for the rest of his life. As early as 1783, when he composed *Théorie du mouvement et de la figure elliptique des planètes*, he elaborated a suggestion that he had advanced in the *Mémoire sur la chaleur* ([1783a]), written jointly with Lavoisier. It expressed his belief that optical refraction, capillary action, the cohesion of solids, their crystalline properties, and even chemical reactions were the results of an attractive force, gravitational in nature and even identical with gravity at bottom ([1784a], xii–xiii; see Section 16). Almost twenty years earlier, near the beginning of his career, he had remarked in the program of the dual probability-gravitation memoir ([1776a, 2°]; see Section 5) that analogy gives us every reason to suppose that gravity operates between all

the particles of matter extending down to the shortest ranges. He repeated the detailed speculation in the first edition of *Exposition du système du monde* (B: [1796], II, 196–198) and looked forward to the day when the law governing the force would be understood and when "we shall be able to raise the physics of terrestrial bodies to the state of perfection to which celestial physics has been brought by the discovery of universal gravitation." In this comment, which is obviously reminiscent of the speculations on molecular forces in the Queries of Newton's *Opticks*, there lay the nucleus of a program that guided Laplace's own research in physics and that of several distinguished pupils until the 1820's.

Nevertheless, it was not until 1805 that Laplace began publishing on problems related to his program. By then, interest in molecular forces treated in the Newtonian manner had been greatly stimulated in France by Berthollet's work on chemical affinity, in particular by the *Essai de statique chimique* (1803), in which chemical reactions were explained in terms of short-range attractive forces, supposedly of a gravitational nature, of precisely the kind postulated by Laplace in his physics. It seems likely that Laplace was strongly influenced both by the *Essai* and by Berthollet himself, whose close friend he had been since the 1780's, and that the influence was mutual and reciprocal. In any event, Laplace's first work in molecular physics was published just two years after the publication of the *Essai*, in Book X of the fourth volume of the *Traité de mécanique céleste* (1805) (see esp. chapter 1, pp. 231–276; *OC*, IV, 233–277) and in two supplements to the book (*86, 87*) published in 1806 and 1807 (*OC*, IV, 349–417, 419–498).

It is a measure of Laplace's closeness to the Newtonian tradition that his first studies of molecular forces were concerned with optical refraction and capillary action. Both were manifestations of action at a distance on the molecular scale which had been of special interest to eighteenth-century Newtonians such as Clairaut and Buffon, as well as to Newton himself. (The work of Clairaut appears to have been especially important for Laplace. See, in particular, Clairaut's "Du système du monde dans les principes de la gravitation universelle," in *MARS* [1745/1749], 329–364. On page 338 of this article Clairaut ascribes "the roundness of drops of fluid, the elevation and depression of liquids in capillary tubes, the bending of rays of light, etc." to gravitational forces that become large at small [molecular] distances.) Both Clairaut and Buffon had raised major theoretical problems to which there was still no satisfactory answer by the end of the eighteenth century. In particular, although it was generally accepted that the force between the particles of ordinary matter (in the case of capillary action) and between the particles of ordinary matter and the particles of light (in the case of refraction) diminishes rapidly with distance, it had proved impossible to determine the law relating force and distance. Clairaut, for example, had tried to account for the intense short-range forces by suggesting that the law of gravitational force should contain a term inversely proportional to the fourth power of the distance, $1/r^4$ (*op. cit.*, 337–339). Buffon, by contrast, had upheld the $1/r^2$ law, although he had observed that such a law would be modified at short range by the shape of the particles of matter ("De la nature. Seconde vue" [1765], in his *Histoire naturelle, générale, et particulière*, 44 vols. [Paris, 1749–1804], XIII, xii–xv). Recognizing the intractability of the problem, Laplace proposed a much simpler solution that could be applied in all branches of molecular physics. In treatments that made good use of mathematical techniques developed in his earlier work on celestial mechanics, he showed that the precise form of the law was unimportant and that perfectly satisfactory theories could be given by simply making the traditional assumption that the molecular forces act only over insensible distances.

The treatment of refraction in Book X of the *Mécanique céleste* centered on the specific problem of atmospheric refraction, a matter of practical as well as theoretical concern to Laplace and his colleagues at the Bureau des Longitudes. The whole discussion was conducted in terms of the corpuscular theory of light, the truth of which was never questioned. According to Laplace, the path of a corpuscle of light passing through the successive layers of the earth's atmosphere is determined by the varying attractive forces exerted on it by the particles of air. The measure of these forces was what Laplace, following Newton, called the refracting force (*force réfringente*), a quantity equal to ($\mu^2 - 1$), where μ is the refractive index of the air. In this analysis, ($\mu^2 - 1$) is proportional to the increase in the square of the velocity of the incident corpuscles of light, and hence, in accordance with the normal laws of dynamics, it measures the force of attraction to which they are subject. In deriving his extremely complicated differential equation for the motion of light through the atmosphere, Laplace had to assume, not only the short-range character of the forces to which light corpuscles were subjected, but also that the re-

fracting force was proportional to the density of the air, ρ. In order to integrate the equation, it was necessary to make further, speculative assumptions concerning the variation of ρ with altitude (the subject of a long and somewhat tentative section) and to allow for the effect on ρ of the air's humidity. The result was a method of calculating the magnitude of atmospheric refraction for which Laplace claimed complete reliability at any but small angles of elevation.

Despite subsequent refinements, much of Laplace's theory of capillary action, as expounded in the two supplements to Book X of the *Mécanique céleste*, survives in modern textbooks (a brief study of Laplace's theory appears in M: Bikerman [1975]). However, its roots lie as firmly in the vain quest for a comprehensive physics of short-range forces as do those of his work on refraction. As in the theory of refraction, it was crucial that the forces exerted by the particles of matter on one another could be ignored at any but insensible distances (although it was equally important that these distances be finite—an assumption that distinguished Laplace's theory from others in which adhesion was seen as the cause of capillary phenomena). Hence Laplace was glad to invoke Hauksbee's observation that the height to which a liquid rises in a capillary tube is independent of the thickness of the walls of the tube.

In each of the two supplements on capillary action Laplace presented a quite distinct version of his theory. In the first, he arrived at a general differential equation of the surface of a liquid in a capillary tube by considering the force acting on an infinitely narrow canal of the liquid parallel to the axis of the tube. In the second, he treated the equilibrium of the column of liquid in a capillary tube by considering the forces acting upon successive cylindrical laminae of the liquid parallel to the sides of the tube. The two versions were in no sense inconsistent, although in a number of applications the second version proved to be somewhat simpler and more fruitful.

Laplace was concerned, above all, to demonstrate the close agreement between his theory and experiment, and much of both supplements was devoted to this task. Among his most striking successes was a proof (obtained by solving the differential equation of the liquid surface in the first version of his theory) that the elevation of a liquid in a capillary tube is very nearly in inverse proportion to the tube's diameter. Using the same version of the theory, he also showed that the insertion of a tube of radius r_1 along the axis of a hollow tube of slightly larger radius r_2 causes the liquid between the tubes to rise to a height equal to that to which it would rise in a circular capillary tube of radius $(r_2 - r_1)$; thus he confirmed a well-known observation made but not explained by Newton. Among the other classic problems treated in the supplements were the behavior of a drop of liquid in capillary tubes of various shapes (including conical tubes), the rise of liquids between parallel or nearly parallel plates, the shape of a drop of mercury resting on a flat surface, and the force drawing together parallel plates separated by a thin film of liquid.

The importance, for Laplace's theory, of the short-range character of the molecular forces cannot be overstressed. Small terms involving the square of the distance were repeatedly ignored, and it is no coincidence that in his concluding remarks to the second supplement Laplace reiterated his belief in the identity of the forces at work in optical refraction, capillary action, and chemical reactions. In accordance with his belief that capillarity is a consequence of intermolecular action at a distance (albeit at a very small distance), he tried to determine the relative magnitude of the attractive force between the particles composing the liquid (F_1) and the force between the particles of the liquid and those of the tube (F_2). Neglecting variations in density near the surface of the liquid and the walls of the tube, he showed that if $F_2 > F_1/2$, the surface must be concave; otherwise it must be convex, being, in the limiting case of $F_2 = 0$, a convex hemisphere.

Even as the supplements on capillary action were being written, the comparison between theory and observation was being carried still further in experiments, performed at Laplace's request, by Gay-Lussac, Haüy, and Jean-Louis Trémery (the experiments are reported in [1806a]; see OC, IV, 403–405). These experiments gave the theory added plausibility, as Laplace himself was always ready to observe; and they certainly helped it to survive the criticism of Laplace's only contemporary rival in the treatment of capillarity, Thomas Young. By comparison, Young's theory ("An Essay on the Cohesion of Fluids," in *Philosophical Transactions of the Royal Society* [1805], 65–87), which was based on the concept of surface tension rather than intermolecular attraction, was obscure and unmathematical. Yet Laplace's theory was not without fault, and its author led the way in making modifications. In a paper that he read to the Academy of Sciences in September 1819, the theory was refined to take account of the effect of heat in reducing the attractive force between the particles

of a liquid ([1819h]); the net attractive force was now taken as the difference between the innate attraction (the only force considered in the supplements to the *Mécanique céleste*) and a repulsive force that was supposed to be caused by the presence of heat. An even more important modification was made in 1831 in Poisson's *Nouvelle théorie de l'action capillaire*, in which Poisson remedied one of the most obvious weaknesses in Laplace's theory by taking account of the variations in density near the surfaces of the liquid and the material of the capillary tube.

24. The Laplacian School. From the time the studies of refraction and capillary action appeared until 1815, Laplace exerted a dominating influence on French physics. Its extent is equally apparent from the problems that younger men were encouraged to investigate (either directly or through prize competitions), from the nature of their answers (which with remarkable frequency served to endorse and extend the Laplacian program), and from educational syllabuses and textbooks, which seldom departed from Laplacian orthodoxy on such matters as the physical reality of the imponderable fluids of heat, light, electricity, and magnetism. Yet at no time was Laplace's control total. There were always those in France who worked outside the Laplacian tradition or even in opposition to it. For example, the paper on the distribution of heat in solid bodies that Fourier read to the First Class of the French Institute in 1807 shows no sign of Laplace's influence, either in its positivistically inclined physics or in its mathematical techniques. (See J: Grattan-Guinness with Ravetz [1972]. A revised version of the paper of 1807 was submitted in 1811 for the prize competition of the First Class. It won the competition but was not published until 1824–1826; see *MASIF*, **4** [1819–1820/1824], 185–555; and **5** [1821–1822/1826, 153–246].) Indeed, Fourier's treatment stands in marked contrast with Laplace's own discussion of the problem, incorporated as a "Note" to his paper on double refraction read to the Institute in January 1809 ([1810a], 326–342; OC, XII, 286–298). In this note Laplace set up a model for heat transfer by reference to the molecular radiation of caloric over insensible distances. Even Poisson's papers of 1811–1813 on electrostatics ("Sur la distribution de l'électricité à la surface des corps conducteurs," in *MI*, **12**, pt. 1 [1811/1812], 1–92; *ibid.*, pt. 2 [1811/1814], 163–274) owed more to Coulomb than to Laplace, although Poisson was close to Laplace at this time and Laplace would certainly have approved of his treatment, in particular his use of the two-fluid theory of electricity. Such instances of non-Laplacian physics leave no doubt that a fruitful union of the mathematical and experimental approaches to physics would have occurred in early-nineteenth-century France quite independently of Laplace. But the fact remains that Laplace did more than any of his contemporaries to foster that union and, at least in the short term, to determine the character of the work that emerged from it.

The years of Laplace's greatest influence in physics were also those in which his personal standing was at its height, outside the scientific community as well as within it; and he seized every opportunity of furthering his scientific interests. It was a simple matter for him to direct the attention of gifted young graduates of the École Polytechnique, such as Gay-Lussac, Biot, Poisson, and Malus, to problems of his own choice, often in return for help in advancing their careers in the teaching institutions of Paris or at the Bureau des Longitudes. And, once he had become Berthollet's next-door neighbor at Arcueil and the joint patron of the Société d'Arcueil in 1806, he could offer his protégés the additional attractions of access to Berthollet's private laboratory and an association with the elite of Parisian science in the weekend house parties that were a feature of Arcueil life until 1813 (J: Crosland [1967], *passim*). The work of Gay-Lussac, Haüy, and Trémery on capillary action (1806), of Biot on the transmission of sound in vapors (1807), and of Arago and Biot on the polarization of light (1811–1812) was very obviously a result of direct influence of this kind.

It was equally important for the course of French physics that Laplace wielded extraordinary power in the First Class of the French Institute. Here his ability to dictate problems and solutions was no less apparent than in the more intimate atmosphere of Arcueil. It was Laplace, for instance, who persuaded the First Class to engage Biot and Arago on the experimental investigation of refraction in gases, which they described to the class in March 1806 ("Mémoire sur les affinités des corps pour la lumière, et particulièrement sur les forces réfringentes des différens gaz," in *MI*, 7, pt. 1 [July 1806], 301–387). It is a measure of his influence that their results, although obviously applicable to the practical problems of astronomical refraction as well, were presented in the context of a highly theoretical discussion of short-range molecular forces and of the affinities between the particles of the eight gases examined and the corpuscles of light. Biot and Arago, in fact,

adopted Laplace's analysis of refraction without question. Although they measured refractive index (μ) in their experiments, they presented their results in terms of refractive power (Laplace's *pouvoir réfringent*), that is, the quantity $(\mu^2 - 1)/\rho$; and they provided the experimental evidence—conspicuously lacking in Book X of the *Mécanique céleste*—that, for any one gas, $\mu^2 - 1$ is proportional to ρ. It is also a mark of their allegiance to the prevailing orthodoxy of Arcueil—although in this case Berthollet was as much the inspiration as Laplace—that they speculated confidently on the analogy that they supposed to exist between chemical affinity and affinity for light, as measured by the refractive power. Such an analogy was consistent with Laplace's view that both types of affinity were gravitational in origin, so that it was highly satisfactory to be able to show that the order in which substances appeared in the two tables of affinity was very roughly similar.

Laplace also used his position at the Institute to good effect in the system of prize competitions. There is little doubt that he was chiefly responsible for the setting of the competition for a mathematical study of double refraction, which was announced in January 1808 and won by Malus, a recent recruit to the Arcueil circle, in January 1810. (For a detailed study of this competition, see M: Frankel [1974], 223–245.) The intention in setting this subject was clearly that Laplace's theoretical treatment of ordinary refraction, as given in the *Mécanique céleste* in 1805, should be extended to embrace double refraction as well; and to this extent the competition was a success.

Double refraction had never been satisfactorily explained either in the corpuscular theory or in Huygens' wave theory. Among the corpuscularians, Newton's brief analysis of the phenomenon in terms of the two "sides" of a ray of light (*Opticks*, 4th ed. [1730], Query 26) was still endorsed in textbooks but vaguely and without conviction; Haüy's *Traité élémentaire de physique* (2nd ed. [Paris, 1806], II, 334–355) is a good illustration of this. Huygens' explanation, as given in the *Traité de la lumière* (1690), not only had obvious weaknesses, particularly in its inability to explain the phenomena associated with crossed double-refracting crystals, but was also too closely allied to the wave theory to carry conviction at a time when—especially in France—the corpuscular theory was dominant.

It seems likely that the immediate stimulus for the competition on double refraction was the news of Wollaston's experimental confirmation of Huygens' construction for the ordinary and extraordinary rays. Huygens had used his wave theory and his notion of secondary wavelets to show that the wave surface of an extraordinary ray was an ellipsoid of revolution, while that of an ordinary ray was a sphere. He had then deduced the properties of the ellipsoid and had established laws governing the path of the extraordinary ray at different angles of incidence. Although Huygens confirmed these laws experimentally, his method, as described in the *Traité*, was obscure; hence the need for Wollaston's systematic confirmation ("On the Oblique Refraction of Iceland Crystal," in *Philosophical Transactions of the Royal Society* [1802], 381–386), described before the Royal Society in June 1802 but, because of the war, inaccessible in France until 1807.

Wollaston's paper appeared as an impressive endorsement of Huygens' construction and, by implication (for Wollaston did not endorse the wave theory), as a challenge to the corpuscularians. The challenge was one that Laplace could not resist, and his enthusiasm for a competition that was clearly intended to yield a corpuscularian counterpart to Huygens' wave theory of double refraction was only heightened by the availability of a candidate of impeccable credentials in Malus. The latter's analytical skills and commitment both to the corpuscular theory and to the doctrine of short-range forces were already apparent in the "Traité d'optique," which he read to the First Class of the Institute in April 1807 (published in *Mémoires présentés à l'Institut national . . . par divers savans . . . Sciences mathématiques et physiques*, 2 [1811], 214–302); hence the endorsement of these principles in his prize-winning paper was, we may assume, no more than the fulfillment of Laplace's expectations.

Laplace followed the course of the competition, and Malus's work in particular, very closely. A report on the paper of December 1808 in which Malus announced his discovery of polarization (*91*) reflects Laplace's admiration not only for the discovery but also for Malus's experimental confirmation of Huygens' law of extraordinary refraction (*OC*, XIV, 322). (When Laplace presented his report to the First Class of the Institute, on 19 December 1808, Malus's confirmation of Huygens' law was still unpublished. See M: Frankel [1974], 233.) At last it was established beyond doubt that any corpuscular theory of double refraction would have to be consistent with the law, and almost immediately Laplace showed how this might be achieved, in the "Mémoire sur le mouvement de

la lumière dans les milieux diaphanes," which he read to the First Class of the Institute in January 1809 ([*1810a*]).

Laplace began by asserting, quite dogmatically, that Huygens' wave theory was inadequate for the explanation of double refraction and that the way ahead lay in devising a new explanation in terms of short-range molecular forces. His own, corpuscular theory rested on the principle of least action and on an arbitrary but plausible assumption concerning the relationship between the velocity of light inside a crystal (v), the velocity of light outside the crystal (c), and the angle (V) between the ray inside the crystal and the crystal's optic axis. Presumably by analogy with Snell's law for ordinary refraction, for which $v^2 = c^2 + a^2$, Laplace put, for the extraordinary ray, $v^2 = c^2 + a^2 \cos^2 V$. Assuming the truth of this equation, he derived expressions relating the direction of the extraordinary ray to the angle of incidence of the ray entering the crystal and the orientation of the optic axis.

Laplace's treatment was remarkably like Malus's. The expressions by which they both described the path of the extraordinary ray were similar in form and, by an adjustment of constants, could even be made identical. Moreover, in arriving at his expression, Malus, like Laplace, leaned heavily on the principle of least action, although he derived the dependence of v on the orientation of the extraordinary ray by assuming, as Laplace had not done, the truth of Huygens' law. The similarity between the two papers was such that the possibility of plagiarism cannot be ruled out. Malus felt that by the time Laplace wrote his paper of January 1809, he already knew the essentials of Malus's theory, which were almost certainly available by late 1808. And, whether or not it was intentional, Laplace's paper certainly had the effect of diminishing Malus's achievement in providing a corpuscular theory of double refraction.

Taken together, the papers of Laplace and Malus could be passed off as yet another triumph for corpuscular optics: now no one could doubt that Huygens' law was consistent with the doctrine of short-range forces and the materiality of light. Yet there were weaknesses. As Young observed, the ellipsoid of revolution, which represented a wave front in Huygens' theory, was reduced in Laplace's paper to a mathematical construct without physical significance (see Young's unsigned review of Laplace's memoir, in *Quarterly Review*, 2 [1809], 337–348, esp. 344); and it was by no means obvious that there really existed molecular forces with the special directional properties required in order to explain extraordinary refraction. But in the period of Laplacian domination of French physics, such objections were readily overlooked.

Laplace's involvement in the prize competition on the specific heats of gases, which was set in January 1811, was equally apparent though less direct. The winning entry, by Delaroche and Bérard ("Mémoire sur la détermination de la chaleur spécifique des différens gaz," in *Annales de chimie*, **85** [1813], 72–110, 113–182), made a decisive contribution to Laplacian physics, and we may be sure that Laplace's wishes were prominent both in the setting of the competition and in the adjudication. The first aim was the acquisition of reliable data in a notoriously uncertain branch of experimental physics. But a quite explicit subsidiary purpose was to decide whether it was possible for some caloric to exist in a body in a combined, or latent, state (that is, without being detected by a thermometer) or whether (as William Irvine, Adair Crawford, and John Dalton had supposed) all of the caloric was present in its "sensible," or free, state and therefore as a contribution to the body's temperature. In their *Mémoire sur la chaleur* ([*1783a*]) Lavoisier and Laplace had provided strong evidence against Irvine's theory, so that it was predictable enough that the winners, Delaroche and Bérard, should use their measurements of the specific heats of elementary and compound gases to endorse what was clearly the Laplacian view. As a result of experiments that they performed entirely at Arcueil, they firmly upheld the distinction between latent and sensible caloric.

So in the competitions on double refraction and the specific heats of gases Laplace was well served, but not all of his attempts to use the system of prize competitions were so successful. The competition on the distribution of heat in solids, which Fourier won in 1811, departed significantly from Laplace's approach to the problem (although, unlike Lagrange, he found much to admire in Fourier's paper); and the competition set in 1809 on the theory of elastic surfaces was for Laplace a failure. Before the closing date for this competition, Laplace added elastic surfaces to the list of phenomena that might be explained in terms of short-range molecular forces ([*1810a*], p. 329), but no entries of sufficient merit were received. The prize was eventually awarded in January 1816 to Sophie Germain, whose paper broke pointedly with the theory of elastic surfaces treated in the Laplacian manner, which Poisson had presented before the First Class of the Institute in 1814. (Germain's

paper was published in an enlarged and modified form as *Recherches sur la théorie des surfaces élastiques* [Paris, 1821]. Poisson's paper appeared as "Mémoire sur les surfaces élastiques," in *MI*, **13**, pt. 2 [1812/1816], 167–225; see esp. 171–172 and 192–225.)

25. Theory of Error. The activity at Arcueil was at its height from 1805 through 1809, after which interval of preoccupation with problems of physics and younger physicists (see Sections 22, 23, 24), Laplace turned back to probability for the intensive effort that culminated in the production of the *Théorie analytique des probabilités* in 1812 and the companion *Essai philosophique sur les probabilités* in 1814. The prelude to these works consists in a pair of memoirs ([*1810b*] and [*1811a*]) and a supplement ([*1810c*]) to the earlier paper, together with a "Notice sur les probabilités," published anonymously in the *Annuaire publié par le Bureau des longitudes* ([*1810d*]) and since forgotten. Laplace presented the first of these papers before the Institute on 9 April 1810 (*95*). We have already seen how prior to that the analysis of probable error had assumed increasing importance for him in Book III of *Mécanique céleste*, particularly in the comparison of spheroidal attraction theory to geodesic data in chapter 5, and how the problem of correcting for instrumental error in physical observations had concerned him in Book X, mainly in relation to barometric and thermometric data (see Section 21).

The greatest novelty in the two analytical papers of 1810 and 1811 is the derivation from what is now called the central limit theorem of the least-square rule for determining the mean value in a series of observations. Legendre had published the rule in 1805 as a method for resolving inconsistencies between linear equations formed with astronomical data. His procedure was not a probabilistic one. In 1809 Gauss did derive the least-square law from an analysis of what is now called the normal distribution (L: Eisenhart [1964]; Plackett [1972]; Sheynin [1977]). It is sometimes said that this opportunity was what drew Laplace back to a preoccupation with the whole theory of probability in these, his advancing years, after the lapse of a quarter century since his initial immersion in its theory, definition, and application to population problems. That is uncertain, however, since it was only in the addendum ([*1810c*]; *OC*, XII, 353) to the earlier memoir that he first mentioned least squares. Moreover, he accompanied these memoirs with the popular "Notice sur les probabilités" (cf. Delambre, in *MI* [1811/1812],

"Histoire," i – ii) in which Laplace enlarged on the lecture he had given before the École Normale in 1795 ([*1800d*]). Most of the passages from this notice he then incorporated verbatim in the methodological and actuarial sections of the first edition of the *Essai philosophique* ([E]). In the *Annuaire* of the Bureau des Longitudes they serve to introduce a set of tables of mortality and feature a verbal statement of the central limit theorem (*op. cit.*, 110 – 111). Perhaps, therefore, it will be prudent to report his own account of the route that he had followed in finally arriving at that theorem.

The opening mathematical paper ([*1810b*]) in the pair under discussion has exactly the same title, "Mémoire sur les approximations des formules qui sont fonctions de très grands nombres," as did the important sequence twenty-five years before ([*1785a*] and [*1786b*]) that had moved probability from analysis of games of chance to population studies (see Section 12). In Laplace's own recollection, it was the lengthy repetition of events encountered in theory of probability that had initially brought home to him the inconvenience of evaluating formulas into which the numbers of these events had to be substituted in order to achieve a numerical solution. He had then attacked the difficulty by seeking a general method for accomplishing transformations of the type that Stirling had discovered for reducing the middle term of a binomial raised to a high power to a convergent series. The method he had given ([*1781a*] and [*1785a*]; see Section 12) transformed the integrals of linear differential or difference equations, whether partial or ordinary, into convergent series when large numbers were substituted in terms under the integral sign, the larger the numbers the more convergent the series. Among the formulas he could thus transform, the most notable was that for the finite difference of the power of a variable. In probability, the conditions of the problem often required restricting consideration to the positive values even though the variable decreases through zero into the negative range.

That was the case in the analysis of the probability that the mean inclination of any number of cometary orbits is contained within a given range. It now appears that Laplace had felt dissatisfied with everything he had so far tried on that problem. He had started it with his youthful analysis of the orbital inclinations of comets in order to determine whether the distribution bespeaks the same cause as the nearly coplanar arrangement of the planets ([*1776b*]; see Section 6). Apparently, he took up the question again soon afterward, for he now says that the problem can be resolved by a method that

he had given in his first comprehensive memoir on probability ([*1781a*]; see Section 11), namely that the required probability could be expressed by the finite difference of the power of a uniformly decreasing variable in a formula where the exponent and the difference are the same as the number of orbits. Unfortunately, a numerical solution was unobtainable in practice, and it is reasonable to surmise that this was the reason that he failed to include the problem in the printed memoir ([*1781a*]). The obstacle stopped him for a long time, he acknowledges. Finally, and this would appear to be the background of the 1810 memoir, he had resolved the difficulty by approaching the problem from another point of view. Assuming in general that the prior probabilities (he now says *facilités*) of inclination serve any law whatever, he succeeded in expressing the required probability in a convergent series. For he had come to see the problem as identical with those in which the probability is required that the mean error in a large number of observations falls within certain limits, which question he had discussed at the end of "Mémoire sur les probabilités" ([*1781a*], Article XIII, 30 – 33]), although without numerical examples. (He does not say so here, but the point of view was also akin to that taken in his calculation that the error in estimating the population of France from a given sample would be within certain limits [*1786c*]; see Section 13.) He could then show that if the observations are repeated an indefinite number of times, their mean result converges on a limit such that, if an equal interval on either side be made as small as one pleases, the probability that the result will be contained therein can be brought so close to certainty that the difference is less than any assignable magnitude. If positive and negative errors are equipossible, this mean term is indistinguishable from the truth. Because the methods he had so far discussed were indirect, Laplace considered it preferable to find a direct approach to evaluating the finite differences of the higher powers of the variable; and he proceeded to apply to error theory a technique that he had published the previous year in *Journal de l'École polytechnique* ([*1809e*]; OC, XIV, 193). The memoir contains refinements of his earlier work on generating functions and on the use of definite integrals for solving certain classes of linear partial differential and difference equations that could not be integrated in finite terms ([*1782a*]). He applied to the present purpose an analysis involving the reciprocity of real and imaginary results, which he had introduced in the first memoir on approximate solutions to formulas containing very large numbers ([1785a]; cf. Section 29).

Thus, it was by way of analyzing the distribution of cometary orbits that Laplace came to the central limit theorem, having perfected methods for evaluating the mathematical expressions developed years before. The opening articles argue the old proposition that neither the mean inclination of the cometary orbits (by now ninety-seven were known, all of which he could now include in the computation), nor the proportion of direct to retrograde motions, can be supposed to result from the same cause as the arrangement of the planetary system. Article VI changes the problem of mean inclination into the problem that the mean error of a number n of observations will be contained within the limits $\pm \dfrac{rh}{\sqrt{n}}$, where r is the sum of the errors. At first, Laplace assumes the equipossibility of error in the interval h, but he goes on to the general case in which the error distribution follows any law, and obtains for the required probability the formula (OC, XII, 325):

$$\frac{2}{\sqrt{\pi}} \sqrt{\frac{k}{2k'}} \int e^{-\frac{k}{2k'} r^2} dr. \qquad (126)$$

When $\phi\left(\dfrac{x}{h}\right)$ is the probability of the error $\pm x$, k is

$$\int_{-h/2}^{h/2} \phi \frac{x}{h} dx,$$

and k' is

$$\int_{-h/2}^{h/2} \frac{x^2}{h^2} \phi\left(\frac{x}{h}\right) dx.$$

Later in 1809 (we do not know precisely when), Laplace composed a brief supplement ([1810c]) in which he returned to the choice of the mean in a series of observations, which task had first attracted him to error theory in the memoir on the probability of cause ([1774c], Article V; see Section 4). He invokes the procedure that he had imagined crudely there and more abstractly in the closing passages of the "Mémoire sur les probabilités" ([1781a], Articles XXX–XXXIII). A curve of probability might be constructed, for which the abscissa defines the "true" instant of the observation—presumably astronomical—and the ordinate is proportional to the probability that the value is correct. The problem is to find the point on the x-axis at which the departure à craindre from the truth is a minimum. Now then, just as in the theory of probability, the loss "to be feared" is multiplied by its probability and the product summed, so in error theory the amount of each error, regardless of sign, is to be multiplied by its probability and the product summed. Supposing that n observations of one sort, with equal possibility of error, result in a mean value of A; that n' of another sort, following a different law of error, result in a mean of $A + q$; that n'' of yet another sort and another distribution result in a mean of $A + q'$, and so on; and that $A + X$ is the mean to be preferred among all these results. From Equation 126 Laplace then derives the proposition that the required value of X will be that for which the function (OC, XII, 353)

$$(pX)^2 + [p'(q-X)]^2 + [p''(q-X)]^2 + \cdots \qquad (127)$$

is a minimum, $p, p', p'', \cdots$, representing the greatest probabilities of the results given by the observations $n, n', n'', \cdots$. That expression gives the sum of the squares of each result multiplied respectively by the greatest ordinate in its curve of error. It is clear from Laplace's comment that the novelty was not in the least-square property itself. He considered its status merely hypothetical, however, when the mean depended on a few observations or on an average among a number of single observations. It became valid generally only when each of the results among which it gave the mean itself depended on a very large number of observations. Its basis had to be statistical (a word that he did not employ), and only then could it be derived from the theory of probability and employed whatever the distributions of error in instruments or observations.

Daniel Bernoulli, Euler, and Gauss are mentioned in this note, albeit rather vaguely, but not Legendre. Hard feelings about priorities in the matter of least squares had meanwhile arisen between Legendre and Gauss. Delambre, now a permanent secretary of the scientific division of the Institute, tried to make peace (MI, 12 [1811/1812], "Histoire," i–xiii). His contemporary account reaches the same conclusion that Laplace himself arrived at when reviewing the origin of least squares in Théorie analytique des probabilités (OC, VII, 353). Gauss had indeed had the idea first and made use of it in private calculation, but Legendre had come upon it independently and published it first. Delambre also reports Gauss's attribution of inspiration to a theorem that he had found in Laplace, namely that the value of the integral $\int e^{-t^2} dt$ taken from $-\infty$ to $+\infty$ is $\sqrt{\pi}$ (cf. Section 12, Equation 62). In fact, so Legendre informed Gauss in their exchange of reproach, the theorem belonged to Euler

(M: Plackett [1972], 250). Otherwise, Laplace escaped unscathed on the fringe of this dispute, never having claimed the least-square rule itself but only the generality that it could assume in virtue of his derivation of it from the probability of cause. His initial procedure would now be called Bayesian.

Laplace followed a different procedure in the second of these papers, "Mémoire sur les intégrales définies . . ." ([1811a]). He opened it also with a historical resume, recalling (what he had never claimed at the time) how the companion discoveries of generating functions ([1782a]) and approximations for formulas containing very large numbers ([1785a]; see Section 12) were really complementary aspects of a single calculus. He reminded his readers that the object of the former was the relation between some function of an indeterminate variable and the coefficients of its powers when the function is expanded in a series, and that generating functions had initially proved most valuable in solving difference equations in which problems of the theory of chance were formulated. The object of the latter, on the other hand, was to express variables that occur in difference equations in the form of definite integrals to be evaluated by rapidly convergent approximations. It turns out, however, that the quantity under the integral sign in such cases is nothing other than the generating function of the variable expressed by the definite integral. That is how the two theories merged in a single approach that he would henceforth call the calculus of generating functions, and that he also thought of as the exponential calculus of differential operators (*caractéristiques*) (*ibid.; OC*, XII, 360). It is valid both in infinitesimal and finite analysis. When a difference equation is expanded in powers of the difference taken as indeterminate but infinitesimal, and higher-order infinitesimals are held to be negligible relative to those of some lower order, the result is a differential equation. But the integral of that equation is also the integral of the difference equation wherein the infinitesimal quantities are similarly held to be negligible relative to the finite quantities. Justifying the neglect of such terms led Laplace into one of his few discussions of the foundations of the calculus and defenses of its rigor.

When first presenting the approximations for formulas containing large numbers ([1785a]), Laplace had shown how to evaluate several classes of the definite integrals that he employed in terms of transcendent quantities. The method depended on the passage from the real to the imaginary and re-sulted in series of sines and cosines. These were special cases, however, and only now was he in a position to give a direct and general method for evaluating any such expressions. That topic occupies the opening article, after which Laplace illustrated the method in three representative problems of the theory of probability. The first concerns a case of duration of play in theory of games of chance. The second is an urn problem. Two vessels contain n balls each. Of the total $2n$, half are black and half white. Each draw consists of taking a ball from each urn and placing it in the other. What is the probability that after r draws there will be x white balls in urn A? Mathematically, Laplace considered this the most interesting of his illustrations of the newly named calculus of generating functions, for his solution involved—so he claimed—the first application of partial differential equations to infinitesimal analysis in the theory of probability (*ibid.; OC*, XII, 361–362).

Nevertheless, he reserved the fullest treatment for the third problem and republished the articles containing its resolution in *Connaissance des temps* ([1811b]). He thus emphasized the method because of its widespread utility in the theory of chance, its object being the mean to choose among the results given by different sets of observations. For a modern mathematician's account of this second, strongly featured presentation of the method of least squares, see Sheynin's excellent article (L: [1977]), nos. 5.1–5.2. The following is a paraphrase of Laplace's own précis, which he intended for readers unversed in probability ([1811a]; *OC*, XII, 362). The idea was to employ the totality of a very large number of observations to correct several elements that are already approximately known. Each observation is a function of these elements, and their approximate value could be substituted in that function. Those values were to be modified by small corrections, which constituted the unknowns. The function was then expanded in a series of powers of those corrections. Squares, products, and higher powers are neglected, and the series is equated to the observed value. Those steps gave an initial equation of condition between the corrections to be applied to the elements. A second equation could be found from a second observation, a third from a third, and so on. If the observations had each been precise, only one equation apiece would have been needed. But since they were subject to error, the effect of which was to be minimized, a very great number of them had to be taken in order that the errors might compensate each other in the values deduced from the total number. There was the core of the problem. How were the equations to be combined?

Here was the point at which probability entered the procedure. Any mode of combination would consist in multiplying each equation by a particular factor and summing all the products. The respective systems of factors employed would yield systems of definitive equations between the corrections of the elements, and as many equations would be needed as there were elements to correct in solving them. It was obvious that the crux consisted in choosing factors such that the probability of error, positive or negative, should be a minimum for each element. Again defining mean error as the product of the amount of each error multiplied by its probability, Laplace then would show that in each equation of condition, when the respective coefficients are varied so that it can be set equal to zero, the sum of the squares is a minimum. As introduced by Legendre and Gauss, the method was limited (in Laplace's view) to finding the definitive equations needed for a solution. In his derivation, it also served to determine the corrections. Thus, once again, this time employing what is now called a linear regression rather than a Bayesian approach, Laplace claimed that a derivation of the method of least squares from theory of probability promoted it from the status of a rule of thumb to that of a mathematical law.

26. Probability: Théorie analytique and Essai philosophique. In the preamble to the "Mémoire sur les intégrales définies" just discussed, Laplace wrote: "The calculus of generating functions is the foundation of a theory that I propose to publish soon on probability" ([*1811a*]; *OC*, XII, 360). Good as his word, he presented the first part of *Théorie analytique des probabilités* to the Institute on 23 March 1812 and the second part on 29 June (*98, 99*). There is a minor bibliographical puzzle here. The complete treatise is a quarto volume of 464 pages in the first edition and is divided into two books, Book I consisting of a "Première partie" and a "Seconde partie." The significance of the partition will be clarified in a moment. What is unclear is whether Laplace had Book I, Part I printed first, and then Book I, Part II together with all of Book II; or whether, after the three-month interval, it was Book II that he saw through the press. The latter conjecture seems more logical, although the *procès-verbaux* of the Institute are confirmed by the "Avertissement" to the second edition, presented on 14 November 1814 (*104*). In either case, the general scheme is similar to that of *Mécanique céleste*. Book I is devoted to the mathematical

methods. In Book II, occupying two-thirds of the volume, they are applied to the solution of problems in probability. There is some difference in the relation of the organization to the sequence of events in Laplace's career, however. In the field of probability, his resolution of a rather larger proportion of the problems than in celestial mechanics had preceded his development of the mathematical techniques incorporated in the finished treatise. That was notably the case in the areas of games of chance and probability of cause and, to a degree, in demography. The areas of application that he explored later tended to be in the realm of error theory, decision theory, judicial probability, and credibility of witnesses.

The first edition contains a brief introduction (pp. 1–3) that was eliminated in the second and third (1820) in favor of the *Essai philosophique*. It is worth notice, nevertheless, for the interest that Laplace claimed for the work in bringing it before the public:

> I am particularly concerned to determine the probability of causes and results, as exhibited in events that occur in large numbers, and to investigate the laws according to which that probability approaches a limit in proportion to the repetition of events. That investigation deserves the attention of mathematicians because of the analysis required. It is primarily there that the approximation of formulas that are functions of large numbers has its most important applications. The investigation will benefit observers in identifying the mean to be chosen among the results of their observations and the probability of the errors still to be apprehended. Lastly, the investigation is one that deserves the attention of philosophers in showing how in the final analysis there is a regularity underlying the very things that seem to us to pertain entirely to chance, and in unveiling the hidden but constant causes on which that regularity depends. It is on the regularity of the mean outcomes of events taken in large numbers that various institutions depend, such as annuities, tontines, and insurance policies. Questions about those subjects, as well as about inoculation with vaccine and decisions of electoral assemblies, present no further difficulty in the light of my theory. I limit myself here to resolving the most general of them, but the importance of these concerns in civil life, the moral considerations that complicate them, and the voluminous data that they presuppose require a separate work.

Laplace never wrote that separate work, although the thought of it may well have been what led him to expand his old lecture for the École Normale into the *Essai philosophique* two years later.

In conformity with the program announced the

preceding year ([*1811a*]), the general subtitle of Book I is "Calcul des fonctions génératrices." It consists almost entirely of a republication, with some revision, of the two cardinal mathematical investigations of the early 1780's. The "Mémoire sur les suites" ([*1782a*]), on generating functions themselves, has now become the basis of its first part, and that on the approximation by definite integrals of formulas containing very large numbers ([*1785a*] and [*1786b*]), the basis of its second part. (For a more detailed and mathematical summary of the latter than is given in our Section 12, see L: Todhunter [1865], nos. 956–968.) The introduction reiterates what Laplace had first stated in the memoir of the preceding year ([*1811a*]), that the two theories are branches of a single calculus, the one concerned with solving the difference equations in which problems of chance events are formulated, the other with evaluating the expressions that result when events are repeated many times.

Laplace says in the introduction that he is now presenting these theories in a more general manner than he had done thirty years before. The chief difference in principle is that the new calculus is held to have emerged along the main line of evolution of the analytical treatment of exponential quantities. In an opening historical chapter, Laplace traces the lineage back through the work of Lagrange, Leibniz, Newton, and Wallis to Descartes's invention of numerical indices for denoting the operations of squaring, cubing, and raising magnitudes to higher integral powers. The principal difference in practice between the two earlier memoirs and their revision in Book I is that Laplace omitted certain passages that had come to appear extraneous in the interval and gave greater prominence to others that now appeared strategic. The most important omission is three articles from the "Mémoire sur les suites" on the solution of second-order partial differential equations, which were important for problems of physics but not for theory of games of chance ([*1782a*], Articles XVIII–XX; *OC*, X, 54–70). On the other hand, Laplace gave greater emphasis than in the earlier memoirs to the passage from the finite to the infinitesimal and also from real to imaginary quantity. He now develops as an argument what he had merely asserted in the immediately preceding memoir on definite integrals ([*1811a*]), namely that rigor is not impaired by the necessity of neglecting in appropriate circumstances infinitesimal quantities relative to finite quantities and higher-order infinitesimals relative to those of lower order. It is in support of this proposition that he brings in the solution to the

problem of vibrating strings from [*1782a*]. It affords a convincing example that discontinuous solutions of partial differential equations are possible under conditions that he specifies (*OC*, VII, 70–80). He attached even greater importance to the fertility that he increasingly found in the process of passing from real to imaginary quantity and discussed those procedures in the transitional section between the first and second parts. The limits of the definite integrals to be converted into convergent series are given by the roots of an equation such that when the signs of the coefficients are changed, the roots become imaginary. But it was precisely this property that led Laplace to the values of certain definite integrals that occur frequently in probability and that depend on the two transcendental quantities π and e. His early methods had been *ad hoc* and indirect, but since that time he had perfected direct methods for evaluating such integrals in a general manner, a procedure that (he acknowledged) Euler had arrived at independently (*OC*, VII, 88).

In Book II, subtitled "Théorie générale des probabilités," Laplace turns from the calculus to probability itself. Indeed, it is fair to say that he constituted the subject, drawing together the main types of problems from the theory of chance already treated by many mathematicians, including himself, in a somewhat haphazard manner, and rehandling them in tandem with problems from the new areas of application in philosophy of science, astronomy, geodesy, instrumentation, error, population, and the procedures of judicial panels and electoral bodies. Unlike the two parts of Book I and much of *Mécanique céleste*, Book II is more than a republication of earlier memoirs with minor and incidental revision. Material from earlier work is incorporated in it, to be sure, but it is revised mathematically and fortified with new material. What is carried over without significant change from the earliest memoirs ([*1774c*] and [*1776a*]) is the point of view from which the subject as a whole is treated and the spirit in which the various topics are approached. It has been said that *Théorie analytique des probabilités* is unsystematic, rather a collection of chapters that might as well be separate than a treatise in the usual sense. Perhaps so. Its organization certainly recapitulates the evolution of the subject matter rather than some logical system within it. It is also difficult to imagine its serving either as a textbook, as the first two volumes of *Mécanique céleste* could do, or as a work of reference, in the way that the third and fourth volumes really did do. Its relation to the subject was different. Rather than drawing together the lifework of a leading contributor to a vast and classical area of science, it was the first full-scale study completely devoted to a new specialty, building out from old and often hackneyed problems into areas where quantification had been nonexistent or chimerical. Later commentators have also sometimes castigated the obscurity and lack of rigor in many passages of the analysis. Once again, it may be so. It is constitutionally and temperamentally very difficult, however, for many mathematicians to enter sympathetically into what was once the forefront of research. Important parts of *Mécanique céleste* were also in the front lines, of course— but that was the location of *Théorie analytique des probabilités* as a whole. What no one has denied is that it was a seminal if not a fully systematic work.

The first chapter gives the general principles and opens with the famous characterization of probability as a branch of knowledge both required by the limitation of the human intelligence and serving to repair its deficiencies in part. The subject is relative, therefore, both to our knowledge and to our ignorance of the laws of a determined universe. After stating the definition of probability itself and the rule for multiplying the probabilities of independent events, Laplace includes as the third basic principle a verbal statement of his theorem on the probability of cause, still without mentioning Bayes. Thereupon, he takes the example of the unsuspected asymmetries of a coin to consider the effect of unequal prior probabilities mistakenly taken for equal. Finally, he distinguishes between mathematical and moral expectation. The basic content of these matters was drawn from the companion memoirs ([*1774c*] and [*1776a*, l°]) composed thirty-nine years previously in 1773 (see Section 4).

The actual problems discussed in the early chapters also consist in part of examples reworked from these and the other early papers on theory of chance. (For a useful mathematical summary of many of them in modern terminology, see L: Sheynin [1976].) Laplace solved them by using generating functions and arranged them, not for their own sake, but to illustrate the typology of problems in probability at large, interspersing new subject matter where the methodology made it appropriate. Chapter 2, which is concerned with the probability of compound events composed of simple events of known probability, is much the most considerable, occupying about one-quarter of Book II. In a discussion of the old problem of de-

termining the probability that all n numbers in a lottery will turn up at least once in i draws when r slips are chosen on each draw, he adduced the case of the French national lottery, composed of ninety numbers drawn five at a time. Laplace went on to other classic problems in direct probability: of odds and evens in extracting balls from an urn, of extracting given numbers of balls of a particular color from mixtures in several urns, of order and sequence in the retrieval of numbered balls, of the division of stakes and of the ruin or victory of one of a pair of gamblers in standard games.

Perhaps it will be useful to trace the sequence in one set of problems as an illustration of how Laplace made the connections between topics. He imagines (no. 13) an urn containing $n + 1$ balls numbered 0, 1, 2, 3, $\cdots$ n. A ball is taken out and returned, and the number noted. What is the probability that after i draws, the sum of the numbers will be s? If t_1, t_2, t_3, $\cdots$ t_i are the numbers of balls taken in the first, second, third, etc. draws, then as long as t_2, t_3, $\cdots$ t_i do not vary,

$$t_1 + t_2 + t_3 + \cdots + t_i = s. \qquad (128)$$

Only that one combination is possible. But if different numbers are taken, so that t_1 and t_2 are varied simultaneously and are capable of taking any value beginning at zero and continuing indefinitely, then (128) will be given by the following number of combinations:

$$s + 1 - t_3 - t_4 \cdots - t_i \qquad (129)$$

since the limits of t_1 are zero, which would give

$$t_2 = s - t_3 - t_4 \cdots - t_i,$$

and $s - t_3 - t_4 \cdots - t_i$, which would give $t_2 = 0$. Negative values are excluded. By like reasoning, Laplace finds that the total number of combinations that can give Equation 128 on the supposition of the indefinite variability of t_1, t_2, t_3, $\cdots$ t_i, always greater than zero, is

$$\frac{(s+i-1)(s+i-2)(s+i-3) \cdots (s+1)}{1 \cdot 2 \cdot 3 \cdots (i-1)}. \qquad (130)$$

By the conditions of the problem, however, these variables cannot exceed n, and the probability of any particular value of t_1 from zero to n is $\frac{1}{n+1}$. Since the probability of t_1 equal to or greater than $(n + 1)$ is nil, it may be represented by the expression $\frac{1 - l^{n+1}}{n+1}$ provided that $l =$ unity. Now then, on condition that l be introduced only when t_i has reached the limit $n + 1$, and that it be equal to unity at the end of the operation, any value of t_1 can be represented by $\dfrac{1 - l^{n+1}}{n+1}$. The same is true for the other variables. Since the probability of (128) is the product of the probabilities of the values $t_1, t_2, t_3, \cdots$, its expression is $\left(\dfrac{1 - l^{n+1}}{n+1}\right)^i$. The number of combinations given by that equation multiplied by their respective probabilities is then

$$\frac{(s+1)(s+2)\cdots(s+i-1)}{1\cdot 2\cdot 3\cdots(i-1)}\left(\frac{1-l^{n+1}}{n+1}\right)^i. \quad (131)$$

In expanding that function, l^{n+1} is to be applied only to combinations in which one variable is beginning to exceed n; l^{n+2} only to combinations in which two of the variables begin to exceed n, and so on. Thus, if it is supposed that t_1 has grown larger than n, then by setting $t_1 = n + 1 + t'_1$, Equation 128 becomes

$$s - n - 1 = t'_1 + t_2 + t_3 + \cdots, \quad (132)$$

where t'_1 increases indefinitely. If two variables, t_1 and t_2, exceed n, then setting $t_1 = n + 1 + t'_1$, and $t_2 = n + 1 + t'_2$, Equation 128 becomes

$$s - 2n - 2 = t'_1 + t'_2 + t_3 + \cdots. \quad (133)$$

The purpose of this manipulation is to decrease s in the function (130) by $n + 1$, relative to the system of variables $t'_1, t_2, t_3 \cdots$, to decrease s by $2n + 2$, relative to the system $t'_1, t'_2, t_3, \cdots$, and so on. In expanding (131) in powers of l, s is to be decreased by the exponent indicating the power of l, and when $l = 1$, the function (131) becomes

$$\frac{(s+1)(s+2)\cdots(s+i-1)}{1\cdot 2\cdot 3\cdots(i-1)(n+1)^i}$$

$$-\frac{i(s-n)(s-n+1)\cdots(s+i-n-2)}{1\cdot 2\cdot 3\cdots(i-1)(n+i)^i}+\frac{i(i-1)}{1\cdot 2}$$

$$\times\frac{(s-2n-1)(s-2n)\cdots(s+i-2n-3)}{1\cdot 2\cdot 3\cdots(i-1)(n+1)^i}-\cdots,$$

$$(134)$$

which series is continued until one factor, $(s - n)$, $(s - 2n - 1)$, $(s - 3n - 2)$, $\cdots$, becomes zero or negative in value.

The formula (134) — to change the problem now — will give the probability of throwing any number s in tossing i dice each with $n + 1$ sides, the smallest number on any side being 1. If s and n are infinite

numbers, (134) becomes the following expression:

$$\frac{1}{1\cdot 2\cdot 3\cdots(i-1)n}\left\{\left(\frac{s}{n}\right)^{i-1}-i\left(\frac{s}{n}-1\right)^{i-1}\right.$$

$$\left.+\frac{i(i-1)}{1\cdot 2}\left(\frac{s}{n}-2\right)^{i-1}\cdots\right\} \quad (135)$$

This expression, proceeds Laplace — affording his reader not so much as a new paragraph to draw breath — can be employed to determine the probability that the sum of the inclinations of orbits to the ecliptic will be contained within given limits on the assumption of equipossibility of inclination between $0°$ and a right angle. If a right angle, $\frac{1}{2}\pi$, is divided into an infinite number n of equal parts, and s contains an infinite number of these parts, then if ϕ is the sum of the inclinations of the orbits,

$$\frac{s}{n} = \frac{\phi}{\frac{1}{2}\pi}. \quad (136)$$

Multiplying (136) by ds, or $\dfrac{nd\phi}{\frac{1}{2}\pi}$, and integrating from $\phi - \epsilon$ to $\phi + \epsilon$, gives

$$\frac{1}{1\cdot 2\cdot 3\cdots i}\left[\begin{array}{l}\left(\dfrac{\phi+\epsilon}{\frac{1}{2}\pi}\right)^i-i\left(\dfrac{\phi+\epsilon}{\frac{1}{2}\pi}-1\right)^i\\[2mm]+\dfrac{i(i-1)}{1\cdot 2}\left(\dfrac{\phi+\epsilon}{\frac{1}{2}\pi}-2\right)^i-\cdots\\[2mm]-\left(\dfrac{\phi-\epsilon}{\frac{1}{2}\pi}\right)^i+i\left(\dfrac{\phi-\epsilon}{\frac{1}{2}\pi}-1\right)^i\\[2mm]-\dfrac{i(i-1)}{1\cdot 2}\left(\dfrac{\phi-\epsilon}{\frac{1}{2}\pi}-2\right)^i+\cdots\end{array}\right]$$

$$(137)$$

Formula 137 expresses the probability that the sum of the inclinations of the orbits is contained within the limits $\phi - \epsilon$ and $\phi + \epsilon$.

We shall not follow Laplace into yet another calculation (his last on this phenomenon) that the orbital arrangement of the planets results from a single cause and that the comets escape its compass, nor from that back to a variation on the original problem, in which any number of balls in the urn may be designated by the same integer, nor even into his derivation by the same method that the sum of the errors in a series of observations will be contained within given limits. Suffice it to indicate the sequence and the virtuosity it bespeaks. But we must notice his earliest venture, this late in life, into judicial probability. Imagine a number i of points along a straight line, at each of which an ordinate is erected. The first ordinate must be at least equal to the second, the second at least equal to the third, and so on; and the sum of these i ordinates is s. The problem is to determine, among all the values that each ordinate can assume, the mean value. For that quantity in the case of the rth ordinate, Laplace obtains the expression (*OC*, VII, 276)

$$\frac{s}{i}\left(\frac{1}{i}+\frac{1}{i+1}+\cdots+\frac{1}{r}\right). \tag{138}$$

Suppose now, however, that an event is produced by one of the i causes A, B, C, $\cdots$, and that a panel of judges is to reach a verdict on which of the causes was responsible. Each member of the panel might write on a ballot the various letters in the order that appeared most probable to him. Formula 138 will now give the mean value of the probability that he assigns to the rth cause (in this application s must amount to certainty and have the value of 1). If all members of the tribunal follow that procedure, and the values for each cause are summed, the largest sum will point to the most probable cause in the view of that panel.

Laplace hastened to add that since electors, unlike judges, are not constrained to decide for or against a candidate but impute to him all degrees of merit in making their choices, the above procedure may not be applied to elections. He proceeded to outline a probabilistic scheme for a preferential ballot that would produce the most mathematically exact expression of electoral will. Unfortunately, however, electors would not in fact make their choices on the basis of merit but would rank lowest the candidate who presented the greatest threat to their own man. In practice, therefore, preferential ballots favor mediocrity and had been abandoned wherever tried.

The third chapter deals with limits, in the sense in which the idea figures in the frequency definitions of the discipline of probability that have developed out of it (L: Molina [1930], 386). In his own terminology, his concern was with the laws of probability that result from the indefinite multiplication of events. No single passage is as clear and definite as his derivation of the central limit theorem in the memoir on approximating the values of formulas containing large numbers ([*1810b*]) that had brought him back to probability several years before, but the examples he adduces are much more various. He begins with a conventional binomial problem. The probabilities of two events a and b are respectively p and $1-p$. The probability that a will occur x times and b will occur x' times in $x+x'$ tries is given by the $(x'+1)$th term of the binomial $[p+(1-p)]^{x+x'}$. Laplace calculates the sum of two terms that are symmetrical on either side of the middle term of the expansion of the binomial. The formula is

$$\frac{2}{\sqrt{\pi}}\frac{\sqrt{n}}{\sqrt{2\pi xx'}}e^{\frac{-nl^2}{2xx'}}, \quad \text{where } n=x+x'.$$

When $t=\frac{l\sqrt{n}}{2xx'}$, the sum of all such pairs is (*OC*, VII, 283–284)

$$\frac{2}{\sqrt{\pi}}e^{-t^2}\,dt+\frac{\sqrt{n}}{\sqrt{2\pi xx'}}e^{-t^2}. \tag{139}$$

Discussing this formula and the reasoning, Laplace points out that two sorts of approximations are involved. The first is relative to the limits of the *a priori* probability (*facilité*) of the event a, and the second to the probability that the ratio of the occurrences of a to the total number of events will be contained within certain limits. As the events are repeated, the latter probability increases so long as the limits remain the same. On the other hand, so long as the probability remains the same, the limits grow closer together. When the number of events reaches infinity, the limits converge in a point and the probability becomes a certainty. Just as he had done in his earliest general memoir on probability ([*1781a*]), Laplace turned to birth records to illustrate how the ratio of boys to girls gives figures from experience for prior probabilities, or *facilités*.

The latter part of the discussion contains another of the many passages scattered throughout his writings that have led modern readers to feel that Laplace must somehow have had an inkling (or perhaps a repressed belief) that random processes occur in nature itself and not merely as a function of our ignorance. The mathematical occasion here is the use, started in ([*1811a*]), of partial differential equations in solving certain limit problems (see Section 25). The concluding example turns on a ring of urns, one containing only white and another only black balls, and the rest mixtures of very different proportions. Laplace proves that if a ball is drawn from any urn and placed in its neighbor, and if that urn is well shaken and a ball drawn from it and placed in the next further on, and so on an indefinite number of times around the circle, the ratio of white to black balls in each urn will eventually be the same as the ratio of white to black balls in all of them. But what Laplace really thought to show by such examples was the tendency of constant forces in nature to bring order into the most chaotic systems.

By comparison to the early probabilistic memoirs of the 1770's and 1780's, the fourth chapter on probability of error certainly represents the most significant development in the subject as a whole. It contains, of course, a derivation (no. 20) of the least-square law for taking the mean in a series of observations, which is given by essentially the same method as in [*1811a*], although in a more detailed and abstract form. There is much more to the discussion of error theory than that, however (see L: Sheynin [1977], no. 6, 25–34, who gives Laplace's formulations in modern notation). The chapter opens (no. 18) with determinations that the sum of errors of a large number of errors—equivalent to the distribution of sums of random variables—will be contained within given limits, on the assumption of a known and equipossible law of errors. It continues (no. 19) with the probability that the sum of the errors (again amounting to random variables), all considered as positive, and of their squares and cubes, will be contained within given limits. This is equivalent to considering the distribution of the sum of moduli. That leads to the problem of correcting values known approximately by the results of a great number of observations, which is to say by least squares, first in the case of a single element (no. 20) and then of two or more elements (no. 21). Mathematically, this involves a discussion of linearized equations with one unknown and with two unknowns, respectively. Laplace includes instructions on application of the analysis to the correction of astronomical data by comparison of the values given in a number of tables. He then considers the case in which the probability of positive and negative error is unequal, and derives the distribution that results (no. 22). The next-to-last section (no. 23) deals with the statistical prediction of error and methods of allowing for it on the basis of experience. At least, that seems to be a fair statement of what Laplace had in mind in speaking of "the mean result of observations large in number and not yet made," on the basis of the mean determined for past observations of which the respective departures from the mean are known (*OC*, VII, 338). The chapter closes with a historical sketch of the methods used by astronomers to minimize error up to the formulation of least squares, in which account Laplace renders Legendre and Gauss each his due (see Section 25).

In the fifth chapter, Laplace discussed the application of probability to the investigation of phenomena themselves and of their causes, wherein it might serve to establish the physical significance of data amid all the complexities of the world. The approach offers practical instances of his sense of the relativity of the subject to knowledge and to ignorance, to science and to nature. In the analysis of error, it is the phenomena that are considered certain, whereas here the existence and boundaries of the phenomena themselves are the object of the calculation. The main example is the daily variation of the barometer, which long and frequent observation shows to be normally at its highest at 9:00 A.M. and lowest at 4:00 P.M., after which it rises to a lower peak at 11:00 P.M. and sinks until 4:00 A.M. Laplace calculated the probability that this diurnal pattern is due to some regular cause, namely the action of the sun, and determined its mean extent. He then raised a further question which, for lack of data, he could not resolve mathematically here, but which is interesting since it came to occupy the very last calculation of his life (see Section 28). For in theory, atmospheric tides would constitute a second and independent cause contributing to the daily variations of barometric pressure. He referred his readers to his discussion of that hypothetical phenomenon, a corollary to the treatment of oceanic tides, in *Mécanique céleste*, Book IV (*OC*, II, 310–314). The detection of such a small effect was not yet possible, although Laplace expressed his confidence that observations would one day become sufficiently extensive and precise to permit its isolation.

In short, it was calculations of this sort that Laplace had in mind when he claimed, as he here remarked again, that on the cosmic scale probability had permitted him to identify the great inequalities of Jupiter and Saturn, even as it had enabled him to detect the minuscule deviation from the vertical of a body falling toward a rotating earth. He even had hopes for its calculus in physiological investigations, imagining that application to a large number of observations might suffice to determine whether electrical or magnetic charges have detectable effects upon the nervous system, and whether animal magnetism reflects reality or suggestibility. In general—he felt confident—the same analysis could in principle be applied to medical and economic questions, and even to problems of morality, for the operations of causes many times repeated are as regular in those domains as in physics. Laplace had no examples to propose, however, and closed the chapter with a mathematical problem extraneous in subject matter but not in methodology. The problem had been imagined by Buffon in order to show the applicability of geometry to probability (L: Sheynin [1976], 152). It consists of tossing a needle onto a grid of parallel lines, and then onto a grid ruled in rectangles, of which the optimal dimensions relative to the length of the needle constitute the problem. Laplace adapted it to a probabilistic, or in this instance a statistical, method for approximating to the value of π. It would be possible, he points out, although not mathematically inviting, to apply a similar approach to the rectification of curves and squaring of surfaces in general.

Chapter 6, "On the Probability of Causes and Future Events, Drawn From Observed Events," is in effect concerned with problems of statistical inference. In practice, the material represents a reworking of his early memoir on probability of cause ([1774c]) and of the application of inverse probability by means of approximations of definite integrals to calculations involving births of boys and girls and also to population problems at large ([1781a], [1786b], and [1786c]). He now had figures for Naples as well as for Paris and London. In calculating the probable error in estimates of the population of France based on the available samples, he made use of the partial census which, at his request, the government had instituted in 1801.

The next, very brief, chapter also starts with old material, to which he gave a new turn. He recurs to his own discovery ([1774c]) of the effect of inequalities in the prior probabilities that are mistakenly supposed to be equal (see Section 4). He always attached great importance to that finding, so much so that he alluded to it in the opening chapter of Book II, where definitions were laid down. The significance was that it brought out the care that needed to be taken when mathematical calculations of probability were applied to physical events. In effect, there are no perfect symmetries in the real world, and what Laplace was saying was that allowance has to be made for slight deviations of parameters from assumed values in making predictions. He discussed the problem in the same connection in which he had started it, in relation to the unfairness to one of two players of unsuspected asymmetries in a coin to be tossed. That could be mitigated, he now suggested, by submitting the chance of asymmetry itself to calculation. He let the probability of throwing heads or tails be $\frac{1 \pm \alpha}{2}$, where α represents the unknown difference between the prior probabilities of throwing one or the other. The probability of throwing heads n times in a row will then be (OC, VII, 410–411)

$$\frac{(1+\alpha)^n + (1-\alpha)^n}{2^{n+1}};\qquad (140)$$

and a player who bets on heads or tails consecu-

tively will have an advantage over one who bets on an alternation. Instead of that, it will be fairer to try tossing two similar coins simultaneously n times running. Then the true value of the probability that the two coins will fall the same way is

$$\frac{1}{2^{n+1}}\ [(1+\alpha\alpha')^n + (1-\alpha\alpha')^n],\qquad (141)$$

which is closer to the equipossible $\frac{1}{2^n}$ than is (140).

In chapters 8, 9, and 10, all of them quite brief, Laplace took up life expectancy, annuities, insurance, and moral expectation (or prudence). We do not know where he obtained his information, but it is reasonable to suppose that some of it must have been derived from occasional service on commissions appointed to review writings in this area and various actuarial schemes submitted to the government. The *procès-verbaux* of the Academy in its last years and of the Institute contain record of his having thus been called on from time to time. Moreover, the "Notice sur les probabilités" ([1810d]) was published as a rationale of the application that it was legitimate to make to tables of mortality. This piece, it will be recalled (see Section 25), was an expansion of his École Normale lecture of 1795 ([1800d]). It was then further expanded to become the first edition of the *Essai philosophique* and concludes with a summons to governments to license and regulate underwriters of insurance, annuities, and tontines, and to encourage investment in soundly managed associations. For an insurance industry and a literature did exist, although Laplace does not refer either to actual practice or to authorities. Comparison of his chapters with both would be required before a judgment could be made of what his contribution may have been.

Mathematically, his model for calculations of the "mean duration," both of life and marriage, is error theory. Given the tables of mortality covering a large population, a value for the mean length of life may be taken and the probability calculated that the mean life of a sample of stated size will fall within given limits. Calculation of life expectancy at any age follows directly. Laplace also gave a calculation for estimating the effect of smallpox on the death rate and of vaccination on life expectancy. The conclusion is that the eradication of smallpox would increase life expectancy by three years, if the growth in the population did not diminish the improvement by outrunning the food supply. Laplace did not give the data or provide numerical examples here, as he had done in his population studies. The succeeding chapter on annuities and tontines is equally abstract and gives expressions for the capital required to create annuities on one or several lives, for the investment needed to build an estate of given size, and for the advantages to be expected from participation in mutual benefit societies.

In the tenth chapter, with which Laplace concluded the first edition, he softened the asperity he had once expressed about Daniel Bernoulli's calculation of a value for moral expectation (see Section 4) in distinguishing that notion from mathematical expectation ([*1776a*, 1°], Article XXV). Bernoulli had proposed that prospective benefits, in practice financial ones, may be quantified as the quotient of their amount divided by the total worth of the beneficiary. Laplace now adopted that principle as a useful guide to conduct—without attributing it this time to Bernoulli. In infinitesimal terms, where x represents the fortune and dx the increment, its benefit will be $\frac{k\,dx}{x}$. If y represents the moral fortune corresponding to the physical value (*OC*, VII, 441),

$$y = k \log x + \log h, \qquad (142)$$

where h is an arbitrary constant to be determined by the ratio of a value of y corresponding to a value of x. But perhaps it will not be necessary to follow the calculation in order to be convinced. Laplace concluded that in the most mathematically advantageous games of chance the odds are always unfavorable over time, and that diversification is a prudent practice in the investment of wealth. On matters of this sort, he wrote more persuasively in the ordinary language of the *Essai philosophique* than in the mathematics of the *Théorie analytique*.

Laplace must have continued straight on to expand the "Notice sur les probabilités" ([*1810d*]) into the *Essai philosophique*. He presented the first edition to the Institute in February 1814 (*102*), a year and a half after finishing the *Théorie analytique*. In August of that year he also read a memoir on the probability of testimony (*103*). Inclusion of these two pieces, the first as the introduction and the second as a new concluding chapter 11, together with three minor mathematical additions (*OC*, VII, 471–493), marks the difference between the first edition of *Théorie analytique des probabilités* and the second, completed by November 1814 (*104*). The two pieces have in common the tendency to move the subject further in the direction of civic relevance, the one in expounding it for laymen, the other in extending the application to concerns of life in society.

The *Essai philosophique sur les probabilités* has certainly had a longer life and almost certainly a larger number of readers than any of Laplace's other writings, including its counterpart in celestial mechanics, *Exposition du système du monde*. The reason for its continuing—indeed, its growing—success has clearly been the importance that probability, statistics, and stochastic analysis have increasingly assumed in science, social science, and philosophy of science. Inevitably, Laplace's technical writings have come to have the same sort of relation to the later development of the discipline of probability that, for example, Newton's *Principia mathematica* had to the later science of mechanics. Even if there were no other reason, that would suffice to explain why most readers who wish to repair to the fountainhead of what is often called the subjective interpretation of probability, in contrast to the frequency view, have recourse to the *Essai philosophique*. But there is a complementary reason, and that is the extreme difficulty of many parts of the *Théorie analytique*.

Given the accessibility of the *Essai philosophique* in many editions and languages, a summary scarcely seems necessary. The work itself is a summary. Instead, a reservation may be ventured, although somewhat hesitantly. If the two famous popularizations are compared in point of intrinsic merit, it is possible to consider the *Exposition du système du monde* the better book. At least, it conveys its subject with altogether greater clarity. For, once the reader is past the epistemological opening passages in the *Essai philosophique*, Laplace's paraphrase of the mathematics of *Théorie analytique* is not very easy to follow. No doubt the subject matter lent itself less well to verbal summary than did astronomy or geodesy. But it may also be worth noting that the order of composition was reversed. Laplace wrote the *Système du monde* as a book in its own right before he compiled the *Mécanique céleste*. The former was an outline or a prospectus for the latter. In the case of the *Essai philosophique*, he wrote all but the epistemological and actuarial sections after the *Théorie analytique*. In its first edition, it was a précis and bears the same relation to the treatise that the initial sections in many of his memoirs do to them, that of a preface written last. Moreover, there is nothing in the epistemology that he had not already said in principle in his lecture at the École Normale in 1795 ([*1800d*]; see Section 20) or indeed in the prolegomena of the youthful probability-gravitation memoir ([*1776a*]; see Section 4). It is true that in the later editions of the *Essai philosophique* he did enlarge upon topics likely to interest a wider public and that his observations on the credibility of witnesses and on the procedures of legislative assemblies and of judicial panels make more comprehensible the calculations of the supplementary material on the same topics added to the second and third editions of the *Théorie analytique*.

Let us consider briefly the approach of the eleventh chapter of *Théorie analytique* (*OC*, VII, 455–470), on the probability of testimony. The inevitable urn containing numbered slips is the model analyzed. A slip is drawn, and a witness reports the number to be *n*. Is he telling the truth? It was Laplace's idea to apply inverse probability to such problems, taking the statement for an event and estimating the probability that it was caused by the truthfulness of the witness. There are four possibilities: (1) he is neither lying nor making a mistake; (2) he is not lying and is mistaken; (3) he is lying and not mistaken; (4) he is both lying and mistaken. With these alternatives, Laplace employs a Bayesian analysis, first for this problem and then for a series of more complicated instances involving several occurrences witnessed by more than one observer. The corresponding discussion in the fourth edition (*117*) of the *Essai philosophique* (*OC*, VII, lxxix–xc) gives numerical examples and goes on to expose what he considered the fallacy in Pascal's wager on the existence of God. The probability of truthfulness in the witnesses who promise infinite felicity to believers is infinitely small. There is also a daunting estimate of the decay of reliability of historical information with the passage of time.

More interesting is the concluding article in the treatise. There the judgment rendered by a tribunal deciding between contradictory assertions is assimilated to the reports of several witnesses about the drawing of a numbered slip from an urn containing only two. The panel consists of *r* judges, and *p* is the probability that each will render a true judgment. The probability of the soundness of a unanimous verdict will then be $\dfrac{p^r}{p^r + (1-p)^r}$. The value of *p* is given by the proportion of unanimous verdicts, denoted by *i*, to the total number of cases *n*. Since $p^r + (1-p)^r = \dfrac{i}{n}$, or very nearly so, solving that equation will give the probability *p* of the veracity of each judge. Laplace then showed that

if the tribunal consists of three magistrates (*OC*, VII, 470),

$$p = \frac{1}{2} \pm \sqrt{\frac{4i - n}{12n}}. \tag{143}$$

Choosing the positive root on the assumption that each judge has a greater propensity for truth than error, Laplace calculated the case of a court half of whose verdicts are unanimous. The probability of veracity in each judge will then be 0.789, and the probability that a verdict sustained on appeal is just will be 0.981 if the finding is unanimous, and 0.789 if the vote is divided. The greater the number of judges and the more enlightened they are, the better the chance that justice will be done—for to do Laplace himself justice, he acknowledged the artificiality of these calculations in introducing the topic in *Essai philosophique*, claiming only that they might provide guidance to common sense (*OC*, VII, lxxix).

Laplace extended the application of inverse probability to the analysis of criminal procedures in a supplement to the *Théorie analytique*, the first of four, composed in 1816 (*107*). For this purpose a condemnation is an event, and the probability is required that it was caused by the guilt of the accused. As always in the probability of cause, prior probabilities had to be known or assumed, and Laplace again supposed that the probability of a truthful juror or judge lies between 1/2 and 1. In a panel of eight members of whom five suffice to convict, the probability of error came to 65/256. He felt that the English jury system with its requirement for unanimity weighted the odds too heavily against the security of society, but that the French criminal code was unjust to the accused. By one provision, if a defendant was found guilty by a majority of 7 to 5 in a court of first instance, it required a vote of 4 to 1 to overturn the verdict in a court of appeal, since a majority of only 3 to 2 there still left a plurality against him in the two courts taken together. That rule was as offensive to common sense as to common humanity (*OC*, VII, 529). In view of the severe strictures that have been passed upon Laplace's political conduct, it should be noted that he took the trouble of publishing a pamphlet expounding on mathematical grounds the urgency of reforming these savage provisions ([*P1816*]); and in the definitive, fourth edition of *Essai philosophique* he gave his considered opinion that a majority of 9 out of 12 for conviction gave the most even balance between the interests of society in protection and in equity (*OC*, VII, xcxix).

Between 1817 and 1819, Laplace investigated the application of probability to sharpening the precision of geodesic data and gathered these studies for publication as the second and third supplements to the third edition (1820) of the *Théorie analytique* (*112, 118*). In recent years scholars concerned with the history of statistics have been especially interested in these two pieces, which Laplace himself saw in the context of his theory of error. His intention was to improve on the method of least squares in the minimization of instrumental and observational error. That had also been his motivation in the opening articles of the First Supplement, where before taking up judicial probabilities, he further developed what he called the "most advantageous" method of combining equations of condition formed from observations of a single element, like those exemplified in his initial justification of the least-squares method ([*1811a*]; see Section 22; cf. *Théorie analytique*, Book II, no. 21; *OC*, VII, 327–335). He then applied the method to estimating the probable error in Bouvard's recent, highly refined calculations of the masses of Uranus, Saturn, and Jupiter (*OC*, VII, 516–520).

In the Second Supplement, Laplace turned to geodesy and compared the results of his method with the so-called method of situation of Bošković (*OC*, VII, 531–580). Stigler considers that this discussion contains the earliest instance of a comparison of two well-elaborated methods of estimation for a general population, in which the conditions that make one of them preferable are specified. He is particularly enthusiastic about the growing statistical sophistication, as he sees it, of Laplace's later work in probability and argues that the analysis here is strikingly similar to that which led R. A. Fisher to the discovery of the concept of sufficiency in 1920 (L: [1973], 441–443; cf. Sheynin [1977], 41–44). In the Third Supplement, Laplace reports the result of applying his method to the extension of the revolutionary Delambre-Méchain survey of the meridian from a base in Perpignan to Formentera in the Balearic Islands. The data were the discrepancies between 180° and the sums of the angles measured for each triangle. There were only twenty-six triangles in the Perpignan-Formentera chain, however, and Laplace preferred to estimate the law of error on the basis of all 700 triangles in the original survey. He could then calculate the probabilities of error of various magnitudes in the length of the meridian by the formulas already developed for his modified, or most advantageous, method of least squares. In a further article on a general method for cases involving several sources of error, Laplace obtained a paradigm equation (129) for formulating equations of condition that relate values for observed elements to the error distributions involved. The equation served him in his later investigation of variations of the barometer as evidence for lunar atmospheric tides, the last he ever undertook (see Section 28).

In Laplace's own life and career, perhaps it is appropriate to see the curve breaking over in 1820 with the publication of the third, and definitive, edition of *Théorie analytique des probabilités*. In 1825 he did compose a fourth supplement, containing a minor modification to the theory of generating functions. By then he was showing signs of age. The minutes of the Institute record that the work was presented by Laplace and by his son.

27. Loss of Influence. It will be recalled (see Section 24) that in January 1816 Sophie Germain won the Institute's prize set in 1809 for the theory of elastic surfaces. Her paper broke sharply with the approach of the Laplacian school, and her successful challenge was one of the first signs that Laplace's power was beginning to wane. But it was by no means the only sign. The slackening of corporate research activity at Arcueil after 1812 and the cessation of regular meetings in 1813 did not augur well, and after 1815 Laplace became an increasingly isolated figure in the scientific community of the Restoration, particularly in the realm of physics. His personal reputation also suffered from the readiness of his accommodation to yet another change of political regime. In the Senate he voted for the overthrow of Napoleon in favor of a restored Bourbon monarchy in 1814. Conveniently absenting himself from Paris during Napoleon's temporary return to power in the Hundred Days—an episode that clearly embarrassed him—he remained loyal to the Bourbons until his death, becoming a bête noire of the liberals, most notably on his refusal in 1826 to sign a declaration of the Académie Française supporting the freedom of the press.

Perhaps the most serious assault on Laplace's physics came with the development of Fresnel's wave theory of light and its championing by Arago, a former member of the Arcueil circle, between 1815 and the early 1820's. In the face of this challenge, the Laplacian position was represented, rather typically, by Laplace's disciples. Thus when Fresnel won the competition of the Academy of Sciences for a study of the theory of diffraction in 1819 ("Mémoire sur la diffraction de la lumière," in *MASIF*, **5** [1821–1822/1826], 339–475), his theory was measured not against any of Laplace's writings but against the corpuscular theory of diffraction which Biot and Pouillet had devised, probably at Laplace's instigation, in 1816 (the theory is expounded in Biot's *Traité de physique expérimentale et mathématique*, 4 vols. [Paris, 1816], IV, 743–775); and it was Biot, not Laplace, who continued the open resistance to the wave theory into the 1820's. Similarly, Laplace did not respond publicly to the growing support for the chemical atomic theory in France after 1815, even though the theory was inconsistent with Berthollet's chemistry of affinities and the whole notion of short-range chemical forces. Nor did he react to the criticism of the caloric theory that was explicit in the work of Petit and Dulong on specific heats (1819) and clearly implied in Fourier's *Théorie analytique de la chaleur* (1822). (See A. T. Petit and P. L. Dulong, "Recherches sur quelques points importans de la théorie de la chaleur," in *Annales de chimie et de physique*, **10** [1819], 395–413, esp. 396–398 and 406–413. The criticisms of Petit and Dulong are discussed in Robert Fox, "The Background to the Discovery of Dulong and Petit's Law," in *British Journal for the History of Science*, **4** [1968–1969], 1–22, esp. 9–16.)

Despite the criticism to which his style of physics was subjected, Laplace never admitted defeat. By the early 1820's few could share his apparently unswerving belief in the physical reality of the imponderable fluids of heat and light, yet between 1821 and 1823 he developed the most elaborate version of his caloric theory of gases. He expounded the theory first in papers published chiefly in the *Connaissance des temps* and then, in a definitive and modified form, in Book XII of the fifth volume of the *Mécanique céleste* (*OC*, V, 97–160).

In all the versions of his theory, Laplace leaned heavily on the treatment of gravitation that he had published in the first volume of the *Mécanique céleste* in 1799. In particular, his expressions for the gravitational forces between spherical bodies proved to be readily applicable to the repulsion that, in accordance with the standard Newtonian model of gas structure, he supposed to exist between the particles of a gas; the modification that the force between the particles was not only repulsive but also inversely proportional to the distance between them was easily made.

In his first paper on caloric theory in the *Connaissance des temps* ([*1821d*]), which was the published version of one that he read to the Academy of Sciences in September 1821 (*123*), Laplace considered the equilibrium of a spherical shell taken at random in a gas. Invoking the condition that the force between the particles is effective only at short range, he showed that the pressure of the gas, P, is proportional to $\rho^2 c^2$, where ρ is its density and c the quantity of heat contained in each of its particles. The argument had a highly speculative cast and rested on the unfounded assumption that the repulsive force between any two adjacent gas particles is proportional to c^2. Even more suspect was Laplace's model of dynamic equilibrium, in which, when the temperature is constant, the particles of a gas constantly radiate and absorb caloric at an equal rate. Postulating the simplest of mechanisms for the process, Laplace pictured the radiation from any particle as resulting from the mechanical detachment of the particle's own caloric by incident radiant caloric, the density of which, $\pi(u)$, was taken as a function of the temperature, u, alone. If the fraction of incident caloric absorbed was put equal to q (a constant depending solely on the nature of the gas) and if it was assumed (quite gratuitously) that the quantity of caloric detached was proportional both to c and to the total "density" of caloric in the gas, ρc, it followed that

$$\rho c^2 = q\pi(u). \qquad (144)$$

Since for Laplace $P \propto \rho^2 c^2$, Boyle's law was an immediate consequence of this equation, as was Dalton's law of partial pressures. It also followed that since the function $\pi(u)$ was independent of the nature of the gas, all gases expand to the same extent for a given increment in temperature, as Dalton (1801) and Gay-Lussac (1802) had observed. The obvious next step, of assuming $\pi(u)$ to be proportional to the (absolute) temperature as measured on the air thermometer, was not taken in [*1821d*] but appeared very soon afterward in a paper published in the November issue of the *Annales de chimie et de physique* ([*1821a*]), and it was axiomatic in the definitive version presented in Book XII of the *Mécanique céleste* (*OC*, V, 125).

The fact that Laplace's theory was consistent with the main gas laws lent it obvious plausibility, but one prediction in particular raised difficulties. It followed from equation (144) that the isothermal compression of a gas to, for example, one-half of its original volume would cause c to decrease by a factor $\sqrt{2}$. Qualitatively, a reduction in the value of c was perfectly consistent with the phenomenon of adiabatic heating, but Laplace showed that a decrease by a factor $\sqrt{2}$ in isothermal compression was too great to account accurately for the error in Newton's expression for the velocity of sound; in fact, it led to the impossibly high figure of 2 for γ. Laplace's immediate solution was to suggest that the alternate compressions and rarefactions occurred slowly enough for there to be some heat exchange with the surroundings, but by December 1821 he had abandoned this hypothesis. In a paper submitted in that month to the Bureau des Longitudes and published the following year in the *Connaissance des temps* ([*1822a*]) he argued that heat exchange did not occur but that the heat "expelled" in excess of that required to reconcile the theoretical and experimental values for the velocity of sound merely becomes latent and so ceases to contribute to the interparticle force. Hence c now represents not the total quantity of heat in a particle of gas but only that part of it that is "sensible" or free; the "total heat" of a particle is Q or $(c + i)$, i being its latent or combined heat.

It was a simple matter for Laplace to restate his fundamental expression for the velocity of sound ($\sqrt{dP/d\rho}$) in a form that involved c, and he did this in [*1822a*]. Assuming $P \propto \rho^2 c^2$, it followed that the velocity of sound is equal to

$$\sqrt{\frac{2P}{\rho}\left(1 + \frac{\rho}{c}\frac{dc}{d\rho}\right)};$$

and this in turn implied that

$$1 + \frac{\rho}{c}\frac{dc}{d\rho}$$

is equal to $\gamma/2$. In a supplement to this paper, which dates almost certainly from early 1822 ([*1822b*]), Laplace also showed how he could express γ in an equation involving Q, ρ, and P. To do this, he assumed that Q was a function of any two of P (that is, $\rho^2 c^2$), ρ, and the absolute temperature, so that in adiabatic conditions ($\Delta Q = 0$)

$$dP\left(\frac{\partial Q}{\partial P}\right)_\rho + d\rho\left(\frac{\partial Q}{\partial \rho}\right)_P = 0, \qquad (145)$$

and

$$\gamma = -(\rho/P)\{(\partial Q/\partial\rho)_P/(\partial Q/\partial P)_\rho\}. \qquad (146)$$

In these ways Laplace showed how the investigation of c and Q, both quantities that were intimately related to his speculations on the state of caloric in bodies and not susceptible to a direct test, could proceed simply through the measurement of γ.

The experiments to determine γ that Gay-Lussac and Welter conducted in 1822 therefore assumed a heightened theoretical significance. Particularly fruitful for Laplace's purpose was the observation that γ remained very nearly constant over a wide range of temperature and pressure. When the condition $\gamma = $ constant was introduced into (145), it followed, by integration, that Q must be a function of $P^{1/\gamma}/\rho$ or, inserting the absolute temperature u, of $uP^{(\frac{1}{\gamma}-1)}$. By postulating the simplest possible relationship between Q and $P^{(\frac{1}{\gamma}-1)}$ — proportionality — Laplace could then show that

$$Q = KuP^{\left(\frac{1}{\gamma}-1\right)}, \qquad (147)$$

where K is an unknown constant, determined by the nature of the gas. In the *Mécanique céleste* (C: V, 128; *OC*, V, 143), Equation (147) appeared as

$$Q = F + KuP^{\left(\frac{1}{\gamma}-1\right)}, \qquad (148)$$

but for Laplace's purposes the two expressions were equivalent. One important result in particular followed with either (147) or (148). This was that the ratio between the volume specific heats of any gas at two different pressures P_0 and P_1, but at the same temperature, is equal to $(P_1/P_0)^{1/\gamma}$. In fact, the volume specific heats in such circumstances should be in the ratio P_0/P_1, but the close agreement with Delaroche and Bérard's erroneous results for the variations of specific heat with pressure only endorsed Laplace's conclusion and the assumptions from which it was derived.

To all appearances, Laplace had secured a major triumph in giving at least one branch of the caloric theory the quantitative character that it had always conspicuously lacked. Yet in important respects the triumph was illusory. There was no independent evidence to confirm his assertions concerning the state of caloric in gases; they were clearly determined by the requirement that the deductions made from them should agree with the gas laws — for discussion of this point, see (M: Fox [1971], 173–174). And logically, despite his elaborate expressions involving the hypothetical entities c and i, much of Laplace's argument rested on far simpler premises than he intimated. In 1823 this point was made implicitly but unmistakably by Laplace's most loyal pupil, Poisson ("Sur la vitesse du son," in *Connaissance des temps* [1826/1823], 257–277; and "Sur la chaleur des gaz et des vapeurs," in *Annales de chimie*, 2nd ser., **23** [1823], 337–352), who reviewed and extended several aspects of Laplace's theory of heat. Most of his results had already been obtained by Laplace, but new ground was also broken. In the first paper Poisson derived the now familiar expressions for adiabatic changes in volume, $TV^{\gamma-1} = $ constant, and $PV^\gamma = $ constant; and in the second he arrived at the false conclusion that the principal specific heats of a gas, c_p and c_v, are equal to $BP^{\left(\frac{1}{\gamma}-1\right)}$ and $\frac{1}{\gamma}BP^{\left(\frac{1}{\gamma}-1\right)}$, where B is a constant. No reader could miss the point that all this was achieved without any mention of Laplace's mechanisms. Poisson merely assumed, as any supporter of the caloric theory would have done, that the heat content of a gas was a function of its pressure and density.

Possibly the most telling evidence of Laplace's diminished status in physics toward the end of his life is the almost total indifference with which his work on caloric was received. It aroused neither overt opposition nor support except, somewhat ambiguously, from Poisson, and it stimulated no further research. Yet in 1824 Laplace appeared as confident as ever that a physics based on imponderable fluids and short-range molecular forces could be achieved. In that year, in the "Avertissement" to the fifth edition of the *Système du monde*, he wrote that he intended to make molecular forces the subject of a special supplement. As it happened, the intention was never fulfilled (see Bibliography, Section H). The physics of the sixth edition of the *Système du monde* (which appeared in 1827, the year of Laplace's death, and again, as a quarto, in 1835) was virtually identical to that of the fourth edition (1813).

So in his last years there were few who endorsed Laplace's approach to physics. The great days of Arcueil were now a distant memory, and the once loyal disciples were no longer involved in the problems that their master had identified. In 1822 Biot virtually retired from the scientific community, following his conflict with Arago over the wave theory of light and his defeat by Fourier in the election for one of the two posts of permanent secretary of the Academy of Sciences. It was left for Poisson to carry on Laplacian physics into the late 1820's and 1830's. But even he was far from being an uncritical admirer. In his *Nouvelle théorie de l'action capillaire* (1831) he criticized and corrected a number of shortcomings in Laplace's theory of capillarity; and in the *Théorie mathématique de la chaleur* (1835), despite a prefatory discussion of the properties of caloric, he totally ignored—as he had in 1823—the model that Laplace had perfected in the early 1820's.

28. The Last Analysis. On the publication of Volume IV of *Mécanique céleste* in 1805, Laplace had undertaken to complete the original plan with an eleventh and final book giving an account of the work of predecessors and contemporaries in the science of astronomy. Instead, he had become immersed in physics and in probability, and by the time in the 1820's when he got down to the histories he had promised, his own work was already beginning to be history. Meanwhile, and notably in 1819 and the early 1820's, he had published other investigations on particular topics of celestial mechanics and decided to collect these pieces and append them to the historical summaries of the areas they concerned. Thus the intended Book XI became Books XI through XVI. Laplace had them printed as they were completed beginning in March 1823 (*125, 126, 129–131, 133*) and assembled them as the fifth volume at the end of 1825. The historical notices are more detailed than the concluding chapters of *Système du monde* and are written in a matter-of-fact rather than an inspirational vein. It would be interesting to know at what point in the great investigations of his own career he had studied the works of his predecessors, for it is clear that he knew them well. His histories are still worth consulting in one respect, for his own sense of what he himself had contributed to the several topics. It is doubtful that many of the new investigations assembled for Volume V made much difference to the further development of celestial mechanics; on the whole, their day was past. Book XI is said to be about the figure and rotation of the earth (cf. [*1818b*], [*1819a*], [*1819b*], [*1820e*], [*1820f*], [*1820g*]); Book XII, about the attraction and repulsion of spheres and the motion of elastic fluids, though it really contains the comprehensive development of Laplace's caloric theory of heat and gases discussed in Section 27 (cf. [*1820h*], [*1821d*], [*1822a*], [*1822b*], [*1822d*]); Book XIII about the oscillation of fluids surrounding the planets (cf. [*1815c*], [*1819d*], [*1819e*], [*1820d*], [*1821a*], [*1823a*]); Book XIV about the rotation of heavenly bodies about their centers of gravity (cf. [*1809d*], [*1824a*]); Book XV about the theory of planetary and cometary motions (cf. [*1813a*], [*1819c*], [*1821c*]); and Book XVI about satellite theory (cf. [*1809c*], [*1812a*], [*1820a*], [*1820b*], [*1820c*], [*1820i*], [*1821b*]). The comprehensive titles are a bit misleading. Most of Volume V consists of minor emendations to the data and improvements on fine points of the analysis of particular phenomena treated under those headings in the four main volumes.

Several novelties and peculiarities are worth signaling, however. Inevitably, Laplace had been in touch with the work of Cuvier, whose position and influence in the biological sciences during the Napoleonic period and afterward paralleled his own eminence in mathematical quarters. The first substantive chapter of Book XI consists of calculations purporting to show how the depth and configuration of the seas can be reconciled with the geological evidence for catastrophic inundations and extreme climatic changes in the history of the earth. Chapter 4 also concerns the theory of the earth, in respect to its cooling. As far back as 1809, Laplace had learned of Fourier's investigations of the diffusion of heat (J: Grattan-Guinness [1972], 444–452) and had referred in print to Fourier's pathbreaking but still unpublished paper of 1807 ([1810a]; OC, XII, 295). Despite the difference in their approaches (which he did not mention), he opened his chapter on the heat of the earth by expressing his pleasure that Fourier's two fundamental equations (OC, V, 82–83),

$$\frac{\partial^2 V}{\partial x^2} + \frac{\partial^2 V}{\partial y^2} + \frac{\partial^2 V}{\partial z^2} = k \frac{\partial V}{\partial t}; \qquad (149)$$

which expresses the diffusion of heat inside the earth, or any comparable body, where V is the heat of any point; and

$$-\frac{\partial V}{\partial r} = fV - fl, \qquad (150)$$

which expresses the transmission of heat through the surface, were simply modifications respectively of his general equation (94) on the attraction of spheroids (the potential function), and of his own Equation 2 in Book III, no. 10 of Mécanique céleste (OC, II, 30). Laplace did not allude to the ambivalence in the background of his further relations with Fourier and with his own disciple, Poisson, bested in the rivalry between the two (J: Grattan-Guinness [1972], 462–463). He went on to analyze the temperature gradient beneath the surface and the rate of cooling of the earth in expressions analogous to those that he had developed years before ([1785b]) for spheroidal attraction theory. His purpose was to estimate whether the shrinkage of the earth on cooling was sufficient to decrease the angular velocity and thus to alter the length of the day detectably. While acknowledging that his parameters were hypothetical, he felt safe in concluding that the effect, if it existed at all, did not amount to 0.01 seconds since the time of Hipparchus.

In Book XIII, Laplace thought to redeem a promise, or an assurance, other than historical. It will be recalled that the atmospheric tides had interested him since the earliest memoirs on the ebb and flow of the seas ([1779b]; see Section 8). He recurred to the subject briefly and inconclusively in Mécanique céleste, Book IV, and more confidently in Book II of Théorie analytique des proba-

bilités. Discussing the significance of data in chapter 5, where the most important example came from barometric readings, Laplace there predicted that one day records would be sufficiently full and accurate to permit detecting the gravitational influence of sun and moon among the other, in effect much larger, causes that determine atmospheric pressure (see Section 23). Now, in 1823, taking his point of departure from his previous analysis of mean sea level, he set out to apply his own version of the least-squares analysis to the detection of significance in the variations of the barometer that could be correlated with the relative positions of earth, sun, and moon ([1823a]). The third supplement (118) to Théorie analytique des probabilités, published in 1820, again described his least-squares method—now somewhat modified—as the "most advantageous." As in the original distinction from Legendre's approach ([1811a]), Laplace meant by "most advantageous" that he combined the equations of condition for the unknowns so as to determine the most probable values (cf. Section 25). In an excellent recent discussion, Stigler (L: [1975]) describes the modification as weighted least squares. Laplace now did have access to a series of barometric measurements recorded at the Observatory in Paris—quite probably at his instigation—three times a day, at 9:00 A.M., noon, and 3:00 P.M. from 1 October 1815 through 1 October 1823. He published his findings in Connaissance des temps ([1823a]) and reprinted them with little change in Volume V (OC, V, 184–188, 262–268).

Laplace's idea was to determine whether the gravitational influence can be detected by comparing variations in barometric pressures over those eight years in the four days surrounding syzygies (when the sun, moon, and earth are in line) and quadratures (when they make a right angle). From the conditions, he formed the linear equations

$$x \cos (2iq) + y \sin (2iq) = E_i;$$
$$y \cos (2iq) - x \sin (2iq) = F_i, \qquad (151)$$

in which x and y are the unknowns to be estimated; i indicates the day of each set of data and has the value -1, 0, $+1$, or $+2$; q represents the synodic motion of the moon; and E_i and F_i are computed from the data by the following formulas:

$$E_i = A_i'' - A_i + B_i - B_i'';$$
$$F_i = \{2A_i' - (A_i + A_i'') - 2B_i' + (B_i + B_i'')\}$$
$$\left(1 + \sin\frac{q}{4}\right). \qquad (152)$$

In these expressions, A_i denotes the eight-year

mean of the 9:00 A.M. measurements for the ith day after syzygy; B_i for the ith day after quadrature; A_i' and B_i' the means for the noon values; and A_i'' and B_i'' for the 3:00 P.M. values. Thus, E_i is the mean barometric change between 9:00 A.M. and 3:00 P.M. for the ith day after syzygy, minus the same change for the ith day after quadrature; while F_i is proportional to the difference between the mean rates of change for those days. These expressions had to be combined by the modification that he had brought to his "most advantageous" method in the Third Supplement to the *Théorie analytique des probabilités* (*OC*, VII, 608–616). He multiplied each of the four equations for E by a factor of three and by the corresponding coefficient of x, and multiplied each of the equations for F by the corresponding coefficient of y, obtaining

$$x\,(8 + \Sigma \cos 4iq) + y\Sigma(\sin 4iq)$$

$$= 3\Sigma E_i \cos 2iq - \Sigma F_i \sin 2iq$$

$$y\,(8 - \Sigma \cos 4iq) + x\Sigma(\sin 4iq)$$

$$= 3\Sigma F_i \sin 2iq + \Sigma F_i \cos 2iq.$$

$$(153)$$

Substituting the data from the observations and calculating x and y (0.10743 and 0.017591 respectively), Laplace found the range of the lunar atmospheric tide to be 0.05443 millimeters of mercury and the time of the maximum tide in syzygy to be 18 minutes and 36 seconds after 3:00 P.M. There then remained the problem of determining the probability that these observations really did exhibit the existence of a lunar atmospheric tide. For it was not enough to compare the variations at syzygy and quadrature with those assumed to follow from irregular or random causes, as he had just done. Unless the probability of error in the conclusion is contained within very narrow limits, it might be that the data exhibit only the overall effects of irregular causes, a fallacy to which the science of meteorology was prone. In what amounted to the application of a central limit theorem (the phrase was never his), Laplace calculated the probability that chance alone would produce a variation in the means no greater than that indicated by the eight-year accumulation of observations. The value was 0.843, an unconvincing figure in the tidal quest. All that could be said was that there would be "some implausibility" (*OC*, V, 268) in attributing the variation to chance alone. To increase to near certainty the probability that tides are responsible, the very small effects detected would need to rest

on something like nine times the 1,584 thrice-daily readings, or approximately 40,000 observations.

In the next four years Bouvard continued the program of recording barometric readings at the Paris Observatory, which data he compared with a comparable series assembled on similar principles by Ramond at Clermont-Ferrand, in the Puy-de-Dôme. Bouvard then recalculated the whole corpus, an enormous labor that led Laplace to take up his theory of lunar atmospheric tides yet again. In this, his last paper ([*1827b*]), composed in his seventy-eighth year, he modified once more his method of calculating probable error. Whether or not he had in the interval become aware of the importance of independence as between E_i and F_i in Equation 152—and Stigler thinks he may well have revised his approach for just that reason (L: [1975], 503)—his new calculation did combine the equations of condition in such a way that terms depending on the same measurements served to determine only one unknown. Moreover, in explaining it, he now put a distance between his approach and that of least squares, for which several mathematicians have given proofs that were "not at all satisfactory" (*OC*, V, 491). The art consists in choosing the factors by which the equations of condition formed from the data are to be multiplied in combining them into a system of final equations. Laplace now compares his procedure with that followed in planetary astronomy. In order to correct the elliptical elements, observed longitudes are equated to theoretical longitudes, each modified by the relevant correction. A large number of equations of condition are thus formed. Each is multiplied by the coefficient of the initial correction. Adding all of them gives the first final equation. The same procedure is followed for each successive correction, until there are as many final equations as there are corrections. But the longitude does not depend on a single observation. It is derived from two observations by different instruments, one giving right ascension and the other declination. The law of errors may not be the same for both or have the same effect on the longitude. It was in determining the most advantageous factors (given all these complications) that his method was superior to least squares, and he referred to the general expression that he had given for it in the Third Supplement to the *Théorie analytique des probabilités* (*OC*, VII, 612):

$$l^{(i)}x + p^{(i)}y + q^{(i)}z + \cdots$$

$$= a^{(i)} + m^{(i)}\gamma^{(i)} + n^{(i)}\lambda^{(i)} + r^{(i)}\delta^{(i)} + \cdots, \quad (154)$$

where l, p, q, a, m, n, and r are coefficients given by the conditions; γ, λ, and δ are errors in the observations arising from different circumstances; and x, y, and z are unknowns to be estimated.

Obviously, his equations of condition (152) for the variations in the lunar tide had been formed in that mold, and now, four years later, he combined them in a manner conformable to the astronomical illustration just given of the "most advantageous" method. Having thus revised the method, Laplace let Bouvard perform the calculation, which yielded values of 0.031758 for x and 0.01534 for y, and a difference of 0.01763 millimeters of mercury for the range of the atmospheric tide. Again, the probability had to be calculated that the results show the existence of a regular cause, in this case the gravitational pull of the moon, rather than mere chance. If the value for x were the effect of chance alone, the probability that it would fall within the limits ± 0.031758 would be $\frac{1}{\sqrt{\pi}} \int g\, e^{-g^2 l^2} \cdot dl$, where g is given by observation, and the integral is evaluated between those same limits. That works out to be only 0.3617, and it would again need to be very close to unity to be convincing evidence of the existence of a lunar tide. The value for y gave even a lower probability, and the detectability of a lunar tide in Paris had, therefore, still to be considered moot despite the additional data (OC, V, 500).

Corollary information proved more amenable to the search for causes. Ramond in his observations in Clermont-Ferrand had discovered — and Bouvard in Paris had confirmed — that the daily variation of the barometer between 9:00 A.M. and 3:00 P.M. varied with the seasons, the mean increase being 0.557 millimeters of mercury in the three months from November through January and 0.940 in the following quarter. In the remaining two quarters, the values were intermediate between those extremes. Did these differences result from cause or chance? Again, only probability could decide, and on making the calculation Laplace found that the two values just cited do argue the existence of a regular cause with a high degree of probability, but that the intermediate values and the annual mean of 0.762 can reasonably be attributed to the effects of chance. Bouvard had also noticed that the mean variation is positive in every month of the year, and in a corollary calculation Laplace found the pattern probabilistically predictable. Readers interested in comparing Laplace's capabilities with the resources of modern statistical science may wish to consult the evaluations of Laplace's handling of this problem by Stigler (L: [1975], 509–515) and by Sheynin (L: [1977], 56–58). The manuscript for this paper, published posthumously ([1827b]) with another on elliptical motion and the calculation of planetary distances, was found among Laplace's papers after his death and was incorporated in further printings of Mécanique céleste, Volume V, as a supplement.

Fourier in his éloge (K: [1835], xii) recalled that Laplace retained his extraordinary memory to a very advanced age. He always ate and drank very lightly and showed no sign of enfeeblement before his last two years. Magendie was his doctor and Bouvard was with him constantly at the end. There is a bust of him by Houdon, and Guérin did his official portrait as president of the senate in 1803. Most likenesses show a thin, pointed face with narrow lips and prominent nose. Later portraits suggest a slight tendency to dewlaps in his final years. Laplace was buried at Père Lachaise. The monument erected to him there was moved to Beaumont-en-Auge in 1878, when his remains were transferred to St. Julien de Mailloc, a small village in the canton of Orbec in Calvados.

PART V: THE LAPLACE TRANSFORM

29. Laplace's Integral Solutions to Partial Differential Equations. Laplace's name is most widely used today by mathematicians when referring to the "Laplace transform" method of solving differential, difference, and integral equations. Thus it is meet to outline here the contexts in which it arises in Laplace's writings and its later development into a systematized theory.

To begin at the end: the modern definition of the Laplace transform $\bar{f}$ of f is

$$\bar{f}(s) = \int_0^\infty e^{-su} f(u)\, du, \quad \mathrm{Re}\,(s) > 0. \quad (155)$$

The essence of Laplace transform theory is to convert the given f-problem via (155) to a problem in $\bar{f}$, solve that, and then convert back to the f-solution. The theory itself includes addition, convolution, and shifting theorems, results on transforms of derivatives and integrals, and especially the inverse theorem by means of which we have a general rule to get back to f from $\bar{f}$:

$$f(x) = \frac{1}{2\pi\sqrt{-1}} \int_C \bar{f}(s)\, e^{sx}\, ds, \quad (156)$$

where C is a certain kind of contour in the s-plane. Note that the problem context mentioned at the beginning, and the various theorems stated after (155), are needed to characterize the theory; integral forms similar to (155) and (156) are not sufficient on their own to earn the name of "Laplace transform."

Let us now trace some of this history. Historians of the calculus are accustomed to finding seeds of later ideas in Euler, and such is the case here. In a paper published in 1744 he examined

$$z = \int X(x) e^{ax} dx \qquad (157)$$

as a possible form of solution of differential equations,[1] and a more extensive discussion was given in 1753.[2] However, his preference was for functional or, to a lesser extent, power-series solutions of differential equations (and sometimes combinations of both), although iterative indefinite integrals of a function would also sometimes be used.[3] Euler's ideas to date on solutions of differential equations were outlined in detail in *Institutiones calculi integralis* (1768–1770); integral solutions of the form of (157) were given some space, as was the similar form[4]

$$\int X(x) x^\lambda dx. \qquad (158)$$

The influence of Euler on Lagrange was very profound; and of particular interest for the subsequent influence on Laplace is Lagrange's 1773 paper on finding the mean of a set of observations (of which Laplace was aware, as we saw in Section 4). Lagrange considered a few special discrete and continuous distributions, and evaluated the probability of errors falling within given limits. This involved him in "Laplace-transform"-looking integrals such as

$$\int X(x) e^{-ax} a^x dx, \qquad (159)$$

where X is a rational function, and their conversion into infinite series.[5] Although we can interpret the results in terms of modern Laplace transform theory, Lagrange, like Euler, did not see his results in quite that way.

The first significant signs of Laplace's interest in such expressions occur in his "Mémoire sur les suites" ([1782a]). There his solution method by successive approximations (see Section 12 above) involved formulas such as

$$u = \sum_{r=1}^{\infty} a_r(s, s_1) \int^{(r)} \phi(s) (ds)^r +$$

$$\sum_{r=1}^{\infty} b_r(s, s_1) \int^{(r)} \psi(s_1) (ds_1)^r, \qquad (160)$$

where ϕ and ψ are "arbitrary" (*OC*, X, 54). This kind of result was already given in his first presentation in [1777a] of the method (*OC*, IX, 24 ff.); but later in [1782a] he came close to a Laplace transform of the form (158) for integral values of μ, for he used iterative integration by parts to obtain

$$\int \phi(z) z^\mu dz =$$
$$C + \sum_{r=0}^{\mu} (-1)^r \mu P r \phi_{r+1}(z) z^{\mu-r}, \qquad (161)$$

where ϕ_r is the rth indefinite integral of ϕ (*OC*, X, 66). However, the purpose was not to explore the properties of (161) for themselves but to obtain this integral solution of a general linear second-order partial differential equation:

$$u = (2x)^{-m/2} \left\{ \int^{x+at} \lrcorner \left(\frac{x+at-z}{2x} \right) \phi(z) dz + \int_0^{x-at} \lrcorner \left(\frac{x-at-z}{2x} \right) \psi(z) dz \right\} \qquad (162)$$

(*ibid.*, 68), where $\lrcorner$ is the solution of a certain second-order ordinary differential equation.

More promising material for our purpose occurs in Laplace's paper [1785a] on approximating to functions of very large numbers. He took the linear difference equation

$$S(s) = \sum_i A_r(s) \Delta^r y(s), \qquad (163)$$

(where Laplace's s is real) and applied two transforms to it:

$$y(s) = \int x^s \phi(x) dx, \qquad (164)$$

akin to (161) and now sometimes called the "Mellin transform," which proved particularly useful when $S \not\equiv 0$; and the "almost-Laplace" transform

$$y(s) = \int e^{-sx} \phi(x) dx, \qquad (165)$$

which is helpful when $S \equiv 0$ (*OC*, X, 212, 236–248). In the course of using these two transforms he derived a few basic properties; for example, from (165) he had a theorem on (forward) differences:

$$\Delta^r y(s) = \int e^{-sx} (e^x - 1)^r \phi(x) dx \qquad (166)$$

(*ibid.*, 236); while (164) provided a similar result for differences,

$$\Delta^r y(s) = \int x^s (x-1)^r \phi(x) dx, \qquad (167)$$

and also one for derivatives,

$$\frac{d^k y(s)}{dx^k} = \int x^s (\log x)^k \phi(x) \, dx \qquad (168)$$

(*ibid.*, 242–247; see also 278–291). "In many circumstances," Laplace commented prophetically, "these forms [(165)] . . . are more useful than the preceding ones [(164)]" (*ibid.*, 248). It is worth noting also that earlier parts of this paper feature integrals the integrands of which involve e^{-t^2}, for the Laplace transform of the error function is of some importance in certain applications.[6] Later in the paper Laplace urged general solutions to differential equations using the form of (164) or (165) (*ibid.*, 253).

It is this work that is normally cited as the origin of the term "Laplace transform"; but we must also look at the effect on Laplace of Fourier's 1807 monograph on heat diffusion. Fourier had found the "diffusion equation," in forms such as

$$\frac{\partial^2 y}{\partial x^2} = \frac{\partial y}{\partial t}, \qquad (169)$$

to represent the physical phenomenon, and the "Fourier series" solution form

$$y = \sum_{r=0}^{\infty} (a_r \cos rx + b_r \sin rx) \, e^{-r^2 t} \qquad (170)$$

to solve it.

A strong controversy ensued at the Institut de France about this work, partly because solutions of the form of (170) had been considered and rejected in the eighteenth century.[7] A particularly relevant criticism to our current discussion is that the initial condition function f is not explicitly encased in the solution (170) — as it is in integral and functional solutions — but appears only in the integrals that define its coefficient; to the mathematical mind of the time, the explicit involvement of f helped to justify the generality of any solution. Lagrange, still alive, remained opposed to (170), as did Poisson and Biot; but Laplace accepted Fourier's results. In [1810a] he constructed a Newtonian intermolecular force model to obtain the heat transfer term in (169) (*OC*, XII, 293). More significantly, in [1809e] he published a miscellany paper on analytical methods that not only related to Fourier's work but also developed techniques presented in "Mémoire sur les suites" ([1782a]) and the paper ([1785a]) on very large numbers.

As a special case of advancing the results of [1782a], Laplace considered Fourier's diffusion equation (169) and solved a problem that is conspicuous by its absence from Fourier's 1807 mono-

graph: to solve (169) for an *infinite* range of values of x, where the periodicity of the trigonometric functions rules out (170). Poisson, already aware in 1806 of the trend of Fourier's work, had offered this power-series solution[8] of (169):

$$y = \sum_{r=0}^{\infty} \frac{x^{2r}}{(2r)!} f^{(r)}(t) +$$
$$\sum_{r=0}^{\infty} \frac{x^{2r+1}}{(2r+1)!} g^{(r)}(t). \qquad (171)$$

In [1809e] Laplace used the same type of solution of (169). Applying the initial condition

$$y = \phi(x), \text{ when } t = 0, \, -\infty \le x \le \infty, \qquad (172)$$

he obtained

$$y = \sum_{r=0}^{\infty} \frac{t^r}{r!} \phi^{(2r)}(x), \qquad (173)$$

and then submitted it to an ingenious manipulation. The result

$$\int_{-\infty}^{\infty} z^{2r} e^{-z^2} \, dz = \frac{(2r)!}{4^r r!} \sqrt{\pi} \qquad (174)$$

— proved in [1785a] see *OC*, X, 269, where "t_{2r}" is misprinted from the original for "t^{2r}"; I have used z for t in (174), although Laplace did not explicitly recall his proof here — and the obvious

$$\int_{-\infty}^{\infty} z^{2r+1} e^{-z^2} \, dz = 0 \qquad (175)$$

converted (173) to

$$y = \frac{1}{\sqrt{\pi}} \int_{-\infty}^{\infty} \sum_{r=0}^{\infty} \frac{(2z\sqrt{t})^r}{r!} \phi^{(r)}(x) \, e^{-z^2} \, dz. \qquad (176)$$

The integrand of (176) contains a Taylor expansion, so that we have finally the integral solution

$$y = \frac{1}{\sqrt{\pi}} \int_{-\infty}^{\infty} \phi(x + 2z\sqrt{t}) \, e^{-z^2} \, dz \qquad (177)$$

(*OC*, XIV, 184–193).

This solution form preserved the tradition of containing the initial condition function ϕ explicitly. Fourier himself now realized that an integral solution would work for an infinite range of values of x, and by ingenious if unrigorous manipulations of infinitesimals he very quickly found the "Fourier transform" and its inverse. They took forms such as

$$\underline{f}(q) = \sqrt{\frac{2}{\pi}} \int_0^{\infty} f(u) \cos qu \, du \qquad (178)$$

and

$$f(x) = \sqrt{\frac{2}{\pi}} \int_0^\infty \underline{f}(q) \cos qx \, dq, \qquad (179)$$

and led to double-integral solutions of the diffusion equation (169) in which, as in (177), the initial condition function f is encased:[9]

$$y = \frac{2}{\pi} \int_0^\infty \int_0^\infty f(u) \cos qu \cos qx \, e^{-q^2 t} \, du \, dq. \quad (180)$$

Thus two new integral (and the Fourier series) solutions of linear partial differential equations were produced in a very short time. During the next decade an intense development of these methods occurred in a variety of physical contexts. Fourier integrals were the most popular, but Poisson used Laplace's form (177) whenever he could. Because Laplace himself was not prominently involved, we shall not pursue the details here;[10] but several of his results of this period are worthy of notice. He used Fourier integrals in [*1810b*], which continued the purpose of [*1785a*] on very large numbers (*OC*, XII, 334–344). In [*1811a*] he returned to another old interest, finding the mean of a set of observations, and derived more Fourier integrals from integrals such as

$$\int_0^\infty e^{-ax} x^{-\omega} e^{\sqrt{-1}\, rx} \, dx \qquad (181)$$

(*OC*, XII, 363; compare the results in [*1785a*] at *OC*, X, 264). Elsewhere in [*1811a*] he may possibly have revealed another influence from Fourier, for he showed that the set of functions

$$\left\{ \frac{(-2)^i}{1 \cdot 3 \cdots (2i-1)\sqrt{\pi}} \int_\infty^\infty e^{-s^2} (\mu + s\sqrt{-1})^{2i} \, ds, \right.$$
$$\left. i = 1, 2, \cdots \right\} \quad (182)$$

was orthogonal over $(-\infty, \infty)$ with respect to the weighting function $e^{-\mu^2}$ (*ibid.*, 382) — an analysis that corresponds closely to Fourier's 1807 demonstration[11] of the orthogonality of the (misnamed) "Bessel functions" $\{J_0(a_i x)\}$; the $\{a_i\}$ are the roots of a certain transcendental equation} with respect to the weighting function x — and an orthogonality expansion similar to Fourier's (*ibid.*, 384). This work constitutes Laplace's anticipation of a form of the "Hermite polynomials" of half a century later (see L: Molina [1930]); the expansion is now misnamed "the Gram-Charlier expansion." Finally in this association of Laplace with Fourier, we recall from Section 28 Laplace's use of Fourier analysis in estimating the age of the earth.

Laplace's *Théorie analytique des probabilités*, which appeared in editions in 1812, 1814, and 1820, also deserves mention; for, as in his earlier work on mathematical probability (see Sections 4 and 11) he included, especially in Book I, part 1, treatments of the generating function in the form

$$\sum_r p_r t^r \qquad (183)$$

rather than as what we now call the moment generating function of the distribution function of the discrete random variable t:

$$\sum_t e^{\lambda t} f(t). \qquad (184)$$

He also used a continuous analogue of (183),

$$y(x) = \int t^{-x} T(t) \, dt, \qquad (185)$$

which harks back to his (164), and at one point adapted his earlier (168) to define the then rather novel fractional derivative of $y(x)$:

$$d^i y(x) / dx^i = \int t^{-x} (\log 1/t)^i T(t) \, dt, \quad (186)$$

where i is *not* necessarily an integer (*OC*, VII, 86). He also used a continuous version of (184),

$$y(x) = \int e^{-xt} f(t) \, dt, \qquad (187)$$

where an inverse transform is attempted (*OC*, VII, 136), and also in treating again the "Hermite polynomials" (in Book II, chapter 3). Various other of his earlier results were given an airing: in Book I, part 2, some Fourier integrals were evaluated, and the use of (164) and (165) in solving difference equations and in developing asymptotic theory was again dealt with. Laplace also made some use of characteristic functions for discrete distributions (for example, in Book I, part 1 and Book II, chapter 4 — and already in [*1810b*] at *OC*, XII, 309 for a uniform distribution).

However, the full relationship between mathematical probability and harmonic analysis does not seem to have been grasped at this time. For example, we now know that the distribution function of a sum of independent random variables is the convolution of the component distribution functions, and that the Laplace transform converts the convolution into the product of its transformed distributions; yet this was not shown, although Poisson was especially aware of the significance of convolutions in Fourier integral solutions of differential equations.[12] Again, the existence of the integral in (185) is better secured by the use of complex variables in defining the characteristic function of f:

$$X(\lambda) = \int_{-\infty}^{\infty} e^{\lambda \sqrt{-1} \lambda t} f(t) \, dt; \qquad (188)$$

but this move had to wait for a time, although Cauchy was very adept at handling complex variable forms of the Fourier integral (178).[13]

Thus we see a number of opportunities that later generations were to grasp. It is appropriate here only to outline the later development of the Laplace transform, which has been our principal theme. The first systematic study of its basic properties was carried out in an 1820's manuscript by Abel, first published in 1839:[14] he started from generating functions, and noted the multivariate transform

$$\phi(x, y, z, \cdots) =$$

$$\int e^{xu + yv + zp + \cdots} f(u, v, p, \cdots) \, du \, dv \, dp \cdots. \quad (189)$$

Meanwhile, in 1833 Robert Murphy had taken the transform in the form

$$g(x) = \int t^{x-1} \phi(t) \, dt, \qquad (190)$$

where ϕ is a rational function, and made explicit this formula for the inverse:[15]

$$\phi(t) = \frac{1}{t} \left(\text{coefficient of } \frac{1}{x} \text{ in } \frac{g(x)}{t^x} \right). \quad (191)$$

It was the difficulty of finding a general formula for the inverse, as well as the difficulty of solving integral equations of any kind, that prevented the Laplace transform from revealing its power for so long;[16] Fourier's quick success in obtaining his inverse transform (179) was crucial to the much more rapid development of his methods. It should be pointed out that when the phrase "Laplace transformation" is found in nineteenth-century mathematical literature, the reference is normally either to Laplace's method of reducing partial differential equations or to his method of cascades (compare Sections 12 and 7 respectively). When progress did come, it was through the aid of Fourier analysis. For example, in 1859 Riemann converted the transform.

$$g(s) = \int_0^\infty h(x) \, x^{-s} \, d(\log x), \quad s = a + b\sqrt{-1}, \quad (192)$$

to a sum of Fourier sine and cosine integrals, and he inverted both, by means of the appropriate versions of (179), to end up with[17]

$$h(y) = \frac{1}{2\pi\sqrt{-1}} \int_{a-\infty\sqrt{-1}}^{a+\infty\sqrt{-1}} g(s) \, y^s \, ds. \quad (193)$$

Dini studied such inversions, in contour form, in 1880, and again Fourier analysis provided the means.[18] Laplace transform theory had to await such events as Poincaré's 1885 analysis of asymptotic solutions to differential equations,[19] and especially the development of Heaviside's operational calculus in the 1890's.[20] Modernly recognizable proofs of the inversion formula were produced early in the twentieth century,[21] and they helped substantially in the exegesis of Heaviside's ideas in the 1920's with the "operational calculus" and its applications. J. R. Carson's work was especially significant in systematizing the operational calculus, based on the Laplace transform, for its use in electrical circuit theory.[22] Thus textbooks on both theory and applications began to appear in the 1930's and early 1940's.[23] Then, with the theory well launched, some of its development was classified during World War II, for it was used in problems such as waveguide design for radar systems. A politically acute man like Laplace would have appreciated that.

NOTES TO SECTION 29

1. See esp. art. 6 of L. Euler, "De constructione aequationum" (1744), in *Opera omnia*, 1st ser., XXII, 150–161.
2. See arts. 6 ff. of L. Euler, "Methodus aequationes differentiales . . ." (1753), in *Opera omnia*, 1st ser., XXII, 181–213.
3. See, for example, esp. art. 28 of L. Euler, "Recherches sur l'intégration de l'équation . . ." (1766), in *Opera omnia*, 1st ser., XXIII, 42–73. On these and other references, see (N: Petrova [1975]).
4. *Institutiones calculi integralis*, II (1769), chs. 3–4 and 5 respectively; in *Opera omnia*, 1st ser., XII.
5. See esp. arts. 37–42 of J. L. Lagrange, "Mémoire sur l'utilité de la méthode. . ." (1773), in *Oeuvres*, II, 171–234.
6. This is well conveyed in, for example, Francis D. Murnaghan, *The Laplace Transformation* (Washington, D.C., 1962).
7. For further details on these matters, see (J: Grattan-Guinness with Ravetz [1972]).
8. S.-D. Poisson, "Mémoire sur les solutions. . .," in *Journal de l'École polytechnique*, cahier 13, **6** (1806), 60–116, esp. 109–111.
9. Fourier's most detailed treatment is in arts. 342–385 of his *Théorie analytique de la chaleur* (1822), in *Oeuvres*, I, 387–448.
10. Some hints are given in n. 7, chs. 21 and 22; and in chs. 6–10, *passim*, of (N: Burkhardt [1908]).
11. See (J: Grattan-Guinness with Ravetz [1972]), ch. 16, note 7.
12. See esp. S.-D. Poisson, "Mémoire sur la théorie des ondes," in *Mémoires de l'Académie royale des sciences de l'Institut de France*, **1** (1816), 71–186.
13. See esp. A.-L. Cauchy, "Sur les intégrales des équations linéaires. . ." (1823), in *Oeuvres*, 2nd ser., I, 275–357; and its continuation by operational means in "Sur l'analogie

des puissances et des différences" (1827), *ibid.*, 2nd ser., VII, 198–254. The form of (188) received some attention in the context of probability in S.-D. Poisson, *Recherches sur la probabilité des jugements. . .* (Paris, 1837), ch. 4.

14. N. H. Abel, "Sur les fonctions génératrices et leurs déterminantes," in *Oeuvres complètes*, B. Holmboe, ed. (1839), II, 77–88–he slightly misstates (189); *Oeuvres complètes*, L. Sylow and S. Lie, eds. (1881), II, 67–81.

15. R. Murphy, "On the Inverse Method of Definite Integrals . . .," in *Transactions of the Cambridge Philosophical Society*, 4 (1833), 353–408; see 362.

16. Literature on this history includes Harry Bateman, *Report on the History and Present State of the Theory of Integral Equations* (London, 1911); and Hans Hahn, "Bericht über die Theorie der linearen Integralgleichungen," in *Jahresbericht der Deutschen Mathematiker-Vereinigung*, 20 (1911), 69–117.

17. B. Riemann, "Ueber die Anzahl der Primzahlen unter einer gegebenen Grösse" (1859), in *Gesammelte mathematische Werke*, 2nd ed. (Leipzig, 1892), 144–155; see 148.

18. See esp. arts. 62–88 *passim*, of Ulisse Dini, *Serie di Fourier. . .* (Pisa, 1880), in his *Opere*, IV.

19. Henri Poincaré, "Sur les équations linéaires . . ." (1885), in *Oeuvres*, I, 226–289. Amusingly, Poincaré misnames it "Bessel transformation" throughout the paper and puts a corrective note at the end. The *Oeuvres* edition silently makes the correction, although the original page numbers are incorrectly given.

The use of the term "Laplace transform" may stem from Boole's advocacy of the form $\int e^{ux} V(x)$ to solve differential equations in his *A Treatise on Differential Equations*, 2nd ed. (Cambridge, 1865), ch. 18, where its advocacy also in J. Petzval's *Integration der linearen Differentialgleichungen . . .*, 2 vols. (Vienna, 1853–1859), I, 38–119, 328–395 (see also II, 369–379) is mentioned. Notice, however, that in ch. 17 Boole uses the phrase "Laplace transformation" to refer to Laplace's method of cascades–and Petzval uses "Laplace's integral" to refer (I, 96) *only* to the equation $\int_0^\infty e^{-x^2} dx = \frac{1}{2}\sqrt{\pi}$, which is a special case of (174).

20. Oliver Heaviside, *Electromagnetic Theory*, 3 vols. (London, 1893–1912).

21. See esp. H. M. MacDonald, "Some Applications of Fourier's Theorem," in *Proceedings of the London Mathematical Society*, 1st ser., 35 (1902–1903), 428–443; H. Mellin, "Abriss einer einheitlichen Theorie. . .," in *Mathematische Annalen*, 68 (1910), 305–337; and T. J. I'A. Bromwich, "Normal Coordinates in Dynamical Systems," in *Proceedings of the London Mathematical Society*, 2nd ser., 15 (1916), 401–448.

22. See esp. J. R. Carson, *Electric Circuit Theory and the Operational Calculus* (New York, 1926; repr. New York, 1953). The book is essentially a reprint of his articles with the same title in *Bell System Technical Journal*, 4 (1925), 685–761; and 5 (1926), 50–95, 336–384; see also his "The Heaviside Operational Calculus," *ibid.*, 1 (1922), pt. 2, 43–55; and "Notes on the Heaviside Operational Calculus," *ibid.*, 9 (1930), 150–162.

23. In German, see esp. G. Doetsch, *Theorie und Anwendung der Laplacesche Transformation* (Berlin, 1937; repr. New York, 1943). In English, for theory see D. V. Widder, *The Laplace Transform* (Princeton, 1946); and for applications, H. S. Carslaw and J. C. Jaeger, *Operational Methods in Applied Mathematics* (Oxford, 1941). For bibliography, see M. F. Gardner and J. L. Barnes, *Transients in Linear Systems Studied by the Laplace Transformation* (New York, 1942), 359–382.

I am indebted to Jock MacKenzie and Stephen Stigler for advice on this article.

I. GRATTAN-GUINNESS

BIBLIOGRAPHY

This bibliography is divided into two major sections and is arranged under the following headings:

ORIGINAL WORKS
  A. Correspondence
  B. *Exposition du système du monde*
  C. *Traité de mécanique céleste*
  D. *Théorie analytique des probabilités*
  E. *Essai philosophique sur les probabilités*
  F. Translations of *Mécanique céleste*
  G. *Oeuvres de Laplace* (1843–1847)
  H. *Oeuvres complètes de Laplace* (1878–1912)
  I. Individual Memoirs
    1. Order of Composition
    2. Order of Publication

SECONDARY LITERATURE
  J. Biographical and General
  K. Celestial Mechanics
  L. Probability
  M. Mathematical Physics
  N. Mathematics

The key to abbreviations will be found in Section I.

ORIGINAL WORKS

A. Correspondence. Laplace conducted an extensive correspondence with leading scientists throughout his lifetime; and it must have been important to him as a record of his thoughts, for he kept copies of his own letters. Unfortunately, it was consumed, along with all the other papers in the possession of the family, by a fire that swept through the château of Mailloc in Normandy in 1925. The property was then owned by his great-great grandson, the comte de Colbert-Laplace. In a letter to Karl Pearson [J] he tells of his intention to publish the Laplace-Lagrange correspondence and of his grandmother's recollections of her grandfather. Also, F. N. David has stated that much personal and scientific material, including all correspondence with English scientists, was destroyed during the British bombardment of Caen in 1944, but no details are given and no authority is cited ("Some Notes on Laplace," in J. Neyman and L. M. LeCam, eds., *Bernoulli, Bayes and Laplace* [Berlin–Heidelberg–New York, 1965], 30–44). In any case, the losses are irreparable, for with one exception (*17a*) the editors of the *Oeuvres complètes*, 14 vols. (Paris, 1878–1912), failed to include anything not already in print.

A few of Laplace's other letters have been printed in editions devoted to his correspondents. There are fourteen letters to Lagrange and twelve from Lagrange in *Oeuvres de Lagrange*, XIV (Paris, 1892); and several others in *Oeuvres de Lavoisier, Correspondance*, René Fric, ed., 3 fascs. to date (Paris, 1955–1964). Occasional documents are to be found at the Bibliothèque de l'Institut de France, MS 2242, and next door at the Archives de l'Académie des Sciences. From the former repository R. Taton has published a few letters and other pieces illustrating Laplace's relations with Lacroix from 1789 until 1815, "Laplace et Sylvestre-François Lacroix," in *Revue d'histoire des sciences*, 6 (1953), 350–360; and from the latter R. Hahn has summarized a fragment on theology, "Laplace's Religious Views," in *Archives internationales d'histoire des sciences*, 8 (1955), 38–40. Yves Laissus has published letters to Alexis Bouvard (20 Feb. 1797) and J.-B. Delambre (29 Jan. 1798), in *Revue d'histoire des sciences*, 14 (1961), 285–296.

In 1886 Charles Henry published six letters from Laplace to Condorcet and d'Alembert, of which the originals are in the Condorcet papers at the Institut de France, and four together with a fragment on the orbits of comets from the papers of the Abbé A.-G. Pingré in the Bibliothèque Sainte-Geneviève, in *Bollettino di bibliografia e storia delle scienze matematiche e fisiche*, 19 (1886), 149–178. These documents are reprinted in *OC*, XIV, 340–371. See below, (*34*).

Two letters by Laplace as minister of the interior, dated 17 frimaire and 26 frimaire an VIII (8 Dec. and 17 Dec. 1799), the latter accompanied by a report, appear in the *Moniteur universel* (an VIII), no. 78 (18 frimaire), 307–308; and no. 87 (27 frimaire), 343–345.

There are scattered autographs of Laplace in other collections. For example, there are reports on his examination of artillery cadets in 1784, 1785, and 1786, and his recommendations for reform of the system in July and August 1789, at the Archives de la Guerre, X^D 249 (Vincennes). There is fragmentary correspondence with Fourier in the Fourier papers, Bibliothèque Nationale, fonds français, MSS 22501, 68–74; and 22529, 122–124. The Library of the American Philosophical Society, Philadelphia, has a few letters to him from Madame de Laplace and their son, and several from Laplace to Giovanni Fabroni in Florence. The Library of the Royal Society of London has a dozen letters to English colleagues, six to Charles Blagden, one to Thomas Young, and five to J. F. W. Herschel. But such glimpses are fleeting, and to a very large extent the history of Laplace's work must be reconstructed from the internal evidence of the published writings, controlled as to chronology by the records of the Académie des Sciences.

It will be convenient to give first the major treatises in the form in which they were published during Laplace's lifetime, followed by details of the translations, the two collected editions, and the individual memoirs. The place of publication is Paris, unless indicated otherwise.

B. Exposition du système du monde, 2 vols. (an IV [1796]); 2nd ed. (an VII [1799]); 3rd ed. (1808); 4th ed. (1813); 5th ed. (1824). An edition printed by de Vroom in Brussels in 1826 and 1827 appears to be a reprint of the 5th ed., even though the latter printing is called *sixième édition* on the title page. It seems probable that the true 6th ed., for which Laplace was reading proof at the end of his life, was delayed until 1835, when it appeared in Paris, prefaced by the *éloge* delivered by Fourier on

15 June 1829 before the Institut de France [J]. This edition occupies vol. VI of [G] and [H] below. For the differences between it and the 5th ed., see the discussion under [H].

C. Traité de mécanique céleste: vols. I and II (an VII [1799]); vol. III (an XI [1802]); vol. IV (an XIII [1805]); vol. V (1823–1825). A 2nd ed. was published in 4 vols. (1829–1839). This work occupies vols. I–V of [G] and [H] below.

D. Théorie analytique des probabilités (1812); 2nd ed. (1814); 3rd ed. (1820). With 3 supps. published in 1816, 1818, and 1820, respectively, this work, with a 4th supp. (1825), occupies vol. VII of [G] and [H] below. A facsimile of the 1st ed. was published by Éditions Culture et Civilisation (Brussels, 1967).

E. Essai philosophique sur les probabilités (1814), originally published as the "Introduction" to the 2nd ed. of [D] above; 2nd ed. (1814); 3rd ed. (1816); 4th ed. (1819); 5th ed. (1825). It is included with [D] above in vol. VII of both [G] and [H] below. A facsimile of the 1st ed. was published by Éditions Culture et Civilisation (Brussels, 1967).

F. Translations of Mécanique céleste: J. C. Burckhardt published a German trans. of vols. I and II as *Mechanik des Himmels*, 2 vols. (Berlin, 1800–1802). There are two early English translations of Book I and Books I and II respectively: by John Toplis (London–Nottingham, 1814) and by Henry Harte, 2 vols. (Dublin, 1822–1827). Both were entirely superseded by the splendid work of Nathaniel Bowditch, *Mécanique céleste by the Marquis de Laplace, Translated With a Commentary*, 4 vols. (Boston, 1829–1839). Bowditch's commentary in the footnotes is an indispensable vade mecum for the study of Laplace, explaining and filling out the demonstrations, and containing a great body of historical as well as mathematical and astronomical elucidation. Bowditch did not translate Volume V of *Mécanique céleste*.

G. Oeuvres de Laplace, 7 vols. (1843–1847), reprints [B], [C], and [D] above, with [E] included as the intro. to [D]. Its publication, initiated by Laplace's widow, was eventually subsidized by the state.

H. Oeuvres complètes de Laplace, 14 vols. (1878–1912), was financed by a bequest from Laplace's son, General the Marquis de Laplace, who died on 7 October 1874. His will entrusted the task to the Académie des Sciences. There is correspondence in the Laplace dossier in its archives concerning the arrangements between his niece, the comtesse de Colbert-Laplace, the permanent secretaries, and the publisher, Gauthier. General Laplace expressly directed that the edition was to contain neither commentary nor extraneous elements. He based this injunction on what he took to be the wishes of his father, who had often said in the last months of his life that no corrections should be made in the works of savants after their death; modifying their writings in any way could only distort the record of their initial thoughts and be prejudicial to the history of science.

In only one respect (apart from correction of typographical errors) was the new edition to depart from [G]

in its printing of the major treatises in the first seven volumes. Before his death, Laplace had begun correcting the proofs for a 6th ed. of *Exposition du système du monde* [B]. His intention had been to return to the 4th ed. and restore its chapters 12 ("De la stabilité et de l'équilibre des mers"), 17 ("Réflexions sur la loi de la pesanteur universelle"), and 18 ("De l'attraction moléculaire"), which he had omitted from the 5th ed. In the foreword to the projected 6th ed. Laplace said that he intended a separate work bringing together "the principal results of the application of analysis to the phenomena due to molecular actions distinct from universal attraction, which had just been much extended." Since he did not have the time for that, his son considered it consistent with his principles to restore these chapters from the 4th ed.

For the rest, Volumes VIII–XII contain the individual memoirs published by the Académie des Sciences through 1793 and by the Institut de France after 1795. Volume XIII contains writings published in *Connaissance des temps* from 1798 until Laplace's death, and Volume XIV, memoirs reprinted from *Journal de l'École polytechnique* (most notably his course on mathematics given at the École Normale in 1795); articles from *Journal de physique, Annales de physique et chimie, Journal des mines,* and so on; scattered items of correspondence; and fragments concerning annuities, rents, and matters of public interest. There is a very inadequate "Table analytique."

Despite their instructions, the editors did modernize much of Laplace's notation, for which reason it is preferable to have recourse to the original printing whenever possible, particularly in the case of the earlier memoirs. Since that is possible only in large research libraries, it has seemed practical to give quotations from the original sources and to make page references to the *Oeuvres complètes* whenever the work in question is contained in them. Unfortunately, however, the edition is not exhaustive; the editors simply went through the journals mentioned above and reprinted what they found seriatim. Thus, they missed Laplace's earliest papers [*1771a, 1771b, 1774a*] published in Leipzig and Turin, as well as one major treatise, *Théorie du mouvement et de la figure elliptique des planètes* (1784), and other, lesser writings. It is quite possible that further publications that escaped their net may also have eluded us.

I. Individual Memoirs. For details of separate printings and also for later editions and translations of the *Système du monde* and *Essai philosophique sur les probabilités,* the reader will do well to have recourse to the Library of Congress, *National Union Catalog,* and the British Museum, *General Catalogue of Printed Books,* as well as to the Bibliothèque Nationale, *Catalogue général des livres imprimés.* The last named contains a phantom that should here be exorcised. It lists among the writings of Laplace *Essai sur la théorie des nombres. Second supplément* (1825). The volume corresponding to that call number (V. **7051**) has "Laplace" penciled on the flyleaf but is in fact Legendre's 2nd

supp. to his *Essai sur la théorie des nombres* (1808). Another copy is bound with the 2nd ed. of that work (1825).

What follows is (1) a chronology of Laplace's work in the order of the composition of particular writings, and (2) a bibliographical listing of his memoirs in the order of publication. As will become evident, the two sequences are not everywhere the same. Prolonged immersion in these confusing details has convinced us that any redundancy in this double listing will be more than compensated by the facility it creates for keeping the problem of tracing the development of Laplace's research distinct from the problem of tracing the history of the influence of his publications. The cross-references make it possible to relate the two sequences at any juncture.

The first list has been established from the records of the Académie des Sciences. The *procès-verbaux,* or minutes of the semiweekly meetings of that body, were transcribed into a register that is conserved in the Archives de l'Académie des Sciences in the Institut de France. Before Laplace was elected to membership, the papers that he submitted were referred to commissions for evaluation, according to the normal practice. The record of these reports is maintained in a separate register (which, however, is not complete); and many of the reports themselves remain in the archives, classified by date. The sequence of these early communications, (*1*)–(*13*) in our numbering, was investigated by Stephen M. Stigler for "Laplace's Early Work: Chronology and Citations," in *Isis,* **69,** no. 247 (June 1978). He has most generously communicated to us a preprint together with notes of his researches in the archives in the summer of 1976. The MSS of the papers themselves were normally returned to the contributor and have not been conserved in the archives. In rare instances, the text was transcribed in the *procès-verbaux.* After Laplace's election to the Academy, the only record we have consists in most instances of the original title of his communications and the date on which he read or simply submitted them. In certain instances he formally requested recognition of priority—*pour prendre date.* Unless otherwise indicated, the dates and titles below (through 1793) are from the *procès-verbaux,* which carry through to the suppression of the Academy on 8 August of that year by the Revolutionary Convention, and thereafter from the published *procès-verbaux* of the Institut de France.

Since the foundation of the Institut de France in 1795, the Académie des Sciences has formed one of its constituent bodies, as its Classe des Sciences Physiques et Mathématiques from 1795 to 1814 and under the name Académie des Sciences since the Restoration. For the period 1795–1835 its *procès-verbaux* have been published together with the reports of committees, which are even more valuable. In the Academy before 1793 and in the Institute after 1795, Laplace served on many commissions concerned with evaluating the work of others or with special projects. We have included in this listing only the reports for which he was primarily responsible as author or spokesman. His other involvements in the affairs of the Institute were manifold, particularly in relation to the prize programs. They may be followed by means of the indexes to each volume of the *procès-verbaux*.

As for the second listing, that of publications, a word is needed about the organization and dating of the Academy's memoirs. Under the old regime, an annual volume was published under the general title *Histoire et mémoires de l'Académie royale des sciences de Paris*. The two sections are separately paginated and for this reason are cited separately (see the table of abbreviations below). The *Histoire* consists of announcements— prizes, distinguished visitors, works received, and so on—together with an abstract of the memoirs prepared by the permanent secretary. The *Mémoires*, which constitute the bulk of each volume, are the scientific papers themselves published by the members. Confusion in dating easily arises, because publication was always two to four years in arrears. Thus the volume for the year 1780 appeared in 1784 and contained memoirs submitted in 1783—or any time between the nominal and publication dates. Our method is to indicate that volume as *MARS* (1780/1784), with the latter date that of publication, and to specify memoirs in the bibliography by the date of publication. The *Connaissance des temps* presents the reverse problem. The volume of this almanac "for 1818," for example, contained the ephemerides for that year but appeared in 1815. Thus, it is cited *CT* (1818/1815), with the latter date still that of publication.

Journals proliferated after 1795, and Laplace then fell into the practice of publishing short papers and abstracts of his long memoirs in the *Connaissance des temps* and other periodicals mentioned in the list of abbreviations. More often than not, he would publish the same piece, sometimes with minor modifications, in several journals. The Laplace entry in the Royal Society of London, *Catalogue of Scientific Papers, 1800–1863*, III (1869), cites all the journals in which each piece appeared, as well as the translations that appeared in Germany and in Britain. We have limited ourselves to the most readily accessible journal; and when more than one is indicated, we have cited the number of the memoir (indicated by *RSC*) as listed in the catalog. The editors took the ostensible date of the various journals at face value and thus cannot always be relied on for their dating.

In addition, Laplace published a few reports concerned with the administration of the Institute and École Polytechnique. Also, the opinions that he delivered in his political capacity as a senator in the Napoleonic regime and a member of the Chambre des Pairs after the Restoration were printed in the proceedings of these bodies. Although we are not noticing his rare interventions in debates, it has seemed practical to include these episodic political and administrative pieces in the chronology of publications, and to distinguish them from the scientific writings by a "*P*" placed before the date.

The following abbreviations are employed:

AC   *Annales de chimie*
AP   *Archives parlementaires*

BSPM   *Bulletin de la Société philomathique de Paris*
CT   *Connaissance des temps*
CX   *Correspondance de l'École polytechnique*
HARS   *Histoire de l'Académie royale des sciences de Paris* (the preface to the corresponding volume of *MARS* below)
JP   *Journal de physique*
JX   *Journal de l'École polytechnique*
MARS   *Mémoires de l'Académie royale des sciences de Paris*
MASIF   *Mémoires de l'Académie royale des sciences de l'Institut de France* (1 [1816/1818]–...).
MI   *Mémoires de l'Institut national des sciences et arts; sciences mathématiques et physiques*, 14 vols. (thermidor an VI [1798]–1818), for the Directory and the Napoleonic period
OC   *Oeuvres complètes de Laplace* [H]
PV   "Registre des procès-verbaux des séances de l'Académie royale des sciences de Paris"
PVIF   Académie des sciences, *Procès-verbaux des séances ... depuis la fondation de l'Institut jusqu'au mois d'août 1835*, 10 vols. (Hendaye, 1910–1922)
RSC   Royal Society of London, *Catalogue of Scientific Papers (1800–1863)*, III (London, 1869), 845–848
SE   *Mémoires de mathématique et de physique, présentés ... par divers sçavans* (often cited *Savants étrangers*), 11 vols. (1750–1786)

I, 1. Individual Memoirs by Order of Composition

(1) 28 Mar. 1770. "Recherches sur les maxima et minima des lignes courbes." Referees: Borda and Condorcet. Report, 28 Apr. 1770, printed in Bigourdan (J: [1931]). Published as [*1774a*] below.

(2) 18 July 1770. "Sur quelques usages du calcul intégral appliqué aux différences finies." Referees: Borda and Bossut. Report, 1 Sept. 1770, is in the archives of the Académie. The last paragraph is printed in Bigourdan (J: [1931]). An early draft of [*1771b*].

(3) 28 Nov. 1770. "Sur une méthode pour déterminer la variation de l'écliptique du mouvement des noeuds et de l'inclinaison de l'orbite des planètes." Referees: Condorcet and Bossut. Report, 12 Dec. 1770, is in the archives of the Académie.

(4) Date unrecorded, but probably Dec. 1770. "Sur la détermination de la variation de l'inclinaison et les mouvements des noeuds de toutes les planètes et principalement la variation de l'obliquité de l'écliptique." Referees: Dionis du Séjour, Bezout, and Condorcet. Report, 9 Jan. 1771, is in the archives. An entry in *PV* for that same date refers to a "Suite" to a memoir with an almost identical title to *(4)* and names d'Alembert and Condorcet as referees. This is probably an error, since *(4)* was itself a sequel to *(3)*; and it is more likely that d'Alembert and Condorcet were referees for *(5)*.

(5) 19 Jan. 1771. "Sur le calcul intégral." No referees recorded in *PV*, and the archives contain no report; but

see *(4)* above. The memoir was translated into Latin and was published in *Nova acta eruditorum*, as per [*1771a*] below.

(6) 13 Feb. 1771. "Sur le calcul intégral, les suites récurrentes, et la détermination de l'orbite lunaire." Referees: Condorcet and Bossut. Report, 20 Mar. 1771, is in the archives. The register of reports further specifies the topics as "1° Sur l'intégration de l'équation linéaire d'un ordre quelconque. 2° Sur une généralisation de la méthode qu'il a déjà employé pour les séries récurrentes. 3° Sur une application des formules de son mémoire sur l'obliquité de l'écliptique à des équations de l'orbite lunaire."

(7) 4 May 1771. "Sur les perturbations du mouvement des planètes causées par l'action de leurs satellites." Referees: Bezout and Bossut. Report, 15 May 1771, is in the archives.

(8) 17 May 1771. "Sur le calcul intégral appliqué aux différences finies à plusieurs variables." Referees: Borda and Bossut. There is a report in the archives, but it is dated the same day as the memoir and is by Condorcet. It describes the memoir as an extension of a previous work, which must be *(2)*, on which Borda and Bossut had reported. Evidently a revised draft of [*1771b*].

(9) 27 Nov. 1771. "Une théorie générale du mouvement des planètes." Referees: d'Alembert, Bezout, and Bossut. The report, 29 Jan. 1772, is in the archives. It describes the paper as concerned with "la théorie Newtonienne des planètes" and is sufficiently full to permit the conclusion that Laplace expanded this memoir to constitute his first general treatise on celestial mechanics, [*1784a*] below.

(10) 5 Feb. 1772. "Sur les suites récurrentes appliquées à la théorie des hasards." Referees: Dionis du Séjour and Le Roi. Report, 26 Feb. 1772, is in the archives. Probably a draft of [*1774b*]. The clerk failed to record the term "recurro-recurrent," although the referees allude to it.

(11) 2 May 1772. "Recherches pour le calcul intégral." Referees: Le Roi and Condorcet. The report, 6 May 1772, is in the archives and identifies the topic as "sur les solutions des équations différentielles non comprises dans l'intégral général." The subject of singular solutions occupies the first part of [*1775a*]. This paper, *(11)*, was probably combined with *(12)* and was superseded by *(14)*.

(12) Date unrecorded in *PV*. "Nouvelles recherches sur les intégrales particulières." Referees: Le Roi and Condorcet. Report, 30 May 1772, is in the archives.

(13) 10 Mar. 1773. "Recherches sur l'intégration des équations différentielles aux différences finies et sur leur application à l'analyse des hasards." Reading continued 17 Mar. Referees: Le Roi, Borda, and Dionis du Séjour. Report, 31 Mar. 1773, is in the archives. Revised version presented "pour retenir date," 7 Dec. 1773. Published as [*1776a*, 1°] below. This was the last memoir that Laplace submitted prior to his election to the Académie on 31 Mar., the very date of the report. The referees were dazzled and wound up their account with the following judgment: "Tel est le mémoire. . . . Nous

en avons dit beaucoup de choses avantageuses dans le courant de notre rapport, et nous sommes persuadés que le petit nombre de savants qui le liront en porteront le même jugement, et nous croions même qu'ils ajouteront à nos éloges. Enfin nous ne craignons pas d'avancer que cet ouvrage donne dès à présent à son auteur un rang très distingué parmi les géomètres."

(14) 14 July 1773. "Recherches sur les solutions particulières des équations différentielles." Reading continued 21 July. Published with *(15)* and *(17)* as [*1775a*].

(15) 27 Apr. 1774. "Une suite du mémoire sur les équations séculaires des planètes." The reference is probably to an early draft of *(17)* and hence of the second part of [*1775a*]. The memoir of which it is said to be the sequel was probably [*1776a*, 2°].

(16) 31 Aug. 1774. "Sur le calcul intégral." Probably the draft of the first part of [*1776c*].

(17) 17 Dec. 1774. "Sur les inégalités séculaires des planètes." Presented "pour retenir date." This memoir must have become the second part of [*1775a*] and may have been a revision of *(15)*.

(17a) 6 Sept. 1775. Report (with d'Alembert, Borda, Bezout, and Vandermonde) on Dionis du Séjour, *Essai sur les phénomènes relatifs aux disparitions périodiques de l'anneau de Saturne* (Paris, 1776); *OC*, XIV, 333–339. It is unclear why the editors of *OC* saw fit to include this one among Laplace's reports from the *registres* of the old Académie—and nothing else.

(18) 28 Feb. 1776. Began reading "Un mémoire sur les nombres." The only trace that exists of what was probably this piece is a remark in a letter from Lagrange thanking Laplace for sending him several memoirs and observing about one of them, "Votre démonstration du théorème de Fermat sur les nombres premiers de la forme 8n + 3 est ingénieuse . . ." (Lagrange to Laplace, 30 Dec. 1776, *Oeuvres de Lagrange*, XIV, 67). See also Laplace's reply, 3 Feb. 1778, acknowledging receipt of a further communication from Lagrange on Fermat's theorem (*ibid.*, 74). The only other recorded involvement of Laplace with number theory was his service as referee, together with Bezout, on two committees reviewing works by the Abbé Genty on prime numbers, 23 Aug. 1780 and 18 July 1781 (*PV*, **99**, fols. 219–220; and **100**, fol. 155); and on a third with Lagrange and Lacroix, 26 Mar. 1802 (*PVIF*, II, 485). See *(78)* below.

(19) 4 Dec. 1776. There is no record in the *PV*, but a marginal note in "Recherches sur le calcul intégral aux différences partielles" [*1777a*] states that the memoir was submitted on this date, having been read in 1773.

(20) 22 Jan. 1777. "Recherches sur la loi de la pesanteur à la surface d'un sphéroïde homogène en équilibre." Laplace deposited the text on 25 Jan. and observed at the outset that this paper was a continuation of what he had begun in [*1776d*]. It is transcribed in full in *PV*, **96**, fols. 17–25; and is virtually identical with the opening section of [*1778a*]; see *OC*, IX, 71–87. The printed version omits an undertaking that Laplace placed at the end of the manuscript memoir. He there proposed in a further memoir to investigate the figure of Saturn and

the law of gravity resulting from the action of its rings. That intention he fulfilled in [*1789a*].

(21) 8 Mar. 1777. "Recherches sur le milieu qu'il faut choisir entre les résultats de plusieurs observations." This memoir is transcribed in *PV*, **96**, fols. 122–142. It has never been published. Arrangements are in hand to print it in a forthcoming issue of *Revue d'histoire des sciences et de leurs applications.*

(22) 9 Apr. 1777. "Sur la nature du fluide qui reste dans le récipient de la machine pneumatique." No trace remains of this piece.

(23) 7 May 1777. "Un mémoire sur les oscillations des fluides qui recouvrent les planètes." On 31 May, Laplace read an addition to this memoir, which he is recorded as having withdrawn. After revision, it was combined with *(20)* in [*1778a*].

(24) 15 Nov. 1777. A marginal note in [*1778a*] records this date for submission of the memoir, combining *(20)* and *(23)*, the first installment of the investigation of tidal phenoma, "Recherches sur plusieurs points du système du monde."

(25) 18 Feb. 1778. "Un mémoire sur le calcul intégral." Probably a draft for all or part of [*1780a*].

(26) 13 May 1778. "Recherches sur les ondes, pour servir à son mémoire imprimé dans le volume de 1775." The reference is to [*1778a*], and this investigation of wave motion was printed as the final article (XXXVII) of the second sequel, [*1779b*]; see *OC*, IX, 301–310.

(27) 7 Oct. 1778. A marginal note in [*1779a*] records the submission of the memoir. No mention in *PV*. This was the first sequel on tides and on the motion of the earth.

(28) 25 Dec. 1778. A marginal note in [*1779b*] specifies the date of submission. See also *(26)*, which was appended. This was the second sequel on tides and on the motion of the earth.

(29) 16 June 1779. A marginal note gives the date for submission of "Mémoire sur l'usage du calcul aux différences partielles dans la théorie des suites" [*1780b*].

(30) 7 July 1779. "Une addition à son mémoire actuellement sous presse sur la précession des équinoxes." The reference is to [*1780c*]. Laplace apparently read the addition before reading the memoir. See *(31)*.

(31) 18 Aug. 1779. "Un mémoire sur la précession des équinoxes." The draft of [*1780c*].

(32) 1 Sept. 1779. "Un écrit où il répond à quelques objections faites contre son mémoire sur la précession des équinoxes, imprimé en 1776" [sic].

(33) 31 May 1780. "Mémoire sur le calcul aux suites appliqué aux probabilités." Draft of [*1781a*], submitted for publication on 31 July according to a marginal note.

(34) 21 Mar. 1781. Read "Un mémoire sur la détermination des orbites des comètes." A draft of the analytical part (Articles I–VII) of [*1784b*]. Laplace evidently revised the calculations *(36)* after learning of Herschel's "comet." It is also likely that the draft read to the Academy did not contain the instructions for application in Article VIII, an early version of which Laplace commu-

nicated to the Abbé Pingré no later than November 1782. It was published with fragments of correspondence by Henry (A: [1886]; *OC*, XIV, 355–368) and is virtually identical with Article VIII of the published memoir ([*1784b*]; *OC*, X, 127–141.

(35) 2 May 1781. "Une application de sa méthode à la comète qui paroît actuellement."

(36) 13 June 1781. "Un mémoire sur une méthode de calculer l'orbite des comètes." The dossier for this session includes a note containing the calculations in Laplace's hand.

(37) 28 July 1781. "Des eléments de la comète de M. Herschel, déterminés par un nouveau calcul." The numerical data are transcribed in *PV*, **100**, fols. 160–161.

(38) 21 Dec. 1781. An entry records on behalf of Lavoisier and Laplace the date on which they deposited the description of a new "pyromètre" by means of which the elongation of solid bodies under the influence of heat could be measured to an accuracy of "0.01 lignes," which is to say about 0.001 inches. Accompanying the account of the instrument, which had been constructed, was a series of experiments on the dilation of glass and metals. These must certainly have been among the earlier experiments carried out in the garden of the Arsenal in 1781 and 1782 that were published after Lavoisier's execution, "De l'action du calorique sur les corps solides, principalement sur le verre et sur les métaux, et du rallongement ou du raccourcissement dont ils sont susceptibles . . ." [*1793c*], in *Oeuvres de Lavoisier*. II (1862), 739–759. This instrument may well have been the one for which Biot reconstructed the design in his *Traité de physique* (1816), aided by the recollections of Laplace and Madame Lavoisier (*Oeuvres de Lavoisier*, II, 760).

(39) 2 Mar. 1782. An entry records on behalf of Lavoisier and Laplace a series of experiments already begun that show that substances passing from the liquid to the gaseous state and from the gaseous to the liquid state emit negative or positive electricity. These experiments were clearly the basis of [*1784c*].

(40) 22 Jan. 1783. "Un mémoire sur la planète d'Herschel." The gist of this memoir, together with the results of the calculations in *(42)*, was evidently incorporated in [*1784a*], pt. I, nos. 14–17, pp. 28–59; but it does not appear that Laplace ever published *(35)*, *(36)*, *(37)*, and *(42)* per se. According to an annotation on a handlist of Laplace's memoirs contained in the dossier at the Académie des Sciences concerning publication of *OC*, there was a memoir on "Eléments de la nouvelle planète Ouranus," in the *Mémoires de l'Académie impériale et royale des sciences et belles-lettres de Bruxelles* in 1788. In fact, there is nothing by Laplace in that collection, but **5** (1788), 22–48, does contain a memoir by F. von Zach (or "de Zach," as he is called there) entitled "Mémoire sur la nouvelle planète Ouranus," presented on 20 May 1785. Laplace and Zach were in frequent correspondence, and Laplace supplied him with the elements of the orbit, pp. 43–44.

(41) 15 Mar. 1783. Report (with Bezout and d'Alem-

bert) on Legendre's memoir on "Attraction des sphéroïdes homogènes." Transcribed in *PV*, **102**, fols. 85–87. A review of the state of the problem. The Legendre memoir was published in *SE*, **10** (1785), 411–434.

(42) 21 May 1783. "Une note d'où il résulte que d'après ses calculs, et ceux de M. Méchain, la planète Herschel est la même chose qu'une étoile observée par Mayer et qui ne se retrouve plus." Data given in *PV*, **102**, fols. 119–120.

(43) 24 May 1783. "Un mémoire sur l'attraction des sphéroïdes elliptiques." Presented in addition on 31 May. This piece almost certainly constituted part II of [*1784a*].

(44) 18 June 1783. "Un mémoire, fait conjointement avec M. Lavoisier, sur une nouvelle méthode de mesurer la chaleur." Laplace is recorded as having read the memoir, published as [*1783a*].

(45) 25 June 1783. Lavoisier and Laplace announced that they had repeated the combustion of combustible air (hydrogen) combined with dephlogisticated air (oxygen) in the presence of several observers, and obtained pure water. This demonstration, which occupied the public meeting of the Academy for St. Martin's Day, took place exactly one week after Laplace had read their joint *Mémoire sur la chaleur* [*1783a*] (*PV*, **102**, fol. 104 [18 June 1783], fol. 144 [25 June 1783]). Lavoisier then published this and other experiments, "Mémoire dans lequel on a pour objet de prouver que l'eau n'est point une substance simple . . . ," in *MARS* (1781/1784), 468–494; also *Oeuvres de Lavoisier*, II (1862), 334–359.

(46) 23 July 1783. Laplace read experiments done in England on the freezing of mercury (*PV*, **102**, fol. 159). It is not clear whose experiments these were, although Laplace's interest in them almost certainly pertained to the work on heat that he continued with Lavoisier through 1783 into 1784, which is reported in "Mémoire contenant les expériences faites sur la chaleur, pendant l'hiver de 1783 à 1784, par P. S. de Laplace & A. L. Lavoisier." Published after Lavoisier's death—see *(38)*—and in *Oeuvres de Lavoisier*, II (1862), 724–738.

(47) 3 Dec. 1783. Laplace requested the appointment of a commission to review his treatise on the motion and figure of the planets [*1784a*]. The referees, Dionis du Séjour, Borda, and Cousin, reported on 31 Jan. 1784, recommending publication under the *privilège* of the Académie, as was necessary for a work issued independently of the *MARS*. The report is given in *PV*, **103**, fols. 72–76.

(48) 11 Aug. 1784. "Un mémoire sur l'équilibre des fluides sphéroïdes." The draft of [*1785b*].

(49) 25 June 1785. A memoir "Sur les probabilités," intended as sequel to his "mémoire de 1782." The reference is to [*1785a*], the memoir on approximate solutions to problems involving functions containing terms raised to very high powers, and the present memoir was the draft of its sequel [*1786b*]. Laplace continued the reading on 28 June.

(50) 19 Nov. 1785. "Un mémoire sur les inégalités séculaires des planètes." Condorcet recorded the memoir on this date, and Laplace read it on 23 Nov. This is the draft of [*1787a*].

(51) 30 Nov. 1785. "Un mémoire sur la population de la France." The draft of [*1786c*].

(52) 6 May 1786. Laplace presented a theorem on the motions of Jupiter and Saturn "pour retenir date." On 10 May he read a draft of the first memoir on the theory of Jupiter and Saturn [*1788a*].

(53) 15 July 1786. "Un 2ᵉ mémoire sur la théorie de Jupiter et de Saturne." The draft of [*1788b*].

(54) 21 July 1787. On behalf of a committee consisting also of Cousin and Legendre, Laplace read a *compte-rendu* of R.-J. Haüy, *Exposition raisonée de la théorie de l'électricité et du magnétisme, d'après les principes d'Aepinus* (Paris, 1787). The account is very appreciative, and the report is transcribed in *PV*, **106**, fols. 290–293.

(55) 19 Dec. 1787. "Un mémoire sur l'équation séculaire de la lune." A first draft of [*1788c*].

(56) 2 Apr. 1788. "Un mémoire sur l'équation séculaire de la lune." Probably a revision rather than an extension of *(55)*, for the memoir [*1788c*] is a brief one.

(57) 26 Apr. 1789. A commission composed of Lagrange, Lalande, and Méchain presented a *compte-rendu* of tables for Jupiter and Saturn prepared by Delambre, which compare the predictions from Laplace's theory of the two planets to the record of observations. The report is transcribed in *PV*, **108**, fols. 92–99.

(58) 18 July 1789. "Un mémoire sur l'inclinaison de l'écliptique." This is probably the draft of Articles II–VII of [*1793a*].

(59) 17 Apr. 1790. "Un mémoire sur la théorie des satellites de Jupiter." The draft of [*1791a*].

(60) 15 Dec. 1790. Laplace began "Un mémoire sur le flux et le reflux de la mer." Delayed in publication [*1797a*].

(61) 21 Jan. 1796 (1 pluviôse an IV). Laplace presented "Un mémoire sur les mouvements des corps célestes autour de leurs centres de gravité." *PVIF*, I, 6. Draft of [*1798a*]. Readied for publication on 5 Jan. 1797 (16 nivôse an V).

(62) 7 Oct. 1796. (16 vendémiaire an V). Report (with Lagrange) on two memoirs by Flaugergues, "De l'aberration de la lumière" and "Du phénomène de l'apparence de l'étoile sur le disque de la lune dans les occultations." *PVIF*, I, 114–115.

(63) 20 Apr. 1797 (1 floréal an V). Read a "Mémoire sur les équations séculaires du mouvement des noeuds et de l'apogée de l'orbite lunaire et sur l'aberration des étoiles." *PVIF*, I, 203. Draft of [*1798b*].

(64) 10 Jan. 1798 (21 nivôse an VI). Read the preamble of a "Mémoire sur les équations séculaires du mouvement de la lune, de son apogée et de ses noeuds." *PVIF*, I, 330. Text of [*1799a*].

(65) 21 Dec. 1798 (1 nivôse an VII). Laplace, Lacépède, and Fourcroy submitted a report on the ques-

tions to be presented to the Institut d'Égypte. The report was combined with those from the 2nd and 3rd classes and was printed in *Histoire de la classe des sciences morales et politiques de l'Institut de France*, **3** (prairial an IX [May–June 1801]), 5–19.

(66) 5 Apr. 1799 (16 germinal an VII). A report (with Lagrange) on several memoirs of Parceval on "le calcul intégral aux différences partielles." *PVIF*, I, 546–547.

(67) 7 Sept. 1799 (21 fructidor an VII). Presented copies of *Exposition du système du monde* and *Mécanique céleste*. *PVIF*, I, 619.

(68) 2 Nov. 1799 (11 brumaire an VIII). A report (with Coulomb and Lefèvre-Gineau—it is not clear that Laplace was the author) on a memoir by Libes on the role of caloric in elasticity. *PVIF*, II, 21–22.

(69) 12 Nov. 1799 (21 brumaire an VIII). A report (with Napoléon Bonaparte and Lacroix) on a memoir of Biot on "les équations aux différences mêlées." *PVIF*, II, 30–32. See also the joint report with Prony (read by the latter on 6 frimaire an VIII [27 Nov. 1799], *PVIF*, II, 45–48), on Biot's memoir "Considérations sur les intégrales des équations aux différences finies," *PVIF*, II, 45–48, published in full, *MI*, **3** (prairial an IX [May–June 1801]), "Histoire," 12–21.

(70) 2 Mar. 1800 (11 ventôse an VIII). Read a "Mémoire sur le mouvement des orbites des satellites de Saturne et d'Uranus." *PVIF*, II, 118. Abstracted [*1800b*]. Draft of [*1801a*].

(71) 15 June 1800 (26 prairial an VIII). Read a "Mémoire sur la théorie de la lune." *PVIF*, II, 177. Draft of [*1801b*].

(72) 20 June 1800 (1 messidor an VIII). Announced Bouvard's application of a new equation contained in the previous memoir *(71)* to observations by Maskelyne, yielding a flattening of 1/314. *PVIF*, II, 179.

(73) 2 Dec. 1800 (11 frimaire an IX). Proposed continuing in the *Mémoires de l'Institut* the notes on the French population contained in the final volumes of the Académie under the old regime. *PVIF*, II, 274.

(74) 10 June 1801 (21 prairial an IX). Read a "Mémoire sur la théorie de la lune." *PVIF*, II, 359. Not separately published. May have been incorporated in *Mécanique céleste*, Book VII (Volume III, 1802).

(75) 12 Nov. 1801 (21 brumaire an X). Report (with Delambre) on a memoir "Sur la théorie de Mars" by Lefrançois-Lalande. *PVIF*, II, 426–429.

(76) 26 Jan. 1802 (6 pluviôse an X). Read a "Mémoire sur une inégalité à longue période, qu'il vient de découvrir dans le mouvement de la lune. . . ." *PVIF*, II, 457. Not separately published at this time. May have been incorporated in *Mécanique céleste*, Book VII (Volume III, 1802). Laplace returned to this topic in [*1811c*] and [*1812a*]. See also *(94)*.

(77) 12 Mar. 1802 (21 ventôse an X). Read a "Mémoire sur la théorie lunaire." *PVIF*, II, 476. Not separately published. May have been incorporated in *Mécanique céleste*, Book VII (Volume III, 1802).

(78) 27 Mar. 1802 (6 germinal an X). Report (with

Lagrange and Lacroix) on a memoir of Genty on number theory. *PVIF*, II, 485.

(79) 17 Nov. 1802 (26 brumaire an XI). Announces measures that the government has adopted to resume making exact estimates of the size of the population by taking samples in various regions and calculating the factor by which the annual number of births is to be multiplied. *PVIF*, II, 595.

(80) 29 Dec. 1802 (8 nivôse an XI). Presented Volume III of *Traité de mécanique céleste*. *PVIF*, II, 606.

(81) 2 May 1803 (12 floréal an XI). Read a set of observations on the tides, upon which a committee consisting of himself, Levêque, and Rochon was appointed. *PVIF*, II, 659. See [*1803a*].

(82) 12 Sept. 1803 (25 fructidor an XI). Read a "Mémoire sur les tables de Jupiter et la masse de Saturne." *PVIF*, II, 703. Draft of [*1804a*].

(83) 27 May 1805 (7 prairial an XIII). Presented Volume IV of *Mécanique céleste* (the minute mistakenly says Volume XIV). *PVIF*, III, 216.

(84) 14 Oct. 1805 (22 vendémiaire an XIV). Read a "Mémoire sur la diminution de l'obliquité de l'écliptique." *PVIF*, III, 262. There is no record of publication.

(85) 23 Dec. 1805 (2 nivôse an XIV). Read a "Mémoire sur les tubes capillaires." *PVIF*, III, 293. Published in part [*1806a*].

(86) 28 Apr. 1806. Presented "Théorie de l'action capillaire." *PVIF*, III, 344. Originally issued (1806) as a separate booklet under the above title, this piece was incorporated in later printings of *Mécanique céleste*, Volume IV, as the first Supplement to Book X. *OC*, IV, 349–417. Abstracted [*1806c*].

(87) 29 Sept. 1806. Read a "Suite à sa théorie de l'action capillaire." *PVIF*, III, 431. Abstracted [*1807a*]. A printed copy, separately issued although sometimes bound with *(86)*, was presented to the Institut on 6 July 1807. *PVIF*, III, 353. This piece was incorporated in later printings of *Mécanique céleste*, Volume IV, as the second Supplement to Book X. *OC*, IV, 419–498.

(88) 24 Nov. 1806. Read a memoir on "L'adhésion des corps à la surface des fluides." *PVIF*, III, 451. Printed in part as [*1806d*].

(89) 21 Mar. 1808. Presented a copy of the 3rd edition of *Exposition du système du monde*. *PVIF*, IV, 36.

(90) 17 Aug. 1808. Presented *Supplément au Traité de mécanique céleste* to the Bureau des Longitudes. This appendix concerns the theory of planetary perturbations developed in Books II and VI, and was incorporated in later printings of Volume III (*OC*, III, 325–350). Laplace also presented a copy to the Institut on 26 Sept. 1808. *PVIF*, IV, 106. The last section (5) corrects an error in the sign in the expressions for the fifth power of the eccentricities and inclinations of the orbits in the theory of the inequalities of Jupiter and Saturn, *OC*, III, 349–350.

(91) 19 Dec. 1808. Report (with Haüy, Chaptal, and Berthollet) on the memoir of Malus, "Sur divers phénomènes de la double réfraction de la lumière." La-

place's report is printed in *PVIF*, IV, 145–147; and in *OC*, XIV, 321–326. *RSC* 22.

(92) 30 Jan. 1809. Read a memoir on "La loi de la réfraction extraordinaire de la lumière dans les milieux transparents." *PVIF*, IV, 159. Abstracted in [*1809b*]. Published as [*1810a*].

(93) 10 Apr. 1809. Reported (with Lacroix) on a memoir of Poisson on "La rotation de la terre." *PVIF*, IV, 190–192.

(94) 18 Sept. 1809. Read a memoir on "La libration de la lune." *PVIF*, IV, 253. This memoir was probably combined with *(76)* in [*1811c*] and [*1812a*].

(95) 9 Apr. 1810. Read a report on "Les probabilités." *PVIF*, IV, 341. A draft of [*1810b*].

(96) 21 May 1810. Reported (with Biot and Arago) on a memoir by Daubuisson on "La mesure des hauteurs par le baromètre." *PVIF*, IV, 350–352.

(97) 29 Apr. 1811. Read a memoir on "Les intégrales définies." *PVIF*, IV, 475. A draft of [*1811a*].

(98) 23 Mar. 1812. Presented the "première partie" of *Théorie analytique des probabilités*. *PVIF*, V, 34.

(99) 29 June 1812. Presented the "seconde partie" of *Théorie analytique des probabilités*. *PVIF*, V, 69. The first edition was thus issued in at least two installments.

(100) 24 May 1813. Presented the 4th edition of *Exposition du système du monde*. *PVIF*, V, 214.

(101) 2 Aug. 1813. Read a memoir on "Les éléments des variations des orbites planétaires." *PVIF*, V, 235. There is no record of publication.

(102) 14 Feb. 1814. Presented *Essai philosophique sur les probabilités* (1814). *PVIF*, V, 316. Incorporated with *(104)* as its Introduction. The version printed in *OC*, VII, v–cliii, is *(117)*, the 4th ed. (1819).

(103) 8 Aug. 1814. Read a memoir on "La probabilité des témoignages." *PVIF*, V, 386. Incorporated in *(104)*, the 2nd ed. of *Théorie analytique des probabilités*, Book II, chapter 11; *OC*, VII, 455–485.

(104) 14 Nov. 1814. Presented the 2nd ed. of *Théorie analytique des probabilités*, incorporating *(102)* and *(103)*, together with three minor additions. *PVIF*, V, 422. *OC*, VII, 471–493.

(105) 10 July 1815. Read a memoir on "Les marées." *PVIF*, V, 527. A draft of [*1815c*].

(106) 18 Sept. 1815. Read a memoir on "Les probabilités, dans lequel il détermine la limite de l'erreur qui peut rester après qu'on a déterminé les valeurs les plus probables des inconnues." *PVIF*, V, 554. The draft of [*1815a*].

(107) 26 Aug. 1816. Presented a supplement to *Théorie analytique des probabilités*. *PVIF*, VI, 73. Incorporated in the 3rd ed. (1820) as Supplement I. *OC*, VII, 497–530. See *(118)*.

(108) 28 Oct. 1816. Read a "Note sur la pendule." *PVIF*, VI, 108. Probably the draft of [*1816a*].

(109) 25 Nov. 1816. Read "Note sur l'action réciproque des pendules et sur la vitesse du son dans les diverses substances." *PVIF*, VI, 113. A draft of [*1816b*].

(110) 23 Dec. 1816. Read a "Note sur la vitesse du son." *PVIF*, VI, 131. Related to [*1816c*] and [*1816d*]. See the marginal note in the latter.

(111) 4 Aug. 1817. Read a memoir on "L'application du calcul des probabilités aux opérations géodésiques." *PVIF*, VI, 208. A draft of [*1817a*].

(112) 2 Feb. 1818. Presented a second Supplement to *Théorie analytique des probabilités*. *PVIF*, VI, 263. The supplement consists of *(111)* together with additions and was incorporated in the 3rd ed., *Théorie analytique des probabilités* (1820). *OC*, VII, 531–580. See *(118)*.

(113) 18 May 1818. Read a "Mémoire sur la rotation de la terre." *PVIF*, VI, 316. The draft of [*1819a*].

(114) 3 Aug. 1818. Read a memoir "Sur la figure de la terre et la loi de la pesanteur à sa surface." *PVIF*, VI, 350. Abstracted in [*1818b*] and published in [*1819b*].

(115) 26 May 1819. Read a memoir "Sur la figure de la terre" before the Bureau des Longitudes; see the marginal note in *CT* (1822/1820), 284. The draft of [*1820e*].

(116) 13 Sept. 1819. Read a memoir "Considérations sur les phénomènes capillaires." *PVIF*, VI, 487. Presumably the draft of [*1819h*].

(117) 25 Oct. 1819. Presented the 4th ed. of *Essai philosophique sur les probabilités*. *PVIF*, VI, 504. Replaced the 1st ed. *(102)* as Introduction to *Théorie analytique des probabilités (104)* in the 3rd ed. (1820). *OC*, VII, v–cliii.

(118) 20 Dec. 1819. Read a "Mémoire sur l'application du calcul des probabilités aux opérations géodésiques," *PVIF*, VI, 515. The draft of what became the 3rd Supplement to the 3rd ed. of *Théorie analytique des probabilités* (1820). *OC*, VII, 581–616. Abstracted in [*1819f*] and printed as [*1819g*].

(119) 19 Jan. 1820. Read a memoir "Sur les inégalités lunaires dues à l'aplatissement de la terre" before the Bureau des Longitudes. See the marginal note in [*1820a*].

(120) 28 Feb. 1820. Presented the 3rd ed. of *Théorie analytique des probabilités*, containing the revised Introduction *(117)* and three supplements *(107)*, *(112)*, and *(118)*.

(121) 29 Mar. 1820. Read "Sur le perfectionnement de la théorie et des tables lunaires" before the Bureau des Longitudes. See the marginal note in [*1820b*].

(122) 12 Apr. 1820. Read "Sur l'inégalité lunaire à longue période, dépendante de la différence des deux hemisphères terrestres" before the Bureau des Longitudes. See the marginal note in [*1820c*].

(123) 10 Sept. 1821. Read a "Mémoire sur l'attraction des corps sphériques et sur la répulsion des fluides élastiques." *PVIF*, VII, 222.

(124) 12 Dec. 1821. Presented a memoir on elastic fluids and the speed of sound to the Bureau des Longitudes. See the marginal note in [*1822a*].

(125) 17 Mar. 1823. Presented Book XI of *Mécanique céleste*. *PVIF*, VII, 457. *OC*, V, 6–96.

(126) 21 Apr. 1823. Presented Book XII of *Mécanique céleste*. *PVIF*, VII, 480. *OC*, V, 99–160.

(127) 8 Sept. 1823. Presented a memoir "Sur le flux et le reflux de la mer." *PVIF*, VII, 538. Published as [*1823a*].

(128) 5 Jan. 1824. Presented the 5th ed. of *Système du monde*. *PVIF*, VIII, 3.

(129) 9 Feb. 1824. Presented Book XIII of *Mécanique céleste*. *PVIF*, VIII, 24. *OC*, V, 164–269.

(130) 26 July 1824. Presented Book XIV of *Mécanique céleste*. *PVIF*, VIII, 117. *OC*, V, 273–323.

(131) 13 Dec. 1824. Presented Book XV of *Mécanique céleste*. *PVIF*, VIII, 162. *OC*, V, 327–387.

(132) 7 Feb. 1825. Laplace, together with his son, presented a fourth supplement to *Théorie analytique des probabilités*. *PVIF*, VIII, 182. *OC*, VII, 617–645.

(133) 16 Aug. 1825. Presented Volume V of *Mécanique céleste*, Book XVI being the final book. *PVIF*, VIII, 261. *OC*, V, 389–465.

(134) 23 July 1827. The Academy received a Supplement to *Mécanique céleste*, Volume V; the MS had been found among Laplace's papers after his death. *PVIF*, VIII, 571. *OC*, V, 469–505.

I, 2. Individual Memoirs by Order of Publication

[*1771a*] "Disquisitiones de calculo integrale," in *Nova acta eruditorum, Anno 1771* (Leipzig, 1771), 539–559; not in *OC*. A draft was presented to the Academy on 19 Jan. 1771; see (5) above.

[*1771b*] "Recherches sur le calcul intégral aux différences infiniment petites, et aux différences finies," in *Mélanges de philosophie et de mathématiques de la Société royale de Turin, pour les années 1766–1769* (*Miscellanea Taurinensia*, IV), date of publication not given but probably 1771, pp. 273–345. A typographical error numbers pp. 273–288 as 173–188. Laplace read an early draft to the Academy on 18 July 1770 and a revised version on 17 May 1771 (2) and (8) above. Not in *OC*. I am indebted to Mr. George Anastaplo for a discussion of this memoir.

[*1774a*] "Disquisitiones de maximis et minimis, fluentium indefinitarum," in *Nova acta eruditorum, Anno 1772* (Leipzig, 1774), 193–213. Not in *OC*. First draft read to the Academy on 28 Mar. 1770 (1) above. I am indebted to Mr. Chikara Sazaki for a discussion of this memoir.

[*1774b*] "Mémoire sur les suites récurro-récurrentes et sur leurs usages dans la théorie des hasards," in SE, 6 (1774), 353–371; *OC*, VIII, 5–24. A draft was presented on 5 Feb. 1772. Referees: Dionis du Séjour and Le Roi, who reported on 26 Feb. 1772 (10) above.

[*1774c*] "Mémoire sur la probabilité des causes par les événements," in *SE*, 6 (1774), 621–656; *OC*, VIII, 27–65. *PV* contains no mention of this memoir. It seems probable, however, that it was composed between March and December 1773, concurrently with the revision of [*1776a*, 1°].

[*1775a*] "Mémoire sur les solutions particulières des équations différentielles et sur les inégalités séculaires des planètes," in *MARS* (1772, pt. 1/1775), 343–377; *OC*, VIII, 325–366. Laplace read the first part (*OC*, VIII, 325–354) on 14 and 21 July 1773 (*14*), having started the topic in a paper of 2 May 1772 (*11*). The second part (*ibid.*, 354–366) was registered on 17 Dec. 1774 (*17*).

[*1775b*] "Addition au mémoire sur les solutions particulières . . .," in *MARS* (1772, pt. 1/1775), 651–656; *OC*, VIII, 361–366.

[*1776a*] "Recherches, 1°, sur l'intégration des équations différentielles aux différences finies, et sur leur usage dans la théorie des hasards. 2°, sur le principe de la gravitation universelle, et sur les inégalités séculaires des planètes qui en dépendent," in *SE* (1773/1776), 37–232; *OC*, printed as two memoirs, VIII, 69–197, 198–275. A note printed in the margin (*SE* [1773/1776], 37) gives 10 Feb. 1773 as the date on which 1° was read. The register of *PV* gives 10 Mar., with reading continued on 17 Mar. See (*13*) above. We do not know when Laplace readied 2° for publication, although it must have been before 27 Apr. 1774, when he presented a further memoir called a "Suite"; see (*15*) and (*17*). As printed, 2° probably contains elements from (*3*), (*4*), (*6*), (*7*), and (*9*) above, but most of it goes beyond anything suggested by these titles.

[*1776b*] "Mémoire sur l'inclinaison moyenne des orbites des comètes, sur la figure de la terre, et sur les fonctions," in *SE* (1773/1776), 503–540; *OC*, VIII, 279–321. There is no record of when Laplace presented these topics.

[*1776c*] "Recherches sur le calcul intégral et sur le système du monde," in *MARS* (1772, pt. 2/1776), 267–376; *OC*, VIII, 369–477. Laplace read the first part on 31 Aug. 1774 (*16*).

[*1776d*] "Additions aux recherches sur le calcul intégral et sur le système du monde," in *MARS* (1772, pt. 2/1776), 533–554; *OC*, VIII, 478–501.

[*1777a*] "Recherches sur le calcul intégral aux différences partielles," in *MARS* (1773/1777), 341–402; *OC*, IX, 5–68. A marginal note says that this memoir was read in 1773 and was submitted for publication on 4 Dec. 1776 (*19*).

[*1778a*] "Recherches sur plusieurs points du système du monde," in *MARS* (1775/1778), 75–182; *OC*, IX, 71–183. A combination of (*20*) and (*23*), the latter revised and submitted on 15 Nov. 1777 (*24*).

[*1779a*] "Recherches sur plusieurs points du système du monde" (Suite), in *MARS* (1776/1779), 177–267; *OC*, IX, 187–280. A marginal note specifies that this continuation of [*1778a*], with which the articles are numbered consecutively, was submitted on 7 Oct. 1778.

[*1779b*] "Recherches sur plusieurs points du système du monde" (Suite), in *MARS* (1776/1779), 525–552; *OC*, IX, 283–310. Submitted on 25 Dec. 1778. See (*26*) and (*28*).

[*1780a*] "Mémoire sur l'intégration des équations différentielles par approximation," in *MARS* (1777/1780), 373–397; *OC*, IX, 357–379. There is no record of anything to which this is more likely to have corresponded than (*25*), read on 18 Feb. 1778.

[*1780b*] "Mémoire sur l'usage du calcul aux différ-

ences partielles dans la théorie des suites," in *MARS* (1777/1780), 99–122; *OC*, IX, 313–335. A marginal note dates the submission 16 June 1779 (*29*).

[*1780c*] "Mémoire sur la précession des équinoxes," in *MARS* (1777/1780), 329–345; *OC*, IX, 339–354. A marginal note is confirmed by the entry in *PV* (*31*) that Laplace read this memoir formally on 18 Aug. 1779, even though he had already read an "addition" to it on 7 July (*30*). Apparently, it elicited some criticism and discussion (*32*).

[*1781a*] "Mémoire sur les probabilités," in *MARS* (1778/1781), 227–232; *OC*, IX, 383–485. On 31 May 1780 Laplace read a "Mémoire sur le calcul aux suites appliqué aux probabilités" (*33*) and submitted the memoir for publication on 19 July, according to a marginal note.

[*1782a*] "Mémoire sur les suites," in *MARS* (1779/1782), 207–309; *OC*, X, 1–89. Not mentioned in *PV*.

[*1783a*] *Mémoire sur la chaleur*, written with Lavoisier. This separate printing issued from the Imprimerie Royale. The memoir as published by the Académie a year later is in *MARS* (1780/1784), 355–408; *OC*, X, 149–200; also in *Oeuvres de Lavoisier*, J. B. Dumas, ed., II (Paris, 1862), 283–333. I am indebted to Mr. Robert Bernstein for discussion of problems arising from the physical chemistry of this memoir.

[*1784a*] *Théorie du mouvement et de la figure elliptique des planètes* (Paris, 1784). Not in *OC*. Part I of this treatise probably represents a revision and expansion of (*9*), together with material on comets from (*35*), (*36*), (*37*), (*40*), and (*42*), and other up-to-date matter. Part II almost surely consists of a memoir "Sur l'attraction des sphéroïdes elliptiques" (*43*) that Laplace read on 24 and 31 May 1783 and no doubt draws also on the Legendre memoir that he discussed in (*41*). Laplace requested a commission of review on 3 Dec. 1783 (*47*). A finished copy was presented to the Académie on 24 Feb. 1784 (*PV*, **103**, fol. 37).

[*1784b*] "Mémoire sur la détermination des orbites des comètes," in *MARS* (1780/1784), 13–72; *OC*, X, 93–146. The same title as (*34*), probably enlarged.

[*1784c*] "Mémoire sur l'électricité qu'absorbent les corps qui se réduisent en vapeurs," written with Lavoisier, in *MARS* (1781/1784), 292–294; *OC*, X, 203–205; also in *Oeuvres de Lavoisier*, II, 374–376.

[*1785a*] "Mémoire sur les approximations des formules qui sont fonctions de trés grands nombres," in *MARS* (1782/1785), 1–88; *OC*, X, 209–291. Not mentioned in *PV*.

[*1785b*] "Théorie des attractions des sphéroïdes et de la figure des planètes," in *MARS* (1782/1785), 113–196; *OC*, X, 341–419. Read on 11 Aug. 1784 (*48*).

[*1786a*] "Mémoire sur la figure de la terre," in *MARS* (1783/1786), 17–46; *OC*, XI, 3–32. Not mentioned in *PV*.

[*1786b*] "Mémoire sur les approximations des formules qui sont fonctions de très grands nombres" (Suite), in *MARS* (1783/1786), 423–467; *OC*, X, 295–338. Laplace read the draft on 25 and 28 June 1785 (*49*).

[*1786c*] "Sur les naissances, les mariages et les morts à Paris, depuis 1771 jusqu'en 1784, et dans toute l'étendue de la France, pendant les années 1781 et 1782," in *MARS* (1783/1786), 693–702; *OC*, XI, 35–46. Read on 30 Nov. 1785 (*51*).

[*1787a*] "Mémoire sur les inégalités séculaires des planètes et des satellites," in *MARS* (1784/1787), 1–50; *OC*, XI, 49–92. Recorded on 19 Nov. 1785 and read on 23 Nov. (*50*).

[*1788a*] "Théorie de Jupiter et de Saturne," in *MARS* (1785/1788), 33–160; *OC*, XI, 95–207. Laplace read the draft on 10 May 1786 (*52*).

[*1788b*] "Théorie de Jupiter et de Saturne" (Suite), in *MARS* (1786/1788), 201–234; *OC*, XI, 211–239. Read on 15 July 1786 (*53*). This memoir is part III of [*1788a*].

[*1788c*] "Sur l'équation séculaire de la lune," in *MARS* (1786/1788), 235–264; *OC*, XI, 243–271. The draft was read on 19 Dec. 1787 (*55*) and was revised on 2 Apr. 1788 (*56*).

[*1789a*] "Mémoire sur la théorie de l'anneau de Saturne," in *MARS* (1787/1789), 249–267; *OC*, XI, 275–292.

[*1789b*] "Mémoire sur les variations séculaires des orbites des planètes," in *MARS* (1787/1789), 267–279; *OC*, XI, 297–306.

[*1790a*] "Sur la théorie des satellites de Jupiter," in *CT* (1792/1790), 273–286. Not in *OC*.

[*1791a*] "Théorie des satellites de Jupiter," in *MARS* (1788/1791), 249–364; *OC*, XI, 309–411. Read on 17 Apr. 1790 (*59*). I am indebted to Mr. Sherwin Singer for a discussion of this memoir.

[*1793a*] "Sur quelques points du système du monde," in *MARS* (1789/1793), 1–87; *OC*, XI, 477–558. On 18 July 1789 Laplace read a paper on the inclination of the plane of the ecliptic (*58*), which may probably have been the draft of Articles II–VII; *OC*, XI, 481–493.

[*1793b*] "Théorie des satellites de Jupiter" (Suite), in *MARS* (1789/1793), 237–296; *OC*, XI, 415–473. Not mentioned in *PV*.

[*1793c*] "De l'action du calorique sur les corps solides, principalement sur le verre et sur les métaux. . .," in *Oeuvres de Lavoisier*, II (1862), 739–759, written by Laplace and Lavoisier. For the original printing, undated but *ca*. 1803, see *Dictionary of Scientific Biography*, VIII, 87. The year assigned here is that in which Lavoisier composed the report of his experiments with Laplace in the winter of 1781–1782 (*38*) and also those reported in [*1793d*]. Not in *OC*.

[*1793d*] "Mémoire contenant les expériences faites sur la chaleur pendant l'hiver de 1783 à 1784," in *Oeuvres de Lavoisier*, II (1862), 724–738, written by Laplace and Lavoisier. See [*1793c*]. Not in *OC*.

[*P1796*] *Discours prononcé aux deux conseils . . . au nom de l'Institut national des sciences et des arts*, 17 Sept. 1796 (1er jour complémentaire an IV). Report on the first year of the Institut. Not in *OC*.

[*1797a*] "Mémoire sur le flux et le reflux de la mer," in *MARS* (1790/1797), 45–181; *OC*, XII, 3–126. Laplace began the reading on 15 Dec. 1790 (*60*).

[*1797b*] "Sur le mouvement de l'apogée de la lune et sur celui de ses noeuds," in *BSPM*, **1** (1797), 22–23. Not in *OC*. *RSC* 1.

[*1797c*] "Sur les équations séculaires du mouvement de la lune," in *BSPM*, **1** (1797), 99–101. Not in *OC*. *RSC* 2.

[*1798a*] "Mémoire sur les mouvements des corps célestes autour de leurs centres de gravité," in *MI*, **1** (an IV [1795–1796]/thermidor an VI [July–Aug. 1798]), 301–376; *OC*, XII, 129–187. Presented on 21 Jan. 1796 (*61*).

[*1798b*] "Sur les équations séculaires des mouvements de l'apogée et des noeuds de l'orbite lunaire," in *CT* (an VIII [1799–1800]/pluviôse an VI [Jan.–Feb. 1798]), 362–370; *OC*, XIII, 3–14. Read to the Institut on 20 Apr. 1797 (*63*). The calculations were deferred to [*1799a*].

[*1798c*] "Mémoire sur la détermination d'un plan qui reste toujours parallèle à lui-même, dans le mouvement d'un système de corps agissant d'une manière quelconque les uns sur les autres et libres de toute action étrangère," in *JX*, **2**, 5ᵉ cahier (prairial an VI [May–June 1798]), 155–159; *OC*, XIV, 3–7.

[*1798d*] "Sur les plus grandes marées de l'an IX," in *CT* (an IX [1800–1801]/fructidor an VI [Aug.–Sept. 1798), 213–218; *OC*, XIII, 15–19.

[*1799a*] "Mémoire sur les équations séculaires des mouvements de la lune, de son apogée et de ses noeuds," in *MI*, **2** (an VII [1798–1799]/fructidor an VII [Aug.–Sept. 1799]), 126–182; *OC*, XII, 191–234; *OC*, XII, 191–234. Read on 10 Jan. 1798 (*64*). The calculations for [*1798b*].

[*1799b*] "Sur la mécanique," in *JX*, **2**, 6ᵉ cahier (thermidor an VII [July–Aug. 1799]), 343–344; *OC*, XIV, 8–9.

[*1799c*] "Sur quelques équations des tables lunaires," in *CT* (an X [1801–1802]/fructidor an VII [Aug.–Sept. 1799]), 361–365; *OC*, XIII, 20–24.

[*1799d*] *Allgemeine geographische Ephemeriden*, **4**, no. 1 (July 1799), 1–6. Laplace supplied the editor, F. X. von Zach, with a proof for the statement in *Exposition du système du monde* (B: [1796], II, 305) that a luminous body 250 times larger than the sun and of comparable density to the earth would exert an attractive power that would prevent the light rays from escaping from its surface and that the largest luminous bodies in the universe may thus be invisible. The proof is translated as Appendix A of S. W. Hawking and G. F. R. Ellis, *The Large-scale Structure of Space-time* (Cambridge, 1973), 365–368. I owe this reference to the kindness of John Stachel. Not in *OC*. Laplace eliminated this passage from later editions of *Système du monde*.

[*1800a*] "Sur l'orbite du dernier satellite de Saturne," in *BSPM*, **2** (1800), 109; not in *OC*.

[*1800b*] "Sur les mouvements des orbites des satellites de Saturne et d'Uranus," in *CT* (an XI [1802–1803]/messidor an VIII [June–July 1800]), 485–489; not in *OC*. Read on 1 Mar. 1800 (*70*); an abstract of [*1801a*].

[*1800c*] "Sur la théorie de la lune," in *CT* (an XI [1802–1803]/1800), 504–506; not in *OC*. An abstract of [*1801b*] on a periodic inequality in the nutation of the lunar orbit.

[*1800d*] "Leçons de mathématiques professées à l'École normale en 1795," in *Séances de l'École normale* (an VIII [1799–1800]), I, 16–32, 268–280, 381–393; (pt. 2), 3–23, 130–134; II, 116–129, 302–318; III, 24–39; IV, 32–70, 223–263; V, 201–219; VI, 32–73; reprinted in *JX*, **2**, 7ᵉ and 8ᵉ cahiers (June 1812), 1–172; *OC*, XIV, 10–177, *RSC* 8.

[*P1800*] *Rapport sur la situation de l'École polytechnique*, 24 Dec. 1800 (3 nivôse an IX). Submitted to the minister of the interior on behalf of the Conseil de Perfectionnement. Not in *OC*.

[*1801a*] "Mémoire sur les mouvements des orbites des satellites de Saturne et d'Uranus," in *MI*, **3** (prairial an IX [May–June 1801]), 107–127; *OC*, XII, 237–253. Read on 1 Mar. 1800 (*70*).

[*1801b*] "Mémoire sur la théorie de la lune," in *MI*, **3** (prairial an IX [May–June 1801]), 198–206; *OC*, XII, 257–263. Read on 15 June 1800 (*71*). *RSC* 11.

[*1801c*] "Sur la théorie de la lune," in *CT* (an XII [1803–1804]/fructidor an IX [Aug.–Sept. 1801]), 493–501; not in *OC*. On an inequality in the lunar parallax; an abstract of [*1801b*].

[*1801d*] "Sur un problème de physique, relatif à l'électricité," in *BSPM*, **3**, no. 51 (prairial an IX [May–June 1801]), 21–23. Not in *OC*. A concluding editor's note reads: "Nous devons au C. Laplace cette application à l'électricité, des formules relatives à la théorie de la figure de la terre."–I.B.

[*1803a*] "Sur les marées," in *BSPM*, **3**, no. 74 (floréal an XI [Apr.–May 1803]), 106; not in *OC*. *RSC* 13. See (*81*).

[*1803b*] "Mémoire sur le mouvement d'un corps qui tombe d'une grande hauteur," in *BSPM*, **3**, no. 75 (prairial an XI [May–June 1803]), 109–115; *OC*, XIV, 267–277.

[*1803c*] Two notes on the relation of pressure to temperature among the molecules of an enclosed gas, contributed to Claude-Louis Berthollet, *Essai de statique chimique*, 2 vols. (1803), I, 245–247, n. 5; I, 522–523, n. 18; *OC*, XIV, 329–332.

[*1804a*] "Sur les tables de Jupiter et sur la masse de Saturne," in *CT* (an XIV [1805–1806]/nivôse an XII [Dec. 1803–Jan. 1804], 435–440; *OC*, XIII, 25–29. Laplace read a draft at the Institut on 12 Sept. 1803 (*82*). *RSC* 16.

[*1804b*] "Sur la théorie de Jupiter et de Saturne," in *CT* (an XV [1806–1807]/frimaire an XIII [Nov.–Dec. 1804], 296–307; *OC*, XIII, 30–40. *RSC* 20.

[*P1805*] "Rapport sur le projet . . . portant rétablissement du calendrier grégorien." Sénat conservateur, 9 Sept. 1805 (22 fructidor an XIII), in *AP*, VIII, 722–723. Not in *OC*.

[*1806a*] "Sur la théorie des tubes capillaires," in *JP*, **62** (Jan. 1806), 120–128; *OC*, XIV, 217–227. An abstract of (*85*), read on 23 Dec. 1805. *RSC* 17.

[*1806b*] "Sur l'attraction et la répulsion apparente des petits corps qui nagent à la surface des fluides," in *JP*, **63** (Sept. 1806), 248–252; *OC*, XIV, 228–232. Read in part on 29 Sept. 1806 (*87*). *RSC* 18.

[*1806c*] "Sur l'action capillaire," in *JP*, **63** (Dec. 1806), 474–477; also *CX*, **1** (1804–1808), 246–256; *OC*, XIV, 233–246. An abstract of (*86*), read on 28 Apr. 1806. *RSC* 15.

[*1806d*] "De l'adhésion des corps à la surface des fluides," in *JP*, **63** (Nov. 1806), 413–418; *OC*, XIV, 247–253. An abstract of (*88*), read on 24 Nov. 1806. *RSC* 19.

[*1807a*] "Supplément à la théorie de l'action capillaire," in *JP*, **65** (July 1807), 88–95; not in *OC*. An abstract of (*87*), read on 29 Sept. 1806.

[*1809a*] "Mémoire sur la double réfraction de la lumière dans les cristaux diaphanes," in *BSPM*, **1**, no. 18 (Mar. 1809), 303–310; *OC*, XIV, 278–287. An abstract of (*92*), read on 30 Jan. 1809. *RSC* 23.

[*1809b*] "Sur la loi de la réfraction extraordinaire de la lumière dans les cristaux diaphanes," in *JP*, **68** (Jan. 1809), 107–111; *OC*, XIV, 254–258. An abstract of the passages of [*1810a*] (*92*) that deal with the application of the principle of least action to double refraction, in consequence of forces of attraction and repulsion acting at undetectable distances. *RSC* 23.

[*1809c*] "Sur l'anneau de Saturne," in *CT* (1811/July 1809), 450–453; *OC*, XIII, 41–43. *RSC* 24.

[*1809d*] "Mémoire sur la diminution de l'obliquité de l'écliptique qui résulte des observations anciennes," in *CT* (1811/July 1809), 429–450; *OC*, XIII, 44–70. *RSC* 30.

[*1809e*] "Mémoire sur divers points d'analyse," in *JX*, **8**, 15e cahier (Dec. 1809), 229–265; *OC*, XIV, 178–214.

[*1810a*] "Mémoire sur le mouvement de la lumière dans les milieux diaphanes," in *MI*, **10** (1809/1810), 300–342; *OC*, XII, 267–298. Read at the Institut on 30 Jan. 1809 (*92*). The date is mistakenly given as 1808 in *OC*, XII, 267n. *RSC* 27.

[*1810b*] "Mémoire sur les approximations des formules qui sont fonctions de très grands nombres, et sur leur application aux probabilités," in *MI*, **10** (1809/1810), 353–415; *OC*, XII, 301–353. Read on 9 Apr. 1810 (*95*). Delambre summarized this paper in *MI*, **11** (1810/1811), "Histoire," iii–v.

[*1810c*] "Supplément au mémoire sur les approximations des formules qui sont fonctions de très grands nombres," in *MI*, **10** (1809/1810), 559–565; *OC*, XII, 349–353.

[*1810d*] "Notice sur les probabilités," in *Annuaire publié par le Bureau des longitudes* (1811/1810), 98–125. Not in *OC*.

[*1810e*] "Sur la dépression du mercure dans une tube de baromètre, due à sa capillarité," in *CT* (1812/July 1810), 315–320; *OC*, XIII, 71–77. Bouvard published corrections to the table of data, which are printed in *OC*, XIII, 334–341. *RSC* 31.

[*1811a*] "Mémoire sur les intégrales définies, et leur application aux probabilités, et spécialement à la recherche du milieu qu'il faut choisir entre les résultats des observations," in *MI*, **11** (1810/1811), 279–347; *OC*, XII, 357–412. Read on 29 Apr. 1811 (*97*). There is a prefatory summary by Delambre, in *MI*, **12** (1811/1812), "Histoire," i–xiii, reviewing the state of the question of least squares.

[*1811b*] "Du milieu qu'il faut choisir entre les résultats d'un grand nombre d'observations," in *CT* (1813/July 1811), 213–223; *OC*, XIII, 78. *RSC* 32.

[*1811c*] "Sur l'inégalité à longue période du mouvement lunaire," in *CT* (1813/July 1811), 223–227; *OC*, XIII, 79–84. Continued in [*1812a*]. See (*76*) and (*94*).

[*1812a*] "Sur l'inégalité à longue période du mouvement lunaire," in *CT* (1815/Nov. 1812), 213–214; *OC*, XIII, 85–87. A continuation of [*1811c*]. See (*76*) and (*94*). *RSC* 33.

[*1813a*] "Sur les comètes," in *CT* (1816/Nov. 1813), 213–220; *OC*, XIII, 88–97.

[*P1814*] Debate on a proposal to authorize the exportation of grain, Chambre des Pairs, 8 Nov. 1814, in *AP*, XIII, 470–471. Laplace's opinion supported free trade. Not in *OC*.

[*1815a*] "Sur l'application du calcul des probabilités à la philosophie naturelle," in *CT* (1818/1815), 361–377; *OC*, XIII, 98–116. Read before the Institut on 18 Sept. 1815 (*106*). *RSC* 34.

[*1815b*] "Sur le calcul des probabilités appliqué à la philosophie naturelle," in *CT* (1818/1815), 378–381; *OC*, XIII, 117–120. Supplement to [*1815a*]. *RSC* 34.

[*1815c*] "Sur le flux et reflux de la mer," in *CT* (1818/1815), 354–361; not in *OC*. Read on 10 July 1815 (*105*). *RSC* 35 mistakenly identifies this with [*1820a*], of which it was a preliminary abstract.

[*1816a*] "Sur la longueur du pendule à secondes," in *AC*, **3** (1816), 92–94. An excerpt from [*1817a*]. Read on 28 Oct. 1816 (*108*).

[*1816b*] "Sur l'action réciproque des pendules et sur la vitesse du son dans les diverses substances," in *AC*, **3** (1816), 162–169; *OC*, XIV, 291–296. Read before the Académie on 25 Nov. 1816 (*109*). *RSC* 36.

[*1816c*] "Sur la transmission du son à travers les corps solides," in *BSPM* (1816), 190–192; *OC*, XIV, 288. An abstract of [*1816b*]. See (*110*). *RSC* 40.

[*1816d*] "Sur la vitesse du son dans l'air et dans l'eau," in *AC*, **3** (1816), 238–241; *OC*, XIV, 297–300. Read at the Académie on 23 Dec. 1816 (*110*). *RSC* 37.

[*P1816*] "Sur une disposition du code d'instruction criminelle." Pamphlet, 15 Nov. 1816. Bibliothèque Nationale Fp. **1187**. On the mathematical equity of majorities required to find an accused guilty, in court of first instance and on appeal. Proposed modification of Article 351 of Code d'Instruction Criminelle as unfair to the accused. Not in *OC*.

[*1817a*] "Sur la longueur du pendule à secondes," in *CT* (1820/1817), 265–280; *OC*, XIII, 121–139. A fuller text than [*1816a*], with which *RSC* 38 mistakenly identifies it. Read on 28 Oct. 1816 (*108*).

[*1817b*] "Addition au mémoire précédent sur la lon-

gueur du pendule à secondes," in *CT* (1820/1817), 441–442; *OC*, XIII, 140–142.

[*P1817*] Recommendation on the cadastre, Chambre des Pairs, debate on the budget of 1817, 21 Mar. 1817, in *AP*, 2nd ser., XIX, 506–507; *OC*, XIV, 372–374. Urged completion of cadastre tied to geodesic survey as the basis for a fair assessment of the land tax.

[*1818a*] "Application du calcul des probabilités aux opérations géodésiques," in *CT* (1820/1818), 422–440. Excerpted in *AC*, *BSPM*, and *JP*. *RSC* 41. Read before the Académie on 4 Aug. 1817 (*111*). Incorporated, with additions (*112*), in *Théorie analytique des probabilités*, 3rd ed. (1820), as Supplement 2; *OC*, VII, 531–580.

[*1818b*] "Sur la figure de la terre, et la loi de la pesanteur à sa surface," in *AC*, **8** (1818), 313–318; *CT* (1821/1819), 326–331. Abstracted from [*1819b*]. Read on 3 Aug. 1818 (*114*). *RSC* 44.

[*1819a*] "Sur la rotation de la terre," in CT (1821/1819), 242–259; *OC*, XIII, 144–164. Read before the Academy on 18 May 1818 (*113*). *RSC* 43.

[*1819b*] "Mémoire sur la figure de la terre," in *MASIF*, **2** (1817/1819), 137–184; *OC*, XII, 415–455. Read on 3 Aug. 1818 (*OC* mistakenly has 4 Aug.). See (*114*). *RSC* 42.

[*1819c*] "Sur l'influence de la grande inégalité de Jupiter et de Saturne, dans le mouvement des corps du système solaire," in *CT* (1821/1819), 266–271; *OC*, XIII, 175–180.

[*1819d*] "Sur la loi de la pesanteur, en supposant le sphéroïde terrestre homogène et de même densité que la mer," in *CT* (1821/1819), 284–290; *OC*, XIII, 165–172.

[*1819e*] "Addition au mémoire précédent," in *CT* (1821/1819), 353; *OC*, XIII, 173–174.

[*1819f*] "Mémoire sur l'application du calcul des probabilités aux observations et spécialement aux opérations du nivellement," in *AC*, **12** (1819), 337–341; *OC*, XIV, 301–304. An abstract of the 3rd Supplement of *Théorie analytique des probabilités*, 3rd ed. (1820); *OC*, VII, 581–616. Read on 20 Dec. 1819 (*118*).

[*1819g*] "Application du calcul des probabilités aux opérations géodésiques de la méridienne de France," in *BSPM* (1819), 137–139; reprinted in *CT* (1822/1820), 346–348. Incorporated in the 3rd Supplement of *Théorie analytique des probabilités*, 3rd ed. (1820); *OC*, VII, 581–585. Cf. *OC*, XIII, 188, for correction of an error of calculation. Read on 20 Dec. 1819 (*118*). *RSC* 47.

[*1819h*] "Considérations sur la théorie des phénomènes capillaires," in *JP*, **89** (Oct. 1819), 292–296; XIV, 259–264. Read on 13 Sept. 1819 (*116*). *RSC* 45.

[*P1819*] Recommendation on the lottery, Chambre des Pairs debate on the budget of 1819, 16 July 1819, in *AP*, 2nd ser., XXV, 683–684; *OC*, XIV, 375–378. Urged suppression of the lottery on the grounds that it was inappropriate to raise public funds by encouraging illusions among the citizens.

[*1820a*] "Sur les inégalités lunaires dues à l'aplatissement de la terre," in *CT* (1823/1820), 219–225; *OC*, XIII, 189–197. Read on 19 Jan. 1820 (119).

[*1820b*] "Sur le perfectionnement de la théorie et des tables lunaires," in *CT* (1823/1820), 226–231; *OC*, XIII, 198–204. Read on 29 Mar. 1820 (*121*). *RSC* 49.

[*1820c*] "Sur l'inégalité lunaire à longue période, dépendante de la différence des deux hémisphères terrestres," in *CT* (1823/1820), 232–239; *OC*, XIII, 205–212. Read on 12 Apr. 1820 (*122*).

[*1820d*] "Mémoire sur le flux et le reflux de la mer," in *MASIF*, **3** (1818/1820), 1–90; *OC*, XII, 473–546. An expansion of [*1815b*].

[*1820e*] "Addition au mémoire sur la figure de la terre, inséré dans le volume précédent," in *MASIF*, **3** (1818/1820), 489–502; *OC*, XII, 459–469. The preceding memoir was [*1819b*]. Also printed under the title "Sur la figure de la terre," in *CT* (1822/1820), 284–293. Read on 26 May 1819 (*115*). Cf. *OC*, XIII, 187.

[*1820f*] "Mémoire sur la diminution de la durée du jour par le refroidissement de la terre," in *CT* (1823/1820), 245–257. Incorporated in *Mécanique céleste*, Volume V, Book XI, chapters 1 and 4. *OC*, V, 24–28, 82–88, 91–96. Cf. *OC*, XIII, 213. *RSC* 48.

[*1820g*] "Addition au mémoire précédent) sur la diminution de la durée du jour. . .," in *CT* (1823/1820), 324–327. Incorporated in *Mécanique céleste*, Volume V, Book XI, chapter 4, 88–91. Cf. *OC*, XIII, 214. *RSC* 48.

[*1820h*] "Sur la densité moyenne de la terre," in *CT* (1823/1820), 328–331; *OC*, XIII, 215–220. *RSC* 50.

[*1820i*] "Éclaircissements sur les mémoires précédents, relatifs aux inégalités lunaires dépendantes de la figure de la terre, et au perfectionnement de la théorie et des tables de la lune," in *CT* (1823/1820), 332–337; *OC*, XIII, 221–228.

[*1821a*] "Éclaircissements de la théorie des fluides élastiques," in *AC*, **18** (1821), 273–280; *OC*, XIV, 305–311.

[*1821b*] "Sur les variations des éléments du mouvement elliptique, et sur les inégalités lunaires à longues périodes," in *CT* (1824/1821), 274–307; *OC*, XIII, 229–264.

[*1821c*] "Sur la détermination des orbites des comètes," in *CT* (1824/1821), 314–320; *OC*, XIII, 265–272. Includes an example of the method applied to the comet of 1805 by Bouvard.

[*1821d*] "Sur l'attraction des sphères et sur la répulsion des fluides élastiques," in *CT* (1824/1821), 328–343; *OC*, XIII, 273–290. Read before the Academy on 10 Sept. 1821 (*123*). *RSC* 51.

[*1821e*] *Précis de l'histoire de l'astronomie* (1821). A separate publication of Book V of *Exposition du système du monde*, from the 4th ed. (1813).

[*P1821*] Debate on Article 351 of Code d'Instruction Criminelle, Chambre des Pairs, 30 Mar. 1821, in *AP*, 2nd ser., XXX, 531–532; *OC*, XIV, 379–381. Recommendations on the most equitable modes of reaching a decision in juries.

[*1822a*] "Développement de la théorie des fluides élastiques et application de cette théorie à la vitesse du son," in *CT* (1825/1822), 219–227; *OC*, XIII,

291–301. Submitted to the Bureau des Longitudes on 12 Dec. 1821. *RSC* 55.

[*1822b*] "Addition au mémoire précédent sur le développement de la théorie des fluides élastiques," in *CT* (1825/1822), 302–323; *OC*, XIII, 302.

[*1822c*] "Sur la vitesse du son," in *CT* (1825/1822), 371–372; *OC*, XIII, 303–304. *RSC* 57.

[*1822d*] "Addition au mémoire sur la théorie des fluides élastiques," in *CT* (1825/1822), 386–387; *OC*, XIII, 305.

[*1823a*] "De l'action de la lune sur l'atmosphère," in *CT* (1826/1823), 308–317. Incorporated in *Mécanique céleste*, Book XIII; *OC*, V, 184–188, 262–268. *RSC* 58.

[*1824a*] "Sur les variations de l'obliquité de l'écliptique et de la précession des équinoxes," in *CT* (1827/1824), 234–237; *OC*, XIII, 307–311.

[*P1824*] Debate on conversion of the public debt, Chambre des Pairs, 1 June 1824, in *AP*, 2nd ser., XLI, 125; *OC*, XIV, 382–383. Calculation of the effects of various schemes of amortization on the cost of servicing the debt.

[*1825a*] "Sur le développement en série du radical qui exprime la distance mutuelle de deux planètes, et sur le développement du rayon vecteur elliptique," in *CT* (1828/1825), 311–321; *OC*, XIII, 312.

[*1825b*] "Sur la réduction de la longueur du pendule, au niveau de la mer," in *AC*, 30 (1825), 381–387; *OC*, XIV, 312–317.

[*P1825*] Debate on the conversion of the government bond issue, Chambre des Pairs, 26 Apr. 1825, in *AP*, 2nd ser., XLV, 144–145; *OC*, XIV, 385–387. Favored reduction of the interest rate and an increase of capital.

[*1826a*] "Mémoire sur les deux grandes inégalités de Jupiter et de Saturne," in *CT* (1829/1826), 236–244; *OC*, XIII, 313–322.

[*1826b*] "Mémoire sur divers points de mécanique céleste: I. Sur les mouvements de l'orbite du dernier satellite de Saturne; II. Sur l'inégalité de Mercure à longue période, dont l'argument est le moyen mouvement de Mercure, moins celui de la terre; III. De l'action des étoiles sur le système planétaire"; in *CT* (1829/1826), 245–251; *OC*, XIII, 323–330.

[*1826c*] "Mémoire sur un moyen de détruire les effets de la capillarité dans les baromètres," in *CT* (1829/1826), 301–302; *OC*, XIII, 331–333.

[*1827a*] "Mémoire sur le développement de l'anomalie vraie et du rayon vecteur elliptique en séries ordonnées suivant les puissances de l'excentricité," in *MASIF, 6* (1823/1827), 61–80; *OC*, XII, 549–566.

[*1827b*] "Mémoire sur le flux et reflux lunaire atmosphérique," in *CT* (1830/1827), 3–18; *OC*, XIII, 342–358. Published in Supplement to *Mécanique céleste*, Volume V; *OC*, V, 489–505.

SECONDARY LITERATURE

J. Biographical and General. The only attempt at a comprehensive account is H. Andoyer, *L'oeuvre scienti-fique de Laplace* (Paris, 1922), a modernized précis that is useful at this level. It is unfair to this unpretentious little (162-page) work to quote here the comment with which the editor of *L'action nationale* prefaced an excerpt from its methodological section (n.s. **18** [Jan.–June 1922], 14–21), but the remark deserves rescue from the oblivion of that journal:

> À l'heure où l'esprit de snobisme et d'aventure, qui semble être la marque de notre temps, croit découvrir dans les théories, peu accessibles mais tapageuses, du mathématicien allemand Einstein, un je ne sais quel nouveau point de départ pour la pensée, une voie insoupçonnée pour la recherche scientifique, il est bon de rappeler l'effort aussi innovateur que parfaitement intelligible de notre Laplace, dont la grande hardiesse s'accompagnait d'une égale modestie.

The most important éloge is Joseph Fourier, "Éloge historique de M. le Marquis de Laplace, prononcé . . . le 15 juin 1829," in *MASIF*, 10 (1831), "Histoire," lxxxi–cii, prefixed to the 1835 printing of the 6th ed. of *Exposition du système du monde* and reprinted in most later eds; there is an English trans. in *Philosophical Magazine*, 2nd ser., 6 (1829), 370–381. J.-B. Biot and S.-D. Poisson delivered eulogies at the funeral, and both texts are prefixed to the 1827 printing of *Exposition du système du monde*. Much later, Biot published a reminiscence of Laplace as scientific father figure that he had delivered before the Académie Française, "Une anecdote relative à M. Laplace," in *Journal des savants* (Feb. 1850), 65–71. François Arago also composed a "Notice," in his *Oeuvres*, III (1859), 459–515; there is an English trans. in *Biographies of Distinguished Scientific Men* (London, 1857), 196–241. In this century innumerable anniversary pieces have appeared, the only ones worthy of record being André Danjon, "Pierre-Simon Marquis de Laplace," in *Notices et discours. Académie des sciences*, 3 (1949–1956) [Paris, 1957], delivered at a 200th anniversary celebration in Caen; René Taton, "Laplace," in *La Nature* (Paris), **77** (1949), 221–223; and E. T. Whittaker, "Laplace," in *Mathematical Gazette*, **33** (1949), 1–12.

It is still useful to consult the articles in certain well-known nineteenth-century biographical encyclopedias; but before doing so, readers should bear in mind that just as entries in these works concerning figures in previous centuries derive from tradition and legend rather than from historical research, so the accounts of near-contemporary persons depend on gossip and reminiscence rather than on scholarship. Hence, the decline of Laplace's personal reputation is the main motif in A. Rabbe, J. Vieilh de Boisjolin, and Sainte-Preuve, *Biographie universelle et portative des contemporains*, 5 vols. (Paris, 1834), III, 151–153; Parisot, in *Biographie universelle, ancienne et moderne*, L. G. Michaud, ed., 85 vols. (Paris, 1811–1862), LXX, 237–260; and E. Merlieux, in *Nouvelle biographie générale*, F. Hoefer, ed., 46 vols. (Paris, 1855–1866), XXIX (1859), cols. 531–548. On Laplace's failure to support the declaration of the Académie Française in favor of the freedom of the press, see also E. Grassier, *Les cinq cents immortels. Histoire de l'Académie française* (Paris, 1906), 148–149.

Notarial records and other official notices are reproduced in B. Boncompagni, "Intorno agli alti di nascità e di morte di Pietro Simone Laplace," in *Bollettino di bibliografia e storia delle scienze matematiche e fisiche*, **15** (1883), 447–465. L. Puisieux, *Notice sur Laplace* (Caen, 1847), may still be consulted. Karl Pearson published extracts from lectures on the life and work of Laplace in *Biometrika*, **21** (1929), 202–216; and appended to it an antiquarian article written at his request by the Abbé G.-A. Simon, "Les origines de Laplace: sa généalogie, ses études," *ibid.*, 217–230. G. Bigourdan, "La jeunesse de Laplace," in *Science moderne*, no. 8 (1931), 377–384, takes him up to his election to the Academy. S.-F. Lacroix, *Essais sur l'enseignement en général et sur celui de mathématiques en particulier*, 3rd ed. (1828), is useful for the context of Laplace's teaching in the 1790's. Laplace joined with Legendre in a report read by the latter (11 nivôse an V [31 Dec. 1976], *PVIF*, I, 154–157) on Lacroix, *Traité de calcul différentiel et intégral*, 2 vols. (1797), and printed in full at the end of Vol. I of that work, pp. 520 ff. There is much biographical information in Maurice Crosland, *The Society of Arcueil* (London, 1967). Of more incidental interest are G. Sarton, "Laplace's Religion," in *Isis*, **33** (1941), 309–312; and D. Duveen and R. Hahn, "Laplace's Succession to Bezout's Post of *Examinateur des élèves de l'artillerie*," *ibid.*, **48** (1957), 416–427.

There is information on Laplace's relations with Fourier, and further bibliography, in Ivor Grattan-Guinness with J. R. Ravetz, *Joseph Fourier, 1768–1830* (Cambridge, Mass., 1972). Paul Marmottan edited the correspondence of Madame de Laplace with Elisa Bonaparte, *Lettres de Madame de Laplace à Élisa Napoléon, princesse de Lucques et de Piombino* (Paris, 1897). They cover mainly the years 1807 and 1808.

K. Celestial Mechanics. It is worthy of remark that in the nineteenth century interest in Laplace centered on his celestial mechanics; that in the twentieth century it shifted to probability; that very recently attention has begun to be paid to his physics, although mainly for its institutional and political implications; and that surprisingly little scholarship has been addressed expressly to his mathematical work, which has been discussed mostly in sections of large-scale works on the evolution of over-all aspects of mathematics.

Of near-contemporary astronomical and physical texts, the most helpful by far is Mary Somerville, *Mechanism of the Heavens* (London, 1831). Her exposition is somewhat more elementary than Bowditch's commentary [F], to which it makes a valuable supplement. Less satisfactory, although still worth mentioning, is Thomas Young, *Elementary Illustrations of the Celestial Mechanics of Laplace* (London, 1821). More valuable historically are two Victorian monuments: Robert Grant, *History of Physical Astronomy From the Earliest Ages to the Middle of the 19th Century* (London, 1852; repr. New York, 1966); and Isaac Todhunter, *A History of the Mathematical Theories of Attraction and the Figure of the Earth From the Time of Newton to That of Laplace*, 2 vols. (London, 1873; repr. New York, 1962). Among more recent works, questions of origin and development bulk much more largely than they did in the writings of Laplace himself. So it is in B. O. Bianco, "Le idee di Lagrange, Laplace, Gauss, e Schiaparelli sull'origine delle comete," in *Memorie della Reale Accademia delle scienze di Torino*, 2nd ser., **63** (1913), 59–110. Jules Vuillemin is both methodological and metaphysical in "Sur la généralisation de l'estimation de la force chez Laplace," in *Thalès*, **9** (1958), 61–76; Jacques Merlau-Ponty is largely metaphysical in "Situation et rôle de l'hypothèse cosmogonique dans la pensée cosmologique de Laplace," in *Revue d'histoire des sciences et de leurs applications*, **29** (1976), 21–49; Stanley L. Jaki is more concrete on the development of Laplace's cosmogonical views, with special reference to the status of the nebular hypothesis in successive editions of the *Système du monde*, "The Five Forms of Laplace's Cosmogony," in *American Journal of Physics*, **44** (1976), 4–11. It has, unfortunately, not been possible to consult the unpublished M.Sc. thesis by Eric J. Aiton, "The Development of the Theory of the Tides in the Seventeenth and Eighteenth Centuries" (University of London, 1953).

L. Probability. The starting place is still Isaac Todhunter, *A History of the Mathematical Theory of Probability From the Time of Pascal to That of Laplace* (London, 1865). Since then the most comprehensive treatment of the subject as a whole is Ivo Schneider, *Die Entwicklung des Wahrscheinlichkeitsbegriffs in der Mathematik von Pascal bis Laplace* (Munich, 1972), a *Habilitationsschrift*. Ian Hacking, *The Emergence of Probability* (Cambridge, 1975), is philosophically motivated and largely nontechnical; in our judgment the resulting account does less than justice to Laplace. Still of interest are the unsigned article by Augustus de Morgan in the form of a review of the *Théorie analytique*, in *Dublin Review*, **2** (1836–1837), 338–354; and **3** (1837), 237–248; and E. Czuber, "Die Entwicklung der Wahrscheinlichkeitstheorie und ihrer Anwendungen," which is *Jahresbericht der Deutschen Mathematikervereinigung*, **7**, no. 2 (1899).

More recent writings are D. van Dantzig, "Laplace probabiliste et statisticien et ses précurseurs," in *Archives internationales d'histoire des sciences*, **8** (1955), 27–37; Churchill Eisenhart, "The Meaning of 'Least' in Least Squares," in *Journal of the Washington Academy of Sciences*, **54** (1964), 24–33; C. C. Gillispie, "Intellectual Factors in the Background of Analysis by Probabilities," in A. C. Crombie, ed., *Scientific Change* (London, 1963), 433–453; and "Probability and Politics: Laplace, Condorcet, and Turgot," in *Proceedings of the American Philosophical Society*, **116**, no. 1 (Feb. 1972), 1–20; H. O. Lancaster, "Forerunners of the Pearson χ^2," in

Australian Journal of Statistics, **8** (1966), 117–126; Wilhelm Lorey, "Die Bedeutung von Laplace für die Statistik," in *Allgemeines statistisches Archiv,* **23** (1934), 398–410; L. E. Maistrov, *Probability Theory; A Historical Sketch,* translated and edited by Samuel Kotz (New York–London, 1974); E. C. Molina, "The Theory of Probability: Some Comments on Laplace's *Théorie analytique,*" in *Bulletin of the American Mathematical Society,* **36** (1930), 369–392, largely in defense of generating functions; R. L. Plackett, "The Discovery of the Method of Least Squares," in *Biometrika,* **59** (1972), 239–251; Ivo Schneider, "Rudolph Clausius' Beitrag zur Einführung wahrscheinlichkeitstheoretischer Methoden in die Physik der Gase nach 1856," in *Archive for History of Exact Sciences,* **14** (1975), 237–261, which deals with Laplace's role in the emergence of the idea of treating kinetic theory by methods of the calculus of probabilities; H. L. Seal, "The Historical Development of the Use of Generating Functions in Probability Theory," in *Mitteilungen der Vereinigung schweizerischer Versicherungs-Mathematiker,* **49** (1949), 209–228; an important group of papers by O. B. Sheynin: "Finite Random Sums," in *Archive for History of Exact Sciences,* **9** (1973), 275–305; "P. S. Laplace's Work on Probability," *ibid.,* **16** (1976), 137–187, which is mainly a summary critique of *Théorie analytique des probabilités;* and "Laplace's Theory of Errors," *ibid.,* **17** (1977), 1–61; an excellent series of papers by Stephen M. Stigler: "Laplace, Fisher, and the Discovery of the Concept of Sufficiency," in *Biometrika,* **60** (1973), 439–455; "Cauchy and the Witch of Agnesi," *ibid.,* **61** (1974), 375–380; "Gergonne's 1815 Paper on the Design and Analysis of Polynomial Regression Experiments," in *Historia mathematica,* **1** (1974), 431–447; "Napoleonic Statistics: The Work of Laplace," in *Biometrika,* **62** (1975), 503–517; and a postscript to the article on Laplace, in J. Tanner and W. Kruskal, eds., *Encyclopedia of Statistics in the Social Sciences* (in press); and E. Yamakazi, "D'Alembert et Condorcet—quelques aspects de l'histoire du calcul des probabilités," in *Japanese Studies in the History of Science,* **10** (1971), 59–93.

M. Mathematical Physics. The indispensable sources for Laplace's work in physical science are J. J. Bikerman, "Theories of Capillary Attraction," in *Centaurus,* **19** (1975), 182–206; Bernard S. Finn, "Laplace and the Speed of Sound," in *Isis,* **55** (1964), 7–19; Robert Fox, *The Caloric Theory of Gases From Lavoisier to Regnault* (London, 1971); and "The Rise and Fall of Laplacian Physics," in *Historical Studies in the Physical Sciences,* **4** (1974), 89–136; Eugene Frankel, "The Search for a Corpuscular Theory of Double Refraction: Malus, Laplace and the Prize Competition of 1808," in *Centaurus,* **18** (1974), 223–245; H. H. Frisinger, "Mathematics in the History of Meteorology: The Pressure-Height Problem From Pascal to Laplace," in *Historia mathematica,* **1** (1974), 263–286; Henry Guerlac, "Chemistry as a Branch of Physics: Laplace's Collaboration With Lavoisier," in *Historical Studies in the Physi-*

cal Sciences, **7** (1976), 193–276; and T. H. Lodwig and W. A. Smeaton, "The Ice Calorimeter of Lavoisier and Laplace and Some of Its Critics," in *Annals of Science,* **31** (1974), 1–18.

N. Mathematics. Much of the discussion in many of the foregoing titles is of necessity mathematical. In addition, help is available from works primarily concerned with topics in the history of mathematics and rational mechanics, notably H. Burckhardt, "Entwicklungen nach oscillirenden Functionen und Integration der Differentialgleichungen der mathematischen Physik," which is *Jahresbericht der Deutschen Mathematikervereinigung,* **10**, no. 2 (1908), an 1,800-page monograph of which Section VI, pp. 398–408, deals especially with Laplace's method for integrating differential equations by means of definite integrals; Florian Cajori, *A History of Mathematical Notations,* 2 vols. (Chicago, 1928–1929), II, *passim;* Theodor Körner, "Der Begriff des materiellen Punktes in der Mechanik des achtzehnten Jahrhunderts," in *Bibliotheca mathematica,* 3rd ser., **5** (1904), 15–62, esp. 52–54; Elaine Koppelmann, "The Calculus of Operations and the Rise of Abstract Algebra," in *Archive for History of Exact Sciences,* **8** (1971), 155–242; E. C. Molina, "An Expansion for Laplacian Integrals," in *Bell System Technical Journal,* **11** (1932), 563–575; Thomas Muir, *The Theory of Determinants in the Historical Order of Development,* 4 vols. (London, 1906–1923); S. S. Petrova, "K istorii metoda kaskadov Laplasa" ("Toward the History of Laplace's Method of Cascades"), in *Istoriko-matematicheskie issledovania,* **19** (1974), 125–131; and "Rannyaya istoria preobrazovania Laplasa" ("The Early History of the Laplace Transform"), *ibid.,* **20** (1975), 246–256; O. B. Sheynin, "O poyavlenii delta-funktsii Diraka v trudakh P. S. Laplasa" ("On the Appearance of Dirac's Delta-Function in the Works of P. S. Laplace"), *ibid.,* 303–308; and Isaac Todhunter, *Elementary Treatise on Laplace's Function, Lamé's Function, and Bessel's Function* (London, 1875).

LA ROCHE, ESTIENNE DE (*fl.* Lyons, France, *ca.* 1520)

La Roche, known as Villefranche, was born in Lyons. A pupil of Nicolas Chuquet, he taught arithmetic for twenty-five years in the commercial center of his native town and was called "master of ciphers."

La Roche's *Larismetique,* published at Lyons in 1520, was long considered the work of an excellent writer who, early in the sixteenth century, introduced into France the Italian knowledge of arithmetic and useful notations for powers and roots. His fame decreased remarkably in 1880, when Aristide Marre published Chuquet's "Triparty," written in 1484 but preserved only in manuscript. The first part of *Larismetique* was then seen to be mostly a copy of the earlier work, with the omission of those striking features that established Chuquet as an algebraist of the first rank. Chuquet, for example, employed a more advanced notation for powers and he introduced zero as an exponent. It is not clear why La Roche failed to publish the "Triparty." He may have suppressed it in order to claim the credit for himself, or perhaps he thought it too far beyond the comprehension of prospective readers. Nevertheless, through *Larismetique* some of Chuquet's innovations influenced such French arithmeticians as Jean Buteo and Guillaume Gosselin.

The second, and greater, part of La Roche's work has, apart from some geometrical calculations at the end, a commercial character. The author states that as a basis he used "the flower of several masters, experts in the art" of arithmetic, such as Luca Pacioli, supplemented by his own knowledge of business practice. The result was a good but traditional arithmetic that presented an outstanding view of contemporary methods of computation and their applications in trade.

BIBLIOGRAPHY

Larismetique nouellement composee par maistre Estienne de la Roche dict Villefranche natif de Lyon sur le Rosne divisée en deux parties ... (Lyons, 1520) was republished as *Larismetique et geometrie de maistre Estienne de la Roche dict Ville Franche, nouuellement imprimee et des faultes corrigee* ... (Lyons, 1538).

See M. Cantor, *Vorlesungen über Geschichte der Mathematik*, II (Leipzig, 1913), 371–374; and N. Z. Davis, "Sixteenth-Century French Arithmetics on the Business Life," in *Journal of the History of Ideas*, **21** (1960), 18–48. On Chuquet and La Roche, see Aristide Marre, "Notice sur Nicolas Chuquet," in *Bullettino di bibliografia e di storia delle scienze matematiche e fisiche*, **13** (1880), esp. 569–580.

J. J. VERDONK

LAURENT, MATTHIEU PAUL HERMANN (*b.* Echternach, Luxembourg, 2 September 1841; *d.* Paris, France, 19 February 1908)

Laurent's father, Auguste, was a noted chemist. After his father's death in 1853, Laurent was sent to the École Polytechnique in Paris and the École d'Application at Metz. He rose to the rank of officer but resigned in 1865 and took his *docteur-ès-sciences* at the University of Nancy with a thesis on the continuity of functions of a complex variable. In 1866 he became *répétiteur* at the École Polytechnique but returned to active military service during the Franco-Prussian War. He resigned to resume the post of *répétiteur* at the École Polytechnique, and in 1871 he was appointed actuary for the Compagnie d'Assurance de l'Union. In 1874 he married Berthe Moutard; in 1883 he became an *examinateur* at the École Polytechnique, and in 1889 he was appointed professor at the École Agronomique in Paris. In 1905 he was made an officer of the Legion of Honor.

Although Laurent's output comprised about thirty books and several dozen papers, his importance lies mainly in the teaching rather than in the development of mathematics. His papers dealt primarily with problems in analysis (especially relating to infinite series, elliptic functions, and Legendre polynomials), the theory of equations, differential equations and their solution, analytic geometry and the theory of curves, and the theory of substitutions and elimination. In the latter field he made one of his most useful contributions by extending some of the known techniques of eliminating variables to find the solutions to equations. Laurent was also noteworthy in developing statistical and interpolation formulas for the calculation of actuarial tables, annuities, and insurance rates; and he gave the name "chremastatistics" to subjects such as insurance and economics. He was a founding member of the Société des Actuaires Français and from 1903 was responsible for the mathematical section of the *Grande encyclopédie*, to which he contributed over 130 articles. He was a member of the editorial boards of the *Journal des mathématiques pures et appliquées* and of the *Nouvelles annales des mathématiques*, contributing articles especially to the latter.

Laurent's first textbook was the short *Traité des séries* (1862), one of the first works devoted entirely to the convergence as well as the summation of series; it was followed by *Traité des résidus* (1865). (It was Pierre Alphonse Laurent who was responsible, in 1843, for the Laurent series.) Of Laurent's later works, the comprehensive seven-volume *Traité d'analyse* (1885–1891) is notable. It is divided into two parts, of two and five volumes respectively, on the differential and integral calculus, and includes not only the standard treatments of the derivative and the integral and their applications to geometry but also substantial sections on the theory of functions, determinants, and elliptic functions. The last three volumes are devoted entirely to the solution and application of ordinary and partial differential equations. Laurent's other books deal with probability, arithmetic and algebra, rational mechanics, and statistics and its applications in economics. In 1895 he published *Traité d'arithmétique* under the names of his friends C. A. Laisant and Émile Lemoine, since arithmetic was part of the curriculum of the École Polytechnique, and he was not allowed as an examiner to publish the work under his own name.

BIBLIOGRAPHY

I. ORIGINAL WORKS. In addition to works mentioned in the text, the following are worthy of note: *Traité du calcul des probabilités* (Paris, 1873); *Théorie élémentaire des fonctions elliptiques* (Paris, 1882); *Traité d'algèbre* (Paris, 1867; 5th ed., 1894); *Traité de mécanique rationnelle*, 2 vols. (Paris, 1889); *Théorie des jeux de hasard* (Paris, 1893); *Théorie des assurances sur la vie* (Paris, 1895); *Opérations financières* (Paris, 1898); *L'élimination* (Paris, 1900); *Petit traité d'économie politique* (Paris, 1902); *Traité de perspective* [intended for artists and draftsmen] (Paris, 1902); *Appendice sur les résidus . . .* (Paris, 1904); *Théorie des nombres ordinaires et algébriques* (Paris, 1904); *La géométrie analytique* (Paris, 1906); and *Statistique mathématique* (Paris, 1908), his last book. A substantial number of his papers on statistical and related matters were published in *Bulletin trimestriel de l'Institut des actuaires français*.

II. SECONDARY LITERATURE. The most comprehensive source of bibliographical and biographical information is a 63-page pamphlet published in 1909 under the title *Hermann Laurent 1841–1908. Biographie—bibliographie*. This work is, however, extremely rare; and a fairly substantial amount of information may be gleaned from Poggendorff, IV, 844; V, 713. A notice on Laurent appeared in the *Grande encyclopédie*, XXI, 1038.

I. GRATTAN-GUINNESS

LAURENT, PIERRE ALPHONSE (*b.* Paris, France, 18 July 1813; *d.* Paris, 2 September 1854)

In 1832, after studying for two years at the École Polytechnique, Laurent graduated among the highest in his class, receiving the rank of a second lieutenant in the engineering corps. When he left the École d'Application at Metz he was sent to Algeria, where he took part in the Tlemcen and Tafna expeditions. He returned to France and participated in the study leading to the enlargement of the port of Le Havre. Laurent spent about six years in Le Havre directing the difficult hydraulic construction projects. His superiors considered him a promising officer; they admired his sure judgment and his extensive practical training.

In the midst of these technical operations Laurent composed his first scientific memoirs. Around 1843 he sent to the Académie des Sciences a "Mémoire sur le calcul des variations." The Academy had set the following problem as the subject of the Grand Prize in the mathematical sciences for 1842: Find the limiting equations that must be joined to the indefinite equations in order to determine completely the maxima and minima of multiple integrals. The prize was won by Pierre Frédéric Sarrus, then dean of the Faculty of Sciences of Strasbourg. A memoir by Delaunay was accorded an honorable mention. Laurent submitted his memoir to the Academy after the close of the competition but before the judges announced their decision. His entry presented great similarities to Sarrus's work. Although some of Laurent's methods could be considered more inductive than rigorous, Cauchy, in his report of 20 May, concluded that the piece should be approved by the Academy and inserted in the *Recueil des savants étrangers*. Laurent's work was never published, however, while Delaunay's memoir appeared in the *Journal de l'Ecole polytechnique* in 1843, and Sarrus's in the *Recueil des savants étrangers* in 1846.

A similar fate befell Laurent's "Extension du théorème de M. Cauchy relatif à la convergence du développement d'une fonction suivant les puissances ascendantes de la variable *x*." The content of this paper is known only through Cauchy's report to the Academy in 1843. Characteristically, Cauchy spoke more about himself than about the author. He stated his own theorem first:

Let *x* designate a real or imaginary variable; a real or imaginary function of *x* will be developable in a convergent series ordered according to the ascending powers of this variable, while the modulus of the variable will preserve a value less than the smallest of the values for which the function or its derivative ceases to be finite or continuous.

While carefully examining the first demonstration of this theorem, Laurent recognized that Cauchy's analysis could lead to a more general theorem, which Cauchy formulated in his report in the following way:

Let *x* designate a real or imaginary variable; a real or imaginary function of *x* can be represented by the sum of two convergent series, one ordered according to the integral and ascending powers of *x*, and the other according to the integral and descending powers of *x*; and the modulus of *x* will take on a value in an interval within which the function or its derivative does not cease to be finite and continuous.

Cauchy thought Laurent's memoir merited approval by the Academy and inclusion in the *Recueil des savants étrangers*, but it too was not published. One can gain an idea of Laurent's methods by his study published posthumously in 1863.

Meanwhile Laurent abandoned research in pure mathematics and concentrated on the theory of light waves. The majority of his investigations in this area appeared in notes published in the *Comptes rendus hebdomadaires des séances de l'Académie des sciences*. Laurent summarized the principal ideas of his research in a letter to Arago. He declared that the theory of polarization was still at the point where Fresnel had left it. He criticized Cauchy's method of finding differential equations to explain this group of phenomena and asserted that the equations were purely empirical. He rejected the use of single material points in determining the equations of motion of light, and employed instead a system combining the spheroids and a system of material points. Cauchy responded vigorously to Laurent's claim that he had thereby proved that the molecules of bodies have finite dimensions.

When Jacobi, a correspondent of the Academy since 1830, was elected a foreign associate member in 1846, Cauchy nominated Laurent for Jacobi's former position, but he was not elected. A short time later Laurent was promoted to major and called to Paris to join the committee on fortifications. While carrying out his new duties, he continued his scientific research. He died in 1854 at the age of forty-two, leaving a wife and three children.

His widow arranged for two more of his memoirs to be presented to the Academy of Sciences. One, on optics, *Examen de la théorie de la lumière dans le système des ondes*, was never published, despite Cauchy's recommendation that it be printed in the *Recueil des savants étrangers*. The other did not appear until 1863, when it was published in the *Journal de l'Ecole polytechnique*. Designating the modulus of a complex number as X and its argument as p, Laurent proposed to study the continuous integrals of the equation

$$dF/dx = 1/(x \sqrt{-1}) \cdot dF/dp,$$

where F is a function of the form $\varphi + \psi \sqrt{-1}$ subject to the condition $F(x, \pi) = F(x, -\pi)$, and which, together with its first order partial derivatives, remains finite and continuous for all x and all p relative to the points of the plane included between two closed curves A and B, each of which encircles the origin of the system of coordinates. If C is a curve encircling the origin, contained between A and B and represented by the polar equation

$$X = P(p), \quad \text{with} \quad P(\pi) = P(-\pi),$$

Laurent demonstrated that the integral

$$I = \int_{-\pi}^{+\pi} dp\, F(P, p)(\sqrt{-1} + 1/P \cdot dP/dp)$$

is independent of the curve C, that is, of the function P. He thus showed that the first variation of I is identically zero when C undergoes an infinitely small variation. He arrived at the same result, moreover, by calculating a double integral following a procedure devised by Cauchy. Laurent deduced his theorem from it by a method analogous to the one Cauchy had employed to establish his own theorem. He showed that if ρ_1 and ρ_2 are the radii of two circles centered at the origin and tangent respectively to the curves A and B, then at every polar coordinate point (X, p) situated in the annulus delimited by these circles:

$$F(X, p)$$

$$= \frac{1}{2\pi} \sum_0^\infty X^n e^{np\sqrt{-1}} \int_{-\pi}^{+\pi} dp'\, F(\rho_2, p') \frac{1}{\rho_2^n e^{np'\sqrt{-1}}}$$

$$+ \frac{1}{2\pi} \sum_0^\infty \frac{1}{X^n e^{np\sqrt{-1}}} \int_{-\pi}^{+\pi} dp'\, F(\rho_1, p')\, \rho_1^n e^{np'\sqrt{-1}}.$$

In the memoir he applied these results to the problem of the equilibrium of temperatures in a body and to the phenomenon of elasticity.

BIBLIOGRAPHY

I. ORIGINAL WORKS. Among Laurent's writings are "Mémoire sur la forme générale des équations aux différentielles linéaires et à coëfficients constants, propre à représenter les lois des mouvements infiniment petits d'un système de points matériels, soumis à des forces d'attraction ou de répulsion mutuelle," in *Comptes rendus hebdomadaires des séances de l'Académie des sciences*, **18** (1844), 294–297; "Equations des mouvements infiniment petits d'un système de sphéroïdes soumis à des forces d'attraction ou de répulsion mutuelle," *ibid.*, 771–774; "Sur la nature des forces répulsives entre les molécules," *ibid.*, 865–869; "Sur la rotation des plans de polarisation dans les mouvements infiniment petits d'un système de sphéroïdes," *ibid.*, 936–940; "Sur les fondements de la théorie mathématique de la polarisation mobile," *ibid.*, **19** (1844), 329–333; "Mémoire sur les mouvements infiniment petits d'une file rectiligne de sphéroïdes," *ibid.*, 482–483; and "Note sur les équations d'équilibre entre des forces quelconques, appliquées aux différents points d'un corps solide libre," in *Nouvelles annales de mathématiques*, IV (1845), 9–14.

See also "Note sur la théorie mathématique de la lumière," in *Comptes rendus hebdomadaires des séances de l'Académie des sciences*, **20** (1845), 560–563, 1076–1082, 1593–1603; "Observations sur les ondes liquides," *ibid.*, **20** (1845), 1713–1716; "Sur les mouvements atomiques," *ibid.*, **21** (1845), 438–443; "Sur les mouvements vibratoires de l'éther," *ibid.*, 529–553; "Recherches sur la théorie mathématique des mouvements ondulatoires," *ibid.*, 1160–1163; "Sur la propagation des ondes sonores," *ibid.*, **22** (1846), 80–84; "Sur les ondes sonores," *ibid.*, 251–253; and "Mémoire sur la théorie des imaginaires, sur l'équilibre des températures et sur l'équilibre d'élasticité," in *Journal de l'École polytechnique*, **23** (1863), 75–204.

II. Secondary Literature. For information on Laurent's work, see the following articles in Augustin Cauchy, *Oeuvres complètes*, 1st ser., VIII (Paris, 1893): "Rapport sur un mémoire de M. Laurent qui a pour titre: Extension du théorème de M. Cauchy relatif à la convergence du développement d'une fonction suivant les puissances ascendantes de la variable *x* (30 Octobre 1843)," pp. 115–117; "Rapport sur un mémoire de M. Laurent relatif au calcul des variations (20 Mai 1844)," pp. 208–210; and "Observations à l'occasion d'une note de M. Laurent (20 Mai 1844)," pp. 210–213.

See also "Mémoire sur la théorie de la polarisation chromatique (27 Mai 1844)," *ibid.*, XI (Paris, 1899), 213–225; and "Rapport sur un mémoire de M. Laurent, relatif aux équations d'équilibre et de mouvement d'un système de sphéroïdes sollicités par des forces d'attraction et de répulsion mutuelles (31 Juillet 1848)," *ibid.*, pp. 73–75; and "Rapport sur deux mémoires de M. Pierre Alphonse Laurent, chef de bataillon du Génie (19 Mars 1855)," *ibid.*, XII (Paris, 1900), pp. 256–258.

For further reference, see Joseph Bertrand, "Notice sur les travaux du Commandant Laurent, lue en Avril 1860 à la séance annuelle de la Société des Amis des Sciences," in *Éloges académiques* (Paris, 1890), pp. 389–393; and I. Todhunter, *A History of the Calculus of Variations* (1861), pp. 476–477.

JEAN ITARD

LAVANHA, JOÃO BAPTISTA (*b.* Portugal, *ca.* 1550; *d.* Madrid, Spain, 31 March 1624)

Lavanha was appointed professor of mathematics at Madrid in 1583. (At that time Spain and Portugal were united under Philip II.) From 1587 he served as chief engineer and several years later became chief cosmographer; although provisionally named to this post in 1591, he did not actually assume its duties until 1596. Responsible for the technical aspects of navigation, he maintained in Lisbon a chair for the teaching of mathematics to sailors and pilots. He also inspected the maps and instruments used in navigation prepared in the cartography workshops and supervised the construction of astrolabes, quadrants, and compasses. In addition he was placed in charge of the examinations required of all who wished to become pilots, cartographers, or instrument makers for the navy.

The best-known of Lavanha's works is undoubtedly the *Regimento nautico* (1595; 2nd ed., 1606), which contains important texts for pilots, including rules for determining latitude and tables of the declination of the sun, corrected by Lavanha himself. Around 1600 Lavanha was the first to prepare tables of azimuths at rising and setting for the observation of magnetic declination by taking the rhumb line of the rising or setting of the sun with the magnetic compass.

As an engineer Lavanha carried out fieldwork for the tracing of topographical maps, the most important of which is the map of the kingdom of Aragon (1615–1618); to determine the coordinates of the fundamental points of the map Lavanha used a goniometer of his own design. This instrument was later perfected and proved very useful in surveying.

BIBLIOGRAPHY

I. Original Works. The *Regimento nautico* underwent two eds. during the author's lifetime (see text). Lavanha's other works are "Tratado da arte de navegar," library of the National Palace, Madrid, MS 1910; still unpublished, this MS contains Lavanha's lectures given at Madrid in 1588; *Naufrágio de nau S. Alberto* (Lisbon, 1597); *Itinerário do reino de Aragon* (Zaragoza, 1895), which contains the notes taken by Lavanha during his travels in the course of preparing the topographical map of Aragon; "Descripción del universo," National Library, Madrid, MS 9251, a brief and carefully done treatise on cosmography dedicated to the crown prince and dating from 1613; *Quarta década da Ásia* (Madrid, 1615), a new ed. of the work of the same title by João de Barros, rev. and completed by Lavanha; and *Viagem da catholica real magestade del rey D. Filipe N. S. ao reyno de Portugal e relação do solene recebimento que nelle se lhe fez* (Madrid, 1622), an account of the festivities held in honor of the visit of Philip II to Portugal. Lavanha also wrote on history and the nobility.

II. Secondary Literature. See Armando Cortesão, *Cartografia e cartógrafos portugueses dos séculos XVI e XVII*, II (Lisbon, 1935), 294–361; and Sousa Viterbo, *Trabalhos nauticos, dos Portugueses nos séculos XVI e XVII* (Lisbon, 1898), pp. 171–183.

LUÍS DE ALBUQUERQUE

LAX, GASPAR (*b.* Sariñena, Aragon, Spain, 1487; *d.* Zaragoza, Spain, 23 February 1560)

After studying the arts and theology in Zaragoza, Lax taught in Paris in 1507 and 1508 at the Collège de Calvi, also known as the "Little Sorbonne." He transferred to the Collège de Montaigu, where he continued to teach and to study under the Scottish master John Maior; in 1517 he returned to the Collège de Calvi. Lax had an agile mind and an excellent memory, but he became so engrossed with the logical subtleties of the nominalist school that he was soon known as "the Prince of the Parisian *sophistae*." A prolific writer, he turned out a series of ponderous tomes on *exponibilia, insolubilia,* and other topics of terminist logic. His student, the humanist Juan Luis Vives, later reported that he heard Lax and his colleague, John Dullaert of Ghent, moan over the years they had spent on such trivialities. Lax taught at Paris until 1523; possibly he returned to Spain in 1524, along with his countryman Juan de Celaya, when foreigners were asked to leave the university. In 1525 he taught mathematics and philosophy at the *studium generale* of Zaragoza. He remained there until his death, at which time he was vice-chancellor and rector.

Lax achieved greater fame as a mathematician than as a logician or as a philosopher. He published his *Arithmetica speculativa* and *Proportiones* at Paris in 1515 (Villoslada adds to these a *De propositionibus arithmeticis,* same place and date). The first is described by D. E. Smith as "a very prolix treatment of theoretical arithmetic, based on Boethius and his medieval successors" (p. 121). The *Proportiones* is a more compact and formalistic treatment of ratios, with citations of Euclid, Jordanus, and Campanus; unlike most sixteenth-century treatises on ratios, however, it does not deal with the velocities of motion in the Mertonian and Parisian traditions. Possibly Lax treated this interesting topic in his *Quaestiones phisicales,* printed at Zaragoza, 1527, according to early lists. (I have searched extensively for this, with no success.)

BIBLIOGRAPHY

None of Lax's works is translated from the Latin, and copies of the originals are rare; positive microfilms of the *Arithmetica speculativa* and various logical works are obtainable from the Vatican Library.

A brief general treatment of Lax is in R. G. Villoslada, S.J., *La universidad de Paris durante los estudios de Francisco de Vitoria (1507–1522).* Analecta Gregoriana XIV (Rome, 1938), pp. 404–407 and *passim.* See also Hubert Élie, "Quelques maîtres de l'université de Paris vers l'an 1500," in *Archives d'histoire doctrinale et littéraire du moyen âge,* **18** (1950–1951), 193–243, esp. 214–216.

Lax's logical and philosophical thought is treated by Marcial Solana, *Historia de la filosofía española, Época del Renacimiento (siglo XVI)* (Madrid, 1941), III, 19–33. His arithmetic is described in D. E. Smith, *Rara arithmetica* (Boston–London, 1908), p. 121.

WILLIAM A. WALLACE, O.P.

LEBESGUE, HENRI LÉON (*b*. Beauvais, France, 28 June 1875; *d*. Paris, France, 26 July 1941)

Lebesgue studied at the École Normale Supérieure from 1894 to 1897. His first university positions were at Rennes (1902–1906) and Poitiers (1906–1910). At the Sorbonne, he became *maître de conférences* (in mathematical analysis, 1910–1919) and then *professeur d'application de la géométrie à l'analyse.* In 1921 he was named professor at the Collège de France and the following year was elected to the Académie des Sciences.

Lebesgue's outstanding contribution to mathematics was the theory of integration that bears his name and that became the foundation for subsequent work in integration theory and its applications. After completing his studies at the École Normale Supérieure, Lebesgue spent the next two years working in its library, where he became acquainted with the work of another recent graduate, René Baire. Baire's unprecedented and successful researches on the theory of discontinuous functions of a real variable indicated to Lebesgue what could be achieved in this area. From 1899 to 1902, while teaching at the Lycée Centrale in Nancy, Lebesgue developed the ideas that he presented in 1902 as his doctoral thesis at the Sorbonne. In this work Lebesgue began to develop his theory of integration which, as he showed, includes within its scope all the bounded discontinuous functions introduced by Baire.

The Lebesgue integral is a generalization of the integral introduced by Riemann in 1854. As Riemann's theory of integration was developed during the 1870's and 1880's, a measure-theoretic viewpoint was gradually introduced. This viewpoint was made especially prominent in Camille Jordan's treatment of the Riemann integral in his *Cours d'analyse* (1893) and strongly influenced Lebesgue's outlook on these matters. The significance of placing integration theory within a measure-theoretic context was that it made it possible to see that a generalization of the notions of measure and measurability carries with it corresponding generalizations of the notions of the integral and integrability. In 1898 Émile Borel was led through his work on complex function theory to introduce radically different notions of measure and measurability. Some mathematicians found Borel's ideas lacking in appeal and relevance, especially since they involved assigning measure zero to some dense sets. Lebesgue, however, accepted them. He completed Borel's definitions of measure and measurability so that they represented generalizations of Jordan's definitions and then used them to obtain his generalization of the Riemann integral.

After the work of Jordan and Borel, Lebesgue's

generalizations were somewhat inevitable. Thus, W. H. Young and G. Vitali, independently of Lebesgue and of each other, introduced the same generalization of Jordan's theory of measure; in Young's case, it led to a generalization of the integral that was essentially the same as Lebesgue's. In Lebesgue's work, however, the generalized definition of the integral was simply the starting point of his contributions to integration theory. What made the new definition important was that Lebesgue was able to recognize in it an analytical tool capable of dealing with—and to a large extent overcoming—the numerous theoretical difficulties that had arisen in connection with Riemann's theory of integration. In fact, the problems posed by these difficulties motivated all of Lebesgue's major results.

The first such problem had been raised unwittingly by Fourier early in the nineteenth century: (1) If a bounded function can be represented by a trigonometric series, is that series the Fourier series of the function? Closely related to (1) is (2): When is the term-by-term integration of an infinite series permissible? Fourier had assumed that for bounded functions the answer to (2) is Always, and he had used this assumption to prove that the answer to (1) is Yes.

By the end of the nineteenth century it was recognized—and emphasized—that term-by-term integration is not always valid even for uniformly bounded series of Riemann-integrable functions, precisely because the function represented by the series need not be Riemann-integrable. These developments, however, paved the way for Lebesgue's elegant proof that term-by-term integration is permissible for any uniformly bounded series of Lebesgue-integrable functions. By applying this result to (1), Lebesgue was able to affirm Fourier's conclusion that the answer is Yes.

Another source of difficulties was the fundamental theorem of the calculus,

$$\int_a^b f'(x)\, dx = f(b) - f(a).$$

The work of Dini and Volterra in the period 1878–1881 made it clear that functions exist which have bounded derivatives that are not integrable in Riemann's sense, so that the fundamental theorem becomes meaningless for these functions. Later further classes of these functions were discovered; and additional problems arose in connection with Harnack's extension of the Riemann integral to unbounded functions because continuous functions with densely distributed intervals of invariability were discovered. These functions provided examples of Harnack-integrable derivatives for which the fundamental theorem is false. Lebesgue

showed that for bounded derivatives these difficulties disappear entirely when integrals are taken in his sense. He also showed that the fundamental theorem is true for an unbounded, finite-valued derivative f' that is Lebesgue-integrable and that this is the case if, and only if, f is of bounded variation. Furthermore, Lebesgue's suggestive observations concerning the case in which f' is finite-valued but not Lebesgue-integrable were successfully developed by Arnaud Denjoy, starting in 1912, using the transfinite methods developed by Baire.

The discovery of continuous monotonic functions with densely distributed intervals of invariability also raised the question: When is a continuous function an integral? The question prompted Harnack to introduce the property that has since been termed absolute continuity. During the 1890's absolute continuity came to be regarded as the characteristic property of absolutely convergent integrals, although no one was actually able to show that every absolutely continuous function is an integral. Lebesgue, however, perceived that this is precisely the case when integrals are taken in his sense.

A deeper familiarity with infinite sets of points had led to the discovery of the problems connected with the fundamental theorem. The nascent theory of infinite sets also stimulated an interest in the meaningfulness of the customary formula

$$L = \int_a^b [1 + (f')^2]^{1/2}$$

for the length of the curve $y = f(x)$. Paul du Bois-Reymond, who initiated an interest in the problem in 1879, was convinced that the theory of integration is indispensable for the treatment of the concepts of rectifiability and curve length within the general context of the modern function concept. But by the end of the nineteenth century this view appeared untenable, particularly because of the criticism and counterexamples given by Ludwig Scheeffer. Lebesgue was quite interested in this matter and was able to use the methods and results of his theory of integration to reinstate the credibility of du Bois-Reymond's assertion that the concepts of curve length and integral are closely related.

Lebesgue's work on the fundamental theorem and on the theory of curve rectification played an important role in his discovery that a continuous function of bounded variation possesses a finite derivative except possibly on a set of Lebesgue measure zero. This theorem gains in significance when viewed against the background of the century-long discussion of the differentiability properties of continuous functions. During roughly the first half of the nineteenth century, it was generally thought that continuous functions are differentiable at "most" points, although continuous functions were frequently assumed to be "piecewise" monotonic. (Thus, differentiability and monotonicity were linked together, albeit tenuously.) By the end of the century this view was discredited, and no less a mathematician than Weierstrass felt that there must exist continuous monotonic functions that are nowhere differentiable. Thus, in a sense, Lebesgue's theorem substantiated the intuitions of an earlier generation of mathematicians.

Riemann's definition of the integral also raised problems in connection with the traditional theorem positing the identity of double and iterated integrals of a function of two variables. Examples were discovered for which the theorem fails to hold. As a result, the traditional formulation of the theorem had to be modified, and the modifications became drastic when Riemann's definition was extended to unbounded functions. Although Lebesgue himself did not resolve this infelicity, it was his treatment of the problem that formed the foundation for Fubini's proof (1907) that the Lebesgue integral does make it possible to restore to the theorem the simplicity of its traditional formulation.

During the academic years 1902–1903 and 1904–1905, Lebesgue was given the honor of presenting the Cours Peccot at the Collège de France. His lectures, published as the monographs *Leçons sur l'intégration* . . . (1904) and *Leçons sur les séries trigonométriques* (1906), served to make his ideas better known. By 1910 the number of mathematicians engaged in work involving the Lebesgue integral began to increase rapidly. Lebesgue's own work—particularly his highly successful applications of his integral in the theory of trigonometric series—was the chief reason for this increase, but the pioneering research of others, notably Fatou, F. Riesz, and Fischer, also contributed substantially to the trend. In particular, Riesz's work on L^p spaces secured a permanent place for the Lebesgue integral in the theory of integral equations and function spaces.

Although Lebesgue was primarily concerned with his own theory of integration, he played a role in bringing about the development of the abstract theories of measure and integration that predominate in contemporary mathematical research. In 1910 he published an important memoir, "Sur l'intégration des fonctions discontinues," in which he extended the theory of integration and differentiation to n-dimensional space. Here Lebesgue introduced, and made fundamental, the notion of a countably additive set function (defined on Lebesgue-measurable sets) and observed in passing that such functions are of bounded variation on sets on which they take a finite value. By thus linking the notions of bounded variation and additivity, Lebesgue's observation suggested to Radon a definition of the integral that would include both the definitions of Lebesgue and Stieltjes as special cases. Radon's paper (1913), which soon led to further abstractions, indicated the viability of Lebesgue's ideas in a much more general setting.

By the time of his election to the Académie des Sciences in 1922, Lebesgue had produced nearly ninety books and papers. Much of this output was concerned with his theory of integration, but he also did significant work on the structure of sets and functions (later carried further by Lusin and others), the calculus of variations, the theory of surface area, and dimension theory.

For his contributions to mathematics Lebesgue received the Prix Houllevigue (1912), the Prix Poncelet (1914), the Prix Saintour (1917), and the Prix Petit d'Ormoy (1919). During the last twenty years of his life, he remained very active, but his writings reflected a broadening of interests and were largely concerned with pedagogical and historical questions and with elementary geometry.

BIBLIOGRAPHY

Lebesgue's most important writings are "Intégrale, longueur, aire," in *Annali di matematica pura ed applicata*, 3rd ser., **7** (1902), 231–359, his thesis; *Leçons sur l'intégration et la recherche des fonctions primitives* (Paris, 1904; 2nd ed., 1928); *Leçons sur les séries trigonométriques* (Paris, 1906); and "Sur l'intégration des fonctions discontinues," in *Annales scientifiques de l'École normale supérieure*, 3rd ser., **27** (1910), 361–450. A complete list of his publications to 1922 and an analysis of their contents is in Lebesgue's *Notice sur les travaux scientifiques de M. Henri Lebesgue* (Toulouse, 1922). Lebesgue's complete works are being prepared for publication by l'Enseignement Mathématique (Geneva).

Biographical information and references on Lebesgue can be obtained from K. O. May, "Biographical Sketch of Henri Lebesgue," in H. Lebesgue, *Measure and the Integral*, K. O. May, ed., (San Francisco, 1966), 1–7. For a discussion of Lebesgue's work on integration theory and its historical background, see T. Hawkins, *Lebesgue's Theory of Integration: Its Origins and Development* (Madison, Wis., 1970).

THOMAS HAWKINS

LEFSCHETZ, SOLOMON (*b*. Moscow, Russia, 3 September 1884; *d*. Princeton, New Jersey, 5 October 1972)

Lefschetz was the son of Alexander Lefschetz,

an importer, and his wife, Vera, who were Turkish citizens. Shortly after his birth the family moved to Paris, where he grew up with five brothers and one sister. French was his native tongue, but he learned Russian and other languages in later years. From 1902 to 1905 Lefschetz studied at the École Centrale, Paris, graduating as *ingenieur des arts et manufactures*. In November 1905 he emigrated to the United States and found a job at the Baldwin Locomotive Works near Philadelphia. In early 1907 he joined the engineering staff of the Westinghouse Electric and Manufacturing Company in Pittsburgh. In November of that year he lost his hands and forearms in a tragic accident.

Lefschetz soon realized that his true bent was mathematics, not engineering. Among his professors at the École Centrale had been Émile Picard and Paul Appell, authors of famous treatises on analysis and analytic mechanics that he now read. In 1910, while teaching apprentices at Westinghouse, Lefschetz determined to make his career in mathematics. He enrolled as a graduate student at Clark University, Worcester, Massachusetts, and obtained the Ph.D. in just one year with a dissertation on a problem in algebraic geometry proposed by W. E. Story. On 17 June 1912 Lefschetz became an American citizen, and on 3 July 1913 he married Alice Berg Hayes, a fellow student at Clark who had received a master's degree in mathematics. She helped him to overcome his handicap, encouraging him in his work and moderating his combative ebullience. They had no children.

From 1911 to 1913 Lefschetz was an instructor at the University of Nebraska, Lincoln, where he taught a heavy load of beginning courses but found ample time to pursue his own work in algebraic geometry. In 1913 he moved to a slightly better position at the University of Kansas in Lawrence. As his work became known in America and Europe, he rose through the ranks to become full professor in 1923. In 1919 he was awarded the Prix Bordin by the Académie des Sciences of Paris and in 1923 the Bôcher Memorial Prize of the American Mathematical Society.

In 1924 Lefschetz accepted a post at Princeton University, where he spent the rest of his life. He had prized the opportunity for solitary research at Nebraska and Kansas, but he welcomed the new world that opened up to him at Princeton. He acquired distinguished geometers as colleagues—James W. Alexander, Luther P. Eisenhart, Oswald Veblen—and met stimulating visitors from abroad, such as Pavel Aleksandrov, Heinz Hopf, M. H. A. Newman, and Hermann Weyl. His first (1926) of some

thirty doctoral students was the topologist-to-be Paul A. Smith, who had followed him to Princeton from Kansas.

From his Ph.D. to his appointment to the faculty of Princeton, Lefschetz worked mainly in algebraic geometry, his most important results being presented in his 1921 paper "On Certain Numerical Invariants of Algebraic Varieties with Application to Abelian Varieties" and in his 1924 monograph *L'analysis situs et la géométrie algébrique*. The study of the properties of families of algebraic curves and surfaces began in the nineteenth century as part of the theory of algebraic functions of complex variables. For Lefschetz, too, curves and surfaces—and, more generally, algebraic varieties—were significant representations of the corresponding functions. He was able to solve some of the problems encountered by his predecessors and to enlarge the scope of the subject by the use of new methods. As he put it, "It was my lot to plant the harpoon of algebraic topology into the body of the whale of algebraic geometry."

In the 1850's G. F. B. Riemann founded the modern theory of complex algebraic curves by considering, for each curve, an associated surface now called the Riemann surface. The theory was further developed by Guido Castelnuovo, Federigo Enriques, Francesco Severi, and especially Émile Picard. (Lefschetz, while at the École Central, had taken Picard's demanding course.) Riemann and these later mathematicians recognized that it is the topological properties of the Riemann surface (the connectedness properties of the surface as a whole rather than its metrical and local properties) that are significant, yet at the time there was no theory of such properties. In the 1890's Henri Poincaré established such a theory (under the name "analysis situs"), and Lefschetz used Poincaré's results to extend the work of Riemann and his successors.

Riemann had used a series of cuts to turn the Riemann surface into an open 2-cell (and the correspondence between the function and the 2-cell then gave the desired results); Lefschetz used a series of cuts to turn a nonsingular algebraic variety of complex dimension d into an open $2d$-cell. This allowed him to answer many questions (for example, he showed that not all orientable manifolds of even dimension are the carrier manifolds of algebraic varieties) and to extend the theory of integrals of the second kind to double and triple integrals on an algebraic variety of any dimension.

Lefschetz took up Poincaré's study of curves on a surface, which he generalized to the study of subvarieties of an algebraic variety. He found necessary and sufficient conditions for an integral (2d-2)-dimensional homology class of variety V of complex dimension d to contain the cycle of a divisor on V. This result and others allowed Lefschetz to make important contributions to the theory of correspondences between curves and to the theory of Abelian varieties. (A much more detailed review by W. V. D. Hodge of Lefschetz's work and influence in algebraic geometry appears in the volume *Algebraic Geometry and Topology.*)

According to Hodge, "Our greatest debt to Lefschetz lies in the fact that he showed us that a study of topology was essential for all algebraic geometers." Lefschetz' work in algebraic geometry also gave great impetus to the study of topology, since its value to other areas of mathematics had been demonstrated. In 1923 Lefschetz turned to the development of Poincaré's topology, calling it algebraic topology to distinguish it from the abstract topology of sets of points.

Almost all of Lefschetz' topology resulted from his desire to prove certain fixed-point theorems. Around 1910 L. E. J. Brouwer proved a basic fixed-point theorem: Every continuous transformation of an n-simplex into itself has at least one fixed point. In a series of papers Lefschetz obtained a much more general result: For any continuous transformation f of a topological space X into itself, there is a number $L(f)$, often called the Lefschetz number, such that if $L(f) \neq 0$, then the transformation f has a fixed point. $L(f)$ is defined as follows: f induces a transformation f_p of the pth homology group H_p of the space X into itself; consider H_p as a vector space over the rational numbers and let $\mathrm{Tr}(f_p)$ be the trace of f_p; then $L(f) = \Sigma\,(-1)^p\,\mathrm{Tr}(f_p)$. For $L(f)$ to be well defined, certain restrictions must be placed on X; Lefschetz succeeded in progressively weakening these restrictions.

Lefschetz used the following simple example to explain his fixed-point theorem. Let f be a continuous transformation of the interval $0 \leq x \leq 1$ into itself. The curve consisting of the points $(x, f(x))$ represents f. (See Figure 1.) The diagonal $0 \leq x = y \leq 1$ represents the identity transformation i, that is, the transformation that sends each point of the interval to itself. The points of intersection (called the coincidences) of f and i are the fixed points of f. We want a number that is the same for all continuous transformations of the interval $0 \leq x \leq 1$. The number of coincidences is not constant; f and g, for example, differ in this respect. But if, for a particular transformation, we count the number of crossings from *above* to below (marked a in the figure) and the number of crossings from *below* to

above (marked b in the figure), and if we subtract the latter from the former, we get a number (here, 1) that is the same for all continuous transformations of an interval into itself. That is, for this space (the interval $0 \leq x \leq 1$), the Lefschetz number $L(f)$ is 1. Since $L(f)$ is not zero, any continuous transformation of $0 \leq x \leq 1$ into itself has a fixed point. (It is intuitively clear that any continuous curve passing from the left side of the square to the right side must intersect the diagonal.)

In 1923 Lefschetz proved this fixed-point theorem for compact orientable manifolds. Since an n-cell is not a manifold, this result did not include the Brouwer fixed-point theorem. By introducing the concept of relative homology groups, Lefschetz in 1927 extended his theorem to manifolds with boundary; his theorem then included Brouwer's. He continued to seek generalizations of the theorem: in 1927 he proved it for any finite complex, and in 1936 for any locally connected space. Lefschetz studied fixed points as part of a more general study of coincidences. If f and g are transformations of space X into space Y, the points x of X such that $f(x) = g(x)$ are called the coincidences of f and g. One can prove that under certain conditions two transformations must have coincidences—for example, in Figure 1, if f and g are continuous and f is above g at 0 and below g at 1, then the number of times f crosses g from above to below (marked α) minus the number of times f crosses g from below to above (marked β) is necessarily 1.

In the course of this work Lefschetz invented many of the basic tools of algebraic topology. He made extensive use of product spaces; he developed intersection theory, including the theory of the intersection ring of a manifold; and he made essential contributions to various kinds of homology theory, notably relative homology, singular homology, and cohomology.

A by-product of Lefschetz' work on fixed points was his duality theorem, which provided a bridge between the classical duality theorems of Poincaré and of Alexander. The Lefschetz duality theorem states that the p-dimensional Betti number of an orientable n-dimensional manifold M with regular boundary L equals the $(n-p)$-dimensional Betti number of M modulo L (that is, without L). Figure 2 shows an oriented 2-manifold M with regular boundary L in three parts, one exterior and two interior. The absolute 1-cycles c_1 and c_2 generate the 1-dimensional Betti group of M with boundary L, and the relative 1-cycles d_1 and d_2 generate the relative 1-dimensional Betti group of M modulo L. Thus the 1-dimensional Betti numbers of M and M

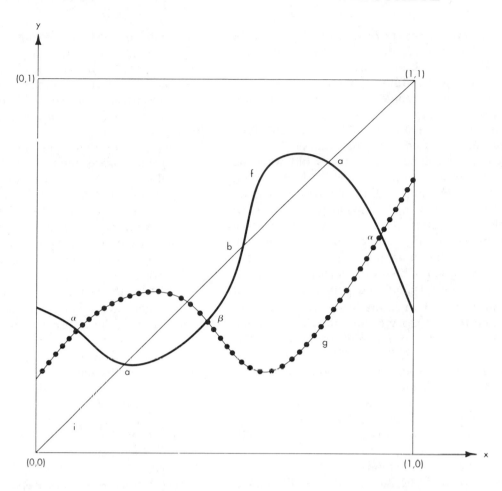

FIGURE 1.

modulo L are both 2. Cuts along d_1 and d_2 turn the 2-manifold into a 2-cell. (A full exposition of Lefschetz' fixed-point theorem and his duality theorem is in his *Introduction to Topology*, 1949.)

During his years as professor at Princeton (1924–1953), Lefschetz was the center of an active group of topologists. His *Topology* (1930) and his *Algebraic Topology* (1942) presented comprehensive accounts of the field and were extremely influential. Indeed, these books firmly established the use of the terms "topology" (rather than "analysis situs") and "algebraic topology" (rather than "combinatorial topology"). (A thorough review by Norman Steenrod of Lefschetz' work and influence in algebraic topology appears in *Algebraic Geometry and Topology*, 1957.)

Lefschetz was an editor of *Annals of Mathematics* from 1928 to 1958, and it was primarily his efforts—insisting on the highest standards, soliciting manuscripts, and securing rapid publication of the most important papers—that made the *Annals* one of the world's foremost mathematical journals. As Steenrod put it, "The importance to American mathematicians of a first-class journal is that it sets high standards for them to aim at. In this somewhat indirect manner, Lefschetz profoundly affected the development of mathematics in the United States."

There was another way in which Lefschetz contributed to the beginning of the publication of advanced mathematics in the United States. As late as the 1930's the American Mathematical Society, whose Colloquium Publications included books by Lefschetz in 1930 and 1942, was almost the only U.S. publisher of advanced mathematics books. However, two important series of advanced mathematics monographs and textbooks began in 1938 and 1940: the Princeton Mathematical Series and the Annals of Mathematics Studies, both initiated by A. W. Tucker, student and colleague of Lefschetz. Lefschetz wrote two important books for the former series (1949, 1953) and wrote or edited six books for the latter.

In 1943 Lefschetz was asked to consult for the U.S. Navy at the David Taylor Model Basin near Washington, D.C. Working with Nicholas Minorsky, he studied guidance systems and the stability of ships, and became acquainted with the work of Soviet mathematicians on nonlinear mechanics and control theory. Lefschetz recognized that the geometric theory of differential equations, which had begun with the work of Poincaré and A. M. Liapunov, could be fruitfully applied, and his background in algebraic geometry and topology proved useful. From 1943 to the end of his life, Lefschetz gave most of his attention to differential equations, doing research and encouraging others.

Lefschetz was almost sixty years old when he turned to differential equations, yet he did important original work. He studied the solutions of analytic differential equations near singular points and gave a complete characterization, for a two-dimensional system, of the solution curves passing through an isolated critical point in the neighborhood of the critical point. Much of his work focused on nonlinear differential equations and on dissipative (as distinct from conservative) dynamic systems. This work contributed to the theory of nonlinear controls and to the study of structural stability of systems. The Russian topologist L. S. Pontriagin, who was a good friend of Lefschetz' both before and after the war, also turned to control theory as a result of his wartime work. (Lawrence Markus' "Solomon Lefschetz: An Appreciation in Memoriam" contains a more detailed account of Lefschetz' work and influence on differential equations.)

In 1946 the newly established Office of Naval Research provided the funding for a differential equations project, directed by Lefschetz, at Princeton. This soon became a leading center for the study of ordinary differential equations, and the project continued at Princeton for five years after Lefschetz'

retirement in 1953. In 1957 he established a mathematics center under the auspices of the Research Institute for Advanced Study (RIAS), a branch of the Glen L. Martin Company of Baltimore (now Martin-Marietta). In 1964 Lefschetz and many of the other mathematicians in his group at RIAS moved to Brown University to form the Center for Dynamical Systems (later named the Lefschetz Center for Dynamical Systems). J. P. LaSalle, who had spent the year 1946–1947 with the differential equations project at Princeton and who was Lefschetz' second in command at RIAS, became director at the Brown center. Lefschetz helped to found the *Journal of Differential Equations* and served as an editor for some fifteen years. He continued his work at Brown until 1970.

Lefschetz translated two Russian books on differential equations into English, and he edited several volumes on nonlinear oscillations. He gave constant encouragement to his younger colleagues, in some cases cajoling them into proving important theorems. His work in differential equations showed the usefulness of geometric and topological methods and helped to raise the intellectual stature of applied mathematics.

Throughout his life Lefschetz loved to travel. In the 1920's and 1930's he made many trips to Europe, especially to France, Italy, and the Soviet Union. During World War II, European travel was impractical, so Lefschetz was visiting professor at the National University of Mexico (1944). Although he did not know Spanish when he arrived there, several weeks later he was giving his lectures in that lan-

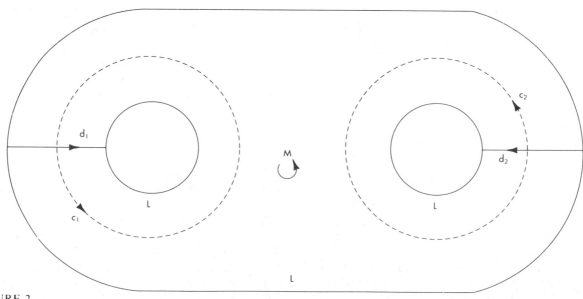

FIGURE 2.

guage. He returned for several months in the academic year 1945–1946, and in the following two decades made many trips to Mexico City, spending most winters there from 1953 to 1966. He helped to build a lively school of mathematics at the National University of Mexico, and in recognition of his efforts the Mexican government in 1964 awarded him the Order of the Aztec Eagle, rarely presented to a foreigner.

Lefschetz was Henry Burchard Fine (research) professor of mathematics at Princeton (1933–1953), succeeding Oswald Veblen, the first holder of the chair (1926–1932). He was chairman of the department of mathematics at Princeton from 1945 until his retirement in 1953. Lefschetz served as president of the American Mathematical Society (1935–1936). The Accademia Nazionale dei Lincei of Rome awarded him the Antonio Feltrinelli International Prize, one of the world's highest mathematical honors, in 1956. In 1964 he was awarded the National Medal of Science by President Johnson "for indomitable leadership in developing mathematics and training mathematicians, for fundamental publications in algebraic geometry and topology, and for stimulating needed research in nonlinear control processes." He was granted honorary degrees by Paris, Prague, Mexico, Clark, Brown, and Princeton. He was a member of the American Philosophical Society and of the National Academy of Sciences, and a foreign member of the Royal Society of London, of the Académie des Sciences of Paris, of the Academia Real de Ciencias of Madrid, and of the Reale Instituto Lombardo of Milan.

BIBLIOGRAPHY

I. ORIGINAL WORKS. Lefschetz' doctoral dissertation (Clark University, 1911). "On the Existence of Loci with Given Singularities," was published in *Transactions of the American Mathematical Society*, **14** (1913), 23–41. Major works include *L'analysis situs et la géométrie algébrique* (Paris, 1924; repr. 1950); *Topology* (New York, 1930; 2nd ed., 1956); *Algebraic Topology* (New York, 1942); *Introduction to Topology* (Princeton, 1949); *Algebraic Geometry* (Princeton, 1953); *Differential Equations: Geometric Theory* (New York, 1957; 2nd ed., 1962); *Stability by Liapunov's Direct Method* (New York, 1961), written with Joseph P. LaSalle; *Stability of Nonlinear Automatic Control Systems* (New York, 1964); and *Applications of Algebraic Topology* (New York, 1975). A vivid self-portrait of Lefschetz is "Reminiscences of a Mathematical Immigrant in the United States," in *American Mathematical Monthly*, **77** (1970), 344–350.

Selected Papers (New York, 1971) brings together "A Page of Mathematical Autobiography," in *Bulletin of the American Mathematical Society*, **74** (1968), 854–879,

awarded the society's 1970 Leroy P. Steele Prize; "On Certain Numerical Invariants of Algebraic Varieties with Application to Abelian Varieties," in *Transactions of the American Mathematical Society*, **22** (1921), 327–482, awarded the society's 1924 Bôcher Memorial Prize and, in its original French version, the 1919 Prix Bordin of the Paris Academy of Sciences; the 1924 monograph cited above; 16 other principal papers; and a bibliography (to 1970). The paper "The Early Development of Algebraic Topology," in *Boletim da Sociedade brasileira de matematica*, **1** (1971), 1–48, summarizes Lefschetz' view of the development of algebraic topology.

Lefschetz' works are listed in Poggendorff, V, 723; VI, 1488; VIIb, 2802–2804.

II. SECONDARY LITERATURE. On Lefschetz and his work see Raymond C. Archibald, *A Semicentennial History of the American Mathematical Society* (New York, 1938), 236–240; R. H. Fox, D. C. Spencer, and A. W. Tucker, eds., *Algebraic Geometry and Topology* (Princeton, 1957), 1–49; Philip Griffiths, Donald C. Spencer, and George W. Whitehead, "Solomon Lefschetz," in *Biographical Memoirs, National Academy of Sciences*, **61** (1990); Sir William Hodge, "Solomon Lefschetz, 1884–1972," in *Biographical Memoirs of Fellows of the Royal Society*, **19** (1973), 433–453, repr. in *Bulletin of the London Mathematical Society*, **6** (1974), 198–217, and in *The Lefschetz Centennial Conference*, pt. 1, *Proceedings on Algebraic Geometry*, D. Sundararaman, ed. (Providence, R.I., 1986), 27–46; and Lawrence Markus, "Solomon Lefschetz: An Appreciation in Memoriam," in *Bulletin of the American Mathematical Society*, **79** (1973), 663–680. These memoirs all contain bibliographies. Markus also cites the reviews of Lefschetz' publications in *Mathematical Reviews*. Other memoirs are Sir William Hodge, "Solomon Lefschetz, 1884–1972," in *American Philosophical Society Year Book, 1974* (1975), 186–193; and Joseph P. LaSalle, "Memorial to Solomon Lefschetz," in *IEEE Transactions on Automatic Control*, **AC-18** (1973), 89–90, and "Solomon Lefschetz: A Memorial Address," in *Dynamical Systems*, I, Lamberto Cesari, Jack K. Hale, and Joseph P. LaSalle, eds. (New York, 1976), xvii–xxi. Also see *National Cyclopedia of American Biography*, LVI (Clifton, N.J., 1975), 503–504.

ALBERT W. TUCKER
FREDERIK NEBEKER

LEGENDRE, ADRIEN-MARIE (*b.* Paris, France, 18 September 1752; *d.* Paris, 9 January 1833)

Legendre, who came from a well-to-do family, studied in Paris at the Collège Mazarin (also called Collège des Quatre-Nations). He received an education in science, especially mathematics, that was unusually advanced for Paris schools in the eighteenth century. His mathematics teacher was the Abbé Joseph-

François Marie, a mathematician of some renown and well-regarded at court. In 1770, at the age of eighteen, Legendre defended his theses in mathematics and physics at the Collège Mazarin. In 1774 Marie utilized several of his essays in a treatise on mechanics.

Legendre's modest fortune was sufficient to allow him to devote himself entirely to research. Nevertheless he taught mathematics at the École Militaire in Paris from 1775 to 1780.

In 1782 Legendre won the prize of the Berlin Academy. The subject of its competition that year concerned exterior ballistics: "Determine the curve described by cannonballs and bombs, taking into consideration the resistance of the air; give rules for obtaining the ranges corresponding to different initial velocities and to different angles of projection." His essay, which was published in Berlin, attracted the attention of Lagrange, who asked Laplace for information about the young author. A few years later the Abbé Marie and Legendre arranged for Lagrange's *Mécanique analytique* (Paris, 1788) to be published and saw it through the press.

Meanwhile, Legendre sought to make himself better known in French scientific circles, particularly at the Académie des Sciences. He conducted research on the mutual attractions of planetary spheroids and on their equilibrium forms. In January 1783 he read a memoir on this problem before the Academy; it was published in the *Recueil des savants étrangers* (1785). He also submitted to Laplace essays on second-degree indeterminate equations, on the properties of continued fractions, on probabilities, and on the rotation of bodies subject to no accelerating force. As a result, on 30 March 1783 he was elected to the Academy as an *adjoint mécanicien*, replacing Laplace, who had been promoted to *associé*.

Legendre's scientific output continued to grow. In July 1784 he read before the Academy his "Recherches sur la figure des planètes." Upon the publication of this memoir, he recalled that Laplace had utilized his works in a study published in the *Mémoires de l'Académie des sciences* for 1782 (published in 1784) but written after his own, which allowed "M. de Laplace to go more deeply into this matter and to present a complete theory of it." The famous "Legendre polynomials" first appeared in these 1784 "Recherches."

The "Recherches d'analyse indéterminée" (1785) contains, among other things, the demonstration of a theorem that allows decision on the possibility or impossibility of solution of every second-degree indeterminate equation; an account of the law of reciprocity of quadratic residues and of its many applications; the sketch of a theory of the decomposi-

tion of numbers into three squares; and the statement of a theorem that later became famous: "Every arithmetical progression whose first term and ratio are relatively prime contains an infinite number of prime numbers."

In 1786 Legendre presented a study on the manner of distinguishing maxima from minima in the calculus of variations. The "Legendre conditions" set forth in this paper later gave rise to an extensive literature. Legendre next published, in the *Mémoires de l'Académie* for 1786, two important works on integrations by elliptic arcs and on the comparison of these arcs; here can be found the rudiments of his theory of elliptic functions.

In the works cited above, Legendre had marked off his favorite areas of research: celestial mechanics, number theory, and the theory of elliptic functions. Although he did take up other problems in the course of his life, he always returned to these subjects.

Legendre's career at the Academy proceeded without any setbacks. On the reorganization of the mechanics section he was promoted to *associé* (1785). In 1787, along with Cassini IV and Méchain, he was assigned by the Academy to the geodetic operations undertaken jointly by the Paris and Greenwich observatories. On this occasion he became a fellow of the Royal Society. His work on this project found expression in the "Mémoire sur les opérations trigonométriques dont les résultats dépendent de la figure de la terre." Here are found "Legendre's theorem" on spherical triangles:

> When the sides of a triangle are very small in relation to the radius of the sphere, it differs very little from a rectilinear triangle. If one subtracts from each of its angles a third of the excess of the sum of the three angles over [the sum of] two right angles, the angles, diminished in this manner, may be considered those of a rectilinear triangle whose sides are equal in length to those of the given triangle.

This memoir also contains his method of indeterminate corrections:

> In these calculations there exist some elements that are susceptible to a slight uncertainty. In order to make the calculation only once, and in order to determine the influence of the errors at a glance, I have supposed the value of each principal element to be augmented by an indeterminate quantity that designates the required correction. These literal quantities, which are considered to be very small, do not prevent one from carrying out the calculation by logarithms in the usual manner.

In the *Mémoires de l'Académie* for 1787 Legendre published an important theoretical work stimulated by Monge's studies of minimal surfaces. Entitled "L'intégration de quelques équations aux différences partielles," it contains the Legendre transformation. Given the partial differential equation

$$R \frac{\partial^2 z}{\partial x^2} + S \frac{\partial^2 z}{\partial x \, \partial y} + T \frac{\partial^2 z}{\partial y^2} = 0.$$

Set $\partial z/\partial x = p$ and $\partial z/\partial y = q$. Suppose R, S, T are functions of p and q only. Legendre is concerned with the plane tangent to the surface being sought: $z = f(x, y)$. The equation of this plane being $pX + qY - Z - v = 0$, he shows that v satisfies the equation

$$R \frac{\partial^2 v}{\partial q^2} - S \frac{\partial^2 v}{\partial p \, \partial q} + T \frac{\partial^2 v}{\partial p^2} = 0.$$

Later, in volume II of his *Traité des fonctions elliptiques* (1826), Legendre employed an analogous procedure to demonstrate "the manner of expressing every integral as an arc length of a curve." If $\int p d\omega$ is the integral in question (p being a function of ω), he shows that the arc length of the envelope of the family of straight lines $x \cos \omega + y \sin \omega - p = 0$ is equal to $\int p d\omega + p'$, where p' is the derivative of p with respect to ω.

In 1789 and 1790 Legendre presented his "Mémoire sur les intégrales doubles," in which he completed his analysis of the attraction of spheroids; a study of the case of heterogeneous spheroids, and some investigations of the particular integrals of differential equations.

In April 1792 Legendre read before the Academy an important study on elliptic transcendentals, a more systematic account of material presented in his first works on the question, dating from 1786. The academies were suppressed in August 1793; consequently he published this study himself, toward the end of the same year, in a quarto volume of more than a hundred pages.

The times were difficult for everyone and for Legendre in particular. He may even have been obliged to hide for a time. In any case his "small fortune" disappeared, and he was obliged to find work, especially since he had married a girl of nineteen, Marguerite Couhin. He later wrote to Jacobi:

> I married following a bloody revolution that had destroyed my small fortune; we had great problems and some very difficult moments, but my wife staunchly helped me to put my affairs in order little by little and gave me the tranquillity necessary for my customary work and for writing new works that have steadily increased my reputation.

On 13 April 1791 Legendre had been named one of the Academy's three commissioners for the astronomical operations and triangulations necessary for determining the standard meter. His colleagues were Méchain and Cassini IV, who four years earlier had participated with him in the geodetic linking of the Paris and Greenwich meridians. On 17 March 1792, however, Legendre had requested to be relieved of this assignment. In ventôse *an* II (February–March 1794) the Commission of Public Instruction of the department of Paris appointed him professor of pure mathematics at the short-lived Institut de Marat, formerly the Collège d'Harcourt. During 1794 he was head of the first office of the National Executive Commission of Public Instruction (the second section, Sciences and Letters). He had eight employees under him and was expected to concern himself with weights and measures, inventions and discoveries, and the encouragement of science.

A tireless worker, during this same period Legendre published his *Éléments de géométrie*. This textbook was to dominate elementary instruction in the subject for almost a century. On 29 vendémiaire *an* II (20 October 1793) the Committee of Public Instruction, of which Legendre soon became senior clerk, commissioned him and Lagrange to write a book entitled *Éléments de calcul et de géométrie*. Actually his work must already have been nearly finished. He had probably been working on it for several years, encouraged perhaps by Condorcet, who stated in 1791, in his *Mémoires sur l'instruction publique:* "I have often spoken of elementary books written for children and for adults, of works designed to serve as guides for teachers. . . . Perhaps it is of some use to mention here that I had conceived the project for these works and prepared the means necessary to execute them. . . ."

In the meantime the decimal system had been adopted for the measurement of angles; and the survey offices, under the direction of Prony, undertook to calculate the sines of angles in ten-thousandths of a right angle, correct to twenty-two decimal places; the logarithms of sines in hundred-thousandths of a right angle, correct to twelve decimal places; and the logarithms of numbers from 1 to 200,000, also to twelve decimal places. In 1802 Legendre wrote: "These three tables, constructed by means of new techniques based principally on the calculus of differences, are one of the most beautiful monuments ever erected to science." Prony had them drawn up rapidly through a division of labor that permitted him to employ people with low qualifications. The work was prepared by a section of analysts headed by Legendre, who devised new formulas for determining the successive differences of the sines. The other sections had only to perform additions. This collective work resulted in two completely independent copies of the tables, which were mutually verified by their identity. These manuscript tables were deposited at the Bureau des Longitudes. An explanatory article appeared in the *Mémoires de l'Institut* (1801).

Legendre figured neither among the professors of the *écoles normales* of *an* III nor among those of the École Polytechnique. He did, however, succeed Laplace, in 1799, as examiner in mathematics of the graduating students assigned to the artillery. He held this position until 1815, when he voluntarily resigned and was replaced by Prony. He was granted a pension of 3,000 francs, equal to half his salary. He lost it in 1824 following his refusal to vote for the official candidate in an election for a seat in the Institute.

Legendre was not one of the forty-eight scholars selected in August 1795 to form the nucleus of the Institut National, but on 13 December he was elected a resident member in the mathematics section. In 1808, upon the creation of the University, he was named a *conseiller titulaire*. A member of the Legion of Honor, he also obtained the title of Chevalier de l'Empire—a minor honor compared with the title of count bestowed on his colleagues Lagrange, Laplace, and Monge. When Lagrange died in 1813, Legendre replaced him at the Bureau des Longitudes, where he remained for the rest of his life.

We now return to Legendre's scientific publications. The first edition of his *Essai sur la théorie des nombres* appeared in 1798. In it he took up in a more systematic and more thorough fashion the topics covered in his "Recherches" of 1785.

His *Nouvelles méthodes pour la détermination des orbites des comètes* (1806) contains, in a supplement, the first statement and the first published application of the method of least squares. Gauss declared in his *Theoria motus corporum coelestium* (1809) that he himself had been using this method since 1795. This assertion, which was true, infuriated Legendre, who returned to the subject in 1811 and 1820.

Legendre had been dismayed once before by Gauss: in 1801 the latter attributed to himself the law of reciprocity of quadratic residues, which Legendre had stated in 1785. Later, in 1827, Legendre wrote to Jacobi: "How has M. Gauss dared to tell you that the majority of your theorems [on elliptic functions] were known to him and that he had discovered them as early as 1808? This excessive impudence is unbelievable in a man who has sufficient personal merit not to have need of appropriating the discoveries of others."

Both Legendre in his indignation and Gauss in his priority claims were acting in good faith. Gauss considered that a theorem was his if he gave the first rigorous demonstration of it. Legendre, twenty-five years his senior, had a much broader and often a hazier sense of rigor. For Legendre, a belated disciple of Euler, an argumentation that was merely plausible often took the place of a proof. Consequently all discussion of priority between the two resembled a dialogue of the deaf.

In "Analyse des triangles tracés sur la surface d'un sphéroïde" (read before the Institute in March 1806), in which he considered the triangles formed by the geodesics of an ellipsoid of revolution, Legendre generalized his theorem concerning spherical triangles. Gauss provided a much broader generalization of this theorem in 1827, in his "Disquisitiones generales circa superficies curvas."

Legendre brought out the second edition of *Essai sur la théorie des nombres* in 1808. He later wrote two supplements to it (1816, 1825).

The "Recherches sur diverses sortes d'intégrales définies" (1809) continued an early study of Eulerian integrals—the term is Legendre's—in particular of the "gamma function." The earlier work appeared in 1793, in *Mémoire sur les transcendantes elliptiques*. The investigations of 1809 were, in turn, revised, completed, and enlarged in later works devoted to elliptic functions (1811, 1816, 1817, 1826).

Volume I of the *Exercices de calcul intégral* (1811) contains a majority of the results that Legendre obtained in the study of elliptic integrals. Volume III was published in 1816. Volume II, which includes the important numerical tables of the elliptic integrals, appeared in 1817.

In 1823 Legendre published "Recherches sur quelques objets d'analyse indéterminée et particulièrement sur le théorème de Fermat" in *Mémoires de l'Académie*. It contains a beautiful demonstration of the impossibility of an integral solution of the equation $x^5 + y^5 = z^5$, followed by an examination of more complicated cases of the theorem. This memoir was reproduced as the second supplement to the *Essai sur la théorie des nombres* (1825).

In 1825 and 1826, in *Traité des fonctions elliptiques*, Legendre took up once more and developed the essential aspects of his 1811 work, including applications to geometry and mechanics. In 1827, however, Jacobi informed Legendre of his own discoveries in this area. The latter, inspired by the contributions of his correspondent and by those of Abel, published three supplements to his *Théorie des fonctions elliptiques* (the title of volume I of the *Traité*) in rapid succession (1828, 1829, 1832).

In May 1830 the third edition of Legendre's

Théorie des nombres appeared. In this two-volume work he developed the material of the *Essai* of 1808, adding new thoughts inspired, to a large extent, by Gauss. Jacobi drew his attention to a weak point in his reasoning, and on 11 October 1830 Legendre presented a corrected memoir that appeared in 1832 in the Academy's *Mémoires*. Shortly before his death he referred to this memoir as a necessary complement and conclusion to his *Traité* and expressed the need for printing it at the end of that work. His wish was not fulfilled.

The "Réflexions sur différentes manières de démontrer la théorie des parallèles ou le théorème sur la somme des trois angles du triangle" appeared in the *Mémoires* in 1833. Legendre had already sent a separately printed copy of it to Jacobi at the end of June 1832.

Legendre died on 9 January 1833, following a painful illness. His health had been failing for several years. His wife, who died in December 1856, made a cult of his memory and until her death displayed a naïve, religious respect for everything that had belonged to him. She left to the village of Auteuil (now part of Paris) the last country house in which they had lived. They had no children.

We shall now return to the three main fields treated in Legendre's works: number theory, elliptic functions, and elementary geometry—more particularly, the theory of parallel lines.

Number Theory. In the introduction to the second edition of his *Théorie des nombres* (1808) Legendre exhibited an admirable concern for rigor. For example, he demonstrated the commutativity of the product of integers by a technique related to Fermat's method of infinite descent. A direct disciple of Euler and Lagrange, he, like them, made frequent use of the algorithm of continued fractions, as much to solve first-degree indeterminate equations as to show that Fermat's equation $x^2 - Ay^2 = 1$ always admits an integral solution.

Moreover, Legendre followed Lagrange step by step in the study of quadratic forms, a study that he completed in some respects. He showed, for example, that every odd number not of the form $8k + 7$ is the sum of three squares. (He had shown this imperfectly as early as 1785 and in a nearly satisfactory manner in 1798.) On the basis of this result, Cauchy, in 1812, demonstrated Fermat's theorem for the case of polygonal numbers.

Legendre's principal contribution was the law of reciprocity of quadratic residues. He stated it as early as 1785, when he produced a very long and imperfect demonstration of it. In 1801 Gauss subjected it to a thorough criticism and was able to declare that

he was the first to have demonstrated the proposition rigorously. In 1808, while preserving his first exposition, improved in 1798, Legendre adopted the proof given by his young critic. In 1830 he added to it that of Jacobi, which he found superior.

We have already mentioned Legendre's contributions to the study of Fermat's great theorem concerning the impossibility of finding an integral solution of the equation $x^n + y^n + z^n = 0$. In this connection he had met Dirichlet, a young mathematician of great promise.

A very skillful calculator, Legendre furnished valuable tables listing the quadratic and linear divisors of quadratic forms and the least solutions of Fermat's equation $x^2 - Ay^2 = \pm 1$. For the latter table, published in 1798 and reproduced in a much abridged form in 1808, he later (1830) utilized the corrections made by the Danish mathematician C. F. Degen.

Legendre should be considered a precursor of analytic number theory. His law of the distribution of prime numbers, outlined in 1798 and made more precise in 1808, took the following form: If y is the number of prime numbers less than x, then $y = \dfrac{x}{\log x - 1.08366}$. He found it, he stated, by induction. In 1830 he pointed out again that it had been found through induction and that "it remains to demonstrate it a priori"; and he developed some observations on this subject in a manner similar to Euler's. About 1793 Gauss intuited the law of the asymptotic distribution of prime numbers, which could have occurred to any attentive reader of Euler. But it was Legendre who first drew attention to this remarkable law, which was not truly demonstrated until 1896 (by Charles de la Vallée Poussin and Jacques Hadamard).

On the other hand, Legendre thought he had demonstrated, as early as 1785, that in every arithmetic progression $ax + b$ where a and b are relative primes, there is an infinite number of primes. He even specified that in giving to b the $\varphi(a)$ values prime to a and less than this number ($\varphi(a)$ being Euler's indicatrix), the prime numbers are distributed almost equally among the $\varphi(a)$ distinct progressions. These propositions were first rigorously demonstrated by Dirichlet in 1837.

Giving a rather broad scope to number theory, Legendre sought in 1830 to present Abel's conceptions concerning the algebraic solution of equations. Legendre thought it had been convincingly proved that such a solution is in general impossible for degrees higher than the fourth. He was also interested in the numerical solution of equations. In particular he studied the separation of roots and their expansion as continued fractions. In 1808 he presented a demonstration of the fundamental theorem of algebra that was quite analogous to that given by J. R. Argand in 1806. These essentially correct analytical demonstrations required only a few restatements to be made rigorous.

It should be noted that in 1806 Legendre's attitude toward Argand was very understanding. He did not publicly adopt the latter's ideas on the geometric representation of complex numbers; but thanks to the letter that he wrote to François Argand concerning his brother's discovery, that discovery was not lost, and in 1813 it reached a large audience through Gergonne's *Annales*.

In note 4 of his *Éléments de géométrie*—a note included in the first editions of the work—Legendre, by employing the algorithm of continued fractions, established Lambert's theorem (1761): the ratio of the circumference of a circle to its diameter is an irrational number. He improved this result by showing that the square of this ratio is also irrational, and added: "It is probable that the number π is not even included in the algebraic irrationals, but it appears to be very difficult to demonstrate this proposition rigorously."

Much attracted throughout his life by number theory, Legendre was well aware of the difficulties it presents and in his last years experienced a sort of disenchantment with it. For example, in 1828 he wrote to Jacobi: "I would advise you not to give too much time to investigations of this nature: they are very difficult and are often fruitless."

Number theory, of course, does not constitute the most significant portion of his *oeuvre*. Instead, he should be considered the founder of the theory of elliptic functions. MacLaurin and d'Alembert had studied integrals expressible by arcs of an ellipse or a hyperbola. Fagnano had shown that to any given ellipse or hyperbola two arcs the difference of which equals an algebraic quantity can be assigned in an infinite number of ways (1716). He had also demonstrated that the arcs of Bernoulli's lemniscate $(x^2 + y^2)^2 = a^2(x^2 - y^2)$ can be multiplied and divided algebraically like the arcs of a circle. This was the first demonstration of the use of the simplest of the elliptic integrals, the one later designated by Legendre as $F(x)$ and considered by him to govern all the others.

In 1761 Euler had found the complete algebraic integral of a differential equation composed of two separate but similar terms, each of which is integrable only by arcs of conics: $\dfrac{dx}{R(x)} + \dfrac{dy}{R(y)} = 0$, R being the square root of a fourth-degree polynomial. This discovery, made almost by chance, allowed Euler to compare—in a more general manner than had ever

been done previously—not only arcs of the same conic section or lemniscate but also, in general, all the transcendentals $\int \dfrac{P\,dx}{R}$, where P is a rational function of x and R is the square root of a fourth-degree polynomial.

In 1768 Lagrange undertook to incorporate Euler's discovery into the ordinary procedures of analysis and, in 1784 and 1785, he presented a general method for finding the integrals $\int \dfrac{P\,dx}{R}$ by approximation. Meanwhile, John Landen had demonstrated in 1775 that every arc of a hyperbola can be measured by two arcs of an ellipse. As a result of this memorable discovery the term "Landen's theorem" was applied not only to this result but also to the first known transformation of elliptic integrals.

Such was the state of research in the theory of elliptic transcendentals in 1786, when Legendre published his works on integration by elliptic arcs. The first portion of these, written before he had become aware of Landen's discoveries, contained new ideas concerning the use of elliptic arcs, notably a method of avoiding the use of hyperbolic arcs by replacing them with a suitably constructed table of elliptic arcs. He then gave a new demonstration of Landen's theorem and proved by the same method that every given ellipse is part of an infinite sequence of ellipses, related in such a way that by the rectification of two arbitrarily chosen ellipses the rectification of all the others is obtained. With this theorem it was possible to reduce the rectification of a given ellipse to that of two others differing arbitrarily little from a circle.

But this topic, and the theory of elliptic transcendentals in general, required a more systematic treatment. This is what Legendre, who was virtually alone in his interest in the problem, attempted to provide in his "Mémoire sur les transcendantes elliptiques" (1793). He proposed to compare all functions of this type, classify them into different species, reduce each one to the simplest possible form, evaluate them by the easiest and most rapid approximations, and create a sort of algorithm from the theory as a whole.

Later research having enabled him to perfect this theory in several respects, Legendre returned to it in the *Exercices* of 1811. On this occasion he gave his theory a trigonometric appearance. Setting $\varDelta = \sqrt{1 - c^2 \sin^2 \varphi}$, with $0 \leqslant c \leqslant 1$, he calls c the modulus of the function. The integral being taken from 0 to φ, φ is called its amplitude; $\sqrt{(1 - c^2)} = b$ is the complement of the modulus. The simplest of the elliptic transcendentals is the integral of the first kind: $F(\varphi) = \int \dfrac{d\varphi}{\varDelta}$. The integral of the second kind, which is representable by an elliptic arc of major axis 1 and eccentricity c, takes the form $E(\varphi) = \int \Delta d\varphi$. The integral of the third kind is

$$\Pi(\varphi) = \int \frac{d\varphi}{(1 + \eta \sin^2 \varphi)\,\Delta},$$

with parameter n. Every elliptic integral can be expressed as a combination of these three types of transcendentals.

Let φ and ψ be two variables linked by the differential equation

$$\frac{d\varphi}{\sqrt{1 - c^2 \sin^2 \varphi}} + \frac{d\psi}{\sqrt{1 - c^2 \sin^2 \psi}} = 0.$$

The integral of the equation is $F(\varphi) + F(\psi) = F(\mu)$, μ being an arbitrary constant. Euler's theorem gives

$$\cos \varphi \cos \psi - \sin \varphi \sin \psi \sqrt{1 - c^2 \sin^2 \mu} = \cos \mu.$$

Thus it allows μ to be found algebraically, such that $F(\varphi) + F(\psi) = F(\mu)$, and then $F(\varphi)$ to be multiplied by an arbitrary number, whole or rational. From these observations Legendre deduced many consequences for each of the three kinds of integrals.

Furthermore, by designating the integral of the first kind with modulus c and amplitude φ as $F(c, \varphi)$, Legendre was able, with the aid of Landen's theorem, to establish the transformation later called quadratic.

Thus, if $\sin(2\varphi' - \varphi) = c \sin \varphi$ and if $c' = \dfrac{2 \sqrt{c}}{1 + c}$, then $F(c', \varphi') = \dfrac{1 + c}{2} F(c, \varphi)$. Through repeated use of this transformation Legendre constructed and published (1817) his tables of elliptic functions. In 1825 he wrote:

> To render the theory wholly useful it remained to construct a series of tables by means of which one could find, in every given case, the numerical value of the functions. These tables have finally been constructed, after a multitude of investigations undertaken with a view toward discovering the methods and formulas most suitable to diminishing the length and difficulty of the calculations.

The work Legendre published in 1826, volume II of *Traité des fonctions elliptiques*, contains nine of these tables. The last one is "the general table of the functions F and E for each [sexagesimal] degree of the amplitude φ and of the angle of the modulus θ ($\sin \theta = c$) to ten decimal places for θ less than $45°$ and nine for θ between $45°$ and $90°$." He wrote to Jacobi regarding these enormous computations that he carried out unassisted: "My goal has always been to introduce into calculation new elements that one can work with in arbitrary numbers, and I devoted myself to an exceedingly long and tedious task in order to construct the tables, a task I do not hesitate to believe is as considerable as that of Briggs's great tables."

Volume II of the *Traité* (1826) includes material on the construction of elliptic functions that is of the greatest interest from the point of view of numerical analysis. In particular Legendre presents a symbolic calculus, inspired by Lagrange, linking the expansion of a function by Taylor's formula with the calculation of its finite differences of various orders. Other investigations of this topic may be found in the analogous studies by Arbogast and Kramp, and by the students of Hindenburg. The same volume of the *Traité* lists—to twelve decimal places—the logarithms of the values of the gamma function $\Gamma(x)$ when x varies in thousandths of an integer and ranges from 1 to 2 inclusively.

In the meantime, around 1825, chance led Legendre to examine two functions F linked by relationships between their moduli, on the one hand, and their amplitudes, on the other—relationships that do not arise in the context of Landen's transformation. In generalizing these relationships Legendre discovered a new transformation closely related to the trisection of the function F. This trisection necessitated the solution of a ninth-degree algebraic equation. The new transformation reduced this solution to that of two third-degree equations.

In 1827, however, Jacobi (whose correspondence with Legendre, always of the greatest scientific and human interest, continued until 1832) communicated to Legendre his own discoveries and also informed him of Abel's. Legendre's attitude in the face of the discoveries of his young rivals was remarkable for its enthusiasm and forthrightness. In the foreword to volume III of his *Traité* he announced:

> A young geometer, M. Jacobi of Koenigsberg, who was not aware of the *Traité* [but who, it should be added, was familiar, like Abel, with the *Exercices* of 1811], has succeeded, through his own investigations, in discovering not only the second transformation, which is related to the number 3, but a third related to the number 5, and he has already become certain that there must exist a similar one for every given odd number.

Legendre also drew attention to Abel's memoirs and analyzed their content. Legendre's first two supplements are devoted primarily to Jacobi's works but also to those of Abel, which contained the first appearance of modern elliptic functions, the inverse functions of the Legendre integrals. Legendre discussed their extension to the complex domain and their double periodicity in his usual somewhat ponderous style. The third supplement deals mainly with Abel and his great theorem. Legendre concluded his work on 4 March 1832: "We have only touched the surface of this subject, but it may be supposed that it will be steadily enriched by the works of mathematicians and that eventually it will constitute one of the most beautiful parts of the analysis of transcendental functions."

In 1869 Charles Hermite made the following judgment concerning Legendre's writings: "Legendre, who for so many reasons is considered the founder of the theory of elliptic functions, greatly smoothed the way for his successors; it is the fact of the double periodicity of the inverse function, immediately discovered by Abel and Jacobi, that is missing and that gave such a restrained analytical character to his *Traité des fonctions elliptiques*."

Legendre's *Éléments de géométrie* long dominated elementary instruction in the subject through its numerous editions and translations. Quite dogmatic in its presentation, this work marked a partial return to Euclid in France. The notes that accompany and enrich the text still have a certain interest. The text itself, virtually unchanged since the first edition, does not take into account the various contributions made by Monge's disciples. The *Éléments* is above all a typical example of the difficulties encountered by the advocates of non-Euclidean geometries in their struggle to gain acceptance for their conceptions. The first published work of János Bolyai dates from 1832 and is thus contemporary with "Réflexions . . . sur la théorie des parallèles . . .," in which Legendre recalled the efforts (all unsuccessful although he was not convinced of this) that he made between 1794 and 1823 to demonstrate Euclid's postulate. Let us first mention two very positive achievements that date from 1800. First: "The sum of the three angles of a rectilinear triangle cannot be greater than two right angles," a proposition he arrived at, of course, by accepting all the axioms, theorems, and postulates preceding the parallel postulate in Euclid's *Elements*. Second: "If there exists a single triangle in which the sum of the angles is equal to two right angles, then in any triangle the sum of the angles will likewise be equal to two right angles."

Yet, aside from these beautiful theorems, demonstrated in an impeccable manner, hardly anything but paralogisms are to be found. Like all the disciples of Newton, Legendre believed in absolute space and in the "absolute magnitude" of the sides of a rectilinear triangle. Taking up again a favorite idea of Lagrange's, outlined by the latter in volume 2 of the *Mémoires de Turin* (1761), he utilized (1794) the "law of homogeneous magnitudes" to establish the theorem of the sum of the angles of a triangle. Suppose a triangle is given with a side a and the adjacent angles B and C. The triangle is then well defined. The third angle A is therefore a function of the given quantities: $A = \varphi(B, C, a)$. But A, B, and C are pure numbers and a is a length. Now, by solving the equation $A = \varphi(B, C, a)$ with a as the unknown, the equation $a = f(A, B, C)$ is obtained "from which it would result that the side a is equal to a pure number without dimension, which is absurd." The law of homogeneous magnitudes therefore requires that this length disappear from the formula at the start and thus that $A = \varphi(B, C)$. By considering a right triangle and its altitude it is easily found that $A + B + C = \pi$.

Until the end of his life Legendre remained convinced of the value of this reasoning, and his other attempts at demonstration held only a purely pedagogical interest for him. They all failed because he always relied, in the last analysis, on propositions that were "evident" from the Euclidean point of view. Among these are the following: two convex contours of opposed concavities intersect at a finite distance; from a point within an angle a straight line cutting the two sides can always be drawn; and through three nonaligned points a circumference of a circle can always be passed.

At the end of his *Réflexions*, Legendre even adopted the pseudodemonstration of Louis Bertrand involving infinite spaces of various orders; and he thought he had improved it by what was actually an even more obscure argument. His virtuosity in spherical geometry and spherical trigonometry did not free him from a blind belief in absolute Euclidean space. "It is nevertheless certain," he wrote in 1832, "that the theorem on the sum of the three angles of the triangle should be considered one of those fundamental truths that are impossible to contest and that are an enduring example of mathematical certitude."

Let us conclude this study by emphasizing the transitional character of Legendre's works, which, in time as well as in spirit, are neither completely of the eighteenth century nor of the nineteenth. His scientific activity, extending from about 1770 to the end of 1832, was divided equally between the two centuries. He was a first-rate disciple of Lagrange and above all of Euler. His writings, like theirs, treat both abstract mathematics and the application of mathematics to the system of the world. Yet his boundless confidence in the powers of abstract science bespeaks a certain naïveté. In 1808 he wrote: "It is remarkable that from integral calculus an essential proposition concerning prime numbers can be deduced." The law in question was that of the distribution of the primes, and his remark is very pertinent. He added: "All the truths of mathematics are linked to each other, and all means of discovering them are equally admissible." One can easily agree with him on this point. But he went further, and here he makes one smile: "Consequently we were led to consider functions in order to demonstrate various basic theorems of geometry and mechanics."

Number theory was a sound and difficult school of logic for Legendre, as for all mathematicians who have worked in that field. Yet on several occasions, as in his studies of Eulerian integrals, he employed disconcerting arguments. For example, having established for positive integral values a certain relationship in which the gamma function occurs, he declares that the relationship is true for every value of this variable because the two members of the relationship are continuous functions. Elsewhere he elaborates on his reasoning: the two members are reduced to the same expression, which he works out; it is an extremely divergent (in the modern sense of the term) series. Still another time he employs an "infinite constant."

Consequently Legendre's writings rapidly became obsolete. Nevertheless he remains a marvelous calculator, a skillful analyst, and, in sum, a good mathematician. In both the theory of elliptic functions and number theory he raised questions that were fruitful subjects of investigation for mathematicians of the nineteenth century.

BIBLIOGRAPHY

I. Original Works. Legendre's writings are *Theses mathematicae ex analysi, geometria, mecanica exerptae, ex collegio Mazarinaeo* (Paris, 1770); Abbé Marie, *Traité de mécanique* (Paris, 1774), which includes several passages by Legendre; *Recherches sur la trajectoire des projectiles dans les milieux résistants* (Berlin, 1782); "Recherches sur la figure des planètes," in *Mémoires de l'Académie des sciences* for 1784, pp. 370 ff.; "Recherches d'analyse indéterminée," *ibid.* for 1785, pp. 465–560; "Mémoire sur la manière de distinguer les maxima des minima dans le calcul des variations," *ibid.* for 1786, pp. 7–37, and 1787, 348–351; German trans. in Ostwalds Klassiker der exacten Wissenschaften, no. 47; "Mémoires sur les intégrations par arcs d'ellipse et sur la comparaison de ces arcs," in *Mémoires de l'Académie des sciences* for 1786, pp. 616, 644–673; "Mémoire sur l'intégration de quelques équations aux différences partielles," *ibid.* for 1787, pp. 309–351; "Mémoire sur les opérations trigonométriques dont les résultats dépendent de la figure de la terre," *ibid.* for 1787, pp. 352 ff.; "Mémoire sur les intégrales doubles," *ibid.* for 1788, pp. 454–486; "Recherches sur les sphéroïdes homogènes," *ibid.* for 1790; and "Mémoire sur les intégrales particulières des équations différentielles," *ibid.* for 1790.

Works published after the establishment of the republic are *Mémoire sur les transcendantes elliptiques* (Paris, 1793);

Éléments de géométrie, avec des notes (Paris, 1794; 12th ed., 1823), new ed. with additions by A. Blanchet (Paris, 1845; 21st ed., 1876)—these eds. often depart from Legendre's text; English trans. by John Farrar (Cambridge, Mass., 1819) and other English eds. until 1890; German trans. by A. L. Crelle (Berlin, 1822); Romanian trans. by P. Poenaru (Bucharest, 1837); *Essai sur la théorie des nombres* (Paris, 1798; 2nd ed., 1808; with supps., 1816, 1825; 3rd ed., 2 vols., Paris, 1830) and German trans. by Maser as *Zahlentheorie* (Leipzig, 1893); *Méthodes analytiques pour la détermination d'un arc de méridien, par Delambre et Legendre* (Paris, 1799); "Nouvelle formule pour réduire en distances vraies les distances apparentes de la lune au soleil ou à une étoile," in *Mémoires de l'Institut national des sciences et arts*, 6 (1806), 30–54; and *Nouvelles méthodes pour la détermination des orbites des comètes . . .* (Paris, 1806).

Subsequent works are "Analyse des triangles tracés sur la surface d'un sphéroïde," in *Mémoires de l'Institut national des sciences et arts*, 7, pt. 1 (1806), 130–161; "Recherches sur diverses sortes d'intégrales définies," *ibid.* (1809), pp. 416–509; "Méthode des moindres carrés pour trouver le milieu le plus probable entre les résultats de différentes observations," *ibid.*, pt. 2 (1810), 149–154, with supp. (Paris, 1820); "Mémoire sur l'attractions des ellipsoïdes homogènes," *ibid.*, pt. 2 (1810), pp. 155–183, read 5 Oct. 1812; *Exercices de calcul intégral*, 3 vols. (Paris, 1811–1817); "Sur une méthode d'interpolation employée par Briggs dans la construction de ses grandes tables trigonométriques," in *Connaissance des temps ou des mouvements célestes pour 1817*, 10 (Paris, 1815), 219–222; "Méthodes diverses pour faciliter l'interpolation des grandes tables trigonométriques," *ibid.*, pp. 302–331, and "Recherches sur quelques objets d'analyse indéterminée et particulièrement sur le théorème de Fermat," in *Mémoires de l'Académie des sciences*, n.s. 6 (1823), 1–60.

Traité des fonctions elliptiques et des intégrales eulériennes, avec des tables pour en faciliter le calcul numérique was published in 3 vols. (Paris, 1825–1828); vol. I contains the theory of elliptic functions and its application to various problems of geometry and mechanics; vol. II contains the methods of constructing the elliptical tables, a collection of these tables, the treatise on Eulerian integrals, and an appendix; and vol. III includes various supplements to the theory of Eulerian functions. The three supplements are dated 12 Aug. 1828, 15 Mar. 1829, and 4 Mar. 1832.

Legendre's last works are "Note sur les nouvelles propriétés des fonctions elliptiques découvertes par M. Jacobi," in *Astronomische Nachrichten*, 6 (1828), cols. 205–208; "Mémoire sur la détermination des fonctions Y et Z qui satisfont à l'équation: $4(x^n - 1) = (x - 1)(Y^2 \pm nZ^2)$," in *Mémoires de l'Académie des sciences*, 11 (1832), 81–99, read 11 Oct. 1830; and "Réflexions sur différentes manières de démontrer la théorie des parallèles ou le théorème sur la somme des trois angles du triangle," *ibid.*, 12 (1833), 367–410.

For Legendre's mathematical correspondence with Jacobi, see C. G. J. Jacobi, *Gesammelte Werke*, I (Berlin,

1881), 386–461. For his correspondence with Abel, see N. H. Abel, *Mémorial publié à l'occasion du centenaire de sa naissance*, pt. 2 (Oslo, 1902): pp. 77–79 (Legendre's letter to Abel, 25 Oct. 1828), pp. 82–90 (Abel's letter to Legendre, 25 Nov. 1828), and pp. 91–93 (Legendre's letter to Abel, 16 Jan. 1829).

II. SECONDARY LITERATURE. On Legendre and his work, see Élie de Beaumont, "Éloge historique d'Adrien-Marie Legendre, lu le 25 mars 1861," in *Mémoires de l'Académie des sciences*, **32** (1864), xxxvii–xciv; J. B. J. Delambre, *Rapport historique sur les progrès des sciences mathématiques depuis 1789, et sur leur état actuel* (Paris, 1810), pp. 7–10, 34, 46–96, 135–137, in which S. F. Lacroix was responsible for everything concerning pure mathematics; A. Birembaut, "Les deux déterminations de l'unité de masse du système métrique," in *Revue d'histoire des sciences et de leurs applications*, **12**, no. 1 (1958), 24–54; C. D. Hellman, "Legendre and the French Reform of Weights and Measures," in *Osiris*, **1** (1936), 314–340; Jacob, "A. M. Legendre," in Hoefer, ed., *Nouvelle biographie générale*, XXX (Paris, 1862), cols. 385–388; Gino Loria, *Storia delle matematiche*, 2nd ed. (Milan, 1950), pp. 768–770; Maximilien Marie, *Histoire des mathématiques*, X (Paris, 1887), 110–148; L. Maurice, "Mémoire sur les travaux et les écrits de M. Legendre," in *Bibliothèque universelle des sciences, belles-lettres et arts. Sciences et arts* (Geneva), **52** (1833), 45–82; and E. H. Neville, "A Biographical Note," in *Mathematical Gazette*, **17** (1933), 200–201.

See also N. Nielsen, *Géomètres français sous la Révolution* (Copenhagen, 1929), pp. 166–174; Maurice d'Ocagne, *Histoire abrégée des mathématiques* (Paris, 1955), pp. 182–187; Parisot, "Legendre," in Michaud, ed., *Biographie universelle ancienne et moderne*, XXIII, 610–615; Poggendorff, I, cols. 1406–1407; Denis Poisson, "Discours prononcé aux funérailles de M. Legendre . . .," in *Moniteur universel* (20 Jan. 1833), p. 162; J. M. Quérard, "Legendre, Adrien-Marie," in *France littéraire*, **5** (1833), 94–95; A. Rabbe, *Biographie universelle et portative des contemporains*, III (Paris, 1834), 234–235; L. G. Simons, "The Influence of French Mathematicians at the End of the Eighteenth Century Upon the Teaching of Mathematics in American Colleges," in *Isis*, **15**, no. 45 (Feb. 1931), 104–123; D. E. Smith, "Legendre on Least Squares," in *A Source Book in Mathematics* (New York, 1929), pp. 576–579; I. Todhunter, *A History of the Progress of the Calculus of Variations* (Cambridge, 1861), ch. 9, pp. 229–253; A. Aubry, "Sur les travaux arithmétiques de Lagrange, de Legendre et de Gauss," in *Enseignement mathématique*, **11** (1909), 430–450; and Ivor Grattan-Guinness, *The Development of the Foundations of Mathematical Analysis from Euler to Riemann* (Cambridge, Mass., 1970), pp. 29, 36–41.

JEAN ITARD

LEIBNIZ, GOTTFRIED WILHELM (*b.* Leipzig, Germany, 1 July 1646; *d.* Hannover, Germany, 14 November 1716)

Leibniz was the son of Friedrich Leibniz, who was professor of moral philosophy and held various administrative posts at the University of Leipzig. His mother, Katherina Schmuck, was also from an academic family. Although the Leibniz family was of Slavonic origin, it had been established in the Leipzig area for more than two hundred years, and three generations had been in the service of the local princes.

Leibniz attended the Nicolai school, where his precocity led his teachers to attempt to confine him to materials thought suitable to his age. A sympathetic relative recognized his gifts and aptitude for self-instruction, and on the death of Friedrich Leibniz, in 1652, recommended that the boy be given unhampered access to the library that his father had assembled. By the time he was fourteen, Leibniz had thus become acquainted with a wide range of classical, scholastic, and even patristic writers, and had, in fact, begun that omnivorous reading that was to be his habit throughout his life. (Indeed, Leibniz' ability to read almost anything led Fontenelle to remark of him that he bestowed the honor of reading on a great mass of bad books.)

At the age of fifteen Leibniz entered the University of Leipzig, where he received most of his formal education, although that institution was at that time firmly entrenched in the Aristotelian tradition and did little to encourage science. In 1663 he was for a brief time a student at the University of Jena, where Erhard Weigel first taught him to understand Euclidean geometry. Leibniz continued his studies at Altdorf, from which he received the doctorate in 1666, with a dissertation entitled *Disputatio de casibus perplexis*. He was invited to remain at that university, but chose instead, during the second half of 1667, to undertake a visit to Holland.

Leibniz reached Mainz, where, through the offices of the statesman J. C. von Boyneburg, he met the elector Johann Philipp von Schönborn, who asked him into his service. Leibniz worked on general legal problems, developed his program for legal reform of the Holy Roman Empire, wrote (anonymously) a number of position papers for the elector, and began a vast correspondence that by 1671 had already brought him into contact with the secretaries of the Royal Society of London and the Paris Academy of Sciences, as well as with Athanasius Kircher in Italy and Otto von Guericke in Magdeburg. He also began work on his calculating machine, a device designed to multiply and divide by the mechanical repetition of adding or subtracting. In 1671 Pierre de Carcavi, royal librarian in Paris, asked Leibniz to send him this machine so that it could be shown to Colbert. The machine was, however, only in the design stage at that time (although a model of it was built in 1672 and demonstrated to the Academy three years later).

In the winter of 1671–1672, Leibniz and Boyneburg set forth a plan to forestall French attacks on the Rhineland. By its terms, Louis XIV was to conquer Egypt, create a colonial empire in North Africa, and build a canal across the isthmus of Suez—thereby gratifying his imperial ambitions at no cost to the Netherlands and the German states along the Rhine. Leibniz was asked to accompany a diplomatic mission to Paris to discuss this matter with the king. He never met Louis, but he did immerse himself in the intellectual and scientific life of Paris, forming a lifelong friendship with Christiaan Huygens. He also met Antoine Arnauld and Carcavi. The official mission came to nothing, however, and in December 1672 Leibniz' patron and collaborator Boyneburg died.

In January 1673 Leibniz went to London with a mission to encourage peace negotiations between England and the Netherlands; while there he became acquainted with Oldenburg, Pell, Hooke, and Boyle, and was elected to the Royal Society. The mission was completed, but the elector Johann Philipp had died, and his successor showed little interest in continuing Leibniz' salary, especially since Leibniz wanted to return to Paris. Leibniz arrived in the French capital in March 1673, hoping to make a sufficient reputation to obtain for himself a paid post in the Academy of Sciences. Disappointed in this ambition, he visited London briefly, where he saw Oldenburg and Collins, and in October 1676 left Paris for Hannover, where he was to enter the service of Johann Friedrich, duke of Brunswick-Lüneburg. En route, Leibniz stopped in Holland, where he had scientific discussions with Jan Hudde and Leeuwenhoek, and, at The Hague between 18 and 21 November, conducted a momentous series of conversations with Spinoza.

By the end of November Leibniz had arrived in Hannover, where he was initially a member of the duke's personal staff. He acted as adviser and librarian, as well as consulting on various engineering projects. (One of these, a scheme to increase the yield of the Harz silver mines by employing windmill-powered pumps, was put into operation in 1679, but failed a few years later, through no fault of the engineering principles involved.) Leibniz was soon formally appointed a councillor at court, and when Johann Friedrich died suddenly in 1679 to be succeeded by his brother Ernst August (in March 1680),

he was confirmed in this office. Sophia, the wife of the new duke, became Leibniz' philosophical confidante; Ernst August commissioned him to write a genealogy of the house of Brunswick, *Annales imperii occidentes Brunsvicenses*, to support the imperial and dynastic claims of that family. Leibniz' researches on this subject involved him in a series of scholarly travels; his princely support opened the doors of archives and libraries, and he was enabled to meet and discuss science with eminent men throughout Europe.

Leibniz left Hannover in October 1687 and traveled across Germany; in Munich he found an indication that the Guelphs were related to the house of Este, an important point for his genealogy. In May 1688 he arrived in Vienna; in October of that year he had an audience with Emperor Leopold I, to whom he outlined a number of plans for economic and scientific reforms. He also sought an appointment at the Austrian court, which was granted only in 1713. He then proceeded to Venice and thence to Rome. He hoped to meet Queen Christina, but she had died; he did become a member of the Accademia Fisico-matematica that she had founded. In Rome, too, Leibniz met the Jesuit missionary Claudio Filippo Grimaldi, who was shortly to leave for China as mathematician to the court of Peking; Grimaldi awakened in Leibniz what was to become a lasting interest in Chinese culture. Returning north from Rome, Leibniz stopped in Florence for a lively exchange on mathematical problems with Galileo's pupil Viviani; in Bologna he met Malpighi.

On 30 December 1689 Leibniz reached Modena, his ultimate destination, and set to work in the ducal archives which had been opened to him. (Indeed, he threw himself into his genealogical research with such fervor that he afflicted himself with severe eyestrain.) He interrupted his work long enough to arrange a marriage between Rinaldo d'Este of Modena and Princess Charlotte Felicitas of Brunswick-Lüneburg (celebrated on 2 December 1695), but by February 1690 he was able to prove the original relatedness of the house of Este and the Guelph line, and his research was complete. He returned to Hannover, making various stops along the way; his efforts were influential in the elevation of Hannover to electoral status (1692) and earned Leibniz himself an appointment as privy councillor.

Elector Ernst August died in January 1698 and his successor, Georg Ludwig, although urging Leibniz to complete the history of his house, nevertheless declined to make any other use of his services. Leibniz found support for his project in other courts, however, particularly through the patronage of Sophia Charlotte, daughter of Ernst August and

Sophia and electress of Brandenburg. At her invitation Leibniz went to Berlin in 1700, in which year, on his recommendation, the Berlin Academy was founded. Leibniz became its president for life. Sophia Charlotte died in 1705; Leibniz made his last visit to Berlin in 1711. He persisted in his efforts toward religious, political, and cultural reforms, now hoping to influence the Hapsburg court in Vienna and Peter the Great of Russia. In 1712 Peter appointed him privy councillor, and from 1712 to 1714 he served as imperial privy councillor in Vienna.

On 14 September 1714 Leibniz returned to Hannover; he arrived there three days after Georg Ludwig had left for England as King George I. Leibniz petitioned for a post in London as court historian, but the new king refused to consider it until he had finished his history of the house of Brunswick. Leibniz, plagued by gout, spent the last two years of his life trying to finish that monumental work. He died on 14 November 1716, quite neglected by the noblemen he had served. He never married.

FREDERICK KREILING

LEIBNIZ: Physics, Logic, Metaphysics

The special problems for any comprehensive treatment of the scientific investigations of Leibniz arise, on the one hand, from the fact that essential parts of his work have not been edited and, on the other hand, from the universality of his scientific interests. In view of this diversity of interests and the fragmentary, or rather encyclopedic, character of his work, the expositor is confronted with the task of achieving, at least in part, what Leibniz himself, following architectonic principles (within the framework of a *scientia generalis*), was unable to accomplish.

Leibniz is a striking example of a man whose universal interests (in his case ranging from physics through theory of law, linguistic philosophy, and historiography to particular questions of dogmatic theology) hindered rather than aided specialized scientific work. On the other hand, this broad interest, insofar as it remained oriented in architectonic principles, led to a concentration on methodological questions. In relation to the structure of a science, these are more important than concrete results. The position of Leibniz at the beginning of modern science is analogous to that of Aristotle at the beginning of ancient science. Leibniz' universality is comparable with that of Aristotle, different only in that it did not, as Aristotle's, remain grounded in essentially unchanged metaphysical distinctions but evolved by degrees from an encyclopedic multiplicity of interests.

Consequently, in the strict sense in which there is an Aristotelian system, there is no Leibnizian system but rather a marked metaphysical and methodological concern that systematically expresses variations on the same theme in the various special fields (such as physics and logic) and underlies Leibniz' quest to establish a unified system of knowledge.

Leibniz' autobiographical statement in a letter to Rémond de Montmort in 1714 explains how, at the age of fifteen, though accepting the mechanical philosophy, his search for the ultimate grounds of mechanism led him to metaphysics and the doctrine of entelechies. This indicates the early orientation of Leibniz' thought towards the ideas of the *Monadologie*. Instead of setting out his philosophy systematically in a *magnum opus*, Leibniz presented piecemeal clarifications of his views in works that, in various ways, were inspired by the publications of others. After reading the papers of Huygens and Wren on collision and the *Elementorum philosophiae* of Hobbes, Leibniz composed his *Hypothesis physica nova*, consisting of two parts, *Theoria motus abstracti* and *Theoria motus concreti*, which in 1671 he presented respectively to the Paris Academy of Sciences and the London Royal Society. At this time, Leibniz owed more to Descartes, whose work he knew only at second hand, than he was later willing to admit. Closer study of the philosophy of Descartes led Leibniz to a more decisive rejection.

In 1686 he published in the *Acta eruditorum* a criticism of Descartes's measure of force, *Brevis demonstratio erroris memorabilis Cartesii et aliorum circa legem naturae*, which started a controversy with Catalan, Malebranche, and Papin lasting until 1691. Also in 1686 Leibniz sent to Arnauld, for his comments, an essay entitled *Discours de métaphysique*, in which he developed the ideas of the later *Théodicée*. The tracts entitled *De lineis opticis, Schediasma de resistentia medii*, and *Tentamen de motuum coelestium causis*, published in the *Acta eruditorum* in 1689, were hurriedly composed by Leibniz after he had read the review of Newton's *Principia* in the same journal, in an attempt to obtain some credit for results which he had derived independently of Newton. In 1692, at the instigation of Pelisson, Leibniz wrote an *Essay de dynamique*, which was read to the Paris Academy by Philippe de la Hire, and in 1695 there appeared in the *Acta eruditorum* an article entitled *Specimen dynamicum*, which contained the clearest exposition of Leibniz' dynamics.

Leibniz' *Nouveaux essais sur l'entendement humain*, completed in 1705 but not published during his lifetime, presented a detailed criticism of Locke's position. By adding *nisi ipse intellectus* to the famous maxim, *Nihil est in intellectu quod non prius fuerit in sensu* (wrongly attributed to Aristotle by Duns Scotus[1]), Leibniz neatly reversed the application of the principle by Locke. According to Leibniz, the mind originally contains the principles of the various ideas which the senses on occasion call forth.

In 1710 Leibniz published his *Essais de Théodicée sur la bonté de Dieu, la liberté de l'homme et l'origine du mal*, a work composed at the instigation of Sophia Charlotte, with whom Leibniz had conversed concerning the views of Bayle. In response to a request from Prince Eugene for an abstract of the *Théodicée*, Leibniz in 1714 wrote the *Principes de la nature et de la grâce fondées en raison* and the *Monadologie*. When in 1715 Leibniz wrote to Princess Caroline of Wales, criticizing the philosophical and theological implications of the work of Newton, she commissioned Samuel Clarke to reply. The ensuing correspondence, containing Leibniz' most penetrating criticism of Newtonian philosophy, was published in 1717.

Rational Physics (Protophysics). In his efforts to clarify fundamental physical principles, Leibniz followed a plan which he called a transition from geometry to physics through a "science of motion that unites matter with forms and theory with practice."[2] He sought the metaphysical foundations of mechanics in an axiomatic structure. The *Theoria motus abstracti*[3] offers a rational theory of motion whose axiomatic foundation (*fundamenta praedemonstrabilia*) was inspired by the indivisibles of Cavalieri and the notion of *conatus* proposed by Hobbes. Both the word *conatus* and the mechanical idea were taken from Hobbes,[4] while the mathematical reasoning was derived from Cavalieri. After his invention of the calculus, Leibniz was able to replace Cavalieri's indivisibles by differentials and this enabled him to apply his theory of *conatus* to the solution of dynamical problems.

The concept of *conatus* provided for Leibniz a path of escape from the paradox of Zeno. Motion is continuous and therefore infinitely divisible, but if motion is real, its beginning cannot be a mere nothing.[5] *Conatus* is a tendency to motion, a mind-like quality having the same relation to motion as a point to space (in Cavalieri's terms) or a differential to a finite quantity (in terms of the infinitesimal calculus). *Conatus* represents virtual motion; it is an intensive quality that can be measured by the distance traversed in an infinitesimal element of time. A body can possess several *conatuses* simultaneously and these can be combined into a single *conatus* if they are compatible. In the absence of motion, *conatus* lasts only an instant,[6] but however weak, its effect is transmitted to infinity in a plenum. Leibniz' doctrine of *conatus*, in which a body is conceived as a momentary mind, that is, a mind without memory, may be regarded as a first sketch of the philosophy of monads.

Mathematically, *conatus* represents for Leibniz accelerative force in the Newtonian sense, so that, by summing an infinity of *conatuses* (that is, by integration), the effect of a continuous force can be measured. Examples of *conatus* given by Leibniz are centrifugal force and what he called the solicitation of gravity. Further clarifications of the concept of *conatus* are given in the *Essay de dynamique* and *Specimen dynamicum*, where *conatus* is compared with static force or *vis mortua* in contrast to *vis viva*, which is produced by an infinity of impressions of *vis mortua*.

Physics (Mechanical Hypothesis). Leibniz soon recognized that the idea of *conatus* could not by itself explain the results of the experiments of Huygens and Wren on collision. Since in the absence of motion *conatus* lasts only an instant, a body once brought to rest in a collision, Leibniz explains, could not then rebound.[7] A new property of matter was needed and this was provided for Leibniz by the action of an ether. As conceived by Leibniz in his *Theoria motus concreti*,[8] the ether was a universal agent of motion, explaining mechanically all the phenomena of the visible world. This essentially Cartesian notion was adopted by Leibniz following a brief attachment to the doctrine of physical atomism defended in the works of Bacon and Gassendi. Leibniz did not, however, become a Cartesian, nor did he aim to construct an entirely new hypothesis but rather to improve and reconcile those of others.[9]

A good example of the way in which Leibniz pursued this goal is provided by the planetary theory expounded in his *Tentamen de motuum coelestium causis*. In this work, Leibniz combined the mechanics of *conatus* and inertial motion with the concept of a fluid vortex to give a physical explanation of planetary motion on the basis of Kepler's analysis of the elliptical orbit into a circulation and a radial motion. Leibniz' harmonic vortex accounted for the circulation while the variation in distance was explained by the combined action of the centrifugal force arising from the circulation and the solicitation of gravity. This solicitation he held to be the effect of a second independent vortex of the kind imagined by Huygens, to whom he described Newton's attraction as "an immaterial and inexplicable virtue," a criticism he made public in the *Théodicée* and repeated in the correspondence with Clarke.

Although Leibniz' planetary theory could be described as a modification of that of Descartes, he did not acknowledge any inspiration from this source. Attributing the idea of a fluid vortex to Kepler and also, but incorrectly, the idea of centrifugal force,

Leibniz claimed that Descartes had made ample use of these ideas without acknowledgment. Leibniz had already, in a letter to Arnauld,[10] rejected the Cartesian doctrine that the essence of corporeal substance is extension. One reason that led him to this rejection was the theological problem of transubstantiation which he studied at the instigation of Baron Boyneburg,[11] but the most important dynamical reason was connected with the relativity of motion. As explained by Leibniz in the *Discours de métaphysique*,[12] since motion is relative, the real difference between a moving body and a body at rest cannot consist of change of position. Consequently, as the principle of inertial motion precludes an external impulse for a body moving with constant speed, the cause of motion must be an inherent force. Another argument against the Cartesian position involves the principle of the identity of indiscernibles. From this principle it follows that, besides extension, which is a property carried by a body from place to place, the body must have some intrinsic property which distinguishes it from others. According to Leibniz, bodies possess three properties which cannot be derived from extension: namely, impenetrability, inertia, and activity. Impenetrability and inertia are associated with *materia prima*, which is an abstraction, while *materia secunda* (the matter of dynamics) is matter endowed with force.

Since, for Leibniz, force alone confers reality to motion, the correct measure of force becomes the central problem of dynamics. Now Descartes had measured what Leibniz regarded as the active force of bodies, that is, the cause of their activity, by their quantity of motion. But, as Leibniz remarked in a letter of 1680,[13] Descartes's erroneous laws of collision implied that his basic principle of the conservation of motion was false. In 1686 Leibniz published his criticism of the Cartesian principle of the conservation of motion in his *Brevis demonstratio erroris mirabilis Cartesii*, thereby precipitating the *vis viva* controversy. According to Leibniz, Descartes had incorrectly generalized from statics to dynamics. In statics or virtual motion, Leibniz explains, the force is as the velocity but when the body has acquired a finite velocity and the force has become live, it is as the square of the velocity. As Leibniz remarked on several occasions, there is always a perfect equation between cause and effect, so that the force of a body in motion is measured by the product of the mass and the height to which the body could rise (the effect of the force). Using the laws of Galileo, this height was shown by Leibniz to be proportional to the square of the velocity, so that the force *(vis viva)* could be expressed as mv^2.

Since *vis viva* was regarded by Leibniz as the ultimate physical reality,[14] it had to be conserved throughout all transformations. Huygens had shown that, in elastic collision, *vis viva* is not diminished. The *vis viva* apparently lost in inelastic collision Leibniz held to be in fact simply distributed among the small parts of the bodies.[15]

Leibniz discovered the principle of the conservation of momentum, which he described as the "quantité d'avancement."[16] Had Descartes known that the quantity of motion is preserved in every direction (so that motion is completely determined, leaving no opportunity for the directing influence of mind), Leibniz remarks, he would probably have discovered the preestablished harmony. But in Leibniz' view, the principle of the conservation of momentum did not correspond to something absolute, since two bodies moving together with equal quantities of motion would have no total momentum. Leibniz' discovery of yet another absolute quantity in the concept of *action* enabled him to answer the Cartesian criticism that he had failed to take time into account in his consideration of *vis viva*. In his *Dynamica de potentia et legibus naturae corporeae*, Leibniz made an attempt to fit this new concept into his axiomatic scheme.

Although succeeding generations described the *vis viva* controversy as a battle of words, there can be no doubt that Leibniz himself saw it as a debate about the nature of reality. Referring to his search for a true dynamics, Leibniz remarked in 1689 that, to escape from the labyrinth, he could find "no other thread of Ariadne than the evaluation of forces, under the supposition of the metaphysical principle that the total effect is always equal to the complete cause."[17]

Scientia Generalis. According to the usual distinctions, the position that Leibniz took in physics, as well as in other fundamental questions, was rationalistic, and to that extent, despite all differences in detail, was related to Descartes's position. Evident confirmation of this may be seen in Leibniz' controversy with Locke; although he does not explicitly defend the Cartesian view, he uses arguments compatible with this position.

It is often overlooked, however, that Leibniz was always concerned to discuss epistemological issues as questions of theoretical science. For example, while Locke speaks of the origins of knowledge, Leibniz speaks of the structure of a science which encompasses that particular field. Thus Leibniz sees the distinction between necessary and contingent truths, so important in the debate with Locke, as a problem of theoretical science which transcends any consideration of the historical alternatives, rationalism and empiricism. Neither an empiricist in the sense of Locke nor yet a rationalist in the sense of Descartes, Leibniz saw the refutation of the empiricist's thesis (experience as the nonconceptual basis of knowledge) not as the problem of a rational psychology as it was then understood (in Cartesian idiom, the assumption of inborn truths and ideas) but as a problem that can be resolved only within the framework of a general logic of scientific research. Nevertheless, he shares with Descartes one fundamental rationalistic idea, namely the notion (which may be discerned in the Cartesian *mathesis universalis)* of a *scientia generalis.* In connection with his theoretical linguistic efforts towards a *characteristica universalis,* this thought appears in Leibniz as a plan for a *mathématique universelle.*[18]

Inspired by the ideas of Lull, Kircher, Descartes, Hobbes, Wilkins, and Dalgarno, Leibniz pursued the invention of an alphabet of thought *(alphabetum cogitationum humanarum)*[19] that would not only be a form of shorthand but a formalism for the creation of knowledge itself. He sought a method that would permit "truths of reason in any field whatever to be attained, to some degree at least, through a calculus, as in arithmetic or algebra."[20] The program of such a *lingua philosophica* or *characteristica universalis* was to proceed through lists of definitions to an elementary terminology encompassing a complete encyclopedia of all that was known. Leibniz connected this plan with others that he had, such as the construction of a general language for intellectual discourse and a rational grammar, conceived as a continuation of the older *grammatica speculativa.*

While Leibniz' programmatic statements leave open the question of just how the basic language he was searching for and the encyclopedia were to be connected (the *characteristica universalis,* according to other explanations, was itself to facilitate a compendium of knowledge), a certain *ars combinatoria,* conceived as part of an *ars inveniendi,* was to serve in the creation of the lists of definitions. As early as 1666, in Leibniz' *Dissertatio de arte combinatoria,* the *ars inveniendi* was sketched out under the name *logica inventiva* (or *logica inventionis)* as a calculus of concepts in which, in marked contrast to the traditional theories of concepts and judgments, he discusses the possibility of transforming rules of inference into schematic deductive rules. Within this framework there is also a complementary *ars iudicandi,* a mechanical procedure for decision making. However, the thought of gaining scientific propositions by means of a calculus of concepts derived from the *ars combinatoria* and a mechanical procedure for decision making remained lodged in a few attempts at the formation of the "alphabet." Leibniz was unable to complete the most important task for this project, namely, the proof of its completeness and irreducibility, nor did he consider this problem in his plans for the *scientia generalis,* a basic part of which was the "alphabet," the *characteristica universalis* in the form of a *mathématique universelle.*

The *scientia generalis* exists essentially only in the "tables of contents," which are not internally consistent terminologically and thus admit of additions at will. Nevertheless, it is clear that Leibniz was thinking here of a structure for a general methodology, consisting, on the one hand, of partial methodologies concerning special sciences such as mathematics, and on the other hand, of procedures for the *ars inveniendi,* such as the *characteristica universalis;* taken together, these were probably intended to replace traditional epistemology as a unified conceptual armory. This was by no means impracticable, at least in part. For example, the analytical procedures in which arithmetical transformations occur independently of the processes to which they refer, employed by Leibniz in physics, may be construed as a partial realization of the concept of a *characteristica universalis.*

Formal Logic. Leibniz produced yet another proof of the feasibility of his plan for schematic operations with concepts. Besides the infinitesimal calculus, he created a logical calculus *(calculus ratiocinator, universalis, logicus,* or *rationalis)* that was to lend the same certainty to deductions concerning concepts as that possessed by algebraic deduction. Leibniz stands here at the very beginning of formal logic in the modern sense, especially in relation to the older syllogistics, which he succeeded in casting into the form of a calculus. A number of different steps may be distinguished in his program for a logical calculus. In 1679 various versions of an arithmetical calculus appeared that permitted a representation of a conjunction of predicates by the product of prime numbers assigned to the individual predicates. In order to solve the problem of negation—needed in the syllogistic modes—negative numbers were introduced for the nonpredicates of a concept. Every concept was assigned a pair of numbers having no common factor, in which the factors of the first represented the predicates and the factors of the second represented the nonpredicates of the concept. Because this arithmetical calculus became too complex, Leibniz replaced it in about 1686 by plans for an algebraic calculus treating the identity of concepts and the inclusion of one concept in another. The components of this calculus were the symbols for predicates, $a, b, c, \ldots$ *(termini),* an operational sign $-$ *(non),* four relational signs $\subset, \not\subset, =, \neq$ (represented in language by *est, non est, sunt idem* or *eadem sunt, diversa sunt)* and the logical particles in vernacular form. To the rules of the calculus *(principia calculi)*—as distinct from the axioms *(propositiones per se verae)* and hypotheses *(propositiones positae)* which constitute its foundation —belong the principles of implication and logical equivalence and also a substitution formula. Among the theses *(propositiones verae)* that can be proved with the aid of the axioms and hypotheses, such as $a \subset a$ (reflexivity of the relation $\subset$) and $a \subset b$ et $b \subset c$ implies $a \subset c$ (transitivity of $\subset$), is the proposition $a \subset b$ et $d \subset c$ implies $ad \subset bc$. This was called by Leibniz the "admirable theorem" *(praeclarum theorema)* and appears again, much later, with Russell and Whitehead.[21]

Leibniz extended this algebraic calculus in various ways, first with a predicate-constant *ens* (or *res*), which may be understood as a precursor of the existential quantifier, and secondly with the interpretation of the predicates as propositions instead of concepts. Inclusion between concepts becomes implication between propositions and the new predicate-constant *ens* appears as the truth value *(verum)*, intensionally designated as *possibile*. These discourses were concluded in about 1690 with two calculi[22] in which a transition is made from an (intensional) logic of concepts to a logic of classes. The first, originally entitled *Non inelegans specimen demonstrandi in abstractis* (a "plus-minus calculus"), is a pure calculus of classes (a dualization of the thesis of the original algebraic calculus) in which a new predicate-constant *nihil* (for *non-ens*) is introduced. The second calculus (a "plus calculus") is an abstract calculus for which an extensional as well as an intensional interpretation is expressly given. Logical addition in the "plus-minus calculus" is symbolized by $+$. In the "plus calculus," logical addition, as well as logical multiplication in the intensional sense, is symbolized by $\oplus$, while the relational sign $=$ *(sunt idem* or *eadem sunt)* is replaced by ∞ and the sign $\neq$ by *non* $A \infty B$. Furthermore, subtraction appears in the "plus-minus calculus," symbolized by $-$ or $\ominus$, and also the relation of incompatibility *(incommunicantia sunt)* together with its negation *(communicantia sunt* or *compatibilia sunt)*. For example, one of the propositions of the calculus states: $A - B = C$ holds exactly, if and only if $A = B + C$, and B and C are incompatible; in modern notation

$$a \sqcup b = c \wedge (b \subset a) \leftrightarrow a = (b \vee c) \wedge (b \mid c).$$

(The condition $b \subset a$ is implicit in Leibniz' use of the symbol $-$).

If we disregard a few syntactical details and observe that Leibniz' work gives an approximation to a complete interpretation of the elements of a logical calculus (including the rules for transformation), we see here for the first time a formal language and thus an actual successful example of a *characteristica universalis*. It is true that Leibniz did not make sufficient distinction between the formal structure of the calculus and the interpretations of its content; for example, the beginnings of the calculus are immediately considered as axiomatic and the rules of transformation are viewed as principles of deduction. Yet it is decisive for Leibniz' program and our appreciation of it that he succeeded at all, in his logical calculus, in the formal reconstruction of principles of deduction concerning concepts.

General Logic. Leibniz' general logical investigations play just as important a role in his systematic philosophy as does his logical calculus. Most important are his analytical theory of judgment, the theory of complete concepts on which this is based, and the distinction between necessary and contingent propositions. According to Leibniz' analytical theory of judgment, in every true proposition of the subject-predicate form, the concept of the predicate is contained originally in the concept of the subject *(praedicatum inest subiecto)*. The *inesse* relation between subject and predicate is indeed the converse of the universal-affirmative relation between concepts, long known in traditional syllogisms (*B inest omni A* is the converse of *omne A est B*).[23] Although it is thus taken for granted that subject-concepts are completely analyzable, it suffices, in a particular case, that a certain predicate-concept can be considered as contained in a certain subject-concept. Fundamentally, there is a theory of concepts according to which concepts are usually defined as combinations of partials, so that analysis of these composite concepts *(notiones compositae)* should lead to simple concepts *(notiones primitivae* or *irresolubiles)*. With these, the *characteristica universalis* could then begin again. When the predicate-concept simply repeats the subject-concept, Leibniz speaks of an identical proposition; when this is not the case, but analysis shows the predicate-concept to be contained implicitly in the subject-concept, he speaks of a virtually identical proposition.

The distinction between necessary propositions or truths of reason *(vérités de raisonnement)* and contingent propositions or truths of fact *(vérités de fait)* is central to Leibniz' theory of science. As contingent truths, the laws of nature are discoverable by observation and induction but they have their rational foundation, whose investigation constitutes for Leibniz the essential element in science, in principles of order and perfection. Leibniz replaces the classical syllogism, as a principle of deduction, by the principle of substitution of equivalents to reduce composite propositions to identical propositions.

Contingent propositions are defined as those that are neither identical nor reducible through a finite number of substitutions to identical propositions.

All contingent propositions are held by Leibniz to be reducible to identical propositions through an infinite number of steps. Only God can perform these steps, but even for God, such propositions are not necessary (in the sense of being demanded by the principle of contradiction). Nevertheless, contingent propositions, in Leibniz' view, can be known *a priori* by God and, in principle, also by man. For Leibniz, the terms *a priori* and *necessary* are evidently not synonymous. It is the principle of sufficient reason that enables us (at least in principle) to know contingent truths *a priori*. Consequently, the deduction of such truths involves an appeal to final causes. On the physical plane, every event must have its cause in an anterior event. Thus we have a series of contingent events for which the reason must be sought in a necessary Being outside the series of contingents. The choice between the possibles does not depend on God's understanding, that is to say, on the necessity of the truths of mathematics and logic, but on his volition. God can create any possible world, but, being God, he wills the best of all possible worlds. Thus the contingent truths, including the laws of nature, do not proceed from logical necessity but from a moral necessity.

Methodological Principles. Logical calculi and the notions mentioned under "General Logic" belong to a general theory of foundations that also encompasses certain important Leibnizian methodological principles. The principle of sufficient reason *(principium rationis sufficientis*, also designated as *principium nobilissimum)* plays a special role. In its simplest form it is phrased "nothing is without a reason" *(nihil est sine ratione)*, which includes not only the concept of physical causality *(nihil fit sine causa)* but also in general the concept of a logical antecedent-consequent relationship. According to Leibniz, "a large part of metaphysics [by which he means rational theology], physics, and ethics" may be constructed on this proposition.[24] Viewed methodologically, this means that, in the principle of sufficient reason, there is a teleological as well as a causal principle; the particular import of the proposition is that both principles may be used in the same way for physical processes and human actions.

Defending the utility of final causes in physics (in opposition to the view of Descartes), Leibniz explained that these often provided an easier path than the more direct method of mechanical explanation in terms of efficient causes.[25] Leibniz had himself in 1682 used a variation of Fermat's principle in an application of his method of maxima and minima to the derivation of the law of refraction. Closely associated with the principle of sufficient reason is the principle of perfection *(principium perfectionis* or *melioris)*. In physics, this principle determines the actual motion from among the possible motions, and in metaphysics leads Leibniz to the idea of "the best of all possible worlds." The clearest expression of Leibniz' view is to be found in his *Tentamen anagogicum*,[26] written in about 1694, where he remarks that the least parts of the universe are ruled by the most perfect order. In this context, the idea of perfection consists in a maximum or minimum quantity, the choice between the two being determined by another architectonic principle, such as the principle of simplicity. Since the laws of nature themselves are held by Leibniz to depend on these principles, he supposed the existence of a perfect correlation between physical explanations in terms of final and efficient causes.

In relation to Leibniz' analytical theory of judgment and his distinction between necessary and contingent propositions, the principle of sufficient reason entails that, in the case of a well-founded connection between, for example, physical cause and physical effect, the proposition that formulates the effect may be described as a logical implication of the proposition that formulates the cause. Generalized in the sense of the analytical theory of truth and falsehood that Leibniz upholds, this means: "nothing is without a reason; that is, there is no proposition in which there is not some connection between the concept of the predicate and the concept of the subject, or which cannot be proved *a priori*."[27] This logical sense of the principle of sufficient reason contains also (in its formulation as a *principium reddendae rationis*) a methodological postulate; propositions are not only capable of being grounded in reasons (in the given analytical manner) but they must be so grounded (insofar as they are formulated with scientific intent).[28]

In addition to the principle of sufficient reason, the principle of contradiction *(principium contradictionis)* and the principle of the identity of indiscernibles *(principium identitatis indiscernibilium)* are especially in evidence in Leibniz' logic. In its Leibnizian formulation, the principle of contradiction, $\neg(A \wedge \neg A)$, includes the principle of the excluded middle, $A \vee \neg A$ *(tertium non datur)*: "nothing can be and not be at the same time; everything is or is not."[29] Since Leibniz' formulation rests on a theory according to which predicates, in principle, can be traced back to identical propositions, he also classes the principle of contradiction as a principle of identity. The principle of the identity of indiscernibles again defines the identity of two subjects, whether concrete or abstract, in terms of the property that the mutual replacement of their complete concepts in any arbitrary statement does not in the least change the truth value of that statement *(salva veritate)*. Two subjects s_1 and s_2 are different when there is a predicate P that is included in the complete concept S_1 of s_1 but not in the complete concept S_2 of s_2, or vice versa. If there is no such predicate, then because of the mutual replaceability of both complete concepts S_1 and S_2, there is no sense in talking of different subjects. This means, however, that the principle of the identity of indiscernibles, together with its traditional meaning ("there are no two indistinguishable subjects"[30]), is synonymous with the definition of logical equality ("whatever can be put in place of anything else, *salva veritate*, is identical to it"[31]).

Metaphysics (Logical Atomism). Since the investigations of Russell and Couturat, it has become clear that Leibniz' theory of monads is characterized by an attempt to discuss metaphysical questions within a framework of logical distinctions. On several occasions, however, Leibniz himself remarks that dynamics was to a great extent the foundation of his system. For example, in his *De primae philosophiae emendatione et de notione substantiae*, Leibniz comments that the notion of force, for the exposition of which he had designed a special science of dynamics, added much to the clear understanding of the concept of substance.[32] This suggests that it was the notion of mechanical energy that led to the concept of substance as activity. Again, it is in dynamics, Leibniz remarks, that we learn the difference between necessary truths and those which have their source in final causes, that is to say, contingent truths,[33] while optical theory, in the form of Fermat's principle, pointed to the location of the final causes in the principle of perfection.[34] Even the subject-predicate logic itself, which forms the rational foundation of Leibniz' metaphysics, seems to take on a biological image, such as the growth of a plant from a seed, when Leibniz writes to De Volder that the present state of a substance must involve its future states and vice versa. It thus appears that physical analogies very probably provided the initial inspiration for the formation of Leibniz' metaphysical concepts.

In the preface to the *Théodicée*, Leibniz declares that there are two famous labryrinths in which our reason goes astray; the one relates to the problem of liberty (which is the principal subject of the *Théodicée*), the other to the problem of continuity and the antinomies of the infinite. To arrive at a true metaphysics, Leibniz remarks in another place, it is necessary to have passed through the labyrinth of the continuum.[35]

Extension, like other continuous quantities, is infinitely divisible, so that physical bodies, however small, have yet smaller parts. For Leibniz, there can be no real whole without real unities, that is, indivisibles,[36] or as he expresses it (repeating a phrase used by Nicholas of Cusa[37]), being and unity are convertible terms.[38] Now the real unities underlying physical bodies cannot be mathematical points, for these are mere nothings. As Leibniz explains, "only metaphysical or substantial points . . . are exact and real; without them there would be nothing real, since without true unities *[les véritables unités]* a composite whole would be impossible."[39] Within the narrower framework of physics, such unities can be understood as the concept of mass-points, but they are meant in the broader sense of the classical concept of substance, to the consideration of which Leibniz had in 1663 devoted his first philosophical essay, *Dissertatio metaphysica de principio individui*. Leibniz' metaphysical realities are unextended substances or monads (a term he used from 1696), whose essence is an intensive quality of the nature of force or mind.

Leibniz consciously adheres to Aristotelian definitions, when he emphasizes that we may speak of an individual substance whenever a predicate-concept is included in a subject-concept, and this subject-concept never appears itself as a predicate-concept. A concept fulfilling this condition may thus be designated as an individual concept *(notion individuelle)* and may be construed as a complete concept, that is, as the infinite conjunction of predicates appertaining to that individual. If a complete subject-concept were itself to appear as a predicate-concept, then according to the principle of the identity of indiscernibles, the predicated individual would be identical to the designated individual. This result of Leibniz is a logical reconstruction of the traditional ontological distinction between substance and quality.

The definition of individual concepts, according to which individual substances are denoted by complete concepts, leads also to the idea, central to the theory of monads, that each monad or individual substance represents or mirrors the whole universe. What Leibniz means is that, given a particular subject, all other subjects must appear, represented by their names or designations, in at least one of the infinite conjunction of predicates constituting the complete concept of that particular subject.

Leibniz describes the inner activity which constitutes the essence of the monad as perception.[40] This does not imply that all monads are conscious. The monad has perception in the sense that it represents the universe from its point of view, while its activity is manifested in spontaneous change from one perception to another. The attribution of perception and appetition to the monads does not mean that they can be sufficiently defined in terms of physiological and psychological processes, although Leibniz does compare them to biological organisms; he was, of course, familiar with the work of Leeuwenhoek, Swammerdam, and Malpighi on microorganisms, which seemed to confirm the theory of preformation demanded by the doctrine of monads. Once again, the logical basis for the theory of perception is that the concept of the monad's inner activity must occur in the concept of the individual monad; for everything that an individual substance encounters "is only the consequence of its notion or complete concept, since this notion already contains all predicates or events and expresses the whole universe."[41]

Within the framework of this conceptual connection between a theory of perception and a theory of individual concepts, sufficient room remains for physiological and psychological discussion and here Leibniz goes far beyond the level of debate in Locke and Descartes. In particular, Leibniz distinguishes between consciousness and self-consciousness, and again, between stimuli which rise above the threshold of consciousness and those that remain below it; he even observes that the summation of sub-threshold stimuli can finally lead to one that emerges over the threshold of consciousness, a clear hint of the existence of the unconscious.

Since, for Leibniz, the real unities constituting the universe are essentially perceptive, it follows that the real continuum must also be a continuum of perception. The infinite totality of monads represent or mirror the universe, of which each is a part, from all possible points of view, so that the universe is at once continuous and not only infinitely divisible but actually divided into an infinity of real metaphysical atoms.[42] As these atoms are purely intensive unities, they are mutually exclusive, so that no real interaction between them is possible. Consequently, Leibniz needed his principle of the preestablished harmony (which, he claimed, avoided the perpetual intervention of God involved in the doctrine of occasionalism) to explain the mutual compatibility of the internal activities of the monads. Leibniz thus evaded the antinomies of the continuum by conceiving reality not as an extensive plenum of matter bound by physical relations but as an intensive plenum of force or life bound by a preestablished harmony.

The monads differ in the clarity of their perceptions, for their activity is opposed and their perceptions consequently confused to varying degrees by the *materia prima* with which every created monad is endowed. As with the *materia prima* of dynamics, that

of the monads is thus associated with passivity. Only one monad, God, is free of *materia prima* and he alone perceives the world with clarity, that is to say, as it really is.

Physical bodies consist of infinite aggregates of monads. Since such aggregates form only accidental unities, they are not real wholes and consequently, in Leibniz' view, not possessed of real magnitude. It is in this sense that Leibniz denies infinite number while admitting the existence of an actual infinite. When an aggregate has one dominant monad, the aggregate appears as the organic body of this monad. Aggregates without a dominant monad simply appear as *materia secunda*, the matter of dynamics. Bodies as such are therefore conceived by Leibniz simply as phenomena, but in contrast to dreams and similar illusions, well-founded phenomena on account of their consistency. For Leibniz then, the world of extended physical bodies is just a world of appearance, a symbolic representation of the real world of monads.

From this doctrine it follows that the forces involved in dynamics are only accidental, or derivative, as Leibniz terms them. The real active force, or *vis primitiva*, which remains constant in each corporeal substance, corresponds to mind or substantial form. Leibniz does not, however, reintroduce substantial forms as physical causes;[43] for in his view, physical explanations involve a *vis derivativa* or accidental force by which the *vis primitiva* or real principle of action is modified.[44] One monad, having more *vis primitiva*, represents the universe more distinctly than another, a difference that can be expressed by the terms active and passive, though there is, of course, no real interaction. In the world of phenomena, this relation is symbolized in the notion of physical causality. The laws of nature, including the principle of the conservation of *vis viva*, thus have relevance only at the phenomenal level, though they symbolize, on the metaphysical plane, an order manifested through the realization of predicates of individual substances in accordance with the preestablished harmony.

In the early stages of the formulation of his metaphysics, Leibniz located the unextended substances, that he later called monads, in points.[45] This presupposed a real space in which the monads were embedded, a view that consideration of the nature of substance and the difficulties of the continuum caused him soon to abandon. In his *Système nouveau*,[46] written in 1695, Leibniz described atoms of substance (that is, monads) as metaphysical points, but the mathematical points associated with the space of physics he described as the points of view of the monads. Physical space, Leibniz explains, consists of relations of order between coexistent things.[47] This may be contrasted with the notion of an abstract space, which consists of an assemblage of possible relations between possible existents.[48] For Leibniz then, space is an assemblage of relations between the monads. By locating the points of space in a quality of the monads, namely their points of view, Leibniz makes space entirely dependent on the monads. Space itself, however, is not a property of the monads, for points are not parts of space. In the sense of distance between points, space is a mere ideal thing, the consideration of which, Leibniz remarks, is nevertheless useful.[49] Distances between points are representations of the differences of the points of view of the monads. Owing to the preestablished harmony, these relations are compatible, so that space is a well-founded phenomenon, an extensive representation of an intensive continuum. Similarly time, as the order of noncontemporaneous events,[50] is also a well-founded phenomenon.

Leibniz' objections to the kind of absolute real space and time conceived by Newton are expressed most completely in his correspondence with Clarke. Real space and time, Leibniz argues, would violate the principle of sufficient reason and the principle of the identity of indiscernibles. For example, a rotation of the whole universe in an absolute space would leave the arrangement of bodies among themselves unchanged, but no sufficient reason could be found why God should have placed the whole universe in one of these positions rather than the other. Again, if time were absolute, no reason could be found why God should have created the universe at one time rather than another.[51]

From the ideal nature of space and time, it follows that motion, in the physical sense, is also ideal and therefore relative.[52] Against Newton, Leibniz maintains the relativity not only of rectilinear motion but also of rotation.[53] Yet Leibniz is willing to admit that there is a difference between what he calls an absolute real motion of a body and a mere change in its position relative to other bodies. For it is the body in which the cause of motion (that is, the active force) resides that is truly in motion.[54] Now it is evidently the *vis primitiva* that Leibniz has in mind, since consideration of the *vis derivativa (conatus* or *vis viva)* does not serve to identify an absolute motion, so that we may interpret Leibniz as saying that true absolute motion appertains to the metaphysical plane, where it can be perceived only by God. Indeed all bodies have an absolute motion in this sense, for since all monads have activity, all aggregates have *vis viva*. The world of phenomena is therefore conceived by Leibniz as a world of bodies in absolute motion (rest being a mere abstraction) but a world in which only relative changes

of position can be observed.

The theory of monads may be seen as a sustained effort to present, in "cosmological" completeness, a systematic unified structure of knowledge on the basis of a logical reconstruction of the concept of substance. Insofar as the central assertion, namely, that because there are composite "substances," there must be simple substances, is not only a cosmological and metaphysical statement, but in addition, an assertion of the priority of synthetic over analytic procedures, his efforts retain their original methodological meaning. As revealed in his plan for a *characteristica universalis*, analysis, for Leibniz, implies synthesis, but a synthesis that must begin with irreducible elements. Where there are no such elements, neither analysis nor synthesis is possible within the framework of Leibniz' constructive methodology. This means that Leibniz, in the course of his protracted efforts to define an individual substance, moved from physical atomism to logical atomism in the modern sense, as represented by Russell. Leibniz believed that he had proved the thesis of an unambiguously defined world, in which the physico-theological theme running through the mechanistic philosophy of his age might once again be seen as a metaphysics in the classical sense.

Influence. The thought of Leibniz influenced the history of philosophy and science in two ways; first, through the mediocre systematization of Christian Wolff known as the "Leibnizo-Wolffian" philosophy, and secondly, through the significance of particular theories in the history of various sciences. While the tradition of the Leibnizo-Wolffian philosophy ended with Kant, the influence of particular theories of Leibniz lasted through the nineteenth and into the twentieth century.

The controversy with Newton and Clarke was not conducive to the reception of Leibniz' work in physics and hindered the objective evaluation of important contributions such as his law of radial acceleration. The *vis viva* controversy arose as a direct result of Leibniz' criticism of Descartes and concerned not only the measure of force but also the nature of force itself. While 'sGravesande and d'Alembert (in his *Traité de mécanique*) judged the dispute to be merely a semantic argument, Kant in 1747 *(Gedanken von der wahren Schätzung der lebendigen Kräfte)* made an ineffective attempt at reconciliation. Leibnizian dynamics was developed further by Bošković, who transformed the concept of dynamic force in the direction of a concept of relational force.

Within the framework of rational physics, Kant contributed some essential improvements, such as the completion of the distinction between necessary and contingent propositions by means of the concept of the synthetic *a priori* and clarification of the principle of causality. Leibniz' protophysical plan, however, remained intact. It was continued later by Whewell, Clifford, Mach, and Dingler, to mention only a few. Insofar as the fundamental concepts of space and time were concerned, the Newtonian ideas of absolute space and time at first prevailed over the Leibnizian ideas of relational space and time. Kant also tried here to mediate between the ideas of Leibniz and Newton, but his own suggestion (space as the origin of the distinction between a nonreflexible figure and its mirror image, such as a pair of gloves) strongly resembled the Newtonian concept of absolute space. Modern relativistic physics has turned the scales in favor of the ideas of Leibniz.

Among the methodological principles of Leibniz, only the principle of sufficient reason has played a prominent role in the history of philosophy. Wolff, disregarding Leibniz' methodological intentions, tried to prove it by ontological means *(Philosophia sive ontologia);* Kant reduced it essentially to the law of causality and in 1813 Schopenhauer drew on it for the elucidation of his four conditions of verification *(Über die vierfache Wurzel des Satzes vom zureichenden Grunde).* On the other hand, the methodological project of a *characteristica universalis* together with the ensuing development of logical calculi has played a most significant role in the history of modern logic. In 1896 Frege, recalling Leibniz, described his *Begriffsschrift* of 1879 as a *lingua characterica* (not just a *calculus ratiocinator*), thus distinguishing it from the parallel efforts of Boole and Peano. De Morgan and Boole tried to carry out what Scholz has described as the "Leibniz program" of the development of a logical algebra of classes. This connection between logic and mathematics, evident also in Peirce and Schröder, was once again weakened by Frege, Peano, and Russell, whose work (especially that of Frege) nevertheless bears the inescapable influence of Leibniz; for even where the differences are greatest, the development of modern logic can be traced back to Leibniz. In this connection, it is fortunate that (in the absence of any publications of Leibniz) there is a tradition of correspondence beginning with letters between Leibniz, Oldenburg, and Tschirnhaus. The emphasis here, as exemplified in the logic theories of Ploucquet, Lambert, and Castillon, is on the intensional interpretation of logical calculi.

While there is an affinity between the theory of monads and Russell's logical atomism, a direct influence of the more metaphysical parts of the theory of monads on the history of scientific thought is difficult to prove. Particular results, such as the biological concept of preformation (accepted by Haller, Bonnet, and Spallanzani) or the discovery of sensory thresholds, though related to the theory of monads in a systematic way, became detached from it and followed their own lines of development. Yet the term "monad" played an important role with Wolff, Baumgarten, Crusius, and, at the beginning, with Kant (as exemplified in his *Monadologica physica* of 1756), then later with Goethe and Solger as well. Vitalism in its various forms, including the "biological romanticism" of the nineteenth century (the Schelling school), embraced in general the biological interpretation of the theory of monads, but this did not amount to a revival of the metaphysical theory. It is more likely that vitalism simply represented a reaction against mechanism, a tradition to which Leibniz also belonged.

NOTES

1. Duns Scotus, *Questiones super universalibus Porphyrii* (Venice, 1512), Quest. 3.
2. L. Couturat, ed., *Opuscules et fragments inédits de Leibniz* (Paris, 1903; Hildesheim, 1966), p. 594.
3. G. W. Leibniz, *Sämtliche Schriften und Briefe*, VI, 2, pp. 258–276.
4. T. Hobbes, *Elementorum philosophiae* (London, 1655), sectio prima: de corpore, pars tertia, cap. 15, §2 and §3.
5. *Sämtliche Schriften und Briefe*, VI, 2, p. 264.
6. *Ibid.*, p. 266.
7. *Ibid.*, p. 231.
8. *Ibid.*, pp. 221–257.
9. *Ibid.*, p. 257.
10. *Sämtliche Schriften und Briefe*, II, 1, p. 172.
11. *Ibid.*, pp. 488–490.
12. G. W. Leibniz, *Die philosophischen Schriften*, C. I. Gerhardt, ed., IV, p. 444; cf. p. 369.
13. *Sämtliche Schriften und Briefe*, II, 1, p. 508.
14. P. Costabel, *Leibniz et la dynamique* (Paris, 1960), p. 106.
15. G. W. Leibniz, *Mathematische Schriften*, C. I. Gerhardt, ed., VI, pp. 230–231. The manuscript called *Essay de dynamique* by Gerhardt is not earlier than 1698.
16. P. Costabel, *op. cit.*, p. 105.
17. *Ibid.*, p. 12.
18. *Sämtliche Schriften und Briefe*, VI, 6, p. 487.
19. L. Couturat, *op. cit.*, p. 430.
20. *Die philosophischen Schriften*, VII, p. 32.
21. *Principia mathematica*, *3. 47.
22. *Die philosophischen Schriften*, VII, pp. 228–247. Cf. L. Couturat, *op. cit.*, pp. 246–270.
23. *Sämtliche Schriften und Briefe*, VI, 1, p. 183.
24. *Die philosophischen Schriften*, VII, p. 301.
25. *Ibid.*, IV, pp. 447–448.
26. *Ibid.*, VII, pp. 270–279.
27. *G. W. Leibniz, Textes inédits*, G. Grua, ed. (Paris, 1948), I, p. 287.
28. *Die philosophischen Schriften*, VII, p. 309. Cf. L. Couturat, *op. cit.*, p. 525.
29. L. Couturat, *op. cit.*, p. 515.
30. *Sämtliche Schriften und Briefe*, VI, 6, p. 230.
31. *Die philosophischen Schriften*, VII, p. 219.
32. *Ibid.*, IV, p. 469.
33. *Ibid.*, III, p. 645.

34. *Ibid.*, IV, p. 447.
35. *Mathematische Schriften*, VII, p. 326.
36. *Die philosophischen Schriften*, II, p. 97.
37. Nicholas of Cusa, *De docta ignorantia*, Bk. II, ch. 7.
38. *Die philosophischen Schriften*, II, p. 304.
39. *Ibid.*, IV, p. 483.
40. *Principes de la nature et de la grâce*, A. Robinet, ed., p. 27.
41. *Discours de métaphysique*, G. le Roy, ed., p. 50.
42. *Die philosophischen Schriften*, I, p. 416.
43. *Ibid.*, II, p. 58.
44. *Mathematische Schriften*, VI, p. 236.
45. *Die philosophischen Schriften*, II, p. 372.
46. *Ibid.*, IV, p. 482.
47. *Ibid.*, IV, p. 491. Cf. II, p. 450.
48. *Ibid.*, VII, p. 415.
49. *Ibid.*, VII, p. 401.
50. *Mathematische Schriften*, VII, p. 18.
51. *Die philosophischen Schriften*, VII, p. 364.
52. *Ibid.*, II, p. 270. Cf. *Mathematische Schriften*, VI, p. 247.
53. *Mathematische Schriften*, II, p. 184.
54. *Die philosophischen Schriften*, VII, p. 404. Cf. IV, p. 444 and L. Couturat, *op. cit.*, p. 594.

JÜRGEN MITTELSTRASS
ERIC J. AITON

LEIBNIZ: Mathematics

Leibniz had learned simple computation and a little geometry in his elementary studies and in secondary schools, but his interest in mathematics was aroused by the numerous remarks on the importance of the subject that he encountered in his reading of philosophical works. In Leipzig, John Kuhn's lectures on Euclid left him unsatisfied, whereas he received some stimulation from Erhard Weigel in Jena. During his student years, he had also cursorily read introductory works on Cossist algebra and the *Deliciae physico-mathematicae* of Daniel Schwenter and Philipp Harsdörffer (1636–1653) with their varied and mainly practical content. At this stage Leibniz considered himself acquainted with all the essential areas of mathematics that he needed for his studies in logic, which attracted him much more strongly. The very modest specialized knowledge that he then possessed is reflected in the *Dissertatio de arte combinatoria* (1666); several additions are presented in the *Hypothesis physica nova* (1671).

In accord with the encyclopedic approach popular at the time, Leibniz limited himself primarily to methods and results and considered demonstrations nonessential and unimportant. His effort to mechanize computation led him to work on a calculating machine which would perform all four fundamental operations of arithmetic.

Leibniz was occupied with diplomatic tasks in Paris from the spring of 1672, but he continued the studies (begun in 1666) on the arithmetic triangle which had appeared on the title page of Apianus' *Arithmetic* (1527) and which was well known in the sixteenth century; Leibniz was still unaware, however, of Pascal's treatise of 1665. He also studied the array of differences of the number sequences, and discovered both fundamental rules of the calculus of finite differences of sequences with a finite number of members. He revealed this in conversation with Huygens, who challenged his visitor to produce the summation of reciprocal triangular numbers and, therefore, of a sequence with infinitely many members. Leibniz succeeded in this task at the end of 1672 and summed further sequences of reciprocal polygonal numbers and, following the work of Grégoire de St.-Vincent (1647), the geometric sequence, through transition to the difference sequence.

As a member of a delegation from Mainz, Leibniz traveled to London in the spring of 1673 to take part in the unsuccessful peace negotiations between England, France, and the Netherlands. He was received by Oldenburg at the Royal Society, where he demonstrated an unfinished model of his calculating machine. Through Robert Boyle he met John Pell, who was familiar with the entire algebraic literature of the time. Pell discussed with Leibniz his successes in calculus of differences and immediately referred him to several relevant works of which Leibniz was not aware—including Mercator's *Logarithmotechnia* (1668), in which the logarithmic series is determined through prior division, and Barrow's *Lectiones opticae* (1669) and *Lectiones geometricae* (1670). (Barrow's works were published in 1672 under the single title *Lectiones opticae et geometricae*.)

Leibniz became a member of the Royal Society upon application, but he had seriously damaged his scientific reputation through thoughtless pronouncements on the array of differences, and still more through his rash promise of soon producing a working model of the calculating machine. Leibniz could not fully develop the calculator's principle of design until 1674, by which time he could take advantage of the invention of direct drive, the tachometer, and the stepped drum.

Through Oldenburg, Leibniz received hints, phrased in general terms, of Newton's and Gregory's results in infinitesimal mathematics; but he was still a novice and therefore could not comprehend the significance of what had been communicated to him. Huygens referred him to the relevant literature on infinitesimals in mathematics and Leibniz became passionately interested in the subject. Following the lead of Pascal's *Lettres de "A. Delonville"* [= *Pascal*] *contenant quelques unes de ses inventions de géométrie* (1659), by 1673 he had mastered the characteristic triangle and had found, by means of a transmutation—

that is, of the integral transformation, discovered through affine geometry,

$$\frac{1}{2}\int_0^{x}\left[y(\bar{x}) - x\frac{dy}{dx}(\bar{x}) \right] \cdot d\bar{x},$$

for the determination of a segment of a plane curve— a method developed on a purely geometrical basis by means of which he could uniformly derive all the previously stated theorems on quadratures.

Leibniz' most important new result, which he communicated in 1674 to Huygens, Oldenburg, and his friends in Paris, were the arithmetical quadrature of the circle, including the arc tangent series, which had been achieved in a manner corresponding to Mercator's series division, and the elementary quadrature of a cycloidal segment (presented in print in 1678 in a form that concealed the method). Referred by Jacques Ozanam to problems of indeterminate analysis that can be solved algebraically, Leibniz also achieved success in this area by simplifying methods, as in the essay on

$$x + y + z = p^2, \; x^2 + y^2 + z^2 = q^4$$

(to be solved in natural numbers). Furthermore, a casual note indicates that at this time he was already concerned with dyadic arithmetic.

The announcement of new publications on algebra provoked Leibniz to undertake a thorough review of the pertinent technical literature, in particular the Latin translation of Descartes's *Géométrie* (1637), published by Frans van Schooten (1659–1661) with commentaries and further studies written by Descartes's followers.

His efforts culminated in four results obtained in 1675: a more suitable manner of expressing the indices (ik in lieu of a_{ik}, for instance); the determination of symmetric functions and especially of sums of powers of the solutions of algebraic equations; the construction of equations of higher degree that can be represented by means of compound radicals; and ingenious attempts to solve higher equations algorithmically by means of radicals, attempts that were not recognized as fruitless because of the computational difficulties involved. On the other hand, Leibniz succeeded in demonstrating the universal validity of Cardano's formulas for solving cubic equations even when three real solutions are present and in establishing that in this case the imaginary cannot be dispensed with. The generality of these results had been frequently doubted because of the influence of Descartes. Through this work Leibniz concluded that the sum of conjugate complex expressions is always real (cf. the well-known example $\sqrt{1 + \sqrt{-3}} + \sqrt{1 - \sqrt{-3}} = \sqrt{6}$). The theorem

named for de Moivre later proved this conclusion to be correct.

In the fall of 1675 Leibniz was visited by Tschirnhaus, who, while studying Descartes's methods (which he greatly overrated), had acquired considerable skill in algebraic computation. His virtuosity aroused admiration in London, yet it did not transcend the formal and led to a mistaken judgment of the new results achieved by Newton and Gregory. Tschirnhaus and Leibniz became friends and together went through the unpublished scientific papers of Descartes, Pascal, and other French mathematicians. The joint studies that emerged from this undertaking dealt with the array of differences and with the "harmonic" sequence $\cdots$, 1/5, 1/4, 1/3, 1/2, 1/1 and was treated by Leibniz as the counterpart of the arithmetic triangle. They then considered the succession of the prime numbers and presented a beautiful geometric interpretation of the sieve of Eratosthenes—which, however, cannot be recognized from the remark printed in 1678 that the prime numbers greater than three must be chosen from the numbers $6n \pm 1$.

When Roberval died in 1675 Leibniz hoped to succeed him in the professorship of mathematics established by Pierre de la Ramée at the Collège de France and also to become a member of the Académie des Sciences. Earlier in 1675 he had demonstrated at the Academy the improved model of his calculating machine and had referred to an unusual kind of chronometer. He was rejected in both cases because his negligence had cost him the favor of his patrons. Nevertheless, his thorough, critical study of earlier mathematical writings resulted in important advances, especially in the field of infinitesimals. He recognized the transcendence of the circular and logarithmic functions, the basic properties of the logarithmic and other transcendental curves, and the correspondence between the quadrature of the circle and the quadrature of the hyperbola. In addition, he considered questions of probability.

In the late autumn of 1675, seeking a better understanding of Cavalieri's quadrature methods (1635), Leibniz made his greatest discovery: the symbolic characterization of limiting processes by means of the calculus. To be sure, "not a single previously unsolved problem was solved" by this discovery (Newton's disparaging judgment in the priority dispute); yet it set out the procedure to be followed in a suggestive, efficient, abstract form and permitted the characterization and classification of the applicable computational steps. In connection with the arrangement in undetermined coefficients, Leibniz sought to clarify the conditions under which an algebraic function can be integrated algebraically. In addition he solved important differential equations: for example, the tractrix problem, proposed to him by Perrault, and Debeaune's problem (1638), which he knew from Descartes's *Lettres* (III, 1667); and which required the curve through the origin determined by

$$\frac{dy}{dx} = \frac{x - y}{a}.$$

He established that not every differential equation can be solved exclusively through the use of quadratures and was immediately cognizant of the far-reaching importance of symbolism and technical terminology.

Leibniz only hinted at his new discovery in vague remarks, as in letters to Oldenburg in which he requested details of the methods employed by Newton and Gregory. He received some results in reply, especially concerning power series expansions—which were obviously distorted through gross errors in copying—but nothing of fundamental significance (Newton's letters to Leibniz of June and October 1676, with further information on Gregory and Pell supplied by Oldenburg). Leibniz explained the new discovery to him personally, but Tschirnhaus was more precisely informed. He did not listen attentively, was troubled by the unfamiliar terminology and symbols, and thus never achieved a deeper understanding of Leibnizian analysis. Tschirnhaus also had the advantage of knowing the answer, written in great haste, to Newton's first letter, where Leibniz referred to the solution of Debeaune's problem (as an example of a differential equation that can be integrated in a closed form) and hinted at the principle of *vis viva*. Leibniz also included the essential elements of the arithmetical quadrature of the circle; yet it was derived not by means of the general transmutation but, rather, through a more special one of narrower virtue. Tschirnhaus did not know that the preliminary draft of this letter contained an example of the method of series expansion through gradual integration (later named for Cauchy [1844] and Picard [1890]) and, in any case, he would not have been able to understand and fully appreciate it. On the other hand, he did see and approve the definitive manuscript (1676) on the arithmetical quadrature of the circle. This work also contains the proof by convergence of an alternating sequence with members decreasing without limit; the rigorous treatment of transmutation and its application to the quadrature of higher parabolas and hyperbolas; the logarithmic series and its counterpart, the arc tangent series, and its numerical representation of $\frac{\pi}{4}$ (Leibniz series);

and the representation of $\frac{ln\,2}{4}$ and $\frac{\pi}{8}$ through omission of members of the series

$$\sum_{n=2}^{\infty} \frac{1}{(n - 1)(n + 1)} = \frac{3}{4}.$$

The planned publication did not occur and subsequently the paper was superseded by Leibniz' own work as well as by that of others, particularly the two Bernoullis and L'Hospital.

Since there was no possibility of obtaining a sufficiently remunerative post in Paris, Leibniz entered the service of Hannover in the fall of 1676. He traveled first to London, where he sought out Oldenburg and the latter's mathematical authority, John Collins. He presented them with papers on algebra, which Collins transcribed and which were transmitted to Newton. A longer discussion with Collins was devoted primarily to algebraic questions although dyadics were also touched upon. Leibniz also made excerpts from Newton's letters and from the manuscript of his *De analysi per aequationes numero terminorum infinitas* (1669), which had been deposited with the Royal Society, and from the extracts procured by Collins of letters and papers of Gregory, only a small selection of which Leibniz had obtained earlier. He then went to Amsterdam, where he called on Hudde, who informed him of his own mathematical works.

In the intellectually limited atmosphere of Hannover there was no possibility of serious mathematical discussion. His talks with the Cartesian A. Eckhardt (1678–1679) on Pythagorean triangles with square measures and related questions were unsatisfying. The correspondence with Oldenburg provided an opportunity, in the early summer of 1677, to communicate the determination of tangents according to the method of the differential calculus, but this exchange ended in the autumn with Oldenburg's death. Huygens was ill and Tschirnhaus was traveling in Italy. Thus, in the midst of his multitudinous duties at court, Leibniz lacked the external stimulus needed to continue his previous studies on a large scale. Instead, he concentrated on symbological investigations, his first detailed draft in dyadics, and studies on pure geometric representation of positional relations without calculation, the counterpart to analytic geometry. Only after the founding of the *Acta eruditorum* (1682) did Leibniz present his mathematical papers to the public. In 1682 he published "De vera proportione circuli ad quadratum circumscriptum in numeris rationalibus" and "Unicum opticae, catoptricae et dioptricae principium," concise summaries of the chief results of the arithmetical quadrature of the circle and a hint regarding the derivation of the law of refraction by means of the extreme value method of the differential calculus. These revelations were followed in 1684 by the method of determining algebraic integrals of algebraic functions, a brief presentation of the differential calculus with a hint concerning the solution of Debeaune's problem by means of the logarithmic curve, and further remarks on the fundamental ideas of the integral calculus.

In 1686 Leibniz published the main concepts of the proof of the transcendental nature of $\int \sqrt{a^2 \pm x^2} \cdot dx$ and an example of integration, the first appearance in print of the integral sign (the initial letter of the word *summa*).

Yet Leibniz did not attract general attention until his public attack on Cartesian dynamics (1686–1688) by reference to the principle of the conservation of *vis viva*, with the dimensions mv^2. In the subsequent controversy with the Cartesians, Leibniz put forth for solution a dynamic problem that was also considered by Huygens (1687) and Jakob Bernoulli (1690): Under what conditions does a point moving without friction in a parallel gravitational field descend with uniform velocity? In this connection, Bernoulli raised the problem of the catenary, which was solved almost simultaneously by Leibniz, Huygens, and Johann Bernoulli (published 1691) and which introduced for debate a series of further subjects of increasing difficulty, stemming primarily from applied dynamics. Two are particularly noteworthy: The first was the determination, requested by Leibniz in 1689, of the isochrona paracentrica. Under what conditions does a point moving without friction under constant gravity revolve with uniform velocity about a fixed point? This problem was solved by Leibniz, Jakob Bernoulli, and Johann Bernoulli (1694). The second was the determination, requested by Johann Bernoulli, of the conditions under which a point moving without friction in a parallel gravitational field descends in the shortest possible time from one given point to another given point below it. This problem, called the brachistochrone, was solved in 1697 by Leibniz, Newton, Jakob Bernoulli, and Johann Bernoulli.

The participants in these investigations revealed only their results, not their derivations. The latter are found, in the case of Leibniz, in the posthumous papers or, in certain instances, in the letters exchanged with Jakob Bernoulli (from 1687), Rudolf Christian von Bodenhausen (from 1690), L'Hospital (from 1692), and Johann Bernoulli (from 1693). These letters, like the papers on pure mathematics that Leibniz published in the scientific journals, were usually hastily written in his few free hours. They were not always well edited and are far from being free of errors. Yet, despite their imperfections, they are extraordinarily rich in ideas. In part the letters were written to communicate original ideas, which were only occasionally pursued later; most of them, however, are drawn from earlier papers or brief notes. The following ideas in the correspondence should be specially mentioned:

(*a*) The determination of the center of curvature for a point of a curve as the intersection of two adjacent normals (1686–1692). Leibniz erroneously assumed that the circle of curvature has, in general, four neighboring points (instead of three) in common with the curve. It was only after some years that he understood, through the detailed explanation of Johann Bernoulli, the objections made by Jakob Bernoulli (from 1692). He immediately admitted his error publicly and candidly, as was his custom (1695–1696).

(*b*) The determination of that reflecting curve in the plane by which a given reflecting curve is completed in such a way that the rays of light coming from a given point are rejoined, after reflection in both curves, in another given point (1689).

(*c*) A detailed presentation of the results of the arithmetical quadrature of the circle and of the hyperbola, combined with communication of the power series for the arc tangent, the cosine, the sine, the natural logarithm, and the exponential function (1691).

(*d*) The theory of envelopes, illustrated with examples (1692, 1694).

(*e*) The treatment of differential equations through arrangement in undetermined coefficients (1693).

(*f*) The determination of the tractrix for a straight path and, following this, a mechanical construction of the integral curves of differential equations (1693), the earliest example of an integraph.

In 1694 Leibniz expressed his intention to present his own contributions and those of other contemporary mathematicians uniformly and comprehensively in a large work to be entitled *Scientia infiniti*. By 1696 Jakob Bernoulli had provided him with some of his own work and Leibniz had composed headings for earlier notes and selected some essential passages, but he did not get beyond this preliminary, unorganized collection of material. Much of his time was now taken up defending his ideas. Nieuwentijt, for example (1694–1696), questioned the admissibility and use of higher differentials. In his defense, Leibniz emphasized that his method should be considered only an abbreviated and easily grasped guide and that everything could be confirmed by strict deductions in the style of Archimedes (1695). On this occasion he revealed the differentiation of exponential functions such as x^x, which he had long known.

Even the originality of Leibniz' method was called

into doubt. Hence, in 1691, Jakob Bernoulli, who was interested primarily in results and not in general concepts, saw in Leibniz' differential calculus only a mathematical reproduction of what Barrow had presented in a purely geometrical fashion in his *Lectiones geometricae*. He also failed to realize the general significance of the symbolism. In England it was observed with growing uneasiness that Leibniz was becoming increasingly the leader of a small but very active group of mathematicians. Moreover, the English deplored the lack of any public indication that Leibniz—as Newton supposed—had taken crucial suggestions from the two great letters of 1676. Representative material from these letters was in Wallis' *Algebra* (1685), and it was expanded in the Latin version (Wallis' *Opera*, II [1693]). Fatio de Duillier, who shortly before had seen copies of Newton's letters and other unpublished writings on methods of quadrature (1676), became convinced that in the treatment of questions in the mathematics of infinitesimals Newton had advanced far beyond Leibniz and that the latter was dependent on Newton. Since 1687 Fatio had been working with Huygens, who did not think much of Leibniz' symbolism, on the treatment of "inverse" tangent problems—differential equations—and in simple cases had achieved a methodical application of integrating factors.

In the preface to Volume I of Wallis' *Opera*, which did not appear until 1695, it is stated that the priority for the infinitesimal methods belongs to Newton. Furthermore, the words are so chosen that it could have been—and in fact was—inferred that Leibniz plagiarized Newton. Wallis, in his concern for the proper recognition of Newton's merits, was unceasing in his efforts to persuade Newton to publish his works on this subject. Beyond this, he obtained copies of several of the letters exchanged between Leibniz and Oldenburg in the years 1673 to 1677 and received permission from Newton and Leibniz to publish the writings in question. He included them in Volume III of his *Opera* (1699). The collection he assembled was based not on the largely inaccessible originals but, rather, on copies in which crucial passages were abbreviated. As a result, it was possible for the reader to gain the impression that Newton possessed priority in having obtained decisive results in the field of infinitesimals (method of tangents, power series in the handling of quadratures, and inverse tangent problems) and that Leibniz was guilty of plagiarism on the basis of what he had taken from Newton. Fatio pronounced this reproach in the sharpest terms in his *Lineae brevissimi descensus investigatio* (1699).

Leibniz replied in 1700 with a vigorous defense of his position, in which he stressed that he had obtained only results, not methods, from Newton and that he had already published the fundamental concepts of the differential calculus in 1684, three years before the appearance of the material that Newton referred to in a similar form in his *Principia* (1687). On this occasion he also described his own procedure with reference to de Moivre's theorem (1698) on series inversion through the use of undetermined coefficients. Leibniz made his procedure more general and easier to grasp by the introduction of numerical coefficients (in the sense of indices). The attack subsided because Fatio, who was excitable, oversensitive, and given to a coarse manner of expression, turned away from science and became a fervent adherent of an aggressive religious sect. He was eventually pilloried.

Wallis' insinuations were repeated by G. Cheyne in his *Methodus* (1703) and temperately yet firmly rebutted in Leibniz' review of 1703. Cheyne's discussion of special quadratures was probably what led Newton to publish the *Quadratura curvarum* (manuscript of 1676) and the *Enumeratio linearum tertii ordinis* (studies beginning in 1667–1668) as appendices to the *Optics* (1704). Newton viewed certain passages of Leibniz' review of the *Optics* (1705) as abusive attacks and gave additional material to John Keill, who, in a paper published in 1710, publicly accused Leibniz of plagiarism. Leibniz' protests (1711) led to the establishment of a commission of the Royal Society, which decided against him (1712) on the basis of the letters printed by Wallis and further earlier writings produced by Newton. The commission published the evidence, together with an analysis that had been published in 1711, in a *Commercium epistolicum* (1713 edition).

The verdict reached by these biased investigators, who heard no testimony from Leibniz and only superficially examined the available data, was accepted without question for some 140 years and was influential into the first half of the twentieth century. In the light of the much more extensive material now available, it is recognized as wrong. It can be understood only in the nationalistic context in which the controversy took place. The continuation of the quarrel was an embarrassment to both parties; and, since it yielded nothing new scientifically, it is unimportant for an understanding of Leibniz' mathematics. The intended rebuttal did not materialize, and Leibniz' interesting, but fragmentary, account of how he arrived at his discovery (*Historia et origo calculi differentialis* [1714]) was not published until the nineteenth century.

The hints concerning mathematical topics in Leibniz' correspondence are especially fascinating.

When writing to those experienced in mathematics, whom he viewed as competitors, he expressed himself very cautiously, yet with such extraordinary cleverness that his words imply far more than is apparent from an examination of the notes and jottings preserved in his papers. For instance, his remarks on the solvability of higher equations are actually an anticipation of Galois's theory. Frequently, material of general validity is illustrated only by simple examples, as is the case with the schematic solution of systems of linear equations by means of number couples (double indices) in quadratic arrangement, which corresponds to the determinant form (1693).

In several places the metaphysical background is very much in evidence, as in the working out of binary numeration, which Leibniz connected with the creation of the world (indicated by 1) from nothingness (indicated by 0). The same is true of his interpretation of the imaginary number as an intermediate entity between Being and Not-Being (1702). His hope of being able to make a statement about the transcendence of π by employing the dyadic presentation (1701) was fruitless yet interesting, for transcendental numbers can be constructed out of infinite dual fractions possessing regular gaps (an example in the decimal system was given by Goldbach in 1729). The attempts to present $\sum_{n=1}^{r} \frac{1}{n}$ (reference in 1682, recognized as false in 1696) and $\sum_{n=1}^{\infty} \frac{1}{n^2}$ (1696) in closed form were unsuccessful, and the claimed rectification of an arc of the equilateral hyperbola through the quadrature of the hyperbola (1676) was based on an error in computation. Against these failures we may set the importance of the recognition of the correspondence between the multinomial theorem (1676) and the continuous differentiation and integration with fractional index that emerged from this observation. During this period (about 1696) Leibniz also achieved the general representation of partial differentiation; the reduction of the differential equation

$$a_{00} + a_{10}x + (a_{01} + a_{11}x)y' = 0$$

by means of the transformation

$$x = p_{11}u + p_{12}v, \; y = p_{21}u + p_{22}v;$$

the solution of

$$y' + p(x)y + q(x) = 0$$

and

$$(y')^2 + p(x)y' + q(x) = 0$$

through series with coefficients in number couples; and the reduction of the equation, which had originated with Jakob Bernoulli,

$$y' = p(x)y + q(x)y^n$$

to

$$y' = P(x)y + Q(x).$$

Leibniz' inventive powers and productivity in mathematics did not begin to slow until around 1700. The integration of rational functions (1702–1703) was, to be sure, an important accomplishment; but the subject was not completely explored, since Leibniz supposed (Johann Bernoulli to the contrary) that there existed other imaginary units besides $\sqrt{-1}$ (for example, $\sqrt[4]{-1}$) which could not be represented by ordinary complex numbers. The subsequent study, which was not published at the time, on the integration of special classes of irrational functions also remains of great interest. The discussion with Johann Bernoulli on the determination of arclike algebraic curves in the plane (1704–1706) resulted in both a consideration of relative motions in the plane and an interesting geometric construction of the arclike curve equivalent to a given curve. This construction is related to the optical essay of 1689 and to the theory of envelopes of 1692–1694, but it cannot readily be grasped in terms of a formula (1706). The remarks (1712) on the logarithms of negative numbers and on the representation of $\sum(-1)^n$ by 1/2 can no longer be considered satisfactory. The description of the calculating machine (1710) indicates its importance but does not give the important details; the first machines of practical application were constructed by P. M. Hahn in 1774 on the basis of Leibniz' ideas.

Leibniz accorded a great importance to mathematics because of its broad interest and numerous applications. The extent of his concern with mathematics is evident from the countless remarks and notes in his posthumous papers, only small portions of which have been accessible in print until now, as well as from the exceedingly challenging and suggestive influential comments expressed brilliantly in the letters and in the works published in his own lifetime.

Leibniz' power lay primarily in his great ability to distinguish the essential elements in the results of others, which were often rambling and presented in a manner that was difficult to understand. He put them in a new form, and by setting them in a larger context made them into a harmoniously balanced and comprehensive whole. This was possible only because in his reading Leibniz was prepared, despite his impatience, to immerse himself enthusiastically and selflessly in the thought of others. He was concerned with formulating authoritative ideas clearly and connecting them, as he did in so exemplary a fashion in the mathematics of infinitesimals. Interesting details were important—they occur often in his notes—but even more important were inner relationships and their comprehension, as this term is employed in the history of thought. He undertook the work required by such an approach for no other purpose than the exploration of the conditions under which new ideas emerge, stimulate each other, and are joined in a unified thought structure.

JOSEPH E. HOFMANN

BIBLIOGRAPHY

I. ORIGINAL WORKS. The following volumes of the *Sämtliche Schriften und Briefe*, edited by the Deutsche Akademie der Wissenschaften in Berlin, have been published: Series I *(Allgemeiner politischer und historischer Briefwechsel)*, vol. 1: 1668–1676 (1923; Hildesheim, 1970); vol. 2: 1676–1679 (1927; Hildesheim, 1970); vol. 3: 1680–1683 (1938; Hildesheim, 1970); vol. 4: 1684–1687 (1950); vol. 5: 1687–1690 (1954; Hildesheim, 1970); vol. 6: 1690–1691 (1957; Hildesheim, 1970); vol. 7: 1691–1692 (1964); vol. 8: 1692 (1970); Series II *(Philosophischer Briefwechsel)*, vol. 1: 1663–1685 (1926); Series IV *(Politische Schriften)*, vol. 1: 1667–1676 (1931); vol. 2: 1677–1687 (1963); Series VI *(Philosophische Schriften)*, vol. 1: 1663–1672 (1930); vol. 2: 1663–1672 (1966); vol. 6: *Nouveaux essais* (1962).

Until publication of the *Sämtliche Schriften und Briefe* is completed, it is necessary to use earlier editions and recent partial editions. The most important of these editions are the following (the larger editions are cited first): L. Dutens, ed., *G. W. Leibnitii opera omnia*, 6 vols. (Geneva, 1768); J. E. Erdmann, ed., *G. W. Leibniz. Opera philosophica quae extant latina gallica germanica omnia* (Berlin, 1840; Aalen, 1959); G. H. Pertz, ed., *G. W. Leibniz. Gesammelte Werke*, Part I: *Geschichte*, 4 vols. (Hannover, 1843–1847; Hildesheim, 1966); A. Foucher de Careil, ed., *Leibniz. Oeuvres*, 7 vols. (Paris, 1859–1875; Hildesheim, 1969); C. I. Gerhardt, ed., *G. W. Leibniz. Mathematische Schriften*, 7 vols. (Berlin–Halle, 1849–1863; Hildesheim, 1962). An index to the edition has been compiled by J. E. Hofmann (Hildesheim, 1971); C. I. Gerhardt, ed., *Die philosophischen Schriften von G. W. Leibniz*, 7 vols. (Berlin, 1875–1890; Hildesheim, 1960–1961); G. E. Guhrauer, ed., *G. W. Leibniz. Deutsche Schriften*, 2 vols. (Berlin, 1838–1840; Hildesheim, 1966); J. G. Eckhart, ed., *G. W. Leibniz. Collectanea etymologica* (Hannover, 1717; Hildesheim, 1970); A. Foucher de Careil, ed., *Lettres et opuscules inédits de Leibniz* (Paris, 1854; Hildesheim, 1971); A. Foucher de Careil, ed., *Nouvelles lettres et opuscules inédits de Leibniz* (Paris, 1857; Hildesheim, 1971); C. Haas, ed. and tr., *Theologisches System* (Tübingen, 1860; Hildesheim, 1966); C. L. Grotefend, ed., *Briefwechsel zwischen Leibniz, Arnauld und dem Landgrafen Ernst von Hessen-Rheinfels* (Hannover, 1846); C. I. Gerhardt, ed., *Briefwechsel zwischen Leibniz und Christian Wolff* (Halle, 1860; Hildesheim, 1963); E. Bodemann, ed., *Die Leibniz-Handschriften der Königlichen öffentlichen Bibliothek zu Hannover* (Hannover, 1889; Hildesheim, 1966); and *Der Briefwechsel des G. W. Leibniz in der Königlichen öffentlichen Bibliothek zu Hannover* (Hannover, 1895; Hildesheim, 1966); C. I. Gerhardt, ed., *Der Briefwechsel von G. W. Leibniz mit Mathematikern* (Berlin, 1899; Hildesheim, 1962); L. Couturat, ed., *Opuscules et fragments inédits de Leibniz* (Paris, 1903; Hildesheim, 1966); E. Gerland, ed., *Leibnizens nachgelassene Schriften physikalischen, mechanischen und technischen Inhalts* (Leipzig, 1906); H. Lestienne, ed., *G. W. Leibniz. Discours de métaphysique* (Paris, 1907, 2nd ed., 1929; Paris, 1952); I. Jagodinskij, ed., *Leibnitiana elementa philosophiae arcanae de summa rerum* (Kazan, 1913); P. Schrecker, ed., *G. W. Leibniz. Lettres et fragments inédits sur les problèmes philosophiques, théologiques, politiques de la réconciliation des doctrines protestantes (1669–1704)* (Paris, 1934); G. Grua, ed., *G. W. Leibniz. Textes inédits*, 2 vols. (Paris, 1948); W. von Engelhardt, ed. and tr., *G. W. Leibniz. Protogaea*, in *Leibniz. Werke* (W. E. Peuckert, ed.), vol. I (Stuttgart, 1949); A. Robinet, ed., *G. W. Leibniz. Principes de la nature et de la grâce fondés en raison. Principes de la philosophie ou monadologie. Publiés intégralement d'après les manuscrits de Hanovre, Vienne et Paris et présentés d'après des lettres inédits* (Paris, 1954); and *Correspondance Leibniz-Clarke. Présentés d'après les manuscrits originales des bibliothèques de Hanovre et de Londres* (Paris, 1957); G. le Roy, ed., *Leibniz. Discours de métaphysique et correspondance avec Arnauld* (Paris, 1957); O. Saame, ed. and tr., *G. W. Leibniz. Confessio philosophi. Ein Dialog* (Frankfurt, 1967); J. Brunschwig, ed., *Essais de Théodicée sur la bonté de Dieu, la liberté de l'homme et l'origine du mal* (Paris, 1969).

There are translations of single works, especially into English and German. English translations (including selections): *Philosophical Works*, G. M. Duncan, ed. and tr. (New Haven, 1890); *The Monadology and Other Philosophical Writings*, R. Latta, ed. and tr. (Oxford, 1898); *New Essays Concerning Human Understanding*, A. G. Langley, ed. and tr. (Chicago, 1916, 1949); *Discourse on Metaphysics*, P. G. Lucas and L. Grint, ed. and tr. (Manchester, 1953; 2nd ed. 1961); *Philosophical Writings*, M. Morris, ed. and tr. (London, 1934, 1968); *Theodicy*, E. M. Huggard and A. Farrer, ed. and tr. (London, 1951); *Selections*, P. P. Wiener, ed. (New York, 1951; 2nd ed. 1971); *Philosophical Papers and Letters*, L. E. Loemker, ed. and tr., 2 vols. (Chicago, 1956; 2nd ed. Dordrecht, 1969); *The Leibniz-Clarke Correspondence*, H. G. Alexander, ed. (Manchester, 1956); *Monadology and Other Philosophical Essays*, P. and A. Schrecker, ed. and tr. (Indianapolis, 1965); *Logical Papers*, G. H. R. Parkinson, ed. and tr. (Oxford, 1966); *The Leibniz-Arnauld Correspondence*,

H. T. Mason, ed. and tr. (Manchester–New York, 1967); *General Investigations Concerning the Analysis of Concepts and Truths*, W. H. O'Brian, ed. and tr. (Athens, Ga., 1968).

German translations (including selections) are *Handschriften zur Grundlegung der Philosophie*, E. Cassirer, ed., A. Buchenau, tr., 2 vols. (Hamburg, 1904; 3rd ed. 1966); *Neue Abhandlungen über den menschlichen Verstand*, E. Cassirer, ed. and tr. (3rd ed., 1915; Hamburg, 1971); the same work, edited and translated by H. H. Holz and W. von Engelhardt, 2 vols. (Frankfurt, 1961); *Die Theodizee*, A. Buchenau, ed. and tr. (Hamburg, 2nd ed., 1968); *Schöpferische Vernunft*, W. von Engelhardt, ed. and tr. (Marburg, 1952); *Metaphysische Abhandlung*, H. Herring, ed. and tr. (Hamburg, 1958); *Fragmente zur Logik*, F. Schmidt, ed. and tr. (Berlin, 1960); *Vernunftprinzipien der Natur und der Gnade. Monadologie*, H. Herring, ed., A. Buchenau, tr. (Hamburg, 1960); *Kleine Schriften zur Metaphysik*, H. H. Holz, ed., 2 vols. (Frankfurt–Vienna, 1966–1967).

Bibliographical material on the works of Leibniz and the secondary literature can be found in E. Ravier, *Bibliographie des oeuvres de Leibniz* (Paris, 1937; Hildesheim, 1966), additional material in P. Schrecker, "Une bibliographie de Leibniz," in *Revue philosophique de la France et de l'Étranger*, **126** (1938), 324–346; Albert Rivaud, *Catalogue critique des manuscrits de Leibniz Fasc. II (Mars 1672–Novembre 1676)* (Poitiers, 1914–1924; repr. New York–Hildesheim, 1972); K. Müller, *Leibniz-Bibliographie. Verzeichnis der Literatur über Leibniz* (Frankfurt, 1967). Bibliographical supplements appear regularly in *Studia Leibnitiana. Vierteljahresschrift für Philosophie und Geschichte der Wissenschaften*, K. Müller and W. Totok, eds., **1** (1969); G. Utermöhlen, "Leibniz-Bibliographie 1967–1968," **1** (1969), 293–320; G. Utermöhlen and A. Schmitz, "Leibniz-Bibliographie. Neue Titel 1968–1970," **2** (1970), 302–320; A. Koch-Klose and A. Hölzer, "Leibniz-Bibliographie. Neue Titel 1969–1971," **3** (1971), 309–320.

II SECONDARY LITERATURE. The literature on Leibniz' philosophy and science is so extensive that a complete presentation cannot be given. In the following selection, more recent works have been preferred, especially those which may provide additional views on the philosophy and science of Leibniz.

H. Aarsleff, "Leibniz on Locke and Language," in *American Philosophical Quarterly*, **1** (1964), 165–188; E. J. Aiton, "The Harmonic Vortex of Leibniz," in *The Vortex Theory of Planetary Motions* (London–New York, 1972); and "Leibniz on Motion in a Resisting Medium," in *Archive for History of Exact Sciences*, **9** (1972), 257–274; W. H. Barber, *Leibniz in France. From Arnauld to Voltaire* (Oxford, 1955); Y. Belaval, *Leibniz critique de Descartes* (Paris, 1960); and *Leibniz. Initiation à sa philosophie* (Paris, 1962; 3rd ed. 1969); A. Boehm, *Le "vinculum substantiale" chez Leibniz. Ses origines historiques* (Paris, 1938; 2nd ed. 1962); F. Brunner, *Études sur la signification historique de la philosophie de Leibniz* (Paris, 1950); G. Buchdahl, *Metaphysics and the Philosophy of Science.*

The Classical Origins—Descartes to Kant (Oxford, 1969); P. Burgelin, *Commentaire du Discours de métaphysique de Leibniz* (Paris, 1959); H. W. Carr, *Leibniz* (London, 1929, 1960); E. Cassirer, *Leibniz' System in seinem wissenschaftlichen Grundlagen* (Marburg, 1902; Darmstadt, 1962); P. Costabel, *Leibniz et la dynamique. Les textes de 1692* (Paris, 1960); L. Couturat, *La logique de Leibniz* (Paris, 1901; Hildesheim, 1961); L. Davillé, *Leibniz historien. Essai sur l'activité et les méthodes historiques de Leibniz* (Paris, 1909); K. Dürr, *Neue Beleuchtung einer Theorie von Leibniz. Grundzüge des Logikkalküls* (Darmstadt, 1930); K. Dürr, "Die mathematische Logik von Leibniz," in *Studia philosophica*, **7** (1947), 87–102; K. Fischer, *G. W. Leibniz. Leben, Werke und Lehre* (Heidelberg, 5th ed. 1920, W. Kabitz, ed.); J. O. Fleckenstein, *G. W. Leibniz. Barock und Universalismus* (Munich, 1958); G. Friedmann, *Leibniz et Spinoza* (Paris, 2nd ed. 1946, 3rd ed. 1963); M. Gueroult, *Dynamique et métaphysique leibniziennes suivi d'une note sur le principe de la moindre action chez Maupertuis* (Paris, 1934, 1967); G. E. Guhrauer, *G. W. Freiherr von Leibniz. Eine Biographie*, 2 vols. (Wrocław, 1846; Hildesheim, 1966); G. Grua, *Jurisprudence universelle et théodicée selon Leibniz* (Paris, 1953); and *La justice humaine selon Leibniz* (Paris, 1956); H. Heimsoeth, *Die Methode der Erkenntnis bei Descartes und Leibniz*, 2 vols. (Giessen, 1912–1914); A. Heinekamp, *Das Problem des Guten bei Leibniz* (Bonn, 1969); K. Hildebrandt, *Leibniz und das Reich der Gnade* (The Hague, 1953); H. H. Golz, *Leibniz* (Stuttgart, 1958); K. Huber, *Leibniz* (Munich, 1951); J. Jalabert, *La théorie leibnizienne de la substance* (Paris, 1947); J. Jalabert, *Le Dieu de Leibniz* (Paris, 1960); J. Guitton, *Pascal et Leibniz* (Paris, 1951); M. Jammer, *Concepts of Force. A Study in the Foundations of Dynamics* (Cambridge, Mass., 1957); W. Janke, *Leibniz. Die Emendation der Metaphysik* (Frankfurt, 1963); H. W. B. Joseph, *Lectures on the Philosophy of Leibniz*, J. L. Austin, ed. (Oxford, 1949); W. Kabitz, *Die Philosophie des jungen Leibniz. Untersuchungen zur Entwicklungsgeschichte seines Systems* (Heidelberg, 1909); F. Kaulbach, *Die Metaphysik des Raumes bei Leibniz und Kant* (Cologne, 1960); R. Kauppi, *Über die leibnizsche Logik. Mit besonderer Berücksichtigung des Problems der Intension und der Extension* (*Acta Philosophica Fennica XII;* Helsinki, 1960); W. Kneale and M. Kneale, *The Development of Logic* (Oxford, 1962); L. Krüger, *Rationalismus und Entwurf einer universalen Logik bei Leibniz* (Frankfurt, 1969); D. Mahnke, "Leibnizens Synthese von Universalmathematik und Individualmetaphysik," in *Jahrbuch für Philosophie und phänomenologische Forschung*, **7** (1925), 305–612 (repr. Stuttgart, 1964); G. Martin, *Leibniz. Logik und Metaphysik* (Cologne, 1960; 2nd ed., Berlin, 1967; English tr. by P. G. Lucas and K. J. Northcott from the 1st ed. : *Leibniz. Logic and Metaphysics* (Manchester–New York, 1964); J. T. Mertz, *Leibniz* (Edinburgh–London, 1884; repr. New York, 1948); R. W. Meyer, *Leibniz and the 17th Century Revolution* (Glasgow, 1956); J. Mittelstrass, *Neuzeit und Aufklärung. Studien zur Entstehung der neuzeitlichen Wissenschaft und Philosophie* (Berlin, 1970); J. Moreau, *L'universe leibnizien* (Paris–Lyons, 1956);

K. Müller and G. Krönert, *Leben und Werk von G. W. Leibniz. Eine Chronik* (Frankfurt, 1969); E. Naert, *Leibniz et la querelle du pur amour* (Paris, 1959); E. Naert, *Mémoire et conscience de soi selon Leibniz* (Paris, 1961); G. H. R. Parkinson, *Logic and Reality in Leibniz' Metaphysics* (Oxford, 1965); G. H. R. Parkinson, *Leibniz on Human Freedom* (*Studia Leibnitiana Sonderheft 2;* Wiesbaden, 1970); C. A. van Peursen, *Leibniz* (Baarn, 1966), tr. into English by H. Hoskins (London, 1969); H. Poser, *Zur Theorie der Modalbegriffe bei G. W. Leibniz* (*Studia Leibnitiana Suppl. VI;* Wiesbaden, 1969); N. Rescher, "Leibniz' Interpretation of His Logical Calculi," in *Journal of Symbolic Logic,* **19** (1954), 1–13; N. Rescher, *The Philosophy of Leibniz* (Englewood Cliffs, N.J., 1967); W. Risse, *Die Logik der Neuzeit II: 1640–1780* (Stuttgart, 1970); A. Robinet, *Malebranche et Leibniz. Relations personelles* (Paris, 1955); A. Robinet, *Leibniz et la racine de l'existence* (Paris, 1962); B. Russell, *A Critical Exposition of the Philosophy of Leibniz* (Cambridge, 1900; 2nd ed., London, 1937); H. Schiedermair, *Das Phänomen der Macht und die Idee des Rechts bei G. W. Leibniz* (*Studia Leibnitiana Suppl. VII;* Wiesbaden, 1970); H. Scholz, "Leibniz" (1942), reprinted in H. Scholz, *Mathesis universalis,* H. Hermes, F. Kambartel and J. Ritter, eds. (Basel, 1961); L. Stein, *Leibniz und Spinoza. Ein Beitrag zur Entwicklungsgeschichte der leibnizischen Philosophie* (Berlin, 1890); G. Stieler, *Leibniz und Malebranche und das Theodizeeproblem* (Darmstadt, 1930); W. Totok and C. Haase, eds., *Leibniz. Sein Leben, sein Wirken, seine Welt* (Hannover, 1966); A. T. Tymieniecka, *Leibniz' Cosmological Synthesis* (Assen, 1964); P. Wiedeburg, *Der junge Leibniz, das Reich und Europa,* pt. I, 2 vols. (Wiesbaden, 1962).

E. Hochstetter, ed., *Leibniz zu seinem 300 Geburtstag 1646–1946,* 8 pts. (Berlin, 1946–1952); G. Schischkoff, ed., *Beiträge zur Leibniz-Forschung* (Reutlingen, 1947); E. Hochstetter and G. Schischkoff, eds., *Zum Gedenken an den 250 Todestag von G. W. Leibniz* (*Zeitschrift für philosophische Forschung,* **20,** nos. 3–4 (Meisenheim, 1966), 377–658; and *Zum Gedenken an den 250 Todestag von G. W. Leibniz* (*Philosophia naturalis,* **10,** no. 2 (1968), 134–293); *Leibniz (1646–1716). Aspects de l'homme et de l'oeuvre (Journées Leibniz, organis. au Centre Int. de Synthèse, 28–30 mai 1966)* (Paris, 1968); *Studia Leibnitiana Supplementa,* vols. I–V (*Akten des Int. Leibniz-Kongresses Hannover, 14–19 November 1966)* (Wiesbaden, 1968–1970).

LEMOINE, ÉMILE MICHEL HYACINTHE (*b.* Quimper, France, 22 November 1840; *d.* Paris, France, 21 December 1912)

Lemoine can be characterized as an amateur mathematician and musician whose work was influential in both areas. Like a number of other famous French mathematicians, he was educated at the École Polytechnique in Paris, from which he was graduated in 1860. He taught there but was forced to resign after five or six years because of poor health.

Subsequently he was a civil engineer, and he eventually became chief inspector for the department of gas supply in Paris. His avocations remained mathematics and music.

In 1860, while he was still at the École Polytechnique, Lemoine and other teachers formed a chamber music group, nicknamed "La Trompette." Camille Saint-Saëns wrote pieces for it.

Lemoine's major mathematical achievements were in geometry. He and John Casey are generally credited with having founded the newer geometry of the triangle.

In 1873, at the meeting of the Association Française pour l'Avancement des Sciences held in Lyons, Lemoine presented a paper entitled "Sur quelques propriétés d'un point remarquable du triangle." In this paper he called attention to the point of intersection of the symmedians of a triangle and described some of its more important properties. He also introduced the special circle named for him.

The point of concurrence of the symmedians of a triangle is called the Lemoine point (in France), the Grebe point (in Germany, after E. W. Grebe), or, most generally, the symmedian point. The last term was coined by the geometer Robert Tucker, of the University College School in London, in the interest of uniformity and amity. It is generally symbolized by K.

The symmedian point had appeared in the work of geometers before Lemoine, but his was the first systematic exposition of some of its interesting properties. Lemoine's concern with the problem of simplifying geometric constructions led him to develop a theory of constructions, which he called geometrography. He presented this system at the meeting of the Association Française pour l'Avancement des Sciences that was held at Oran, Algeria, in 1888.

Briefly, Lemoine reduced geometric constructions to five elementary operations: (1) placing a compass end on a given point; (2) placing a compass end on a given line; (3) drawing a circle with the compass so placed; (4) placing a straightedge on a given point; (5) drawing a line once the straightedge has been placed. The number of times any one of these five operations was performed he called the "simplicity" of the construction. The number of times operation (1), (2), or (4) was performed he called the "exactitude" of the construction. By a suitable examination of the operations involved in a construction, it is usually possible to reduce the simplicity. For example, it is possible to reduce the simplicity of the construction of a circle tangent to three given circles (Apollonius' problem) from over 400 steps to 199 steps.

This system had a mixed reception in the mathematical world. It appears to help reduce the number of steps required for constructions but generally requires more geometrical sophistication and ingenuity on the part of the constructor. It is now generally ignored.

Lemoine also wrote on local probability and on transformations involving geometric formulas. Concerning these transformations, he showed that it is always possible, by a suitable exchange of line segments, to derive from one formula a second formula of the same nature. Thus, from the formula for the radius of the incircle of a triangle, it is possible to derive formulas for the radii of the excircles of the same triangle.

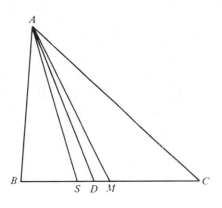

FIGURE 1

His mathematical work ceased after about 1895, but Lemoine's interest in the field continued. In 1894 he helped C. A. Laisant to found the periodical *Intermédiare des mathématiciens* and was its editor for many years.

Lemoine's reputation rests mainly on his work with the symmedian point. Briefly (see Figure 1), if,

in triangle *ABC*, cevian *AM* is the median from vertex *A* and cevian *AD* is the bisector of the same angle, then cevian *AS*, which is symmetric with *AM* in respect to *AD*, is the symmedian to side *BC*. Among the results presented by Lemoine were that the three symmedians of a triangle are concurrent and that each symmedian divides the side to which it is drawn in the ratio of the squares of the other two sides.

If (see Figure 2) lines are drawn through the given symmedian point *K* parallel to the sides of the given triangle, these lines meet the sides of the triangle in six points lying on a circle. This circle is called the first Lemoine circle. The center of the circle is the midpoint of the line segment, *OK*, joining the circumcenter and symmedian point of the triangle. The distances of *K* from the sides of the triangle are proportional to the lengths of the sides. The line segments cut from the sides by the first Lemoine circle have lengths proportional to the cubes of the sides. If antiparallels are drawn to the sides through *K*, they meet the sides of the triangle in six concyclic points. The circle thus determined, called the second Lemoine circle, has its center at *K*. Since their introduction by Lemoine, many properties of the symmedian point and the Lemoine circles have been discovered.

BIBLIOGRAPHY

I. ORIGINAL WORKS. Lemoine's papers are listed in Poggendorff, III, 793; IV, 864; V, 727–728; and in the Royal Society *Catalogue of Scientific Papers*, VIII, 200–201; X, 560–561; XVI, 699–700. See esp. "Note sur un point remarquable du plan d'un triangle," in *Nouvelles annales de mathématiques*, 2nd ser., **12** (1873), 364–366; "Quelques questions de probabilités résolues géométriquement," in *Bulletin de la Société mathématique de France*, **11** (1883), 13 25; and "Sur une généralisation des propriétés relative au cercle de Brocard et au point de Lemoine," in *Nouvelles annales de mathématiques*, 3rd ser., **4** (1885), 201–223, repr. as "Étude sur le triangle et certains points de géométrographie," in *Proceedings of the Edinburgh Mathematical Society*, **13** (1895), 2–25.

II. SECONDARY LITERATURE. On Lemoine and his work see *La grande encyclopédie*, XXI (Paris, n.d.), 1197; F. Cajori, *A History of Mathematics*, 2nd ed. (London, 1919), 299–300; J. L. Coolidge, *A History of Geometrical Methods* (Oxford, 1940), p. 58, and *passim;* and R. A. Johnson, *Modern Geometry* (Boston–New York, 1929), *passim.*

SAMUEL L. GREITZER

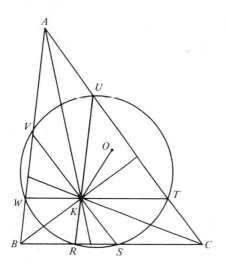

FIGURE 2

LEO (*fl.* Athens, first half of fourth century B.C.)

Leo was a minor mathematician of the Platonic school. All that is known of him comes from the following passage in the summary of the history of geometry reproduced in Proclus' commentary on the first book of Euclid's *Elements*:[1]

> Younger than Leodamas [of Thasos] were Neoclides and his pupil Leo, who[2] added many things to those discovered by their predecessors, so that Leo was able to make a collection of the elements more carefully framed both in the number and in the utility of the things proved, and also found *diorismoi*, that is, tests of when the problem which it is sought to solve is possible and when not.

Proclus' source immediately adds that Eudoxus of Cnidus was "a little younger than Leo"; and since he has earlier made Leodamas contemporary with Archytas and Theaetetus, this puts the active life of Leo in the first half of the fourth century B.C. It is not stated in so many words that he lived in Athens; but since all the other persons mentioned belonged to the Platonic circle, this is a fair inference.

Leo had been preceded in the writing of *Elements* by Hippocrates of Chios. His book has not survived and presumably was eclipsed by Euclid's. He is the first Greek mathematician who is specifically said to have occupied himself with conditions of the possibility of solutions of problems; but the Greek word[3] does not necessarily mean that he discovered or invented the subject—and indeed it is clear that there must have been *diorismoi* before his time. From the earliest days it must have been realized that a triangle could be constructed out of three lines only if the sum of two was greater than the third, as is explicitly stated in Euclid I.22. This was certainly known to the Pythagoreans, and the more sophisticated *diorismos* in Euclid VI.28 is also probably Pythagorean: a parallelogram equal to a given rectilineal figure can be "applied" to a given straight line so as to be deficient by a given figure only if the given figure is not greater than the parallelogram described on half the straight line and is similar to the defect.[4] There is also a *diorismos* in the second geometrical problem in Plato's *Meno*; and if its latest editor, R. S. Bluck, is right in dating that work to about 386–385 B.C., it probably preceded Leo's studies.[5] Nevertheless, Leo must have distinguished himself in this field to have been so singled out for mention by Eudemus, if he is Proclus' ultimate source; it is probable that he was the first to recognize *diorismoi* as a special subject for research, and he may have invented the name.[6]

NOTES

1. Proclus, *In primum Euclidis*, Friedlein ed., pp. 66.18–67.1.
2. The Greek word is in the plural.
3. It is εὑρεῖν, which in its primary sense means no more than "to find." T. L. Heath, *A History of Greek Mathematics* (Oxford, 1921), I, 303, 319, takes it to mean that Leo "invented" *diorismoi*—which he rightly regards as an error—but this is to read too much into the word in this context.
4. The problem is equivalent to the solution of the quadratic equation

$$ax - (b/c)x^2 = A,$$

which has a real root only if

$$A \not> (c/b) \cdot (a^2/4).$$

See T. L. Heath, *The Thirteen Books of Euclid's Elements*, 2nd ed. (Cambridge, 1925; repr. Cambridge–New York, 1956), II, 257–265.
5. See R. S. Bluck, *Plato's Meno* (Cambridge, 1961), pp. 108–120, for the date and app., pp. 441–461, for a discussion of this much-debated problem with full documentation.
6. Primarily signifying "definition," διορισμός came to have two technical meanings in Greek mathematics: (1) the particular enunciation of a Euclidean proposition, that is, a closer definition of the thing sought in relation to a particular figure; and (2) an examination of the conditions of possibility of a solution. Pappus uses the word in the latter sense only, but Proclus knows both meanings (*In primum Euclidis*, Friedlein ed., pp. 202.2–5, 203.4, 9–10). It is easy to see how one meaning merges into the other. See T. L. Heath, *The Thirteen Books of Euclid's Elements*, I, 130–131; and Charles Mugler, *Dictionnaire historique de la terminologie géométrique des grecs*, pp. 141–142.

IVOR BULMER-THOMAS

LEO THE MATHEMATICIAN, also known as **Leo the Philosopher** (*b.* Constantinople[?], *ca.* 790; *d.* Constantinople[?], after 869)

Leo, who is often confused both by medieval and modern scholars with Emperor Leo VI the Wise (886–912) and with the patrician Leo Choerosphactes (*b. ca.* 845–850; *d.* after 919), belonged to a prominent Byzantine family, as is indicated by the fact that his cousin, John VII Morocharzianus the Grammarian, had been patriarch (837–843). The rather conflicting sources attest that Leo obtained a rudimentary education in rhetoric, philosophy, and arithmetic from a scholar on the island of Andros but that his more advanced knowledge of these subjects, and of geometry, astronomy, and astrology was gained through his own researches among the manuscripts that he found in monastic libraries.

In the 820's Leo began to give private instruction at Constantinople; one of the students who had read Euclid's *Elements* with him was captured by the Arab army in 830 or 831, and his enthusiastic report of his master's accomplishments caused the caliph al-Ma'mûn (813–833) to invite Leo to Baghdad. The

Byzantine emperor Theophilus (829–842), learning of this invitation, responded by charging Leo with the task of providing public education at the Church of the Forty Martyrs in Constantinople. While he was in Theophilus' service, Leo supervised the construction of a series of fire-signal stations between Loulon, located north of Tarsus and close to the Arab border, and the capital. A message could be transmitted over these stations in less than an hour; by establishing theoretically synchronized chronometers at either end, Leo was able to provide for the transmission of twelve different messages depending on the hour at which the first fire was lit.

From the spring of 840 until the spring of 843 Leo served as archbishop of Thessalonica, a post he received presumably because of his political influence rather than his holiness. He was promptly deposed when the iconodule Methodius I succeeded his iconoclast cousin John as patriarch in 843. Leo apparently returned to private teaching in Constantinople until about 855, when he was appointed head of the "Philosophical School" founded by Caesar Bardas (d. 866) in the Magnaura Palace, where arithmetic, geometry, and astronomy, as well as grammar and philosophy, were taught. The last notice of him is in a chronicle recording an astrological prediction that he made in Constantinople in 869.

From ninth-century manuscripts Leo is known to have been involved in the process of transcribing texts written in majuscule script into minuscule; this activity may well have included some editorial work, although its nature and extent are uncertain. In any case, he was connected with the transcription of at least some of the Tetralogies of Plato's works, of the larger part of the corpus of Archimedes' works, and of Ptolemy's Almagest; it is likely that he was also concerned with the collection of mathematical and astronomical writings known as the Little Astronomy. Arethas' copy of Euclid's Elements contains, at VI.5, a "school note" by Leo on the addition and subtraction of fractions, in which he uses the Greek alphabetical symbols for numbers as the denominators. Finally, from some of his poems preserved in the Palatine Anthology, it is known that he possessed copies of the Mechanics of Cyrinus and Marcellus, the Conics of Apollonius, the Introduction of the astrologer Paul of Alexandria, the romance of Achilles Tatius, as well as works of Theon on astronomy and Proclus on geometry.

His own surving scientific works are astrological. His "Scholia on the Hourly Motion," which claims to correct an error in an example given in Porphyrius' commentary on Ptolemy's Apotelesmatics, in fact refers to one in Pancharius' commentary on Ptolemy III 11, 8–11, as cited by Hephaestio of Thebes, Apotelesmatics II 11, 39–40 (Pingree, p. 124); his solution is absurdly taken from an entirely different example in the anonymous commentary on Ptolemy III 11, 10 (Wolf, p. 114). This proves that his technical mastery of astrology was very shaky indeed. His treatise "On the Solar Eclipse in the Royal Triplicity" is lifted from Lydus' On Omens 9 (Wachsmuth, pp. 19–21) and from Hephaestio I 21, 12–32 (Pingree, pp. 54–62). The short works on political astrology attributed to him in some manuscripts seem to be derived from the eleventh-century Byzantine translation of an Arabic astrological compendium of one Aḥmad, in which they are II 123–125. It is at present impossible to judge the authenticity of the other brief tracts on divination by thunder, earthquakes, the lords of the weekdays, and the gospels and psalms that are found in Byzantine manuscripts, but skepticism seems to be called for.

It remains, then, that Leo was important for his role in the transmission of Greek scientific literature and in the restoration of Byzantine learning after a long period of decline. He made few, if any, original contributions to science.

BIBLIOGRAPHY

I. Original Works. 1. A homily delivered at Thessalonica on 25 March 842, is in V. Laurent, ed., Mélanges Eugène Tisserant, II (Vatican City, 1964), 281–302.

2. "Scholia on the Hourly Motion," F. Cumont, ed., in Catalogus codicum astrologorum graecorum (hereafter cited as CCAG), I (Brussels, 1898), p. 139.

3. "On the Solar Eclipse in the Royal Triplicity," F. C. Hertlein, ed., in Hermes, 8 (1874), 173–176; cf. F. Boll in CCAG, VII (Brussels, 1908), 150–151.

4. Twelve poems in the Palatine Anthology (IX 200–203, 214, 361, and 578–581; XV 12; and XVI [Planudean Anthology] 387 C). IX 1–358 was edited by P. Waltz (Paris, 1957), and XV by F. Buffière (Paris, 1970); the rest may be found in the ed. by F. Dübner, 2 vols. (Paris, 1864–1877).

5. A group of poems was attributed to Leo and edited by J. F. Boissonade, in Anecdota graeca, II (Paris, 1830), 469 ff.; the first, on old age, may indeed be his.

The following are of doubtful authenticity:

6–7. "How to Know the Lengths of the Reigns of Kings and Rulers, and What Happens in Their Reigns" and "On the Appearance of the Ruler," F. Cumont, ed., in CCAG, IV (Brussels, 1903), 92–93; it has been noted previously that these are taken from Aḥmad.

8. "Thunder Divination According to the Course of the Moon," an unpublished treatise found on fols. 1–2 of

A 56 sup. in the Ambrosian Library, Milan. The index to *CCAG*, III (Brussels, 1901), incorrectly ascribes to Leo that text edited by A. Martini and D. Bassi on pp. 25–29.

9. "Divination From the Holy Gospel and Psalter," on fols. 28v–30 of Laurentianus graecus 86, 14, Florence.

10. "On a Sick Man," a treatise on medical astrology preserved on fols. 137v–138 of Vaticanus graecus 952.

11. A work on astrological predictions from the lords of the weekdays, accompanied by a "portrait" of Leo, on fols. 284v–285v of codex 3632 of the University Library, Bologna.

12. "Earthquake Omens," A. Delatte, ed., *CCAG*, X (Brussels, 1924), 132–135, is attributed to the Emperor Leo (Leo VI the Wise); but the attribution could possibly be a mistake for Leo the Mathematician.

13. "Gnomic Sayings," M. A. Šangin, ed., in *CCAG*, XII (Brussels, 1936), 105.

14. A poem edited by P. Matranga, *Anecdota graeca*, II (Rome, 1850), 559, is sometimes—and probably erroneously—ascribed to Leo; it follows some pieces by Leo's student Constantine, attacking him for studying pagan science, *ibid.*, 555–559.

II. SECONDARY LITERATURE. The best source is now P. Lemerle, *Le premier humanisme byzantin* (Paris, 1971), pp. 148–176; Lemerle gives references to almost all the earlier literature and is weak only in his discussion of Leo's astrological tracts.

DAVID PINGREE

LEODAMAS OF THASOS (*b.* Thasos, Greece; *fl.* Athens, *ca.* 380 B.C.)

Leodamas is treated as a contemporary of Plato in the summary of the history of geometry which Proclus reproduces in his commentary on the first book of Euclid's *Elements:*

> At this time also lived Leodamas of Thasos, Archytas of Tarentum and Theaetetus of Athens, by whom the theorems were increased in number and brought together in a more scientific grouping.[1]

Thasos, the birthplace of Leodamas, is an island in the northern Aegean off the coast of Thrace; but it would appear from the linking of his name with that of Archytas and Theaetetus that he spent his productive years in the Academy at Athens. This association with Archytas and Theaetetus suggests that he must have been a considerable mathematician; but the only other fact known about him is that Plato, according to Diogenes Laertius, "explained" (εἰσηγήσατο) to him the method of analysis[2] or, according to Proclus, "communicated" (παρεδέδωκεν) it to him.[3] Proclus describes analysis as carrying that which is sought up to an acknowledged first principle;

he says it is the most elegant of the methods handed down for the discovery of lemmas in geometry, and he adds that by means of it Leodamas discovered many things in geometry.[4] These passages have led some to suppose that Plato invented the method of mathematical analysis, but this is possibly due to confusion with Plato's emphasis in the *Republic* on philosophical analysis. Mathematical analysis is clearly the same as reduction, of which Hippocrates had given a notable example in the reduction of the problem of doubling the cube to that of finding two mean proportionals; and the method must have been in use even earlier among the Pythagoreans.[5]

NOTES

1. Proclus, *In primum Euclidis*, Friedlein ed. (Leipzig, 1873, repr. Hildesheim, 1967), p. 66.14–18.
2. Diogenes Laertius, III.24. If this sentence is to be read in conjunction with the one preceding, Diogenes' authority is Favorinus.
3. Proclus, *op. cit.*, p. 211.21–22.
4. The fact that at this point Proclus waxes so eloquent about the merits of analysis is regarded by T. L. Heath, in *A History of Greek Mathematics*, I (Oxford, 1921), 120, as proof that he could not himself have been the author of the summary of geometry, and it is virtually certain that the ultimate source of this part of the summary is Eudemus.
5. In the same passage Diogenes Laertius, relying on Favorinus, attributes to Plato the first use of the word "element"—which is obviously untrue, since Democritus must have used it before him.

BIBLIOGRAPHY

See Kurt von Fritz, "Leodamas," in Pauly-Wissowa, Supp. VII (Stuttgart, 1940), cols. 371–373.

IVOR BULMER-THOMAS

LEONARDO DA VINCI (*b.* Vinci, near Empolia, Italy, 15 April 1452; *d.* Amboise, France, 2 May 1519)

The reader may find helpful a preliminary word of explanation on the treatment being given the work of Leonardo da Vinci. The range of his knowledge was such as to recommend individual treatment of specific areas, but it is not that which is exceptional about the article that follows, for other articles in this *Dictionary* have been divided among several scholars specializing in appropriate disciplines. But the case of

Leonardo is *sui generis* even in the context of the Renaissance, hospitable though its climate was to the growth of personal legends. It would be well to agree, before trying to penetrate Leonardo's sensibility, that it is anachronistic to ask whether he was a "scientist" and, although we may use the word "science" for convenience, it is largely irrelevant to wonder what he contributed toward its development. Strictly speaking, a thing cannot be a contribution unless it is known; and until the notebooks came to light, much was rumored but very little known of Leonardo's work except for his surviving paintings and (perhaps) certain features of his engineering practice, together with the well-founded tradition that he was learned in anatomy.

Rather than attributing this or that "discovery" to Leonardo, the interesting matter is to learn what Leonardo knew and how he knew it. It is to fulfill that purpose that the present article was composed. The task is important because it measures the scope of an extraordinary intellect and sensibility. Beyond that, it is rewarding because the study of Leonardo enables us to estimate what could be known at that particular juncture. Indeed, the opportunity is unique in the history of science, at least in its extent, for scientists and philosophers who advance their subjects by completing and communicating their work normally obscure in the process the elements with which they began. Not so Leonardo, whose art in drawing and artlessness in writing open windows to the knowledge latent in the civilization of the Renaissance.

The editors consider that they have been fortunate in persuading Dr. Kenneth D. Keele to write an introductory section on the lineaments of Leonardo's career together with a more detailed treatment of his studies in anatomy and physiology. Drs. Ladislao Reti, Marshall Clagett, Augusto Marinoni, and Cecil Schneer then develop in comparable detail the aspects of Leonardo's work that pertain to technology and engineering, to the science of mechanics, to mathematics, and to geology.

CHARLES C. GILLISPIE

LIFE, SCIENTIFIC METHODS, AND ANATOMICAL WORKS

Leonardo da Vinci was the illegitimate son of Piero da Vinci, a respected Florentine notary, and a peasant girl named Caterina. The year that Leonardo was born, his father was rapidly married off to a girl of good family, Albiera di Giovanni Amadori.

Genetically it is of some interest that Piero's youngest legitimate son, Bartolommeo, an enthusiastic admirer of his half-brother Leonardo, deliberately repeated his father's "experiment" by marrying a woman of Vinci and, as Vasari relates, "prayed God to grant him another Leonardo." In fact he produced Pierino da Vinci, a sculptor of sufficient genius to win himself the name of "Il Vinci" long before he died at the age of twenty-two.

Young Leonardo's education at Vinci was conventionally limited to reading and writing. His early manifested gifts for music and art induced his father to apprentice him, about 1467, to Andrea del Verrocchio, in whose workshop he studied painting, sculpture, and mechanics. During this period in Florence, Leonardo's activities appear to have been directed predominantly toward painting and sculpture; the earliest of his pictures still extant, the "Baptism of Christ," was painted in collaboration with Verrocchio in 1473. The "Adoration of the Magi" was still incomplete when he left for Milan in 1482, to enter the employ of Ludovico Sforza (Ludovico il Moro), duke of Milan. In his application to Ludovico, Leonardo revealed that a great deal of his attention had already been devoted to military engineering; only in concluding did he mention his achievements in architecture, painting, and sculpture, which could "well bear comparison with anyone else."

Leonardo lived at Milan in the duke's service until 1499. During these years his interest in the problems of mechanics and the physics of light grew steadily while his artistic output reached a peak in the fresco "The Last Supper" (1497) and in the clay model of his great equestrian statue of Francesco Sforza (1493). The notebooks of this period show the increase of his interest in mathematics, the physics of light, the physiology of vision, and numerous mechanical problems, including those of flight. Four projects for books—separate treatises on painting, architecture, mechanics, and the human figure—appear in his notes. These studies were to occupy him for the rest of his life. During his last years in Milan he collaborated with the mathematician Luca Pacioli on his *Divina proportione*; Leonardo drew the figures for the first book.

After the capture of the duke of Milan by the French, Leonardo left for Venice, eventually returning to Florence. He then entered the service of Cesare Borgia and was employed for about a year as chief inspector of fortifications and military engineer in the Romagna. Following this he was responsible for an unsuccessful attempt to divert the Arno near Pisa. While in Florence he began the portrait "Mona Lisa" and also the ill-fated fresco "Battle of Anghiari." During these years in Florence, from 1500 to 1506, Leonardo began his systematic researches into human anatomy. Mathematics and the mechanical sciences, too, increasingly occupied his time; and he began to couple his study of the problem of human flight with intensive research on bird flight and meteorology. His studies on the movement of water, a lifelong preoccupation, were later compiled into the *Treatise on the Movement and Measurement of Water*.

In June 1506 Leonardo returned to Milan, where Charles d'Amboise, the French governor, showed him the keenest appreciation he had yet experienced. During this period he produced most of his brilliant anatomical drawings, perhaps stimulated for a short while by the young Pavian anatomist Marcantonio della Torre. Leonardo had now come to feel that mathematics held the key to the "powers" of nature; and his work in hydrology, geology, meteorology, biology, and human physiology was increasingly devoted to a search for the geometrical "rules" of those powers through visual experience, experiment, and reason.

After the French were expelled from Milan in 1513, Leonardo left for Rome, hoping that the Medici Pope Leo X and his brother Giuliano would provide him with encouragement and a good working environment. Nothing came of this hope; and in 1516 he resumed the French liaison, this time with Francis I, with whom he traveled to Amboise in 1516. He died there after a stroke.

Problems of Evaluating Leonardo's Scientific Thought. There are many different opinions concerning Leonardo's stature as a scientist. The essential reason that this is so lies in the grossly abbreviated form in which his work has come down to posterity. Leonardo himself noted that "abbreviators of works do harm to knowledge . . . for certainty springs from a complete knowledge of all the parts which united compose the whole" (*Windsor Collection*, fol. 19084r, in I. A. Richter, *Selections . . .*, p. 3). Unhappily, his extant notes are both abbreviated and confused. It is therefore necessary to assess these defects before evaluating Leonardo's work in the history of science.

The Losses of Leonardo's Manuscripts. Although Leonardo clearly intended to write treatises on painting, architecture, mechanics, and anatomy, he brought none to publication. Two known works are published under his name, the *Treatise on Painting* and *Treatise on the Movement and Measurement of Water*; both were compiled after his death from his notes. These remain of great value, although their respective compilers, Francesco Melzi and Luigi Arconati, constructed them according to their own ideas, rather than Leonardo's. The great mass of

surviving data consists of some 6,000 sheets of Leonardo's manuscript notes. It is difficult to estimate what proportion of the whole these represent. Reti has calculated that 75 percent of the material used by Melzi for his compilation of the *Treatise on Painting* has since been lost. If only a corresponding proportion of Leonardo's scientific notes are extant, this is indeed a severe truncation. The qualitative loss is probably even greater, since there is no trace of a number of "books" to which Leonardo frequently referred in his notes as "completed," and which he used as references, among them an "Elements of Mechanics," and a "Book on Water"—not to mention fifteen "small books" of anatomical drawings.

Sources of Confusion in the Notes. The notes that remain are in great confusion, in part because Leonardo himself made no effort to integrate them, and in part because after his death they underwent almost every conceivable kind of disarrangement and mutilation—as is illustrated by the great scrapbook of sheets composing the *Codex Atlanticus*. Thus the thousands of pages that do survive resemble the pieces of a grossly incomplete jigsaw puzzle.

Leonardo's mode of expressing himself often challenges interpretation. Apart from his "mirror"

FIGURE 1. The diversity of subjects on a single page of Leonardo's notes, of which this is an example, raises problems of interpretation (*Windsor Collection*, fol. 12283. Reproduced by gracious permission of Her Majesty Queen Elizabeth II).

script, he habitually presented his thoughts visually, sometimes covering an astonishing range of phenomena with very few words, as in *Windsor Collection*, fol. 12283 (Figure 1). This page contains segments of circles, a geometrical study for the "rule of diminution" of a straight line when curved, a study of curly hair (with a note on its preparation), and drawings of grasses curling around an arum lily, an old man with curly hair, trees, billowing clouds, rippling waves in a pool, a prancing horse, and a screw press. All can be seen as studies of curves, viewed from different aspects, each of which is developed in detail in various parts of his notes. The sheet provides a good example of Leonardo's visual approach to any problem—by integration—a mode which has until recently been frowned upon by orthodox science. Interpretation of the meaning of many of the drawings must necessarily be speculative; but it is always dangerous to call any drawing a "doodle," since some of Leonardo's most interesting scientific concepts appear as casual, small, inartistic figures.

A further source of confusion in Leonardo's notes derives from his habit of periodically returning to the same subject. This often resulted in incompatible statements in different notes, which Leonardo himself recognized, referring in 1508 to his notes as "a collection without order taken from many papers . . . for which O reader blame me not because the subjects are many, and memory cannot retain them . . . because of the long intervals between one time of writing and another" (*Codex Arundel*, fol. 1r).

Leonardo's thinking was intensely progressive during these "long intervals" of time. A note made in 1490 may therefore differ markedly from one on the same subject from 1500 or 1510. With this understanding, contradictory statements can often be transformed into sources of comprehension if they can be dated—a means of tracing the progress of Leonardo's thought that has only recently become available.

In 1936, with the facsimile production of the Forster codices, it was thought that publication of extant Leonardo notes was complete. Nevertheless, in 1967 two further codices, containing 340 folios, were found in Madrid. These still await publication; and one wonders how many more will be found.

Leonardo's Scientific Method. Leonardo lived at a time when theology was the queen of the sciences. Theological thinking emphasizes the divine incomprehensibility and mystery of natural phenomena; even the Neoplatonic thought of Leonardo's contemporary Marsilio Ficino focused on a direct, revealed link between the mind of man and God and was not concerned with the visual exploration of natural phenomena. Leonardo, on the other hand, declared that faith that is the foundation of all science: there is a logic in natural phenomena detectable by the senses and comprehensible to the mathematical logic of the human mind. Beyond this he postulated God as the creator of all.

Leonardo felt his way to his scientific outlook through his study of the theory of painting, which led him to analyze visual phenomena. As he declared,

> Painters study such things as pertain to the true understanding of all the forms of nature's works, and solicitously contrive to acquire an understanding of all these forms as far as possible. For this is the way to understand the Creator of so many admirable things, and this is the way to love such a great Inventor. In truth great love is born of great knowledge of the thing that is loved [*Treatise on Painting*, para. 80].

For Leonardo the world of nature was created by God, and the science or theory of painting "is a subtle invention which with philosophical and ingenious speculation takes as its theme all the various kinds of forms, airs and scenes, plants, grasses and flowers which are surrounded by light and shade. And this truly is a science and the true-born daughter of Nature" (MS *Ashburnham* 2038, fol. 20r, in E. MacCurdy, *Notebooks*, II, 229).

Science for Leonardo was basically visual: "The eye, the window of the soul, is the chief means whereby the understanding can most fully and abundantly appreciate the infinite works of Nature; and the ear is second" (MS *Ashburnham* 2038, fol. 20r, in E. MacCurdy, *Notebooks*, II, 227). He asserted his belief that the patterns of natural phenomena can conform with the patterns of form created in the human mind—"Painting compels the mind of the painter to transform itself into the very mind of Nature to become an interpreter between Nature and the art. It explains the causes of Nature's manifestations as compelled by its laws. . ." (*Treatise on Painting*, para. 55). These are "laws of necessity the artificer of nature—the bridle, the law and the theme" (*Codex Forster*, III, fol. 43v), while "Necessity constrains all effects to the direct result of their causes" (*Codex Atlanticus*, fol. 345v-b). For Leonardo these causes, effects, and laws could be expressed visually in the form of a geometry that includes the movement of things as well as their resting forms.

Leonardo's Mathematics of Science. Leonardo defined science as "that mental analysis which has its origin in ultimate principles beyond which nothing in nature can be found which is part of that science" (*Treatise on Painting*, para. 1). Geometry was such a science, in which "the point is that than which nothing can be smaller. Therefore the point is the first principle of geometry and nothing in nature or the human mind can be the origin of the point" (*ibid.*). He differentiated between the "natural" point, which has the characteristics of an atom, and the "conceptual" point of geometry: "The smallest natural point is larger than all mathematical points, because a natural point is a continuous quantity and as such is infinitely divisible, while the mathematical point is indivisible, having no quantity" (quoted from J. P. Richter, *Literary Works of Leonardo*, 44). In this way he linked geometry with physics and denied the term "science" to any investigation that is not capable of "mathematical" demonstration, such as the so-called sciences that "begin and end in the mind" and are "without the test of experience." He proclaimed the necessity for both geometry and experience, taking as his example astronomy, which was all "visual lines, which enclose all the different shapes of bodies created by nature, and without which the art of geometry is blind" (*Treatise on Painting*, para. 15). Thus, via geometry, human experience could interpret nature.

Leonardo divided his inquiry into three coincident parts: the geometry of vision, the geometry of nature, that is, physics or "natural philosophy," and pure geometry. His investigation of vision was the first of his physiological researches; it pertained primarily to perception and derived largely from the traditional concept of a cone of vision. (Pure geometry—that is, Euclidean geometry—is discussed in the mathematics section, below.)

The Geometry of Vision. Without the test of visual experience there could be no science for Leonardo, for "the observer's mind must enter into nature's mind" (*Treatise on Painting*, para. 40). The problem of vision involved his concept of the spread of light from its source. This he conceived of by analogy to the transverse wave-spread set up by dropping a stone into a still pond. "Just as a stone flung into water becomes the centre and cause of many circles . . . so

any object placed in the luminous atmosphere diffuses itself in circles and fills the surrounding air with images of itself" (MS *A*, fol. 9r). These images spread out in circles from the surfaces of the object with steady diminution of power to the eye (Figure 2). As pond waves spread by the power of percussion, so the light wave varies in power with the force of percussion and inversely with its distance in the form of an infinite number of pyramids (like perspective), diminishing as they approach the eye (Figure 3). The

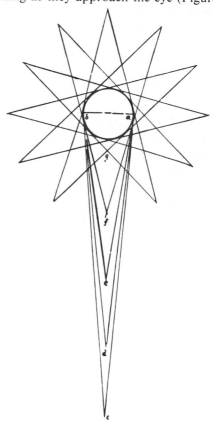

FIGURE 3. The pyramidal spread of light from a luminous object, *ab*, in all directions. "The circle of equidistant converging rays of the pyramid will give angles, and objects to the eye of equal size" (MS *Ashburnham* 2038, fol. 6b).

pyramidal form which Leonardo used to represent this decline of power has the characteristic that

> . . . if you cut the pyramid at any stage of its height by a line equidistant from its base you will find that the proportion of the height of this section from its base to the total height of the pyramid will be the same as the proportion between the breadth of this section and the breadth of the whole base [MS *M*, fol. 44r].

Leonardo thus represented the power of percussion by the base or diameter of a cone or pyramid, and its

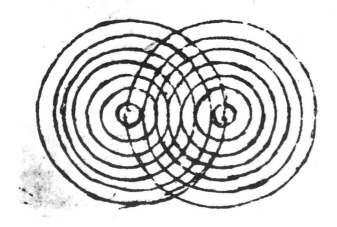

FIGURE 2. The intersection of waves produced by two stones dropped into a pond. Leonardo used this as an analogy for the spread of all powers produced by percussion, in which he included light and sound (MS *A*, fol. 61r).

decline by its breadth at any height of the pyramid. When the spreading light image reaches the pupil, it finds not a point but a circle, which in its turn contracts or expands with the power of light reaching it and forms the base of another cone or pyramid of light rays directed by refraction through the lens system of the eye to the optic nerve (Figure 4). The image then travels via the central foramen up the nerve to the "imprensiva" of the brain, wherein the percussion is impressed. Here it joins with the impressions made by the "percussions" from the nerves that serve the senses of hearing, smell, touch, and pain—all of which are activated by similar percussive mechanisms following similar pyramidal laws.

Thus in the imprensiva a spatiotemporal verisimilitude of the external environment is produced, while a truly mathematical, geometrically conditioned model of reality is experienced by the "senso commune" in

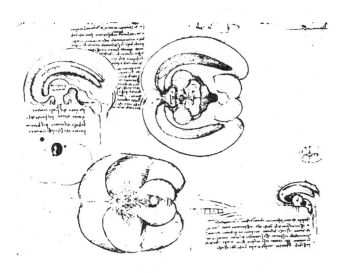

FIGURE 5. Wax casts of the cerebral ventricles. In the figure at left the lateral ventricle is labeled "imprensiva"; the third ventricle, "senso commune"; and the fourth ventricle, "memoria" (*Quaderni d'anatomia*, fol. 7r. Reproduced by gracious permission of Her Majesty Queen Elizabeth II).

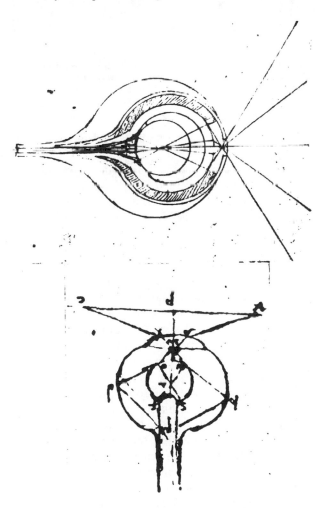

FIGURE 4. The dioptrics of the lens system of the eye. In the upper figure rays are shown crossing once at the pupil and again in the lens, to which the optic nerve is in apposition (*Codex Atlanticus*, fol. 337r-a). Below, rays are reflected from the retina, which acts as a mirror (MS *D*, fol. 10).

the third ventricle where all these sensations come together (Figure 5). "Experience therefore does not ever err, it is only your judgment that errs in promising itself results which are not caused by your experiments" (*Codex Atlanticus*, fol. 154r). Leonardo later located the imprensiva in the lateral ventricles of the brain when he discovered them. "Memory" and "judgment" he located in the fourth and third ventricles, respectively. Thus his distinction between sensory "experience" and "judgment" have physiological as well as psychological connotations.

Leonardo recognized that errors of sensory observation can occur. He attributed these to "impediments"—the resulting experience "partaking of this impediment in a greater or less degree in proportion as this impediment is more or less powerful."

The Geometry of Nature. The pyramidal form that Leonardo imposed upon the propagation of visual images he further applied to the propagation of the four "powers" of nature: "movement, force, weight, and percussion." He saw it as perspectival, i.e., simple, pyramidal proportion. It was in this form, therefore, that he quantified these powers, whether dealing with light and vision, as above, or with other forms of the powers of nature, as, for example, weights, levers, the movements of water, and power transmission in machines, including the human heart or limbs. For example, he described the force of a spring as "pyramidal because it begins at a point or instant and with each degree of movement and time it acquires size and speed" (MS *G*, fol. 30r); he further described the movement of compound pulleys as "pyramidal since it proceeds to slowness with uniform diminution of uniformity down to the last rope" (*ibid.*, fol. 87v); see mechanics section, below. Such phrasing is reminiscent of the terminology of the Merton School and reminds one that the names "Suisset" and "Tisber" occur in Leonardo's notes.

Leonardo's close relationship with Luca Pacioli in Milan strongly stimulated his interest in mathematics. At this time he made an intensive study of algebra and the "manipulation of roots," describing algebra as "the demonstration of the equality of one thing with another" (MS *K*, II, fol. 27b). He does not, however, appear to have applied this concept of algebraic equations to his scientific work. On the other hand, he did apply square roots to the calculation of wingspan in relation to the weight of the human flying machine. His formula ran thus: "If a pelican of weight 25 pounds has a wingspan of 5 braccia, then a man of weight 400 pounds will require a wingspan of $\sqrt{400} = 20$ braccia" (*Codex Atlanticus*, fol. 320r-b). This calculation was made about the time of his final attempt at flight (1504). Leonardo never applied the inverse-square law to any "power" or "force."

Leonardo's Methods of Observation and Experiment. Leonardo's acquisition of "experience" was remarkable for three main methods: measurement, models, and markers. From about 1490, when he concluded that the "powers" of nature had geometrical relationships, Leonardo attempted to quantify his observations and experiments. Measurement entered into all his observations; measurements of weights, distances, and velocities. His notes from about this time contain descriptions of hodometers, anemometers, and hygrometers, as well as balances of various ingenious types.

In general one is struck, however, by the crudity of his measurements of both space and time. He rarely mentioned any spatial measurement other than the braccio (approximately twenty-four inches). For small intervals of time, such as the heart rate, he used musical tempi. Here he explained, "of which tempi an hour contains 1080" (*Quaderni d'anatomia*, II, 11r). For timing he used sandglasses and water clocks. Although he certainly did not invent the balance, he did use balances in a highly original way—for example, by placing a man in one pan and observing whether the downward movement of a levered wing to which he was attached would raise him or not, and by weighing objects at different temperatures.

Models were Leonardo's favorite form of experi-

mental demonstration. He used them particularly for observations of the flow of water or blood currents. Perhaps his smallest model was a glass cast of an aorta with its valves (Figure 6); the largest was one of

FIGURE 6.   Upper right, a glass cast of an aorta with instructions for casting. The figures on the left margin are also schemes for aortic models (*Quaderni d'anatomia*, II, fol. 12r. Reproduced by gracious permission of Her Majesty Queen Elizabeth II).

the Mediterranean, which he built to demonstrate the effects of the rivers entering it.

Markers were another favorite method for visualizing the movements of water, both in Leonardo's models and in actual rivers. His models for this purpose consisted of tanks with three glass sides through which he could view the seeds, bits of paper, or colored inks used as markers; he had a special set of floats, each designed to be suspended at a different depth. With such observations and experiments he accumulated an enormous mass of data regarding the directions and velocities of water movements, their angles of reflection, the effects of percussion, and the movements of suspended solids. He traced the movements of sand and stones in water and their mode of deposition, as well as the action of water on surrounding surfaces—for instance, the erosion of river banks. He also applied these results to such problems as the movement of lock gates or aortic valves. He extended the marker method to the other "elements," particularly to the movement of solid bodies in air, including projectiles, dust, and "birds" (models).

Leonardo frequently advocated the repetition of experiments, "for the experiment might be false whether it deceived the investigator or not" (MS *M*, fol. 57r). If a confirmed experiment did not agree with a suggested mathematical "rule," he discarded the rule. By this means, and clearly to his surprise, he had to reject the Aristotelian "rule" that "if a power moves a mobile object with a certain speed, it will move half this mobile object twice as swiftly." By experiment Leonardo tested the rule, comparing the movements of "atoms" of dust in air with those of large objects fired from a mortar; and from his observations he drew a moral—mistrust those who have used nothing but their imagination and have not verified their statements by experiment. For Leonardo mathematical rules had to give way to experimental verification or refutation.

Leonardo applied his experimental or mathematical results only to visual space. Unlike such medieval antecedents as Oresme, he refused to quantify such abstract qualities as beauty or glory; he specifically stated that geometry and arithmetic "are not concerned with quality, the beauty of nature's creations, or the harmony of the world" (*Treatise on Painting*, para. 15). He honored the precept that these are fields for the creative arts rather than for the creative sciences.

Leonardo's "Rules." Not only did Leonardo advocate repetition of experiments, but he performed experiments in series, each repeated with one slight variation to resemble continuous change. For example, on investigating flight with model birds, he wrote: "Suppose a suspended body resembling a bird and that the tail is twisted to different angles. By means of this you will be able to derive a general rule as to the various movements of birds occasioned by bending their tails" (MS *L*, fol. 61v). Demonstrating the distribution of weight of a beam suspended by two cords, he wrote: "I make my figures so that you shall know all the cases that are placed under one simple rule" (*Codex Atlanticus*, fol. 274r-b). The statement is carried out in the following three pages of patient depiction of all the variable distributions of weight (*ibid.*, fols. 274r-b, r-a, v-b).

Thus by repeated observation, repeated experiment, and calculatedly varying his experiments, Leonardo built up quantitative data into limited generalized "rules." "These rules," he wrote, "are the causes of making you know the true from the false" (*ibid.*, fol. 119v-a). Since the rule is mathematical in form, he averred, "There is no certainty where one cannot apply any of the mathematical sciences" (MS *G*, fol. 96v); and clearly it follows that "No man who is not a mathematician should read the elements of my work" (*Windsor Collection*, fol. 19118v, in I. A. Richter, *Selections . . .*, p. 7).

The Four Powers. Leonardo's notes contain long debates on the nature of movement, weight, force, and percussion, all in the context of the Aristotelian elements of earth, air, fire, and water. From this debate emerged the statement: "Weight, force, together with percussion, are to be spoken of as the producers of movement as well as being produced by it" (*Codex Arundel*, fol. 184v). He finally saw weight as an accidental power produced by a displaced element "desiring" to return to its natural place in its own element. Thus "gravity" and "levity" were two aspects of the same drive. Force was caused by violent movement stored within bodies. Sometimes Leonardo called force "accidental weight," using the Aristotelian meaning of "accidental." Movement of an object from one point to another could be natural, accidental, or participating. Impetus was derived movement arising from primary movement when the movable thing was joined to the mover. He defined percussion as "an end of movement created in an indivisible period of time, because it is caused at the point which is the end of the line of movement" (*Codex Forster*, III, fol. 32r. in I. A. Richter, *Selections . . .*, p. 77).

This remarkable simplification of his experiences of "nature" was applied by Leonardo to all fields of investigation and practical creation, that is, to science and its derived art of invention. Clearly these four powers were both derived from, and most applicable to, mechanics. "Mechanics is the paradise of mathematical science because here one comes to the fruits of mathematics" (MS *E*, fol. 8v). This statement was generalized when Leonard asserted: "Proportion is not only found in numbers and measurements but also in sounds, weights, times, spaces, and whatsoever powers there be" (MS *K*, 497, Ravaisson-Mollien). From these two statements his essentially integrative approach to all problems can be glimpsed. In each field of investigation he built up, from quantitative observation and experiment, defined mathematical "rules" which he applied to the particular problem occupying him. For example, with regard to the flight of the bird, when discussing the problem of its being overturned, he set out the forces concerned and then stated: "This is proved by the first section of the Elements of Machines which shows how things in equilibrium which are percussed outside their center of gravity send down their opposite sides . . ." (*Codex on Flight . . .*, fol. 8r). He continued, "And in this way it will return to a position of equilibrium. This is proved by the fourth of the third, according to which that object is more overcome that is acted on by the greater forces; also by the fifth of the third, according to which a resistance is weaker the farther it is from its fixed point" (*ibid.*, fol. 9r). In this way Leonardo's "rules" were built into the structure of his thought about all the powers of nature, imparting a remarkable consistency in all fields, whether mechanics, light, sound, architecture, botany, or human physiology. Unfortunately, the books to which he refers in this way, showing how he reached these generalizations, have been lost.

Leonardo's Achievements in Science. Leonardo's achievements in art and science depended primarily on his remarkable acuity of vision, and his particular sensitivity to the geometrical consequences of that vision. These gifts he combined with the creative technology of the engineer and the artist. These creative aspects emerge in his achievements in scientific technology.

Mathematics. Leonardo's approach to mathematics was predominantly physical. Even when appearing abstract, as in his "Book on Transmutation" (of forms), his practical object was revealed by his reference to the metalworker or sculptor. Typical of his contribution to mathematics were proportional and parabolic compasses. His explorations of the properties of the pyramid were, as is to be expected, thorough. As a result of an experimental investigation of the center of gravity of a tetrahedron, he discovered that the center of gravity is at "a quarter of the axis of that pyramid" (MS *F*, fol. 51r). (For his development of pure mathematics, see the section on mathematics.)

Mechanics. (Here brief mention is made only of the main areas studied by Leonardo. For fuller development of these, see the section on mechanics.) Leonardo's point of departure for statics was Archimedes' work on the lever, of the principles of which he had some understanding. His appreciation that equilibrium of a balance depends arithmetically upon the weights and their distances from the fulcrum gave him many examples of pyramidal (arithmetical) proportion.

Leonardo never quite reached the concepts of mass or inertia, as opposed to weight. He still used the "halfway" concept of impetus when he said, "All moved bodies continue to move as long as the impression of the force of their motors remains in them" (*Codex on Flight . . .*, fol. 12r). This is as near as he came to Newton's first law. And although Leonardo disproved the Aristotelian relationship between force, weight, and velocity, he did not reach the concept of acceleration resulting from action of the force on a moving body. Newton's third law, however, Leonardo did state clearly in his concrete way and apply persistently. For example, "An object offers as much resistance to the air as the air does to the object" (*Codex Atlanticus*, fol. 381v-a). And after a repetition of this statement he added: "And it is the same with water, which a similar circumstance has shown me acts in the same way as air" (*Codex Atlanticus*, fol. 395r). One can see here the process by which he built up to one of his "rules"—Newton's third law.

Gravity for Leonardo was the force of weight which is exerted "along a central line which with straightness is imagined from the thing to the center of the world" (MS *I*, fol. 22v). In his investigations of it Leonardo dropped weights from high towers. For example, he dropped two balls of similar weight together and observed at the bottom whether they still touched (MS *M*, fol. 57r). From such experiments he noted: "In air of uniform density the heavy body which falls at each degree of time acquires a degree of movement more than the degree of preceding time . . . the aforesaid powers are all pyramidal, seeing that they commence in nothing and proceed to increase in degrees of arithmetical proportion" (*ibid.*, fol. 44r). He concluded that the velocity is proportional to the time of fall but, incorrectly, that the distance of fall is also proportional directly to the time, not to its square.

Leonardo appreciated and used the concepts of resolving and compounding of forces. He described the parallelogram of forces, although he did not draw it, in analyzing the flight of the bird (*Codex on Flight*, fol. 5r); and he resolved the movement of a weight down an inclined plane into two components (MS *G*, fol. 75r). Such movement led him to study friction, a force which, like so many others, he divided into simple and compound. Leonardo appreciated the importance of the pressure or weight factor and the nature of the surface and their independence of area. Thus, for "a polished smooth surface" he found a coefficient of friction of 0.25. He was aware that such friction produces heat.

Hydrodynamics. All the "rules" described above were carried into Leonardo's studies of the movement of water. Here two phenomena received particular attention: wave formation and eddies. He found the velocity of flow of water to be inversely proportional to the dimension of the passage, whether rivers or blood vessels are being discussed. Currents of water, as observed by his marker experiments, percussed so that the angles of incidence and reflection were equal, similar to those made by bouncing balls. The formation of the transverse wave from the percussion of a stone in water was similarly explained. The cohesion of a drop of water against the force of gravity led Leonardo to postulate a force "like that of a magnet," which was also responsible for capillary attraction. The extent of his studies of water is reflected in the *Codex Leicester*, where he draws "732 conclusions as to water" (*Codex Leicester*, fol. 26v).

Cosmology. Water, more than the other elements, led Leonardo to compare "the greater and the lesser world." The macrocosm–microcosm analogy was very real to him, since he believed that similar laws governed both the cosmos and the body of man. He considered at one time, for example, that the movement of the waters of the earth, particularly to the tops of mountains, was analogous to the movement of blood to the head, both being produced by heat. At first he postulated that water was drawn up by the heat of the sun; later he suggested that the heat arose from subterranean fires, from volcanos in the earth. He posited such subterranean fires as an analogy to the human heart, which he saw not only as the percussor of blood to the periphery but also as a source of heat to the body through the friction of the blood in its chambers (Figure 7).

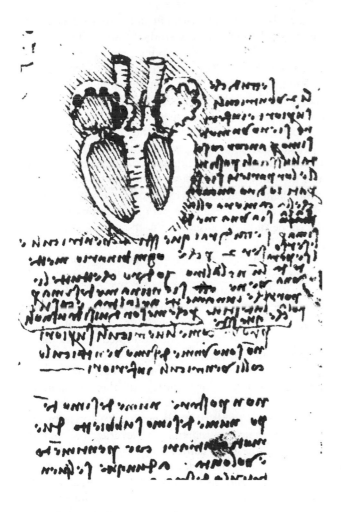

FIGURE 7. The heart as a percussion and heat-producing instrument. Blood from the atria, above, is propelled into the ventricles, below, from which part of the blood is propelled into the blood vessels and part back into the atria, producing heat by friction (*Quaderni d'anatomia,* II, fol. 3v. Reproduced by gracious permission of Her Majesty Queen Elizabeth II).

FIGURE 8. "The Arsenal," one of the many studies of the external powers of the human body, here being exerted to create a power transformation into the projectile force of a cannon (*Windsor Collection,* fol. 12647. Reproduced by gracious permission of Her Majesty Queen Elizabeth II).

Leonardo saw the land of the world as emerging from its surrounding element of water by a process of growth. Mountains, the skeleton of the world, were formed by destructive rain, frost, and snow washing the soft earth down into the rivers. Where large landslides occurred, inland seas were formed, from which the waters eventually broke through gorges to reach the sea, their "natural" level. No better summary of Leonardo's neptunist concept of these geological changes can be found than the background of his "Mona Lisa."

Biology. From about 1489 to 1500 Leonardo investigated the physiology of vision and the external powers of the human body. During this period he applied the principles of the "four powers"—movement, force, weight, and percussion—to every conceivable human activity. Many of the drawings of men in action found in the *Treatise on Painting* date from this period, during which he also completed a book, now lost, on the human figure. He drew men sitting, standing, running, digging, pushing, pulling, and so on, all with such points of reference as the center of gravity or the leverage of the trunk and limbs. These simple movements he elaborated into studies of men at work and so to the transformation of human power into machines at work, the field of many of his technological inventions (Figure 8). (For Leonardo's development of this field, see the section on technology.)

Anatomy. Leonardo later investigated the internal powers of the human body. He described his approach to human anatomy and physiology in a passage headed "On Machines":

> Why Nature cannot give movement to animals without mechanical instruments is shown by me in this book, *On the Works of Motion Made by Nature in Animals.* For this I have set out the rules on the 4 powers of nature without which nothing can through her give local motion to these animals. Therefore we shall first describe this local motion, and how it produces and is produced by each of the other three powers. . . .

He then briefly defined these powers (*Quaderni d'anatomia*, I, fol. 1r) and added an admonition: "Arrange it so that the book of the elements of mechanics with examples shall precede the demonstration of the movement and force of man and other animals, and by means of these you will be able to prove all your propositions" (*Anatomical Folio A*, fol. 10r).

As usual, Leonardo gave intense thought to his methods of approaching the problem of man the machine. "I shall describe the function of the parts from every side, laying before your eyes the knowledge of the whole healthy figure of man in so far as it has local motion by means of its parts" (*Quaderni d'anatomia*, I, fol. 2r). He applied his gift of visual artistry and his concepts of the four powers to the human body with results that remain unique. The mechanics of the musculoskeletal system were displayed and explained, such complex movements as pronation and supination being correctly analyzed and demonstrated.

In his anatomical writings Leonardo, always fastidious, noted his intense dislike of "passing the night hours in the company of corpses, quartered and flayed, and horrible to behold."

Human Anatomy. On several occasions Leonardo laid out comprehensive plans for demonstrating the anatomy of the human body. In all of them he put great stress on the necessity for presenting the parts of the body from all sides. He stated, moreover, that each part must be dissected specifically to demonstrate vessels, nerves, or muscles:

> . . . you will need three [dissections] in order to have a complete knowledge of the veins and arteries, destroying all the rest with very great care; three others for a knowledge of the membranes, three for the nerves, muscles and ligaments, three for the bones and cartilages . . . . Three must also be devoted to the female body, and in this there is a great mystery by reason of the womb and its fetus.

Leonardo thus hoped to reveal "in fifteen entire figures . . . the whole figure and capacity of man in so far as it has local movement by means of its parts" (*Quaderni d'anatomia*, I, fol. 2r). His extant anatomical drawings show that he was in fact able to carry out a large part of this extensive program.

In addition to conventional methods of dissection, Leonardo brought to his study of anatomy his own particular skill in modelmaking. He discovered the true shape and size of the cerebral ventricles through making wax casts of them, and he came to appreciate the actions of the ventricles of the heart and the aortic valves by making casts of the cardiac atria and ventricles and glass models of the aorta.

Since his approach was primarily mechanical, Leonardo regarded the bones of the skeleton as levers and their attached muscles as the lines of force acting upon them. A firm knowledge of these actions could not be reached without a detailed demonstration of the shapes and dimensions of both bones and muscles. About 1510, Leonardo executed for this purpose a series of drawings, which constitute a large part of the collection *Anatomical Folio A*. Here he systematically illustrated all the main bones and muscles of the body, often accompanying the drawings with mechanical diagrams to show their mode of action. In these drawings Leonardo frequently adopted the technique of representing muscles by narrow bands, corresponding to what he called their "lines of force" (Figure 9), thus facilitating demonstration of their mechanical powers. Since an understanding of the mode of articulation of joints is clearly necessary to an appreciation of their movements in leverage, Leonardo illustrated these structures by an exploded view, whereby the joint surfaces are separated and the surrounding tendons of muscles are severed to show their exact lines of action in moving the joints. Such illustrations permitted Leonardo to demonstrate, for example, the subtleties of the movements of the upper cervical spine and the shoulder joint.

Possibly because the visual sense was so overwhelmingly important to him, Leonardo appears to have made his earliest anatomical studies on the optic nerves, cranial nerves, spinal cord, and peripheral nervous system. In the course of these studies he traced back the optic nerves, beautifully illustrating the optic chiasma and the optic tracts. In his attempts to elucidate the central distribution of sensory tracts in the brain, he injected the cerebral ventricles with wax, thereby ascertaining and demonstrating their approximate shape, size, and situation. On this discovery he based his own mechanical theory of sensation through percussion.

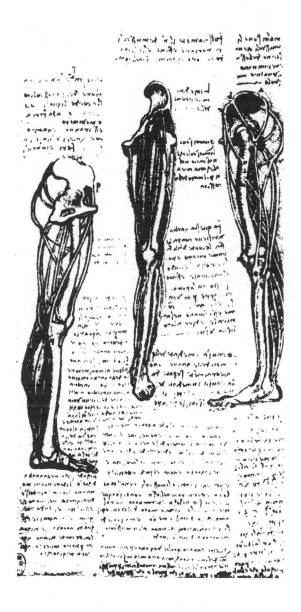

FIGURE 9. The muscles of the leg, one of the many studies of the internal powers of the human body; here the accurately dissected muscles are represented by their "central lines of force," showing their mechanical leverage on the joints (*Quaderni d'anatomia*, V, fol. 4r. Reproduced by gracious permission of Her Majesty Queen Elizabeth II).

Leonardo conceived the eye itself to be a camera obscura in which the inverted image, formed by light penetrating the pupil, is reinverted by the action of the lens. By constructing a glass model of the eye and lens, into which he inserted his own head with his own eye in the position corresponding to that of the optic nerve, he came to the conclusion that the optic nerve was the sensitive visual receptor organ. Here his own experimental brilliance deceived him.

On pithing a frog he noted, "The frog instantly dies when the spinal cord is pierced, and previous to this it lived without head, heart, bowels, or skin. Here therefore it would seem lies the foundation of movement and life" (*Quaderni d'anatomia*, V, fol. 21v). He here contradicted both Aristotelian and Galenic concepts, and opened the way for his own mechanical theory of sensation and movement.

Leonardo's interest in the alimentary tract arose with his dissection of the "old man" in the Hospital of Santa Maria Nuova in Florence. From this dissection he made drawings of the esophagus, stomach, liver, and gallbladder, and drew a first approximation of the distribution of the coils of small and large intestines in the abdomen. Perhaps most notable of all was a detailed sketch of the appendix (its first known representation) accompanied by the hypothesis that it served to take up superfluous wind from the bowel. The heat necessary for digestive coction of the food, Leonardo held, was derived from the heat of the heart—not from the liver, as the Galenists stated. The movement of food and digested products down the bowel was, in Leonardo's view, brought about by the descent of the diaphragm and the pressure produced by contraction of the transverse muscles of the abdomen. Since he did not vivisect, he did not observe peristalsis. Always aware of the necessity of feedback mechanisms to preserve the equilibrium of life, Leonardo was greatly concerned with the fate of superfluous blood, since blood was thought to be continuously manufactured by the liver. Superfluous blood, Leonardo thought, was dispersed through the bowel, contributing largely to the formation of the feces.

Leonardo understood in principle the mechanism of respiration, clearly described by Galen. Describing the movements of the ribs, he wrote, ". . . since there is no vacuum in nature the lung which touches the ribs from within must necessarily follow their expansion; and the lung therefore opening like a pair of bellows draws in the air" (*Anatomical Folio A*, fol. 15v). He considered, however, that the most powerful muscle of inspiration is the diaphragm, the "motor of food and air," as he called it, since by its descent it draws in air and presses food down the gut. After a long debate Leonardo decided that expiration is mostly passive, induced by the diaphragm rising with contraction of the abdominal muscles, and subsidence of the ribs.

Leonardo's studies of the heart and its action occupy more anatomical sheets than those of any other organ. By tying off the atria and ventricles and injecting them with air (later wax), he obtained an accurate idea of their shape and volume. He thus came to recognize that the atria are the contracting chambers of the heart which propel blood into the ventricles, a discovery to which he devoted pages of discussion and verification because it was entirely opposed to Galenic physiology. He applied the same technique to the root of the aorta to discover the aortic sinuses, subsequently named after the anatomist Antonio Maria Valsalva. Having established the shape and position of the valve cusps, Leonardo applied the same marker technique which he used so often in his studies of rivers and water currents. To a glass model of the aorta, containing the aortic valve ring and cusps of an ox, he attached the ventricle (or a bag representing it), which he squeezed so that water passed through the valve. The water contained the seeds of panic grass, which served to demonstrate the directional flow of the currents passing the valve cusps. From these experiments Leonardo showed that the aortic valve cusps close in vertical, not horizontal, apposition—that is, from the side, by pressure of eddying currents, not from above, by direct reflux. Although much modern evidence confirms this view, such action has not yet been directly visualized through angiocardiography.

Other features of Leonardo's study of the anatomy of the heart include his detailed demonstration of the coronary vessels and of the moderator band which some have named after him. By observation of the movements of the "spillo," the instrument that slaughterers used to pierce the heart of a pig, Leonardo deduced the relation of systole to the production of the pulse and apex beat. He considered that the force of cardiac percussion propelling the blood was exhausted by the time the blood reached the periphery of the body, however, and thus missed the Harveian concept of its circulation.

Although his drawings of the kidney, ureter, and bladder are relatively sophisticated, Leonardo's mechanistic physiology did not take him far beyond Galen's views on urology. He saw the kidney as acting as a kind of filter, as did Vesalius after him. His representation of the uterus as a single cavity marks a great advance, particularly in his drawing of a five-month *fetus in utero*, although even in this drawing Leonardo showed the cotyledons of the bovine uterus.

His drawings of male and female genitalia that pertain to coitus show an austere emphasis on procreation that is perhaps reflected in his comment: "The act of procreation and the members employed therein are so repulsive that if it were not for the beauty of the faces and the adornments of the actors and the pent-up impulse, nature would lose the human species" (*Anatomical Folio A*, fol. 10r).

Comparative Anatomy. Although Leonardo concentrated his anatomical investigations on the human body, he by no means confined them to that field. From the artistic point of view, he was equally interested in the structural mechanics of the horse; and from the point of view of the ever-present problem of flying, the anatomy of the bird and bat took priority.

There are scattered through Leonardo's extant notebooks illustrations and notes on the anatomy of horses, birds, bats, oxen, pigs, dogs, monkeys, lions, and frogs. Most of these were studies undertaken to solve particular "power" problems. His anatomy of the horse, however, forms an important exception, for Lomazzo, Vasari, and Rubens all refer to the existence of Leonardo's "book on the anatomy of the horse," which has since been lost. Possible remnants of it remain in some of the drawings of the proportions of the horse in the Royal Library, Windsor, the *Codex Huygens*, and the musculoskeletal sketches in MS K, folios 102r and 109v. But perhaps the best-known comparative study of the hind limbs of the horse and the legs of man has come down to us in his drawing on *Quaderni d'anatomia*, V, fol. 22r, where he wrote: "Show a man on tiptoe so that you may compare man with other animals."

In a number of cases Leonardo repeated Galen's mistakes in substituting animal for human parts. These mistakes diminished as his increasing knowledge of anatomy revealed to him surprising variation of form in organs serving similar physiological functions. He then turned to such variations to gain knowledge of the function. Such was the basis of his numerous studies of the shapes of the pupils of the eye in men, cats, and different birds. And it was by dissection of the lion that Leonardo came to say:

> I have found that the constitution of the human body among all the constitutions of animals is of more obtuse and blunt sensibilities, and so is formed of an instrument less ingenious and of parts less capable of receiving the power of the senses. I have seen in the leonine species how the sense of smell forming part of the substance of the brain descends into a very large receptacle to meet the sense of smell. . . . The eyes of the leonine species have a great part of the head as their receptacle, so that the optic nerves are in immediate conjunction with the brain. With man the contrary is

seen to be the case, for the cavities of the eye occupy a small part of the head, and the optic nerves are thin, long and weak [*Anatomical Folio B*, fol. 13v].

That Leonardo appreciated the importance of these studies in comparative anatomy is evinced in his note "Write of the varieties of the intestines of the human species, apes, and such like; then of the differences found in the leonine species, then the bovine, and lastly the birds; and make the description in the form of a discourse" (*Anatomical Folio B*, fol. 37r). His awareness of homologous structures was most pronounced in relation to the limbs, the form and power of which in both man and animals were of outstanding artistic and scientific importance to him. "Anatomize the bat, study it carefully and on this construct your machine," he enjoins on MS *F*, folio 41v. Comparing the arm of man and the wing of the bird, he pointed out: "The sinews and muscles of a bird are incomparably more powerful than those of man because the whole mass of so many muscles and of the fleshy parts of the breast go to aid and increase the movement of the wings, while the breastbone is all in one piece and consequently affords the bird very great power" (*Codex on Flight* . . . , fol. 16r). To elucidate this problem he embarked on a comparative mechanical anatomy of the proportions of the wings of the bat, the eagle, and the pelican, and the arm of man. He even reduced the forelimb to a three-jointed model of levers representing humerus, forearm, and hand, manipulating this artificial limb by pulley mechanisms. He was clearly using comparative anatomy as a means of solving the great problem of human flight.

Such comparisons led Leonardo to suggest repeatedly that he should represent the hands and feet of "the bear, monkey, and certain birds" in order to see how they differ from those of man. Examples of such completed work are scattered in the notes.

From such studies Leonardo came to realize the anatomical significance of "the movements of animals with four feet, amongst which is man, who likewise in his infancy goes on four feet, and who moves his limbs crosswise, as do other four-footed animals, for example the horse in trotting" (MS *E*, fol. 16r; *Codex Atlanticus*, fol. 297r).

From such steps Leonardo reached the generalization: "All terrestrial animals have a similarity of their parts, that is their muscles, nerves and bones, and these do not vary except in length and size, as will be demonstrated in the book of Anatomy. . . . Then there are the aquatic animals which are of many varieties, concerning which I shall not persuade the painter that there is any rule, since they are of almost infinite variety, as are insects" (MS *G*, fol. 5v). "Man

differs from animals," concludes Leonardo, "only in what is accidental, and in this he is divine. . . ." (*Anatomical Folio B*, fol. 13v). After referring to skill in drawing, knowledge of the geometry of the four powers, and patience as being necessary for completing his anatomical researches, he finally wrote of his work: "Considering which things whether or no they have all been found in me, the hundred and twenty books which I have composed will give their verdict, yes or no. In these I have not been hindered either by avarice or negligence, but only by want of time. Farewell" (*Quaderni d'anatomia*, I, fol. 13r).

Botany. Leonardo's botanical studies developed, as it were, in miniature along lines similar to those of his anatomy, with the important difference that in this field he had no predecessors like Galen and Mondino to aid (or impede) his personal observations. These studies commenced in his early years with representation of the external forms of flowering plants, and it was not long before evidence appeared of his interest in plant physiology. About 1489, on a page containing two of his most beautiful designs for cathedrals, he presented a series of four botanical diagrams, one being described by the words: "If you strip off a ring of bark from the tree, it will wither from the ring upwards and remain alive from there downwards" (MS *B*, fol. 17v). Experiments and observations on the movement of sap and growth of plants and trees continued. They reached a climax about 1513, when he was in Rome. Many of these are gathered together in MS *G* and book VI of the *Treatise on Painting*. For many years Leonardo saw movement of sap in the plant as analogous to the movement of blood in the animal and water in the living earth. It is drawn upward by the heat of the sun and downward by its own "natural" weight:

> Heat that is poured into animated bodies moves the humours which nourish them. The movement made by this humour is the conservation of itself. The same cause moves the water through the spreading veins of the earth as that which moves the blood in the human species. . . . In the same way so does the water that rises from the low roots of the vine to its lofty summit and falling through the severed branches upon the primal roots mounts anew [*Codex Arundel*, fols. 234r, 235].

Incidentally, he postulated this same mechanism for the absorption of food from the human intestine by the portal veins.

Leonardo described an experiment with a gourd:

> The sun gives spirit and life to plants and the earth nourishes them with moisture. In this connection I once made an experiment of leaving only one very small

root on a gourd and keeping it nourished with water and the gourd brought to perfection all the fruits that it could produce, which were about sixty. And I set myself diligently to consider the source of its life; and I perceived that it was the dew of the night which penetrated abundantly with its moisture through the joints of its great leaves to nourish this plant with its offspring, or rather seeds which have to produce its offspring. . . . The leaf serves as a nipple or breast to the branch or fruit which grows in the following year [MS *G*, fol. 32v].

Thus Leonardo reached a concept of the necessity of sunlight "giving spirit and life" through its leaves to a plant, while the moisture of its sap came from both root and leaf. He also perceived upward and downward movement of sap. He located the cambium when he stated: "The growth in thickness of trees is brought about by the sap which in the month of April is created between the 'camicia' [cambium] and the wood of the tree. At that time this cambium is converted into bark and the bark acquires new cracks" (*Treatise on Painting*, pt. VI, McMahon ed., p. 893).

Appreciating this seasonal growth of wood from the cambium, Leonardo came to recognize its part in the annual ring formation in trees. He wrote: "The age of trees which have not been injured by men can be counted in years by their branching from the trunk. The trees have as many differences in age as they have principal branches. . . . The circles of branches of trees which have been cut show the number of their years, and also show which years were wetter or drier according to their greater or lesser thickness . . ." (*ibid.*, p. 900). In these words Leonardo showed himself to be the originator of dendrochronology.

Leonardo's observation on the growth of the tree trunk and the patterns of its branches and leaves, combined with his views on plant nutrition, initiated his study of phyllotaxy:

> The lower trunks of trees do not keep their roundness of size when they approach the origin of their branches or roots. And this arises because the higher and lower branches are the organs [membra] by which the plants (or trees) are nourished; that is to say, in summer they are nourished from above by the dew and rain through the leaves and in winter from below through the contact which the earth has with their roots. . . . Larger branches do not grow toward the middle of the tree. This arises because every branch naturally seeks the air and avoids shadow. In those branches which turn to the sky, the course of the water and dew descends . . . and keeps the lower part more humid than the upper, and for this reason the branches have more abundant nourishment there, and therefore grow more [*ibid.*, p. 885].

Thus the trunk of the tree, being most nourished, is the thickest part of the tree. Leonardo saw here the mechanical implications of the force of winds on trees: "The part of the tree which is farthest from the force which percusses it is most damaged by this percussion because of its greater leverage. Thus nature has provided increased thickness in that part, and most in such trees as grow to great heights like pines" (*Codex Arundel*, fol. 277v). Leonardo asserted that the branch pattern of a plant or tree follows its leaf pattern: "The growth of the branches of trees on their principal trunk is like that of the growth of their leaves, which develop in four ways, one above the other. The first and most general is that the sixth leaf above always grows above the sixth below; and the second is for the third pair of leaves to be above the third pair below; the third way is that for the third leaf to be above the third below" (*Treatise on Painting*, McMahon ed., p. 889). This whole pattern of trunk, branch, and leaf Leonardo saw as designed to catch maximum sun, rain, and air—the leaves and branches were arranged "to leave intervals which the air and sun can penetrate, and drops that fall on the first leaf can also fall on the fourth and sixth leaves, and so on" (*ibid.*).

"All the flowers that see the sun mature their seed and not the others, that is, those that see only the reflection of the sun" (MS *G*, fol. 37v). And of seeds he wrote, "All seeds have the umbilical cord which breaks when the seed is ripe; and in like manner they have matrix [uterus] and secundina [membranes], as is shown in herbs and seeds that grow in pods" (*Quaderni d'anatomia*, III, fol. 9v). These words, written on a page of drawings of the infant in the womb, vividly reveal Leonardo's integrating mode of thought.

KENNETH D. KEELE

TECHNOLOGY

A statistical analysis of his extant writings suggests that technology was the most important of Leonardo's varied interests. Indeed, it is revealing to compare the volume of his technological writings with that of his purely artistic work. Of his paintings, fewer than ten are unanimously authenticated by art scholars. This evident disinclination to paint, which even his contemporaries remarked upon, contrasts strongly with the incredible toil and patience that Leonardo lavished upon scientific and technical studies, particularly in geometry, mechanics, and engineering.

Documentary evidence indicates that in his appointments Leonardo was always referred to not only as an artist but also as an engineer. At the court of Ludovico il Moro he was "Ingeniarius et pinctor," while Cesare Borgia called him his most beloved

"Architecto et Engegnero Generale" (1502). When Leonardo returned to Florence, he was immediately consulted as military engineer and sent officially "a livellare Arno in quello di Pisa e levallo del letto suo" (1503).[1] In 1504 he was in Piombino, in the service of Jacopo IV d'Appiano, working on the improvement of that little city-state's fortifications.[2] For Louis XII he was "notre chier et bien aimé Léonard de Vinci, notre paintre et ingénieur ordinaire" (1507).[3] When in Rome, from 1513 to 1516, his duties clearly included technical work, as documented by drafts of letters to his patron Giuliano de' Medici, found in the *Codex Atlanticus*. Even his official burial document refers to him as "Lionard de Vincy, noble millanois, premier peinctre et ingenieur et architecte du Roy, mescanichien d'Estat ..." (1519).[4] The surviving notebooks and drawings demonstrate Leonardo's lifelong interest in the mechanical arts and engineering.

Leonardo's scientific and technological activities were well known to his early biographers, even if they did not approve of them. Paolo Giovio's short account on Leonardo's life (*ca.* 1527) contains a significant phrase: "But while he was thus spending his time in the close research of subordinate branches of his art he carried only very few works to completion."

Another biographer, the so-called "Anonimo Gaddiano" or "Magliabechiano," writing around 1540, said that Leonardo "was delightfully inventive, and was most skillful in lifting weights, in building waterworks and other imaginative constructions, nor did his mind ever come to rest, but dwelt always with ingenuity on the creation of new inventions."

Vasari's biography of Leonardo, in his *Lives of the Painters, Sculptors and Architects* (1550; 2nd ed., 1568), reflects the widespread sentiments of his contemporaries who were puzzled by the behavior of a man who, unconcerned with the great artistic gifts endowed upon him by Providence, dedicated himself to interesting but less noble occupations.

Vasari's testimony concerning Leonardo's widespread technological projects (confirmed by Lomazzo) is important in assessing the influence of Leonardo on the development of Western technology:

> He would have made great profit in learning had he not been so capricious and fickle, for he began to learn many things and then gave them up ... he was the first, though so young, to propose to canalise the Arno from Pisa to Florence. He made designs for mills, fulling machines, and other engines to go by water. ... Every day he made models and designs for the removal of mountains with ease and to pierce them to pass from one place to another, and by means of levers, cranes and winches to raise and draw heavy weights; he devised a

method for cleansing ports, and to raise water from great depths, schemes which his brain never ceased to evolve. Many designs for these motions are scattered about, and I have seen numbers of them. ... His interests were so numerous that his inquiries into natural phenomena led him to study the properties of herbs and to observe the movements of the heavens, the moon's orbit and the progress of the sun.

(It is characteristic of Leonardo's contemporary critics that Vasari, giving an account of Leonardo's last days, represents him as telling Francis I "the circumstances of his sickness, showing how greatly he had offended God and man in not having worked in his art as he ought.")

Lomazzo, in his *Trattato della pittura* (Milan, 1584), tells of having seen many of Leonardo's mechanical projects and praises especially thirty sheets representing a variety of mills, owned by Ambrogio Figino, and the automaton in the form of a lion made for Francis I. In his *Idea del tempio della pittura* (Milan, 1590), Lomazzo mentions "Leonardo's books, where all mathematical motions and effects are considered" and of his "projects for lifting heavy weights with ease, which are spread over all Europe. They are held in great esteem by the experts, because they think that nobody could do more, in this field, than what has been done by Leonardo." Lomazzo also notes "the art of turning oval shapes with a lathe invented by Leonardo," which was shown by a pupil of Melzi to Dionigi, brother of the Maggiore, who adopted it with great satisfaction.

Leonardo's actual technological investigations and work still await an exhaustive and objective study. Many early writers accepted all the ingenious mechanical contrivances found in the manuscripts as original inventions; their claims suffer from lack of historical perspective, particularly as concerns the work of the engineers who preceded Leonardo. The "inventions" of Leonardo have been celebrated uncritically, while the main obstacle to a properly critical study lies in the very nature of the available evidence, scattered and fragmented over many thousands of pages. Only in very recent times has the need for a chronological perspective been felt and the methods for its adoption elaborated.[5] It is precisely the earliest—and for this reason the least original—of Leonardo's projects for which model makers and general authors have shown a predilection. On the other hand, the preference for these juvenile projects is fully justified: they are among the most beautiful and lovingly elaborated designs of the artist-engineer. The drawings and writings of MS *B*, the *Codex Trivulzianus*, and the earliest folios of the *Codex Atlanticus* date from this period (*ca.* 1478–1490). Similar themes in the almost contemporary manuscripts of Francesco di Giorgio Martini offer ample opportunity to study Leonardo's early reliance on traditional technological schemes (Francesco di Giorgio himself borrowed heavily from Brunelleschi and especially from Mariano di Jacopo, called Taccola, the "Archimedes of Siena"); the same comparison serves to demonstrate Leonardo's originality and his search for rational ways of constructing better machines.

While he was still in Florence, Leonardo acquired a diversified range of skills in addition to the various crafts he learned in the workshop of Verrocchio, who was not only a painter but also a sculptor and a goldsmith. Leonardo must therefore have been familiar with bronze casting, and there is also early evidence of his interest in horology. His famous letter to Ludovico il Moro, offering his services, advertises Leonardo's familiarity with techniques of military importance, which, discounting a juvenile self-confidence, must have been based on some real experience.

Leonardo's true vocation for the technical arts developed in Milan, Italy's industrial center. The notes that he made during his first Milanese period (from 1481 or 1482 until 1499) indicate that he was in close contact with artisans and engineers engaged in extremely diversified technical activities—with, for example, military and civil architects, hydraulic engineers, millers, masons and other workers in stone, carpenters, textile workers, dyers, iron founders, bronze casters (of bells, statuary, and guns), locksmiths, clockmakers, and jewelers. At the same time that he was assimilating all available traditional experience, Leonardo was able to draw upon the fertile imagination and innate technological vision that, combined with his unparalleled artistic genius in the graphic rendering of the most complicated mechanical devices, allowed him to make improvements and innovations.

From about 1492 on (as shown in MS *A*; *Codex Forster*; *Codex Madrid*, I; MS *H*, and a great number of pages of the *Codex Atlanticus*), Leonardo became increasingly involved in the study of the theoretical background of engineering practice. At about that time he wrote a treatise on "elementi macchinali" that he returned to in later writings, citing it by book and paragraph. This treatise is lost, but many passages in the *Atlanticus* and *Arundel* codices may be drafts for it. *Codex Madrid*, I (1492–1497), takes up these matters in two main sections, one dealing with matters that today would be called statics and kinematics and another dedicated to applied mechanics, especially mechanisms.

Our knowledge of the technical arts of the fourteenth to sixteenth centuries is scarce and fragmentary. Engineers were reluctant to write about their experience; if they did, they chose to treat fantastic possibilities rather than the true practices of their time. The books of Biringuccio, Agricola, and, in part, Zonca are among the very few exceptions, although they deal with specialized technological fields. The notes and drawings of Leonardo should therefore be studied not only to discover his inventions and priorities, as has largely been done in the past, but also—and especially—for the insight they give into the state of the technical arts of his time. Leonardo took note of all the interesting mechanical contrivances he saw or heard about from fellow artists, scholars, artisans, and travelers. Speaking of his own solutions and improvements, he often referred to the customary practices. Thus his manuscripts are among the most important sources for medieval and Renaissance technology. In all other manuscripts and books of machines by authors of the periods both preceding and following Leonardo, projects for complete machines are presented, without any discussion of their construction and efficiency.[6] The only exception previous to the eighteenth-century authors Sturm, Leupold, and Belidor is represented by the work of Simon Stevin, around 1600.

As far as the evidence just mentioned shows, the mechanical engineering of times past was limited by factors of two sorts: various inadequacies in the actual construction of machines produced excessive friction and wear, and there was insufficient understanding of the possibilities inherent in any mechanical system. Leonardo's work deserves our attention as that of the first engineer to try systematically to overcome these shortcomings; most important, he was the first to recognize that each machine was a composition of certain universal mechanisms.

In this, as in several other respects, Leonardo anticipated Leupold, to whom, according to Reuleaux, the foundations of the science of mechanisms is generally attributed.[7] Indeed, of Reuleaux's own list of the constructive elements of machines (screws, keys or wedges, rivets, bearings, plummer blocks, pins, shafts, couplings, belts, cord and chain drives, friction wheels, gears, flywheels, levers, cranks, connecting rods, ratchet wheels, brakes, pipes, cylinders, pistons, valves, and springs), only the rivets are missing from Leonardo's inventories.

In Leonardo's time and even much later, engineers were convinced that the work done by a given prime mover, be it a waterwheel or the muscles of men or animals, could be indefinitely increased by means of suitable mechanical apparatuses. Such a belief led fatally to the idea of perpetual motion machines, on whose development an immense amount of effort was wasted, from the Middle Ages until the nineteenth century. Since the possibility of constructing a perpetual motion machine could not, until very recent times, be dismissed by scientific arguments, men of science of the first order accepted or rejected the underlying idea by intuition rather than by knowledge.

Leonardo followed the contemporary trend, and his earliest writings contain a fair number of perpetual motion schemes. But he gave up the idea around 1492, when he stated "It is impossible that dead [still] water may be the cause of its own or of some other body's motion" (MS *A*, fol. 43r), a statement that he later extended to all kinds of mechanical movements. By 1494 Leonardo could say that

> . . . in whatever system where the weight attached to the wheel should be the cause of the motion of the wheel, without any doubt the center of the gravity of the weight will stop beneath the center of its axle. No instrument devised by human ingenuity, which turns with its wheel, can remedy this effect. Oh! speculators about perpetual motion, how many vain chimeras have you created in the like quest. Go and take your place with the seekers after gold! [*Codex Forster*, II₂, fol. 92v].

Many similar statements can be found in the manuscripts, and it is worth noting that Leonardo's argument against perpetual motion machines is the same that was later put forth by Huygens and Parent.

Another belief common among Renaissance engineers was that flywheels (called "rote aumentative") and similar energy-storing and equalizing devices are endowed with the virtue of increasing the power of a mechanical system. Leonardo knew that such devices could be useful, but he also knew that their incorporation into a machine caused an increase in the demand of power instead of reducing it (*Codex Atlanticus*, fol. 207v-b; *Codex Madrid*, I, fol. 124r).

A practical consequence of this line of thought was Leonardo's recognition that machines do not perform work but only modify the manner of its application. The first clear formulation of this was given by Galileo,[8] but the same principle permeates all of Leonardo's pertinent investigations. He knew that mechanical advantage does not go beyond the given power available, from which the losses caused by friction must be deducted, and he formulated the basic concepts of what are known today as work and power. Leonardo's variables for these include force, time, distance, and weight (*Codex Forster*, II₂, fol. 78v; *Codex Madrid*, I, fol. 152r). One of the best examples is folio 35r of *Codex Madrid*, I, where Leonardo compares the performance of two lifting systems;

the first is a simple windlass moved by a crank, capable of lifting 5,000 pounds; the second is also moved by a crank, but a worm gear confers upon it a higher mechanical advantage, raising its lifting capacity to 50,000 pounds. Leonardo affirms that operators of both machines, applying twenty-five pounds of force and cranking with the same speed, will have the load of 50,000 pounds raised to the same height at the end of one hour. The first instrument will raise its load in ten journeys, while the second will lift it all at once. The end result, however, will be the same.

In the same codex Leonardo established rules of general validity: "Among the infinite varieties of instruments which can be made for lifting weights, all will have the same power if the motions [distances] and the acting and patient weights are equal" (*Codex Madrid*, I, fol. 175r). Accordingly, "It is impossible to increase the power of instruments used for weight-lifting, if the quantity of force and motion is given" (*ibid.*, fol. 175v).

That Leonardo had an intuitive grasp of the principle of the conservation of energy is shown in many notes dispersed throughout the manuscripts. He tried to measure the different kinds of energy known to him (muscle power, springs, running and falling water, wind, and so forth) in terms of gravity—that is, using dynamometers counterbalanced by weights, anticipating Borelli and Smeaton. He even tried to investigate the energetic equivalent of gunpowder, weighing the propellant and the missile and measuring the range. The missile was then shot from a crossbow spanned with a given weight, which was then correlated with the quantity of gunpowder used in the first experiment (*ibid.*, fol. 60r).

Leonardo was aware that the main impediment to all mechanical motions was friction. He clearly recognized the importance of frictional resistance not only between solid bodies but also in liquids and gases. In order to evaluate the role of friction in mechanical motions, he devised ingenious experimental equipment, which included friction banks identical to those used by Coulomb 300 years later. From his experiments Leonardo derived several still-valid general principles—that frictional resistance differs according to the nature of the surfaces in contact, that it depends on the degree of smoothness of those surfaces, that it is independent of the area of the surfaces in contact, that it increases in direct proportion to the load, and that it can be reduced by interposing rolling elements or lubricating fluids between the surfaces in contact. He introduced the concept of the coefficient of friction and estimated that for "polished and smooth" surfaces the ratio F/P was 0.25, or one-fourth of the weight. This value is reasonably accurate for hardwood on hardwood, bronze on steel, and for other materials with which Leonardo was acquainted.[9]

Leonardo's main concern, however, was rolling friction. Realizing that lubrication alone could not prevent rapid wear of an axle and its bearing, Leonardo suggested the use of bearing blocks with split, adjustable bushings of antifriction metal ("three parts

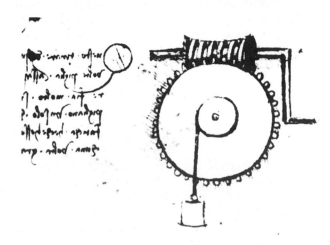

FIGURE 1. Worm gear, shaped to match the curve of the toothed wheel it drives. Designed by Leonardo in 1495 (*Codex Madrid*, I, 17v). It was reinvented by the English engineer Henry Hindley, *ca.* 1740.

of copper and seven of tin melted together"). He was also the first to suggest true ball and roller bearings, developing ring-shaped races to eliminate the loss due to contact friction of the individual balls in a bearing. Leonardo's thrust bearings with conical pivots turning on cones, rollers, or balls (*ibid.*, fol. 101v) are particularly interesting. He also worked persistently to produce gearings designed to overcome frictional resistance. Even when they are not accompanied by geometrical elaborations, some of his gears are unmistakably cycloidal. Leonardo further introduced various new gear forms, among them trapezoidal, helical, and conical bevel gears; of particular note is his globoidal gear, of which several variants are found in the *Codex Atlanticus* and *Codex Madrid*, I, one of them being a worm gear shaped to match the curve of the toothed wheel it drives, thus overcoming the risk inherent in an endless screw that engages only a single gear tooth (*ibid.*, fols. 17v-18v). This device was rediscovered by Henry Hindley around 1740.

Leonardo's development of complicated gear systems was not motivated by any vain hope of obtaining limitless mechanical advantages. He warned the makers of machines:

The more wheels you will have in your instrument, the more toothing you will need, and the more teeth, the greater will be the friction of the wheels with the spindles of their pinions. And the greater the friction, the more power is lost by the motor and, consequently, force is lacking for the orderly motion of the entire system [*Codex Atlanticus*, fol. 207v-b].

Leonardo's contribution to practical kinematics is documented by the devices sketched and described in his notebooks. Since the conversion of rotary to alternating motion (or vice versa) was best performed with the help of the crank and rod combinations, Leonardo sketched hundreds of them to illustrate the kinematics of such composite machines as sawmills, pumps, spinning wheels, grinding machines, and blowers. In addition he drew scores of ingenious combinations of gears, linkages, cams, and ratchets, designed to transmit and modify mechanical movements. He used the pendulum as an energy accumulator in working machines as well as an escapement in clockwork (*Codex Madrid*, I, fol. 61v).

Although simple cord drives had been known since the Middle Ages, Leonardo's belt techniques, including tightening devices, must be considered as original. His manuscripts describe both hinged link chains and continuous chain drives with sprocket wheels (*ibid.*, fol. 10r; *Codex Atlanticus*, fol. 357r-a).

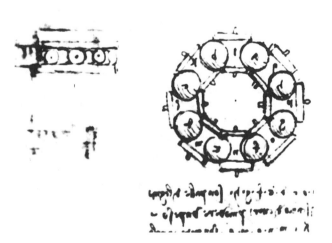

FIGURE 2. Antifriction balls designed by Leonardo for a ball bearing. Reinvented in 1920 (*Codex Madrid*, I, 101v).

Leonardo's notes about the most efficient use of prime movers deserve special attention. His particular interest in attaining the maximum efficiency of muscle power is understandable, since muscle power represented the only motor that might be used in a flying machine, a project that aroused his ambition as early as 1487 and one in which he remained interested until the end of his life. Since muscles were also the most common source of power, it was further important to establish the most effective ways to use them in performing work.

Leonardo estimated the force exerted by a man turning a crank as twenty-five pounds. (Philippe de La Hire found it to be twenty-seven pounds, while Guillaume Amontons, in similar experiments, confirmed Leonardo's figure; in 1782 Claude François Berthelot wrote that men cannot produce a continuous effort of more than twenty pounds, even if some authors admitted twenty-four.)[10] Such a return seemed highly unsatisfactory. Leonardo tried to find more suitable mechanical arrangements, the most remarkable of which employ the weight of men or animals instead of muscle power. For activating pile drivers (*Codex Leicester*, fol. 28v [*ca.* 1505]) or excavation machines (*Codex Atlanticus*, fols. 1v-b, 331v-a), Leonardo used the weight of men, who by running up ladders and returning on a descending platform, would raise the ram or monkey. Leonardo used the same system for lifting heavier loads with cranes, the counterweight being "one ox and one man"; lifting capacity was further increased by applying a differential windlass to the arm of the crane (*ibid.*, fol. 363v-b [*ca.* 1495]).

Until the advent of the steam engine the most popular portable prime mover was the treadmill, known since antiquity. Leonardo found the conventional type, in which men walk inside the drum, in the manner of a squirrel cage, to be inherently less efficient than one employing the weight of the men on the outside of the drum. While he did not invent the external treadmill, he was the first to use it rationally— the next scholar to analyze the efficiency of the treadmill mathematically was Simon Stevin (1586).

Leonardo also had very clear ideas about the advantages and the limitations of waterpower. He rejected popular hydraulic perpetual motion schemes, "Falling water will raise as much more weight than its own as is the weight equivalent to its percussion... But you have to deduce from the power of the instrument what is lost by friction in its bearings" (*ibid.*, fol. 151r-a). Since the weight of the percussion, according to Leonardo, is proportional to height, and therefore to gravitational acceleration ("among natural forces, percussion surpasses all others... because at every stage of the descent it acquires more momentum"), this represents the first, if imperfect, statement of the basic definition of the energy potential $Ep = mgh$.

Leonardo describes hydraulic wheels on many pages of his notebooks and drawings, either separately or as part of technological operations. He continually sought improvements for systems currently in use. He evaluated all varieties of prime movers, vertical as well as horizontal, and improved on the traditional Lombard mills by modifying the wheels and their races and introducing an adjustable wheel-raising device (MS *H*; *Codex Atlanticus*, fols. 304r-b, v-d [*ca.* 1494]).

In 1718 L. C. Sturm described a "new kind" of mill constructed in the Mark of Brandenburg, "where a lot of fuss was made about them, although they were not as new as most people in those parts let themselves be persuaded...." They were, in fact, identical to those designed by Leonardo for the country estate of Ludovico il Moro near Vigevano around 1494.

It is noteworthy that in his mature technological projects Leonardo returned to horizontal waterwheels for moving heavy machinery (*Codex Atlanticus*, fol. 2r-a and b [*ca.* 1510]), confirming once more the high power output of such prime movers. His papers provide forerunners of the reaction turbine (*Codex Forster*, I₂) and the Pelton wheel (*Codex Madrid*, I, fol. 22v); drawings of completely encased waterwheels appear on several folios of the *Codex Atlanticus*.

There is little about wind power in Leonardo's writings, probably because meteorological conditions limited its practical use in Italy. Although it is erroneous to attribute the invention of the tower mill to Leonardo (as has been done), the pertinent sketches are significant because they show for the first time a brake wheel mounted on the wind shaft (MS *L*, fol. 34v). (The arrangement reappears, as do many other ideas of Leonardo's, in Ramelli's book of 1588 [plate cxxxiii].) Windmills with rotors turning on a vertical shaft provided with shield walls are elaborated on folios 43v, 44r, 74v, 75r, and 55v of *Codex Madrid*, II; and there can be no doubt that Leonardo became acquainted with them through friends who had seen them in the East.

In contrast with Leonardo's scant interest in wind power, he paid constant attention to heat and fire as possible sources of energy. His experiments with steam are found on folios 10r and 15r of the *Codex Leicester*. His approximate estimation of the volume of steam evolved through the evaporation of a given quantity of water suggests a ratio 1 : 1,500, the correct figure being about 1 : 1,700. Besson in 1569 still believed that the proportion was 1 : 10, a ratio raised to 1 : 255 in the famous experiments of Jean Rey; it was not until 1683 that a better estimate— 1 : 2,000—was made by Samuel Morland. Leonardo's best-known contribution to the utilization of steam power was his "Architronito" (MS *B*, fol. 33r), a steam cannon. The idea is not as impractical as generally assumed, since steam cannons were used in the American Civil War and even in World War II (Holman projectors). It was Leonardo, and not Branca (1629), who described the first impulse turbine moved by a jet of steam (*Codex Leicester*, fol. 28v).

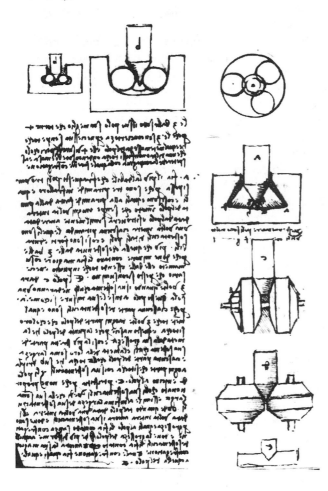

FIGURE 3. Ring-shaped race for a ball bearing with independent separation devices, *ca.* 1494 (*Codex Madrid*, I, 20v). Reinvented in the eighteenth century.

One of Leonardo's most original technological attempts toward a more efficient prime mover is the thermal engine drawn and described on folio 16v of MS *F* (1508–1509), which anticipates Huygens' and Papin's experiments. In 1690 Papin arrived at the idea of the atmospheric steam engine after Huygens' experiments with a gunpowder engine (1673) failed to give consistent results. Leonardo's atmospheric thermal motor, conceived "to lift a great weight by means of fire," like those of Huygens and Papin, consisted of cylinder, piston, and valve, and worked in exactly the same way.[11]

Leonardo's studies on the behavior and resistance of materials were the first of their kind. The problem was also attacked by Galileo, but an adequate treatment of the subject had to wait until the eighteenth century. One of Leonardo's most interesting observations was pointed out by Zammattio and refers to the bending of an elastic beam, or spring. Leonardo recognized clearly that the fibers of the beam are lengthened at the outside of the curvature and shortened at the inside. In the middle, there is an area which is not deformed, which Leonardo called the "linea centrica" (now called the neutral axis). Leonardo suggested that similar conditions obtained in the case of ropes bent around a pulley and in single as well as intertwisted wires (*Codex Madrid*, I, fols. 84v, 154v). More than two centuries had to pass before this model of the internal stresses was proposed again by Jakob Bernoulli.

Leonardo's notebooks also contain the first descriptions of machine tools of some significance, including plate rollers for nonferrous metals (MS *I*, fol. 48v), rollers for bars and strips (*Codex Atlanticus*, fol. 370v-b; MS *G*, fol. 70v), rollers for iron staves (*Codex Atlanticus*, fol. 2r-a and b), semiautomatic wood planers (*ibid.*, fol. 38v-b), and a planer for iron (*Codex Madrid*, I, fol. 84v). His thread-cutting machines (*Codex Atlanticus*, fol. 367v-a) reveal great ingenuity, and their principle has been adopted for modern use.

Not only did Leonardo describe the first lathe with continuous motion (*ibid.*, *fol.* 381r-b) but, according to Lomazzo, he must also be credited with the invention of the elliptic lathe, generally attributed to Besson (1569). Leonardo described external and internal grinders (*ibid.*, fols. 7r-b, 291r-a) as well as disk and belt grinding machines (*ibid.*, fols. 320r-b, 380v-b, 318v-a). He devoted a great deal of attention to the development of grinding and polishing wheels for plane and concave mirrors (*ibid.*, fols. 32r-a, 396v-f, 401r-a; *Codex Madrid*, I, fol. 163v, 164r; MS *G*, fol. 82v, for examples). Folio 159r-b of the *Codex Atlanticus* is concerned with shaping sheet metal by stamping (to make chandeliers of two or, better, four parts). The pressure necessary for this operation was obtained by means of a wedge press.

Leonardo's interest in water mills has already been mentioned. Of his work in applied hydraulics, the improvement of canal locks and sluices (miter gates and wickets) is an outstanding example. He discussed the theory and the practice of an original type of centrifugal pump (MS *F*, fols. 13r, 16r) and the best ways of constructing and moving Archimedean screws. Some of these methods were based on coiled pipes (MS *E*, fols. 13v, 14r) like those seen by Cardano at the waterworks of Augsburg in 1541.

Leonardo left plans for a great number of machines which were generally without parallel until the eighteenth and nineteenth centuries. Some of these are the improved pile drivers (*Codex Forster*, II, fol. 73v; MS *H*, fol. 80v; *Codex Leicester*, fol. 28v) later described by La Hire (1707) and Belidor (1737), a cylindrical bolter activated by the main drive of a grain mill (*Codex Madrid*, I, fols. 21v, 22r), and a mechanized wedge press (*ibid.*, 46v, 47r), which in the eighteenth century became known as the Dutch press. Particularly original are Leonardo's well-known canal-building machines, scattered through the *Codex Atlanticus*—in Parsons' opinion, "had Leonardo contributed nothing more to engineering than his plans and studies for the Arno canal, they alone would place him in the first rank of engineers for all time." The knowledge that most of those projects were executed in the Romagna during Leonardo's service with Cesare Borgia makes little difference.

Leonardo also designed textile machinery. Plans for spinning machines, embodying mechanical principles which did not reappear until the eighteenth century, are found on folio 393v-a of the *Codex Atlanticus*, as well as in the *Codex Madrid*, I (fols. 65v, 66r). The group represented in the *Codex Atlanticus* includes ropemaking machines of advanced design (fol. 2v-a and b), silk doubling and winding machines (fol. 36v-b), gig mills whose principle reappears in the nineteenth century (fols. 38r-a, 161v-b, 297r-a), shearing machines (fols. 397r-a, 397v-a), and even a power loom (fols. 317v-b, 356r-a, 356v-a).

Leonardo was also interested in the graphic arts and in 1494 presented details of the contemporary printing press, antedating by more than fifty years the first sensible reproduction of such an instrument. Even earlier (around 1480) he had tried to improve the efficiency of the printing press by making the motion of the carriage a function of the motion of the pressing screw. Leonardo's most interesting innovation in this field, however, was his invention of a technique of relief etching, permitting the printing of text and illustration in a single operation (*Codex Madrid*, II, fol. 119r [1504]). The technique was reinvented by William Blake in 1789 and perfected by Gillot around 1850.[12]

Leonardo's work on flight and flying machines is too well known to be discussed here in detail. The most positive part of it consists of his studies on the flight of birds, found in several notebooks, among them *Codex on Flight* . . .; MSS *K*, *E*, *G*, and *L*; *Codex Atlanticus*; and *Codex Madrid*, II, etc. Leonardo's flying machines embody many interesting mechanical features, although their basic conception as ornithopters makes them impractical. Only later did Leonardo decide to take up gliders, as did Lilienthal 400 years later. Although the idea of the parachute and of the so-called helicopter may antedate Leonardo, he was the first to experiment with true airscrews.

Leonardo's interest in chemical phenomena (for example, combustion) embraced them as such, or in relation to the practical arts. He made some inspired projects for distillation apparatus, based on the "Moor's head" condensation system that was universally adopted in the sixteenth century. Descriptions of water-cooled delivery pipes may also be found among his papers, as may a good description of an operation for separating gold from silver (*Codex Atlanticus*, fol. 244v [*ca.* 1505]). Some of the most original of the many practical chemical operations that are described in Leonardo's notebooks are concerned with making decorative objects of imitation agate, chalcedony, jasper, or amber. Leonardo began with proteins—a concentrated solution of gelatin or egg-white—and added pigments and vegetable colors. The material was then shaped by casting in ceramic molds or by extrusion; after drying, the objects were polished and then varnished for stability (MS *I*, fol. 27v; MS *F*, fols. 42r, 55v, 73v, 95v; MS *K*, fols. 114–118). By laminating unsized paper impregnated with the same materials and subsequently drying it, he obtained plates "so dense as to resemble bronze"; after varnishing, "they will be like glass and resist humidity" (MS *F*, fol. 96r). Leonardo's notes thus contain the basic operations of modern plastic technology.[13]

Of Leonardo's projects in military engineering and weaponry, those of his early period are more spectacular than practical. Some of them are, however, useful in obtaining firsthand information on contemporary techniques of cannon founding (*Codex Atlanticus*, fol. 19r-b) and also provide an interesting footnote on the survival, several centuries after the introduction of gunpowder, of such ancient devices as crossbows, ballistae, and mangonels. Leonardo did make some surprisingly modern suggestions; he was a stout advocate (although not the inventor) of breech-loading guns, he designed a water-cooled barrel for a rapid-fire gun, and, on several occasions, he proposed ogive-headed projectiles, with or without directional fins. His designs for wheel locks (*ibid.*, fols. 56v-b, 353r-c, 357r-a) antedate by about fifteen years the earliest known similar devices, which were constructed in Nuremberg. His suggestion of prefabricated cartridges consisting of ball, charge, and primer, which occurs on folio 9r-b of the *Codex Atlanticus*, is a very early (*ca.* 1480) proposal of a system introduced in Saxony around 1590.

Several of Leonardo's military projects are of importance to the history of mechanical engineering because of such details of construction as the racks used for spanning giant crossbows (*ibid.*, fol. 53r-a and b [*ca.* 1485]) or the perfectly developed universal joint on a light gun mount (*ibid.*, fol. 399v-a [*ca.* 1494]).

Leonardo worked as military architect at the court of Ludovico il Moro, although his precise tasks are not documented. His activities during his short stay in the service of Cesare Borgia are, however, better known. His projects for the modernization of the fortresses in the Romagna are very modern in concept, while the maps and city plans executed during this period (especially that of Imola in *Windsor Collection*, fol. 12284) have been called monuments in the history of cartography.

One of the manuscripts recently brought to light, *Codex Madrid*, II, reveals an activity of Leonardo's unknown until 1967—his work on the fortifications of Piombino for Jacopo IV d'Appiano (1504). Leonardo's technological work is characterized not only by an understanding of the natural laws (he is, incidentally, the first to have used this term) that govern the functioning of all mechanical devices but also by the requirement of technical and economical efficiency. He was not an armchair technologist, inventing ingenious but unusable machines; his main goal was practical efficiency and economy. He continually sought the best mechanical solution for a given task; a single page of his notes often contains a number of alternative means. Leonardo abhorred waste, be it of time, power, or money. This is why so many double-acting devices—ratchet mechanisms, blowers, and pumps—are found in his writings. This mentality led Leonardo toward more highly automated machines, including the file-cutting machine of *Codex Atlanticus,* folio 6r-b, the automatic hammer for gold-foil work of *Codex Atlanticus*, folios 8r-a, 21r-a, and 21v-a, and the mechanized printing press, rope-making machine, and power loom, already mentioned.[14]

According to Beck, the concept of the transmission of power to various operating machines was one of the most important in the development of industrial machinery. Beck thought that the earliest industrial application of this type is found in Agricola's famous *De re metallica* (1550) in a complex designed for the mercury amalgamation treatment of gold ores.[15] Leonardo, however, described several projects of the same kind, while on folios 46v and 47r of *Codex Madrid*, I, he considered the possibility of running a complete oil factory with a single power source. No fewer than five separate operations were to be performed in this combine—milling by rollers, scraping,

pressing in a wedge press, releasing the pressed material, and mixing on the heating pan. This project is further remarkable because the power is transmitted by shafting; the complex thus represents a complete "Dutch oil mill," of which no other record exists prior to the eighteenth century.

Leonardo's interest in practical technology was at its strongest during his first Milanese period, from 1481 or 1482 to 1499. After that his concern shifted from practice to theory, although on occasion he resumed practical activities, as in 1502, when he built canals in the Romagna, and around 1509, when he executed works on the Adda River in Lombardy. He worked intensively on the construction of concave mirror systems in Rome, and he left highly original plans for the improvement of the minting techniques in that city (1513–1516). He was engaged in hydraulic works along the Loire during his last years.

NOTES

1. Luca Beltrami, *Documenti e memorie riguardanti la vita e le opere di Leonardo da Vinci* (Milan, 1919), nos. 66, 117, 126, 127.
2. *Codex Madrid*, II, *passim.*
3. Beltrami, op. cit., no. 189.
4. Beltrami, op. cit., no. 246.
5. G. Calvi, *I manoscritti di Leonardo da Vinci* (Bologna, 1925); A. M. Brizio, *Scritti scelti di Leonardo da Vinci* (Turin, 1952); Kenneth Clark, *A Catalogue of the Drawings of Leonardo da Vinci at Windsor Castle* (Cambridge, 1935; 2nd rev. ed., London, 1968–1969); C. Pedretti, *Studi Vinciani* (Geneva, 1957).
6. Kyeser (1405), Anonymous of the Hussite Wars (*ca.* 1430), Fontana (*ca.* 1420), Taccola (*ca.* 1450), Francesco di Giorgio (*ca.* 1480), Besson (1569), Ramelli (1588), Zonca (1607), Strada (1617–1618), Veranzio (*ca.* 1615), Branca (1629), Biringuccio (1540), Agricola (1556), Cardano (1550), Lorini (1591), Böckler (1661), Zeising (1607–1614).
7. F. Reuleaux, *The Kinematic of Machinery* (New York, 1876; repr. 1963); R. S. Hartenberg and J. Denavit, *Kinematic Synthesis of Linkages* (New York, 1964).
8. G. Galilei, *Le meccaniche* (*ca.* 1600), trans. with intro. and notes by I. E. Drabkin and Stillman Drake as *Galilei on Motion and on Mechanics* (Madison, Wis., 1960).
9. G. Canestrini, *Leonardo costruttore di macchine e veicoli* (Milan, 1939); L. Reti, "Leonardo on Bearings and Gears," in *Scientific American*, **224** (1971), 100.
10. E. S. Ferguson, "The Measurement of the 'Man-Day,'" in *Scientific American*, **225** (1971), 96. The writings of La Hire and Amontons are in *Mémoires de l'Académie . . .*, **1** (1699).
11. L. Reti, "Leonardo da Vinci nella storia della macchina a vapore," in *Rivista di ingegneria* (1956–1957).
12. L. Reti, "Leonardo da Vinci and the Graphic Arts," in *Burlington Magazine*, **113** (1971), 189.
13. L. Reti, "Le arti chimiche di Leonardo da Vinci," in *Chimica e l'industria*, **34** (1952), 655, 721.
14. B. Dibner, "Leonardo: Prophet of Automation," in C. D. O'Malley, ed., *Leonardo's Legacy* (Berkeley–Los Angeles, 1969).
15. T. Beck, *Beiträge zur Geschichte des Maschinenbaues* (Berlin, 1900), pp. 152–153.

LADISLAO RETI

MECHANICS

Although Leonardo was interested in mechanics for most of his mature life, he would appear to have turned more and more of his attention to it from 1508 on. It is difficult to construct a unified and consistent picture of his mechanics in detail, but the major trends, concepts, and influences can be delineated with some firmness.[1] Statics may be considered first, since this area of theoretical mechanics greatly attracted him and his earliest influences in this field probably came from the medieval science of weights. To this he later added Archimedes' *On the Equilibrium of Planes*, with a consequent interest in the development of a procedure for determining the centers of gravity of sundry geometrical magnitudes.

In his usual fashion Leonardo absorbed the ideas of his predecessors, turned them in practical and experiential directions, and developed his own system of nomenclature—for example, he called the arms of balances "braccia" while in levers "lieva" is the arm of the lever to which the power is applied and "contralieva" the arm in which the resistance lies. Influenced by the Scholastics, he called the position of horizontal equilibrium the "sito dell'equalità" (or sometimes the position "equale allo orizzonte"). Pendent weights are simply "pesi," or "pesi attacati," or "pesi appiccati"; the cords supporting them—or, more generally, the lines of force in which the weights or forces act or in which they are applied—are called "appendicoli." Leonardo further distinguished between "braccia reali o linee corporee," the actual lever arms, and "braccia potenziali o spirituali o semireali," the potential or effective arms. The potential arm is the horizontal distance to the vertical (that is, the "linea central") through the center of motion in the case of bent levers, or, more generally, the perpendicular distance to the center of motion from the line of force about the center of motion. He often called the center of motion the "centro del circunvolubile," or simply the "polo."

The classical law of the lever appears again and again in Leonardo's notebooks. For example, *Codex Atlanticus*, folio 176v-d, states, "The ratio of the weights which hold the arms of the balance parallel to the horizon is the same as that of the arms, but is an inverse one." In *Codex Arundel*, folio 1v, the law appears formulaically as $W_2 = (W_1 \cdot s_1)/s_2$: "Multiply the longer arm of the balance by the weight it supports and divide the product by the shorter arm, and the result will be the weight which, when placed on the shorter arm, resists the descent of the longer arm, the arms of the balance being above all basically balanced."

A few considerations that prove the influence of the medieval science of weights upon Leonardo are in order. The medieval science of weights consisted essentially of the following corpus of works:[2] Pseudo-Euclid, *Liber de ponderoso et levi*, a geometrical treatment of basic Aristotelian ideas relating forces, volumes, weights, and velocities; Pseudo-Archimedes, *De ponderibus Archimenidis* (also entitled *De incidentibus in humidum*), essentially a work of hydrostatics; an anonymous tract from the Greek, *De canonio*, treating of the Roman balance or steelyard by reduction to a theoretical balance; Thābit ibn Qurra, *Liber karastonis*, another treatment of the Roman balance; Jordanus de Nemore, *Elementa de ponderibus* (also entitled *Elementa super demonstrationem ponderum*), a work existing in many manuscripts and complemented by several reworked versions of the late thirteenth and the fourteenth centuries, which was marked by the first use of the concept of positional gravity *(gravitas secundum situm)*, by a false demonstration of the law of the bent lever, and by an elegant proof of the law of the lever on the basis of the principle of virtual displacements; an anonymous *Liber de ponderibus* (called, by its modern editor, Version P), which contains a kind of short Peripatetic commentary to the enunciations of Jordanus; a *Liber de ratione ponderis*, also attributed to Jordanus, which is a greatly expanded and corrected version of the *Elementa* in four parts and is distinguished by a more correct use of the concept of positional gravity, by a superb proof of the law of the bent lever based on the principle of virtual displacements, by the same proof of the law of the straight lever given in the *Elementa*, and by a remarkable and sound proof of the law of the equilibrium of connected weights on adjacent inclined planes that is also based on the principle of virtual displacements—thereby constituting the first correct statement and proof of the inclined plane law—and including a number of practical problems in statics and dynamics, of which the most noteworthy are those connected with the bent lever in part III; and Blasius of Parma, *Tractatus de ponderibus*, a rather inept treatment of the problems of statics and hydrostatics based on the preceding works.

The whole corpus is marked methodologically by its geometric form and conceptually by its use of dynamics (particularly the principle of virtual velocities or the principle of virtual displacements in one form or another) in application to the basic statical problems and conclusions inherited from Greek antiquity. Leonardo was much influenced by the corpus' general dynamical approach as well as by particular conclusions of specific works. Reasonably conclusive evidence exists to show that Leonardo had read Pseudo-Archimedes, *De canonio,* and Thābit ibn Qurra, while completely conclusive evidence reveals his knowledge of the *Elementa, De ratione ponderis,* and Blasius. It is reasonable to suppose that he also saw the other works of the corpus, since they were so often included in the same manuscripts as the works he did read.

The two works upon which Leonardo drew most heavily were the *Elementa de ponderibus* and the *Liber de ratione ponderis.* The key passage that shows decisively that Leonardo read both of them occurs in *Codex Atlanticus,* folios 154v-a and r-a. In this passage, whose significance has not been properly recognized before, Leonardo presents a close Italian translation of all the postulates from the *Elementa* (E.01–E.07) and the enunciations of the first two propositions (without proofs), together with a definition that precedes the proof of proposition E.2.[3] He then shifts to the *Liber de ratione ponderis* and includes the enunciations of all the propositions of the first two parts (except R2.05) and the first two propositions of the third part.[4] It seems likely that Leonardo made his translation from a single manuscript that contained both works and, after starting his translation of the *Elementa,* suddenly realized the superiority of the *De ratione ponderis.* He may also have translated the rest of part III, for he seems to have been influenced by propositions R3.05 and R3.06, the last two propositions in part III, and perhaps also by R3.04 in passages not considered here (see MS *A,* fols. 1r, 33v). Another page in *Codex Atlanticus,* folio 165v-a and v-c, contains all of the enunciations of the propositions of part IV (except for R4.07, R4.11–12, and R4.16). The two passages from the *Codex Atlanticus* together establish that Leonardo had complete knowledge of the best and the most original work in the corpus of the medieval science of weights.

The passages cited do not, of course, show what Leonardo did with that knowledge, although others do. For example in MS *G,* folio 79r, Leonardo refutes the incorrect proof of the second part of proposition E.2 (or of its equivalent, R1.02). The proposition states: "When the beam of a balance of equal arm lengths is in the horizontal position, if equal weights are suspended [from its extremities], it will not leave the horizontal position, and if it should be moved from the horizontal position, it will revert to it."[5] The second part is true for a material beam supported from above, since the elevation of one of the arms removes the center of gravity from the vertical line through the fulcrum and, accordingly, the balance beam returns to the horizontal position as the center of gravity seeks the vertical. The medieval proof in E.2 and

R1.02, however, treats the balance as if it were a theoretical balance (with weightless beam) and attempts to show that it would return to the horizontal position. Based on the false use of the concept of positional gravity, it asserts that the weight above the line of horizontal equilibrium has a greater gravity according to its position than the weight depressed below the line, for if both weights tended to move downward, the arc on which the upper weight would move intercepts more of the vertical than the arc on which the lower weight would tend to move. Leonardo's refutation is based on showing that because the weights are connected, the actual arcs to be compared are oppositely directed and so have equal obliquities—and thus the superior weight enjoys no positional advantage. In MS *E,* folio 59r, Leonardo seems also to give the correct explanation for the return to horizontal equilibrium of the material beam.

A further response to the *Liber de ratione ponderis* is in *Codex Atlanticus,* folio 354v-c, where Leonardo again translates proposition R1.09 and paraphrases proposition R1.10 of the medieval work: "The equality of the declination conserves the equality of the weights. If the ratios of the weights and the obliquities on which they are placed are the same but inverse, the weights will remain equal in gravity and motion" ("La equalità della declinazione osserva la equalità de' pesi. Se le proporzioni de' pesi e dell' obbliqua dove si posano, saranno equali, ma converse, essi pesi resteranno equali in gravità e in moto"). The equivalent propositions from the *Liber de ratione ponderis* were "R1.09. Equalitas declinationis identitatem conservat ponderis" and "R1.10. Si per diversarum obliquitatum vias duo pondera descendant, fueritque declinationum et ponderum una proportio eodum ordine sumpta, una erit utriusque virtus in descendendo."[6] While Leonardo preserved R1.09 exactly in holding that positional weight on the incline is everywhere the same as long as the incline's declination is the same, his rephrasing of R1.10 indicates that he adopted a different measure of "declination."

R. Marcolongo believed that Leonardo measured obliquity by the ratio of the common altitude of the inclines to the length of the incline (that is, by the sine of the angle of inclination), while Jordanus had measured obliquity by the length of the incline that intercepts the common altitude (that is, by the cosecant of the angle).[7] Thus, if p_1 and p_2 are connected weights placed on the inclined planes that are of lengths l_1 and l_2, respectively, with common altitude h, then, according to Marcolongo's view of Leonardo's method, $p_1/p_2 = (h/l_2)/(h/l_1)$, and thus $p_1/p_2 = l_1/l_2,$

as Jordanus held. Hence, if Marcolongo is correct, Leonardo had absorbed the correct exposition of the inclined plane problem from the *Liber de ratione ponderis*. Perhaps he did, but it is not exhibited in this passage, for the figure accompanying the passage (Figure 1), with its numerical designations of 2 and 1

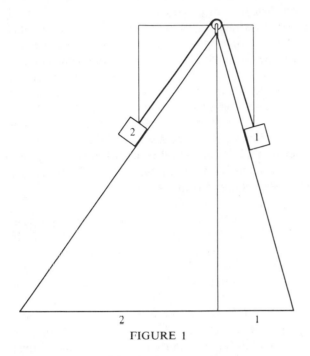

FIGURE 1

on the bases cut off by the vertical, shows that Leonardo believed the weights on the inclines to be inversely proportional to the tangents of the angles of inclination rather than to the sines—and such a solution is

clearly incorrect. The same incorrect solution is apparent in MS *G*, folio 77v, where again equilibrium of the two weights is preserved when the weights are in the same ratio as the bases cut off by the common altitude (thus implying that the weights are inversely proportional to the tangents).

Other passages give evidence of Leonardo's vacillating methods and confusion. One (*Codex on Flight*, fol. 4r) consists of two paragraphs that apply to the same figure (Figure 2). The first is evidently an explanation of a proposition expressed elsewhere (MS *E*, fol. 75r) to the effect that although equal weights balance each other on the equal arms of a balance, they do not do so if they are put on inclines of different obliquity. It states:

> The weight *q*, because of the right angle *n* [perpendicularly] above point *e* in line *df*, weighs 2/3 of its natural weight, which was 3 pounds, and so has a residual force ["che resta in potenzia"] [along *nq*] of 2 pounds; and the weight *p*, whose natural weight was also 3 pounds, has a residual force of 1 pound [along *mp*] because of right angle *m* [perpendicularly] above point *g* in line *hd*. [Therefore, *p* and *q* are not in equilibrium on these inclines.]

The bracketed material has been added as clearly implicit, and so far this analysis seems to be entirely correct. It is evident from the figure that Leonardo has applied the concept of potential lever arm (implying static moment) to the determination of the component of weight along the incline, so that $F_1 \cdot dn = W_1 \cdot de$, where F_1 is the component of the natural weight W_1 along the incline, *dn* is the potential lever arm through which F_1 acts around fulcrum *d*, and *de* is the lever

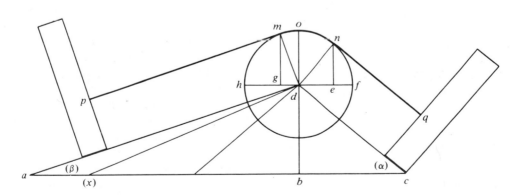

FIGURE 2

arm through which W_1 would act when hanging from n. Hence, $F_1 = W_1 \cdot (de/dn) = W_1 \cdot \sin \angle dne$. But $\angle dne = \angle \alpha$, and so we have the correct formulation $F_1 = W_1 \cdot \sin \alpha$. In the same way for weight p, it can be shown that $F_2 = W_2 \cdot \sin \beta$. And since Leonardo apparently constructed $de = 2df/3$, $dg = hd/3$, and $W_1 = W_2 = 3$, obviously $F_1 = 2$ and $F_2 = 1$ and the weights are not in equilibrium.

In the second paragraph, which also pertains to the figure, he changes p and q, each of which was initially equal to three pounds, to two pounds, and one pound, respectively, with the object of determining whether the adjusted weights would be in equilibrium:

> So now we have one pound against two pounds. And because the obliquities da and dc on which these weights are placed are not in the same ratio as the weights, that is, 2 to 1 [the weights are not in equilibrium]; like the said weights [in the first paragraph?], they alter natural gravities [but they are not in equilibrium] because the obliquity da exceeds the obliquity dc, or contains the obliquity dc, $2\frac{1}{2}$ times, as is demonstrated by their bases ab and bc, whose ratio is a double sesquialterate ratio [that is, 5:2], while the ratio of the weights will be a double ratio [that is, 2:1].

It is abundantly clear, at least in the second paragraph, that Leonardo was assuming that for equilibrium the weights ought to be directly proportional to the bases (and thus inversely proportional to the tangents); and since the weights are not as the base lines, they are not in equilibrium. In fact, in adding line $d[x]$ Leonardo was indicating the declination he thought would establish the equilibrium of p and q, weights of two pounds and one pound, respectively, for it is obvious that the horizontal distances $b[x]$ and bc are also related as 2 : 1. This is further confirmation that Leonardo measured declination by the tangent.

Assuming that both paragraphs were written at the same time, it is apparent that Leonardo then thought that both methods of determining the effective weight on an incline—the method using the concept of the lever and the technique of using obliquities measured

by tangents—were correct. A similar confusion is apparent in his treatment of the tensions in strings. But there is still another figure (Figure 3), which has accompanying it in MS *H*, folio 81(33)v, the following brief statement: "On the balance, weight ab will be as weight cd." If Leonardo was assuming that the weights are of the same material with equal thickness and, as it seems in the figure, that they are of the same width, with their lengths equal to the lengths of the vertical and the incline, respectively, thus producing weights that are proportional to these lengths, then he was indeed giving a correct example of the inclined-plane principle that may well reflect proposition R1.10 of the *Liber de ratione ponderis*. There is one further solution of the inclined-plane problem, on MS *A*, folio 21v, that is totally erroneous and, so far as is known, unique. It is not discussed here; the reader is referred to Duhem's treatment, with the caution that Duhem's conclusion that it was derived from Pappus' erroneous solution is questionable.[8]

As important as Leonardo's responses to proposition R1.10 are his responses to the bent-lever proposition, R1.08, of the *Liber de ratione ponderis*. In *Codex Arundel*, folio 32v, he presents another Italian translation of it (in addition to the translation already noted in his omnibus collection of translations of the enunciations of the medieval work). In this new translation he writes of the bent-lever law as "tested": "Tested. If the arms of the balance are unequal and their juncture in the fulcrum is angular, and if their *termini* are equally distant from the central [that is, vertical] line through the fulcrum, with equal weights applied there [at the *termini*], they will weigh equally [that is, be in equilibrium]"—or "Sperimentata. Se le braccia della bilancia fieno inequali, e la lor congiunzione nel polo sia angulare, se i termini lor fieno equalmente distanti alla linea centrale del polo, li pesi appiccativi, essendo equali, equalmente peseranno," a translation of the Latin text, "R1.08. Si inequalia fuerint brachia libre, et in centro motus angulum fecerint, si termini eorum ad directionem hinc inde equaliter accesserint, equalia appensa, in hac dispositione equaliter ponderabunt."[9] Other, somewhat confused passages indicate that Leonardo had indeed absorbed the significance of the passage he had twice translated.[10]

More important, Leonardo extended the bent-lever law beyond the special case of equal weights at equal horizontal distances, given in R1.08, to cases in which the more general law of the bent lever—"weights are inversely proportional to the horizontal distances"—is applied. He did this in a large number of problems to which he applied his concept of "potential lever arm." The first passage notable for this concept is in

FIGURE 3. (Note: The horizontal base line and the continuation of the line from point c beyond the pulley wheel to the balance beam are in Leonardo's drawing but should be deleted.)

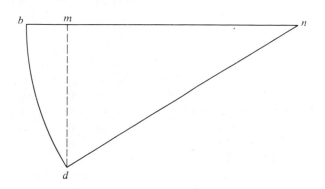

FIGURE 4. (Note: This is the essential part of a more detailed drawing.)

MS *E*, folio 72v, and probably derives from proposition R3.05 of the *Liber de ratione ponderis*.[11] Here Leonardo wrote (see Figure 4): "The ratio that space *mn* has to space *nb* is the same as the ratio that the weight which has descended to *d* has to the weight it had in position *b*. It follows that, *mn* being 9/11 of *nb*, the weight in *d* is 9/10 (! 9/11) of the weight it had in height *b*." In this passage *n* is the center of motion and *mn* is the potential lever arm of the weight in position *d*. His use of the potential lever arm is also illustrated in

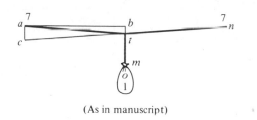

(As in manuscript)

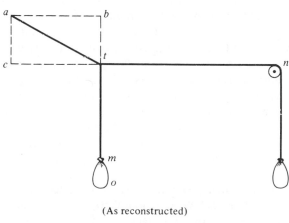

(As reconstructed)

FIGURE 5

a passage that can be reconstructed from MS *E*, folio 65r, as follows (Figure 5). A bar *at* is pivoted at *a*; a weight *o* is suspended from *t* at *m* and a second weight acts on *t* in a direction *tn* perpendicular to that of the first weight. The weights at *m* and *n* necessary to keep the bar in equilibrium are to be determined. In this determination Leonardo took *ab* and *ac* as the potential lever arms (and so labeled them), so that the weights *m* and *n* are inversely proportional to the potential lever arms *ab* and *ac*. The same kind of problem is illustrated in a passage in *Codex Atlanticus*, folio 268v-b, which can be summarized by reference to Figure 6. Cord *ab* supports a weight *n*, which is

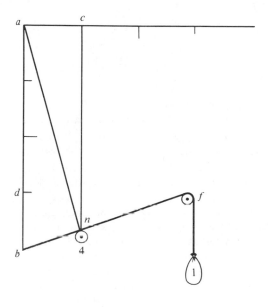

FIGURE 6

pulled to the position indicated by a tangential force along *nf* that is given a value of 1 and there keeps *an* in equilibrium. The passage indicates that weight 1, acting through a distance of four units (the potential lever arm *an*), keeps in equilibrium a weight *n* of 4, acting through a distance of one unit (the potential counterlever *ac*). A similar use of "potential lever arm" is found in problems like that illustrated in Figure 7, taken from MS *M*, folio 40r. Here the potential lever arm is *an*, the perpendicular drawn from the line of force *fp* to the center of motion *a*. Hence the weights suspended from *p* and *m* are related inversely as the distances *an* and *am*. These and similar problems reveal Leonardo's acute awareness of the proper factors of horizontal distance and force determining the static moment about a point.

The concept of potential lever arm also played a crucial role in Leonardo's effort to analyze the tension

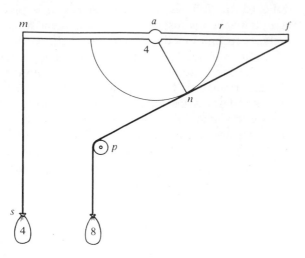

FIGURE 7

in strings. Before examining that role, it must be noted that Leonardo often used an incorrect rule based on tangents rather than sines, a rule similar to that which he mistakenly applied to the problem of the inclined plane. An example of the incorrect procedure appears in MS *E*, folio 66v (see Figure 8):

> The heavy body suspended in the angle of the cord divides the weight to these cords in the ratio of the angles included between the said cords and the central [that is, vertical] line of the weight. Proof. Let the angle of the said cord be *bac*, in which is suspended heavy body *g* by cord *ag*. Then let this angle be cut in the position of equality [that is, in the horizontal direction] by line *fb*. Then draw the perpendicular *da* to angle *a*

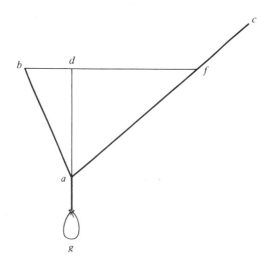

FIGURE 8

and it will be in the direct continuation of cord *ag*, and the ratio which space *df* has to space *db*, the weight [that is, tension] in cord *ba* will have to the weight [that is, tension] in cord *fa*.

Thus, with *da* the common altitude and *df* and *db* used as the measures of the angles at *a*, Leonardo is actually measuring the tensions by the inverse ratio of the tangents. This same incorrect procedure appears many times in the notebooks (for instance, MS *E*, fols. 67v, 68r, 68v, 69r, 69v, 71r; *Codex Arundel*, fol. 117v; MS *G*, fol. 39v).

In addition to this faulty method Leonardo in some instances employed a correct procedure based on the concept of the potential lever arm. In *Codex Arundel*, folio 1v, Leonardo wrote that "the weight 3 is not distributed to the real arms of the balance in the same [although inverse] ratio of these arms but in the [inverse] ratio of the potential arms" (see Figure 9).

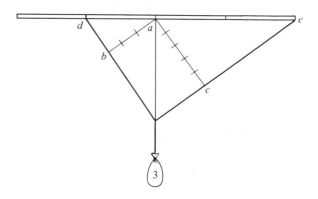

FIGURE 9

The cord is attached to a horizontal beam and a weight is hung from the cord. In the figure *ab* and *ac* are the potential arms. This is equivalent to a theorem that could be expressed in modern terms as "the moments of two concurrent forces around a point on the resultant are mutually equal." Leonardo's theorem, however, does not allow the calculation of the actual tensions in the strings. By locating the center of the moments first on one and then on the other of the concurrent forces, however, Leonardo discovered how to find the tensions in the segments of a string supporting a weight. In *Codex Arundel*, folio 6r (see Figure 10), he stated:

> Here the potential lever *db* is six times the potential counterlever *bc*. Whence it follows that one pound placed in the force line "appendiculo" *dn* is equal in power to six pounds placed in the semireal force line

In these last examples the weight hangs from the center of the cord. But in *Codex Arundel*, folio 6v, the same analysis is applied to a weight suspended at a point other than the middle of the cord (Figure 12).

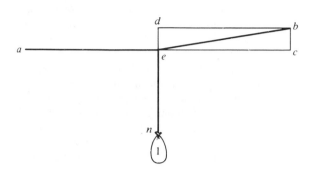

FIGURE 10

ca, and to another six pounds of power conjoined at *b*. Therefore, the cord *aeb* by means of one pound placed in line *dn* has the [total] effect of twelve pounds.

All of which is to say that Leonardo has determined that there are six pounds of tension in each segment of the cord. The general procedure is exhibited in MS *E*, folio 65r (see Figure 11). Under the figure is the caption "*a* is the pole [that is, fulcrum] of the angular balance [with arms] *ad* and *af*, and their force lines ['appendiculi'] are *dn* and *fc*." This applies to the figure on the left and indicates that *af* and *da* are the lever arms on which the tension in *cb* and the weight hanging at *b* act. Leonardo then went on to say: "The greater the angle of the cord which supports weight *n* in the middle of the cord, the smaller becomes the potential arm [that is, *ac* in the figure on the right] and the greater becomes the potential counter-arm [that is, *ba*] supporting the weight." Since Leonardo has drawn the figure so that *ab* is four times *ac* and has marked the weight of *n* as 1, the obvious implication is that the tension in cord *df* will be 4.

Here the weight *n* is supported by two different forces, *mf* and *mb*. Now it is necessary to find the potential levers and counterlevers of these two forces *bm* and *fm*. For the force [at] *b* [with *f* the fulcrum of the potential lever] the [potential] lever arm is *fe* and the [potential] counterlever is *fa*. Thus for the lever arm *fe* the force line ["appendiculo"] is *eb* along which the motor *b* is applied; and for the counterlever *fa* the force line is *an*, which supports weight *n*. Having arranged the balance of the power and resistance of motor and weight, it is necessary to see what ratio lever *fe* has to counterlever *fa;* which lever *fe* is 21/22 of counterlever *fa*. Therefore *b* suffers 22 [pounds of

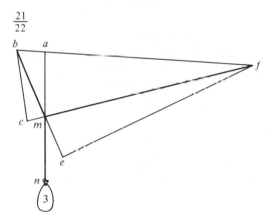

FIGURE 12. (Note: There is some discrepancy between Leonardo's text and the figure as concerns the relative length of the lines.)

tension] when *n* is 21. In the second disposition [with *b* instead of *f* as the fulcrum of a potential lever], *bc* is the [potential] lever arm and *ba* the [potential] counter-lever. For *bc* the force line is *cf* along which the motor *f* is applied and weight *n* is applied along force line *an*. Now it is necessary to see what ratio lever *bc* has to counterlever *ba*, which counterlever is 1/3 of the lever. Therefore, one pound of force in *f* resists three pounds of weight in *ba;* and 21/22 of the three pounds in *n*, when placed at *b*, resist twenty-two placed in *ba*. . . . Thus is completed the rule for calculating the unequal arms of the angular cord.

In a similar problem in *Codex Arundel*, folio 4v, Leonardo determined the tensions of the string segments; in this case the strings are no longer attached or fixed to a beam but are suspended from two pulley wheels from which also hang two equal weights (Figure 13). Here *abc* is apparently an equilateral

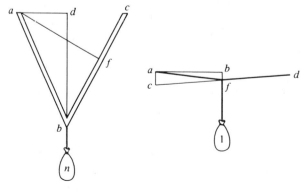

FIGURE 11

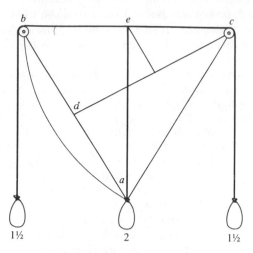

FIGURE 13

triangle, *cd* is the potential arm for the tension in string *ba* acting about fulcrum *c* and *ec* is the potential counterlever through which the weight 2 at *a* acts. If an equilateral triangle was intended, then, by Leonardo's procedure, the tension in each segment of the string ought to be $2/\sqrt{3} = 1.15$, rather than 1.5, as Leonardo miscalculated it. It is clear from all of these examples in which the tension is calculated that Leonardo was using a theorem that he understood as: "The ratio of the tension in a cord segment to the weight supported by the cord is equal to the inverse ratio of the potential lever arms through which the tension and weight act, where the fulcrum of the potential bent lever is in the point of support of the other segment of the cord." This is equivalent to a theorem in the composition of moments: "If one considers two concurrent forces and their resultant, the moment of the resultant about a point taken on one of the two concurrent forces is equal to the moment of the other concurrent force about the same point." The discovery and use of this basic concept in analyzing string tensions was Leonardo's most original development in statics beyond the medieval science of weights that he had inherited. Unfortunately, like most of Leonardo's investigations, it exerted no influence on those of his successors.

Another area of statics in which the medieval science of weights may have influenced Leonardo was that in which a determination is made of the partial forces in the supports of a beam where the beam itself supports a weight. Proposition R3.06 in the *Liber de ratione ponderis* states: "A weight not suspended in the middle [of a beam] makes the shorter part heavier according to the ratio of the longer part to the

shorter part."[12] The proof indicates that the partial forces in the supports are inversely related to the distances from the principal weight to the supports. In *Codex Arundel*, folio 8v (see Figure 14), Leonardo arrived at a similar conclusion:

> The beam which is suspended from its extremities by two cords of equal height divides its weight equally in each cord. If the beam is suspended by its extremities at an equal height, and in its midpoint a weight is hung, then the gravity of such a weight is equally distributed to the supports of the beam. But the weight which is moved from the middle of the beam toward one of its extremities becomes lighter at the extremity away from which it was moved, or heavier at the other extremity, by a weight which has the same ratio to the total weight as the motion completed by the weight [that is, its distance moved from the center] has to the whole beam.

Leonardo also absorbed the concept, so prevalent in the medieval science of weights (particularly in the *De canonio*, in Thābit ibn Qurra's *Liber karastonis*, and in part II of the *Liber de ratione ponderis*), that a

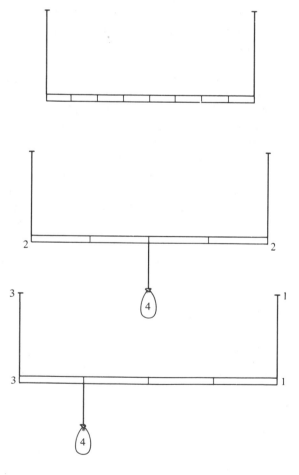

FIGURE 14

segment of a solid beam may be replaced by a weight hung from the midpoint of a weightless arm of the same length and position. For example, see Leonardo's exposition in MS *A*, folio 5r (see Figure 15):

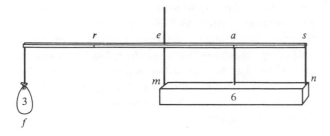

FIGURE 15

If a balance has a weight which is similar [that is, equal] in length to one of its arms, the weight being *mn* of six pounds, how many pounds are to be placed in *f* to resist it [that is, which will be in equilibrium with it]? I say that three pounds will suffice, for if weight *mn* is as long as one of its arms, you could judge that it may be replaced in the middle of the balance arm at point *a;* therefore, if six pounds are in *a*, another six pounds placed at *r* would produce resistance to them [that is, be in equilibrium with them], and, if you proceed as before in point *r* [but now] in the extremity of the balance, three pounds will produce the [necessary] resistance to them.

This replacement doctrine was the key step in solving the problem of the Roman balance in all of the above-noted tracts.[13]

The medieval science of weights was not the only influence upon Leonardo's statics, however, since it may be documented that he also, perhaps at a later time, read book I of Archimedes' *On the Equilibrium of Planes*. As a result he seems to have begun a work on centers of gravity in about 1508, as may be seen in a series of passages in *Codex Arundel*. Since these passages have already been translated and analyzed in rather complete detail elsewhere,[14] only their content and objectives will be given here. Preliminary to Leonardo's propositions on centers of gravity are a number of passages distinguishing three centers of a figure that has weight (see *Codex Arundel*, fol. 72v): "The first is the center of its natural gravity, the second [the center] of its accidental gravity, and the third is [the center] of the magnitude of this body." On folio 123v of this manuscript the centers are defined:

The center of the magnitude of bodies is placed in the middle with respect to the length, breadth and thickness of these bodies. The center of the accidental gravity of these bodies is placed in the middle with respect to

the parts which resist one another by standing in equilibrium. The center of natural gravity is that which divides a body into two parts equal in weight and quantity.

It is clear from many other passages that the center of natural gravity is the symmetrical center with respect to weight. Hence, the center of natural gravity of a beam lies in its center, and that center would not be disturbed by hanging equal weights on its extremities. If unequal weights are applied, however, there is a shift of the center of gravity, which is now called the center of accidental gravity, the weights having assumed accidental gravities by their positions on the unequal arms. The doctrine of the three centers can be traced to Scholastic writings of Nicole Oresme, Albert of Saxony, Marsilius of Inghen (and, no doubt, others).[15] In all of these preliminary considerations Leonardo assumed that a body or a system of bodies is in equilibrium when supported from its center of gravity (be it natural or accidental). It should also be observed that Leonardo assumed the law of the lever as being proved before setting out to prove his Archimedean-like propositions.

The first Archimedean passage to note is in *Codex Arundel*, folio 16v, where Leonardo includes a series of statements on equilibrium that is drawn in significant part from the postulates and early propositions of book I of *On the Equilibrium of Planes*. His terminology suggests that when Leonardo wrote this passage, he was using the translation of Jacobus Cremonensis (*ca.* 1450).[16]

More important than this passage are the propositions and proofs on centers of gravity, framed under the influence of Archimedes' work, which Leonardo specifically cites in a number of instances. The order for these propositions that Leonardo's own numeration seems to suggest is the following:

1. *Codex Arundel*, folio 16v, "Every triangle has the center of its gravity in the intersection of the lines which start from the angles and terminate in the centers of the sides opposite them." This is proposition 14 of book I of *On the Equilibrium of Planes*, and Leonardo included in his "proof" an additional proof of sorts for Archimedes' proposition 13 (since that proposition is fundamental for the proof of proposition 14), although the proof for proposition 13 ignores Archimedes' superb geometrical demonstration. Depending, as it does, on balance considerations, Leonardo's proof is more like Archimedes' second proof of proposition 13. Leonardo's proof of proposition 14 is for an equilateral triangle, but at its end he notes that it applies as well to scalene triangles.

2. *Codex Arundel*, folio 16r: "The center of gravity of any two equal triangles lies in the middle of the

line beginning at the center of one triangle and terminating in the center of gravity of the other triangle." This is equivalent to proposition 4 of *On the Equilibrium of Planes*, but Leonardo's proof differs from Archimedes' in that it merely shows that the center of gravity is in the middle of the line because the weights would be in equilibrium about that point. Archimedes' work is here cited (under the inaccurate title of *De ponderibus*, since the Pseudo-Archimedean work of that title was concerned with hydrostatics rather than statics).

3. *Codex Arundel*, folio 16r: "If two unequal triangles are in equilibrium at unequal distances, the greater will be placed at the lesser distance and the lesser at the greater distance." This is similar to proposition 3 of Archimedes' work. Leonardo, however, simply employed the law of the lever in his proof, which Archimedes did not do, since he did not offer a proof of the law until propositions 6 and 7.

4. *Codex Arundel*, folio 17v: "The center of gravity of every square of parallel sides and equal angles is equally distant from its angles." This is a special case of proposition 10 of *On the Equilibrium of Planes*; but Leonardo's proof, based once more on a balancing procedure, is not directly related to either of the proofs provided by Archimedes.

5. *Codex Arundel*, folio 17v: "The center of gravity of every corbel-like figure [that is, isosceles trapezium] lies in the line which divides it into two equal parts when two of its sides are parallel." This is similar to Archimedes' proposition 15, which treated more generally of any trapezium. Leonardo made a numerical determination of where the center of gravity lies on the bisector. Although his proof is not close to Archimedes', like Archimedes he used the law of the lever in his proof.

6. *Codex Arundel*, folio 17r: "The center of gravity of every equilateral pentagon is in the center of the circle which circumscribes it." This has no equivalent in Archimedes' work. The proof proceeds by dividing the pentagon into triangles that are shown to balance

about the center of the circle. Again Leonardo used the law of the lever in his proof, much as he had in his previous propositions. The proof is immediately followed by the determination of the center of gravity of a pentagon that is not equilateral, in which the same balancing techniques are again employed. Leonardo here cited Archimedes as the authority for the law of the lever, and the designation of Archimedes' proposition as the "fifth" is perhaps an indication that he was using William of Moerbeke's medieval translation of *On the Equilibrium of Planes* instead of that of Jacobus Cremonensis, in which the equivalent proposition is number 7. Although these exhaust those propositions of Leonardo's that are directly related to *On the Equilibrium of Planes*, it should be noted that Leonardo used the same balancing techniques in his effort to determine the center of gravity of a semicircle (see *Codex Arundel*, fols. 215r-v).

It should also be noted that Leonardo went beyond Archimedes' treatise in one major respect—the determination of centers of gravity of solids, a subject taken up in more detail later in the century by Francesco Maurolico and Federico Commandino. Two of the propositions investigated by Leonardo may be presented here to illustrate his procedures. Both propositions concern the center of gravity of a pyramid and appear to be discoveries of Leonardo's. The first is that the center of gravity of a pyramid (actually, a regular tetrahedron) is, at the intersection of the axes, a distance on each axis of 1/4 of its length, starting from the center of one of the faces. (By "axis" Leonardo understood a line drawn from a vertex to the center of the opposite face.) In one place (*Codex Arundel*, fol. 218v) he wrote of the intersection of the pyramidal axes as follows: "The inferior [interior?] axes of pyramids which arise from [a point lying at] 1/3 of the axis of their bases [that is, faces] will intersect in [a point lying at] 1/4 of their length [starting] at the base."

Despite the confusion of singulars and plurals as well as of the expression "inferior axes," the prop-

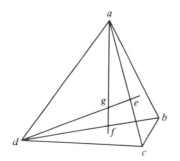 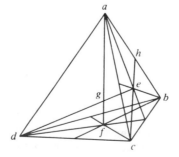 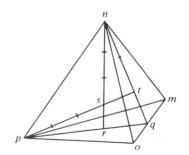

FIGURE 16

osition is clear enough, particularly since Leonardo provided both the drawing shown in Figure 16 and its explanation and, in addition, the intersection of the pyramidal axes is definitely specified as the center of gravity in another passage (fol. 193v): "The center of gravity of the [pyramidal] body of four triangular bases [that is, faces] is located at the intersection of its axes and it will be in the 1/4 part of their length." The proof of this is actually given on the page of the original quotation about the intersection of the axes (fol. 218v), but only as a proof following a more general statement about pyramids and cones:

> The center of gravity of any pyramid—round, triangular, square, or [whose base is] of any number of sides—is in the fourth part of its axis near the base. Let the pyramid be *abcd* with base *bcd* and apex *a*. Find the center of the base *bcd*, which you let be *f*, then find the center of face *abc*, which will be *e*, as was proved by the first [proposition]. Now draw line *af*, in which the center of gravity of the pyramid lies because *f* is the center of base *bcd* and the apex *a* is perpendicularly above *f* and the angles *b*, *c* and *d* are equally distant from *f* and [thus] weigh equally so that the center of gravity lies in line *af*. Now draw a line from angle *d* to the center *e* of face *abc*, cutting *af* in point *g*. I say for the aforesaid reason that the center of gravity is in line *de*. So, since the center is in each [line] and there can be only one center, it necessarily lies in the intersection of these lines, namely in point *g*, because the angles *a*, *b*, *c* and *d* are equally distant from this *g*.

As noted above, the proof is given only for a regular tetrahedron, none being given for the cone or for other pyramids designated in the general enunciation. It represents a rather intuitive mechanical approach, for Leonardo abruptly stated that because the angles *b*, *c*, and *d* weigh equally about *f*, the center of gravity of the base triangle, and *a* is perpendicularly above *f*, the center of gravity of the whole pyramid must lie in line *af*. This is reminiscent of Hero's demonstration of the equilibrium of a triangle supported at its center with equal weights at the angles. This kind of reasoning, then, seems to be extended to the whole pyramid by Leonardo at the end of the proof in which he declared that each of the four angles is equidistant from *g* and, presumably, equal weights at the angles would therefore be in equilibrium if the pyramid were supported in *g*. It is worth noting that a generation later Maurolico gave a very neat demonstration of just such a determination of the center of gravity of a tetrahedron by the hanging of equal weights at the angles.[17] Finally, one additional theorem (without proof), concerning the center of gravity of a tetrahedron, appears to have been Leonardo's own discovery (*Codex Arundel*, fol. 123v):

> The pyramid with triangular base has the center of its natural gravity in the [line] segment which extends from the middle of the base [that is, the midpoint of one edge] to the middle of the side [that is, edge] opposite the base; and it [the center of gravity] is located on the segment equally distant [from the termini] of the [said] line joining the base with the aforesaid side.

Despite Leonardo's unusual and imprecise language (an attempt has been made to rectify it by bracketed additions), it is clear that he has here expressed a neat theorem to the effect that the center of gravity of the tetrahedron lies at the intersection of the segments joining the midpoint of each edge with the midpoint of the opposite edge and that each of these segments is bisected by the center of gravity. Again, it is possible that Leonardo arrived at this proposition by considering four equal weights hung at the angles. At any rate the balance procedure, whose refinements he learned from Archimedes, no doubt played some part in his discovery, however it was made.

Leonardo gave considerable attention to one other area of statics, pulley problems. Since this work perhaps belongs more to his study of machines, except for a brief discussion in the section on dynamics, the reader is referred to Marcolongo's brief but excellent account.[18]

Turning to Leonardo's knowledge of hydrostatics, it should first be noted that certain fragments from William of Moerbeke's translation of Archimedes' *On Floating Bodies* appear in the *Codex Atlanticus*, folios 153v-e, 153r-b, and 153r-c.[19] These fragments (which occupy a single sheet bound into the codex) are not in Leonardo's customary mirror script but appear in normal writing, from left to right. Although sometimes considered by earlier authors to have been written by Leonardo, they are now generally believed to be by some other hand.[20] Whether the sheet was once the property of Leonardo or whether it was added to Leonardo's material after his death cannot be determined with certainty—at any rate, the fragments can be identified as being from proposition 10 of book II of the Archimedean work. Whatever Leonardo's relationship to these fragments, his notebooks reveal that he had only a sketchy and indirect knowledge of Archimedean hydrostatics, which he seems to have drawn from the medieval tradition of *De ponderibus Archimenidis*. Numerous passages in the notebooks reveal a general knowledge of density and specific weight (for instance, MS *C*, fol. 26v, MS *F*, fol. 70r; MS *E*, fol. 74v). Similarly, Leonardo certainly knew that bodies weigh less in water than in air (see MS *F*, fol. 69r), and in one passage (*Codex Atlanticus*, fol. 284v) he proposed to measure the relative resistance of water as compared with air by plunging the weight on one arm of a balance held in aerial equilibrium into water and then determining how much extra weight must be added to the weight in the water to maintain the balance in equilibrium. See also MS *A*, folio 30v: "The weight in air exhibits the truth of its weight, the weight in water will appear to be less weight by the amount the water is heavier than the air."

So far as is known, however, the principle of Archimedes as embraced by proposition 7 of book I of the genuine *On Floating Bodies* was not precisely stated by Leonardo. Even if he did know the principle, as some have suggested, he probably would have learned it from proposition 1 of the medieval *De ponderibus Archimenidis*. As a matter of fact, Leonardo many times repeated the first postulate of the medieval work, that bodies or elements do not have weight amid their own kind—or, as Leonardo put it (*Codex Atlanticus*, fol. 365r-a; *Codex Arundel*, fol. 189r), "No part of an element weighs in its element" (cf. *Codex Arundel*, fol. 160r). Still, he could have gotten the postulate from Blasius of Parma's *De ponderibus*, a work that Leonardo knew and criticized (see MS *Ashburnham* 2038, fol. 2v). It is possible that since Leonardo knew the basic principle of floating bodies—that a floating body displaces its weight of liquid (see *Codex Forster* II₂, fol. 65v)—he may have gotten it directly from proposition 5 of book I of *On Floating Bodies*. But even this principle appeared in one manuscript of the medieval *De ponderibus Archimenidis* and was incorporated into John of Murs' version of that work, which appeared as part of his widely read *Quadripartitum numerorum* of 1343.[21] So, then, all of the meager reflections of Archimedean hydrostatics found in Leonardo's notebooks could easily have been drawn from medieval sources, and (with the possible exception of the disputed fragments noted above) nothing from the brilliant treatments in book II of the genuine *On Floating Bodies* is to be found in the great artist's notebooks. It is worth remarking, however, that although Leonardo showed little knowledge of Archimedean hydrostatics he had considerable success in the practical hydrostatic questions that arose from his study of pumps and other hydrostatic devices.[22]

The problems Leonardo considered concerning the hydrostatic equilibrium of liquids in communicating vessels were of two kinds: those in which the liquid is under the influence of gravity alone and those in which the liquid is under the external pressure of a piston in one of the communicating vessels. In connection with problems of the first kind, he expressly and correctly stated the law of communicating vessels in *Codex Atlanticus*, folio 219v-a: "The surfaces of all

liquids at rest, which are joined together below, are always of equal height." Leonardo further noted in various ways that a quantity of water will never lift another quantity of water, even if the second quantity is in a narrower vessel, to a level that is higher than its own, whatever the ratio between the surfaces of the two communicating vessels (*Codex Atlanticus*, fol. 165v)—although he never gave, as far as can be seen, the correct explanation: the equality of the air pressure on both surfaces of the water in the communicating vessels. In some but not all passages (see *Codex Leicester*, fol. 25r; *Codex Atlanticus*, fol. 321v-a) Leonardo did free himself from the misapplication to hydrostatic equilibrium of the principle of the equilibrium of a balance of equal arms bearing equal weights (*Codex Atlanticus*, fol. 206r-a; *Codex Arundel*, fol. 264r). His own explanations are not happy ones, however. He also correctly analyzed the varying levels that would result if, to a liquid in a U-tube, were added a specifically lighter liquid which does not mix with the initial liquid (see Figure 17). In MS *E*, folio

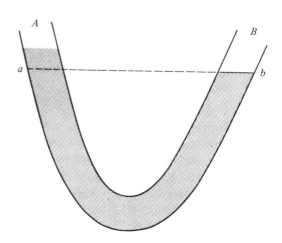

FIGURE 17

74v, he indicated that if the specific weight of the initial liquid were double that of the liquid added, the free surface of the heavier liquid in limb *B* would be at a level halfway between the level of the free surface of the lighter liquid and the surface of contact of the two liquids (the last two surfaces being in limb *A*).

In problems of the second kind, in which the force of a piston is applied to the surface of the liquid in one of the communicating vessels (Figure 18), despite some passages in which he gave an incorrect or only partially true account (see MS *A*, fol. 45r; *Codex Atlanticus*, fol. 384v-a), Leonardo did compose an entirely correct and generally expressed applicable statement or rule (*Codex Leicester*, fol. 11r). Assuming the tube on the right to be vertical and cylindrical, Leonardo observed that the ratio between the pressing weight of the piston and the weight of water in the tube on the right, above the upper level of the water in the vessel on the left, is equal to the ratio between the area under pressure from the piston and the area

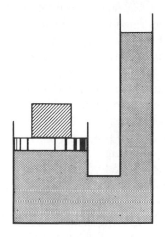

FIGURE 18

of the tube on the right (see *Codex Atlanticus*, fols. 20r, 206r-a, 306v-c; *Codex Leicester*, fol. 26r). And indeed, in a long explanation accompanying the rule in *Codex Leicester*, folio 11r, Leonardo approached, although still in a confused manner, the concept of pressure itself (a concept that appears in no other of his hydrostatic passages, so far as is known) and that of its uniform transmission through a liquid. Leonardo did not, however, generalize his observations to produce Pascal's law, that any additional pressure applied to a confined liquid at its boundary will be transmitted equally to every point in the liquid. Incidentally, the above-noted passage in *Codex Leicester*, folio 11r, also seems to imply a significant consequence for problems of the first kind: that the pressure in an enclosed liquid increases with its depth below its highest point.

Any discussion of Leonardo's knowledge of hydrostatics should be complemented with a few remarks regarding his observations on fluid motion. From the various quotations judiciously evaluated by Truesdell, one can single out some in which Leonardo appears as the first to express special cases of two basic laws of fluid mechanics. The first is the principle of continuity, which declares that the speed of steady flow varies inversely as the cross-sectional area of the channel. Leonardo expressed this in a number of passages, for example, in MS *A*, folio 57v, where he

stated: "Every movement of water of equal breadth and surface will run that much faster in one place than in another, as [the water] may be less deep in the former place than in the latter" (compare MS *H*, fol. 54(6)v; *Codex Atlanticus*, fols. 80r-b, 81v-a; and *Codex Leicester*, fols. 24r and, particularly, 6v). He clearly recognized the principle as implying steady discharge in *Codex Atlanticus*, folio 287r-b: "If the water is not added to or taken away from the river, it will pass with equal quantities in every degree of its breadth [length?], with diverse speeds and slownesses, through the various straitnesses and breadths of its length."

The second principle of fluid motion enunciated by Leonardo was that of equal circulation. In its modern form, when applied to vortex motion, it holds that the product of speed and length is the same on each circle of flow. Leonardo expressed it, in *Codex Atlanticus*, folio 296v-b, as:

The helical or rather rotary motion of every liquid is so much the swifter as it is nearer to the center of its revolution. This that we set forth is a case worthy of admiration; for the motion of the circular wheel is so much the slower as it is nearer to the center of the rotating thing. But in this case [of water] we have the same motion, through speed and length, in each whole revolution of the water, just the same in the circumference of the greatest circle as in the least. . . .

It could well be that Leonardo's reference to the motion of the circular wheel was suggested by either a statement in Pseudo-Aristotle's *Mechanica* (848A)—that on a rotating radius "the point which is farther from the fixed center is the quicker"—or by the first postulate of the thirteenth-century *Liber de motu* of Gerard of Brussels, which held that "those which are farther from the center or immobile axis are moved more [quickly]. Those which are less far are moved less [quickly]."[23] At any rate, it is worthy of note that Leonardo's statement of the principle of equal circulation is embroidered by an unsound theoretical explanation, but even so, one must agree with Truesdell's conclusion (p. 79): "If Leonardo discovered these two principles from observation, he stands among the founders of western mechanics."

The analysis can now be completed by turning to Leonardo's more general efforts in the dynamics and kinematics of moving bodies, including those that descend under the influence of gravity. In dynamics Leonardo often expressed views that were Aristotelian or Aristotelian as modified by Scholastic writers. His notes contain a virtual flood of definitions of gravity, weight, force, motion, impetus, and percussion:

1. MS *B*, folio 63r: "Gravity, force, material motion and percussion are four accidental powers

with which all the evident works of mortal men have their causes and their deaths."

2. *Codex Arundel*, folio 37r: "Gravity is an invisible power which is created by accidental motion and infused into bodies which are removed from their natural place."

3. *Codex Atlanticus*, folio 246r-a: "The power of every gravity is extended toward the center of the world."

4. *Codex Arundel*, folio 37v: "Gravity, force and percussion are of such nature that each by itself alone can arise from each of the others and also each can give birth to them. And all together, and each by itself, can create motion and arise from it" and "Weight desires [to act in] a single line [that is, toward the center of the world] and force an infinitude [of lines]. Weight is of equal power throughout its life and force always weakens [as it acts]. Weight passes by nature into all its supports and exists throughout the length of these supports and completely through all their parts."

5. *Codex Atlanticus*, folio 253r-c: "Force is a spiritual essence which by accidental violence is conjoined in heavy bodies deprived of their natural desires; in such bodies, it [that is, force], although of short duration, often appears [to be] of marvelous power. Force is a power that is spiritual, incorporeal, impalpable, which force is effected for a short life in bodies which by accidental violence stand outside of their natural repose. 'Spiritual,' I say, because in it there is invisible life; 'incorporeal' and 'impalpable,' because the body in which it arises does not increase in form or in weight."

6. MS *A*, folio 34v: "Force, I say to be a spiritual virtue, an invisible power, which through accidental, external violence is caused by motion and is placed and infused into bodies which are withdrawn and turned from their natural use. . . ."

On the same page as the last Leonardo indicated that force has three "offices" ("ofizi") embracing an "infinitude of examples" of each. These are "drawing" ("tirare"), "pushing" ("spignere"), and "stopping" ("fermare"). Force arises in two ways: by the rapid expansion of a rare body in the presence of a dense one, as in the explosion of a gun, or by the return to their natural dispositions of bodies that have been distorted or bent, as manifested by the action of a bow.

Turning from the passages on "force" to those on "impetus," it is immediately apparent that Leonardo has absorbed the medieval theory that explains the motion of projectiles by the impression of an impetus into the projectile by the projector, a theory outlined in its most mature form by Jean Buridan and repeated by many other authors, including Albert of Saxony, whose works Leonardo had read.[24] Leonardo's dependence on the medieval impetus theory is readily shown by noting a few of his statements concerning it:

1. MS *E*, folio 22r: "Impetus is a virtue ["virtù"] created by motion and transmitted by the motor to the mobile that has as much motion as the impetus has life."

2. *Codex Atlanticus*, folio 161v-a: "Impetus is a power ["potenzia"] of the motor applied to its mobile, which [power] causes the mobile to move after it has separated from its motor."

3. MS *G*, folio 73r: "Impetus is the impression of motion transmitted by the motor to the mobile. Impetus is a power impressed by the motor in the mobile. . . . Every impression tends toward permanence or desires to be permanent."

In the last passage Leonardo's words are particularly reminiscent of Buridan's "inertia-like" impetus. On the other hand, Buridan's quantitative description of impetus as directly proportional to both the quantity of prime matter in and the velocity of the mobile is nowhere evident in Leonardo's notebooks. In some passages Leonardo noted the view held by some of his contemporaries (such as Agostino Nifo) that the air plays a supplementary role in keeping the projectile in motion (see *Codex Atlanticus*, fol. 168v-b): "Impetus is [the] impression of local motion transmitted by the motor to the mobile and maintained by the air or the water as they move in order to prevent a vacuum" (cf. *ibid.*, fol. 219v-a). In *Codex Atlanticus*, folio 108r-a, however, he stressed the role of the air in resisting the motion of the projectile and concluded that the air gives little or no help to the motion. Furthermore, in *Codex Leicester*, folio 29v, he gives a long and detailed refutation of the possible role of the air as motor, as Buridan had before him. And not only is it the air as resistance that weakens the impetus in a projectile; the impetus is also weakened and destroyed by the tendency to natural motion. For example, in MS *E*, folio 29r, Leonardo says: "But the natural motion conjoined with the motion of a motor [that is, arising from the impetus derived from the motor] consumes the impetus of the motor."

Leonardo also applied the impetus theory to many of the same inertial phenomena as did his medieval predecessors—for instance, to the stability of the spinning top (MS *E*, fol. 50v), to pendular and other kinds of oscillating motion (*Codex Arundel*, fol. 2r), to impact and rebound (*Codex Leicester*, fols. 8r, 29r), and to the common medieval speculation regarding a ball falling through a hole in the earth to the center and rising on the other side before falling back and oscillating about the center of the earth (*Codex Atlanticus*, fol. 153v-b). In a sense, all of these last are embraced by the general statement in MS

E, folio 40v: "The impetus created in whatever line has the power of finishing in any other line."

In the overwhelming majority of passages, Leonardo applied the impetus theory to violent motion of projection. In some places, however, he also applied it to cases of natural motion, as did his medieval predecessors when they explained the acceleration of falling bodies through the continuous impression of impetus by the undiminished natural weight of the body. For example, in *Codex Atlanticus*, folio 176r-a, Leonardo wrote: "Impetus arises from weight just as it arises from force." And in the same manuscript (fol. 202v-b) he noted the continuous acquisition of impetus "up to the center [of the world]." Leonardo was convinced of the acceleration of falling bodies (although his kinematic description of that fall was confused); hence, he no doubt believed that the principal cause of such acceleration was the continual acquisition of impetus.

One last aspect of Leonardo's impetus doctrine remains to be discussed—his concept of compound impetus, defined in MS *E*, folio 35r, as that which occurs when the motion "partakes of the impetus of the motor and the impetus of the mobile." The example he gave is that of a spinning body moved by an external force along a straight line. When the impetus of the primary force dominates, the body moves along a simple straight line. As that impetus dies, the rotary motion of the spinning body acts with it to produce a

composite-curved motion. Finally, all of the impetus of the original motion is dissipated and a simple circular motion remains that arises only from the spinning body. A series of passages (*Codex Arundel*, fols. 143r–144v) are further concerned with the relationship of transversal and natural motions, which, if the passages and diagrams have been understood correctly, concur to produce resultant composite motions. It appears later in the same manuscript (fol. 147v) that Leonardo thought that the first part of a projectile path was straight until the primary impetus diminished enough for the natural motion to have an effect:

> The mobile is [first] moved in that direction ["aspetto"] in which the motion of its motor is moved. The straightness of the transversal motion in the mobile lasts so long as the internal power given it by the motor lasts. Straightness is wanting to the transversal motion because [that is, when] the power which the mobile acquired from its motor diminishes.

A beautiful instance of compound motion upon which Leonardo reported more than once is that of an arrow or stone shot into the air from a rotating earth, which arrow or stone would fall to the ground with rectilinear motion with respect to the rotating earth because it receives a circular impetus from the earth. But with respect to a stationary frame, the descent is said to be spiral, that is, compounded of

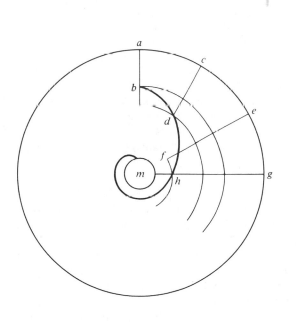

(As in manuscript)

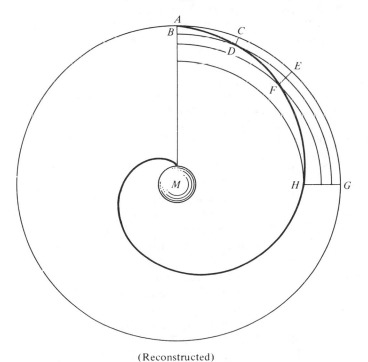

(Reconstructed)

FIGURE 19

rectilinear and circular motions. The longer of the passages in which Leonardo described this kind of compound motion is worth quoting (MS *G*, fol. 55r; see Figure 19):

> On the heavy body descending in air, with the elements rotating in a complete rotation in twenty-four hours. The mobile descending from the uppermost part of the sphere of fire will produce a straight motion down to the earth even if the elements are in a continuous motion of rotation about the center of the world. Proof: let *b* be the heavy body which descends through the elements from [point] *a* to the center of the world, *m*. I say that such a heavy body, even if it makes a curved descent in the manner of a spiral line, will never deviate in its rectilinear descent along which it continually proceeds from the place whence it began to the center of the world, because when it departs from point *a* and descends to *b*, in the time in which it has descended to *b*, it has been carried on to [point] *d*, the position of *a* having rotated to *c*, and so the mobile finds itself in the straight line extending from *c* to the center of the world, *m*. If the mobile descends from *d* to *f*, the beginning of motion, *c*, is, in the same time, moved from *c* to *f* [!*e*]. And if *f* descends to *h*, *e* is rotated to *g*; and so in twenty-four hours the mobile descends to the earth [directly] under the place whence it first began. And such a motion is a compounded one.
>
> [In margin:] If the mobile descends from the uppermost part of the elements to the lowest point in twenty-four hours, its motion is compounded of straight and curved [motions]. I say "straight" because it will never deviate from the shortest line extending from the place whence it began to the center of the elements, and it will stop at the lowest extremity of such a rectitude, which stands, as if to the zenith, under the place from which the mobile began [to descend]. And such a motion is inherently curved along with the parts of the line, and consequently in the end is curved along with the whole line. Thus it happened that the stone thrown from the tower does not hit the side of the tower before hitting the ground.

This is not unlike a passage found in Nicole Oresme's *Livre du ciel et du monde*.[25]

In view of the Aristotelian and Scholastic doctrines already noted, it is not surprising to find that Leonardo again and again adopted some form of the Peripatetic law of motion relating velocity directly to force and inversely to resistance. For example, MS *F*, folios 51r-v, lists a series of Aristotelian rules. It begins "1° if one power moves a body through a certain space in a certain time, the same power will move half the body twice the space in the same time. . . ." (compare MS *F*, fol. 26r). This law, when applied to machines like the pulley and the lever, became a kind of primitive conservation-of-work principle, as it had been in antiquity and the Middle Ages. Its sense was

that "there is in effect a definite limit to the results of a given effort, and this effort is not alone a question of the magnitude of the force but also of the distance, in any given time, through which it acts. If the one be increased, it can only be at the expense of the other."[26] In regard to the lever, Leonardo wrote (MS *A*, fol. 45r): "The ratio which the length of the lever has to the counterlever you will find to be the same as that in the quality of their weights and similarly in the slowness of movement and in the quality of the paths traversed by their extremities, when they have arrived at the permanent height of their pole." He stated again (*E*, fol. 58v):

> By the amount that accidental weight is added to the motor placed at the extremity of the lever so does the mobile placed at the extremity of the counterlever exceed its natural weight. And the movement of the motor is greater than that of the mobile by as much as the accidental weight of the motor exceeds its natural weight.

Leonardo also applied the principle to more complex machines (MS *A*, fol. 33v): "The more a force is extended from wheel to wheel, from lever to lever, or from screw to screw, the greater is its power and its slowness." Concerning multiple pulleys, he added (MS *E*, fol. 20v):

> The powers that the cords interposed between the pulleys receive from their motor are in the same ratio as the speeds of their motions. Of the motions made by the cords on their pulleys, the motion of the last cord is in the same ratio to the first as that of the number of cords; that is, if there are five, the first is moved one braccio, while the last is moved 1/5 of a braccio; and if there are six, the last cord will be moved 1/6 of a braccio, and so on to infinity. The ratio which the motion of the motor of the pulleys has to the motion of the weight lifted by the pulleys is the same as that of the weight lifted by such pulleys to the weight of its motor. . . .

It is not difficult to see why Leonardo, so concerned with this view of compensating gain and loss, attacked the speculators on perpetual motion (*Codex Forster* II₂, fol. 92v): "O speculators on continuous motion, how many vain designs of a similar nature have you created. Go and accompany the seekers after gold." One area of dynamics that Leonardo treated is particularly worthy of note, that which he often called "percussion." In this area he went beyond his predecessors and, one might say, virtually created it as a branch of mechanics. For him the subject included not only effects of the impacts of hammers on nails and other surfaces (as in MS *C*, fol. 6v; MS *A*, fol.

53v) but also rectilinear impact of two balls, either both in motion or one in motion and the other at rest (see the various examples illustrated on MS *A*, fol. 8r), and rebound phenomena off a firm surface. In describing impacts in *Codex Arundel*, folio 83v, Leonardo wrote: "There are two kinds ["nature"] of percussion: the one when the object [struck] flees from the mobile that strikes it; the other when the mobile rebounds rectilinearly from the object struck." In one passage (MS *I*, fol. 41v), a problem of impacting balls is posed: "Ball *a* is moved with three degrees of velocity and ball *b* with four degrees of velocity. It is asked what is the difference ["varietà"] in such percussion [of *a*] with *b* when the latter ball would be at rest and when it [*a*] would meet the latter ball [moving] with the said four degrees of velocity."

In some passages Leonardo attempted to distinguish and measure the relative effects of the impetus of an object striking a surface and of the percussion executed by a resisting surface. For example, in *Codex Arundel*, folio 81v, he showed the rebound path as an arc (later called "l'arco del moto refresso") and indicated that the altitude of rebound is acquired only from the simple percussion, while the horizontal distance traversed in rebound is acquired only from the impetus that the mobile had on striking the surface, so that "by the amount that the rebound is higher than it is long, the power of the percussion exceeds the power of the impetus, and by the amount that the rebound's length exceeds its height, the percussion is exceeded by the impetus."

What is perhaps Leonardo's most interesting conclusion about rebound is that the angle of incidence is equal to that of rebound. For example, in *Codex Arundel*, folio 82v, he stated: "The angle made by the reflected motion of heavy bodies becomes equal to the angle made by the incident motion." Again, in MS *A*, folio 19r (Figure 20), he wrote:

> Every blow struck on an object rebounds rectilinearly at an angle equal ["simile"] to that of percussion. This proposition is clearly evident, inasmuch as, if you would strike a wall with a ball, it would rise rectilinearly at an angle equal to that of the percussion. That is, if

the ball *b* is thrown at *c*, it will return rectilinearly through the line *cb* because it is constrained to produce equal angles on the wall *fg*. And if you throw it along line *bd*, it will return rectilinearly along line *de*, and so the line of percussion and the line of rebound will make one angle on wall *fg* situated in the middle between two equal angles, as *d* appears between *m* and *n*. [See also *Codex Atlanticus*, fol. 125r-a.]

The transfer, and in a sense the conservation, of power and impetus in percussion is described in *Codex Leicester*, folio 8r:

> If the percussor will be equal and similar to the percussed, the percussor leaves its power completely in the percussed, which flees with fury from the site of the percussion, leaving its percussor there. But if the percussor—similar but not equal to the percussed—is greater, it will not lose its impetus completely after the percussion but there will remain the amount by which it exceeds the quantity of the percussed. And if the percussor will be less than the percussed, it will rebound rectilinearly through more distance than the percussed by the amount that the percussed exceeds the percussor.

Leonardo is here obviously groping for adequate laws of impact.

The last area to be considered is Leonardo's treatment of the kinematics of moving bodies, especially the kinematics of falling bodies. In *Codex Arundel*, folio 176v, he gave definitions of "slower" and "quicker" that rest ultimately on Aristotle:[27] "That motion is slower which, in the same time, acquires less space. And that is quicker which, in the same time, acquires more space." The description of falling bodies in respect to uniform acceleration is, of course, more complex. It should be said at the outset that Leonardo never succeeded in freeing his descriptions from essential confusions of the relationships of the variables involved. Most of his passages imply that the speed of fall is not only directly proportional to the time of fall, which is correct, but that it is also directly proportional to the distance of fall, which is not. In MS *M*, folio 45r, he declared that "the gravity [that is, heavy body] which descends freely, in every degree of time, acquires a degree of motion, and, in every degree of motion, a degree of speed." If, like Duhem, one interprets "degree of motion," that is, quantity of motion, to be equivalent not to distance but to the medieval impetus, then Leonardo's statement is entirely correct and implies only that speed of fall is proportional to time of fall. One might also interpret the passage in MS *M*, folio 44r, in the same way (see Figure 21):

> Prove the ratio of the time and the motion together with the speed produced in the descent of heavy bodies

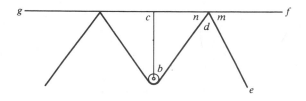

FIGURE 20

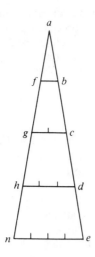

FIGURE 21

by means of the pyramidal figure, for the aforesaid powers ["potenzie"] are all pyramidal since they commence in nothing and go on increasing by degrees in arithmetic proportion. If you cut the pyramid in any degree of its height by a line parallel to the base, you will find that the space which extends from the section to the base has the same ratio as the breadth of the section has to the breadth of the whole base. You see that [just as] *ab* is 1/4 of *ae* so section *fb* is 1/4 of *ne*.

As in mathematical passages, Leonardo here used "pyramidal" where "triangular" is intended.[28] Thus he seems to require the representation of the whole motion by a triangle with point *a* the beginning of the motion and *ne* the final speed, with each of all the parallels representing the speed at some and every instant of time. In other passages Leonardo clearly coordinated instants in time with points and the whole time with a line (see *Codex Arundel*, fols. 176r-v). His triangular representation of quantity of motion is reminiscent of similar representations of uniformly difform motion (that is, uniform acceleration) in the medieval doctrine of configurations developed by Nicole Oresme and Giovanni Casali; Leonardo's use of an isosceles triangle seems to indicate that it was Casali's account rather than Oresme's that influenced him.[29] It should be emphasized, however, that in applying the triangle specifically to the motion of fall rather than to an abstract example of uniform acceleration, Leonardo was one step closer to the fruitful use to which Galileo and his successors put the triangle. Two similar passages illustrate this—the first (MS *M*, fol. 59v) again designates the triangle as a pyramidal figure, while in the second, in *Codex Madrid* I, folio 88v (Figure 22)[30] the triangle is divided into sixteen

equally spaced sections. Leonardo explained the units on the left of the latter figure by saying that "these unities are designated to demonstrate that the excesses of degrees are equal." Lower on the same page he noted that "the thing which descends acquires a degree of speed in every degree of motion and loses a degree of time." By "every degree of motion" he may have meant equal vertical spaces between the parallels into which the motion is divided. Hence, this phrase would be equivalent to saying "in every degree of time." The comment about the loss of time merely emphasizes the whole time spent during the completion of the motion.

All of the foregoing comments suggest a possible, even plausible, interpretation of Leonardo's concept of "degree of motion" in these passages. Still, one should examine other passages in which Leonardo seems also to hold that velocity is directly proportional to distance of fall. Consider, for example, MS *M*, folio 44v: "The heavy body ["gravità"] which descends, in every degree of time, acquires a degree of motion more than in the degree of time preceding, and similarly a degree of speed ["velocità"] more than

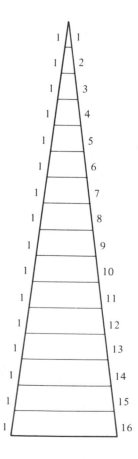

FIGURE 22

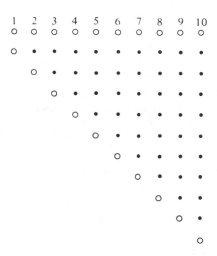

FIGURE 23

in the preceding degree of motion. Therefore, in each doubled quantity of time, the length of descent ["lunghezza del discenso"] is doubled and [also] the speed of motion." The figure accompanying this passage (Figure 23) has the following legend: "It is here shown that whatever the ratio that one quantity of time has to another, so one quantity of motion will have to the other and [similarly] one quantity of speed to the other." There seems little doubt from this passage that Leonardo believed that in equal periods of time, equal increments of space are being acquired. One last passage deserves mention because, although also ambiguous, it reveals that Leonardo believed that the same kinds of relationships hold for motion on an incline as in vertical fall (MS *M*, fol. 42v): "Although the motion be oblique, it observes, in its every degree, the increase of the motion and the speed in arithmetic proportion." The figure (Figure 24) indicates that the motion on the incline is represented by the triangular section *ebc*, while the vertical fall is represented by *abc*. Hence, with this figure Leonardo clearly intended that the velocities at the end of both vertical and oblique descents are

equal (that is, both are represented by *bc*) and also that the velocities midway in these descents are equal (that is, *mn* = *op*). The figure also shows that the times involved in acquiring the velocities differ, since the altitude of △*ebc* is obviously greater than the altitude of △ *abc*.

So much, then, for the most important aspects of Leonardo's theoretical mechanics. His considerable dependence on earlier currents has been noted, as has his quite significant original extension and development of those currents. It cannot be denied, however, that his notebooks, virtually closed as they were to his successors, exerted little or no influence on the development of mechanics.

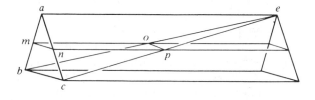

FIGURE 24

NOTES

1. The many passages from Leonardo's notebooks quoted here can be found in the standard eds. of the various MSS. Most of them have also been collected in Uccelli's ed. of *I libri di meccanica*. The English trans. (with only two exceptions) are my own.
2. The full corpus has been published in E. A. Moody and M. Clagett, *The Medieval Science of Weights* (Madison, Wis., 1952; repr., 1960). Variant versions of the texts have been studied and partially published in J. E. Brown, "The 'Scientia de ponderibus' in the Later Middle Ages" (dissertation, Univ. of Wis., 1967).
3. Moody and Clagett, *op. cit.*, pp. 128–131. Incidentally, the definition that precedes the proof is the sure sign that Leonardo translated the postulates and first two enunciations from the *Elementa* rather than from version P (where the enunciations are the same), since the definition was not included in Version P.
4. *Ibid.*, pp. 174–207.
5. *Ibid.*, pp. 130–131.
6. *Ibid.*, pp. 188–191. Leonardo's translation of these same propositions in *Codex Atlanticus*, fols. 154v-a-r-a, is very literal: "La equalità della declinazione conserva la equalità del peso. Se per due vie di diverse obliquità due pesi discendano, e sieno medesimo proporzione, se della d[eclinazione] de' pesi col medesimo ordine presa sarà ancora una medesima virtù dell'una e d[ell'altra in discendendo]." The bracketed material has been added from the Latin text.
7. Marcolongo, *Studi vinciani*, p. 173.
8. Duhem, *Les origines de la statique*, I, 189–190.
9. Moody and Clagett, *op. cit.*, pp. 184–187. Leonardo's more literal translation of Rl.08 in *Codex Atlanticus*, fol. 154v-a, runs: "Se le braccia della libra sono inequali e nel centro del moto faranno un angolo, s'e' termini loro s'accosteranno parte equalmente alla direzione, e' pesi equali in questa disposizione equalmente peseranno."
10. Marcolongo, *op. cit.*, p. 149, discusses one such passage (*Codex Arundel*, fol. 67v); see also pp. 147–148, discussing the figures on MS *Ashburnham* 2038, fol. 3r; and *Codex Arundel*, fol. 32v (in the passage earlier than the one noted above in the text).
11. Moody and Clagett, *op. cit.*, pp. 208–211.
12. *Ibid.*, pp. 210–211.
13. *Ibid.*, pp. 64–65, 102–109, 192–193.
14. Clagett, "Leonardo da Vinci . . .," pp. 119–140.
15. *Ibid.*, pp. 121–126.
16. *Ibid.*, p. 126.
17. Archimedes, *Monumenta omnia mathematica, quae extant . . . ex traditione Francisci Maurolici* (Palermo, 1685), *De*

momentis aequalibus, bk. IV, prop. 16, pp. 169–170. Maurolico completed the *De momentis aequalibus* in 1548.

18. Marcolongo, *op. cit.*, pp. 203–216.

19. See Clagett, "Leonardo da Vinci . . .," pp. 140–141. That account is here revised, taking into account the probability that the fragments were not copied by Leonardo.

20. *Ibid.*, p. 140, n. 65, notes the opinion of Favaro and Schmidt that the fragments are truly in Leonardo's hand. But Carlo Pedretti, whose knowledge of Leonardo's hand is sure and experienced, is convinced they are not. Arredi, *Le origini dell'idrostatica*, pp. 11–12, had already recognized that the notes were not in Leonardo's hand.

21. M. Clagett, *The Science of Mechanics in the Middle Ages* (Madison, Wis., 1959; repr., 1961), pp. 124–125.

22. Here Arredi's account is followed closely.

23. Clagett, *The Science of Mechanics*, p. 187.

24. *Ibid.*, chs. 8–9.

25. *Ibid.*, pp. 601–603.

26. Hart, *The Mechanical Investigations*, pp. 93–94.

27. Clagett, *The Science of Mechanics*, pp. 176–179.

28. Clagett, "Leonardo da Vinci . . .," p. 106, quoting MS *K*, fol. 79v.

29. M. Clagett, *Nicole Oresme and the Medieval Geometry of Qualities* (Madison, Wis., 1968), pp. 66–70.

30. I must thank L. Reti, editor of the forthcoming ed. of the Madrid codices, for providing me with this passage.

MARSHALL CLAGETT

MATHEMATICS

Leonardo's admiration for mathematics was unconditional, and found expression in his writings in such statements as "No certainty exists where none of the mathematical sciences can be applied" (MS *G*, fol. 96v). It is therefore useful to consider the development of his mathematical thought, drawing upon the whole of his manuscripts in order to reconstruct its principal stages; such a study will also serve to illustrate the sources for much of his work.

Leonardo particularly valued the rigorous logic implicit in mathematics, whereby the mathematician could hope to attain truth with the same certitude as might a physicist dealing with experimental data. (Students of the moral and metaphysical sciences, on the other hand, had no such expectation, since they were forced to proceed from unascertainable and infinitely arguable hypotheses.) His predilection did not, however, presuppose a broad mathematical culture or any real talent for calculation. Certainly, his education was that of an artisan rather than a mathematician, consisting of reading, writing, and the practical basics of calculus and geometry, together with the considerable body of practical rules that had been accumulated by generations of craftsmen and artists.

The effects of his early education may be seen in Leonardo's literary style (he preferred aphorisms and definitions to any prolonged organic development of ideas) and in his mathematics, which contains grave oversights not entirely due to haste. An example of the latter is his embarrassment when confronted with square and cube roots. In *Codex Arundel* (fol. 200r) he proposed, as an original discovery, a simple method for finding all roots "both irrational and rational," whereby the "root" is defined as a fraction of which the numerator alone is multiplied by itself one or two times to find the square or cubic figure. Thus the square root of 2 is obtained by multiplying 2/2 by 2/2 to find 4/2, or simply 2; while the cube root of 3 is reached by taking $3/9 \times 3/9 \times 3/9 = 27/9$, or 3. He applied this erroneous method several times in his later work; however absurd they might be, Leonardo seems to have been prouder of his discoveries in mathematics than in any other field.

When he was in his late thirties, Leonardo began to try to fill the gaps in his education and took up the serious study of Latin and geometry, among other subjects. At the same time he began to write one or more treatises. He wished to write for scientists, although scholars of the period were not prepared to admit the knowledge possessed by an artist as science. (An illustration of this occurs in Alberti's definition of the "principles" of geometry, in which he stated that he could not use truly scientific terms because he was addressing himself to painters.) It was only after Leonardo entered the Sforza service in Milan and became associated with philosophers and men of letters on a basis of mutual esteem that he took up his theory of the supremacy of painting. This theory was in part incorporated into the *Treatise on Painting* compiled by Leonardo's disciple Francesco Melzi, who, however, omitted Leonardo's definitions of the geometric "principles" of point, line, and area— definitions that Leonardo had drawn up with great care, since he wished them to be read by mathematicians rather than artists.

As a painter, Leonardo was, of course, concerned with proportion and also with "vividness of the actions" (this is how he translated Ficino's definition of beauty as "actus vivacitas"). In his pursuit of the latter, Leonardo inclined toward physics, seeking motions that could be studied experimentally. Perspective, too, had an important place in the treatise on painting, but Leonardo was more concerned with aerial perspective (chiaroscuro) than with linear. MS *C* (1490) is rich in geometrical drawings, although limited to the depiction of the projection of rays of light; it contains no organic system of theorems.

Aside from those in MS *C*, the pages dedicated to geometry in other early manuscripts are few; there are nine in MS *B* (*ca.* 1489) and nineteen in MS *A* (1492). The prevalent matter in all of these is the division of the circumference of the circle into equal parts, a prerequisite for the construction of polygons and for various other well-known procedures. The notes set down are not connected with each other and represent elementary precepts that were common knowledge to all "engineers." Because of these limitations, it is impossible to accept Caversazzi's thesis concerning MS *B*, folios 27v and 40r, wherein Leonardo explained how to divide a circumference into equal parts by merely "opening the compass"; Caversazzi sees this as an "exquisite geometric discovery," one that may be applied to solve Euclidean problems of the first and second degree. But since at this time Leonardo had not yet begun to study Euclid, it is probable that he was referring to precepts known to all draftsmen.

Seven pages are devoted to geometry in *Codex Forster* III (1493–1495) and, again, these contain only elementary formulas, expressed in language more imaginative than scientific (the volume of a sphere, for example, is described as "the air enclosed within a spherical body"). Only in *Codex Forster* II$_1$, written between 1495 and 1497, are there the first signs of a concentrated interest in geometrical problems, particularly those that were deeply to concern Leonardo in later years—lunes and the equivalence of rectilinear and curvilinear surfaces. An additional seventeen pages of this manuscript are devoted to the theory of proportion.

The two manuscripts that mark the close of Leonardo's first sojourn in Milan—MS *M* and MS *I*—are of far greater importance. The first thirty-six pages of MS *M* contain translations of Euclid ("Petitioni" and "Conceptioni") as well as derivations of propositions 1–42 (with a few omissions) of book I of the *Elements*, together with a group of propositions from the tenth book. Propositions 43–46 of book I appear in the first sixteen folios of MS *I* (which must for that reason be considered as being of a later date than MS *M*), as do propositions 1–4 and 6–10 of book II, selections from book III, and occasional references to book X. These evidences of Leonardo's systematic study of Euclid may be related to his friendship and collaboration with Luca Pacioli.

Leonardo must have read the *Elements* and acquired some deeper knowledge of geometry before undertaking the splendid drawings of solid bodies with which he illustrated the first book of Pacioli's *Divina proportione*. His interest in this work is probably reflected in the pages of *Codex Forster* II$_1$ on proportion; it would also explain his study of the tenth book of the *Elements*, the book least read because of its difficulty and its practical limitation to the construction of regular polygons. Pacioli was thus responsible for arousing Leonardo's enthusiasm for geometry and for introducing him to Euclid's work; indeed, he may

have helped him read Euclid, since the text would have been extremely difficult for a man as relatively unlettered as Leonardo. (It is interesting to note that MS *I* also contains some first principles of Latin, copied from Perotti's grammar.) Pacioli's influence on Leonardo was probably also indirect, through his *Summa arithmetica* and perhaps through his translation of the *Elements*.

That Leonardo had at hand the Latin text of the *Elements* of 1482 or 1491 can be seen through the identity of some of his drawings with those texts as well as by certain verbal correspondences. At the same time, his method was not to transcribe sentences from the text he was studying but to attempt to present geometrical ideas graphically. Each page of his geometrical notes represents an aid to memorizing Euclid's text, rather than a compendium; hence it is not always easy to trace the specific passages studied. For example, Leonardo would often begin with a sketch, a number, or occasionally a word which he must have used initially to impress upon his mind some of the intricacies of Euclid's theses and later to recall the whole content. In MS *M*, folio 29v, three figures appear: a point and a line; the same point and line with an additional transversal line; and two parallel lines joined by the transversal, the original point having disappeared. The correspondence with the Euclidean thesis, together with the coincidence of similar notes on the preceding and following pages to propositions 27, 28, 29, 30, and 32, respectively, prove this to be Euclid's book I, proposition 31.

Notes on Euclid's first books also appear in certain folios of the *Codex Atlanticus*, where they are set out in better order and in a more complete form. On folio 169r-b, for instance, the "Petitioni" and "Conceptioni" are presented symbolically, while on folio 177v-a proposition 1.7 is transformed into a series of thirteen drawings.

Leonardo continued to work with Pacioli after they both left Milan in 1499. In the *Codex Atlanticus* he stated that he would learn "the multiplication of roots" from his friend "master Luca" (fol. 120r-d), and he had in fact transcribed all the rules for operations with fractions from the *Summa arithmetica* (fol. 69, a–b). Pietro da Novellara recorded in 1503 that Leonardo was neglecting painting in favor of geometry; this activity is reflected in MS *K*, *Codex Madrid*, II, and *Codex Forster* I$_1$, as well as in many folios of the *Codex Atlanticus*.

Two-thirds of MS *K*$_1$ (1504) are devoted to Euclid. From folio 15v to folio 48v Leonardo copied, in reverse order, almost all the marginal figures of books V and VI of the *Elements*. He transcribed none of the text, although the drawings are accompanied by unmistakable signs of his contemplation of the theory of proportion. MS K_2 contains notes similar to those in MS *M* and MS *I*; here they refer to the whole of the second book of the *Elements*, to a few propositions of books I, II, and III, and to nine of the first sixteen definitions of book V.

Leonardo's interest in the theory of proportion is further evident in *Codex Madrid*, II, folios 46v–50, in which he summarizes and describes the treatise "De proportionibus et proportionalitatibus" that is part of Pacioli's *Summa arithmetica*. A drawing on folio 78 of the same manuscript, graphically illustrating all the various kinds of proportions and proportionalities, is also taken from Pacioli's book, while Euclid reappears in the last five pages of the manuscript proper. In the latter portion Leonardo transcribed, in an elegant handwriting, the first pages of an Italian version of the *Elements*, the author of which is not known (the list of Leonardo's books cites only "Euclid, in Italian, that is, the first three books"). Folio 85r contains the ingenious illustration of Euclid's so-called algorithm (VII.2, X.2–3) that is repeated in more detail in *Codex Atlanticus*, folio 207r-b.

It is thus clear from manuscript sources that from the time that Leonardo began to collaborate with Pacioli on the *Divina proportione*, he concentrated on books I and II of Euclid—an indispensable base—and on books V and VI, the theory of proportion that had also been treated by Pacioli in the *Summa arithmetica*. The few references to book X deal with the ratios of incommensurate quantities; therefore there can be no doubt that the subject of proportions and proportionalities remained a constant center of Leonardo's interest.

There is no evidence of a similar study of the last books of Euclid, but it must not be forgotten that about two-thirds of Leonardo's writings have been lost. There is, moreover, no lack of practical applications of the propositions of the last books in Leonardo's writings. But *Codex Madrid,* II, is of particular importance because it demonstrates that Leonardo, after conducting a modest study of Euclid from approximately 1496 to 1504, began to conduct ambitious personal research. Having copied out the first pages of the *Elements* as, perhaps, a model, Leonardo wrote on folios 111r and 112r two titles indicative of the plan of his work, "The Science of Equiparation" and "On the Equality of Unequal Areas." For this new science he wrote on folio 107v a group of "Petitioni" and "Conceptioni" based upon Euclid's. Here Leonardo's chief concern lay in the squaring of curvilinear surfaces, which he generally divided into "falcates" (triangles with one, two, or

three curved sides) and "portions" (circular segments formed by an arc and a chord, which could also be the side of a polygon inscribed in a circle). He carried out the transformation of these figures into their rectilinear equivalents by various means, some of which (such as superimposition and motion, or rotation) were mechanical.

The use of mechanical solutions, rarely accepted by Euclid, may perhaps be attributable to Leonardo's engineering background; he would almost seem to have recognized the unorthodoxy of his procedures in applying to himself Giordano's words: "This method is not simply geometrical but is subordinated to, and participates in, both philosophy and geometry, because the proof is obtained by means of motion, although in the end all mathematical sciences are philosophical speculations" (*Codex Madrid*, II, fol. 107r). Leonardo noted, however, that the squaring of curvilinear surfaces could be accomplished by more orthodox geometrical methods, provided the curved sides of the figure form parts of circles proportional among themselves (*Codex Atlanticus*, fol. 139v-a).

It is a short step from squaring falcates to squaring the circle, and Leonardo proposed several solutions to the latter problem. Again, some of them were mechanical and were suggested to him by studying Vitruvius. These consist in, for example, measuring the rectilinear track left by a wheel of which the width is one-quarter of the wheel's diameter (MS *G*, fol. 61r; also MS *E*, fol. 25v, where the width of the wheel that makes "a complete revolution" is mistakenly given as being equal to the radius). The circumference is obtained by winding a thread around the wheel, then withdrawing and measuring it (MS *K*, fol. 80r).

Leonardo was also well acquainted with the method for the "quadratura circuli per lunulas," which he knew from the *De expetendis et fugiendis rebus* of Giorgio Valla. A drawing corresponding to this method appears in MS *K*, folio 61r. (The identity of "Zenophont" or "Zenophonte," a mathematician criticized by Leonardo on the previous page of the same manuscript, is probably resolvable as Antiphon,

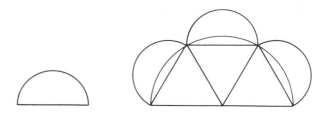

FIGURE 1. The quaᴅratura circuli per lunulas.

whose method of quadrature was also criticized by Valla.)

Leonardo of course knew Archimedes' solution to squaring the circle; Clagett has pointed out that he both praised and criticized it without ever having understood it completely. He accepted Archimedes' first proposition, which establishes the equivalence of a circle and a rectangular triangle of which the shorter sides are equal to the radius and the circumference of the circle, respectively; he remained unsatisfied with the third proposition, which fixes the approximate ratio between the circumference (taken as an element separating two contiguous classes of polygons) and the diameter as 22:7. Leonardo tried to take this approximation beyond the ninety-six-sided polygon; it is in this attempt at extension ad infinitum that the value of his effort lies.

Valla provided Leonardo with a starting point when, in describing the procedure of squaring "by lunes," he recommended "trapezium dissolvatur in triangula." Leonardo copied Valla's drawing, dividing the trapezium inscribed in a semicircle into three triangles; he extended the concept in MS K, folio 80r, in which he split the circle into sixteen triangles, rectified the circumference, then fitted the triangles together like gear teeth, eight into eight, to attain a rectangle equivalent to the circle. He took a further step in *Codex Madrid*, II, folio 105v, when departing from Euclid II.2 (circles are to each other as the squares of their diameters), he took two circles, having diameters of 1 and 14, respectively, and divided the larger into 196 sectors, each equivalent to the whole of the smaller circle.

In *Codex Atlanticus*, folio 118v-a, Leonardo dealt with circles of the ratio 1:1,000 and found that when the larger was split into 1,000 sectors, the "portion" (the difference between the sector and the triangle) was an "imperceptible quantity similar to the mathematical point." By logical extension, if each sector were "a millionth of its circle, it would be a straight portion" or "almost plane, and thus we would have carried out a squaring nearer the truth than Archimedes'" (*Codex Madrid*, II, fol. 105v). In *Codex Arundel*, folio 137v, Leonardo squared the two diameters, writing "one by one is one" and "one million by one million is one million"; his disappointment in seeing that the squares did not increase suggested the variant "four million by four million is sixteen million" (that he corrected his error in *Codex Atlanticus*, fol. 118r-a, writing "a million millions," reveals a poor grasp of calculation).

Leonardo was clearly proud of his discovery of the quadrature, and in *Codex Madrid*, II, folio 112r he recorded the exact moment that it came to him—on the night of St. Andrew's day (30 November), 1504, as hour, light, and page drew to a close. In actual fact, however, Leonardo's discovery amounted only to affirming the equivalence of a given circle to an infinitesimal part of another without calculating any measure; to have made the necessary calculations, he would have had to use Archimedes' formula 22:7, which he rejected. Leonardo characterized Archimedes' method of squaring as "ben detta e male data" (*Codex Atlanticus*, fol. 85r-a), that is, "well said and badly given." It would seem necessary to describe his own solution simply as "detta," not "data."

The presumed discovery on St. Andrew's night did, however, encourage Leonardo to pursue his geometrical studies in the hope of making other new breakthroughs. MS K_3, MS F, and a large number of pages in the *Codex Atlanticus* demonstrate his continuous and intense work in transforming sectors, "falcates," and "portions" into rectilinear figures. Taking as given that curved lines must have equal or proportional radii, Leonardo practiced constructing a series of squares doubled in succession, in which he inscribed circles proportioned in the same way; to obtain quadruple circles, he doubled the radii. To obtain submultiple circles, he divided a square constructed on the diameter of the circle into the required number of rectangles, transforming one into a square and inscribing the submultiple circle therein. In order to double the circle, however, instead of using the diagonal of the square constructed on the diameter, he turned to arithmetic calculus to increase proportionally the measure of the radius, adopting a ratio of 1:3/2, which is somewhat greater than the true one of 1:$\sqrt{2}$. To obtain a series of circles doubling one another, he divided the greatest radius into equal parts, forgetting that arithmetic progression is not the same as geometric (*Codex Madrid*, II, fols. 117v, 132).

Alternating with the many pages in the *Codex Atlanticus* devoted to the solution of specific problems are others giving the fundamental rules of Leonardo's new science of comparison. Within the same sphere falls a group of pages in *Codex Madrid*, II, which are concerned with transforming rectilinear figures into other equivalent figures or solids into other solids. These sections of the two collections, presumably together with pages that are now lost, are preparatory to the short treatise on stereometry contained in *Codex Forster* I_1 (1505) and entitled "Book on Transformation, That Is, of One Body Into Another Without Decrease or Increase of Substance." In his study of this treatise, Marcolongo judges it to be suitable "for draftsmen more skilled in handling rule, square, and compass than in making numerical calculations"—Leonardo's viewpoint was often that of the engineer.

One of the problems to which Leonardo chose to apply his new science was that of how to transform a parallelepiped into a cube, or how to double the volume of a cube and then insert two proportional means between two segments. In the *Summa arithmetica*, Pacioli had solved the problem and had described how to find the cube root of 8 by geometrical methods, although he provided no geometrical demonstrations. Leonardo, in *Codex Atlanticus*, folio 58r, stated that if the edge of a cube is 4, the edge of the same cube doubled will be 5 plus a fraction that is "inexpressible and easier to make than to express." By 1504 Leonardo also possessed Valla's book, which gave the solution of the problem, with numerous demonstrations from the ancients. Leonardo copied various figures from Valla (in *Codex Arundel*, fols. 78r–79v, where the last one is, however, Pacioli's) and transcribed a vernacular translation of the part of Valla's book referring to the demonstrations of Philoponus and Parmenius. (That, having the Latin text at hand, Leonardo felt the need to translate or to have translated the two pages that interested him confirms his difficulty in reading Latin directly— Clagett and Marcolongo have both pointed out many mistakes in the translation of this passage which, if uncorrected, distort the text.)

Leonardo repeatedly expressed his dissatisfaction with the solution reported by Valla. He particularly objected to having to make the rule swing until the compass has fixed two points of intersection; this "negotiation," he stated (*Codex Atlanticus*, fol. 218v-b), seemed to him "dubious and mechanical." Since Valla attributed this procedure to Plato, Leonardo further stated, in MS *F* (1508), folio 59r, that "the proof given by Plato to the inhabitants of Delo is not geometrical." He continued to look for other, more truly "geometrical," means to double the cube or find the cube root.

In folios 50v–59v of MS *F* and in the similar folios 159r-a and b of the *Codex Atlanticus*, Leonardo tried, in opposition to the "ancient system," to resolve the problem by decomposing and rebuilding a cube; he further attempted to apply Pythagoras' theorem by substituting three cubes for three squares constructed on the sides of a right triangle. Since every square is equal to half the square constructed on its diagonal, he attempted to halve each cube with a diagonal cut, on the assumption that the face of a doubled cube could be obtained through manipulating the rectangular face formed by the cut. He arranged nine cubes in the form of a parallelepiped upon which he analyzed the diagonals that he supposed to represent the square

and cube roots, respectively (*Codex Atlanticus*, fols. 159r-b, 303r-b; *Windsor Collection*, fol. 19128). He forgot, however, that the progression of squares and cubes does not correspond to the natural series of numbers. Although he studied the proportions between the areas that "cover" a cube and those of the same cube doubled, he realized that he could not apply "the science of cubes based on surfaces, but based on bodies [volumes]" (*Codex Arundel*, fol. 203r). He was thus aware that his formulation of the problem was inaccurate.

Leonardo finally arrived at a solution. He recorded in *Codex Atlanticus*, folios 218v-b, 231r-b, that in order to "avoid the difficulty of the mechanical system" taught by Plato and other ancients, he had

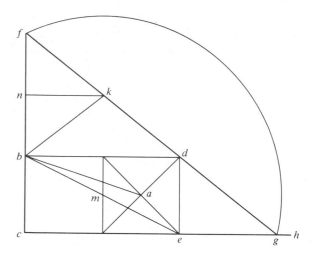

FIGURE 2. $bc : eg = eg : bf = bf : bd$
$eg = fk = kd = kb$
$ab = bf$ (*Codex Atlanticus*, 218v-b).

eliminated the compass and the imprecise movement of the rule in favor of placing two sides of the rectangle in the ratio $b = 2a$ (thereby unknowingly reestablishing the ratio used in the Greek text). Step by step, then, his procedure was to join two faces of a cube to make a rectangle, connect the upper-left angle to the center of the right square, then carry the line obtained to the upper extension of side *a*; from the extreme point thus reached, he drew a line that, touching the upper-right angle of the rectangle, cut the extension of its base. On this line Leonardo was able to determine the measure of the edge of the doubled cube, a measure that is to be found four times in the figure thus constructed. His results are reasonably accurate; with $a = 2$, Leonardo obtained a cube root for 16 as little as 0.02967 in excess of its true value.

Leonardo was unable to demonstrate the truth of his "new invention" save through criticism of the "mechanical test" of the compass, which after "laborious effort" helped the ancients to discover the proportional means—whereas now, Leonardo claimed, "without effort I use it to confirm that my experiment was confirmed by the ancients"—which, he added, "could not be done before our time." What Leonardo had discovered was that the third proportional number, used to determine the second, coincides with a line that can be more accurately constructed inside the rectangle; he thereby simplified the classical procedure without in any way discussing its scientific demonstrations, which he took for granted. He must, however, have checked his results experimentally and judged them with his unerring eye.

Other pages of the *Codex Atlanticus* contain summaries of problems to be solved, as, for example, folio 139r-a, which is entitled "Curvilinear Geometrical Elements." This, together with other titles—"On Transformation," folio 128r-a; "Book on Equation," folio 128r-a; and "Geometrical Play" ("De ludo geometrico"), folios 45v-a, 174v-b, 184v-c, and 259v-a —including the previously mentioned "Science of Equiparation"—might suggest that Leonardo had actually written systematic books and treatises that are now lost. But it is known that he cherished projects that he did not complete; and it is unlikely that he composed treatises using methods and forms different from those set out in, for example, *Codex Forster* I₂. The titles of treatises projected but unwritten do provide some record of the stages of his mathematical work, in addition to which Leonardo has recorded some specific dates for his successes.

Leonardo's discovery on St. Andrew's night has already been mentioned; in the same manuscript, *Codex Madrid*, II, on folio 118r, he further mentioned that a certain invention had been given to him "as a gift on Christmas morning 1504." In *Windsor Collection*, folio 19145, he claimed to have discovered, after prolonged research, a way of squaring the angle of two curved sides on Sunday, 30 April 1509. (Folio 128r-a of the *Codex Atlanticus*, the beginning of the "Book of Equation," is concerned with the squaring of a "portion" of a single curved side and promises a second book devoted to the new procedure.)

Although the last discovery is exactly dated, Leonardo's explanation of it is not very clear. (This is often the case in Leonardo's work, since the manuscripts are marked by incomplete and fragmentary discussions, geometrical figures unaccompanied by any explanation of the construction, and the bare statements of something proved elsewhere.) His accomplishment is, however, apparent—he had learned how to vary a "portion" in infinite figures,

decomposing and rebuilding it in many different ways. The examples drawn on the *Windsor Collection* page cited reappear, with variations, in hundreds of illustrations scattered or collected in the *Codex Atlanticus*. The reader can only be dismayed by their complexity and monotony.

The mathematical pages of the *Codex Atlanticus* (to which all folio numbers hereafter cited refer) provide an interesting insight into the late developments of Leonardo's method. On folio 139r-a, among other places, he confirmed his proposal to vary "to infinity" one or more surfaces while maintaining the same quantity. It is clear that he received from the elaboration of his geometric equations the same pleasure that a mathematician derives from the development of algebraic ones. If, at the beginning of his research on the measure of curvilinear surfaces, his interest would seem to have been that of an engineer, his later work would seem to be marked by a disinterested passion for his subject. Indeed, the title of the last book that he planned— "Geometrical Play," or "De ludo geometrico"—which he began on folio 45v-a and worked on up to the last years of his life, indicates this.

For example, one of Leonardo's basic exercises consists of inscribing a square within a circle, then joining the resultant four "portions" in twos to get

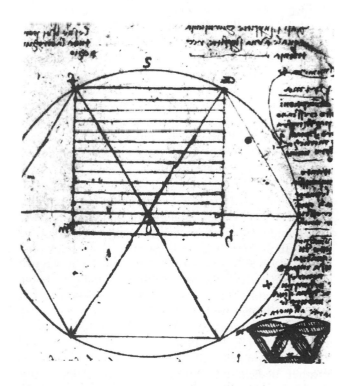

FIGURE 3. The square of proportionality (*Codex Atlanticus*, 111v-b).

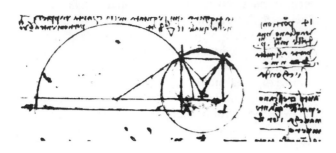

FIGURE 4. (*Codex Atlanticus*, 111v-b).

"bisangoli." The "bisangles" can then be broken up, subdivided, and distributed within the circumference to create full and empty spaces which are to each other as the inscribed square is to the four "portions" of the circumscribed circle. An important development of this is Leonardo's substitution of a hexagon for the square, the hexagon being described as the most perfect division of the circle (fols. 111v-a and b [Figs. 3, 4]). This leaves six "portions" for subsequent operations, and Leonardo recommended their subdivision in multiples of six. (On the splendid folio 110v-a [Fig. 5], he listed and calculated the first fifty multiples of six, but through a curious oversight the product of 34×6 is given as 104, rather than 204; and all the following calculations are thus incorrect.)

To obtain the exact dimensions of submultiple "portions," Leonardo devised the "square of proportionality" (fol. 107v-a), which he constructed on the side of the hexagon inscribed within the circle and then subdivided into the required number of equal rectangles. He next transformed one such rectangle into the equivalent square, the side of which is the radius of the submultiplied circle, the side of the corresponding inscribed hexagon, and the origin or chord of the minor "portions." These were then joined in pairs ("bisangoli"), combined into rosettes or stars, and distributed inside the circumference of the circle in a fretwork of full and empty spaces, of which the area of all full spaces is always equal to that of the six greater "portions" and the area of all the empty spaces to the area of the inscribed hexagon. The result is of undoubted aesthetic value and may be taken as the culmination of the geometrical adventure that began for Leonardo with Pacioli's *Divina proportione*.

Although Leonardo remained faithful throughout his life to the idea of proportion as the fundamental structure of reality, the insufficient and inconstant rigor of his scientific thesis precludes his being considered a mathematician in the true sense of the word. His work had no influence on the history of math-

ematics; it was organic to his reflections as an artist and "philosopher" (as he wished to call himself and as he was ultimately called by the king of France). In his geometrical research he drew upon Archimedes and the ancients' doctrine of lunes to develop the most neglected parts of Euclid's work—curvilinear angles, the squaring of curvilinear areas, and the infinite variation of forms of unaltered quantity. Thus, in Leonardo's philosophy, does nature build and infinitely vary her forms, from the simplest to the most complex; and even the most complex have a rational structure that defines their beauty. It was Leonardo's profound intuition that "Necessity . . . bridle and eternal rule of Nature" must have a mathematical foundation and that the infinite forms found in nature must therefore be the infinite variations of a fundamental "equation."

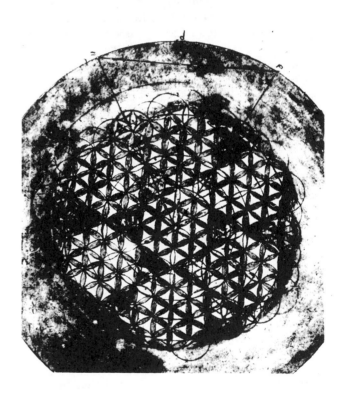

FIGURE 5. (*Codex Atlanticus*, 110v-a).

Leonardo thus expressed a Pythagorean or Platonic conception of reality, common to many artists of the Renaissance. It was at the same time a revolutionary view, inasmuch as it identified form as function and further integrated into the concept of function the medieval notion of substance. Leonardo did not formulate his conception of reality in the abstract terms of universal scientific law. Rather, as the purpose of his painting was always to render the most subtle designs of natural structures, his last geometric constructions were aimed at discovering the mathematical structure of nature.

AUGUSTO MARINONI

GEOLOGY

In the later years of his life Leonardo da Vinci described the configuration of the earth's crust as the result of actual processes, principally fluvial, operating over immense periods of time—a system of geology which Duhem described as "perhaps his most complete and lasting invention" (Duhem, II, p. 342).

For Leonardo, the study of the great world was related to the study of man. "Man is the model of the world" (*Codex Arundel*, fol. 156v; De Lorenzo, p. 8), he wrote, ". . . called by the ancients a microcosm . . ., composed like the earth itself, of earth, water, air and fire; as man contains within himself bones, the supports and armature of the flesh, the world has rocks, the supports of the earth: as man has in him the lake of blood which the lungs swell and decrease in breathing, the body of the earth has its oceanic sea which also swells and diminishes every six hours in nourishing the world" (MS *A*, fol. 55v).

Leonardo's geologic perceptions date back to his earliest apprenticeship in Florence. Horizontally stratified rocks in the foreground and pyramidal peaks above a background sea in the *Baptism of Christ* (Uffizi, Florence), which he worked on with his master Verrocchio in 1472, reflect the influence of Van Eyck on Florentine landscape conventions (Castelfranco, p. 472).

Leonardo's earliest dated work (1473), probably drawn in the field, is a sketch of the valley of the Arno (Uffizi). It displays similar characteristics—horizontal strata with waterfalls in the right foreground, and eroded hills above a broad alluvial valley behind.

In subsequent drawings and paintings, rocks may be thrown into cataclysmic contortions but at the same time are folded and fractured realistically. (Leonardo's infrequent mentions of earthquakes [*Codex Leicester*, fol. 10v], volcanoes [*Codex Arundel*, fol. 155r; and Richter, 1939], and internal heat betray a lack of firsthand familiarity with Italy from Naples south. His idea of catastrophe was of storm, avalanche, and flood, and his apocalyptic essays do not alter the essential actualism of his system. He pointedly neglects the plutonist orogenic ideas of Albertus Magnus for the gradualist-neptunism of Albert of Saxony [Duhem, II, p. 334].) The cliffs rising from a harbor in the background to the

Annunciation (Uffizi) are not unlike views from above Lake Como or Lake Maggiore in the gathering mists. But the ultimate expression of Leonardo's visual apprehension of topography and the true measure of the extent of his journey from the first sketch of 1473 is in the Windsor drawings of the Alps above the plains of the Po (*Windsor Collection*, folios 12410, 12414). They were done in the final years of his life in Italy at about the same time that he formulated his geologic system (Calvi, p. xiii, places the composition of the geologic notes in Tuscany before his Alpine studies). In these notes Leonardo boldly rejected Judeo-Christian cosmology for the secular naturalism of the classical tradition as demonstrated by natural processes and by the actual configuration of the material world. Leonardo estimated that 200,000 years were required for the Po to lay down its plain ([Muentz, p. 34]; he had clearly abandoned the Judeo-Christian time scale for one that was two to three orders of magnitude greater [cf. Duhem, II, p. 335; and Richter, p. 915]).

In Leonardo's system, the highest peaks of the Alps and the Apennines were former islands in an ancient sea. Mountains are continually eroded by winds and rains. Every valley is carved by its river, which is proven by the concordance of the stratigraphic column across the valley walls (*Codex Leicester*, fol. 10r) and the proportionality of river size to valley breadth (*Codex Atlanticus*, fol. 321b). The foothills and plains made by alluvial deposition continually extend the area of land at the expense of the sea. Mountains made lighter by erosion rise slowly to maintain the earth's center of gravity at the center of the universe, bringing up petrified marine strata with their accompanying fauna and flora to be eroded into mountains in their turn.

Such great lakes as the Black Sea are impounded by the collapse of mountains and then, as streams breach the barriers, they drain down one into the other. In this way the Arno was seen to be cutting through its own flood plain, the Po to have filled in the great north Italian triangle from the Alps and Apennines to Venice, and the Nile from Memphis to Alexandria. The Mediterranean itself, the "greatest of rivers," is being filled by the expanding deltas of its tributaries. When the future extension of the Nile erodes through the barrier of the Pillars of Hercules, it will drain what remains of the Mediterranean. Its bottom, relieved of the weight of the superincumbent sea, will rise isostatically (not to be confused with the modern concept of isostasy) to become the summits of mountains.

Just as Leonardo turned to dissection to study anatomy, so he dissected the earth—first in Milan during the years that he spent with Ludovico Sforza (il Moro); later as architect and engineer-general to Cesare Borgia and in land reclamation in Tuscany and for Leo X—for a period of 33 years from 1482 until 1515. Excavations for canals, moats, and roadways in Lombardy, Tuscany, Emilia, and the Romagna were carried out under his direct supervision during most of his career. He constructed plans and relief maps requiring exact measurements as well as litho-logic and structural insight. His designs for surveying and drafting instruments; his numerous sketches, notes, and calculations of costs, manpower, and time; and his meticulous plans of machines for excavation and hydraulic controls all attest to the extent of his occupation with practical geology. The maps them-selves—"bird's-eye" topographic constructions, relief maps, and outline plans of drainage and culture—are the geological analogues of his anatomical drawings, transcending sixteenth-century technics and science.

Leonardo was familiar with classical geological traditions through the works of Albertus Magnus and Cecco d'Ascoli, Vincent of Beauvais, Ramon Lull, Isidore of Seville, Jan de Mandeville, and, above all, Albert of Saxony. Yet his demonstrations of the organic origins of fossils *in situ*, the impossibility of the biblical deluge, and the natural processes of petrifaction are based on meticulous observations—for example, of growth lines on shells (*Codex Leicester*, fol. 10a; Richter, p. 990).

"When I was casting the great horse at Milan. . . .," he wrote, "some countrymen brought to my workshop a great sack of cockles and corals that were found in the mountains of Parma and Piacenza" (*Codex Leicester*, fol. 9v). Was it his experience with the process of casting that led him ultimately to discuss the origins of the fossils and their casts; of worm tracks; *glossopetrae*; fragmented and complete shells; paired and single shells; leaves; tufa; and conglom-erates? Did this casting experience lead to a discussion of the relationship of velocity of flow to the sedi-mentary gradation from the mountains to the sea, of coarse gravels and breccias to the finest white potter's clay?

Leonardo also observed and discussed turbidity currents (*Codex Leicester*, fol. 20r); initial horizontality (MS *F*, fol. 11v); the relationship of sedimentary textures to turbulence of flow, graded bedding, the formation of evaporites (*Codex Atlanticus*, fol. 160); and the association of folded strata with mountains (*Codex Arundel*, fol. 30b, Richter, 982). After numer-ous false starts, he arrived at an understanding of the hydrologic cycle (MS *E*, fol. 12a and Richter, 930); he dismissed the Pythagorean identification of the forms of the elements with the Platonic solids (MS *F*

and Richter, 939); and he recorded the migration of sand dunes (MS *F*, fol. 61a and Richter, 1087).

After the period as engineer with Cesare Borgia, Leonardo had returned to Florence, then proceeded to Rome, and finally found sanctuary in Milan in 1508. Here he made the geologic notes of MS *F* under the heading *De mondo ed acque*. It is from this period also that the red chalk Windsor drawings of the Alps date, reflecting his interest in, and excursions into, the nearby Alps (Clark, p. 134).

Leonardo brought not only his experience and his scientific principles to his landscapes, but also his sense of fantasy (Castelfranco, p. 473). The foreground of the two versions of the *Virgin of the Rocks* (Louvre and National Gallery) appears to be alternately horizontal, vertical, and horizontal strata, with caves widening into tunnels so that the roofs form natural bridges, some of them falling in. Such hollowing out from underneath and falling in of the back is the same mechanism used by Nicholas Steno in his *Prodromus* of 1669 to account for the inclination of strata.

Duhem has argued cogently that Leonardo's ideas were transmitted through Cardano and Palissy to the modern world. There are many similarities which suggest a connection also with the highly influential *Telliamed* of Benoit de Maillet (1749). The notebooks were in part accessible well in advance of the modern development of a natural geology. G. B. Venturi's studies of the geologic material in the notebooks were published in 1797 when catastrophic views of earth history were dominant. This was the year of birth of Charles Lyell, whose *Principles of Geology* in 1830 first formally established actualism as geologic orthodoxy. (In later editions of the *Principles*, Lyell wrote that his attention was called to the Venturi studies by H. Hallam. G. Libri's notes on Leonardo's geology also date to the decade of Lyell's *Principles*. By contrast, the diluvial doctrine which Leonardo had demolished was seriously defended by William Buck-land in his *Reliquiae diluvianae* as late as 1823, and catastrophism persisted well into the second half of the nineteenth century.)

Unfortunately, Leonardo rarely if ever sketched an indubitable fossil. He discussed but never il-lustrated the vivid Lake Garda *ammonitico rosso*—a Jurassic red marble with striking spiral ammonites used extensively in Milan. Leonardo's realistic strata, especially in the *Virgin and St. Anne* of the Louvre, closely resemble these limestones as they weather in the Milanese damp. How is it possible that his "ineffable left hand" traced no illustrations of his comments—those comments which in their freshness, their simplicity, and vivid detail are a warranty of firsthand observation and an actualistic geologic position not achieved again for centuries? "The understanding of times past and of the site of the world is the ornament and the food of the human mind," he wrote (*Codex Atlanticus*, fol. 365v).

CECIL J. SCHNEER

BIBLIOGRAPHY

Arbitrary Collections

1.	*Codex Atlanticus*	1478–1518
2.	*Windsor Collection*	1478–1518
3.	*Codex Arundel*	1480–1518

Notebooks

4.	*Codex Forster*, I$_2$ (fols. 41–55)	1480–1490
5.	MS *B*	*ca.* 1489
6.	*Codex Trivulzianus*	*ca.* 1489
7.	MS *C*	1490
8.	*Codex Madrid*, II (fols. 141–157)	1491–1493
9.	MS *A*	1492
10.	*Codex Madrid*, I	1492–1497
11.	*Codex Forster*, II$_1$, II$_2$, III	1493–1495
12.	MS *H*	1493–1494
13.	MS *M*	*ca.* 1495
14.	MS *I*	1495–1499
15.	MS *L*	1497; 1502–1503
16.	*Codex Madrid*, II (fols. 1–140)	1503–1505
17.	MS *K$_1$*	1504
18.	MS *K$_2$*	1504–1509
19.	*Codex Forster*, I$_1$	1505
20.	*Codex on Flight* . . .	1505
21.	*Codex Leicester*	*ca.* 1506
22.	MS *D*	*ca.* 1508
23.	MS *F*	1508–1509
24.	MS *K$_3$*	1509–1512
25.	*Anatomical Folio A*	*ca.* 1510
26.	MS *G*	1510–1516
27.	MS *E*	1513–1514

Note: Not all scholars are in agreement as to the years given above. It is, however, a matter of plus or minus one or two years.

I. ORIGINAL WORKS. Published treatises (compilations) are *Treatise on Painting* (abr.), pub. by Rafaelle du Fresne (Paris, 1651), complete treatise, as found in *Codex Urbinas latinus* 1270, trans. into English, annotated, and published in facs. by Philip A. McMahon (Princeton, 1956); and *Il trattato del moto e misura dell'acqua* . . ., pub. from *Codex Barberinianus* by E. Carusi and A. Favoro (Bologna, 1923).

Published MSS are *Codex Atlanticus*, facs. ed. (Milan, 1872 [inc.], 1894–1904), consisting of 401 fols., each containing one or more MS sheets (*Codex* is in the Biblioteca Ambrosiana, Milan); MSS *A–M* and *Ashburnham 2038* and *2037* (in the library of the Institut de France), 6 vols., Charles Ravaisson-Mollien, ed. (Paris, 1881–1891), con-

sisting of 2,178 facs. reproducing the 14 MSS in the Institut de France and Bibliothèque Nationale, with transcription and French trans.; *Codex Trivulzianus*, transcription and annotation by Luca Beltrami (Milan, 1891), containing 55 fols.; *Codex on the Flight of Birds*, 14 fols. pub. by Theodore Sabachnikoff, transcribed by Giovanni Piumati, translated by C. Ravaisson-Mollien (Paris, 1893, 1946); *The Drawings of Leonardo da Vinci at Windsor Castle*, cataloged by Kenneth Clark, 2nd ed., rev. with the assistance of Carlo Pedretti (London, 1968), containing 234 fols.: repros. of all the drawings at Windsor, including the anatomical drawings (notes are not transcribed or translated where this has been done in other works—such as the selections of J. P. Richter, *Anatomical Folios A and B*, and the *Quaderni d'anatomia*; see below); *Dell'anatomia fogli A*, pub. by T. Sabachnikoff and G. Piumati (Turin, 1901); *Dell'anatomia fogli B*, pub. by T. Sabachnikoff and G. Piumati (Turin, 1901); *Quaderni d'anatomia*, 6 vols., Ove C. L. Vangensten, A. Fonahn, and H. Hopstock, eds. (Christiania, 1911–1916), all the anatomical drawings not included in *Folios A and B; Codex Leicester* (Milan, 1909), 36 fols., pub. by G. Calvi with the title *Libro originale della natura peso e moto delle acque* (*Codex* is in the Leicester Library, Holkham Hall, Norfolk); *Codex Arundel*, a bound vol. marked *Arundel 263*, pub. by the Reale Commissione Vinciana, with transcription (Rome, 1923–1930), containing 283 fols. (*Codex* is in British Museum); and *Codex Forster*, 5 vols., 304 fols., pub. with transcription by the Reale Commissione Vinciana (Rome, 1936) (*Codex* is in the Victoria and Albert Museum, London).

MSS are J. P. Richter, *The Literary Works of Leonardo da Vinci*, 2 vols. (London, 1970), containing a transcription and English translation of a wide range of Leonardo's notes used as a reference work in Clark's *Catalogue of the Drawings at Windsor Castle;* and E. MacCurdy, *The Notebooks of Leonardo da Vinci*, 2 vols. (London, 1939; 2nd ed., 1956), the most extensive selection of Leonardo's notes.

II. SECONDARY LITERATURE. The following works can be used to obtain a general picture of Leonardo's scientific work: Mario Baratta, *Leonardo da Vinci ed i problemi della terra* (Turin, 1903); Elmer Belt, *Leonardo the Anatomist* (Lawrence, Kan., 1955); Girolamo Calvi, *I manoscritti di Leonardo da Vinci* (Rome, 1925); B. Dibner, *Leonardo da Vinci, Military Engineer* (New York, 1946), and *Leonardo da Vinci, Prophet of Automation* (New York, 1969); Pierre Duhem, *Études sur Léonard de Vinci* (Paris, 1906–1913; repr. 1955); Sigrid Esche-Braunfels, *Leonardo da Vinci, das anatomische Werk* (Basel, 1954); Giuseppe Favoro, *Leonardo da Vinci, i medici e la medicina* (Rome, 1923), and "Leonardo da Vinci e l'anatomia," in *Scientia*, no. 6 (1952), 170–175; Bertrand Gille, *The Renaissance Engineers* (London, 1966); I. B. Hart, *The World of Leonardo da Vinci* (London, 1961); L. H. Heydenreich, *Leonardo da Vinci* (Berlin, 1944), also trans. into English (London, 1954); K. D. Keele, *Leonardo da Vinci on the Movement of the Heart and Blood* (London, 1952); "The Genesis of Mona Lisa," in *Journal of the History of Medicine*, **14**

(1959), 135; and "Leonardo da Vinci's Physiology of the Senses," in C. D. O'Malley, ed., *Leonardo's Legacy* (Berkeley–Los Angeles, 1969); E. MacCurdy, *The Mind of Leonardo da Vinci* (New York, 1928); J. P. McMurrich, *Leonardo da Vinci, the Anatomist* (Baltimore, 1930); Roberto Marcolongo, *Studi vinciani: Memorie sulla geometria e la meccanica di Leonardo da Vinci* (Naples, 1937); and A. Marinoni, "The Manuscripts of Leonardo da Vinci and Their Editions," in *Leonardo saggi e ricerche* (Rome, 1954).

See also C. D. O'Malley, ed., *Leonardo's Legacy—an International Symposium* (Berkeley–Los Angeles, 1969); C. D. O'Malley and J. B. de C. M. Saunders, *Leonardo da Vinci on the Human Body* (New York, 1952); Erwin Panofsky, *The Codex Huygens and Leonardo da Vinci's Art Theory* (London, 1940); A. Pazzini, ed., *Leonardo da Vinci. Il trattato della anatomia* (Rome, 1962); Carlo Pedretti, *Documenti e memorie riguardanti Leonardo da Vinci a Bologna e in Emilia* (Bologna, 1953); *Studi vinciani* (Geneva, 1957); and *Leonardo da Vinci on Painting—a Lost Book (Libro A)* (London, 1965); *Raccolta vinciana*, "Commune di Milano, Castello Sforzesco," I–XX (Milan, 1905–1964); Ladislao Reti, "Le arti chimiche di Leonardo da Vinci," in *Chimica e l'industria*, **34** (1952), 655–721; "Leonardo da Vinci's Experiments on Combustion," in *Journal of Chemical Education*, **29** (1952), 590; "The Problem of Prime Movers," in *Leonardo da Vinci, Technologist* (New York, 1969); and "The Two Unpublished Manuscripts of Leonardo da Vinci in Madrid," *ibid.*; I. A. Richter, *Selections From the Notebooks of Leonardo da Vinci* (Oxford, 1962); Vasco Ronchi, "Leonardo e l'ottica," in *Leonardo saggi e ricerche* (Rome, 1954); George Sarton, *Léonard de Vinci, ingénieur et savant. Colloques internationaux* (Paris, 1953), pp. 11–22; E. Solmi, *Scritti vinciani*, papers collected by Arrigo Solmi (Florence, 1924); K. T. Steinitz, *Leonardo da Vinci's Trattato della pittura* (Copenhagen, 1958); Arturo Uccelli, *I libri di meccanica di Leonardo da Vinci nella ricostruzione ordinata da A. Uccelli* (Milan, 1940); Giorgio Vasari, *Lives of the Painters and Architects* (London, 1927); and V. P. Zubov, *Leonardo da Vinci*, trans. from the Russian by David H. Kraus (Cambridge, Mass., 1968).

The remainder of the bibliography is divided into sections corresponding to those in the text: Technology, Mechanics, Mathematics, and Geology.

Technology. On Leonardo's work in technology, the following should be consulted: T. Beck, *Beiträge zur Geschichte des Maschinenbaues*, 2nd ed. (Berlin, 1900), completed in *Zeitschrift des Vereines deutscher Ingenieure* (1906), 524–531, 562–569, 645–651, 777–784; I. Calvi, *L'architettura militare di Leonardo da Vinci* (Milan, 1943); G. Canestrini, *Leonardo costruttore di macchine e veicoli* (Milan, 1939); B. Dibner, *Leonardo da Vinci, Military Engineer* (New York, 1946); F. M. Feldhaus, *Leonardo der Techniker und Erfinder* (Jena, 1922); R. Giacomelli, *Gli scritti di Leonardo da Vinci sul volo* (Rome, 1936); C. H. Gibbs Smith, "The Flying Machine of Leonardo da Vinci," in *Shell Aviation News*, no. 194 (1954); *The Aeroplane* (London, 1960); and *Leonardo da Vinci's Aeronautics*

(London, 1967); B. Gille, *Engineers of the Renaissance* (Cambridge, Mass., 1966); I. B. Hart, *The Mechanical Investigations of Leonardo da Vinci* (London, 1925; 2nd ed., with a foreword by E. A. Moody, Berkeley–Los Angeles, 1963), and *The World of Leonardo da Vinci* (London, 1961); *Léonard de Vinci et l'expérience scientifique au XVI siècle* (Paris, 1952), a collection of articles; *Leonardo da Vinci* (New York, 1967), a collection of articles originally pub. in 1939; R. Marcolongo, *Leonardo da Vinci artista-scienziato* (Milan, 1939); W. B. Parsons, *Engineers and Engineering in the Renaissance* (Baltimore, 1939; 2nd ed., Cambridge, Mass., 1968); L. Reti, "Leonardo da Vinci nella storia della macchina a vapore," in *Rivista di ingegneria* (1956–1957); L. Reti and B. Dibner, *Leonardo da Vinci, Technologist* (New York, 1969); G. Strobino, *Leonardo da Vinci e la meccanica tessile* (Milan, 1953); C. Truesdell, *Essays in the History of Mechanics* (New York, 1968); L. Tursini, *Le armi di Leonardo da Vinci* (Milan, 1952); A. Uccelli, *Storia della tecnica . . .* (Milan, 1945), and *I libri del volo di Leonardo da Vinci* (Milan, 1952); A. P. Usher, *A History of Mechanical Inventions*, rev. ed. (Cambridge, Mass., 1954); and V. P. Zubov, *Leonardo da Vinci* (Cambridge, Mass., 1968).

Mechanics. Particularly useful as a source collection of pertinent passages on mechanics in the notebooks is A. Uccelli, ed., *I libri di meccanica . . .* (Milan, 1942). The pioneer analytic works were those of P. Duhem, *Les origines de la statique*, 2 vols. (Paris, 1905–1906), and *Études sur Léonard de Vinci* (Paris, 1906–1913; repr. 1955). These works were the first to put Leonardo's mechanical works into historical perspective. Their main defect is that a full corpus of Leonardo's notebooks was not available to Duhem. They are less successful in interpreting Leonardo's dynamics. Far less perceptive than Duhem's work is F. Schuster's treatment of Leonardo's statics, *Zur Mechanik Leonardo da Vincis* (Erlangen, 1915), which also suffered because the sources available to him were deficient. A work that ordinarily follows Schuster (and Duhem) is I. B. Hart, *The Mechanical Investigations of Leonardo da Vinci* (London, 1925; 2nd ed., with foreword by E. A. Moody, Berkeley–Los Angeles, 1963). It tends to treat Leonardo in isolation, although the 2nd ed. makes some effort to rectify this deficiency. The best treatment of Leonardo's mechanics remains R. Marcolongo, *Studi vinciani: Memorie sulla geometria e la meccanica di Leonardo da Vinci* (Naples, 1937). It is wanting only in its treatment of Leonardo's hydrostatics and the motion of fluids. For a brief but important study of Leonardo's hydrostatics, see F. Arredi, *Le origini dell'idrostatica* (Rome, 1943), pp. 8–16. For an acute appraisal of Leonardo's mechanics in general and his fluid mechanics in particular, see C. Truesdell, *Essays in the History of Mechanics* (New York, 1968), pp. 1–83, esp. 62–79. Finally, for the influence of Archimedes on Leonardo, see M. Clagett, "Leonardo da Vinci and the Medieval Archimedes," in *Physis*, **11** (1969), 100–151, esp. 108–113, 119–140.

Mathematics. The most thorough study of Leonardo's mathematical works was carried out in the first part of the twentieth century by R. Marcolongo, whose most important writings are: "Le ricerche geometrico-meccaniche di Leonardo da Vinci," in *Atti della Società italiana delle scienze, detta dei XL*, 3rd ser., **23** (1929), 49–100; *Il trattato di Leonardo da Vinci sulle trasformazioni dei solidi* (Naples, 1934); and *Leonardo da Vinci artista-scienziato* (Milan, 1939). The cited article of C. Caversazzi, "Un'invenzione geometrica di Leonardo da Vinci," is in *Emporium* (May 1939), 317–323. Important articles are M. Clagett, "Leonardo da Vinci and the Medieval Archimedes," in *Physis*, **11** (1969), 100–151; and C. Pedretti, "The Geometrical Studies," in K. Clark, *The Drawings of Leonardo da Vinci at Windsor Castle*, 2nd ed., rev. (London, 1968), I, xlix–liii; and "Leonardo da Vinci: Manuscripts and Drawings of the French Period, 1517–1518," in *Gazette des beaux-arts* (Nov. 1970), 185–318.

The following studies by A. Marinoni provide a detailed analysis of some of Leonardo's works: "Le operazioni aritmetiche nei manoscritti vinciani," in *Raccolta vinciana*, XIX (Milan, 1962), 1–62; "La teoria dei numeri frazionari nei manoscritti vinciani. Leonardo e Luca Pacioli," *ibid.*, XX (Milan, 1964), 111–196; and "L'aritmetica di Leonardo," in *Periodico di matematiche* (Dec. 1968), 543–558. See also Marinoni's *L'essere del nulla* (Florence, 1970) on the definitions of the "principles" of geometry in Leonardo, and "Leonardo da Vinci," in *Grande antologia filosofica* (Milan, 1964), VI, 1149–1212, on the supposed definition of the principle of inertia.

Geology. On Leonardo's work in geology, see the following: Mario Baratta, *Leonardo da Vinci ed i problemi della terra* (Turin, 1903); *I disegni geografici di Leonardo da Vinci conservati nel Castello di Windsor* (Rome, 1941); Girolamo Calvi, *Introduction, Codex Leicester* (Rome, 1909); Giorgio Castelfranco, "Sul pensiero geologico e il paesaggio di Leonardo," in Achille Marazza, ed., *Saggi e Ricerche* (Rome, 1954), app. 2; Kenneth Clark, *Leonardo da Vinci* (Baltimore, 1963); Giuseppe De Lorenzo, *Leonardo da Vinci e la geologia* (Bologna, 1920); Pierre Duhem, *Études sur Léonard de Vinci*, 3 vols. (Paris, 1906–1913; repr. 1955); Eugène Muentz, *Leonardo da Vinci, Artist, Thinker, and Man of Science* (New York, 1898); and J. P. Richter, ed., *The Notebooks of Leonardo da Vinci* (New York, 1970).

LE PAIGE, CONSTANTIN (*b*. Liège, Belgium, 9 March 1852; *d*. Liège, 26 January 1929)

Le Paige, the son of Jeanne Jacques and Constantin Marie Le Paige, received his secondary education at Spa and Liège. After taking a course in mathematics with V. Falisse, he entered the University of Liège in 1869, where he attended the lectures of E. Catalan, to whom we owe a special form of determinants, the so-called circulants. After his graduation on 28 July 1875, Le Paige began teaching the theory of determinants and higher analysis at the university. He was appointed extraordinary professor of mathematics

in 1882, and ordinary professor in 1885, which post he retained until his retirement in 1922; he was appointed professor emeritus in 1923. His wife was the former Marie Joséphine Ernst.

Le Paige began work at a time when the theory of algebraic forms, initiated by Boole in 1841 and developed by Cayley and Sylvester in England, Hermite in France, and Clebsch and Aronhold in Germany, had drawn the attention of the geometers. This theory studies the properties of such forms, which remain unchanged under linear substitutions. Le Paige's investigations touched mainly upon the geometry of algebraic curves and surfaces, and the theory of invariants and involutions. He coordinated and generalized the extensions which at that time had been tried. His best-known achievement was the construction of a cubic surface given by nineteen points. Starting from the construction of a cubic surface given by a straight line, three groups of three points on a line, and six other points, Le Paige comes to the construction of a cubic surface given by three lines and seven points. From this he proceeds to the construction of a cubic surface given by a line, three points on a line, and twelve other points, and by means of the construction of a cubic surface given by three points on a line and sixteen other points, he arrives at a surface given by nineteen points.

Steiner's theorem, that a conic section can be generated by the intersection of two projective pencils, had been extended by Chasles to plane algebraic curves. Le Paige also studied the generation of plane cubic and quartic curves, and the construction of a plane cubic curve given by nine points is presented in his memoir "Sur les courbes du troisième ordre" (*Mémoires de l'Académie royale de Belgique*, 43 [1881] and 45 [1882]), written with F. Folie.

Besides writing on algebraic geometry, Le Paige was also a historian of mathematics. He published the correspondence of Sluse, canon of Liège, with Pascal, Huygens, Oldenburg, and Wallis. His "Notes pour servir à l'histoire des mathématiques dans l'ancien pays de Liège" (*Bulletin de l'Institut archéologique liégeois*, 21 [1890]), devotes a large section to the Belgian astronomer Wendelin, and in "Sur l'origine de certains signes d'opération" (*Annales de la Société scientifiques de Bruxelles*, 16 [1891–1892]) Le Paige explains the origin of the symbols of operation. After his appointment as director of the Institut d'Astrophysique de Cointe-Sclessim in 1897 Le Paige wrote a number of astronomical treatises.

Le Paige was elected a member of the Royal Academy of Sciences of Belgium in 1885. His international reputation is attested by the following partial list of his affiliations: member of the Royal Society of Sciences of Liège (1878) and of the Royal Society of Bohemia; corresponding member of the Pontificia Accademia dei Nuovi Lincei (1881) and of the Royal Academy of Sciences of Lisbon (1883); and honorary member of the Mathematical Society of Amsterdam (1886).

BIBLIOGRAPHY

In addition to the works mentioned in the text, Le Paige published the following astronomical works: "Sur la réduction au lieu apparent. Termes dus à l'aberration," in *Mémoires de la Société royale des Sciences de Liège*, **3** (1901); and "Étude sur les visées au bain de mercure," *ibid.*

A fuller account of Le Paige's work and a complete list of his publications is given in L. Godeaux, "Notice sur Constantin le Paige," in *Annuaire de l'Académie royale de Belgique*, **105** (1939), 239–270.

H. L. L. Busard

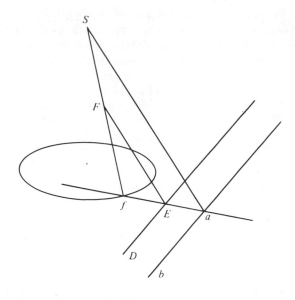

FIGURE 1

LE POIVRE, JACQUES-FRANÇOIS (*fl.* France, early eighteenth century)

A minor figure in the early history of projective geometry, Le Poivre is known only by his short treatise, *Traité des sections du cylindre et du cône considérées dans le solide et dans le plan, avec des démonstrations simples & nouvelles* (Paris, 1704). According to the review of this work in the *Journal des sçavans*, he lived in Mons and worked on the treatise for three years; nothing more is known about him.

Aimed both at presenting the conic sections in a form readily understandable to the novice and at offering new results to specialists, the *Traité* is divided into two parts. The first examines the ellipse by means of the parallel projection of a circle from one plane to another and, by inversion of the projection, within the same plane. Although primarily interested here in the tangent properties of the curve, Le Poivre also proves several theorems concerning its conjugate axes in a much simpler way than had been achieved earlier.

Part 2 is more interesting for its greater generality. Here Le Poivre generates the conic sections by means of the central projection of a circle. Taking a circle as base and a point S (at first assumed to be off the plane of the circle) as summit, he draws two parallel lines ab and DE in the plane of the circle (see Fig. 1). He then draws through any point f on the circle an arbitrary line intersecting DE at E and ab at a. Having drawn Sa, he draws EF parallel to it and intersecting Sf at F. Point F, he then shows, lies on a conic section, the precise nature of which depends on the location of line ab: if ab lies wholly outside the circle, the section is an ellipse; if ab is tangent to the circle, the

section is a parabola; if ab cuts the circle, the section is a hyperbola. The theorems that he goes on to prove are nevertheless independent of the specific position of ab and hence apply to conic sections in general.

If one views ab and DE as the intersections of two parallel planes with the plane of the circle, and Sf as an element of the cone determined by point S and the circle, then Le Poivre's construction reduces to that of Apollonius. But the construction itself does not rely on that visualization of a solid, nor does it require that S in fact be off the plane of the circle. Hence the theorems also hold for central projections in the same plane.

In reviewing Le Poivre's *Traité* for the *Acta eruditorum*, Christian Wolff spoke warmly of its elegance and originality. The anonymous reviewer of the *Journal des sçavans*, however, insisted on Le Poivre's omission of several important conic properties, in particular the focal properties, and on the extent to which he had failed to go beyond (or even to equal) the methods of Philippe de La Hire. In fact, Le Poivre's method of central projection is essentially that employed by La Hire in Part 2 of his *Nouvelle méthode en géométrie, pour les sections des superficies coniques et cylindriques* (Paris, 1673). Whether independent of La Hire or not, Le Poivre's work was apparently lost in his shadow, not to be brought to light again until Michel Chasles's survey of the history of geometry in 1837.

BIBLIOGRAPHY

Le Poivre's *Traité* is quite rare. The above description of it is taken from the reviews in the *Acta eruditorum*

(Mar. 1707), 132–133 (the identification of Wolff as reviewer is from a contemporary marginal in the Princeton copy); and the *Journal des sçavans*, **32** (1704), 649–658. Chasles, who felt that Le Poivre belonged in a class with Desargues, Pascal, and La Hire, discusses his work in pars. 31–34 of ch. 3 of the *Aperçu historique sur l'origine et le développement des méthodes en géométrie, particulièrement de celles qui se rapportent à la géométrie moderne* (Brussels, 1837); German trans. by L. A. Sohncke (Halle, 1839; repr. Wiesbaden, 1968). The entry for Le Poivre in the *Nouvelle biographie générale*, XXX (Paris, 1862), 852, stems entirely from Chasles.

MICHAEL S. MAHONEY

LERCH, MATHIAS (*b.* Milínov, near Sušice, Bohemia, 20 February 1860; *d.* Sušice, Czechoslovakia, 3 August 1922)

Lerch studied mathematics in Prague and, in 1884 and 1885, at the University of Berlin under Weierstrass, Kronecker, and Lazarus Fuchs. In 1886 he became a *Privatdozent* at the Czech technical institute in Prague and in 1896 full professor at the University of Fribourg. He returned to his native country in 1906, following his appointment as full professor at the Czech technical institute in Brno. In 1920 Lerch became the first professor of mathematics at the newly founded Masaryk University in Brno. He died two years later, at the age of sixty-two. In 1900 he received the grand prize of the Paris Academy for his *Essais sur le calcul du nombre des classes de formes quadratiques binaires aux coefficients entiers* [199].

Of Lerch's 238 scientific writings, some of which are quite comprehensive, 118 were written in Czech. About 150 deal with analysis and about forty with number theory; the rest are devoted to geometry, numerical methods, and other subjects. Lerch's achievements in analysis were in general function theory, general and special infinite series, special functions (particularly the gamma function), elliptic functions, and integral calculus. His works are noteworthy with regard to methodology. In particular he described and applied to concrete questions new methodological principles of considerable importance: the principle of the introduction of an auxiliary parameter for meromorphic functions [203] and the principle of most rapid convergence [210]. Lerch's best-known accomplishments include the Lerch theory on the generally unique solution φ of the equation $J(a) = \int_0^\infty \exp(-ax)\, \varphi(x)\, dx$—[73, 180]—which is fundamental in modern operator calculus; and the Lerch formula [101, 105, 116, 124], obtained originally from the theory of Malmsténian series, for the derivative of the Kummerian trigonometric development of log $\Gamma(v)$:

$$\sum_{k=1}^{\infty} \sin(2k+1)\, v\pi \cdot \log \frac{k}{k+1}$$
$$= (\log 2\pi - \Gamma'[1]) \sin v\pi$$
$$+ \frac{\pi}{2} \cos v\pi + \frac{\Gamma'(v)}{\Gamma(v)} \sin v\pi \ (0 < v < 1).$$

BIBLIOGRAPHY

I. ORIGINAL WORKS. A complete, chronological bibliography of Lerch's scientific works was published by J. Škrášek in *Czechoslovak Mathematical Journal*, **3** (1953), 111–122. The numbers in text in square brackets refer to works so numbered in Škrášek's listing.

II. SECONDARY LITERATURE. An extensive discussion of Lerch's work in mathematical analysis was published by O. Borůvka *et al.* in *Práce Brněnské základny Československé akademie věd*, **29** (1957), 417–540. A detailed biography of Lerch can be found in an article by L. Frank in *Časopis pro pěstování matematiky*, **78** (1953), 119–137.

O. BORŮVKA

LE ROY, ÉDOUARD (*b.* Paris, France, 18 June 1870; *d.* Paris, 9 November 1954)

Le Roy's father worked for the Compagnie Transatlantique for several years and then established his own business outfitting ships in Le Havre. Le Roy studied at home under the guidance of a tutor and was admitted in 1892 to the École Normale Supérieure. He became an *agrégé* in 1895 and earned a doctor of science degree in 1898; his thesis attracted the attention of Henri Poincaré. Until 1921 he taught mathematics classes that prepared students for the leading scientific schools. From 1924 to 1940 he was *chargé de conférences* at the Faculty of Sciences in Paris.

Although trained as a mathematician, Le Roy's enthusiastic discovery of the "new philosophy" of Bergson, to which he devoted a book in 1912, led him to teach philosophy. Bergson appointed Le Roy his *suppléant* in the chair of modern philosophy at the Collège de France (1914–1920). Named professor in 1921, Le Roy taught there until 1941; several of his published works are transcriptions of his courses. He was elected to the Académie des Sciences Morales et Politiques in 1919, and he entered the Académie Française as Bergson's successor in 1945.

A Catholic and a scientist, Le Roy had, in his youth, put forth theses in the philosophy of religion and the philosophy of science that provoked lively polemics. In "Qu'est-ce qu'un dogme?" (*La quinzaine*, 16 Apr. 1905) he emphasized the opposition between dogma and the body of positive knowledge. Dogma, he asserted, has a negative sense: it excludes and condemns certain errors rather than determining the truth in a positive fashion. Above all a dogma has a practical sense—that is its primary value.

Le Roy was thus involved in the quarrels precipitated by "modernist philosophy," which was condemned in the encyclical *Pascendi* by Pope Pius X in 1907, and his *Le problème de Dieu* (1929) was placed on the Index in June 1931. In the philosophy of science, Le Roy had proclaimed, in articles in *Revue de métaphysique et de morale* (1899, 1900), that facts are less established than constituted and that, far from being received passively by the mind, they are to some extent created by it. These paradoxical statements excited a certain interest through Poincaré's criticism of them in *La valeur de la science* (Paris, 1906, ch. 10).

While wishing to defend and justify the Bergsonian notion of creative evolution, Le Roy set forth his own philosophy of life, a "doctrine of authentically spiritualist inspiration" that sought a "restoration of finality" and respected the idea of creation. Le Roy's views were similar in many ways to those of his friend Teilhard de Chardin. According to Le Roy, there exists at the basis of life—as the major cause of its changes and progress—a psychic factor, a genuine power of invention. To recapture the activity of this factor one must consider the sole contemporary being —that is, Man—in which the power of creative evolution is still vital. Man must be observed in his capacity as inventor in order to return, by means of retrospective analogy, to the paleontological past. Biosphere and noosphere are the great moments of evolution. At the origin of the noosphere we must conceive a phenomenon *sui generis* of vital transformation affecting the entire biosphere: hominization. Humanity then appears as a new order of reality, sustaining a relationship with the lower forms of life analogous to that between these lower forms and inanimate matter. Man then no longer seems a paradoxical excrescence but becomes the key to transformist explanations. According to the "lesson that emerges from Christianity," man's intuition of a spiritual beyond and the ideal of an interior and mystic life show that we must form a concept of *Homo spiritualis* distinct from *Homo faber* and *Homo sapiens*.

In analyzing the history and philosophy of science, Le Roy likewise accorded a central position to the notion of invention, itself intimately linked to that of intuition, since intuitive thought is always, to some extent, inventive. True mathematical intuition is operative intuition; and the analyst should everywhere attempt to bring to consciousness the operative action perceived in its dynamic indivisibility. The transition from physics to microphysics clearly illuminates "the primary role of a factor of inventive energy in the innermost recesses of thought." Reason itself is in a state of becoming and must gradually be invented.

What will regulate this invention? An absolutely primary foundation must be sought which will be indisputable in every regard and, at the same time, dynamic and vital. Synthesizing twenty-five years of teaching, Le Roy in the *Essai d'une philosophie première*, his last course at the Collège de France, presented the major steps of such a search, the chief concern of which is to satisfy "the demands of idealism."

BIBLIOGRAPHY

I. ORIGINAL WORKS. Le Roy's principal publications are "Sur l'intégration des équations de la chaleur," in *Annales scientifiques de l'École normale supérieure*, **14** (1897), 379–465, and *ibid.*, **15** (1898), 9–178, his doctoral diss.; *Dogme et critique* (Paris, 1906); *Une philosophie nouvelle: Henri Bergson* (Paris, 1912); *L'exigence idéaliste et le fait de l'évolution* (Paris, 1927); *Les origines humaines et l'évolution de l'intelligence* (Paris, 1928); *La pensée intuitive*, 2 vols. (Paris, 1929–1930); *Le problème de Dieu* (Paris, 1929); and *Introduction à l'étude du problème religieux* (Paris, 1944).

After Le Roy's death his son, Georges Le Roy, published the lectures his father had given at the Collège de France as *Essai d'une philosophie première, l'exigence idéaliste et l'exigence morale*, 2 vols. (Paris, 1956–1958); and *La pensée mathématique pure* (Paris, 1960). The "Notice bibliographique," in *Études philosophiques* (Apr. 1955), 207–210, records many of Le Roy's works.

II. SECONDARY LITERATURE. See the following, listed chronologically: S. Gagnebin, *La philosophie de l'intuition. Essai sur les idées de Mr Édouard Le Roy* (Paris, 1912); L. Weber, "Une philosophie de l'invention. M. Édouard Le Roy," in *Revue de métaphysique et de morale*, **39** (1932), 59–86, 253–292; F. Olgiati, *Édouard Le Roy e il problema di Dio* (Milan, 1929); J. Lacroix, "Édouard Le Roy, philosophe de l'invention," in *Études philosophiques* (Apr. 1955), 189–205; G. Maire, "La philosophie d'Edouard Le Roy," *ibid.*, **27** (1972), 201–220; M. Tavares de Miranda, *Théorie de la vérité chez Édouard Le Roy* (Paris–Recife, Brazil, 1957); and G. Bachelard, *L'engagement rationaliste* (Paris, 1972), 155–168.

Biographical information is in E. Rideau, "Édouard Le Roy," in *Études*, no. 245 (April 1945), 246–255; and in the addresses delivered at the Académie Française by A. Chaumeix at the time of Le Roy's reception on 18 Oct. 1945, in *Institut de France, Publications diverses*, no. 18 (1945); and by H. Daniel-Rops when he succeeded Le Roy at the Academy, *ibid.*, no. 8 (1956).

On Le Roy's religious philosophy, see the article by E. Rideau cited above and A.-D. Sertillanges, *Le christianisme et les philosophes*, II (Paris, 1941), 402–419.

In an app. to *Bergson et Teilhard de Chardin* (Paris, 1963), pp. 655–659, M. B. Madaule discusses Le Roy's friendship with Teilhard, the large area of agreement in their views, and their correspondence.

Concerning the polemic with Poincaré, the ways in which Le Roy weakened his first statements, and his final homage to Poincaré, see J. Abelé, "Le Roy et la philosophie des sciences," in *Études*, no. 284 (April 1955), 106–112.

M. Serres discusses Le Roy's *La pensée mathématique pure* in "La querelle des anciens et des modernes," in his *Hermès ou la communication* (Paris, 1968), pp. 46–77. While terming the work a "monument of traditional epistemology," he shows how Le Roy, in applying his method of analysis to a mathematics that was already outdated, failed completely to consider "modern mathematics."

E. COUMET

LEŚNIEWSKI, STANISŁAW (*b.* Serpukhov, Russia, 18 March 1886; *d.* Warsaw, Poland, 13 May 1939)

After studying philosophy at various German universities, Leśniewski received the Ph.D. under Kazimierz Twardowski at Lvov in 1912. From 1919 until his death he held the chair of philosophy of mathematics at the University of Warsaw and, with Jan Łukasiewicz, inspired and directed research at the Warsaw school of logic. As a student Leśniewski studied the works of John Stuart Mill and Edmund Husserl, but through the influence of Łukasiewicz he soon turned to mathematical logic and began to study the *Principia* and the writings of Gottlob Frege and Ernst Schröder. A thorough and painstaking analysis of Russell's antinomy of the class of all those classes which are not members of themselves led Leśniewski to the construction of a system of logic and of the foundations of mathematics remarkable for its originality, elegance, and comprehensiveness. It consists of three theories, which he called protothetic, ontology, and mereology.

The standard system of protothetic, which is the most comprehensive logic of propositions, is based on a single axiom; and the functor of equivalence, "if and only if," occurs in it as the only undefined term. The directives of protothetic include (1) three rules of inference: substitution, detachment, and the distribution of the universal quantifier; (2) the rule of protothetical definition; and (3) the rule of protothetical extensionality. Protothetic presupposes no more fundamental theory, whereas all other deductive theories which are not parts of protothetic must be based on it or on a part of it.

Ontology is obtained by subjoining ontological axioms to protothetic, adapting the directives of protothetic to them, and allowing for a rule of ontological definition and a rule of ontological extensionality. The standard system of ontology is based on a single ontological axiom, in which the functor of singular inclusion, the copula "is," occurs as the only undefined term. Ontology comprises traditional logic and counterparts of the calculus of predicates, the calculus of classes, and the calculus of relations, including the theory of identity.

By subjoining mereological axioms to ontology and adapting the ontological directives to them, we obtain mereology, which is a theory of part-whole relations. The standard system of mereology, with the functor "proper or improper part of" as the only undefined term, can then be based on a single mereological axiom. No specifically mereological directives are involved. While ontology yields the foundations of arithmetic, mereology is the cornerstone of the foundations of geometry.

Leśniewski formulated the directives of his systems with unprecedented precision. In the art of formalizing deductive theories he has remained unsurpassed. Yet the theories that he developed never ceased for him to be interpreted theories, intended to embody a very general, and hence philosophically interesting, description of reality.

BIBLIOGRAPHY

I. ORIGINAL WORKS. Leśniewski's writings include "O podstawach matematyki" ("On the Foundations of Mathematics"), in *Przegląd filozoficzny*, **30** (1927), 164–206; **31** (1928), 261–291; **32** (1929), 60–101; **33** (1930), 77–105, 142–170, with a discussion of the Russellian antinomy and an exposition of mereology; "Grundzüge eines neuen Systems der Grundlagen der Mathematik," in *Fundamenta mathematicae*, **14** (1929), 1–81, which gives an account of the origin and development of protothetic and contains the statement of protothetical directives; "Über die Grundlagen der Ontologie," in *Comptes rendus des séances de la Société des sciences et des lettres de Varsovie*, Cl. III, **23** (1930), 111–132, containing the statement of the directives of ontology; "Über Definitionen in der sogenannten Theorie der Deduktion," *ibid.*, **24** (1931), 289–309, with the statement of the rules of inference and the rule of definition for a system of the classical calculus of propositions; and *Einleitende Bemerkungen zur Fortsetzung meiner Mitteilung u.d. T.* "*Grundzüge eines neuen Systems der Grundlagen der Mathematik*" (Warsaw, 1938), which includes a discussion of certain problems concerning protothetic. The last two works are available in an English trans. in Storrs McCall, ed., *Polish Logic 1920–1939* (Oxford, 1967), pp. 116–169, 170–187. *Grundzüge eines neuen Systems der Grundlagen der Mathematik §12* (Warsaw, 1938) offers the deduction of an axiom system of the classical calculus of propositions from a single axiom of protothetic.

II. SECONDARY LITERATURE. See T. Kotarbiński, *La logique en Pologne* (Rome, 1959); C. Lejewski, "A Contribution to Leśniewski's Mereology," in *Polskie towarzystwo naukowe na obszyźnie. Rocznik*, 5 (1955), 43–50; "A New Axiom of Mereology," *ibid.*, 6 (1956), 65–70; "On Leśniewski's Ontology," in *Ratio*, 1 (1958), 150–176; "A Note on a Problem Concerning the Axiomatic Foundations of Mereology," in *Notre Dame Journal of Formal Logic*, 4 (1963), 135–139; "A Single Axiom for the Mereological Notion of Proper Part," *ibid.*, 8 (1967), 279–285; and "Consistency of Leśniewski's Mereology," in *Journal of Symbolic Logic*, 34 (1969), 321–328; E. C. Luschei, *The Logical Systems of Leśniewski* (Amsterdam, 1962), a comprehensive and reliable presentation of the foundations of the systems constructed by Leśniewski; J. Słupecki, "St. Leśniewski's Protothetics," in *Studia logica*, 1 (1953), 44–112; "S. Leśniewski's Calculus of Names," *ibid.*, 3 (1955), 7–76, which concerns ontology; "Towards a Generalised Mereology of Leśniewski," *ibid.*, 8 (1958), 131–163; B. Sobociński, "O kolejnych uproszczeniach aksjomatyki 'ontologji' Prof. St. Leśniewskiego" ("On Successive Simplifications of the Axiom System of Prof. S. Leśniewski's 'Ontology' "), in *Fragmenty filozoficzne* (Warsaw, 1934), pp. 144–160, available in English in Storrs McCall, ed., *Polish Logic 1920–1939* (Oxford, 1967), pp. 188–200; "L'analyse de l'antinomie Russellienne par Leśniewski," in *Methodos*, 1 (1949), 94–107, 220–228, 308–316; 2 (1950), 237–257; "Studies in Leśniewski's Mereology," in *Polskie towarzystwo naukowe na obczyźnie. Rocznik*, 5 (1955), 34–43; "On Well-Constructed Axiom Systems," *ibid.*, 6 (1956), 54–65; "La génesis de la escuela polaca de lógica," in *Oriente Europeo*, 7 (1957), 83–95; and "On the Single Axioms of Protothetic," in *Notre Dame Journal of Formal Logic*, 1 (1960), 52–73; 2 (1961), 111–126, 129–148, in progress; and A. Tarski, "O wyrazie pierwotnym logistyki," in *Przegląd filozoficzny*, 26 (1923), 68–89, available in English in A. Tarski, *Logic, Semantics, Metamathematics* (Oxford, 1956), pp. 1–23, important for the study of protothetic.

CZESŁAW LEJEWSKI

LE TENNEUR, JACQUES-ALEXANDRE (*b.* Paris, France; *d.* after 1652)

Described as a patrician of Paris on the title page of his principal book, little else is known of Le Tenneur, friend of Mersenne and correspondent of Gassendi. Probably a resident of Paris until the mid-1640's, he was at Clermont-Ferrand (near Puy-de-Dôme) late in 1646, and in 1651 he was counselor to a provincial senate. C. De Waard identifies him as counselor to the Cour des Aydes of Guyenne, but without indicating dates.

All modern authorities agree in attributing to Le Tenneur the *Traité des quantitez incommensurables*, whose author identified himself on its title page only

by the letters I.N.T.Q.L.[1] Mersenne mentioned the *Traité* as in preparation on 15 January 1640 and sent a copy to Haak on 4 September, indicating that it was "by one of my friends." It was directed against Stevin's *L'arithmétique* (Leiden, 1585; ed. A. Girard, 1625), particularly opposing Stevin's treatment of unity as a number. Although Le Tenneur's arguments now seem elementary and conservative, they go to the heart of the foundations of algebra, standing as a final attempt to preserve the classical Greek separation of arithmetic from geometry that Descartes abandoned in 1637. The basic question is whether the unit may properly be considered as divisible. Against Stevin's affirmative answer, Le Tenneur took the view that this would in effect either merely substitute a different unit or deny the existence of any unit relevant to the problem at hand. The bearing of this analysis on the problems of indivisibles and infinitesimals that were then coming to the fore is evident; but a rapid and widespread acceptance of algebraic geometry doomed the classic distinctions, and the book was neglected. Aware of Viète's work and of the need to give symbolic treatment to incommensurables in the classic sense, Le Tenneur included a paraphrase of book X of Euclid's *Elements*, in which he gave the symbolic operations for each proposition. The book ends with an essay, addressed to the Académie Française, proposing that French should be used in science and outlining methods for the coining of terms, reminiscent of Stevin's earlier argument for the use of Dutch.

In January 1648 Mersenne wrote to Le Tenneur asking him to perform the barometric experiment at Puy-de-Dôme later done by F. Perier at Pascal's request. Le Tenneur, who had moved to Tours, replied that it could not be done in winter and expressed the view that, in any event, the level of mercury would not be changed by the ascent.

The importance of Le Tenneur to the history of science, however, depends on another book, *De motu naturaliter accelerato . . .* (1649), in which he showed himself to be the only mathematical physicist of the time who understood precisely Galileo's reasoning in rejecting the proportionality of speeds in free fall to the distances traversed. This subject was hotly debated in the late 1640's between Gassendi and two Jesuits, Pierre Cazré and Honoré Fabri. In 1647 Fermat, who had previously questioned the validity of Galileo's odd-number rule for distances traversed, wrote out for Gassendi a rigorous demonstration of the impossibility of space proportionality, believing that Galileo had deliberately withheld his own. Le Tenneur, who appears not to have seen Fermat's proof, perceived and illustrated the nature of Galileo's use of one-to-one correspondence between the speeds in a given fall from rest and those in its first half.

Le Tenneur's interest in the matter began with a request from Mersenne for a discussion of Cazré's *Physica demonstratio* (1645), which in turn had arisen from his letters to Gassendi opposing the latter's *De motu impresso a motore translato* of 1642. Le Tenneur's critique of Cazré took the form of a *Disputatio physico-mathematicus* sent in manuscript form to Mersenne, probably in mid-1646, and also sent to Cazré or forwarded to him by Mersenne. Gassendi published his own reply to Cazré as *De proportione qua gravia decidentia accelerantur* (1646) and sent a copy to Le Tenneur. Writing on 24 November 1646 to acknowledge this gift, Le Tenneur sent Gassendi a copy of his *Disputatio*. Gassendi replied on 14 December, and on 16 January 1647 Le Tenneur wrote him that Mersenne had mentioned some other Jesuit than Cazré. This was Honoré Fabri, whose *Tractatus physicus de motu locali* (1646) acknowledged the correctness of Galileo's rules for sensible distances only, explaining this in terms of the space–proportionality of insensible quanta of impetus. Baliani had (also in 1646) advanced a similar hypothesis. Two days later, Le Tenneur wrote that Cazré had meanwhile replied to his earlier *Disputatio* and sent the reply to Gassendi with his own rebuttal.

On 12 April 1647 Le Tenneur wrote out a refutation of Fabri's position in the form of a long letter to Mersenne. Fabri contended that the hypotenuse in Galileo's triangle was in ultimate reality a discrete step function (a denticulated line, as he called it) and that the space quanta traversed in true physical instants progressed as the positive integers rather than as the observed odd numbers. Le Tenneur opposed any analysis by physical instants (the medieval *minima naturalia*) on the grounds that if indivisible, such instants implied Galileo's law, whereas if divisible, they fell under Galileo's phrase "in any parts of time" and excluded Fabri's hypothetical increments of velocity added discretely (*simul*).

Mersenne appears to have communicated this letter to Fabri, who published it as an appendix to a new book in 1647, with critical comments. Finally, Le Tenneur wrote out a long reply to Fabri and composed a further treatise of his own in support of Galileo's laws against all his opponents. On 1 January 1649 he submitted it to Gassendi with the idea of publishing it together with his previous writings on the subject if Gassendi approved. Gassendi had meanwhile moved to Aix-en-Provence for his health and did not receive the material until Easter. His enthusiastic letter of endorsement was sent to Le Tenneur on 17 May 1649 and was included as the final item in *De motu accelerato*.

Of all the participants in this wordy dispute, only Le Tenneur correctly reconstructed Galileo's original argument. His book is of further interest for its inclusion of a strictly mathematical derivation of Galileo's odd-number rule by the young Christiaan Huygens, which had been sent by his father to Mersenne. Le Tenneur published it together with a postil predicting great things from Huygens. *De motu accelerato* is of further historical importance for its refutation of Fabri's dictum that no physical instant could be identical with a mathematical point in time, the last stand of orthodox Aristotelian physics and impetus theory against the continuity concept introduced by Galileo. Even Descartes had rejected the idea that in reaching any given speed from rest, a body must first have passed through every lesser speed. His letters to Mersenne on this point may have been the occasion for its having been called to the attention of Le Tenneur.

The only other books by Le Tenneur related to controversies with Jean-Jacques Chifflet over French history and royal genealogy. He sent one of these to Gassendi and in an accompanying letter seems to have considered himself more a historian than a scientist, despite his valuable if neglected contributions to fundamental issues of mathematics and physics in the seventeenth century.

NOTE

1. The attribution, although probably correct, is not yet certain. No early reference to this book includes more than the family name of the author, and the title page suggests the possibility that there may have been an I. N. (or J. N.) Le Tenneur; Gassendi mentioned a brother of Jacques-Alexandre who has not been identified. In the preface, the author expressed his intention of identifying himself after hearing comments on his book; if the same author wrote *De motu accelerato* (1649) mention of the earlier book would be expected in it. Moreover, the vigorous argument for the use of French hardly fits J.-A. Le Tenneur, who thereafter published only in Latin.

BIBLIOGRAPHY

I. Original Works. Le Tenneur's writings are *Traité des quantitez incommensurables* (Paris, 1640); *De motu naturaliter accelerato tractatus physico-mathematicus* (Paris, 1649), one section of which had appeared under the author's initials in H. Fabri (P. Mousnier, ed.), *Metaphysica demonstrativa* (Lyons, 1647); *Veritas vindicata adversus . . . Joan. Jac. Chifletii* (Paris, 1651); and *De sacra ampulla remensi tractatus apologeticus adversus Joan. Jac. Chifletum* (Paris, 1652). Some correspondence between Gassendi and Le Tenneur was published in Gassendi,

Opera omnia, VI (Lyons, 1658). See Adam and Tannery, eds., *Oeuvres de Descartes,* V (Paris, 1903); L. Brunschvig and P. Boutroux, eds., *Oeuvres de B. Pascal,* II (Paris, 1908). Some of Le Tenneur's letters are preserved at Vienne, France, and at the Bibliothèque Nationale, Paris.

II. SECONDARY LITERATURE. For references to and notes about Le Tenneur see *Correspondance du P. Marin Mersenne,* P. Tannery and C. De Waard, eds., IX–XI; most letters between the two men have not yet been published and were not accessible for this article. See also H. Brown, *Scientific Organization in 17th Century France* (New York, 1967), pp. 54–56; S. Drake in *Isis,* **49** (1958), 342–346; **49** (1958), 409–413; *British Journal of the History of Science,* **5** (1970), 34–36; and *Galileo Studies* (Ann Arbor, Mich., 1970), 235–236; W. E. K. Middleton, *History of the Barometer* (Baltimore, 1964), 40, which gives references to papers on the Pascal controversy published by Felix Matthieu in the *Revue de Paris* (1906).

STILLMAN DRAKE

LEURECHON, JEAN (*b.* Bar-le-Duc, France, *ca.* 1591; *d.* Pont-à-Mousson, France, 17 January 1670)

Leurechon was a Jesuit who taught theology, philosophy, and mathematics in the cloister of his order at Bar-le-Duc, Lorraine. Very little is known of his personal life. In his earlier years he wrote several tracts on astronomy and an inconsequential work on geometry.

Leurechon is remembered chiefly for his collection of mathematical recreations, some of which were published under other names. Issued at a time when interest in recreational mathematics was rapidly rising, this work obviously appealed to popular fancy, for it passed through some thirty editions before 1700. Based largely on the work of Bachet de Méziriac, it included, besides many original problems, some taken from Cardano. It served in turn as a foundation for the works of Mydorge, Ozanam, Montucla, and Charles Hutton. For the most part Leurechon borrowed only Bachet's simpler and easier problems, completely bypassing the more significant sections. Leurechon's work was characterized by Montucla as "a pathetic jumble" and by D. E. Smith as "a poor collection of trivialities."

BIBLIOGRAPHY

I. ORIGINAL WORKS. Leurechon's tracts on astronomy include *Pratiques de quelques horloges et du cylindre* (Pont-à-Mousson, 1616); *Ratio facillima describendi quamplurima et omnis generis horologia brevissimo tempore* (Pont-à-Mousson, 1618); and *Discours sur les observations de la comète de 1618* (Paris–Rheims, 1619). His work on geom-

etry was *Selectae propositiones in tota sparsim mathematica pulcherrime propositae* (Pont-à-Mousson, 1622).

His collection of mathematical recreations, published under the pseudonym Hendrik van Etten, was *La récréation mathématique ou entretien facétieux sur plusieurs plaisants problèmes, en fait arithmétique* . . . (Pont-à-Mousson, 1624); 2nd ed., rev. and enl. (Paris, 1626). Many subsequent eds. and translations appeared: the first English trans., by William Oughtred, was *Mathematicall Recreations* (London, 1633).

II. SECONDARY LITERATURE. On Leurechon and his work, see Moritz Cantor, *Vorlesungen über Geschichte der Mathematik,* II (Leipzig, 1913), 673–674; 768–769; and Poggendorff, I, 1438. See also H. Zeitlinger, *Bibliotheca chemico-mathematica* (London, 1921), I, 61; II, 536.

WILLIAM L. SCHAAF

LEVI BEN GERSON (*b.* Bagnols, Gard, France, 1288; *d.* 20 April 1344)

Levi was also called RaLBaG (a monogram of Rabbi Levi ben Gerson) by the Jewish writers and Gersoni, Gersonides, Leo de Bannolis or Balneolis, Leo Judaeus, and Leo Hebraeus (not to be confused with Leone Ebreo [*d.* 1521/1535], author of the *Dialoghi d'Amore*) by Latin writers. He lived in Orange and Avignon, which were not affected by the expulsion of the Jews from France in 1306 by the order of King Philip the Fair. He seems to have maintained good relations with the papal court—the Latin translations of *De sinibus, chordis et arcubus* and *Tractatus instrumenti astronomie* were dedicated to Clement VI in 1342—and with eminent French and Provençal personalities: his *Luḥot* and *De harmonicis numeris* were written at the request of a group of Jews and Christian noblemen and at the request of Philip of Vitry, bishop of Meaux, respectively. It has been insinuated, without foundation, that he embraced Christianity. It is possible that he practiced medicine, although the evidence is scant. He probably knew neither Arabic nor Latin and thus had to base his work on available Hebrew translations.

In 1321 or 1322 Levi finished the *Sefer ha mispar* ("Book of Number"), also called *Maʿaseh ḥosheb* ("Work of the Computer"; see Exodus 26:1). It deals with general principles of arithmetic and algebra and their applications to calculation: summations of series and combinatorial analysis (permutations and combinations). He used mathematical induction in his demonstrations earlier than Francesco Maurolico (1575) and Pascal (*ca.* 1654). He explained place value notation, but instead of figures, he uses Hebrew letters according to their numerical value, as well as sexagesimal fractions.

In 1342 Levi wrote *De harmonicis numeris*, of which only the Latin translation survives. Its purpose was to demonstrate that, except for the pairs 1-2, 2-3, 3-4, and 8-9, it is impossible for two numbers that follow each other to be composed of the factors 2 and 3.

Levi's trigonometrical work is in *De sinibus, chordis et arcubus* (dated 1343) based on the Hebrew text of his *Sefer Tekunah*. He uses chords, sines, versed sines, and cosines but no tangents (known in Europe since 1126). Following Ptolemaic methods, he calculated sine tables with great precision. He also formulated the sine theorem for plane triangles; this theorem had been known in the Orient since the end of the tenth century, but it is not clear whether Levi rediscovered it independently or knew it through Jābir ibn Aflaḥ (twelfth century).

Levi wrote two geometrical works: a commentary on books I–V of Euclid's *Elements* that used the Hebrew translation by Moses ibn Tibbon (Montpellier, 1270)—an attempt to construct a geometry without axioms—and the treatise *Ḥibbur ḥokmat ha-tishboret* ("Science of Geometry"), of which only a fragment has been preserved.

The greatest work by Levi ben Gerson is philosophical in character. It is entitled *Milḥamot Adonai* ("The Wars of the Lord") and is divided into six books. The fifth book deals with astronomy and is composed of three treatises, the first of which is known as *Sefer Tekunah* ("Book of Astronomy"). Completed in 1328 and revised in 1340, it was translated into Latin in the fourteenth century. It is divided into 136 chapters and includes two works that are frequently found separately in the manuscripts: the *Luḥot* (chapter 99), astronomical tables calculated

for the meridian of Ezob (Izop; Orange) in 1320, and his description of the construction and use of the instrument called the Jacob's staff (chapters 4-11). Levi treated this instrument not only in the chapters mentioned (which were translated into Latin by Peter of Alexandria in 1342) but also in two Hebrew poems. In these versions it is called *kelī* ("instrument") and *megalleh 'amūqqōt* ("secretum revelator"; see Job 12:22); on the other hand, one of these two poems bears the subtitle "'al ha-maqel" ("Concerning the Staff") and in it he refers to Jacob's staff (Genesis 32:10). This is the origin of the expression *baculus Jacobi*, used in some Latin manuscripts, and of the misunderstanding that he wanted to attribute his invention to someone called Jacob. The instrument is also called *baculus geometricus, baculus astronomicus*, or *balestilha*. It consists of a graduated rod and a plate that moves along the rod perpendicular to it. In order to measure an angle, the observer must look at both ends of the plate. The angle α is determined solving triangle *ABC*. This instrument helped Levi in his attempts to determine the center of vision in the eye; unfortunately the experiment was not sufficiently precise and Levi concluded that the center of vision is in the crystalline lens, thus agreeing with Galen and Ibn al-Haytham.

Levi's astronomical system began with a critique of the *Almagest* and of al-Biṭrūjī's *Kltāb al-hay'a* (translated into Hebrew in the thirteenth century). His principal sources were al-Battānī (whom he could have known through Abraham bar Ḥiyya), the *Islāh al-Majisṭī* of Jābir ibn Aflaḥ (translated by Moses ibn Tibbon in 1274), Ibn Rushd, and Abraham ibn 'Ezra. He followed the doctrine of al-Farghānī (Hebrew translation by Jacob Anatoli, *ca.* 1231–1235) concerning the motion of the solar apogee. He rejected the planetary systems of Ptolemy and al-Biṭrūjī because he did not feel that they conformed with the data obtained by observation, as in the variations in the apparent sizes of the planets. Thus Levi observed that, according to Ptolemy, the apparent size of Mars must vary sixfold while, according to his own observations, it varies twice. The Ptolemaic epicycles also did not agree with observations (accepting the one of the moon would imply that we see both sides alternately). In the same way Levi rejected the theory of the trepidation of the equinoxes. This theoretical work was accompanied by many years of well-defined observation (1321–1339) in which Levi used his staff and the camera obscura. The use of the camera obscura in astronomy dates back to Ibn al-Haytham and was known in Europe in the second half of the thirteenth century; Levi is distinguished for his careful instructions on how the observations

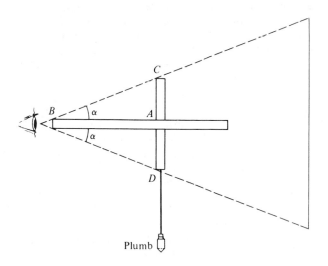

FIGURE 1. Jacob's staff.

should be performed and for his explanation of the theoretical basis of the camera obscura.

The planetary system conceived by Levi contains a mixture of technical considerations with others of a metaphysical character. He postulates the existence of forty-eight spheres, some concentric with the earth and others not. The movement is transmitted from the innermost sphere to the outermost by means of an intermediate nonresistant fluid. The stars are affixed to the last sphere of their own system, and each sphere or system of spheres is moved by an immaterial intelligence. The number of spirits that move the heavens is, then, forty-eight or eight. Within this general framework, Levi investigated particularly the sun and the moon. His lunar model eliminated the use of epicycles; its results were practically equivalent to those of Ptolemy's model at syzygy and quadrature (where Levi believed them to be adequate enough) but an entirely new correction was introduced by him at the octants (where Ptolemaic theory could not be accepted because of systematic discrepancies with observation): there is no evidence to suggest a relationship between Levi and Tycho Brahe concerning the latter's discovery of variation (an inequality that reaches its maximum at octant). It is also clear that Levi's model represented the two first lunar inequalities better than Ptolemy's model did. Finally he eliminated practically all the variations in lunar distance from the earth, for which he rightly criticized Ptolemy's model.

The movements of the planets were less extensively dealt with (chapters 103–135). Levi carefully studied the controversial question concerning the places of Venus and Mercury with respect to the sun (chapters 129–135) without arriving at any definitive conclusion. Finally, one of his greatest contributions to medieval astronomy was his extraordinary enlargement of the Ptolemaic universe—for example, the maximum distance of Venus (Ptolemy, 1,079 earth radii; Levi, 8,971,112 earth radii); the distance of the fixed stars from the center of the earth (Ptolemy, 20,000 earth radii; Levi, $159 \times 10^{12} + 6,515 \times 10^8 + 1,338 \times 10^4 + 944$ earth radii); and the diameter of first-magnitude stars (Ptolemy, $4.5 + 1/20$ earth radii; Levi, more than 328×10^8 earth radii).

A few astrological treatises of Levi have been preserved, including a prediction addressed to Pope Benedict XII in 1339 and his *Prognosticon de conjunctione Saturni et Jovis (et Martis) a.D. 1345*, left unfinished at his death (the Latin translation by Peter of Alexandria and Solomon ben Gerson, Levi's brother, is extant). This conjunction of the three superior planets was also the subject of predictions by John of Murs and Firminus de Bellavalle (Firmin de Beauval). At the outbreak of the black plague of 1348 the conjunction was believed, retrospectively, to be the celestial cause that had corrupted the air.

Levi's work was influential in Europe until the eighteenth century. In the fourteenth century his astronomical tables were used by Jacob ben David Yomtob in constucting his own tables (Perpignan, 1361). It influenced the astrological work of Symon de Covino (*d.* 1367), as well as the astronomical work of Immanuel ben Jacob of Tarascon (*fl. ca.* 1340–1377). In the fifteenth century the *Sefer Tekunah* was praised by Abraham Zacuto (*ca.* 1450–1510); and the treatise *De sinibus* was the model for the *De triangulis* of Regiomontanus (1464; published 1533). The latter, as well as his disciples Bernhard Walther (1430–1504) and Martin Behaim (*d.* 1507), used the Jacob's staff, and it continued to be widely used in navigation, with various improvements, until the middle of the eighteenth century. In the seventeenth century Kepler wrote to his friend Johannes Ramus, asking him to send a copy of the *Sefer Tekunah* to him. There is also a curious cosmographical treatise written in Hebrew by an unknown Roman Jew who cites Levi as being among the greatest authors of the past.

BIBLIOGRAPHY

I. ORIGINAL WORKS. Gerson Lange, *Die Praxis des Rechners* (Frankfurt, 1909), contains an edited German trans. of the *Ma'aseh Ḥosheb;* Joseph Carlebach, *Lewi als Mathematiker* (Berlin, 1910), has an ed. of the *De numeris harmonicis* on pp. 125–144. Maximilian Curtze, "Die Abhandlungen des Levi ben Gerson über Trigonometrie und den Jacobstab," in *Bibliotheca mathematica*, 2nd ser., **12** (1898), 97–112, is a Latin trans. of the *De sinibus* and the *Tractatus instrumenti astronomie*. The eds. of the *Milḥamot Adonai* do not include the *Sefer Tekunah*, which traditionally is considered as a separate work. On the latter see Ernest Renan, "Les écrivains juifs français du XIVe siècle," in *Histoire littéraire de la France*, XXXI (Paris, 1893), 586–644—see esp. pp. 624–641, the Hebrew and Latin texts of the intro. and table of contents of the *Sefer Tekunah;* see also Baldassarre Boncompagni, "Intorno ad un trattato d'aritmetica stampato nel 1478," in *Atti dell' Accademia Pontificia dei Nuovi Lincei* (1863), 741–753, a textual study of three Latin MSS from the above-mentioned work plus some short fragments. Goldstein ("Levi ben Gerson's Lunar Model" quoted below) gives an English translation of the significant passages concerning Levi's lunar theory. On the MSS of the *Sefer Tekunah*, as well as the remaining unpublished works by Levi, see Moritz Steinschneider, *Mathematik bei den Juden* (Leipzig, 1893–1899; Frankfurt, 1901; Hildesheim, 1964).

II. SECONDARY LITERATURE. See F. Cantera Burgos, *El*

judío salamantino Abraham Zacut. Notas para la historia de la astronomía en la España medieval (Madrid, n.d.), pp. 53, 55, 153, 189–190; Pamela H. Espenshade, "A Text on Trigonometry by Levi ben Gerson," in *Mathematics Teacher*, **60** (1967), 628–637; Bernard R. Goldstein, "The Town of Ezob/Aurayca," in *Revue des études juives*, **126** (1967), 269–271; "Preliminary Remarks on Levi ben Gerson's Contributions to Astronomy," in *Proceedings of the Israel Academy of Sciences and Humanities*, **3**, no. 9 (1969), 239–254; *Al-Biṭrūji: On the Principles of Astronomy*, I (New Haven–London, 1971), 40–43; "Levi ben Gerson's Lunar Model," in *Centaurus*, **16** (1972), 257–283; and "Theory and Observation in Medieval Astronomy," in *Isis*, **63** (1972), 39–47; Isidore Loeb, "La ville d'Hysope," in *Revue des études juives*, **1** (1880), 72–82; D. C. Lindberg, "The Theory of Pinhole Images in the Fourteenth Century," in *Archives for History of Exact Sciences*, **6** (1970), 299–325, esp. pp. 303 ff.; José M. Millás Vallicrosa and David Romano, *Cosmografía de un judío romano del siglo XVII* (Madrid–Barcelona, 1954), pp. 20, 33, 65, 70, 76–77, 85, 87; B. A. Rosenfeld, "Dokazatelstva piatogo postulata Evklida srednevekovykh matematikov Khasana Ibn al-Khaisana i Lva Gersonida" ("The Proofs of Euclid's Fifth Postulate by the Medieval Mathematicians Ibn al-Haytham and Levi ben Gerson"), in *Istoriko-matematicheskie issledovaniya*, **11** (1958), 733–782; George Sarton, *Introduction to the History of Science*, III (Baltimore, 1947–1948), 594–607, and the bibliography given there— see also pp. 129, 886, 1116, 1516, 1518; and Lynn Thorndike, *A History of Magic and Experimental Science*, III (New York–London, 1934), 38, 303–305, 309–311.

JULIO SAMSÓ

LEVI-CIVITA, TULLIO (*b*. Padua, Italy, 29 March 1873; *d*. Rome, Italy, 20 December 1941)

The son of Giacomo Levi-Civita, a lawyer who from 1908 was a senator, Levi-Civita was an outstanding student at the *liceo* in Padua. In 1890 he enrolled in the Faculty of Mathematics of the University of Padua. Giuseppe Veronese and Gregorio Ricci Curbastro were among his teachers. He received his diploma in 1894 and in 1895 became resident professor at the teachers' college annexed to the Faculty of Science at Pavia. From 1897 to 1918 Levi-Civita taught rational mechanics at the University of Padua. His years in Padua (where in 1914 he married a pupil, Libera Trevisani) were scientifically the most fruitful of his career. In 1918 he became professor of higher analysis at Rome and, in 1920, of rational mechanics. In 1938, struck by the fascist racial laws against Jews, he was forced to give up teaching.

The breadth of his scientific interests, his scruples regarding the fulfillment of his academic responsibilities, and his affection for young people made Levi-Civita the leader of a flourishing school of mathematicians.

Levi-Civita's approximately 200 memoirs in pure and applied mathematics deal with analytical mechanics, celestial mechanics, hydrodynamics, elasticity, electromagnetism, and atomic physics. His most important contribution to science was rooted in the memoir "Sulle trasformazioni delle equazioni dinamiche" (1896), which was characterized by the use of the methods of absolute differential calculus that Ricci Curbastro had applied only to differential geometry. In the "Méthodes de calcul différentiel absolus et leurs applications," written with Ricci Curbastro and published in 1900 in *Mathematische Annalen*, there is a complete exposition of the new calculus, which consists of a particular algorithm designed to express geometric and physical laws in Euclidean and non-Euclidean spaces, particularly in Riemannian curved spaces. The memoir concerns a very general but laborious type of calculus that made it possible to deal with many difficult problems, including, according to Einstein, the formulation of the general theory of relativity.

Although Levi-Civita had expressed certain reservations concerning relativity in the first years after its formulation (1905), he gradually came to accept the new views. His own original research culminated in 1917 in the introduction of the concept of parallelism in curved spaces that now bears his name; it furnishes a simple law for transporting a vector parallel to itself along a curve in a space of *n* dimensions. With this new concept, absolute differential calculus, having absorbed other techniques, became tensor calculus, now the essential instrument of the unitary relativistic theories of gravitation and electromagnetism. Two of the concept's many applications and generalizations were in the "geometry of paths," which extends the concept of Riemannian variety, and in the theory of spaces with affine and projective connections, which is used with the geometry for a complete representation of electromagnetic phenomena in the framework of general relativity.

In studying the stability of the phenomena of motion, Levi-Civita used a general method, which, by means of a periodic solution of a first-order differential system, restores stability or instability to the study of certain point transformations. He ascertained that periodic solutions, in a first approximation of apparent stability, prove instead to be unstable. Another of Levi-Civita's contributions to analytical mechanics was the general theory of stationary motions, in which moving bodies passing the same spot always do so at the same speed. The theory enabled him to find with a uniform method all the known cases of stationary motion and also to discover new ones.

From 1906 Levi-Civita's memoirs in hydrodynamics, his favorite field, deal with the resistance of a liquid to the translational motion of an immersed solid; he resolved the problem through the general integration of the equations for irrotational flows past a solid body, allowing for the formation of a cavity behind it. His general theory of canal waves originated in a memoir written in 1925.

In related memoirs (1903–1916) Levi-Civita contributed to celestial mechanics in the study of the three-body problem: the determination of the motion of three bodies, considered as reduced to their centers of mass and subject to mutual Newtonian attraction. In 1914–1916 he succeeded in eliminating the singularities presented at the points of possible collisions, past or future. His results furnished a rigorous solution to the classic problem—which, by indirect method and by transcending dynamic equations, Karl F. Sundmann had reached in 1912, as Levi-Civita himself admitted.

His research in relativity led Levi-Civita to mathematical problems suggested by atomic physics, which in the 1920's was developing outside the traditional framework: the general theory of adiabatic invariants, the motion of a body of variable mass, the extension of the Maxwellian distribution to a system of corpuscles, and Schrödinger's equations.

BIBLIOGRAPHY

I. ORIGINAL WORKS. All of Levi-Civita's memoirs and notes published between 1893 and 1928 were collected in his *Opere matematiche. Memorie e note*, 4 vols. (Bologna, 1954–1960). Other works include *Questioni di meccanica classica e relativistica* (Bologna, 1924), also in German trans. (Berlin, 1924); *Lezioni di calcolo differenziale assoluto* (Rome, 1925); *Lezioni di meccanica razionale*, 2 vols. (Bologna, 1926–1927; 2nd ed., 1930), written with Ugo Amaldi; and *Fondamenti di meccanica relativistica* (Bologna, 1928).

II. SECONDARY LITERATURE. See the following, listed chronologically: Corrado Segre, "Relazione sul concorso al premio reale per la matematica, del 1907," in *Atti dell'Accademia nazionale dei Lincei. Rendiconti delle sedute solenni*, **2** (1908), 410–424; Albert Einstein, "Die Grundlage der allgemeinen Relativitätstheorie," in *Annalen der Physik*, 4th ser., **49** (1916), 769; "Tullio Levi-Civita," in *Annuario della Pontificia Accademia delle Scienze*, **1** (1936–1937), 496–511, with a complete list of his memberships in scientific institutions and of his academic honors; and Ugo Amaldi, "Commemorazione del socio Tullio Levi-Civita," in *Atti dell'Accademia nazionale dei Lincei, Rendiconti. Classe di scienze fisiche, matematiche e naturali*, 8th ser., **1** (1946), 1130–1155, with a complete bibliography.

MARIO GLIOZZI

LEVINSON, NORMAN (*b*. Boston, Massachusetts, 11 August 1912; *d*. Boston, 10 October 1975)

Levinson entered the Massachusetts Institute of Technology in 1929, having graduated from Revere High School earlier that year. In June 1934 he received the B.S. and M.S. degrees in electrical engineering. At that time he had completed practically every graduate course offered by the department of mathematics and had obtained results that H. B. Phillips, head of the department, described as "sufficient for a doctor's thesis of unusual excellence." Among these courses was Fourier series and integrals, given in the fall of 1933–1934 by Norbert Wiener. Wiener had given Levinson a copy of the unpublished manuscript "Fourier Transforms in the Complex Domain," by R. E. A. C. Paley and Wiener, for revision. When Levinson found a gap in a proof and was able to prove a lemma that corrected it, Wiener typed the proof, affixed Levinson's name to the paper, and submitted it to a journal for him.

This incident began a friendship that lasted the rest of their lives. Wiener and Phillips arranged an MIT Redfield traveling fellowship for Levinson for the year 1934–1935, which Levinson spent at Cambridge University, where he studied under the distinguished mathematical analyst G. H. Hardy. In June 1935 he received the doctorate in mathematics from MIT. Levinson was then awarded a National Research Council fellowship for the years 1935–1937, which he spent at the Institute for Advanced Study and Princeton University under the supervision of John von Neumann. Upon being offered an instructorship in mathematics at MIT, Levinson was released from his fellowship, went to MIT in February 1937, and remained there for the rest of his life, except for periods on leave. In February 1938 he married Zipporah Wallman.

Levinson's early work centers on results related to the Paley-Wiener book (published in 1934). Levinson sharpened many results and obtained significant new ones. In 1940 the American Mathematical Society published his work in this area as *Gap and Density Theorems*. After its appearance Levinson decided to shift his field to nonlinear differential equations. He soon obtained substantial mathematical results, and his outstanding contributions to differential equations were recognized by the American Mathematical Society in 1954 when it awarded him the Bôcher Prize. In addition, Levinson's work touched many areas of mathematical analysis and its applications. In the period 1946–1947 he wrote two papers that simplified and explained Wiener's work on stationary time series, which had a significant impact on random signal theory in general and on geophysical signal processing in particular. His work contributed to some of the improved petroleum prospecting methods that made possible the discovery of virtually all the offshore oil fields found since 1960, as well as most of the onshore discoveries.

Levinson did work in probability, quantum mechanics, complex programming, and analytic number theory. In 1967 he became the fortieth mathematician to be elected to the National Academy of Sciences, and in 1971 he was appointed Institute professor at MIT. Also in 1971 he was awarded the Chauvenet Prize of the Mathematical Association of America. The paper for which he received this prize was in analytical number theory and served as a precursor to the papers he wrote on the Riemann hypothesis. Levinson greatly advanced this theory and was on the threshold of perhaps his greatest achievement in mathematics at the time of his death.

BIBLIOGRAPHY

I. ORIGINAL WORKS. "A Heuristic Exposition of Wiener's Mathematical Theory of Prediction and Filtering," in *Journal of Mathematics and Physics*, **26** (1947), 110–119; "The Wiener RMS (Root Mean Square) Error Criterion in Filter Design and Prediction," in *J. Math. Phys.*, **25** (1947), 261–278; and *Gap and Density Theorems* (New York, 1940).

II. SECONDARY LITERATURE. E. A. Robinson, "A Historical Perspective of Spectrum Estimation," in *Proceedings of the IEEE*, **70**, no. 9 (1982), 885–907.

ENDERS A. ROBINSON

LÉVY, MAURICE (*b.* Ribeauvillé, France, 28 February 1838; *d.* Paris, France, 30 September 1910)

Maurice Lévy had a distinguished career as a practicing engineer, teacher, and researcher. He studied at the École Polytechnique from 1856 to 1858 and at the École des Ponts et Chaussées. After graduating he served for several years in the provinces and continued his studies. In 1867 he was awarded the *docteur ès sciences* and in 1872 was assigned to the navigation service of the Seine in the region of Paris. In 1880 he became chief government civil engineer and, in 1885, inspector general. At the same time Lévy pursued an academic career. From 1862 to 1883 he served as *répétiteur* in mechanics at the École Polytechnique. In 1875 he was appointed professor of applied mechanics at the École Centrale des Arts et Manufactures, and in 1885 he became professor of analytic and celestial mechanics at the

Collège de France. Lévy was elected to the Académie des Sciences in 1883 and served as president of the Société Philomatique in 1880.

Lévy's research ranged over projective and differential geometry, mechanics, kinematics, hydraulics, and hydrodynamics. Of his two theses, the first, influenced by the work of Gabriel Lamé, deals with orthogonal curvilinear coordinates; the second is on the theory and application of liquid motion. He often returned to the question of elasticity, and his writings on the subject include a book published in 1873. His other works include theoretical treatises on energy and hydrodynamics, as well as more practical ones on boat propulsion.

Lévy considered his most significant work to be that on graphical statics (1874), which was an attempt to apply the methods of projective geometry, particularly the theory of geometric transformations, to problems of statics. It was directed toward engineers and was very popular, going through three editions.

BIBLIOGRAPHY

I. ORIGINAL WORKS. A complete bibliography is in Poggendorff, III, 804–805; IV, 876–877; and V, 737. Lévy's two theses are "Sur une transformation des coordonnées curvilignes orthogonales, et sur les coordonnées curvilignes comprenant une famille quelconque de surfaces du second ordre," in *Journal de l'École polytechnique*, **26** (1870), 157–200; and *Essai théorique et appliqué sur le mouvement des liquides*, published separately (Paris, 1867). His books are *Étude d'un système de barrage mobile* (Paris, 1873); *Application de la théorie mathématique de l'élasticité à l'étude de systèmes articulés* (Paris, 1873); *La statique graphique et ses applications aux constructions*, with atlas (Paris, 1874; 2nd ed., 4 vols., Paris, 1886–1888; 3rd ed., 1913–1918); *Sur le principe d'énergie* (Paris, 1890), written with G. Pavie; *Étude des moyens mécanique et électrique de traction des bateaux, Partie I: Halage funiculaire* (Paris, 1894); *Théorie des marées* (Paris, 1898); and *Éléments de cinématique et de mécanique* (Paris, 1902).

II. SECONDARY LITERATURE. There is very little available beyond the article in *La grande encyclopédie*, XXII, 148; and the obituary by Émile Picard in *Comptes rendus hebdomadaires des séances de l'Académie des sciences*, **151** (1910), 603–606.

ELAINE KOPPELMAN

LEXELL, ANDERS JOHAN (*b.* Åbo, Sweden [now Turku, Finland], 24 December 1740; *d.* St. Petersburg, Russia, 11 December 1784)

Lexell was the son of Jonas Lexell, a city councillor and jeweler, and his wife, Magdalena Catharina

Björckegren. He graduated from the University of Åbo in 1760 as bachelor of philosophy and became assistant professor of Uppsala Nautical School in 1763 and professor of mathematics in 1766. Invited to work at the St. Petersburg Academy of Sciences on the recommendation of the Swedish astronomer P. W. Wargentin in 1768, he was appointed adjunct in 1769 and professor of astronomy in 1771. His research soon made him well-known. In 1775 the Swedish government offered him a professorship at the University of Åbo which would permit him to proceed with his work in St. Petersburg until 1780; but Lexell preferred to remain in Russia. He spent 1780–1782 traveling in Western Europe; and his letters to J. A. Euler, permanent secretary of the Academy, contain valuable information on scientific life in Germany, France, and England. (These letters are kept at the Archives of the U.S.S.R. Academy of Sciences, Leningrad.)

After Leonhard Euler's death in 1783, Lexell for a short time held Euler's professorship of mathematics, but Lexell himself died the following year. Lexell was a member of the Academy of Sciences in Stockholm, the Society of Sciences in Uppsala (1763), and a corresponding member of the Paris Académie des Sciences (1776).

At St. Petersburg Lexell immediately became one of the closest associates of Leonhard Euler. Under the famous mathematician's supervision he and W.-L. Krafft and J. A. Euler helped to prepare Euler's *Theoria motuum lunae, nova methodo pertractata* (1772) for publication. Euler's influence upon Lexell's scientific activity was considerable; but the latter's works were carried out independently.

On 3 June 1769 the St. Petersburg Academy conducted observations of the transit of Venus at many sites in Russia. Lexell took an active part in the organization and processing of the observations. Using L. Euler's method he calculated (1) the solar parallax to be $8''.68$ (compared to today's value of $8''.80$). No less interesting was Lexell's determination of the orbits of the 1769 comet (2) and especially of the comet discovered in 1770 by Messier (3). Lexell established the period of the latter on its elliptical orbit as five and a half years; this was the first known short revolution-period comet. Passing near Jupiter and its satellites the comet exerted no influence upon their motion; Lexell thus concluded that the masses of comets are rather small in spite of their enormous sizes. Lexell's comet, which had not been observed before 1770, has not been seen again; probably it lost its gaseous coat and become invisible. Still more important was Lexell's investigation of the orbit of the moving body discovered by W. Herschel on 13 March

1781 and initially regarded as a comet. Lexell's calculations showed that this heavenly body was a new planet (Uranus), nearly twice as far from the sun as Saturn (4). Moreover, Lexell pointed out that perturbations in the new planet's motion could not be explained by the action of the known members of the solar system and stated the hypothesis that they must be caused by another, more remote planet. This hypothesis proved correct when Neptune was discovered in 1846 on the basis of the calculations of J. Adams and U. Le Verrier.

Lexell's mathematical works are devoted to problems of analysis and geometry. Following Euler he elaborated the method of integrating factor as applied to higher order differential equations (1771). He gave a solution of linear systems of second order differential equations with constant coefficients (1778, 1783); suggested a classification of elliptic integrals (1778); calculated integrals of some irrational functions by reducing them to integrals of rational functions (1785).

Lexell for the first time constructed a general system of polygonometry (5), e.g., of trigonometrical solution of plane n-gons on the given $2n - 3$ sides and angles between them, provided that at least $n - 2$ elements are sides. These investigations formed a natural sequel to and generalization of the works on trigonometrical solution of quadrangles published shortly before by J.-H. Lambert (1770), J. T. Mayer (1773), and S. Björnssen (1780). Lexell based solutions of all the problems on two principal equations obtained when the sides of a polygon are projected on the two normal (to one another) axes situated in its plane, provided that one of them coincides with some side. From these equations he deduced others effective in the solution of triangles and quadrangles on certain given elements, suggested analogous formulae for pentagons, hexagons, and heptagons and stated considerations relevant to classification and solution of problems in the general case. He also considered, though in less detail, the problem of solution of n-gons on diagonals and on angles they form with sides. After Lexell polygonometry was also worked out by S. L'Huillier (1789).

Lexell considerably enriched spherical geometry and trigonometry. Especially brilliant is his theorem discovered no later than 1778 but published only in 1784: the geometric locus of the vertices of spherical triangles with the same base and equal area are arcs of two small circles whose extremities are points diametrically opposite to the extremities of the common base (6).

In his two articles which were published posthumously (7, 8), Lexell established other properties of small circles on the sphere and deduced a number of new propositions of spherical trigonometry in which he generalized Heron's and Ptolemy's theorems for the sphere and suggested elegant formulae for defining the radii of circumference of circles inscribed in spherical triangles or quadrangles and circumscribed about them. Works by St. Petersburg academicians N. Fuss and F. T. Schubert on spherical geometry and trigonometry were close to these investigations.

Five unpublished papers on geometry by Lexell are preserved in the Archives of the Academy of Sciences in Leningrad (18).

BIBLIOGRAPHY

I. Original Works.

1. *Disquisitio de investiganda vera quantitate parallaxeos Solis ex transitu Veneris ante discum solis anno 1769* (St. Petersburg, 1772).

2. *Recherches et calculs sur la vraie orbite elliptique de la comète de l'an 1769 et son temps périodique* (St. Petersburg, 1770), written with L. Euler.

3. *Réflexions sur le temps périodique des comètes en général et principalement sur celui de la comète observée en 1770* (St. Petersburg, 1772).

4. *Recherches sur la nouvelle planète découverte par Mr Herschel* (St. Petersburg, 1783).

5. "De resolutione polygonorum rectilineorum," in *Novi Commentarii Ac. Sc. Petropolitanae*, **19** (1774), 1775, 184–236; **20** (1775), 1776, 80–122.

6. "Solutio problematis geometrici ex doctrina sphaericorum," in *Acta Ac. Sc. Petropolitanae*, **5**, 1 (1781), 1784, 112–126.

7. "De proprietatibus circulorum in superficie sphaerica descriptorum," *ibid.*, **6**, 1 (1782), 1786, 58–103.

8. "Demonstratio nonnullorum theorematum ex doctrina sphaerica," *ibid.*, **6**, 2 (1782), 1786, 85–95.

II. Secondary Literature.

9. "Précis de la vie de M. Lexell," in *Nova acta Ac. Sc. Petropolitanae*, **2** (1784), 1788, 12–15.

10. J.-C. Poggendorf, *Biographisch-Literarisches Handwörterbuch zur Geschichte der exacten Wissenschaften*, 1 (Leipzig, 1863), 1444–1446, contains bibliography. (See also 13.)

11. *Nordisk Familjebok Konversationslexikon och realencyklopedi*, IX (Stockholm, 1885), 1189–1191.

12. M. Cantor, *Vorlesungen über Geschichte der Mathematik*, IV (Leipzig, 1908), see Index.

13. O. V. Dinze and K. I. Shafranovski, *Matematika v izdaniakh Akademii nauk* ("Mathematical Works Published by Academy of Sciences") (Moscow–Leningrad, 1936).

14. *Svenska män och kvinnor. Biografisk uppslagswork*, IV (Stockholm, 1948), 553.

15. *Istoria Akademii nauk SSSR* ("History of the Academy of Sciences of the U.S.S.R."), I (Moscow–Leningrad, 1958), see Index.

16. V. I. Lysenko, "Raboty po poligonometrii v Rossii XVIII v." ("Works on Polygonometry in Russia in the XVIII Century"), in *Istorico-matematicheskie issledovania*, **12** (1959), 161–178.

17. *Idem*, "O rabotakh peterburgskikh akademikov A. I. Lexella, N. I. Fussa u F. I. Shuberta po sfericheskoi geometrii i sfericheskoi trigonometrii" ("On the Works of Petersburg Academicians A. I. Lexell, N. I. Fuss, and F. T. Schubert on Spherical Geometry and Trigonometry"), in *Trudy Instituta istorii estestvoznania i tekhniki*, **34** (1960), 384–414.

18. *Idem*, "O neopublikovannykh rukopisiakh po geometrii akademikov A. I. Lexella i N. I. Fussa" ("On the Unpublished Works of Academicians A. I. Lexell and N. I. Fuss on Geometry"), in *Voprosy istorii estestvoznania i tekhniki*, **9** (1960), 116–120.

19. *Idem*, "Iz istorii pervoi peterburgskoi matematicheskoi shkoly" ("On the History of the First Mathematical School in St. Petersburg"), in *Trudy Instituta istorii estestvoznania i tekhniki*, **43** (1961), 182–205.

20. A. P. Youschkevitch, *Istoria matematiki v Rossii do 1917 goda* ("History of Mathematics in Russia Until 1917") (Moscow, 1968), see Index.

A. T. Grigorian
A. P. Youschkevitch

L'HOSPITAL (L'HÔPITAL), GUILLAUME-FRANÇOIS-ANTOINE DE (Marquis de Sainte-Mesme, Comte d'Entremont) (*b.* Paris, France, 1661; *d.* Paris, 2 February 1704)

The son of Anne-Alexandre de L'Hospital and of Elizabeth Gobelin, L'Hospital served for a time as a cavalry officer but resigned from the army because of nearsightedness. From that time onwards he devoted his energies entirely to mathematics. He married Marie-Charlotte de Romilley de La Chesnelaye, who bore him one son and three daughters.

L'Hospital's mathematical talents were recognized when he was still a boy. It is reported that when he was only fifteen years of age he solved, much to the surprise of his elders, a problem on the cycloid which had been put forward by Pascal. Later he contributed solutions to several problems posed by Jean (Johann) Bernoulli, among them the problem of the brachistochrone, which was solved at the same time by three others—Newton, Leibniz, and Jacques (Jakob) Bernoulli. His memory has survived in the name of the rule for finding the limiting value of a fraction whose numerator and denominator tend to zero. However, in his own time, and for several generations after his death, his fame was based on his book *Analyse des infiniment petits pour l'intelligence des lignes courbes* (1st ed., 1696, 2nd ed. 1715). Following the classical custom, the book starts with a set of definitions and axioms. Thus, a *variable* quantity is defined as one that increases or decreases continuously while a *constant* quantity remains the same while others change. The *difference* (differential) is defined as the infinitely small portion by which a variable quantity increases or decreases continuously. Of the two axioms, the first postulates that quantities which differ only by infinitely small amounts may be substituted for one another, while the second states that a curve may be thought of as a polygonal line with an infinite number of infinitely small sides such that the angle between adjacent lines determines the curvature of the curve. Following the axioms, the basic rules of the differential calculus are given and exemplified. The second chapter applies these rules to the determination of the tangent to a curve in a given point. While many examples are given, the approach is perfectly general, that is, it applies to arbitrary curves or to the relation between two arbitrary curves. The third chapter deals with maximum-minimum problems and includes examples drawn from mechanics and from geography. Next comes a treatment of points of inflection and of cusps. This involves the introduction of higher-order differentials, each supposed infinitely small compared to its predecessor. Later chapters deal with evolutes and with caustics. L'Hospital's rule is given in chapter 9.

The *Analyse des infiniment petits* was the first textbook of the differential calculus. The existence of several commentaries on it—one by Varignon (1725)—attests to its popularity. The question of its intellectual ownership has been much debated. Jean Bernoulli, who is known to have instructed L'Hospital in the calculus about 1691, complained after L'Hospital's death that he (Bernoulli) had not been given enough credit for his contributions. L'Hospital himself, in the introduction to his books, freely acknowledges his indebtedness to Leibniz and to the Bernoulli brothers. On the other hand, he states that he regards the foundations provided by him as his own idea, although they also have been credited by some to Jean Bernoulli. However, these foundations can be found, less explicitly, also in Leibniz, although Leibniz made it clear that he did not accept L'Hospital's Platonistic views on the reality of infinitely small and infinitely large quantities.

At his death L'Hospital left the completed manuscript of a second book, *Traité analytique des sections coniques et de leur usage pour la résolution des équations dans les problèmes tant déterminés qu'indéterminés.* It was published in 1720. L'Hospital had also planned to write a continuation to his *Analyse des infiniment petits* which would have dealt with the integral calculus, but he dropped this project in deference to Leibniz, who had let him know that he had similar intentions.

L'Hospital was a major figure in the early development of the calculus on the continent of Europe. He advanced its cause not only by his scientific works but also by his many contacts, including correspondence with Leibniz, with Jean Bernoulli, and with Huygens. Fontenelle tells us that it was he who introduced Huygens to the new calculus.

According to the testimony of his contemporaries, L'Hospital possessed a very attractive personality, being, among other things, modest and generous, two qualities which were not widespread among the mathematicians of his time.

BIBLIOGRAPHY

L'Hospital's principal works are *Analyse des infiniment petits pour l'intelligence des lignes courbes* (Paris, 1696; 2nd ed., 1715); and the posthumous *Traité analytique des sections coniques et de leur usage pour la résolution des équations dans les problèmes tant déterminés qu'indéterminés* (Paris, 1720).

On his life and work, see the *éloge* by Fontenelle in the *Histoires* of the Paris Academy of Sciences for 1704, p. 125, and in Fontenelle's *Oeuvres diverses*, III (The Hague, 1729); J. E. Montucla, *Histoire des mathématiques*, II (Paris, 1758), 396; O. J. Rebel, *Der Briefwechsel zwischen Johann (I.) Bernoulli und dem Marquis de l'Hospital* (Heidelberg, 1932); and P. Schafheitlin, ed., *Die Differentialrechnung von Johann Bernoulli aus den Jahren 1691–1692*, Ostwalds Klassiker der Exacten Wissenschaften no. 211 (Leipzig, 1924).

ABRAHAM ROBINSON

L'HUILLIER (or LHUILIER), SIMON-ANTOINE-JEAN (*b.* Geneva, Switzerland, 24 April 1750; *d.* Geneva, 28 March 1840)

L'Huillier, the fourth child of Laurent L'Huillier and his second wife, Suzanne-Constance Matte, came from a family of jewelers and goldsmiths originally from Mâcon. In 1691 they became citizens of Geneva, where they had found refuge at the time of the revocation of the Edict of Nantes. Attracted to mathematics at an early age, L'Huillier refused a relative's offer to bequeath him a part of his fortune if the young man consented to follow an ecclesiastical career. After brilliant secondary studies he attended the mathematics courses given at the Calvin Academy by Louis Bertrand, a former student of Leonhard Euler. He also followed the physics courses of Georges-Louis Le Sage, his famous relative, who gave him much advice and encouragement. Through Le Sage he obtained a position as tutor in the Rilliet-Plantamour family, with whom he stayed for two years. At Le Sage's prompting, in 1773 he sent to the *Journal encyclopédique* a "Lettre en réponse aux objections élevées contre la gravitation newtonienne."

Le Sage had had as a student and then as a collaborator Christoph Friedrich Pfleiderer, who later taught mathematics at Tübingen. In 1766, on the recommendation of Le Sage, Pfleiderer was named professor of mathematics and physics at the military academy in Warsaw recently founded by King Stanislaus II. He was subsequently appointed to the commission in charge of preparing textbooks for use in Polish schools. In 1775 he sent the commission's plans for a textbook contest to Le Sage, who tried to persuade L'Huillier to submit a proposal for a physics text, but the latter preferred to compete in mathematics. He rapidly drew up an outline, sent it to Warsaw, and won the prize. The king sent his congratulations to the young author, and Prince Adam Czartoryski offered him a post as tutor to his son, also named Adam, at their residence in Puławy.

L'Huillier accepted and spent the best years of his life in Poland, from 1777 to 1788. His pedagogical duties did not prevent him from writing his mathematics course, which he put in finished form with the aid of Pfleiderer, and which was translated into Polish by the Abbé Andrzej Gawroński, the king's reader. L'Huillier had an unusually gifted pupil and proved to be an excellent teacher. He had numerous social obligations arising from his situation (including hunting parties), but he still found time to compose several memoirs and to compete in 1786 in the Berlin Academy's contest on the theory of mathematical infinity. The jury, headed by Lagrange, awarded him the prize.

L'Huillier returned home in 1789 and found his native country in a state of considerable agitation. Fearing revolutionary disturbances, he decided to stay with his friend Pfleiderer in Tübingen, where he remained until 1794. Although offered a professorship of mathematics at the University of Leiden in 1795, L'Huillier entered the competition for the post left vacant in Geneva by his former teacher Louis Bertrand. In 1795 he was appointed to the Geneva Academy (of which he soon became rector) and held the chair of mathematics without interruption until his retirement in 1823. Also in 1795 he married Marie Cartier, by whom he had one daughter and one son.

Whereas the Poles found L'Huillier distinctly puritanical, his fellow citizens of Geneva reproached him for his lack of austerity and his whimsicality, although the latter quality never went beyond putting geometric theorems into verse and writing ballads on the number three and on the square root of minus one. Toward the end of his career Charles-François Sturm was among his students.

L'Huillier was also involved in the political life of Geneva. He was a member of the Legislative Council, over which he presided in 1796, and a member of the Representative Council from its creation. His scientific achievements earned him membership in the Polish Educational Society, corresponding memberships in the academies of Berlin, Göttingen, and St. Petersburg, and in the Royal Society, and an honorary professorship at the University of Leiden.

L'Huillier's extensive and varied scientific work bore the stamp of an original intellect even in its most elementary components; and while it did not possess the subtlety of Sturm's writings, it surpassed those of Bertrand in its vigor. L'Huillier's excellent textbooks on algebra and geometry were used for many years in Polish schools. His treatise in Latin on problems of maxima and minima greatly impressed the geometer Jacob Steiner half a century later. L'Huillier also considered the problem, widely discussed at the time, of the minimum amount of wax contained in honeycomb cells. While in Poland he sent articles to the Berlin Academy, as well as the prize-winning memoir of 1786: *Exposition élémentaire des principes des calculs supérieurs*. Printed at the Academy's expense, the memoir was later discussed at length by Montucla in his revised *Histoire des mathématiques* and was examined in 1966 by E. S. Shatunova. In this work, which L'Huillier sent to Berlin with the motto "Infinity is the abyss in which our thoughts vanish," e presented a pertinent critique of Fontenelle's conceptions and even of Euler's, and provided new insights into the notion of limit, its interpretation, and its use. Baron J. F. T. Maurice recognized the exemplary rigor of L'Huillier's argumentation, although he regretted, not unjustifiably, that it "was accompanied by long-winded passages that could have been avoided."

In 1796 L'Huillier sent to the Berlin Academy the algebraic solution of the generalized Pappus problem. Euler, Fuss, and Lexell had found a geometric solution in 1780, and Lagrange had discovered an algebraic solution for the case of the triangle in 1776. L'Huillier based his contribution on the method used by Lagrange. More remarkable, however, were the four articles on probabilities, written with Pierre Prévost, that L'Huillier published in the *Mémoires de l'Académie de Berlin* of 1796 and 1797. Commencing with the problem of an urn containing black and white balls that are withdrawn and not replaced, the authors sought to determine the composition of the contents of the urn from the balls drawn. In this type of question concerning the probabilities of causes, they turned to the works of Jakob Bernoulli, De Moivre, Bayes and Laplace, their goal being clearly to find a demonstration of the principle that Laplace stated as follows and that L'Huillier termed the etiological principle: "If an event can be produced by a number n of different causes, the probabilities of the existence of these causes taken from the event are among themselves as the probabilities of the event taken from these causes." The four articles are of considerable interest, and Isaac Todhunter mentions them in his *History of the Mathematical Theory of Probability.*

The two-volume *Éléments raisonnés d'algèbre* that L'Huillier wrote for his Geneva students in 1804 was really a sequel to his texts for Polish schools. The first volume, composed of eight chapters, was concerned solely with first- and second-degree equations. One chapter was devoted to an account of Diophantine analysis. Volume II (chapters 9–22) treated progressions, logarithms, and combinations and went as far as fourth-degree equations. A chapter on continued fractions was based on the works of Lagrange and of Legendre; another concerned the method of indeterminate coefficients. Questions of calculus were discussed in an appendix. The main value of these two volumes lay in the author's clear exposition and judicious selection of exercises, for some of which he furnished solutions.

L'Huillier's last major work appeared in 1809 in Paris and Geneva. Dedicated to his former pupil Adam Czartoryski, who was then minister of public education in Russia, it dealt with geometric loci in the plane (straight line and circle) and in space (sphere). Between 1810 and 1813 L'Huillier was an editor of the *Annales de mathématiques pures et appliquées* and wrote seven articles on plane and spherical geometry and the construction of polyhedrons.

BIBLIOGRAPHY

I. ORIGINAL WORKS. L'Huillier's writings include *Éléments d'arithmétique et de géométrie* . . . (Warsaw, 1778), partly translated by Gawroński as *Geometrya dla szkoł narodowych* (Warsaw, 1780) and *Algiebra dla szkoł narodowych* (Warsaw, 1782); "Mémoire sur le minimum de cire des alvéoles des abeilles, et en particulier un minimum minimorum relatif à cette matière," in *Mémoires de l'Académie Royale des sciences et belles-lettres de Berlin* (1781), 277–300; *De relatione mutua capacitatis et terminorum figurarum seu de maximis et minimis* (Warsaw, 1782); "Théorème sur les solides plano-superficiels," in *Mémoires de l'Académie Royale des sciences et belles-lettres de Berlin* (1786–1787), 423–432; *Exposition élémentaire des principes des calculs supérieures,* . . . (Berlin, 1787); "Sur la décomposition en facteurs de la somme et de la différence de deux puissances à exposants quelconques de la base des logarithmes hyperboliques . . .," in *Mémoires de l'Académie Royale des sciences et belles-lettres de Berlin* (1788–1789), 326–368; *Polygonométrie et abrégé d'isopérimétrie élémentaire* (Geneva, 1789); *Examen du mode*

d'élection proposé à la Convention nationale de France et adopté à Genève (Geneva, 1794); and *Principiorum calculi differentialis et integralis expositio elementaris* (Tübingen, 1795).

See also "Solution algébrique du problème suivant: A un cercle donné, inscrire un polygone dont les côtés passent par des points donnés," in *Mémoires de l'Académie Royale des sciences et belles-lettres de Berlin* (1796), 94–116; "Sur les probabilités," *ibid.,* Cl. de math., 117–142, written with Pierre Prévost; "Mémoire sur l'art d'estimer les probabilités des causes par les effets," *ibid.,* Cl. de phil. spéc., 3–24, written with Pierre Prévost; "Remarques sur l'utilité et l'étendue du principe par lequel on estime la probabilité des causes," *ibid.,* 25–41, written with Pierre Prévost; "Mémoire sur l'application du calcul des probabilités à la valeur du témoignage," *ibid.* (1797), Cl. de phil. spéc., 120–152, written with Pierre Prévost; *Précis d'arithmétique par demandes et réponses à l'usage des écoles primaires* (Geneva, 1797); *Éléments raisonnés d'algèbre publiés à l'usage des étudiants en philosophie,* 2 vols. (Geneva, 1804); *Éléments d'analyse géométrique et d'analyse algébrique* (Geneva–Paris, 1809); and "Analogies entre les triangles, rectangles, rectilignes et sphériques," in *Annales de mathématiques pures et appliquées,* **1** (1810–1811), 197–201.

II. SECONDARY LITERATURE. The first articles on L'Huillier, which appeared during his lifetime, were Jean Sénebier, *Histoire littéraire de Genève,* III (Geneva, 1786), 216–217; and J.-M. Quérard, *France littéraire,* V (Paris, 1833), 295. Shortly after his death there appeared Auguste de La Rive, *Discours sur l'instruction publique* (Geneva, 1840); and "Discours du prof. de Candolle à la séance publique de la Société des arts du 13 août 1840," in *Procès-verbaux des séances annuelles de la Société pour l'avancement des arts,* **4** (1840), 10–15. Brief articles are in Haag, *France protestante,* VII (Paris, 1857), 85; and A. de Montet, *Dictionnaire biographique des Genevois et des Vaudois,* II (Lausanne, 1878), 66–68.

The best account of L'Huillier's life and work is Rudolf Wolf, *Biographien zur Kulturgeschichte der Schweiz,* I (Zurich, 1858), 401–422. See also L. Isely, *Histoire des sciences mathématiques dans la Suisse française* (Neuchâtel, 1901), pp. 160–167.

More recent publications are Samuel Dickstein, "Przyczynek do biografji Szymona Lhuiliera (1750–1840)," in *Kongres matematyków krajów słowiańskich. sprawozdanie* (Warsaw, 1930), pp. 111–118; Émile L'Huillier, *Notice généalogique sur la famille L'Huillier de Genève* (Geneva, 1957); Emanuel Rostworowski, "La Suisse et la Pologne au XVIIIe siècle," in *Échanges entre la Pologne et la Suisse du XIVe au XIXe siècle* (Geneva, 1965), pp. 182–185; and E. S. Shatunova, "Teoria grani Simona Luilera" ("Simon L'Huillier's Theory of Limits"), in *Istoriko-matematicheskie issledovaniya,* **17** (1966), 325–331.

A. P. Youschkevitch discusses L'Huillier's 1786 prizewinning memoir in an essay, "The Mathematical Theory of the Infinite," in Charles C. Gillispie, *Lazare Carnot, Savant* (Princeton, 1971), 156–158.

PIERRE SPEZIALI

LI CHIH, also called **LI YEH** (*b*. Ta-hsing [now Peking], China, 1192; *d*. Hopeh province, China, 1279)

Li Chih (literary name, Jen-ch'ing; appellation, Ching-chai) has been described by George Sarton as one of the greatest mathematicians of his time and of his race. His father, Li Yü, served as an attaché under a Jurchen officer called by the Chinese name Hu Sha-hu. Li Yü later sent his family back to his home in Luan-ch'eng, Hopeh province. Li Chih went alone to the Yüan-shih district in the same province for his education.

In 1230 Li Chih went to Loyang to take the civil service examination; after he passed, he was appointed registrar in the district of Kao-ling, Shensi province. Before he reported for duty, however, he was made governor of Chün-chou (now Yü-hsien), Honan province. In 1232 the Mongols captured the city of Chün-chou, and Li Chih was forced to seek refuge in Shansi province. The kingdom of the Jurchen fell into the hands of the Mongols in 1234. From that time on, Li Chih devoted himself to serious study, frequently living in poverty. It was during this period that he wrote his most important mathematical work, the *Ts'e-yüan hai-ching* ("Sea Mirror of the Circle Measurements").

About 1251 Li Chih, finding himself in an improved financial position, returned to the Yüan-shih district of Hopeh province and settled near Feng-lung, a mountain in that district. Although he continued to lead the life of a scholarly recluse, he counted Chang Te-hui and Yüan Yü among his friends; the three of them became popularly known as "the Three Friends of [Feng-]Lung Mountain." In 1257 Kublai Khan sent for Li Chih and asked him about the government of the state, the selection and deployment of scholars for civil service, and the reasons for earthquakes. Li Chih completed another mathematical text, the *I-ku yen-tuan* ("New Steps in Computation") in 1259. Kublai Khan ascended the throne in 1260 and the following year offered Li Chih a government post, which was politely declined with the plea of ill health and old age. In 1264 the Mongolian emperor set up the Han-lin Academy for the purpose of writing the official histories of the kingdoms of Liao and Jurchen, and the following year Li Chih was obliged to join it. After a few months he submitted his resignation, again pleading infirmity and old age. He returned to his home near Feng-lung, and many pupils came to study under him.

Li Chih changed his name to Li Yeh at some point in his life because he wished to avoid having the same name as the third T'ang emperor, whose dynastic title was T'ang Kao-tsung (650–683). This circum-stance has given rise to some confusion as to whether Li Yeh was a misprint for Li Chih.

Besides the *Ts'e-yüan hai-ching* and the *I-ku yen-tuan*, Li Chih wrote several other works, including the *Fan shuo*, the *Ching-chai ku-chin chu*, the *Wen chi*, and the *Pi-shu ts'ung-hsiao*. Before his death Li Chih told his son, Li K'e-hsiu, to burn all his books except the *Ts'e-yüan hai-ching*, because he felt that it alone would be of use to future generations. We do not know to what extent his wishes were carried out; but the *I-ku yen-tuan* survived the fire, and the *Ching-chai ku-chin chu* has also come down to us. His other works are now lost, although some passages from the *Fan shuo* are quoted in the *Ching-chai ku-chin chu*. Only the *Ts'e-yüan hai-ching* and the *I-ku yen-tuan* will be further described here, since the other extant work has neither mathematical nor scientific interest.

Originally called the *Ts'e-yüan hai-ching hsi-ts'ao* and completed in 1248, the *Ts'e-yüan hai-ching* was not published until some thirty years later, at about the same time as the *I-ku yen-tuan*. From a preface written by Wang Te-yüan, it appears that there was a second edition in 1287. In the late eighteenth century the *Ts'e-yüan hai-ching* was included in the imperial encyclopedia, the *Ssu-k'u ch'üan-shu*. It came from a copy preserved in the private library of Li Huang (*d*. 1811). A handwritten copy of the book was made by Juan Yuan (1764–1849) from the version in the *Ssu-k'u ch'üan-shu*. Later Ting Chieh presented a handwritten fourteenth-century copy of the *Ts'e-yüan hai-ching hsi-ts'ao* with the seal of Sung Lien (1310–1381) to Juan Yuan. This is probably the copy that is now preserved in the Peking Library. At the request of Juan Yuan, the Ch'ing mathematician Li Jui (1768–1817) collated the two versions in 1797. This has become the most widely circulated edition of the *Ts'e-yüan hai-ching* that exists today. In 1798 Li Jui's version was incorporated in the *Chih-pu-tsu-chai ts'ung-shu* collection, and in 1875 in the *Pai-fu-t'ang suan-hsüeh ts'ung-shu* collection. The modern reproduction in the *Ts'ung-shu chi-ch'eng* series is based on the version in the *Chih-pu-tsu-chai ts'ung-shu* collection.

The *Ts'e-yüan hai-ching* was studied by many eighteenth- and nineteenth-century Chinese mathematicians, such as K'ung Kuang-shen (1752–1786) and Li Shan-lan (1811–1882). A detailed analysis of the work was made by Li Yen (1892–1963), but it has not yet been translated.

The *I-ku yen-tuan* was completed in 1259 and was published in 1282. It has been regarded as a later version of a previous mathematical text, the *I-ku-chi*, which is no longer extant. The *I-ku yen-tuan* is incorporated in both the *Chih-pu-tsu-chai ts'ung-shu* and the *Pai-fu-t'ang suan-hsüeh ts'ung-shu* collections. The modern reproduction of the *I-ku yen-tuan* in the *Ts'ung-shu chi-ch'eng* series is based on the version in the *Chih-pu-tsu-chai ts'ung-shu* collection. It has been translated into French by L. van Hée.

Li Chih introduced an algebraic process called the *t'ien yüan shu* ("method of the celestial elements" or "coefficient array method") for setting up equations to any degree. The *t'ien yüan shu* occupied a very important position in the history of mathematics in both China and Japan. From the early fourteenth century until algebra was brought to China from the West by the Jesuits, no one in China seemed to understand this method. Algebra enabled Chinese mathematicians of the eighteenth century, especially Mei Ku-ch'eng, to recognize the algebra of the *t'ien yüan shu* and the *ssu yüan shu* of Chu Shih-chieh despite their unfamiliar notation. Knowing that algebra originally entered Europe from the East, some enthusiastic Chinese scholars of that time went so far as to claim that the *t'ien yüan shu* had gone from China to the West and there became known as algebra. The *t'ien yüan shu* also exerted a profound influence in Japan, where it became known as the *tengenjutsu*. The seventeenth-century Japanese mathematician Seki Takakazu (also known as Seki Kōwa), for example, developed from the algebra of Li Chih and Chu Shih-chieh a formula for infinite expansion, which is now arrived at by means of the infinitesimal calculus.

Li Chih did not claim to be the originator of the *t'ien yüan shu*. From his *Ching-chai ku-chin chu* it appears that he had copied the method from a certain mathematician in Taiyuan (in modern Shansi) named P'eng Che (literary name, Yen-ts'ai), of whom we

know little. Chu Shih-chieh wrote in the early fourteenth century that one of Li Chih's friends, the famous poet Yuan Hao-wen, was also versed in the method of the celestial element. In the *t'ien yüan shu* method the absolute term is denoted by the character *t'ai* and the unknown by *yüan*, or element. An equation is arranged in a vertical column in which the term containing the unknown is set above the absolute term, the square of the unknown above the unknown, then the cube, and so on in increasing powers. Reciprocals or negative powers can also be placed in descending order after the absolute term. Thus the equation

$$- x^2 + 8640 + 652320x^{-1} + 4665600x^{-2} = 0$$

is represented on the countingboard as in Figure 1a, with its equivalent in Arabic numerals shown in Figure 1b. It is sufficient to indicate one position of the unknown and one of the absolute term by writing the words *yüan* and *t'ai*. It is curious that Li Chih reversed the process of expressing algebraic equations in his *I-ku yen-tuan* by writing the unknown below the absolute, the square below the unknown, and so on. For example, the equation $1700 - 80x - 0.25x^2 = 0$ is shown in Figure 1c and in Arabic numerals in Figure 1d. Li Chih's method was followed by later Chinese mathematicians.

Li Chih indicated negative quantities by drawing an oblique line over the final digit of the number concerned. He also used the zero symbol as his contemporary Ch'in Chiu-shao did, although there is no evidence that the two ever met or even heard of each other. It is likely that the zero symbol was used earlier in China, and it has even been suggested by Yen Tun-chieh that although the dot (*bindu*) was introduced from India in the eighth century and the circle for

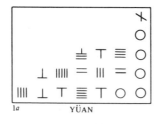

FIGURE 1a

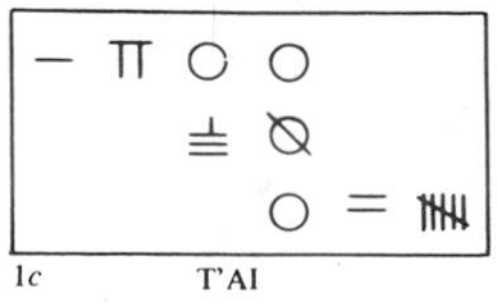

FIGURE 1b

FIGURE 1c

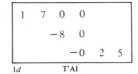

FIGURE 1d

zero appeared in a magic square brought from the area of Islamic culture in the thirteenth century, the circle was nevertheless evolved independently in China from the square denoting zero sometime during the twelfth century.

Li Chih made use of numerical equations up to the sixth degree. He did not describe the procedure of solving such equations, which omission indicates that the method must have been well known in China during his time. This method must be similar to that rediscovered independently by Ruffini and Horner in the early nineteenth century, as described by Ch'in Chiu-shao. Li Chih stabilized the terminology used in connection with equations of higher degrees in the form

$$+ax^6 + bx^5 + cx^4 + dx^3 + ex^2 + fx + g = 0.$$

The absolute term g is called by the general term *shih*, or by the more specific terms *p'ing shih, fang shih, erh ch'eng fang shih, san ch'eng fang shih, shih ch'eng fang shih*, and *wu ch'eng fang shih* for linear equations, quadratic equations, cubic equations, quartic equations, and equations of the fifth and sixth degrees, respectively. The coefficient of the highest power of x (in this case, a) in the equation is called *yü, yü fa*, or *ch'ang fa*. The coefficient of the lowest power of x (in this case, f) is called *ts'ung* or *ts'ung fang*. All coefficients between the lowest and the highest powers are described by the word *lien*. For a cubic equation the coefficient of x^2 is known by the term *lien*. For a quartic equation the coefficient of x^2 is called *ti i lien*, that is, the first *lien*, and the coefficient of x^3 is *ti erh lien*, that is, the second *lien*. Hence, in the sixth-degree equation above we have e, *ti i lien* (first *lien*); d, *ti erh lien* (second *lien*); c, *ti san lien* (third *lien*); and b, *ti shih lien* (fourth *lien*).

All the above, except in the case of the absolute term, apply only to positive numbers. To denote negative numbers, Li Chih added either the word *i* or the word *hsü* before the terms applying to coefficients of the highest and lowest powers of x and before the word *lien*. He did not use different terms to distinguish between positive and negative absolute terms and, unlike Ch'in Chiu-shao, he did not make it a rule that the absolute term must be negative.

It is interesting to see how Li Chih handled the remainder in extracting a square root. An example is encountered in the equation

$$-22.5x^2 - 648x + 23002 = 0,$$

which occurred in the fortieth problem of his *I-ku yen-tuan*. He put $y = nx$, where $n = 22.5$, and transformed the equation into

$$-y^2 - 648y + 517545 = 0.$$

From the above, $y = 465$, and hence $x = 20^2/_3$. The same method was also used by Ch'in Chiu-shao.

The *Ts'e-yüan hai-ching* includes 170 problems dealing with various situations based on a circle inscribed in or circumscribing a right triangle. The same question is asked in all these problems and the same answer obtained. The book begins with a diagram showing a circle inscribed in a right triangle, ABC (Fig. 2). The square $CDEF$ circumscribing the

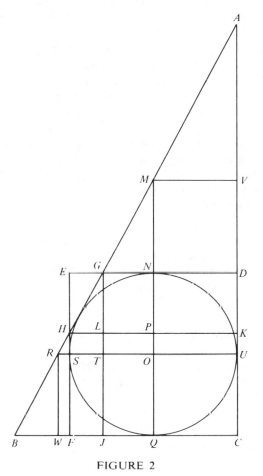

FIGURE 2

circle lies along the base and height of $\triangle ABC$ and intersects the hypotenuse AB at G and H, from which perpendiculars GJ and HK are dropped on BC and AC, respectively. GJ and HK intersect at L. Through O, the center of the circle, $MNPOQ$ is drawn parallel to AC, meeting AB at M and BC at Q and cutting ED at N and HK at P. Also through O is drawn $RSTOU$, parallel to BC, meeting AB at R and AC at U and cutting EF at S and GJ at T. Finally, MV is drawn parallel to BC, meeting AC at V, and RW is drawn parallel to AC, meeting BC at W.

Special terms are then given for the three sides of each of the fifteen triangles in the diagram. These are followed by a list of relationships between the sides of some of these triangles and the circle. For example: the sides of $\triangle ABC$ and the diameter of the inscribed circle have the relationship $D = 2ab/(a + b + c)$; the sides of $\triangle ARU$ and the diameter of a circle with its center at one of the sides and touching the other two sides have the relationship $D = 2ar/(r + u)$; and the sides of $\triangle AGD$ and the diameter of an escribed circle touching the side ED and the sides AG and AD produced have the relationship $D = 2ag/(g + d - a)$. Similarly, for $\triangle MBQ$, $D = 2mb/(m + q)$; for $\triangle HBF$, $D = shb/(h + f - b)$; for $\triangle MRO$; $D = 2mr/o$; for $\triangle GHE$, $D = 2hg/(h + g - e)$; for $\triangle MGN$, $D = 2mg/(n - m)$; and for $\triangle HRS$, $D = 2hr/(s - r)$.

All the above are given in chapter 1 of the book. In the subsequent chapters Li Chih showed how these results can be applied to various cases. For example, the second problem in chapter 2 says:

> Two persons, A and B, start from the western gate [of a circular city wall]. B [first] walks a distance of 256 *pu* eastward. Then A walks a distance of 480 *pu* south before he can see B. Find [the diameter of the wall] as before.

The equation for $\triangle MBQ$ was then applied directly to give the diameter of the circular city wall.

Li Chih showed how to solve a similar problem by the use of a cubic equation. The fourth problem in chapter 3 says:

> A leaves the western gate [of a circular city wall] and walks south for 480 *pu*. B leaves the eastern gate and walks straight ahead a distance of 16 *pu*, when he just begins to see A. Find [the diameter of the city wall] as before.

Here Li Chih found x, the diameter of the city wall, by solving the cubic equation

$$x^3 + cx^2 - 4cb^2 = 0,$$

where $c = 16$ *pu* and $b = 480$ *pu*. This obviously came from the quartic equation

$$x^4 + 2cx^3 + c^2x^2 - 4cb^2x - 4c^2b^2 = 0,$$

which can be derived directly from the equation for $\triangle MBQ$. In doing this Li Chih had discarded the factor $(x + c)$, knowing that the answer $x = -c$ was inadmissible. It is interesting to compare this with the tenth-degree equation used by Ch'in Chiu-shao for the same purpose.

All the 170 problems in the *Ts'e-yüan hai-ching* have been studied by Li Yen. To illustrate Li Chih's

method of solving these problems, we shall follow step by step the working of problem 18 in chapter 11, which says:

> 135 *pu* directly out of the southern gate [of a circular city wall] is a tree. If one walks 15 *pu* out of the northern city gate and then turns east for a distance of 208 *pu*, the tree becomes visible. Find [the diameter of the city wall] as before. [The answer says 240 *pu* as before.]

Using modern conventions but following the traditional Chinese method of indicating the cardinal points in such a way that south is at the top, north at the bottom, east to the left, and west to the right, the problem is as illustrated in Figure 3.

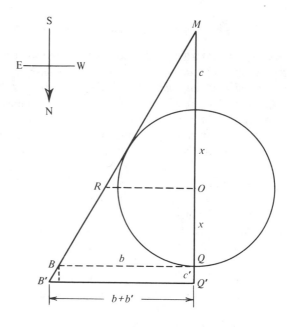

FIGURE 3

First, the method is given:

> Take the product of the distance to the east and that to the south [that is, $c(b + b')$], square it, and make it the *shih* [that is, $c^2(b + b')^2$ is taken as the absolute term]. Square the distance to the east, multiply it by the distance to the south, and double it to form the *ts'ung* [that is, the coefficient of x, the radius, is $2c(b + b')^2$]. Put aside the square of the distance to the east [that is, $(b + b')^2$]; add together the distance to the south and north, subtract the sum from the distance to the east, square the result, and subtract this from the distance to the east [that is, $(b + b')^2 - \{(b + b') - (c + c')\}^2$]; put aside this value. Again add together the distances to the south and north, multiply the sum first by the distance to the east and then by 2 [that is, $2(b + b')(c + c')$]; subtracting from this the amount just set aside gives the *tai i i lien* [that is, the coefficient of x^2 is $-2\{(b + b')(c + c')\} - [(b + b')^2 - \{(b + b') -$

$(c + c')\}^2]]$. Multiply the distance to the east by 4 and put this aside [that is, $4(b + b')$]; add the distances to the south and north, subtract the sum from the eastward distance and multiply by 4 [that is, $4\{(b + b') + (c + c')\}$]; subtracting this result from the amount put aside gives the *tai erh i lien* [that is, the coefficient of x^3 is $-4(b + b') - 4\{(b + b') + (c + c')\}$]. Take 4 times the *hsü yü* [that is, $-4x^4$]. Solving the quartic equation gives the radius.

The procedure is as follows:

Set up one celestial element to represent the radius. (This is the *kao kou*.) Adding to this the distance to the south gives Figure 4a (below), which represents the

FIGURE 4a

kao hsien (that is, the vertical side MO in MRO in Figure 3 is $x + 135$). Put down the value for the *ta kou* (base of $MB'Q'$) of 208 and multiply it by the *kao hsien* ($x + 135$); the result is $208x + 28080$ (Figure 4b).

FIGURE 4b

Dividing this by the *kao kou* gives $208 + 28080x^{-1}$ (Figure 4c).

FIGURE 4c

This is the *ta hsien* (the hypotenuse MB' of $\triangle MB'Q'$), and squaring this yields $43264 + 11681280x^{-1} + 788486400x^{-2}$ (Figure 4d).

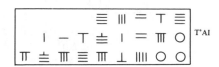

FIGURE 4d

The above is temporarily set aside. Take 2 as the celestial element and add this to the sum of the distances to the south and north, giving $2x + 150$ (Figure 4e),

FIGURE 4e

or the *ta ku* (the vertical side MQ' of $\triangle MB'Q'$). Subtracting from this the value of the *ta kou*, 208, $2x - 58$ is obtained (Figure 4f).

FIGURE 4f

This is known as the *chiao*. Squaring it gives the *chiao mi*, $4x^2 - 232x + 3364$, shown in Figure 4g.

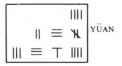

FIGURE 4g

Subtracting the *chiao mi* from the quantity set aside (Figure 4d) yields $-4x^2 + 232x + 39900 + 11681280x^{-1} + 788486400x^{-2}$ (Figure 4h).

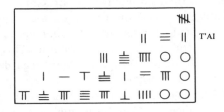

FIGURE 4h

This value, known as *erh-chih-chi*, is set aside at the lefthand side of the countingboard. Next multiply the *ta ku* (*MQ'*) by the *ta kou* (*B'Q'*), which yields $416x + 31200$ (Figure 4i).

FIGURE 4i

This is the *chih chi*, which, when doubled, gives $832x + 62400$ (Figure 4j).

FIGURE 4j

This value is the same as that set aside at the left (that is, the value represented by Figure 4h). Equating the two values, one obtains $-4x^4 - 600x^3 - 22500x^2 + 11681280x + 788486400 = 0$ (Figure 4k).

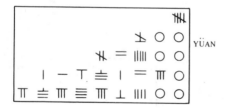

FIGURE 4k

Note that the position of the celestial element is no longer indicated here.

Solving this as a quartic equation, one obtains 120 *pu*, the radius of the circular city wall, which corresponds with the required answer.

Although written much later than the *Ts'e-yüan hai-ching*, the *I-ku yen-tuan* is considerably simpler in its contents. It is thought that Li Chih took this opportunity to explain the *t'ien yüan shu* method in a less complicated manner after finding his first book too difficult for people to understand. This second mathematical treatise has also been regarded as a later version of another work, *I-ku chi*, published between 1078 and 1224 and no longer extant. According to a preface in Chu Shih-chieh's *Ssu-yüan yu-chien*, the *I-ku chi* was written by a certain Chiang

Chou of P'ing-yang. Out of a total of sixty-four problems in the *I-ku yen-tuan*, twenty-one are referred to as the "old method" (*chiu shu*), which presumably means the *I-ku chi*. Sixteen of these twenty-one problems deal with the quadratic equation

$$ax^2 + bx - c = 0,$$

where $a > 0$ or $a < 0$, $b > 0$ and $c > 0$. When $c > 0$ and $b > 0$, they are called by the terms *shih* and *ts'ung*, respectively. When $a > 0$, it is known as *lien* instead of the more general term *yü*, and when $a < 0$, it is also known as *lien*, but is followed by the words *chien ts'ung*.

Divided into three chapters, the *I-ku yen-tuan* deals with the combination of a circle and a square or, in a few cases, a circle and a rectangle. A full translation of the first problem in chapter 1 is given below:

A square farm with a circular pool of water in the center has an area 13 *mou* and 7 1/2 tenths of a *mou* [that is, 13.75 *mou*]. The pool is 20 *pu* from the edge [1 *mou* = 240 square *pu*]. Find the side of the square and the diameter of the pool.

Answer: Side of square = 60 *pu*, diameter of pool = 20 *pu*.

Method: Put down one [counting rod] as the celestial element to represent the diameter of the pool. By adding twice the distance from the edge of the pool to the side of the farm, the side of the square farm is given by $x + 40$ [Figure 5a].

FIGURE 5a

The square of the side gives the area of the farm and the circular pool. That is, the total area is given by $x^2 + 80x + 1600$ [Figure 5b].

Again, put down one [counting rod] as the celestial element to denote the diameter of the pool. Squaring the diameter, and multiplying the result by 3 [the ancient approximate value of π], then dividing the

FIGURE 5b

result by 4, yields the area of the pool: $0.75x^2$ [Figure 5c].

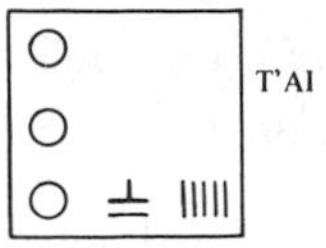

FIGURE 5c

Subtracting the area of the pool from the total area gives $0.25x^2 + 80x + 1600$ [Figure 5d].

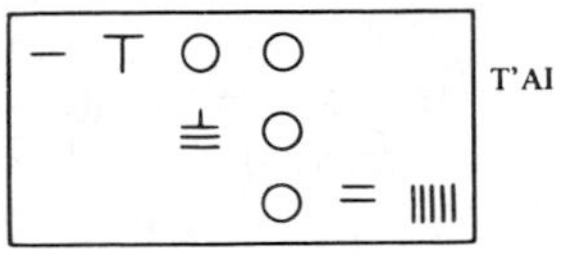

FIGURE 5d

The given area is 3,300 [square] *pu*. Equating this with the above yields $-0.25x^2 - 80x + 1700 = 0$ [Figure 5e].

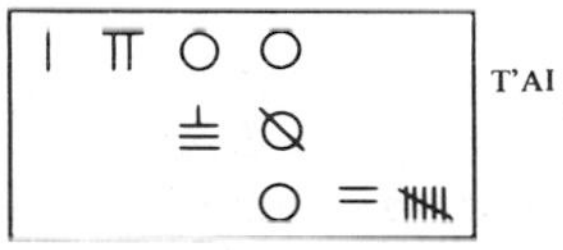

FIGURE 5e

Applying the method of solving quadratic equations shows the diameter of the pool to be 20 *pu*. If the distance from the side of the square to the edge of the pool is doubled and added to the diameter of the pool, the side of the farm is found to be 60 *pu*.

The first ten problems in the *I-ku yen-tuan* deal with a circle in the center of a square, each with different given parameters; the next ten problems are concerned with a square inside a circle. Problems 21 and 22, the last two problems in chapter 1, are concerned only with squares. In chapter 2, problems 23–29, we have the combination of a square with a circumscribed circle, while problem 30 gives the combination of two circles. Problem 31 concerns a rectangle with a circle in the center, and problems 32–37 give a circle with a rectangle at its center. In problem 38 two rectangles are given. Problems 39–42 treat various cases of a circle inside a rectangle. Problem 43, the first in chapter 3, deals with the three different values of π: the ancient value $\pi = 3$, the "close" value $\pi = 22/7$, and Liu Hui's value $\pi = 3.14$. Problem 44 is concerned with a trapezium, problem 45 with a square inside another square, problem 46 with a

circle set outside but along the extended diagonal of a square, problem 47 with a square within a rectangle, and problem 48 with a rectangle within a square. In problems 49–52 a square is placed in the center of a larger square so that the diagonal of one is perpendicular to two sides of the other. In problems 53 and 54 the central square is replaced by a rectangle. Problems 55 and 56 are concerned with the annulus, and problems 57 and 58 with a rectangle inside a circle. In problem 59 a square encloses a circle, which in turn encloses another square at the center; and in problem 60 a circle encloses a square, which in turn encloses a circle at the center. Problem 62 concerns a square placed diagonally at a corner of another square. Problem 63 concerns a circle and two squares with another circle enclosed in one of them. The last problem, 64, has an annulus enclosed by a larger square.

Li Chih and Ch'in Chiu-shao were contemporaries, but they never mentioned each other in their writings. Li Chih lived in the north and Ch'in Chiu-shao in the south during the time when China was ruled in the south by the Sung dynasty and in the north first by the Jurchen Tartars and later by the Mongols. It is very likely that the two never even heard of each other. The terminology they used for equations of higher degree is similar but not identical. They also employed the so-called celestial element in different ways. Li Chih used it to denote the unknown quantity; but to Ch'in Chiu-shao the celestial element was a known number, and he never used the term in connection with his numerical equations. Ch'in Chiu-shao went into great detail in explaining the process of root extraction of numerical equations, but he did not describe how such equations were constructed by algebraic considerations from the given data in the problems. On the contrary, Li Chih concentrated on the method of setting out such equations algebraically without explaining the process of solving them. Thus Li Chih was indeed, as George Sarton says, essentially an algebraist.

BIBLIOGRAPHY

Works that may be consulted for further information on Li Chih and his writings are Ch'ien Pao-tsung, *Chung-kuo suan hsüeh-shih* ["History of Chinese Mathematics"] (Peking, 1932), pp. 116–124; Ch'ien Pao-tsung *et al.*, *Sung Yuan shu-hsüeh-shih lun-wen-chi* ["Collection of Essays on Chinese Mathematics in the Periods of Sung and Yuan"] (Peking, 1966), pp. 104–148; L. van Heé, "Li Yeh, mathématicien chinois du XIIIe siècle," in *T'oung Pao*, **14** (1913), pp. 537–568; Juan Yuan, *Ch'ou-jen chuan* ["Biographies of Mathematicians and Astronomers"] (Shanghai, 1935); Li Yen, *Chung-kuo shu-hsüeh ta-kang* ["Outline of Chinese

Mathematics"], I (Shanghai, 1931), pp. 141–156; *Chung-kuo suan-hsüeh-shih* ["History of Chinese Mathematics"] (Shanghai, 1937), pp. 99–100; and "Chung-suan-shih lunts'ung," in *Gesammelte Abhandlungen über die Geschichte der chinesischen Mathematik*, **4**, no. 1 (1947), 15–251; Li Yen and Tu Shih-jan, *Chung-kuo ku-tai shu-hsüeh chienshih* ["Concise History of Ancient Chinese Mathematics"], II (Peking, 1964), pp. 145, 147; Yoshio Mikami, *The Development of Mathematics in China and Japan* (Leipzig, 1913), pp. 79–84; Joseph Needham, *Science and Civilisation in China*, III (Cambridge, 1959), esp. pp. 40–41; George Sarton, *Introduction to the History of Science*, 3 vols. (Baltimore, 1927–1947), esp. vol. 2, pp. 627–628; Sung Lien *et al.*, *Yuan shih* ["Official History of the Yuan Dynasty"] (*ca.* 1370), ch. 160; and Alexander Wylie, *Notes on Chinese Literature* (Shanghai, 1902), p. 116.

HO PENG-YOKE

LIE, MARIUS SOPHUS (*b.* Nordfjordeide, Norway, 17 December 1842; *d.* Christiania [now Oslo], Norway, 18 February 1899)

Sophus Lie, as he is known, was the sixth and youngest child of a Lutheran pastor, Johann Herman Lie. He first attended school in Moss (Kristianiafjord), then, from 1857 to 1859, Nissen's Private Latin School in Christiania. He studied at Christiania University from 1859 to 1865, mainly mathematics and sciences. Although mathematics was taught by such people as Bjerknes and Sylow, Lie was not much impressed. After his examination in 1865, he gave private lessons, became slightly interested in astronomy, and tried to learn mechanics; but he could not decide what to do. The situation changed when, in 1868, he hit upon Poncelet's and Plücker's writings. Later, he called himself a student of Plücker's, although he had never met him. Plücker's momentous idea to create new geometries by choosing figures other than points—in fact straight lines—as elements of space pervaded all of Lie's work.

Lie's first published paper brought him a scholarship for study abroad. He spent the winter of 1869–1870 in Berlin, where he met Felix Klein, whose interest in geometry also had been influenced by Plücker's work. This acquaintance developed into a friendship that, although seriously troubled in later years, proved crucial for the scientific progress of both men. Lie and Klein had quite different characters as humans and mathematicians: the algebraist Klein was fascinated by the peculiarities of charming problems; the analyst Lie, parting from special cases, sought to understand a problem in its appropriate generalization.

Lie and Klein spent the summer of 1870 in Paris, where they became acquainted with Darboux and Camille Jordan. Here Lie, influenced by the ideas of the French "anallagmatic" school, discovered his famous contact transformation, which maps straight lines into spheres and principal tangent curves into curvature lines. He also became familiar with Monge's theory of differential equations. At the outbreak of the Franco-Prussian war in July, Klein left Paris; Lie, as a Norwegian, stayed. In August he decided to hike to Italy but was arrested near Fontainebleau as a spy. After a month in prison, he was freed through Darboux's intervention. Just before the Germans blockaded Paris, he escaped to Italy. From there he returned to Germany, where he again met Klein.

In 1871 Lie was awarded a scholarship to Christiania University. He also taught at Nissen's Private Latin School. In July 1872 he received his Ph.D. During this period he developed the integration theory of partial differential equations now found in many textbooks, although rarely under his name. Lie's results were found at the same time by Adolph Mayer, with whom he conducted a lively correspondence. Lie's letters are a valuable source of knowledge about his development.

In 1872 a chair in mathematics was created for him at Christiania University. In 1873 Lie turned from the invariants of contact transformations to the principles of the theory of transformation groups. Together with Sylow he assumed the editorship of Niels Abel's works. In 1874 Lie married Anna Birch, who bore him two sons and a daughter.

His main interest turned to transformation groups, his most celebrated creation, although in 1876 he returned to differential geometry. In the same year he joined G. O. Sars and Worm Müller in founding the *Archiv för mathematik og naturvidenskab*. In 1882 the work of Halphen and Laguerre on differential invariants led Lie to resume his investigations on transformation groups.

Lie was quite isolated in Christiania. He had no students interested in his research. Abroad, except for Klein, Mayer, and somewhat later Picard, nobody paid attention to his work. In 1884 Klein and Mayer induced F. Engel, who had just received his Ph.D., to visit Lie in order to learn about transformation groups and to help him write a comprehensive book on the subject. Engel stayed nine months with Lie. Thanks to his activity the work was accomplished, its three parts being published between 1888 and 1893, whereas Lie's other great projects were never completed. F. Hausdorff, whom Lie had chosen to assist him in preparing a work on contact transformations and partial differential equations, got interested in quite different subjects.

This happened after 1886 when Lie had succeeded Klein at Leipzig, where, indeed, he found students, among whom was G. Scheffers. With him Lie published textbooks on transformation groups and on differential equations, and a fragmentary geometry of contact transformations. In the last years of his life Lie turned to foundations of geometry, which at that time meant the Helmholtz space problem.

In 1889 Lie, who was described as an open-hearted man of gigantic stature and excellent physical health, was struck by what was then called neurasthenia. Treatment in a mental hospital led to his recovery, and in 1890 he could resume his work. His character, however, had changed greatly. He became increasingly sensitive, irascible, suspicious, and misanthropic, despite the many tokens of recognition that were heaped upon him.

Meanwhile, his Norwegian friends sought to lure him back to Norway. Another special chair in mathematics was created for him at Christiania University, and in September 1898 he moved there. He died of pernicious anemia the following February. His papers have been edited, with excellent annotations, by F. Engel and P. Heegaard.

Lie's first papers dealt with very special subjects in geometry, more precisely, in differential geometry. In comparison with his later performances, they seem like classroom exercises; but they are actually the seeds from which his great theories grew. Change of the space element and related mappings, the lines of a complex considered as solutions of a differential equation, special contact transformations, and trajectories of special groups prepared his theory of partial differential equations, contact transformations, and transformation groups. He often returned to this less sophisticated differential geometry. His best-known discoveries of this kind during his later years concern minimal surfaces.

The crucial idea that emerged from his preliminary investigations was a new choice of space element, the contact element: an incidence pair of point and line or, in n dimensions, of point and hyperplane. The manifold of these elements was now studied, not algebraically, as Klein would have done—and actually did—but analytically or, rather, from the standpoint of differential geometry. The procedure of describing a line complex by a partial differential equation was inverted: solving the first-order partial differential equation

$$F\left(x, x_1, \cdots, x_{n-1}, \frac{\partial r}{\partial x_1}, \cdots, \frac{\partial x}{\partial x_{n-1}}\right) = 0$$

means fibering the manifold $F(x, x_1, \cdots, x_{n-1}, p_1, \cdots, p_{n-1}) = 0$ of $(2n-1)$-space by n-submanifolds on which the Pfaffian equation $dx = p_1 dx + \cdots + p_{n-1} dx_{n-1}$ prevails. This Pfaffian equation was

interpreted geometrically: it means the incidence of the contact elements $\ulcorner x, x_1, \cdots, x_{n-1}, p_1, \cdots, p_{n-1} \urcorner$ and $\ulcorner x + dx, x_1 + dx_1, \cdots, x_{n-1} + dx_{n-1}, p_1 + dp_1, \cdots, p_{n-1} + dp_{n-1} \urcorner$. This incidence notion was so strongly suggested by the geometry of complexes (or, as one would say today, by symplectic geometry) that Lie never bothered to state it explicitly. Indeed, if it is viewed in the related $2n$-vector space instead of $(2n + 1)$-projective space, incidence means what is called conjugateness with respect to a skew form. It was one of Lie's idiosyncrasies that he never made this skew form explicit, even after Frobenius had introduced it in 1877; obviously Lie did not like it because he had missed it. It is another drawback that Lie adhered mainly to projective formulations in $(2n - 1)$-space, which led to clumsy formulas as soon as things had to be presented analytically; homogeneous formulations in $2n$-space are more elegant and make the ideas much clearer, so they will be used in the sequel such that the partial differential equation is written as $F(x_1, \cdots, x_n, p_1, \cdots p_n) = 0$, with $p_1 dx_1 + \cdots + p_n dx_n$ as the total differential of the nonexplicit unknown variable. Then the skew form (the Frobenius covariant) has the shape $\sum(\delta p_i dx_i - dp_i \delta x_i)$.

A manifold $z = f(x_1, \cdots, x_n)$ in $(n + 1)$-space, if viewed in the $2n$-space of contact elements, makes $\sum p_i dx_i$ a complete differential, or, in geometrical terms, neighboring contact elements in this manifold are incident. But there are more such n-dimensional *Elementvereine*: a k-dimensional manifold in $(n + 1)$-space with all its n-dimensional tangent spaces shares this property. It was an important step to deal with all these *Elementvereine* on the same footing, for it led to an illuminating extension of the differential equation problem and to contact transformations. Finding a complete solution of the differential equation now amounted to fibering the manifold $F = 0$ by n-dimensional *Elementvereine*. In geometrical terms the Lagrange-Monge-Pfaff-Cauchy theory (which is often falsely ascribed to Hamilton and Jacobi) was refashioned: to every point of $F = 0$ the skew form assigns one tangential direction that is conjugate to the whole $(2n - 1)$-dimensional tangential plane. Integrating this field of directions, or otherwise solving the system of ordinary differential equations

$$\frac{dx_i}{dt} = \frac{\partial F}{\partial p_i}, \ \frac{dp_i}{dt} = -\frac{\partial F}{\partial x_i},$$

one obtains a fibering of $F = 0$ into curves, the "characteristic strips," closely connected to the Monge curves (touching the Monge cones). Thus it became geometrically clear why every complete solution also had to be fibered by characteristic strips.

Here the notion of contact transformation came in. First suggested by special instances, it was conceived of as a mapping that conserves the incidence of neighboring contact elements. Analytically, this meant invariance of $\sum p_i dx_i$ up to a total differential. The characteristic strips appeared as the trajectories of such a contact transformation:

$$(F, \cdot) = \sum \left(\frac{\partial F}{\partial p_i} \frac{\partial}{\partial x_i} - \frac{\partial F}{\partial x_i} \frac{\partial}{\partial p_i} \right).$$

Thus characteristic strips must be incident everywhere as soon as they are so in one point. This led to a geometric reinterpretation of Cauchy's construction of one solution of the partial differential equation. From one $(n-1)$-dimensional *Elementverein* on $F = 0$, which is easily found, one had to issue all characteristic strips. But even a complete solution was obtained in this way: by cross-secting the system of characteristics, the figure was lowered by two dimensions in order to apply induction. Solving the partial differential equation was now brought back to integrating systems of ordinary equations of, subsequently, 2, 4, $\cdots$, $2n$ variables. In comparison with older methods, this was an enormous reduction of the integration job, which at the same time was performed analytically by Adolph Mayer.

With the Poisson brackets $(F, \cdot)$ viewed as contact transformations, Jacobi's integration theory of systems

$$F_j(x_1, \cdots, x_n, p_1, \cdots p_n) = 0$$

was reinterpreted and simplified. Indeed, $(F, \cdot F_j)$ is nothing but the commutator of the related contact transformations. The notion of transformation group, although not yet explicitly formulated, was already active in Lie's unconscious. The integrability condition $(F_i, F_j) = \sum \rho_{ij}^k F_k$ (where the ρ_{ij}^k are functions) was indeed closely connected to group theory ideas, and it is not surprising that Lie called such a system a group. The theory of these "function groups," which was thoroughly developed for use in partial differential equations and contact transformations, was the last stepping-stone to the theory of transformation groups, which was later applied in differential equations.

Lie's integration theory was the result of marvelous geometric intuitions. The preceding short account is the most direct way to present it. The usual way is a rigmarole of formulas, even in the comparatively excellent book of Engel and Faber. Whereas transformation groups have become famous as Lie groups, his integration theory is not as well known as it deserves to be. To a certain extent this is Lie's own fault. The nineteenth-century mathematical public often could not understand lucid abstract ideas if they were not expressed in the analytic language of that time, even if this language would not help to make things clearer. So Lie, a poor analyst in comparison with his ablest contemporaries, had to adapt and express in a host of formulas, ideas which would have been said better without them. It was Lie's misfortune that by yielding to this urge, he rendered his theories obscure to the geometricians and failed to convince the analysts.

About 1870 group theory became fashionable. In 1870 C. Jordan published his *Traité des substitutions,* and two years later Klein presented his *Erlanger Programm.* Obviously Klein and Lie must have discussed group theory early. Nevertheless, to name a certain set of (smooth) mappings of (part of) n space, depending on r parameters, a group was still a new way of speaking. Klein, with his background in the theory of invariants, of course thought of very special groups, as his *Erlanger Programm* and later works prove. Lie, however, soon turned to transformation groups in general—finite continuous groups, as he christened them ("finite" because of the finite number of parameters, and "continuous" because at that time this included differentiability of any order wanted). Today they are called Lie groups. In the mid-1870's this theory was completed, although its publication would take many years.

Taking derivatives (velocity fields) at identity in all directions creates the infinitesimal transformations of the group, which together form the infinitesimal group. The first fundamental theorem, providing a necessary and sufficient condition, tells how the derivatives at any parameter point $a_1, \cdots, a_r$ are linearly combined from those at identity. The second fundamental theorem says that the infinitesimal transformations will and should form what is today called a Lie algebra,

$$[X_i, X_j] = X_i X_j - X_j X_i = \sum_k c_{ij}^k X_k,$$

with some structure constants c_{ij}^k. Antisymmetry and Jacobi associativity yield the relations

$$c_{ij}^k + c_{ji}^k = 0,$$

$$\sum_k (c_{ij}^k c_{kl}^m + c_{jl}^k c_{ki}^m + c_{li}^k c_{kj}^m) = 0$$

between the structure constants. It cost Lie some trouble to prove that these relations were also sufficient.

From these fundamental theorems the theory was developed extensively. The underlying abstract group, called the parameter group, showed up. Differential invariants were investigated, and automorphism groups of differential equations were used as tools of solution. Groups in a plane and in 3-space were classified. "Infinite continuous" groups were also considered, with no remarkable success, then and afterward. Lie dreamed of a Galois theory of differential equations but did not really succeed, since he could not explain what kind of *ausführbare* operations should correspond to the rational ones of Galois theory and what solving meant in the case of a differential equation with no nontrivial automorphisms. Nevertheless, it was an inexhaustible and promising subject.

Gradually, quite a few mathematicians became interested in the subject. First, of course, was Lie's student Engel. F. Schur then gave another proof of the third fundamental theorem (1889–1890), which led to interesting new views; L. Maurer refashioned the proofs of all fundamental theorems (1888–1891); and Picard and Vessiot developed Galois theories of differential equations (1883, 1891). The most astonishing fact about Lie groups, that their abstract structure was determined by the purely algebraic phenomenon of their structure constants, led to the most important investigations. First were those of Wilhelm Killing, who tried to classify the simple Lie groups. This was a tedious job, and he erred more than once. This made Lie furious, and according to oral tradition he is said to have warned one of his students who was leaving: "Farewell, and if ever you meet that s.o.b., kill him." Although belittled by Lie and some of his followers, Killing's work was excellent. It was revised by Cartan, who after staying with Lie wrote his famous thesis (1894). For many years Cartan—gifted with Lie's geometric intuition and, although trained in the French tradition, as incapable as Lie of explaining things clearly—was the greatest, if not the only, really important mathematician who continued Lie's tradition in all his fields. But Cartan was isolated. Weyl's papers of 1922–1923 marked the revival of Lie groups. In the 1930's Lie's local approach gave way to a global one. The elimination of differentiability conditions in Lie groups took place between the 1920's and 1950's. Chevalley's development of algebraic groups was a momentous generalization of Lie groups in the 1950's. Lie algebras, replacing ordinary associativity by Jacobi associativity, became popular among algebraists from the 1940's. Lie groups now play an increasingly important part in quantum physics. The joining of topology to algebra on the most primitive level, as Lie did, has shown its creative power in this century.

In 1868 Hermann von Helmholtz formulated his space problem, an attempt to replace Euclid's foundations of geometry with group-theoretic ones, although

in fact groups were never explicitly mentioned in that paper. In 1890 Lie showed that Helmholtz's formulations were unsatisfactory and that his solution was defective. His work on this subject, now called the Helmholtz-Lie space problem, is one of the most beautiful applications of Lie groups. In the 1950's and 1960's it was reconsidered in a topological setting.

BIBLIOGRAPHY

I. ORIGINAL WORKS. Lie's collected papers were published as *Gesammelte Abhandlungen*, F. Engel and P. Heegaard, eds., 6 vols. in 11 pts. (Leipzig–Oslo, 1922–1937). His writings include *Theorie der Transformationsgruppen*, 3 vols. (Leipzig, 1888–1893), on which Engel collaborated; *Vorlesungen über Differentialgleichungen mit bekannten infinitesimalen Transformationen* (Leipzig, 1891), written with G. Scheffers; *Vorlesungen über continuierliche Gruppen mit geometrischen und anderen Anwendungen* (Leipzig, 1893), written with G. Scheffers; and *Geometrie der Berührungstransformationen* (Leipzig, 1896), written with G. Scheffers.

II. SECONDARY LITERATURE. Works on Lie or his work are F. Engel, "Sophus Lie," in *Jahresbericht der Deutschen Matematiker-Vereinigung*, **8** (1900), 30–46; and M. Noether, "Sophus Lie," in *Mathematische Annalen*, **53** (1900), 1–41.

HANS FREUDENTHAL

LINDELÖF, ERNST LEONHARD (*b*. Helsingfors, Sweden [now Helsinki, Finland], 7 March 1870; *d*. Helsinki, 4 June 1946)

Lindelöf was the son of the mathematician Leonard Lorenz Lindelöf, who was a professor in Helsingfors from 1857 to 1874. He studied in Helsingfors from 1887 to 1900, and spent the year 1891 in Stockholm, 1893 and 1894 in Paris, and 1901 in Göttingen. He passed his university examination in 1895 in Helsingfors and then gave courses in mathematics as a docent. In 1902 he became assistant professor and in 1903 full professor of mathematics. From 1907 he belonged to the editorial board of the *Acta Mathematica*, and he was a member of many learned academies and societies. He received honorary doctoral degrees from the Universities of Uppsala, Oslo, and Stockholm, and he was also named honorary professor by the University of Helsinki. He retired in 1938.

At the beginning of his career Lindelöf published a remarkable work on the theory of differential equations, in which he investigated the existence of solutions ("Sur l'intégration de l'équation différentielle de Kummer," in *Acta Societatis Scientiae Fennicae*, 19

[1890], 1). He soon turned his attention to function theory, and in this area solved some fundamental problems in the theory of analytic functions. His primary field of interest, however, was in entire functions. He considered the mutual dependency between the growth of the function and the coefficients of the Taylor expansion. He also treated the behavior of analytic functions in the neighborhood of a singular point. The investigations concern questions which arise from Picard's problem. Together with Phragmén he developed a general principle that he applied to function theory. His works are characterized by clarity and purity of method as well as elegance of form.

Lindelöf's investigations of analytic continuation with the help of summation formulas had far-reaching results, which are set down in his excellent book *Le calcul des résidus*. In it he examines the role which residue theory (Cauchy) plays in function theory as a means of access to modern analysis. In this endeavor he applies the results of Mittag-Leffler. Moreover, he considers series analogous to the Fourier summation formulas and applications to the gamma function and the Riemann function. In addition, new results concerning the Stirling series and analytic continuation are presented. The book concludes with an asymptotic investigation of series defined by Taylor's formula. The method of successive correction and the examination of this procedure following the studies of Picard and Schwarz is characteristic of Lindelöf's work. His last works dealt with conformal mapping.

Lindelöf early abandoned creative scientific research and devoted himself enthusiastically to his duties as a professor; he was always available to researchers and colleagues. He laid the foundations for the study of the history of mathematics in Finland and trained many students. In an interesting festschrift published in honor of Lindelöf's sixtieth birthday fourteen authors presented papers on function theory, diophantine equations, correlation theory, and number theory.

Lindelöf devoted his last years mainly to publishing textbooks which were noted for their lucidity and comprehensible style. Of his publications, eight deal with the theory of differential equations, twenty-three with function theory, four with the theory of error in harmonic analysis, and five with other fields.

BIBLIOGRAPHY

A listing of Lindelöf's mathematical works may be found in P. J. Myrberg, "Ernst Lindelöf in memoriam," in *Acta Mathematica*, **79** (Uppsala, 1947), i–iv. Lindelöf's major textbooks are *Le calcul des résidus et ses applications à la théorie des fonctions* (Paris, 1905; New York, 1947); *Inledning til högre Analysen* (Stockholm, 1912), translated into Finnish as *Johdatus korkeampaan analysiin* (Helsinki, 1917, new ed., 1956), and German as *Einführung in die höhere Analysis* (Berlin, 1934); *Differentiaali- ja integraali-laska ja sen sovellutukset* ("Differential and Integral Calculus and their Application"), 4 vols. (Helsinki, 1920–1946); and *Johdatus funktioteoriaan* ("Introduction to Function Theory"; Helsinki, 1936).

The festschrift, *Commentationes in honorem Ernesti Leonardi Lindelöf. Die VII Mensis Martii A MCMXXX Sexagenarii*, edited by his students, is in *Suomalaisen tiedeakatemiam toimituksia*, ser. A, **32** (Helsinki, 1929).

HERBERT OETTEL

LINDEMANN, CARL LOUIS FERDINAND (*b.* Hannover, Germany, 12 April 1852; *d.* Munich, Germany, 6 March 1939)

Lindemann studied in Göttingen, Erlangen, and Munich from 1870 to 1873. He was particularly influenced by Clebsch, who pioneered in invariant theory. Lindemann received the doctorate from Erlangen in 1873, under the direction of F. Klein. His dissertation dealt with infinitely small movements of rigid bodies under general projective mensuration. He then undertook a year-long academic journey to Oxford, Cambridge, London, and Paris, where he met Chasles, J. Bertrand, C. Jordan, and Hermite. In 1877 Lindemann qualified as lecturer at Würzburg. In the same year he became assistant professor at the University of Freiburg. He became full professor in 1879. In 1883 he accepted an appointment at Königsberg and finally, ten years later, one at Munich, where he was for many years also active on the administrative board of the university. He was elected an associate member of the Bavarian Academy of Sciences in 1894, and a full member in 1895.

Lindemann was one of the founders of the modern German educational system. He emphasized the development of the seminar and in his lectures communicated the latest research results. He also supervised more than sixty doctoral students, including David Hilbert. In the years before World War I, he represented the Bavarian Academy in the meetings of the International Association of Academies of Sciences and Learned Societies.

Lindemann wrote papers on numerous branches of mathematics and on theoretical mechanics and spectrum theory. In addition, he edited and revised Clebsch's geometry lectures following the latter's untimely death (as *Vorlesungen über Geometrie* [Leipzig, 1876–1877]).

Lindemann's most outstanding original research is

his 1882 work on the transcendence of π. This work definitively settled the ancient problem of the quadrature of the circle; it also redefined and reanimated fundamental questions in the mathematics of its own time.

In the nineteenth century mathematicians had realized that not every real number was necessarily the root of an algebraic equation and that therefore non-algebraic, so-called transcendental, numbers must exist. Liouville stated certain transcendental numbers, and in 1873 Hermite succeeded in demonstrating the transcendence of the base e of the natural logarithms. It was at this point that Lindemann turned his attention to the subject.

The demonstration of the transcendence of π is based on the proof of the theorem that, except for trivial cases, every expression of the form $\sum_{i=1}^{n} A_i e^{a_i}$, where A_i and a_i are algebraic numbers, must always be different from zero. Since the imaginary unity i, as the root of the equation $x^2 + 1 = 0$, is algebraic, and since $e^{\pi i} + e^0 = 0$, then πi and therefore also π cannot be algebraic. So much the less then is π a root, representable by a radical, of an algebraic equation; hence the quadrature of the circle is impossible, inasmuch as π cannot be constructed with ruler and compass.

Lindemann also composed works in the history of mathematics, including a "Geschichte der Polyder und der Zahlzeichen" (in *Sitzungsberichte der mathematisch-physikalischen Klasse der Bayrischen Akademie der Wissenschaften* [1896]). He and his wife collaborated in translating and revising some of the works of Poincaré. Their edition of his *La science et l'hypothèse* (as *Wissenschaft und Hypothese* [Leipzig, 1904]) contributed greatly to the dissemination of Poincaré's ideas in Germany.

BIBLIOGRAPHY

I. ORIGINAL WORKS. In addition to the works cited in the text, see especially "Über die Ludolphsche Zahl," in *Sitzungsberichte der Preussischen Akademie der Wissenschaften zu Berlin*, math.-phys. Klasse, **22** (1882); and "Über die Zahl π," in *Mathematische Annalen*, **25** (1882).

II. SECONDARY LITERATURE. See "Druckschriften-Verzeichnis von F. Lindemann," in *Almanach der Königlich Bayrischen Akademie der Wissenschaften zum 150. Stiftungsfest* (Munich, 1909), 303–306; "F. von Lindemanns 70. Geburtstag," in *Jahresberichte der Mathematikervereinigung*, **31** (1922), 24–30; and C. Carathéodory, "Nekrolog auf Ferdinand von Lindemann," in *Sitzungsberichte der mathematisch-naturwissenschaftlichen Abteilung der Bayrischen Akademie der Wissenschaften zu München*, no. 1 (1940), 61–63.

H. WUSSING

LINNIK, IURII VLADIMIROVICH (*b*. Belaia Tserkov', Ukraine, Russia, 21 January 1915; *d*. Leningrad, U.S.S.R., 30 June 1972)

Linnik's parents, Vladimir Pavlovitch Linnik and Maria Abramovna Yakerina, were schoolteachers. His father later became a famous scientist in the field of optics and a member of the U.S.S.R. Academy of Sciences. After graduation from secondary school in 1931, Linnik, having worked for a year as a laboratory assistant, entered Leningrad University, where he studied theoretical physics and mathematics. He graduated from the university in 1938 and received the doctorate in mathematics in 1940, joining the staff of the Leningrad branch of the V. A. Steklov Institute of Mathematics of the U.S.S.R. Academy of Sciences. From 1944 he was simultaneously a professor in the Mathematics Department of Leningrad University. Linnik organized the chair of probability theory and mathematical statistics and founded the Leningrad school of probability and statistics.

Linnik's principal fields of endeavor were number theory, probability theory, and mathematical statistics. A characteristic feature of his work was the use of very advanced analytical techniques. His early works were devoted to analytic number theory. He began with the problem of the representation of an integer by positive ternary quadratic forms. Linnik next developed a powerful new method of investigating similar problems, the so-called ergodic method in number theory. A short paper (1941) served as a beginning of another powerful method now known as the large sieve method. In the 1950's Linnik developed a new strong method of analytic number theory. This method made it possible to solve some problems of additive number theory that cannot be treated by earlier methods. This method, which also uses some ideas of probability theory, is known as the dispersion method in number theory.

In the late 1940's Linnik began to work in probability theory and statistics. He immediately became famous because of his papers on probability limit theorems. Most important here was his work on probability of large deviations, where he found a new understanding of the problem. In the 1950's Linnik advanced the arithmetic of probability distributions, which had ceased to develop at the end of the 1930's. He did very important research in mathematical statistics and was one of the first to use the powerful analytical apparatus of the modern function theory for the solution of statistical problems. In a sense he created analytical statistics. He solved such difficult problems of statistics as characterization problems, the Behrens-Fisher problem, and the minimax property of the Hotelling T^2 test. Linnik was elected a member of the U.S.S.R. Academy of Sciences in 1964. He was also a member of the Swedish Academy and of many other societies and held an honorary doctorate from the University of Paris. For many years he was president of the Leningrad Mathematical Society.

BIBLIOGRAPHY

I. Original Works. Works by Linnik that are available in English are *Method of Least Squares and Principles of the Theory of Observations*, Regina C. Erlandt, trans., N. L. Johnson, ed. (New York, 1961); *The Dispersion Method in Binary Additive Problems*, S. Schur, trans. (Providence, R.I., 1963); *The Decomposition of Probability Distributions*, S. J. Taylor, ed. (New York, 1964); *Elementary Methods in Analytic Number Theory*, A. Feinstein, trans., rev. and ed. by L. J. Mordell (Chicago, 1965), written with A. Gelfond; "Characterization of Tests of the Bartlett-Schaffé Type" and "On the Construction of Optimal . . . Solutions of the Behrens-Fischer Problem," in *Articles on Mathematical Statistics and the Theory of Probability*, Proceedings of the Steklov Institute of Mathematics no. 79 (1966); *Ergodic Properties of Algebraic Fields*, M. S. Keane, trans. (New York, 1968); *Statistical Problems with Nuisance Parameters* (Providence, R.I., 1968); *Independent and Stationary Sequences of Random Variables*, J. F. C. Kingman, ed. (Groningen, 1971), written with I. A. Ibragimov; "Nonlinear Statistics and Random Linear Forms," written with A. A. Zinger, and "Gamma Distribution and Partial Sufficiency of Polynomials," written with A. L. Ruhin and S. I. Strelic, in *Theoretical Problems in Mathematical Statistics*, Proceedings of the Steklov Institute of Mathematics no. 111 (1972); *Characterization Problems in Mathematical Statistics*, B. Ramachandran, trans. (New York, 1973), written with A. M. Kagan and C. Radhakrishna Rao; and *Decomposition of Random Variables and Vectors*, Judah Rosenblatt, ed. (Providence, R.I., 1977), written with I. V. Ostrovskii.

II. Secondary Literature. Bibliographies are in *Uspekhi matematicheskikh nauk*, **20**, no. 2 (1965), 229–236, and **28**, no. 2 (1973), 210–213.

I. A. Ibragimov

LIOUVILLE, JOSEPH (*b.* St.-Omer, Pas-de-Calais, France, 24 March 1809; *d.* Paris, France, 8 September 1882)

Liouville is most famous for having founded and directed for almost forty years one of the major mathematical journals of the nineteenth century, the *Journal de Liouville*. He also made important contributions in pure and applied mathematics and exerted a fruitful influence on French mathematics through his teaching.

The few articles devoted to Liouville contain little biographical data. Thus the principal stages of his life and career must be reconstructed on the basis of original documentation. There is no exhaustive list of Liouville's works, which are dispersed in some 400 publications—the most nearly complete is that in the Royal Society's *Catalogue of Scientific Papers*. His work as a whole has been treated in only two original studies of limited scope, those of G. Chrystal and G. Loria. On the other hand, certain of Liouville's works have been analyzed in greater detail, such as those on geometry. In view of the limited space available, this study cannot hope to provide a thorough account of Liouville's work but will attempt instead to present its major themes.

Life. Liouville was the second son of Claude-Joseph Liouville (1772–1852), an army captain, and Thérèse Balland, both originally from Lorraine. Liouville studied in Commercy and then in Toul. In 1831 he married a maternal cousin, Marie-Louise Balland (1812–1880); they had three daughters and one son. Liouville lived a calm and studious life, enlivened by an annual vacation at the family house in Toul. His scientific career was disturbed only by a brief venture into politics, during the Revolution of 1848. Already known for his democratic convictions, he was elected on 23 April 1848 to the Constituent Assembly as one of the representatives from the department of the Meurthe. He voted with the moderate democratic party. His defeat in the elections for the Legislative Assembly in May 1849 marked the end of his political ambitions.

Admitted to the École Polytechnique in November 1825, Liouville transferred in November 1827 to the École des Ponts et Chaussées, where, while preparing for a career in engineering, he began original research in mathematics and mathematical physics. Between June 1828 and November 1830 he presented before the Académie des Sciences seven memoirs, two of which dealt with the theory of electricity, three with the analytic theory of heat, and two with mathematical analysis. Although Academy reporters expressed certain reservations, these first works were on the whole very favorably received; and their partial publication in the *Annales de chimie et de physique*, in Gergonne's *Annales*,[1] and in Férussac's *Bulletin* gained their author a certain reputation. In order to secure as much freedom as possible to pursue his research, Liouville soon thought of changing professions. In 1830, upon graduating from the École des Ponts et Chaussées, he refused the position of engineer that he was offered, hoping that his reputation would permit him to obtain a teaching post fairly soon.

In November 1831 Liouville was selected by the Council on Instruction of the École Polytechnique to replace P. Binet as *répétiteur* in L. Mathieu's course in analysis and mechanics. This was the beginning of a brilliant career of some fifty years, in the course of which Liouville taught pure and applied mathematics in the leading Paris institutions of higher education.

In 1838 Liouville succeeded Mathieu as holder of one of the two chairs of analysis and mechanics at the École Polytechnique, a position that he resigned in 1851, immediately after his election to the Collège de France. From 1833 to 1838 Liouville also taught mathematics and mechanics, but at a more elementary level, at the recently founded École Centrale des Arts et Manufactures. In March 1837 he was chosen to teach mathematical physics at the Collège de France as *suppléant* for J. B. Biot. He resigned in March 1843 to protest the election of Count Libri-Carrucci to the chair of mathematics at that institution.

Liouville did not return to the Collège de France until the beginning of 1851, when he succeeded Libri-Carrucci, who had left France.[2] This chair had no fixed program, and so for the first time Liouville could present his own research and discuss current topics. He took advantage of this to present unpublished works, some of which were developed by his students before he himself published them.[3] Appreciating the interest and flexibility of such teaching, he remained in the post until 1879, when he arranged for O. Bonnet to take over his duties.

Liouville also wished to teach on the university level. Toward this end he had earned his doctorate with a dissertation on certain developments in Fourier series and their applications in mathematical physics (1836). He was therefore eligible for election, in 1857, to the chair of rational mechanics at the Paris Faculty of Sciences, a position vacant since the death of Charles Sturm. In 1874, he stopped teaching there and arranged for his replacement by Darboux.

Parallel with this very full academic career, Liouville was elected a member of the astronomy section of the Académie des Sciences in June 1839, succeeding M. Lefrançois de Lalande; and in 1840 he succeeded Poisson as a member of the Bureau des Longitudes. From this time on, he participated regularly in the work of these two groups. For forty years he also passionately devoted himself to another particularly burdensome task, heading an important mathematical journal. The almost simultaneous demise, in 1831, of the only French mathematical review, Gergonne's *Annales de mathématiques pures et appliquées*, together with one of the principal science reviews, Férussac's *Bulletin des sciences mathématiques, astronomiques, physiques et chimiques*, deprived French-language mathematicians of two of their favorite forums. Liouville understood that the vigor of French mathematical writings demanded the creation of new organs of communication. Despite his youth and inexperience in the problems of editing and publishing, he launched the *Journal de mathématiques pures et appliquées* in January 1836. He published the first thirty-nine volumes (the twenty of the first series [1836–1855] and the nineteen of the second series [1856–1874]), each volume in twelve fascicles of thirty-two to forty pages. Finally, at the end of 1874, he entrusted the editorship to H. Résal.

Open to all branches of pure and applied mathematics, the publication was extremely successful and was soon called the *Journal de Liouville*. Its first volume contained articles by Ampère, Chasles, Coriolis, Jacobi, Lamé, V.-A. Lebesgue, Libri-Carrucci, Plücker, Sturm, and Liouville himself. Although not all the tables of contents are as brilliant as that of the first, the thirty-nine volumes published by Liouville record an important part of the mathematical activity of the forty years of the mid-nineteenth century. In fact, Liouville secured regular contributions from a majority of the great mathematicians of the era and maintained particularly warm and fruitful relations with Jacobi, Dirichlet, Lamé, Coriolis, and Sturm. At the same time he sought to guide and smooth the way for the first works of young authors, notably Le Verrier, Bonnet, J. A. Serret, J. Bertrand, Hermite, and Bour. But his outstanding qualities as an editor are most clearly displayed in his exemplary effort to assimilate as perfectly as possible the work of Galois. He imposed this task on himself in order to establish in an irreproachable fashion the texts he published in volume 11 of the *Journal de mathématiques*.

During the first thirty years of his career Liouville, while maintaining a very special interest in mathematical analysis, also did research in mathematical physics, algebra, number theory, and geometry. Starting in 1857, however, he considerably altered the orientation of his studies, concentrating more and more on particular problems of number theory. Departing in this way from the most fruitful paths of mathematical research, Liouville saw his influence decline rapidly. Yet it was the abandonment of the editorship of his *Journal* in 1874 that signaled the real end of his activity. His publications, which had been appearing with decreasing frequency since 1867, stopped altogether at this time. Simultaneously he gave up his courses at the Sorbonne, where his *suppléants* were Darboux and then Tisserand. He still attended the sessions of the Académie des Sciences and of the Bureau des Longitudes and still lectured at the Collège de France; but he no longer really participated in French mathematical life.

Mathematical Works. Liouville published thirty-nine volumes of the *Journal de mathématiques*, republished a work by Monge, and published a treatise by Navier; but he never composed a general work of his own. He did write nearly 400 memoirs, articles, and notes on a great many aspects of pure and applied mathematics. Despite its great diversity, this literary output is marked by a limited number of major themes, the majority of which were evident in his first publications. Liouville also published numerous articles correcting, completing, or extending the results of others, especially of articles that had appeared in the *Journal de mathématiques*. Other articles by him were summaries of or extracts from courses he gave at the Collège de France.

The divisions used below tend to obscure one of the main characteristics of Liouville's works, their interdisciplinary nature. Yet they are indispensable in the presentation of such a diverse body of work. References generally will be limited to the year of publication; given that information, further details can rapidly be found by consulting the *Catalogue of Scientific Papers.*

Mathematical Analysis. It was in mathematical analysis that Liouville published the greatest number and the most varied of his works. Composed mainly from 1832 to 1857, they number about one hundred. It is thus possible to mention only the most important and most original of these contributions, including some that were virtually ignored by contemporaries. To grasp their significance fully, it must be noted that these apparently disordered investigations were actually guided—for lack of an overall plan—by a few governing ideas. It is also important to view each of them in the context of the studies carried out at the same time by Gauss, Jacobi, Cauchy, and Sturm. It should be remembered that in his courses at the Collège de France, Liouville treated important questions that do not appear among his writings and that he inspired many disciples.

Certain of Liouville's earliest investigations in mathematical analysis should be viewed as a continuation of the then most recent works of Abel and Jacobi. The most important are concerned with attempts to classify all algebraic functions and the simplest types of transcendental functions, with the theory of elliptic functions, and with certain types of integrals that can be expressed by an algebraic function.

Following the demonstration by Abel and Galois

of the impossibility of algebraically solving general equations higher than the fourth degree, Liouville devoted several memoirs to determining the nature of the roots of algebraic equations of higher degree and of transcendental equations. One of the results he obtained was that according to which the number e cannot be the root of any second- or fourth-degree equation (1840). In 1844 he discovered a specific characteristic of the expansion as a continued fraction of every algebraic number, and showed that there are continued fractions that do not possess this characteristic. This discovery ("Liouville's transcendental numbers") is set forth in a memoir entitled "Sur des classes très-étendues de nombres dont la valeur n'est ni algébrique, ni même réductible à des irrationnelles algébriques" (*Journal de mathématiques*, **16** [1851], 133–142). It was not until 1873 that G. Cantor demonstrated the existence of much more general transcendental numbers.

In 1844 Liouville took up the study of all the functions possessing—like the elliptic functions—the property of admitting two periods. He set forth his theory to Joachimsthal and Borchardt (1847) before presenting it at the Collège de France (1850–1851). Thus, although he published little on the subject, the theory itself rapidly became widely known through the publications of Borchardt and the *Théorie des fonctions doublement périodiques* (1859) of Briot and Bouquet. Liouville made important contributions to the theory of Eulerian functions. He also sought to develop the theory of differential equations and of partial differential equations. In addition to numerous memoirs treating particular types of differential equations, such as Riccati's equation, and various technical questions, Liouville also worked on general problems, such as the demonstration (1840) of the impossibility, in general, of reducing the solution of differential equations either to a finite sequence of algebraic operations and indefinite integrations or—independently of Cauchy—to a particular aspect of the method of successive approximations (1837–1838). His contributions in the theory of partial differential equations were also of considerable value, even though a large portion of his "discoveries" had been anticipated by Jacobi. Much of his research in this area was closely linked with rational mechanics, celestial mechanics, and mathematical physics.

Pursuing the pioneer investigations of Leibniz, Johann Bernoulli, and Euler, Liouville devoted a part of his early work (1832–1836) to an attempt to enlarge as far as possible the notions of the differential and the integral, and in particular to establish the theory of derivatives of arbitrary index. Assuming a function $f(x)$ to be representable as a series of exponentials

$$f(x) = \sum_{n=0}^{n=+\infty} (c_n e^{a_n x}),$$

he defined its derivative of order s (s being an arbitrary number, rational or irrational, or even complex) by the series

$$D_s f(x) = \sum_{n=0}^{n=+\infty} c_n a_n^s \, e^{a_n x}.$$

This definition does in fact extend the ordinary differential calculus of integral indexes, but its generality is limited: not every function admits an expansion of the type proposed; and the convergence and uniqueness of the expansion are not guaranteed for all values of s. Despite its weaknesses and deficiencies, Liouville's endeavor, one of the many efforts that led to the establishment of functional calculus, shows his great virtuosity in handling the analysis of his time.

Liouville and Sturm published an important series of memoirs in the first two volumes of the *Journal de mathématiques* (1836–1837). Bourbaki (*Éléments d'histoire des mathématiques*, 2nd ed., pp. 260–262) shows that these investigations, which extended the numerous earlier works devoted to the equation of vibrating strings, permitted the elaboration of a general theory of oscillations for the case of one variable. He also shows that they are linked to the beginning of the theory of linear integral equations that contributed to the advent of modern ideas concerning functional analysis.

This constitutes only a broad outline of Liouville's chief contributions to analysis. The principal works mentioned below in connection with mathematical physics should for the most part be considered direct applications—or even important elements—of Liouville's analytical investigations.

Mathematical Physics. Under the influence of Ampère and of Navier, whose courses he had followed at the Collège de France and at the École des Ponts et Chaussées from 1828 to 1830, Liouville directed his first investigations to two areas of mathematical physics of current interest: the theory of electrodynamics and the theory of heat. After these first studies he never returned to the former topic. On the other hand he later (1836–1838, 1846–1848) devoted several memoirs to the theory of heat, but only for the purpose of employing new analytic methods, such as elliptic functions. Similarly, it was to demonstrate the power of analysis that he considered certain aspects of the theory of sound (1836, 1838) and the distribution of electricity on the surface of conductors (1846, 1857).

Celestial Mechanics. Liouville came in contact with celestial mechanics in 1834, through a hydrodynamical problem: finding the surface of equilibrium of a homogeneous fluid mass in rotation about an axis. He showed that with Laplace's formulas one can demonstrate Jacobi's theorem concerning the existence among these equilibrium figures of an ellipsoidal surface with unequal axes. Between 1839 and 1855 Liouville returned to this topic on several occasions, confirming the efficacy of the Laplacian methods while verifying the great power of the new procedures. From 1836 to 1842 he wrote a series of memoirs on classical celestial mechanics (perturbations, secular variations, the use of elliptic functions). Subsequently, although he was active in the Bureau des Longitudes, he devoted only a few notes to the problem of attraction (1845) and to particular cases of the three-body problem (1842, 1846).

Rational Mechanics. Rational mechanics held Liouville's interest for only two short periods. From 1846 to 1849, influenced by the work of Hamilton and Jacobi, he sought to erect a theory of point dynamics. He did not return to related subjects until 1855 and 1856, when he published, respectively, two studies of the differential equations of dynamics and an important note on the use of the principle of least action.

Algebra. Although Liouville wrote only a few memoirs dealing with algebraic questions, his contributions in this field merit discussion in some detail.

In 1836, with his friend Sturm, Liouville demonstrated Cauchy's theorem concerning the number of complex roots of an algebraic equation that are situated in the interior of a given contour, and in 1840 he gave an elegant demonstration of the fundamental theorem of algebra. From 1841 to 1847 he took up, on new bases, the problem of the elimination of an unknown from two equations in two unknowns, and applied the principles brought to light in this case to the demonstration of various properties of infinitesimal geometry. In 1846 he presented a new method for decomposing rational functions, and in 1863 he generalized Rolle's theorem to the imaginary roots of equations.

Liouville's most significant contribution by far, however, was concerned with the theory of algebraic equations and group theory. He published very little on these questions, but from 1843 to 1846 he conducted a thorough study of Galois's manuscripts in order to prepare for publication, in the October and November 1846 issues of his *Journal de mathématiques*, the bulk of the work of the young mathematician who tragically had died in 1832. Liouville's brief "Avertissement" (pp. 381–384) paid fitting homage to the value of Galois's work, but the second part of the

Oeuvres, announced for the following volume of the *Journal*, was not published until 1908 by J. Tannery. According to J. Bertrand, Liouville invited a few friends, including J. A. Serret, to attend a series of lectures on Galois's work.[1] Although he did not publish the text of these lectures, Liouville nevertheless contributed in large measure to making known a body of work whose extraordinary innovations were to become more and more influential. He thus participated, indirectly, in the elaboration of modern algebra and of group theory.

Geometry. Liouville's work in geometry, the subject of an excellent analysis by Chasles (*Rapport sur les progrès de la géométrie* [Paris, 1870], pp. 127–130), consists of about twenty works written over the period from 1832 to 1854. The majority of them are applications or extensions of other investigations and are more analytic than geometric in their inspiration.

In 1832 Liouville showed that his "calculus of differentials of arbitrary index" could facilitate the study of certain questions of mechanics and geometry. In 1841 and 1844 he demonstrated and extended, by employing elimination theory, numerous metric properties of curves and surfaces that were established geometrically by Chasles. In 1844 Liouville published a new method for determining the geodesic lines of an arbitrary ellipsoid, a problem that Jacobi had just reduced to one involving elliptic transcendentals. In 1846 he proposed a direct demonstration of the so-called Joachimsthal equation and generalized the study of polygons of maximal or minimal perimeter inscribed in or circumscribed about a plane or spherical conic section to geodesic polygons traced on an ellipsoid. Finally, in 1847, prompted by a note of W. Thomson concerning the distribution of electricity on two conducting bodies, Liouville undertook an analytic study of inversive geometry in space, which he called "transformation by reciprocal vector rays." He showed that the inversion is the only conformal nonlinear spatial transformation and pointed out its applications to many questions of geometry and mathematical physics.

When Liouville published the fifth edition of Monge's *Application de l'analyse à la géométrie* (1850), he added to it Gauss's famous memoir *Disquisitiones generales circa superficies curvas*. He also appended to it seven important related notes of his own; these dealt with the theory of space curves, the introduction of the notions of relative curvature and geodesic curvature of curves situated on a surface, the integration of the equation of geodesic lines, the notion of total curvature, the study of the deformations of a surface of constant curvature, a particular type of representation of one surface on another, and the theory of vibrating strings.

Liouville returned to certain aspects of the general theory of surfaces in later works and in his lectures at the Collège de France—for instance, the determination of the surface the development of which is composed of two confocal quadrics (1851). Although they treat rather disparate topics, these works on infinitesimal geometry exerted a salutary influence on research in this field, confirming the fruitfulness of the analytic methods of Gauss's school.

Number Theory. Liouville entered the new field of number theory in 1840 with a demonstration that the impossibility of the equation $x^n + y^n = z^n$ entails that of the equation $x^{2n} + y^{2n} = z^{2n}$. He returned to this field only occasionally in the following years, publishing a comparison of two particular quadratic forms (1845) and a new demonstration of the law of quadratic reciprocity (1847). In 1856, however, he began an impressive and astonishing series of works in this area, abandoning—except for some brief notes on analysis—the important investigations he was carrying out in other branches of mathematics. At first he took an interest in quite varied questions, including the sum of the divisors of an integer; the impossibility, for integers, of the equation $(p - 1)! + 1 = p^m$, p being a prime number greater than 5; and the number $\varphi(n)$ of integers less than n that are prime to n. From 1858 to 1865, in eighteen successive notes published in the *Journal de mathématiques* under the general title "Sur quelques formules générales qui peuvent être utiles dans la théorie des nombres," Liouville stated without demonstration a series of theorems—a list is given in volume II of L. E. Dickson, *History of the Theory of Numbers*—that constitute the foundations of "analytic" number theory.

But from 1859 to 1866 Liouville devoted the bulk of his publications—nearly 200 short notes in the *Journal de mathématiques*—to a monotonous series of particular problems in number theory. These problems are reducible to two principal types: the exposition of certain properties of prime numbers of a particular form and their products (properties equivalent to the existence of integral solutions of equations having the form $ax + by = c$, the numbers a, b, c being of a given form); and the determination of different representations of an arbitrary integer by a quadratic form of the type $ax^2 + by^2 + cz^2 + dt^2$, where a, b, c, and d are given constants.

L. E. Dickson mentions the examples Liouville studied in this series and the demonstrations that were published later: Liouville's notes contain only statements and numerical proofs. One may well be astonished at his singular behavior in abandoning his other research in order to amass, without any real demonstration, detailed results concerning two specialized topics in number theory. He never explained this in his writings. Hence one may wonder, as did G. Loria, whether he may have justified his apparently mysterious choice of examples in the course of his lectures at the Collège de France. Bôcher, more severe, simply considers these last publications to be mediocre.

Four hundred memoirs, published mainly in the *Journal de mathématiques* and the *Comptes rendus hebdomadaires des séances de l'Académie des sciences*, and 340 manuscript notebooks[5] in the Bibliothèque de l'Institut de France, Paris—this is the mass of documents that must be carefully analyzed in order to provide an exhaustive description of Liouville's work. To complete this account, it would also be necessary to trace more exactly his activity as head of the *Journal de mathématiques*, to assemble the greatest amount of data possible on the courses he taught, above all at the Collège de France, and to ascertain his role in the training of his students and in their publications.

NOTES

1. This, Liouville's second publication—he was then twenty-one—appeared in *Annales de mathématiques pures et appliquées* (**21**, nos. 5 and 6 [Nov. and Dec. 1830]). The second of these issues also contains two short notes by Evariste Galois, whose work Liouville published in *Journal de mathématiques pures et appliquées*, **11** (1846). But this circumstance obviously is not sufficient to prove that the two knew each other. A note by Gergonne, following Liouville's memoir, severely criticizes its style and presentation. The editor of the *Annales* denied all hope of a future for the young man who, five years later, succeeded him by creating the *Journal de mathématiques*. See also Liouville's "Note sur l'électro-dynamique," in *Bulletin des sciences mathématiques* . . ., **15** (Jan. 1831), 29–31, which is omitted from all bibliographies.
2. In 1843 the election for the chair of mathematics left vacant by the death of S. F. Lacroix saw three opposing candidates, all members of the Académie des Sciences: Cauchy, Liouville, and Libri-Carrucci. At the time Liouville was engaged in a violent controversy with Libri-Carrucci, whose abilities he publicly disputed. He therefore resigned as soon as he learned that the Council of the Collège de France was recommending that the Assembly vote for Libri-Carrucci. In 1850, when this chair became vacant, following Libri-Carrucci's dismissal, Cauchy and Liouville again were candidates. The particular circumstances of the votes that resulted in Liouville's finally being chosen (18 Jan. 1851) gave rise to vigorous protests by Cauchy.
3. Thus the works on doubly periodic functions that Liouville had presented privately (1847) or in public lectures (1851) were used by Borchardt and Joachimsthal and also by Briot and Bouquet. Similarly, Lebesgue published in his *Exercices d'analyse numérique* (1859) Liouville's demonstration, unpublished until then, of Waring's theorem for the case of biquadratic numbers.
4. J. Bertrand (*Éloges académiques*, II [Paris, 1902], 342–343) wrote that it was out of deference to Liouville, who had taught him Galois's discoveries, that J. A. Serret mentioned

these discoveries in neither the first (1849) nor the second edition (1859) of his *Cours d'algèbre supérieure*, but only in the third (1866).
5. A rapid examination of some of these notebooks shows that they consist mainly of outlines and final drafts of the published works, but the whole collection would have to be gone over very thoroughly before a definitive evaluation could be made.

BIBLIOGRAPHY

I. ORIGINAL WORKS. Liouville published only two of his works in book form: his thesis, *Sur le développement des fonctions ou parties de fonctions en séries de sinus et de cosinus, dont on fait usage dans un grand nombre de questions de mécanique et de physique* . . . (Paris, 1836); and a summary of a course he gave at the École Centrale des Arts et Manufactures in 1837–1838, *Résumé des leçons de trigonométrie. Notes pour le cours de statique* (Paris, n.d.). He edited and annotated Gaspard Monge, *Application de l'analyse à la géométrie*, 5th ed. (Paris, 1850); and H. Navier, *Résumé des leçons d'analyse données à l'École polytechnique* . . ., 2 vols. (Paris, 1856).

Liouville published the first 39 vols. of the *Journal de mathématiques pures et appliquées*: 1st ser., **1–20** (1836–1855); 2nd ser., **1–19** (1856–1874). He also wrote approximately 400 papers, of which the majority are cited in the Royal Society's *Catalogue of Scientific Papers*, IV (1870), 39–49 (nos. 1–309 for the period 1829–1863, plus three articles written in collaboration with Sturm); VIII (1879), 239–241 (nos. 310–377 for the period 1864–1873); X (1894), 606 (nos. 378–380 for the period 1874–1880). See also Poggendorff, I, cols. 1471–1475 and III, p. 818.

The list of Liouville's contributions to the *Journal de mathématiques* is given in the tables of contents inserted at the end of vol. **20**, 1st ser. (1855), and at the end of vol. **19**, 2nd ser. (1874). (The articles in the *Journal de mathématiques* signed "Besge" are attributed to Liouville by H. Brocard, in *Intermédiaire des mathématiciens*, **9** [1902], 216.) The memoirs and notes that Liouville presented to the Académie des Sciences are cited from 1829 to July 1835 in the corresponding vols. of the *Procès-verbaux des séances de l'Académie des sciences* (see index) and after July 1835 in the vols. of *Tables des Comptes rendus hebdomadaires de l'Académie des sciences*, published every 15 years.

J. Tannery edited the *Correspondance entre Lejeune-Dirichlet et Liouville* (Paris, 1910), a collection of articles published in the *Bulletin des sciences mathématiques*, 2nd ser., **32** (1908), pt. 1, 47–62, 88–95; and **33** (1908–1909), pt. 1, 47–64.

Liouville's MSS are in the Bibliothèque de l'Institut de France, Paris. They consist of 340 notebooks and cartons of various materials, MS 3615–3640. See also the papers of Evariste Galois, MS 2108, folios 252–285.

II. SECONDARY LITERATURE. Liouville's biography is sketched in the following articles (listed chronologically): Jacob, in F. Hoefer, ed., *Nouvelle biographie générale*, XXXI (Paris, 1872), 316–318; G. Vapereau, *Dictionnaire universel des contemporains*, 5th ed. (Paris, 1880), 1171–

1172; H. Faye and E. Laboulaye, in *Comptes rendus hebdomadaires des séances de l'Académie des sciences,* **95** (1882), 467–471, a speech given at his funeral; David, in *Mémoires de l'Académie des sciences, inscriptions et belles-lettres de Toulouse,* 8th ser., **5** (1883), 257–258; A. Robert and G. Cougny, *Dictionnaire des parlementaires français,* II (Paris, 1890), 165; H. Laurent, in *Livre du centenaire de l'École polytechnique,* I (Paris, 1895), 130–133; and L. Sagnet, in *La grande encyclopédie,* XXII (Paris, 1896), 305; and *Intermédiaire des mathématiciens,* **9** (1902), 215–217; **13** (1906), 13–15; **14** (1907), 59–61.

The principal studies dealing with Liouville's work as a whole are G. Chrystal, "Joseph Liouville," in *Proceedings of the Royal Society of Edinburgh,* **14** (1888), 2nd pagination, 83–91; and G. Loria, "Le mathématicien J. Liouville et ses oeuvres," in *Archeion,* **18** (1936), 117–139, translated into English as "J. Liouville and His Work," in *Scripta mathematica,* **4** (1936), 147–154 (with portrait), 257–263, 301–306.

Interesting details and comments concerning various aspects of Liouville's work are in J. Bertrand, *Rapport sur les progrès les plus récents de l'analyse mathématique* (Paris, 1867), pp. 2–5, 32; M. Chasles, *Rapport sur les progrès de la géométrie* (Paris, 1870), 127–140; N. Saltykow, "Sur le rapport des travaux de S. Lie à ceux de Liouville," in *Comptes rendus hebdomadaires des séances de l'Académie des sciences,* **137** (1903), 403–405; M. Bôcher, "Mathématiques et mathématiciens français," in *Revue internationale de l'enseignement,* **67** (1914), 30–31; F. Cajori, *History of Mathematics,* rev. ed. (New York, 1919), see index; L. E. Dickson, *History of the Theory of Numbers,* 3 vols. (Washington, D.C., 1919–1923), see index; and N. Bourbaki, *Éléments d'histoire des mathématiques,* 2nd ed. (Paris, 1964), 260–262.

RENÉ TATON

LIPSCHITZ, RUDOLF OTTO SIGISMUND (*b.* near Königsberg, Germany [now Kaliningrad, R.S.F.S.R.], 14 May 1832; *d.* Bonn, Germany, 7 October 1903)

Lipschitz was born on his father's estate, Bönkein. At the age of fifteen he began the study of mathematics at the University of Königsberg, where Franz Neumann was teaching. He then went to Dirichlet in Berlin, and he always considered himself Dirichlet's student. After interrupting his studies for a year because of illness, he received his doctorate from the University of Berlin on 9 August 1853. After a period of training and teaching at the Gymnasiums in Königsberg and Elbing, Lipschitz became a *Privatdozent* in mathematics at the University of Berlin in 1857. In the same year he married Ida Pascha, the daughter of a neighboring landowner. In 1862 he became an associate professor at Breslau, and in 1864 a full professor at Bonn, where he was examiner for the dissertation of nineteen-year-old Felix Klein in 1868. He rejected an offer to succeed Clebsch at

Göttingen in 1873. Lipschitz was a corresponding member of the academies of Paris, Berlin, Göttingen, and Rome. He loved music, especially classical music.

Lipschitz distinguished himself through the unusual breadth of his research. He carried out many important and fruitful investigations in number theory, in the theory of Bessel functions and of Fourier series, in ordinary and partial differential equations, and in analytical mechanics and potential theory. Of special note are his extensive investigations concerning *n*-dimensional differential forms and the related questions of the calculus of variations, geometry, and mechanics. This work—in which he drew upon the developments that Riemann had presented in his famous lecture on the basic hypotheses underlying geometry—contributed to the creation of a new branch of mathematics.

Lipschitz was also very interested in the fundamental questions of mathematical research and of mathematical instruction in the universities. He gathered together his studies on these topics in the two-volume *Grundlagen der Analysis.* Until then a work of this kind had never appeared in German, although such books existed in French. The work begins with the theory of the rational integers and goes on to differential equations and function theory. The foundation of mathematics is also considered in terms of its applications.

In basic analysis Lipschitz furnished a condition, named for him, which is today as important for proofs of existence and uniqueness as for approximation theory and constructive function theory: If f is a function defined in the interval $\langle a, b \rangle$, then f may be said to satisfy a Lipschitz condition with the exponent α and the coefficient M if for any two values x, y in $\langle a, b \rangle$, the condition

$$|f(y) - f(x)| \leqslant M\,|y - x|^{\alpha}, \qquad \alpha > 0,$$

is satisfied.

In his algebraic number theory investigations of sums of arbitrarily many squares, Lipschitz obtained certain symbolic expressions from real transformations and derived computational rules for them. In this manner he obtained a hypercomplex system that is today termed a Lipschitz algebra. In the case of sums of two squares, his symbolic expressions go over into the numbers of the Gaussian number field; and in that of three squares, into the Hamiltonian quaternions. Related studies were carried out by H. Grassmann.

Lipschitz's most important achievements are contained in his investigations of forms on *n* differentials which he published, starting in 1869, in numerous articles, especially in the *Journal für die reine und angewandte Mathematik*. In this area he was one of the direct followers of Riemann, who in his lecture of 1854, before the Göttingen philosophical faculty, had formulated the principal problems of differential geometry in higher-dimension manifolds and had begun the study of the possible metric structures of an *n*-dimensional manifold. This lecture, which was not exclusively for mathematicians and which presented only the basic ideas, was published in 1868, following Riemann's death. A year later Lipschitz published his first work on this subject. With E. B. Christoffel, he was one of the first to employ cogredient differentiation; and in the process he created an easily used computational method. He showed that the vanishing of a certain expression is a necessary and sufficient condition for a Riemannian manifold to be Euclidean. The expression in question is a fourth-degree curvature quantity. Riemann knew this and had argued it in a work submitted in 1861 to a competition held by the French Academy of Sciences. Riemann did not win the prize, however; and the essay was not published until 1876, when it appeared in his collected works.

Lipschitz was especially successful in his investigations of the properties of Riemannian submanifolds V_m of dimension m in a Riemannian manifold V_n of dimension n. He showed flexure invariants for V_m in V_n, proved theorems concerning curvature, and investigated minimal submanifolds V_m in V_n. He was also responsible for the chief theorem concerning the mean curvature vector that yields the condition for a minimal submanifold: A submanifold V_m of V_n is a minimal submanifold if and only if the mean curvature vector vanishes at every point. Thus a manifold V_m is said to be a minimal manifold in V_n if, the boundary being fixed, the variation of the content of each subset bounded by a closed V_{m-1} vanishes. The definition of the mean curvature vector of a submanifold V_m is based on the fundamental concept of the curvature vector of a nonisotropic curve in V_m. This vector can be described with the help of Christoffel's three index symbols. Its length is the first curvature of the curve and vanishes for geodesics in V_m.

Lipschitz's investigations were continued by G. Ricci. The latter's absolute differential calculus was employed, beginning in 1913, by Einstein, who in turn stimulated interest and further research in the differential geometry of higher-dimension manifolds.

BIBLIOGRAPHY

Lipschitz's books are *Grundlagen der Analysis*, 2 vols. (Bonn, 1877–1880); and *Untersuchungen über die Summen von Quadraten* (Bonn, 1886). He also published in many German and foreign journals, especially the *Journal für die reine und angewandte Mathematik* (from 1869). There is a bibliography in Poggendorff, IV, 897.

A biographical article is H. Kortum, "Rudolf Lipschitz," in *Jahresberichte der Deutschen Matematiker-Vereinigung*, **15** (1906), 56–59.

BRUNO SCHOENEBERG

LITTLEWOOD, JOHN EDENSOR (*b*. Rochester, England, 9 June 1885; *d*. Cambridge, England, 6 September 1977)

Littlewood was the eldest son of Edward Thornton Littlewood and Sylvia Ackland. His father, a graduate of Peterhouse, Cambridge, took his family to South Africa in 1892 when he became headmaster of a school at Wynberg, near Cape Town. John spent the years 1900 to 1903 at St. Paul's School in London, where his mathematics master was Francis Sowerby Macaulay, himself a creative mathematician.

Littlewood went to Cambridge as a scholar at Trinity College in October 1903. At this time the physical sciences were in a very strong position in Cambridge. As a result mathematics was looked upon as ancillary to physical science, which meant that the emphasis was on special functions and differential equations, where the treatment was far from rigorous. Moreover, great emphasis was put on manipulative skill. All this was not to Littlewood's taste: "I wasted my time except for rare interludes for the first two academic years." He did, however, value lectures given by Alfred North Whitehead on the foundations of mechanics.

Littlewood's research began during the long vacation of 1906. His tutor and director of studies was E. W. Barnes, who later left Cambridge for a career in the Anglican church and became better known as bishop of Birmingham. In 1907 Littlewood accepted the post of lecturer at Manchester University. He returned to Cambridge in 1910 and succeeded Whitehead as college lecturer at Trinity College.

It would be wrong to give the impression that Littlewood was concerned solely with mathematics; he had very wide interests. He was strong, somewhat shorter than average, and a very able athlete. He rowed for his college in Cambridge and later was very active in rock climbing and skiing. He also had a strong interest in music and was a good raconteur. However, his absorbing passion was mathematics, and although he was by no means averse to applied mathematics (indeed, he made important contributions to ballistics; *Collected Papers*, p. 21), his real interest was in analysis. Thus any account of Littlewood must be largely occupied with his contributions to pure mathematics. The mathematically inclined reader will find an excellent account in J. C. Burkill et al. (1978).

At the time Littlewood began his research, Barnes had studied entire functions of nonzero order, but his methods did not extend to functions of zero order, so he suggested that Littlewood might work on those functions. Littlewood later said, "I rather luckily struck oil at once (by switching to more elementary methods) and after that never looked back." In fact the "switch" was a big leap forward. He was able to establish for general functions a relation between the maximum and minimum moduli of these functions on large circles extending to infinity. Barnes had worked with special functions. There was a curious sequel that reveals much about analysis in Cambridge at the time. Barnes now suggested a problem on the zero of a certain analytic function. This was the notorious Riemann zeta function, which is very important in prime number theory. In 1859 Georg Friedrich Riemann had conjectured that all its complex zeros have real part 1/2. This is the famous Riemann hypothesis, which has never been proved. That Barnes should suggest this problem even to a very brilliant pupil shows that he could have had no idea of what was involved. Although Littlewood failed to prove the Riemann hypothesis, his investigations bore fruit. His work on the Riemann zeta function had great permanent value and led to his maxim "Never be afraid to tackle a difficult problem, however difficult it may appear. You may not solve it, but it could lead you on to something else."

Littlewood's second achievement about this time was the discovery of his famous Tauberian theorem (*Collected Papers*, p. 757). Sometime before, an earlier but less deep Tauberian theorem had been proved by G. H. Hardy, and the common interest of these two mathematicians in Tauberian theory was an important factor in initiating their lifelong collaboration. Hardy and Littlewood had very different personalities—indeed, they had little in common apart from the fact that they were both mathematicians working in Cambridge. Their joint work was collected in the papers of Hardy, and some three-quarters of the papers in the first three volumes of his papers were written jointly with Littlewood. During some of the most fruitful years, Littlewood was in Cambridge and Hardy in Oxford; they worked by correspondence. However, after Hardy's return to Cambridge, they still preferred to work in this way even though they were both at Trinity College.

This remarkable collaboration between two equally outstanding scientists was probably the greatest ever between two mathematicians. Harald Bohr states that it was not started without misgivings. It was important to them that their collaboration not cramp either of their styles or encroach on their freedom:

> Therefore as a safety measure . . . they amused themselves by formulating some so-called axioms . . . . The first of them said that, when one wrote to the other it was completely indifferent whether what they wrote was right or wrong. As Hardy put it, otherwise they could not write completely as they pleased, but would have to feel a certain responsibility thereby. The second axiom was to the effect that, when one received a letter from the other he was under no obligation whatsoever to read it, let alone to answer it, . . . it might be that the recipient . . . would prefer not to work at that particular time, or perhaps he was just interested in other problems. The third axiom was to the effect that, although it did not really matter if they both simultaneously thought about the same detail, still it was preferable that they should not do so. And finally, the fourth and perhaps the most important axiom, stated that it was quite indifferent if one of them had not contributed the least bit to the contents of a paper under their common names; otherwise . . . now one and then the other, would oppose being named as co-author. *(Collected Works,* I, p. xxviii)

The contribution of Hardy and Littlewood to analysis was enormous. It extended over a vast range including Diophantine approximation, additive number theory, Waring's problem, the Riemann zeta function, prime number theory, inequalities, and Fourier series. In many cases their results are the best known to date, and work is still being done on many of their problems. Much of this is dealt with adequately by Titchmarsh et al., so we mention only the work on the rearrangement of functions and the Hardy-Littlewood maximal function, which has become fundamental in harmonic analysis (Stein and Weiss, p. 53).

Littlewood's work on the Riemann zeta function was outstanding and of great permanent value. An account of it and the subsequent developments is given by Montgomery in the Royal Society biographical memoir. Littlewood did not approve the Riemann hypothesis and became increasingly skeptical about it. Indeed, he privately expressed the opinion that it was false, but that the first zero in the critical script not on the critical line would be so far removed as to be beyond computation even by the most sophisticated methods, thereby rendering the problem unsolvable in the foreseeable future. This view was partly the result of his work on the functions $\pi(x)$ and li(x) discussed by

Montgomery.

Littlewood collaborated with other mathematicians besides Hardy. He and Harald Bohr prepared a book on the Riemann zeta function, but when it was completed, they were too exhausted to send it to the publisher. The manuscript was passed on to Ingham and Edward Charles Titchmarsh, and later incorporated in their larger works. Littlewood collaborated with Dame Mary Cartwright on differential equations, with A. C. Offord on random equations and entire functions, and with R. E. A. C. Paley on Fourier analysis. The differential equations considered in the work with Cartwright arose in the study of electric circuits. A brief account with further developments is given by Peter Swinnerton-Dyer in Littlewood's *Collected Papers* (p. 295) and by Cartwright (1974). Following the work with Offord, there is now a considerable literature on zeros of polynomials and related matters. There is a brief account of the developments by Bollobas in Littlewood's *Collected Papers* (pp. 1343, 1421) and further development by Kleitman.

Littlewood's work with Paley represents one of the most far-reaching advances in Fourier analysis. In terms of its one-dimensional Fourier series, they define the dyactic decomposition of a function and, by employing the Poisson integral, a certain nonlinear operator they called the g function. The Littlewood-Paley theory was based on complex variable methods and thus was limited to one dimension. It was later realized that an n-dimensional result could be deduced from the one-dimensional theory, and this led in turn to some of the most exciting developments in analysis. There is a brief account by Brannan in Littlewood's *Collected Papers* (p. 664) and also by E. M. Stein in *Singular Integrals* (pp. 81–94) and *Topics in Harmonic Analysis*.

At the age of eighty-two, Littlewood gave a lecture at Rockefeller University entitled "The Mathematician's Art of Work." After reading this and *A Mathematician's Miscellany*, it seems fair to say that few mathematicians have told us so much about themselves and their style of work as has Littlewood.

BIBLIOGRAPHY

I. ORIGINAL WORKS. Littlewood's writings are brought together in his *Collected Papers* (Oxford, 1982) and in G. H. Hardy, *Collected Papers*, 7 vols. (Oxford, 1966–1979). See also Littlewood's *A Mathematician's Miscellany* (London, 1953); and "The Mathematician's Work of Art," in *Rockefeller University Review*, **5** (1967), 1–7.

II. SECONDARY LITERATURE. Harald Bohr, *Collected Mathematical Works*, I (Copenhagen, 1952); J. C. Burkill, W. K. Hayman, H. L. Montgomery, A. Zygmund, and A. C. Offord, "John Edensor Littlewood," in *Biographical Memoirs of Fellows of the Royal Society*, **24** (1978), 323–367; Mary L. Cartwright, in *Bulletin of the Institute of Mathematics and Its Applications*, **10** (1974), 329; D. J. Kleitman, "Some New Results on the Littlewood-Offord Problem," in *Journal of Combinatorial Theory*, **A20** (1976), 89–113; Elias M. Stein, *Singular Integrals and Differentiability Properties of Functions* (Princeton, 1970), *Topics in Harmonic Analysis Related to the Littlewood-Paley Theory* (Princeton, 1970), and *Introduction to Fourier Analysis on Euclidean Spaces* (Princeton, 1971), with Guido Weiss; and E. C. Titchmarsh et al., "Godfrey Harold Hardy," in *Journal of the London Mathematical Society*, **25** (1950), 81–138.

A. C. OFFORD

LIU HUI (*fl.* China, *ca.* A.D. 250)

Nothing is known about the life of Liu Hui, except that he flourished in the kingdom of Wei toward the end of the Three Kingdoms period (A.D. 221–265). His mathematical writings, on the other hand, are well known; his commentary on the *Chiu-chang suan-shu* ("Nine Chapters on the Mathematical Art") has exerted a profound influence on Chinese mathematics for well over 1,000 years. He wrote another important, but much shorter, work: the *Hai-tao suan-ching* ("Sea Island Mathematical Manual").

Some scholars believe that the *Chiu-chang suan-shu*, also called the *Chiu-chang suan-ching* ("Mathematical Manual in Nine Chapters"), was already in existence in China during the third century B.C. Ch'ien Pao-tsung, in his *Chung-kuo suan-hsüeh-shih*, and Chang Yin-lin (*Yenching Hsüeh Pao*, **2** [1927], 301) have noted that the titles of certain officials mentioned in the problems date from Ch'in and earlier (third and early second centuries B.C.). There are also references which must indicate a taxation system of 203 B.C. According to Liu Hui's preface, the book was burned during the time of Emperor Ch'in Shih-huang (221–209 B.C.); but remnants of it were later recovered and put in order. In the following two centuries, commentaries on this book were written by Chang Ts'ang (*fl.* 165–142 B.C.) and Keng Shou-ch'ang (*fl.* 75–49 B.C.). In a study by Ch'ien Pao-tsung (1963) it is suggested, from internal textual evidence, that the *Chiu-chang suan-shu* was written between 50 B.C. and A.D. 100 and that it is doubtful whether Chang Ts'ang and Keng Shou-ch'ang had anything to do with the book. Yet Li Yen and Tu Shih-jan, both colleagues of Ch'ien Pao-tsung, still believed Liu Hui's preface when they wrote about the *Chiu-chang suan-shu* in the same year.

During the seventh century both the *Chiu-chang suan-shu* and the *Hai-tao suan-ching* (A.D. 263) were included in *Suan-ching shih-shu* ("Ten Mathematical Manuals," A.D. 656), to which the T'ang mathematician and astronomer Li Shun-feng (602–670) added his annotations and commentaries. These works then became standard texts for students of mathematics; official regulations prescribed that three years be devoted to the works of Liu Hui. Liu Hui's works also found their way to Japan with these ten mathematical manuals. When schools were established in Japan in 702 and mathematics was taught, both the *Chiu-chang suan-shu* and the *Hai-tao suan-ching* were among the prescribed texts.

According to Ch'eng Ta-wei's mathematical treatise, the *Suan-fa t'ung-tsung* ("Systematic Treatise on Arithmetic"; 1592), both the *Chiu-chang suan-shu* and the *Hai-tao suan-ching* were first printed officially in 1084. There was another printed version of them by Pao Huan-chih in 1213. In the early fifteenth century they were included, although considerably rearranged, in the vast Ming encyclopedia, the *Yung-lo ta-tien* (1403–1407). In the second part of the eighteenth century Tai Chen (1724–1777) reconstructed these two texts after having extracted them piecemeal from the *Yung-lo ta-tien*. They were subsequently included by K'ung Chi-han (1739–1787) in his *Wei-po-hsieh ts'ung-shu* (1773). Three years later Ch'ü Tseng-fa printed them separately with a preface by Tai Chen.

Other reproductions based on Tai Chen's reconstruction in the *Wei-po-hsieh ts'ung-shu* are found in the *Suan-ching shih-shu* ("Ten Mathematical Manuals") of Mei Ch'i-chao (1862) and in the *Wan-yu-wen-k'u* (1929–1933) and *Ssu-pu ts'ung-k'an* series (1920–1922; both of the Commercial Press, Shanghai). Two nineteenth-century scholars, Chung Hsiang and Li Huang, discovered that certain passages in the text had been rendered incomprehensible by Tai Chen's attempt to improve on the original text of the *Chiu-chang suan-shu*. A fragment of the early thirteenth-century edition of the *Chiu-chang suan-shu*, consisting of only five chapters, was found during the seventeenth century in Nanking, in the private library of Huang Yü-chi (1629–1691). This copy was seen by the famous Ch'ing scholar Mei Wen-ting (1633–1721) in 1678, and it later came into the possession of K'ung Chi-han (1739–1784) and then Chang Tun-jen (1754–1834); finally it was acquired by the Shanghai Library, where it is now kept. In 1684, Mao I (1640–after 1710) made a handwritten copy of the original text found in the library of Huang Yü-chi. This copy was later acquired by the emperor during the Ch'ien-lung reign (1736–1795). In 1932 it was reproduced

in the *T'ien-lu-lin-lang ts'ung-shu* series.

In 1261 Yang Hui wrote the *Hsiang-chieh chiu-chang suan-fa* ("Detailed Analysis of the Mathematical Rules in the Nine Chapters") to elucidate the problems in the *Chiu-chang suan-shu*. Ch'ien Pao-tsung in 1963 collated the text of the *Chiu-chang suan-shu* from Tai Chen's version, the fragments of the late Sung edition as reproduced in the *T'ien-lu-lin-lang ts'ung-shu* series, and Yang Hui's *Hsiang-chieh chiu-chang suan-fa*.

As for the *Hai-tao suan-ching*, only the reconstructed version by Tai Chen remains. It was reproduced in the *Wu-ying-tien* palace edition (before 1794), the "Ten Mathematical Manuals" in K'ung Chi-han's *Wei-po-hsieh ts'ung-shu*, and the appendix to Chü Tseng-fa's *Chiu-chang suan-shu*.

The *Chiu-chang suan-shu* was intended as a practical handbook, a kind of aide-mémoire for architects, engineers, officials, and tradesmen. This is the reason for the presence of so many problems on building canals and dikes, city walls, taxation, barter, public services, etc. It consists of nine chapters, with a total of 246 problems. The chapters may be outlined as follows:

(1) *Fang-t'ien* ("Land Surveying") contains the rules for finding the areas of triangles, trapezoids, rectangles, circles, sectors of circles, and annuli. It gives rules for addition, subtraction, multiplication, and division of fractions. There is an interesting but inaccurate formula for the area of the segment of a circle, where the chord c and the sagitta s are known, in the form $s(c + s)/2$. This expression later appeared during the ninth century in Mahāvīra's *Gaṇitasāra-sangraha*.

Of special interest is the value of the ratio of the circumference of a circle to its diameter that Liu Hui used. The ancient value of π used in China was 3, but since the first century Chinese mathematicians had been searching for a more accurate value. Liu Hsin (d. A.D. 23) used 3.1547, while Chang Heng (78–139) gave $\sqrt{10}$ and 92/29. Wang Fan (219–257) found 142/45, and then Liu Hui gave 3.14. The most important names in this connection are, however, those of Tsu Ch'ung-chih (430–501), a brilliant mathematician, astronomer, and engineer of the Liu Sung and Ch'i dynasties, and his son, Tsu Cheng-chih. Tsu Ch'ung-chih gave two values for π, first an "inaccurate" one (*yo lü*), equal to 22/7, given earlier by Archimedes, and then a "more accurate" one (*mi lu*), 355/113 (3.1415929). He even looked for further approximations and found that π lies between 3.1415926 and 3.1415927. His method was probably described in the *Chui Shu*, which he and his son wrote but is now lost. Tsu Ch'ung-chih's value of 355/113 for π disappeared for many centuries in China until

it was again taken up by Chao Yu-ch'in (*fl. ca.* 1300).
Liu Hui obtained the accurate value 3.14 by taking
the ratio of the perimeter of a regular polygon of
ninety-six sides to the diameter of a circle enclosing
this polygon. Let us begin with a regular hexagon of
side L_6. The ratio of the perimeter of the hexagon to
the diameter of the circle enclosing it is 3. If we change
the hexagon to a regular polygon of twelve sides, as
shown in Figure 1—noting that $L_6 = r$, the radius of
the circumscribed circle—then the side of the twelve-
sided polygon is given by

$$L_{12} = \sqrt{2r\left[r - \sqrt{r^2 - \left(\frac{L_6}{2}\right)^2}\right]}.$$

Hence, if L_n is known, then L_{2n} can be found from
the expression

$$L_{2n} = \sqrt{2r\left[r - \sqrt{r^2 - \left(\frac{L_n}{2}\right)^2}\right]}.$$

Taking $r = 1$, the following values can be found:
$L_6 = 1$; $L_{12} = 0.517638$; $L_{24} = 0.261052$; $L_{48} = 0.130806$; $L_{96} = 0.065438$.

The perimeter of a regular polygon of $n = 96$
and $r = 1$ is $96 \times 0.065438 = 6.282048$. Hence
$\pi = 6.282048/2 = 3.141024$, or approximately 3.14.
Liu Hui also used a polygon of 3,072 sides and
obtained his best value, 3.14159.

(2) *Su-mi* ("Millet and Rice") deals with percent-
ages and proportions. Indeterminate equations are
avoided in the last nine problems in this chapter by
the use of proportions.

(3) *Ts'ui-fen* ("Distribution by Progression") concerns distribution of properties among partners
according to given rates. It also includes problems
in taxation of goods of different qualities, and others
in arithmetical and geometrical progressions, all
solved by use of proportions.

(4) *Shao-kuang* ("Diminishing Breadth") involves
finding the sides of a rectangle when the area and one
of the sides are given, the circumference of a circle
when its area is known, the side of a cube given its
volume, and the diameter of a sphere of known
volume. The use of the least common multiple in
fractions is shown. It is interesting that unit fractions
are used, for example, in problem 11 in this chapter.
The given width of a rectangular form is expressed as

$$1 + 1/2 + 1/3 + 1/4 + 1/5 + 1/6 + 1/7 + 1/8 + 1/9 + 1/10 + 1/11 + 1/12.$$

The problems in this chapter also lead to the extraction of square roots and cube roots; problem 13,
for example, involves finding the square root of

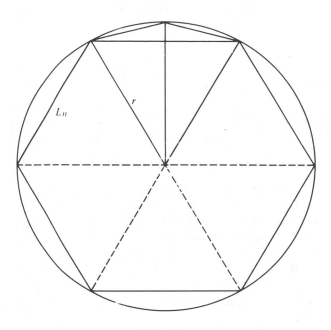

FIGURE 1

25,281. According to the method given in the *Chiu-
chang suan-shu*, this number, known as the *shih*
(dividend), is first placed in the second row from the
top of the counting board. Next, one counting rod,
called the preliminary *chieh-suan*, is put on the bottom
row of the counting board in the farthest right-hand
digit column. This rod is moved to the left, two places
at a time, as far as it can go without overshooting the
farthest left digit of the number in the *shih* row. With
its new place value this rod is called the *chieh-suan*.
It is shown in Figure 2a.

		fang		1
2 5 2 8 1		*shih*		1 5 2 8 1
		fa		1 0 0 0 0
1		*chieh-suan*		1

FIGURE 2a   FIGURE 2b

The first figure of the root is found to lie between
100 and 200. Then 1 is taken as the first figure of the
root and is placed on the top row in the hundreds
column. The top row is called *fang*. The *chieh-suan*
is multiplied by the first figure of the root. The
product, called *fa*, is placed in the third row. The
shih (25,281) less the *fa* (10,000) leaves the "first
remainder" (15,281), which is written on the second
row, as shown in Figure 2b. After the division has
been made, the *fa* is doubled to form the *ting-fa*. This

is moved one digit to the right, while the *chieh-suan* is shifted two digits to the right, as shown in Figure 2c.

1
1 5 2 8 1
2 0 0 0
1

fang
1st / 2nd re.
ting-fa
chieh-suan

2 7 8 1
2 5 0 0
1

FIGURE 2c　　　　　　FIGURE 2d

The second figure, selected by trial and error, is found to lie between 5 and 6. The tens' digit is therefore taken to be 5 and will be placed in its appropriate position on the top row in Figure 2e. The *chieh-suan* (which is now 100) is multiplied by this second figure and the product is added to the *ting-fa*, which becomes 2,500. The *ting-fa* multiplied by 5 is subtracted from the first remainder, which gives a remainder of 2,781 (15,281 − 2,500 × 5 = 2,781), as shown in Figure 2d. The *ting-fa* is next shifted one digit to the right and the *chieh-suan* two places (see Figure 2e). The third figure, again selected by trial and error, is found to be 9. This unit digit is placed in its appropriate position on the top row. The *chieh-suan*, which is now 1, is multiplied by this third figure and the product is added to the *ting-fa*, which becomes 259. The second remainder is divided by the *ting-fa*, which leaves a remainder of zero (2,781 ÷ 259 = 9 + 0). Hence the answer is 159 (see Figure 2f).

1 5
2 7 8 1
2 5 0
1

fang
2nd / last re.
ting-fa
chieh-suan

1 5 9
0
2 5 9
1

FIGURE 2e　　　　　　FIGURE 2f

(5) *Shang-kung* ("Consultations on Engineering Works") gives the volumes of such solid figures as the prism, the pyramid, the tetrahedron, the wedge, the cylinder, the cone, and the frustum of a cone:

(*a*) Volume of square prism = square of side of base times height.

(*b*) Volume of cylinder = 1/12 square of circumference of circle times height (where π is taken to be approximately 3).

(*c*) Volume of truncated square pyramid = 1/3 the height times the sum of the squares of the sides of the upper and lower squares and the product of the sides of the upper and lower squares.

(*d*) Volume of square pyramid = 1/3 the height

times the square of the side of the base.

(*e*) Volume of frustum of a circular cone = 1/36 the height times the sum of the squares of the circumferences of the upper and lower circular faces and the product of these two circumferences (where π is taken to be approximately 3).

(*f*) Volume of circular cone = 1/36 the height times the square of the circumference of the base (where π is taken to be approximately 3).

(*g*) Volume of a right triangular prism = 1/2 the product of the width, the length, and the height.

(*h*) Volume of a rectangular pyramid = 1/3 the product of the width and length of the base and the height.

(*i*) Volume of tetrahedron with two opposite edges perpendicular to each other = 1/6 the product of the two perpendicular opposite edges and the perpendicular common to these two edges.

(6) *Chün-shu* ("Impartial Taxation") concerns problems of pursuit and alligation, especially in connection with the time required for taxpayers to get their grain contributions from their native towns to the capital. It also deals with problems of ratios in connection with the allocation of tax burdens according to the population. Problem 12 in this chapter says:

> A good runner can go 100 paces while a bad runner goes 60 paces. The bad runner has gone a distance of 100 paces before the good runner starts pursuing him. In how many paces will the good runner catch up? [Answer: 250 paces.]

(7) *Ying pu-tsu* or *ying-nü* ("Excess and Deficiency"). *Ying*, referring to the full moon, and *pu-tsu* or *nü* to the new moon, mean "too much" and "too little," respectively. This section deals with a Chinese algebraic invention used mainly for solving problems of the type $ax + b = 0$ in a rather roundabout manner. The method came to be known in Europe as the rule of false position. In this method two guesses, x_1 and x_2, are made, giving rise to values c_1 and c_2, respectively, either greater or less than 0. From these we have the following equations:

$$(1) \qquad ax_1 + b = c_1$$
$$(2) \qquad ax_2 + b = c_2.$$

Multiplying (1) by x_2 and (2) by x_1, we have

$$(1') \qquad ax_1x_2 + bx_2 = c_1x_2$$
$$(2') \qquad ax_1x_2 + bx_1 = c_2x_1$$
$$(3) \qquad \therefore b(x_2 - x_1) = c_1x_2 - c_2x_1.$$

From (1) and (2),

$$(4) \qquad a(x_2 - x_1) = c_2 - c_1$$

$$\therefore \frac{b}{a} = \frac{c_1 x_2 - c_2 x_1}{c_2 - c_1}.$$

Hence

(5) $$x = -\frac{b}{a} = \frac{c_1 x_2 - c_2 x_1}{c_1 - c_2}.$$

Problem 1 in this chapter says:

In a situation where certain things are purchased jointly, if each person pays 8 [units of money], the surplus is 3 [units], and if each person pays 7, the deficiency is 4. Find the number of persons and the price of the things brought. [Answer: 7 persons and 53 units of money.]

According to the method of excess and deficiency, the rates (that is, the "guesses" 8 and 7) are first set on the counting board with the excess (3) and deficiency (−4) placed below them. The rates are then cross multiplied by the excess and deficiency, and the products are added to form the dividend. Then the excess and deficiency are added together to form the divisor. The quotient gives the correct amount of money payable by each person. To get the number of persons, add the excess and deficiency and divide the sum by the difference between the two rates. In other words, x and a are obtained using equations (5) and (4) above.

Sometimes a straightforward problem may be transformed into one involving the use of the rule of false position. Problem 18 in the same chapter says:

There are 9 [equal] pieces of gold and 11 [equal] pieces of silver. The two lots weigh the same. One piece is taken from each lot and put in the other. The lot containing mainly gold is now found to weigh less than the lot containing mainly silver by 13 ounces. Find the weight of each piece of gold and silver.

Here two guesses are made for the weight of gold. The method says that if each piece of gold weighs 3 pounds, then each piece of silver would weigh 2 5/11 pounds, giving a deficiency of 49/11 ounces; and if each piece of gold weighs 2 pounds, then each piece of silver would weigh 1 7/11 pounds, giving an excess of 15/11 ounces. Following this, the rule of false position is applied.

(8) *Fang-ch'eng* ("Calculation by Tabulation") is concerned with simultaneous linear equations, using both positive and negative numbers. Problem 18 in this chapter involves five unknowns but gives only four equations, thus heralding the indeterminate equation. The process of solving simultaneous linear equations given here is the same as the modern procedure for solving the simultaneous system

$$a_1 x + b_1 y + c_1 z = d_1$$
$$a_2 x + b_2 y + c_2 z = d_2$$
$$a_3 x + b_3 y + c_3 z = d_3,$$

except that the coefficients and constants are arranged in vertical columns instead of being written horizontally:

a_1	a_2	a_3
b_1	b_2	b_3
c_1	c_2	c_3
d_1	d_2	d_3.

In this chapter Liu Hui also explains the algebraic addition and subtraction of positive and negative numbers. (Liu Hui denoted positive numbers and negative numbers by red and black calculating rods, respectively.)

(9) *Kou-ku* ("Right Angles") deals with the application of the Pythagorean theorem. Some of its problems are as follows:

A cylindrical piece of wood with a cross-section diameter of 2 feet, 5 inches, is to be cut into a piece of plank 7 inches thick. What is the width? [problem 4] There is a tree 20 feet high and 3 feet in circumference. A creeper winds round the tree seven times and just reaches the top. Find the length of the vine. [problem 5] There is a pond 7 feet square with a reed growing at the center and measuring 1 foot above the water. The reed just reaches the bank at the water level when drawn toward it. Find the depth of the water and the length of the reed. [problem 6] There is a bamboo 10 feet high. When bent, the upper end touches the ground 3 feet away from the stem. Find the height of the break. [problem 13]

It is interesting that a problem similar to 13 appeared in Brahmagupta's work in the seventh century.

Problem 20 has aroused even greater interest:

There is a square town of unknown dimension. A gate is at the middle of each side. Twenty paces out of the north gate is a tree. If one walks 14 paces from the south gate, turns west, and takes 1,775 paces, the tree will just come into view. Find the length of the side of the town.

The book indicates that the answer can be obtained by evolving the root of the quadratic equation

$$x^2 + (14 + 20)x = 2(1775 \times 20).$$

The method of solving this equation is not described. Mikami suggests that it is highly probable that the root extraction was carried out with an additional term in the first-degree coefficient in the unknown and that this additional term was called *tsung*, but in his literal translation of some parts of the text concerning root extractions he does not notice that the successive steps correspond closely to those in Horner's method. Ch'ien Pao-tsung and Li Yen have both tried to compare the method described in the *Chiu-chang suan-shu* with that of Horner, but they have not clarified the textual obscurities. Wang Ling and Needham say that it is possible to show that if the text of the *Chiu-chang suan-shu* is very carefully followed, the essentials of the methods used by the Chinese for solving numerical equations of the second and higher degrees, similar to that developed by Horner in 1819, are present in a work that may be dated in the first century B.C.

The *Hai-tao suan-ching*, originally known by the name *Ch'ung ch'a* ("Method of Double Differences"), was appended to the *Chiu-chang suan-shu* as its tenth chapter. It was separated from the main text during the seventh century, when the "Ten Mathematical Manuals" were chosen, and was given the title *Hai-tao suan-ching*. According to Mikami, the term *ch'ung ch'a* was intended to mean double, or repeated, application of proportions of the sides of right triangles. The name *Hai-tao* probably came from the first problem of the book, which deals with an island in the sea. Consisting of only nine problems, the book is equivalent to less than one chapter of the *Chiu-chang suan-shu*.

In its preface Liu Hui describes the classical Chinese method of determining the distance from the sun to the flat earth by means of double triangulation. According to this method, two vertical poles eight feet high were erected at the same level along the same meridian, one at the ancient Chou capital of Yan-ch'eng and the other 10,000 *li* (1 *li* = 1,800 feet) to the north. The lengths of the shadows cast by the sun at midday of the summer solstice were measured, and from these the distance of sun could be derived. Liu Hui then shows how the same method can be applied to more everyday examples. Problem 1 says:

> A sea island is viewed from a distance. Two poles, each 30 feet high, are erected on the same level 1,000 *pu* [1 *pu* = 6 ft.] apart so that the pole at the rear is in a straight line with the island and the other pole. If one moves 123 *pu* back from the nearer pole, the top of the island is just visible through the end of the pole if he views it from ground level. Should he move back 127 *pu* from the other pole, the top of the island is just visible through the end of the pole if viewed from ground level. Find the elevation of the island and its distance from the [nearer] pole. [Answer: The elevation of the island is 4 *li*, 55 *pu*. The distance to the [nearer] pole is 102 *li*, 150 *pu* (300 *pu* = 1 *li*).]

The rule for solving this problem is given as follows:

> Multiply the height of the pole by the distance between the poles and divide the product by the difference between the distances that one has to walk back from the poles in order to view the highest point on the island. Adding the height of the pole to the quotient gives the elevation of the island. To find the distance from the nearer pole to the island, multiply the distance walked back from that pole by the distance between the poles. Dividing the product by the difference between the distances that one has to walk back from the poles gives that distance.

Problem 7 is of special interest:

> A person is looking into an abyss with a piece of white rock at the bottom. From the shore a crossbar is turned to lie on the side that is normally upright [so that its base is vertical]. If the base is 3 feet and one looks at the surface of the water [directly above the rock] from the tip of the base, the line of sight meets the height of the crossbar at a distance of 4 feet, 5 inches; and when one looks at the rock, the line of sight meets the height of the crossbar at a distance of 2 feet, 4 inches. A similar crossbar is set up 4 feet above the first. If one looks from the tip of the base, the line of sight to the water surface [directly above the rock] would meet the height of the crossbar at a distance of 4 feet; and if one looks at the rock, it will be 2 feet, 2 inches. Find the depth of the water.

In Figure 3, if P is the water surface above the white rock, R, and BC and FG are the two crossbars, then $BC = FG = 3$ feet; $GC = 4$ feet; $AC = 4$ feet, 5 inches; $DC = 2$ feet, 4 inches; $EG = 4$ feet; and $HG = 2$ feet, 2 inches. The depth of the water, PR, is sought. To obtain the answer, Liu Hui gives the following rule:

$$PR = GC \frac{EG(DC - HG) - HG(AC - EG)}{(DC - HG)(AC - EG)}.$$

Liu Hui has not taken into account here the refractive index of water. The rule given is an extension of that used in solving problem 4, which uses the same method for determining the depth of a valley:

> A person is looking at a deep valley. From the edge of the valley a crossbar is turned to lie on the side that is normally upright [so that its base is vertical]. The base is 6 feet long. If one looks at the bottom of the valley from the edge of the base, the line of sight meets the vertical side at a distance of 9 feet, 1 inch. Another crossbar is set 30 feet directly above the first. If the bottom of the valley is observed from the edge of the base, the line of sight will meet the vertical side at a distance of 8 feet, 5 inches. Find the depth of the valley.

$$CS = \frac{GC \cdot HG}{(DC - HG)} - CB.$$

PR is derived from the difference between *CS* and *CQ*.

As for the other problems, problem 2 concerns finding the height of a tree on a hill; problem 3 deals with the size of a distant walled city; problem 5 shows how to measure the height of a tower on a plain as seen from a hill; problem 6 gives a method for finding the width of a gulf seen from a distance on land; problem 8 is a case of finding the width of a river seen from a hill; and problem 9 seeks the size of a city seen from a mountain.

BIBLIOGRAPHY

A modern ed. of the *Chiu-chang suan-shu* is vol. 1121 in the *Ts'ung-Shu Chi-Chêng* series (Shanghai, 1936).

Works dealing with Liu Hui and his writings are Ch'ien Pao-tsung, *Suan-ching shih-shu* ("Ten Mathematical Manuals"), 2 vols. (Peking, 1963), 83–272; and *Chung-kuo suan-hsüeh-shih* ("History of Chinese Mathematics") (Peking, 1964), 61–75; L. van Hée, "Le Hai Tao Suan Ching de Lieou," in *T'oung Pao*, **20** (1921), 51–60; Hsü Shunfang, *Chung-suan-chia te tai-shu-hsüeh yen-chiu* ("A Study of Algebra by Chinese Mathematicians") (Peking, 1955), 1–8; Li Yen, *Chung-kuo shu-Hsüeh ta-kang* ("Outline of Chinese Mathematics"), I (Shanghai, 1931); and *Chung-kuo suan-hsüeh-shih* ("History of Chinese Mathematics") (Shanghai, 1937; rev. ed., 1955), 16, 19, 21; Li Yen and Tu Shih-jan, *Chung-kuo ku-tai shu-hsüeh chien-shih* ("Brief History of Ancient Chinese Mathematics"), I (Peking, 1963), 45–77; Yoshio Mikami, *The Development of Mathematics in China and Japan* (New York, 1913); Joseph Needham, *Science and Civilisation in China*, III (Cambridge, 1959), 24–27; George Sarton, *Introduction to the History of Science*, 3 vols. (Baltimore, 1927–1947), esp. I, 338; Wang Ling, "The Chiu Chang Suan Shu and the History of Chinese Mathematics During the Han Dynasty," a doctoral diss. (Cambridge Univ., 1956); Wang Ling and Joseph Needham, "Horner's Method in Chinese Mathematics; Its Origins in the Root-Extraction Procedure of the Han Dynasty," in *T'oung Pao*, **43** (1955), 345–401; and Alexander Wylie, *Chinese Researches* (Shanghai, 1897; repr. Peking, 1936, and Taipei, 1966), 170–174.

Some important special studies on the *Chiu-chang suan-shu* are E. I. Berezkina, "Drevnekitaysky traktat matematika v devyati knigach" ("The Ancient Chinese Mathematical Treatise in Nine Books"), in *Istoriko-matematicheskie issledovaniya*, **10** (1957), 423–584, a Russian trans. of the *Chiu-chang suan-shu;* Kurt Vogel, *Neun Bücher arithmetischer Technik* (Brunswick, 1968), a German trans. and study of the work; and A. P. Youschkevitsch, *Geschichte der Mathematik im Mittelalter* (Leipzig, 1964), 1–88 ("Die Mathematik in China"), translated from the Russian.

Access to old biographical notes and bibliographical citations concerning mathematical works are Hu Yü-chin, *Ssu-K'u-T'i-Yao Pu-Chêng* ("Supplements to the *Ssu-K'u-T'i-yao*"), 2 vols. (Taipei, 1964–1967); and Ting Fu-pao

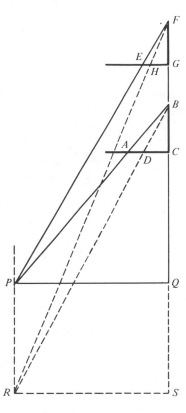

FIGURE 3

If we refer again to Figure 3, ignoring the broken lines, we have $CB = GF = 6$ feet; $CG = 30$ feet; $AC = 9$ feet, 1 inch; $EG = 8$ feet, 5 inches; and CQ is the depth. From similar triangles *ABC* and *PBQ*,

$$QB \cdot AC = PQ \cdot CB;$$

and from similar triangles *EFG* and *PFQ*,

$$QF \cdot EG = PQ \cdot GF.$$

Since $CB = GF$, and $QF = QB + BF$,

$$QB \cdot AC = (QB + BF)\, EG,$$

$$QB(AC - EG) = BF \cdot EG = GC \cdot EG,$$

that is,

$$(CQ + CB)(AC - EG) = GC \cdot EG.$$

Hence,

$$CQ = \frac{GC \cdot EG}{AC - EG} - CB.$$

In problem 7 one can also obtain the distance from the bank to the bottom of the abyss (*CS* in Figure 3) from the expression and Chou Yün-ch'ing, *Ssu-Pu-Tsung-Lu Suan-Fa-Pien* ("Bibliography of Mathematical Books to Supplement the *Ssu-K'u-Ch'uan-Shu* Encyclopedia"; Shanghai, 1956).

More information on the *Suan-Ching Shi-Shu* can be found in Needham, *Science and Civilisation in China*, III, 18; and in A. Hummel, *Eminent Chinese of the Ch'ing Period* (Washington, 1943), p. 697.

The two extant volumes of the *Yung-Lo Ta-Tien* encyclopedia have been reproduced photographically (Peking, 1960); they show that the arrangement was according to mathematical procedures and not by authors.

HO PENG-YOKE

LOBACHEVSKY, NIKOLAI IVANOVICH (*b.* Nizhni Novgorod [now Gorki], Russia, 2 December 1792; *d.* Kazan, Russia, 24 February 1856)

Lobachevsky was the son of Ivan Maksimovich Lobachevsky, a clerk in a land-surveying office, and Praskovia Aleksandrovna Lobachevskaya. In about 1800 the mother moved with her three sons to Kazan, where Lobachevsky and his brothers were soon enrolled in the Gymnasium on public scholarships. In 1807 Lobachevsky entered Kazan University, where he studied under the supervision of Martin Bartels, a friend of Gauss, and, in 1812, received the master's degree in physics and mathematics. In 1814 he became an adjunct in physical and mathematical sciences and began to lecture on various aspects of mathematics and mechanics. He was appointed extraordinary professor in 1814 and professor ordinarius in 1822, the same year in which he began an administrative career as a member of the committee formed to supervise the construction of the new university buildings. He was chairman of that committee in 1825, twice dean of the department of physics and mathematics (in 1820–1821 and 1823–1825), librarian of the university (1825–1835), rector (1827–1846), and assistant trustee for the whole of the Kazan educational district (1846–1855).

In recognition of his work Lobachevsky was in 1837 raised to the hereditary nobility; he designed his own familial device (which is reproduced on his tombstone), depicting Solomon's seal, a bee, an arrow, and a horseshoe, to symbolize wisdom, diligence, alacrity, and happiness, respectively. He had in 1832 made a wealthy marriage, to Lady Varvara Aleksivna Moisieva, but his family of seven children and the cost of technological improvements for his estate left him with little money upon his retirement from the university, although he received a modest pension. A worsening sclerotic condition progressively affected his eyesight, and he was blind in his last years.

Although Lobachevsky wrote his first major work,

Geometriya, in 1823, it was not published in its original form until 1909. The basic geometrical studies that it embodies, however, led Lobachevsky to his chief discovery—non-Euclidean geometry (now called Lobachevskian geometry)—which he first set out in "Exposition succincte des principes de la géométrie avec une démonstration rigoureuse du théorème des parallèles," and on which he reported to the Kazan department of physics and mathematics at a meeting held on 23 February 1826. His first published work on the subject, "O nachalakh geometrii" ("On the Principles of Geometry"), appeared in the *Kazanski vestnik*, a journal published by the university, in 1829–1830; it comprised the earlier "Exposition."

Some of Lobachevsky's early papers, too, were on such nongeometrical subjects as algebra and the theoretical aspects of infinite series. Thus, in 1834 he published his paper "Algebra ili ischislenie konechnykh" ("Algebra, or Calculus of Finites"), of which most had been composed as early as 1825. The first issue of the *Uchenye zapiski* ("Scientific Memoirs") of Kazan University, founded by Lobachevsky, likewise carried his article "Ob ischezanii trigonometricheskikh strok" ("On the Convergence of Trigonometrical Series"). The chief thrust of his scientific endeavor was, however, geometrical, and his later work was devoted exclusively to his new non-Euclidean geometry.

In 1835 Lobachevsky published a long article, "Voobrazhaemaya geometriya" ("Imaginary Geometry"), in the *Uchenye zapiski*. He also translated it into French for Crelle's *Journal für die reine und angewandte Mathematik*. The following year he published, also in the *Uchenye zapiski*, a continuation of this work, "Primenenie voobrazhaemoi geometrii k nekotorym integralam" ("Application of Imaginary Geometry to Certain Integrals"). The same period, from 1835 to 1838, also saw him concerned with writing *Novye nachala geometrii s polnoi teoriei parallelnykh* ("New Principles of Geometry With a Complete Theory of Parallels"), which incorporated a version of his first work, the still unpublished *Geometriya*. The last two chapters of the book were abbreviated and translated for publication in Crelle's *Journal* in 1842. *Geometrische Untersuchungen zur Theorie der Parallellinien*, which he published in Berlin in 1840, is the best exposition of his new geometry; following its publication, in 1842, Lobachevsky was, on the recommendation of Gauss, elected to the Göttingen Gesellschaft der Wissenschaften. His last work, *Pangéométrie*, was published in Kazan in 1855–1856.

Lobachevskian Geometry. Lobachevsky's non-Euclidean geometry was the product of some two millennia of criticism of the *Elements*. Geometers had historically been concerned primarily with Euclid's fifth postulate: If a straight line meets two other straight lines so as to make the two interior angles on one side of the former together less than two right angles, then the latter straight lines will meet if produced on that side on which the angles are less than two right angles (it must be noted that Euclid understood lines as finite segments). This postulate is equivalent to the statement that given a line and a point not on it, one can draw through the point one and only one coplanar line not intersecting the given line. Throughout the centuries, mathematicians tried to prove the fifth postulate as a theorem either by assuming implicitly an equivalent statement (as did Posidonius, Ptolemy, Proclus, Thābit ibn Qurra, Ibn al-Haytham, Saccheri, and Legendre) or by directly substituting a more obvious postulate for it (as did al-Khayyāmī, al-Ṭūsī, and Wallis).

In his early lectures on geometry, Lobachevsky himself attempted to prove the fifth postulate; his own geometry is derived from his later insight that a geometry in which all of Euclid's axioms except the fifth postulate hold true is not in itself contradictory. He called such a system "imaginary geometry," proceeding from an analogy with imaginary numbers. If imaginary numbers are the most general numbers for which the laws of arithmetic of real numbers prove justifiable, then imaginary geometry is the most general geometrical system. It was Lobachevsky's merit to refute the uniqueness of Euclid's geometry, and to consider it as a special case of a more general system.

In Lobachevskian geometry, given a line *a* and a point *A* not on it (see Fig. 1), one can draw through *A* more than one coplanar line not intersecting *a*. It

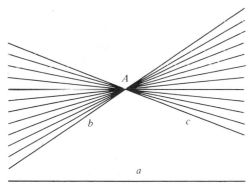

FIGURE 1

follows that one can draw infinitely many such lines which, taken together, constitute an angle of which the vertex is *A*. The two lines, *b* and *c*, bordering that

angle are called parallels to *a*, and the lines contained between them are called ultraparallels, or diverging lines; all other lines through *A* intersect *a*. If one measures the distance between two parallel lines on a secant equally inclined to each, then, as Lobachevsky proved, that distance decreases indefinitely, tending to zero, as one moves farther out from *A*. Consequently, when representing Lobachevskian parallels in the Euclidean plane, one often draws them conventionally as asymptotic curves (see Fig. 2). The

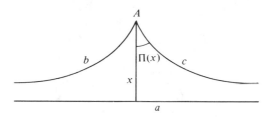

FIGURE 2

angle $\Pi(x)$ between the perpendicular *x* from point *A* to line *a* and a parallel drawn through *A* is a function of *x*. Lobachevsky showed that this function, named after him, can be expressed in elementary terms as

$$\cot \frac{\Pi(x)}{2} = e^x;$$

clearly, $\Pi(0) = \pi/2$, and, for $x > 0$, $\Pi(x) < \pi/2$. Lobachevsky later proved that the distance between two diverging lines, where distance is again measured on a secant equally inclined to each, tends to infinity as one moves farther out from *A*; the distance has a minimum value when the secant is perpendicular to each line, and this perpendicular secant is unique.

A comparison of Euclidean and Lobachevskian geometry yields several immediate and interesting contrasts. In the latter, the sum of the angles of the right triangle of which the vertices are the point *A*, the foot of the perpendicular *x* on *a*, and a point on *a* situated at such a distance from *x* that the hypotenuse of the triangle lies close to a parallel through *A* is evidently less than two right angles. Lobachevsky proved that indeed for all triangles in the Lobachevskian plane the sum of the angles is less than two right angles.

In addition to pencils of intersecting lines and pencils of parallel lines, which are common to both the Euclidean and Lobachevskian planes, the latter also contains pencils of diverging lines, which consist of all perpendiculars to the same line. In both planes, the circle is the orthogonal trajectory of a pencil of intersecting lines, but the orthogonal trajectories of the other pencils differ in the Lobachevskian plane.

That of a pencil of parallel lines (see Fig. 3) is called

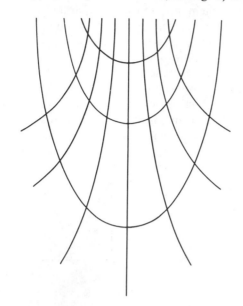

FIGURE 3

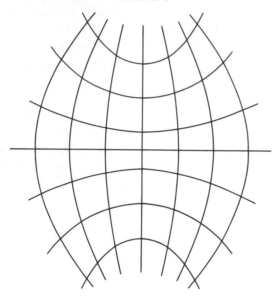

FIGURE 4

a horocycle, or limit circle; as the name implies, it is the curve toward which the circular trajectory of a pencil of intersecting lines tends as the intersection point tends to infinity. The orthogonal trajectory of a pencil of diverging lines (see Fig. 4) is called an equidistant, or hypercycle; it is the locus of points of the Lobachevskian plane that are equally distant from the common perpendicular of the diverging lines in the pencil, and this perpendicular is called the base of the equidistant.

On the basis of these orthogonal trajectories, Lobachevsky also constructed a space geometry. By

rotating the circle, the horocycle, and the equidistant about one of the orthogonal lines, he obtained, respectively, a sphere, a horosphere (or limit sphere), and an equidistant surface, the last being the locus of the points of space equally distant from a plane. Although geometry on the sphere does not differ from that of Euclidean space, the geometry on each of the two sheets of the equidistant surface is that of the Lobachevskian plane, the geometry on the horosphere that of the Euclidean plane.

Working from the geometry (and, hence, trigonometry) of the Euclidean plane on horospheres, Lobachevsky derived trigonometric formulas for triangles in the Lobachevskian plane. In modern terms these formulas are:

$$\cosh \frac{a}{q} = \cosh \frac{b}{q} \cosh \frac{c}{q} - \sinh \frac{b}{q} \sinh \frac{c}{q} \cos A,$$

$$\frac{\sinh \frac{a}{q}}{\sin A} = \frac{\sinh \frac{b}{q}}{\sin B} = \frac{\sinh \frac{c}{q}}{\sin C},$$

$$\cos A = -\cos B \cos C + \sin B \sin C \cosh \frac{a}{q}, \quad (1)$$

where q is a certain constant of the Lobachevskian plane.

Comparing these formulas with those of spherical trigonometry on a sphere of radius r, that is,

$$\cos \frac{a}{r} = \cos \frac{b}{r} \cos \frac{c}{r} + \sin \frac{b}{r} \sin \frac{c}{r} \cos A,$$

$$\frac{\sin \frac{a}{r}}{\sin A} = \frac{\sin \frac{b}{r}}{\sin B} = \frac{\sin \frac{c}{r}}{\sin C},$$

$$\cos A = -\cos B \cos C + \sin B \sin C \cos \frac{a}{r}, \quad (2)$$

Lobachevsky discovered that the formulas of trigonometry in the space he defined can be derived from formulas of spherical trigonometry if the sides a, b, c of triangles are regarded as purely imaginary numbers or, put another way, if the radius r of the sphere is considered as purely imaginary. Indeed, (2) is transformed into (1) if it is supposed that $r = qi$ and the correlations $\cos ix = \cosh x$ and $\sin ix = \sinh x$ are employed. In this Lobachevsky saw evidence of the noncontradictory nature of the geometry he had discovered. This idea can be made quite rigorous by introducing imaginary points of Euclidean space, producing the so-called complex Euclidean space; defining in that space the sphere of purely imaginary radius; and considering a set of points on that sphere that have real rectangular coordinates x and y and purely imaginary coordinate z. (Such a set of points in the complex Euclidean space was first considered in 1908 by H. Minkowski, in connection with Einstein's special principle of relativity; it is now called pseudo-Euclidean space.) The sphere of the imaginary radius in this space thus appears to be a hyperboloid of two sheets, each of which is a model of the Lobachevskian plane, while construction of this model proves it to be noncontradictory in nature.

Lobachevskian geometry is further analogous to spherical geometry. The area of triangle S in Lobachevsky's plane is expressed through its angles (in radian measure) by the formula

$$S = q^2(\pi - A - B - C), \qquad (3)$$

whereas the area of spherical triangle S is expressed through its angles (by the same measure) as

$$S = r^2(A + B + C - \pi). \qquad (4)$$

Formula (3) is transformed into formula (4) if $r = qi$.

Lines of the Lobachevskian plane are represented on the sphere of imaginary radius of the pseudo-Euclidean space by sections with planes through the center of the sphere. Intersecting lines can then be represented by sections with planes intersecting on a line of purely imaginary length; parallel lines by sections with planes intersecting on lines of zero length (isotropic lines); and diverging lines by sections with planes intersecting on lines of real length. Circles, horocycles, and equidistants of the Lobachevskian plane are represented by sections of the sphere of imaginary radius with planes that do not pass through its center.

If the sides a, b, c of the triangle are very small or the numbers q and r very large, it is necessary to consider only the first members in the series

$$\cosh x = 1 + \frac{x^2}{2} + \frac{x^4}{4!} + \cdots,$$

$$\sinh x = x = \frac{x^3}{3!} + \frac{x^5}{5!} + \cdots,$$

$$\cos x = 1 - \frac{x^2}{2} + \frac{x^4}{4!} - + \cdots,$$

$$\sin x = x - \frac{x^3}{3!} + \frac{x^5}{5!} - + \cdots. \qquad (5)$$

If it is assumed for formulas (1) and (2), above, that $\sinh x = x$ and $\cosh x = \cos x = 1$, $\sin x = x$ or $\cosh x = 1 + \frac{x^2}{2}$ and $\cos x = 1 - \frac{x^2}{2}$, these formulas become

$$a^2 = b^2 + c^2 - 2bc \cos A,$$

$$\frac{a}{\sin A} = \frac{b}{\sin B} = \frac{c}{\sin C},$$

$$A + B + C = \pi, \qquad (6)$$

in the Euclidean plane. Euclidean geometry may then be considered as a limiting case of both spherical and Lobachevskian geometry as r and q tend to infinity, or as a particular case for $r = q = \infty$. In analogy to the number $\frac{1}{r^2}$, which represents the curvature of the sphere, the number $-\frac{1}{q^2}$ is called the curvature of the Lobachevskian plane; the constant q is called the radius of curvature of this plane.

Lobachevsky recognized the universal character of his new geometry in naming it "pangeometry." He nevertheless thought it necessary to establish experimentally which geometry—his or Euclid's—actually occurs in the real world. To this end he made a series of calculations of the sums of the angles of triangles of which the vertices are two diametrically opposed points on the orbit of the earth and one of the fixed stars Sirius, Rigel, or 28 Eridani. Having established that the deviation of these sums from π is no greater than might be due to errors in observation, he concluded that the geometry of the real world might be considered as Euclidean, whence he also found "a rigorous proof of the theorem of parallels" as set out in his work of 1826. In explaining his calculations (in "O nachalakh geometrii" ["On the Principles of Geometry"]), Lobachevsky noted that it is possible to find experimentally the deviation from π of the sum of the angles of cosmic triangles of great size; in a later work (*Novye nachala geometrii s polnoi teoriei parallelnykh* ["New Principles of Geometry With a Complete Theory of Parallels"]) he moved to the opposite scale and suggested that his geometry might find application in the "intimate sphere of molecular attractions."

In his earlier papers Lobachevsky had defined imaginary geometry on an a priori basis, beginning with the supposition that Euclid's fifth postulate does not hold true and explaining the principle tenets of his new geometry without defining it (although he did describe the results of his experiment to prove his theorem of parallels). In "Voobrazhaemaya geometriya" ("Imaginary Geometry"), however, he built up the new geometry analytically, proceeding from its inherent trigonometrical formulas and considering the derivation of these formulas from spherical trigonometry to guarantee its internal consistency. In the sequel to that paper, "Primenenie voobrazhaemoi geometrii k nekotorym integralam" ("Application of Imaginary Geometry to Certain Integrals"), he applied geometrical considerations in Lobachevskian space to the calculation of known integrals (in order to make sure that their application led to valid results), then to new, previously uncalculated integrals.

In *Novye nachala geometrii s polnoi teoriei par-*

allelnykh ("New Principles of Geometry With a Complete Theory of Parallels"), Lobachevsky, after criticizing various demonstrations of the fifth postulate, went on to develop the idea of a geometry independent of the fifth postulate, an idea presented in his earliest *Geometriya* (of which a considerable portion was encompassed in the later work). The last two chapters of the book—on the solution of triangles, on given measurements, and on probable errors in calculation—were connected with his attempts to establish experimentally what sort of geometry obtains in the real world. Lobachevsky's last two books, *Geometrische Untersuchungen* and *Pangéométrie*, represent summaries of his previous geometrical work. The former dealt with the elements of the new geometry, while the latter applied differential and integral calculus to it.

At the same time as Lobachevsky, other geometers were making similar discoveries. Gauss had arrived at an idea of non-Euclidean geometry in the last years of the eighteenth century and had for several decades continued to study the problems that such an idea presented. He never published his results, however, and these became known only after his death and the publication of his correspondence. Jànos Bolyai, the son of Gauss's university comrade Farkas Bolyai, hit upon Lobachevskian geometry at a slightly later date than Lobachevsky; he explained his discovery in an appendix to his father's work that was published in 1832. (Since Gauss did not publish his work on the subject, and since Bolyai published only at a later date, Lobachevsky clearly holds priority.)

It may be observed that Lobachevsky's works in other areas of mathematics were either directly relevant to his geometry (as his calculations on definite integrals and probable errors of observation) or results of his studies of foundations of mathematics (as his works on the theory of finites and the theory of trigonometric series). His work on these problems again for the most part paralleled that of other European mathematicians. It is, for example, worth noting that in his algebra Lobachevsky suggested a method of separating roots of equations by their repeated squaring, a method coincident with that suggested by Dandelin in 1826 and by Gräffe in 1837. His paper on the convergence of trigonometric series, too, suggested a general definition of function like that proposed by Dirichlet in 1837. (Lobachevsky also gave a rigorous definition of continuity and differentiability, and pointed out the difference between these notions.)

Recognition of Lobachevskian Geometry. Lobachevsky's work was little heralded during his lifetime. M. V. Ostrogradsky, the most famous mathematician of the St. Petersburg Academy, for one, did not understand Lobachevsky's achievement, and published an uncomplimentary review of "O nachalakh geometrii" ("On the Principles of Geometry"); the magazine *Syn otechestva* soon followed his lead, and in 1834 issued a pamphlet ridiculing Lobachevsky's paper. Although Gauss, who had received a copy of the *Geometrische Untersuchungen* from Lobachevsky, spoke to him flatteringly of the book, studied Russian especially to read his works in their original language, and supported his election to the Göttingen Gesellschaft der Wissenschaften, he never publicly commented on Lobachevsky's discovery. His views on the new geometry became clear only after the publication, in 1860–1865, of his correspondence with H. C. Schumacher. Following this, in 1865, the English algebraist Cayley (who had himself paved the way for the theory of projective metrics in 1859 with his "Sixth Memoir Upon Quantics") brought out his "A Note Upon Lobachevsky's Imaginary Geometry," from which it is evident that he also failed to understand Lobachevsky's work.

The cause of Lobachevskian geometry was, however, furthered by Hoüel, one of its earliest proponents, who in 1866 brought out a French translation of *Geometrische Untersuchungen*, with appended extracts from the Gauss-Schumacher correspondence. The following year he also published Bolyai's appendix on non-Euclidean geometry, which was translated into Italian by Battaglini in 1867. Hoüel's own *Notices sur la vie et les travaux de N. I. Lobachevsky* appeared in 1870. In the meantime, Lobachevsky's *Geometrische Untersuchungen* had been translated into Russian by A. V. Letnikov; it was published in 1868 in the newly founded Moscow magazine *Matematichesky sbornik*, together with Letnikov's article "O teorii parallelnykh linii N. I. Lobachevskogo" ("On the Theory of Parallel Lines by N. I. Lobachevsky").

These translations and reviews were soon augmented by extensions of Lobachevskian geometry itself. In 1858 Beltrami published in the *Giornale di matematiche* his "Saggio di interpretazione della geometria non-euclidea," in which he established that the intrinsic geometry of the pseudosphere and other surfaces of constant negative curvature coincides with the geometry of part of the Lobachevskian plane and that an interpretation of the whole Lobachevskian plane can be constructed in the interior of a circle in the Euclidean plane. This interpretation can be derived by projecting a hemisphere of imaginary radius in pseudo-Euclidean space from its center onto a Euclidean plane tangent to this hemisphere. The article was translated into French by Hoüel in 1869 for publication in the *Annales scientifiques de l'École Normale Supérieure*.

In 1870 Weierstrass led a seminar on Lobachevsky's geometry at the University of Berlin; the young Felix Klein was one of the participants. Weierstrass' own contribution to the subject, the so-called Weierstrass coordinates, are essentially rectangular coordinates of a point on a hemisphere of imaginary radius in pseudo-Euclidean space. Klein compared Lobachevskian geometry with Cayley's projective metrics to establish that Lobachevsky's geometry is in fact one of Cayley's geometries, which Cayley himself (although he was acquainted with Lobachevskian geometry) had failed to notice. The Lobachevskian plane can be regarded as the interior domain of a conic section on a projective plane; when this conic section is a circle, representation of the Lobachevskian plane on the projective plane coincides with Beltrami's interpretation. It thus follows that motions of the Lobachevskian plane are represented in Beltrami's interpretation by projective transformations of the plane mapping a circle into itself. Lines of the Lobachevskian plane are represented in Beltrami's interpretation by chords of the circle, while parallel lines are represented by chords intersecting on the circumference, and diverging lines by non-intersecting chords. There are analogous interpretations for three-dimensional and multidimensional Lobachevskian spaces, in which Beltrami's circle or Klein's conic section is replaced by a sphere or oval quadric, e.g., ellipsoid.

Poincaré made two important contributions to Lobachevskian geometry at somewhat later dates. In 1882 he suggested an interpretation of the Lobachevskian plane in terms of a Euclidean semiplane; in this intrepretation, motions of the Lobachevskian plane are represented by inversive transformations, mapping the border of the semiplane into itself, while Lobachevskian lines are mapped by perpendiculars to this border or by semicircles with centers on it. An important property of this interpretation is that angles in the Lobachevskian plane are mapped conformally. Taking as given that inversive transformations on the plane are represented as fractional linear functions of a complex variable, Poincaré used such an interpretation for the theory of automorphic functions.

Poincaré's interpretation is often described in other terms, as when a semiplane is mapped by inversive transformation into the interior of a circle. An interpretation in terms of the circle can also be presented by projecting the hemisphere of imaginary radius in pseudo-Euclidean space from one of its points onto the Euclidean plane perpendicular to the radius through this point. This projection is analogous to stereographic projection, through which the preservation of angles in Poincaré's interpretation is explained. In 1887 Poincaré suggested a second interpretation of the Lobachevskian plane, this one in terms of a two-sheeted hyperboloid coinciding with that on the hemisphere of imaginary radius as already defined.

A further important development of Lobachevsky's geometry came from Riemann, whose address of 1854, *Uber die Hypothesen, welche der Geometrie zu Grundliegen,* was published in 1866. Developing Gauss's idea of intrinsic geometry of a surface, Riemann presented a notion of multidimensional curved space (now called Riemannian space). Riemannian space of constant positive curvature (often called Riemannian elliptic space) is represented by the geometry on a sphere in fourth-dimensional or multidimensional Euclidean space or in the space with a projective metric in which an imaginary quadric plays the part of a conic section (or Klein's quadric). It subsequently, then, became clear that Lobachevskian space (often called hyperbolic space) is the Riemannian space of constant negative curvature. It was with this in mind that Klein, in his memoir of 1871, "Über die sogenannte nicht-euklidische Geometrie," chose to consider all three geometries—Euclidean, elliptic, and hyperbolic—from a single standpoint, whereby groups of motions of all three are subgroups of the group of projective transformations of projective space.

Here the extension of the concept of space, which was introduced by Lobachevsky and Riemann, merges with the concept of group, which was introduced by Galois, a synthesis that Klein developed further in 1872 in *Vergleichende Betrachtungen über neuere geometrische Forschungen* (also known as the *Erlanger Programm*) in which he arrived at a general view of various geometries as theories of invariants of various continuous groups of transformations. A new stage in the development of mathematics thus began, one in which the mathematics of antiquity and the Middle Ages (that is, the mathematics of constant magnitudes) and the mathematics of early modern times (that is, the mathematics of variable magnitudes) were replaced by modern mathematics—the mathematics of many geometries, of many algebras, and of many mathematical systems having no classical analogues. A number of these systems found applications in modern physics—pseudo-Euclidean geometry, one of the projective metrics, figures in the special theory of relativity; Riemannian geometry appears in the general theory of relativity; and group theory is significant to quantum physics.

The presence of specifically Lobachevskian geometry is felt in modern physics in the isomorphism of the group of motions of Lobachevskian space and the Lorentz group. This isomorphism opens the possibility of applying Lobachevskian geometry to the solution of a number of problems of relativist quantum physics. Within the framework of the general theory of relativity, the problem of the geometry of the real world, to which Lobachevsky had devoted so much attention, was solved; the geometry of the real world is that of variable curvature, which is on the average much closer to Lobachevsky's than to Euclid's.

BIBLIOGRAPHY

I. ORIGINAL WORKS. Lobachevsky's writings have been brought together in *Polnoe sobranie sochinenii* ("Complete Works"), 5 vols. (Moscow–Leningrad, 1946–1951): vols. I–III, geometrical works; vol. IV, algebraical works; vol. V, works on analysis, the theory of probability, mechanics, and astronomy. His geometrical works were also collected as *Polnoe sobranie sochinenii po geometrii* ("Complete Geometrical Works"), 2 vols. (Kazan, 1883–1886): vol. I, works in Russian; vol. II, works in French and German.

Translations include J. Hoüel, *Études géométriques sur la théorie des parallèles* (Paris, 1866; 2nd ed., 1900); G. B. Halsted, *Geometrical Researches on the Theory of Parallels*, Neomonic ser. no. 4 (Austin, Tex., 1892; repr. Chicago–London, 1942); and *New Principles of Geometry With Complete Theory of Parallels*, Neomonic ser. no. 5 (Austin, Tex., 1897); F. Engel, *Zwei geometrische Abhandlungen* (Leipzig, 1898); F. Mallieux, *Nouveaux principes de la géométrie avec une théorie complète des parallèles* (Brussels, 1901); and H. Liebmann, *Imaginäre Geometrie und Anwendungen der imaginären Geometrie auf einige Integrale* (Leipzig, 1904).

II. SECONDARY LITERATURE. Among works on Lobachevsky are the following: A. A. Andronov, "Gde i kogda rodilsya N. I. Lobachevsky?" ("Where and When Was Lobachevsky born?"), in *Istoriko-matematicheskie issledovaniya*, 9 (1956); R. Bonola, *La geometria non-euclidea: Esposizione storico-critico del suo sviluppo* (Bologna, 1906); translated into German as *Die nicht-euklidische Geometrie. Historisch-kritische Darstellung ihrer Entwicklung*, 3rd ed. (Leipzig, 1921); translated into Russian as *Neevklidova geometriya. Kritiko-istoricheskoe issledovanie e razvitiya* (St. Petersburg, 1910); translated into English as *Non-Euclidean Geometry. A Critical and Historical Study of Its Developments* (New York, 1955); J. L. Coolidge, *The Elements of Non-Euclidean Geometry* (Oxford, 1909); H. S. M. Coxeter, *Non-Euclidean Geometry*, 3rd ed. (Toronto, 1957); V. M. Gerasimova, *Ukazatel literatury po geometrii Lobachevskogo i razvitiyu e idei* ("A Guide to Studies on Lobachevskian Geometry and the Development of Its Ideas"; Moscow, 1952); B. V. Gnedenko, "O rabotakh N. I. Lobachevskogo po teorii veroyatnostei" ("On Lobachevsky's Works on the Calculus of Probabilities"), in *Istoriko-matematicheskie issledovaniya*, 2 (1949); N. I. Idelson, "Lobachevskii-astronom" ("Lobachevsky as an Astronomer"), *ibid.*

Also of value are V. F. Kagan, *Lobachevsky*, 2nd ed. (Moscow–Leningrad, 1948); and *Osnovaniya geometrii* ("Foundations of Geometry"), 2 vols. (I, Moscow–Leningrad, 1949; II, Moscow, 1956); E. K. Khilkevich, "Iz istorii rasprostraneniya i razvitiya idei N. I. Lobachevskogo v 60-70-kh godakh XIX stoletiya" ("The History of the Spread and Development of N. I. Lobachevsky's Ideas in the 60th to 70th Years of the Nineteenth Century"), in *Istoriko-matematicheskie issledovaniya*, 2 (1949); F. Klein, *Vorlesungen über nichteuklidische Geometrie*, 3rd ed. (Berlin, 1928), also translated into Russian as *Neevklidova geometriya* (Moscow–Leningrad, 1936); B. L. Laptev, "Teoriya parallelnykh pryamykh v rannikh rabotakh Lobachevskogo" ("Theory of Parallel Lines in Lobachevsky's Early Works"), in *Istoriko-matematicheskie issledovaniya*, 4 (1951); H. Liebmann, *Nicht-euclidische Geometrie*, 3rd ed. (Berlin, 1923); G. L. Luntz, "O rabotakh N. I. Lobachevskogo po matematicheskomu analizu" ("On N. I. Lobachevsky's Work in Mathematical Analysis"), in *Istoriko-matematicheskie issledovaniya*, 2 (1949); M. B. Modzalevsky, *Materialy dlya biografii N. I. Lobachevskogo* ("Materials for N. I. Lobachevsky's Biography"; Moscow–Leningrad, 1948); V. V. Morozov, "Ob algebraicheskikh rukopisyakh N. I. Lobachevskogo" ("On Algebraic Manuscripts of N. I. Lobachevsky"), in *Istoriko-matematicheskie issledovaniya*, 4 (1951); and A. P. Norden, ed., *Ob osnovaniyakh geometrii. Sbornik klassicheskikh rabot po geometrii Lobachevskogo i razvitiyu e idei* ("On Foundations of Geometry. Collection of Classic Works on Lobachevskian Geometry and the Development of Its Ideas"; Moscow, 1956).

See also B. A. Rosenfeld, *Neevklidovy geometrii* (Moscow, 1955); "Interpretacii geometrii Lobachevskogo" ("Interpretations of Lobachevskian Geometry"), in *Istoriko-matematicheskie issledovaniya*, 9 (1956); and *Neevklidovy prostranstva* ("Non-Euclidean Spaces"; Moscow, 1968); D. M. Y. Sommerville, *Bibliography of Non-Euclidean Geometry* (London, 1911); and *The Elements of Non-Euclidean Geometry* (London, 1914); S. A. Yanovskaya, "O mirovozzrenii N. I. Lobachevskogo" ("On N. I. Lobachevsky's Outlook"), in *Istoriko-matematicheskie issledovaniya*, 4 (1951); and A. P. Youschkevitch and I. G. Bashmakova, " 'Algebra ili vychislenie konechnykh' N. I. Lobachevskogo" (" 'Algebra or Calculus of Finites' by N. I. Lobachevsky"), in *Istoriko-matematicheskie issledovaniya*, 2 (1949).

B. A. ROSENFELD

LÖWENHEIM, LEOPOLD (*b.* Krefeld, Germany, 26 June 1878; *d.* East Berlin, German Democratic Republic, 5 May 1957)

The son of Elise Röhn, a writer, and Detmold Louis (Ludwig) Löwenheim, a mathematics teacher at the Krefeld Polytechnic until 1881 and a private scholar thereafter, Lowenheim received his secondary education in Berlin at the Königliche Luisen-Gymnasium, from which he graduated in 1896. That same year he showed inclinations to philosophical and social thought by joining the Deutsche Gesellschaft für Ethische Kultur (to which his father had belonged). He studied mathematics and natural science from 1896 to 1900 at Friedrich Wilhelm University in Berlin and at the Technische Hochschule in Charlottenburg (then an autonomous neighboring city of Berlin). Having qualified in 1901 as a teacher of mathematics and physics in the upper grades, and of chemistry and mineralogy in the middle grades, Löwenheim was appointed *Oberlehrer* at the Jahn-Realgymnasium in Berlin in 1904, after a year of postgraduate training and a year as a probationary teacher. In 1915 he was given the title *professor*, and in 1919 he became *Studienrat*.

Although in subsequent years much of his time was taken up by teaching obligations, Löwenheim not only managed to revise and edit his father's unfinished work on Democritus (it was published in 1914) but also began his most fruitful period of study and research in mathematical logic, a field with which he had become acquainted through review articles and Ernst Schröder's *Vorlesungen über die Algebra der Logik* (1890–1905). In 1906 Löwenheim joined the Berlin Mathematical Society, to which he read his first paper in 1907, and became a member of the reviewers' staff of the *Jahrbuch über die Fortschritte der Mathematik*. In spite of World War I, during which Löwenheim served in France, Hungary, and Serbia from August 1915 to December 1916 (after which he returned to teaching in Berlin), it was between 1908 and 1919 that he published his most important papers on the algebra of logic, continuing and adding to the work of C. S. Peirce, Schröder, and Alfred North Whitehead.

In papers of 1908 and 1910, Löwenheim analyzed and improved upon the customary methods for solving equations in the calculus of classes or domains (that is, set theory in its Peirce-Schröderian setting) and proved what is now known as Löwenheim's general development theorem for functions of functions. The techniques employed admit of extension to the Peirce-Schröder calculus of relatives, a form of the logic of relations shown by Löwenheim, in a paper of 1913, to be expandable into a calculus of $m \times n$ "matrices of domains" similar to the now customary theory of matrices, especially regarding the representation of transformations by matrices. Löwenheim greatly simplified some of Whitehead's results on substitutions and proved that every theorem about transformations of any arbitrary object is valid if its validity can be shown for transformations of domains.

In his 1915 paper "Über Möglichkeiten im Relativkalkül," Löwenheim reported three results considered classic today. He proved that in classic first-order quantificational logic (with equality, but this is an unnecessary restriction), every formula without free individual variables that is satisfiable at all is already satisfiable in a denumerable (a finite or denumerably infinite) domain. The importance of this theorem of Löwenheim lies in its demonstration that one cannot "implicitly define" the domain of objects satisfying an axiom system formulated in first-order logic, or even the structure of such domains. For example, an axiom system for the real numbers (a nondenumerable domain, as Georg Cantor had shown in 1874) also has a denumerable model, and therefore at least two nonisomorphic models: the intended "standard" one consisting of the reals and the denumerable, "nonstandard" model shown to exist by Löwenheim's theorem.

This situation has been called the Löwenheim-Skolem paradox, but Thoralf Skolem, who extended Löwenheim's theorem in 1920 and 1923, and developed general methods for constructing nonstandard models, pointed out that the result was not paradoxical; rather, it indicated a limit to the characterizability of structures by formal systems and revealed the relativity of (for example, set-theoretical) concepts defined within them. Besides this result, the 1915 paper contained a decision procedure for monadic quantificational logic (that is, with only one-place predicates) and a reduction of the decision problem for full quantificational logic (that is, of finding an algorithmic procedure that effectively decides between satisfiability or nonsatisfiability of an arbitrary formula of the theory) to the decision problem for the subtheory with one- and two-place predicates.

Löwenheim's later papers in mathematical logic have not so far proved to be of equal importance, and in fact his interests broadened to a more philosophical and existential outlook in which questions of mathematical education maintained a prominent place.

In 1931 Löwenheim married Johanna Rassmussen Teichert. His professional life came to an abrupt (but temporary) end in 1934, when he had to accept forced retirement as a 25 percent non-Aryan. He subsequently supported himself by teaching eurythmy and geometry at the Anthroposophic School of Eurythmy in Berlin. A further blow was the loss of all his belongings, including 1,100 geometrical drawings and some geometrical models, and unpublished manuscripts on logic, geometry, music, and the history of art, in the bombing of Berlin on 23 August 1943. Löwenheim managed to survive, however, and again taught mathematics at the Pestalozzi-Schule and the Franz-Mehring-Schule, both in Berlin-Lichtenberg, from 1946 to 1949. Professional logicians (among whom Paul Bernays, Heinrich Scholz, and Alfred Tarski had visited Löwenheim in the 1930's) were convinced that he had not survived the war.

It seems that Löwenheim did not know of the publication of his paper "On Making Indirect Proofs Direct" (translated from the German by Willard Van Orman Quine) in 1946. He left to his stepson, Johannes Teichert, some manuscripts to be used for instruction in schools of eurythmy and for the training of teachers in Waldorf schools, some autobiographical notes, and the sheet proofs of an unpublished sequel to his paper of 1915, written for publication in the 1939 volume of *Fundamenta mathematicae*.

BIBLIOGRAPHY

I. ORIGINAL WORKS. "Über das Auflösungsproblem im logischen Klassenkalkül," in *Sitzungsberichte der Berliner mathematischen Gesellschaft*, **7** (1908), 89–94; "Über die Auflösung von Gleichungen im logischen Gebietekalkül," in *Mathematische Annalen*, **68** (1910), 169–207; "Über Transformationen im Gebietekalkül," *ibid.*, **73** (1913), 245–272; "Über eine Erweiterung des Gebietekalküls, welche auch die gewöhnliche Algebra umfasst," in *Archiv für systematische Philosophie und Soziologie*, **21** (1915), 137–148; "Über Möglichkeiten im Relativkalkül," in *Mathematische Annalen*, **76** (1916), 447–470, translated by Stefan Bauer-Mengelberg as "On Possibilities in the Calculus of Relatives," in Jean van Heijenoort, ed., *From Frege to Gödel: A Source Book in Mathematical Logic, 1879–1931* (Cambridge, Mass., 1967), 228–251; "Einkleidung der Mathematik in Schröderschen Relativkalkül," in *Journal of Symbolic Logic*, **5** (1940), 1–15; and "On Making Indirect Proofs Direct," Willard V. Quine, trans., in *Scripta mathematica*, **12**, no. 2 (1946), 125–147.

II. SECONDARY LITERATURE. Gottlob Frege, *Wissenschaftlicher Briefwechsel*, Felix Meiner, Gottfried Gabriel, et al., eds. (Hamburg, 1976), 157–161; Thoralf Skolem, "Sur la portée du théorème de Löwenheim-Skolem," in Ferdinand Gonseth, ed., *Les entretiens de Zurich sur les fondaments et la méthode des sciences mathématiques, 6–9 décembre 1938* (Zurich, 1941), 25–52; and Christian Thiel, "Leben und Werk Leopold Löwenheims (1878–1957): Teil I, Biographisches und Bibliographisches," in *Jahresbericht der Deutschen Mathematiker-Vereinigung*, **77** (1975), 1–9, with portrait; "Leopold Löwenheim: Life, Work, and Early Influence," in R. O. Gandy and J. M. E. Hyland, eds., *Logic Colloquium 76* (Amsterdam, 1977), 235–252, with bibliography; "Gedanken zum hundertsten Geburtstag Leopold Löwenheims," in *Teorema*, **8** (1978), 263–267, with portrait; and "Löwenheim, Leopold," in Jürgen Mittelstrass, ed., *Enzyklopädie Philosophie und*

Wissenschaftstheorie, II (Mannheim, 1984), 715f.

CHRISTIAN THIEL

LOEWNER, CHARLES (KARL) (*b.* Lany, Bohemia [now Czechoslovakia], 29 May 1893; *d.* Stanford, California, 8 January 1968)

Loewner was the son of Sigmund and Jana Loewner. He studied mathematics with G. Pick at the German University of Prague and received the Ph.D. in 1917. From 1917 to 1922 he was an assistant at the German Technical University of Prague; from 1922 to 1928, assistant and *Privatdozent* at the University of Berlin; from 1928 to 1930, extraordinary professor at the University of Cologne; and from 1930 to 1939, full professor at Charles University in Prague, which he left when the Nazis occupied Czechoslovakia. From 1939 to 1944 he was lecturer and assistant professor at the University of Louisville, Kentucky; from 1945 to 1946, associate professor, and from 1946 to 1951, full professor at Syracuse University; and from 1951 until his retirement in 1963, full professor at Stanford University.

Loewner was married to Elizabeth Alexander, who died in 1955; they had one daughter. Of short stature, soft-spoken, modest, shy (but exceedingly kind to his acquaintances), he had a large number of research students, even after his retirement. His knowledge of mathematics was broad and profound, and included significant parts of mathematical physics. His originality was remarkable; he chose as his problems far from fashionable topics.

One idea pervades Loewner's work from his Ph.D. thesis: applying Lie theory concepts and methods to semigroups, and applying semigroups to unexpected mathematical situations. This led him in 1923 to a sensational result (4): the first significant contribution to the Bieberbach hypothesis. (A *schlicht* function $f(z) = \sum a_n z^n$ in the unit circle with $a_0 = 0$, $a_1 = 1$, has $|a_n| \leq n$—the case $n = 2$ was Bieberbach's and Loewner proved it for $n = 3$; in its totality the problem is still open.) In 1934 Loewner defined nth-order real monotonic functions by the property of staying monotonic if extended to nth-degree symmetric matrices (7) and characterized ∞th-order monotonic functions as functions which, analytically extended to the upper half-plane, map it into itself. The semigroups of first- and second-order monotonic mappings are infinitesimally generated; this property breaks down for orders greater than 2 (28, 32). The infinitesimally generated closed subsemigroup of monotonic mappings of infinite order is characterized by *schlicht* extensions to the upper half-plane (21). Loewner studied minimal semigroup extensions of Lie groups; for the group of the real projective line there are two: that of monotonic mappings of infinite order, and its inverse (21). In higher dimensions the question becomes significant under a suitable definition of monotony (30). Loewner also studied semigroups in a more geometrical context: deformation theorems for projective and Moebius translations (19), and infinitesimally generated semigroups invariant under the non-Euclidean or Moebius group (19), particularly if finite dimensionality and minimality are requested (22).

Among Loewner's other papers, many of which deal with physics, one should be mentioned explicitly: his non-Archimedean measure in Hilbert space (8), which despite its startling originality (or rather because of it) has drawn little attention outside the circle of those who know Loewner's work.

BIBLIOGRAPHY

Loewner's works are

(1) "Untersuchungen über die Verzerrung bei konformen Abbildungen des Einheitskreises, die durch Funktionen mit nichtverschwindender Ableitung geliefert werden," in *Berichte über die Verhandlungen der Sächsischen Akademie der Wissenschaften zu Leipzig*, Math.-phys. Klasse, **69** (1917), 89–106;

(2) "Über Extremumsätze bei der konformen Abbildung des Äusseren des Einheitskreises," in *Mathematische Zeitschrift*, **3** (1919), 65–77;

(3) "Eine Anwendung des Koebeschen Verzerrungssatzes auf ein Problem der Hydrodynamik," *ibid.*, 78–86, written with P. Frank;

(4) "Untersuchungen über schlichte konforme Abbildungen des Einheitskreises," in *Mathematische Annalen*, **89** (1923), 103–121;

(5) "Bemerkung zu einem Blaschkeschen Konvergenzsatze," in *Jahresbericht der Deutschen Mathematikervereinigung*, **32** (1923), 198–200, written with T. Rado;

(6) Chapters 3 and 16 in P. Frank and R. von Mises, eds., *Die Differential- und Integralgleichungen der Mechanik und Physik* (Brunswick, 1925), ch. 3, 119–192, and ch. 16, 685–737;

(7) "Über monotone Matrixfunktionen," in *Mathematische Zeitschrift*, **38** (1934), 177–216;

(8) "Grundzüge einer Inhaltslehre im Hilbertschen Raume," in *Annals of Mathematics*, **40** (1939), 816–833;

(9) "A Topological Characterization of a Class of Integral Operators," *ibid.*, **49** (1948), 316–332;

(10) "Some Classes of Functions Defined by Difference or Differential Inequalities," in *Bulletin of the American Mathematical Society*, **56** (1950), 308–319;

(11) *A Transformation Theory of the Partial Differential Equations of Gas Dynamics*, NACA Technical Report no. 2065 (New York, 1950);

(12) "Generation of Solutions of Systems of Partial Differential Equations by Composition of Infinitesimal Baecklund Transformations," in *Journal d'analyse mathématique*, **2** (1952–1953), 219–242;

(13) "On Generation of Solutions of the Biharmonic Equation in the Plane by Conformal Mappings," in *Pacific Journal of Mathematics*, **3** (1953), 417–436;

(14) "Conservation Laws in Compressible Fluid Flow and Associated Mappings," in *Journal of Rational Mechanics and Analysis*, **2** (1953), 537–561;

(15) "Some Bounds for the Critical Free Stream Mach Number of a Compressible Flow Around an Obstacle," in *Studies in Mathematics and Mechanics Presented to Richard von Mises* (New York, 1954), 177–183;

(16) "On Some Critical Points of Higher Order," Technical Note no. 2, Air Force Contract AF 18(600)680 (1954);

(17) "On Totally Positive Matrices," in *Mathematische Zeitschrift*, **63** (1955), 338–340;

(18) "Continuous Groups," mimeographed notes, University of California at Berkeley (1955);

(19) "On Some Transformation Semigroups," in *Journal of Rational Mechanics and Analysis*, **5** (1956), 791–804;

(20) "Advanced Matrix Theory," mimeographed notes, Stanford University (1957);

(21) "Semigroups of Conformal Mappings," in *Seminar on Analytic Functions, Institute for Advanced Study*, I (Princeton, N.J., 1957), 278–288;

(22) "On Some Transformation Semigroups Invariant Under Euclidean and non-Euclidean Isometries," in *Journal of Mathematics and Mechanics*, **8** (1959), 393–409;

(23) "A Theorem on the Partial Order Derived From a Certain Transformation Semigroup," in *Mathematische Zeitschrift*, **72** (1959), 53–60;

(24) "On the Conformal Capacity in Space," in *Journal of Mathematics and Mechanics*, **8** (1959), 411–414;

(25) "On Some Compositions of Hadamard Type in Classes of Analytic Functions," in *Bulletin of the American Mathematical Society*, **65** (1959), 284–286, written with E. Netanyahu;

(26) "A Group Theoretical Characterization of Some Manifold Structures," Technical Report no. 2 (1962);

(27) "On Some Classes of Functions Associated With Exponential Polynomials," in *Studies in Mathematical Analysis and Related Topics* (Stanford, Calif., 1962), 175–182, written with S. Karlin;

(28) "On Generation of Monotonic Transformations of Higher Order by Infinitesimal Transformations," in *Journal d'analyse mathématique*, **11** (1963), 189–206;

(29) "On Some Classes of Functions Associated With Systems of Curves or Partial Differential Equations of First Order," in *Outlines of the Joint Soviet-American Symposium on Partial Differential Equations* (Novosibirsk, 1963);

(30) "On Semigroups in Analysis and Geometry," in *Bulletin of the American Mathematical Society*, **70** (1964), 1–15;

(31) "Approximation on an Arc by Polynomials With Restricted Zeros," in *Proceedings of the Koninklijke Neder-*

landse Akademie van Wetenschappen, Section A, **67** (1964), 121–128, written with J. Korevaar;

(32) "On Schlicht-monotonic Functions of Higher Order," in *Journal of Mathematical Analysis and Applications*, **14** (1966), 320–326;

(33) "Some Concepts of Parallelism With Respect to a Given Transformation Group," in *Duke Mathematical Journal*, **33** (1966), 151–164;

(34) "Determination of the Critical Exponent of the Green's Function," in *Contemporary Problems in the Theory of Analytic Functions* (Moscow, 1965), pp. 184–187;

(35) "On the Difference Between the Geometric and the Arithmetic Mean of *n* Quantities," in *Advances in Mathematics*, **5** (1971), 472–473, written with H. B. Mann; and

(36) *Theory of Continuous Groups*, with notes by H. Flanders and M. H. Protter (Cambridge, Mass., 1971).

HANS FREUDENTHAL

LOEWY, ALFRED (*b*. Rawitsch, Germany [now Rawicz, Poznan, Poland], 20 June 1873; *d*. Freiburg im Breisgau, Germany, 25 January 1935)

Loewy studied from 1891 to 1895 at the universities of Breslau, Munich, Berlin, and Göttingen. He earned his Ph.D. in 1894 at Munich; was granted his *Habilitation* as *Privatdozent* at Freiburg in 1897; and became extraordinary professor in 1902. Not until 1919 was he appointed a full professor at Freiburg. In 1935 he was forced into retirement because he was a Jew. From about 1920 he was troubled with poor eyesight and he died totally blind.

Loewy published some seventy papers in mathematical periodicals and a few books. He edited German translations of works by Abel, Fourier, and Sturm; and the greater portion of the first part of Pascal's *Repertorium* was his work. His publications were concerned mainly with linear groups, with the algebraic theory of linear and algebraic differential equations, and with actuarial mathematics.

BIBLIOGRAPHY

I. ORIGINAL WORKS. Loewy's writings include *Versicherungsmathematik*, Göschen collection, 180 (Leipzig, 1903); *Lehrbuch der Algebra* (Leipzig, 1915); and *Mathematik des Geld- und Zahlungsverkehrs* (Leipzig, 1920).

Translations edited by Loewy or to which he contributed are N. H. Abel, *Abhandlung über eine besondere Klasse algebraisch auflösbarer Gleichungen*, Ostwald's Klassiker no. 111 (Leipzig, 1900); J. B. Fourier, *Die Auflösung der bestimmten Gleichungen*, Ostwald's Klassiker no. 127 (Leipzig, 1902); C. Sturm, *Abhandlung über die Auflösung der numerischen Gleichungen*, Ostwald's Klassiker no. 143 (Leipzig, 1904); and E. Pascal, ed., *Repertorium der*

höheren Mathematik, P. Epstein and M. E. Timerding, eds., 2nd ed., I (Leipzig, 1910).

II. SECONDARY LITERATURE. See S. Breuer, "Alfred Loewy," in *Versicherungsarchiv*, **6** (1935), 1–5; and A. Fraenkel, "Alfred Loewy," in *Scripta mathematica*, **5** (1938), 17–22, with portrait.

HANS FREUDENTHAL

LOOMIS, ELIAS (*b*. Willington, Connecticut, 7 August 1811; *d*. New Haven, Connecticut, 15 August 1889)

Loomis graduated from Yale College in 1830, and was a tutor there from 1833 to 1836. He became professor of mathematics and natural philosophy at Western Reserve College, in Hudson, Ohio, in 1836, although he spent the first year of his appointment in further study in Paris. From 1844 to 1860 he was professor at the University of the City of New York. In 1860 he accepted a call to Yale, where he stayed until the end of his life. After the early death of his wife, Loomis led a rather isolated life, centered around his work, his only diversion being the compilation of an extensive genealogy of the Loomis family. He was member of the National Academy of Sciences and of scientific societies in the United States and Europe.

Loomis' interest was divided among several branches of science. Most of his scientific achievements were of a practical, rather than a theoretical, nature. His work, reflecting his conviction that the laws governing natural phenomena can be uncovered only by studying observed data, was carried out with utmost precision, and his research, although not always original, was highly valued because of its great reliability. In his own time, however, Loomis was better known for the publication of a large number of textbooks on mathematics, astronomy, and meteorology than for his scientific investigations.

Loomis made his most important contributions in the field of meteorology. In 1846 he published the first "synoptic" weather map, a new method of data representation that in the following decades exerted a profound influence on the formulation of theories of storms. This method became of fundamental importance in the development of weather prediction. The weather maps presented in Loomis' paper brought clarification to the heated controversy between J. P. Espy and W. C. Redfield concerning the surface wind pattern in storms. Later, Loomis essentially followed Espy in regarding thermal convection, reinforced by the latent heat released during condensation of water vapor, as the chief factor in storm formation. As soon as weather maps began to be published on a daily basis in the United States, in 1871, Loomis embarked on a long series of meticulous statistical investigations of cyclones and anticyclones. His results effectively supported the convection theory of cyclones.

Throughout his life Loomis was strongly interested in geomagnetism. In 1833–1834 he conducted a series of hourly observations of the earth's magnetic field and mapped his results for the United States. In 1860 Loomis prepared the first map of the frequency distribution of auroras and pointed out that the oval belt of most frequent auroras was not centered on the geographic pole but approximately paralleled the lines of equal magnetic dip.

Loomis devoted much of his time to astronomical investigations. These studies dealt mainly with the observation of meteors and the determination of longitude and latitude of various localities. Together with D. Olmsted he rediscovered Halley's comet on its return in 1835 and computed its orbit.

BIBLIOGRAPHY

I. ORIGINAL WORKS. Loomis published a large number of his papers in the *American Journal of Science and Arts*, including his investigations on the aurora borealis (1859–1861) and a series of twenty-three papers entitled "Contributions to Meteorology" (1874–1889). A complete bibliography of Loomis' works is to be found in H. A. Newton, "Biographical Memoir of Elias Loomis," in *Biographical Memoirs. National Academy of Sciences*, **3** (1895), 213–252. Collections of Loomis' papers and correspondence are to be found in the Manuscripts and Archives Department of the Beinecke Rare Book and Manuscript Library at Yale University.

II. SECONDARY LITERATURE. The most complete biographical notice is H. A. Newton, cited above. See also F. Waldo, "Some Remarks on Theoretical Meteorology in the United States, 1855 to 1890," in *Report of the International Meteorological Congress, Chicago*, August 21–24, 1893, edited by O. L. Fassig as *Bulletin. Weather Bureau, United States Department of Agriculture* **2**, pt. 2 (1895), 318–325.

GISELA KUTZBACH

LORIA, GINO (*b*. Mantua, Italy, 19 May 1862; *d*. Genoa, Italy, 30 January 1954)

After graduating in 1883 from Turin University, where higher geometry was taught by Enrico D'Ovidio, Loria attended a postgraduate course at Pavia University taught by Beltrami, Bertini, and F. Casorati. Loria became D'Ovidio's assistant in November 1884; on 1 November 1886 he was ap-

pointed extraordinary professor of higher geometry at Genoa University, becoming full professor in 1891. He held the chair of higher geometry at Genoa for forty-nine years, until he retired in 1935; he also taught the history of mathematics, descriptive geometry, and mathematics education. He wrote a number of treatises on descriptive geometry that were appreciated for their simplicity, elegant constructions, and generality. In them he introduced elements of photogrammetry. He was a member of the Accademia Nazionale dei Lincei and of various other academies.

Loria's geometrical research, at first carried out in cooperation with Corrado Segre, was especially concerned with new applications of algebraic concepts to the geometry of straight lines and spheres, with hyperspatial projective geometry, with algebraic correspondence between fundamental forms, and with Cremona transformations in space. But the field in which Loria's scientific activity was most extensive was the history of mathematics from antiquity down to his own time.

Special mention should be made of *Le scienze esatte nell'antica Grecia* (1914), a reworking of the articles which appeared in the *Memorie della Regia Accademia di scienze, lettere e arti in Modena* in 1893–1902. It constitutes a rich source of information on Greek mathematics. *Storia della geometria descrittiva* (1921) shows Loria's liking for the subject. *Guida allo studio della storia delle matematiche* (last ed., 1946) is methodological in character and places at scholars' disposal the rich source materials and collections on the subject with which he had worked for years. Full bibliographical information is in *Il passato e il presente delle principali teorie geometriche*, updated in the editions of 1897, 1907, and 1931.

Loria devoted two works to special algebraic and transcendental curves which have attracted the attention of mathematicians. The first of these works was published in German in 1902, and only much later (1930–1931) in Italian, with the title *Curve piane speciali algebriche e trascendenti*; the other is *Le curve sghembe speciali algebriche e trascendenti* (1925). As F. Enriques has pointed out, the curves studied by Loria are of special interest because the study of particular cases often leads to general results.

Many of Loria's writings are biographical, notably those on Archimedes, Newton, Cremona, Beltrami, and Tannery. With G. Vassura he edited the largely unpublished writings of Torricelli (E. Torricelli, *Opere*, 4 vols. [Faenza, 1919–1944]). In 1897 Loria recognized, in one of Torricelli's manuscripts, the first known rectification of a curve: the logarithmic spiral.

Some of Loria's works have been collected in the volume *Scritti, conferenze e discorsi sulla storia delle matematiche* (1937); and an overall view of the evolution of mathematical thought, from ancient times to the end of the nineteenth century, is provided in his *Storia delle matematiche* (2nd ed., 1950).

Loria's library, containing many works on the history of mathematics, was left to the University of Genoa.

BIBLIOGRAPHY

I. ORIGINAL WORKS. A list of Loria's works is in the commemorative address delivered by A. Terracini at the Accademia dei Lincei (see below) and includes 386 writings. Some of his more important articles are: "Sur les différentes espèces de complexes du second degré des droites qui coupent harmoniquement deux surfaces du second ordre," in *Mathematische Annalen*, **23** (1883), 213–235, written with C. Segre; "Sulle corrispondenze proiettive fra due piani e fra due spazi," in *Giornale di matematiche*, **22** (1883), 1–16; "Ricerche intorno alla geometria della sfera e loro applicazione allo studio ed alla classificazione delle superficie di quarto ordine aventi per linea doppia il cerchio immaginario all'infinito," in *Memorie della Reale Accademia delle scienze di Torino*, 2nd ser., **36** (1884), 199–297; "Sulla classificazione delle trasformazioni razionali dello spazio, in particolare sulle trasformazioni di genere uno," in *Rendiconti dell'Istituto lombardo di scienze e lettere*, 2nd ser., **23** (1890), 824–834; "Della varia fortuna d'Euclide in relazione con i problemi dell'insegnamento della geometria elementare," in *Periodico di matematica per l'insegnamento secondario*, **8** (1893), 81–113; "Evangelista Torricelli e la prima rettificazione di una curva," in *Atti dell'Accademia nazionale dei Lincei, Rendiconti*, 5th ser., **6**, no. 2 (1897), 318–323; "Eugenio Beltrami e le sue opere matematiche," in *Bibliotheca mathematica*, 3rd ser., **2** (1901), 392–440; "Commemorazione di L. Cremona," in *Atti della Società ligustica di scienze naturali e geografiche*, **15** (1904), 19; "Necrologio. Paolo Tannery," in *Bollettino di bibliografia e storia delle scienze matematiche pubblicato per cura di Gino Loria*, **8** (1905), 27–30; and "La storia della matematica vista da un veterano," in *Bollettino dell'Unione matematica italiana*, 3rd ser., **5** (1950), 165–170.

His books include *Spezielle algebraische und transscendente ebene Curven* (Leipzig, 1902), trans. by author as *Curve piane speciali algebriche e trascendenti*, 2 vols. (Milan, 1930–1931); *Le scienze esatte nell'antica Grecia* (Milan, 1914); *Newton* (Rome, 1920); *Storia della geometria descrittiva dalle origini sino ai nostri giorni* (Milan, 1921); *Le curve sghembe speciali algebriche e trascendenti*, 2 vols. (Bologna, 1925); *Archimede* (Milan, 1928); *Storia delle matematiche*, 2 vols. (Torino, 1929–1931; 2nd ed., Milan, 1950); *Il passato e il presente delle principali teorie geometriche* (Padua, 1931), an updating of arts. In *Memorie della Reale Accademia delle scienze di Torino*, sers. 2, **38** (1887);

Scritti, conferenze e discorsi sulla storia delle matematiche (Padua, 1937); and *Guida allo studio della storia delle matematiche* (Milan, 1946).

II. SECONDARY LITERATURE. See A. Terracini, "Gino Loria. Cenni commemorativi," in *Atti dell'Accademia delle scienze di Torino*, **88** (1953–1954), 6–11; and "Commemorazione del socio Gino Loria," in *Atti della Accademia Nazionale dei Lincei, Rendiconti*, 8th ser., Classe di scienze fisiche, matematiche e naturali, **17** (1954), 402–421, with bibliography.

ETTORE CARRUCCIO

LOTKA, ALFRED JAMES (*b.* Lemberg, Austria [now Lvov, Ukrainian S.S.R.], 2 March 1880; *d.* Red Bank, New Jersey, 5 December 1949)

Born of American parents, Lotka received his primary education in France and Germany, took science degrees at the University of Birmingham, England, and subsequently attended graduate courses in physics at Leipzig and Cornell. At various times he worked for the General Chemical Company, the U.S. Patent Office, the National Bureau of Standards, and from 1911 to 1914 was editor of the *Scientific American Supplement*. In 1924, after having spent two years at Johns Hopkins University composing his magnum opus, *Elements of Physical Biology*, he joined the statistical bureau of the Metropolitan Life Insurance Company in New York. There he spent the remainder of his working life (eventually becoming assistant statistician). In 1935 he married Romola Beattie; they had no children. During 1938–1939 he was president of the Population Association of America, and in 1942 he was president of the American Statistical Association.

Lotka's cardinal interests lay in the dynamics of biological populations, and this stemmed from his being struck, as a young physicist, by the similarities between chemical autocatalysis and the proliferation of organisms under specified conditions. He soon developed an "analytical" theory of population that was a function of birthrate, deathrate, and age distribution. His model was more realistic than earlier models; nevertheless he was admirably cautious about its predictive value. He also paid attention to interspecies competition. Building on some mathematical work of Volterra's (in 1926), he formulated a growth law for two competing populations, expressing the process in terms of two interlocking differential equations.

Lotka took a broad culture-conscious view of the quantification of biological change and devoted much thought to the ecologic influence of industrial man. The *Elements of Physical Biology* is an ambitious work, treating the whole biological world from a mathematico-physical standpoint. Later, during his service in the insurance business, he collaborated in writing about life expectancy and allied topics.

BIBLIOGRAPHY

Lotka's most important work, *Elements of Physical Biology* (Baltimore, 1925), was reissued with the title *Elements of Mathematical Biology* (New York, 1956). This ed. carries a full 94-item bibliography of Lotka's scientific and technical papers. With Louis I. Dublin he published three books: *The Money Value of a Man* (New York, 1930); *Length of Life* (New York, 1936); and *Twenty-Five Years of Health Progress* (New York, 1937). The most thorough exposition of his views on population change and evolution is to be found in *Théorie analytique des associations biologiques* (Paris, 1934; 1939), an English trans. of which he was working on at the time of his death. Almost all modern books on population theory mention Lotka's contributions.

NORMAN T. GRIDGEMAN

LOVE, AUGUSTUS EDWARD HOUGH (*b*. Weston-super-Mare, England, 17 April 1863; *d*. Oxford, England, 5 June 1940)

Love was one of four children and the second son of John Henry Love, a surgeon of Somersetshire. He was educated at Wolverhampton Grammar School, and his subsequent career owed much to his mathematical master, the Reverend Henry Williams.

He entered St. John's College, Cambridge, in 1882. He was a fellow of St. John's College from 1886 to 1889 and held the Sedleian chair of natural philosophy at Oxford from 1899 on. He was elected a fellow of the Royal Society of London in 1894. Love was secretary of the London Mathematical Society for fifteen years and president in 1912–1913. He was noted as a quiet, unassuming, brilliant scholar, with a logical and superbly tidy mind. He liked traveling, was interested in music, and played croquet. He never married; a sister, Blanche, kept house for him.

Love's principal research interests were the theory of deformable media, both fluid and solid, and theoretical geophysics. He also contributed to the theory of electric waves and ballistics, and published books on theoretical mechanics and the calculus.

Love's first great work, *A Treatise on the Mathematical Theory of Elasticity*, appeared in two volumes in 1892–1893. A second edition, largely rewritten, appeared in 1906 and was followed by further editions in 1920 and 1927. This treatise, translated into several foreign languages, served as the world's standard source on the subject for nearly half a century. It is a masterpiece of exposition and stands as a classic in the literature of mathematical physics. It continues to be much referred to by workers in the field.

While Love's contribution to the pure theory of elasticity rests principally on his expository powers, his excursions into theoretical geophysics led to far-reaching discoveries about the structure of the earth. His second work, *Some Problems of Geodynamics*, won the Adams Prize at Cambridge in 1911. The work includes contributions on isostasy, tides of the solid earth, variation of latitude, effects of compressibility in the earth, gravitational instability, and the vibrations of a compressible planet. Many of his contributions are basic in current geophysical research, especially Love waves and Love's numbers, the latter being key numbers in tidal theory.

Developing the theory of Love waves was probably his greatest contribution. Formal theory on the transmission of primary (P) and secondary (S) waves in the interior of an elastic body had been worked out by Poisson and Stokes (1830–1850). In 1885 Rayleigh had shown that waves (Rayleigh waves) could be transmitted over the surface of an elastic solid. Rayleigh's theory concerned a semi-infinite, uniform, perfectly elastic, isotropic solid with an infinite plane boundary over which the waves travel.

According to Rayleigh the only permissible surface waves under these conditions are polarized so that the SH component of the particle motions is absent; this is the component which lies in the plane of the surface and is at right angles to the direction of wave advance. A second property of the waves is that for any general initial disturbance they advance unchanged in form: there is no dispersion—no spreading out into sine wave constituents over time.

When surface seismic waves were first detected in studies of earthquake records (some time after 1900), they were found to be discordant with the above two properties of Rayleigh waves. Love set out to investigate a suggestion that the earth's crust is responsible for the discordances. He examined a mathematical model consisting of Rayleigh's uniform medium overlain by a uniform layer of distinct elastic properties and density, and found that this model both permits the transmission of SH waves and requires the waves to be dispersed. These waves are now called Love waves. Love was thus the first to satisfy the general observational requirements of seismology with respect to surface waves.

Love's analysis also supplied a relation between periods and group velocities of surface waves, which became a powerful tool in estimating crustal thicknesses in various geographical regions of the earth: it led *inter alia* to the first evidence of the large differences in crustal structures below continents and oceans.

BIBLIOGRAPHY

Love published forty-five research papers over the period 1887–1929. A full list is given in the *Obituary Notices of Fellows of the Royal Society*. **3** (1939–1941), 480–482.

Love's books are *A Treatise on the Mathematical Theory of Elasticity*, 2 vols. (Cambridge, 1892–1893; 2nd ed., 1906; 3rd ed., 1920; 4th ed., 1927); *Theoretical Mechanics* (Cambridge, 1897; 2nd ed., 1906; 3rd ed., 1921); *Elements of the Differential and Integral Calculus* (Cambridge, 1909); *Some Problems of Geodynamics* (Cambridge, 1911).

K. E. BULLEN

LUCAS, FRANÇOIS-ÉDOUARD-ANATOLE (*b.* Amiens, France, 1842; *d.* Paris, France, 3 October 1891)

Educated at the École Normale in Amiens, he was first employed as an assistant at the Paris Observatory. After serving as an artillery officer in the Franco-Prussian War, he became professor of mathematics at the Lycée Saint-Louis and the Lycée Charlemagne, both in Paris. He was an entertaining teacher. He died as a result of a trivial accident at a banquet; a piece of a dropped plate flew up and gashed his cheek, and within a few days he succumbed to erysipelas.

In number theory his research interest centered on primes and factorization. He devised what is essentially the modern method of testing the primality of Mersenne's numbers, his theorem being as follows: The number $M_p = 2^p - 1$, in which p is a prime, is itself prime if and only if $S_{p-1} \equiv 0 \bmod M_p$, where S belongs to the sequence $S_1 = 4$; $S_n = S_{n-1}^2 - 2$. Using this he was able in 1876 to identify $2^{127} - 1$ as a prime.

The first new Mersenne prime discovered in over a century, it is the largest ever to be checked without electronic help. He loved calculating, wrote on the history of mechanical aids to the process, and worked on plans (never realized) for a large-capacity binary-scale computer. He did some highly original work on the arithmetization of the elliptic functions and on Fibonacci sequences, and he claimed to have made substantial progress in the construction of a proof of Fermat's last theorem.

Lucas' many contributions to number theory were balanced by extensive writings on recreational mathematics, and his four-volume book on the subject remains a classic. Perhaps the best-known of the problems he devised is that of the tower of Hanoi, in which n distinctive rings piled on one of three pegs on a board have to be transferred, in peg-to-peg single steps, to one of the other pegs, the final ordering of the rings to be unchanged.

BIBLIOGRAPHY

I. ORIGINAL WORKS. A comprehensive bibliography of 184 items is appended to Duncan Harkin, "On the Mathematical Works of François-Édouard-Anatole Lucas," in *Enseignement mathématique*, 2nd ser., **3** (1957), 276–288. Only the 1st vol. of Lucas' projected multivolume *Théorie des nombres* (Paris, 1891) was published. See also *Récréations mathématiques*, 4 vols. (Paris, 1891–1894; repr. Paris, 1960).

II. SECONDARY LITERATURE. Lucas' most important contributions to number theory are synopsized in L. E. Dickson, *History of the Theory of Numbers*, 3 vols. (Washington, 1919–1923)—see esp. vol. I, ch. 17. Harkin's article (see above) is also informative in this respect.

NORMAN T. GRIDGEMAN

LUEROTH (or LÜROTH), JAKOB (*b.* Mannheim, Germany, 18 February 1844; *d.* Munich, Germany, 14 September 1910)

Lueroth's first scientific interests lay in astronomy. He began making observations while he was still in secondary school, but since he was hampered by bad eyesight he took up the study of mathematics instead. He attended the universities of Heidelberg, Berlin, and Giessen from 1863 until 1866; he had already, in 1865, written his doctoral dissertation on the Pascal configuration. In 1867 he became *Privatdozent* at the University of Heidelberg, and two years later, when he was still only twenty-five years old, he was appointed professor ordinarius at the Technische Hochschule in Karlsruhe. From 1880 until 1883 he taught at the Technische Hochschule of Munich, and from the latter year until his death, at the University of Freiburg.

Lueroth's first mathematical publications were concerned with questions in analytical geometry, linear geometry, and theory of invariants, a development of the work of his teachers Hesse and Clebsch. His name is associated with three specific contributions to science. The first of these, a covariant of a given ternary form of fourth degree, is called the "Lueroth quartic," and Lueroth discovered it when he examined, following Clebsch, the condition under which a ternary quartic form may be represented as a sum of five fourth-powers of linear forms. In 1876 he demonstrated the "Lueroth theorem," whereby each uni-rational curve is rational—Castelnuovo in 1895 proved the analogous but more difficult theorem for surfaces. Finally, the "Clebsch-Lueroth method" may be employed in the construction of a Riemann surface for a given algebraic curve in the complex plane.

In addition, Lueroth worked in other areas of mathematics far removed from algebraic geometry. He obtained partial proof of the topological invariance of dimension (proved in 1911 by L. Brouwer) and, following the work of Staudt, did research in complex geometry. He was also involved in the logical researches of his friend Schröder and published two books in applied mathematics and mechanics. These were *Grundriss der Mechanik*, in which he used the vector calculus for the first time, and *Vorlesungen über numerisches Rechnen*. Lueroth collaborated in editing the collected works of Hesse and Grassmann.

BIBLIOGRAPHY

I. ORIGINAL WORKS. A complete bibliography of Lueroth's works may be found in the Brill and Noether obituary (see below). The papers containing his main discoveries are "Einige Eigenschaften einer gewissen Gattung von Kurven 4. Ordnung," in *Mathematische Annalen*, **2** (1869), 37–53; "Das Imaginäre in der Geometrie und das Rechnen mit Würfen," *ibid.*, **8** (1875), 145–214, "Beweis eines Satzes über rationale Kurven," *ibid.*, **9** (1876), 163–165; and "Über die kanonischen Querschnitte einer Riemannschen Fläche," in *Sitzungsberichte der physikalisch-medizinischen Sozietät in Erlangen*, **15** (1883), 24–30. He also published *Grundriss der Mechanik* (Munich, 1881), and *Vorlesungen über numerisches Rechnen* (Leipzig, 1900).

II. SECONDARY LITERATURE. An obituary is A. Brill and M. Noether, "Jacob Lueroth," in *Jahresberichte der Deutschen Mathematikervereinigung*, **20** (1911), 279–299.

WERNER BURAU

ŁUKASIEWICZ, JAN (*b*. Lvov, Austrian Galicia [now Ukrainian S.S.R.], 21 December 1878; *d*. Dublin, Ireland, 13 February 1956)

Łukasiewicz' father, Paul, was a captain in the Austrian army; his mother, the former Leopoldine Holtzer, was the daughter of an Austrian civil servant. The family was Roman Catholic, and the language spoken at home was Polish. Young Łukasiewicz studied mathematics and philosophy at the University of Lvov, earning his doctorate *sub auspiciis imperatoris*, a rare honor (1902). At the same institution he received his *Habilitation* (1906) and lectured in logic and philosophy, as *Privatdozent* until 1911, then as extraordinary professor. In 1915 Łukasiewicz accepted an invitation to lecture at the University of Warsaw, then in German-occupied territory.

Between the world wars, as a citizen of independent Poland, Łukasiewicz was minister of education (1919), professor at the University of Warsaw (1920–1939), twice rector of that institution, an active member of scientific societies, and the recipient of several honors. He and Stanislaw Leśniewski founded the Warsaw school of logic, which A. Tarski helped make world famous. Viewing mathematical logic as an instrument of inquiry into the foundations of mathematics and the methodology of empirical science, Łukasiewicz succeeded in making it a required subject for mathematics and science students in Polish universities. His lucid lectures attracted students of the humanities as well.

The sufferings endured by Łukasiewicz and his wife (the former Regina Barwinska) during World War II are poignantly recalled in an autobiographical note. (See Sobociński's "In Memoriam," cited below.) In 1946 Łukasiewicz, then an exile in Belgium, accepted a professorship at the Royal Irish Academy, Dublin, where he remained until his death.

After some early essays on the principles of non-contradiction and excluded middle (1910), Łukasiewicz arrived by 1917 at the conception of a three-valued propositional calculus. His subsequent researches on many-valued logics is regarded by some as his greatest contribution. He viewed these "non-Aristotelian" logics as representing possible new ways of thinking, and he experimented with interpreting them in modal terms and in probability terms. The nonstandard systems he developed have value independently of the philosophy that inspired them or of the usefulness of those interpretations. Lukasiewicz created the elegant "Łukasiewicz system" for two-valued propositional logic and the parenthesis-free "Polish notation."

The metalogic (a term he coined on the model of Hilbert's terminology) of propositional calculi, notably the theory of their syntactic and semantic completeness, owes much to Łukasiewicz and his school. He regarded these studies as a prelude to analogous investigations for the rest of logic, which were then carried out by Tarski.

Using modern formal techniques, Łukasiewicz reconstructed and reevaluated ancient and medieval logic. Through his work in this area, we have changed our view of the history of logic.

During his last years in Ireland, Łukasiewicz published important studies on modal and intuitionistic logic, and he again made logical history with a detailed and novel study of Aristotle's syllogistic. Essentially he interpreted syllogisms in Aristotle to be theorems of logic, not rules of derivations.

ical Philosophy: A Survey and a Comparison with British Analytical Philosophy (New York, 1967), 56–72.

GEORGE GOE

BIBLIOGRAPHY

I. ORIGINAL WORKS. Most of Łukasiewicz' contributions were first presented in short notes, often in Polish, or in his university lectures. A list of all, or almost all, of his publications is appended to Andrzej Mostowski's "L'oeuvre scientifique de Jan Łukasiewicz dans le domaine de la logique mathématique," in *Fundamenta mathematicae*, **44** (1957), 1–11. His following writings present important results systematically: *Elementy logiki matematycznej* ("Elements of Mathematical Logic"; Warsaw, 1929; 2nd ed., 1958), translated by Olgierd Wojtasiewicz as *Elements of Mathematical Logic* (New York, 1963); "Philosophische Bemerkungen zu mehrwertigen Systemen des Aussagenkalküls," in *Comptes rendus des séances de la Société des sciences et des lettres de Varsovie*, Cl. III, **23** (1930), 51–77, written with Alfred Tarski; "Untersuchungen über den Aussagenkalkül," *ibid.*, 30–50; "Zur Geschichte der Aussagenlogik," in *Erkenntnis*, **5** (1935–1936), 111–131; "A System of Modal Logic," in *Journal of Computing Systems*, **1** (1953), 111–149; and *Aristotle's Syllogistic From the Stand-Point of Modern Formal Logic*, 2nd ed. (Oxford, 1957).

II. SECONDARY LITERATURE. The following two articles jointly constitute a valuable survey of Łukasiewicz' life-work as a logician, philosopher, and historian of logic: L. Borkowski and J. Słupecki, "The Logical Works of Jan Łukasiewicz," in *Studia logica*, **8** (1958), 7–56; and Tadeusz Kotarbiński, "Jan Łukasiewicz's Works on the History of Logic," *ibid.*, 57–62. Shorter general treatments of Łukasiewicz's work are the Mostowski article cited above; Bolesław Sobociński, "In Memoriam Jan Łukasiewicz," in *Philosophical Studies* (Maynooth, Ireland), **6** (1956), 3–49, which contains an autobiographical note, "Curriculum vitae of Jan Łukasiewicz," and a bibliography; and Heinrich Scholz, "In Memoriam Jan Łukasiewicz," in *Archiv für mathematische Logik und Grundlagenforschung*, **3** (1957), 3–18, which contains an excellent summary of the technical aspects of Łukasiewicz' contributions.

Łukasiewicz' exegesis of Aristotle's syllogistic is disputed in Arthur N. Prior, "Łukasiewicz's Symbolic Logic," in *Australasian Journal of Philosophy*, **30** (1952), 33–46, and is discussed in Gunther Patzig, *Die Aristotelische Syllogistik: Logisch-philologische Untersuchungen über das Buch A der "Ersten Analytiken"* (Göttingen, 1959); English trans. by J. Barnes, *Aristotle's Theory of the Syllogism: A Logico-philological Study of Book A of the Prior Analytics* (Dordrecht, 1968), *passim*, esp. 196–202.

For a general evaluation of Łukasiewicz' philosophical and logical ideas, see Henryk Skolimowsky, *Polish Analyt-*

LULL, RAMON (*b.* Ciutat de Mallorques [now Palma de Mallorca], *ca.* 1232; *d.* Ciutat de Mallorques [?], January/March [?] 1316)

A Catalan encyclopedist, Lull invented an "art of finding truth" which inspired Leibniz's dream of a universal algebra four centuries later. His contributions to science are understandable only when examined in their historical and theological context. The son of a Catalan nobleman of the same name who participated in the reconquest of Mallorca from the Moors, Lull was brought up with James the Conqueror's younger son (later crowned James II of Mallorca), whose seneschal he became. About six years after his marriage to Blanca Picany (1257) he was converted from a courtly to a religious way of life, following a series of visions of Christ crucified. He never took holy orders (although he may have become a Franciscan tertiary in 1295), but his subsequent career was dominated by three religious resolutions: to become a missionary and attain martyrdom, to establish colleges where missionaries would study oriental languages, and to provide them with "the best book[s] in the world against the errors of the infidel."[1]

Lull's preparations lasted a decade; his remaining forty years (from 1275, when he was summoned by Prince James to Montpellier, where he lectured on the early versions of his Art) were spent in writing, preaching, lecturing, and traveling (including missionary journeys to Tunis in 1292; Bougie, Algeria, in 1307; and Tunis late in 1315), and in attempts to secure support from numerous kings and four successive popes for his proposed colleges. During Lull's lifetime only James II of Mallorca established such a foundation (1276, the year of his accession); when he lost Mallorca to his elder brother, Peter III of Aragon, the college at Miramar apparently was abandoned (*ca.* 1292). In Lull's old age his proposals were finally approved by the Council of Vienne (1311–1312); and colleges for the study of Arabic, Hebrew, and Chaldean were founded in Rome, Bologna, Paris, Salamanca, and Oxford after Lull's death. Pious tradition has it that he died after being stoned by Muslims in Bougie (January 1316[?]), although his actual death is variously said to have occurred in Bougie, at sea, or in Mallorca; modern scholars doubt the historicity of his martyrdom. As for his third resolution, it led to the various versions of Lull's Art—and all his scientific contributions were by-products of this enterprise.

James the Conqueror's chief adviser, the Dominican Saint Ramon de Penyafort, dissuaded Lull from studying in Paris, where his age and lack of Latin would have told against him; he therefore studied informally in Mallorca (1265[?]–1273[?]). His thought was thus not structured at the formative stage by the Scholastic training which molded most other late medieval Christian thinkers; this fostered the development of his highly idiosyncratic system by leaving his mind open to numerous non-Scholastic sources. These included cabalism (then flourishing in learned Jewish circles in both Catalonia and Italy), earlier Christian writers discarded by Scholasticism (for instance, John Scotus Eriugena, whose ninth-century *De divisione naturae* influenced Lullian cosmological works, notably the *Liber chaos*, either directly or indirectly—and hence also his Art), and probably also Arabic humoral medicine and astrology. The Augustinian Neoplatonism of the Victorines also proved important, partly because of its continuing prominence but mainly because its marked coincidences with both Islamic and cabalistic Neoplatonism favored the creation of a syncretistic system which was firmly grounded in doctrines equally acceptable to Christians, Jews, and Muslims.

This fusion occurred after the eight years Lull spent in Mallorca studying Latin, learning Arabic from a slave, reading all texts available to him in either tongue, and writing copiously. One of his earliest works was a compendium of the logic of al-Ghazālī in Arabic (1270[?]); it has since been lost, although two later compendia with similar titles survive—one in Latin, the other in Catalan mnemonic verse. In all, Lull wrote at least 292 works in Catalan, Arabic, or Latin over a period of forty-five years (1270–1315); most of them have been preserved, although no Arabic manuscripts have yet been traced and many Catalan and Latin works remain unpublished. His initial awkwardness in Latin, coupled with his desire that knowledge be made available to non-Latin-speaking sectors of society, made Lull the first person to mold Catalan into a literary medium. He used it not only in important mystical works, poetry, and allegorical novels (none of which concerns us here) but also to deal with every learned subject which engaged his attention: theology and philosophy; arithmetic, geometry, and astronomy (often mainly astrology), which, together with music, formed the quadrivium (the higher division of the seven liberal arts); grammar, rhetoric, and logic (the trivium); law; and medicine. Thus, Lull created a fully developed learned vocab-ulary in Catalan almost a century before any other Romance vernacular became a viable scholarly medium. Almost all Lull's works in such nonliterary fields were connected in some way with his Art, because the "art of finding truth" which he developed to convert "the infidel" proved applicable to every branch of knowledge. Lull himself pioneered its application to all subjects studied in medieval universities—except for music—and also constructed one of the last great medieval encyclopedias, the *Arbor scientiae* (1295–1296), in accordance with its basic principles.

Yet the Art can be understood correctly only when viewed in the light of Lull's primary aim: to place Christian apologetics on a rational basis for use in disputations with Muslims, for whom arguments *de auctoritate* grounded on the Old Testament—widely used by Dominicans in disputations with the Jews—carried no weight. The same purpose lay behind the *Summa contra gentiles* of Aquinas, written at the request of his fellow Dominican Penyafort, whose concern for the conversion of all non-Christians (but particularly those in James the Conqueror's dominions) thus inspired the two chief thirteenth-century attempts in this direction; the *Summa contra gentiles* was finished during the interval between Lull's discovery of his own calling and his interview with Penyafort. But whereas Aquinas distinguished categorically between what reason could prove and that which, while not contrary to reason, needed faith in revelation, Lull advanced what he called necessary reasons for accepting dogmas like the Trinity and the Incarnation. This gave his Art a rationalistic air that led to much subsequent criticism. Lull himself described his Art as lying between faith and logic, and his "necessary reasons" were not so much logical proofs as reasons of greater or lesser congruence which could not be denied without rejecting generally accepted principles. In this respect they were not appreciably more "rationalistic" than Aquinas's "proofs" that the truths of faith were not incompatible with reason. But the differences between the two apologetic systems are far more striking than their resemblances.

Lull regarded his Art as divinely inspired and hence infallible (although open to improvement in successive versions). Its first form, the *Ars compendiosa inveniendi veritatem* or *Ars maior*[2] (1273–1274[?]), was composed after a mystical "illumination" on Mount Randa, Mallorca, in which Lull saw that everything could be systematically related back to God by examining how Creation was structured by the active manifestation of the divine attributes—which he called Dignities and used as the absolute principles of his Art. Examining their manifestations involved using a set of relative principles; and both sets could be visualized in combinatory diagrams, known as Figures *A* and *T*. The original Figure *A* had sixteen Dignities, lettered *BCDEFGHIKLMNOPQR*; the original Figure *T* had five triads, only three of which (*EFG* + *HIK* + *LMN*) were strictly principles of relation, the others being sets of subjects (God + Creature + Operation, *BCD*) and possible judgments (Affirmation + Doubt + Negation, *OPQ*). All early versions had a proliferation of supplementary visual aids, which always included diagrams showing the four elements, and—with the obvious exception of Figure *T*—most features of the system were grouped into sets of sixteen items, lettered like the Dignities.

This quaternary base seems to provide the key to the origins of the Art's combinatory aspect, apparently modeled on the methods used to calculate combinations of the sixteen elemental "grades" (four each for fire, air, water, and earth) in both astrology and humoral medicine. A major simplification in the *Ars inventiva* (*ca.* 1289) eliminated the elemental features, reduced the diagrams to four (unchanged thereafter), reduced Figure *T* to the nine actual relative principles (Difference + Concordance + Contradiction, Beginning + Middle + End, and Majority + Equality + Minority) and the sixteen original Dignities to the nine shown in Figure 1. In still later versions the symbolic letters *BCDEFGHIK* acquired up to six meanings that were ultimately set out in the gridlike "alphabet" of the *Ars generalis ultima* and its abridgment, the *Ars brevis* (both 1308),

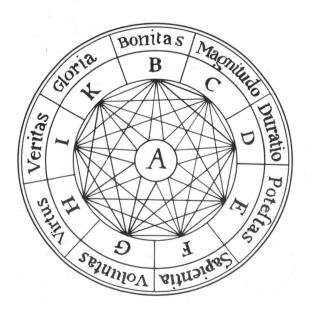

FIGURE 1. The Lullian "Dignities."

from which Figure 2 is reproduced. The traditional seven virtues and seven vices have been extended to sets of nine, to meet the requirements of the ternary system; the last two of ten *quaestiones* (a series connected with the ten Aristotelian categories) had to share the same compartment, since the set of fundamental questions could not be shortened and still be exhaustive.

The most distinctive characteristic of Lull's Art is clearly its combinatory nature, which led to both the use of complex semimechanical techniques that sometimes required figures with separately revolving concentric wheels—"volvelles," in bibliographical parlance (see Figure 3)—and to the symbolic notation of its alphabet. These features justify its classification among the forerunners of both modern symbolic logic and computer science, with its systematically exhaustive consideration of all possible combinations of the material under examination, reduced to a symbolic coding. Yet these techniques taken over from nontheological sources, however striking, remain ancillary, and should not obscure the theocentric basis of the Art. It relates everything to the exemplification of God's Dignities, thus starting out from both the monotheism common to Judaism, Christianity, and Islam and their common acceptance of a Neoplatonic exemplarist world picture, to argue its way up and down the traditional ladder of being on the basis of the analogies between its rungs—as becomes very obvious in Lull's *De ascensu et descensu intellectus* (1305). The lowest rung was that of the elements, and Lull probably thought that the "model" provided by the physical doctrines of his time constituted a valid "scientific" basis for arguments projected to higher levels. Since this physical basis would be accepted in the scientific field by savants of all three "revealed religions," he doubtless also hoped that the specifically Christian conclusions which he drew in the apologetic field would be equally acceptable. It even seems likely that what hit him with the force of a divine "illumination" on Mount Randa was his sudden recognition of such a possibility.

There is no evidence that Lull's Art ever converted anybody, but his application of the combinatory method to other disciplines (begun in the four *Libri principiorum*, *ca.* 1274–1275) was followed by numerous later Lullists; the Art's function as a means of unifying all knowledge into a single system remained viable throughout the Renaissance and well into the seventeenth century. As a system of logical inquiry (see Lull's *Logica nova* [1303] for the strictly logical implications, disentangled from other aspects), its method of proceeding from basic sets of preestablished concepts by the systematic exploration of their

	1. Essentia 2. Unitas 3. Perfect o										
	A	B	C	D	E	F	G	H	I	K
Alphabetum seu principia huius artis sunt aut	Praedicata	Absoluta	Bonitas	Magnitudo	Æternitas seu Duratio	Potestas	Sapientia	Voluntas	Virtus	Veritas	Gloria
		T. Relata seu respectus	Differentia	Concordantia	Contrarietas	Principium	Medium	Finis	Maioritas	Æqualitas	Minoritas
	Q. Quaestiones		Vtrum?	Quid?	De quo?	Quare?	Quantum?	Quale?	Quando?	Vbi?	Quomodo? Cum quo?
	S. Subiecta		Deus	Angelus	Coelum	Homo	Imaginatio	Sensitiua	Vegetatiua	Elementatiua	Instrumentatiua
	V. Virtutes		Iustitia	Prudentia	Fortitudo	Temperantia	Fides	Spes	Charitas	Patientia	Pietas
	V. Vitia		Auaritia	Gula	Luxuria	Superbia	Acidia	Inuidia	Ira	Mendacium	Inconstantia

FIGURE 2.   The "alphabet" of Lull's *Ars brevis* (1303).

combinations—in connection with any question on any conceivable subject—can be succinctly stated in terms taken from the *Dissertatio de arte combinatoria* (1666) of Leibniz, which was inspired by the Lullian Art: "A proposition is made up of subject and predicate; hence all propositions are combinations. Hence the logic of inventing [discovering] propositions involves solving this problem: 1. given a subject, [finding] the predicates; 2. given a predicate, finding the subjects [to which it may] apply, whether by way of affirmation or negation."[3]

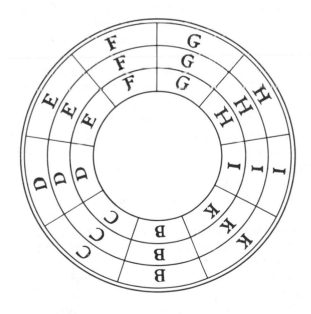

FIGURE 3.   The fourth figure of the later Art: the inner wheels rotate independently, allowing all possible ternary combinations of the letters *BCDEFGHIK* to be read off.

Recent research has concentrated on the clarification of Lull's ideas, the identification of their sources, and the nature of their influence on later thinkers—especially Nicholas of Cusa and Giordano Bruno. Major advances in all these fields have taken place since the 1950's, but much more research is still required. The specific origins of Lull's doctrines regarding the elements, whose importance has been fully recognized only since 1954 (see Yates), are particularly significant. A proper exploration of the antecedents of his *Opera medica* is a prerequisite for establishing Lull's final place in the history of Western science. In this connection it must be mentioned that although Lull himself was opposed to alchemy (but not to astrology, a "science" he sought to improve in the *Tractatus novus de astronomia* [1297]), his methods had obvious applications in the alchemical field—and they were so applied in a host of pseudo-Lullian alchemical works, most of them composed more than fifty years after his death. These works explain the traditional (but false) "scientific" view which made him "Lull the Alchemist."

NOTES

1. *Vida coëtanea.* The Latin (dictated by Lull [?], probably 1311) says "book," which doubtlessly agreed with Lull's original resolve; the plural, in the fourteenth-century Catalan text (modernized in *Obres essencials*, see I, 36), would better fit the series of "improved" versions of the Art itself, which first took shape almost ten years after Lull's conversion.

2. References to an *Ars magna* in later centuries are usually either to the definitive *Ars magna generalis ultima* (1308) or to Lull's system in general. The alternative title of the first version recalls Roger Bacon's *Opus maius* (1267); the connections between Lull and Bacon have yet to be

investigated, but many resemblances may well be due to common Arabic sources.

3. "Propositio componitur ex subiecto et praedicato, omnes igitur propositiones sunt combinationes. Logicae igitur inventivae propositionum est hoc problema solvere: 1. Dato subiecto praedicata. 2. Dato praedicato subiecta invenire, utraque cum affirmative, tum negative" (G. W. Leibniz, *op. cit.* [in text], no. 55, in *Sämtliche Schriften und Briefen*, 2nd ser., I [Darmstadt, 1926], 192).

BIBLIOGRAPHY

I. ORIGINAL WORKS. The larger of the standard eds. in Catalan is *Obres de Ramon Lull*, 21 vols., with 9 more planned (Palma de Mallorca, 1901–   ), cited below as *ORL. Obres essencials*, 2 vols. (Barcelona, 1957–1960), cited below as *Ob es*, contains the chief literary works; the modernized text has many errata, but there are excellent general introductions and a select bibliography.

Collections in Latin are Beati Raymundi Lulli, *Opera omnia*, I. Salzinger, ed., vols. I-VI, IX (VII and VIII unpublished) (Mainz, 1721–1742), contains 48 works, repr. Minerva GMBH, cited below as *MOG;* reprint of *Quattuor libri principiorum* from *MOG* I (Paris–The Hague, 1969), cited below as *QLP; Opera parva*, 3 vols. (Palma, 1744–1746), 15 works, 12 of which are not in *MOG;* and *Opera medica* (Palma, 1742)—it and *Opera parva* are to be issued in Gerstenberg Reprints. A modern critical ed. is *Raymundi Lulli Opera latina*, 5 vols., of 30 planned (Palma, 1961–   ), thus far previously unpublished works, cited below as *ORL*.

Major scientific works and versions of the Art are *Ars compendiosa inveniendi veritatem/Ars maior* (1273–1274[?]), *MOG* I; *Ars Universalis* (1274–1275[?]), *MOG* I; *Liber principiorum theologiae, Liber principiorum philosophiae, Liber principiorum juris, Liber principiorum medicinae* (1274–1275[?]), *MOG* I, *QLP; Liber chaos* (1275–1276[?]), *MOG III; Ars compendiosa medicinae* (1275–1276[?]), *Opera medica; Logica Algazalis* (*ca.* 1281), which is related to the Catalan verse *Logica del Gatzel* (after 1282[?]), *ORL* XIX; *Ars inventiva [veritatis]* (1289[?]), *MOG* V; *De levitate et ponderositate elementorum* (1293), *Opera medica; Arbor scientiae* (29 Sept. 1295–1 Apr. 1296), in various rare eds., in Catalan as *Arbre de ciencia* (simultaneous[?]), *ORL* XI-XIII, *Ob es* I; *Tractatus novus de astronomia* (1297; unpublished), Latin text discussed in Yates (1954; see below), Catalan MS is British Museum, Add. 16434, to appear in *ORL;* and *Liber de geometria [nova et compendiosa]* (1299), ed. by J. M. Millás-Vallicrosa (Barcelona, 1953), considered unreliable—see R. D. F. Pring-Mill, "La geometría luliana," in *Estudios Lulianos,* 2 (1958), 341–342.

Other works by Lull are *Liber de natura* (1301) (Palma, 1744); *Logica nova* (Palma, 1744); *Liber de regionibus sanitatis et infirmitatis* (1303), *Opera medica; De ascensu et descensu intellectus* (1305) (Palma, 1744); *Ars brevis* (1308), *Opera parva* I; *Ars generalis ultima/Ars magna [generalis ultima]* (1305–1308), in L. Zetzner, *Raymundi Lulli opera ea quae ad . . . artem . . . pertinent* (Strasbourg, 1598, 1609, 1617, 1651); and *Vita coëtanea* (dictated [?]

1311), B. de Gaiffier, ed., in *Analecta Bollandiana,* **48** (1930), 130–178, in Catalan as *Vida coëtania, Ob es*.

II. SECONDARY LITERATURE. See E. Colomer, S.J., *Nikolaus von Kues und Raimund Lull* (Berlin, 1961); C. E. Dufourcq, *L'Espagne catalane et le Maghreb aux XIIIᵉ et XIVᵉ siècles* (Paris, 1966); J. N. Hillgarth, *Ramon Lull and Lullism in Fourteenth-Century France* (Oxford, 1971); Erhard-Wolfram Platzeck, O.F.M., *Raimund Lull, sein Leben, seine Werke, die Grundlagen seines Denkens,* 2 vols. (Düsseldorf, 1961–1964), vol. II contains the fullest bibliography of Lull's writings and Lullian studies; and Frances A. Yates, "The Art of Ramon Lull: An Approach to It Through Lull's Theory of the Elements," in *Journal of the Warburg and Courtauld Institutes,* **17** (1954), 115–173; and "Ramon Lull and John Scotus Erigena," *ibid.,* **23** (1960), 1–44; but see R. D. F. Pring-Mill, in *Estudios Lulianos,* **7** (1963), 167–180.

See also *Estudios Lulianos,* which began publication in 1957, and E. W. Platzeck's comprehensive survey of research from 1955 to 1969 in *Antonianum,* **45** (1970), 213–272.

R. D. F. PRING-MILL

LUZIN, NIKOLAI NIKOLAIEVICH (*b.* Tomsk, Russia, 9 December 1883; *d.* Moscow, U.S.S.R., 28 February 1950)

Luzin was the son of a trade official, Nikolai Mitrofanovich Luzin, and Olga Nikolaievna. He completed his secondary schooling at Tomsk in 1901 and entered the mathematics division of the Physics-Mathematics Faculty of Moscow University. Here he became an active member of the circle of science students headed by N. E. Zhukovsky and studied mathematics under the guidance of D. F. Egorov. He spent the winter and spring of 1906 in Paris, where he attended lectures at the Sorbonne and the Collège de France. At the end of 1906 Luzin completed the course at Moscow University and remained there to prepare for a professorship. In 1910, after passing the examinations for the master's degree, he was appointed assistant professor at Moscow University but did not take up his duties there; he was sent to Göttingen and Paris for further study in those fields that had interested him for several years—the theory of functions of a real variable, integration theory, and the theory of trigonometric series. Luzin's first memoirs, published in 1911–1913 in *Matematicheskii sbornik* and the *Comptes rendus* of the Paris Academy of Sciences, immediately attracted the attention of the scientific world. In the spring of 1914, upon his return to Moscow, Luzin started lecturing, one of his courses being on function theory; he also organized a special research seminar on the subject. In 1915 he submitted a monograph entitled

Integral i trigonometrichesky ryad ("Integrals and the Trigonometric Series"), published in *Matematicheskii sbornik*, and defended it at the Physics-Mathematics Faculty as his master's thesis. On the basis of its outstanding merits, the scientific council awarded Luzin the doctorate in pure mathematics, and in 1917 he became a professor.

During the period 1914–1924 Luzin, a brilliant lecturer and scientific organizer, was the center of a Moscow school of function theory which greatly influenced the subsequent development of mathematics, both in the Soviet Union and abroad. Such outstanding mathematicians as P. S. Alexandrov, A. Y. Khinchin, D. E. Menshov, M. Y. Suslin, A. N. Kolmogorov, N. K. Bari, and P. S. Novikov were his pupils.

Luzin was a member of the Moscow Mathematical Society, of the Moscow Society of Explorers of Nature, and of the Cracow Academy of Sciences; an honorary member of the Calcutta Mathematical Society and of the Belgian Mathematical Society; and was elected vice-president of the International Mathematical Congress held at Bologna in 1928. In 1927 Luzin was elected a corresponding member of the Soviet Academy of Sciences, and in 1929 he became an academician.

After 1930 Luzin devoted less time to teaching and worked mainly at the Soviet Academy of Sciences: the Mathematical Institute (1929–1936; 1941–1950) and the Institute of Automatics and Telemechanics (1936–1950).

Luzin's mathematical creativity relates mostly to the theory of functions of a real variable in its two branches, metric and descriptive. Insofar as the first is concerned, Luzin's thesis (Moscow, 1915) is paramount, since it contains important results on the structure of measurable sets and functions, on primitive functions, on convergence of trigonometric series, and on representability of functions by trigonometric series. Cited in the thesis are examples of power series with coefficients tending to zero and nevertheless diverging everywhere on the boundary of the circle of convergence (1912), as well as a trigonometric series with coefficients tending to zero that nevertheless diverges almost everywhere (1912). These examples stimulated many later investigations. Luzin later showed that every measurable function can, in a certain sense, be represented as a trigonometric series that may be summable almost everywhere to that function by the methods of Poisson and Riemann.

Another important result obtained by Luzin on absolute convergence resides in the fact that when a trigonometric series converges absolutely at two points, the distance between which is incommensurable with respect to π, this series converges absolutely over an everywhere dense set and therefore will either converge everywhere or diverge everywhere.

The investigation of the structure of measurable sets and functions led Luzin to prove the so-called C property: that is, that every measurable function which is almost everywhere finite over a given segment can be made continuous over the segment by varying its value on a set of arbitrarily small measure (1912). In Luzin's hands this theorem was a most important means of investigation; by resorting to it he managed to solve completely a number of cardinal problems: finding a primitive function, the representability of a function as a trigonometric series, and finding a harmonic function that is holomorphic inside a circle and takes given values on the circumference.

In the theory of integration, Luzin solved the problem of how to distinguish the Lebesgue integral or the Denjoy integral from the other primitives of the given function. For this purpose he introduced a new concept of complete variation of a function for a perfect set. The metric theory of functions was applied by Luzin to the study of boundary properties of analytical functions.

After 1915 Luzin turned to the descriptive theory of functions. Having investigated the so-called B sets studied by Borel, Baire, and Lebesgue, Luzin raised questions concerning the power of B sets and the construction of sets that are not B sets without resorting to Zermelo's axiom, to which many mathematicians objected. Both of the problems were solved by Luzin's pupils; M. Y. Suslin constructed a more extended class of sets than that of B sets, called analytical or A sets. Luzin introduced new definitions of both A sets and B sets, as well as the "sieving process," which became very important in the theory of A sets. Through the use of this process, Luzin also showed that a segment may be represented as a sum of pairwise disjoint B sets. It is to date the strongest result in the theory of sets that is not based upon Zermelo's axiom. Luzin also created a theory of "projective" sets (1925), which are obtained from B sets by successively performing the operation of projection and taking a complement. Through the introduction of this concept, some difficulties of a mathematical and logical nature came to light and were studied by his successors.

Luzin also provided decisive results in the solution of the problem of bending on the main base (1938) that dated back to K. M. Peterson, and the evaluation of the convergence of S. A. Chaplygin's method of approximate solution of differential equations (1932). He also wrote brilliant articles on Euler and

Newton (1933, 1943). Luzin's many manuals and textbooks on mathematical analysis and the theory of functions of a real variable went through many editions and are still used by students in the Soviet Union.

BIBLIOGRAPHY

I. ORIGINAL WORKS. Luzin's writings were brought together in *Sobranie sochinenii* ("Collected Works"), 3 vols. (Moscow, 1953–1959). Individual works include *Leçons sur les ensembles analytiques et leurs applications* (Paris, 1930); and *Integral i trigonometrichesky ryad* ("Integrals and Trigonometric Series"), new ed. (Moscow-Leningrad, 1951), with biography of Luzin by V. V. Golubev and N. K. Bari, pp. 11–31; an analysis of his work by Bari and L. A. Lusternik, pp. 32–45; detailed commentary by Bari and D. E. Menshov, pp. 389–537; and a bibliography, pp. 538–547.

II. SECONDARY LITERATURE. See N. K. Bari and L. A. Lusternik, "Raboti N. N. Luzina po metricheskoy teorii funktsy" ("The Works of N. N. Luzin in the Metric Theory of Functions"), in *Uspekhi matematicheskikh nauk*, **6**, no. 6 (1951), 28–46; V. S. Fedorov, "Trudi N. N. Luzina po teorii funktsy kompleksnogo peremennogo" ("The Works of N. N. Luzin in the Theory of Functions of a Complex Variable"), *ibid.*, **7**, no. 2 (1952), 7–16; V. K. Goltsman and P. I. Kuznetsov, "Raboti N. N. Luzina po differentsialnim uravneniam i po vychislitelnim metodam" ("The Works of N. N. Luzin in Differential Equations and in Computational Methods"), *ibid.*, 17–30; L. V. Keldysh and P. S. Novikov, "Raboti N. N. Luzina v oblasti deskriptivnoy teorii mnozhestv" ("The Works of N. N. Luzin in the Area of the Descriptive Theory of Sets"), *ibid.*, **8**, no. 2 (1953), 93–104; and A. P. Youschkevitch, *Istoria matematiki v Rossii* ("The History of Mathematics in Russia"; Moscow, 1968), 565–577.

A. B. PAPLAUSCAS

LYAPUNOV, ALEKSANDR MIKHAILOVICH (b. Yaroslavl, Russia, 6 June 1857; d. Odessa, U.S.S.R., 3 November 1918)

Lyapunov was a son of the astronomer Mikhail Vasilievich Lyapunov, who worked at Kazan University from 1840 until 1855 and was director of the Demidovski Lyceum in Yaroslavl from 1856 until 1863; his mother was the former Sofia Aleksandrovna Shilipova. Lyapunov's brother Sergei was a composer; another brother, Boris, was a specialist in Slavic philology and a member of the Soviet Academy of Sciences.

Lyapunov received his elementary education at home and later with an uncle, R. M. Sechenov, brother of the physiologist I. M. Sechenov. With R.

M. Sechenov's daughter Natalia Rafailovna (whom he married in 1886), he prepared for the Gymnasium. In 1870 Lyapunov's mother moved to Nizhny Novgorod (now Gorky) with her children. After graduating from the Gymnasium in Nizhny Novgorod in 1876, Lyapunov enrolled in the Physics and Mathematics Faculty of St. Petersburg University, where P. L. Chebyshev greatly influenced him.

Upon graduating from the university in 1880, Lyapunov remained, upon the recommendation of D. K. Bobylev, in the department of mechanics of St. Petersburg University in order to prepare for a professorial career. In 1881 he published his first two scientific papers, which dealt with hydrostatics: "O ravnovesii tyazhelykh tel v tyazhelykh zhidkostyakh, soderzhashchikhsya v sosude opredelennoy formy" ("On the Equilibrium of Heavy Bodies in Heavy Liquids Contained in a Vessel of a Certain Shape") and "O potentsiale gidrostaticheskikh davleny" ("On the Potential of Hydrostatic Pressures").

In 1882 Chebyshev posed the following question: "It is known that at a certain angular velocity ellipsoidal forms cease to be the forms of equilibrium of a rotating liquid. In this case, do they not shift into some new forms of equilibrium which differ little from ellipsoids for small increases in the angular velocity?" Lyapunov did not solve the question at the time, but the problem led him to another that became the subject of his master's dissertation, *Ob ustoychivosti ellipsoidalnykh form ravnovesia vrashchayushcheysya zhidkosti* ("On the Stability of Ellipsoidal Forms of Equilibrium of a Rotating Liquid"; 1884), which he defended at St. Petersburg University in 1885.

In the autumn of that year Lyapunov began to teach mechanics at Kharkov University as a *Privatdozent*. For some time he was completely occupied by the preparation of lectures and by teaching, but in 1888 his papers on the stability of the motion of mechanical systems having a finite number of degrees of freedom began to be published. In 1892 he published the classic *Obshchaya zadacha ob ustoychivosti dvizhenia* ("The General Problem of the Stability of Motion"), and in the same year he defended it as his doctoral dissertation at Moscow University; N. E. Zhukovsky was one of the examiners. Lyapunov studied this field until 1902.

In 1893 Lyapunov became a professor at Kharkov. In addition to mechanics he taught mathematics courses. He was also active in the Kharkov Mathematical Society. From 1891 until 1898 he was its vice-president, and from 1899 until 1902 its president and the editor of its *Soobshchenia* ("Reports").

At Kharkov, Lyapunov conducted investigations

in mathematical physics (1886–1902) and the theory of probability (1900–1901) and obtained outstanding results in both. At the beginning of 1901 he was elected an associate member of the St. Petersburg Academy of Sciences, and at the end of that year he became an academician in applied mathematics, a chair which had remained vacant for seven years, since the death of Chebyshev.

In St. Petersburg, Lyapunov devoted himself completely to scientific work. He returned to the problem that Chebyshev had placed before him and, in an extensive series of papers which continued until his death, developed the theory of figures of equilibrium of rotating heavy liquids and of the stability of these figures.

In 1908 Lyapunov attended the Fourth International Congress of Mathematicians in Rome. He was involved in the publication of the complete collected works of Euler *(L. Euleri Opera omnia)* and was an editor of volumes XVIII and XIX of the first (mathematical) series, which appeared in 1920 and 1932. Lyapunov's scientific work received wide recognition. He was elected an honorary member of the universities of St. Petersburg, Kharkov, and Kazan, a foreign member of the Accademia dei Lincei (1909) and of the Paris Academy of Sciences (1916), and a member of many other scientific societies.

In the summer of 1917 Lyapunov went to Odessa with his wife, who suffered from a serious form of tuberculosis. He began to lecture at the university; but in the spring of the following year his wife's condition rapidly deteriorated and she died on 31 October 1918. On that day Lyapunov shot himself and died three days later, without regaining consciousness. In accordance with a wish stated in a note that he had left, he was buried with his wife.

Lyapunov and A. A. Markov, who had been schoolmates at St. Petersburg University and, later, colleagues at the Academy of Sciences, were Chebyshev's most prominent students and representatives of the St. Petersburg mathematics school. Both were outstanding mathematicians and both exerted a powerful influence on the subsequent development of science. Lyapunov concentrated on three fields: the stability of equilibrium and motion of a mechanical system having a finite number of degrees of freedom; the stability of figures of equilibrium of a uniformly rotating liquid; the stability of figures of equilibrium of a rotating liquid.

Lyapunov's papers on the stability of systems having a finite number of degrees of freedom, among which his doctoral dissertation occupies a central position, belong equally to mathematics and to mechanics. They contain thorough analyses of a great many problems in the theory of ordinary differential equations.

The mathematical formulation of a problem closely related historically to investigations in celestial mechanics of the eighteenth and nineteenth centuries (the problem of the stability of the solar system) is the following: Given a system of n ordinary, first-order differential equations for n functions $x_k(t)$ of the independent variable t (time). It is assumed that the equations are solved with respect to the derivative dx_k/dt on the left side and that the right sides are power series with respect to $x_1, x_2, \cdots, x_n$ without free members, such that the equations have the obvious null solution $x_1 = x_2 = \cdots = x_n = 0$. The coefficients of the series can depend on t. The solution of the system is completely defined by assignment of the values of the unknown functions x_k for some value $t = t_0$. The stability of the null solution, according to Lyapunov, is stability in the infinite time interval $t \geq t_0$, with respect to the initial data. In other words, stability consists in the fact that, for $t \geq t_0$, the solution of the system $x_k(t)$ will be sufficiently small in absolute value for sufficiently small absolute values of the initial data $x_k(t_0)$. The mechanical systems described above, often called dynamic systems, play a fundamental role in dynamics.

When the corresponding system of differential equations is integrated and its solution is found in simple form, the investigation of stability presents no difficulty. As a rule, however, this integration is impracticable. Therefore, mathematicians generally use the approximation method, which consists in replacing the right sides of the equations by the system of linear members of their expansions into power series. In this manner the task devolves into a study of the stability of a linear system of differential equations; this substantially simplifies the problem, especially when the coefficients of the linear system are constants. It remained unclear, however, whether the replacement of the given system by a linear one was valid and, if valid, under what conditions. Use of a second- or somewhat higher-order approximation (that is, the retention of second- or somewhat higher-order members on the right side) enables one to improve the accuracy of knowledge about functions $x_k(t)$ in a finite time interval but gives no new basis for any conclusions about stability in the infinite interval $t \geq t_0$. As Lyapunov noted, the only attempt at a rigorous solution of the question had been made by Poincaré a short time earlier in the special cases of second-order and, in part, third-order systems.

With the aid of new methods that he had created, Lyapunov himself solved, for extremely general assumptions, the question of when the first approximation solves the problem of stability. He thoroughly examined the cases, especially important in practice, when the coefficients of the series on the right side of the equations are constants (the "established motion") or are periodic functions of time t, having one and the same period. For example, if, given constant coefficients, the real parts of all the roots of the system's characteristic equation (an nth degree, "secular" algebraic equation) are negative, the solution of the initial system is stable; if, however, there is among the roots one having a positive real part, then the solution is unstable. The first approximation, however, does not permit one to solve the problem of stability if the characteristic equation, while not having roots with positive real numbers, has roots the real parts of which are equal to zero. Here, the cases when the characteristic equation has one root equal to zero, or when it has two purely imaginary conjugate roots, are of special interest; these cases were exhaustively investigated by Lyapunov. In the case of periodic coefficients Lyapunov examined the possibilities arising in two especially interesting instances: when one of the roots of the characteristic equation is equal to unity and when two imaginary conjugate roots have a modulus equal to unity.

Among many other results is the proof of the theorem of the instability of motion if the force function of the forces acting on the system is not a maximum. Several of Lyapunov's articles dealing with a detailed analysis of the solution of homogeneous linear second-order equations having periodic coefficients (1896–1902) have the same orientation.

The ideas of this cycle of papers, especially Lyapunov's doctoral dissertation, are related to Poincaré's investigation. Specific results obtained by both these scholars coincide, but they do not deal with the basic content or the basic methods of their works. In particular, Poincaré made wide use of geometrical and topological concepts, while Lyapunov used purely analytical methods. Both Poincaré's papers and Lyapunov's works are fundamental to the qualitative theory of ordinary differential equations. At first Lyapunov's theory of the stability of mechanical systems did not receive the wide response given to Poincaré's more general ideas. But, from the early 1930's the number of papers directly related to Lyapunov's investigations increased very rapidly, especially with the growth of the significance of problems concerning the stability of motion in modern physics and engineering, primarily because of the study of fluctuations in various mechanical and physical systems. Problems of stability arise in the determination of the work regimen of various machines, in the construction of airplanes, electrical engineering, and ballistics.

Lyapunov studied figures of equilibrium of a uniformly rotating liquid over a period of thirty-six years. In the lecture "O forme nebesnykh tel" ("On the Shape of Celestial Bodies"; 1918) he said:

> According to a well-known hypothesis, each such body was initially in a liquid state; it took its present form before solidification, having previously received an unchanging form as the result of internal friction. Assuming this, the shape of a celestial body must be one of those which can be assumed by a rotating liquid mass, the particles of which mutually attract one another according to Newton's law, or, at least, must differ little from such a figure of equilibrium of a rotating liquid [*Izbrannye trudy*, p. 303].

Lyapunov mentioned the mathematical difficulty of studying equilibrium figures, a study which entails the solution of nonlinear integral equations.

It was Newton, his eighteenth-century successors Maclaurin and d'Alembert, and others who established that ellipsoids of rotation could be figures of equilibrium of homogeneous rotating liquids. Later, Jacobi demonstrated that certain triaxial ellipsoids could also be such figures. Other scholars also studied this problem. When, in 1882, Chebyshev placed before Lyapunov the question concerning the possibility of the existence of other equilibrium figures that are close to ellipsoidal, Lyapunov could solve the problem only in the first approximation. Believing it impossible to judge the existence of new figures according to the first approximation, he put off a definitive solution to the question. In his master's thesis of 1884 he guardedly mentioned that certain algebraic surfaces which were close to earlier-known ellipsoids of equilibrium, satisfy the conditions of equilibrium in the first approximation. On the other hand, in this thesis he examined the problem of the stability of the Maclaurin and Jacobi ellipsoids, injecting clarity and rigor into the statement of the problem, defining for the first time the concept of stability for a continuous medium.

In a series of papers written between 1903 and 1918, Lyapunov moved deeply into the investigation of Chebyshev's problem and related questions. In *Recherches dans la théorie de la figure des corps célestes* and *Sur l'équation de Clairaut*... he proved the existence of nearly spherical figures of equilibrium for a sufficiently slowly rotating nonhomogeneous liquid, and investigated the solutions to the integral-differential equations arising from this, which contain the unknown function both under the integral sign and under the sign of the derivatives; the first of these equations is "Clairaut's equation." In *Sur un pro-*

blème de Tchébycheff and *Sur les figures d'équilibre peu différentes des ellipsoids* . . . it was established that among ellipsoids of equilibrium there are "ellipsoids of bifurcation" and that, in addition to ellipsoidal figures close to these, there also exist close, nonellipsoidal figures of equilibrium. A number of methods are entailed in the consistent determination of the equations of these figures. Finally, in the posthumously published *Sur certaines séries de figures d'équilibre d'un liquide hétérogène en rotation,* it is proved that each Maclaurin and Jacobi ellipsoid differing from the ellipsoids of bifurcation engenders new figures of equilibrium that are close to the Maclaurin and Jacobi ellipsoids in form; their density is not considered constant but, rather, as weakly varying.

In *Problème de minimum dans une question de stabilité des figures d'équilibre d'une masse fluide en rotation,* Lyapunov further developed and made more precise the theory of stability stated in his master's thesis and investigated the stability of the new, nearly ellipsoidal, figures of equilibrium that he had previously found.

In solving all these problems and the corresponding nonlinear integral and integral-differential equations, Lyapunov had to overcome great mathematical difficulties. To this end he devised delicate methods of approximation, the convergence of which he proved with the rigor of contemporary mathematics; generalized the concept of the integral (in the direction of the Stieltjes-Riemann integral); and proved a number of new theorems on spherical functions.

Lyapunov's works again approach those of Poincaré. At a certain angular velocity, figures of equilibrium that Poincaré called "pear-shaped" branch off from Jacobi ellipsoids. The astronomer G. H. Darwin encountered the problem of the stability of pear-shaped forms in his hypothesis concerning the origin of double stars arising from the division of a rotating liquid mass into two bodies. Poincaré, who examined the question within the limits of the second approximation, stated the hypothesis that these forms were stable; and Darwin, using Poincaré's general theory, seemingly confirmed this opinion, which was indispensable to his cosmogonical hypothesis, by calculations. Lyapunov's calculations, which were based on precise formulas and evaluations, led him to the opposite conclusion—that the pear-shaped figures were unstable. In 1911 Poincaré stated that he was not sure of the correctness of his prior opinion, but that to solve the question would require one to begin the very complex computations again. In 1912 Lyapunov published the necessary calculations in the third part of *Sur certaines séries de figures d'équilibre*

. . ., but no one sought to verify them. In 1917 Sir James Jeans confirmed Lyapunov's results, having discovered the defect in Darwin's computations.

During the period 1886–1902, Lyapunov devoted several works to mathematical physics; *Sur certaines questions qui se rattachent au problème de Dirichlet* (1898) is fundamental among these. Here, for the first time, a number of the basic properties of the potentials of simple and double layers were studied with utter rigor and the necessary and sufficient conditions, under which the function that solves Dirichlet's problem within a given range has normal derivatives over the limiting range of the surface, were indicated. These investigations created the foundation of a number of classic methods for solving boundary-value problems. In addition, Lyapunov's works on mathematical physics brought that area of analysis to the attention of a number of Kharkov mathematicians, especially V. A. Steklov, Lyapunov's student.

Finally, in two works that arose from a course in the theory of probability taught by Lyapunov, he substantially generalized Laplace's limit theorem in application to sums of random independent values. Chebyshev gave the first such generalization of this theorem in 1887, indicating the possibility of its proof, in the form given by him, by the method of moments; and Markov carried out the full proof on this basis in 1898. In "Sur une proposition de la théorie des probabilités" (1900) and "Nouvelle forme du théorème sur la limite de probabilité" (1901), Lyapunov proved the central limit theorem by the method of characteristic functions, which has subsequently assumed a fundamental place in the theory of probability; moreover, he did so under much broader conditions than Markov had used. Some time later, however, Markov proved the central limit theorem under Lyapunov's conditions by using the method of moments. These works by Lyapunov also served as the starting point for many later investigations.

BIBLIOGRAPHY

I. ORIGINAL WORKS. A complete list of Lyapunov's works is in *Aleksandr Mikhailovich Lyapunov. Bibliografia,* compiled by A. M. Lukomskaya, V. I. Smirnov, ed. (Moscow–Leningrad, 1953). Collections of his writings are *A. M. Lyapunov, Izbrannye trudy* ("Selected Works"; Moscow–Leningrad, 1948), with a bibliography compiled by A. M. Lukomskaya; and his *Sobranie sochineny* ("Collected Works"), 5 vols. (Moscow, 1954–1965), which includes Russian translations of all works written in French.

Individual works are *Ob ustoychivosti ellipsoidalnykh form ravnovesia vrashchayushcheysya zhidkosti* ("On the

Stability of Ellipsoidal Forms of Equilibrium of a Rotating Liquid"; St. Petersburg, 1884), his master's thesis, translated into French as "Sur la stabilité des figures ellipsoidales d'équilibre d'un liquide animé d'un mouvement de rotation," in *Annales de la Faculté des sciences de l'Université de Toulouse*, 2nd ser., **6** (1904), 5–116; *Obshchaya zadacha ob ustoychivosti dvizhenia* ("The General Problem of the Stability of Motion"; Kharkov, 1902; 2nd ed., Moscow–Leningrad, 1935; 3rd ed., 1950), his doctoral dissertation, translated into French as "Problème générale de la stabilité du mouvement," in *Annales de la Faculté des sciences de l'Université de Toulouse*, 2nd ser., **9** (1907), 203–474, reprinted as no. 17 in the Annals of Mathematics series (Princeton, 1947); *Recherches dans la théorie de la figure des corps célestes* (St. Petersburg, 1903); *Sur l'équation de Clairaut et les équations plus générales de la théorie de la figure des planètes* (St. Petersburg, 1904); *Sur un problème de Tchebycheff* (St. Petersburg, 1905); *Sur les figures d'équilibre peu différentes des ellipsoids d'une masse liquide homogène douée d'un mouvement de rotation*, 4 vols. (St. Petersburg, 1906–1914); and *Problème de minimum dans une question de stabilité des figures d'équilibre d'une masse fluide en rotation* (St. Petersburg, 1908).

Published posthumously were *Sur certaines séries de figures d'équilibre d'un liquide hétérogène en rotation*, 2 vols. (Leningrad, 1925–1927); and *Raboty po teorii potentsiala* ("Papers on the Theory of Potentials"; Moscow–Leningrad, 1949), with a biographical essay by V. A. Steklov.

II. Secondary Literature. See Y. L. Geronimus, *Ocherki o rabotakh korifeev russkoy mekhaniki* ("Essays on the Works of the Leading Figures of Russian Mechanics"; Moscow, 1952); A. T. Grigorian, *Ocherki istorii mekhaniki v Rossii* ("Essays on the History of Mechanics in Russia"; Moscow, 1961), 139–148, 219–225; V. I. Smirnov, "Ocherk nauchnykh trudov A. M. Lyapunova" ("Essay on the Scientific Works of A. M. Lyapunov"), in V. I. Smirnov, ed., *A. M. Lyapunov, Izbrannye trudy* (see above), 495–538; "Ocherk zhizni A. M. Lyapunova" and "Obzor nauchnogo tvorchestva A. M. Lyapunova" ("Essay on the Life of A. M. Lyapunov" and "A Survey of the Creative Scientific Work of A. M. Lyapunov"), in *Aleksandr Mikhailovich Lyapunov. Bibliografia* (see above), 469–478, 479–532; and "Iz perepiski P. Appelya, Z. Adamara, G. Burkkhardta, V. Volterra, P. Dyugema, K. Zhordana, A. Puankare i N. Rado s akademikom A. M. Lyapunovym" ("From the Correspondence of P. Appell, J. Hadamard, H. Burckhardt, V. Volterra, P. Duhem, C. Jordan, H. Poincaré, and N. Rado With Academician A. M. Lyapunov"), in *Trudy Instituta istorii estestvoznania i tekhniki. Akademia nauk SSSR*, **19** (1957), 690–719; V. A. Steklov, *Aleksandr Mikhailovich Lyapunov. Nekrolog* (Petrograd, 1919), repr. in *Obshchaya zadacha ustoychivosti dvizhenia*, 2nd ed. (see above), 367–388 and in Lyapunov's *Raboty po teorii potentsiala* (see above), 7–32; and A. P. Youschkevitch, *Istoria matematiki v Rossii do 1917 goda* ("The History of Mathematics in Russia Before 1917"; Moscow, 1968), 448–458.

A. T. Grigorian

MACAULAY, FRANCIS SOWERBY (*b.* Witney, England, 11 February 1862; *d.* Cambridge, England, 9 February 1937)

The son of a Methodist minister, Macaulay was educated at Kingswood School, Bath, a school for the sons of the Methodist clergy, and at St. John's College, Cambridge. After graduating with distinction, he taught mathematics for two years at Kingswood and, from 1885 to 1911, at St. Paul's School, London, where he worked with senior pupils who were preparing to enter a university. He was remarkably successful: two of his many pupils who became eminent mathematicians were G. N. Watson and J. E. Littlewood. In *A Mathematician's Miscellany*, Littlewood gives a vivid picture of Macaulay's methods: there was little formal instruction; students were directed to read widely but thoroughly, encouraged to be self-reliant, and inspired to look forward to pursuing research in mathematics.

In recognition of his own researches, which he had steadily carried on despite his heavy teaching responsibilities, in 1928 Macaulay was elected a fellow of the Royal Society, a distinction very seldom attained by a schoolmaster. Apart from some elementary articles in the *Mathematical Gazette* and a school text on geometrical conics, he wrote some fourteen papers on algebraic geometry and a Cambridge tract on modular systems, otherwise polynomial ideals. The earlier papers concerned algebraic plane curves, their multiple points and intersections, and the Noether and Riemann-Roch theorems. This work led to later papers on the theory of algebraic polynomials and of modular systems. Much of this was pioneering work with an important influence on subsequent research in algebraic geometry, and it was directed toward the construction of a firm and precise basis of algebra on which geometrical theorems could be safely erected.

BIBLIOGRAPHY

I. Original Works. Macaulay's books are *Geometrical Conics* (Cambridge, 1895); and *The Algebraic Theory of Modular Systems*, Cambridge Mathematical Tracts, no. 19 (Cambridge, 1916). A list of Macaulay's papers follows the obituary notice by H. F. Baker cited below.

II. Secondary Literature. See H. F. Baker's notice of Macaulay in *Journal of the London Mathematical Society*, **13** (1938), 157–160; and J. E. Littlewood, *A Mathematician's Miscellany* (London, 1953), 66–83—the paragraphs relevant to Macaulay are quoted in Baker's notice.

T. A. A. Broadbent

McCOLL, HUGH (*b.* 1837; *d.* Boulogne-sur-Mer, France, 27 December 1909)

McColl's contributions to mathematical logic and its symbolic expression helped to clarify the subject in the particular period which may be said to begin with Boole's *An Investigation of the Laws of Thought...* (1854) and reach a climax in the *Principia Mathematica* (1950) of Whitehead and Russell.

The logical calculus of propositions has a certain analogy to that of classes, with implication in the former corresponding to inclusion in the latter. Thus, for propositions p, q, r, we have that if p implies q and q implies r, then p implies r, while for classes A, B, C, the dual statement is that if A is contained in B and B is contained in C, then A is contained in C. But the duality is not complete. If p implies q or r, then p implies q or p implies r, but if A is contained in B or C, with "or" in its usual inclusive sense, then we cannot say that either A is contained in B or A is contained in C. The ambiguity is to be seen in Boole's *Laws of Thought*, where he is aware of the duality but is not always quite clear about which interpretation of his symbolic calculus he is using. Since the duality is not perfect, the question arises as to which calculus is the more basic. In his papers, chiefly in the period 1880–1900, discussing many points of the symbolic logic then in process of formation, McColl takes the view, which has much to commend it, that implication and propositions have a more fundamental character than inclusion and classes. His arguments are forceful; but his logical position would have been clearer had he distinguished between a propositional function containing an indeterminate such as "x is a prime number," and a proposition, which is the form assumed by a propositional function when the indeterminate receives a specific value. The proposition is then a statement which is either true or false, whereas no truth-value can be assigned to a propositional function. The distinction was hinted at by Peano, but seems to have been first clearly drawn by Russell.

BIBLIOGRAPHY

McColl's main writings on symbolic logic are "On the Calculus of Equivalent Statements," in *Proceedings of the London Mathematical Society*, 1st ser. **9, 10, 11, 13**; "Symbolic Reasoning," in *Mind* (1880, 1897, 1900); and "La logique symbolique et ses applications," in *Bibliothèque du Congrès International de Philosophie*, III (Paris, 1901).

T. A. A. BROADBENT

MACLAURIN, COLIN (*b.* Kilmodan, Scotland, February 1698; *d.* Edinburgh, Scotland, 14 January 1746)

Maclaurin was the youngest of the three sons of John Maclaurin, minister of the parish of Kilmodan and a man of profound learning. John, the eldest son, followed in his father's footsteps and became a noted divine. The father died when Maclaurin was only six weeks old and after the death of his mother nine years later, Maclaurin was cared for by an uncle, Daniel Maclaurin, a minister of Kilfinnan.

In 1709 Maclaurin entered the University of Glasgow where he read divinity for a year. At Glasgow he became acquainted with Robert Simson, professor of mathematics. Simson, who tried to revive the geometry of the ancients, particularly the *Elements* of Euclid, stimulated Maclaurin's interest in this aspect of mathematics.

In 1715 Maclaurin defended the thesis "On the Power of Gravity," for which he was awarded a master of arts degree. It led to his appointment, in 1717, as professor of mathematics at Marischal College, Aberdeen, although he was still only in his teens. This appointment marked the beginning of a brilliant mathematical career which was to continue without interruption until the end of his life.

In 1719 Maclaurin visited London, where he was well received in the scientific circles of the capital and where he met Newton. On a second visit he met and formed a lasting friendship with Martin Folkes, who became president of the Royal Society in 1741, Maclaurin was meanwhile actively working on his *Geometrica organica*, which was published in 1720 with Newton's imprimatur.

Geometrica organica, sive descriptio linearum curvarum universalis dealt with the general properties of conics and of the higher plane curves. It contained proofs of many important theorems which were to be found, without proof, in Newton's work, as well as a considerable number of others which Maclaurin had discovered while at the university. Following traditional geometrical methods, Maclaurin showed that the higher plane curves, the cubic and the quartic, could be described by the rotation of two angles about their vertices. Newton had shown that the conic sections might all be described by the rotation of two angles of fixed size about their vertices S and C as centers of rotation. If the point of intersection of two of the arms lie on a fixed straight line, the intersection of the other two arms will describe a conic section which will pass through S and C.

In 1722 Maclaurin left Scotland to serve as companion and tutor to the son of Lord Polwarth, plenipotentiary of Great Britain at Cambrai. They visited

Paris, then went on to Lorraine, where Maclaurin, during a period of intense mathematical activity, wrote *On the Percussion of Bodies.* It won him the prize offered by the French Academy of Sciences in 1724.

In the same year, the sudden death of Maclaurin's pupil caused him to return to Aberdeen. As a result of three years' absence, however, his chair had been declared vacant. Maclaurin then moved to Edinburgh, where he acted as deputy for the elderly James Gregory. There is no doubt that Maclaurin owed his appointment to a strong recommendation from Newton, who wrote to him:

> I am very glad to hear that you have a prospect of being joined to Mr. James Gregory in the Professorship of the Mathematics at Edinburgh, not only because you are my friend, but principally because of your abilities, you being acquainted as well with the new improvements of mathematics as with the former state of these sciences. I heartily wish you good success and shall be very glad of hearing of your being elected.

In a further letter to the lord provost of Edinburgh, Newton wrote:

> I am glad to understand that Mr. Maclaurin is in good repute amongst you, for I think he deserves it very well: And to satisfy you that I do not flatter him, and also to encourage him to accept the place of assisting Mr. Gregory, in order to succeed him, I am ready (if you will please give me leave) to contribute twenty pounds per annum towards a provision for him till Mr. Gregory's place becomes void, if I live so long.

Maclaurin was appointed to the Edinburgh chair when it fell vacant. He assumed its duties in 1725, lecturing on a wide range of topics that included twelve books of Euclid, spherical trigonometry, the conics, the elements of fortification, astronomy, and perspective, as well as a careful exposition of Newton's *Principia.*

Maclaurin was elected a fellow of the Royal Society in 1719. He was also influential in persuading the members of the Edinburgh Society for Improving Medical Knowledge to widen its scope. The society's name was thus changed to the Philosophical Society and Maclaurin became one of its secretaries. (In 1783 the organization was granted incorporation by George III as the Royal Society of Edinburgh.) In 1733 Maclaurin married Anne, daughter of Walter Stewart, solicitor general for Scotland. Of their seven children, two sons and three daughters survived him.

Maclaurin's *Treatise of Fluxions* (1742) has been described as the earliest logical and systematic publication of the Newtonian methods. It stood as a model of rigor until the appearance of Cauchy's *Cours d'analyse* in 1821. Maclaurin, a zealous disciple

of Newton, hoped to silence criticism of the latter's doctrine of "prime and ultimate ratios," which proved something of a stumbling block to even Newton's staunchest supporters. In the *Treatise* Maclaurin tried to provide a geometrical framework for the doctrine of fluxions; in this way he hoped to refute his critics, the most vociferous of whom was George Berkeley, Bishop of Cloyne. In 1734 Berkeley had published *The Analyst. A Letter Addressed to an Infidel Mathematician,* in which he derided Newton's conception of "prime and ultimate ratios." (The "infidel mathematician" himself was Halley, who had piloted the first edition of the *Principia* through the press.) Berkeley maintained that it was not possible to imagine a finite ratio between two evanescent quantities. "What are these fluxions?" he asked. "The velocities of evanescent increments? They are neither finite quantities, nor quantities infinitely small, nor yet nothing. May we not call them the ghosts of departed quantities?"

In the preface to the *Treatise,* Maclaurin gave his reasons for replying to Berkeley:

> A Letter published in the year 1734 under the Title of *The Analyst,* first gave occasion to the ensuing Treatise, and several Reasons concurred to induce me to write on the subject at so great length. The Author of that piece had represented the Method of Fluxions as founded on false Reasoning, and full of Mysteries. His objections seemed to have been occasioned by the concise manner in which the Elements of this method have been usually described, and their having been so much misunderstood by a Person of his abilities appeared to me to be a sufficient Proof that a fuller account of the grounds of this was required.

He took up the question of fluxions almost immediately and defended Newton's methods:

> In explaining the notion of Fluxions I have followed Sir Isaac Newton in the First Book imagining there can be no difficulty in conceiving Velocity wherever there is motion, nor do I think I have departed from his sense in the Second Book, and in both I have endeavoured to avoid several expressions which though convenient, might be liable to exceptions and perhaps occasion disputes. . . .
> There were some who disliked the making much use of infinites and infinitesimals in geometry. Of this number was Sir Isaac Newton (whose caution was almost as distinguishing a part of his character as his invention) especially after he saw that this liberty was growing to so great a height. In demonstrating the grounds of the method of fluxions he avoided them, establishing it in a way more agreeable to the strictness of geometry.

Maclaurin followed Newton in abandoning the

view that variable quantities were made up of infinitesimal elements and in approaching the problem from kinematical considerations. Moreover, he consistently followed the Newtonian notation, although the Leibnizian notation was by this time well established on the Continent. Thus he wrote (in the *Treatise*, p. 738), "The fluxion of xy is $x\dot{y} + \dot{x}y$."

The *Treatise* is otherwise noteworthy for the solution of a great number of problems in geometry, statics, and the theory of attractions. It contains an elaborate discussion on infinite series, including Maclaurin's test for convergence, as well as a remarkable investigation of curves of quickest descent and various isoperimetrical problems. It describes his series for the expansion of a function of x, namely,

$$f(x) = f(0) + xf'(0) + \frac{x^2}{2!} f''(0) + \frac{x^3}{3!} f'''(0) + \cdots .$$

Maclaurin also elaborated many of the principles enunciated by Newton in the *Principia* in this work, including problems in applied geometry and physics, founded on the geometry of Euclid.

Maclaurin's discussion of the attraction of an ellipsoid on an internal point is particularly significant. His interest in this subject began in 1740 when he submitted an essay "On the Tides" (*De causa physica fluxus et refluxus maris*) for a prize offered by the Académie des Sciences. Maclaurin shared the award with Daniel Bernoulli and Euler; all three men based their work upon proposition 24 of the *Principia*, on the flux and reflux of the sea. Maclaurin's original essay was hastily assembled, but he developed his ideas much further in the *Treatise* (II, article 686). He showed that a homogeneous fluid mass revolving uniformly about an axis under the action of gravity must assume the form of an ellipsoid of revolution. Clairaut was so impressed with Maclaurin's exposition that in his *Théorie de la figure de la terre* (1743), he abandoned analytical techniques and attacked the problem of the shape of the earth by purely geometrical methods.

In the *Treatise* Maclaurin presented for the first time the correct theory for distinguishing between maximum and minimum values of a function; he further indicated the importance of this distinction in the theory of multiple points of curves. In Chapter IX of Volume I, article 238, "Of the Greatest and Least Ordinates, of the points of contrary flexion and reflexion of various kinds, and of other affections of curves that are defined by a common or by a fluxional equation," he wrote that "There are hardly any speculations in Geometry more useful or more entertaining than those which relate to the *Maximum* and *Minimum*."

Maclaurin's persistent defense of the Newtonian methods was not without harmful consequences for the progress of mathematics in Great Britain. National pride induced Englishmen to follow the geometrical methods which Newton had employed in the *Principia*, and to neglect the analytical methods which were being pursued with such conspicuous success on the Continent. As a result, English mathematicians came to think that the calculus was not really necessary. This unfortunate neglect persisted for a century or more. It was said that during the eighteenth century Maclaurin and Matthew Stewart, who succeeded him in the mathematical chair at Edinburgh, were the only prominent mathematicians in Great Britain. Writing toward the end of the century, J. Lalande, in his *Life of Condorcet*, maintained that in 1764 there was not a single first-rate analyst in the whole of England.

Maclaurin's advice was sought nevertheless on many topics, not all of them mathematical. He was a skilled experimentalist, and he devised a variety of mechanical appliances. He made valuable astronomical observations and did actuarial computations for the use of insurance societies. He also took an active part in improving maps of the Orkney and Shetland Islands, with a view to discovering a northeast polar passage from Greenland to the southern seas, and prepared an extensive memorial upon this subject for the government. (Since the government was at that time primarily interested in finding a northwest passage, the matter was dropped.)

When a Highland army marched upon Edinburgh in the uprising of 1745, Maclaurin wholeheartedly organized the defenses of the city. With tireless energy, he planned and supervised the hastily erected fortifications, and, indeed, drove himself to a state of exhaustion from which he never recovered. The city fell to the Jacobites and Maclaurin was forced to flee to England. He reached York and sought refuge with Thomas Herring, the archbishop. He returned to Edinburgh once it became clear that the Jacobites were not going to occupy the city, but the rigors he had endured had very severely undermined his health. He died soon after, at the age of forty-eight. Only a few hours before his death he dictated the concluding passage of his work on Newton's philosophy, in which he affirmed his unwavering belief in a future life.

At the meeting of the university following Maclaurin's death, his friend, Alexander Munro, professor of anatomy at the University of Glasgow, paid tribute to him: "He was more nobly distinguished from the bulk of mankind by the qualities of the heart: his sincere love of God and men, his universal benevolence and unaffected piety together with a warmth and constancy in his friendship that was in a manner peculiar to himself."

BIBLIOGRAPHY

I. Original Works. Maclaurin's works are *Geometrica organica, sive descriptio linearum curvarum universalis* (London, 1720); *The Treatise of Fluxions*, 2 vols. (Edinburgh, 1742); and *A Treatise of Algebra* (1748), a somewhat elementary posthumous work on the application of algebra to geometry, to which is joined a Latin tract, "De linearum geometricarum proprietatibus generalibus" (1756), printed from a manuscript written and corrected in Maclaurin's own hand. *An Account of Sir Isaac Newton's Philosophical Discoveries* (London, 1748) has a prefatory memoir on Maclaurin, "An Account of the Life and Writings of the Author," by Patrick Murdoch.

Maclaurin's papers published in the *Philosophical Transactions of the Royal Society* are: "Of the Construction and Measure of Curves," no. 356 (1718); "A New Universal Method of Describing All Curves of Every Order by the Assistance of Angles and Right Lines," no. 359 (1719); "A Letter . . . to Martin Folkes Esq. Concerning Equations with Impossible Roots (May 1726)," no. 394; "A Second Letter . . . to Martin Folkes Concerning the Roots of Equations, With the Demonstration of Other Rules in Algebra," no. 408 (1729); "On the Description of Curve Lines With an Account of Further Improvements, and a Paper Dated at Nancy, 27 Nov. 1722," no. 439; and "An Abstract of What Has Been Printed Since the Year 1721, as a Supplement to a Treatise Concerning a Description of Curve Lines, Published in 1719, and to Which the Author Proposes to Add to That Supplement," 39.

Further papers published in the *Philosophical Transactions* are "An Account of the Treatise of Fluxions," no. 467 and continued in no. 469; "A Rule for Finding the Meridional Parts to a Spheroid With the Same Exactness as a Sphere," no. 461 (1711); "A Letter From Mr. Colin Maclaurin . . . to Mr. John Machin Concerning the Description of Curve Lines. Communicated to the Royal Society December 21. 1732"; "An Observation of the Eclipse of the Sun, on February 18, 1737 Made at Edinburgh, in a Letter to Martin Folkes," 40, 177; "Of the Basis of Cells Wherein Bees Deposit Their Honey," no. 471 (1743).

Maclaurin also left a large number of manuscripts and unfinished essays on a variety of subjects, mathematical and nonmathematical.

II. Secondary Literature. Further information on Maclaurin's life and work may be found in W. W. R. Ball, *A Short Account of the History of Mathematics* (1912), 359–363; Florian Cajori, *History of Mathematics* (1919); Moritz Cantor, *Vorlesungen über Geschichte der Mathematik* (1884–1908); J. P. Montucla, *Histoire des Mathématiques*, 4 vols. (1799–1802); H. W. Turnbull, "Colin Maclaurin," in *American Mathematical Monthly*, 54, no. 6 (1947).

J. F. Scott

MacMAHON, PERCY ALEXANDER (*b.* Malta, 26 September 1854; *d.* Bognor Regis, England, 25 December 1929)

MacMahon was the son of Brigadier General P. W. MacMahon. He entered the army in 1871, rising to the rank of major in 1889. He served as instructor in mathematics at the Royal Military Academy from 1882 to 1888, as assistant inspector at Woolwich arsenal to 1891, and as professor of physics at the Artillery college until his retirement in 1898. Afterward, he was deputy warden of standards at the Board of Trade from 1906 to 1920. A fellow of the Royal Society in 1890, he was president of the London Mathematical Society in 1894–1896, and president of the Royal Astronomical Society in 1917.

MacMahon was a master of classical algebra, who had remarkable insight into algebraic form and structure, together with a power of rapid and precise calculation. His early work dealt with invariants, following the studies of Cayley and Sylvester. He noticed that the partial differential equation for semi-invariants is fundamentally the same as that for general symmetric functions. MacMahon made use of the concept of generating functions, and of U. Hammond's symbolic calculus of differential operators in connection with symmetric functions. His power of calculation helped him in the work of tabulation and enumeration.

The study of symmetric functions led to MacMahon's interest in partitions and to the enumeration of Euler's Latin squares. His presidential address to the London Mathematical Society gave a survey of combinatorial analysis, and his two-volume treatise of 1915–1916 is a classic in this field. It identified and clarified the master theorems, and indicated a wealth of applications. An introductory version was published in 1920.

MacMahon's interest in repeating patterns and space-filling solids began in his childhood with observations of piles of shot found in his military environment. He revived this interest in latter years, writing a book on mathematical pastimes.

BIBLIOGRAPHY

I. Original Works. The presidential address on combinatorial analysis is printed in the *Proceedings of the London Mathematical Society*, 1st ser., 28 (1897). Some ninety research papers are listed in the obituary notice by H. F. Baker, cited below. Works by MacMahon were *Combinatorial Analysis*, I–II (Cambridge, 1915–1916); *An Introduction to Combinatorial Analysis* (Cambridge, 1920); and *New Mathematical Pastimes* (Cambridge, 1921).

II. Secondary Literature. The obituary notice by H. F. Baker in the *Journal of the London Mathematical*

Society, **5** (1930), 305–318, gives a brief sketch of MacMahon's life and a substantial account and analysis of his mathematical work.

T. A. A. BROADBENT

MACMILLAN, WILLIAM DUNCAN (*b.* La Crosse, Wisconsin, 24 July 1871; *d.* St. Paul, Minnesota, 14 November 1948)

William Macmillan was the son of Duncan D. Macmillan and Mary Jean MacCrea. He attended Lake Forest College, the University of Virginia, and Fort Worth University, from which he received the B.A. in 1898. He then went to the University of Chicago, where he spent most of his working life. He took the M.A. there in 1906 and the Ph.D. in 1908. A pupil of F. R. Moulton, he became a research assistant, first in geology (1907–1908) and then in mathematics and astronomy (1908–1909). He held a succession of posts in astronomy at the university, becoming professor emeritus in 1936.

Macmillan's interests centered around cosmogony and related topics in applied mathematics. Probably his most widely known works were his textbooks of theoretical mechanics. He made a number of original contributions to potential theory, the theory of differential equations with periodic coefficients, and the theory of automorphic functions. He took an active part in the then controversial discussions of the theory of relativity, contributing to *A Debate on the Theory of Relativity* (New York, 1927) with R. D. Carmichael, H. T. Davis, and others.

One of Macmillan's most influential pieces of work was an attempt to remove the supposed paradox of P. L. de Cheseaux (1744) and H. W. M. Olbers (1823), whereby, with the hypothesis of an infinite and uniform distribution of stars throughout space, the night sky would shine with a brightness corresponding to their average surface brightness. In 1918 and 1925 Macmillan proposed a form of continual material creation (*Astrophysical Journal*, **48** (1918), 35, and *Science*, **62** (1925), 63–72, 96–99, 121–127). His main concern was with the formation of the planets and stars. Among his so-called postulates he included two according to which the universe maintains a steady state, and another according to which the energy of a large region of the universe, supposedly unbounded, is conserved. He acknowledged that matter is converted to energy in stellar interiors, and explained away the De Cheseaux-Olbers paradox as a disappearance or dissipation of the radiation traversing empty space. (This radiation was to reappear in the form of hydrogen atoms.) Subsequently, R. A.

Millikan, one of Macmillan's colleagues at Chicago, used his theory to account for the origin of cosmic rays, but by 1935 A. H. Compton proved that it could not account for the high energies of much cosmic radiation. The theory was then abandoned. It should be noted that, unlike more recent steady-state theories, Macmillan's identified a source from which the mass or energy of the created particle was drawn. He did not suggest creation *ex nihilo*.

BIBLIOGRAPHY

Macmillan collaborated with F. R. Moulton, C. S. Slichter, *et al.*, in *Contributions to Cosmogony and the Fundamental Problems of Geology. The Tidal and Other Problems* (Washington, D.C., 1909), and with Moulton, F. R. Longley, *et al.*, in *Periodic Orbits*, Carnegie Institution of Washington publ. no. 161 (Washington, D.C., 1920). His best-known work was *Theoretical Mechanics*, 3 vols. (New York, 1927–1936). On the background to Macmillan's writings on cosmogony, see J. D. North, *The Measure of the Universe* (Oxford, 1965), esp. 18, 198–199, and 260–261.

J. D. NORTH

MAGINI, GIOVANNI ANTONIO (*b.* Padua, Italy, 13 June 1555; *d.* Bologna, Italy, 11 February 1617)

Magini graduated with a degree in philosophy from the University of Bologna in 1579; in 1588 he was appointed to one of the two chairs of mathematics there, having been preferred for that post to his younger contemporary Galileo. (The other chair was held by Pietro Cataldi, a mathematician of great prestige.) Magini alternated lectures on Euclid with classes in astronomy, which, stimulated by his passion for astrology, was actually his chief scholarly interest. Astrology itself had been taught at Bologna since 1125. Its study produced results occasionally useful to astronomers, as, for example, the more accurate calculation of celestial movements. Magini wrote several astrological works that were admired in their time, and also served the Gonzaga prince of Mantua as judicial astrologer (with varying results). For this reason he spent long periods of time in that city.

Like his astrological works, Magini's writings on astronomy remain of only historical interest, due in large part to his adherence to Ptolemaic principles. He rejected the Copernican theory, which was then being vindicated by Galileo; the conservatism of his thought indeed made him Galileo's enemy, and Magini more or less openly lent his support to libels against the younger man. Within the boundaries of his Ptolemaicism, Magini drew up complex theories, among them the multiplication of Ptolemaic spheres and orbits, and also performed some useful calculations. He was, in fact, much more skilled in calculation than in theory, and his ephemerides remained valid for a long time.

Magini's mathematical work was essentially practical. In 1592 he published his *Tabula tetragonica*, a table of the squares of natural numbers which was designed to permit the determination of the products of two factors as the difference between two squares. In 1609 he brought out extremely accurate trigonometric tables, in which he introduced new terms for what are now called cosines, cotangents, and cosecants. Magini's nomenclature enjoyed some currency, and was later adopted by Cavalieri, who succeeded him at Bologna. Magini made further contributions to practical geometry, including works on the geometry of the sphere and the applications of trigonometry, for which he invented certain calculating devices that may be reconstructed from his texts. Of his lectures on Euclid, some notes relating to the third book are extant in the Ambrosian Library in Milan.

Although Magini's fame in his own century rested upon these and other accomplishments (including his studies on mirrors and especially the concave spherical mirrors that he fabricated, one of which he presented to the emperor Rudolf II), he is today remembered chiefly as a geographer and cartographer. One of his earliest works was a commentary on Ptolemaic geography, in which he took up the problem of the topographical representation of the earth. He then embarked upon the ambitious project that, with interruptions, occupied him the rest of his life—an atlas of Italy, providing maps of each region (showing the borders of each state) with exact nomenclature and historical notes. The most complete edition of this atlas was published by his son, Fabio, in 1620, three years after Magini's death. Unfortunately, even this edition represents only a small part of Magini's actual work, since his notes for a greater volume, together with much of his library (particularly astrological works), were confiscated by the Roman Inquisition and apparently lost or destroyed.

BIBLIOGRAPHY

I. ORIGINAL WORKS. Magini wrote in Latin and most of his works were then translated into Italian. The major works are *Ephemerides coelestium motuum* (Venice, 1582); *Novae coelestium orbium Theoricae congruentes cum observationibus N. Copernici* (Venice, 1589); *De planis triangulis liber unicus et de dimitiendi ratione per quadrentem et geometricum quadratum libri quinque* (Venice, 1592); *Tabula tetragonica, seu quadratorum numerorum cum suis radicibus* (Venice, 1592); *Geographiae universae* (Venice, 1596); *Tabulae primi mobilis, quas directionum vulgo dicunt* (Venice, 1604). His later works include *Continuatio Ephemeridum coelestium motuum* (Venice, 1607); *Ephemeridum coelestium motuum, ab anno Domini 1608 usque ad annum 1630* (Frankfurt, 1608); *Tabulae generales ad Primum Mobile spectantes, et primo quidem sequitur magnus canon mathematicus* (Bologna, 1609); *Breve instruttione sopra l'apparenze et mirabili effetti dello specchio concavo sferico* (Bologna, 1611); *Geographiae universae* (Venice, 1616); *Tabulae novae iuxta Tychonis rationes elaboratae* (Bologna, 1619); and his atlas, *Italia* (Bologna, 1620).

II. SECONDARY LITERATURE. The best biography of Magini is A. Favaro, *Carteggio inedito di Ticone Brahe, Giovanni Keplero e di altri celebri astronomi e matematici dei secoli XVI e XVII con Giovanni Antonio Magini* (Bologna, 1886). Other works are R. Almagia, *L'Italia di G. A. Magini e la cartografia dell'Italia nei secoli XVI e XVII* (Naples, 1922); and G. Loria, *Storia delle matematiche* (Milan, 1950), pp. 380, 400, 422–425.

LUIGI CAMPEDELLI

MAGNITSKY, LEONTY FILIPPOVICH (*b.* Ostashkov, Russia, 19 June 1669; *d.* Moscow, Russia, 30 October 1739)

No precise information exists on Magnitsky's origins and early years. It is possible that he studied in Moscow at the Slavonic, Greek, and Latin Academy founded in 1687. It is also possible that he acquired his broad knowledge, which included many foreign languages, independently. In 1701 Peter the Great founded the Navigation School in Moscow, and it soon became the breeding ground for the technical intelligentsia. Peter brought Magnitsky there to teach in 1702. Magnitsky worked there for the rest of his life, and was named director in 1715.

Magnitsky's *Arithmetic* (1703) was the first guide to mathematics published in Russia. Its first edition of 2,400 copies was extraordinarily large for that time and it served as the basic textbook of mathematics in Russia for half a century. The founder of Russian science, Lomonosov, called it, along with one grammar book, "our gateways to learning." Magnitsky's textbook successfully combined the tradition of Russian mathematical literature of the seventeenth century with that of the western European mathematical schools. In the first section a detailed exposition of mathematical problems is given. The second section, almost an encyclopedia of the natural sciences of the time, contains information on algebra and its geometrical applications, the computation of trigonometric tables of sines, tangents, and secants, and information on navigational astronomy, geodesy, and navigation.

There are also tables of magnetic declination, tables of latitude of the points of rising and setting of the sun and moon, and coordinates of the most important ports with their times of high and low tide.

Magnitsky also participated in the preparation of a Russian edition (1703) of the logarithmic tables of Vlacq (1628).

BIBLIOGRAPHY

Magnitsky's one published work was *Arifmetika, sirech nauka chislitelnaya. Tablitsy sinusov, tangensov i sekansov i logarifma sinusov i tangensov* ("Arithmetic, Called the Computational Science. Tables of Sines, Tangents, and Secants and Logarithms of Sines and Tangents"; Moscow, 1703).

Works about Magnitsky are: A. P. Denisov, *Leonty Filippovich Magnitsky* (Moscow, 1967); D. D. Galanin, *Leonty Filippovich Magnitsky i yego "Arifmetika"* ("Leonty Filippovich Magnitsky and his 'Arithmetic' "), 3 vols. (Moscow, 1914); and A. P. Youschkevitch, *Istoria matematika v Rossii do 1917 goda* ("History of Mathematics in Russia Until 1917"; Moscow, 1968).

S. PLOTKIN

AL-MĀHĀNĪ, ABŪ 'ABD ALLĀH MUHAMMAD IBN 'ĪSĀ (*b.* Mahan, Kerman, Persia; *fl.* Baghdad, *ca.* 860; *d. ca.* 880)

Our main source of information on al-Māhānī's life consists of quotations from an unspecified work by al-Māhānī in Ibn Yūnus' *Hakimite Tables.* Here Ibn Yūnus cites observations of conjunctions and lunar and solar eclipses made by al-Māhānī between 853 and 866. Al-Māhānī remarked, in connection with the lunar eclipses, that he calculated their beginnings with an astrolabe and that the beginnings of three consecutive eclipses were about half an hour later than calculated.

Al-Māhānī's main accomplishments lie in mathematics; in the *Fihrist* he is mentioned only as geometer and arithmetician. Al-Khayyāmī states that al-Māhānī was the first to attempt an algebraic solution of the Archimedean problem of dividing a sphere by a plane into segments the volumes of which are in a given ratio (*On the Sphere and the Cylinder* II, 4). Al-Māhānī expressed this problem in a cubic equation of the form $x^3 + a = cx^2$, but he could not proceed further. According to al-Khayyāmī, the problem was thought unsolvable until al-Khāzin succeeded by using conic sections. In Leiden there exists a manuscript copy of a commentary to al-Māhānī's treatise, probably by al-Qūhī.

Al-Māhānī wrote commentaries to books I, V, X,

and XIII of Euclid's *Elements.* Of these, the treatise on the twenty-six propositions of book I that can be proved without a *reductio ad absurdum* has been lost. Part of a commentary on book X, on irrational ratios; an explanation of obscure passages in book XIII; and three (different?) treatises on ratio (book V) are extant. Since book V, on the theory of proportion, was presented in a synthetic form which did not reveal how the doctrine of proportions had come into being, Arabic mathematicians were dissatisfied with definition 5, the fundamental one. They did not deny its correctness, however, and accepted it as a principle. Gradually they replaced the Euclidean "equimultiple" definition by the pre-Eudoxian "anthyphairetic" definition, which compared magnitudes by comparing their expansion in continued fractions. The "anthyphairetic" conception appears in explicit form in al-Māhānī's treatise, in which he referred to Thābit ibn Qurra. Al-Māhānī regarded ratio as "the mutual behavior of two magnitudes when compared with one another by means of the Euclidean process of finding the greatest common measure." Two pairs of magnitudes were for him proportional when "the two series of quotients appearing in that process are identical." Essentially the same theory was worked out later by al-Nayrīzī. Neither established a connection with Euclid's definition, which was first done by Ibn al-Haytham.

At the request of some geometers al-Māhānī wrote an improved edition of the *Sphaerica* of Menelaus—of book I and part of book II—which has been lost. His improvements consisted of inserting explanatory remarks, modernizing the language (with special consideration given to technical terms), and remodeling or replacing obscure proofs. This edition was revised and finished by Ahmad ibn Abī Sa'īd al-Harawī in the tenth century. Al-Tūsī, who wrote the most widely known Arabic edition, considered al-Māhānī's and al-Harawī's improvements valueless and used the edition by Abū Nasr Mansūr ibn 'Irāq.

BIBLIOGRAPHY

I. ORIGINAL WORKS. C. Brockelmann, *Geschichte der arabischen Literatur,* supp. I (Leiden, 1937), 383, lists the available MSS of al-Māhānī. Information on al-Māhānī is also given in H. Suter's translation of the *Fihrist* in *Das Mathematiker-Verzeichniss im Fihrist des Ibn abī Ja'kūb al-Nadīm,* in *Abhandlungen zur Geschichte der Mathematik,* VI (Leipzig, 1892), 25, 58. Partial translations and discussions of al-Māhānī's work are in M. Krause, *Die Sphärik von Menelaos aus Alexandrien* (Berlin, 1936), 1, 13, 23–26; G. P. Matvievskaya, *Uchenie o chisle na srednevekovom Blizhnem i Srednem Vostoke* ("Studies on

Number in the Medieval Near and Middle East"; Tashkent, 1967), ch. 6, which deals with commentaries on Euclid X; and E. B. Plooij, *Euclid's Conception of Ratio* (Rotterdam, 1950), 4, 50, 61.

II. SECONDARY LITERATURE. On al-Māhānī's observations, see "Ibn Yūnus, *Le livre de la grande Table Hakémite*, trans. by J. J. A. Caussin de Perceval in *Notices et extraits de la Bibliothèque nationale*, 7 (1804), 58, 80, 102–112, 164. Information on al-Māhānī as a mathematician, especially his treatment of the Archimedean problem, is in F. Woepcke, *L'algèbre d'Omar Alkhayyāmī* (Paris, 1851), 2, 40–44, 96. On the anthyphairetic theory, see O. Becker, "*Eudoxos Studien I*," in *Quellen und Studien zur Geschichte der Mathematik, Astronomie und Physik*, Abt. B, 2 (1933), 311–333.

YVONNE DOLD-SAMPLONIUS

MAHĀVĪRA (*fl.* Mysore, India, ninth century)

Mahāvīra, a Jain, wrote during the reign of Amoghavarṣa, the Rāṣṭrakūṭa monarch of Karṇāṭaka and Mahārāṣṭra between 814/815 and about 880. Nothing else of his life is known. His sole work was a major treatise on mathematics, the *Gaṇitasārasaṅgraha* (see essay in Supplement), in nine chapters:

1. Terminology.
2. Arithmetical operations.
3. Operations involving fractions.
4. Miscellaneous operations.
5. Operations involving the rule of three.
6. Mixed operations.
7. Operations relating to the calculations of areas.
8. Operations relating to excavations.
9. Operations relating to shadows.

There is one commentary on this work by a certain Varadarāja, and another in Kannaḍa, entitled *Daivajñavallabha*.

BIBLIOGRAPHY

The *Gaṇitasārasaṅgraha* was edited, with an English trans. and notes, by M. Raṅgācārya (Madras, 1912); and with a Hindi *anuvāda* by Lakṣmīcandra Jaina as *Jīvarāma Jaina Granthamālā* 12 (Solāpura, 1963). There are discussions of various aspects of this work (listed chronologically) by D. E. Smith, "The Ganita-Sara-Sangraha of Mahāvīrācārya," in *Bibliotheca mathematica*, 3, no. 9 (1908–1909), 106–110; B. Datta, "On Mahāvīra's Solution of Rational Triangles and Quadrilaterals," in *Bulletin of the Calcutta Mathematical Society*, 20 (1932), 267–294; B. Datta, "On the Relation of Mahāvīra to Śrīdhara," in *Isis*, 17 (1932), 25–33; B. Datta and A. N. Singh, *History of Hindu Mathematics*, 2 vols. (Lahore, 1935–1938; repr. in 1 vol., Bombay, 1962), *passim;* E. T. Bell, "Mahavira's

Diophantine System," in *Bulletin of the Calcutta Mathematical Society*, **38** (1946), 121–122; and A. Volodarsky, "O traktate Magaviry 'Kratky kurs matematiki,' " in *Fiziko-matematicheskie nauki v stranakh vostoka*, II (Moscow, 1969), 98–130.

DAVID PINGREE

MAIOR (or **MAIORIS**), **JOHN** (frequently cited as **JEAN MAIR**) (*b.* Gleghornie, near Haddington, Scotland, 1469; *d.* St. Andrews, Scotland, 1550)

Maior received his early education in Haddington, whence he passed to God's House (later Christ's College), Cambridge, and then to the University of Paris, where he enrolled at the Collège Ste. Barbe about 1492; he completed his education at the Collège de Montaigu. He received the licentiate in arts in 1495 and the licentiate and doctorate in theology in 1506. In 1518 Maior returned to Scotland, where he occupied the first chair of philosophy and theology at Glasgow; in 1522 he was invited to the University of St. Andrews to teach logic and theology. Attracted back to Paris in 1525, he taught there until 1531, when he returned again to St. Andrews. He became provost of St. Salvator's College in 1533 and, as dean of the theological faculty, was invited to the provincial council of 1549, although he could not attend because of advanced age.

Maior spent most of his productive life in Paris, where he formed a school of philosophers and theologians whose influence was unparalleled in its time. Himself taught by nominalists such as Thomas Bricot and Geronymo Pardo and by the Scotist Peter Tartaret, Maior showed a special predilection for nominalism while remaining open to realism, especially that of his *conterraneus* (countryman) John Duns Scotus. To this eclecticism Maior brought a great concern for positive sources, researching and editing with his students many terminist and Scholastic treatises and even contributing to history with his impressive *Historiae Majoris Britanniae, tam Angliae quam Scotiae* (Paris, 1521). His students included the Spaniards Luis Coronel and his brother Antonio and Gaspar Lax; the Scots Robert Caubraith, David Cranston, and George Lokert; and Peter Crokart of Brussels and John Dullaert of Ghent. They and their students quickly diffused Maior's ideals of scholarship through the universities of Spain, Britain, and France, and ultimately throughout Europe. In theology Maior was unsympathetic to the Reformers (he taught the young John Knox while at Glasgow) and remained faithful to the Church of Rome until his death.

Maior's importance for physical science derives

from his interest in logic and mathematics and their application to the problems of natural philosophy. He became an important avenue through which the writings of the fourteenth-century Mertonians, especially Bradwardine, Heytesbury, and Swineshead, exerted an influence in the schools of the sixteenth century, including those at Padua and Pisa, where the young Galileo received his education. Among Maior's logical writings the treatise *Propositum de infinito* (1506) is important for its anticipation of modern mathematical treatments of infinity; in it he argues in favor of the existence of actual infinities *(infinita actu)* and discusses the possibilities of motion of an infinite body.

Maior also composed series of questions on all of Aristotle's physical works (Paris, 1526), based on "an exemplar sent to me from Britain" and thus probably written between 1518 and 1525; it is a balanced, if somewhat eclectic, exposition of the main positions that were then being argued by the nominalists and realists. Maior's commentaries on the *Sentences* are significant for their treatment of scientific questions in a theological context; they were used and cited, generally favorably, until the end of the sixteenth century.

BIBLIOGRAPHY

I. ORIGINAL WORKS. Hubert Élie, ed., *Le traité "De l'infini" de Jean Mair* (Paris, 1938), is a Latin ed. of the *Propositum de infinito* with French trans., intro., and notes. Some of Maior's works are listed in the *Dictionary of National Biography*, XII (1921–1922), 830–832. That list has been emended by R. G. Villoslada, S.J., "La universidad de Paris durante los estudios de Francisco de Vitoria, O.P. (1507–1522)," in *Analecta Gregoriana*, **14** (1938), 121–164; and by Élie, *op. cit.*, pp. v–xix. Villoslada also analyzes Maior's philosophical and theological writings and provides a guide to bibliography.

II. SECONDARY LITERATURE. See Hubert Élie, "Quelques maîtres de l'université de Paris vers l'an 1500," in *Archives d'histoire doctrinale et littéraire du moyen âge*, **18** (1950–1951), 193–243, esp. 205–212; and William A. Wallace, O.P., "The Concept of Motion in the Sixteenth Century," in *Proceedings of the American Catholic Philosophical Association*, **41** (1967), 184–195; also A. B. Emden, *A Biographical Register of The University of Cambridge to 1500* (Cambridge, 1963), 384–385.

WILLIAM A. WALLACE, O.P.

MALEBRANCHE, NICOLAS (*b.* Paris, France, 5 August 1638; *d.* Paris, 13 October 1715)

Malebranche's life spanned the same years as Louis XIV's, and a famous contemporary, Antoine Arnauld, termed his philosophy *"grand et magnifique,"* adjectives historians often apply to that monarch's reign. The grandeur of his philosophy consists in the way he assimilated the whole of the Cartesian heritage and attempted to elaborate, on theological foundations, an original, rationalist-oriented speculative system. The passage of time and the recently concluded publication of his works have restored to Malebranche the stature of a remarkable intellect, for whom the polemics in which he ceaselessly engaged were merely occasions to buttress his "search for truth." Yet, while his personality can be understood in terms of the profound—and religious—unity of his thought and life, the influence of his work is not free from paradox: Voltaire honored him as one of the greatest speculative thinkers, and d'Alembert placed his portrait above his writing table. A discussion of Malebranche would be incomplete without an attempt to comprehend why Enlightenment philosophers accorded him this praise, suspect as it was in the eyes of theologians.

The youngest son of a large family, Malebranche was born with a delicate constitution. Through his father, a royal counsellor, he was linked to the rural bourgeoisie. His mother, Catherine de Lauson, belonged to the minor nobility; her brother, Jean de Lauson, was governor of Canada. His family's modest wealth allowed him to pursue a special program of studies adapted to his physical disability. It was not until age sixteen that he entered the Collège de la Marche of the University of Paris. He received the master of arts degree there in 1656 after having attended the lectures of the renowned Peripatetic M. Rouillard. His piety inclined him toward the priesthood, and for three years he studied theology at the Sorbonne. It seems, however, that he was no more satisfied with this instruction than he had been with commentaries on Aristotle. He entered the Congregation of the Oratory on 20 January 1660, no doubt attracted by its reputation for liberty and culture in the service of the inner life. The impression he made on his new teachers was not altogether favorable. Although he was judged to be suited for the religious life and endowed with the virtues required in communal life, his was considered an "undistinguished intellect."

The explanation of this judgment may well be that, during his four years of Oratorian training, Malebranche, who was ordained priest on 20 September 1664, does not seem to have been sympathetic to the newest elements of the curriculum: an interest in history and erudition, and a passion for positive theology founded on critical study of the Scriptures. Malebranche was taught by the leaders of this tendency,

Richard Simon and Charles Lecointe, but did not adopt their views. However that may be, he did become acquainted at the Oratory with the ideas of St. Augustine and Plato.

The stimulus for Malebranche's independent intellectual development came from Descartes, during the first year of his priesthood. It was said that this change resulted from his reading of the newly published *Traité de l'homme*, whose editors had sought to emphasize the broad area of agreement between Descartes and Augustine that was revealed by this posthumous work. Whatever the event that decided Malebranche in favor of this disputed book, it is certain that within three or four years he had completely redone his studies and had made the Cartesian legacy an integral part of his thought. Evidence for this assertion is to be found in *De la recherche de la vérité*, begun as early as 1668. The title itself reveals the inspiration he drew from the manuscripts generously made available to him by the circle around Claude Clerselier. Indeed, the content of the first volume exhibits this inspiration so clearly that Malebranche became involved in difficulties with the censors and had to postpone publication until 1674.

The following year, 1675, saw the publication of a revised edition of the first volume, the second volume, and Jean Prestet's *Élémens des mathématiques*. The simultaneous appearance of these three books is significant. Prestet, a young man with no resources, owed everything to Malebranche and was evidently his pupil even before the Congregation decided officially in 1674 to recognize Malebranche as professor of mathematics at the seminary. The extremely gifted Prestet rapidly accomplished what Malebranche himself was unable to achieve while he was embroiled in difficulties over his philosophical writings. It was Malebranche, however, who was responsible for the simultaneous publication of 1675, for he wished to place before the public an original philosophical and mathematical synthesis attesting the vitality of Cartesianism.

The general impression given by this synthesis—an impression that accounts for its success—was not deceptive. It was indeed from Descartes that Malebranche attempted to discover a science and a method of reasoning founded on clear and distinct ideas. Later he himself declared that what Augustine lacked was the opportunity to learn from Descartes that bodies are not seen in themselves. From the beginning of his philosophical career Malebranche let it be known that he considered this a fundamental lesson. Rejecting sensible qualities, he held, like Descartes, that things are to be judged solely by the ideas that represent them to us according to their intelligible essence.

All the same the *Recherche de la vérité* touches on various subjects that are not at all Cartesian: primacy of religious goals, refutation of the doctrine of innate ideas, negation of composite substance, union of the problems of error and sin, explanation of the creation by God's love for himself, and affirmation that God acts in the most simple ways, that he is the sole efficient cause, and that natural causes are only "occasional" causes. The list of new branches that Malebranche grafted onto the Cartesian trunk and that corresponded to his hope of establishing a truly Christian philosophy could be expanded; but at this stage of his career it was a matter of possible materials for a new doctrine rather than such a doctrine itself.

Progress toward this goal is represented by *Conversations chrétiennes* (1677) and the third volume of the *Recherche* (1678), "containing several elucidations concerning the principal difficulties of the preceding volumes." But it was with the *Traité de la nature et de la grâce* (Amsterdam, 1680) that Malebranche emerged as the creator of a new system of the world. Inspired by a discussion with Arnauld in 1679, the book's immediate goal was to refute Jansenist ideas concerning grace and predestination. But in order to untangle this essentially religious problem, he transferred the debate to the philosophical plane, thus demonstrating to what extent he disagreed with Descartes on the value of extending rational reflection to questions of theology.

In examining this book one grasps the essential difference between the two thinkers. A believer and a philosopher, Malebranche did not experience the hyperbolic doubt expressed in the first Cartesian *Méditation;* he did not confront the "Cogito" as the initial indubitable existence; he did not have to seek to escape from a structure of thought closed in upon itself by discovering a God who could guarantee the universality and immutability of truth. For Malebranche, as for Descartes, God was undoubtedly the keystone and foundation of all truth, but for the former he was not the God reached by philosophical speculation whose essence is demonstrated by his existence. Rather, he is Augustine's God *intimior intimo meo*, whose presence in man is the source of the believer's daily meditation and from whom all light descends. He is also the God of wisdom, creator of a universe ordered according to laws that are both perfectly simple and perfectly intelligible—the God who, acting uniquely for his own glory, created man that he might live in union with him and participate in his reason, in his word itself.

Thus, whereas Descartes refused as a vain undertaking any speculation on divine motivations, Malebranche found in this realm something on which he could base the exercise of human reason. In his doctrine the union of man and God is not only the goal of the religious life, it is also the means of attaining a vision, in God, in which there occurs the fullest possible communication of wisdom and intelligibility. Of course, Malebranche does not claim that this communication, the supreme guarantee against error, is a blessing easily obtained or permanently assured. But he does assert that in making the effort to discern the coherence of rational discourse, sinful man, whether Christian or atheist, always obtains some reflection of the universal reason, even if he is unaware of or actually denies its divine nature. Indeed Malebranche contends that attention is a *natural prayer* that God has established as the occasional cause of our knowledge.

The term and the notion of occasional cause are not due to Malebranche, but his use of them and the importance he gave to them were incontestably original. Assigning the source of all effective action to God, he took causality in the strict sense out of the created world. This world is indeed regulated by divine wisdom, but as a function of relationships that carry in themselves no necessity whatever. Moreover, the means that man has received to make it intelligible could only be indirect, that is, occasional. Malebranche thus arrived at a philosophical system that goes far beyond the theological problem that was, so to say, the occasion for its own complete formulation.

When the *Traité* appeared, it was already several years since Malebranche had been assigned any specific duties. Starting in 1680 he devoted all his time to writing and to his role as mediator between theology and Cartesian natural philosophy. He was assailed by polemics that obliged him to review, correct, and improve his system. It is impossible to recount this highly complicated story in a few lines or to discuss in detail the modifications he made in response to a flood of objections and difficulties. However interesting the debates in which Malebranche found himself involved (for example, over the coordination of the two different perfections represented by the divine laws and the divine work) and whatever accusations he was forced to counter (destroying Providence, excluding miracles, minimizing grace to the advantage of liberty), he did not need to modify for the scientific public the basic positions of his philosophy as outlined above.

It should be merely noted in passing that Malebranche, who was more skillful in the art of revising his texts than in that of controversy, rapidly alienated a number of people, even in the Oratory. In Arnauld's opinion he was incapable of maintaining a suitable degree of detachment, and Bossuet judged him severely. Most important, he failed to escape papal censure: the *Traité* was placed on the Index in 1690 while he

was in the midst of preparing the third edition. He was sincerely troubled by the decision of the hierarchy, but it did not stop him. The seventh and last edition appeared in 1712, along with the sixth edition of the *Recherche*.

These figures are revealing. Malebranche was read in his own time as much by admirers as by opponents. So much is evident. What most clearly appears in this record of publication, however, is a tireless capacity for modifying his positions and a mind always receptive to suggestions, two rare qualities that testify to his character and intelligence. Malebranche owed his position in the scientific movement of his time to this harmony of his personal qualities with his doctrine of occasionalism.

It is not difficult to understand why occasionalism was a conception particularly conducive to the advance of experimental science. To the degree that nature appeared, to Malebranche, as simply a sphere of relations, the dialogue between reason and experience became for him, inevitably, the fundamental stimulus in the pursuit of knowledge. For when reason was supported by metaphysics, as it was in Descartes, it had much too great a tendency to declare what should be, a priori, and to call upon experience solely for confirmation. In his view, however, the only means of discovery available to the human mind are occasional causes, that is, causes which could have been totally different and which are the reflection not of some ontological necessity but only of the Creator's will. Consequently, experience is indispensable. Of course, it must be intimately conjoined with the exercise of reason in order to attain knowledge of the relations that God has established in his Creation in fact, and not involuntarily, as it were, to comply with some metaphysical imperative. While Malebranche's philosophy provided, above all, a rationale for the study of physics, what is striking is the way in which he was led to grasp this fact himself and to work simultaneously in very different disciplines.

As noted above, the simultaneous publication of Prestet's *Élémens* and the first edition of the *Recherche* suggests that Malebranche was sufficiently well-versed in Cartesian mathematics to have been capable of inspiring a highly talented disciple and to have worked with him on an up-to-date textbook. John Wallis in his *Treatise of Algebra* (1684) did not hesitate to attribute to Malebranche the authorship of the *Élémens* and to reproach the work for being merely a compilation, one that failed to cite its sources other than Descartes and Viète. In replying to this accusation, Prestet clearly implied that he was not annoyed at the attribution of his book to "a person more skillful than he," but he ironically asserted his astonishment that anyone could have supposed he had read so many specialized works. Dating his own initiation in mathematics to 1671, he artlessly stated that Descartes was virtually his only source and that, moreover, he was completely dissatisfied with the few other books that had come to his attention. These remarks would be as true of Malebranche as of Prestet himself.

It is likely that Malebranche's duties as a professor of mathematics lasted only a short while. In any case they have left no further trace. Moreover, when Leibniz met Prestet at Malebranche's residence during his stay in Paris, he was well aware of their respective roles, as is evident from his later correspondence with Malebranche. The disciple, who clearly surpassed his master in the technical realm, was entrusted with the actual mathematical portion of the work; but the master directed the research, and his orientation of it consisted in giving the greatest possible development to Cartesian mathematics.

The *Élémens* consisted of two parts. The first was devoted to arithmetic and algebra, the second to analysis, that is, the application of the two former disciplines to the resolution of all problems concerned with magnitude *(grandeur)*. By magnitude, the author specified that he meant not only what is susceptible of extension in various dimensions but, more generally, everything "susceptible of more and less" *(de plus et de moins)*—in other words, everything that could enter, according to Archimedean logic, into the formal rules of relations. The plan of the work corresponded to one of the aspects of the intelligibility that Malebranche promised to the exercise of the human mind. Prestet added: "We do not attempt to understand or even to reason about the infinite," a point of view which was in accord with Descartes's thinking and to which he always remained faithful. The authors cited in the section on analysis were Diophantus, Viète, and Descartes. In his view, however, Descartes's method was "the most general, the most fruitful, and the most simple of all." In utilizing this method he completed Descartes's effort, notably with regard to equations of the fourth and fifth degree, an area in which he fancied that he had made a theoretical advance.

As to that, he deluded himself a bit, but he did at least provoke Leibniz' curiosity and interest in the subject. Leibniz was disappointed to learn from Malebranche in 1679 that Prestet, who had entered the Oratory and was busy preparing for the priesthood, had not pursued his investigations. This circumstance explains why the theory of equations and the analytic expression of roots constituted the grounds on which Leibniz chose to attack Malebranche. In telling Malebranche that this was the area that most clearly demonstrated the insufficiency and limitations of the

Cartesian method, Leibniz was on the right track. Between 1680 and 1690 Malebranche progressively detached himself from Prestet, whose teaching at the University of Angers during these years was marked by painful conflicts with the Jesuits.

True, a new person in Malebranche's immediate entourage, the Abbé Catelan, lent Prestet a hand in assimilating English mathematics and in attempting to attach Barrow's method and Wallis' arithmetic of the infinitesimals to Cartesian mathematics. But Malebranche also became acquainted with a young gentleman, the Marquis de L'Hospital, whom he considered more receptive to the changes that he suspected might be necessary. Prestet died in 1691 after having published two volumes of *Nouveaux élémens* (1689), leaving in manuscript a third volume on geometry that was never published because of Malebranche's unfavorable opinion. For a few months Catelan sought to continue Prestet's work, but the cause was already lost. From 1690 to 1691 Malebranche devoted all his attention to the compromise that L'Hospital had worked out and then ardently followed what the latter was learning from Johann I Bernoulli in 1692. The arrival in Paris of this messenger of Leibniz' new calculus was the "occasion" that completely rearranged the mathematical landscape. Malebranche left to his Oratorian collaborators the task of completing the fair copy of the manuscript recording the mathematical reform elaborated by L'Hospital the preceding year, and the two of them became converts to the movement emanating from Hannover.

This rapid sequence of events within the space of only two or three years undoubtedly reproduced, in a certain way, the situation of 1671–1675. Malebranche assimilated the innovations, pen in hand, and convinced himself of the necessity of encouraging research in the new direction. L'Hospital was the real mathematician, the one who mastered the material and proceeded faster. He soon asserted his own independence from Malebranche; in 1696 he published his *Analyse des infiniment petits* virtually without consulting him. This independence, moreover, was the sign of a new reality. The rapidity with which mathematics was developing reflected the fruitfulness of analysis, which combined consideration of the infinite with the operational procedures of the differential and integral calculus. And the rapid pace accentuated the distinction between those who truly deserved to be considered mathematicians, and the partisans who could only follow, more or less closely, with greater or less difficulty. Malebranche henceforth belonged in the second category.

All the same, he possessed the valuable assets of freshness and enthusiasm. In this regard Leibniz said he had to laugh to see how Malebranche was so enamored of algebra, so enchanted with its operational effectiveness. The enchantment that Malebranche found in the mathematics of the infinitesimal analysis attests to the same naïveté. He failed to distinguish clearly between the respective roles of logic and calculation. Believing that the new mathematics was within striking distance of perfection, he could not understand what restrained the great masters from placing their discoveries before the public. What diminishes Malebranche's standing as a mathematician in the eyes of the specialists, his naïveté, was the same quality that made his advocacy more effective.

In the fifth edition of the *Recherche de la vérité* (1700), Malebranche replaced all the mathematical references he had previously given with L'Hospital's *Analyse* and a work on integral calculus that his former secretary, Louis Carré, had just compiled from material in the archives of the Oratory. Fully aware of its deficiencies, Malebranche expressed the hope that a better work would shortly appear and hinted that the required effort was under way. He had good reason for doing so, because in 1698 he had, in effect, assigned this task to the Oratorian Charles-René Reyneau, Prestet's successor at Angers. And to the extent that this outstanding teacher encountered great difficulties in absorbing the infinitesimal methods, there were grounds for thinking that the result of his labor would correspond to the conditions required for the dissemination of the new ideas in the schools and would, in short, constitute a good textbook.

The enterprise was marked by many vicissitudes and was not completed until 1708, after the happy conclusion at the Académie des Sciences of the polemic provoked by Michel Rolle against the infinitesimals. (Malebranche played the most active role in bringing about this happy ending.) Although Reyneau's *Analyse démontrée* appeared in 1708, later than expected, it answered all the more fully to the hopes placed in it. The first textbook of the new mathematics, it fulfilled the important social function indispensable to all reform. It was from one of this work's posthumous editions that d'Alembert learned the subject.

It is evident that Malebranche holds no place in the history of mathematics by virtue of any specific discovery, nor any claim to be considered a true mathematician. Nevertheless, the history of mathematics at the end of the seventeenth century—at least in France—cannot be described without referring to his activity. The mainspring of the spread and development of Cartesian mathematics, Malebranche successively insisted on the need for reform and fostered the introduction of Leibnizian mathematics. Throughout these changes, moreover, he was concerned with their implications for teaching.

While the importance of intelligibility in his philosophy accounts for his special interest in mathematics, it was, rather, toward physics and the natural sciences that Malebranche turned his attention. The first edition of the *Recherche* clearly demonstrates that this vast subject attracted Malebranche's interest from the start and that he had already read extensively in it. In the realm of physics, Rohault's recent publication seemed to Malebranche both adequate and faithful to the Cartesian method. The only topic in which Malebranche felt obliged to make a personal contribution was that of the laws of collision. It is also the question to which he returned in 1692 in publishing a small volume entitled *Des loix de la communication des mouvements*.

The date 1692 in itself is significant, but to understand fully Malebranche's statement that this short treatise was written in order to meet Leibniz' criticisms, it is not sufficient to consider only the mathematical developments outlined above. It must also be recalled that in 1686–1687 Leibniz had launched an attack in the *Acta eruditorum* against the Cartesian identification of force with the quantity of motion and had thereby provoked a bitter controversy with Catelan, who was then friendly with Malebranche. Moreover, in 1692 Malebranche was the recipient of a manuscript copy of Leibniz' *Essay de dynamique*. The brief work that he brought out almost simultaneously shows that Malebranche was able to assimilate criticism without capitulating to it.

Although Malebranche agreed to revise the whole of his presentation of the subject, he did not consent to abandon any more of the Cartesian legacy than he had already done in dropping the principle that a force inheres in the state of rest. Further, he assumed that he had answered Leibniz' objections by distinguishing three types of laws, corresponding to the "different suppositions that may be held relating to colliding bodies and to the surrounding medium." On this occasion, moreover, he gave greater importance to the notion of elasticity. Nevertheless, his conclusion, presented with highly interesting remarks on the respective roles of theoretical speculation and experiment, makes clear that he was not satisfied with his work and was ready for a more radical revision. He undertook such a revision in several steps in the years 1698 to 1700, characterizing his own publication of 1692 as a "wretched little treatise."

In the course of this tumultuous development of his ideas Malebranche made his most original contribution to the scientific movement—and did so in his capacity as speculative philosopher. In his exposition of the third law of impact, he invested collision theory with a clarity that was lacking in Mariotte's *Traité de la percussion ou chocq des corps* (1673). After concisely expressing the principles of research, he judiciously chose numerical examples and then stated a position that he firmly maintained in the following years: the scientist's duty is to begin with the diversity of observations and then to establish laws. These laws, when submitted to mathematical operations, should reflect natural effects step by step. It was in this connection that Malebranche was dissatisfied with Mariotte's propositions. The latter had, it is true, clearly distinguished between two operations. First, he disregarded elasticity and treated the bodies as if they were soft. Second, he superimposed the effect of elasticity, which consisted in assigning the respective velocities in inverse ratio to the masses. But in Malebranche's view the first operation was unintelligible, since bodies without elasticity were, he supposed, necessarily hard. And the second operation ran into serious logical difficulties, for taking the force to be the absolute quantity of motion led to paradoxical results. Malebranche satisfied himself with regard to the first point in 1698–1699 by means of a modification of the concept of matter, the subject of his "Mémoire sur la lumière, les couleurs etc." He attempted to overcome the second problem by considering the property of reciprocity, which Mariotte's laws assumed, to be a "revelation" of the experiment, the sort of principle of intelligibility to which all rational effort must be subject. While correcting the proofs for the fifth edition of the *Recherche*, he was rewarded by the discovery that the whole question became clarified if the absolute quantity of motion were replaced by the algebraic quantity, that is, if the sign were taken into account.

This discovery led to the final corrections, which now furnished an original way of demonstrating, without paralogism or *petitio principii*, the laws of elastic collision. Moreover, this method of improving Mariotte's presentation avoided adopting Leibniz' point of view and preserved as much as possible of Descartes's conception.

Convinced that he had found a solution, Malebranche turned his attention all the more resolutely toward other problems. The memoir alluded to above won him membership in the Académie des Sciences at the time of its reorganization in 1699. Henceforth, Malebranche actively participated in scientific life, while gathering the material he was to incorporate in the sixth edition of the *Recherche* (1712), in which he made the necessary revisions, corrections, and additions in those sections devoted to all the topics in which he thought science bore on his philosophy.

It is most important to note that certain authors have erred in ridiculing the patching up of the Cartesian vortices that Malebranche is supposed to have begun. To be sure, he speaks of subtle matter and vortices, but his system arises from a syncretism that borrowed much from recent advances in physics and especially from the work of Huygens. Malebranche's subtle matter is a unique primary substance that, forced to move at high speed in a closed universe, is obliged to whirl in vortices the dimensions of which can decrease without limit, a property predicated on the supposition that no vacuum can exist. The formula for centrifugal force then requires that these small vortices, which are actually the universal material of all physical entities, be not only perfectly elastic but capable, as well, of releasing a "fearful" force upon breaking up. A theoretical model of this sort is not a trivial invention.

Nor is there anything trivial about the manner in which Malebranche utilized this model to study luminous phenomena and to provide an account of universal gravitation, of planetary motion, and of gravity. This model, considered in itself as the seat of action in the universe, inspired his idea that light consists of vibration in a medium under pressure. And considered in all its ramifications, it led him to conceive of the gross matter accessible to our senses as the result of a condensation in the neighborhood of a vortical center. This picture was imposed by the inapplicability to the case of large vortices of a homogeneous mechanical model centered on a point with invariant properties for distances near to or far from the center.

Although all this theoretical effort must be granted a certain originality, none of it was adopted by eighteenth-century science. It was not until much later that scientists again took up the idea that frequency is characteristic of colors or the idea that orthography can help establish the laws of central systems of small diameter—and when they did they were unaware that Malebranche had advocated such views.

Nor did anything come either of the hours that Malebranche spent at the microscope or of his botanical observations. Despite the importance he accorded to the experimental method after 1700, he never considered himself more than an amateur, concerned simply to grasp what it was that the specialization of others was accomplishing. The only experiment that we can confidently attribute to his own efforts—before his reading of Newton's *Opticks*—concerned the virtual equivalence of air and of the vacuum produced in the air pump as mediums for the propagation of light. It was a perfect example of the ambiguity of so-called crucial experiments. Malebranche's improvements in methods for observing generation in eggs in the hatchery were trivial and presupposed confirmation of the ovist theory. Even though the science of life seemed to him a realm apart, incomprehensible without the idea of finality, he applied to it what is now known as the notion of structure, deriving from his mathematical critique of being and extension. That is why he advocated the doctrine of the *emboîtement des germes.*

It has to be admitted that Malebranche came to a scientific career, in the broad sense, too late in life. It was unusual enough that at age sixty he was able to carry out experimental research which showed a greater command of the subject than he could have won from books alone; and more should not be asked of him. Faithful to his speculative temperament, he was ardently concerned to preserve from his Cartesian past those values he thought enduring and to bequeath a system reconciling this past with the science of his day. This arduous enterprise condemned him to be a follower, not a leader, and it is not surprising that his work failed to exhibit intimate knowledge of the most advanced developments of contemporary science. The reformulation of results that have become common knowledge always requires the discovery of new results, if it is to incite interest. Malebranche failed to go beyond the reexpression of either the sine law of refraction of light or the inverse-square law of gravitation, and he left his vibratory theory of colors in only a rudimentary state.

Still, the high level of reflection he demanded from his readers exerted an influence on the most diverse thinkers both in France and abroad. As in the case of mathematics, Malebranche has a claim to be remembered in the history of physics, a science the autonomy of which was scarcely recognized in the last years of the seventeenth century and which had to formulate a charter for itself. In this respect Malebranche indisputably answered to the needs of his time, and his efforts were not in vain.

Thus, to the extent that Malebranche enriched theoretical speculation and worked to fashion a suitable basis for the union of the rational and the experimental, he made a genuine contribution to the autonomy of science. His activity was always inspired by his religious philosophy and, reciprocally, his results appeared to him to provide support for it. Others could complete the separation, retaining the autonomy and discarding the philosophy.

In preparing this account the author has sought to adhere to the facts available to him. This same fidelity, however, obliges him to restore to Malebranche something beyong the authorship of a body of thought that advanced an enlightened rationalism. The restitution concerns the virtues that Malebranche constantly displayed during his life: a capacity to correct himself, a sensitivity to the difficulties of the ordinary reader

and to the needs of his time, and a perseverance in educating himself in many fields. In Malebranche, the man is inseparable from the thinker, and the man was wholly imbued with Christian faith. One may, of course, not share this faith, and then the separation of science from belief is easy to effect. But whoever accepts the lesson to be learned in contemplating the total, integrated image of a life will no less easily perceive the violence of such an act. This is why, after several centuries, the message offered by Malebranche endures.

BIBLIOGRAPHY

I. ORIGINAL WORKS. The complete works of Malebranche, published under the direction of André Robinet as *Oeuvres complètes*, 20 vols. (Paris, 1958–1968), include correspondence and MSS. For his scientific work, see esp. vol. III, *Éclaircissements de la recherche de la vérité* (1678–1712); and vol. XVII, pt. 1, *Lois du mouvement* (1675–1712); and pt. 2, *Mathematica,* containing unpublished mathematical and other works, with critical annotations by P. Costabel.

Six eds. of *De la recherche de la vérité* were published, at Paris, during Malebranche's lifetime: the first three, in 2 vols. (1674–1675, 1675, 1677–1678); the 4th and 5th, in 3 vols. (1678–1679, 1700); and the 6th, in 4 vols. (1712). The *Traité de la nature et de la grâce* (Amsterdam, 1680) was followed in 1681 by *Éclaircissement, ou la suite du Traité* ....

II. SECONDARY LITERATURE. Works on Malebranche and his work include V. Delbos, *Étude de la philosophie de Malebranche* (Paris, 1924); G. Dreyfus, *La volonté selon Malebranche* (Paris, 1958); H. Gouhier, *La vocation de Malebranche* (Paris, 1926); and *La philosophie de Malebranche et son expérience religieuse* (Paris, 1926); M. Gueroult, *Malebranche*, 3 vols. (Paris, 1955–1959); A. Robinet, *Malebranche, de l'Académie des sciences* (Paris, 1970); and G. Rodis-Lewis, *Nicolas Malebranche* (Paris, 1963). See also *Malebranche—l'homme et l'oeuvre* (Paris, 1966), published by the Centre International de Synthèse.

PIERRE COSTABEL

MALFATTI, GIAN FRANCESCO (*b.* Ala, Trento, Italy, 1731; *d.* Ferrara, Italy, 9 October 1807)

After completing his studies in Bologna under the guidance of Francesco Maria Zanotti, Gabriele Manfredi, and Vincenzo Riccati, Malfatti went to Ferrara in 1754, where he founded a school of mathematics and physics. In 1771, when the University of Ferrara was reestablished, he was appointed professor of mathematics. He held this post for about thirty years, teaching all phases of mathematics from Euclidean geometry to calculus.

Malfatti became famous for his paper "De aequationibus quadrato-cubicis disquisitio analytica" (1770), in which, given an equation of the fifth degree, he constructed a resolvent of the equation of the sixth degree, that is, the well-known Malfatti resolvent. If the root is known, the complete resolution of the given equation may be deduced. The latter, however, cannot be obtained by means of rational root expressions; rather, as Brioschi later demonstrated, it is obtained by means of elliptical transcendents.

Malfatti also demonstrated that a memoir on the theory of probability, published by Lagrange in 1774 and proclaimed by Poisson as "one of Lagrange's most beautiful works," nevertheless required explanation at one point.

In a brief treatise entitled *Della curva cassiniana* (1781), Malfatti demonstrated that a special case of Cassini's curve, the lemniscate, has the property that a mass point moving on it under gravity goes along any arc of the curve in the same time as it traverses the subtending chord.

In 1802 Malfatti gave the first, brilliant solution of the problem that bears his name: "Describe in a triangle three circumferences that are mutually tangent, each of which touches two sides of the triangle." Many illustrious mathematicians had dealt with this problem. Jacques Bernoulli (1654–1705) had earlier dealt with the special case in which the triangle is isosceles. An elegant geometric solution was supplied by Steiner (*Crelle's Journal*, vol. 1, 1826), while Clebsch, dealing with the same problem in 1857, made an excellent application of the elliptical functions (*Crelle's Journal*, vol. 53, 1857).

In a letter to A. M. Lorgna (27 April 1783), Malfatti gave the polar equation concerning the squaring of the circle.

BIBLIOGRAPHY

I. ORIGINAL WORKS. Among Malfatti's works are "De aequationibus quadrato-cubicis disquisitio analytica," in *Atti dell'Accademia dei Fisiocritici di Siena* (1770); *Memorie della Società italiana delle scienze detta dei XL*, **3**; *Della curva cassiniana* (Pavia, 1781); *Memorie della Società italiana delle scienze detta dei XL*, **10** (1802); and his letter to Lorgna, in *Bullettino di bibliografia e di storia delle scienze matematiche e fisiche*, **9** (1876), 438.

II. SECONDARY LITERATURE. For further information on Malfatti and his work, see G. B. Biadego, "Intorno alla vita e agli scritti di Gianfrancesco Malfatti, matematico del sec. XVIII°," in *Bullettino di bibliografia e storia delle matematiche del Boncompagni*, **9** (1876); E. Bortolotti, "Sulla risolvente di Malfatti," in *Atti dell'Accademia di Modena*, 3rd ser., **7** (1906); "Commemorazione di G. F. Malfatti," in *Atti della XIX riunione della Società italiana per il progresso delle scienze* (1930). Also see article on Malfatti in *Enciclopedia italiana* (Milan, 1934), XXII, 16; F. Brioschi, "Sulla risolvente di Malfatti," in *Memorie dell'Istituto lombardo di scienze e lettere*, **9** (1863); Gino Loria, *Curve piane speciali: Teoria e storia* (Milan, 1930), I, 265, and II, 23; and *Storia delle matematiche*, 2nd ed. (Milan, 1950), *passim*; A. Procissi, "Questioni connesse al problema di Malfatti e bibliografia," in *Periodico di matematiche*, 4th ser., **12** (1932); and A. Wittstein, *Geschichte des Malfatti'schen Problems* (Munich, 1871).

A. NATUCCI

MALTSEV (or **Malcev**), ANATOLY IVANOVICH (*b.* Misheronsky, near Moscow, Russia, 27 November 1909; *d.* Novosibirsk, U.S.S.R., 7 July 1967)

The son of a glassblower, Maltsev graduated in 1931 from Moscow University and completed his graduate work there under A. N. Kolmogorov. He received his M.S. in 1937 and the D.S. in 1941 and became professor of mathematics in 1944. He was a corresponding member of the Academy of Sciences of the U.S.S.R. from 1953 and was elected a member in 1958.

From 1932 to 1960 Maltsev taught mathematics at the Ivanovo Pedagogical Institute in Moscow, rising from assistant to head of the department of algebra. He worked at the Mathematical Institute of the Academy in Moscow from 1941 to 1960, when he became head of the department of algebra at the Mathematical Institute of the Siberian branch of the Academy in Novosibirsk as well as head of the chair of algebra and mathematical logic at the University of Novosibirsk. He received the State Prize in 1946 for his work in algebra and, in 1964, the Lenin Prize for his work in the application of mathematical logic to algebra and in the theory of algebraic systems. In 1956 he was named Honored Scientist of the Russian Federation and in 1963 was elected president of the Siberian Mathematical Society.

Maltsev's most important work was in algebra and mathematical logic. In his first publication (1936), which dealt with a general method for obtaining local theorems in mathematical logic, he provided such a theorem for the limited calculus of predicates of arbitrary signature. By means of this theorem an arbitrary set of formulas of this calculus is noncontradictory when—and only when—any finite subset of this set is noncontradictory. In this work the theorem of the extension of infinite models was also proved. Both theorems are important in mathematical logic and in the theory of models, the creation of which Maltsev himself was largely responsible for. His local method enabled him to prove (1941) a series of important theorems of the theory of groups and other algebraic systems. In 1956 he generalized his local theorems to cover many classes of models. Ideas similar to those presented in the last of these works led A. Robinson to formulate his nonstandard analysis, in which actual infinitesimally small and great magnitudes obtained an original substantiation.

Maltsev's most important works in algebra dealt with the theory of Lie groups. He proved (1940, 1943) that for a Lie group to have an exact linear representation, linear representability of the radical of this Lie group and the corresponding factor group constitutes a necessary and sufficient condition. In 1941 he proved that Cartan's theorem of the inclusion of an arbitrary local Lie group into a full Lie group cannot be generalized for local general topological groups. In 1944 he described all semisimple subgroups of simple Lie groups of infinite classes and exceptional classes *G* and *F*, and proved the conjugateness of semisimple factors in Levi's decomposition of Lie groups and algebras.

The following year Maltsev defined the rational submodulus of Lie algebra, characterizing the Lie group by the finite-leaved covering; and he discovered the criteria for a subgroup of a Lie group, corresponding to a given subalgebra of Lie algebra, to be closed. He also proved that maximal compact subgroups of a connected Lie group are conjugate (Cartan's problem) and that a Lie group is homeomorphic to a direct product of such a subgroup by Euclidean space. In 1948 he obtained important results in the theory of nilpotent manifolds, i.e. homogeneous manifolds the fundamental groups of which are nilpotent Lie groups. In 1951 he proved the so-called Maltsev-Kolchin theorem of solvable linear groups and studied properties of solvable groups of integer matrices and new classes of solvable groups. In 1955 he constructed an alternative analogue of Lie groups and a corresponding analogue of Lie algebras that are now called Maltsev algebras. In 1957 he constructed the general theory of free topological algebras as being a generalization of topological groups.

In the last ten years of his life Maltsev obtained important results in the theory of algebraic systems and models and in the synthesis of algebra and mathematical logic, which he described in a series of papers and in the posthumous *Algebraicheskie sistemy* ("Algebraic Systems," 1970). His results in the theory of algorithms are presented in the monograph *Algoritmy i rekursivnye funktsii* ("Algorithms and Recursive Functions," 1965). Maltsev was the author of an important textbook of algebra, *Osnovy lineynoy algebry* ("Foundations of Linear Algebra," 1948), founded the journal *Algebra i logika. Seminar*, and was editor-in-chief of *Sibirskii matematicheskii zhurnal*.

BIBLIOGRAPHY

A bibliography of 96 works follows the obituary of Maltsev by P. S. Aleksandrov *et al.*, in *Uspekhi matematicheskikh nauk*, **23**, no. 3 (1968), 159–170. Works referred to above are "Untersuchungen aus dem Gebiete der mathematischen Logik," in *Matematicheskii sbornik*, **1** (1936), 323–326; "Ob izomorfnom predstavlenii beskonechnykh grupp matritsami" ("On the Isomorphic Representation of Infinite Groups by Means of Matrices"), *ibid.*, **8** (1940), 405–422; "Ob odnom obshchem metode polucheniya lokalnykh teorem teorii grupp" ("On a General Method for Obtaining Local Theorems of the Theory of Groups"), in *Uchenye zapiski Ivanovskogo pedagogicheskogo instituta*, Fiz.-mat. fak., **1**, no. 1 (1941), 3–9; "O lokalnykh i polnykh topologicheskikh gruppakh" ("On Local and Full Topological Groups"), in *Doklady Akademii nauk SSSR*, **32**, no. 9 (1941), 606–608; "O lineyno svyaznykh lokalno zamknutykh gruppakh" ("On Linearly Connected Locally Closed Groups"), *ibid.*, **41**, no. 8 (1943), 108–110; "O poluprostykh podgruppakh grupp Li" ("On Semisimple Subgroups of Lie Groups"), in *Izvestiya Akademii nauk SSSR*, Ser. mat., **8** (1944), 143–174; "On the Theory of the Lie Groups in the Large," in *Matematicheskii sbornik*, **16** (1945), 163–190; **19** (1946), 523–524; *Osnovy lineynoy algebry* ("Foundations of Linear Algebra"; Moscow–Leningrad, 1948; 2nd ed., Moscow, 1956; 3rd ed., Moscow, 1970); "Ob odnom klasse odnorodnykh prostranstv" ("On One Class of Homogenous Spaces"), in *Izvestiya Akademii nauk SSSR*, Ser. mat., **13** (1949), 9–32; "O nekotorykh klassakh beskonechnykh razreshimykh grupp" ("On Certain Classes of Infinite Solvable Groups"), in *Matematicheskii sbornik*, **28** (1951), 567–588; "Analiticheskie lupy" ("Analytical Loops"), *ibid.*, **36** (1955), 569–576; "O predstavleniyakh modeley" ("On Representations of Models"), in *Doklady Akademii nauk SSSR*, **108**, no. 1 (1956), 27–29; "Svobodnye topologicheskie algebry" ("Free Topological Algebras"), in *Izvestiya Akademii nauk SSSR*, Ser. mat., **21** (1957), 171–198; "Modelnye sootvetstviya" ("Model Correspondences"), *ibid.*, **23** (1959), 313–336; "Regulyarnye proizvedenia modeley" ("Regular Products of Models"), *ibid.*, 489–502; "Konstruktivnye algebry" ("Constructive Algebras"), in *Uspekhi matematicheskikh nauk*, **16**, no. 3 (1961), 3–60; *Algoritmy i rekursivnye funktsii* ("Algorithms and Recursive Functions"; Moscow, 1965); and *Algebraicheskie sistemy* ("Algebraic Systems"; Moscow, 1970).

B. A. Rosenfeld

MANNHEIM, VICTOR MAYER AMÉDÉE (*b.* Paris, France, 17 July 1831; *d.* Paris, 11 December 1906)

A follower of the geometric tradition of Poncelet

and Chasles, Amédée Mannheim, like his predecessors, spent most of his professional career associated with the École Polytechnique, which he entered in 1848. In 1850 he went to the École d'Application at Metz. While still a student he invented a type of slide rule, a modified version of which is still in use. After graduation as a lieutenant, he spent several years at various provincial garrisons. In 1859 he was appointed *répétiteur* at the École Polytechnique; in 1863, examiner; and in 1864, professor of descriptive geometry. He attained the rank of colonel in the engineering corps, retiring from the army in 1890 and from his teaching post in 1901. He was a dedicated and popular teacher, strongly devoted to the École Polytechnique, and was one of the founders of the Société Amicale des Anciens Élèves de l'École.

Mannheim worked in many branches of geometry. His primary interest was in projective geometry, and he was influenced by Chasles's work on the polar reciprocal transformation, which he further investigated with respect to metric properties. He applied these studies in his work in kinematic geometry, which he defined as the study of motion, independent of force, time, and any elements outside the moving figure. He also made significant contributions to the theory of surfaces, primarily in regard to Fresnel's wave surfaces. Most of his results can be found in his texts, *Cours de géométrie descriptive de l'École Polytechnique* (1880) and *Principes et développements de la géométrie cinématique* (1894), which, although he was an enthusiast for the synthetic method in geometry, contained much differential geometry, as well as a good summary of that subject. In recognition of his contributions to the field of geometry Mannheim was awarded the Poncelet Prize in 1872.

BIBLIOGRAPHY

I. ORIGINAL WORKS. Mannheim's early works on the polar reciprocal transformation include his *Théorie des polaires réciproques* (Metz, 1851); and *Transformation de propriétés métriques des figures à l'aide de la théorie des polaires réciproques* (Paris, 1857). His work in kinematic geometry is found primarily in *Cours de géométrie descriptive de l'École Polytechnique comprenant les éléments de la géométrie cinématique* (Paris, 1880; 2nd ed. 1886); and *Principes et développements de la géométrie cinématique; ouvrage contenant de nombreuses applications à la théorie des surfaces* (Paris, 1894). A complete list of his works is in Poggendorff, III, 865–866; IV, 952; and V, 801; and in the article by Loria cited below. For a list of his important papers in the theory of surfaces, see G. Loria, *Il passato ed il presente delle principali teorie geometriche*, 2nd ed. (Turin, 1896), 115.

II. SECONDARY LITERATURE. For an account of Mann-heim's life, see C. A. Laisant, "La vie et les travaux d'Amédée Mannheim," in *L'enseignement mathématique*, **9** (1907), 169–179. A much fuller account of his work is G. Loria, "L'opera geometrica di A. Mannheim," in *Rendiconti de Circolo matematico di Palermo*, **26** (1908), 1–63, and "A. Mannheim—Soldier and Mathematician," in *Scripta Mathematica*, **2** (1934), 337–342. Mannheim's works on the wave surface is considered in C. Niven, "On M. Mannheim's Researches on the Wave Surface," in *Quarterly Journal of Pure and Applied Mathematics*, **15** (1878), 242–257.

ELAINE KOPPELMAN

MANSION, PAUL (*b.* Marchin, near Huy, Belgium, 3 June 1844; *d.* Ghent, Belgium, 16 April 1919)

Mansion was a professor at the University of Ghent, member of the Royal Academy of Belgium, and director of the Journal *Mathesis*. He entered the École Normale des Sciences at Ghent in 1862; and by the age of twenty-three he was teaching advanced courses. He held an eminent position in the scientific world of Belgium despite his extreme narrow-mindedness. In 1874 he founded, with Eugène-Charles Catalan and J. Neuberg, the *Nouvelle correspondance mathématique*; this title was chosen in memory of the *Correspondance mathématique et physique*, edited by Garnier and Adolphe Quetelet. Through the efforts of Mansion and Neuberg, who were encouraged by Catalan himself, the *Nouvelle correspondance* was succeeded in 1881 by *Mathesis*. Mansion retired in 1910.

Alphonse Demoulin's notice on Mansion (1929) includes a bibliography of 349 items, some of which were published in important foreign compendia. Several others appeared in German translation. Mansion's own French translations of works by Riemann, Julius Plücker, Clebsch, Dante, and even Cardinal Manning attest to the extent of his interests. Among other subjects, he taught the history of mathematics and of the physical sciences, in which field he wrote in particular on Greek astronomy, Copernicus, Galileo, and Kepler. His desire to justify the positions of Catholic orthodoxy is evident.

BIBLIOGRAPHY

A bibliography of Mansion's works is in the notice by A. Demoulin, in *Annuaire de l'Académie royale de Belgique*, **95** (1929), 77–147. On Mansion's life and work see L. Godeaux, in *Biographie nationale publiée par l'Académie royale de Belgique*, XXX (Brussels, 1959), 540–542; and in *Florilège des sciences en Belgique pendant le 19ᵉ siècle et le début du 20ᵉ siècle* (Brussels, 1968), 129–132.

J. PELSENEER

MANṢŪR IBN ʿALĪ IBN ʿIRĀQ, ABŪ NAṢR (*fl.* Khwarizm [now Kara-Kalpakskaya, A.S.S.R.]; *d.* Ghazna [?] [now Ghazni, Afghanistan], *ca.* 1036)

Abū Naṣr was probably a native of Gīlān (Persia); it is likely that he belonged to the family of Banū ʿIrāq who ruled Khwarizm until it fell to the Maʾmūnī dynasty in A.D. 995. He was a disciple of Abuʾl Wafāʾ al-Būzjānī and the teacher of al-Bīrūnī. Abū Naṣr passed most of his life in the court of the monarchs ʿAlī ibn Maʾmūn and Abuʾl-ʿAbbās Maʾmūn, who extended their patronage to a number of scientists, including al-Bīrūnī and Ibn Sīnā. About 1016, the year in which Abuʾl-ʿAbbās Maʾmūn died, both Abū Naṣr and al-Bīrūnī left Khwarizm and went to the court of Sultan Maḥmūd al-Ghaznawī in Ghazna, where Abū Naṣr spent the rest of his life.

Abū Naṣr's fame is due in large part to his collaboration with al-Bīrūnī. Although this collaboration is generally considered to have begun in about 1008, the year in which al-Bīrūnī returned to Khwarizm from the court of Jurjān (now Kunya-Urgench, Turkmen S.S.R.), there is ample evidence for an earlier date. For example, in his *Al-Āthār al-bāqiya* ("Chronology"), finished in the year 1000, al-Bīrūnī refers to Abū Naṣr as *Ustādhī*—"my master," while Abū Naṣr dedicated his book on the azimuth, written sometime before 998, to his pupil.

This collaboration also presents grave difficulties in assigning the authorship of specific works. A case in point is some twelve works that al-Bīrūnī lists as being written "in my name" (*bismī*), a phrase that has led scholars to consider them to be of his own composition. Nallino has, however, pointed out that *bismī* might also mean "addressed to me" or "dedicated to me"—by Abū Naṣr—and there is considerable evidence in support of this interpretation. For instance, the phrase is used in this sense in both medieval texts (the *Mafātīḥ al-ʿulūm* of Muḥammad ibn Aḥmad al-Khwārizmī of 977) and modern ones of which there is no doubt of the authorship. The incipits and explicits of the works in question make it clear, moreover, that they were written by Abū Naṣr in response to al-Bīrūnī's request for solutions to specific problems that had arisen in the course of his more general researches. Indeed, in some of al-Bīrūnī's own books he mentioned Abū Naṣr by name and stated that his book incorporates the results of some investigations that the older man carried out at his request. Al-Bīrūnī gave Abū Naṣr full credit for his discoveries—as, indeed, he gave full credit to each of his several collaborators, including Abū Sahl al-Masīḥī, a certain Abū ʿAli al-Ḥasan ibn al-Jīlī (otherwise unidentified) and Ibn Sīnā, who wrote answers to philosophical questions submitted to him by al-Bīrūnī.

The extent of the collaboration between Abū Naṣr and al-Bīrūnī may be demonstrated by the latter's work on the determination of the obliquity of the ecliptic. Al-Bīrūnī carried out observations in Khwarizm in 997, and in Ghazna in 1016, 1019, and 1020. Employing the classical method of measuring the meridian height of the sun at the time of the solstices, he computed the angle of inclination as 23°35′. On the other hand, however, al-Bīrūnī became acquainted with a work by Muḥammad ibn al-Ṣabbāḥ, in which the latter described a method for determining the position, ortive amplitude, and maximum declination of the sun. Since al-Bīrūnī's copy was full of apparent errors, he gave it to Abū Naṣr and asked him to correct it and to prepare a critical report of Ibn al-Ṣabbāḥ's techniques.

Abū Naṣr thus came to write his *Risāla fi ʾl-barāhīn ʿalā ʿamal Muḥammad ibn al-Ṣabbāḥ* ("A Treatise on the Demonstration of the Construction Devised by Muḥammad Ibn al-Ṣabbāḥ"), in which he took up Ibn al-Ṣabbāḥ's method in detail and demonstrated that it must be in error to the extent that it depended on the hypothesis of the uniform movement of the sun on the ecliptic. According to Ibn al-Ṣabbāḥ, the ortive amplitude of the sun at solstice (a_t) may be obtained by making three observations of the solar ortive amplitude (a_1, a_2, a_3) at thirty day intervals within a single season of the year. He thus reached the formula:

$$2 \sin a_t = \frac{2 \sin a_2 \sqrt{(2 \sin a_2)^2 - 2 \sin a_1\, 2 \sin a_3}}{\sqrt{(2 \sin a_2)^2 - (\sin a + \sin a_3)^2}}.$$

The same result may also be obtained from only two observations (a_1, a_2) if the distance (d) covered by the sun on the ecliptic over the period between the two observations is known:

$$2 \sin a_t = \frac{R \sqrt{\dfrac{R^2(\sin a_1 + \sin a_2)^2}{\cos^2 \dfrac{d}{2}} - 4 \sin a_1 \sin a_2}}{\sin \dfrac{d}{2}}.$$

The value of a_t is thus extractable in two ways, and the value of the maximum declination can then be discovered by applying the formula of al-Battānī and Ḥabash:

$$\sin \text{ort. ampl.} = \frac{\sin \partial x R}{\cos \varphi}.$$

Al-Bīrūnī then took up Abū Naṣr's clarification of Ibn al-Ṣabbāḥ's work, citing it in his own *Al-Qānūn al-Masʿūdī* and *Taḥdīd*. He remained, however, primarily interested in obtaining the angle of inclination, and simplified Ibn al-Ṣabbāḥ's methods to that end. He thus, within the two formulas, substituted three and two, respectively, observations of the declination of the sun for the three and two observations of solar ortive amplitude. By this method he obtained values for the angle of inclination of 23°25′19″ and 23°24′16″, respectively. These values are clearly at odds with that then commonly held (23°35′) and confirmed by al-Bīrūnī's own observations. Al-Bīrūnī then returned to Abū Naṣr's work, and explained the discrepancy as being due to Ibn al-Ṣabbāḥ's supposition of the uniform motion of the sun on the ecliptic, as well as to the continuous use of sines and square roots.

Abū Naṣr's contributions to trigonometry are more direct. He is one of the three authors (the others being Abu'l Wafāʾ and Abū Maḥmūd al-Khujandī) to whom al-Ṭūsī attributed the discovery of the sine law whereby in a spherical triangle the sines of the sides are in relationship to the sines of the opposite angles as

$$\frac{\sin a}{\sin A} = \frac{\sin b}{\sin B} = \frac{\sin c}{\sin C},$$

or, in a plane triangle, the sides are in relationship to the sines of the opposite angles as

$$\frac{a}{\sin A} = \frac{b}{\sin B} = \frac{c}{\sin C}.$$

The question of which of these three mathematicians was actually the first to discover this law remains unresolved, however. Luckey has convincingly argued against al-Khujandī, pointing out that he was essentially a practical astronomer, unconcerned with theoretical problems. Both Abū Naṣr and Abu'l Wafāʾ, on the other hand, claimed discovery of the law, and while it is impossible to determine who has the better right, two considerations would seem to corroborate Abū Naṣr's contention. First, he employed the law a number of times throughout his astronomical and geometrical writings; whether or not it was his own finding, he nevertheless dealt with it as a significant novelty. Second, Abū Naṣr treated the demonstration of this law in two of his most important works, the *Al-Majisṭī al-Shāhī* ("Almagest of the Shah") and the *Kitāb fī 'l-sumūt* ("Book of the Azimuth"), as well as in two lesser ones, *Risāla fī maʿrifat al-qisiyy al-falakiyya* ("Treatise on the Determination of Spherical Arcs") and *Risāla fī 'l-jawāb ʿan masāʾil handasiyya suʾila ʿanhā* ("Treatise in Which Some Geometrical Questions Addressed to Him are Answered").

The *Al-Majisṭī al-Shāhī* and the *Kitāb fī 'l-sumūt* have both been lost. It is known that the latter was written at the request of al-Bīrūnī, as well as dedicated to him, and that it was concerned with various proce-

dures for calculating the direction of the *qibla*. Abū Naṣr's other significant work, the most complete Arabic version of the *Spherics* of Menelaus, is, however, still extant (although the original Greek text is lost). Of the twenty-two works that are known to have been written by Abū Naṣr, a total of seventeen remain, of which sixteen have been published.

In addition to the books cited above, the remainder of Abū Naṣr's work consisted of short monographs on specific problems of geometry or astronomy. These lesser writings include *Risāla fī ḥall shubha ʿaraḍat fī 'l-thālitha ʿashar min Kitāb al-Uṣūl* ("Treatise in Which a Difficulty in the Thirteenth Book of the *Elements* is Solved"); *Maqāla fī iṣlāḥ shakl min kitāb Mānālāwus fī 'l-kuriyyāt ʿadala fīhi muṣalliḥū hādha 'l-kitāb* ("On the Correction of a Proposition in the *Spherics* of Menelaus, in Which the Emendators of This Book Have Erred"); *Risāla fī ṣanʿat al-asṭurlāb bi 'l-ṭarīq al-ṣināʿī* ("Treatise on the Construction of the Astrolabe in the Artisan's Manner"); *Risāla fī 'l-asṭurlāb al-sarṭānī al-muŷannaḥ fī ḥaqīqatihi bi 'l-ṭarīq al-sināʿi* ("Treatise on the True Winged Crab Astrolabe, According to the Artisan's Method"); and *Faṣl min kitāb fī kuriyyat al-samāʾ* ("A Chapter From a Book on the Sphericity of the Heavens").

BIBLIOGRAPHY

I. Original Works. Abū Naṣr's version of the *Spherics* of Menelaus exists in an excellent critical edition, with German trans., by Max Krause, "Die Sphärik von Menelaos aus Alexandrien in der Verbesserung von Abū Naṣr Manṣūr ibn ʿAlī ibn ʿIrāq. Mit Untersuchungen zur Geschichte des Textes bei den islamischen Mathematikern," in *Abhandlungen der K. Gesellschaft der Wissenschaften zu Göttingen*, Phil.-hist. Kl., no. 17 (Berlin, 1936). Most of the rest of his extant work has been badly edited as *Rasāʾil Abī Naṣr Manṣūr ilā 'l-Bīrūnī*. Dāʾirat al-Maʿārif al-ʿUthmāniyya (Hyderabad, 1948); six of the same treatises are trans. into Spanish in Julio Samsó, *Estudios sobre Abū Naṣr Manṣūr* (Barcelona, 1969).

II. Secondary Literature. On Abū Naṣr and his work, see D. J. Boilot, "L'oeuvre d'al-Beruni: essai bibliographique," in *Mélanges de l'Institut dominicain d'études orientales*, 2 (1955), 161–256; "Bibliographie d'al-Beruni. Corrigenda et addenda," *ibid.*, 3 (1956), 391–396; E. S. Kennedy and H. Sharkas, "Two Medieval Methods for Determining the Obliquity of the Ecliptic," in *Mathematical Teacher*, 55 (1962), 286–290; Julio Samsó, *Estudios sobre Abū Naṣr Manṣūr b. ʿAlī b. ʿIrāq* (Barcelona, 1969); "Contribución a un análisis de la terminología matemático-astronómica de Abū Naṣr Manṣūr b. ʿAlī b. ʿIrāq," in *Pensamiento*, 25 (1969), 235–248; Paul Luckey, "Zur Entstehung der Kugeldreiectsrechnung," in *Deutsche Mathematik*, 5 (1940–1941), 405–446; Muḥammad Shafī, "Abū Naṣr ibn ʿIrāq aur us kā sanah wafāt" ("Abū

Naṣr ibn 'Irāq and the Date of his Death"), in Urdu with English summary, in *60 doğum münasebetyle Zeki Velidi Togan'a armağan. Symbolae in honorem Z. V. Togan* (Istanbul, 1954–1955), 484–492; Heinrich Suter, "Zur Trigonometrie der Araber," in *Bibliotheca Mathematica*, 3rd ser., X (1910), 156–160; and K. Vogel and Max Krause, "Die Sphärik von Menelaus aus Alexandrien in der Verbesserung von Abū Naṣr b. 'Ali ibn 'Irāq," in *Gnomon*, **15** (1939), 343–395.

JULIO SAMSÓ

MARCI OF KRONLAND, JOHANNES MARCUS

(*b*. Lanškroun, Bohemia [now Czechoslovakia], 13 June 1595; *d*. Prague, Bohemia [now Czechoslovakia], 10 April 1667)

Marci, whose father was clerk to an aristocrat, received his early education at the Jesuit college in Jindřichův Hradec, then studied philosophy and theology in Olomouc and, from 1618 on, medicine in Prague. He took the M.D. in 1625, then began to lecture at the Prague Faculty of Medicine. He achieved considerable renown as a physician, becoming physician to the Kingdom of Bohemia and personal attendant to two emperors, Ferdinand III and Leopold I.

Although it is recorded that Marci wished to become a priest and a Jesuit, and although he took a staunchly Catholic position during the forced civil re-Catholicization of Bohemia and Moravia (1625–1626), he nevertheless represented the anti-Jesuit party in the affairs of Prague University. To gain support at the Vatican for his party's purpose, which was to prevent the Jesuits from gaining control of the medical and legal faculties (since they already held the faculties of philosophy and theology), Marci undertook a diplomatic trip to Italy, which had important results in his scientific life. During this trip, which he made in 1639, Marci met Paul Guldin and Athanasius Kircher, with whom he corresponded for a long time, and also read Galileo's *Discorsi*, although he did not meet Galileo.

Marci's political activities did not injure his career. He was professor of medicine at Prague University from about 1620 to 1660. In 1648 he took active part in defending the city against the Swedes; he was knighted for merit in 1654. He retained his academic position even after the Prague Charles University merged with the Jesuit institution to become Charles-Ferdinand University, a unification that greatly favored Jesuit pretensions. Marci became rector of the university in 1662; according to Jesuit sources he was admitted to the Society shortly before his death.

As a scientist, Marci worked in considerable iso-

lation. The Catholic Counter-Reformation, exploited by the Hapsburg rulers, had gradually strangled scientific life in Bohemia, and access to the works of foreign scientists was severely limited. Marci's knowledge of the researches of his contemporaries was therefore at best random, and his own work shows evidences of the ideological pressures of his own Prague environment. Marci studied many scientific subjects, including astronomy and mathematics; in the latter he was probably stimulated by the work of the Jesuit Grégoire de Saint-Vincent, who taught at Prague.

Marci's most important work was, however, accomplished in medicine and physics. His 1639 book, *De proportione motus*, contained his theory of the collision of bodies (particularly elastic bodies) and gave an account of the experiments whereby he reached it. Although these experiments are described precisely, Marci was unable to formulate general quantitative laws from them, since his results were not drawn from exact measurements of either of the sizes and weights of the spheres that he employed or of the direction and velocity of their motion. Rather, he was content with simple comparisons of the properties that he investigated, characterizing them as being "smaller," "bigger," or "the same" as each other; his allegations of their proportionalities are thus unproven. Some of his concepts, too (for example that of impulse), lack exact definition, but despite these shortcomings, his observations and conclusions are generally right. He was able to distinguish different qualities of spheres and to state the concepts of solid bodies and of quantity of motion.

The section on the collision of bodies in *De proportione motus* is only one of those in which Marci dealt in problems of mechanics. He also stated the correct relationship between the duration of the oscillation of a pendulum and its length and proposed using a pendulum for measuring short periods of time (for example, for taking the pulse of a patient). He further described the properties of free fall. Here the question of the influence on Marci of Galileo's *Discorsi* must arise. The *Discorsi* was published a year before *De proportione motus*, and Marci certainly read it before publishing his own book, but the exact extent to which he drew upon it remains unknown. Certainly Marci had less skill than Galileo in reducing mechanics to mathematical forms; but if, in later years, he chose to emphasize the divergence of his opinions from Galileo's, he may well have been influenced by the attitude of the church toward the latter's writings.

Marci also carried out research in optics, setting down most of his results in *Thaumantias liber de arcu coelesti* (1648). In his optical experiments, designed to explain the phenomenon of the rainbow, Marci placed himself in the line of such Bohemian and Moravian investigators as Kepler, Christophe Scheiner, Baltasar Konrád, and Melchior Haněl. In his experiments on the decomposition of white light, for which he employed prisms, Marci described the spectral colors and recorded that each color corresponded to a specific refraction angle. He also stated that the color of a ray is constant when it is again refracted through another prism (*Thaumantias liber de arcu coelesti*, pp. 99–100). He did not mention the reconstitution of the spectrum into white light (a result that is first to be found in the work of Newton), although he did study the "mixture" of colored rays. He also made inconclusive experiments on light phenomena on thin films. In general, Marci's optical works are not successful in speculation, since his attempts to deduce the properties of light and to explain the causes of observed phenomena on the basis of his optical knowledge become entangled in the philosophical notions of his time.

Marci's medical works also become involved in philosophical as well as theoretical problems. It is interesting to note that he devoted particular attention to questions of what would now be termed neurology, psychology, and psychophysiology, in treatises that have not yet been fully evaluated. His work on epilepsy is, however, worthy of special note, since in it Marci tried to adopt a purely medical approach to the disease and to analyze critically both previous descriptions of epileptic fits and existing theories of their origin. From these data he drew, in obscure and symbolic terms, the conclusion that epilepsy is, in fact, a nervous disease; this result is in keeping with his theories of perception, memory, and imagination, in which his method was observational and his guiding principle that later formulated by Locke as "nihil est in intellectu quod non prius fuerit in sensu."

It is thus apparent that philosophical considerations figured importantly in Marci's scientific work; it is perhaps less obvious that his philosophy was in turn colored by developments in the natural sciences. Marci's philosophy represented a sometimes incoherent fusion of Aristotelian and Platonic ideas with Catholic mysticism. From these elements he derived a speculative pantheism, based on a "world soul"—uniting the macrocosmos and the microcosmos—and a "virtus plastica sive seminalis," or an "active idea." He attempted to confirm his mystical beliefs by means of then newly established and often subjectively interpreted tenets of natural science; he further called upon these new discoveries to answer such philosophical questions as the relationship between mind and body and to elaborate a general view of the world and nature. (In so doing he drew close to the later systems of *Naturphilosophie*.) Marci's philosophical ideas probably had some influence on such Prague philosophers as Hirnheim (and perhaps even on the young Spinoza), while some of his ideas were taken up by the Cambridge Platonists, among them Ralph Cudworth and, in particular, Francis Glisson.

BIBLIOGRAPHY

Marci's principal works are *De proportione motus figurarum rectilinearum et circuli quadratura ex motu* (Prague, 1639), repr. in *Acta historiae rerum naturalium necnon technicarum*, special issue 3 (1967), 131–258; *Thaumantias liber de arcu coelesti deque colorum apparentium natura, ortu et causis, in quo pellucidi opticae fontes a sua scaturigine, ab his vero colorigeni rivi derivantur* (Prague, 1648; repr. 1968); *Lithurgia mentis seu disceptatio medico-philosophica et optica de natura epilepsiae* ... (Regensburg, 1678); and *Ortho-Sophia seu philosophia impulsus universalis* (Prague, 1683).

Bibliographies of writings by and about Marci are Dagmar Ledrerová, "Bibliographie de Johannes Marcus Marci," in *Acta historiae rerum naturalium necnon technicarum*, special issue 3 (1967), 39–50; and "Bibliografie Jana Marka Marci," in *Zprávy Čs. společnosti pro dějiny věd a techniky*, nos. 9–10 (1968), 107–119.

Luboš Nový

MARKOV, ANDREI ANDREEVICH (*b*. Ryazan, Russia, 14 June 1856; *d*. Petrograd [now Leningrad], U.S.S.R., 20 May 1922)

Markov's father, Andrei Grigorievich Markov, a member of the gentry, served in St. Petersburg in the Forestry Department and managed a private estate. His mother, Nadezhda Petrovna, was the daughter of a state employee. Markov was in poor health and used crutches until he was ten years old. He early manifested a talent for mathematics in high school but was not diligent in other courses. In 1874 Markov entered the mathematics department of St. Petersburg University and enrolled in a seminar for superior students, led by A. N. Korkin and E. I. Zolotarev. He had met them in his high school days after presenting a paper on integration of linear differential equations (which contained results already known). He also attended lectures by the head of the St. Petersburg mathematical school, P. L. Chebyshev, and afterward became a consistent follower of his ideas.

In 1878 Markov graduated from the university with a gold medal for his thesis, "Ob integrirovanii differentsialnykh uravnenii pri pomoshchi neprryvnykh drobei" ("On the Integration of Differential Equations by Means of Continued Fractions") and remained at the university to prepare for a professorship. In 1880 he defended his master's thesis, "O binarnykh kvadratichnykh formakh polozhitelnogo opredelitelia" ("On the Binary Quadratic Forms With Positive Determinant"; *Izbrannye trudy*, pp. 9–83), and began teaching in the university as a docent. In 1884 he defended his doctoral dissertation, devoted to continued fractions and the problem of moments. In 1883 he married Maria Ivanovna Valvatyeva, the daughter of the proprietress of the estate managed by his father. They had been childhood friends, and Markov had helped her to learn mathematics. Later he proposed to her, but her mother agreed to the marriage only after Markov strengthened his social position.

For twenty-five years Markov combined research with intensive teaching at St. Petersburg University. In 1886 he was named extraordinary professor and in 1893, full professor. In this period he studied many questions: number theory, continued fractions, functions least deviating from zero, approximate quadrature formulas, integration in elementary functions, the problem of moments, probability theory, and differential equations. His lectures were distinguished by an irreproachable strictness of argument, and he developed in his students that mathematical cast of mind that takes nothing for granted. He included in his courses many recent results of investigations, while often omitting traditional questions. The lectures were difficult, and only serious students could understand them. He stated his opinions in a peremptory manner and was extremely exacting with his associates. During his lectures he did not bother about the order of equations on the blackboard, nor about his personal appearance. He was also a faculty adviser for a student mathematical circle. Nominated by Chebyshev, Markov was elected in 1886 an adjunct of the St. Petersburg Academy of Sciences; in 1890 he became an extraordinary academician and in 1896 an ordinary academician. In 1905, after twenty-five years of teaching, Markov retired to make room for younger mathematicians. He was named professor emeritus, but still taught the probability course at the university, by his right as an academician. At this time his scientific interests concentrated on probability theory and in particular on the chains later named for him.

A man of firm opinions, Markov participated in the liberal movement in Russia at the beginning of the twentieth century. In a series of caustic letters to academic and state authorities, he protested against the overruling, at the czar's order, of the election in 1902 of Maxim Gorky to the St. Petersburg Academy, he refused to receive decorations (1903), and he repudiated his membership in the electorate after the illegal dissolution of the Second State Duma by the government (1907). The authorities preferred not to respond to these declarations, considering them the extravagances of an academician. In 1913, when officials pompously celebrated the three-hundredth anniversary of the House of Romanov, Markov organized a celebration of the two-hundredth anniversary of the law of large numbers (in 1713 Jakob I Bernoulli's *Ars conjectandi* was posthumously published).

In September 1917 Markov asked the Academy to send him to the interior of Russia, and he spent the famine winter in Zaraisk, a little country town. There he voluntarily taught mathematics in a secondary school without pay. Soon after his return to Petrograd, his health declined sharply and he had an eye operation. In 1921 he continued lecturing, scarcely able to stand. He died after several months of intense suffering.

Markov belonged to Chebyshev's scientific school and, more than others, was faithful to the creed and the principles of his master. He inherited from Chebyshev an interest in concrete problems; a simplicity of mathematical procedures; a need to solve problems effectively, whether simple or algorithmic; and a desire to obtain exact limits for asymptotic results. These views coexisted with an underestimation of the role of some new general concepts in contemporary mathematics, namely of the axiomatic method and of the theory of functions of complex variables. Characteristic of Markov was the adherence to a chosen method of investigation and maintenance of his own view of what is valuable in science. He once said, "Mathematics is that which Gauss, Chebyshev, Lyapunov, Steklov, and I study" (N. M. Guenter, "O pedagogicheskoi deyatelnosti A. A. Markov," p. 37).

The principal aim of most of Markov's works in number theory and function theory was to evaluate the exact upper or lower bounds for various quantities (quadratic forms, integrals, derivatives). In probability theory it was at first to apply the bounds for integrals to the proof of the central limit theorem outlined by Chebyshev; later it was to discover new phenomena satisfying this theorem. Markov's work in various branches of mathematics is also united by systematic use of Chebyshev's favorite method of continued fractions, which became the principal instrument in Markov's investigations.

Markov's work in number theory was devoted mostly to the problem of arithmetical minima of indefinite quadratic forms studied previously in Russia by Korkin and Zolotarev (the topic goes back to Gauss and Hermite). These two authors had shown that if one excludes the form $f(x, y) = x^2 - xy - y^2$ (and the forms equivalent to it) for which $\min |f| = \sqrt{\frac{1}{5}d}$, then for the remaining binary forms $f(x, y) = ax^2 + 2bxy + cy^2$ with $d = b^2 - ac > 0$, one has $\min |f| \leqslant \sqrt{\frac{1}{2}d}$. By means of continued fractions Markov showed in his master's thesis (*Izbrannye trudy*, pp. 9–83) that 4/5 and 1/2 are the first two terms of an infinite decreasing sequence $\{N_k\}$ converging to 4/9, such that (1) for every N_k there exists a finite number of nonequivalent binary forms whose minimum is equal to $\sqrt{N_k d}$ and (2) if the minimum of any indefinite binary form is more than $\sqrt{\frac{4}{9}d}$, then it is equal to one of the values of $\sqrt{N_k d}$. To the limiting value $\sqrt{\frac{4}{9}d}$ there correspond infinitely many nonequivalent forms. Following the traditions of the Petersburg mathematical school, Markov also computed the first twenty numbers of $\{N_k\}$ and the forms corresponding to them. In 1901–1909 he returned to the problem of extrema of indefinite quadratic forms. He found the first four extremal forms of three variables (one of them was known to Korkin) and two extremal forms of four variables, and published a long list of ternary forms with $d \leqslant 50$. Markov's works on indefinite forms were continued both in the Soviet Union and in the West. Another problem of number theory was considered by Markov in his paper "Sur les nombres entiers dépendents d'une racine cubique d'un nombre entier ordinaire" (*Izbrannye trudy*, pp. 85–133). Following Zolotarev's ideas, Markov here obtained the final result for decomposition into ideal prime factors in the field generated by $\sqrt[3]{A}$ and calculated the units of these fields for all $A \leqslant 70$.

The next area of Markov's work concerned the evaluation of limits of functions, integrals, and derivatives. The problem of moments was the most notable among these topics. From a work of J. Bienaymé presented to the Paris Academy of Sciences in 1833 (republished in Liouville's *Journal de mathématiques pures et appliquées* in 1867), Chebyshev borrowed the problem of finding the upper and lower bounds of an integral

$$(1) \qquad \int_a^x f(x)\, dx$$

of a nonnegative function f with given values of its moments

$$(2) \quad m_k = \int_A^B x^k f(x)\, dx \qquad (k = 0, 1, \cdots, N)$$

and the idea of applying the solution of this problem of moments to prove limit laws in probability theory. In 1874 Chebyshev published, without proofs, inequalities providing upper and lower bounds for integral (1) for some special values of a and $x(A < a < x < B)$. These bounds were expressed through the convergents of the continued fraction into which the series $\sum m_k/Z^{k+1}$ formally decomposes. The proofs of Chebyshev's inequalities appeared in 1884 in Markov's memoir "Démonstration de certaines inégalités de M. Tchebycheff" (*Izbrannye trudy po teorii nepreryvnykh drovei . . .*, pp. 15–24). The same inequalities with the same proofs were published at almost the same time by the Dutch mathematician Stieltjes. Markov claimed priority, to which Stieltjes replied that he could not have known of Markov's paper and that Chebyshev's work had indeed escaped his attention. Later Markov and Stieltjes studied the problem of moments largely side by side and sometimes one would find new proofs of the other's already published results. Both used continued fractions in their investigations and developed their theory further; but a difference in their methodological approaches manifested itself: Markov was mostly interested in the case of finite numbers of given moments and he studied the problem entirely within the limits of classical calculus; Stieltjes paid more attention to the problem of given infinite sequences of moments, and, seeking the most adequate formulation of the problem, introduced a generalization of the classical integral—the so-called Stieltjes integral.

In his doctoral dissertation Markov solved the question of the upper and lower bounds of integral (1) in the case when the first N moments are known. In subsequent papers he generalized the problem by allowing the appearance of an additional factor $\Omega(x)$ under integral (1); allowing, instead of power moments (2), moments relative to arbitrary functions $\lambda_k(x)$; and substituting the condition $c \leqslant f(x) \leqslant C$ for $f(x) \geqslant 0$. In other papers he investigated the distribution of the roots of the denominators of the convergents of the continued fraction mentioned above and the convergence of this fraction. The last question is closely related to the uniqueness of the solution of the Stieltjes problem of moments (finding a function, given its infinite sequence of power moments). In 1895, in his memoir "Deux démonstrations de la convergence de certaines fractions continues" (*Izbrannye trudy po teorii nepreryvnykh drovei . . .*, pp. 106–119), Markov obtained the following sufficient condition for the convergence, and therefore for the uniqueness of the Stieltjes problem, of functions defined on $[0, \infty)$: $\varlimsup_{k \to \infty} \sqrt[k]{m_k} < \infty$. Further results were obtained by O. Perron, H. Hamburger, F. Riesz, and T. G. Carleman.

Markov solved in 1889 another problem on extremal values which arose from the needs of chemistry in "Ob odnom voprose D. I. Mendeleeva" ("On a Question of D. I. Mendeleev"; *Izbrannye trudy po teorii nepreryvnykh drovei . . .*, pp. 51–75). Here Markov found the maximum possible value of the derivative $f'(z)$ of a polynomial $f(z)$ of degree $\leqslant n$ on an interval [a, b], provided that $|f(z)| \leqslant L$ on [a, b]. (This maximum value is equal to $2n^2L/(b - a)$.) Markov's result was generalized in 1892 by his younger brother Vladimir (who died five years afterward), and it was later extended for other cases by S. N. Bernstein and N. I. Akhiezer. Markov also worked on some other, practical extremal problems, namely the mapping of a part of a surface of revolution onto a plane with minimal deformations and the joining of two straight lines with a smooth curve having minimal curvature. The question of Mendeleev can be reformulated as a question about the maximum deviation of the polynomial $f(z)$ from zero, and it is therefore closely related to Chebyshev's theory of polynomials deviating least from zero and to some other topics connected with this theory, such as orthogonal polynomials (particularly Hermite and Legendre polynomials and the distribution of their roots), interpolation, and approximate quadrature formulas.

Markov obtained new results in all these areas; but unlike Chebyshev, who also studied quadrature formulas, Markov found in his formulas the expression of the remainder term. For example, in his doctoral dissertation he derived the remainder term of a quadrature formula originating with Gauss. Among other topics related to approximation calculus, Markov considered summation and improving the convergence of series. Evidence of Markov's liking for computation are his tables of the integral of probabilities calculated to eleven decimal places. Markov paid much attention to interpolation, summation, transformations of series, approximate calculation of integrals, and calculation of tables in his *Ischislenie konechnykh raznostei* ("Calculus of Finite Differences"). The difference equations themselves occupy a modest place in this book, which contains characteristic connections with the work of Briggs, Gauss, and Euler and many carefully calculated examples. Markov also obtained some results in the theory of differential equations—on Lamé's equation and the equation of the hypergeometric series—partly overlapping results of Felix Klein, and results concerning the possibility of expressing integrals in terms of elementary functions.

Markov's work in probability theory produced the greatest effect on the development of science. The basic achievements in probability theory by the middle of the nineteenth century were the law of large numbers, presented in its simplest version by Jakob I Bernoulli, and the central limit theorem (as it is now called) of de Moivre and Laplace. Satisfactory proofs under sufficiently wide assumptions had not been found, however, nor had the limits of their applicability. Through their closely interrelated works on these two laws Chebyshev, Markov, and Lyapunov created

the foundation for the modernization of probability theory. In 1867 Chebyshev had found an elementary proof of the law of large numbers and turned to demonstrating the central limit theorem, using the solution of the problem of moments. The Bienaymé–Chebyshev problem mentioned above, translated into probability language, becomes a problem about the exact limits for the distribution function $F_\xi(x)$ of a random variable ξ with N given first moments $m_k = E\xi^k$. Let $\xi_1, \xi_2, \cdots, \xi_n, \cdots$ be a sequence of independent random variables with zero means (the case of nonzero $E\xi_n$ can be easily reduced to the considered one). According to Chebyshev's approach, one must show (a) that for every k the kth moment m_k of the normalized sum

$$\zeta_n = \frac{\xi_1 + \cdots + \xi_n}{\mathrm{var}(\xi_1 + \cdots + \xi_n)}$$

tends to the corresponding moment μ_k of the standard Gaussian distribution

$$\Phi(x) = \frac{1}{\sqrt{2\pi}} \int_{-\infty}^{x} e^{-\frac{y^2}{2}} \, dy$$

if $n \to \infty$, and (b) that if $m_k \to \mu_k$ for all k, then $F_{\zeta_n}(x) \to \Phi(x)$. When Markov published (1884) the proofs of Chebyshev's inequalities concerning the moments, Chebyshev began to work faster. In 1886 he showed that if $m_k = \mu_k$, then $F(x) = \Phi(x)$ (for him, but not for Markov, it was equivalent to assertion [b]); and in 1887 he published a demonstration of point (a) based on incorrect manipulations with divergent series.

Markov decided to turn Chebyshev's argument into a correct one and fulfilled this aim in 1898 in the paper "Sur les racines de l'équation $e^{x^2}(d^n e^{-x^2}/dx^n) = 0$" (*Izbrannye trudy po teorii nepreryvnykh drovei* ..., pp. 231–243; *Izbrannye trudy*, pp. 253–269) and in his letters to Professor A. V. Vassilyev at Kazan University, entitled "Zakon bolshikh chisel i sposob naimenshikh kvadratov" ("The Law of Large Numbers and the Method of Least Squares"; *Izbrannye trudy*, pp. 231–251). In the first of his letters Markov defined his aim thus:

The theorem which Chebyshev is proving ... has been regarded as true for a long time, but is established by an extremely inaccurate procedure. I do not say proved because I do not recognize inaccurate proofs.... The known derivation of the theorem is inaccurate but simple. The derivation by Chebyshev on the contrary is very complicated, for it is based on preliminary investigations. ... Therefore the question arises as to whether Chebyshev's derivation differs from the previous one only by its intricacy but is analogous to it in essentials, or whether one can make this derivation accurate. Your essay on Chebyshev's works strengthened my long-standing desire to simplify and at the same time to make quite accurate Chebyshev's analysis" [*Izbrannye trudy*, p. 231].

In his letters to Vassilyev, Markov established an arithmetical proof of convergence $m_k \to \mu_k$ (assertion [a]) under the following conditions: (1) for every k the sequence $E\xi_1^k, E\xi_2^k, \cdots$ is bounded and (2) $\text{var}(\xi_1 + \cdots + \xi_n) \geqslant cn$ for all n and some fixed $c > 0$. The corresponding calculation based on the expansion of the polynomial $(x_1 + \cdots + x_n)^k$ is maintained in all subsequent works by Markov on the limit theorem. In the article "Sur les racines ..." Markov proved that $F(x) \to \Phi(x)$ if $m_k \to \mu_k$ (assertion [b]) by means of further analysis of Chebyshev's inequalities and continued fractions. He showed by examples that assumption (2), the need for which was unnoticed by Chebyshev, cannot be omitted.

In 1900 Markov published *Ischislenie veroyatnostei* ("Probability Calculus"). This book played an important role in modernizing probability theory. Characteristic features of the book are the inclusion of recent results obtained by Markov, rigorous proofs, elaborate references to classical works of the eighteenth century which for Markov had contemporary as well as historical importance, many numerical examples, and a polemical tone (Markov never missed an opportunity to mention an incorrectly solved example from another author and to correct the error).

But the triumph of the method of moments lasted only a short time. In 1901 Lyapunov, who was less influenced by their master, Chebyshev, and prized more highly the "transcendental" means (in Chebyshev's words) of the complex variable, played on Markov what he termed "a great dirty trick" (V. A. Steklov, "A. A. Markov," p. 178). Lyapunov discovered a new way to obtain and prove the limit theorems —the method of characteristic functions. The principal idea of this much more flexible method consists in assigning to the distribution of a random variable ξ not the sequence of moments $\{m_k\}$ but the characteristic function $\varphi(t) = Ee^{it\xi}$ and deducing the convergence of distributions from convergence of characteristic functions. Lyapunov proved the central limit theorem (for independent summands with zero means) by his method under the conditions that (1) all moments $d_n = E\,|\,\xi_n\,|^{2+\delta}$ are finite for some $\delta > 0$, and

$$(2) \qquad \lim_{n\to\infty} \frac{[\text{var}(\xi_1 + \cdots + \xi_n)]^{2+\delta}}{(d_1 + \cdots + d_n)^2} = \infty,$$

which are near to necessary and sufficient ones.

Although the second conditions of Markov and Lyapunov are of a similar character (both require rapid growth of the variance of the sum), the first condition of Lyapunov is incomparably wider than Chebyshev-Markov's, because it does not require even the existence of moments of the third and subsequent orders.

Markov struggled for eight years to rehabilitate the method of moments and was at last successful. In the memoir "Teorema o predele veroyatnosti dlya sluchaev akademika A. M. Lyapunova" ("Theorem About the Limit of Probability for the Cases of Academician A. M. Lyapunov"; *Izbrannye trudy*, pp. 319–337), included in the third edition of his *Ischislenie veroyatnostei*, Markov proved Lyapunov's result by using the new procedure of truncating the distributions, thus permitting one to reduce the general case to the case of bounded moments of every order. This procedure is still a useful device, but the method of moments could not stand the competition of the simpler and more universal method of characteristic functions. Also in the third edition of *Ischislenie veroyatnostei*, Markov showed, by means of truncating, that the law of large numbers is true for a sequence $\xi_1, \xi_2, \cdots, \xi_n, \cdots$ of independent random variables if for any $p > 1$ the moments $E\,|\,\xi_n\,|^p$ are bounded. (Chebyshev had proved the case $p = 2$.) Markov also deduced here the convergence of distributions from the convergence of moments for the cases when the limiting distribution is not Gaussian but has the density $Ae^{-x^2}\,|\,x\,|^\nu$ or $Ae^{-x}x^\delta$ $(x \geqslant 0)$. (The theorem was demonstrated for other continuous limiting distributions in 1920 by M. Pólya.)

In his efforts to establish the limiting laws of probability in the most general situation and to enlarge the applications of the method of moments, Markov began a systematic study of sequences of mutually dependent variables, and selected from among them an important class later named for him. A sequence $\{\xi_n\}$ of random variables (or random phenomena of some other kind) is called a Markov chain if, given the value of the present variable ξ_n, the future ξ_{n+1} becomes independent of the past $\xi_1, \xi_2, \cdots, \xi_{n-1}$. If the conditional distribution of ξ_{n+1} given ξ_n (defined by transition probabilities at time n) does not depend on n, then the chain is called homogeneous. The possible values of ξ_n are the states of the chain. Such chains appeared for the first time in 1906 in Markov's paper "Rasprostranenie zakona bolshikh chisel na velichiny, zavisyashchie drug ot druga" ("The Extension of the Law of Large Numbers on Mutually Dependent Variables"; *Izbrannye trudy*, pp. 339–361). Markov started with the statement that if the variance of the sum $(\xi_1 + \cdots + \xi_n)$ grows more slowly than n^2, then the law of large numbers is true for the sequence $\{\xi_n\}$, no matter how the random variables depend on each other. He also gave examples of dependent variables satisfying this condition, among them a homogeneous chain with a finite number of states. Markov obtained the necessary estimation of the variance from the convergence as $n \to \infty$ of the distribution of ξ_n to some final distribution independent of the values of ξ_1 (the "ergodic" property of the chain).

In his next paper, "Issledovanie zamechatelnogo sluchaya zavisimykh ispytanii" ("Investigation of a Remarkable Case of Dependent Trials"; in *Izvestiya Peterburgskoi akademii nauk*, 6th ser., **1**, no. 3 [1907], 61–80), Markov proved the central limit theorem for the sums $\xi_1 + \cdots + \xi_n$, where $\{\xi_n\}$ is a homogeneous chain with two states, 0 and 1. In 1908, in the article "Rasprostrancnie predelnykh theorem ischislenia veroyatnostei na summu velichin, svyazannykh v tsep" ("The Extension of the Limit Theorems of Probability Calculus to Sums of Variables Connected in a Chain"; *Izbrannye trudy*, pp. 365–397), he generalized this result to arbitrary homogeneous chains with finite numbers of states, whose transition probabilities satisfy some restrictions. The proof, as in all of Markov's works, was obtained by the method of moments. In "Issledovanie obshchego sluchaya ispytanii svyazannykh v tsep" ("Investigation of the General Case of Trials Connected in a Chain"; *Izbrannye trudy* [1910], pp. 467–507), Markov demonstrated the central limit theorem for nonhomogeneous chains with two states under the condition that all four transition probabilities remain in a fixed interval (c_1, c_2) $(0 < c_1 < c_2 < 1)$. In other articles, published in 1911–1912, he studied various generalizations of his chains (compound chains where ξ_n depends on several previous variables, so-called Markov-Bruns chains, partly observed chains) and deduced for them the central limit theorem under some restrictions.

Markov arrived at his chains starting from the internal needs of probability theory, and he never wrote about their applications to physical science. For him the only real examples of the chains were literary texts, where the two states denoted the vowels and the consonants (in order to illustrate his results he statistically worked up the alternation of vowels and consonants in Pushkin's *Eugene Onegin* (*Ischislenie veroyatnostei*, 4th ed., pp. 566–577). Nevertheless, the mathematical scheme offered by Markov and extended later to families of random variables $\{\xi_t\}$ depending on continuous time t (which are called Markov processes, as suggested by Khinchin) has proved very fruitful and has found many applications. The development of molecular and statistical physics, quantum theory, and genetics showed that a deterministic approach is

insufficient in natural sciences, and forced physicists to turn to probabilistic concepts. Through this evolution of scientific views, the Markov principle of statistical independence of future from past if the present is known, appeared to be the necessary probabilistic generalization of Huygens' principle of "absence of after effect." The far-reaching importance of such a generalization is shown by the fact that although Markov was the first to study the chains as a new, independent mathematical object, a number of random phenomena providing examples of Markov chains or processes were considered by other scientists before his work or concurrently with it. In 1889 the biologist Francis Galton studied the problem of survival of a family by means of a model reducing to a Markov chain with a denumerable number of states. An example of a Markov chain was considered in 1907 by Paul and T. Ehrenfest as a model of diffusion. In 1912 Poincaré, in the second edition of his *Calcul des probabilités*, in connection with the problem of card shuffling, proved the ergodic property for a chain defined on a permutation group and mentioned the possibility of an analogous approach to problems of statistical physics. An important example of a continuous Markov process was studied on a heuristic level in 1900–1901 by L. Bachelier in the theory of speculation. The same process appeared in 1905–1907 in works of Einstein and M. Smoluchowski on Brownian motion.

Markov's studies on chains were continued by S. N. Bernstein, M. Fréchet, V. I. Romanovsky, A. N. Kolmogorov, W. Doeblin, and many others. The first rigorous treatment of a continuous Markov process, the process of Brownian motion, was provided in 1923 by Wiener. The foundations of the general theory of Markov processes were laid down in the 1930's by Kolmogorov. The modern aspect of the theory of Markov processes, which became an intensively developing autonomous branch of mathematics, resulted from work by W. Feller, P. Lévy, J. Doob, E. B. Dynkin, K. Ito, and other contemporary probabilists.

Markov also studied other topics in probability: the method of least squares, the coefficient of variance, and some urn schemes.

BIBLIOGRAPHY

I. ORIGINAL WORKS. The most significant of Markov's papers are republished in *Izbrannye trudy po teorii nepreryvnykh drovei . . .* and *Izbrannye trudy*, with modern commentaries; the latter contains a complete bibliography of original and secondary works to 1951. The earlier collection of his writings is *Izbrannye trudy po teorii nepreryvnykh drovei i teorii funktsii naimenee uklonyaiushchikhsya ot nulya*, N. I. Akhiezer, ed. ("Selected Works on Continued

Fractions Theory and Theory of Functions Least Deviating From Zero"; Moscow, 1948), with comments by the ed. One of the memoirs was translated into English: "Functions Generated by Developing Power Series in Continued Fractions," in *Duke Mathematical Journal*, **7** (1940), 85–96. The later collection is *Izbrannye trudy. Teoria chisel. Teoria veroyatnostei*, Y. V. Linnik, ed. ("Selected Works. Number Theory. Probability Theory"; Moscow–Leningrad, 1951), which contains an essay on the papers in the volume and comments by the editor, and N. A. Sapogov, O. V. Sarmanov, and V. N. Timofeev; the most detailed biography of Markov, by his son A. A. Markov; and a full bibliography.

Individual works by Markov are *O nekotorykh prilozheniakh algebraicheskikh nepreryvnykh drobei* ("On Some Applications of Algebraic Continued Fractions"; St. Petersburg, 1884), his doctoral dissertation; *Tables des valeurs de l'intégrale $\int_x^\infty e^{-t^2}\, dt$* (St. Petersburg, 1888); *Ischislenie konechnykh raznostei* ("Differential Calculus"), 2 vols. (St. Petersburg, 1889–1891; 2nd ed., Odessa, 1910), also translated into German as *Differenzenrechnung* (Leipzig, 1896); and *Ischislenie veroyatnostei* ("Probability Calculus"; St. Petersburg, 1900; 2nd ed., 1908; 3rd ed., 1913; 4th ed., Moscow, 1924), posthumous 4th ed. with biographical note by A. S. Bezikovich, also translated into German as *Wahrscheinlichkeitsrechnung* (Leipzig–Berlin, 1912).

II. SECONDARY LITERATURE. Besides the biography in *Izbrannye trudy*, there is basic information in V. A. Steklov, "Andrei Andreevich Markov," in *Izvestiya Rossiiskoi akademii nauk*, **16** (1922), 169–184. See also *ibid.*, **17** (1923), 19–52; Y. V. Uspensky, "Ocherk nauchnoi deyatelnosti A. A. Markova" ("An Essay on the Scientific Work of A. A. Markov"); N. M. Guenter, "O pedagogicheskoi deyatelnosti A. A. Markova" ("On the Pedagogical Activity of A. A. Markov"); and A. Bezikovich, "Raboty A. A. Markova po teorii veroyatnostei" ("Markov's Works in Probability").

Various aspects of Markov's work are discussed in *Nauchnoe nasledie P. L. Chebysheva* ("The Scientific Heritage of P. L. Chebyshev"), I (Moscow–Leningrad, 1945), which compares Chebyshev's results in various fields with those of Markov, Lyapunov, and their followers in papers by N. I. Akhiezer (pp. 22–39), S. N. Bernstein (pp. 53–66), and V. L. Goncharov (pp. 154–155); and B. N. Delone, *Peterburgskaya shkola teorii chisel* ("The Petersburg School of Number Theory"; Moscow–Leningrad, 1947), which has a detailed exposition of Markov's master's thesis and a summary of further development of associated topics, pp. 141–193.

General surveys of Markov's life and work include B. V. Gnedenko, *Ocherki po istorii matematiki v Rossii* ("Essays on the History of Mathematics in Russia"; Moscow, 1946), pp. 125–133; *Istoria otechestvennoi matematiki* ("History of Russian Mathematics"), II (Kiev, 1967), with an essay on Markov by I. B. Pogrebyssky, pp. 328–340; and A. P. Youschkevitch, *Istoria matematiki v Rossii do 1917 goda* ("History of Mathematics in Russia Until 1917"; Moscow, 1968), pp. 357–363, 395–403.

Post-Markov development of the theory of his chains is discussed by M. Fréchet, *Théorie des événements en chaine dans le cas d'un nombre fini d'états possible*, in *Recherches théoriques modernes sur le calcul des probabilités*, II (Paris, 1938); J. G. Kemeny and J. L. Snell, *Finite Markov Chains* (Princeton, 1960); and V. I. Romanovski, *Diskretnye tsepi Markova* ("Discrete Markov Chains"; Moscow, 1949).

An introduction to the modern theory of Markov processes is M. Loève, *Probability Theory* (Princeton, 1955), ch. 12.

ALEXANDER A. YOUSCHKEVITCH

MARTIANUS CAPELLA (*b.* Carthage; *fl.* Carthage, *ca.* A.D. 365–440)

Martianus may have been a secondary school teacher or a rhetorician, and he appears to have pleaded cases as a *rhetor* or advocate. He was the author of *De nuptiis philologiae et Mercurii*, the most popular textbook in the Latin West during the early Middle Ages. Cast in the form of an allegory of a heavenly marriage, in which seven bridesmaids present a compendium of each of the liberal arts, this book became the foundation of the medieval curriculum of the trivium (books III–V) and quadrivium (VI–IX). The setting (I–II) became a model of heavenly journeys as late as Dante and contributed greatly to the popularity of the book. Although Martianus understood little more of the subject matter of the disciplines than what he presented in digest form, he was a key figure in the history of rhetoric, education, and science for a thousand years.

Owing to the disappearance in the early Middle Ages of Varro's book on the mathematical disciplines (*Disciplinae*, IV–VII), Martianus' quadrivium books, inspired by Varro's archetypal work, provide the best means of reconstructing the ancient Roman mathematical disciplines. Book VI, *De geometria*, proves to be not a book on geometry but a conspectus of *terra cognita*, reduced from the geographical books of Pliny the Elder's *Natural History* (III–VI) and the *Collectanea rerum memorabilium* of Solinus. Martianus closes with a ten-page digest of Euclidean geometry, drawn from some Latin primer in the Varronian tradition. This digest assumes importance as a rare sample of pre-Boethian Latin geometry. Book VII, *De arithmetica*, was the second most important treatise on arithmetic after Boethius' *De institutione arithmetica*. Martianus' ultimate sources were Nicomachus' *Introduction to Arithmetic* and Euclid's *Elements* VII–IX, but his immediate sources were Latin primers based upon these works. A. Dick cites the original passages in the apparatus of his edition. Martianus' arithmetic proper consists of classifications and definitions of the kinds of numbers (largely Nicomachean, with some Euclidean material) and Latin translations of the enunciations of thirty-six Euclidean arithmetical propositions. Euclid developed his proofs geometrically; Martianus used numerical illustrations.

Book VIII, *De astronomia*, is the best extant ancient Latin treatise on astronomy. Because of its systematic, proportionate, and comprehensive treatment, it is the only one that bears comparison with such popular Greek handbooks as Geminus' *Introduction to Phenomena*. Its excellence indicates that Greek traditions, transmitted to the Latin world by Varro, were fairly well preserved in digest form. Martianus deals with all the conventional topics: the celestial circles; northern and southern constellations; hours of daylight at the various latitudes; anomalies of the four seasons; and a discussion of the orbits of each of the planets, including the sun and moon. Martianus was the only Latin author to give a clear exposition of Heraclides' theory of the heliocentric motions of Venus and Mercury and was commended for this by Copernicus.

Book IX, *De harmonia*, largely drawn from Aristides Quintilianus' *Peri mousikes*, book I, is important for its Latin definitions of musical terms that have long puzzled medieval musicologists. Next to Boethius, Martianus was the most important ancient Latin authority on music.

BIBLIOGRAPHY

I. ORIGINAL WORKS. The best ed. of *De nuptiis* is that of A. Dick (Leipzig, 1925). A new ed., to be published about 1976, is being prepared for the Teubner Library by J. A. Willis. A trans. of the complete work, with commentary, is W. H. Stahl, *Martianus Capella and the Seven Liberal Arts* (New York, 1971).

II. SECONDARY LITERATURE. See W. H. Stahl, *The Quadrivium of Martianus Capella; a Study of Latin Traditions in the Mathematical Sciences from 50 B.C. to A.D. 1250* (New York, 1969); and *Roman Science; Origins, Development, and Influence to the Later Middle Ages* (Madison, Wis., 1962), which contains a chapter on Martianus and places him in the stream of Latin scientific writings. C. Leonardi's book-length census of Martianus' MSS describes 243 MSS and excerpts and discusses his influence in later ages: "I codici di Marziano Capella," in *Aevum*, **33** (1959), 443–489; **34** (1960), 1–99, 411–524.

W. H. STAHL

MASCHERONI, LORENZO (*b*. Castagneta, near Bergamo, Italy, 13 May 1750; *d*. Paris, France, 14 July 1800)

Mascheroni was the son of Paolo Mascheroni dell'Olmo, a prosperous landowner, and Maria Ciribelli. He was ordained a priest at seventeen and at twenty was teaching rhetoric and then, from 1778, physics and mathematics at the seminary of Bergamo. His *Nuove ricerche su l'equilibrio delle vòlte* (1785) led to his appointment as professor of algebra and geometry at the University of Pavia in 1786. In 1789 and 1793 he was rector of the university and, from 1788 to 1791, was head of the Accademia degli Affidati. Mascheroni was a member of the Academy of Padua, of the Royal Academy of Mantua, and of the Società Italiana delle Scienze. In his *Adnotationes ad calculum integrale Euleri* (1790) he calculated Euler's constant, sometimes called the Euler-Mascheroni constant, to thirty-two decimal places; the figure was corrected from the twentieth decimal place by Johann von Soldner in 1809.

In 1797 Mascheroni was appointed deputy to the legislative body in Milan. Sent to Paris by a commission to study the new system of money and of weights and measures, he published his findings in 1798 but was prevented from returning home by the Austrian occupation of Milan in 1799. Also a poet, Mascheroni dedicated his *Geometria del compasso* (1797) to Napoleon in verse; his celebrated *Invito a Lesbia Cidonia* (1793) glorifies the athenaeum of Pavia. He died after a brief illness, apparently from the complications of a cold. The poet Monti mourned his death in the *Mascheroniana*.

Mascheroni's *Nuove ricerche* is a well-composed work on statics, and the *Adnotationes* shows a profound understanding of Euler's calculus. He is best known, however, for his *Geometria del compasso*, in which he shows that all plane construction problems that can be solved with ruler and compass can also be solved with compass alone. It is understood that the given and unknowns are points; in particular, a straight line is considered known if two points of it are known.

In the preface Mascheroni recounts the genesis of his work. He was moved initially by a desire to make an original contribution to elementary geometry. It occurred to him that ruler and compass could perhaps be separated, as water can be separated into two gases; but he was also assailed by doubts and fears often attendant upon research. He then chanced to reread an article on the way Graham and Bird had divided their great astronomical quadrant, and he realized that the division had been made by compass alone, although, to be sure, by trial and error. This encouraged him, and he continued his work with two purposes in mind: to give a theoretical solution to the problem of constructions with compass alone and to offer practical constructions that might be of help in making precision instruments. The second concern is shown in the brief solutions of many specific problems and in a chapter on approximate solutions.

The theoretical solution (see especially §191) depends on the solution of the following problems: (1) to bisect a given circular arc of given center; (2) to add and subtract given segments; (3) to find the fourth proportional to three given segments; (4) to find the intersection of two given lines; and (5) to find the intersection of a given line and given circle.

In 1906 August Adler applied the theory of inversion to the Mascheroni constructions. Since this theory places lines and circles on an equal footing, it sheds light on Mascheroni's problem; but the solution via inversion is not as elegant—and certainly not as simple or as brief—as Mascheroni's.

Mascheroni's theory is but a chapter in the long history of geometrical constructions by specified means. The limitation to ruler and compass occurs in book I of Euclid's *Elements*—at least the first three postulates have been called the postulates of construction; and there are even reasons to suppose that Euclid's so-called axiomatic procedure is really only an axiomatization of the Euclidean constructions.

Euclid, of course, had inherited a tradition of restricting construction to ruler and compass. Oenopides is credited by Proclus with the construction for dropping a perpendicular (*Elements* I.12) and with the method of transferring an angle (I.23). The tradition itself appears to be of religious origin (see Seidenberg, 1959, 1962).

About 980, the Arab mathematician Abu'l-Wafā' proposed using a ruler and a compass of fixed opening, and in the sixteenth century da Vinci, Dürer, Cardano, Tartaglia, and Ferrari were also concerned with this restriction. In 1672 Georg Mohr showed that all the construction problems of the first six books of the *Elements* can be done with compass alone. Lambert in 1774 discussed the problem "Given a parallelogram, construct, with ruler only, a parallel to a given line."

Poncelet, who mentions Mascheroni in this connection, showed in 1822 that in the presence of a given circle with given center, all the Euclidean constructions can be carried out with ruler alone. This has also been credited to Jacob Steiner, although he had heard of Poncelet's result, or "conjecture," as he called it. Poncelet and others also studied constructions with ruler alone; abstractly, his result is related to the axiomatic introduction of coordinates in the projective plane. Johannes Trolle Hjelmslev and others have studied the analogue of the Mascheroni constructions in non-Euclidean geometry.

The question has recently been posed whether the notion of two points being a unit apart could serve as the sole primitive notion in Euclidean plane geometry. An affirmative answer was given, based on a device of Peaucellier's for converting circular motion into rectilineal motion.

In 1928 Mohr's *Euclides danicus*, which had fallen into obscurity, was republished with a preface by Hjelmslev, according to whom Mascheroni's result had been known and systematically expounded 125 years earlier by Mohr. The justice of this judgment and the question of the independence of Mascheroni's work will now be examined.

The term "independent invention" is used in two different but often confused senses. Anthropologists use it in reference to the appearance of identical, or similar, complex phenomena in different cultures. A controversy rages, the opposing positions of which, perhaps stripped of necessary qualifications, can be put thus: According to the "independent inventionists," the appearance of identical social phenomena in different cultures (especially in New World and Old World cultures) is evidence for the view that the human mind works similarly under similar circumstances; for the "diffusionists," it is evidence of a historical connection, but not necessarily a direct one.

The historian, dealing with a single community, uses the term in a different sense. When he says two inventions are independent, he means that each was made without direct reliance on the other. Simultaneous and independent solutions of outstanding problems that are widely published in the scholarly press are no more surprising than the simultaneous solutions by schoolboys of an assigned problem; and the simultaneous development in similar directions of a common fund of knowledge can also be expected. Even so, examples of independent identical innovations are rare and difficult to establish.

Although five centuries separate Abu'l-Wafā' and Leonardo, presumably no one will doubt that the Italians got the compass problem of a single opening from the Arabs (or, possibly, that both got it from a third source).

When the works of Mascheroni and Mohr are compared, it is apparent that the main ideas of their solutions of individual problems are in most cases quite different. In particular, this can be said for the bisection of a given segment. Moreover, the problem of bisection plays no role in Mascheroni's general solution, whereas it is central in Mohr's constructions. Still more significantly, the general problem is not formulated in Mohr's book. Thus, any suggestion of Mascheroni's direct reliance on Mohr would be quite inappropriate. Of course, the possibility cannot be excluded that Mascheroni, who explicitly denied knowledge that anyone had previously treated the matter, had heard of a partial formulation of the problem.

It appears that Hjelmslev's judgment is not entirely accurate. Mohr's book is quite remarkable and contains the basis for a simple proof of Mascheroni's result, but there is no evidence within the book itself that Mohr formulated the problem of constructions with compass alone in complete generality.

BIBLIOGRAPHY

I. ORIGINAL WORKS. Mascheroni's mathematical works are *Nuove ricerche su l'equilibrio delle vòlte* (Bergamo, 1785); *Adnotationes ad calculum integrale Euleri* (Pavia, 1790); and *Geometria del compasso* (Pavia, 1797). A nonmathematical work is *Invito a Lesbia Cidonia* (Pavia, 1793).

II. SECONDARY LITERATURE. Biographical details are presented in A. Fiamazzo, *Nuovo contributo alla biografia di L. Mascheroni*, 2 vols. (Bergamo, 1904); J. W. L. Glaisher, "History of Euler's Constant," in *Messenger of Mathematics*, **1** (1872), 25–30; G. Loria and C. Alasia, "Bibliographie de Mascheroni," in *Intermédiaire des mathématiciens*, **19** (1912), 92–94; and G. Natali, "Mascheroni," in *Enciclopedia italiana*, XXII (Rome, 1934), 496.

Adler's application of the theory of inversion to Mascheroni's constructions is presented in his *Theorie der geometrischen Konstruktionen* (Leipzig, 1906).

Support for the view that Euclid's so-called axiomatic procedure is merely an axiomatization of Euclidean constructions may be found in A. Seidenberg, "Peg and Cord in Ancient Greek Geometry," in *Scripta mathematica*, **24** (1959), 107–122; and "The Ritual Origin of Geometry," in *Archive for History of Exact Sciences*, **1** (1962), 488–527. Opposition to the above view is presented in T. L. Heath's ed. of Euclid's *Elements*, I, 124; and A. D. Steele, "Über die Rolle von Zirkel und Lineal in der griechischen Mathematik," in *Quellen und Studien zur Geschichte der Mathematik, Astronomie und Physik*, Abt. B, **3** (1936), 287–369. W. M. Kutta, "Zur Geschichte der Geometrie mit constanter Zirkelöffnung," in *Nova acta Academiae Caesarae Leopoldino Carolinae*, **71** (1898), 71–101, discusses the use of a ruler and a compass of fixed opening.

Georg Mohr's *Euclides danicus* was translated into German by J. Pál and provided with a foreword by J. Hjelmslev (Copenhagen, 1928). Lambert's work is referred to in R. C. Archibald, "Outline of the History of Mathematics," in *American Mathematical Monthly*, **56**, no. 1, supp. (1949), note 277, 98.

Poncelet's and Steiner's contributions can be found in Poncelet's *Traité des propriétés projectives des figures*, 2nd ed. (Paris, 1865), I, 181–184, 413–414; and in Steiner's *Geometrical Constructions With a Ruler*, translated by M. E. Stark and edited by R. C. Archibald (New York, 1950), p. 10.

Analogues of Mascheroni's work in non-Euclidean geometry are discussed in J. Hjelmslev, "Om et af den danske Matematiker Georg Mohr udgivet skrift *Euclides Danicus*," in *Matematisk tidsskrift*, B (1928), 1–7; and in articles by A. S. Smogorzhevsky, V. F. Rogachenko, and K. K. Mokrishchev that are reviewed in *Mathematical Reviews*, **14** (1953), 576, 1007; **15** (1954), 148; and **17** (1956), 885, 998.

The question of whether the notion of two points being a unit apart can be the sole primitive notion in Euclidean plane geometry is discussed in R. M. Robinson, "Binary Relations as Primitive Notions in Elementary Geometry," in Leon Henkin, Patrick Suppes, and Alfred Tarski, eds., *The Axiomatic Method With Special Reference to Geometry and Physics* (Amsterdam, 1959), 68–85.

A. SEIDENBERG

MASERES, FRANCIS (*b.* London, England, 15 December 1731; *d.* Reigate, Surrey, England, 19 May 1824), *mathematics*.

Maseres was the son of a physician who was descended from a family that had been forced to flee France by the revocation of the Edict of Nantes. At Clare College, Cambridge, he obtained his B.A. degree in 1752 with highest honors in both classics and mathematics. Upon receiving the M.A. and a fellowship from his college, he moved to the Temple and was later called to the bar. After spending a few years in the practice of law with little success, he was appointed attorney general for Quebec, in which post he served until 1769. His career in the new world was distinguished "by his loyalty during the American contest and his zeal for the interests of the province." Upon his return to England he was appointed cursitor baron of the Exchequer, an office which he held until his death at the age of ninety-three. During this period of his life he was generally known as Baron Maseres. In addition he was at different times deputy recorder of London and senior judge of the sheriff's court.

Three aspects of Maseres' career are noteworthy. The first is his interest in political matters, particularly in the affairs of Canada and the American colonies. Of a considerable number of essays along these lines from Maseres' pen, the following are typical: (1) "Considerations on the expediency of admitting Representatives from the American Colonies to the House of Commons" (1770); (2) "Account of Proceedings of British and other Protestants of the Province of Quebec to establish a House of Assembly" (anon.), (1775); (3) "The Canadian Freeholder, a Dialogue shewing the Sentiments of the Bulk of the Freeholders on the late Quebeck Act" (1776–1779); (4) "Select Tracts on Civil Wars in England, in the

Reign of Charles I" (1815).

A second aspect of Maseres' long career is the peculiar nature of his mathematical contributions, reflecting his complete lack of creative ability together with naive individualism. For a proper perspective, one must recall that Maseres' works were written about a century and a half after Viète and Harriot had ushered in the period of "symbolic algebra." While Viète had rejected negative roots of equations, certain immediate precursors of Maseres, notably Cotes, De Moivre, Taylor, and Maclaurin, had gone far beyond this stage, as had his contemporaries on the Continent: Lambert, Lagrange, and Laplace. Despite these advances, some quirk in the young Maseres compelled him to reject that part of algebra which was not arithmetic, probably because he could not understand it, although by his own confession others might comprehend it. Unfortunately this prejudice against "negative and impossible quantities" affected much of his later work. Thus in one of his earliest publications, *Dissertation on the Use of the Negative Sign in Algebra* (1758), he writes as follows.

> If any single quantity is marked either with the sign + or the sign − without affecting some other quantity ... the mark will have no meaning or signification; thus if it be said that the square of −5, or the product of −5 into −5, is equal to +25, such an assertion must either signify no more than 5 times 5 is equal to 25 without any regard to the signs, or it must be mere nonsense or unintelligible jargon.

Curiously enough, in addition to Maseres, two other contemporary mathematicians opposed the generalized concept of positive and negative integers: William Frend, father-in-law of De Morgan, and Robert Simson. Maseres unfortunately influenced the teaching of algebra for several decades, as may be seen from textbooks of T. Manning (1796); N. Vilant (1798); and W. Ludlam (1809).

Perhaps the many publications with which he strove to bring mathematics to a much wider public were the most notable aspect of Maseres' legacy. Some were original works; others were reprints of the works of distinguished mathematicians. His original books are characterized by extreme prolixity, occasioned by his rejection of algebra, and the consequent proliferation of particular cases. For example, in the *Dissertation* alluded to above, which is virtually a treatise on elementary algebra, the discussion of basic rules and the solution of quadratic and cubic equations occupy three hundred quarto pages.

Of the reprints that Maseres made at his own expense, the most significant is the *Scriptores logarithmici* (1791–1807), six volumes devoted to the subject of logarithms, including the works of Kepler, Napier, Snellius, and others, interspersed with original tracts on related subjects. Other republications include the following: (1) *Scriptores optici* (1823), a reprint of the optical essays of James Gregory, Descartes, Schooten, Huygens, Halley, and Barrow; (2) Jakob I Bernoulli's tract on permutations and combinations; (3) Colson's translation of Agnesi's *Analytical Institutions*; (4) Hale's Latin treatise on fluxions (1800); and (5) several tracts on English history. Presumably a number of authors were indebted to Maseres for financial assistance of this sort. There can be little doubt of his sincerity and generosity, even if somewhat misplaced.

BIBLIOGRAPHY

I. Original Works.
(1) *A Dissertation on the Use of the Negative Sign in Algebra: containing a demonstration of the rules usually given concerning it; and shewing how quadratic and cubic equations may be explained, without the consideration of negative roots. To which is added, as an appendix, Mr. Machin's quadrature of the circle* (London, 1758).

(2) *Elements of Plane Trigonometry ... with a dissertation on the nature and use of logarithms* (London, 1760).

(3) *A proposal for establishing life-annuities in parishes for the benefit of the industrious poor* (London, 1772).

(4) *Principles of the Doctrine of Life Annuities explained in a familiar manner so as to be intelligible to persons not acquainted with the Doctrine of Chances, and accompanied with a variety of New Tables, accurately computed from observations* (London, 1783).

(5) *Scriptores Logarithmici, or a collection of several curious Tracts on the Nature and Construction of Logarithms, mentioned in Dr. Hutton's Historical Introduction to his New Edition of Sherwin's Mathematical Tables*, 6 vols. (London, 1791–1807).

(6) *The Doctrine of Permutations and Combinations, being an essential and fundamental part of the Doctrine of Chances; as it is delivered by Mr. James Bernoulli, in his excellent Treatise on the Doctrine of Chances, intitled, Ars Conjectandi, and by the celebrated Dr. John Wallis, of Oxford, in a tract intitled from the subject, and published at the end of his Treatise on Algebra; in the former of which tract is contained, a Demonstration of Sir Isaac Newton's famous Binomial Theorem, in the cases of integral powers, and of the reciprocals of integral powers. Together with some other useful mathematical tracts* (London, 1795).

(7) "An Appendix by F. Maseres," in William Frend, *The Principles of Algebra*, 2 vols. in 1 (London, 1796–1799), 211–456. Also "Observations on Mr. Raphson's method of resolving affected equations of all degrees by approximation," *ibid.*, vol. 2, 457–581.

(8) *Tracts on the Resolution of Affected Algebraick Equations by Dr. Halley's, Mr. Raphson's and Sir I. Newton's, Methods of Approximation* [with those of W. Frend

and *J. Kersey*] (London, 1800).

(9) *Tracts on the Resolution of Cubick and Biquadratick Equations* (London, 1803).

II. Secondary Literature.

(10) *The Penny Cyclopaedia of the Society for the Diffusion of Useful Knowledge*, **14** (London, 1837), 480–481.

(11) *The Gentlemen's Magazine* (June 1824); contains a list of Maseres' political writings.

(12) Moritz Cantor, *Vorlesungen über die Geschichte der Mathematik*, IV (Leipzig, 1913), 80, 86–87, 92, 149–151, 271, 302; references to some periodical articles published by Maseres.

William L. Schaaf

MATHEWS, GEORGE BALLARD (*b.* London, England, 23 February 1861; *d.* Liverpool, England, 19 March 1922)

Born of a Herefordshire family, Mathews was educated at Ludlow Grammar School; at University College, London; and at St. John's College, Cambridge. In 1883 he headed the list in the Cambridge mathematical tripos. In 1884 he was elected a fellow of St. John's, but in the same year he was appointed to the chair of mathematics at the newly established University College of North Wales at Bangor. He resigned the Bangor chair in 1896 and returned to lecture at Cambridge. He gave up this appointment in 1911, when he was appointed to a special lectureship at Bangor. He was elected to the Royal Society in 1897.

Mathews was an accomplished classical scholar; and besides Latin and Greek he was proficient in Hebrew, Sanskrit, and Arabic. He also possessed great musical knowledge and skill. His versatility led a colleague at Bangor to assert that Mathews could equally well fill four or more chairs at the college.

In mathematics Mathews' main interest was in the classical theory of numbers, and most of his research papers deal with topics in this field. His book on the theory of numbers, of which only the first of two promised volumes appeared, discusses in detail the Gaussian theory of quadratic forms and its developments by Dirichlet, Eisenstein, and H. J. S. Smith; it also contains a chapter on prime numbers that is concerned largely with describing Riemann's memoir, at that time little known in England. Since the book was published in 1892, it was not possible to mention the proofs of the prime number theorem, first given by Hadamard and Vallée Poussin in 1896. In a related field, his 1907 tract on algebraic equations gave a clear exposition of the Galois theory in relation to the theory of groups.

A collaboration with Andrew Gray, then professor

of physics at Bangor, produced a book on Bessel functions, the first substantial text on this subject in English. The theory is developed carefully and rigorously, but throughout the book stress is laid on applications to electricity, hydrodynamics, and diffraction; in this respect the book retained its value even after the publication in 1922 of Watson's standard treatise on the theory of these functions.

Mathews' book on projective geometry had two main aims: first, to develop the principles of projective geometry without any appeal to the concept of distance and on the basis of a simple but not minimal set of axioms; and second, to expound Staudt's theory of complex elements as defined by real involutions. Much material on the projective properties of conics and quadrics is included. The topics were relatively novel in English texts, although the first volume of Oswald Veblen and J. W. Young's *Projective Geometry* had just become available.

Mathews' research papers advanced the study of higher arithmetic, and his books were equally valuable, since they gave English readers access to fields of study not then adequately expounded for the English-speaking world.

BIBLIOGRAPHY

I. Original Works. Mathews' books are *Theory of Numbers* (Cambridge, 1892); *A Treatise on Bessel Functions and Their Applications to Physics* (London, 1895; 2nd ed., rev. by T. M. MacRobert), written with A. Gray; *Algebraic Equations*, Cambridge Mathematical Tracts, no. 6 (Cambridge, 1907; 3rd ed., rev. by W. E. H. Berwick); and *Projective Geometry* (London, 1914). The 2nd ed. of R. F. Scott's *Theory of Determinants* (London, 1904) was revised by Mathews.

Most of Mathews' research papers were published in *Proceedings of the London Mathematical Society* and *Messenger of Mathematics*.

II. Secondary Literature. See the obituary notices by W. E. H. Berwick, in *Proceedings of the London Mathematical Society*, 2nd ser., **21** (1923), xlvi–l; and A. Gray, in *Mathematical Gazette*, **11** (1922), 133–136.

T. A. A. Broadbent

MATHIEU, ÉMILE LÉONARD (*b.* Metz, France, 15 May 1835; *d.* Nancy, France, 19 October 1890)

Mathieu showed an early aptitude for Latin and Greek at school in Metz; but in his teens he discovered mathematics, and while a student at the École Polytechnique in Paris he passed all the courses in eighteen months. He took his *docteur ès sciences* in March 1859, with a thesis on transitive functions, but had to work as a private tutor until 1869, when he was appointed to a chair of mathematics at Besançon. He moved to Nancy in 1874, where he remained as professor until his death.

Although Mathieu showed great promise in his early years, he never received such normal signs of approbation as a Paris chair or election to the Académie des Sciences. From his late twenties his main efforts were devoted to the then unfashionable continuation of the great French tradition of mathematical physics, and he extended in sophistication the formation and solution of partial differential equations for a wide range of physical problems. Most of his papers in these fields received their definitive form in his projected *Traité de physique mathématique*, the eighth volume of which he had just begun at the time of his death. These volumes and a treatise on analytical dynamics can be taken as the basis for assessing his achievements in applied mathematics, for they contain considered versions, and often extensions, of the results that he had first published in his research papers. Mathieu's first major investigation (in the early 1860's) was an examination of the surfaces of vibration that arise as disturbances from Fresnel waves by considering the dispersive properties of light. His later interest in the polarization of light led him to rework a number of problems in view of certain disclosed weaknesses in Cauchy's analyses.

One of Mathieu's main interests was in potential theory, in which he introduced a new distinction between first and second potential. "First potential" was the standard idea, defined, for example, at a point for a body V by an expression of the form

$$\int_V \frac{1}{r} f(x, y, z)\, dv; \qquad (1)$$

but Mathieu also considered the "second potential"

$$\int_V r f(x, y, z)\, dv, \qquad (2)$$

the properties of which he found especially useful in solving the fourth-order partial differential equation

$$\nabla^2 \nabla^2 w = 0. \qquad (3)$$

His interest in (3) arose especially in problems of elasticity; and in relating and comparing his solutions with problems in heat diffusion (where he had investigated various special distributions in cylindrical bodies), he was led to generalized solutions for partial differential equations and to solutions for problems of the elasticity of three-dimensional bodies, especially those of anisotropic elasticity or subject to

noninfinitesimal deformations. Mathieu applied these results to the especially difficult problem of the vibration of bells, and he also made general applications of his ideas of potential theory to the study of dielectrics and magnetic induction. In his treatment of electrodynamics he suggested that the traversal of a conductor by an electric current gave rise to a pair of neighboring layers of electricity, rather than just a single layer.

Mathieu introduced many new ideas in the study of capillarity, improving upon Poisson's results concerning the change of density in a fluid at its edges. His most notable achievement in this field was to analyze the capillary forces acting on an arbitrary body immersed in a liquid, but in general his results proved to be at variance with experimental findings.

In celestial mechanics Mathieu extended Poisson's results on the secular variation of the great axes of the orbits of planets and on the formulas for their perturbation; he also analyzed the motion of the axes of rotation of the earth and produced estimates of the variation in latitude of a point on the earth. Mathieu studied the three-body problem and applied his results to the calculation of the perturbations of Jupiter and Saturn. In analytical mechanics, he gave new demonstrations of the Hamiltonian systems of equations and of the principle of least action, as well as carrying out many analyses of compound motion, especially those that took into account the motion of the earth.

In all his work Mathieu built principally on solution methods introduced by Fourier and problems investigated by Poisson, Cauchy, and Lamé. The best-known of his achievements, directly linked with his name, are the "Mathieu functions," which arise in solving the two-dimensional wave equation for the motion of an elliptic membrane. After separation of the variables, both space variables satisfy an ordinary differential equation sometimes known as Mathieu's equation:

$$\frac{d^2 u}{dz^2} + (a + 16b \cos 2z)u = 0, \qquad (4)$$

whose solutions are the Mathieu functions $ce_n(z, b)$, $se_n(z, b)$. These functions are usually expressed as trigonometric series in z, each of which takes an infinite power series coefficient in b; but many of their properties, including orthogonality, can be developed from (4) and from various implicit forms. Both equation (4) and the functions were an important source of problems for analysis from Mathieu's initial paper of 1868 until the second decade of the twentieth century. The functions themselves are a special case of the hypergeometric function, and

Mathieu's contributions to pure mathematics included a paper on that function. He also wrote on elliptic functions and especially on various questions concerned with or involving higher algebra—the theory of substitutions and transitive functions (his earliest work, and based on extensions to the results of his thesis) and biquadratic residues. In fact, his earliest work was in pure mathematics; not until his thirties did applied mathematics assume a dominant role in his thought.

Mathieu's shy and retiring nature may have accounted to some extent for the lack of worldly success in his life and career; but among his colleagues he won only friendship and respect. Apart from a serious illness in his twenty-eighth year, which seems to have prevented him from taking over Lamé's lecture courses at the Sorbonne in 1866, he enjoyed good health until the illness that caused his death.

BIBLIOGRAPHY

I. Original Works. The 7 vols. of Mathieu's *Traité de physique mathématique* were published at Paris: *Cours de physique mathématique* (1874); *Théorie de la capillarité* (1883); *Théorie du potentiel et ses applications à l'électrostatique et au magnetisme*, 2 vols. (1885–1886), also trans. into German (1890); *Théorie de l'électrodynamique* (1888); and *Théorie de l'élasticité des corps solides*, 2 vols. (1890). The 3 vols. that were still projected at his death were to have dealt with optics, the theory of gases, and acoustics. His other book was *Dynamique analytique* (Paris, 1878). His papers were published mostly in *Journal de physique*, *Journal für die reine und angewandte Mathematik*, and especially in *Journal des mathématiques pures et appliquées*. A comprehensive list of references can be found in Poggendorff, IV, 1972.

II. Secondary Literature. The two principal writings are P. Duhem, "Émile Mathieu, His Life and Works," in *Bulletin of the New York Mathematical Society*, **1** (1891–1892), 156–168, translated by A. Ziwet; and G. Floquet, "Émile Mathieu," in *Bulletin . . . de la Société des sciences de Nancy*, 2nd ser., **11** (1891), 1–34. A good treatment of Mathieu's equation and functions may be found in E. T. Whittaker and G. N. Watson, *A Course of Modern Analysis* (Cambridge, 1928), ch. 19.

I. Grattan-Guinness

MAUPERTUIS, PIERRE LOUIS MOREAU DE (*b.* St.-Malo, France, 28 September 1698; *d.* Basel, Switzerland, 27 July 1759)

It was said of Maupertuis, in the official eulogy by Samuel Formey, that "Madame Moreau idolized her son rather than loved him. She could not refuse him anything." It seems highly probable that the spoiled child inevitably developed some of those personality characteristics that later made him not only proud but intransigent and incapable of bearing criticism, traits that ultimately led to great unpleasantness in his life and, quite literally, to his undoing.

After private schooling Maupertuis went to Paris at the age of sixteen to study under Le Blond, but he found ordinary philosophical disciplines quite distasteful. In 1717 he began to study music; but he soon developed a strong interest in mathematics, which he pursued under the tutelage of Guisnée and, later, Nicole. Maupertuis was elected to the Academy of Sciences in 1723, at the age of twenty-five, and presented a dissertation, "Sur la forme des instruments de musique." This was soon followed by a mathematical memoir on maxima and minima, some biological observations on a species of salamander, and two mathematical works of much promise: "Sur la quadrature et rectification des figures formées par le roulement des polygones reguliers" and "Sur une nouvelle manière de développer les courbes."

In 1728 Maupertuis made a trip to London that was to exert a major influence upon his subsequent career. From a conceptual world of Cartesian vortices he was transported into the scientific milieu of Newtonian mechanics, and he was quickly converted to these views. From this time on, Maupertuis was the foremost proponent of the Newtonian movement in France and a convinced defender of Newton's ideas about the shape of the earth. After returning to France he visited Basel, where he was befriended by the Bernoullis.

While pursuing, in conjunction with Clairaut, further studies in mathematics—resulting in a steady flow of notable memoirs—Maupertuis was readying his first work on Newtonian principles, "Discours sur les différentes figures des astres" (1732). It brought him the attention of the Marquise du Châtelet and of Voltaire, both of whom he instructed in the new doctrines. His position as the leading Continental Newtonian was confirmed the following year by his "Sur la figure de la terre et sur les moyens que l'astronomie et la géographie fournissent pour la déterminer," which was accompanied by a complementary memoir by Clairaut.

Thus it came about that in 1735 France sent an expedition to Peru under the leadership of La Condamine and another to Lapland under the leadership of Maupertuis. Clairaut, Camus, and other scientists accompanied the latter. The mission of each expedition was to measure as accurately as possible the length of a degree along the meridian of longitude. If, indeed, the earth is flattened toward the poles, as Newton had predicted, the degree of latitude should be shorter in far northern latitudes than near the equator. The voyage began on 2 May 1736 and lasted over a year. The local base for the expedition's fieldwork was Torneå, in northern Sweden—then, according to Maupertuis, a town of fifty or sixty houses and wooden cabins. On the return journey the ship was wrecked in the Baltic Sea, but without loss of life, instruments, or records.

Maupertuis reached Paris on 20 August 1737, only to meet with a rather chilly reception. Envy and jealousy were already at work; he had few Newtonian supporters in France except Voltaire; and La Condamine's expedition had not yet returned from Peru. At this time Maupertuis found respite at Saint-Malo and at Cirey, where Mme du Châtelet and Voltaire made him welcome. He stayed only briefly at Cirey, however, intending to revisit Basel. There he met Samuel König, a young student of Johann I Bernoulli. He persuaded König to accompany him back to Cirey, where König behaved so arrogantly that he angered Mme du Châtelet, who through this episode became temporarily estranged from Maupertuis.

The laborious analysis of the data on the length of the arc of a meridional degree at various latitudes took much time and created much controversy. The measurements made in France had to be corrected. In December 1739 Maupertuis announced to the Academy the value found for the distance along the meridian between Paris and Amiens. The expedition to Peru having returned after an arduous three years, the degree between Quito and Cuenca was added to the comparisons. Still later (1751) measurements made by Lacaille at the Cape of Good Hope permitted a fourth comparison.

In a final revision of the reports on the "Opérations pour déterminer la figure de la terre" (*Oeuvres*, IV, 335) Maupertuis summarized the corrected measurements for a degree of longitude as follows:

	Latitude	Toises
Peru	0°30′	56,768
Cape of Good Hope	33°18′	56,994
France	49°23′	57,199
Lapland	66°10′	57,395

In 1738 Voltaire recommended Maupertuis to Frederick the Great, who was eager to rehabilitate the academy of sciences at Berlin. Frederick commenced overtures to Maupertuis, who visited Berlin after publication of his new, anonymously printed *Éléments de géographie* and his reconciliation with Mme du Châtelet. In Berlin he met Francesco Algarotti and the family of M. de Borck, whose daughter he was later to marry. After the outbreak of the War of the Austrian Succession, Maupertuis joined Frederick in Silesia, only to be captured when his horse bolted into the enemy lines. For a time he was feared dead by his friends, but Maupertuis soon emerged safely in Vienna; ominously, he took offense at the jests of Voltaire regarding his military exploit.

Maupertuis was elected to the Académie Française in 1743. In 1744 he presented the memoir "Accord de différentes lois de la nature" and published "Dissertation sur le nègre blanc." The latter was the precursor of the *Vénus physique* of 1745, which was an enlarged and more fully analyzed argument against the then-dominant biological theory of the preformation of the embryo. Maupertuis argued convincingly that the embryo could not be preformed, either in the egg or in the animalcule (spermatozoon), since hereditary characteristics could be passed down equally through the male or the female parent. He rejected the vitalistic notion that some "essence" from one of the parents could affect the preformed fetus in the other parent, or that maternal impressions could mold the characteristics of the offspring. A strict mechanist, although a believer in the epigenetic view of the origin of the embryo, he looked for some corporeal contribution from each parent as a basis of heredity.

In the middle of 1745 Maupertuis finally accepted Frederick's invitation and took up residence in Berlin. In the same year he married Mlle de Borck; and on 3 March 1746 he was installed as president of the Academy. His first contribution was the brief paper "Les lois du mouvement et du repos," in which he set forth the famous principle of least action, which he regarded as his own most significant scientific contribution. It states simply that "in all the changes that take place in the universe, the sum of the products of each body multiplied by the distance it moves and by the speed with which it moves is the least possible" (*Oeuvres*, II, 328). That is, this quantity tends to a minimum. This principle was later clarified and expounded by Euler, developed by Hamilton and Lagrange, and incorporated in modern times into quantum mechanics and the biological principle of homeostasis. As Maupertuis himself said:

> The laws of movement thus deduced [from this principle], being found to be precisely the same as those observed in nature, we can admire the application of it to all phenomena, in the movement of animals, in the vegetation of plants, in the revolution of the heavenly bodies: and the spectacle of the universe becomes so much the grander, so much the more beautiful, so much worthier of its Author. . . .

These laws, so beautiful and so simple, are perhaps the only ones which the Creator and Organizer of things has established in matter in order to effect all the phenomena of the visible world [*Oeuvres*, I, 44–45].

Maupertuis clearly was successful in attracting to Berlin scientific luminaries who greatly enhanced the luster of the new Academy. Euler, one of the greatest mathematicians of the day, was already there. La Mettrie came in 1748; Mérian and Meckel in 1750; and, in the same year, after the death of Mme du Châtelet, Voltaire arrived in Berlin. With others the brusque impatience of Maupertuis rendered his efforts less successful. On the whole, however, matters were going well when the celebrated "affaire König" erupted. Samuel König, a protégé of Maupertuis, after having been elected a member of the Academy, visited Berlin, was warmly received by Maupertuis, and shortly thereafter submitted a dissertation attacking the validity of the principle of least action and then—most strangely for a devoted adherent of Leibniz—ascribed the discredited law to the latter, citing a letter from Leibniz to Hermann. Maupertuis was incensed. He demanded that the letter be produced. König produced a copy but stated that the original was in the hands of a certain Swiss named Henzi, who had been decapitated at Bern following involvement in a conspiracy. After exhaustive search no trace of the letter was found in Henzi's belongings. Maupertuis then demanded that the Academy take action against König.

At the same time Maupertuis was embroiled in a controversy between Haller and La Mettrie. The latter had dedicated to Haller, much to Haller's dismay, his *L'homme machine* (1748). La Mettrie had, in response to Haller's rejection, responded with a diatribe. Haller demanded an apology; but inasmuch as La Mettrie died at just that time, Maupertuis tried —without success—to assuage Haller with a polite letter. The episode certainly contributed to the extraordinary bitterness and tension that Maupertuis experienced in 1751.

Nevertheless, at this very time Maupertuis was able to publish one of his most significant works, later called *Système de la nature*. A sequel to the *Vénus physique*, it was a theoretical speculation on the nature of biparental heredity that included, as evidence, an account of a study of polydactyly in the family of a Berlin barber-surgeon, Jacob Ruhe, and the first careful and explicit analysis of the transmission of a dominant hereditary trait in man. Not only did Maupertuis demonstrate that polydactyly is transmitted through either the male or the female parent, but he also made a complete record of all normal as well as abnormal members of the family. He furthermore calculated the mathematical probability that the trait would occur coincidentally in the three successive generations of the Ruhe family had it

not been inherited.

On the basis of this study, Maupertuis founded a theory of the formation of the fetus and the nature of heredity that was at least a century ahead of its time. He postulated the existence of hereditary particles present in the semen of the male and female parents and corresponding to the parts of the fetus to be produced. They would come together by chemical attraction, each particle from the male parent joining a corresponding particle from the female parent. Chemical affinity would also account for the proper formation of adjacent parts, since particles representing adjacent parts would be more alike than those of remote parts. At certain times the maternal character would dominate; at others the paternal character. The theory was applied to explain the nature of hybrids between species and their well-known sterility; and it was extended to account for aberrations with extra structures as well as to those characterized by a missing part. The origin of new sorts of particles, as well as the presence of those representing ancestral types, was envisaged. Finally, Maupertuis thought it possible that new species might originate through the geographical isolation of such variations.

During 1752 the König affair reached a climax and a hearing was held, from which Maupertuis absented himself. The letter cited by König was held to be unauthentic and undeserving of credence, and König resigned from the Academy—only to issue a public appeal and defense. Voltaire had already run afoul of Maupertuis, and jealousy existed between them regarding their influence with the king. Maupertuis had shown scant enthusiasm for a proposed monumental dictionary of metaphysics, to be developed by the Academy as a counterpoise to the *Encyclopédie*, for Maupertuis considered the talents of the Berlin Academy insufficient to keep such a work from being superficial. In September 1752 Voltaire attacked Maupertuis, charging him not only with plagiarism and error but also with persecution of honest opponents and with tyranny over the Academy. In the *Diatribe du Docteur Akakia*, Voltaire poured invective on the ideas that Maupertuis had expressed in his *Lettre sur le progrès des sciences* (1752) and *Lettres* (1752)—in which, among other daring speculations regarding the future course of science, Maupertuis had included his most substantial account of the investigation of polydactyly in the Ruhe family and of his own breeding experiments with Iceland dogs. In *Micromégas* Voltaire made fun of the voyage to Lapland undertaken to measure the arc of the meridian and lampooned Maupertuis's amorous adventures in the North. His mockery made a great contrast with the grandiloquent words that he had once inscribed beneath a portrait of Maupertuis. In vain Frederick supported Maupertuis and tried to restore good feeling. Maupertuis was crushed, his health gave way, and he requested a leave to recuperate at Saint-Malo. Pursued by an unceasing volley of Voltaire's most savage satires, Maupertuis withdrew. He remained at Saint-Malo until the spring of 1754, when he returned to Berlin at Frederick's insistence. Here he delivered the eulogy of his friend Montesquieu, who died at Paris early in 1755. He departed again for France, a very sick man, in May 1756. Greatly distressed by the outbreak of the Seven Years' War, he decided to return home by way of Switzerland. He went to Toulouse, whence he set out again in May 1758. At Basel, too ill to proceed, he was received warmly by his old friend Johann Bernoulli. On 27 July 1759, before his wife could reach him, he died and was buried in Dornach.

Maupertuis was a man of singular aspect. He was very short. His body was always in motion; he had numerous tics. He was careless of his apparel. Perhaps he was always endeavoring to attract attention. Perhaps he shared the Napoleonic complex of little men. Certainly he was both highly original and possessed of qualities that attracted friends, especially among the ladies; the Marquise du Châtelet and many other Frenchwomen corresponded regularly with him. He could be gay as well as fiery and violent. Above all he was proud, both of his intelligence and of his accomplishments, and to attack either was to wound him deeply. Above all, he could not understand the character of König, whom he had sponsored and who then gratuitously attacked him, or of Voltaire, whose adulation and friendship so quickly turned to malice and vituperation.

A philosopher as well as a scientist, Maupertuis proved himself a powerful and original thinker in *Essai de cosmologie* (1750). According to A. O. Lovejoy, he anticipated Beccaria and Bentham and, along with Helvétius, represents "the headwaters of the important stream of utilitarian influence which became so broad and sweeping a current through the work of the Benthamites" (*Popular Science Monthly*, **65** [1904], 340). He rejected the favorite eighteenth-century argument in favor of God—the argument from design—and instead, like Hume, he formulated a view of adaptation based on the elimination of the unfit. He recognized that Newton's laws are insufficient to explain chemistry, and even more so life, and turned to Leibniz for ideas about the properties of consciousness. In the *Système de la Nature* we may, with Ernst Cassirer (*Philosophy of the Enlightenment*, p. 86), see an attempt to "reconcile the two great opponents of

the philosophy of nature of the seventeenth century," Newton and Leibniz. Yet in it must also be recognized a highly original work based on his own investigations of heredity. In his effort to introduce a calculus of pleasure and pain, in order to evaluate the good life and to measure happiness, Maupertuis proposed that the amount of pleasure or pain is a product of intensity and duration. This formulation is strictly analogous to his principle of least action in the physical world and shows how he extended his philosophy of nature into a philosophy of life.

BIBLIOGRAPHY

The works of Maupertuis are collected in *Oeuvres*, 4 vols. (Lyons, 1756). For his life see Grandjean de Fouchy, "Éloge de Maupertuis," in L. Angliviel de la Beaumelle, *Vie de Maupertuis* (Paris, 1856); Damiron, *Mémoires sur Maupertuis* (Paris, 1858); and P. Brunet, *Maupertuis*, I. *Étude Biographique* (Paris, 1929).

See also B. Glass, "Maupertuis, Pioneer of Genetics and Evolution," in B. Glass, O. Temkin, and W. Straus, Jr., eds., *Forerunners of Darwin, 1745–1859* (Baltimore, 1959); and Ernst Cassirer, *The Philosophy of the Enlightenment* (Princeton, 1951).

BENTLEY GLASS

MAUROLICO, FRANCESCO (*b.* Messina, Italy, 16 September 1494; *d.* near Messina, 21 or 22 July 1575)

Maurolico's name is variously transcribed as Maurolyco, Marulì, Marulli, and, in Latin, Maurolicus, Maurolycus, and Maurolycius. He was the son of Antonio Maurolico, master of the Messina mint, and his wife, Penuccia or Ranuccia. The family came from Greece, from which they had fled to Sicily to escape the Turks; Maurolico learned Greek, as well as astronomy, from his father. In 1521 he was ordained priest; he later became a Benedictine. Except for short sojourns in Rome and Naples, he lived his whole life in Sicily.

Maurolico's patrons included Giovanni de Vega, Charles V's viceroy of Sicily, who entrusted him with the mathematical education of one of his sons; and Giovanni Ventimiglia and his son, Simon, both marquises of Geraci and princes of Castelbuono and governors ("stradigò") of Messina. In 1550 Simon conferred upon Maurolico the abbey of Santa Maria del Parto (today also known as the Santuario di San Guglielmo), near Castelbuono. Maurolico also held a number of civil commissions in Messina; he served as head of the mint, he was in charge (with the architect Ferramolino) of maintaining the fortifications of the city on behalf of Charles V, and he was appointed to write a history of Sicily, which, as *Sicanicarum rerum compendium*, was published in Messina in 1562. Most important, he gave public lectures on mathematics at the University of Messina, where he was appointed professor in 1569.

Although Maurolico himself referred to a vast literary production (in his *Cosmographia* and *Opuscula*), only a few of his works were printed, although these are enough to show him as an outstanding scholar. In addition to writing his own books, Maurolico translated, commented upon, reconstructed, and edited works by a number of ancient authors. His first work in this vein, published in Messina in 1558, included treatises on the sphere by Theodosius of Bythinia "ex traditione Maurolyci"; by Menelaus of Alexandria "ex traditione eiusdem"; and by Maurolico himself. The book also contained a work by Autolycus of Pitane on the moving sphere, translations of the *De habitationibus* of Theodosius and the *Phaenomena* of Euclid, trigonometric tables, a mathematical compendium, and a work entitled "Maurolyci de sphaera sermo."

This early book is especially noteworthy for two reasons. First, the Neapolitan mathematician Giuseppe d'Auria furthered the dissemination of Maurolico's work by including his annotations in later editions of Autolycus' *Sphaera* and Theodosius' *De habitationibus* (Rome, 1588), as well as of Euclid's *Phaenomena* (Rome, 1591). Second, J. B. J. Delambre, in his *Histoire de l'astronomie du moyen âge*, stated that Maurolico had been the first to make use of the trigonometric function of the secant. Maurolico did give a table of numerical values for the secants of 0° to 45° (the "tabella benefica"), but Copernicus had certainly preceded him in its use.

Maurolico's two other major books on ancient mathematics—one on Apollonius' *Conics*, and the other a collection of the works of Archimedes—were published only after his death. In *Emendatio et restitutio conicorum Apollonii Pergaei* (Messina, 1654), Maurolico attempted to reconstruct books V and VI of the *Conics* from the brief references to them that Apollonius provided in his preface to the entire work. In Maurolico's time, only the first four books were known in the Greek original; he completed his restoration in 1547, and a similar reconstruction of book V was published by Vincenzo Viviani in 1659. (Although Maurolico's work is less famous than Viviani's, both Libri and Gino Loria cite it as an example of his genius.) Maurolico's collection of Archimedes' works, *Admirandi Archimedis Syracusani monumenta omnia mathematica quae extant . . . ex traditione doctissimi viri D. Francisci Maurolici* (Palermo, 1685), was based upon an earlier partial

edition by Borelli (Messina, 1670–1672), which was almost completely lost.

Among the most important of Maurolico's extant books are *Cosmographia* (Venice, 1543), written in the form of three dialogues; *Opuscula mathematica* (Venice, 1575), a collection of eight treatises; *Photismi de lumine et umbra ad perspectivam et radiorum incidentiam facientes* (possibly Venice, 1575, and certainly Naples, 1611); and *Problemata mechanica . . . et ad magnetem et ad pixidem nauticam pertinentia* (Messina, 1613). In addition to these, a number of Maurolico's manuscripts held by the Bibliothèque Nationale, Paris, were published by Federico Napoli in 1876; these include a letter of 8 August 1556, in which Maurolico reported on his mathematical studies to his patron Giovanni de Vega; a brief treatise, previously thought to be lost, entitled "Demonstratio algebrae"; books I and II of a 1555 "Geometricarum quaestionum"; and a "Brevis demonstratio centri in parabola," dated 1565.

Of the mathematical works edited by Napoli, the "Demonstratio algebrae" is elementary in its concerns, dealing with simple second-degree problems and derivations from them. "Geometricarum quaestionum" is primarily devoted to trigonometry and solid geometry, but touches upon geodesy in offering a proposal for a new method for measuring the earth, a method previously discussed in the *Cosmographia* and later taken up by Jean Picard for measuring the meridian (1669–1671). In the "Brevis demonstratio centri in parabola," Maurolico chose to deal with a problem related to mechanics—which he also treated in his edition of Archimedes—the determination of the center of gravity of a segment of a paraboloid of revolution cut off by a plane perpendicular to its axis.

The greatest number of Maurolico's mathematical writings are gathered in the *Opuscula mathematica;* indeed, the second volume of that work, "Arithmeticorum libri duo," is wholly devoted to that subject and contains, among other things, some notable research on the theory of numbers. This includes, in particular, a treatment of polygonal numbers that is more complete than that of Diophantus, to which Maurolico added a number of simple and ingenious proofs. L. E. Dickson has remarked upon Maurolico's argument that every perfect number is hexagonal, and therefore triangular, while Baldassarre Boncompagni noted his proof of a peculiarity of the succession of odd numbers. That property had been enunciated by Nicomachus of Gerasa, Iamblichus, and Boethius, among others.

Among the topics related to mathematics in the *Opuscula* are chronology (the treatise "Computus ecclesiasticus") and gnomonics (in two treatises, both entitled "De lineis horariis," one of which also discusses conics). The work also contains writing on Euclid's *Elements* (for which see also the unpublished Bibliothèque Nationale, Paris, manuscript Fonds Latin 7463). Of particular interest, too, is a passage on a correlation between regular polyhedrons, which was commented upon by J. H. T. Müller, and later by Moritz Cantor. The balance of Maurolico's known mathematical work is contained in three manuscripts, mostly on geometrical problems, in the Biblioteca Nazionale Centrale Vittorio Emanuele in Rome; they have been described by Luigi De Marchi.

Maurolico's work in astronomy includes the first treatise collected in the *Opuscula*, "De sphaera liber unus," in which he criticized Copernicus. In another item of the collection, "De instrumentis astronomicis," Maurolico described the principal astronomical instruments and discussed their theory, use, and history—a subject similar to that treated in one of his first publications, the rare and little-known tract *Quadrati fabrica et eius usus* (Venice, 1546). In practical astronomy, Maurolico observed the nova that appeared in the constellation Cassiopeia in 1572. Until recently all that was known of this observation was contained in the short extracts from an unknown work by Maurolico that were published by Clavius in his *In Sphaeram Ioannis de Sacro Bosco commentarius* (Rome, 1581). In 1960, however, C. Doris Hellman published an apograph manuscript that she had found in the Biblioteca Nazionale of Naples. This manuscript contains a full account of Maurolico's observation; it is dated 6 November 1572, and is clear evidence that Maurolico's observation preceded by at least five days the more famous one made by Tycho Brahe.

Maurolico also did important work in optics; indeed, according to Libri, "it is in his research on optics, above all, that Maurolico showed the most sagacity" (*Histoire*, III, 116). The chief record of this research is *Photismi de lumine et umbra*, in which Maurolico discussed the rainbow, the theory of vision, the effects of lenses, the principal phenomena of dioptrics and catoptrics, radiant heat, photometry, and caustics. Maurolico's work on caustics was anticipated by that of Leonardo da Vinci (as was his research on centers of gravity), but Leonardo's work was not published until long after Maurolico's. Libri further characterized the *Photismi de lumine et umbra* as "full of curious facts and ingenious research" (*Histoire*, III, 118), and Sarton suggested that it might be the most remarkable optical treatise of the sixteenth century outside the tradition of Alhazen, or even the best optical book of the Renaissance (*Six Wings*, 84, 85).

Maurolico applied his broad scientific knowledge to a number of other fields. One treatise in the *Opuscula*, "Musicae traditiones," is devoted to music. The *Problemata mechanica* published in 1613 is concerned with mechanics and magnetism, as is, to some degree, the "Brevis demonstratio." His contributions to geodesy have already been discussed; he made an additional contribution to geography with a map of Sicily, drawn about 1541 at the request of Jacopo Gastaldo (who published it in 1575)—this map was also incorporated by Abraham Ortelius in his *Theatrum orbis terrarum*. Maurolico wrote on the fish of Sicily, in a letter to Pierre Gilles d'Albi, dated 1 March 1543 and published by Domenico Sestini in 1807, and on the eruption of Mt. Etna, in a letter to Cardinal Pietro Bembo, dated 4 May 1546 and published by Giuseppe Spezi in 1862. Finally, he enjoyed some contemporary fame as a meteorologist, based upon a weather prediction that he made for John of Austria upon the latter's departure from Messina prior to the Battle of Lepanto (1571).

BIBLIOGRAPHY

I. ORIGINAL WORKS. Almost all of Maurolico's writings have been mentioned in the text. For further information see Pietro Riccardi, *Biblioteca matematica italiana* (Modena, 1870–1928; repr. Milan, 1952), articles "Archimede," "Auria," "Maurolico"; and Federico Napoli, "Intorno alla vita ed ai lavori di Francesco Maurolico," pref. to "Scritti inediti di Francesco Maurolico," in *Bullettino di bibliografia e di storia delle scienze matematiche e fisiche*, **9** (1876), 1–121, on p. 5 of which is a list of codices of the Bibliothèque Nationale, Paris, containing autographs by Maurolico (Fonds Latin, nos. 6177, 7249, 7251, 7459, 7462–7468, 7471, 7472A, 7473). On this see also Federico Napoli, "Nota intorno ad alcuni manoscritti di Maurolico della Biblioteca Parigina," in *Rivista sicula di scienze, letteratura ed arti*, **8** (1872), 185–192.

See also Luigi De Marchi, "Di tre manoscritti del Maurolicio che si trovano nella Biblioteca Vittorio Emanuele di Roma," in Eneström's *Bibliotheca mathematica* (1885), cols. 141–144, 193–195. In the codices described by De Marchi (marked 32, 33, 34; formerly S. Pantaleo 115, 116, 117), there is a letter from Maurolico to Prince Barresi di Pietraperzia, dated 11 Sept. 1571, which was published by De Marchi in "Una lettera inedita di Francesco Maurolico a proposito della battaglia di Lepanto," in *Rendiconti dell'Istituto lombardo di scienze e lettere*, **16** (1883), 464–467; this letter, De Marchi observes, may be considered as Maurolico's scientific will.

Maurolico's letter to Cardinal Bembo of 4 May 1546 is in Giuseppe Spezi, *Lettere inedite del Card. Pietro Bembo e di altri scrittori del secolo XVI, tratte da codici Vaticani e Barberiniani* (Rome, 1862), pp. 79–84. A letter from Maurolico to Cardinal Antonio Amulio dated 1 Dec. 1568 is in Baldassarre Boncompagni, "Intorno ad una proprietà de' numeri dispari," in *Bullettino di bibliografia e di storia delle scienze matematiche e fisiche*, **8** (1875), 51–62, see pp. 55–56, where a MS on arithmetic by Maurolico is cited (Codex Vat. lat. no. 3131) and the dedicatory letter which precedes it is published.

The work on the nova of 1572 is in "Maurolyco's 'Lost' Essay on the New Star of 1572," transcribed, translated, and edited by C. Doris Hellman, in *Isis*, **51** (1960), 322–336; the MS, in the Biblioteca Nazionale of Naples (cod. I E 56, fols. 2r–10r), perhaps a copy of an autograph version, is entitled "Super nova stella: Que hoc anno iuxta Cassiopes apparere cepit considerationes."

The work on Sicilian fish is in Domenico Sestini, *Viaggi e opuscoli diversi* (Berlin, 1807), 285–302, with notes on pp. 303–313 and mention of the MS used on p. xiii; see also *Tractatus per epistolam Francisci Maurolici ad Petrum Gillium de piscibus siculis Codice manu auctoris exarato, Aloisius Facciolà messanensis nunc primum edidit* (Palermo, 1893). An English translation of the *Photismi* is *The Photismi de Lumine of Maurolycus. A Chapter in Late Medieval Optics*, Henry Crew, trans. (New York, 1940).

The rare pamphlet on the quadrant is in the personal library of Dr. Carlo Viganò, Brescia, Italy. Its full title is *Quadrati fabrica et eius usus, ut hoc solo instrumento, caeteris praetermissis, uniusquisq. mathematicus, contentus esse possit, per Franciscum Maurolycum nuper edita. Illustriss. D. D. Ioanni Vigintimillio Ieraciensium Marchioni, D.* (Venice, 1546). In colophons to various parts of the text Maurolico gives the dates 6 Apr. 1541, 18 Apr. 1541, and 11 Jan. 1542. The work consists of eleven numbered pages and one unnumbered page with a table of stars.

II. SECONDARY LITERATURE. Older biographies and bibliographies on Maurolico include Francesco della Foresta, *Vita dell'abbate del Parto D. Francesco Maurolyco* (Messina, 1613), written by the nephew and namesake of the subject; Antonino Mongitore, "Maurolico," in *Biblioteca sicula*, I (Palermo, 1707), 226–227; Domenico Scinà, *Elogio di Francesco Maurolico* (Palermo, 1808); and Girolamo Tiraboschi, "Maurolico," in *Storia della letteratura italiana*, VII (Milan, 1824), 728–734.

Two valuable monographs from the late nineteenth century are Giuseppe Rossi, *Francesco Maurolico e il risorgimento filosofico e scientifico in Italia nel secolo XVI* (Messina, 1888); and Giacomo Macrì, "Francesco Maurolico nella vita e negli scritti," in R. Accademia Peloritana, *Commemorazione del IV centenario di Francesco Maurolico MDCCCXCIV* (Messina, 1896), p. iii–iv, 1–198. The latter volume also contains "Ricordi inediti di Francesco Maurolico," illustrated by Giuseppe Arenaprimo di Montechiaro, p. 199–230, with three plates reproducing handwritten items by Maurolico.

Maurolico is discussed in the following standard histories of mathematics: J. E. Montucla, *Histoire des mathématiques*, 2 vols. (Paris, 1758), I, 563, 571–572, 695–698; Guglielmo Libri, *Histoire des sciences mathématiques en Italie*, 3 vols. (Paris, 1837–1841), III, 102–118; Moritz Cantor, *Vorlesungen über Geschichte der Mathematik*, 4 vols. (Leipzig, 1880–1908), II, 558–559, 575, *passim*; and David Eugene Smith, *History of Mathematics*, 2 vols. (Boston, 1924–1925), I, 301–302, and II, 622. See also

Florian Cajori, *A History of Mathematical Notations*, 2 vols. (La Salle, Ill., 1928–1929), I, 349, 362, 402, and II, 150.

Maurolico's work on mathematicians of antiquity is discussed in Vincenzo Flauti, "Sull'Archimede e l'Apollonio di Maurolico. Osservazioni storico-critiche," in *Memorie della Accademia delle scienze di Napoli*, **2** (1855–1857), lxxxiv–xciv; and Gino Loria, *Le scienze esatte nell'antica Grecia* (Milan, 1914), 219, 354, 434, 435, 502, 510, 511, 513, 515. On Maurolico as editor of Autolycus, see the following works by Joseph Mogenet: "Pierre Forcadel traducteur de Autolycus," in *Archives internationales d'histoire des sciences* (1950), 114–128; and "Autolycus de Pitane: Histoire du texte, suivie de l'édition critique des traités De la sphère en mouvement et Des levers et couchers," in Université de Louvain, *Recueil de travaux d'histoire et de philologie*, 3rd ser., fasc. 37 (1950), 23, 26, 27, 30–36, 38–42, 48–50, 176.

Arithmetic is treated in Mariano Fontana, "Osservazioni storiche sopra l'aritmetica di Francesco Maurolico," in *Memorie dell'Istituto nazionale italiano* (Bologna), Fis.-mat. cl., **2**, pt. 1 (1808), 275–296; Baldassarre Boncompagni, "Intorno ad una proprietà de' numeri dispari" (see above); and Leonard Eugene Dickson, *History of the Theory of Numbers* (Washington, D.C., 1919; repr. New York, 1952, 1966), I, 9, 20, and II, 5, 6.

On the use of the principle of mathematical induction by Maurolico, anticipated by Euclid, see the following writings by Giovanni Vacca: "Maurolycus, the First Discoverer of the Principle of Mathematical Induction," in *Bulletin of the American Mathematical Society*, **16** (1909–1910), 70–73; "Sulla storia del principio d'induzione completa," in Loria's *Bollettino di bibliografia e storia delle scienze matematiche*, **12** (1910), 33–35; and "Sur le principe d'induction mathématique," in *Revue de métaphysique et de morale*, **19** (1911), 30–33. See also W. H. Bussey, "The Origin of Mathematical Induction," in *American Mathematical Monthly*, **24** (1917), 199–207; Léon Brunschvicg, *Les étapes de la philosophie mathématique*, 3rd ed. (Paris, 1929), 481–484; and Hans Freudenthal, "Zur Geschichte der vollständigen Induktion," in *Archives internationales d'histoire des sciences* (1953), 17–37.

Maurolico's geometry is treated in Michel Chasles, *Aperçu historique sur l'origine et le développement des méthodes en géometrie*, 2nd ed. (Paris, 1875), 120, 291, 293, 345, 496, 516; J. H. T. Müller, "Zur Geschichte des Dualismus in der Geometrie," in Grunert's *Archiv der Mathematik und Physik*, **34** (1860), 1–6; and Federico Amodeo, "Il trattato sulle coniche di Francesco Maurolico," in Eneström's *Bibliotheca mathematica*, 3rd ser., **9** (1908–1909), 123–138.

On centers of gravity, see Margaret E. Baron, *The Origins of the Infinitesimal Calculus* (Oxford, 1969), 90–94.

Astronomy is discussed in J. B. J. Delambre, *Histoire de l'astronomie du moyen âge* (Paris, 1819; repr. New York, 1965), 437–441; J. L. E. Dreyer, *A History of Astronomy From Thales to Kepler* (New York, 1953), 257, 295, 356–357, formerly entitled *History of the Planetary Systems*

From Thales to Kepler (Cambridge, 1906); Lynn Thorndike, *A History of Magic and Experimental Science*, V (New York, 1941), 304, 360, 421, 426, and VI (New York, 1941), 27, 74, 179–180, 382; and Edward Rosen, "Maurolico's Attitude Toward Copernicus," in *Proceedings of the American Philosophical Society*, **101** (1957), 177–194.

On Maurolico's contributions to geodesy, see Pietro Riccardi, "Cenni sulla storia della geodesia in Italia dalle prime epoche fin oltre alla metà del secolo XIX," in *Memorie della Accademia delle scienze di Bologna*, 3rd ser., **10** (1879), 431–528, see 518–519; and "Sopra un antico metodo per determinare il semidiametro della terra," *ibid.*, 4th ser., **7** (1887), 17–22; and Ottavio Zanotti-Bianco, "Sopra una vecchia e poco nota misura del semidiametro terrestre," in *Atti della Accademia delle scienze di Torino*, **19** (1883–1884), 791–794.

On optics, besides works by Libri, Crew, and Sarton already cited, see the following writings of Vasco Ronchi: *Optics, the Science of Vision*, trans. and rev. by Edward Rosen (New York, 1957), 39–40, 265; "L'optique au XVIᵉ siècle," in *La science au seizième siècle. Colloque international de Royaumont, 1–4 juillet 1957* (Paris, 1960), 47–65, and *The Nature of Light*, trans. by V. Barocas (London, 1970), 78, 99ss., 223. See also A. C. Crombie, "The Mechanistic Hypothesis and the Scientific Study of Vision," in S. Bradbury and G. L'E. Turner, eds., *Historical Aspects of Microscopy* (Cambridge, 1967), 3–112 (see 43–46), and in *Proceedings of the Royal Microscopical Society*, 2, pt. 1 (1967).

On music, see Salvatore Pugliatti, "Le *Musicae traditiones* di Francesco Maurolico" in *Atti dell'Accademia peloritana*, **48** (1951–1967). On p. 336 is mentioned a MS, which contains three papers of Maurolico: "De divisione artium," "De quantitate," "De proportione." This MS was recently found by Monsignor Graziano Bellifemine in the Library and Museum of the Seminario Vescovile at Molfetta.

On Maurolico as a man of letters, historian, and philosopher, see G. Macrì, "Francesco Maurolico nella vita e negli scritti" (see above), pp. 48–62, 123–151; Valentino Labate, "Le fonti del *Sicanicarum rerum compendium* di Francesco Maurolico," in *Atti dell'Accademia peloritana*, **13** (1898–1899), 53–84; and L. Perroni-Grande, "F. Maurolico professore dell'Università messinese e dantista," in R. Accademia Peloritana, *CCCL anniversario della Università di Messina. Contributo storico* (Messina, 1900), 15–41, which includes the notarial act containing the nomination of Maurolico as professor at the University of Messina.

Other writings to be consulted are Luigi De Marchi, "Sull'ortografia del nome del matematico messinese Maurolicio," in Eneström's *Biblioteca mathematica* (1886), cols. 90–92; and several biobibliographical writings by Edward Rosen: "The Date of Maurolico's Death," in *Scripta mathematica*, **22** (1956), 285–286; "Maurolico Was an Abbot," in *Archives internationales d'histoire des sciences* (1956), 349–350; "De Morgan's Incorrect Description of Maurolico's Books," in *Papers of the Bibliographical Society of America*, **51** (1957), 111–118; "Was Mauro-lico's Essay on the Nova of 1572 Printed?," in *Isis*, **48** (1957), 171–175; "The Title of Maurolico's *Photismi*," in *American Journal of Physics*, **25** (1957), 226–228; and "The Editions of Maurolico's Mathematical Works," in *Scripta mathematica*, **24** (1959), 56–76.

ARNALDO MASOTTI

MAYER, CHRISTIAN GUSTAV ADOLPH (*b.* Leipzig, Germany, 15 February 1839; *d.* Gries bei Bozen, Austria [now Bolzano, Italy], 11 April 1908)

The son of a wealthy Leipzig merchant family, Mayer studied mathematics and physics from 1857 to 1865 at Leipzig, Göttingen, Heidelberg, and chiefly at Königsberg under F. Neumann. In 1861 he received his doctorate from Heidelberg and qualified to lecture there in 1866. He became assistant professor in 1871 and full professor in 1890. In 1872 Mayer married Margerete Weigel. Poor health caused him to suspend his teaching activities early in 1908.

As a professor, Mayer enjoyed great respect from his colleagues and students. His activity as a researcher, which earned him membership in numerous learned societies, dealt essentially with the theory of differential equations, the calculus of variations, and theoretical mechanics. In his work, following Lagrange and Jacobi, he was capable of bringing out the inner relationship of these fields through emphasis on the principle of least action. Mayer achieved important individual results concerning the theory of integration of partial differential equations and the criteria for maxima and minima in variation problems. This work quickly brought him into close contact with the investigations on partial differential equations that Lie had under way at about the same time. Through subsequent works of Mayer, Lie's achievements became famous relatively quickly. Despite a great variety of methods and an outstanding mastery of calculation, Mayer was unable to develop the rigor necessary for the existence theorems of the calculus of variations; such rigor was displayed in exemplary fashion at approximately the same time by Weierstrass.

BIBLIOGRAPHY

Among Mayer's works are *Beiträge zur Theorie der Maxima und Minima einfacher Integrale* (Leipzig, 1866); *Geschichte des Prinzips der kleinsten Aktion* (Leipzig, 1877); and "Unbeschränkt integrable Systeme von linearen totalen Differentialgleichungen und die simultane Integration linearer partieller Differentialgleichungen," in *Mathematische Annalen*, **5** (1872), 448–470. Also see the obituary notice by O. Holder, in *Berichte* *über die Verhandlungen der sächsischen Akademie der Wissenschaften zu Leipzig*, Math.-phys. Kl., **60** (1908), 353–373.

H. WUSSING

MAZURKIEWICZ, STEFAN

MAZURKIEWICZ, STEFAN (*b*. Warsaw, Poland, 25 September 1888; *d*. Grodżisk Mazowiecki, near Warsaw, 19 June 1945)

Mazurkiewicz was, with Zygmunt Janiszewski and Wacław Sierpiński, a founder of the contemporary Polish mathematical school and, in 1920, of its journal *Fundamenta mathematicae*, which is devoted to set theory and to related fields, including topology and foundations of mathematics.

The son of a noted lawyer, Mazurkiewicz received his secondary education at the lyceum in Warsaw. He passed his baccalaureate in 1907, studied mathematics at the universities of Cracow, Lvov, Munich, and Göttingen, and was awarded a Ph.D. in 1913 by the University of Lvov for his thesis, done under Sierpiński, on curves filling the square ("O krzywych wypełniajacych kwadrat"). Named professor of mathematics in 1915 at the University of Warsaw, he held this chair until his death. He was several times elected dean of the Faculty of Mathematical and Natural Sciences and, in 1937, prorector of the University of Warsaw. He was a member of the Polish Academy of Sciences and Letters; of the Warsaw Society of Sciences and Letters, which elected him its secretary-general in 1935; of the Polish Mathematical Society, which elected him its president for the years 1933–1935; and member of the editorial boards of *Fundamenta mathematicae* and the *Monografie matematyczne* from their beginnings. His book on the theory of probability was written in Warsaw during the German occupation of Poland. The manuscript was destroyed in 1944 when the Germans burned and destroyed Warsaw before their retreat; it was partly rewritten by Mazurkiewicz and published in Polish eleven years after his death. Gravely ill, Mazurkiewicz shared the lot of the people of Warsaw. He died in the outskirts of the city during an operation for gastric ulcer.

Mazurkiewicz' scientific activity was in two principal areas: topology with its applications to the theory of functions, and the theory of probability. The topology seminar given by him and Janiszewski, beginning in 1916, was probably the world's first in this discipline. He exerted a great influence on the scientific work of his students and collaborators by the range of the ideas and problems in which he was interested, by the inventive spirit with which he treated them, and by the diversity of the methods that he applied to them.

As early as 1913 Mazurkiewicz gave to topology an ingenious characterization of the continuous images of the segment of the straight line, known today as locally connected continua. He based it on the notions of the oscillation of a continuum at a point and on that of relative distance; the latter concept, which he introduced, was shown to be valuable for other purposes. This characterization therefore differs from those established at about the same time by Hans Hahn and by Sierpiński, which were based on other ideas. It is also this characterization that is linked with the Mazurkiewicz-Moore theorem on the arcwise connectedness of continua.

Mazurkiewicz' theorems, according to which every continuous function that transforms a compact linear set into a plane set with interior points takes the same value in at least three distinct points (a theorem established independently by Hahn), while every compact plane set that is devoid of interior point is a binary continuous image, enabled him to define the notion of dimension of compact sets as follows: the dimension of such a set C is at most n when n is the smallest whole number for which there exists a continuous function transforming onto C a nondense compact linear set and taking the same value in at most $n + 1$ distinct points of this set. This definition preceded by more than seven years that of Karl Menger and Pavel Uryson, to which it is equivalent for compact sets.

In a series of later publications Mazurkiewicz contributed considerably to the development of topology by means of solutions to several fundamental problems posed by Sierpiński, Karl Menger, Paul Alexandroff, Pavel Uryson, and others, through which he singularly deepened our knowledge, especially of the topological structure of the Euclidean plane. In solving the problem published by Sierpiński (in *Fundamenta mathematicae*, **2** [1921], 286), he constructed on the plane a closed connected set which is the sum of a denumerable infinity of disjoint closed sets (1924) and which, in addition, has the property that all these summands except one are connected; at the same time he showed (independently of R. L. Moore) that on the plane the connectedness of all the summands in question is impossible, although, according to a result of Sierpiński's, it ought to be possible in space. Mazurkiewicz also solved, affirmatively, Alexandroff's problem (1935) on the existence of an indecomposable continuum (that is, one which is the sum of not fewer than $2^{\aleph_0}$ subcontinua different from itself) in every continuum of more than one dimension; that of Menger (1929) on the existence, for every positive integer n, of weakly

n-dimensional sets; and that of Uryson (1927) on the existence, for every integer $n > 1$, of separable complete n-dimensional spaces devoid of connected subsets containing more than one point. He also showed (1929) that if R is a region in n-dimensional Euclidean space and E is a set of $n - 2$ dimensions, then the difference $R - E$ is always connected and is even a semicontinuum.

Mazurkiewicz also contributed important results concerning the topological structure of curves, in particular concerning that of indecomposable continua, as well as an ingenious demonstration, by use of the Baire category method, that the family of hereditarily indecomposable continua of the plane, and therefore that the continua of less paradoxical structure occur in it only exceptionally (1930).

By applying the same method to the problems of the theory of functions, Mazurkiewicz showed (1931) that the set of periodic continuous functions f, for which the integral $\int_0^1 t^{-1}f(x + t) + f(x - t) - 2f(x)dt$ diverges everywhere, is of the second Baire category in the space of all continuous real functions, and that the same is true with the set of continuous functions which are nowhere differentiable. In addition he provided the quite remarkable result that the set of continuous functions transforming the segment of the straight line into plane sets which contains Sierpiński's universal plane curve (universality here designating the presence of homeomorphic images of every plane curve) is also of the second Baire category. Among Mazurkiewicz' other results on functions are those concerning functional spaces and the sets in those spaces that are called projective (1936, 1937), as well as those regarding the set of singular points of an analytic function and the classical theorems of Eugène Roché, Julius Pál, and Michael Fekete.

In the theory of probability, Mazurkiewicz formulated and demonstrated, in a work published in Polish (1922), the strong law of large numbers (independently of Francesco Cantelli); established several axiom systems of this theory (1933, 1934); and constructed a universal separable space of random variables by suitably enlarging that of the random variables of the game of heads or tails to a complete space (1935). These results and many others were included and developed in his book on the theory of probability.

BIBLIOGRAPHY

I. ORIGINAL WORKS. Among the 130 of Mazurkiewicz' mathematical publications listed in *Fundamenta mathematicae*, **34** (1947), 326–331, the most important are "Sur les points multiples des courbes qui remplissent une aire plane," in *Prace matematyczno-fizyczne*, **26** (1915), 113–120; "Teoria zbiorów G_δ" ("Theory of G_δ Sets"), in *Wektor*, **7** (1918), 1–57; "O pewnej nowej formie uogólnienia twierdzenia Bernoulli'ego" ("On a New Generalization of Bernoulli's Theorem"), in *Wiadomości aktuarjalne*, **1** (1922), 1–8; "Sur les continus homogènes," in *Fundamenta mathematicae*, **5** (1924), 137–146; "Sur les continus plans non bornés," *ibid.*, 188–205; "Sur les continus absolument indécomposables," *ibid.*, **16** (1930), 151–159; "Sur le théorème de Rouché," in *Comptes rendus de la Société des sciences et des lettres de Varsovie*, **28** (1936), 78, 79; and "Sur les transformations continues des courbes," in *Fundamenta mathematicae*, **31** (1938), 247–258. See also the posthumous works *Podstawy rachunku prawdopodobieństwa* ("Foundations of the Calculus of Probability"), J. Łoś, ed., *Monografie Matematyczne*, no. 32 (Warsaw, 1956); and *Travaux de topologie et ses applications* (Warsaw, 1969), with a complete bibliography of Mazurkiewicz' 141 scientific publications.

II. SECONDARY LITERATURE. See P. S. Alexandroff, "Sur quelques manifestations de la collaboration entre les écoles mathématiques polonaise et soviétique dans le domaine de topologie et théorie des ensembles," in *Roczniki Polskiego towarzystwa matematycznego*, 2nd ser., *Wiadomości matematyczne*, **6** (1963), 175–180, a lecture delivered at the Polish Mathematical Society, Warsaw, 18 May 1962; and C. Kuratowski, "Stefan Mazurkiewicz et son oeuvre scientifique," in *Fundamenta mathematicae*, **34** (1947), 316–331, repr. in S. Mazurkiewicz, *Travaux de topologie et ses applications* (Warsaw, 1969), pp. 9–26.

B. KNASTER

MELLO, FRANCISCO DE (*b.* Lisbon, Portugal, 1490; *d.* Évora, Portugal, 27 April 1536)

The son of a nobleman, Manuel de Mello, and Beatriz de Silva, Mello was a protégé of the Portuguese king Manuel I, who sent him to Paris to study. Mello graduated in theology and mathematics; his teacher was Pierre Brissot, who gave him a thorough grounding in the works of Euclid and Archimedes. On his return to Portugal, Mello was appointed tutor to the king's children. He may have served in an official capacity in navigating the Atlantic in order to determine the boundaries of the Spanish and Portuguese territories as defined by the Holy See. He was also to some degree involved in Portuguese politics, and shortly before his death was rewarded with the bishopric of Goa (it is not known whether he actually accepted this post, although it is certain that he never went there).

Mello enjoyed considerable fame as a scientist; as such, Gil Vicente dedicated to him some verses in the introduction to the *Auto da feira*. He was also firmly within the humanistic tradition of his time; his friends included Nicolás Clenard, Juan Luis Vives, and his fellow mathematician Gaspar de Lax. Many of his own works were destroyed by the fire that followed the Lisbon earthquake of 1755. Among his mathematical writings are "De videndi ratione atque oculorum forma," a commentary on Euclid's *Optica*; "De incidentibus in humidis," a commentary on Archimedes' hydrostatics; and an "Elements of Geometry," which would seem to be derived from Jābir ibn Aflaḥ. His nonscientific writings included translations from Latin authors and funerary poems.

Mello should not be confused with the great historian Francisco Manuel de Mello (1611–1667), who also wrote on mathematics.

BIBLIOGRAPHY

On Mello and his work see M. Bataillon, "Erasme et la cour de Portugal," in *Études sur le Portugal au temps de l'humanisme* (Coimbra, 1952), 49–100; Diego Barbosa Machado, *Bibliotheca Lusitana* (Lisbon, 1747), 197–198; Felipe Picatoste y Rodríguez, *Apuntes para una biblioteca científica española del siglo XVI* (Madrid, 1891), 167; Antonio Ribeiro dos Santos, *Memoria da vida e escritos de Don Francisco de Mello*, Memórias de literatura portuguesa publicadas pela Academia Real das sciencias de Lisboa, VII (Lisbon, 1806), 237–249; and Inocencio Francisco da Silva, *Diccionario bibliografico portugues*, III (Lisbon, 1859), 8–10.

JUAN VERNET

MENABREA, LUIGI FEDERICO (*b.* Chambéry, Savoy, 4 September 1809; *d.* St. Cassin [near Chambéry], France, 24 May 1896)

Menabrea is known to scientists as one of the most important men in the development of energy methods in the theory of elasticity and structures, and to others as a distinguished general and statesman, each group being generally little aware of Menabrea's accomplishments in the other fields. Indeed, it is remarkable that he was able to make significant contributions in both types of activities.

Menabrea first studied engineering and then mathematics at the University of Turin. Upon graduation he entered the army corps of engineers. When Charles Albert acceded to the throne in 1831, Cavour resigned his army commission, and Menabrea replaced Cavour at the Alpine fortress of Bardo. Menabrea soon left to become professor of mechanics and construction at the Military Academy of the Kingdom of Sardinia at

Turin and at the University of Turin. To this early period belongs his exposition and extension of Babbage's invention of a mechanical calculator to be published in 1842.

His political career started at this time. Between the years 1848 and 1859 King Charles Albert entrusted Menabrea with diplomatic missions to Modena and Parma. Menabrea then entered Parliament (where he championed proposals for Alpine tunneling) and was attached successively to the ministries of war and foreign affairs. At the same time he attained the rank of major general and was commander in chief of the army engineers in the Lombard campaigns of 1859. He directed siege and fortification works and also the artifical flooding of the plains between the Dora Baltea and the Sesia rivers to obstruct the Austrian advance.

During this time (1857–1858) Menabrea's early scientific papers were published, in which he gave the first precise formulation of the methods of structural analysis based on the "virtual work principle" earlier examined by A. Dorna. He studied an elastic truss in these papers and enunciated his "principle of elasticity," calling it also "principle of least work." He stated that when an elastic system attains equilibrium under external forces, the work done by the tensions and compressions in the internal members of the system is a minimum.

Menabrea's political and military advance continued. In 1860 he became lieutenant-general, conducted sieges at Ancona, Capua, and Gaeta, was appointed senator, and was granted the title of count. He was minister of the navy under Ricasoli from June 1861 to May 1862 and from January to April 1863 and minister of public works from December 1862 to September 1864 (under Farini and Minghetti). He was named Italian plenipotentiary for the peace negotiations with Austria in 1866. In October 1867 he succeeded Rattazzi as premier, holding simultaneously the portfolio of foreign minister, and remained in these posts in three cabinets until December 1869. During this turbulent period he was faced with the difficult situation created by Garibaldi's invasion of the Papal States. Menabrea issued the famous proclamation of 27 October 1868, in which he disavowed Garibaldi, against whom he instituted judicial proceedings. He protested against the pope's temporal power, insisted on the Italian prerogative of interference in Rome, and contended against infringement of Italian rights in repeated negotiations with Napoleon III and the pope.

In 1868 Menabrea published a new demonstration of his principle of least work, which, although superior to the preceding one, still failed to note the independence of the variations of the internal forces and of the elongations of the members of the structure. This oversight was criticized by Sabbia, Genocchi, and Castigliano, giving rise to a controversy lasting until 1875, which is described in the article on Castigliano. In 1870 Menabrea published jointly with the French mathematician J. L. F. Bertrand (1822–1900) a note that advanced the first valid proof of his principle.

In order to deprive Menabrea of influence as aide-de-camp to King Victor Emmanuel II, and to get him out of the country, Giovanni Lanza, his successor as premier, appointed him ambassador to London, and in 1882 to Paris. In 1875 he was made marquis of Valdora; he retired from public life in 1892.

Menabrea's place in the history of Italy is assured; his role in the introduction of concepts of work and energy into analytical mechanics and engineering has been overshadowed by the greater fame of Castigliano. In the United States, for example, Menabrea is hardly mentioned, although in Continental and particularly Italian textbooks the correct distinction between Menabrea's and Castigliano's theorems is generally made. Menabrea's methods placed these concepts for the first time very clearly before the engineering profession and thus started the essential work of education which was completed by Castigliano.

BIBLIOGRAPHY

I. ORIGINAL WORKS. Menabrea's principal scientific works consist of seven papers, as follows: "Notions sur la machine analytique de Charles Babbage," in *Bibliothèque Universelle de Genève*, n.s. **41** (1842), 352–376; "Principio generale per determinare le tensioni e le pressioni in un sistema elastico," a seminar presented to the Reale Accademia delle Scienze di Torino in 1857, which was then printed as "Nouveau principe sur la distribution des tensions dans les systèmes élastiques," in *Comptes rendus hebdomadaires des séances de l'Académie des sciences*, **46** (1858), 1056. Then followed "Étude de Statique Physique —Principe général pour déterminer les pressions et les tensions dans un système élastique," in *Memorie della Reale Accademia delle scienze di Torino*, 2nd ser., **25** (1868), 141. An abstract of Bertrand's letter to General Menabrea was published jointly by Menabrea and Bertrand in *Atti della Reale Accademia delle scienze*, **5** (1 May 1870), 702.

The last two contributions are the reply to criticism in "Un'ultima lettera sulle peripezie della serie di Lagrange in risposta al Prof. Angelo Genocchi per L. F. Menabrea, A. D. B. Boncompagni," in *Bullettino di bibliografia e di storia delle scienze matematiche e fisiche*, **6** (October 1873), 435, and the memoir which raised the dispute with Castigliano, i.e., "Sulla determinazione delle tensioni e delle pressioni ne sistemi elastici," in *Atti della Reale Accademia dei Lincei*, 2nd ser., **2** (1875), 201.

II. SECONDARY LITERATURE. The reader is referred to the article on Alberto Castigliano for a listing of pertinent

works, and to Menabrea's autobiography, covering the years up to 1871, published as *Memorie*, L. Briguglio and L. Bulferetti, eds. (Florence, 1971).

BRUNO A. BOLEY

MENAECHMUS (*fl.* Athens and Cyzicus, middle of fourth century B.C.)

In the summary of the history of Greek geometry given by Proclus, derived at this point from Eudemus, it is stated that "Amyclas of Heraclea, one of the friends of Plato, and Menaechmus, a pupil of Eudoxus and associate of Plato, and his brother Dinostratus made the whole of geometry still more perfect."[1] There is no reason to doubt that this Menaechmus is to be identified with the Manaechmus who is described in the *Suda Lexicon* as "a Platonic philosopher of Alopeconnesus, or according to some of Proconnesus, who wrote works of philosophy and three books on Plato's *Republic*."[2] Alopeconnesus was in the Thracian Chersonese, and Proconnesus (the Island of Marmara) was in the Propontis (the Sea of Marmara), no great distance from it; and both were near Cyzicus (Kapidaği Yarimadasi, Turkey), where Eudoxus took up his abode and where Helicon, another pupil, was born.[3] This dating of Menaechmus, about the middle of the fourth century B.C., accords with an agreeable anecdote reproduced by Stobaeus from the grammarian Serenus; when Alexander the Great requested Menaechmus to teach him geometry by an easy method, Menaechmus replied: "O king, for traveling through the country there are private roads and royal roads, but in geometry there is one road for all."[4] A similar story is told of Euclid and Ptolemy I;[5] but it would be natural to transfer it to the more famous geometer, and the attribution to Menaechmus is to be preferred. If true, it would suggest that Menaechmus was the mathematical tutor of Alexander. He could have been introduced to Alexander by Aristotle, who had close relations with the mathematicians of Cyzicus.[6] A phrase used by Proclus in two places—οἱ περὶ Μέναιχμον μαθηματικοί—implies that Menaechmus had a school;[7] and Allman has argued cogently that this was the mathematical school of Cyzicus, of which Eudoxus and Helicon (probably) were heads before him and Polemarchus and Callippus after him.[8]

According to Proclus, Menaechmus differentiated between two senses in which the word στοιχεῖον, "element," is used.[9] In one sense it means any proposition leading to another proposition, as Euclid I.1 is an element in the proof of I.2, or I.4 is in that of I.5; and in this sense propositions may be said to be elements of each other if they can be established reciprocally—for example, the relation between the sum of the interior angles of a rectilineal figure and the sum of the exterior angles. In the second sense an element is a simple constituent of a composite entity, and in this sense not every proposition is an element but only those having a primordial relation to the conclusion, as the postulates have to the theorems. As Proclus notes, this is the sense in which "element" is used by Euclid, and Menaechmus may have helped to fix this terminology.

In another passage Proclus shows that many so-called conversions of propositions are false and are not properly called conversions, that is, not every converse of a proposition is true.[10] As an example he notes that every hexagonal number is triangular but not every triangular number is hexagonal, and he adds that these matters have not escaped the notice of the mathematicians in the circle of Menaechmus and Amphinomus.

In yet another passage Proclus discusses the division of propositions into problems and theorems.[11] While the followers of Speusippus and Amphinomus held that all propositions were theorems, the school of Menaechmus maintained that they were all problems but that there were two types of problems: at one time the aim is to find the thing sought, at another to see what some definite thing is, or to what kind it belongs, or what change it has undergone, or what relation it has to something else. Proclus considers that both schools were right; it might be argued with equal justice that both were wrong and that the distinction between theorem and problem is valid.

It is clear from these references that Menaechmus gave much attention to the philosophy and technology of mathematics. He must also have applied himself to mathematical astronomy, for Theon of Smyrna records that Menaechmus and Callippus introduced the system of "deferent" and "counteracting" spheres into the explanation of the movements of the heavenly bodies (οἱ τὰς μὲν φερούσας, τὰς δὲ ἀνελιττούσας εἰσηγήσαντο).[12] The terms mean that one of the spheres bears the heavenly body; the other corrects its motion so as to account for the apparent irregularities of their paths. Eudoxus was the first to devise a mathematical model to explain the motions of the sun and planets, and he did so by a highly ingenious system of concentric spheres, the common center being the center of the earth. The sun, moon, and planets were each regarded as fixed on the equator of a moving sphere; the poles of that sphere were themselves borne round on a larger concentric sphere moving about two different poles with a different speed; and so on. For the sun and moon Eudoxus postulated three spheres; for the planets, four. The

modifications in this system made by Callippus are known in some detail. For example, he added one sphere for each planet except Jupiter and Saturn and two spheres for the sun and the moon—five in all. Nothing more is known of Menaechmus' contribution than what Theon relates, but he would appear to have been working on the same lines as Callippus. T. H. Martin conjectured that Menaechmus made his contribution in his commentary on Plato's *Republic* when dealing with the passage on the distaff of the Fates.[13]

It is not, however, on these achievements but on the discovery of the conic sections that the fame of Menaechmus chiefly rests. Democritus had speculated on plane sections of a cone parallel to the base and very near to each other,[14] and other geometers must have cut the cone (and cylinder) by sections not parallel to the base; but Menaechmus is the first who is known to have identified the resulting sections as curves with definite properties.

The discovery was a by-product of the search for a method of duplicating the cube. Hippocrates had shown that this could be reduced to the problem of finding two mean proportionals between two lines, and Menaechmus showed that the two means could be obtained by the intersection of a parabola and a hyperbola. His solution is given in a collection of such solutions preserved by Eutocius in his commentary on Archimedes' *On the Sphere and the Cylinder*.[15] Another of the solutions, by Eratosthenes, is introduced by a letter purporting to be from Eratosthenes to Ptolemy Euergetes.[16] The letter is spurious, but it quotes a genuine epigram by Eratosthenes written on a votive pillar to which was attached a device for effecting the solution mechanically. The epigram included the lines:[17]

Try not to do the difficult task of the cylinders of Archytas, or to cut the cones in the triads of Menaechmus or to draw such a pattern of lines as is described by the god-fearing Eudoxus.

Proclus, in a passage derived from Geminus, also attributes the discovery of the conic sections to Menaechmus and cites a line from the verses of Eratosthenes in the form Μὴ δὲ Μεναιχμίους κωνοτομεῖν τριάδας.[18] He notes again in his commentary on Plato's *Timaeus* that Menaechmus solved the problem of finding two means by "conic lines" but says that he prefers to transcribe Archytas' solution.[19]

Eratosthenes' epigram implies not only that Menaechmus was aware of the conic sections but that he was aware of all three types and saw them as sections of a cone—that is, not as plane curves that he later identified with sections of a cone. The proof itself shows also that he knew the properties of the asymptotes of a hyperbola,[20] at least of a rectangular hyperbola, which is astonishing when it is remembered that Apollonius does not introduce the asymptotes until his second book, after the properties of the diameter and ordinates have been proved. There are no signs of any knowledge of the conic sections before Menaechmus, but with him it suddenly blossomed forth into full flower.[21]

The proof as we have it cannot reproduce the words of Menaechmus himself and no doubt has been recast by Eutocius in his own language, or by someone earlier.[22] It uses the terms παραβολή and ὑπερβολή, although these words were first coined by Apollonius; and we have the evidence of Geminus, as transmitted by Eutocius, that "the ancients" (οἱ παλαιοί) used the names "section of a right-angled cone" for the parabola, "section of an obtuse-angled cone" for the hyperbola, and "section of an acute-angled cone" for the ellipse.[23] This is undeniable evidence that at the time of "the ancients" the three curves were conceived as sections of three types of cone. But how ancient were "the ancients"? Pappus gives a similar account to that of Geminus but says these names were given by Aristaeus;[24] and there is some reason to believe that the name used by Menaechmus for the ellipse was θυρεός, because its oval shape resembled a shield.[25] The question of name is not so important as the question behind it: whether Menaechmus discovered his curves as sections of cones or whether he investigated them as plane curves, which were only later (by Aristaeus?) identified with the curves obtained by plane sections of a cone. It will be necessary to return to this question later.

The term ἀσύμπτωτοι, employed by Eutocius, would also not have been used by Menaechmus, who probably used the expression αἱ ἔγγιστα εὐθεῖαι τῆς τοῦ ἀμβλυγωνίου κώνου τομῆς, or simply αἱ ἔγγιστα, which is found in Archimedes, who also employed the old names for the sections. Other terms that Menaechmus would not have used are ἄξων, "axis," and ὀρθία πλευρά, or *latus rectum*.

By way of introduction to Menaechmus' proof it may be pointed out that if *x*, *y* are two mean proportionals between *a*, *b*, so that

$$a : x = x : y = y : b,$$

then

$$x^2 = ay$$

and

$$xy = ab.$$

These are easily recognized today as the equations of a parabola referred to a diameter and a tangent at its extremity as axes and the equation of a hyperbola referred to its asymptotes as axes; the means may therefore be obtained as the intercepts on the axes of a point of intersection of a parabola and hyperbola, but Menaechmus had to discover *ab initio* that there were such curves and to ascertain their properties.

He proceeded by way of analysis and synthesis.

Suppose the problem solved. Let *a*, *b* be the given straight lines and *x*, *y* the mean proportionals—where the letters both indicate the lines and are a measure of

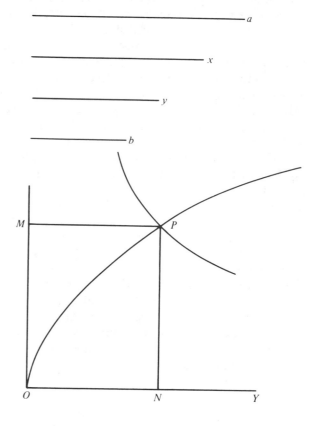

FIGURE 1

their length—so that $a : x = x : y = y : b$. On a straight line OY given in position and terminating at O, let $ON = y$ be cut off, and let there be drawn perpendicular to it at N the straight line $PN = x$. Because $a : x = x : y$, it follows that $ay = x^2$ or $a \cdot ON = x^2$, that is, $a \cdot ON = PN^2$, so that P lies on a parabola through O. Let the parallels PM, OM be drawn. Since xy is given, being equal to ab, $PM \cdot PN$ is also given; and therefore P lies on a hyperbola in the asymptotes OM, ON. P is therefore determined as the intersection of the parabola and hyperbola.

In the synthesis the straight lines a, b are given, and OY is given in position with O as an end point. Through O let there be drawn a parabola having OY as its axis and *latus rectum* a. Then the squares on the ordinates drawn at right angles to OY are equal to the rectangle contained by the *latus rectum* and the abscissa. Let OP be the parabola, let OM be drawn perpendicular to OY, and in the asymptotes OM, OY let there be drawn a hyperbola such that the rectangle contained by the straight lines drawn parallel to OM, ON is equal to the rectangle contained by a, b (that is, $PM \cdot PN = ab$). Let it cut the parabola at P, and let the perpendiculars PM, PN be drawn. Then by the property of the parabola

$$PN^2 = a \cdot ON,$$

that is,

$$a : PN = PN : ON,$$

and by the property of the hyperbola

$$ab = PN \cdot PM$$
$$= PN \cdot ON.$$

Therefore

$$a : PN = ON : b,$$

and

$$a : PN = PN : ON = ON : b.$$

Let a straight line x be drawn equal to PN and a straight line y equal to ON. Then a, x, y, b are in continuous proportion.

This solution is followed in the manuscripts of Eutocius by another solution introduced with the

word $"A\lambda\lambda\omega\varsigma,$ "Otherwise," in which the two means are obtained by the intersection of two parabolas. In the figure, AO, BO are the two given straight lines, the two parabolas through O intersect at P, and it is easily shown that

$$BO : ON = ON : OM = OM : OA,$$

or

$$a : x = x : y = y : b.$$

The proof is established by analysis and synthesis as in the first proof, and it corresponds to the equations

$$x^2 = ay$$
$$y^2 = bx.$$

It has hitherto been assumed by all writers on the subject that this second proof is also by Menaechmus, but G. J. Toomer has discovered as proposition 10 of the Arabic text of Diocles' *On Burning Mirrors* a solution of the problem of two mean proportionals by the intersection of two parabolas with axes at right angles to each other, and with *latera recta* equal to the two extremes, which looks remarkably like the second solution;[26] and it is followed as proposition 11 by another solution which is identical in its mathematical content with that attributed to Diocles by Eutocius. Toomer believes that the second solution should therefore be attributed to Diocles, not to Menaechmus. A final judgment must await publication of his edition of Diocles, but it may at once be noted that there are differences as well as resemblances. In particular, in the Arabic text Diocles starts from the focus-directrix property of the parabola—of which Menaechmus shows no awareness—and in order to get his means deduces from it the property that the ordinate at any point is a mean proportional between the abscissa and the *latus rectum*. It could be that Diocles found his solution independently, or he may have made a conscious adaptation of Menaechmus' solution in order to start from the focus-directrix property.

C. A. Bretschneider first showed how Menaechmus could have investigated the curves, and his suggestion has been generally followed.[27] In a semicircle the perpendicular from any point on the circumference to the diameter is a mean proportional between the segments of the diameter. This property would have been familiar before Menaechmus, and Bretschneider thinks it probable that he would have sought some similar property for the conic sections. We know from Geminus, as transmitted by Eutocius, that "the ancients" generated the conic sections by a plane section at right angles to one side (generator) of the cone, getting different curves according to whether

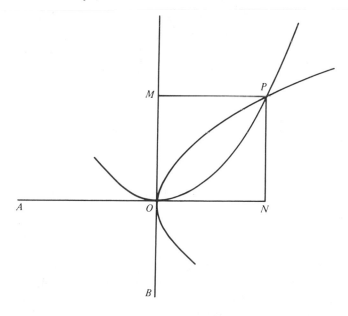

FIGURE 2

the cone was right-angled, obtuse-angled, or acute-angled.[28] If *ABC* is a right-angled cone and *DEF* is a plane section at right angles at *D* to the generator *AC*, the resulting curve where the plane intersects the cone is a parabola. Let *J* be any point in *DE*, and through *J* let there be drawn a plane parallel to the base of the cone. It will cut the cone in a circle. Let it meet the parabola at *K*. The planes *DEF* and *HKG* are both perpendicular to the plane *BAC,* and their line of

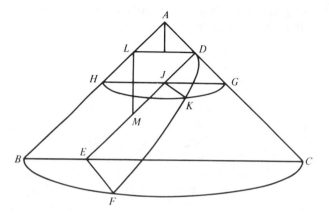

FIGURE 3

intersection *JK* is thus perpendicular to the diameter *HG.* Therefore,

$$JK^2 = HJ \cdot JG$$
$$= LD \cdot JG$$
$$= DJ \cdot DM,$$

because *JDG* and *DLM* are similar triangles. That is to say, the square on the ordinate of the parabola is equal to the rectangle contained by the abscissa and a given straight line *(latus rectum),* which is the fundamental property of the curve. Bretschneider demonstrates in similar manner the corresponding properties for the ellipse and hyperbola.

Despite Eratosthenes' epigram, the clear statement of Geminus, and the evidence of the early names, it has been doubted whether Menaechmus first obtained the curves as sections of a cone. Charles Taylor suggests that they were discovered as plane loci in investigations of the problem of doubling the cube.[29] In support he argues that Menaechmus used a machine for drawing conics, that in his solutions he uses only the parabola and hyperbola, and that the ellipse—the most obvious of the sections of a cone—is treated last by Apollonius; but he agrees that the conception of a conic as a plane locus was immediately lost. If it be the case that such names as "section of a right-angled cone" were introduced by

Aristaeus after the time of Menaechmus, this raises a slight presumption that Menaechmus did not obtain the curves as sections of a cone; but it can hardly outweigh the evidence of Eratosthenes and Geminus.[30]

Allman believes that Menaechmus was led to his discovery by a study of Archytas' solution of the problem of doubling the cube. "In the solution of Archytas the same conceptions are made use of and the same course of reasoning is pursued, which, in the hands of his successor and contemporary Menaechmus, led to the discovery of the three conic sections."[31] This is more than likely. The brilliant solution of Archytas must have made a tremendous splash in the mathematical pool of ancient Greece.

If it be granted that Menaechmus knew how to obtain a hyperbola by a section of an obtuse-angled cone perpendicular to a generator, how did he obtain the rectangular hyperbola required for his proof? H. G. Zeuthen showed how this could be done.[32] In Figure 4, *TKC* is a plane section through the axis

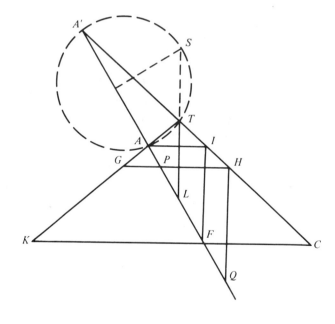

FIGURE 4

of an obtuse-angled cone, *AP* is a perpendicular to the generator *TK,* and a plane section through *A* parallel to the base meets *TC* at *I*. If *P* is the foot of an ordinate to the hyperbola with value *y*, then

$$y^2 = GP \cdot PH$$
$$= AP \cdot PQ$$
$$= AP \cdot \frac{AF}{A'A} \cdot A'P$$
$$= \frac{2AL}{A'A} \cdot x \cdot x',$$

where $AP = x$ and $A'P = x'$.

The hyperbola will be rectangular if $A'A = 2AL$. The problem is therefore as follows: Given a straight line $A'A$, and AL along $A'A$ produced equal to $A'A/2$ to find a cone such that L is on its axis and the section through AL perpendicular to the generator through A is a rectangular hyperbola with $A'A$ as transverse axis. That is to say, the problem is to find a point T on the straight line through A perpendicular to $A'A$ such that TL bisects the angle that is the supplement of $A'TA$. Suppose that T has been found. The circle circumscribing the triangle $A'AT$ will meet LT produced in some point S; and because the angle $A'AT$ is right, $A'T$ is its diameter. Therefore $A'SL$ is right and S lies on the circle having $A'L$ as its diameter. But

$$\angle AA'S = \text{supplement of } \angle ATS$$
$$= \angle ATL$$
$$= \angle LTC$$
$$= \angle A'TS,$$

whence it follows that the segments AS, $A'S$ are equal and S lies on the perpendicular to the midpoint of $A'A$. Therefore S is determined as the intersection of the perpendicular to the midpoint of $A'A$ with the circle drawn on $A'L$ as diameter; and if SL is drawn, T, the vertex of the cone, is obtained as the intersection of SL with the perpendicular to $A'A$ at A.

Some writers, such as Allman, have doubted whether Menaechmus could have been aware of the asymptotes of a hyperbola;[33] but unless it is held that Eutocius rewrote Menaechmus' proof so completely that it really ceased to be Menaechmus, the evidence is compelling. It is easy to see (again following Zeuthen) how in the case of a rectangular hyperbola Menaechmus could have deduced the asymptote property from the axial property without difficulty.[34]

Let AA' be the transverse axis of a rectangular hyperbola, and CE, CE' its asymptotes meeting at right angles at C. Let P be any point on the curve and N the foot of the perpendicular to AA' (the principal ordinate). Let PF, PF' be drawn perpendicular to the asymptotes. Then

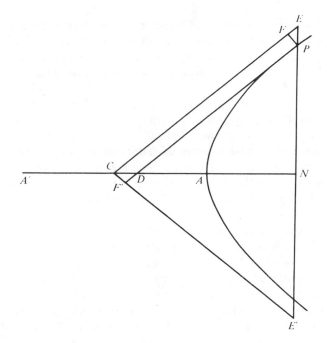

FIGURE 5

$$CA^2 = CN^2 \quad PN^2, \text{ by the axial property}$$
$$= CN \cdot NE - PN \cdot ND$$
$$= 2(\triangle CNE - \triangle PND)$$
$$= 2 \text{ quadrilateral } CDPE$$
$$- 2 \text{ rectangle } CF'PF, \text{ since } \triangle PEF = \triangle CDF',$$
$$= 2PF \cdot PF'.$$
$$\therefore PF \cdot PF' = \tfrac{1}{2}CA^2, \text{ which is the asymptote property.}$$

Alternatively,

$$CA^2 = CN^2 - PN^2$$
$$= EN^2 - PN^2$$
$$= (EN - PN)(EN + PN)$$
$$= (EN - PN)(PN + NE')$$
$$= EP \cdot PE'$$
$$= \sqrt{2}PF \cdot \sqrt{2}PF', \text{ because } \angle PEF \text{ is } 45°.$$
$$\therefore PF \cdot PF' = \tfrac{1}{2}CA^2.$$

The letter of the pseudo-Eratosthenes to Ptolemy Euergetes says that certain Delians, having been commanded by an oracle to double one of their altars, sent a mission to the geometers with Plato in the Academy. Archytas solved the problem by means of half-cylinders, and Eudoxus by means of the so-called curved lines. Although they were able to solve the problem theoretically, none of them except Menaechmus was able to apply his solution in practice—and Menaechmus only to a small extent and with difficulty.[35] According to Plutarch, Plato censured

Eudoxus, Archytas, Menaechmus, and their circle for trying to reduce the doubling of the cube to mechanical devices, for in this way geometry was made to slip back from the incorporeal world to the things of sense.[36]

Despite this emphatic evidence, Bretschneider considers it doubtful whether Menaechmus had an instrument for drawing his curves.[37] He notes that it is possible to find a series of points on each curve but agrees that this is a troublesome method of obtaining a curve without some mechanical device. Allman develops this hint and believes that by the familiar Pythagorean process of the "application" ($\pi\alpha\rho\alpha\beta o\lambda\dot{\eta}$) of areas, which later gave its name to the parabola, Menaechmus could have found as many points as he pleased—"with the greatest facility"—on the parabola $y^2 = px$; that, having solved the Delian problem by the intersection of two parabolas, he later found it easier to employ one parabola and the hyperbola $xy = a^2$, "the construction of which by points is even easier than that of the parabola"; and that this was the way by which in practice he drew the curves.[38] He also implies that this was what the pseudo-Eratosthenes and Plutarch had in mind. The evidence, however, seems inescapable that Menaechmus attempted to find some mechanical device for tracing the curves. Bretschneider's objection that no trace of any such instrument has survived is not substantial. Centuries later, Isidorus of Miletus is said to have invented a compass, $\delta\iota\alpha\beta\dot{\eta}\tau\eta s$, for drawing the parabola in Menaechmus' first solution.[39] Every schoolchild knows, of course, how to draw the conic sections with a ruler, string, and pins;[40] but this easy method was not open to Menaechmus, since it depends upon the focus-directrix property.

There is a possible solution to this dilemma, so simple that apparently it has not hitherto been propounded, although Heath came near to doing so. In Eutocius' collection of solutions to the problem of doubling the cube is a mechanical solution attributed to Plato.[41] It is now universally agreed that it cannot be by Plato because of his censure of mechanical solutions, which fits in with his whole philosophy. M. Cantor, however, thought it possible that he worked it out in a spirit of contempt, just to show how easy such things were in comparison with the real business of the philosopher.[42] The lines between which it is desired to find two means are placed at right angles, as AB, BC. The dotted figure $FGLK$ is an instrument in which a ruler KL moves in slots in the two vertical sides so as to be always parallel to the base FG. The instrument is moved so that FG is made to pass through C, and F lies on AB produced. The ruler is then moved so that KL passes through A.

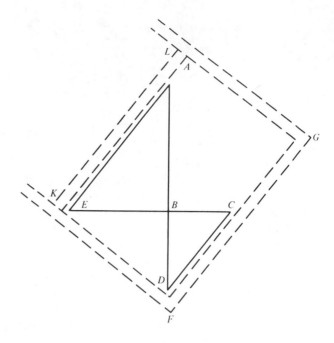

FIGURE 6

If K does not then lie on CB produced, the instrument is manipulated until the four following conditions are all fulfilled: FG passes through C; F lies on AB produced; KL passes through A; K lies on CB produced. The conditions can be satisfied with difficulty—$\delta\nu\sigma\chi\epsilon\rho\hat{\omega}s$, as the pseudo-Eratosthenes says—and when it is done,

$$AB : BE = BE : BD = BD : BC,$$

so that EB, BD are the required means.

The arrangement of the extremes and the means in Figure 6 is exactly the same as in the second solution attributed to Menaechmus. "Hence," says Heath, "it seems probable that someone who had Menaechmus' second solution before him worked to show how the same representation of the four straight lines could be got by a mechanical construction as an alternative to the use of conics."[43] But why not Menaechmus himself? If he was the author, it would be easy for the tradition to refer it to his master, Plato. This cannot be proved or disproved, but it would be the simplest explanation of all the facts.

NOTES

1. Proclus, *In primum Euclidis*, G. Friedlein, ed. (Leipzig, 1873; repr. Hildesheim, 1967), 67.8–12. An English trans. is Glenn R. Morrow, *Proclus: A Commentary on the First Book of Euclid's Elements* (Princeton, 1970), 55–56. For Dinostratus see *Dictionary of Scientific Biography*, IV, 103–105.
2. *Suda Lexicon*, A. Adler, ed., *M.* No. 140, I, pt. 3 (Leipzig,

1933), 317–318. It is entirely in character that the *Suda* not only misspells Menaechmus' name but omits his most important achievement. The *Suda* is followed by Eudocia, *Violarium*, No. 665, H. Flach, ed. (Leipzig, 1880), p. 494.3–5.

3. Also Athenaeus of Cyzicus, if that is the correct interpretation of the name in Proclus, *op. cit.*, 67.16, as seems probable, but it could possibly be understood as Cyzicinus of Athens.

4. Stobaeus, *Anthologium*, C. Wachsmuth, ed., II (Leipzig, 1884), 228.30–33.

5. Proclus, *op. cit.*, 68.13–17.

6. G. J. Allman, *Greek Geometry From Thales to Euclid* (Dublin–London, 1889), 154, n. 2, 179 and n. 42.

7. *Op. cit.*, 78.9, 254.4.

8. *Op. cit.*, 171–172.

9. *Op. cit.*, 72.23–73.14. This passage is subjected to an elaborate analysis by Malcolm Brown in "A Pre-Aristotelian Mathematician on Deductive Order," in *Philosophy and Humanism: Essays in Honor of Paul Oskar Kristeller* (New York, in press). Brown sees Menaechmus as the champion of the relativity of mathematical principles and Aristotle as the champion of their absolute character.

10. *Ibid.*, 253.16–254.5.

11. *Ibid.*, 77.6–79.2.

12. *Liber de astronomia*, T. H. Martin, ed. (Paris, 1849; repr. Groningen, 1971), 330.19–332.3; *Expositio rerum mathematicarum ad legendum Platonem utilium*, E. Hiller, ed. (Leipzig, 1878), 201.22–202.2.

13. *Liber de astronomia*, "Dissertatio," 59–60; *Republic*, X, 616–617.

14. Plutarch, *De communibus notitiis contra Stoicos* 39.3, 1079E, M. Pohlenz and H. Westman, eds., in *Plutarchi Moralia*, VI, fasc. 2 (Leipzig, 1959), 72.3–11. Plutarch writes on the authority of Chrysippus.

15. *Commentarii in libros De sphaera et cylindro*, in *Archimedis opera omnia*, J. L. Heiberg, ed., 2nd ed., III (Leipzig, 1915; repr. Stuttgart, 1972), 54.26–106.24.

16. For Eratosthenes there is now available P. M. Fraser, *Eratosthenes of Cyrene* (London, 1971), which was the 1970 "Lecture on a Master Mind" of the British Academy.

17. Eutocius, *op. cit.*, 96.16–19; διήση is the conjecture of Ulrich von Wilamowitz-Moellendorff for the solecism διζηαι of the MS.

18. *Op. cit.*, 111.20–23.

19. *In Platonis Timaeum ad* 32A, B, E. Diehl, ed. (Leipzig, 1914), pp. 33.29–34.4. The promise to transcribe Archytas is not redeemed in this work.

20. Allman, *op. cit.*, is skeptical on this point. "Menaechmus may have discovered the asymptotes; but, in my judgement, we are not justified in making this assertion, on account of the fact, which is undoubted, that the solutions of Menaechmus have not come down to us in his own words" (p. 170). "There is no evidence, however, for the inference that Menaechmus . . . knew of the existence of the asymptotes of the hyperbola, and its equation in relation to them" (p. 177).

21. The first historian of Greek mathematics, J. E. Montucla, was deeply impressed by this fact. Writing of the proof by means of the parabola and hyperbola between asymptotes he notes, "Cette dernière montre même qu'on avoit fait à cette époque quelque chose de plus que les premiers pas dans cette théorie" (*Histoire des mathématiques*, I [Paris, 1758], 178). And again, "On ne peut y méconnoître une théorie déjà assez sçavante de ces courbes" (p. 183).

22. This appears to have been first recognized by N. T. Reimer, *Historia problematis de cubi duplicatione* (Göttingen, 1798), 68, n.

23. *Commentaria in Conica*, in *Apollonii Pergaei quae . . . exstant . . .*, J. L. Heiberg, ed., II (Leipzig, 1893), 168.17–170.27.

24. *Collectio*, F. Hultsch, ed., II (Berlin, 1877), VII.30–31, pp. 672.20–24, 674.16–19; Hultsch attributes the second

passage to an interpolator.

25. In the following passages of Greek authors θυρεός and ἔλλειψις are used interchangeably: Eutocius, *Commentaria in Conica*, Heiberg, ed., II, 176.6; Proclus, *In primum Euclidis*, Friedlein, ed., 103.6, 9, 10, 111.6 (citing Geminus), 126.19, 20–21, 22. The name appears also to have been familiar to Euclid, for in the preface to the *Phaenomena*, in *Euclidis opera omnia*, J. L. Heiberg and H. Menge, eds., VIII (Leipzig, 1916), 6.5–7, he says: "If a cone or cylinder be cut by a plane not parallel to the base, the section is a section of an acute-angled cone which is like a shield (θυρεός)." From such passages Heiberg concluded that θυρεός was the term used for the ellipse by Menaechmus ("Nogle Bidrag til de graeske Mathematikeres Terminologi," in *Philologisk-historiske Samfunds Mindeskrift*, XXVI [Copenhagen, 1879], 7; *Litterärgeschichtliche Studien über Euklid* [Leipzig, 1882], 88). The primary meaning of θυρεός is "stone put against a door" (to keep it shut)—so H. G. Liddell and R. Scott, *A Greek-English Lexicon*, new ed., H. Stuart Jones (Oxford, 1940)—whence it comes to mean "oblong shield" (shaped like a door).

26. Dublin, Chester Beatty Library, Chester Beatty MS Arabic no. 5255, fols. 1–26.

27. *Die Geometrie und die Geometer vor Euklides* (Leipzig, 1870), 157–158.

28. *Commentaria in conica*, Heiberg, ed., II, 168.17–170.18.

29. *Introduction to the Ancient and Modern Geometry of Conics* (Cambridge, 1881), xxxi, xxxiii, xliii.

30. There is a similar uncertainty about the term "solid loci" (στερεοὶ τόποι). According to Pappus (*Collectio*, VII.30, Hultsch, ed., II, 672.21), Aristaeus wrote five books of *Solid loci* connected with (or continuous with) the *Conics*. This implies that "solid loci" were conics; and the name suggests that when it was given, the curves were regarded as sections of a solid, in contrast with "plane loci" such as straight lines and "linear loci," which were higher curves. But there can be no certainty that the name is older than Aristaeus. T. L. Heath, *A History of Greek Mathematics*, II (Oxford, 1921), 117–118, gives an alternative explanation, deriving plane, solid, and linear loci from plane, solid, and linear problems; but he concedes that it would be natural to speak of the conic sections as solid loci, "especially as they were in fact produced from sections of a solid figure, the cone."

31. *Op. cit.*, 115. In detail he writes:
   In each investigation two planes are perpendicular to an underlying plane; and the intersection of the two planes is a common ordinate to two curves lying one in each plane. In one of the intersecting planes the curve is in each case a semi-circle, and the common ordinate is, therefore, a mean proportional between the segments of its diameter. So far the investigation is the same for all. Now, from the consideration of the figure in the underlying plane—which is different in each case—it follows that:—in the first case—the solution of Archytas—the ordinate in the second intersecting plane is a mean proportional between the segments of its base, whence it is inferred that the extremity of the ordinate in this plane also lies on a semi-circle; in the second case—the section of the right-angled cone—the ordinate is a mean proportional between a given straight line and the abscissa; and, lastly, in the third case—the section of an acute-angled cone—the ordinate is proportional to the geometric mean between the segments of the base [p. 169].

32. *Die Lehre von den Kegelschnitten im Altertum*, R. von Fischer-Benzon, ed. (Copenhagen, 1886), repr. with foreword and index by J. E. Hofmann (Hildesheim, 1966), 464–465. T. L. Heath, who followed Zeuthen's method in *Apollonius of Perga* (Cambridge, 1896), xxvi–xxviii, gives a different method in *A History of Greek Mathematics*, II, 113–114, for determining *T*. He shows that *T* is on the circle which is the locus of all points such that their distances

from A', A are in the ratio 3:1, and T is determined as the intersection of the perpendicular to $A'A$ at A with this circle.

33. See n. 20.
34. *Op. cit.*, 463–464.
35. Eutocius, *Commentarii in libros De sphaera et cylindro*, in *Archimedis opera omnia*, J. L. Heiberg, ed., III, 88.23–90.11. There are similar accounts of the Delian mission in other authors. Plutarch, *De genio Socratis*, 7, 579A–D, P. H. De Lacy and B. Einarson, eds., Loeb Classical Library (London–Cambridge, Mass., 1959), 396.17–398.22, says that Plato referred the Delians to Eudoxus of Cnidus and Helicon of Cyzicus; John Philoponus, *Commentary on the Posterior Analytics of Aristotle*, 1.vii, 75b12, M. Wallies, ed., *Commentaria in Aristotelem Graeca*, XIII, pt. 3 (Berlin, 1909), p. 102.7–18, is in general agreement but omits the references to the geometers. Theon of Smyrna, *Expositio*, E. Hiller, ed., 2.3–12, quoting a lost work of Eratosthenes entitled *Platonicus*, says the god gave this oracle to the Delians, not because he wanted his altar doubled but because he wished to reproach the Greeks for their neglect of mathematics and contempt for geometry. Plutarch also in another work, *De E apud Delphos*, c. 6, 386E, F. C. Babbitt, ed., Loeb Classical Library, Plutarch's *Moralia*, V (London–Cambridge, Mass., 1936), p. 210.6–11 agrees that the god was trying to get the Greeks to pursue geometry rather than to have his altar doubled.
36. Plutarch, *Quaestiones conviviales*, viii.2.1, 718E–F, E. L. Minar, W. C. Helmbold, and F. H. Sandbach, eds., Loeb Classical Library, *Plutarch's Moralia*, IX, trans. as *Table Talk* (London–Cambridge, Mass., 1961), pp. 120.20–122.7. The same censure of Eudoxus and Archytas is repeated in Plutarch, "Vita Marcelli," xiv.5–6, *Plutarch's Lives*, B. Perrin, ed., V, Loeb Classical Library (London–Cambridge, Mass., 1917; repr. 1961), pp. 470.17–472.6, but here there is no mention of Menaechmus.
37. *Op. cit.*, 162.
38. *Op. cit.*, 176–177.
39. [Eutocius], *Commentarii in libros De sphaera et cylindro*, in *Archimedis opera omnia*, Heiberg, ed., III, 84.7–11. The words are bracketed by Heiberg and are no doubt an interpolation made by one of the pupils of Isidorus, who revised Eudocius' text.
40. Charles Smith, *Geometrical Conics* (London, 1894), 32, 84, 125.
41. Eutocius, *Commentarii in libros De sphaera et cylindro*, in *Archimedis opera omnia*, Heiberg, ed., III, 56.13–58.14.
42. *Vorlesungen über Geschichte der Mathematik*, 3rd ed., I (Leipzig, 1907), 234.
43. T. L. Heath, *A History of Greek Mathematics*, I (Oxford, 1921), 256.

BIBLIOGRAPHY

Menaechmus is known to have written a commentary on Plato's *Republic* in three books and other philosophical works, and he must have written at least one work in which he described his discovery of the conic sections. (Whether he wrote a separate book on the subject has been doubted, since Pappus, *Collectio*, F. Hultsch, ed., II [Berlin, 1877], VII 30, p. 672, does not mention any treatise on conics before those of Euclid and Aristaeus.) None of his works has survived. The fragments relating to his life and work are collected in Max C. P. Schmidt, "Die Fragmente des Mathematikers Menaechmus," in *Philologus*, **42** (1884), 77–81. Malcolm Brown (see below) believes that a passage in Proclus, *op. cit.*, 72.23–73.9, may be a quotation by

Menaechmus.

The most complete account of Menaechmus is still that of G. J. Allman, *Greek Geometry From Thales to Euclid* (Dublin–London, 1889), 153–179, reproducing an article which appeared in *Hermathena*, no. 12 (July 1886), 105–130. Other accounts to which reference may profitably be made are C. A. Bretschneider, *Die Geometrie und die Geometer vor Eukleides* (Leipzig, 1870), 155–163; H. G. Zeuthen, *Keglesnitslaeren i Oldtiden* (Copenhagen, 1885), German trans. *Die Lehre von den Kegelschnitten im Altertum*, R. von Fischer-Benzon, ed. (Copenhagen, 1886), repr. with foreword and index by J. E. Hofmann (Hildesheim, 1966), 457–467; T. L. Heath, *Apollonius of Perga* (Cambridge, 1896), xvii–xxx; and *A History of Greek Mathematics* (Oxford, 1921), I, 251–255, II, 110–116; J. L. Coolidge, *A History of the Conic Sections and Quadric Surfaces* (Oxford, 1945), 1–5; Malcolm Brown, "A Pre-Aristotelian Mathematician on Deductive Order," in *Philosophy and Humanism: Essays in Honor of Paul Oskar Kristeller* (New York, in press).

IVOR BULMER-THOMAS

MENELAUS OF ALEXANDRIA (*fl.* Alexandria and Rome, A.D. 100)

Ptolemy records that Menelaus made two astronomical observations at Rome in the first year of the reign of Trajan, that is, A.D. 98.[1] This dating accords with Plutarch's choice of him as a character in a dialogue supposed to have taken place at or near Rome some time after A.D. 75.[2] He is called "Menelaus of Alexandria" by Pappus and Proclus.[3] Nothing more is known of his life.

The first of the observations that Ptolemy records was the occultation of the star Spica by the moon at the tenth hour in the night (that is, 4 A.M. in seasonal hours or 5 A.M. in standard hours) of the fifteenth-sixteenth of the Egyptian month Mechir and its emergence at the eleventh hour.[4] In the second observation Menelaus noticed that at the eleventh hour in the night of 18–19 Mechir the southern horn of the moon appeared to fall in line with the middle and southern stars in the brow of Scorpio, while its center fell to the east of this straight line and was as distant from the star in the middle of Scorpio as the middle star was from the southern, and the northern star of the brow was occulted.[5] Both these observations took place in year 845 of the era of Nabonassar (reigned 747–734 B.C.). By comparing the position of the stars as observed by Timocharis in year 454 of the era of Nabonassar, Ptolemy (and presumably Menelaus before him) concluded that the stars had advanced to the east by 3°55' in 391 years, from which he confirmed the discovery originally made by

Hipparchus that the equinox was moving westward at the rate of 1° a century. (The true figure is 1° in about seventy-two years.) It was by comparing the position of Spica in his day with that recorded by Timocharis that Hipparchus had been led to postulate the precession of the equinoxes.

A list of works attributed to Menelaus is given in the register of mathematicians in the *Fihrist* ("Index") of Ibn al-Nadīm (second half of tenth century). His entry reads:[6]

> He lived before Ptolemy, since the latter makes mention of him. He composed: *The Book on Spherical Propositions. On the Knowledge of the Weights and Distribution of Different Bodies*, composed at the commission of Domitian.[7] Three books on the *Elements of Geometry*, edited by Thābit ibn Qurra. The *Book on the Triangle*. Some of these have been translated into Arabic.

From references by the Arabic writers al-Battānī (*d.* 929), al-Ṣūfī (*d.* 986), and Ḥajjī-Khalīfa it has been deduced that Menelaus composed a catalog of the fixed stars, but there is some uncertainty whether the observations that he undoubtedly made were part of a full catalog.[8]

According to Pappus, Menelaus wrote a treatise on the settings of the signs of the zodiac.[9] Hipparchus had shown "by numbers" that the signs of the zodiac take unequal times to rise, but he had not dealt with their settings. Menelaus appears to have remedied the omission.[10] The work has not survived, nor did Pappus redeem his promise to examine it later, not at least in any surviving writings.

The problem can be solved rigorously only by the use of trigonometry,[11] and it is on his contributions to trigonometry that the fame of Menelaus chiefly rests. Theon of Alexandria noted that Hipparchus had treated chords in a circle in twelve books and Menelaus in six.[12] Almost certainly this means that Menelaus, like Hipparchus before him, compiled a table of sines similar to that found in Ptolemy. For the Greeks, if *AB* is a chord of a circle, sin *AB* is half the chord subtended by double of the arc *AB* and a table of chords is, in effect, a table of sines. Menelaus' work has not survived.

Menelaus' major contribution to the rising science of trigonometry was contained in his *Sphaerica*, in three books. It is this work which entitles him to be regarded as the founder of spherical trigonometry and the first to have disengaged trigonometry from spherics and astronomy and to have made it a separate science. The work has not survived in Greek; but it was translated into Arabic, probably through a lost Syriac rendering, and from Arabic into Latin and

Hebrew. There have been three printed Latin versions; and although it is debatable how much of them is due to Menelaus and how much to their editors, a modern study in German by A. A. Björnbo and a critical edition of the Arabic text with German translation by Max Krause make the content of Menelaus' work tolerably clear.[13]

Book I opens with the definition "A spherical triangle is the space included by arcs of great circles on the surface of a sphere," subject to the limitation that "these arcs are always less than a semicircle." This is the earliest known mention of a spherical triangle. Since the Arabic tradition makes Menelaus address a prince with the words, "O prince, I have discovered a splendid form of demonstrative reasoning," it would appear that he was claiming originality. This is, indeed, implied in a reference by Pappus, who, after describing how a spherical triangle is drawn, says, "Menelaus in his *Sphaerica* calls such a figure a *tripleuron* [τρίπλευρον]."[14] Euclid (in *Elements* I, defs. 19, 20) had used τρίπλευρον for plane rectilinear figures having three sides—that is, triangles—but in the body of his work, beginning with proposition 1, he regularly employed the term τρίγωνον, "triangle." Menelaus' deliberate choice of *tripleuron* for a spherical triangle shows a consciousness of innovation.

In book I Menelaus appears to make it his aim to prove for a spherical triangle propositions analogous to those of Euclid for a plane triangle in *Elements* I. In proposition 11 it is proved that the three angles of a spherical triangle are together greater than two right angles. Menelaus did not always use Euclid's form of proof even where it can be adapted to the sphere, and he avoided the use of indirect proofs by *reductio ad absurdum*. Sometimes his treatment, as of the "ambiguous case" in the congruence of triangles (prop. 13), is more complete than Euclid's.

Book I is an exercise in spherics in the old sense of that term—the geometry of the surface of the sphere—and book II consists only of generalizations or extensions of Theodosius' *Sphaerica* needed in astronomy; the proofs, however, are quite different from those of Theodosius. It is in book III that spherical trigonometry is developed. It opens (prop. 1) with the proposition long since known as "Menelaus' theorem." This is best known from the proof in Ptolemy's *Syntaxis mathematica*, along with preliminary lemmas, but it is not there attributed by name to Menelaus.[15] According to the Arabic of Manṣūr ibn 'Irāq as contained in a Leiden manuscript, the proof runs:[16]

Between two arcs of great circles *ADB* and *AEC* let two other arcs of great circles intersect in *Z*. All four

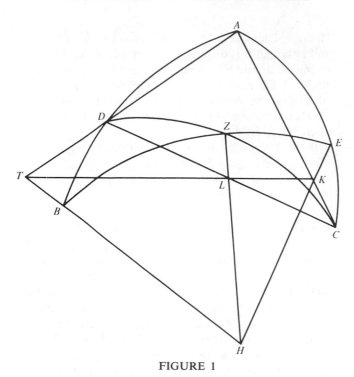

FIGURE 1

$$\frac{\sin CA}{\sin AE} = \frac{\sin CD}{\sin DZ} \cdot \frac{\sin ZB}{\sin BE}.$$

Björnbo observed that Menelaus proved the theorem in its most general and most concise form; Ptolemy proved only what he needed, and Theon loaded his pages with superfluous cases. But A. Rome challenged this view.[17] He considered that Ptolemy really covered all cases, that the completeness of Menelaus' treatment may have been due to subsequent amplification, and that Theon's prolixity was justified by the fact that he was lecturing to beginners.

In Ptolemy's *Syntaxis*, Menelaus' theorem is fundamental. For Menelaus himself it led to several interesting propositions, of which the most important is book III, proposition 5; it is important not so much in itself as in what it assumes. The proposition

arcs are less than a semicircle. It is required to prove

$$\frac{\sin CE}{\sin EA} = \frac{\sin CZ}{\sin ZD} \cdot \frac{\sin DB}{\sin BA}.$$

Let H be the center of the circle and let HZ, HB, HE be drawn. AD and BH lie in a plane and, if they are not parallel, let AD meet BH in the direction of D at T. Draw the straight lines AKC, DLC, meeting HE in K and HZ in L, respectively. Because the arc EZB is in one plane and the triangle ACD is in another plane, the points K, L, T lie on the straight line which is the line of their intersection. (More clearly, because HB, HZ, HE, which are in one plane, respectively intersect the straight lines AD, DC, CA, which are also in one plane, in the points T, L, K, these three points of intersection must lie on the straight line in which the two planes intersect.) Therefore, by what has become known as Menelaus' theorem in plane geometry (which is proved by Ptolemy, although not here),

$$\frac{CK}{KA} = \frac{CL}{LD} \cdot \frac{DT}{TA}.$$

But, as Ptolemy also shows,

$$\frac{CK}{KA} = \frac{\sin CE}{\sin EA}, \quad \frac{CL}{LD} = \frac{\sin CZ}{\sin ZD}, \quad \frac{DT}{TA} = \frac{\sin DB}{\sin BA},$$

and the conclusion follows.

Menelaus proceeds to prove the theorem for the cases where AD meets HB in the direction of A and where AD is parallel to HB. He also proves that

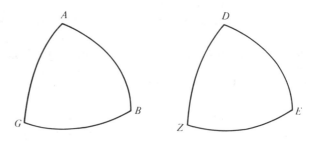

FIGURE 2

is that if in two spherical triangles ABG, DEZ, the angles A, D are both right, and the arcs AG, DZ are each less than a quarter of the circumference,

$$\frac{\sin(BG + GA)}{\sin(BG - GA)} = \frac{\sin(EZ + ZD)}{\sin(EZ - ZD)},$$

from which may be deduced the modern formula

$$\frac{\sin(a + b)}{\sin(a - b)} = \frac{1 + \cos C}{1 - \cos C},$$

or

$$\tan b = \tan a \cos C.$$

In the proof Menelaus casually assumes (to use modern lettering) that if four great circles drawn through any point O on a sphere are intersected in A, B, C, D and A', B', C', D' by two other great circles (transversals), then

$$\frac{\sin AD}{\sin DC} \cdot \frac{\sin BC}{\sin AB} = \frac{\sin A'D'}{\sin D'C'} \cdot \frac{\sin B'C'}{\sin A'B'}.$$

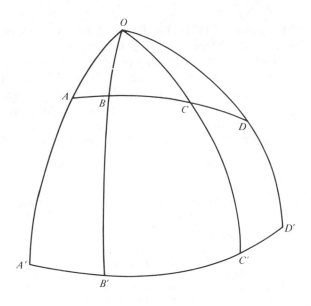

FIGURE 3

This is the anharmonic property, the property that the cross ratio or double ratio of the range $(A, D : B, C)$ is unaltered by projection on to another great circle. There is, of course, a corresponding property for four concurrent lines in a plane cut by a transversal.

It is possible that Menelaus did not prove this property and the preliminary lemmas needed for book III, proposition 1, because he had done so in another work; but the balance of probability is that they were well known in his time and had been discovered by some earlier mathematician. The fact that Menelaus' theorem is proved, not as a proposition about a spherical triangle, but as a proposition about four arcs of great circles, suggests that this also was taken over from someone else. It would not be the first time that credit has been given to the publicist of a discovery rather than to the discoverer. If this is so, it is tempting to think that both Menelaus' theorem and the anharmonic property go back to Hipparchus. This conjecture is reinforced by the fact that the corresponding plane theorems were included by Pappus as lemmas to Euclid's *Porisms* and therefore presumably were assumed by Euclid as known.[18]

When Ptolemy in the former of his two references to Menelaus called him "Menelaus the geometer,"[19] he may have had his trigonometrical work in mind, but Menelaus also contributed to geometry in the narrower sense. According to the *Fihrist*, he composed an *Elements of Geometry* which was edited by Thābit ibn Qurra (d. 901) and a *Book on the Triangle*. None of the former has survived, even in Arabic, and only a small part of the latter in Arabic;[20] but it was probably in one of these works that Menelaus gave

the elegant alternative proof of Euclid, book I, proposition 25, which is preserved by Proclus.[21]

Euclid's enunciation is as follows: "If two triangles have the two sides equal to two sides respectively, but have [one] base greater than the base [of the other], they will also have [one of] the angle[s] contained by the equal straight lines greater [than the other]." He proved the theorem by *reductio ad absurdum*. Menelaus' proof was direct and is perhaps further evidence of his distaste for indirect proofs already manifested in the *Sphaerica*. Let the two triangles be ABC, DEF, with $AB = DE$, $AC = DF$, and $BC > EF$. From BC cut off BG equal to EF. At B make the angle GBH on the side of BC remote from A equal to angle DEF. Draw BH equal to DE. Join HG and produce HG to meet AC at K. Then the triangles BGH, DEF are congruent and $HG = DF = AC$. Now HK is greater than HG or AC, and therefore greater than AK. Thus angle KAH is greater than angle KHA. And since $AB = BH$, angle $BAH =$ angle BHA. Therefore, by addition, angle BAC is greater than angle BHG, that is, greater than angle EDF.

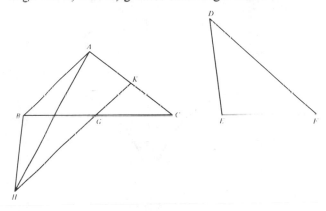

FIGURE 4

The *Liber trium fratrum de geometria*, written by Muḥammad, Aḥmad, and al-Ḥasan, the three sons of Mūsā ibn Shākir (Banū Mūsā) in the first half of the ninth century,[22] states that Menelaus' *Elements of Geometry* contained a solution of the problem of doubling the cube, which turns out to be Archytas' solution.

This bears on a statement by Pappus that Menelaus invented a curve which he called "the paradoxical curve" ($\gamma\rho\alpha\mu\mu\grave{\eta}\ \pi\alpha\rho\acute{\alpha}\delta o\xi o\varsigma$).[23] Pappus, writing of the so-called "surface loci," says that many even more complicated curves having very remarkable properties were discovered by Demetrius of Alexandria in his *Notes on Curves* and by Philo of Tyana as a result of weaving together plektoids[24] and other surfaces of all kinds. Several of the curves, he continues, were considered by more recent writers to be worthy of a longer treatment, in particular the curve called "paradoxical" by Menelaus.

If Menelaus really did reproduce Archytas' solution, which relies on the intersection of a tore and a cylinder, this lends support to a conjecture by Paul Tannery that the curve was none other than Viviani's curve of double curvature.[25] In 1692 Viviani set the learned men of Europe the problem "how to construct in a hemispherical cupola four equal windows such that when these areas are taken away, the remaining part of the curved surface shall be exactly capable of being geometrically squared." His own solution was to take through O, the center of the sphere, a diameter BC and to erect at O a perpendicular OA to the plane $BDCO$. In the plane $BACO$ semicircles are described on the radii BO, CO, and on each a right half-cylinder is described. Each half-cylinder will, of course, touch the sphere internally; and the two half-cylinders will cut out of the hemispherical surface the openings BDE, CDF, with corresponding openings on the other side. The curve in which the half-cylinders

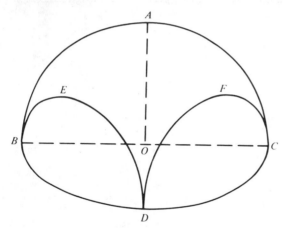

FIGURE 5

intersect the hemisphere is classified as a curve of the fourth order and first species, and it is a particular case of the *hippopede* used by Eudoxus to describe the motion of a planet. The portion left on the hemispherical surface is equal to the square on the diameter of the hemisphere, and Tannery conjectures that the property of this area being squarable was considered at that time, when the squaring of the circle was much in the air, to be a paradox. It is an attractive conjecture but incapable of proof on present evidence.

According to several Arabic sources[26] Menelaus wrote a book on mechanics, the title of which was something like *On the Nature of Mixed Bodies*.[27] This is presumably to be identified with the unnamed work by Menelaus on which al-Khāzinī draws in his *Kitāb mīzān al-ḥikma* ("Book of the Balance of Wisdom," 1121/1122). The fourth chapter of the first book quotes theorems by Menelaus respecting weight and lightness; the first chapter of the fourth book describes Archimedes' balance on the evidence of Menelaus; and the second and third chapters of the same book describe the balance devised by Menelaus himself and his use of it to analyze alloys, with a summary of the values he found for specific gravities.[28]

NOTES

1. *Syntaxis mathematica*, VII, 3, in *Claudii Ptolemaei opera quae exstant omnia*, J. L. Heiberg, ed., I, pt. 2 (Leipzig, 1903), pp. 30.18–19, 33.3–4.
2. Plutarch, *De facie quae in orbe lunae apparet*, 17, 930A, H. Cherniss and William C. Helmbold, eds., in *Moralia*, Loeb Classical Library, XII (London–Cambridge, Mass., 1957), 106.7–15. Lucius is the speaker and says, "In your presence, my dear Menelaus, I am ashamed to confute a mathematical proposition, the foundation, as it were, on which rests the subject of catoptrics. Yet it must be said that the proposition, 'All reflection occurs at equal angles,' is neither self-evident nor an admitted fact." Menelaus is not allowed by Plutarch to speak for himself, and it would be rash to assume from this reference that he made any contribution to optics. Cherniss thinks that "the conversation was meant to have taken place in or about Rome some time—and perhaps quite a long time—after A.D. 75" (p. 12).
3. Pappus, *Collectio*, VI.110, F. Hultsch, ed., II (Berlin, 1877), p. 102.1; Proclus, *In primum Euclidis*, G. Friedlein, ed. (Leipzig, 1873; repr. Hildesheim, 1967), 345.14; English trans., G. R. Morrow (Princeton, 1970).
4. Ptolemy, *op. cit.*, 30.18–32.3.
5. *Ibid.*, 33.3–34.8.
6. Heinrich Suter, "Das Mathematiker Verzeichniss im *Fihrist* des Ibn Abî Ja'kûb an-Nadim (Muhammad Ibn Ishāk)," in *Abhandlungen zur Geschichte der Mathematik*, no. 6 (Leipzig, 1892), 19.
7. This is unlikely to be correct and is probably an embroidering of the reference to Trajan in Ptolemy.
8. A. A. Björnbo, "Hat Menelaos einen Fixsternkatalog verfasst?" in *Bibliotheca mathematica*, 3rd ser., **2** (1901), 196–212.
9. Pappus, *op. cit.*, VI.110, vol. II, 600.25–602.1.
10. This at least is what the text of Pappus as we have it implies, but there is some reason to doubt whether the text can be correct. See Hultsch's note at the point.
11. The inequality of the times was already known to Euclid, *Phaenomena*, *Euclidis opera omnia*, J. L. Heiberg and H. Menge, eds., VIII (Leipzig, 1916), props. 9, 12, 13, pp. 44, 62, 78; and Hypsicles (q.v.) attempted to calculate the times by an arithmetical progression. When Hipparchus is said to have solved the problem "by numbers," it presumably means that he was the first to have given a correct solution by trigonometrical methods.
12. *Commentary on the Syntaxis mathematica of Ptolemy*, A. Rome, ed., in the series Studi e Testi, LXXII (Vatican City, 1936), I.10, p. 451.4–5. For further discussion see A. Rome, "Premiers essais de trigonométrie rectiligne chez les Grecs," in *L'antiquité classique*, **2**, fasc. 1 (1933), 177–192; and a brief earlier note by the same author with the same title in *Annales de la Société scientifique de Bruxelles*, ser. A, **52**, pt. 1 (1932), 271–274.
13. The trans. and eds. are summarized by George Sarton, *Introduction to the History of Science*, I (Baltimore, 1927; repr. 1968), 253–254; and are more fully examined by A. A. Björnbo, *Studien über Menelaos' Sphärik* (Leipzig, 1902), 10–22, and Max Krause, *Die Sphärik von Menelaos*

aus Alexandrien (Berlin, 1936), 1–116. See also the bibliography at the end of this article.

14. Pappus, *op. cit.*, VI.1, p. 476.16–17. This is part of the evidence for the genuineness of the definitions even though they do not appear in Gerard's Latin trans.

15. Ptolemy, *Syntaxis mathematica*, I.13, J. L. Heiberg, ed., I, pt. 1 (Leipzig, 1898), pp. 68.14–76.9. See also the commentary of Theon of Alexandria with the valuable notes of A. Rome, ed., *Commentaires de Pappus et de Théon d'Alexandrie sur l'Almageste*, II, *Théon d'Alexandrie*, which is Studi e Testi, LXXII (Vatican City, 1936), 535–570.

16. A. A. Björnbo, *Studien*, 88–92. Menelaus omits a general enunciation (πρότασις) and goes straight to the particular enunciation (ἔκθεσις). Björnbo (p. 92) regards this as partial evidence that the proposition was taken from some other work; but Rome, "Les explications de Théon d'Alexandrie sur le théorème de Ménélas," in *Annales de la Société scientifique de Bruxelles*, ser. A, **53**, pt. 1 (1933), 45, justly says that the length and complexity of a general enunciation, as given by Theon writing for his pupils, is a sufficient reason for the omission.

17. Björnbo, *Studien*, 92. A. Rome, "Les explications de Théon d'Alexandrie sur la théorème de Ménélas" (see n. 16), 39–50; and *Commentaires de Pappus et de Théon d'Alexandrie sur l'Almageste*, II, 554, n. 1 ("L'on est tenté de conclure que le complément de preuve établissant le théorème de Ménélas pour tous les cas, a été inventé à une date située entre Théon et les auteurs arabes qui nous font connaître les Sphériques.")

18. Pappus, *op. cit.*, VII.3–19, props. 129, 136, 137, 140, 142, 145, Hultsch ed., vol. II, pp. 870.3–872.22, 880.13–882.16, 882.17–884.9, 886.23–888.8, 890.3–892.2, 894.14–28. M. Chasles, "Aperçu historique sur l'origine et le développement des méthodes en géométrie," in *Mémoires couronnés par l'Académie royale des sciences et des belles-lettres de Bruxelles*, **2** (1837), 33, 39; and *Les trois livres de Porismes d'Euclide* (Paris, 1860), 11, 75–77, was the first to recognize the anharmonic property in the lemmas of Pappus and to see that "les propositions d'Euclide étaient de celles auxquelles conduisaient naturellement les développements et les applications de la notion du rapport anharmonique, devenu fondamentale dans la géométrie moderne." Actually, in prop. 129 Pappus does not use four concurrent lines cut by two transversals but three concurrent lines cut by two transversals issuing from the same point. (The generality is not affected.) Props. 136 and 142 are the converse; prop. 137 is a particular case and prop. 140 its converse; prop. 145 is another case of prop. 129.

19. Ptolemy, *op. cit.*, 30.18.

20. M. Steinschneider, *Die arabischen Uebersetzungen aus dem Griechischen*, 2. Abschnitt, Mathematik §111–112, in *Zeitschrift der Deutschen morgenländischen Gesellschaft*, **50** (1896), 199.

21. Proclus, *op. cit.*, 345.9–346.13.

22. M. Curtze first edited Gerard of Cremona's trans. in *Nova acta Academiae Caesareae Leopoldino Carolinae germanicae naturae curiosorum*, **49** (1885), 105–167. This is now superseded by the later and better ed. of M. Clagett, *Archimedes in the Middle Ages*, I (Madison, Wis., 1964), 223–367, see particularly 334–341, 365–366.

23. Pappus, *op. cit.*, IV.36, vol. I, p. 270.17–26.

24. A plektoid (πλεκτοειδὴς ἐπιφάνεια) is a twisted surface; the only other example of the word, also in Pappus, suggests that it may mean a conoid.

25. Paul Tannery, "Pour l'histoire des lignes et surfaces courbes dans l'antiquité," in *Bulletin des sciences mathématiques*, 2nd ser., **7** (1883), 289–291, repr. in his *Mémoires scientifiques*, II (Toulouse–Paris, 1912), 16–18. On Viviani's curve see *Acta eruditorum* (Leipzig, 1692), "Aenigma geometricum de miro opificio testudinis quadrabilis hemispherica a D. Pio Lisci Posillo geometra propositum die 4 April. A. 1692," pp. 274–275, also pp. 275–279, 370–371; Moritz

Cantor, *Vorlesungen über Geschichte der Mathematik*, III (Leipzig, 1898), 205.

26. Among them the *Fihrist*, see n. 7.

27. In *Codex Escurialensis* 905 the title is given as *Liber de quantitate et distinctione corporum mixtorum* and in *Codex Escurialensis* 955 as *De corporum mistorum quantitate et pondere;* but J. G. Wenrich, *De auctorum graecorum versionibus et commentariis Syriacis, Arabicis, Persicisque* (Leipzig, 1842), 211, gives *De cognitione quantitatis discre'ae corporum permixtorum.*

28. N. Khanikoff, "Analysis and Extracts of the Book of the Balance of Wisdom," in *Journal of the American Oriental Society*, **6** (1859), 1–128, especially pp. 34, 85. Unfortunately Khanikoff does not translate the passage referring to Menelaus, but the whole Arabic text has since been published—*Kitāb mīzān al-ḥikma* (Hyderabad, 1940). For further information see *Dictionary of Scientific Biography*, VII.

BIBLIOGRAPHY

I. ORIGINAL WORKS. Menelaus wrote a work on spherics (the geometry of the surface of a sphere) in three books (the third treating spherical trigonometry); a work on chords in the circle, which would have included what is now called a table of sines; an elements of geometry, probably in three books; a book on the triangle, which may or may not have been a publication separate from the last-mentioned one; possibly a work on transcendental curves, including one called "paradoxical" that he discovered himself; a work on hydrostatics, dealing probably with the specific gravities of mixtures; a treatise on the setting of the signs of the zodiac; and a series of astronomical observations which may or may not have amounted to a catalog of the fixed stars.

None of these has survived in Greek, but after earlier efforts the *Sphaerica* was translated into Arabic by Isḥāq ibn Ḥunayn (*d.* 910/911), or possibly by his father, Ḥunayn ibn Isḥāq (*d.* 877), and the translation was revised by several eds., notably by Manṣūr ibn 'Irāq (1007/1008), whose redaction survives in the University library at Leiden as *Codex Leidensis* 930, and by Naṣir al Dīn al-Ṭūsī (1265), whose work exists in many manuscripts. From Arabic the work was translated into Latin by Gerard of Cremona (*d.* 1187), and his trans. survives to varying extents in some 17 MSS; in many of them the author is called Mileus. The work was rendered into Hebrew by Jacob ben Māḥir ibn Tibbon (*ca.* 1273). The first printed ed. was a Latin version by Maurolico (Messina, 1558) from the Arabic; based on a poor MS, it is replete with interpolations. Nor was the Latin version of Mersenne (Paris, 1644) much better. Halley produced a Latin version which was published posthumously (Oxford, 1758) with a preface by G. Costard. Halley made some use of Arabic MSS, but in the main he has given a free rendering of the Hebrew version, with some mathematical treatment of his own. It held the field until Axel Anthon Björnbo produced his "Studien über Menelaos' Sphärik. Beiträge zur Geschichte der Sphärik und Trigonometrie der Griechen," in *Abhandlungen zur Geschichte der Mathematischen Wissenschaften*, **40** (1902), 1–154. After the introductory matter this amounts to a free German rendering of the *Sphaerica* based mainly on

Halley's ed. and *Codex Leidensis* 930. It was the best work on Menelaus that existed for many years, but as a doctoral thesis, the work of a young man who had to rely on secondhand information, it had many deficiencies. The need for a satisfactory ed. of the Arabic text with a German trans. and notes on the history of the text was finally met when Max Krause, basing his work on the same Leiden MS, published "Die Sphärik von Menelaos aus Alexandrien in der Verbesserung von Abū Naṣr Manṣūr b. 'Alī b. 'Irāq mit Untersuchungen zur Geschichte des Textes bei den islamischen Mathematikern," in *Abhandlungen der Gesellschaft der Wissenschaften zu Göttingen*, Phil.-Hist. Klasse, 3rd ser., no. 17 (1936).

None of Menelaus' other works survives even in trans. except for a small part of his *Book on the Triangle* (if this is different from his *Elements of Geometry*). For notes on the Arabic translations, see M. Steinschneider, "Die arabischen Uebersetzungen aus dem Griechischen, 2. Abschnitt, Mathematik 111–112," in *Zeitschrift der Deutschen Morgenländischen Gesellschaft*, **50** (1896), 196–199.

It is possible that the proof of Menelaus' theorem given by Ptolemy, *Syntaxis mathematica*, in *Claudii Ptolemaei opera quae exstant omnia*, J. L. Heiberg, ed., I, pt. 1 (Leipzig, 1898), 74.9–76.9, reproduces, at least to some extent, the language of Menelaus; but in the absence of direct attribution there can be no certainty.

II. SECONDARY LITERATURE. The various references to Menelaus by Plutarch, Pappus, Proclus, and Arabic authors are given in the notes above. The chief modern literature is A. A. Björnbo, "Studien über Menelaos' Sphärik," mentioned above; and his "Hat Menelaos einen Fixsternkatalog verfasst?" in *Bibliotheca mathematica*, 3rd ser., **2** (1901), 196–212; Thomas Heath, *A History of Greek Mathematics*, II (Oxford, 1921), 260–273; A. Rome, "Premiers essais de trigonométrie rectiligne chez les Grecs," in *Annales de la Société scientifique de Bruxelles*, ser. A, **52**, pt. 2 (1932), 271–274; an expanded version with the same title is in *L'antiquité classique*, II, fasc. 1 (Louvain, 1933), 177–192; "Les explications de Théon d'Alexandrie sur le théorème de Ménélas," in *Annales de la Société scientifique de Bruxelles*, ser. A, **53**, pt. 1 (1933), 39–50; and *Commentaires de Pappus et de Théon d'Alexandrie sur l'Almageste*, II, *Théon d'Alexandrie*, Studi e Testi, LXXII (Vatican City, 1936), 535–570; and Max Krause, *Die Sphärik von Menelaos aus Alexandrien* (mentioned above).

IVOR BULMER-THOMAS

MENGOLI, PIETRO (*b*. Bologna, Italy, 1625; *d*. Bologna, 1686)

Mengoli's name appears in the register of the University of Bologna for the years between 1648 and 1686. He studied with Cavalieri, whom he succeeded in the chair of mathematics, and also took a degree in philosophy in 1650 and another in both civil and canon law in 1653. He was in addition ordained to the priesthood and from 1660 until his death served the parish of Santa Maria Maddalena, also in Bologna.

Mengoli's mathematics were superficially conservative. He did not subscribe to the innovations of Torricelli, and his own discoveries were set out in an abstruse Latin that made his works laborious to read. His books were nevertheless widely distributed in the seventeenth century, and were known to Collins, Wallis, and Leibniz; they were then almost forgotten, so that Mengoli's work has been studied again only recently. His significance to the history of science lies in the transitional position of his mathematics, midway between Cavalieri's method of indivisibles and Newton's fluxions and Leibniz' differentials.

In *Novae quadraturae arithmeticae* (Bologna, 1650), Mengoli took up Cataldi's work on infinite algorithms. As Eneström (1912) and Vacca (1915) have pointed out, he was the first to sum infinite series that were not geometric progressions and to demonstrate the existence of a series which, although its general term tends to zero, has a sum that can be greater than any number. In particular, he showed the divergence of the harmonic series

$$\sum_{n=1}^{\infty} \frac{1}{n} = 1 + \frac{1}{2} + \frac{1}{3} + \frac{1}{4} + \cdots,$$

preceding Jakob Bernoulli's demonstration of it by nearly forty years (it was known to Oresme in the fourteenth century). From this, Mengoli made the general deduction that any series formed from the reciprocals of the terms of an arithmetic progression must diverge.

Mengoli also considered the series of the reciprocals of the triangular numbers

$$\frac{1}{3} + \frac{1}{6} + \frac{1}{10} + \cdots \frac{1}{\frac{n(n+1)}{2}} + \cdots,$$

and said that the sum is 1, because the sum of the first *n* terms is $n/(n+2)$, which (for suitably large *n*) differs from 1 by less than any given quantity. He then demonstrated the convergence of the series of the reciprocals of the numbers $n(n + r)$ to the result that

$$\sum_n \frac{1}{n(n+r)} = \frac{1}{n}\left(1 + \frac{1}{2} + \frac{1}{3} + \cdots + \frac{1}{r}\right),$$

and summed the reciprocals of the solid numbers,

$$\sum \frac{1}{n(n+1)(n+2)} = \frac{1}{4}.$$

In the *Geometriae speciosae elementa* (1659), Mengoli set out a logical arrangement of the concepts of limit and definite integral that anticipated the work of nineteenth-century mathematicians. In establishing a rigorous theory of limits, he considered a variable quantity as a ratio of magnitudes and hence needed to consider only positive limits. He then made the following definitions: a variable quantity that can be greater than any assignable number is called "quasi-infinite"; a variable quantity that can be smaller than any positive number is "quasi-nil"; and a variable quantity that can be both smaller than any number larger than a given positive number a and greater than any number smaller than a is "quasi-a."

Using these precise concepts of the infinite, the infinitesimal, and the limit, and working from simple inequalities valid between numerical ratios, he demonstrated (as Agostini recognized by translating his obscure exposition into modern symbols and terminology) the properties of the limit of the sum and the product, and showed that the properties of proportions are conserved also at the limit. The proofs obtain when such limits are neither 0 nor ∞; for this case Mengoli set out the properties of the infinitesimal calculus and the calculus of infinites some thirty years before Newton published them in his *Principia*.

Mengoli's predecessors (among them Archimedes, Kepler, Valerio, and Cavalieri) had assumed as intuitively evident that a plane figure has an area. By contrast, he proved the existence of the area by dividing an interval of the continuous figure $f(x)$ into n parts and considering, alongside the figure to be squared (which he called the "form"), the figures formed by parallelograms constructed on each segment of the interval and having the areas (in modern notation):

$$s_n = \sum_{i=1}^{n} l_i(x_{i+1} - x_i), \quad \text{(inscribed figure)}$$

$$S_n = \sum_{i=1}^{n} L_i(x_{i+1} - x_i), \quad \text{(circumscribed figure)}$$

$$\left.\begin{array}{l} \sigma_n = \sum_{i=1}^{n} f(x_i)(x_{i+1} - x_i), \text{ or} \\[2ex] \sigma'_n = \sum_{i=1}^{n} f(x_{i+1})(x_{i+1} - x_i), \end{array}\right\} \text{(adscribed figure)}$$

where l_i and L_i denote, respectively, the minimum and maximum of $f(x)$ on the interval (x_i, x_{i+1}). Drawing upon the theory of limits that had worked so well in the study of series, Mengoli demonstrated that the sequences of the s_n and S_n tend to the same limit to which the sequences of the σ_n and σ'_n, compressed

between them, also tend. Hence, since the figure to be squared is always compressed between the s_n and the S_n, it follows that this common limit is the area of the figure itself.

Mengoli also used this method to integrate the binomial differentials $Z^s(a - x)^r dx$ with whole and positive exponents. (He had, preceding Wallis, already integrated these some time before by the method of indivisibles.) Before publishing his results, however, he wished to give a rigorous basis to the method of indivisibles or to develop in its stead another method that would be immune to criticism. He therefore set out a purely arithmetic theory of logarithms; having given a definition of the logarithmic ratio similar to Euclid's definition of ratio between magnitudes, he then extended Euclid's book V to encompass his own logarithmic ratio. Mengoli also did significant work in logarithmic series (thirteen years before N. Mercator published his *Logarithmotecnia*).

In a short work of 1672, entitled *Circolo*, Mengoli calculated the integrals of the form

$$\int_0^1 x^{\frac{m}{2}}(1 - x)^{\frac{n}{2}}\, dx,$$

finding for $n/2$ the same infinite product that had already been given by Wallis. Mengoli published other, minor mathematical writings; in addition he was interested in astronomy, and wrote a short vernacular book on music, published in 1670.

BIBLIOGRAPHY

I. ORIGINAL WORKS. Mengoli's writings include *Novae quadraturae arithmeticae* (Bologna, 1650); *Geometriae speciosae elementa* (Bologna, 1659); *Speculazioni di musica* (Bologna, 1670); and *Circolo* (Bologna, 1672).

II. SECONDARY LITERATURE. On Mengoli and his work, see A. Agostini, "La teoria dei limiti in Pietro Mengoli," in *Periodico di matematiche*, 4th ser., **5** (1925), 18–30; "Il concetto di integrale definito in Pietro Mengoli," *ibid.*, 137–146; and "Pietro Mengoli," in *Enciclopedia italiana*, XXII (Milan, 1934), 585; E. Bortolotti, *La storia della matematica nella università di Bologna* (Bologna, 1947), 98–101, 137–138; G. Eneström, "Zur Geschichte der unendlichen Reihen in die Mitte des siebzehnten Jahrhunderte," in *Bibliotheca mathematica* (1912), 135–148; and G. Vacca, "Sulle scoperte di Pietro Mengoli," in *Atti dell'Accademia nazionale dei Lincei. Rendiconti* (Dec. 1915), 512.

A. NATUCCI

MÉRAY, HUGUES CHARLES ROBERT (*b.* Chalon-sur-Saône, France, 12 November 1835; *d.* Dijon, France, 2 February 1911)

Méray entered the École Normale Supérieure in 1854. After teaching at the lycée of St. Quentin from 1857 to 1859 he retired for seven years to a small village near Chalon-sur-Saône. In 1866 he became a lecturer at the University of Lyons and, in 1867, professor at the University of Dijon, where he spent the remainder of his career.

In his time he was a respected but not a leading mathematician. Méray is remembered for having anticipated, clearly and with only minor differences of style, Cantor's theory of irrational numbers, one of the main steps in the arithmetization of analysis.

Méray first expounded his theory in an article entitled "Remarques sur la nature des quantités définies par la condition de servir de limites à des variables données" (1869). His precise formulation in the framework of the terminology of the time and the place is of considerable historical interest.

> I shall now reserve the name number or quantity to the integers and fractions; I shall call *progressive variable* any quantity v which takes its several values successively in unlimited numbers.
>
> Let v_n be the value of v of rank n: if as n increases to infinity there exists a number V such that beginning with a suitable value of n, $V - v_n$ remains smaller than any quantity as small as might be supposed, one says that V is the limit of v and one sees immediately that $v_{n+p} - v_n$ has zero for limit whatever the simultaneous laws of variation imposed on n and p.
>
> If there is no such number it is no longer legitimate, analytically speaking, to claim that v has a limit; but if, in this case, the difference $v_{n+p} - v_n$ still converges to zero then the nature of v shows an extraordinary similarity with that of the variables which really possess limits. We need a special term in order to express the remarkable differentiation with which we are concerned: I shall say that the progressive variable is *convergent*, whether or not a numerical limit can be assigned to it.
>
> The existence of a limit to a convergent variable permits greater ease in stating certain of its properties which do not depend on this particular question [i.e., whether or not there exists a numerical limit] and which frequently can be formulated directly only with much greater difficulty. One sees therefore that it is advantageous, in cases where there is no limit, to retain the same abbreviated language which is used properly when a limit exists, and in order to express the convergence of the variable one may say simply that *it possesses a fictitious limit*.
>
> Here is a first example of the usefulness of this convention: if, when m and n both increase to infinity, the difference $u_m - v_n$ between two convergent variables tends to zero for a certain mutual dependence between the subscripts, then one proves easily that it remains infinitely small also for any other law [i.e., law of dependence between m and n]: I shall then say that the

variables u and v are *equivalent*, and one sees immediately that two variables which are equivalent to a third variable are equivalent to each other [*loc. cit.* p. 284, in translation].

In this paper Méray also discussed the question of how to assign values to a given function for irrational values of the argument or arguments, and he suggested that this problem could always be solved by a passage to the limit. In this connection, as well as elsewhere in his writings, he did in fact assume a somewhat constructive point of view of the notion of a function, taking it for granted that a function can always be obtained constructively either by rational operations or by limiting processes.

The paper marked the first appearance in print of an "arithmetical" theory of irrational numbers. Some years earlier Weierstrass had, in his lectures, introduced the real numbers as sums of sequences or, more precisely, indexed sets, of rational numbers; but he had not published his theory and there is no trace of any influence of Weierstrass' thinking on Méray's. Dedekind also seems to have developed his theory of irrationals at an earlier date, but he did not publish it until after the appearance of Cantor's relevant paper in 1872. In that year Méray's *Nouveau précis d'analyse infinitésimale* was published in Paris. In the first chapter the author sketches again his theory of irrationals and remarks that however peculiar it might appear to be, compared with the classical traditions, he considers it more in agreement with the nature of the problem than the physical examples required in other approaches.

The *Nouveau précis* had as its principal aim the development of a theory of functions of complex variables based on the notion of a power series. Thus here again, Méray followed unconsciously in the footsteps of Weierstrass; consciously, he was developing the subject in the spirit of Lagrange but felt—rightly—that he could firmly establish what Lagrange had only conjectured. The book is in fact written with far greater attention to rigor than was customary in Méray's time.

Little regard was paid to Méray's main achievement until long after it was first produced, partly because of the obscurity of the journal in which it was published. But even in his review (1873) of the *Nouveau précis*, H. Laurent pays no attention to the theory, while gently chiding the author for using too narrow a notion of a function and for being too rigorous in a supposed textbook. At that time there was not in France—as there was in Germany—a sufficient appreciation of the kind of problem considered by Méray, and not until much later was it realized that he had produced a theory of a kind that had added luster to the names of some of the greatest mathematicians of the period.

Although Méray's theory of irrationals stands out above the remainder of his work, his development of it may be regarded as more than an accident. For elsewhere he also showed the same critical spirit, the same regard to detail, and the same independence of thought that led him to his greatest discovery.

BIBLIOGRAPHY

I. ORIGINAL WORKS. Méray's theory was published as "Remarques sur la nature des quantités définies par la condition de servir de limites à des variables données," in *Revue des sociétés savantes des départements*, Section sciences mathématiques, physiques et naturelles, 4th ser., **10** (1869), 280–289. Among his many treatises and textbooks are *Nouveaux éléments de géométrie* (Paris, 1874); *Exposition nouvelle de la théorie des formes linéaires et des déterminants* (Paris, 1884); and *Sur la convergence des développements des intégrales ordinaires d'un système d'équations différentielles totales ou partielles*, 2 vols. (Paris, 1890), written with Charles Riquier.

II. SECONDARY LITERATURE. Laurent's review of the *Nouveau précis* was published in *Bulletin des sciences mathématiques*, **4** (1873), 24–28. See also the biography of Méray in *La grande encyclopédie* XXIII (Paris, 1886), 692; and J. Molk, "Nombres irrationels et la notion de limite," in *Encyclopédie des sciences mathématiques pures et appliquées,* French ed., I (Paris, 1904), 133–160, after the German article by A. Pringsheim.

ABRAHAM ROBINSON

MERCATOR, NICOLAUS (Kauffman, Niklaus)

(*b.* Eutin [?], Schleswig-Holstein, Denmark [now Germany], *ca.* 1619; *d.* Paris, France, 14 January [?] 1687)

His father was probably the Martin Kauffman who taught school at Oldenburg in Holstein from 1623 and died there in 1638. Doubtless educated in boyhood at his father's school, Nicolaus graduated from the University of Rostock and was appointed to the Faculty of Philosophy in 1642. At Copenhagen University in 1648 he superintended a "Disputatio physica de spiritibus et innato calido" and over the next five years produced several short textbooks on elementary astronomy and spherical trigonometry; one of his title pages at this time describes him as "mathematician and writer on travels to the Indies."

His tract on calendar improvement (1653) caught Cromwell's eye in England and, whether invited or not, he subsequently left Denmark for London. There he resided for almost thirty years and came universally to be known by his latinized name, an "anglicization"

which he himself soon adopted. Unable to find a position in a university, Mercator earned a living as a mathematical tutor, but soon he made the acquaintance of Oughtred, Pell, Collins, and other practitioners. In November 1666, on the strength of his newly invented marine chronometer, he was elected a fellow of the Royal Society; earlier, in Oldenburg's *Philosophical Transactions of the Royal Society*, he had wagered the profits (seemingly nonexistent) from his invention against anyone who could match his expertise in the theory of Gerard Mercator's map. Through his Latin version (1669) of Kinckhuysen's Dutch *Algebra*, commissioned by Collins at Seth Ward's suggestion, he came into contact with Newton, and the two men later exchanged letters on lunar theory. Aubrey portrays Mercator at this time as "of little stature, perfect; black haire, . . . darke eie, but of great vivacity of spirit . . . of a soft temper . . . (*amat Venerem aliquantum*): of a prodigious invention, and will be acquainted (familiarly) with nobody." In September 1676 Hooke unsuccessfully proposed Mercator as Mathematical Master at Christ's Hospital. In 1683 he accepted Colbert's commission to plan the waterworks at Versailles, but died soon afterward, having fallen out with his patron.

Mercator's early scientific work is known only through the university textbooks which he wrote in the early 1650's; if not markedly original, they show his firm grasp of essentials. His *Trigonometria sphaericorum logarithmica* (1651) gives neat logarithmic solutions of the standard cases of right and oblique triangles and tabulates the logarithms of sine, cosine, tangent, and cotangent functions (his "Logarithmus," "Antilogarithmus," "Hapsologarithmus," and "Anthapsologarithmus") at $1'$ intervals. His *Cosmographia* (1651) and *Astronomia* (1651) deal respectively with the physical geography of the earth and the elements of spherical astronomy. In his *Rationes mathematicae* (1653) he insists on drawing a basic distinction between rational and irrational numbers: the difference in music is that between harmony and dissonance; in astronomy that between a Keplerian "harmonice mundi" and the observable solar, lunar, and planetary motions. In the tract *De emendatione annua* (1653[?]) he urges the reform of the 365-day year into months of (in sequence) 29, 29, 30, 30, 31, 31, 32, 31, 31, 31, 30, and 30 days.

Mercator's first published book in England, *Hypothesis astronomica nova* (1664), in effect combines Kepler's hypothesis (that planets travel in elliptical orbits round the sun, with the sun at one focus) with his vicarious hypothesis (in which the equant circle is centered in the line of apsides at a distance from the sun roughly 5/8 times the doubled eccentricity):

Mercator sets this ratio exactly equal to the "divine section" ($\sqrt{5} - 1)/2$, with an error even in the case of Mars of less than 2'. (Here a mystical streak in his personality gleams through, for he compares his hypothesis to a knock-kneed man standing with arms outstretched, a "living image of Eternity and the Trinity." He later expounded similar insights in an unpublished manuscript on *Astrologia rationalis*.) Subsequently, in 1670, he showed his skill in theoretical astronomy by demolishing G. D. Cassini's 1669 method for determining the lines of apsides of a planetary orbit, given three solar sightings. He showed that it reduced to the Boulliau-Ward hypothesis of mean motion round an upper-focus equant and pointed out its observational inaccuracy. (His enunciation of the "true" Keplerian hypothesis, that time in orbit is proportional to the focal sector swept out by the planet's radius vector, may well have been the source of Newton's knowledge of this basic law.) The two books of his *Institutiones astronomicae* (1676) offered the student an excellent grounding in contemporary theory, and Newton used them to fill gaps in his rather shaky knowledge of planetary and lunar theory. Some slight hint of the practical scientist is afforded by the barometric measurements made during the previous half year, which Mercator registered at the Royal Society in July 1667. No working drawings are extant of the Huygenian pendulum watch—which he designed in 1666—or of its marine mounting (by gimbal suspension), but an example "of a foote diameter" was made.

Mercator is remembered above all as a mathematician. In 1666 he claimed to be able to prove the identity of "the Logarithmical Tangent-line beginning at 45 deg." with the "true Meridian-line of the Sea-Charte" (Mercator map). This declaration is not authenticated but not necessarily empty. It is difficult to determine how far his researches into finite differences—which were restricted to the advancing-differences formula—were independent of Harriot's unpublished manuscripts on the topic, to which Mercator perhaps had access. In his best-known work, *Logarithmotechnia* (1668), he constructed logarithms from first principles (if $a^b = c$, then $b = \log_a c$), making ingenious use of the inequality

$$\left(\frac{a + px}{a - px}\right) < \left(\frac{a + x}{a - x}\right)^p, \qquad p = 1/2, 1/3, \cdots,$$

while in supplement (a late addition to the manuscript submitted in 1667) he used the St. Vincent-Sarasa hyperbola-area model to establish, independently of Hudde and Newton, the series expansion

$$\operatorname{lognat}(1 + x) = \int_0^x 1/(1 + x) \cdot dx$$
$$= x - \tfrac{1}{2}x^2 + \tfrac{1}{3}x^3 \cdots.$$

The circulation by Collins of the "De analysi," composed hurriedly by Newton as a riposte, seems to have effectively blocked Mercator's plans to publish a complementary *Cyclomathia* with allied expansions (on Newtonian lines) of circle integrals. The "Introductio brevis" which he added in 1678 to Martyn's second edition of the anonymous *Euclidis elementa geometrica* commendably sought to simplify the Euclidean definitions for the beginner by introducing motion proofs: a circle is generated as the ripple on the surface of a stagnant pool when a stone is dropped at its center, a line as the instantaneous meet of two such congruent wave fronts. His *Hypothesis astronomica nova* contains the first publication of the polar equation of an ellipse referred to a focus.

BIBLIOGRAPHY

I. ORIGINAL WORKS. The trio of textbooks put out by Mercator at Danzig in 1651 appeared under the titles *Cosmographia, sive descriptio coeli et terrae in circulos . . .; Trigonometria sphaericorum logarithmica, . . . cum canone triangulorum emendatissimo . . .;* and *Astronomia sphaerica decem problematis omnis ex fundamento tradita.* They were reissued shortly afterward at Leipzig . . . *Conformatae ad exactissimas docendi leges pro tironibus, . . . privatis hactenus experimentis comprobatae.* At Copenhagen Mercator published in 1653 his study on mathematical rationality, *Rationes mathematicae subductae,* and also his propagandist tract on calendar improvement, *De emendatione annua diatribae duae. . . .*

During the next ten years he apparently wrote nothing for the press, but at length produced his *Hypothesis astronomica nova, et consensus ejus cum observationibus* (London, 1664). His wager regarding the logarithmic nature of the Mercator map was announced in "Certain Problems Touching Some Points of Navigation," in *Philosophical Transactions of the Royal Society*, **1**, no. 13 (4 June 1666), 215–218. In 1668 appeared his major work, *Logarithmotechnia: sive methodus construendi logarithmos nova, accurata, & facilis; scripto antehàc communicata, anno sc. 1667 nonis Augusti: cui nunc accedit vera quadratura hyperbolae, & inventio summae logarithmorum* (London, 1668), later reprinted in F. Maseres, *Scriptores logarithmici*, I (London, 1791), 169–196; to Wallis' "account" of it in *Philosophical Transactions of the Royal Society*, **3**, no. 38 (17 Aug. 1668), 753–759, Mercator added "Some further Illustration," *ibid.*, 759–764. For a page-by-page analysis of the bk. see J. E. Hofmann, "Nicolaus Mercators *Logarithmotechnia* (1668)," in *Deutsche Mathematik*, **3** (1938), 446–466. His "Some Considerations . . . Concerning the Geometrick and direct Method of Signior Cassini for finding the Apogees,

Excentricities and Anomalies of the Planets; as that was printed in the *Journal des sçavans* of *Septemb. 2. 1669*" appeared in *Philosophical Transactions of the Royal Society*, **5**, no. 57 (25 Mar. 1670), 1168–1175.

His astronomical compendium, *Institutionum astronomicarum libri duo, de motu astrorum communi & proprio, secundum hypotheses veterum & recentiorum praecipuas* ... came out at London in 1676 (reissued Padua, 1685): Newton's lightly annotated copy is now at Trinity College, Cambridge, NQ.10.152. In an app. to the compendium Mercator reprinted his earlier *Hypothesis nova* (the preface excluded). His "Introductio brevis, qua magnitudinum ortus ex genuinis principiis, & ortarum affectiones ex ipsa genesi derivantur" was adjoined in 1678 to John Martyn's repr. of the "Jesuit's Euclid," in *Euclidis elementa geometrica, novo ordine ac methodo fere, demonstrata* (London, 1666).

None of Mercator's correspondence with his contemporaries seems to have survived, although that with Newton (1675–1676) on lunar vibration is digested in the *Institutiones astronomicae*, 286–287; compare the remark added by Newton to the third bk. of the third ed. of his *Principia*, Propositio XVII (London, 1726), 412. The MS (Bodleian, Oxford, Savile G.20⁴) of Mercator's Latin rendering of Kinckhuysen's *Algebra ofte Stelkonst* (Haarlem, 1661) is reproduced in *The Mathematical Papers of Isaac Newton*, II (Cambridge, 1968), 295–364, followed by Newton's "Observations" upon it, *ibid.*, 364–446.

Thomas Birch in his biography in *A General Dictionary Historical and Critical*, VII (London, 1738), 537–539 [= J. G. de Chaufepié, *Nouveau Dictionnaire historique et critique*, III (Amsterdam, 1753), 79], records the existence in Shirburn Castle of "a manuscript containing Theorems relating to the Resolution of Equations, the Method of Differences, and the Construction of Tables; and another, intitled, *Problema arithmeticum ad doctrinam de differentialium progressionibus pertinens*"; these are now in private possession. Birch also lists (*ibid.*, 539) the section titles of Mercator's unpublished "Astrologia rationalis, argumentis solidis explorata" (now Shirburn 180.F.34). Details of his chronometer are given by Birch in his *History of the Royal Society*, II (London, 1756), 110–114, 187, and in Oldenburg's letter to Leibniz of 18 December 1670 (C. I. Gerhardt, *Die Briefwechsel von G. W. Leibniz*, I [Berlin, 1899], 48). References to the lost treatise on circle quadrature, *Cyclomathia*, occur in John Collins' contemporary correspondence with James Gregory (see the *Gregory Memorial Volume* [London, 1939], 56, 60, 153).

II. SECONDARY LITERATURE. J. E. Hofmann's *Nicolaus Mercator (Kauffman), sein Leben und Wirken, vorzugsweise als Mathematiker* (in *Akademie der Wissenschaften und der Literatur in Mainz [Abh. der Math.-Nat. Kl.]*, no. 3 [1950]) is the best recent survey of Mercator's life and mathematical achievement. On his personality and habits see John Aubrey, *Letters ... and Lives of Eminent Men*, II (London, 1813), 450–451, 473, or *Brief Lives* (London, 1949), 135, 142, 153–154. J.-B. Delambre gives a partially erroneous estimate of Mercator's equant hypothesis of planetary motion in his *Histoire de l'astronomie moderne*, II (Paris,

1821), 539–546; see also Curtis Wilson, "Kepler's Derivation of the Elliptical Path," in *Isis*, **59** (1968), 5–25, esp. 23.

D. T. WHITESIDE

MERSENNE, MARIN (*b.* Oizé, Maine, France, 8 September 1588; *d.* Paris, France, 1 September 1648)

> The sciences have sworn among themselves an inviolable partnership; it is almost impossible to separate them, for they would rather suffer than be torn apart; and if anyone persists in doing so, he gets for his trouble only imperfect and confused fragments. Yet they do not arrive all together, but they hold each other by the hand so that they follow one another in a natural order which it is dangerous to change, because they refuse to enter in any other way where they are called. ....[1]

Mersenne's most general contribution to European culture was this vision of the developing community of the sciences. It could be achieved only by the cultivation of the particular:

> Philosophy would long ago have reached a high level if our predecessors and fathers had put this into practice; and we would not waste time on the primary difficulties, which appear now as severe as in the first centuries which noticed them. We would have the experience of assured phenomena, which would serve as principles for a solid reasoning; truth would not be so deeply sunken; nature would have taken off most of her envelopes; one would see the marvels she contains in all her individuals. ....[1]

These complaints had long been heard, yet "most men are glad to find work done, but few want to apply themselves to it, and many think that this search is useless or ridiculous."[1] He offered his scientific study of music as a particular reparation of a general fault.

Born into a family of laborers, Mersenne entered the new Jesuit *collège* at La Flèche in 1604 and remained there until 1609. After two years of theology at the Sorbonne, in 1611 he joined the Order of Minims and in 1619 returned to Paris to the Minim Convent de l'Annonciade near Place Royale, now Place des Vosges. There he remained, except for brief journeys, until his death in 1648.[2] The Minims recognized that Mersenne could best serve their interests through an apostolate of the intellect. He made his entry upon the European intellectual scene in his earliest publications, with a discussion of ancient and modern science in support of a characteristic theological argument. He aimed to use the certifiable successes of natural science as a demonstration of truth against contemporary errors dangerous to religion and the morals of youth. In his vast and diffuse *Quaestiones in Genesim* (1623) he defended orthodox theology against "atheists, magicians, deists and suchlike,"[3] especially Francesco Giorgio, Telesio, Bruno, Francesco Patrizzi, Campanella, and above all his contemporary Robert Fludd, by attacking atomism and the whole range of Hermetic, Cabalist, and "naturalist" doctrines of occult powers and harmonies and of the Creation. In the same volume he included a special refutation of Giorgio,[4] and he continued his attack on this group in *L'impiété des déistes, athées, et libertins de ce temps* (1624). This attack on magic and the occult in defense of the rationality of nature attracted the attention of Pierre Gassendi, whom he met in 1624 and who became his closest friend.[5]

Mersenne's next work, the *Synopsis mathematica* (1626), was a collection of classical and recent texts on mathematics and mechanics. After that came *La vérité des sciences, contre les sceptiques ou Pyrrhoniens*, a long defense of the possibility of true human knowledge against the Pyrrhonic skepticism developed especially by Montaigne. Thus religion and morality had some rational basis. Yet while he stood with Aristotle in arguing that nature was both rational and knowable, he denied that theologians had to be tied to Aristotle.[6] Against the qualitative, verbal Aristotelian physics he came to argue that nature was rational, its actions limited by quantitative laws, because it was a mechanism.[7]

From about 1623 Mersenne began to make the careful selection of *savants* who met at his convent in Paris or corresponded with him from all over Europe and as far afield as Tunisia, Syria, and Constantinople. His regular visitors or correspondents came to include Peiresc, Gassendi, Descartes,[8] the Roman musicologist Giovanni Battista Doni, Roberval, Beeckman, J. B. van Helmont, Fermat, Hobbes, and the Pascals. It was in Mersenne's quarters that in 1647 the young Blaise Pascal first met Descartes.[9] Mersenne's role as secretary of the republic of scientific letters, with a strong point of view of his own, became institutionalized in the Academia Parisiensis, which he organized in 1635.[10] His monument as an architect of the European scientific community is the rich edition of his *Correspondance* published in Paris in the present century.

Mersenne developed his mature natural philosophy in relation to two fundamental questions. The first was the validity in physics of the axiomatic theory of truly scientific demonstration described in Aristotle's *Posterior Analytics* and exemplified in contemporary discussions especially by Euclid's geometry. Mersenne entered in the wake of the sixteenth-century debate on skepticism. The second question was the accept-ability of a strictly mechanistic conception of nature. Opinions about these two questions decided what was believed to be discoverable in nature and what any particular inquiry had discovered. Opinions about the second also decided how to deal with the relationship of perceiver to world perceived, and so with the information communicated, especially through vision and hearing.

Mersenne's approach to these problems represents a persistent style in science. He took up his characteristic position on the first in the course of the debate over the new astronomy. He treated the decree of 1616 against Copernicus with Northern independence and moved in his early writings from rejection of the hypothesis of the earth's motions because sufficient evidence was lacking,[11] to preference for it as the most plausible. Copernicus' hypothesis, he said, had been neither refuted nor demonstrated: "I have never liked the attitude of people who want to look for, or feign, or imagine reasons or demonstrations where there are none; it is better to confess our ignorance than abuse the world."[12] But Mersenne reacted strongly against theologically sensitive extensions of the new cosmology, especially the doctrines of a plurality of worlds and of the infinity of the universe.[13] He took particular exception to Giordano Bruno: "one of the wickedest men whom the earth has ever supported . . . who seems to have invented a new manner of philosophizing only in order to make underhand attacks on the Christian religion."[14] He maintained that ecclesiastics had the right to condemn opinions likely to scandalize their flocks and merely advised moderation in censorship, because in the end "the true philosophy never conflicts with the belief of the Church."[15]

Through the Christian philosopher defending true knowledge against the skeptic in *La vérité des sciences*, and in later essays, Mersenne defined the kind of rational knowledge he held to be available. He found in Francis Bacon a program for real scientific knowledge, but he reproached him for failing to keep abreast of the "progress of the sciences" and for proposing the impossible goal of penetrating "the nature of things."[16] Only God knew the essences of things. God's inscrutable omnipotence, which denied men independent rational knowledge of his reasons, and the logical impossibility of demonstrating causes uniquely determined by effects reduced the order of nature for men simply to an order of contingent fact. Mersenne concluded that the only knowledge of the physical world available to men was that of the quantitative externals of effects, and that the only hope of science was to explore these externals by means of experiment and the most probable hypotheses. But this was true knowledge, able to guide men's actions, even though theology and logic showed it to be less than that claimed to be possible by Aristotle.[17]

In 1629, after some earlier approaches, Mersenne wrote to Galileo, offering his services in publishing "the new system of the motion of the earth which you have perfected, but which you cannot publish because of the prohibition of the Inquisition."[18] Galileo did not reply to this generous offer—nor, indeed, to any of Mersenne's later letters to him. But Mersenne was not put off. He had come to see in Galileo's work a supreme illustration of the rationality of nature governed by mechanical laws and, so far as these laws went, of the true program for natural science.[19] In 1633 he published his first critique of Galileo's *Dialogo* (1632) in his *Traité des mouvemens et de la cheute des corps pesans et de la proportion de leurs différentes vitesses, dans lequel l'on verra plusieurs expériences très exactes.*[20] His first response to hearing of Galileo's condemnation in that year was to agree with the need for the Church to preserve Scripture from error;[21] yet he came forward at once with a French version (with additions of his own) of Galileo's unpublished early treatise on mechanics under the title *Les méchaniques de Galilée* (1634), and with a summary account of the first two days of the *Dialogo* and of the trial in *Les questions théologiques, physiques, morales, et mathématiques* (1634).

Mersenne's mature natural philosophy appeared in *Les questions* and three other works in the same year: *Questions inouyës, Questions harmoniques,* and *Les préludes de l'harmonie universelle.*[22] He made it plain that Galileo had not been condemned for heresy; and although he wrote later that he would not be prepared to risk schism for the new astronomy,[23] in 1634 he planned to write a defense of Galileo.[24] He gave this up. Mersenne disagreed with Galileo's claim to "necessary demonstrations" on the general ground that no physical science had "the force of perfect demonstration;"[25] and like most of his contemporaries he was unconvinced by the dynamical arguments so far produced by Galileo or anyone else. Yet while he saw the question of the earth's motion as undecided, he encouraged the search for fresh quantitative evidence which alone would make it possible "to distinguish the way nature acts in these movements, and to make a decision about it."[26]

Mersenne's conclusion that an inescapable "ignorance of true causes"[27] was imposed by the human situation gave him a scientific style interestingly different from that of Galileo and of Descartes. They aimed at certainty in physical science; Mersenne, disbelieving in the possibility of certainty, aimed at precision. Galileo's lack of precision in his first published mention of his experiments on acceleration down an inclined plane in the *Dialogo* led Mersenne to doubt whether he had really performed them. His own carefully repeated experiments, using a seconds pendulum to measure time, confirmed the "duplicate proportion" between distance and time deduced by Galileo but gave values nearly twice as great for the actual distances fallen. He commented that "one should not rely too much only on reasoning."[28] On many occasions Mersenne's too close attention to the untidy facts of observation may have deprived him of theoretical insight; but his insistence on the careful specification of experimental procedures, repetition of experiments, publication of the numerical results of actual measurements as distinct from those calculated from theory, and recognition of approximations marked a notable step in the organization of experimental science in the seventeenth century. Amid many words and some credulity, the works of his maturity, especially on acoustics and optics, contain models of "expériences bien reglées et bien faites"[29] and of rational appreciation of the limits of measurement and of discovery.

While strict demonstration was beyond natural science, Mersenne maintained that the imitation of God's works in nature by means of technological artifacts gave experimental natural philosophy an opening into possible explanations of phenomena. In this way he linked his experimental method with the second fundamental question for his natural philosophy—the conception of nature as a mechanism—and with the method of the hypothetical model. Characteristically it was through theological issues that he developed the central idea that living things were automatons. He used it as a weapon in his campaign for the uniqueness of human reason and of its power to grasp true knowledge and moral responsibility, against the false doctrines both of "les naturalistes,"[30] who asserted human participation in a world soul, and of the skeptics, who threw doubt on human superiority over the animals. After his visit to Beeckman, Descartes, and J. B. van Helmont in the Netherlands in 1630,[31] Mersenne came to hold that, on the analogy of sound, light was a form of purely corporeal propagation. Although he remained unconvinced by the evidence for any of the current theories of light and sound and changed his views several times, his restriction of the choice to physical motions gave him (like Descartes) a method of asking how these motions affected a sentient being.[32] He disposed finally of the arguments against the uniqueness of man by declaring animals to be simply automatons, explicitly first in *Les préludes de l'harmonie universelle* (1634):

... for the animals, which we resemble and which

would be our equals if we did not have reason, do not reflect upon the actions or the passions of their external or internal senses, and do not know what is color, odor or sound, or if there is any difference between these objects, to which they are moved rather than moving themselves there. This comes about by the force of the impression that the different objects make on their organs and on their senses, for they cannot discern if it is more appropriate to go and drink or eat or do something else, and they do not eat or drink or do anything else except when the presence of objects, or the animal imagination [*l'imagination brutalle*], necessitates them and transports them to their objects, without their knowing what they do, whether good or bad; which would happen to us just as to them if we were destitute of reason, for they have no enlightenment except what they must have to take their nourishment and to serve us for the uses to which God has destined them.[33]

So one could say of the animals that they knew nothing of the world impinging upon them, "that they do not so much act as be put into action, and that objects make an impression on their senses such that it is necessary for them to follow it just as it is necessary for the wheels of a clock to follow the weights and the spring that pulls them."[34] Yet Mersenne did not say, like Descartes, that animals were machines identical in kind with the artificial machines made by men. He wrote that the movements of the heart would be understood without mystery if one could discover its mechanism,[35] but men could imitate God's productions in nature only externally and quantitatively. The essence remained hidden. Nevertheless, men's artificial imitations could become testable hypotheses or models for explaining natural phenomena.[36] The quantitative relations within natural phenomena represented the rational and stable *harmonie universelle* that God had chosen to exhibit, both within the structure of his physical creation and in the information about it that men were in a position to discover and communicate.

Mersenne selected for his own particular field of positive inquiry, and for the elimination of magic and the irrational, the mode of operation of vision and of heard sound, and of the languages of men and animals. His first original contributions to acoustics (on vibrating strings), as well as analyses of ancient and modern musical theory and optics, appeared in *Quaestiones in Genesim* (1623). In the same year he announced in his *Observationes*[37] on Francesco Giorgio's plans for a systematic science of sound, "le grand oeuvre de la musique,"[38] which henceforth became his chief intellectual preoccupation. The first sketches appeared in the *Traité de l'harmonie universelle* (1627),[39] *Questions harmoniques* (1634), and *Les*

préludes de l'harmonie universelle (1634). Meanwhile, by 1629 Mersenne had planned and soon afterward began writing simultaneously two sets of treatises, in French and in Latin, which together form his great systematic work and were published as the two parts of *Harmonie universelle, contenant la théorie et la pratique de la musique* (1636, 1637), and the eight books of *Harmonicorum libri* with *Harmonicorum instrumentorum libri IV* (1636).[40] Before the final sections of *Harmonie universelle* were in print, he read in Paris, in the winter of 1636–1637, a manuscript of the first day of Galileo's *Discorsi* (1638) containing an account of conclusions about acoustics and the pendulum similar to his own.[41] Mersenne's next work on these subjects was his French summary and critical discussion of Galileo's book in *Les nouvelles pensées de Galilée* (1639). Later he published the results of further acoustical researches in three related works, *Cogitata physico-mathematica* (1644), *Universae geometriae mixtaeque mathematicae synopsis* (1644), and *Novarum observationum physico-mathematicarum tomus III* (1647). The last contains a summary of his contributions to the science of sound.

Parallel discussions of light and vision, beginning in *Quaestiones in Genesim* and Mersenne's correspondence from this time, run especially through *Harmonie universelle* and *Harmonicorum libri*, the *Cogitata*, and *Universae geometriae synopsis*. The inclusion in the optical section of *Universae geometriae synopsis* of unpublished work by Walter Warner, and of a version of Hobbes's treatise on optics with its mechanistic psychology, reflects Mersenne's close English connections at this time. His final contributions to optics, including experimental studies of visual acuity and binocular vision and a critical discussion of current hypotheses on the nature of light, appeared posthumously in *L'optique et la catoptrique* (1651).

Mersenne's scientific analysis of sound and of its effects on the ear and the soul began with the fundamental demonstration that pitch is proportional to frequency and hence that the musical intervals (octave, fifth, fourth, and so on) are ratios of frequencies of vibrations, whatever instrument produces them. The essential propositions were established by G. B. Benedetti (*ca.* 1563), Galileo's father, Vincenzio Galilei (1589–1590), Beeckman (1614–1615), and, finally, Mersenne (1623–1634). Mersenne gave an experimental proof by counting the slow vibrations of very long strings against time measured by pulse beats or a seconds pendulum. He then used the laws he had completed (now bearing his name), relating frequency to the length, tension, and specific gravity of strings, to calculate frequencies too rapid to count. Similar relations were established for wind and percussion instruments. The demonstration of these propositions made it possible to offer quantitative physical explanations of consonance, dissonance, and resonance.[42]

An allied outstanding discovery apparently made first by Mersenne was the law that the frequency of a pendulum is inversely proportional to the square root of the length. His first statement of this was printed by 30 June 1634, about a year before Galileo's was written.[43] Exploring further acoustical quantities, Mersenne pioneered the scientific study of the upper and lower limits of audible frequencies, of harmonics, and of the measurement of the speed of sound, which he showed to be independent of pitch and loudness. He established that the intensity of sound, like that of light, is inversely proportional to the distance from its source.[44] Mersenne's discussions, after his visit to Italy in 1644, of the Italian and later French experiments with a Torricellian vacuum helped to make a live issue of this whole subject and its bearing on the true medium of sound and on the existence of atmospheric pressure.[45] Besides these contributions to science, collaboration with Doni on an ambitious plan for a comprehensive historical work on the theory and practice of ancient and modern music[46] yielded a rich collection of descriptions and illustrations of instruments, making *Harmonie universelle* and its Latin counterpart essential sources for musicology.

In keeping with his empirical philosophy, Mersenne looked for purely rational explanations of the motions and dispositions of the soul brought about by music. He aimed to put an end to all ideas of magical and occult powers of words and sounds.[47] At the same time he offered a rational analysis of language, arguing that if it was language that chiefly distinguished men from animals, this was a fundamental distinction, for language meant conscious understanding of meaning. The speech and jargon of animals was a kind of communication, but not language, for they mindlessly emitted and responded to messages simply as automatons.[48] Mersenne soon rejected any idea that there were natural names revealing the natures of things and firmly proposed a purely rational theory of language that made words simply conventional physical signs. Because all men possessed reason, they had developed languages in which spoken or written words signified meanings. But just as the effects of music varied with temperament, race, period, and culture, so different groups of men had come to express their common understanding of meaning in a variety of languages diversified by their different historical experiences, environments, needs, temperaments, and customs.[49] In this analysis of common elements Mersenne saw a means of inventing a perfect universal language that could convey information without error. Basing his linguistic experiments on a calculus of permutations and combinations, he proposed a system that would convey the only knowledge of things available to men, that of their quantitative externals. Such a language of quantities "could be called natural and universal"[50] and would be a perfect means of philosophical communication.

Descartes's famous comment that this perfect language could be achieved only in an earthly paradise[51] was true in a way perhaps not intended, for "le bon Père Mersenne" seems to have lived mentally in just such a paradise. "A man of simple, innocent, pure heart, without guile," Gassendi wrote three days after his friend had died in his arms. "A man than whom none was more painstaking, inquiring, experienced. A man whom all the arts and sciences to whose advance he tirelessly devoted himself, by investigating or by deliberating or by stimulating others, will justly mourn."[52] With almost his last breath Mersenne asked for an autopsy to discover the cause of his death. *Maxime de Minimis*.[53] He illustrates the creativeness of gifts of personality distinct from those of sheer originality in the scientific movement.

NOTES

1. Mersenne, *Les préludes de l'harmonie universelle* (Paris, 1634), 135–139.
2. Lenoble, *Mersenne*, 15 ff.
3. Mersenne, *Quaestiones celeberrime in Genesim, cum accurata textus explicatione. In hoc volumine athei, et deistae impugnantur, et expurgantur, et Vulgata editio ab haereticorum calumniis vindicatur. Graecorum et Hebraeorum musica instauratur. . . . Opus theologis, philosophis, medicis, iuriconsultis, mathematicis, musicis vero, et catoptricis praesertim utile . . .* (Paris, 1623), preface.
4. Mersenne, *Observationes et emendationes ad Francisci Georgii Veneti problemata* (Paris, 1623).
5. Mersenne, *Correspondance*, I, 190–193; Lenoble, *Mersenne*, xviii, 28.
6. *Quaestiones in Genesim*, preface.
7. Mersenne, *Les méchaniques de Galilée* (1634), "Épistre dédicatoire," ch. 1.
8. It seems likely that he met Descartes in either 1623 or 1625, before or after the latter's journey to Italy: see *Correspondance*, I, 149; and Lenoble, *Mersenne*, 1, 17, 31, 314–316, for the improbability of their friendship at La Flèche as boys separated by seven and a half years in age, and other misconceptions of their relationship promulgated by Descartes's biographer Adrien Baillet.
9. A. Baillet, *La vie de Monsieur Des-Cartes*, II (1691), 327–328; Jacqueline Pascal's letter of 25 Sept. 1647, in Blaise Pascal, *Oeuvres*, L. Brunschvicg, P. Boutroux, and F. Gazier, eds., II (Paris, 1908), 39–48. Pascal in his "Histoire de la roulette" gave Mersenne the credit for being the first to consider, about 1615, the curve produced by "le roulement des roues": *Oeuvres*, VIII (1914), 195; cf. Mersenne, *Correspondance*, I, 13, 183–184, and II, 598–599.
10. *Correspondance*, I, xliii–xliv, V, 209–211, 371; Lenoble, *Mersenne*, 1, 35–36, 48, 233–234, 586–594. Mersenne had

for more than a decade been a member of the Cabinet des Frères Dupuy; for this and the various proposals he made beginning in 1623 for national and international cooperation through academies of theology in which scientific and other experts assisted, of science and mathematics, and of music, see the *Correspondance*, I, 45, 106–107, 129, 136–137, 169–172, V, 301–302; *Quaestiones in Genesim*, preface, dedication, and cols. 1510–1511, 1683–1687; *La vérité des sciences*, 206–224, 751–752, 913–914: *Traité de l'harmonie universelle*, 50, 255–256.

11. *Quaestiones in Genesim*, preface and cols. 841–850, 879–920. He gave considerable attention to Kepler, whom he supported against Fludd: cf. cols. 1016, 1556–1562; *Correspondance*, I, 131–132, 147–148; Lenoble, *Mersenne*, 224–225, 367–370, 394–413.

12. *L'impiété des déistes*, II, 200–201; cf. 198.

13. *Quaestiones in Genesim*, cols. 57, 85, 892–893, 903–904, 1081–1096, 1164; cf. *Correspondance*, I, 130–135.

14. *L'impiété*, I, 230–231; cf. II, 326–342, 363–364, 475.

15. *La vérité*, 111; cf. *L'impiété*, II, 479, 494–495.

16. *La vérité*, 109, 212–213; cf. 913–914.

17. *Ibid.*, 13–15, 226; *Les questions théologiques* (1634), "Épistre" and pp. 9–11, 16–19, 116–117, 123–124, 178–183, 229; *Questions inouyës* (1634), 69–78, 130–131, 153–154; see notes 25–27.

18. *Correspondance*, II, 175.

19. Cf. note 7.

20. *Correspondance*, III, 437–439, 561–568, 630–633.

21. Letter of 8 Feb. 1634, *ibid.*, IV, 37–38.

22. *Ibid.*, IV, 76–78, 156–157; cf. III, 570–572.

23. Mersenne to Martinus Ruarus, 1 Apr. 1644, in Ruarus' *Epistolarum selectarum centuria* (Paris, 1677), 269; Lenoble, *Mersenne*, 413.

24. *Correspondance*, IV, 226, 232, 267–268, 406–407, 411–412, V, 106, 127, 214; note 22. Cf. Descartes's letters to Mersenne during 1633–1635 on Galileo: *ibid.*, III, 557–560; IV, 26–29, 50–52, 97–99, 297–300; V, 127.

25. *Les questions théologiques*, 116–117; cf. 18–19, 43–44, 164.

26. *Harmonie universelle* (1636), "Traitez de la nature des sons et des mouvemens," I, prop. xxxiii, p. 76; cf. II, props. xix, xxi, pp. 149–150, 154–155. The same attitude appears in the *Cogitata physico-mathematica* (1644), "Hydraulica," 251, 260, and "Ballistica," 81–82; in the *Universae geometriae synopsis* (1644), "Cosmographia," preface, 258; and in Roberval's dedication to his "Aristarchus," printed in Mersenne's *Novarum observationum tomus III* (1647).

27. *Les questions théologiques*, 18–19; cf. *Harmonie universelle*, "Première preface générale"; see notes 20, 29.

28. *Harmonie universelle*, "Traitez . . . des sons," II, prop. vii, coroll. 1, p. 112; cf. prop. i, pp. 85–88, and prop vii, pp. 108–112; and for his seconds pendulum, prop. xv, pp. 135–137, prop. xxii, coroll. 9, p. 220; *Correspondance*, IV, 409–411; A. Koyré, "An Experiment in Measurement." These criticisms may have provoked Galileo to describe his experiment in more detail in the *Discorsi* (1638); Mersenne again repeated the experiment and wrote in *Les nouvelles pensées de Galilée* (1639) that, with a ball heavy enough not to be significantly affected by air resistance, he found "les mesmes proportions" (pp. 188–189).

29. *Harmonie universelle*, "Traitez . . . des sons," III, prop. v, p. 167; cf. *Novarum observationum . . . tomus III*, 113, on reason guiding the senses.

30. *Les préludes*, 118; cf. *Quaestiones in Genesim*, cols. 130, 937–948, 1262–1272; *L'impiété*, II, 360–378, 390–391, 401–437; *La vérité*, 15–20, 25–36, 179–189; *Les questions théologiques*, 229–232.

31. See for this visit, *Correspondance*, II, 486, 506–507, 522–525.

32. See for discussions about light and sound, *ibid.*, I, 329–330, 333–335, II, 107–108, 116–124, 248–249, 282–283, 293–296, 353, 456–459, 467–477, 669–670, III, 35–42, 48–49; *Quaestiones in Genesim*, cols. 742, 1561, 1892; *La vérité*, 69–72;

Traité de l'harmonie universelle, preface and p. 7; *Les questions théologiques*, 67–69, 105–106, and 164 of the expurgated ed. (Lenoble, *Mersenne*, xx, 399–401, 518; *Correspondance*, IV, 74–76, 203–206, 267–271); *Harmonie universelle*, "Traitez de la nature des sons," I, props. i–ii, viii–x, xxv, xxxii, pp. 1–6, 14–19, 44–48, 73–74; *Harmonicorum libri*, I, props. ii–vi, pp. 1–3; *Cogitata physico-mathematica*, "Harmonia," 261–271, "Ballistica," preface and pp. 74–82 (on Hobbes, etc.); *Universae geometriae . . . synopsis*, "Praefatio utilis in synopsim mathematicam," sec. x, and pp. 471 bis–487, 548, 567–571 (by Hobbes); *L'optique et la catoptrique* (1651), 1–3, 49–54, 77–92; Lenoble, *Mersenne*, 107–108, 317–318, 370–371, 414–418, 421–424, 478–486; note 44.

33. *Les préludes*, 156–159. Their correspondence and Mersenne's publications leave uncertain what Mersenne knew at this time of the earlier ideas developed by Descartes in the *Regulae*, left unfinished in 1629, and *Le monde* and *L'homme*, begun in the same year.

34. *Harmonie universelle* (1637), "Traitez de la voix," I, prop. lii, p. 79; cf. note 47.

35. *Les questions théologiques*, 76–81; cf. 183. Mersenne sent a copy of William Harvey's *De motu cordis* (1628) together with a set of Fludd's works to Gassendi in Dec. 1628 and discussed the circulation of the blood with Descartes: *Correspondance*, II, 181–182, 189, 268; III, 346, 349–350; VIII, 296.

36. *La vérité*, preface; *Harmonie universelle*, "Traitez de la voix," II, prop. xxii, pp. 159–160, "Nouvelles observations physiques et mathématiques," I, coroll. 5, pp. 7–8.

37. Cols. 439–440; see note 4.

38. *La vérité*, 567; cf. preface and 370–371, 579, 981.

39. "Sommaire"; cf. *Correspondance*, I, 195–196, 204.

40. Mersenne created a major bibliographical problem by writing these treatises simultaneously with numerous revisions and repetitions, and by having the different sections printed separately: scarcely any two of the extant copies have the same contents in the same order; cf. Lenoble, *Mersenne*, xxi–xxvi; see note 41.

41. Galileo Galilei, *Opere*, A. Favaro, ed., XVI (Florence, 1905), 524, XVII (1907), 63–64, 80–81; Mersenne, *Correspondance*, VI, 83–84, 241–243, cf. 216, 237; *Harmonie universelle* (1637), "Seconde observation"; cf. *Les nouvelles pensées de Galilée* (1639), preface and 66–67, 72, 92, 96–99, 104–105, 109–110; cf. *Correspondance*, VII, 107–109, 317–320; see note 42.

42. *Quaestiones in Genesim*, cols. 1556–1562, 1699, 1710; *La vérité*, 370–371, 567, 614–620; *Traité de l'harmonie universelle*, 147–148, 447; *Harmonicorum libri*, I, prop. ii, II, props. vi–viii, xvii–xxi, xxxiii–xxxv, IV, prop. xxvii; *Harmonie universelle*: "Traité des instrumens," I, props. v, xii, xvi, III, props. vii, xvii; "Traitez . . . des sons," I, props. i, vii, xiii, III, props. i, v, vi, xv; "Traitez de la voix," I, prop. lii; "Traitez des consonances," I, props. vi, x, xii, xvii, xviii, xix, xxii, II, prop. x. Mersenne wrote from Paris on 20 Mar. 1634 to Peiresc in Aix-en-Provence that after more than ten years of work he had finished his "grand oeuvre de l'*Harmonie universelle*," of which he sent "le premier cayer" (*Correspondance*, IV, 81–82). The earliest section in which he gave an extensive analysis of the physical quantities determining the notes and intervals produced by vibrating strings, bells, and pipes, and used this to explain resonance, consonance, and dissonance seems to have been the "Traitez des consonances," I, "Des consonances." This was in print by 2 Feb. 1635 (Mersenne to Doni, *Correspondance*, V, 40–41). Internal references and the *Correspondance*, IV–V, indicate that he was writing at the same time, during 1634, the "Traité des instrumens" (I–III) and the *Harmonicorum libri* (I–IV); see Crombie, *Galileo and Mersenne* (forthcoming).

43. Mersenne published this law first in one of his original additions to *Les méchaniques de Galilée*, 7th addition, p. 77.

The "privilège du roy" gives 30 June 1634 as the date on which the printing was completed: cf. Mersenne, *Correspondance*, IV, 76–77, 207–212, and the new ed. of *Les méchaniques* by Rochot (1966). The work was bound with Mersenne's *Les questions théologiques* and presumably sent with that to Doni by way of Peiresc in 1634 (Mersenne to Peiresc, 28 July 1634; Doni to Mersenne, 8 Nov. 1634; *Correspondance*, IV, 267, 384–385, appendix III, 444–455). Élie Diodati sent a copy of *Les méchaniques* from Paris to Galileo on 10 Apr. 1635 (*ibid.*, V, 132; cf. VI, 242). For Mersenne's use of this pendulum law, and his possible derivation of it from the law of falling bodies, see also *Harmonicorum libri*, II, props. xxvi–xxix; *Harmonie universelle*, "Traitez des instrumens," I, props. xix–xx; "Traitez . . . des sons," III, "Du mouvement," props. xxi, xxiii. Galileo's correspondence with Fulgenzio Micanzio in Venice between 19 Nov. 1634 and 7 Apr. 1635 (*Opere*, XVI, 163, 177, 193, 200–201, 203, 208–210, 214, 217–233, 236–237, 239–244, 254) indicates that he had not written the last part of the first day of the *Discorsi* (in which he discussed the pendulum and acoustics) by the latter date. His letter of 9 June 1635 to Diodati, saying that he had sent a copy to Giovanni Pieroni, and subsequent correspondence (*Opere*, XVI, 272–274, 300–304, 359–361) establishes this as the latest date of composition. This copy survives in Biblioteca Nazionale Centrale, Florence, MS Banco Raro 31; cf. note 40.

44. For these subjects see, respectively, *Harmonie universelle*, "Traitez des instrumens," I, prop. xix, III, prop. xvii, "Traitez . . . des sons," III, prop. vi, "Traitez de la voix," I, prop. lii; *Harmonicorum libri*, II, props. xviii, xxxiii; *Harmonie universelle*, "Traitez des instrumens," IV, prop. ix, VI, prop. xlii, VII, prop. xviii, "Nouvelles observations," IV; *Harmonicorum instrumentorum libri IV*, I, prop. xxxiii, III, prop. xxvii; cf. *Quaestiones in Genesim*, col. 1560; *Harmonie universelle*, "Traitez . . . des sons," I, props. vii, viii, xiii, xvii, xxi, III, prop. xxii, "De l'utilité de l'harmonie," prop. ix; *Novarum observationum . . . tomus III*, "Reflectiones physico-mathematicae," ch. 20, *Harmonie universelle*, "Traitez . . . des sons," I, props. xii, xv, cf. props. iii, iv (coroll. 30), and III, prop. xxi, coroll. 4; *Harmonicorum libri*, II, prop. xxxix.

45. *Novarum observationum . . . tomus III*, "Praefatio ad lectorem," "Praefatio secunda," and pp. 84–96, 216–218; cf. de Waard, *L'expérience barométrique*, 117–131; Lenoble, *Mersenne*, xxx, 431–436; Middleton, *The History of the Barometer*, 33–54.

46. Cf. *Correspondance*, III, 395, 512–513, IV, 80, 345, 368, VII, 393–394; G. D. Doni, *Annotazioni sopra il compendio de' generi, e de' modi della musica* (Rome, 1640), 277–280.

47. *Quaestiones in Genesim*, cols. 1619–1624; *La vérité*, 16–17, 32, 69–72; *Les préludes*, 212, 219–222; *Questions harmoniques*, 91–99; *Harmonie universelle*, "Préface générale au lecteur," "Traitez . . . des sons," I, props. i–ii, "Traitez de la voix," I, "Traitez des consonances," I, prop. xxxiii; *Harmonicorum libri*, I, prop. ii; Lenoble, *Mersenne*, 522–531.

48. *Harmonie universelle*, "Traitez de la voix," I, prop. xxxix, pp. 49–52; cf. props. vii–xii, xxxviii; cf. note 33.

49. *Quaestiones in Genesim*, cols. 23–24, 470–471, 702–704, 1197–1202, 1217, 1383–1398, 1692; MS continuation, Bibliothèque Nationale, Paris, MS lat. 17, 262, pp. 511, 536 (Lenoble, *Mersenne*, xiii–xiv, 514–517); *L'impiété*, 167; *La vérité*, 67–76, 544–580; *Traité de l'harmonie universelle*, "Sommaire," item 9; *Questions inouyes*, 95–101, 120–122; *Harmonie universelle*, "Préface générale au lecteur" and "Traitez de la voix," preface, I, II, props. vii–xii; *Harmonicorum libri*, VII; Mersenne's discussions from 1621 to 1640 with Guillaume Bredeau, Descartes, Jean Beaugrand, Peiresc, Gassendi, Comenius, and others are in *Correspondance*, I, 61–63, 102–103; II, 323–329, 374–375; III, 254–262; IV, 329; V, 136–140; VI, 4–6; VII,

447–448; X, 264–274; Lenoble, *Mersenne*, 96–109, 514–521.

50. *Les questions théologiques*, quest. xxxiv, "Peut-on inventer une nouvelle science des sons, qui se nomme psophologie?" p. 158 (expurgated ed.); *Harmonie universelle*, "Traitez . . . des sons," I, prop. xxiv (language played on a lute), "Traitez de la voix," I, props. xii, xlvii–l (artificial rational languages), "De l'utilité de l'harmonie," prop. ix (symbolic language, acoustical telegraph). Cf. his proposals for methods of imitating human speech with instruments and for teaching deaf-mutes to speak and communicate: *Harmonie universelle*, "Traitez de la voix," I, props. x–xi, li, "Traitez des instrumens," II, prop. ix; cf. *Correspondance*, III, 354, 358–359, 375, 378, IV, 258–259, 262–263, 280, 289, 294 (1633–1634). On instruments for imitating human speech see "Traitez des instrumens," VI, props. xxxi–xxxii, xxxvi, VII, prop. xxx; *Correspondance*, III, 2–9, 538–553, 578–597, V, 269–272, 293–294, 299–300, 410–415, 478–482 (1631–1635).

51. Descartes to Mersenne, 20 Nov. 1629, in Mersenne, *Correspondance*, II, 323–329; cf. 374–375, IV, 329, 332, V, 134–140, VI, 4, 6.

52. Gassendi to Louis de Valois, 4 Sept. 1648, *Opera*, VI (Lyons, 1658), 291; Lenoble, *Mersenne*, 596, cf. 58; cf. Coste, *Vie*, 13, 99–101; Mersenne, *Correspondance*, I, xxx.

53. Constantijn Huygens, in a poem cited by Thuillier, *Diarium . . .*, II, 104; cf. Lenoble, *Mersenne*, 597, who also quotes a poem by Hobbes on Mersenne.

BIBLIOGRAPHY

I. Original Works. A list of Mersenne's published and unpublished writings is in R. Lenoble, *Mersenne ou la naissance du mécanisme* (Paris, 1943), "Bibliographie," which also contains a list of publications on Mersenne from the seventeenth century. His main books are named in the text; all were published at Paris. There is a recent edition of *Les méchaniques de Galilée* by B. Rochot (Paris, 1966); and Mersenne's own copy of *Harmonie universelle*, with his annotations made during 1637–1648, has been reprinted in facsimile by the Centre National de la Recherche Scientifique (Paris, 1965). Above all there is Mersenne's *Correspondance*, C. de Waard, R. Pintard, and B. Rochot, eds. (Paris, 1932–   ), which includes information about his publications and MSS.

II. Secondary Literature. The first biography was the valuable study written immediately after Mersenne's death by a fellow Minim, Hilarion de Coste, *La vie du R. P. Marin Mersenne, théologien, philosophe et mathématicien, de l'Ordre des Pères Minim* (Paris, 1649). A second main source for his life is René Thuillier, *Diarium patrum, fratrum et sororum Ordinis Minimorum Provinciae Franciae sive Parisiensis qui religiose obierunt ab anno 1506 ad annum 1700* (Paris, 1709). The critical problems are discussed in the *Correspondance*, I (1932), xix–lv; in this his career, publications, and relations with his contemporaries can be followed in detail from 1617.

The major study of Mersenne's life and thought is Lenoble's *Mersenne*. A valuable monograph is H. Ludwig, *Marin Mersenne und seine Musiklehre* (Halle–Berlin, 1935). For particular aspects there are C. de Waard, *L'expérience barométrique* (Thouars, 1936), and W. E. K. Middleton, *The History of the Barometer* (Baltimore, 1964), on the Torricellian vacuum; Mario M. Rossi, *Alle fonti del deismo e del materialismo moderni* (Florence, 1942), on his relation to deism; A. Koyré, "An Experiment in Measurement," in *Proceedings of the American Philosophical Society*, **97** · (1953), 222–237, repr. in his *Metaphysics and Measurement* (London, 1968), on his critique of Galileo's experiments on acceleration; R. H. Popkin, *The History of Scepticism From Erasmus to Descartes* (Assen, Netherlands, 1964), on his relation to contemporary skepticism; F. A. Yates, *Giordano Bruno and the Hermetic Tradition* (London, 1964), on his relation to Hermeticism; A. C. Crombie, "Mathematics, Music and Medical Science," in *Actes du XIIᵉ Congrès international d'histoire des sciences: Paris 1968* (Paris, 1971), 295–310, on his science of sound; and W. L. Hine, "Mersenne and Copernicanism," in *Isis*, **64** (1973), 18–32. A further substantial discussion of his natural philosophy, with special reference to vision, heard sound and language, is included in A. C. Crombie, with the collaboration of A. Carugo, *Galileo and Mersenne: Science, Nature and the Senses in the Sixteenth and Early Seventeenth Centuries*, 2 vols. (forthcoming).

A. C. CROMBIE

MESHCHERSKY, IVAN VSEVOLODOVICH (*b.* Arkhangelsk, Russia, 10 August 1859; *d.* Leningrad, U.S.S.R., 7 January 1935)

Meshchersky was born into a family of modest means, but succeeded in obtaining a good education. He was enrolled in the Arkhangelsk Gymnasium in 1871, and graduated from it with a gold medal after seven years. He entered St. Petersburg University in 1878, and undertook the study of mathematics, attending the lectures of Chebyshev, A. N. Korkin, and A. Possé; he simultaneously studied mechanics. He graduated in 1882 but remained at the university to begin his own academic career. He passed the examinations for the master's degree in applied mathematics in 1889 and became a *Privatdozent* the following year.

In 1891 Meshchersky was appointed to the chair of mechanics at the St. Petersburg Women's College, a post that he retained until 1919, when the college was incorporated into the university. In 1897 he defended a dissertation entitled *Dinamika tochki peremennoy massy* ("The Dynamics of a Point of Variable Mass") before the Physics and Mathematics Faculty of St. Petersburg University and was awarded a doctorate in applied mathematics. In 1902 Meshchersky was invited to head the department of applied mathematics at the newly founded St. Petersburg Polytechnic Institute (now the Leningrad M. I. Kalin Polytechnic Institute), for which he had helped to develop a curriculum.

Meshchersky taught at St. Petersburg University for twenty-five years and at the Polytechnic Institute

for thirty-three. He was a conscientious and innovative pedagogue. Among other things, he was concerned with drafting a scientific-methodological guide to the teaching of mathematics and mechanics; his *Prepodavanie mekhaniki .i mekhanicheskie kollektsii v nekotorykh vysshikh uchebnykh zavedeniakh Italii, Frantsii, Shveytsarii i Germanii* ("The Teaching of Mechanics and Mechanics Collections in Certain Institutions of Higher Education in Italy, France, Switzerland, and Germany"; 1895) contributed significantly toward raising the standards of the teaching of mechanics in Russia. Meshchersky's own course in theoretical mechanics became famous, while his textbook on that subject, *Sbornik zadach po teoreticheskoy mekhanike* ("A Collection of Problems in Theoretical Mechanics"), published in 1914, went through twenty-four editions and became a standard work.

Meshchersky's purely scientific work was devoted to the motion of bodies of variable mass. He reported the results of his first investigations of the problem at a meeting of the St. Petersburg Mathematical Society held on 27 January 1893, then made it the subject of the doctoral dissertation that he presented four years later. He began the thesis *Dinamika tochki peremennoy massy* with a discussion of the many instances in which the mass of a moving body changes, citing as examples the increase of the mass of the earth occasioned by meteorites falling on it; the increase of the mass of an iceberg with freezing and its decrease with thawing; the increase of the mass of the sun through its gathering of cosmic dust and its decrease with radiation; the decrease of the mass of a rocket as its fuel is consumed; the decrease of the mass of a balloon as its ballast is discarded; and the increase of the mass of a captive balloon as it draws its tether with it in rising.

Having defined the problem, Meshchersky considered it physically. He established that if the mass of a point changes during motion, then Newton's second law of motion must be replaced by an equation of the motion of a point of variable mass wherein

$m \dfrac{d\bar{v}}{dt} = \bar{F} + \bar{R}$ ($\bar{F}$ and $\bar{R}$ being the given and the reactive forces, respectively), where $\bar{F}$ and $\bar{R} = \dfrac{dm}{dt}\,\bar{U}_r$.

This natural generalization of the equation of motion of classical mechanics is now called Meshchersky's equation. In his second important work, "Uravnenia dvizhenia tochki peremennoy massy v obshchem sluchae" ("Equations of the Motion of a Point of Variable Mass in the General Case," 1904), Meshchersky gave his theory a definitive and elegant expression, establishing the general equation of motion of a point of which the mass is changing by the simultaneous incorporation and elimination of particles.

In developing the theoretical foundations of the dynamics of a point of variable mass, Meshchersky opened a new area of theoretical mechanics. He also examined a number of specific problems, including the ascending motion of a rocket and the vertical motion of a balloon. His exceptionally thorough general investigation of the motion of a point of variable mass under the influence of a central force led to a new celestial mechanics; he was further concerned with the motions of comets. He was, moreover, the first to formulate, from given external forces and given trajectories, the so-called inverse problems in determining the law for the change of mass.

Meshchersky published a number of papers on general mechanics. In "Differentsialnye svyazi v sluchae odnoy materialnoy tochki" ("Differential Ties in the Case of One Material Point"; 1887), he examined the motion of a point subjected to a nonholonomic tie, which is neither ideal nor linear. In "O teoreme Puassona pri sushchestvovanii uslovnykh uravneny" ("On Poisson's Theorem on the Existence of Conditional Arbitrary Equations"; 1890), he took up the integration of dynamical equations, while in "Sur un problème de Jacobi" (1894), he gave a generalization of Jacobi's results. A paper of 1919, "Gidrodinamicheskaya analogia prokatki" ("A Hydrodynamic Analogue of Rolling"), is of particular interest because it contains Meshchersky's ingenious attempt to elucidate the equations of motion rolling bodies in terms of those for a viscous fluid.

Meshchersky's work on the motion of bodies of variable mass remains his most important contribution to science. His pioneering studies formed the basis for much of the rocket technology and dynamics that was developed rapidly following World War II.

BIBLIOGRAPHY

I. ORIGINAL WORKS. Meshchersky's writings include "Davlenie na klin v potoke neogranichennoy shiriny dvukh izmereny" ("The Pressure on a Wedge in a Two-Dimensional Stream of Unbounded Width"), in *Zhurnal Russkago fiziko-khimicheskago obshchestva pri Imperatorskago St.-Peterburskago universitete*, **18** (1886); "Differentsialnye svyazi v sluchae odnoy materialnoy tochki" ("Differential Bonds in the Case of One Material Point"), in *Soobshchenie Kharkovskogo matematicheskogo obshchestva* (1887), 68–79; *Prepodavanie mekhaniki i mekhanicheskie kollektsii v nekotorykh vysshikh uchebnykh zavedeniakh Italii, Frantsii, Shveytsarii i Germanii* ("The Teaching of Mechanics and

Mechanics Collections in Certain Institutions of Higher Education in Italy, France, Switzerland, and Germany"; St. Petersburg, 1895); *Dinamika tochki peremennoy massy* ("The Dynamics of a Point of Variable Mass"; St. Petersburg, 1897); and *O vrashchenii tyazhelogo tverdogo tela s razvertyvayushcheysya tyazheloy nityu okolo gorizontalnoy osi* ("On the Rotation of a Heavy Solid Body Having an Unwinding Heavy Thread About Its Horizontal Axis"; St. Petersburg, 1899).

Later writings include "Über die Integration der Bewegungsgleichungen im Probleme zweier Körper von veränderlicher Masse," in *Astronomische Nachrichten*, **159**, no. 3807 (1902); "Uravnenia dvizhenia tochki peremennoy massy v obshchem sluchae" ("Equations of the Motion of a Point of Variable Mass in the General Case"), in *Izvestiya S-Peterburgskago politekhnicheskago instituta Imperatora Petra Velikago*, **1** (1904); *Sbornik zadach po teoreticheskoy mekhanike* ("Collection of Problems in Theoretical Mechanics"; St. Petersburg, 1914); "Zadachi iz dinamiki peremennoy massy" ("Problems From the Dynamics of a Variable Mass"), in *Izvestiya S-Peterburgskago politekhnicheskago instituta Imperatora Petra Velikago*, **27** (1918); and "Gidrodinamicheskaya analogia prokatki" ("A Hydrodynamic Analogue of Rolling"), *ibid.*, **28** (1919).

II. SECONDARY LITERATURE. See Y. L. Geronimus, "Ivan Vsevolodovich Meshchersky (1859–1935)," in *Ocherki o rabotakh korifeev russkoy mekhaniki* ("Essays on the Works of the Leading Figures of Russian Mechanics"; Moscow, 1952); A. T. Grigorian, "Ivan Vsevolodovich Meshchersky (k 100-letiyu so dnya rozhdenia)" ("Ivan Vsevolodovich Meshchersky [on the Centenary of His Birth]"), in *Voprosy istorii estestvoznaniya i tekhniki* (1959), no. 7; and "Mekhanika tel peremennoy massy I. V. Meshcherskogo" ("I. V. Meshchersky's Mechanics of Bodies of Variable Mass"), in *Evolyutsia mekhaniki v Rossii* ("The Evolution of Mechanics in Russia"; Moscow, 1967); A. A. Kosmodemyansky, "Ivan Vsevolodovich Meshchersky (1859–1935)," in *Lyudi russkoy nauki* ("People of Russian Science"; Moscow, 1961), 216–222; and F. I. Nikolai, "Prof. I. V. Meshchersky [Nekrolog]," in *Prikladnaya matematika i mekhanika*, **3**, no. 1 (1936).

A. T. GRIGORIAN

METIUS, ADRIAEN (*b.* Alkmaar, Netherlands, 3 December 1571; *d.* Franeker, Frisia [now Netherlands], 1635)
[METIUS], ADRIAEN ANTHONISZ (*b.* Alkmaar [?], Netherlands, *ca.* 1543; *d.* Alkmaar [?], 20 November 1620)
METIUS, JACOB (*b.* Alkmaar, Netherlands; *d.* Alkmaar, June 1628)

The father, Adriaen Anthonisz, was a cartographer and military engineer for the States of Holland, and between 1582 and 1601 he was burgomaster of

Alkmaar several times. In an unpublished pamphlet *Tegens de quadrature des circkels van Mr. Simon van Eycke* (1584), he gave, according to his son Adriaen (1625), the value of 355/113 for what we now denote by π, stating that it differs from the true value by less than 1/100,000. He obtained it by averaging numerators and denominators of the values 377/120 and 333/106. (This value had already been obtained by Tsu Chung-chih in the fifth century.) Anthonisz built fortifications in the war against Spain, drew charts of cities and military works, and wrote on sundials and astronomical problems. In the receipt for his burial the name Metius, adopted by some of his sons, is mentioned. The origin of the name is uncertain: some derive it from Metz, others from the family name Schelven (*schelf = rick =* Latin *meta*), it may also simply be related to *metiri* (to measure). Anthonisz and his wife Suida Dircksd. had one daughter and six sons, of whom two, Adriaen and Jacob, became widely known.

The second son, Adriaen, educated at the Latin school in Alkmaar, entered the recently founded University of Franeker in Frisia in 1589, and in 1594 continued his studies at the University of Leiden. Among his teachers in Leiden were the mathematicians Rudolf Snellius and Van Ceulen. Like his townsman Blaeu, Adriaen worked under Tycho Brahe at his observatory on the island of Hven; he then went to Rostock and Jena, where in 1595 he gave his first lectures. He returned to the Netherlands where he assisted his father in his military engineering until, in 1598, he was appointed professor extraordinarius at Franeker; in the same year he published his first book, *Doctrina spherica*.

Adriaen became professor ordinarius of mathematics, surveying, navigation, military engineering, and astronomy at Franeker in 1600, a position he held until his death. He bought mathematical and astronomical instruments, observed sunspots, and showed familiarity with the telescope, of which his brother Jacob was a coinventor. He especially appreciated its use for measuring instruments. In his *Geometria practica* (Franeker, 1625) he described a triangulation of part of Frisia, made shortly after Rudolf Snellius' son Willebrord had published his triangulation of the west Netherlands in *Eratosthenes batavus* (1617). Adriaen was a popular and efficient teacher who stressed the training of Frisian surveyors. His lectures were well attended by an international audience including, in 1629, Descartes. In 1625 Adriaen received an honorary doctorate in medicine from Franeker. He was married twice, first to Jetske Andreae, and then to Cecelia Vertest. He left no children. His motto was "Simpliciter et sine strepitu."

Adriaen's books cover all fields that he taught, and although they show little originality, they were widely used in his time. He followed Tycho Brahe's theory of the solar system, but also showed respect for the Copernican system. While not accepting astrology, he did believe in alchemy, and spent money in the search for the transmutation of metals.

His brother Jacob was as shy as Adriaen was sociable. He became an instrument maker in Alkmaar, specializing in the grinding of lenses. He made several inventions but rarely showed them to others, even to his brother. He was one of the claimants to the invention of the telescope, and is mentioned as such by Descartes in his *Dioptrique* (1637). Jacob was indeed one of the first to bring a concave and a convex lens together in a tube, thus constructing a telescope. In 1608 he applied for a patent on such an instrument but unfortunately a similar request had been made a few weeks earlier by H. Lippershey of Middelburg. This disappointment may have intensified Jacob's shyness. Adriaen, in several of his books after 1614, refers to his brother's "perspicilla" (telescope). He expresses the hope that he would allow others to share in his discoveries, but Jacob remained secretive. Before his death he destroyed his instruments so that, as a contemporary said, "the perfection of his art has died and been buried with him."

BIBLIOGRAPHY

I. ORIGINAL WORKS. A satisfactory bibliography of Adriaen Metius' works does not exist. Boeles lists seventeen titles, de Waard eighteen, and Bierens De Haan thirty-three, but some are reprints, trans., or collections. Boeles also lists a map of Frisia and a celestial globe from J. Janssonius' cartographic workshop (1648). Some titles are *Institutiones astronomiae et geographicae*, found together with *Geographische Onderwysinghe, waer in ghehandeld wordt die Beschryvinghe ende Afmetinghe des Aertsche Globe* (Franeker, 1614; Amsterdam, 1621); *Arithmetica et geometrica nova* (Franeker, 1625); *Arithmeticae libri II et geometriae libri VI. Hic adiungitur trigonometriae planorum methodus succincta* (Leiden, 1626); *Geometria practica* (Franeker, 1625), which states that "Parens P. M. illustrium D. D. Ordinum Confoederatarum Belgiae Provinciarum Geometra" found $\pi - 355/113$ (pp. 88–89; "P. M." is clearly "pia memoria"—Anthonisz died in 1620—and not P. Metius, as has occasionally been claimed to justify the term "ratio of Metius"); *Maet-constigh Lineael . . . alsmede de Stercken-Bouwinghe ofte Fortificatie* (Franeker, 1626), which is a trans. of part of *Arithmeticae libri II . . .*, in which is described an early form of a calculating mechanism; *Eeuwighe Handt-calendrier* (Amsterdam, 1627; Rotterdam, 1628); *Tafelen van de Declinatie des Sons* (Franeker, 1627); *Astronomische ende Geogra-*

phische Onderwysinghe (Amsterdam, 1632); *Manuale arithmeticae et geometriae practica* (Franeker, 1633; 1646); *Opera omnia astronomia* (Amsterdam, 1632–1633), which contains the *canon sinuum, tangentium et secantium ad radium* 10,000,000.

II. SECONDARY LITERATURE. On the father and sons see C. de Waard, "Anthonisz" and "Metius," in *Nieuw Neder-landsch Biographisch Woordenboek*, I (Leiden, 1911), 155–158, 1325–1329 (in Dutch). In "Anthonisz," he gives an account of Anthonisz' MSS and published material. On Anthonisz' value of π see D. Bierens De Haan, "Adriaan Metius," in *Bouwstoffen voor de geschiedenis der wis- en natuurkundige wetenschappen in de Nederlanden*, XII, repr. from *Verslagen en Mededeelingen K. Akademie van Weten-schappen Amsterdam, Afdeling Natuurkunde*, 2nd ser., **12** (1878), 1–35. The same author's *Bibliographie neerlandaise historique et scientifique sur les sciences mathématiques et physiques* (Rome, 1883; Nieuwkoop, 1960) lists thirty-three works of Adriaen; this is a reprint of articles in *Bullettino di bibliografia e di storia delle scienze matematiche*, **14** (1881), and **15** (1882), esp. 258–259. Also see his "Notice sur quelques quadrateurs du cercle dans les Pays-Bas," *ibid.*, **7** (1874), 99–104; and "Notice sur un pamphlet mathéma-tique hollandais," *ibid.*, **11** (1878), 383–452. On Adriaen also see W. B. S. Boeles, *Frieslands Hoogeschool*, II (Leeuwarden, 1879), 70–75; and H. K. Schippers, "Fuot-printen fan in mannich Fryske stjerrekundigen," in *Beaken*, **24** (1962), 77–104 (in Frisian). On Jacob, see C. de Waard, *De uitvinding der verrekijkers* (The Hague, 1906).

D. J. STRUIK

MEUSNIER DE LA PLACE, JEAN-BAPTISTE-MARIE-CHARLES (*b.* Tours, France, 19 June 1754; *d.* Mainz, Germany, 17 June 1793)

Meusnier was the son of Jean-Baptiste Meusnier and Anne le Normand Delaplace. The family was for generations engaged in law and administration; the father was a counsel attached to a court (*présidial*) at Tours. He tutored his son, and only during his last years at Tours did Meusnier go to school.

From 1771 to 1773 Meusnier was privately tutored at Paris for entrance into the military academy at Mézières, where he studied in 1774–1775 and graduated as second lieutenant in the Engineering Corps. His mathematics teacher was Gaspard Monge, under whom Meusnier did his only published mathematical work, on the theory of surfaces.

His paper, read at the Paris Academy of Sciences in 1776, supposedly led d'Alembert to state: "Meusnier commence comme je finis." It also led to Meusnier's election, at twenty-one, as a corresponding member of the Academy. He was placed in charge of continuing the descriptions of machines approved by the Academy, and in February 1777 he presented to the

Academy the seventh volume of the *Recueil des machines approuvées par l'Académie*. During 1777, now a first lieutenant, he was sent to Verdun to study mining and sapping. From 1779 to 1788 he worked as a military engineer on the harborworks of Cherbourg, where he displayed great ingenuity and perseverance, despite red tape and intrigues, in the building of the breakwater and the fortification of Île Pelée. To provide drinking water for this island he spent much time on experiments on the desalinization of seawater. In March 1783 Meusnier, sent into debt by his work, presented his machine to the Academy.

During 1783 the first balloon ascensions took place. Meusnier, on leaves of absence from Cherbourg, began to study the theory of this new field, aero-station. In December 1783 he read before the Academy his "Mémoire sur l'équilibre des machines aéro-statiques." The next month he was elected a full member of the Academy and was immediately appointed to a committee on aerostation, other members of which were Lavoisier, Berthollet, and Condorcet. The results of his work on this committee were presented in November 1784 in "Précis des travaux faits à l'Académie des sciences pour la perfection des machines aérostatiques," with a theory and detailed construction plans for dirigible balloons. It led to no practical results at the time.

During this period Meusnier began a collaboration with Lavoisier on the synthesis and analysis of water; Meusnier was especially interested in the production of hydrogen in quantity from water. On 21 April 1784 they presented to the Academy a continuation of the paper presented in June 1783 by Lavoisier and Laplace on the synthesis of water from oxygen and hydrogen: "Mémoire où l'on prouve par la décom-position de l'eau que ce fluide n'est point une substance simple . . . ." It was also a heavy blow against the phlogiston theory, which Berthollet and others soon abandoned in favor of Lavoisier's "théorie française." Meusnier also collaborated with Lavoisier on the improvement of oil lamps for city street illumination. Their ideas were contemporary with those of Aimé Argand and perhaps inspired the construction of his lamp.

In May 1787 Meusnier became a captain; in July 1788, he was promoted to *aide-maréchal général des logis au corps de l'État Major* and major.

From then on his career was with the army, and in July 1789 he became a lieutenant colonel. With his friends Monge and Berthollet he joined the Jacobins in 1790. With many other academicians he was appointed to the Bureau de Consultation Pour les Arts et Métiers to study inventions useful to the state. Meusnier invented a machine for engraving assignats that greatly reduced the possibility of producing counterfeit notes. In February 1792 he was appointed colonel, then *adjutant général colonel*, and in September 1792 field marshal. Sent in February 1793 to the armies of the Rhine commanded by Custine, he participated in the defense of the fortress of Kassel during the siege of Mainz by the Prussians. He was wounded on 5 June and died twelve days later. His remains were brought to Paris (Goethe witnessed the procession leaving Mainz; see his *Kampagne in Frankreich*), and were later transferred to Tours, where in 1888 a bust was erected on a pedestal containing his ashes.

The "Mémoire sur la courbure des surfaces," read in 1776 and published in 1785, was written after Monge had shown him Euler's paper on this subject (*Mémoires de l'Académie des Sciences* [Berlin, 1760]). In the "Mémoire" Meusnier derived "Meusnier's theorem" on the curvature, at a point of a surface, of plane sections with a common tangent and also found, as special solutions of Lagrange's differential equation of the minimal surfaces (1760), the catenoid and the right helicoid. His results can be found in any book on differential geometry. In the "Mémoire" on aerostation (1783) Meusnier presented a theory of the equilibrium of a balloon, the dynamics of ascension, and the rules for maneuvering a balloon. To maintain appropriate altitude even with the disposal of ballast he proposed a balloon filled with hydrogen containing a smaller balloon filled with air (known as *ballonet d'air*); he also suggested a model with air in the larger balloon and hydrogen in the smaller. In the "Précis" of 1784, the result of a great many test experiments, Meusnier gave a detailed plan for the construction of a dirigible balloon in the form of an elongated ellipsoid with another balloon inside. For propulsion he suggested revolving air screws worked by a crew. He described two possibilities: a small dirigible 130 feet long carrying six men and one 260 feet long (130 feet minor axis) with a crew of thirty and food for sixty days, able to fly around the earth. In his formula for the stability of the balloon,

$$ n = \left(\frac{P + E}{P} \right) \times \frac{3}{2} \left(\frac{l^2 - h^2}{h^2} \right) \times \frac{(h - x)^2}{3h - 2x} , $$

n is the distance from the metacenter to the center of the balloon, P the weight of the objects collected at the center of the gondola, E the weight of the balloon as concentrated at the center, l and h the major and minor axes of the balloon, and x the height of the hydrogen when the balloon is on earth, the hydrogen rising above the air in the balloon.

The principle of the revolving screw had also occurred to David Bushnell of Connecticut in the construction of his submarine (1776–1777). Meusnier knew of Bushnell's invention.

After Cavendish had shown nonquantitatively in 1781 that the combination of oxygen and hydrogen yields water, Lavoisier and Laplace in 1783 presented to the Academy an account of their work on the synthesis of water; Monge had also performed this experiment. Meusnier suggested more exact measurements to Lavoisier and constructed precision instruments for this purpose. Their "Mémoire" of April 1784 showed how they had decomposed water into its components; the hydrogen was obtained as a gas and the oxygen in the form of an iron oxide. For many this famous experiment carried convincing evidence against the phlogiston theory.

BIBLIOGRAPHY

I. Original Works. "Mémoire sur la courbure des surfaces" appeared in *Mémoires de mathématique et de physique présentés par divers sçavans*, **10** (1785), pt. 2, 477–510. The "Mémoire" and the "Précis" on aerostation were published, with other material, by G. Darboux in *Mémoires de l'Académie des sciences*, 2nd ser., **51** (1910), 1–128. This includes the "Atlas de dessins relatifs à un projet de machine aérostatique" of 1784, presented in a photographic reproduction to the Academy in 1886 by General Perrier. The "Mémoire où l'on prouve par la décomposition de l'eau . . .," written with Lavoisier, is in *Mémoires de l'Académie royale des sciences pour 1781* (1784), 269–283. See also "Description d'un appareil propre à manoeuvrer différentes espèces d'air dans les expériences qui exigent des volumes considérables," *ibid., 1782* (1785), 466; "Sur les moyens d'opérer l'entière combustion de l'huile et d'augmenter la lumière des lampes," *ibid., 1784* (1787), 390–398. There is MS material in the Archives of the Académie des Sciences, the Institut de France, the Archives Historiques de la Guerre, and the Bibliothèque du Génie, all in Paris. Details are given by J. Laissus (see below).

II. Secondary Literature. "Notice sur le général Meusnier," in *Revue rétrospective*, 2nd ser., **4** (1835), 77–99, contains biographical notes on Meusnier by Monge and others, the originals of which have not been found. Partly based on these is Darboux's "Notice historique sur le général Meusnier," in his *Éloges académiques et discours* (Paris, 1912), 218–262, also in *Mémoires de l'Académie des Sciences*, 2nd ser., **51** (see above). In it are many particulars on Meusnier's work in Cherbourg and in the army of the Revolution. See also L. Louvet, in *Nouvelle biographie générale*, XXXV (1865), cols. 264–267. Bibliographical details based on independent research in the printed and MS materials are in J. Laissus, "Le général Meusnier de la Place, membre de l'Académie royale des sciences," in *Comptes rendus du 93ᵉ Congrès national des sociétés savantes, Tours, 1968*, Section des Sciences, II (Paris, 1971),

75–101. Meusnier's work on decomposition of water can be studied in books on Lavoisier. His works on aerostation have been analyzed by F. Letonné, "Le général Meusnier et ses idées sur la navigation aérienne," in *Revue du génie militaire*, **2** (1888), 247–258; and by Voyer, "Les lois de Meusnier," *ibid.*, **23** (1902), 421–430; "Le ballonet de Meusnier," *ibid.*, 521–532; and "Le général Meusnier et les ballons dirigibles," *ibid.*, **24** (1902), 135–156—German trans. in *Illustrierte aeronautische Mitteilungen*, **9** (1905), 137–144, 353–361, 373–387. The third of these papers gives a proof of Meusnier's stability formula. See also G. Béthuys, *Les aérostations militaires* (Paris, 1894), 137–146. On the Argand lamp see S. T. McCoy, *French Inventions of the Eighteenth Century* (Lexington, Ky., 1952), 52–56.

On the papers relating to the collaboration between Lavoisier and Meusnier, see also D. I. Duveen and H. S. Klickstein, *Bibliography of the Works of Antoine Laurent Lavoisier 1743–1794* (London, 1954), index, p. 462. On Bushnell see D. J. Struik, *Yankee Science in the Making* (New York, 1962), 83, 453.

D. J. STRUIK

MEYER, WILHELM FRANZ (*b.* Magdeburg, Germany, 2 September 1856; *d.* Königsberg, Germany [now Kaliningrad, U.S.S.R.], 11 June 1934)

Meyer studied in Leipzig and Munich, where he received his doctorate in 1878. He studied further in Berlin, where at that time Weierstrass, Kummer, and Kronecker were active. In 1880 he qualified for lecturing at the University of Tübingen, and in 1888 he became full professor at the Bergakademie of Clausthal–Zellerfeld. From October 1897 until October 1924, when he retired, he taught at the University of Königsberg.

Meyer was a many sided and very knowledgeable mathematician, whose list of writings includes 136 titles. His principal field of interest, however, was geometry, especially algebraic geometry and the related projective invariant theory. His *Habilitationsschrift*, which was published in 1883 as *Apolarität und rationale Kurven*, shows this direction of his research. In this work he extended the apolarity theory, created by Reye, to a multidimensional projective geometry based on the theory of rational curves. At the time such considerations were not completely obvious.

Other of Meyer's works from this period deal with algebraic curves and their production, and with related algebraic questions. He early showed himself to be one of the leading experts on invariant theory. In 1892 he composed for the Deutsche Mathematiker-vereinigung a long report on this subject, which was translated into French, Italian, and Polish. In this work he presented the development of invariant theory from its beginning in the middle of the nineteenth century to the end of the century and the appearance of the decisive finiteness theorems of Gordan and Hilbert. Meyer also made many individual contributions to invariant theory. This area of research went somewhat out of fashion during his lifetime, however, chiefly as a result of Hilbert's work.

Meyer was one of the founders of the *Encyklopädie der mathematischen Wissenschaften*. He, H. Weber, and F. Klein were responsible for planning this project. The *Encyklopädie*, which was conceived on a large scale, was supported from 1895 by a syndicate of German academies. From the turn of the century until the 1930's some twenty volumes appeared; they treated all fields of mathematics and their applications. Meyer wrote the articles on potential theory (with H. Burkhardt), invariant theory, the new geometry of the triangle (with G. Berkhan), third-order surfaces, and surfaces of the fourth and higher orders.

The editing of such a vast work required great effort and presupposed considerable knowledge. In this regard Meyer benefited from his extensive familiarity with the literature, gained in large measure through the 2,000 reviews that he wrote for *Fortschritte der Mathematik*; his knowledge of foreign languages was also very useful to him. Of special note are the articles on third- and fourth-degree surfaces, which he composed at an advanced age. At that period, around 1930, Meyer was the only German mathematician who still possessed a comprehensive view of the abundant material, produced mainly in the nineteenth century, on special algebraic curves and surfaces. Meyer conducted investigations in geometry of the triangle, handled in the spirit of Klein's Erlangen program, and gave lectures discussing the essential aspects of mathematical research in the spirit of the time and emphasizing the importance of simple algebraic identities, the symmetries of group theory, and transformation principles as a source of geometric theorems.

Meyer was an excellent teacher who had many students. Most East Prussian mathematics teachers at the beginning of the twentieth century were trained by him.

BIBLIOGRAPHY

An extensive listing of Meyer's writings can be found in Poggendorff, IV, 1001–1002; V, 841; and VI, 1714. They include *Apolarität und rationale Kurven, eine systematische Voruntersuchung zu einer allgemeinen Theorie der linearen Räume* (Tübingen, 1883); "Bericht über den gegenwärtigen Stand der Invariantentheorie," in *Jahresberichte der*

Deutschen Mathematiker-vereinigung, **1** (1892), 79–292; and the following articles in *Encyklopädie der mathematischen Wissenschaften:* "Invariantentheorie," I, pt. 1, 320–403; "Potentialtheorie," II-A, pt.7-b, 464–503, written with H. Burkhardt; "Neuere Dreiecksgeometrie," III, pt.1-b, 1173–1276, written with G. Berkhan; "Flächen 3. Ordnung," III-C, pt. 10-a, 1437–1532; and "Flächen 4. und höherer Ordnung," III-C, 1533–1779.

An article on Meyer is B. Arndt, "W. F. Meyer zum Gedächtnis," in *Jahresberichte der Deutschen Mathematiker-vereinigung*, **45** (1935), 99–113.

W. BURAU

MILHAUD, GASTON (*b.* Nîmes, France, 10 August 1858; *d.* Paris, France, 1 October 1918)

Milhaud, a village near Nîmes, once belonged to the bishop of Nîmes and thus was able to shelter a Marrano community. Gaston Milhaud's ancestors came from this locality. He was the third of the famous trio with the same Christian name who brought fame to Nîmes during the nineteenth century; the other two were the historian Gaston Boissier and the mathematician Gaston Darboux, whose student he was at the École Normale Supérieure.

In 1878 Milhaud qualified for both the École Normale Supérieure and the École Polytechnique; he chose the former. *Agrégé* in mathematics in 1881, he then taught mathematics at Le Havre for ten years. His meeting with Pierre Janet and the fruitful collaboration that followed during this period induced a shift in his interests. He translated du Bois-Reymond's *Théorie générale des fonctions*; wrote a number of articles for such journals as *Revue scientifique, Revue des études grecques*, and *Revue philosophique de la France et de l'étranger*; and was henceforth concerned with the philosophy of mathematics.

Appointed professor of mathematics at Montpellier in 1891, Milhaud gave a series of lectures on the origins of Greek science (published in 1893). In 1894, at Paris, he defended a Ph.D. dissertation on the conditions and limits of logical certainty. This remarkable work was decisive for his career. He was appointed to the chair of philosophy at the Faculty of Letters of Montpellier in 1895 and rapidly became, through his lectures and publications, a respected authority in a field that was then quite new. He also arranged meetings between investigators in various disciplines. In 1909 a chair was created for Milhaud at the Sorbonne in the history of philosophy in relation to science. Despite the decline in his health, which had always been delicate, he continued to be active and held this chair with distinction until his death.

It has been observed that the end of the nineteenth century witnessed two complementary movements in response to the crisis in the foundations of science: that of philosophers becoming scientists and that of scientists becoming philosophers. Milhaud is one of the best representatives of the latter trend. He modestly presented himself as a teacher who wished to do useful work in the history of science, which he conceived of as "inseparable from a critical examination of fundamental notions and inseparable from philosophical views that, underneath the precise data that are constantly accumulating, attempt to appear and to evaluate the progressive and continuous work being accomplished" (quoted in Pierre Janet, "Notice," p. 57).

Acutely aware of the effort required to amass and criticize data, Milhaud declared that he was not learned in this respect. Nevertheless, his many works on Greek science show that he accepted the burdens of scholarship; and his study of the arguments of Zeno of Elea is important and still worth consulting. He was also responsible for renewing knowledge of Descartes as a scientist, and his writings on this subject remain a reliable source. It was Milhaud's second son, Gérard, who with Charles Adam produced an improved edition of Descartes's correspondence.

Milhaud oriented the study of the history of science more toward philosophy. Certain of his views, although representative of his time, are now outmoded, notably those of continuous progress and the analysis of the conditions, role, and scope of demonstration in mathematics and physics. But his writings on logical contradiction, the limits of the affirmations that it appears to permit, and the critique of scientifically inspired deterministic metaphysical systems are still of interest and justify the considerable influence he has exerted. Milhaud also illustrated his contention that "science progresses in proportion to the disinterestedness with which it is pursued." Émile Boutroux said in proposing Milhaud's election to the Académie des Sciences Morales et Politiques in 1918: "By the soundness and originality of his findings in both the theoretical and the historical domains regarding a question of paramount importance, that of the relation between certainty and truth, this conscientious, modest, and penetrating investigator has performed a lasting service to science and to philosophy" (Pierre Janet, "Notice," p. 58).

BIBLIOGRAPHY

I. ORIGINAL WORKS. Milhaud's books include *Leçons sur les origines de la science grecque* (Paris, 1893); *Essai sur les conditions et les limites de la certitude logique* (Paris, 1894; 4th ed., 1924); *Le rationnel* (Paris, 1898); *Les philo-*

sophes géomètres de la Grèce: Platon et ses prédécesseurs (Paris, 1900; 2nd ed., 1934); Le positivisme et le progrès de l'esprit (Études critiques sur Auguste Comte) (Paris, 1902); Études sur la pensée scientifique chez les Grecs et chez les modernes (Paris, 1906); Nouvelles études sur l'histoire de la pensée scientifique (Paris, 1911); Descartes savant (Paris, 1921); Études sur Cournot (Paris, 1927); and La philosophie de Charles Renouvier (Paris, 1927).

Among Milhaud's many articles, the following appeared in Revue de métaphysique et de morale: "Le concept du nombre chez les Pythagoriciens" (1893), 140–156; "Réponse à Brochard" (1893), 400–404, concerning Zeno of Elea; "L'idée d'ordre chez Auguste Comte" (1901), 385–406; "Le hasard chez Aristote et chez Cournot" (1902), 667–681; and "La science et l'hypothèse par H. Poincaré" (1903), 773–781. See also "Science et religion chez Cournot," in Bulletin de la Société française de philosophie (Apr. 1911), 83–104.

II. SECONDARY LITERATURE. See André Bridoux, "Souvenirs concernant Gaston Milhaud," in Bulletin de la Société française de philosophie, 55, no. 2 (1960), 109–112; Edmond Goblot, "Gaston Milhaud (1858–1918)," in Isis, 3 (1921), 391–395; Pierre Janet, "Notice sur Gaston Milhaud," in Annuaire des anciens élèves de l'École normale supérieure (1919), pp. 56–60; André Nadal, "Gaston Milhaud (1858–1918)," in Revue d'histoire des sciences . . . (Paris), 12, no. 2 (1959), 97–110; Dominique Parodi, La philosophie contemporaine en France (Paris, 1919), pp. 211–216; and René Poirier, Philosophes et savants français du XXᵉ siècle, II, La philosophie de la science (Paris, 1926), 55–80; and "Meyerson, Milhaud et le problème de l'épistémologie," in Bulletin de la Société française de philosophie, 55, no. 2 (1960), 65–94.

PIERRE COSTABEL

MILLER, GEORGE ABRAM (b. Lynnville, Pennsylvania, 31 July 1863; d. Urbana, Illinois, 10 February 1951)

The description of Miller's rise to prominence in the world of mathematics is one of those Horatio Alger stories with which American intellectual history of the late nineteenth century is studded. He was the son of Nathan and Mary Sittler Miller and a descendant of one Christian Miller who had emigrated from Switzerland around 1720. Unable to continue his education without self-support, he began to teach school at the age of seventeen. He studied at Franklin and Marshall Academy in Lancaster during 1882–1883, then enrolled at Muhlenberg College, where he received the baccalaureate with honorable mention in 1887, the master of arts in 1890, and an honorary doctor of letters in 1936. Miller served as principal of the schools in Greeley, Kansas, during the year 1887–1888 and as professor of mathematics at Eureka College (Illinois) from 1888 to 1893.

Cumberland University in Lebanon, Tennessee, granted him a doctorate in 1892; it was then possible to do course work by correspondence, and examinations in advanced courses were an acceptable substitute for thesis requirements. Miller was offering the same courses toward a doctorate to his students at Eureka. He spent the summers of 1889 and 1890 at the Johns Hopkins University and the University of Michigan but probably did not come under Frank Nelson Cole's influence until 1893, when he became an instructor at Michigan for three years and lived in Cole's home during the first two years of that period. It was Cole who inspired him to pursue the research in group theory that was to engage his talents for the rest of his life. Cole, incidentally, had been a pupil of Felix Klein, who had made groups basic in his "Erlanger Programm."

Miller spent the years 1895–1897 in Europe, attending the lectures of Sophus Lie at Leipzig and Camille Jordan in Paris. He soon was publishing papers independent of their specializations, although Lie had become instrumental in Miller's study of commutators and commutator subgroups and Jordan's interest in questions of primitivity and imprimitivity was reflected in Miller's investigations of those problems throughout his career.

Upon Miller's return to the United States, his European experience and mathematical productivity gained him an assistant professorship at Cornell (1897–1901). This was followed by an associate professorship at Stanford University (1901–1906), and in 1906 an appointment at the University of Illinois, an affiliation that lasted for the rest of his life—first as associate professor, then as professor, and finally as professor emeritus. His retirement in 1931 was from classroom responsibilities only, for he continued his research and writing in his office at the university. The university undertook, as "a fitting memorial of his contributions to mathematical scholarship and to the renown of the University," the collection and reprinting of Miller's studies in the theory of finite groups as well as other studies. It is said that of the more than 800 titles that appeared in some twenty periodicals over forty years approximately 400 made direct scientific contributions to that theory. Other papers were written in the hope that teachers of elementary and secondary mathematics might be inspired to study advanced mathematics. Miller himself aided in the preparation of these memorial volumes.

This was not the only legacy that Miller left to the University of Illinois. To the great surprise of the colleagues who knew him well, the university found itself after his death the beneficiary of a bequest valued at just under one million dollars, the accumulation of judicious investments. His wife, the former Cassandra Boggs of Urbana, had predeceased him in 1949 and there were no children.

Miller's interest in the history of mathematics was second only to that in the theory of finite groups. His articles on the history of his own subject were of particular significance and value. He became a severe critic of historical methodology in mathematics and was zealous in rooting out error in conjecture or assumed fact. His letters in the David Eugene Smith collection at Columbia University offer ample evidence of this missionary fervor. His "History of Elementary Mathematics" remained unpublished, although there was originally the intention to include it in a volume of the *Collected Papers*.

Miller was elected to the National Academy of Sciences in 1921 and was a fellow of the American Academy of Arts and Sciences. In 1900, for his work in group theory, the Academy of Sciences of Cracow awarded him a prize that had not been given for fourteen years. This is said to have been the Academy's first award to an American for work in pure mathematics. He was a member of the London Mathematical Society, the Société Mathématique de France, and the Deutsche Mathematiker-Vereinigung, an honorary life member of the Indian Mathematical Society, and a corresponding member of the Real Sociedad Matemática Española. He was an active member and served in various high offices of the American Mathematical Society and the Mathematical Association of America, serving also as an editor of the latter's *American Mathematical Monthly* (1909–1915).

BIBLIOGRAPHY

I. ORIGINAL WORKS. Miller's writings were brought together in *The Collected Works of George Abram Miller*, 5 vols. (Urbana, Ill., 1935–1959). Two of his books are *Determinants* (1892) and *Historical Introduction to Mathematical Literature* (New York, 1916). A more detailed bibliography is in Poggendorff, IV, 1013; V, 855–857; and VI, 1737–1738. *Theory and Application of Finite Groups* (New York, 1916; repr. 1961) was written in collaboration with H. F. Blichfeldt and L. E. Dickson.

II. SECONDARY LITERATURE. See H. R. Brahana, "George Abram Miller (1863–1951)," in *Biographical Memoirs. National Academy of Sciences*, 30 (1957), 257–312, with a complete bibliography of Miller's writings (1892–1947) on 277–312. E. T. Bell makes occasional reference to Miller's work in "Fifty Years of Algebra in America, 1888–1938," in *American Mathematical Society Semicentennial Publications*, II, as does Florian Cajori in his *History of Mathematics*. See also J. W. A. Young, *Monographs on Topics of Modern Mathematics Relevant*

to the *Elementary Field* (New York, 1911, 1915, 1927; repr. 1955); *American Men of Science* (New York, 1906), 219–220; and *National Cyclopedia of American Biography*, XVI (New York, 1918), 388.

CAROLYN EISELE

MILLER, WILLIAM HALLOWES (*b*. Llandovery, Carmarthenshire, Wales, 6 April 1801; *d*. Cambridge, England, 20 May 1880)

His father, Captain Francis Miller, who served in the American war, had a long military ancestry. By his first wife Captain Miller had three sons, all of whom entered the army, and two daughters. After losing his estate near Boston, Massachusetts, he retired to Wales to the small estate of Velindre near Llandovery and in 1800 married Ann Davies, the daughter of a Welsh vicar. William was the only child of this second marriage; his mother died a few days after his birth, but his father lived to the age of eighty-six, dying in 1820.

William was educated privately until he entered St. John's College, Cambridge, where he graduated B.A. as fifth wrangler in mathematics in 1826. In 1829 he became a fellow of St. John's and in 1831 published his first book—written in his characteristically lucid but terse style—*The Elements of Hydrostatics and Hydrodynamics*, which survived as a standard, though difficult, textbook into the fifties. Another mathematical textbook, *An Elementary Treatise on the Differential Calculus*, appeared in 1833 and passed through several editions. By then Miller had, in 1832, succeeded William Whewell as professor of mineralogy. He was elected F.R.S. in 1838. In 1841 came a curious diversion: the statutes of St. John's College required all fellows to proceed in time to holy orders except for four who should be doctors of medicine, and in order to retain his fellowship, Miller prepared himself for and took the M.D. He was obliged to vacate his fellowship on his marriage (5 November 1844) to Harriet Susan Minty, the daughter of R. V. Minty, a retired civil servant. They had two sons and four daughters. In 1875 he became a fellow of St. John's again under new statutes. In 1876 he suffered a stroke, which effectively brought his scientific life to a close four years before his death.

Miller's significant contribution to crystallography was made in *A Treatise on Crystallography* published in 1839 (translated into French by H. de Senarmont [1842], and into German with two new chapters by J. Grailich [1856], and again into German in abbreviated form by P. Joerres [1864]). Miller started with the fundamental assertion that crystallographic reference axes should be parallel to possible crystal edges; his system of indexing, a derivative from Whewell

(*Philosophical Transactions of the Royal Society*, 1825), was based on a parametral plane (111) making intercepts *a*, *b*, *c* on such reference axes and was such that indices (*hkl*) were assigned to a plane making intercepts on the reference axes in the ratio $a/h : b/k : c/l$, where *h*, *k*, *l* are integers. The established German school of C. F. Naumann and C. S. Weiss had, to use the same nomenclature, assigned indices (*hkl*) to a plane making intercepts in the ratio $ah : bk : cl$ on reference axes not restricted to parallelism with possible crystal edges. The algebraic advantages of "Millerian indices" were immediately apparent; the crystallographic superiority of Miller's reciprocal indices over Weiss's direct indices did not become apparent until Bravais's development of Haüy's rudimentary lattice concept in 1848, and not fully appreciated until Bragg's interpretation of the diffraction of X rays by crystals in 1912. But Miller's notation had quickly found favor with his contemporaries on grounds of convenience and had already served to codify an immense corpus of morphological observations in a thoroughly well-understood manner.

In the *Treatise* Miller had little to say about symmetry, but he explored crystal geometry to the full. The zone law of Weiss was simplified by the new notation, and zone symbols were defined in familiar form; the equations to the normal and the $\cos \theta$ formula were developed; and the rational sine ratio, which was to be further developed in *A Tract on Crystallography* (1863), made its first appearance here. For the representation of three-dimensional angular relationships Miller followed F. E. Neumann in using spherical projection, but the stereographic projection, which subsequently acquired greater currency, and the gnomonic projection were discussed in the final chapter.

The new edition (1852) of William Phillips' *Elementary Introduction to Mineralogy* by H. J. Brooke and W. H. Miller was an entirely new book largely written, as Brooke states in the preface, by Miller, and it represents his principal contribution to mineralogy. It incorporated a vast amount of accurate goniometric data provided by Miller himself; it followed the *Treatise* in using spherical projection; and it made a tentative start in the use of polarized light for the characterization of transparent minerals. The *Introduction*, like the *Treatise*, soon eclipsed its contemporaries; it inspired Des Cloizeaux to produce his more elaborate *Manuel de minéralogie* (Paris, 1862–1893), and determined the form of all subsequent texts on descriptive mineralogy.

In 1843 Miller branched out into a new field on appointment to the parliamentary committee concerned with the preparation of new standards of length and weight consequent on the destruction of the old standards in the burning of the Houses of Parliament in 1834. His exceptionally accurate work was responsible for the construction of the new standard of weight (*Philosophical Transactions of the Royal Society*, 1856). In 1870 he was appointed to the Commission Internationale du Mètre.

Many honors fell to Miller in his lifetime. He was president of the Cambridge Philosophical Society (1857–1859) and foreign secretary of the Royal Society (1856–1873), being awarded a Royal Medal in 1870.

The exceptional breadth of Miller's scientific knowledge was recognized by his contemporaries. He was generous and hospitable to a point, yet remarkably spartan in his way of life. His ingenuity in constructing surprisingly accurate apparatus from simple, often homely, materials was notable. While no great traveler, he obviously enjoyed his trips to Paris for meetings of the Meter Commission, and he regularly holidayed in the Italian Tirol, where he simply enjoyed the scenery while his wife sketched it.

BIBLIOGRAPHY

I. ORIGINAL WORKS. Miller's works include *The Elements of Hydrostatics and Hydrodynamics* (Cambridge, 1831); *An Elementary Treatise on the Differential Calculus* (Cambridge, 1833); *A Table of Mineralogical Species* (Cambridge, 1833); *A Treatise on Crystallography* (Cambridge, 1839); and William Phillips, *An Elementary Introduction to Mineralogy*, new ed. by H. J. Brooke and W. H. Miller (London, 1852).

II. SECONDARY LITERATURE. On Miller or his work see N. Storey Maskelyne, *Nature*, **22** (1880), 247–249; T. G. Bonney, *Proceedings of the Royal Society*, **31** (1881), ii–vii; and J. P. Cooke, *Proceedings of the American Academy of Arts and Sciences*, **16** (1881), 460–468. Memorial of William Hallowes Miller by his wife (privately printed, Cambridge, 1881[?]).

DUNCAN MCKIE

MINDING, ERNST FERDINAND ADOLF (or **Ferdinand Gotlibovich**) (*b.* Kalisz, Poland, 23 January 1806; *d.* Dorpat, Russia [now Tartu, Estonian S.S.R.], 13 May 1885)

Minding was a son of the town lawyer in Kalisz. After graduation in 1824 from the Gymnasium at Hirschberg (now Jelenia Góra, Poland), where the family had moved in 1807, Minding studied philology, philosophy, and physics at the universities of Halle and Berlin. In mathematics he was a self-taught amateur. After graduating from Berlin University in 1827, Minding taught mathematics in Gymnasiums for several years. In 1829 he received at Halle the doctorate in philosophy for his thesis on approximating the values of double integrals; from 1831 to 1843 he lectured on mathematics at Berlin University and from 1834 also at the Berlin Bauschule. At the university he lectured in 1831 and 1834 on the history of mathematics and gave a general introduction to the foundations and goals of the mathematical sciences. During these years he published thirty works, including several textbooks. Despite intensive pedagogical and scientific activity, Minding's position at Berlin was unsatisfactory; and he eagerly accepted an invitation to the University of Dorpat, where in 1842 the chair of mathematics of the Faculty of Philosophy was divided between one of pure mathematics, which was occupied by K. E. Senff, and one of applied mathematics, which was vacant. From 1843 to 1883 Minding was at the University of Dorpat as a full professor, giving both general and special courses in algebra, analysis, geometry, theory of probability, mechanics, and physics. In 1850 the Faculty of Philosophy was divided into that of physicomathematics and that of history-philology, and in 1851 Minding was elected to a four-year term as dean of the former division. In 1864 Minding and his family became Russian citizens. (In 1838 he had married Augusta Regler, and they had several children.) In the same year he was elected a corresponding member, and in 1879 an honorary member, of the St. Petersburg Academy of Sciences.

Minding's most important discoveries were in the differential geometry of surfaces; in these works he brilliantly continued the researches of Gauss, which had been published in 1828. In his first paper (1830), which dealt with the isoperimetric problem of determining on a given surface the shortest closed curve surrounding a given area (on the plane it is the circumference of a circle), he introduced the concept of geodesic curvature. It was independently discovered in 1848 by O. Bonnet, and it was he who named it geodesic curvature. Minding soon proved, as did Bonnet after him, the invariance of the geodesic curvature under bending of the surface. Neither of them knew that the same results had been presented in an earlier, unpublished paper of Gauss's (1825).

Minding's studies on the bending or the applicability of surfaces were especially remarkable. He first examined the bending of a particular class of surfaces (1838); incidentally, in the case of surfaces of revolution, he studied an example of the "applicability on a principal basis," which later became a preferred research topic for his disciple K. M. Peterson and for Peterson's followers in Moscow. He then proceeded to the general problem of determining the conditions for applicability of surfaces. Gauss had discovered (1828) that if one surface can be isometrically applied to another (so that the bending does not alter the lengths of curves), then the total curvature will be the same at all corresponding points.

In his article "Wie sich entscheiden lässt, ob zwei gegebene krumme Flächen auf einander abwickelbar sind oder nicht . . ." (1839), Minding stated the following sufficient condition for applicability: Two given surfaces of equal constant total curvature are applicable to one another isometrically, and this can be done in infinitely many different ways. He also investigated the corresponding problem for surfaces with a variable total curvature. Today "Minding's theorem" is found in all textbooks of differential geometry. Minding's papers, as well as Gauss's work of 1828, were great influences on the development of this branch of mathematics. In the article "Beiträge zur Theorie der kürzesten Linien auf krummen Flächen," which was published in Crelle's *Journal für die reine und angewandte Mathematik* (1840), Minding pointed out that when the trigonometric functions are replaced by corresponding hyperbolic ones, the trigonometric formulas in spherical trigonometry for the geodesic triangles on the surfaces with constant positive curvature are converted into the hyperbolic formulas for the surfaces with negative curvature. In 1837, Lobachevski showed (in an article that also appeared in Crelle's *Journal*) that the same relation exists between the trigonometric formulas for the sphere and the formulas in his "imaginary" (hyperbolic) geometry. The confrontation of these results might have led to the conclusion that two-dimensional hyperbolic geometry can be (partly) interpreted as the geometry of geodesics on a surface of constant negative curvature; but it was not until 1868 that Beltrami established this connection.

Starting from Euler's ideas, Minding proposed the method of solving the differential equation $M(x, y)\, dx + N(x, y)\, dy = 0$, where M and N are polynomials of some degree, based on determining the integrating factor by means of particular integrals of the equation. Minding's method, expounded in the paper "Beiträge zur Integration der Differential-gleichungen erster Ordnung zwischen zwei Veränder-lichen," for which he received in 1861 the Demidov Prize of the St. Petersburg Academy of Sciences, was developed further by A. N. Korkin and others. Darboux (1878) worked independently, followed by E. Picard and others, in the same direction. Minding also published works on algebra (the elimination problem), the theory of continued fractions, the theory of algebraic functions, and analytic mechanics.

BIBLIOGRAPHY

I. ORIGINAL WORKS. Minding's writings include "Ueber die Curven kürzesten Perimeters auf krummen Flächen," in *Journal für die reine und angewandte Mathematik*, **5** (1830), 297–304; "Bemerkung über die Abwickelung krummer Linien von Flächen," *ibid.*, **6** (1830), 159–161; "De valore integralium duplicum quam proxime inveniendo" (his doctoral diss., in the archives of the University of Halle), pub. with minor modifications as "Ueber die Berechnung des Näherungswertes doppelter Integrale," *ibid.*, 91–95; *Anfangsgründe der höheren Arithmetik* (Berlin, 1832); *Handbuch der Differential- und Integralrechnung nebst Anwendung auf die Geometrie* (Berlin, 1836); *Handbuch der Differential- und Integralrechnung und ihrer Anwendungen auf Geometrie und Mechanik. Zweiter Teil, enthaltend die Mechanik* (Berlin, 1838); "Ueber die Biegung gewisser Flächen," in *Journal für die reine und angewandte Mathematik*, **18** (1838), 297–302; "Wie sich entscheiden lässt, ob zwei gegebene krumme Flächen auf einander abwickelbar sind oder nicht; nebst Bemerkungen über die Flächen von unverändlichem Krümmungsmasse," *ibid.*, **19** (1839), 370–387; "Beiträge zur Theorie der kürzesten Linien auf krummen Flächen," *ibid.*, **20** (1840), 323–327; and "Beiträge zur Integration der Differentialgleichungen erster Ordnung zwischen zwei Veränderlichen," in *Mémoires de l'Académie des sciences de St. Petersbourg*, 7th ser., **5**, no. 1 (1863), 1–95, also pub. separately in Russian trans. (St. Petersburg, 1862).

II. SECONDARY LITERATURE. See R. I. Galchenkova *et al.*, *Ferdinand Minding. 1806–1885* (Leningrad, 1970), which includes a complete list of Minding's works, pp. 205–210 (nos. 1–72), and extensive secondary literature, pp. 210–220 (nos. 73–289); A. Kneser, "Übersicht der wissenschaftlichen Arbeiten Ferdinand Minding's nebst biographischen Notizen," in *Zeitschrift für Mathematik und Physik*, Hist.-lit. Abt., **45** (1900), 113–128; I. Z. Shtokalo, ed., *Istoria otechestvennoy matematiki*, II (Kiev, 1967); A. Voss, "Abbildung und Abwickelung zweier Flächen auf einender abwickelbarer Flächen," in *Encyklopädie der mathematischen Wissenschaften*, III, pt. 6a (Leipzig, 1903), 355–440; and A. P. Youschkevitch, *Istoria matematiki v Rossii do 1917 g.* (Moscow, 1968).

A. YOUSCHKEVITCH

MINEUR, HENRI (*b.* Lille, France, 7 March 1899; *d.* Paris, France, 7 May 1954)

Although he was first on the admissions list of the École Normale Supérieure in 1917, Mineur enlisted in the army and did not enter the school until after the end of World War I. After passing the *agrégation* in mathematics in 1921, he taught at the French *lycée* in Düsseldorf while pursuing the mathematical research he had begun in 1920. He received his doctorate in science in 1924 for his work on functional equations, in which he established an addition theorem for Fuchsian functions.

Mineur had been interested in astronomy from his youth, and in 1925 he left his teaching post to become astronomer at the Paris observatory. He made important contributions to several fields related to mathematical astronomy: celestial mechanics, analytic mechanics, statistics, and numerical calculus. His treatise on the method of least squares has become a classic.

It was in stellar astronomy, however, that Mineur's work was most sustained and fruitful. In particular, he detected the variation in the speed of near stars according to the distance from the galactic plane and the retrograde rotation of the system of globular clusters. He also corrected the coordinates of the galactic center and studied interstellar absorption. As early as 1944 he showed that an important correction had to be made in the zero of the period-luminosity relation of the Cepheids; this change led to a doubling of the scale of distances in the universe. All these results have been confirmed by recent investigations.

Mincur was a brilliant and unusual person who became thoroughly involved in many areas. Between 1940 and 1944 he was a member of the Resistance. He was a founder of the Centre National de la Recherche Scientifique and of the observatory of Saint-Michel in Haute-Provence. At his initiative the Institute d'Astrophysique was created at Paris in 1936; he was its director until his death, which occurred after five years of a serious heart and liver ailment. Mineur twice won prizes of the Académie des Sciences.

BIBLIOGRAPHY

I. ORIGINAL WORKS. In kinematics and stellar dynamics Mineur's principal writings are "Rotation de la galaxie," in *Bulletin astronomique*, **5** (1925), 505–543; "Étude de mouvements propres moyens d'étoiles," *ibid.*, **6** (1930), 281–304; "Recherches sur les vitesses radiales résiduelles . . . ," *ibid.*, **7** (1931), 321–352, written with his wife; *Éléments de statistique . . . stellaire*, Actualités Scientifiques et Industrielles, no. 116 (Paris, 1934); *Photographie stellaire . . .*, *ibid.*, no. 141 (Paris, 1934); *Dénombrement d'étoiles . . .*, *ibid.*, no. 225 (Paris, 1935); "Recherches sur la distribution de la matière absorbante . . . ," in *Annales d'astrophysique*, **1** (1938), 97–128; "Sur la rotation galactique . . . ," *ibid.*, 269–281; "Équilibre des nuages galactiques . . . ," *ibid.*, **2** (1939), 1–244; "Zéro de la relation période-luminosité . . . ," *ibid.*, **7** (1944), 160–186; and "Recherches théoriques sur les accélérations stellaires," *ibid.*, **13** (1950), 219–242. Some of these investigations are summarized in *L'espace interstellaire* (Paris, 1947).

In celestial and analytical mechanics, see especially "La mécanique des masses variables . . . ," in *Annales scientifiques de l'École normale supérieure*, 3rd ser., **50** (1933),

1–69; "Étude théorique du mouvement séculaire de l'axe terrestre," in *Bulletin astronomique*, **13** (1947), 197–252; "Quelques propriétés ... équations de la mécanique," *ibid.*, **13** (1948), 309–328; and "Recherche ... dans le groupe canonique linéaire," *ibid.*, **15** (1950), 107–141.

In statistics and numerical calculus, see *Technique de la méthode des moindres carrés* (Paris, 1938); "Nouvelle méthode de lissage ... période d'un phénomène," in *Annales d'astrophysique*, **6** (1943), 137–158; "Sur la meilleure représentation d'une variable aléatoire ...," *ibid.*, **7** (1944), 17–30; and *Techniques de calcul numérique* (Paris, 1952).

His works in analysis include his doctoral dissertation, "Théorie analytique des groupes continus finis," in *Journal de mathématiques pures et appliquées*, 9th ser., **4** (1925), 23–108; and "Calcul différentiel absolu," in *Bulletin des sciences mathématiques*, 2nd ser., **52** (1928), 63–76.

II. SECONDARY LITERATURE. See D. Barbier, "Henri Mineur," in *Annales d'astrophysique*, **17** (1954), 239–242; and J. Dufay, "Henri Mineur," in *Astronomie*, **70** (1956), 235–238.

JACQUES R. LÉVY

MINKOWSKI, HERMANN (*b.* Alexotas, Russia [now Lithuanian S.S.R.], 22 June 1864; *d.* Göttingen, Germany, 12 January 1909)

Minkowski was born of German parents who returned to Germany and settled in Königsberg [now Kaliningrad, R.S.F.S.R.] when the boy was eight years old. His older brother Oskar became a famous pathologist. Except for three semesters at the University of Berlin, he received his higher education at Königsberg, where he became a lifelong friend of both Hilbert, who was a fellow student, and the slightly older Hurwitz, who was beginning his professorial career. In 1881 the Paris Academy of Sciences had announced a competition for the Grand Prix des Sciences Mathématiques to be awarded in 1883, the subject being the number of representations of an integer as a sum of five squares of integers; Eisenstein had given formulas for that number but without proof. The Academy was unaware that in 1867 H. J. Smith had published an outline of such a proof, and Smith now sent a detailed memoir developing his methods. Without knowledge of Smith's paper, the eighteen-year-old Minkowski, in a masterly manuscript of 140 pages, reconstructed the entire theory of quadratic forms in *n* variables with integral coefficients from Eisenstein's sparse indications. He gave an even better formulation than Smith's because he used a more natural and more general definition of the genus of a form. The Academy, unable to decide between two equally excellent, and substantially equivalent, works, awarded the Grand Prix to both

Smith and Minkowski.

Minkowski received his doctorate in 1885 at Königsberg; he taught at Bonn until 1894, then returned to Königsberg for two years. In 1896 he went to Zurich, where he was Hurwitz' colleague until 1902; Hilbert then obtained the creation of a new professorship for him at Göttingen, where Minkowski taught until his death.

From his Grand Prix paper to his last work Minkowski never ceased to return to the arithmetic of quadratic forms in *n* variables ("*n*-ary forms"). Ever since Gauss's pioneering work on binary quadratic forms at the beginning of the nineteenth century, the generalization of his results to *n*-ary forms had been the goal of many mathematicians, including Eisenstein, Hermite, Smith, Jordan, and Poincaré. Minkowski's most important contributions to the theory were (1) for quadratic forms with rational coefficients, a characterization of equivalence of such forms under a linear transformation with rational coefficients, through a system of three invariants of the form and (2) in a paper of 1905, the completion of the theory of reduction for positive definite *n*-ary quadratic forms with real coefficients, begun by Hermite. The latter had defined a process yielding in each equivalence class (for transformations with integral coefficients) a finite set of "reduced" forms; but it was still possible for this set to consist in more than one form. Minkowski presented a new process of "reduction" giving a unique reduced form in each class. In the space of *n*-ary quadratic forms (of dimension $n(n + 1)/2$), the "fundamental domain" of all reduced forms proves to be a polyhedron; Minkowski made a detailed investigation of the relation of this domain to its neighbors and computed its volume, which enabled him to obtain asymptotic formulas for the number of equivalence classes of a given determinant, when the value of that determinant tends to infinity.

This 1905 paper was greatly influenced by the geometric outlook that Minkowski had developed fifteen years earlier—the "geometry of numbers," as he called it, his most original achievement. He was led to it by the theory of ternary quadratic forms. Following brief indications given by Gauss, Dirichlet had developed a geometrical method of reduction of positive definite ternary forms; Minkowski's brilliant idea was to use the concept of volume in conjunction with this geometric method, thus obtaining far better estimates than had been possible before. To make matters simpler, consider a binary positive definite quadratic form $F(x, y) = ax^2 + 2bxy + cy^2$. To say that F takes a value m when $x = p, y = q$ are integers, means, geometrically, that the ellipse E_m of equation

$F(x, y) = m$ passes through the point (p, q). To find the minimum M of all such values m, obtained for p, q not both 0, Minkowski observed that for small α, certainly the ellipse E_α will not contain any such points; if one considers the ellipse $\frac{1}{2}E_\alpha$ and translates it by sending its center to every point (p, q) with integral coordinates, one obtains an infinite pattern of ellipses which do not touch each other. When α increases and reaches the value M, some of the corresponding ellipses will touch each other but no two will overlap. Now, if $A = ac - b^2$ is the area of the ellipse E_1, the ellipse $\frac{1}{2}E_M$ has area $AM^2/4$, $AM^2/4$ and the total area of the nonoverlapping ellipses which are translations of $\frac{1}{2}E_M$ and which have centers at the points (p, q) with $|p| \leqslant n$ and $|q| \leqslant n$ is $(2n + 1)^2(AM^2/4)$. It is easy to see, however, that there is a constant $c > 0$ independent of n, such that all these ellipses are contained in a square of center 0 and of side $2n + 1 + c$, so that

$$(2n + 1)^2(AM^2/4) \leqslant (2n + 1 + c)^2;$$

letting n grow to infinity gives the inequality

$$\frac{AM^2}{4} \leqslant 1 \quad \text{or} \quad M \leqslant \frac{2}{\sqrt{A}}.$$

Not only can this argument be at once extended to spaces of arbitrary finite dimension, but Minkowski had a second highly original idea: He observed that in the preceding geometric argument, ellipses could be replaced by arbitrary convex symmetric curves (and, in higher-dimensional spaces, by symmetric convex bodies). By varying the nature of these convex bodies with extreme ingenuity (polyhedrons, cylinders), he immediately obtained far-reaching discoveries in many domains of number theory. For instance, by associating to an algebraic integer x in a field of algebraic numbers K of degree n over the rationals, the point in n dimensions having as coordinates the rational integers which are the coefficients of x with respect to a fixed basis, Minkowski gave lower bounds for the discriminant of K, which in particular proved that when $n > 1$, the discriminant may never be equal to 1 and that there are only a finite number of fields of discriminants bounded by a given number.

Minkowski's geometric methods also enabled him to reach a far better understanding of the theory of continued fractions and to generalize it into an algorithm which, at least theoretically, gives a criterion for a number to be algebraic. It was similar in principle to Lagrange's well-known criterion that quadratic irrationals are characterized by periodic continued fractions; but Minkowski also showed that, for his criterion, periodicity occurs in only a small number of cases, which he characterized completely. Finally, if, for instance, one considers (as above, but in three dimensions) an ellipsoid $F(x, y, z) = 1$ in relation to the lattice L of points with integral coordinates, the largest possible number M will be obtained when the translated ellipsoids are "packed together" as closely as possible. If one makes a linear transformation of the space transforming the ellipsoid in a sphere, L is transformed into another lattice consisting of linear combinations with integral coefficients of three vectors. The problem of finding the largest M, then, is equivalent to the "closest packing of spheres" in space, when the centers are at the vertices of a lattice L'; one has to find the lattice L' that gives this closest packing. Minkowski began the study of that difficult problem (which extends to any n-dimensional space) and of corresponding problems when spheres are replaced by some other type of convex set (particularly polyhedrons); they have been the subject of fruitful research ever since.

The intensive use of the concept of convexity in his "geometry of numbers" led Minkowski to investigate systematically the geometrical properties of convex sets in n-dimensional space, a subject that had barely been considered before. He was the first to understand the importance of the notion of hyperplane of support (both geometrically and analytically), and he proved the existence of such hyperplanes at each point of the boundary of a convex body. Long before the modern conception of a metric space was invented, Minkowski realized that a symmetric convex body in an n-dimensional space defines a new notion of "distance" on that space and, hence, a corresponding "geometry." His ideas thus paved the way for the founders of the theory of normed spaces in the 1920's and became the basis for modern functional analysis.

The evaluation of volumes of convex bodies led Minkowski to the very original concept of "mixed volume" of several convex bodies: when K_1, K_2, K_3 are three convex bodies in ordinary space and t_1, t_2, t_3 are three real numbers $\geqslant 0$, the points $t_1x_1 + t_2x_2 + t_3x_3$, when x_j varies in K_j for $j = 1, 2, 3$, fill a new convex body, written $t_1K_1 + t_2K_2 + t_3K_3$. When the volume of this new convex body is computed, it is seen to be a homogeneous polynomial in t_1, t_2, t_3 and the mixed volume $V(K_1, K_2, K_3)$ is the coefficient of $t_1t_2t_3$ in that polynomial. Minkowski discovered remarkable relations between these new quantities and more classical notions: if K_1 is a sphere of radius 1, then $V(K_1, K, K)$ is one third of the area of the convex surface bounding K; and $V(K_1, K_1, K)$ is one third of the mean value of the mean curvature of that surface.

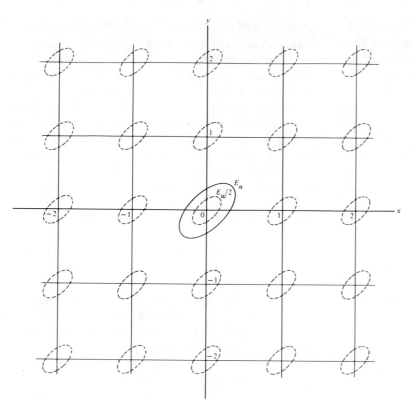

FIGURE 1

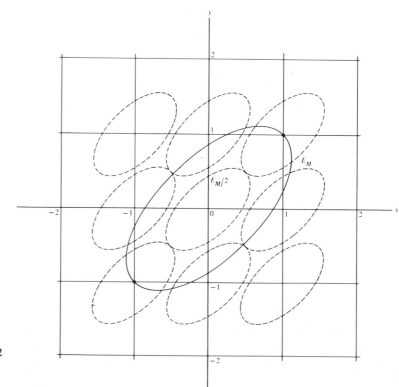

FIGURE 2

He also proved the inequality between mixed volumes

$$V(K_1, K_2, K_3)^2 \geqslant V(K_1, K_1, K_3)\, V(K_2, K_2, K_3),$$

from which he derived a new and simple proof of the isoperimetric property of the sphere. As a beautiful application of his concepts of hyperplane of support and of mixed volumes, Minkowski showed that a convex polyhedron having a given number m of faces is determined entirely by the areas and directions of the faces, a theorem that he generalized to convex surfaces by a passage to the limit. He also determined all convex bodies having constant width.

Minkowski was always interested in mathematical physics but did not work in that field until the last years of his life, when he participated in the movement of ideas that led to the theory of relativity. He was the first to conceive that the relativity principle formulated by Lorentz and Einstein led to the abandonment of the concept of space and time as separate entities and to their replacement by a four-dimensional "space-time," of which he gave a precise definition and initiated the mathematical study; it became the frame of all later developments of the theory and led Einstein to his bolder conception of generalized relativity.

BIBLIOGRAPHY

Minkowski's writings were collected in *Gesammelte Abhandlungen*, D. Hilbert, ed., 2 vols. (Leipzig–Berlin, 1911). Among his books are *Geometrie der Zahlen* (Leipzig, 1896; 2nd ed., 1910); and *Diophantische Approximationen* (Leipzig, 1907; repr. New York, 1957).

On Minkowski's work, see Harris Hancock, *Development of the Minkowski Geometry of Numbers* (New York, 1939); and Frederick W. Lanchester, *Relativity. An Elementary Explanation of the Space-Time Relations As Established by Minkowski* (London, 1935).

J. DIEUDONNÉ

MISES, RICHARD VON (*b.* Lemberg, Austria [now Lvov, U.S.S.R.], 19 April 1883; *d.* Boston, Massachusetts, 14 July 1953)

Von Mises was the second son of Arthur Edler von Mises, a technical expert with the Austrian state railways, and Adele von Landau. His elder brother, Ludwig, became a prominent economist; the younger brother died in infancy. After earning his doctorate in Vienna in 1907, Richard taught at universities in Europe and Turkey and then, from 1939, in the United States. In 1944 he became Gordon McKay professor of aerodynamics and applied mathematics at Harvard. During his European period, he married Hilda Pollaczek-Geiringer, one of his pupils. Proud to call himself an applied mathematician, he was the founder and editor, from 1921 to 1933, of the well-known *Zeitschrift für angewandte Mathematik und Mechanik*. He was a scholar with wide interests, who wrote perceptively on the philosophy of science from a positivist point of view, and who was also an authority on the poet Rilke.

Von Mises' early preoccupation with fluid mechanics led him into aerodynamics and aeronautics, subjects that in the years immediately before 1914 had received a major fillip from the success of heavier-than-air flying machines. He himself learned to fly and in the summer of 1913 gave what is believed to be the first university course on the mechanics of powered flight. After the outbreak of World War I he helped develop an Austrian air arm, and in 1915 the team he led produced a giant 600-horsepower military plane with an original wing profile of his own design (wing theory was perhaps his specialty).

In 1916 he published a booklet on flight, under the auspices of the Luftfahrarsenal in Vienna. It went into many enlarged editions and is the basis of *Theory of Flight*, published with collaborators in English toward the end of World War II. Other, allied topics to which he contributed were elasticity, plasticity, and turbulence. He also worked in various branches of pure mathematics, particularly numerical analysis.

Von Mises' concern with the border areas of mathematics and the experimental sciences was reflected in his giving much thought to probability and statistics. In 1919 he published two papers that, although little noticed at the time, inaugurated a new look at probability that was destined to become famous. The background to this contribution was the slow buildup, during the nineteenth century, of a frequency theory of probability, in contrast to the received classical theory of Laplace. The fathers of the frequency theory, Poisson in France and Ellis in England, had identified the probability of a given event in specified circumstances with the proportion of such events in a set of exactly similar circumstances, or trials. The weakness of this position is the necessary finiteness of the set, and there is no obvious way of extending the idea to those very large or infinite sets that in practice must be sampled for probabilistic information. The Cambridge logician John Venn improved the theory in 1866 by equating probability with the relative frequency of the event "in the long run," thereby introducing a mathematical limit and the infinite set. Nevertheless, even this reformation failed to make the theory compelling enough to tempt mathematicians to put it into rigorous terms; and

Keynes in his *Treatise on Probability* (1921) expressed his inability to assess the frequency theory adequately because it had never been unambiguously formulated. This was the deficiency that Von Mises attempted to correct.

What Von Mises did was to splice two familiar notions, that of the Venn limit and that of a random sequence of events. Let us consider the matter in terms of a binary trial, the outcome of which is either a "success" or otherwise. Given an endless sequence of such trials, in the sense of Bernoulli binomial sampling, what can we say about it probabilistically? A meaningful answer, said Von Mises, is possible only if we postulate (1) the mathematical existence of a limiting value to the fraction successes/trials, and (2) the invariance of this limit for all possible infinite subsequences formed by any rule of place selection of trials that is independent of their outcomes. Then the limit can be called the probability of a success in the particular system. It then follows that the probability of a single event is formally meaningless; random sampling is a *sine qua non*; and the sequence (otherwise collective or sample space) must be clearly defined before any discussion of probability—in this strictly operational sense—can be undertaken.

The intuitive appeal of Von Mises' limiting-frequency theory is strong, and its spirit has influenced all modern statisticians. Remarkably, however, the mathematics of the theory, even after sophistication by leading probabilists, has never been rendered widely acceptable, and some authorities today do not mention Von Mises. In advanced work, the measure-theoretic approach initiated by Kolmogorov in 1933 is most favored. On the practical side, his statistical writings suffered from a foible: he denied the importance of small-sample theory. Von Mises' *Probability, Statistics, and Truth*, published in German in 1928 and in English in 1939, is not a pedagogic text but a semipopular account, very subjective in tone, good on the historic side, and in general notably stimulating.

BIBLIOGRAPHY

I. ORIGINAL WORKS. The core of Von Mises' work is to be found in the following six books: *Probability, Statistics and Truth* (New York, 1939; 2nd ed., 1957); *Theory of Flight* (New York, 1945); *Positivism, a Study in Human Understanding* (Cambridge, Mass., 1951); *Mathematical Theory of Compressible Fluid Flow* (New York, 1958), completed by Hilda Geiringer and G. S. S. Ludford; *Selected Papers of Richard von Mises*, Philipp P. Frank *et al.*, eds. (Providence, R.I., 1963); and *Mathematical Theory of Probability and Statistics* (New York, 1964), edited and complemented by Hilda Geiringer. His first papers on probability are "Fundamentalsätze der Wahrscheinlich-keitsrechnung," in *Mathematische Zeitschrift*, **4** (1919), 1–97; and "Grundlagen der Wahrscheinlichkeitsrechnung," *ibid.*, **5** (1919), 52–99. A good bibliography of 143 works is in Garrett Birkhoff, Gustav Kuerti, and Gabor Szego, eds., *Studies in Mathematics and Mechanics Presented to Richard von Mises* (New York, 1954), which contains a portrait.

II. SECONDARY LITERATURE. The opening chapters of *Mathematical Theory of Probability and Statistics* (see above) contain a survey by Hilda Geiringer of other workers' developments of Von Mises' controversial theory, as well as a synopsis of Kolmogorov's rival theory and its relation to that of Von Mises. A critical essay review of this book by D. V. Lindley is in *Annals of Mathematical Statistics*, **37** (1966), 747–754. W. Kneale, *Probability and Induction* (London, 1949), marshals some logical arguments against limiting-frequency theories. On the other hand, H. Reichenbach, *The Theory of Probability* (Berkeley, 1949); Rudolf Carnap, *Logical Foundations of Probability* (Chicago, 1950); and Karl Popper, *The Logic of Scientific Discovery* (New York, 1958), are all, in different ways and with various emphases, derivative and sympathetic.

NORMAN T. GRIDGEMAN

MITTAG-LEFFLER, MAGNUS GUSTAF (GÖSTA)

(*b.* Stockholm, Sweden, 16 March 1846; *d.* Stockholm, 7 July 1927)

Mittag-Leffler was the eldest son of John Olaf Leffler and Gustava Wilhelmina Mittag. His father was a school principal and from 1867 to 1870 a deputy in the lower house of the Swedish parliament. The atmosphere at home was intellectually stimulating, and Mittag-Leffler's aptitude for mathematics was recognized and encouraged at an early age.

Mittag-Leffler entered the University of Uppsala in 1865 and obtained the doctorate in 1872. He remained at the university as a lecturer for a year, but in 1873 left on a traveling scholarship for Paris, Göttingen, and Berlin. On the advice of Hermite, whom he met in Paris, he went to study under Weierstrass in Berlin. Weierstrass exerted a decisive influence on his subsequent development.

In 1877 Mittag-Leffler wrote his *Habilitationsschrift* on the theory of elliptic function and, in consequence, was appointed professor of mathematics at the University of Helsinki. In 1881 he left Helsinki for Stockholm, where he became professor of mathematics at the newly established Högskola (later the University of Stockholm). He twice served as rector. Among his colleagues there were Sonya Kovalewsky and E. Phragmén. Mittag-Leffler was an excellent lecturer. Among his students were I. O. Bendixson, Helge von Koch, and E. I. Fredholm.

Mittag-Leffler was not among the mathematical giants of his time, but he did contribute several methods and results that have found a lasting place in the mathematical literature. His most important contributions clearly reflect Weierstrass' influence. Thus, where Weierstrass had given formulas for the representation of entire functions and of elliptic functions, Mittag-Leffler set himself the task of finding a representation for an arbitrary meromorphic function $f(z)$ which would display its behavior at its poles. The answer is of classical simplicity. Let $\{z_n\}$ be the set of poles of $f(z)$ so that $\{z_n\}$ is either finite or is infinite and possesses a limit point at infinity. In the former case the answer is trivial since $f(z)$ differs from an entire function only by the sum of its principal parts, $\sum h_n(z - z_n)$. In the latter case, this sum is infinite and may diverge. Convergence is reestablished by adding to the individual terms of the sums certain suitable polynomials.

A generalization of this result, also due to Mittag-Leffler, is concerned with the case where the set $\{z_n\}$ while still consisting of isolated points may have limit points also in the finite plane. Another field that was pioneered by Mittag-Leffler is that of the representation of an analytic function $f(z)$ beyond the circle of convergence of its power series round a given point. Taking this point, without loss of generality, as the origin, one defines the (principal) Mittag-Leffler star of the function with respect to the origin as the union of the straight segments extending from the origin to the first singularity of the function in that direction (or to infinity). Mittag-Leffler developed analytic expressions that represent $f(z)$ in the entire Mittag-Leffler star. The later evolutions of this subject led to its being subsumed under the heading of the theory of summability, where certain infinite matrices are now known as Mittag-Leffler matrices.

Mittag-Leffler was a prolific writer, and the list of his publications includes 119 items. But his importance as a research worker is overshadowed by his prominence as an organizer in many spheres of scientific activity. He was the founder and, for many years, the chief editor of the highly influential *Acta mathematica*, to which he attracted important contributions by men such as E. Borel, G. Cantor, J. Hadamard, D. Hilbert, J. Jensen, V. Volterra, H. Weber, and above all H. Poincaré.

Mittag-Leffler's relationship with Cantor is of particular interest. Mittag-Leffler himself said of his work on meromorphic functions and of its generalizations that it had been his endeavor to subsume Weierstrass' and Cantor's approaches to analysis under a single point of view. And Cantor regarded Mittag-Leffler as one of his most influential friends

and supporters in a hostile world.

Mittag-Leffler was very conscious of the importance of maintaining a record of the contemporary history of mathematics for posterity, and the pages of *Acta mathematica* contains reprints of many exchanges of letters between notable mathematicians of the period. He wrote a moving account of the relationship between Weierstrass and Sonya Kovalewsky.

He was one of the organizers of the first and of subsequent international congresses of mathematicians and was the recipient of many honors, including doctorates from the universities of Bologna, Oxford, Cambridge, Christiania (Oslo), Aberdeen, and St. Andrews.

Mittag-Leffler was married to Signe af Lindfors in 1882.

BIBLIOGRAPHY

Articles by Mittag-Leffler include "Sur la représentation analytique des fonctions monogènes uniformes d'une variable indépendante," in *Acta mathematica*, **4** (1884), 1–79, and "Weierstrass et Sonja Kowalewsky," *ibid.*, **39** (1923), 133–198. A complete bibliography is in N. E. G. Nörlund, "G. Mittag-Leffler," *ibid.*, **50** (1927), I–XXIII. See also A. Schoenflies, "Die Krisis in Cantor's mathematischem Schaffen," *ibid.*, 1–23, with "Zusätzliche Bemerkungen," by Mittag-Leffler, *ibid.*, 25–26; and E. Hille, "In Retrospect," 1962 Yale Mathematical Colloquium (mimcographed).

ABRAHAM ROBINSON

MÖBIUS, AUGUST FERDINAND (*b.* Schulpforta, near Naumburg, Germany, 17 November 1790; *d.* Leipzig, Germany, 26 September 1868)

Möbius was the only child of Johann Heinrich Möbius, a dancing teacher in Schulpforta until his death in 1793, and the former Johanne Catharine Christiane Keil, a descendant of Luther. His father's unmarried brother succeeded him as dancing teacher and as provider for the family until his own death in 1804. Möbius was taught at home until his thirteenth year, by which time he had already shown an interest in mathematics. He pursued formal education from 1803 to 1809 in Schulpforta, where he studied mathematics under Johann Gottlieb Schmidt. In 1809 he entered Leipzig University with the intention of studying law, but his early love for mathematics soon came to dominance. Consequently he studied mathematics under Moritz von Prasse, physics with Ludwig Wilhelm Gilbert, and astronomy with Mollweide, whose assistant he became.

Having been selected for a traveling fellowship,

he left Leipzig in May 1813, a few months before the Battle of Leipzig, and went to Göttingen, where he spent two semesters studying theoretical astronomy with Gauss. He then proceeded to Halle for studies in mathematics with Johann Friedrich Pfaff. When in 1814 Prasse died, Mollweide succeeded him as mathematics professor, thereby opening up the position in astronomy at Leipzig. The position was given to Möbius, who received his doctorate from Leipzig in 1814 and qualified for instruction in early 1815 with his *De peculiaribus quibusdam aequationum trigonometricarum affectionibus.* In the same year he published his doctoral thesis entitled *De computandis occultationibus fixarum per planetas.* In spring 1816 he became extraordinary professor of astronomy at Leipzig and also observer at the observatory. In preparation for these duties he visited a number of the leading German observatories and eventually made recommendations for the refurbishing and reconstruction of the observatory at Leipzig; these were carried out by 1821. Other instruments were added later, including a six-foot Fraunhofer refractor.

In 1820 Möbius' mother, who had come to live with him, died. Shortly thereafter he married Dorothea Christiane Johanna Rothe, whose subsequent blindness did not prevent her from raising a daughter, Emilie, and two sons, Theodor and Paul Heinrich, both of whom became distinguished literary scholars. The former is best known for his research on Scandinavian and Icelandic literature; the latter is sometimes confused with Paul Julius Möbius the neurologist, who was Möbius' grandson.

Although Möbius was offered attractive positions as an astronomer at Greifswald in 1816 and as a mathematician at Dorpat in 1819, he refused them both to remain at Leipzig. In 1829 he became a corresponding member of the Berlin Academy of Sciences, but it was not until 1844, after he had been invited to succeed J. F. Fries at Jena, that Leipzig promoted him to ordinary professor of astronomy and higher mechanics. The slowness of his promotion and his modest salary have been attributed to his quiet and reserved manner, while his refusal to leave Leipzig stemmed from his love for his native Saxony and the quality of Leipzig University. In 1848 Möbius became director of the observatory, and d'Arrest became the observer and eventually his son-in-law. Möbius rarely traveled, and in general his life centered around his study, the observatory, and his family. His writings were fully developed and original; he was not widely read in the mathematical literature of his day and consequently found at times that others had previously discovered ideas presented in his writings. Also his investigations were frequently

aimed not so much at finding new results, but rather at developing more effective and simpler means for treating existing areas. In 1868, not long after having celebrated his fiftieth year of teaching at Leipzig, Möbius died; his wife's death had come nine years earlier.

Möbius' scientific contributions may be divided into two areas—astronomy and mathematics. Like his contemporaries Gauss and W. R. Hamilton, Möbius was employed as an astronomer but made his most important contributions to mathematics.

His early publications were in astronomy; two short papers on Juno and Pallas were followed by the separate publication in 1815 of his doctoral dissertation on occultation phenomena (see above) and in 1816 by his *De minima variatione azimuthi stellarum circulos parallelos uniformiter describentium commentatio.* By 1823 his observational activities had borne fruit to the extent that he published his only work of that sort, his *Beobachtungen auf der Königlichen Universitäts-Sternwarte zu Leipzig.* He published a few observational papers in later decades and in the 1830's made measurements on terrestrial magnetism. He also published two popular treatises on the path of Halley's comet (1835) and on the fundamental laws of astronomy (1836), the latter having gone through many editions. His greatest contribution to astronomy was his *Die Elemente der Mechanik des Himmels* (1843), wherein he gave a thorough mathematical treatment of celestial mechanics without the use of higher mathematics. Although astronomical amateurs could therefore read the book, it nevertheless contained results important to professionals. Moreover he introduced (for the first time, he thought) the use of vectorial addition and subtraction to represent velocities and forces and effectively showed the computational usefulness of that very ancient mathematical device, the epicycle.

When Mollweide died in 1825, Möbius hoped to follow his example by exchanging his own position in astronomy for that in mathematics, but in 1826 M. W. Drobisch was selected. In the following year Möbius published his greatest work, which later became a mathematical classic. Möbius' *Der barycentrische Calcul: Ein neues Hülfsmittel zur analytischen Behandlung der Geometrie* (1827) was not only his most important mathematical publication, but also the source of much of his later work. He had come upon the fundamental ideas for his barycentric calculus in 1818 and by 1821 decided that they merited book-length treatment. In an appendix to his 1823 astronomical treatise, he had given a first discussion of his new method. As he stated in the foreword to his 1827 treatise, the concept of the centroid had been recognized by Archimedes as a useful tool for geometrical investigations.

Möbius proceeded from the well-known law of mechanics, that a combination of weights positioned at various points can be replaced by a single weight of magnitude equal to the sum of the individual weights and positioned at the center of gravity of the combination. Thus Möbius constructed a mathematical system, the fundamental entities of which were points, to each of which a weight or numerical coefficient was assigned. The position of any point could be expressed in this system by varying the numerical coefficients of any four or more noncoplaner points. Thus Möbius used an equation such as $aA + bB + cC \equiv D$, where a, b, c are numerical coefficients (positive or negative), and A, B, C, D are points, to express the fact that if A, B, C are not collinear, then D must lie in the plane of A, B, C. Möbius went on in his treatise to apply this method with noteworthy success to many important geometrical problems. Since barycentric coordinates are a form of homogeneous coordinates, their creator is recognized with Feuerbach and Plücker, whose publications were independent and nearly simultaneous, as a discoverer of homogeneous coordinates.

Moreover Möbius developed important results in projective and affine geometry and also was among the first fully to appreciate the principle of duality and to give a thorough treatment of the cross ratio. He was the first mathematician to make use of a system wherein geometrical entities, such as lines, plane figures, and solids, were consistently treated as spatially oriented and to which a positive or negative sign could be affixed. Moreover he presented in this work the construction now known as the Möbius net. Finally at one point in the treatise he commented that two equal and similar solid figures, which are however mirror images of each other, could be made to coincide, if one were "able to let one system make a half revolution in a space of four dimensions. But since such a space cannot be conceived, this coincidence is impossible in this case" (*Werke*, I, 172).

Nearly all of Möbius' subsequent mathematical publications appeared in Crelle's *Journal für die reine und angewandte Mathematik* and from 1846 in either the *Abhandlungen . . .* or the *Berichte der Königlichen Sächsischen Gesellschaft der Wissenschaften zu Leipzig*. Some of these merit special attention. An 1828 paper discussed two tetrahedrons which mutually circumscribe and inscribe each other; such tetrahedrons are now known as Möbius tetrahedrons. Two dioptrical papers appeared in 1830 wherein Möbius used continued fractions to develop his results; another optical paper appeared in 1855 based on the concept of collineation. The Möbius function in number theory was presented in an 1832 paper, but most of his energies during the 1830's went into a series of papers on statics, which culminated in his 1837 two-volume *Lehrbuch der Statik*, wherein he treated the subject, following Poinsot, through combining individual forces with couples of forces and introduced the concept of a null system.

It is frequently stated that in 1840 Möbius posed for the first time the four-color conjecture, that is, that four colors are sufficient for the unambiguous construction of any map, no matter how complex, on a plane surface. This attribution is, however, incorrect; its source lies in the correct statement that in 1840 Möbius presented a lecture in which he posed the problem of how a kingdom might be divided into five regions in such a way that every region would border on each of the four other regions. In 1846 Möbius published a treatment of spherical trigonometry based on his barycentric calculus and in 1852 a paper on lines of the third order. His 1855 "Theorie der Kreisverwandschaft in rein geometrischer Darstellung" is the culmination of a number of studies on circular transformations, which are now frequently called Möbius transformations.

Möbius had been visited in 1844 by a high school teacher, Hermann Grassmann, whose now famous *Ausdehnungslehre* of 1844 contained among other things results similar to Möbius' point system of analysis. Grassmann requested Möbius to review the book, but Möbius failed to appreciate it, as did many others. When Grassmann in 1846 won the prize in a mathematical contest, which he had entered at Möbius' suggestion, Möbius did agree to write a commentary on the prize-winning essay. This 1847 work was the only significant published analysis of Grassmann's ideas until the late 1860's, when their significance was realized. Möbius was stimulated in the early 1860's to write his own treatise, "Ueber geometrische Addition und Multiplication," but this was not published until nineteen years after his death.

Möbius is now most frequently remembered for his discovery of the one-sided surface called the Möbius strip, which is formed by taking a rectangular strip of paper and connecting its ends after giving it a half twist (*Werke*, II, 484–485). The Paris Academy had offered a prize for research on the geometrical theory of polyhedrons, and in 1858 Möbius began to prepare an essay on this subject. The results of his essay were for the most part given in two important papers: his "Theorie der elementaren Verwandtschaft" of 1863 and his "Ueber die Bestimmung des Inhaltes eines Polyëders" of 1865. The latter contains his discovery of the "Möbius strip" and proof that there are polyhedrons to which no volume can be assigned. Curt Reinhardt has shown from an examination of Möbius' notebooks that he discovered this surface around September 1858 (*Werke*, II, 517–521); this date is significant, since it is now known that Johann Benedict Listing discovered the same surface in July 1858 and published his discovery in 1861. Listing and Möbius, who worked independently of each other, should thus share the credit for this discovery.

BIBLIOGRAPHY

I. ORIGINAL WORKS. Möbius' main publications, including his three long books, are collected in R. Baltzer, F. Klein, and W. Scheibner, eds., *Gesammelte Werke*, 4 vols. (Leipzig, 1885–1887). The second and fourth volumes contain previously unpublished writings, and the fourth contains a useful discussion of Möbius' manuscripts by C. Reinhardt.

II. SECONDARY LITERATURE. The best discussion of Möbius' life and astronomical activities is contained in C. Bruhns, *Die Astronomen auf der Pleissenburg* (Leipzig, 1879). The best treatment of his mathematical work is by R. Baltzer in Möbius, *Werke*, I, v–xx. See also H. Gretschel, "August Ferdinand Möbius," in *Archiv der Mathematik und Physik*, **49**, *Literarischer Bericht*, CLXXXXV (1869), 1–9; and M. Cantor, "Möbius," in *Allgemeine deutsche Biographie*, XX (1885), 38–43. A useful discussion of his barycentric calculus is R. E. Allardice, "The Barycentric Calculus of Möbius," in *Proceedings of the Edinburgh Mathematical Society*, **10** (1892), 2–21, and selections from his treatise on this subject are given in English in D. E. Smith, ed., *A Source Book in Mathematics*, II (New York, 1959), 525–526, 670–676. K. O. May in his "The Origin of the Four-Color Conjecture," in *Mathematics Teacher*, **60** (1967), 516–519, clarifies Möbius' relationship to this conjecture, and M. Crowe, in *A History of Vector Analysis* (Notre Dame, Ind., 1967), treats Möbius' relationship to vectorial analysis and to Grassmann. See also E. Kötter, "Die Entwickelung der synthetischen Geometrie," in *Jahresbericht der Deutschen Mathematikervereinigung*, **5**, pt. 2 (1901), 1–486.

MICHAEL J. CROWE

MOERBEKE, WILLIAM OF, also known as **Guillelmus de Moerbeka** (*b*. Moerbeke, Belgium [?], *ca*. 1220–1235; *d*. before 26 October 1286)

Moerbeke, a Dominican, was one of the most productive and eminent translators from Greek into Latin of philosophical and scientific works written between the fourth century B.C. and the sixth century A.D. A spectacular widening and increase of the Greek sources for study and speculation in the second half of the thirteenth century and later times were due to Moerbeke's insatiable desire to pass on to Latin-reading students the yet undiscovered or rediscovered treasures of Greek civilization, his extensive linguistic knowledge, his indefatigable search for first-class works, and his philosophical vision.

There is little evidence concerning Moerbeke's life apart from some names of places and dates at which he produced a particular translation: they are enough, however, to suggest reasons why he did not have much time to write original works. He was at Nicaea, Asia Minor, in the spring of 1260, and in Thebes—where Dominicans had been present at least since 1253—in December of that same year. He was at Viterbo, then a papal residence, in November 1267, May 1268, and June 1271. From 1272, at the latest, until April 1278 Moerbeke held the office of chaplain and penitentiary to the pope: in this capacity he visited the courts of Savoy and France pleading for help with the Ninth Crusade (March 1272), absolved an Augustinian prior from excommunication (1272, from Orvieto, seat of the papal curia), and authorized Albertus Magnus to absolve two abbeys in Cologne from censures (November 1274). In the same period (May–July 1274) he took part in the Second Council of Lyons, which was meant to bring about the reunion with the Greek Church; there, with Greek dignitaries, he sang the Creed in Greek in a pontifical mass. In October 1277 he was active at Viterbo. From April 1278 until his death he was archbishop of Corinth.

The three or four contemporaries with whom it is definitely known that Moerbeke had some contact were all scientists. The Silesian Witelo, who was in Viterbo toward the end of 1268, dedicated his *Perspectiva* to Moerbeke. In the introduction Witelo sheds some light on Moerbeke's philosophical doctrines and explains that they were never put in writing because Moerbeke was kept too busy by his ecclesiastical and pastoral duties and by his work as a translator. Henry Bate of Malines, a distinguished astronomer, was asked by Moerbeke, whom he met at Lyons in 1274, to write a treatise on the astrolabe; Henry immediately obliged and dedicated his *Magistralis compositio astrolabii* to his compatriot (October 1274). The physician Rosellus of Arezzo, who may have attended Pope Gregory X at his deathbed in Arezzo (1276), is the addressee of Moerbeke's dedication of his version of Galen's *De alimentis* (Viterbo, October 1277). Finally, some evidence seems to suggest that Moerbeke met the mathematician and astronomer Campanus of Novara at the papal curia.

Moerbeke may well have been in touch with

Aquinas at or near Rome before 1269 or between 1271 and 1274, but there is no reliable direct evidence of any personal relationship. It is a commonplace, repeated *ad nauseam* by almost all historians and scholars concerned with either Aquinas or Moerbeke, that the latter was prompted by the former to undertake his work as a translator, especially as a translator of Aristotle. This is most probably nothing more than a legend originating in hagiography, when "evidence" was offered by William of Tocco, a confrère of Aquinas, for the latter's canonization, about forty years after his death. What remains true is that Aquinas, like other philosophers of his time, used some—by no means all—of Moerbeke's translations soon after they were made.

Works. Only one original work by Moerbeke is preserved, under the title *Geomantia* ("Divination From Earth"). It was dedicated to his nephew Arnulphus and seems to have been quite popular: several manuscripts in Latin and one manuscript of a French translation made in 1347 by Walter of Brittany are still extant, but the treatise does not seem to have been studied by modern scholars. The authenticity of the attribution has been doubted on the ground that a "faithful follower of Aquinas" could not have written a treatise on matters condemned by the master, but the premise is unfounded. There is no reason to believe that the *Geomantia* is a translation from the Greek or Arabic. Witelo's evidence strongly supports the evidence for the attribution found in the manuscripts. Addressing himself to Moerbeke in the introduction to his *Perspectiva*, he says:

> As an assiduous investigator of the whole of reality, you saw that the intelligible being which proceeds from the first principles is connected in a causal way with individual beings; and when you were inquiring into the individual causes of these individual beings, it occurred to you that there is something wonderful in the way in which the influence of divine power flows into things of the lower world passing through the powers of the higher world . . .; you saw that what is acted upon varies not only in accordance with the variety of the acting powers, but also in accordance with the variety of the modes of action; consequently you decided to dedicate yourself to the "occult" inquiry of this state of affairs.

Preliminary studies of the *Geomantia* have shown a vocabulary consistent with Moerbeke's translations; explicit mentions of the causal chain from God through the heavens to events on earth, of the occult nature of at least some part of geomancy, as indicated by Witelo; and attribution to "Frater Guillelmus de Moerbeka domini pape penitentiarius." MCCCLXXXVII in some manuscripts should be MCCLXXVI because of

Moerbeke's death date, Witelo's statements, and the description "penitentiarius" and not "archiepiscopus Corinthiensis."

We do not know whether Moerbeke wrote any other original works; but we still possess many, if not all, of the translations which he made from the Greek. He undertook this activity, he says, "in spite of the hard work and tediousness which it involves, in order to provide Latin scholars with new material for study" and "in order that my efforts should add to the light to which Latins have access." His knowledge of the Greek language, perhaps scanty when he first embarked on translations, improved greatly in the course of the more than twenty years which he devoted partly to them. In this field Moerbeke was a very exacting scholar and philologist, comparable only, in the thirteenth century, with Robert Grosseteste. The unfavorable criticism brought against his versions— even against his latest and best—does not take into account two facts: first, that Greek scholarship among Latins in the thirteenth century was not the product of a long tradition and well-organized schools but the hard-won possession of isolated individuals; and second, that a very sound philosophy of language, accompanied by the need for detailed, literal interpretation of authoritative texts—biblical, legal, scientific, philosophical—required that translations should be strictly faithful, word by word, to the original. Within these limits Moerbeke was often excellent, although, like all translators, he made mistakes. He was meticulous in his quest for exactitude; he would search the Latin vocabulary with a sound critical sense and great knowledge, in order to find words which could convey to the intelligent reader the meaning of the Greek terms. If his search failed to produce the necessary results, he would form new Latin words by compounding two terms, or adding prefixes and suffixes on the Greek pattern, or even combining Greek and Latin elements: a typical example would be his rendering of $\alpha \dot{\upsilon} \tau o \kappa \dot{\iota} \nu \eta \tau o \nu$ by "automobile." In extreme cases he would resort to that great source of enrichment of a language, the transliteration, with slight adaptations, of foreign—in his case Greek—words. A test of Moerbeke's care in trying to pass on as much as possible of Aristotle's "light" can be found in his revisions, based on Greek manuscripts, of translations produced by such scholars as Boethius and James of Venice: in most cases where he introduced a change, a misinterpretation was put right, a serious mistake corrected, or a more appropriate shade of meaning introduced if his predecessor had missed a finer point. His scientific attitude toward language is also revealed by his attempt to reproduce the exact Greek sounds (mainly those of Byzantine Greek) in his transliteration of names or of newly introduced technical terms, for instance, by using "kh" for the Greek Χ.

Moerbeke applied his interest and gifts as a translator to four aims: (a) completing and improving the Latins' knowledge of Aristotle's works in all their encyclopedic extent; (b) making available to Latin readers some of the most valuable and comprehensive elaborations of Aristotle's treatises on logic, philosophy of nature, and psychology which had been written between about A.D. 200 and 550; (c) propagating the doctrines of Proclus, the greatest systematizer of Neoplatonic philosophy, on which Moerbeke's own philosophy so much depended; (d) introducing into the Latin West a more exact and extensive knowledge of Archimedes' achievements in mathematics and physics. He also contributed in a smaller measure to the knowledge of Greek medical literature and of works by Ptolemy, Hero, Alexander of Aphrodisias, and Plato.

Evidence for Moerbeke's authorship of the versions ascribed to him varies in strength. In a number of instances—all concerning works by Aristotle—he only revised, more or less thoroughly, versions made by earlier scholars. In the following survey two asterisks indicate the titles of translations for which the evidence of authorship is direct (the translator's name accompanying the text itself); a single asterisk indicates the titles of versions for which evidence is elicited from a linguistic analysis. Dates and places where the translations were made are given only in the relatively few instances for which the evidence is found at the end of the translation itself. Within square brackets is a short indication of the best existing edition, whenever this has been ascertained, or of one old edition (original or a reprint). Some additional information on editions will be found in the bibliography.

The translations or revisions so far identified and ascribed with some degree of probability to Moerbeke are the following:

I. Plato (see Proclus).

II. Aristotle.

(1) Works never before translated into Latin:
*Politica, *one version of bks. I–II.11 [P. Michaud-Quantin, Bruges, 1961] and **one complete [F. Susemihl, Leipzig, 1872; bks. I–III.8, with Aquinas' commentary, H. F. Dondaine and L. Bataillon, Rome, 1972].
*Poetica, 1278 [L. Minio-Paluello, Brussels, 1968].
**Metaphysica, bk. XI [Venice, 1562, and with Aquinas' commentary].
**De motu animalium* [L. Torraca, Naples, 1958].
**De progressu animalium* [unpublished].

(2) Works never before translated into Latin from the Greek:
**Historia animalium* [bk. I, G. Rudberg, Uppsala, 1908; bk. X.6, Rudberg, Uppsala, 1911; bks. II–IX unpublished].
***De partibus animalium*, Thebes, 1260 [unpublished].
**De generatione animalium*, two recensions [H. J. Drossaart Lulofs, Bruges, 1966].
**Meteorologica, bks. I–III [with Aquinas].
*De caelo, bks. III–IV [with Aquinas].

(3) Works of which Latin translations from the Greek already existed and which were translated anew by Moerbeke:
*Categoriae, 1266 [L. Minio-Paluello, Bruges, 1961; also (first half) A. Pattin, Louvain, 1971].
**De interpretatione*, 1268 [G. Verbeke and L. Minio-Paluello, Bruges, 1965].
**Meteorologica, bk. IV [with Aquinas' commentary].
*De caelo, bks. I–II [with Aquinas' commentary].
**Rhetorica, *first recension [unpublished]; **second recension [L. Spengel, Leipzig, 1867].

(4) Works translated from the Greek by other scholars and revised by Moerbeke:
**Analytica posteriora*, translated by James of Venice [L. Minio-Paluello and B. G. Dod, Bruges, 1968].
**De sophisticis elenchis*, translated by Boethius [B. G. Dod and L. Minio-Paluello, in press].
*Physica, translated by James of Venice [with Aquinas' commentary].
**De generatione et corruptione*, translated by an unknown scholar [with Aquinas].
*De anima, translated by James of Venice [with Aquinas].
*Parva naturalia, translated by various scholars: *De sensu and *De memoria [with Aquinas]; **De somno et vigilia* [H. J. Drossaart Lulofs, n.p., 1943]; **De insomniis et De divinatione* [H. J. Drossaart Lulofs, Leiden, 1947]; *De longitudine, *De iuventute, *De morte, *De respiratione [Venice, 1496].
*De coloribus, incomplete, translated by an unknown scholar [E. Franceschini, Louvain, 1955].
**Metaphysica, bks. I–X and XII–XIV [Venice, 1562] and I–X, XII [with Aquinas].
**Ethica Nicomachea*, translated by Robert Grosseteste [R.-A. Gauthier, Leiden–Brussels, 1973].

III. Commentators on Aristotle.

(1) Alexander of Aphrodisias:

**In meteorologica*, Nicaea, 1260 [A. J. Smet, Louvain, 1968]; *In De sensu* [C. Thurot, Paris, 1875].

(2) Themistius:

In De anima, Viterbo, 1267 [G. Verbeke, Louvain, 1957].

(3) Ammonius:

In De interpretatione, 1268 [G. Verbeke, Louvain, 1961].

(4) Philoponus:

In De anima, bks. I.3 and **III.4–9, 1268 [G. Verbeke, Louvain, 1966].

(5) Simplicius:

In categorias, 1266 [Venice, 1516; also (first half) A. Pattin, Louvain, 1971]; **In De caelo*, Viterbo, 1271 [Venice, 1540].

IV. Proclus.

**Elementatio theologica*, Viterbo, 1268 [C. Vansteenkiste, 1951].

**De decem dubitationibus*, **De providentia et fato*, **De malorum subsistentia*, Corinth, 1280 [H. Boese, Berlin, 1960].

In Platonis Parmenidis priorem partem commentarium, including Plato's *Parmenides* as far as 142A (shortly before 1286; authenticated by Henry Bate) [extensive sections edited by V. Cousin, Paris, 1820; last section, lost in Greek, and Plato's text edited by R. Klibansky and L. Labowsky, London, 1953].

In Platonis Timaeum commentarium, extracts, containing also a few passages from Plato's *Timaeus* [G. Verbeke, Louvain, 1953].

V. Alexander of Aphrodisias (see also above, under Commentators on Aristotle).

De fato ad imperatores and *De fato*, which is *De anima*, bk. II (authorship authenticated by the surviving Greek manuscript owned by Moerbeke and carrying his autograph title of possession) [P. Thillet, Paris, 1963].

VI. Archimedes.

De quam pluribus theorematibus, which is *De lineis spiralibus*, 1269 [J. L. Heiberg, Leipzig, 1890].

De centris gravium, which is *De planis aeque repentibus*, 1269 [N. Tartaglia, Venice, 1543].

Quadratura parabolae, 1269 [L. Gauricus, Venice, 1503].

Dimensio circuli, 1269 [L. Gauricus, Venice, 1503; partly, J. L. Heiberg, Leipzig, 1890].

De sphaera et cylindro, 1269 [introduction to bks. I and II, J. L. Heiberg, Copenhagen, 1887, and Leiden, 1890, respectively].

De conoidalibus et sphaeroidalibus, 1269 [unpublished].

De insidentibus aquae, 1269 [bk. I, N. Tartaglia, Venice, 1543; both books, Curtius Troianus, Venice, 1565; collations by J. L. Heiberg, Leipzig, 1890; several sections edited by Heiberg, Leipzig, 1913].

VII. Commentator on Archimedes and Eutocius.

On the De sphaera et cylindro, 1269 [a small section edited by J. L. Heiberg, Leipzig, 1890];

On the De centris gravium, 1269 [unpublished].

VIII. Hero of Alexandria.

Catoptrica, which is Pseudo-Ptolemy, *De speculis*, 1269 [W. (G.) Schmidt, Leipzig, 1901].

IX. Ptolemy.

De Analemmate, 1269 [J. L. Heiberg, Leipzig, 1907].

X. Galen.

**De alimentis*, Viterbo, 1277 [Venice, 1490].

XI. Pseudo-Hippocrates.

**De prognosticationibus aegritudinum secundum motum lunae*, which is (?) *Astronomia* [Padua, 1483].

Some Latin translations attributed at different times to Moerbeke have been proved or can be proved not to be by him. Among them are the Pseudo-Aristotelian *Rhetorica ad Alexandrum* (by Anaximenes of Lampsacus) and *Oeconomica* and Hero of Alexandria's [?] *Pneumatica* or *De aquarum conductibus*.

Influence. Moerbeke's influence can be assessed from different points of view.

1. The popularity of many of his Aristotelian translations is evidenced by the surviving manuscripts of the thirteenth to the fifteenth centuries; printed editions of the fifteenth, sixteenth, and later centuries; and versions or adaptations into French, English, Greek, and Spanish made in the fourteenth, sixteenth, nineteenth, and twentieth centuries. From about 100 to nearly 300 manuscripts and up to a dozen printed editions exist of works which had never before been translated into Greek, or older translations of which had been superseded or revised. This means that these works became accessible—and to a large extent comprehensible—to most Latin-reading students of philosophy, and that the philosophical

language adopted by Moerbeke (and in some cases his interpretations) has influenced philosophical culture since the thirteenth century.

2. The introduction into the Western Latin world—and the consequent extensive study in universities and ecclesiastical and monastic schools, or the less extensive but still very influential study by specialists—of works of Aristotle, Proclus, and Archimedes which had been practically lost sight of for several centuries. An extreme example is provided by Aristotle's *Politica*, which had never been the object of more than exceptional study—and that only among Greeks before the fifth and in the eleventh century—and was almost discovered for the world at large, and introduced as one of the basic classics of political thought, by Moerbeke through his translation. Again, it was through Moerbeke's translations that some of Proclus' works were taken up by eminent philosophers and became essential ingredients of philosophical outlooks which affected the background and contents of some of the great schools of thought of the later Middle Ages, Renaissance, and more recent times. This is particularly true for the *Elementatio theologica*, in which Moerbeke discovered the original text of those propositions which formed the nucleus of the *De causis*, possibly the most influential carrier of Neoplatonic doctrines, transmitted via the Arabic to the Latin schools of the late twelfth and following centuries; it is also true of Proclus' *In Platonis Parmenidis . . . commentarium* and *De providentia et fato*. A similar influence was exerted by the translations of Themistius' and Philoponus' commentaries on the *De anima*, of Simplicius' on the *Categoriae* and *De caelo*, and of Ammonius' on the *De interpretatione*. The importance of Moerbeke's translations of Archimedes has been sketched in a masterly way by M. Clagett in his article on Archimedes in vol. I of this Dictionary.

3. A better knowledge of the actual Greek texts of several works came about through Moerbeke's versions. In a few cases they are the only evidence for lost Greek texts (the whole of Hero's *Catoptrica* and Pseudo-Hippocrates' *De prognosticationibus secundum motum lunae*; an important section of Proclus' *Commentary on the Parmenides*; and some sections of Proclus' smaller treatises and of Archimedes' *De insidentibus aquae*). Apart from two instances, Moerbeke used for his translations manuscripts now lost or not yet identified; on many points some of them provide us with better evidence of the Greek originals than the known Greek manuscripts: this is especially the case for Aristotle's *Politica*. For every single work Moerbeke's translations add to our knowledge of the tradition and history of the Greek texts.

BIBLIOGRAPHY

I. ORIGINAL WORKS. Abundant bibliographical information can be found in G. Lacombe, L. Minio-Paluello *et al.*, *Aristoteles Latinus, Codices: Pars prior* (Rome, 1939; Bruges, 1957), 21–38; *Pars posterior et supplementa* (Cambridge, 1955), 773–782, 1277; and *Supplementa altera* (Bruges, 1961), 7–17. See also M. Grabmann, *Guglielmo di Moerbeke O.P., il traduttore delle opere di Aristotele*, vol. II of *I papi del duecento e l'Aristotelismo*, Miscellanea Historiae Pontificiae, XI (no. 20) (Rome, 1946), *passim*; and in the relevant sections of *Bulletin thomiste* and *Bulletin de théologie ancienne et médiévale*.

The existing MSS of translations from Aristotle and his commentators are listed and described in the 3 vols. cited above of *Aristoteles Latinus, Codices*; those of Archimedes in V. Rose, *Deutsche Literaturzeitung* (1884), 210–213, and J. L. Heiberg, "Neue Studien zu Archimedes," in *Abhandlungen zur Geschichte der Mathematik*, **5** (1890), 1–84; for Pseudo-Hippocrates, see H. Diels, "Die Handschriften der antiken Aerzte I," in *Abhandlungen der Preussischen Akademie der Wissenschaften* (1905). Most scholarly eds. contain additional information on the MSS. No survey was made of the printed eds. of Latin versions of Aristotle, accompanied or not accompanied by commentaries by Ibn Rushd, Aquinas, or others. The *Gesamtkatalog der Wiegendrucke* contains, under "Aristoteles" and the names of commentators, short descriptions of most eds. printed, or thought to have been printed, before 1501 but does not give sufficient identifications of the authors of the translations. The oldest eds. of some of Moerbeke's Aristotelian translations are found in fifteenth- and sixteenth-century printed texts. The eds. of Aristotelian writings mentioned in the text and carrying dates later than 1960 are contained in the series Aristoteles Latinus (part of the Corpus Philosophorum Medii Aevi); those of Aristotelian commentaries cited in the text dated 1957 and later are part of the Corpus Latinum Commentariorum in Aristotelem Graecorum; and most of those mentioned as being "with Aquinas" are found in the modern critical ed. of Aquinas' works, the Leonine ed. (Rome, 1882–). A critical ed. of all the translations from Archimedes and Eutocius based on Moerbeke's autograph is in vol. II of M. Clagett, *Archimedes in the Middle Ages*. The MSS of the *Geomantia* known to date are listed in L. Thorndike and P. Kibre, *A Catalog of Incipits of Mediaeval Scientific Writings in Latin* (1963).

II. SECONDARY LITERATURE. By far the most exhaustive study of Moerbeke's life and the best collection of evidence, information on the works which he translated and on the opinions expressed on them through the centuries, and references to modern scholarly studies is Grabmann's *Guglielmo di Moerbeke, il traduttore . . .* (cited above). This work suffers, however, from the wartime circumstances in which the material was being assembled and from the fact that it was left to be edited and translated into "Germitalian" by rather incompetent hands; the misprints affecting essential data are far too numerous. Its extreme bias in favor of Aquinas' and the popes' share in providing Moerbeke with the initiatives which were in fact his own is all-pervasive and misleading. Among the older works mention should be made of the article on Moerbeke in I. Quétif and I. Échard, *Scriptores ordinis praedicatorum*, I (Paris, 1791), 388–391. The best modern, concise, and critical survey listing Moerbeke's translations and their more important eds. is in P. Thillet's version of Alexander of Aphrodisias' *De fato* (cited in text); unfortunately, he ascribes to Moerbeke more recent Latin translations of Archimedes and Eutocius. For Moerbeke's early stay in Greece, see O. van der Vat, *Die Anfänge der Franziskaner Mission . . . im nahen Orient . . .* (Werl, 1934); B. Altaner's two long articles on the missionaries' linguistic knowledge in the Middle East, in *Zeitschrift für Kirchengeschichte*, **53** (1934) and **55** (1936); V. Laurent, "Le Pape Alexandre IV et l'empire de Nicée," in *Échos d'Orient*, **38** (1935), 26–55; K. M. Setton, "The Byzantine Background to the Italian Renaissance," in *Proceedings of the American Philosophical Society*, **100** (1956), esp. 31–35.

On Witelo and Bate, see C. Baeumker, *Witelo, ein Philosoph . . .*, III, pt. 2 of *Beiträge zur Philosophie des Mittelalters* (Münster, 1908); G. Wallerand, "Henri Bate de Malines et Thomas d'Aquin," in *Revue néoscolastique de philosophie*, **36** (1934), 387–410, and his ed. of the first part of Bate's *Speculum*, *Les philosophes belges*, XI, pt. 1 (Louvain, 1931). On the question of Aquinas' influence on Moerbeke, the best critical assessment is in R.-A. Gauthier's intro. to *Sententia libri ethicorum*, I, which is vol. XLVIII of *S. Thomae de Aquino opera omnia* (Rome, 1969), 232*–235*, 264*–265*. A page from Moerbeke's holograph of his Archimedes is reproduced in B. Kattenbach *et al.*, *Exempla scripturarum*, II (Rome, 1929), pl. 20; and his autograph inscription of property of the Greek MS of Alexander's *De fato* is reproduced in L. Labowsky, "William of Moerbeke's Manuscript of Alexander of Aphrodisias," in *Mediaeval and Renaissance Studies*, n.s. **5** (1961), 155–162.

Studies on Moerbeke's works and on their influence have been directed mainly to aspects of his method as a translator, particularly to his vocabulary, often for the purpose of ascertaining or suggesting his authorship or of distinguishing his version from those by other scholars. Apart from the extensive "indices verborum" which accompany most modern eds. of his texts (esp. the vols. in Aristoteles Latinus and Corpus Latinum Commentariorum Graecorum and the eds. by Drossaart Lulofs and Thillet cited in text as well as the forthcoming vol. II of Clagett's *Archimedes*) and linguistic analyses in some of the introductions (again by Clagett, Lulofs, Thillet, Verbeke, Vansteenkiste, and Rudberg), there are many special inquiries: F. H. Fobes, "Mediaeval Versions of Aristotle's *Meteorology*," in *Classical Philology*, **10** (1915), 297–314; F. Pelster, "Die griechisch-lateinischen Metaphysikuebersetzungen des Mittelalters," in *Beiträge zur Geschichte der Philosophie des Mittelalters*, supp. **2** (1923), 89–118; L. Minio-Paluello, "Guglielmo di Moerbeke traduttore della 'Poetica' d'Aristotele, 1278," in *Rivista di filosofia neoscolastica*, **39** (1947), 1–17; "Henri Aristippe, Guillaume de Moerbeke et les traductions latines médiévales des *Météorologiques* et du *De generatione et corruptione*,"

in *Revue philosophique de Louvain*, **45** (1947), 206–235; D. J. Allan, "Mediaeval Versions of Aristotle *De caelo* and the *Commentary* of Simplicius," in *Mediaeval and Renaissance Studies*, **2** (1950), 82–120.

Various points and aspects of Moerbeke's influence, the dates of his translations in relation to the dates of works in which use was made of them, and commentaries based on his versions have been the object of scholarly study in many books and articles devoted to wider issues. To those already mentioned one may add D. A. Callus, "Les sources de Saint Thomas," in *Aristote et Saint-Thomas d'Aquin: Journées d'études* (Louvain–Paris, 1957), 93–174; A. Dondaine, reviews in *Bulletin Thomiste* (1924 ff.); R. A. Gauthier's intro. to Thomas Aquinas, *Contra gentiles, livre premier* (Paris, 1961); B. Geyer, "Die Uebersetzungen der aristotelischen Metaphysik bei Albertus Magnus und Thomas . . .," in *Philosophisches Jahrbuch*, **30** (1917), 392–415; J. Isaac, *Le Peri Hermeneias en Occident de Boèce à Saint Thomas* (Paris, 1953); R. Klibansky, "Ein Proklosfund und seine Bedeutung," in *Sitzungsberichte der Heidelberger Akademie der Wissenschaften*, Phil.-hist. Kl., **5** (1928–1929); and "Plato's *Parmenides* in the Middle Ages and the Renaissance," in *Mediaeval and Renaissance Studies*, **1** (1943), 281–330; H. Lohr, "Mediaeval Latin Aristotle Commentaries," in *Traditio*, **23** (1967 ff.); A. Mansion, "Le commentaire de Saint Thomas sur le *De sensu et sensato* d'Aristote," in *Mélanges Mandonnet* (Paris, 1930), 83–102; C. Martin, "The Commentaries on the *Politics* of Aristotle in the Late Thirteenth and Early Fourteenth Centuries" (D. Phil. thesis, Oxford University, 1949; copy at the Bodleian Library, Oxford); and B. Schneider, *Die mittelalterlichen griechisch-lateinischen Uebersetzungen der Aristotelischen Rhetorik* (Berlin, 1971).

The study of the Greek tradition through Moerbeke's texts has been carried out extensively both in the process of editing the Greek texts—see, for instance, Heiberg's ed. of Archimedes and Eutocius (Leipzig, 1910–1915) and W. L. Newman's ed. of Aristotle's *Politica* (Oxford, 1887) —and as part of the Aristoteles Latinus (every vol. contains the results of this study). Many separate studies were devoted to problems in this field, including E. Lobel, "The Medieval Latin Poetics," in *Proceedings of the British Academy*, **17** (1931), 309–334, and the work of B. Schneider cited above.

Lorenzo Minio-Paluello

MOHR, GEORG (*b.* Copenhagen, Denmark, 1 April 1640; *d.* Kieslingswalde, near Görlitz, Germany, 26 January 1697)

Mohr was the son of David Mohrendal (or Mohrenthal), a hospital inspector and tradesman. His parents taught him reading, writing, and basic arithmetic, but his love for mathematics could not be satisfied in Denmark, and in 1662 he went to Holland, where Huygens was teaching, and later to England

and France. He returned to Denmark, but about 1687 he went again to Holland, this time because of a difference with King Christian V. Wishing to be scientifically independent, he remained aloof from official positions; but Tschirnhausen finally persuaded him to come to Kieslingswalde to participate in his mathematical projects. Mohr went there in 1695, accompanied by his wife, whom he had married in 1687, and by his three-year-old son. Only one of his works, the *Euclides danicus* (1672), a valuable short work, is known today; but his son claimed that he wrote three books on mathematics and philosophy that were well received by scholars.

Mohr is often mentioned in the intellectual correspondence of the day. He corresponded with Leibniz, with Pieter van Gent, and with Ameldonck Bloeck, a member of Spinoza's circle. In 1675 Oldenburg sent Leibniz a work of Mohr's on the root extraction of $A + \sqrt{B}$. Leibniz, in a letter of 1676 to Oldenburg in which he refers to "Georgius Mohr Danus, in geometria et analysi versatissimus," mentions that he learned from Mohr that Collins had the expansions for sin x and arcsin x. Unfortunately, little else of Mohr's scientific activity is known.

In 1928 Mohr's *Euclides danicus*, which had fallen into obscurity, was republished with a preface by J. Hjelmslev. Hjelmslev recognized that in 1672 Mohr had been dealing with a problem made famous 125 years later by Mascheroni, namely, that of making constructions with compass alone.

The book has two parts: the first consists of the constructions of the first six books of Euclid; the second, of various constructions. The problem of finding the intersection of two lines, which is of some theoretical importance, is solved incidentally in the second part in connection with the construction of a circle through two given points and tangent to a given line.

Hjelmslev made the acute observation that a minor variant of Mohr's constructions enables one to add and subtract segments on the sphere and in the hyperbolic plane.

The obscurity that befell Mohr and his book can be attributed, in some degree, to the presentation of the material. In the body of the book, Mohr does not state the issue until the very last paragraph, although the lines are referred to as "imagined" *(gedachte)*. In the dedication to Christian V, he does say that he believes he has done something new, and on the title page the issue is explicitly stated. Still, it would be easy for an inattentive reader to misjudge the value of the book.

According to Hjelmslev, Mascheroni's result—that all ruler and compass constructions can be done by compass alone—was already known and systematically expounded by Mohr. (The justice of this judgment and the question of the independence of Mascheroni's work are examined in the article on Mascheroni.)

The laconic Mohr tells us nothing about the genesis of his ideas. A guess is that the fundamental problem stems from a similar problem, that of the compass of a single opening, which was posed in the contests of the great Renaissance mathematicians. This conjecture might be supported by a historical study of the problems in the second part of the book: νεύσεις (inclinations) problems; maxima-minima problems; the problem of Pothenot, solved in 1617 by Snellius in his *Eratosthenes batavus;* and problems in perspective.

BIBLIOGRAPHY

Mohr's *Euclides danicus* (Amsterdam, 1672) was translated into German by J. Pál, with a foreword by J. Hjelmslev (Copenhagen, 1928).

Hjelmslev has written two articles on Mohr: "Om et af den danske matematiker Georg Mohr udgivet skrift *Euclides Danicus*," in *Matematisk Tidsskrift*, B (1928), 1–7; and "Beiträge zur Lebenabschreibung von Georg Mohr (1640–1697)," in *Kongelige Danske Videnskabernes Selskabs Skrifter, Math.-fysiske Meddelelser*, **11** (1931), 3–23.

A. SEIDENBERG

MOISEEV, NIKOLAY DMITRIEVICH (*b*. Perm, Russia, 16 December 1902; *d*. Moscow, U.S.S.R., 6 December 1955)

After graduating from the Perm Gymnasium in 1919, Moiseev entered the Faculty of Physics and Mathematics of Perm State University, where he also worked as a laboratory assistant. In 1922 he transferred to Moscow University, from which he graduated in 1923, having specialized in astronomy. In 1922 he became a junior scientific co-worker at the State Astrophysics Institute (since 1931 part of the P. K. Sternberg Astronomical Institute). After completing his graduate work there, in 1929 Moiseev defended his dissertation "O nekotorykh osnovnykh voprosakh teorii proiskhozhdenia komet, meteorov i kosmicheskoy pyli" ("On Certain Basic Questions of the Theory of the Origin of Comets, Meteors, and Cosmic Dust"). From 1929 to 1947 he taught mathematics at the N. E. Zhukovsky Military Air Academy. In 1935 he was awarded the degree of doctor of physics and mathematical sciences and the title of professor. He was director of the department of celestial mechanics at the University of Moscow from 1938 to 1955 and was head of the P. K. Sternberg Astronomical Institute from 1939 to 1943.

The recognized leader of the Moscow school of celestial mechanics, Moiseev published more than 120 works on the mechanical theory of cometary forms; the cosmogony of comets, meteors, and cosmic dust; theoretical gravimetry, including an original method (the "nonregularized earth") used in the theory of determining the forms of geoids from gravimetric observations; and dynamic cosmogony. To the study of the general characteristics of the trajectories of celestial bodies he applied qualitative methods based on the use of differential equations of movement and certain known integrals. He introduced qualitative regional characteristics of the trajectory, such as its contacts with certain given curves and surfaces and its longitudinal and transversal stability.

Moiseev applied qualitative methods to problems of certain specific celestial bodies, and his investigations of the characteristics of stability of orbital motion found many applications in problems of airplane and missile dynamics. His 1949 monograph *Ocherki razvitia teorii ustoychivosti* ("Essays of the Development of the Theory of Stability") presented a historical analysis of the subject from antiquity to the twentieth century.

From 1940 to 1955 Moiseev published the results of his investigations on secular and periodic perturbations and the motions of celestial bodies. He developed concepts of the internal and external environments and twofold averaging. Moiseev established his own, interpolational-average scheme to supplement those of Gauss and Delaunay. Approximate empirical integrals of motion, deduced from observations of celestial bodies, were used for averaging the force function. This method allows the integration of the averaged differential equations of motion and the computation of the ephemerides of perturbation of motion.

Moiseev's chief contributions to mathematics were his two new methods of solving systems of linear differential equations: the method of determinant integrals and the interational method.

BIBLIOGRAPHY

I. ORIGINAL WORKS. Moiseev's early writings are "O vychislenii kometotsentricheskikh koordinat chastitsy kometnogo khvosta" ("On the Computation of the Comet-centered Coordinates of the Particles of the Comet Tail"), in *Russkii astronomicheskii zhurnal*, **1**, pt. 2 (1924), 79–86; "O khvoste komety 1901 I" ("On the Tail of the Comet of 1901 I"), *ibid.*, **2**, pt. 1 (1925), 73–84; "O vychislenii effektivnoy sily i momenta izverzhenia chastitsy

kometnogo khvosta" ("On the Computation of the Effective Force and Moment of Ejection of the Particles of a Comet Tail"), *ibid.*, **2**, pt. 2 (1925), 54–60; and "O stroenii sinkhronnykh konoidov" ("On the Structure of Synchronic Conoids"), *ibid.*, **4**, pt. 3 (1927), 184–190.

Subsequent works are "Über einige Grundfragen der Theorie des Ursprungs der Kometen, Meteoren und des kosmischen Staubes (Kosmogonische Studien)" in *Trudy Gosudarstvennogo astrofizicheskogo instituta*, **5**, no. 1 (1930), 1–87; *Trudy Gosudarstvennogo astronomicheskogo instituta im P. K. Sternberga*, **5**, no. 2 (1933), 1–63; *Astronomicheskii Zhurnal*, **9**, nos. 1–2 (1932), 30–52; and *Trudy Gosudarstvennogo astronomicheskogo instituta im P. K. Sternberga*, **6**, no. 1 (1935), 5–28, 50–58; "Intorno alla legge di resistenza al moto dei corpi in un mezzo pulviscolare," in *Atti dell'Accademia nazionale dei Lincei. Rendiconti*, **15** (1932), 135–139, 377–381, 443–447; "Sulle curve definite da un sistema di equazioni differenziali di secondo ordine," *ibid.*, Ser. 6a, **20** (1934), 178–182, 256–265, 321–327; "O nekotorykh obshchikh metodakh kachestvennogo izuchenia form dvizhenia v problemakh nebesnoy mekhaniki" ("On Certain General Methods of Qualitative Study of the Forms of Motion in Problems of Celestial Mechanics"), in *Trudy Gosudarstvennogo astronomicheskogo instituta im P. K. Sternberga*, 7, pt. 1 (1936), 5–127; **9**, pt. 2 (1939), 5–45, 47–81, 165–166; **14**, pt. 1 (1940), 7–68; **15**, pt. 1 (1945), 7–26; and "O nekotorykh svoystvakh traektory v ogranichennoy probleme trekh tel" ("On Certain Properties of Trajectories in a Limited Three-Body Problem"), *ibid.*, **7**, pt. 1 (1936), 129–225; **9**, pt. 1 (1936), 44–71; **9**, pt. 2 (1939), 82–114, 116–131, 167–170; **15**, pt. 1 (1945), 27–74.

Also published in the 1930's were "Über die Relativkrümmung der zwei benachbarten Trajektorien. Zum Frage über die Stabilität nach Jacobi," in *Astronomicheskii Zhurnal*, **13**, no. 1 (1936), 78–83; "Su alcune proposizioni di morfologia dei movimenti nei problemi dinamichi analoghi a quello del tre corpi," in *Revista de ciencias* (Lima), **39** (1937), 45–50; "Über Stabilität Wahrscheinlichkeitsstrehnung," in *Mathematische Zeitschrift*, **42**, no. 4 (1937), 513–537; "O postroenii oblastey sploshnoy ustoychivosti i neustoychivosti v smysle Lyapunova" ("On the Construction of Areas of Continuous Stability and Instability in Lyapunov's Sense"), in *Doklady Akademii nauk SSSR*, **20**, no. 6 (1938), 419–422; and "O fazovykh oblastyakh sploshnoy ustoychivosti i neustoychivosti" ("On Phase Areas of Continuous Stability and Instability"), *ibid.*, 423–425.

Moiseev's later works are "O nekotorykh osnovnykh uproshchennykh skhemakh nebesnoy mekhaniki, poluchaemykh pri pomoshchi osredenenia raznykh variantov problemy trekh tel" ("On Certain Basic Simplified Schemes of Celestial Mechanics Obtained With the Aid of Averaging Different Variants of the Problem of Three Bodies"), in *Trudy Gosudarstvennogo astronomicheskogo instituta im Sternberga*, **15**, pt. 1 (1945), 75–117; **20** (1951), 147–176; **21** (1952), 3–18; **24** (1954), 3–16; and in *Vestnik Moskovskogo gosudarstvennogo universiteta*, no. 2 (1950), 29–37; "A. M. Lyapunov i ego trudy po teorii ustoychivosti"

("A. M. Lyapunov and His Works on the Theory of Stability"), in *Uchenya zapiski Moskovskogo gosudarstvennogo universiteta*, no. 91 (1947), 129–147; "Kosmogonia" ("Cosmogony"), in the collection of papers, *Astronomia v SSSR za 30 let* ("Astronomy in the U.S.S.R. for Thirty Years"; Moscow–Leningrad, 1948), 184–191; *Ocherki razvitia teorii ustoychivosti* ("Essays of the Development of the Theory of Stability"; Moscow–Leningrad, 1949); and "Obshchii ocherk razvitia mekhaniki vo Rossii i v SSSR" ("A General Sketch of the Development of Mechanics in Russia and in the U.S.S.R."), in the collection of papers, *Mekhanika v SSSR za 30 let* ("Mechanics in the U.S.S.R. for Thirty Years"; Moscow–Leningrad, 1950), 11–57.

The following were published posthumously: "Ob ortointerpolyatsionnom osrednennom variante ogranichennoy zadachi trekh tochek" ("On the Orthointerpolational Averaging Variant of the Limited Problem of Three Points"), in *Trudy Gosudarstvennogo astronomicheskogo instituta im P. K. Sternberga*, **28** (1960), 9–24; and *Ocherk razvitia mekhaniki* ("Essay of the Development of Mechanics"; Moscow, 1961).

II. Secondary Literature. On Moiseev and his work, see (listed in chronological order) the obituary in *Astronomicheskii tsirkulyar Akademii nauk SSSR*, no. 166 (1956), 24–25; and the biographies in *Trudy Gosudarstvennogo astronomicheskogo instituta im P. K. Shternberga*, **28** (1960), 5–9, with a list of 15 of Moiseev's works; *Ocherk razvitia mekhaniki* (cited above), 4–11, with bibliography of 21 works; and E. N. Rakcheev, in *Vestnik Moskovskogo gosudarstvennogo universiteta*, Seria matematika, mekhanika, no. 4 (1961), 71–77, published on the fifth anniversary of his death, with bibliography of 49 works. See also M. S. Yarov-Yarovoy, "Raboty v oblasti nebesnoy mekhaniki v MGU za 50 let (1917–1967 gg.)" ("Works in the Area of Celestial Mechanics at Moscow State University for Fifty Years"), in *Trudy Gosudarstvennogo astronomicheskogo instituta im P. K. Sternberga*, **41** (1968), 86–103.

P. G. Kulikovsky

MOIVRE, ABRAHAM DE (*b.* Vitry-le-François, France, 26 May 1667; *d.* London, England, 27 November 1754)

De Moivre was one of the many gifted Protestants who emigrated from France to England following the revocation of the Edict of Nantes in 1685. His formal education was French, but his contributions were made within the Royal Society of London. His father, a provincial surgeon of modest means, assured him of a competent but undistinguished classical education. It began at the tolerant Catholic village school and continued at the Protestant Academy at Sedan. After the latter was suppressed for its profession of faith, De Moivre had to study at Saumur. It is said that he read mathematics on the side, almost

in secret, and that Christiaan Huygens' work on the mathematics of games of chance, *De ratiociniis in ludo aleae* (Leiden, 1657), formed part of this clandestine study. He received no thorough instruction in mathematics until he went to Paris in 1684 to read the later books of Euclid and other texts under the supervision of Jacques Ozanam.

His Protestant biographers say that De Moivre, like so many of his coreligionists, was imprisoned during the religious tumult of 1685 and not released until 1688. Other, nearly contemporary sources report him in England by 1686. There he took up his lifelong, unprofitable occupation as a tutor in mathematics. On arrival in London, De Moivre knew many of the classic texts, but a chance encounter with Newton's *Principia* showed him how much he had to learn. He mastered the book quickly; later he told how he cut out the huge pages and read them while walking from pupil to pupil. Edmond Halley, then assistant secretary of the Royal Society, was sufficiently impressed to take him up after meeting him in 1692; it was he who communicated De Moivre's first paper, on Newton's doctrine of fluxions, to the Royal Society in 1695 and saw to his election by 1697. (In 1735 De Moivre was elected fellow of the Berlin Academy of Sciences, but not until 1754 did the Paris Academy follow suit.)

Once Halley had made him known, De Moivre's talents became esteemed. He was able to dedicate his first book, *The Doctrine of Chances*, to Newton; and the aging Newton would, it is said, turn students away with "Go to Mr. De Moivre; he knows these things better than I do." He was admired in the verse of Alexander Pope ("Essay on Man" II, 104) and was appointed to the grand commission of 1710, by means of which the Royal Society sought to settle the Leibniz-Newton dispute over the origin of the calculus. Yet throughout his life De Moivre had to eke out a living as tutor, author, and expert on practical applications of probability in gambling and annuities. Despite his powerful friends he found little patronage. He canvassed support in England and even begged Johann I Bernoulli to get Leibniz to intercede on his behalf for a chair of mathematics at Cambridge, but to no avail. He was left complaining of the waste of his time spent walking between the homes of his pupils. At the age of eighty-seven De Moivre succumbed to lethargy. He was sleeping twenty hours a day, and it became a joke that he slept a quarter of an hour more every day and would die when he slept the whole day through.

De Moivre's masterpiece is *The Doctrine of Chances*. A Latin version appeared as "De mensura sortis" in *Philosophical Transactions of the Royal Society*

(1711). Successively expanded versions under the English title were published in 1718, 1738, and 1756. The only systematic treatises on probability printed before 1711 were Huygens' *De ratiociniis in ludo aleae* and Pierre Rémond de Montmort's *Essay d'analyse sur les jeux de hazard* (Paris, 1708). Problems which had been posed in these two books prompted De Moivre's earliest work and, incidentally, caused a feud between Montmort and De Moivre on the subject of originality and priority.

The most memorable of De Moivre's discoveries emerged only slowly. This is his approximation to the binomial probability distribution, which, as the normal or Gaussian distribution, became the most fruitful single instrument of discovery used in probability theory and statistics for the next two centuries. In De Moivre's own time his discovery enormously clarified the concept of probability. At least since the fifteenth century there had been substantial work on games of chance that recognized the existence of stable frequencies in nature. But in the classic work of Huygens and even in that of Montmort, the reader was usually given, in the context of a game or lottery, a set of events of equal probability—a set of what were often called "chances"—and he was asked to derive further probabilities or expectations from this fundamental set. No one had a clear mathematical formulation of how "chances" and stable frequencies are related. Jakob I Bernoulli provided a first answer in part IV of his *Ars conjectandi* (Basel, 1713), where he proved what is now called the weak law of large numbers; De Moivre's approximation to the binomial distribution was conceived as an attempt to improve on Bernoulli.

In some experiment, let the ratio of favorable to unfavorable "chances" be p. In n repeated trials of the experiment, let m be the number of successes. Consider any interval around p, bounded by two limits. Bernoulli proved that the probability that m/n should lie between these limits increases with increasing n and approaches 1 as n grows without bound. But although he could establish the fact of convergence, Bernoulli could not tell at what rate the probability converges. He did obtain some idea of this rate by computing numerical examples for particular values of n and p, but he was unable to state the principles that underlie his discovery. That was left for De Moivre.

De Moivre's solution was published as a Latin pamphlet dated 13 November 1733. Introducing his translation of, and comments on, this work at the end of the last edition of *The Doctrine of Chances*, he took "the liberty to say, that this is the hardest Problem that can be proposed on the Subject of Chance" (p. 242). In this problem the probability of getting exactly m successes in n trials is expressed by the mth term in the expansion of $(a + b)^n$—that is, $\binom{n}{m} a^m b^{n-m}$, where a is the given ratio of chances and $b = 1 - a$. Hence the probability of obtaining a proportion of successes lying between the two limits is a problem in "approximating the Sum of the Terms of the Binomial $(a + b)^n$ expanded into a Series" (p. 243).

Working first with the binomial expansion of $(1 + 1)^n$, De Moivre obtained what is now recognized as $n!$ approximated by Stirling's formula—that is, $cn^{n+\frac{1}{2}}e^{-n}$. He knew the constant c only as the limiting sum of an infinite series: "I desisted in proceeding farther till my worthy and learned Friend Mr. James Stirling, who had applied after me to that inquiry," discovered that $c = \sqrt{2\pi}$ (p. 244). Hence what is now called Stirling's formula is at least as much the work of De Moivre as of Stirling.

With his approximation of $n!$ De Moivre was able, for example, to sum the terms of the binomial from any point up to the central term. This summation is equivalent to the modern normal approximation and is, indeed, the first occurrence of the normal probability integral. He even appears to have perceived, although he did not name, the parameter now called the standard deviation σ. It was left for Laplace and Gauss to construct the equation of the normal curve in its form

$$\int \frac{1}{\sigma \sqrt{2\pi}} e^{-\frac{1}{2}(\frac{x-\mu}{\sigma})^2} \, dx;$$

but De Moivre obtained, in a series of examples, expressions that are logically equivalent to this. He understood the rate of the convergence that Bernoulli had discovered and saw that the "error"—that is, the likely difference of the observed frequency from the true ratio of "chances"—decreases in inverse proportion to the square of the number of trials.

De Moivre's approximation is a theorem in probability theory: given the initial law about the distribution of chances, he could approximate the probability that observed frequencies should lie within any two assigned limits. Unlike some later workers, he did not imagine that his result would solve the converse statistical problem—namely, given the observed frequencies, to approximate the probability that the initial law about the ratio of chances lies within any two limits. But he did think his theorem bore on statistics. After summarizing his theorem, he reasoned:

Conversely, if from numberless Observations we find the Ratio of the Events to converge to a determinate quantity, as to the Ratio of P to Q; then we conclude that this Ratio expresses the determinate Law according to which the Event is to happen. For let that Law be expressed not by the ratio P : Q, but by some other, as R : S; then would the Ratio of the Events converge to this last, and not to the former: which contradicts our *Hypothesis* [p. 251].

Nowhere in *The Doctrine of Chances* is this converse reasoning put to any serious mathematical use, yet its conceptual value is great. For De Moivre, it seemed to resolve the philosophical paradox of finding regularities within events postulated to be random. As he expressed it in the third edition, "altho' Chance produces Irregularities, still the Odds will be infinitely great, that in process of Time, those Irregularities will bear no proportion to the recurrency of that Order which naturally results from ORIGINAL DESIGN" (p. 251).

All the mathematical problems treated by De Moivre before setting out his approximation to the binomial distribution are closely related to earlier work by Huygens and Montmort. They include the first intimation of another approximation to the binomial distribution, now usually named for Poisson. In the normal approximation, the given ratio of chances is constant at p; and as n increases, so does np. In the Poisson approximation, np is constant, so that as n grows, p tends to zero. It is useful in studying the probabilities of rather infrequent events. Although De Moivre worked out a particular case of the Poisson approximation, he does not appear to have guessed its subsequent uses in probability theory.

Also included in *The Doctrine of Chances* are great advances in problems concerning the duration of play; a clearer formulation of combinatorial problems about chances; the use of difference equations and their solutions using recurring series; and, as illustrated by the work on the normal approximation, the use of generating functions, which, by the time of Laplace, came to play a fundamental role in probability mathematics.

Although no statistics are found in *The Doctrine of Chances*, De Moivre did have a great interest in the analysis of mortality statistics and the foundation of the theory of annuities. Perhaps this originated from his friendship with Halley, who in 1693 had written on annuities for the Royal Society, partly in protest at the inane life annuities still being sold by the British government, in which the age of the annuitant was not considered relevant. Halley had very meager mortality data from which to work; but his article, together with the earlier "political arith-metic" of John Graunt and William Petty, prompted the keeping of more accurate and more relevant records. By 1724, when De Moivre published the first edition of *Annuities on Lives*, he could base his computations on many more facts. Even so, he found it convenient to base most of his computations on Halley's data, derived from only five years of observation in the city of Breslau; he claimed that other results confirmed the substantial accuracy of those data. In his tables De Moivre found it convenient to suppose that the death rate is uniform after the age of twelve. He did not pretend that the rate is absolutely uniform, as a matter of objective fact, but argued for uniformity partly because of its mathematical simplicity and partly because the mortality records were still so erratically collected that precise curve fitting was unwarranted.

De Moivre's contribution to annuities lies not in his evaluation of the demographic facts then known but in his derivation of formulas for annuities based on a postulated law of mortality and constant rates of interest on money. Here one finds the treatment of joint annuities on several lives, the inheritance of annuities, problems about the fair division of the costs of a tontine, and other contracts in which both age and interest on capital are relevant. This mathematics became a standard part of all subsequent commercial applications in England. Yet the authorship of this work was a matter of controversy. De Moivre's first edition appeared in 1725; in 1742 Thomas Simpson published *The Doctrine of Annuities and Reversions Deduced From General and Evident Principles*. De Moivre republished in the next year, bitter at what, with some justice, he claimed to be the plagiarization of his work. Since the sale of his books was a real part of his small income, money must have played as great a part as pride in this dispute.

Throughout his life De Moivre published occasional papers on other branches of mathematics. Most of them offered solutions to fairly ephemeral problems in Newton's calculus; in his youth some of this work led him into yet another imbroglio about authorship, involving some minor figures from Scotland, especially George Cheyne. In these lesser works, however, there is one trigonometric equation the discovery of which is sufficiently undisputed that it is still often called De Moivre's theorem:

$$(\cos \varphi + i \sin \varphi)^n = \cos n\varphi + i \sin n\varphi.$$

This result was first stated in 1722 but had been anticipated by a related formula in 1707. It entails or suggests a great many valuable identities and thus became one of the most useful steps in the early development of complex number theory.

BIBLIOGRAPHY

I. ORIGINAL WORKS. De Moivre's two books are *The Doctrine of Chances* (London, 1718; 2nd ed., 1738; 3rd ed., 1756; photo. repr. of 2nd ed., London, 1967; photo. repr. of 3rd ed., together with the biography by Helen M. Walker, New York, 1967); and *A Treatise of Annuities on Lives* (London, 1725), repr. in the 3rd ed. of *The Doctrine of Chances*. Mathematical papers are in *Philosophical Transactions of the Royal Society* between 1695 and 1744 (nos. 216, 230, 240, 265, 278, 309, 329, 341, 345, 352, 360, 373, 374, 451, 473). "De mensura sortis" is no. 329; the trigonometric equation called De Moivre's formula is in 373 and is anticipated in 309. *Approximatio ad summam terminorum binomii* $(a + b)^n$ *in seriem expansi* is reprinted by R. C. Archibald, "A Rare Pamphlet of De Moivre and Some of His Discoveries," in *Isis*, **8** (1926), 671–684. Correspondence with Johann I Bernoulli is published in K. Wollenshläger, "Der mathematische Briefwechsel zwischen Johann I Bernoulli und Abraham de Moivre," in *Verhandlungen der Naturforschenden Gesellschaft in Basel*, **43** (1933), 151–317. I. Schneider (below) lists all known publications and correspondence of De Moivre.

II. SECONDARY LITERATURE. Ivo Schneider, "Der Mathematiker Abraham de Moivre," in *Archive for History of Exact Sciences*, **5** (1968–1969), 177–317, is the definitive study of De Moivre's life and work. For other biography, see Helen M. Walker, "Abraham de Moivre," in *Scripta mathematica*, **2** (1934), 316–333, reprinted in 1967 (see above), and Mathew Maty, *Mémoire sur la vie et sur les écrits de Mr. Abraham de Moivre* (The Hague, 1760).

For other surveys of the work on probability, see Isaac Todhunter, *A History of Probability From the Time of Pascal to That of Laplace* (London, 1865; photo. repr. New York, 1949), 135–193; and F. N. David, *Gods, Games and Gambling* (London, 1962), 161–180, 254–267.

IAN HACKING

MOLIN, FEDOR EDUARDOVICH (*b.* Riga, Russia, 10 September 1861; *d.* Tomsk, U.S.S.R., 25 December 1941)

Molin graduated from the same Gymnasium in Riga at which his father was a teacher. He then entered the Faculty of Physics and Mathematics at Dorpat University (now Tartu University), from which he graduated in 1883 with the rank of candidate and remained in the department of astronomy to prepare for a teaching career. In the same year he was sent to Leipzig University, where he attended the lectures of Felix Klein and Carl Neumann. Under the guidance of Klein he wrote his master's thesis ("Über die lineare Transformation der elliptischen Functionen"), which he defended in 1885 at Dorpat, where he then became *Dozent*.

During this period Molin became acquainted with the works of Sophus Lie and began to study hypercomplex systems. His most profound results in this field were presented in his doctoral dissertation, which he defended in 1892. Despite his outstanding work, Molin was unable to obtain a professorship at Dorpat and in 1900 moved to Tomsk, in west-central Siberia, where he found himself cut off from centers of scientific activity. He occupied the chair of mathematics at Tomsk Technological Institute and from 1918 was professor at Tomsk University. In 1934 he received the title Honored Worker of Science.

Molin obtained fundamental results in the theory of algebras and the theory of representation of groups. In his doctoral dissertation, which concerned the structure of an arbitrary algebra of finite rank over a field of complex numbers C, he showed that a simple algebra over C is isomorphic to a complete ring of matrices. He also introduced the concept of a radical (the term was introduced by Frobenius) and showed that the structure of an arbitrary algebra is reduced essentially into the case where factor algebra by a radical decomposes into a direct sum of simple algebras. Cartan later obtained the same results, which he introduced into the case of an algebra over a field of real numbers. In 1907 Wedderburn extended Molin's and Cartan's results into the case of an algebra over an arbitrary field.

Studying the theory of representation of groups, Molin explicitly introduced a group ring and showed that it is a semisimple algebra broken into the direct sum of S simple algebras, where S is the order of the center. This proved the decomposability of the regular representation into irreducible parts. Molin showed that every irreducible representation of the group is contained in the regular representation. He also demonstrated that representations of groups up to equivalence are determined by their traces. At the same time analogous results were obtained in a different way by Frobenius, who later became acquainted with Molin's research and valued it highly.

BIBLIOGRAPHY

I. ORIGINAL WORKS. Molin's writings include "Über die lineare Transformation der elliptischen Functionen" (Dorpat, 1885), his master's thesis; "Über Systeme höherer complexer Zahlen," in *Mathematische Annalen*, **41** (1893), 83–156, his doctoral dissertation; "Eine Bemerkung über endlichen linearen Substitutionsgruppen," in *Sitzungsbe-*

richte der Naturforscher-Gesellschaft bei der Universität Jurjew, no. 11 (1896–1898), 259–276; "Über die Anzahl der Variabelen einer irreductibelen Substitutionsgruppen," ibid., 277–288; and "Über die Invarianten der linearen Substitutionsgruppen," in Sitzungsberichte der Preussischen Akademie der Wissenschaften zu Berlin, 52 (1897), 1152–1156.

II. SECONDARY LITERATURE. See N. Bourbaki, Éléments d'histoire des mathématiques (Paris, 1969), 152, 154; and N. F. Kanunov, O rabotakh F. E. Molina po teorii predstavlenia grupp ("On the Works of F. E. Molin on the Theory of the Representation of Groups"), no. 17 in the series Istoriko-Matematicheskie Issledovania ("Historical–Mathematical Research"), G. F. Rybkin and A. P. Youschkevitch, eds. (Moscow, 1966), 57–88.

J. G. BASHMAKOVA

MOLLWEIDE, KARL BRANDAN (b. Wolfenbüttel, Germany, 3 February 1774; d. Leipzig, Germany, 10 March 1825)

Mollweide graduated from the University of Halle, then became a teacher of mathematics in the Pädagogium of the Franckesche Stiftung there. In 1811 he was appointed to a position at Leipzig University, where he worked in the astronomical observatory that had been established in the old castle of Pleissenburg; the post carried with it the title of professor, and the following year he was made full professor of astronomy. In 1814 Mollweide was appointed to the chair of mathematics, one of the old and privileged university posts that carried with it the right to become dean or rector; he was twice dean during his eleven-year tenure at Leipzig.

Mollweide's two professorships left him little time to make astronomical observations—during term he usually gave four courses that met for fourteen to sixteen hours weekly. In his astronomy courses he emphasized the fixing of stellar positions, although he also treated the other branches of the subject; his mathematical courses comprised arithmetic, algebra, analysis, stereometry, trigonometry, analytical geometry, conics, and the theory of probability. He nevertheless was able to publish a number of scientific works; some of them represented his own researches, others were editions of standard authors and logarithmic tables.

Certain trigonometrical formulas and a conformal map projection are named for Mollweide. He is also known for his youthful dispute with Goethe over the latter's Farbenlehre, in which he defended the Newtonian theory of colors that Goethe was never able to accept.

BIBLIOGRAPHY

A more complete list of Mollweide's writings is in Poggendorff, II, cols. 180–181. They include "Beweis dass die Bonne'sche Entwerfungsart die Länder ihrem Flächeninhalt auf der Kugel gemäss darstellt," in Monatliche Correspondenz zur Beförderung der Erd- und Himmelskunde, 13 (1806); "Analytische Theorie der stereographische Projektion," ibid., 14 (1806); "Einige Projektionsarten der sphäroidischen Erde," ibid., 16 (1807); Prüfung der Farbenlehre des Herrn von Göthe und Verteidigung des Newtonschen Systems gegen dieselbe (Halle, 1810); Darstellungen der optischen Irrtümer in Herrn von Göthes Farbenlehre (Halle, 1811); Commentatio mathematico-philologica (Leipzig, 1813); Kurzgefasste Beschreibung der künstliche Erd- und Himmelskugel ... (Leipzig, 1818); Multiplex et continuus seriorum transformatio exemplo quodem illustratur (Leipzig, 1820); and Formula valorem praesentem pensionum annuarum comptandi recognitio et disputatio (Leipzig, 1823).

A short biography of Mollweide by Siegmund Günther is in Allgemeine deutsche Biographie, XXII (Leipzig, 1885), 151–154.

H.-CHRIST. FREIESLEBEN

MONGE, GASPARD (b. Beaune, France, 9 May 1746; d. Paris, France, 28 July 1818)

Monge revived the study of certain branches of geometry, and his work was the starting point for the remarkable flowering of that subject during the nineteenth century. Beyond that, his investigations extended to other fields of mathematical analysis, in particular to the theory of partial differential equations, and to problems of physics, chemistry, and technology. A celebrated professor and peerless chef d'école, Monge assumed important administrative and political responsibilities during the Revolution and the Empire. He was thus one of the most original mathematicians of his age, while his civic activities represented the main concerns of the Revolution more fully than did those of any other among contemporary French scientists of comparable stature.

The elder son of Jacques Monge, a merchant originally of Haute-Savoie, and the former Jeanne Rousseaux, of Burgundian origin, Monge was a brilliant student at the Oratorian collège in Beaune. From 1762 to 1764 he completed his education at the Collège de la Trinité in Lyons, where he was placed in charge of a course in physics. After returning to Beaune in the summer of 1764, he sketched a plan of his native city. The high quality of his work attracted the attention of an officer at the École Royale du Génie at Mézières, and this event determined the course of his career.

Created in 1748, the École Royale du Génie at Mézières had great prestige, merited by the quality of the scientific and practical training that it offered. Admitted to the school at the beginning of 1765 in the very modest position of draftsman and technician, Monge was limited to preparing plans of fortifications and to making architectural models, tasks he found somewhat disappointing. But barely a year after his arrival he had an opportunity to display his mathematical abilities. The result was the start of a career worthy of his talents.

Monge was requested to solve a practical exercise in defilading—specifically, to establish a plan for a fortification capable of shielding a position from both the view and the firepower of the enemy no matter what his location. For the very complicated method previously employed he substituted a rapid graphical procedure inspired by the methods of what was soon to become descriptive geometry. This success led to his becoming *répétiteur* to the professor of mathematics, Charles Bossut. In January 1769 Monge succeeded the latter, even though he did not hold the rank of professor. The following year he succeeded the Abbé Nollet as instructor of experimental physics at the school. In this double assignment, devoted partially to practical ends, Monge showed himself to be an able mathematician and physicist, a talented draftsman, a skilled experimenter, and a first-class teacher. The influence he exerted until he left the school at the end of 1784 helped to initiate several brilliant careers of future engineering officers and to give the engineering corps as a whole a solid technical training and a marked appreciation for science. The administrators of the school recognized his ability and, after obtaining for him the official title of "royal professor of mathematics and physics" (1775), steadily increased his salary.

Parallel to this brilliant professional career, Monge very early commenced his personal work. His youthful investigations (1766–1772) were quite varied but exhibit several characteristics that marked his entire output: an acute sense of geometric reality; an interest in practical problems; great analytical ability; and the simultaneous examination of several aspects of a single problem: analytic, geometric, and practical.

This was the period in which Monge developed descriptive geometry. He systematized its basic principles and applied it to various graphical problems studied at the École du Génie—problems taken, for example, from fortification, architecture, and scaffolding. That Monge left only a few documents bearing on this work is not surprising, since he was essentially coordinating and rationalizing earlier knowledge, rather than producing really original

material. Elements of descriptive geometry appeared very early in his teaching—to the degree that his familiarity with the graphical procedures currently in use and with the various branches of geometry allowed him to make the necessary synthesis. The documents from this period record the many investigations inspired by his readings in the rich collections of the library of the École du Génie. This research dealt with topics in infinitesimal calculus, infinitesimal geometry, analytic geometry, and the calculus of variations. His first important original work was "Mémoire sur les développées, les rayons de courbure et différents genres d'inflexions des courbes à double courbure." He published an extract from it in June 1769 in the *Journal encyclopédique*, and in October 1770 he finished a more complete version that he read before the Académie des Sciences in August 1771; the latter, however, was not published until 1785 (*Mémoires de mathématiques et de physique présentés à l'Académie . . . par divers sçavans . . .*, **10**, 511–550). By then some of the most important ideas in the memoir no longer seemed so original, because Monge had employed them in other works published in the intervening years. Nevertheless, this memoir is of exceptional interest, for it presents most of the new conceptions that Monge developed in his later works, as well as his very personal method of exposition, which combined pure geometry, analytic geometry, and infinitesimal calculus.

Wishing to make himself known and to have his work discussed, Monge sought out d'Alembert and Condorcet at the beginning of 1771. On the latter's advice, he later in the same year presented before the Paris Academy four memoirs corresponding to the main areas of his research. The first, which was not published, dealt with a problem to which he never returned: the extension of the calculus of variations to the study of extrema of double integrals. The second was the memoir on infinitesimal geometry mentioned above. The fourth treated a problem in combinatorial analysis related to a card trick.

In the third memoir Monge entered a field of study that was to hold his interest for many years: the theory of partial differential equations. In particular he undertook the parallel examination of certain equations of this type and of the families of corresponding surfaces. The geometric construction of a particular solution of the equations under consideration allowed him to determine the general nature of the arbitrary function involved in the solutions of a partial differential equation. Moreover, this finding enabled him to take a position on a question then being disputed by d'Alembert, Euler, and Daniel Bernoulli. Monge developed the ideas set forth in this memoir in two others sent to the Academy in 1772. The work presented in these papers was extended in four publications dating from 1776; two of these appeared in the *Mémoires* of the Academy of Turin and two in the *Mémoires* of the Paris Academy. In another paper (1774) Monge discussed the nature of the arbitrary functions involved in the integrals of finite difference equations. He also considered the equation of vibrating strings, a topic he later investigated more fully.

In May 1772 the Academy of Sciences elected Monge to be Bossut's correspondent. At this time he became friendly with Condorcet and Vandermonde. The latter's influence was probably responsible for two unpublished memoirs Monge wrote during this period, on the theory of determinants and on the knight's moves on a chessboard.

In 1775 Monge returned to infinitesimal geometry. Working on the theory of developable surfaces outlined by Euler in 1772, he applied it to the problem of shadows and penumbrae and treated several problems concerning ruled surfaces. A memoir composed in 1776 on Condorcet's prompting (and reworked in 1781 on the basis of a more thorough understanding) is of major importance, although not for its contributions to the practical problem of cuts and fills that served as its point of departure. Its great interest lies in its introduction of lines of curvature and congruences of straight lines.

Although in 1776 Monge was still interested in Lagrange's memoir on singular integrals, his predilection for mathematics was meanwhile slowly yielding to a preference for physics and chemistry. In 1774, while traveling in the Pyrenees, he had collaborated with the chemist Jean d'Arcet in making altitude measurements with the aid of a barometer. Having some instruments at his disposal in Mézières and working with Vandermonde and Lavoisier during his stays in Paris, Monge carried out experiments on expansion, solution, the effects of a vacuum, and other phenomena; acquired an extensive knowledge of contemporary physics; and participated in the elaboration of certain theories, including the theory of caloric and triboelectricity.

In 1777 Monge married Catherine Huart. They had three daughters, the two elder of whom married two former members of the National Convention, N.-J. Marey and J. Eschassériaux: the two present branches of Monge's descendants are their issue.

During the period 1777–1780 Monge was interested primarily in physics and chemistry and arranged for a well-equipped chemistry laboratory to be set up at the École du Génie. Moreover, having for some time been responsible for supervising the operation of a forge belonging to his wife, he had become interested in metallurgy.

His election to the Academy of Sciences as *adjoint géomètre* in June 1780 altered Monge's life, obliging him to stay in Paris on a regular basis. Thus for some years he divided his time between the capital and Mézières. In Paris he participated in the Academy's projects and presented memoirs on physics, chemistry, and mathematics. He also substituted for Bossut in the latter's course in hydrodynamics (created by A.-R.-J. Turgot in 1775) and in this capacity trained young disciples such as S. F. Lacroix and M. R. de Prony. At Mézières, where he arranged for a substitute to give some of his courses—although he kept his title and salary—Monge conducted research in chemistry. In June–July 1783 he synthesized water. He then turned his attention to collecting stores of hydrogen and to the outer coverings of balloons. Finally, with J. F. Clouet he succeeded in liquefying sulfur dioxide.

In October 1783 Monge was named examiner of naval cadets, replacing Bézout. He attempted to reconcile his existing obligations with the long absences required by this new post, but it proved to be impossible. In December 1784 he had to give up his professorship at Mézières, thus leaving the school at which he had spent twenty of the most fruitful years of his career. From 1784 to 1792 Monge divided his time between his tours of inspection of naval schools and his stays in Paris, where he continued to participate in the activities of the Academy and to conduct research in mathematics, physics, and chemistry. A list of the subjects of his communications to the Academy attests to their variety: the composition of nitrous acid, the generation of curved surfaces, finite difference equations, and partial differential equations (1785); double refraction and the structure of Iceland spar, the composition of iron, steel, and cast iron, and the action of electric sparks on carbon dioxide gas (1786); capillary phenomena (1787); and the causes of certain meteorological phenomena; and a study in physiological optics (1789).

Meanwhile, with other members of the Academy, Monge assisted Lavoisier in certain experiments. For example, in February 1785 he participated in the analysis and synthesis of water. In fact, he was one of the first to accept Lavoisier's new chemical theory. After having collaborated with Vandermonde and Berthollet on a memoir on "iron considered in its different metallurgical states" (1786), he participated in several investigations of metallurgy in France. In 1788 he joined in the refutation, instigated by Lavoisier, of a treatise by the Irish chemist Kirwan, who was a partisan of the phlogiston theory. That Monge was among the founders of the *Annales de chimie* testifies to his standing in chemistry. During this period Monge's position as naval examiner obliged him to write a course in mathematics to replace Bézout's. Only one volume was published, *Traité élémentaire de statique* (1788).

When the Revolution began in 1789, Monge was among the most widely known of French scientists. A very active member of the Academy of Sciences, he had established a reputation in mathematics, physics, and chemistry. As an examiner of naval cadets he directed a branch of France's military schools, which were then virtually the only institutions offering a scientific education of any merit. This position also placed him in contact, in each port he visited, with bureaucracy that was soon to come under his administration. It also enabled him to visit iron mines, foundries, and factories, and thus to become an expert on metallurgical and technological questions. Furthermore, the important reform of teaching in the naval schools that he had effected in 1786 prepared him for the efforts to renew scientific and technical education that he undertook during the Revolution.

Although Monge was a resolute supporter of the Revolution from the outset, his political role remained discreet until August 1792. He joined several revolutionary societies and clubs but devoted most of his time to tours of inspection as examiner of naval cadets and to his functions as a member of the Academy, particularly to the work of the Academy's Commission on Weights and Measures.

After the fall of the monarchy on 10 August 1792, a government was created to carry on the very difficult struggle imposed on the young republic by adherents of the *ancien régime*. On the designation of the Legislative Assembly, Monge accepted the post of minister of the navy, which he held for eight months. Although not outstanding, his work showed his desire to coordinate all efforts to assure the nation's survival and independence. His politics, however, were judged by some to be too moderate; and attacked from several sides and exhausted by the incessant struggle he had to wage, he resigned on 10 April 1793. Henceforth he never played more than a minor political role. A confirmed republican, he associated with Jacobins such as Pache and Hassenfratz; but he never allied himself with any faction or participated in any concrete political action. On the other hand, he was an ardent patriot, who placed all his energy, talent, and experience in the service of the nation, and he played a very important role in developing the manufacture of arms and munitions, and in estab-

lishing a new system of scientific and technical education.

Monge resumed his former activities for a short time; but after the suppression of the Academy of Sciences on 8 August 1793 his work came under the direct control of the political authorities, especially of the Committee of Public Safety. From the beginning of September 1793 until October 1794, he took part in the work of the Committee on Arms. He wrote, with Vandermonde and Berthollet, a work on the manufacture of forge and case-hardened steels, drew up numerous orders concerning arms manufacture for Lazare Carnot and C. L. Prieur, supervised Paris arms workshops, assembled technical literature on the making of cannons, gave "revolutionary courses" on this latter subject (February–March 1794), and wrote an important work on it. He also was involved in the extracting and refining of saltpeter and the construction and operation of the great powderworks of Paris. In addition, he participated in the development of military balloons.

Monge also engaged in tasks of a different sort. After the suppression of the Academy he joined the Société Philomatique; participated in the work of the Temporary Commission on Weights and Measures, which continued the projects of the Academy's commission; and took part in the activities of the Commission on the Arts, which was responsible for preserving the nation's artistic and cultural heritage. He was also active in the projects for educational reform then under discussion. His experience at the École de Mézières and in the naval schools explains the special interest that the renewal of scientific and technical instruction held for him. At the elementary level, he prepared for the department of Paris a plan for schools for artisans and workers that the Convention adopted on 15 September 1793 but rejected the next day. At a more advanced level, he was convinced of the value of creating a single national school for training civil and military engineers. Consequently, when he was appointed by the Convention (11 March 1794) to the commission responsible for establishing an École Centrale des Travaux Publics, he played an active role in its work. The memoir that Fourcroy prepared in September 1794 to guide the first steps of the future establishment ("Développements sur l'enseignement . . .") shows the influence of Monge's thinking, which derived from his experience at Mézières. Appointed instructor of descriptive geometry on 9 November 1794, Monge supervised the operation of the training school of the future *chefs de brigade*, or foremen, taught descriptive geometry in "revolutionary courses" designed to complete the training of the future students, and was one of the most active members of the governing council. After a two-month delay caused by political difficulties, the school—soon to be called the École Polytechnique—began to function normally in June 1795. Monge's lectures, devoted to the principles and applications of infinitesimal geometry, were printed on unbound sheets; these constituted a preliminary edition of his *Application de l'analyse à la géométrie*.

Monge was also one of the professors at the ephemeral École Normale de l'An III. From 20 January to 20 May 1795 this school brought together in Paris 1,200 students, who were to be trained to teach in the secondary schools then being planned. The lectures he gave, assisted by his former student S.-F. Lacroix and by J. Fournier, constituted the first public course in descriptive geometry. Like those of the other professors, the lectures were taken down by stenographers and published in installments in the *Journal des séances des écoles normales*.

Monge, who regretted the suppression of the Academy of Sciences, actively participated in the meetings held from December 1795 to March 1796 to prepare its rebirth as the first section of the Institut National, created by the Convention on 26 October 1795. But just when Monge's activities seemed to be returning to normal, events intervened that prevented this from happening.

Monge was named, along with his friend Berthollet, one of the six members of the Commission des Sciences et des Arts en Italie, set up by the Directory to select the paintings, sculptures, manuscripts, and valuable objects that the victorious army was to bring back. He left Paris on 23 May 1796. His mission took him to many cities in northern and central Italy, including Rome, and allowed him to become friendly with Bonaparte. At the end of October 1797 Monge returned to Paris, officially designated, with General Louis Berthier, to transmit to the Directory the text of the Treaty of Campoformio.

Immediately after returning, Monge resumed his former posts, as well as a new one, that of director of the École Polytechnique. But his stay in Paris was brief; at the beginning of February 1798 the Directory sent him back to Rome to conduct a political inquiry. While there, Monge took an active interest in the organization of the short-lived Republic of Rome. The following month, at the request of Bonaparte, he took part in the preparations for the Egyptian expedition. Although reluctant at first, he finally agreed to join the expedition. His boat left Italy on 26 May 1798, joining Bonaparte's squadron two weeks later. Monge arrived in Cairo on 21 July and was assigned various administrative and technical tasks. As president of the Institut d'Égypte, created on 21 August, he played an important role in the many scientific and technical projects undertaken by this body. He accompanied Bonaparte on a brief trip in the Suez region, on the disastrous Syrian expedition (February–June 1799), and, after another brief stay in Cairo, on his return voyage to France (17 August–16 October). During this period of three and a half years, in which he was for almost the whole time away from France, Monge's correspondence and communications to the Institut d'Égypte show that he was working on new chapters of his *Application de l'analyse à la géométrie*. Moreover, the observation of certain natural phenomena, such as mirages, and the study of certain techniques, including metallurgy and the cultivation of the vine, provided him with fruitful sources for thought. Meanwhile, at the request of his wife and without his knowledge, his *Géométrie descriptive* was published in 1799 by his friend and disciple J. N. Hachette, who limited himself to collecting Monge's École Normale lectures previously published in the *Séances*.

On his return to Paris, Monge resumed his duties as director of the École Polytechnique but relinquished them two months later when, following the *coup d'état* of 18 Brumaire, Bonaparte named him senator for life. By accepting this position Monge publicly attached himself to the Consulate. Although this decision may seem to contradict his republican convictions and revolutionary faith, it can be explained by his esteem for and admiration of Bonaparte and by his dissatisfaction with the defects and incompetence of the preceding regime. Dazzled by Napoleon, Monge later rallied to the Empire with the same facility and accepted all the honors and gifts the emperor bestowed upon him: grand officer of the Legion of Honor in 1804, president of the Senate in 1806, count of Péluse in 1808, among others.

Monge had to divide his time among his family, his teaching of infinitesimal geometry at the École Polytechnique, and his obligations as a member of the Academy of Sciences and of the Conseil de Perfectionnement of the École Polytechnique, and his duties as a senator. Further tasks were soon added. He was founder of the Société d'Encouragement pour l'Industrie Nationale and vice-president of the commission responsible for supervising the preparation and publication of the material gathered on the Egyptian expedition, *Description de l'Égypte*. Even though his duties as senator took him away on several occasions from his courses at the École Polytechnique, he maintained his intense concern for the school. He kept careful watch over the progress of the students, followed their research, and paid close attention to the curriculum and the teaching.

Most of Monge's publications in this period were written for the students of the École Polytechnique. The wide success of the *Géométrie descriptive* was responsible for the rapid spread of this new branch of geometry both in France and abroad. It was reprinted several times; the edition of 1811 contained a supplement by Hachette; and the fourth, posthumous edition, published in 1820 by Barnabé Brisson, included four previously unpublished lectures on perspective and the theory of shadows.

In 1801 Monge published *Feuilles d'analyse appliquée à la géométrie*, an expanded version of his lectures on infinitesimal geometry of 1795. In 1802, working with Hachette, he prepared a brief exposition of analytic geometry that was designed to replace the few remarks on the subject contained in the *Feuilles*. Entitled *Application de l'algèbre à l'analyse*, it was published separately in 1805; in 1807 it became the first part of the final version of *Feuilles d'analyse*, now entitled *Application de l'analyse à la géométrie*. This larger work was republished in 1809 and again in 1850 by J. Liouville, who appended important supplements.

Aside from new editions of the *Traité élémentaire de statique*, revised by Hachette beginning with the fifth edition (1810), and some physical and technical observations made in Italy and Egypt and published in 1799, Monge's other publications during this period dealt almost exclusively with infinitesimal and analytic geometry. For the most part they were gradually incorporated into successive editions of his books. His production of original scientific work began to decline in 1805.

A decline likewise occurred in Monge's other activities. Suffering from arthritis, he stopped teaching at the École Polytechnique in 1809, arranging for Arago to substitute for him and then to replace him. Although he wrote a few more notes on mathematics and several official technical reports, his creative period had virtually come to an end. In November 1812, overwhelmed by the defeat of the Grande Armée, he suffered a first attack of apoplexy, from which he slowly recovered. At the end of 1813 he was sent to his senatorial district of Liège to organize its defenses but fled a few weeks later before the advancing allied armies. Absent from Paris at the moment of surrender, he did not participate in the session of 3 April 1814, in which the Senate voted the emperor's dethronement. He returned shortly afterward and resumed a more or less normal life. In 1815, during the Hundred Days, he renewed his contacts with Napoleon and even saw him several times after Waterloo and the abdication. In October 1815, fearing for his freedom, Monge left France

for several months. A few days after his return to Paris, in March 1816, he was expelled from the Institut de France and harassed politically in other ways. Increasingly exhausted physically, spiritually, and intellectually, he found his last two years especially painful. Upon his death, despite government opposition, many current and former students at the École Polytechnique paid him tribute. Throughout the nineteenth century mathematicians acknowledged themselves as his disciples or heirs.

Scientific Work. Monge's scientific work encompasses mathematics (various branches of geometry and mathematical analysis), physics, mechanics, and the theory of machines. His principal contributions to these different fields will be discussed in succession, even though his mathematical work constitutes a coherent ensemble in which analytic developments were closely joined with material drawn from pure, descriptive, analytic, and infinitesimal geometry, and even though his investigations in physics, mechanics, and the theory of machines were also intimately linked.

Descriptive and Modern Geometry. Elaborated during the period 1766–1775, Monge's important contribution is known from his *Géométrie descriptive*, the text of his courses at the École Normale de l'An III (1795), and from the manuscript of his lectures given that year at the École Polytechnique. Before him various practitioners, artists, and geometers, including Albrecht Dürer, had applied certain aspects of this technique. Yet Monge should be considered the true creator of descriptive geometry, for it was he who elegantly and methodically converted the group of graphical procedures used by practitioners into a general uniform technique based on simple and rigorous geometric reasoning and methods. Within a few years this new discipline was being taught in French scientific and technical schools and had spread to several other Continental countries.

Monge viewed descriptive geometry as a powerful tool for discovery and demonstration in various branches of pure and infinitesimal geometry. His persuasive example rehabilitated the study and use of pure geometry, which had been partially abandoned because of the success of Cartesian geometry. Monge's systematic use of cylindrical projection and, more discreetly, that of central projection, opened the way to the parallel creation of projective and modern geometry, which was to be the work of his disciples, particularly J.-V. Poncelet. The definition of the orientation of plane areas and volumes, the use of the transformation by reciprocal polars, and the discreet introduction in certain of his writings of imaginary elements and of elements at infinity confirms the importance of his role in the genesis of modern geometry.

Analytic and Infinitesimal Geometry. Analytic and infinitesimal geometry overlap so closely in Monge's work that it is sometimes difficult to separate them. Whereas from 1771 to 1809 he wrote numerous memoirs on the infinitesimal geometry of space, it was not until 1795, in his lectures at the École Polytechnique, that he specifically developed analytic geometry.

Nevertheless, even in his earliest works, Monge sought to remedy the chief weaknesses of analytic geometry, although this discipline was then for him only an auxiliary of infinitesimal geometry. Rejecting the restrictive Cartesian point of view that was still dominant, he considered analytic geometry as an autonomous branch of mathematics, parallel to pure geometry and independent of it. Consonant with this approach, as early as 1772 and at the same time as Lagrange, Monge systematically introduced into the subject the elements defined by first-degree equations (straight lines and planes) that had previously not been part of it. He also solved the basic problems posed by this extension. Parallel with this endeavor, he sought, following Clairaut and Euler, to make up for the long delay in the development of three-dimensional analytic geometry. In addition Monge introduced an absolute symmetry into the use of the coordinate axes. He showed great analytic virtuosity in his calculations, some of which display, except for the symbolism, a skillful handling of determinants and of certain algorithms of vector calculus. His ability in this regard very early allowed him to establish the foundations of the geometry of the straight line (in Plücker's sense), which he systematized in 1795.

The first two editions (1795 and 1801) of Monge's course in "analysis applied to geometry" at the École Polytechnique contain as an introduction a brief statement of the principles and fundamental problems of this renewed analytic geometry, which was soon taught in upper-level French schools. With his disciple J. N. Hachette, Monge published in 1802 an important memoir, "Application de l'algèbre à la géométrie," which completed the preceding study, notably regarding the theory of change of coordinates and the theory of quadrics. In 1805 Monge collected these various contributions to analytic geometry in a booklet entitled *Application de l'algèbre à la géométrie*, which in 1807 became the first part of his great treatise *Application de l'analyse à la géométrie*. The many articles that Monge and his students devoted to individual problems of analytic geometry (change of coordinates, theory of conics and quadratics, among others) in the *Journal de l'École polytechnique*

and in the *Correspondance sur l'École polytechnique* attest to the interest stimulated by the discipline's new orientation.

Throughout his career infinitesimal geometry remained Monge's favorite subject. Here his investigations were directed toward two main topics: families of surfaces defined by their mode of generation, which he examined in connection with the corresponding partial differential equations, and the direct study of the properties of surfaces and space curves. Since the first topic is discussed below, only the principal research relating to the second topic will be presented here. In 1769 Monge defined the evolutes of a space curve and showed that these curves are the geodesics of the developable envelope of the family of planes normal to the given curve. In 1774, after having returned to this question in a memoir presented in 1771, Monge completed the study of developable surfaces outlined by Euler. Concurrently utilizing geometric considerations and analytic arguments, he established the distinction between ruled surfaces and developable surfaces; gave simple criteria for judging, from its equation, whether a given surface is developable; applied these results to the theory of shadows and penumbrae; and solved various problems concerning surfaces. In particular, he determined by means of descriptive geometry the ruled surface passing through three given space curves. Still more important is the memoir on cuts and fills, of which Monge made two drafts (1776 and 1781). The point of departure was a technical problem: to move a certain quantity of earth, determining the trajectory of each molecule in such a way that the total work done is a minimum. Through repeated schematizations he derived the formulation of a question concerning the theory of surfaces that he examined very generally, introducing such important notions as the congruence of straight lines, line of curvature, normal, and focal surface. This memoir served as a starting point for several of Monge's later works, as well as for important investigations by Malus in geometrical optics and by Dupin in infinitesimal geometry.

Several memoirs written between 1783 and 1787 contain numerous studies of families of surfaces and some new results relating to the general theory of surfaces and to the properties of certain space curves.

In *Feuilles d'analyse appliquée à la géométrie* (1795 and 1801) Monge assembled, along with general considerations regarding the theory of surfaces and the geometric interpretation of partial differential equations, monographs on about twenty families of surfaces defined by their mode of generation.

Application de l'analyse à la géométrie (1807) includes some supplementary material, notably attempts to find families of surfaces when one of the nappes of their focal surface is known. The manuscript of Monge's course for 1805–1806 also contains important additional findings (transformations by reciprocal polars, conoids, etc.). The richness and originality in Monge's lectures, qualities evident in this manuscript and confirmed by the testimony of former students, explain why so many French mathematicians can be considered his direct followers. Among them we may cite Tinseau and Meusnier at the École de Mézières, Lacroix, Fourier, and Hachette at the École Normale, and Lancret, Dupin, Livet, Brianchon, Malus, Poncelet, Chasles, Lamé, and still others at the École Polytechnique. Certain aspects of their writings show the direct influence of Monge, who thus emerges as a true *chef d'école*.

Mathematical Analysis. The theory of partial differential equations and that of ordinary differential equations occupies—often in close connection with infinitesimal geometry—an important place in Monge's work. Yet, despite his great mastery of the techniques of analysis and the importance and originality of certain of the new methods he introduced, his writings in this area are sometimes burdened by an excessive number of examples and are blemished by insufficiently rigorous argumentation.

As early as 1771 the memoirs presented to the Academy and the letters to Condorcet reflect two of the guiding ideas of Monge's work: the geometric determination of the arbitrary function involved in the general solution of a partial differential equation, and the equivalence established between the classification of families of surfaces according to their mode of generation and according to their partial differential equation. He returned to these questions several times between 1771 and 1774, developing many examples and extending his study to finite difference equations. Also, in the memoir of 1775 on developable surfaces he discussed the partial differential equation of developable surfaces and that of ruled surfaces.

From 1773 to 1786 Monge carried out new research in this area. In seven memoirs of varying importance he presented flawlessly demonstrated results, and a progressively elaborated outline of very fruitful new methods. His essentially geometric inspiration drew upon the ideas of his earliest papers and on the division, introduced by Lagrange, of the integral surfaces of a first-order partial differential equation into a complete integral, a general integral, and a singular integral. By means of his theory of characteristics Monge gave a geometric interpretation of the method of the variation of parameters. In addition he introduced such basic notions as characteristic curve, integral curve, characteristic developable, trajectory of characteristics, and characteristic cone. Monge was also interested in second-order partial differential equations.

In particular he created the theory of "Monge equations"—equations of the type

$$Ar + Bs + Ct + D = 0,$$

where A, B, C, D are functions of x, y, z, p, q, and where p, q, r, s, and t have the classical meanings—and solved the equation of minimal surfaces. Investigating the theory of partial differential equations from various points of view, Monge—despite some errors and a somewhat disorganized and insufficiently rigorous presentation contributed exceptionally fruitful methods of approaching this topic. For example, he demonstrated the geometric significance of the total differential equations that do not satisfy the condition of integrability, thus anticipating J. F. Pfaff's treatment of the question in 1814–1815. Monge also introduced contact transformations, the use of which was generalized by Lie a century later. In addition he determined the partial differential equations of many families of surfaces and perfected methods of solving and studying various types of partial differential equations.

Monge resumed his research in this area in 1795–1796 and in 1803–1807, when he completed his courses in infinitesimal geometry at the École Polytechnique, with a view toward their publication. He perfected the theories sketched in 1783–1786, corrected or made certain arguments more precise, and studied the area of their application.

Mechanics, Theory of Machines, and Technology. From the time he came to Mézières, Monge was interested in the structure, functioning, and effects of machines; in the technical and industrial problems of fortification and construction; and in local industry, particularly metallurgy. He held that technical progress is a key factor governing the happiness of humanity and depends essentially on the rational application of theoretical science. His interest in physics, mechanics, and the theory of machines derived in part from his view that they are the principal factors of industrial progress and, therefore, of social progress.

Monge discussed the theory of machines in his course in descriptive geometry at the École Polytechnique (end of 1794). His ideas, employed by Hachette in *Traité élémentaire des machines* (1809), were derived from the principle that the function of every machine is to transform a motion of a given type into a motion of another type. Although this overly restrictive conception has been abandoned, it played an important role in the creation of the theory of machines in the nineteenth century.

Monge's *Traité élémentaire de statique* (1788) was a useful textbook, and its successive editions recorded the latest developments in the subject, for example the theory of couples introduced by Poinsot. The fifth edition (1810) included important material on the reduction of an arbitrary system of forces to two rectangular forces.

The unusual experience that Monge had acquired in metallurgy was frequently drawn upon by the revolutionary government and then by Napoleon.

Physics and Chemistry. Although the details regarding Monge's contributions to physics are poorly known, because he never published a major work in this field, his reputation among his contemporaries was solid. His main contributions concerned caloric theory, acoustics (theory of tones), electrostatics, and optics (theory of mirages).

In 1781 Monge was selected to be editor of the *Dictionnaire de physique* of the *Encyclopédie méthodique*. He did not complete this task, but he did write certain articles.

His most important research in chemistry dealt with the composition of water. As early as 1781 he effected the combination of oxygen and hydrogen in the eudiometer, and in June–July and October 1783 he achieved the synthesis of water—at the same time as Lavoisier and independently of him. Although Monge's apparatus was much simpler, the results of his measurements were more precise. On the other hand, his initial conclusions remained tied to the phlogiston theory, whereas Lavoisier's conclusions signaled the triumph of his new chemistry and the overthrow of the traditional conception of the elementary nature of water. Monge soon adhered to the new doctrine. In February 1785 he took part in the great experiment on the synthesis and analysis of water; he was subsequently an ardent propagandist for the new chemistry and actively participated in its development.

In the experimental realm, in 1784 Monge achieved, in collaboration with Clouet, the first liquefaction of a gas, sulfurous anhydride (sulfur dioxide). Finally, between 1786 and 1788 Monge investigated with Berthollet and Vandermonde the principles of metallurgy and the composition of irons, cast metals, and steels. This research enabled them to unite previous findings in these areas, to obtain precise theoretical knowledge by means of painstaking analyses, and to apply this knowledge to the improvement of various techniques.

BIBLIOGRAPHY

I. ORIGINAL WORKS. A partial list of Monge's works is given in Poggendorff, II, 184–186. More precise and more complete bibliographies are in L. de Launay, *Un grand français: Monge* . . . (Paris, 1933), pp. 263–276, which includes a list of MSS and portraits; and in R. Taton, *L'oeuvre scientifique de Gaspard Monge* (Paris, 1951), pp. 377–393, which contains lists of MSS, scientific correspondence, and memoirs presented to the Académie des Sciences.

Works that were published separately are *Traité élémentaire de statique* (Paris, 1788; 8th ed., 1846), trans. into Russian, German, and English; *Avis aux ouvriers en fer sur la fabrication de l'acier* (Paris, 1794), written with Berthollet and Vandermonde; *Description de l'art de fabriquer les canons* . . . (Paris, 1794); *Géométrie descriptive* . . . (Paris, 1799), a collection in 1 vol. of the lectures given in 1795 at the École Normale de l'An III and published in the *Séances des écoles normales* . . . (7th ed., Paris, 1847; repr. 1922), trans. into German, Italian, English, Spanish, and Russian; *Feuilles d'analyse appliquée à la géométrie* . . . (Paris, 1801), a collection, with various additions, of lectures given at the École Polytechnique, which were published on separate sheets in 1795; *Application de l'algèbre à la géométrie* (Paris, 1805), written with Hachette; and *Application de l'analyse à la géométrie* (Paris, 1807), a new ed. of the *Feuilles d'analyse appliquée à la géométrie*, preceded, with special pagination, by *Application de l'algèbre à la géométrie* (new ed., 1809; 5th ed., 1850), J. Liouville, ed., with several appendixes, including Gauss's *Disquisitiones circa superficies curvas;* trans. into Russian, with commentary (Moscow, 1936).

II. SECONDARY LITERATURE. The most recent biography of Monge is P.-V. Aubry, *Monge, le savant ami de Napoléon: 1746–1818* (Paris, 1954). The most complete study of his scientific work is R. Taton, *L'oeuvre scientifique de Gaspard Monge* (Paris, 1951).

A few older monographs are still worth consulting, in particular the following, listed chronologically: C. Dupin, *Essai historique sur les services et les travaux scientifiques de Gaspard Monge* (Paris, 1819; repr. 1964); F. Arago, "Biographie de Gaspard Monge . . .," in *Oeuvres de François Arago, Notices biographiques*, II (Paris, 1853; repr. 1964), 426–592, trans. into German, English, and Russian; E. F. Jomard, *Souvenirs sur Gaspard Monge et ses rapports avec Napoléon* . . . (Paris, 1853); L. de Launay, *Un grand français: Monge, fondateur de l'École polytechnique* (Paris, 1933); and E. Cartan, *Gaspard Monge, sa vie, son oeuvre* (Paris, 1948).

A very complete bibliography of other works dealing with Monge is given in R. Taton, *L'oeuvre scientifique*, pp. 396–425. This list should be completed by some more recent studies, listed chronologically: C. Bronne, "La sénatorerie de Monge," in *Bulletin de la Société belge d'études napoléoniennes*, no. 9 (1953), 14–19; Y. Laissus, "Gaspard Monge et l'expédition d'Égypte (1798–1799)," in *Revue de synthèse*, **81** (1960), 309–336; R. Taton, "Quelques lettres scientifiques de Monge," in *84e Congrès* *des sociétés savantes. Dijon, Section des sciences* (Paris, 1960), pp. 81–86; J. Duray, "Le sénateur Monge au château de Seraing (près de Liège)," in *Bulletin de la Société belge d'études napoléoniennes*, no. 36 (1961), 5–17; A. Birembaut, "Deux lettres de Watt, père et fils, à Monge," in *Annales historiques de la Révolution française*, **35** (1963), 356–358; J. Booker, "Gaspard Monge and His Effect on Engineering Drawing and Technical Education," in *Transactions of the Newcomen Society*, **34** (1961–1962), 15–36; and R. Taton, "La première note mathématique de Gaspard Monge," in *Revue d'histoire des sciences*, **19** (1966), 143–149.

RENÉ TATON

MONTE, GUIDOBALDO, MARCHESE DEL (*b.* Pesaro, Italy, 11 January 1545; *d.* Montebaroccio, 6 January 1607)

[He is known as Guidobaldo del Monte, although his signature reads Guidobaldo dal Monte. The form Guido Ubaldo (from the Latinized version) is often used, Ubaldo being taken incorrectly as the family name.]

Guidobaldo was born into a noble family in the territory of the dukes of Urbino. While at the University of Padua in 1564 he studied mathematics and befriended the poet Torquato Tasso. Later Guidobaldo served in campaigns against the Turks and in 1588 was appointed visitor general of the fortresses and cities of the grand duke of Tuscany. Soon afterward Guidobaldo retired to the family castle of Montebaroccio near Urbino, where he pursued his scientific studies until his death.

Guidobaldo was a prominent figure in the renaissance of the mathematical sciences. At Urbino he was a friend and pupil of Federico Commandino and an intimate of Bernardino Baldi, the mathematical historian. In 1588 Guidobaldo saw Commandino's Latin translation of Pappus through the press at Pesaro. The autograph transcript had initially been sent to the Venetian mathematician Barocius for publication; but Barocius, having refused to edit the work without making extensive changes, sent the manuscript to Guidobaldo, who published the text exactly as he found it. Concerning Pappus, Guidobaldo also corresponded with the Venetian senator Jacomo Contarini, who helped Guidobaldo secure an appointment at Padua for Galileo. Guidobaldo's correspondence with these and other friends is an important source for the history of the mathematics of the period.

Guidobaldo's first book, the *Liber mechanicorum* (1577), was regarded by contemporaries as the greatest work on statics since the Greeks. It was intended as a return to classical Archimedean models of rigorous mathematical proof and as a rejection of the "barbaric" medieval proofs of Jordanus de Nemore (revived by Tartaglia in his *Quesiti* of 1546), which mixed dynamic principles with mathematical analysis.

The *Liber* may be seen as a forceful argument that statics and dynamics are entirely separate sciences; hence no unified science of mechanics is possible. This attitude is evident in Guidobaldo's treatment of equilibrium in the simple machines, which he terms the case where the power sustains the weight. He stresses that a greater power is needed to move the weight than to sustain it and that the power which moves has a greater ratio to the weight moved than does the power which sustains to the weight sustained. Consequently, the same principle and proportions cannot hold good for both moving and sustaining.

Galileo overcame this objection to a unified mechanics by positing that an insensibly greater amount of power was needed to move, than to sustain, a given weight. Guidobaldo had scorned the use of *insensibilia* in mechanics, probably because they were not susceptible of precise mathematical definition. Like his contemporary Benedetti, Guidobaldo attacked Jordanus, Cardano, and Tartaglia for assuming that the lines of descent of heavy bodies were parallel rather than convergent to the center of the earth. The answer of both Tartaglia and Galileo to this demand for unreasonable exactitude in mechanics was that, at a great distance from the center, the difference between the parallel and convergent descents was insensible.

This extreme concern for precision led Guidobaldo to reject the valid inclined-plane theorem of Jordanus in favor of the erroneous theorem of Pappus. Pappus' premise that a definite amount of force was needed to move a body horizontally was in accord with the view of Guidobaldo that more power was required to move than to sustain the body. Moreover, Jordanus' theorem seemed vitiated by its neglect of the angle of convergence of the descents. By supposing against Pappus (whom he named) and Guidobaldo (whom he did not name) that an insensible amount of power was required to move a body horizontally, Galileo was able to apply the principle of virtual displacements to both static and dynamic cases and was able to frame useful principles of virtual work and inertia. Guidobaldo's quest for mathematical rigor may have barred such imaginative concepts from his mind.

The most fruitful section of the *Liber mechanicorum* deals with pulleys, reducing them to the lever. This analysis—which is far superior to that of Benedetti—was adopted by Galileo. In two subsequent mechanical works Guidobaldo developed other ideas of this first book. These works were the *Paraphrase of Archimedes: Equilibrium of Planes* (1588), a copy of which was sent to Galileo, and the posthumous *De cochlea* (1615).

Guidobaldo was Galileo's patron and friend for twenty years and was possibly the greatest single influence on the mechanics of Galileo. In addition to giving Galileo advice on statics, Guidobaldo discussed projectile motion with him, and both scientists reportedly conducted experiments together on the trajectories of cannonballs. In Guidobaldo's notebook (Paris MS 10246), written before 1607, it is asserted that projectiles follow parabolic paths; that this path is similar to the inverted parabola (actually a catenary) which is formed by the slack of a rope held horizontally; and that an inked ball that is rolled sideways over a near perpendicular plane will mark out such a parabola. Remarkably the same two examples are cited by Galileo at the end of the *Two New Sciences*, although only as postscripts to his main proof—which is based on the law of free fall—of the parabolic trajectory.

Among Guidobaldo's nonmechanical works are three manuscript treatises on proportion and Euclid; two astronomical books, the *Planisphaeriorum* (1579) and the posthumous *Problematum astronomicorum* (1609); and the best Renaissance study of perspective (1600).

Guidobaldo helped to develop a number of mathematical instruments, including the proportional compass, the elliptical compass, and a device for dividing the circle into degrees, minutes, and seconds.

BIBLIOGRAPHY

I. ORIGINAL WORKS. Guidobaldo's published works are *Liber mechanicorum* (Pesaro, 1577; repr. Venice, 1615); Italian trans. by Filippo Pigafetta, *Le mechanice* (Venice, 1581; repr. Venice, 1615); *Planisphaeriorum universalium theorica* (Pesaro, 1579; repr. Cologne, 1581); *De ecclesiastici kalendarii restitutione opusculum* (Pesaro, 1580); *In duos Archimedis aequeponderantium libros paraphrasis* (Pesaro, 1588); *Perspectivae libri sex* (Pesaro, 1600); *Problematum astronomicorum libri septem* (Venice, 1609); and *De cochlea libri quatuor* (Venice, 1615).

MS works of Guidobaldo are the *Meditatiunculae*, Bibliothèque Nationale (Paris), MS Lat. 10246; *In quintum Euclidis elementorum commentarius* and *De proportione composita opusculum*, Biblioteca Oliveriana (Pesaro), respectively MSS 630 and 631; and a treatise on the reform of the calendar, Biblioteca Vaticana, MS Vat. Lat. 7058. A collection of drawings of machines by Francesco di Giorgio Martini in the Biblioteca Marciana (Venice), MS Lat. VIII 87(3048), was formerly owned by Guidobaldo. The present location of the MS *In nonnulla Euclidis elementorum expositiones* (item 194 bis in the Boncompagni Sale Catalogue of 1898) is not known.

Guidobaldo's letters (some are copies) are scattered: Biblioteca Nazionale Centrale (Florence), MSS Galileo 15, 16, 88; Biblioteca Comunale "A. Saffi" (Forlì), MSS Autografi Piancastelli Nos. 755, 1508; Archivio di Stato (Mantua), Corrispondenza Estera, E.XXVIII, 3; Biblioteca Ambrosiana (Milan), MSS D.34 inf., J.231 inf., R.121 sup.; Bodleian Library (Oxford), MS Canon. Ital. 145; Bibliothèque Nationale (Paris), MS 7218 Lat.; Biblioteca Oliveriana (Pesaro), MSS 193 Ter.; 211/ii; 426; 1580 (MS 1538 = Tasso to Guidobaldo); Archivum Pontificiae Universitatis Gregorianae (Rome), Cassetta 1, MSS 529-530; Biblioteca Comunale degli Intronati (Siena), MS K.XI.52; Biblioteca Universitaria (Urbino), MS Carità Busta 47, Fasc. 6; and Biblioteca Nazionale Marciana (Venice), MS Ital. IV, 63 (Rari V.259).

Favaro has printed the Galileo correspondence in the *Opere* of Galileo, vol. X; and the two Marciana letters in *Due Lettere*. Rose, *Origins*, prints Ambrosiana MS J.231 inf., and Arrighi, *Un grande*, has six letters from Oliveriana MS 426, with the prefaces of MSS 630 and 631. Most of *Le mechanice* is translated in Drake and Drabkin, *Mechanics*. Important pages from Paris MS 10246 are in Libri, *Histoire*, IV, 369–398.

II. SECONDARY LITERATURE. A bibliog. is in Paul Lawrence Rose, "Materials for a Scientific Biography of Guidobaldo del Monte," in *Actes du XIIe congrès international d'histoire des sciences, Paris, 1968*, **12** (1971), 69–72. The earliest biography is the short note by Guidobaldo's friend Bernardino Baldi, *Cronica de' matematici* (Urbino, 1707), 145–147. Baldi's full *Vita* has disappeared. Giuseppe Mamiani, *Elogi storici di Federico Commandino, G. Ubaldo del Monte . . .* (Pesaro, 1828), is informative, although few references are given. The Guidobaldo section was earlier published in the *Giornale arcadico*, vols. IX, X (Senigallia, 1821). The 1828 ed. is reprinted in Mamiani, *Opuscoli scientifici* (Florence, 1845).

On Guidobaldo's mechanics see Antonio Favaro, "Due lettere inedite di Guidobaldo del Monte a Giacomo Contarini," in *Atti del Istituto veneto di scienze, lettere ed arti*, **59** (1899–1900), 303–312. Pierre Duhem, *Les origines de la statique*, I (Paris, 1905), 209–226, was very critical of Guidobaldo. Stillman Drake and I. E. Drabkin, *Mechanics in Sixteenth Century Italy* (Madison, Wis., 1969), 44–52 and *passim*, are more favorably disposed.

Guidobaldo's astronomical interests are illustrated in Gino Arrighi, "Un grande scienziato italiano; Guidobaldo dal Monte . . .," in *Atti dell' Accademia lucchese di scienze, lettere ed arti*, n.s. **12** (1965), 183–199.

For mathematical instruments see Paul Lawrence Rose, "The Origins of the Proportional Compass," in *Physis*, **10** (1968), 54–69, and "Renaissance Italian Methods of Drawing the Ellipse and Related Curves," in *Physis*, **12** (1970), 371–404.

See also Guillaume Libri, *Histoire des sciences mathématiques en Italie*, IV (Paris, 1841), 79–84, 369–398; and Antonio Favaro, "Galileo e Guidobaldo del Monte," (*Scampoli Galileani 146*), in *Atti dell' Accademia di scienze, lettere ed arti di Padova*, **30** (1914), 54–61.

PAUL LAWRENCE ROSE

MONTEL, PAUL (*b*. Nice, France, 29 April 1876; *d*. Paris, France, 22 January 1975)

Paul Montel was the son of Aristide and Anaïs (Magiolo) Montel. His father was a photographer. He was educated in the Lycée of Nice, and in 1894 he was admitted to the École Normale Supérieure in Paris. After graduation in 1897 he taught classes in several provincial lycées preparing students for the competitive entrance examinations to the École Polytechnique and other engineering schools. He enjoyed teaching and liked a quiet life with plenty of leisure to devote to literature and travel, and he might have remained all his life a lycée professor if his friends had not urged him not to waste his talents and to start writing a thesis. He therefore returned to Paris to work on a doctorate, which he obtained in 1907. He did not become a university professor in Paris until 1918, occupying in the interim several teaching jobs in lycées and technical schools. During the German occupation he was dean of the Faculty of Science, and he was able to uphold the dignity of the French university in spite of the arrogance of the occupiers and the servility of their collaborators. Montel retired in 1946. He married late in life and had no children.

Most of Montel's mathematical papers are concerned with the theory of analytic functions of one complex variable, a very active field among French mathematicians between 1880 and 1940. The idea of compactness had emerged as a fundamental concept in analysis during the nineteenth century: provided a set is bounded in $\mathbf{R}^n$, it is possible to define for any sequence (x_n) of points of the set a subsequence (x_{n_k}) which converges to a point of $\mathbf{R}^n$ (the Bolzano-Weierstrass theorem). Riemann had sought to extend this extremely useful property to sets E of functions of real variables, but it soon appeared that boundedness of E was not sufficient.

Around 1880 G. Ascoli introduced the additional condition of equicontinuity of E, which implies that E has again the Bolzano-Weierstrass property. But at the beginning of the twentieth century Ascoli's theorem had very few applications, and it was Montel who made it popular by showing how useful it could be for analytic functions of a complex variable. His fundamental concept is what he called a normal family, which is a set H of functions defined in a domain $D \subset C$, taking their values in the Riemann sphere S and meromorphic in D, and satisfying the following condition: from any sequence of functions of H it is possible to extract a subsequence that, in every compact subset of D, converges uniformly either to a holomorphic function or to the point ∞ of S.

Montel's central observation is that if H consists of uniformly bounded holomorphic functions in D, it is a normal family; this is a consequence of the Cauchy integral and of Ascoli's theorem. From this criterion follow many others; for instance, if the values of the functions of a set H belong to a domain Δ that can be mapped conformally on a bounded domain, then H is a normal family. This is the case in particular when Δ is the complement of a set of two points in the complex plane $\mathbf{C}$.

Montel showed how the introduction of normal families may bring substantial simplifications in the proofs of many classical results of function theory, such as the mapping theorem of Riemann and Hadamard's characterization of entire functions of finite order. An ingenious application is to the proof of Picard's theorem on essential singularities: suppose O is an essential singularity of a function f holomorphic in $\Delta : O < |z| \le 1$. Then Picard's theorem asserts that $f(z)$ takes on all finite complex values, with one possible exception, as z ranges through Δ. It can be proved by observing that if there are two values that f does not take in Δ, then the family of functions $f_n(z) = f(z/2^n)$ in the ring $\Gamma : \frac{1}{2} \le |z| \le 1$ would be a normal family, and there would be either a subsequence (f_{n_k}) with $|f_{n_k}(z)| \le M$ in Γ, or a subsequence with $|f_{n_k}(z)| \ge 1/M$ in Γ, contradicting the assumption that O is an essential singularity of f.

Other applications made by Montel and his students concern univalent and multivalent functions and algebroid functions. He also investigated what he called quasi-normal families H, which are such that in the domain of definition D each point has a neighborhood in which H is a normal family, with the exception of a finite number of "irregular" points; the consideration of quasi-normal families leads to other applications to complex function theory.

Montel was also interested in the relations between the coefficients of a polynomial and the location of its zeros in the complex plane. For instance, if in a polynomial

$$1 + a_1 x + \cdots + a_{p-1}x^{p-1} + x^p + a_{n_1}x^{n_1} + \cdots + a_{n_k}x^{n_k}$$

the number p and the number k are given (but the a_j and the n_i are arbitrary), then the polynomial always has a root of absolute value at most

$$\binom{k+p}{p}^{1/p}$$

Montel often was invited to lecture in countries where most mathematicians understood French, such as Belgium and Egypt, and in South America. He was especially honored in Rumania, which he visited often and where he had several students. He was the recipient of many honors and was elected a member of the French Academy of Sciences in 1937.

BIBLIOGRAPHY

Selecta, 1897–1947: Cinquantenaire scientifique (Paris, 1947); F. J. Beer, ed., *Paul Montel, mathématicien niçois* (Nice, 1966).

JEAN DIEUDONNÉ

MONTMORT, PIERRE RÉMOND DE (*b.* Paris, France, 27 October 1678; *d.* Paris, 7 October 1719)

Montmort was the second of the three sons of François Rémond and Marguerite Ralle. On the advice of his father he studied law, but tired of it and ran away to England. He toured extensively there and in Germany, returning to France only in 1699, just before his father's death. He had a substantial inheritance, which he did not exploit frivolously.

Having recently read, and been much impressed by, the work of Nicolas Malebranche, Montmort began study under that philosopher. With Malebranche he mastered Cartesian physics and philosophy, and he and a young mathematician, François Nicole, taught themselves the new mathematics. When Montmort visited London again in 1700, it was to meet English scientists; he duly presented himself to Newton. On his return to Paris, his brother persuaded him to become a canon at Notre Dame de Paris. He was a good ecclesiastic until he bought an estate at Montmort and went to call on the grand lady of the neighborhood, the duchess of Angoulême. He fell in love with her niece, and in due course gave up his clerical office and married. It is said to have been an exceptionally happy household.

Montmort's book on probability, *Essay d'analyse sur les jeux de hazard*, which came out in 1708, made his reputation among scientists and led to a fruitful collaboration with Nikolaus I Bernoulli. The Royal Society of London elected Montmort fellow when he was visiting England in 1715 to watch the total eclipse of the sun in the company of the astronomer royal, Edmond Halley. The Académie Royale des Sciences made him an associate member the following year— he could not be granted full membership because he did not reside in Paris. He died during a smallpox epidemic in 1719.

It is not clear why Montmort undertook a systematic

exposition of the theory of games of chance. Gaming was a common pastime among the lesser nobility whom he frequented, but it had not been treated mathematically since Christiaan Huygens' monograph of 1657. Although there had been isolated publications about individual games, and occasional attempts to come to grips with annuities, Jakob I Bernoulli's major work on probability, the *Ars conjectandi*, had not yet been published. Bernoulli's work was nearly complete at his death in 1705; two obituary notices give brief accounts of it. Montmort set out to follow what he took to be Bernoulli's plan.

One obituary gave a fair idea of Bernoulli's proof of the first limit theorem in probability, but Montmort, a lesser mathematician, was not able to reach a comparable result unaided. He therefore continued along the lines laid down by Huygens and made analyses of fashionable games of chance in order to solve problems in combinations and the summation of series. For example, he drew upon the game that he calls "treize," in which the thirteen cards of one suit are shuffled and then drawn one after the other. The player who is drawing wins the round if and only if a card is drawn in its own place, that is, if the *n*th card to be drawn is itself the card *n*. In the generalized game, the pack consists of *m* cards marked in serial order. The chance of winning is shown to be

$$\sum_{i=1}^{i=m} \frac{(-1)^{i-1}}{i!}.$$

A 1793 paper by Leibniz provided Montmort with a rough idea of the limit to which this tends as *m* increases, but Euler was the first to state it as $1 - e^{-1}$.

The greatest value of Montmort's book lay perhaps not in its solutions but in its systematic setting out of problems about games, which are shown to have important mathematical properties worthy of further work. The book aroused Nikolaus I Bernoulli's interest in particular and the 1713 edition includes the mathematical correspondence of the two men. This correspondence in turn provided an incentive for Nikolaus to publish the *Ars conjectandi* of his uncle Jakob I Bernoulli, thereby providing mathematics with a first step beyond mere combinatorial problems in probability.

The work of De Moivre is, to say the least, a continuation of the inquiries of Montmort. Montmort put the case more strongly—he accused De Moivre of stealing his ideas without acknowledgment. De Moivre's *De mensura sortis* appeared in 1711 and Montmort attacked it scathingly in the 1713 edition of his own *Essay*. Montmort's friends tried to soothe him, and largely succeeded. He tried to correspond with De Moivre, but the latter seldom replied. In 1717 Montmort told Brook Taylor that two years earlier he had sent ten theorems to De Moivre; he implied that De Moivre could be expected to publish them.

Taylor was doing his best work at this time. He and Montmort had struck up a close friendship in 1715, and corresponded about not only mathematics but also general questions of philosophy, Montmort mildly defending Cartesian principles against the sturdy Newtonian doctrines of Taylor. Montmort's only other mathematical publication, an essay on summing infinite series, has an appendix by Taylor. It is notable that in this period of vigorous strife between followers of Newton and Leibniz, Montmort was able to remain on the best of terms with both the Bernoullis and the Englishmen.

BIBLIOGRAPHY

I. Original Works. Montmort's mathematical writings are *Essay d'analyse sur les jeux de hazard* (Paris, 1708), 2nd ed. revised and augmented with correspondence between Montmort and N. Bernoulli (Paris, 1713; 1714); and "De seriebus infinitis tractatus," in *Philosophical Transactions of the Royal Society*, **30** (1720), 633–675. Part of Montmort's correspondence with Taylor is in William Young, ed., Brook Taylor, *Contemplatio philosophica* (London, 1793).

II. Secondary Literature. See "Éloge de M. de Montmort," in *Histoire de l'Académie royale des sciences pour l'année 1719* (1721), 83–93.

Ian Hacking

MONTUCLA, JEAN ÉTIENNE (*b.* Lyons, France, 5 September 1725; *d.* Versailles, France, 19 December 1799)

Montucla, the son of a merchant, attended the Jesuit *collège* in Lyons, where he received a thorough education in mathematics and ancient languages. Following the death of his father in 1741 and of his grandmother, who was caring for him, in 1745, he began legal studies at Toulouse. On their completion he went to Paris, drawn by the many opportunities for further training. Soon after his arrival there he undertook the study of the history of mathematics. His work on the quadrature of the circle (1754) brought him a corresponding membership in the Berlin Academy. In the same year he announced the forthcoming publication of what was to be his masterpiece, *Histoire des mathématiques*. The exchange of ideas in the literary circle that had formed around the bookseller and publisher Charles Antoine Jombert (1712–1784), which included Diderot, d'Alembert, and Lalande, was very valuable to him. Before the

appearance of *Histoire des mathématiques*, Montucla published, in collaboration with the physician Pierre Joseph Morisot-Deslandes, a collection of sources on smallpox vaccination (1756).

From 1761 Montucla held several government posts. His first appointment was as secretary of the intendance of Dauphiné in Grenoble, where in 1763 he married Marie Françoise Romand. In 1764–1765 he was made royal astronomer and secretary to Turgot on a mission to Cayenne. After his return, Montucla became inspector of royal buildings (1766–1789) and, later, royal censor (1775). From this period date his new edition of Ozanam's *Récréations mathématiques* (1778) and his translation of Jonathan Carver's account of travels in North America (1784).

As a result of the Revolution, Montucla lost his posts and most of his wealth. He was again given public office in 1795—examination of the treaties deposited in the archives of the Ministry of Foreign Affairs—but the salary was not sufficient to meet his expenses, so he also worked in an office of the national lottery. During these years Montucla, at the insistence of his friends, began to prepare an improved and much enlarged edition of *Histoire des mathématiques*. The first two volumes appeared in August 1799, four months before his death, just when he had been promised a pension of 2,400 francs.

Montucla's major work, the first classical history of mathematics, was a comprehensive and, relative to the state of contemporary scholarship, accurate description of the development of the subject in various countries. The account also included mechanics, astronomy, optics, and music, which were then considered subdivisions of mathematics; these branches *(mathématiques mixtes)* receive a thorough treatment in both editions, and only a third of the space is devoted to pure mathematics. The first volume of the two-volume edition of 1758 covers the beginnings, the Greeks (including the Byzantines), and the West until the start of the seventeenth century; the second volume is devoted entirely to the latter century. Montucla originally planned to take his work up to the middle of the eighteenth century in a third volume but could not do so, principally because of the abundance of material. In the second edition, extended to cover the whole of the eighteenth century, he was able to reach this goal. Much remained unfinished, however, since Montucla died during the printing of the third volume. Lalande, his friend from childhood, assisted by others, completed volumes III (pure mathematics, optics, mechanics) and IV (astronomy, mathematical geography, navigation) and published them in 1802.

Many authors before Montucla—beginning with

Proclus and al-Nadīm—had written on the history of mathematics. Their accounts can be found in the citations of ancient authors, in the prefaces to many mathematical works of the sixteenth through eighteenth centuries, in university addresses (for example, that of Regiomontanus at Padua in 1464), and in two earlier books that, as their titles indicate, were devoted to the history of mathematics: G. I. Vossius' *De universae mathesios natura et constitutione* (1650) and J. C. Heilbronner's *Historia matheseos universae* (1742). All these early efforts constituted only a modest beginning, containing many errors and legends, and the latter two works give only a jumble of names, dates, and titles. Montucla was familiar with all this material and saw what was required: a comprehensive history of the development of mathematical ideas, such as had been called for by Bacon and Montmor. Inspired by them Montucla undertook the immense labor, the difficulty of which he recognized and which he carried out with his own research in and mastery of the original texts.

Montucla had no successor until Moritz Cantor. The *Histoire des mathématiques* is, of course, obsolete—as, in many respects, is Cantor's *Vorlesungen*. Yet even today the expert can, with the requisite caution, go back to Montucla, especially with regard to the mathematics of the seventeenth century.

BIBLIOGRAPHY

I. ORIGINAL WORKS. Montucla's writings include *Histoire des recherches sur la quadrature du cercle* (Paris, 1754); *Recueil de pièces concernant l'inoculation de la petite vérole et propres à en prouver la sécurité et l'utilité* (Paris, 1756), written with Morisot-Deslandes; *Histoire des mathématiques*, 2 vols. (Paris, 1758; 2nd ed., 4 vols., Paris, 1799–1802); a new ed. of Ozanam's *Récréations mathématiques et physiques* (Paris, 1778); and a translation, from the 3rd English ed., of Jonathan Carver, *Voyages dans les parties intérieures de l'Amérique septentrionale, pendant les années 1766, 1767, et 1768* (Paris, 1784).

II. SECONDARY LITERATURE. See the following, listed chronologically: Auguste Savinien Le Blond, "Sur la vie et les ouvrages de Montucla. Extrait de la notice historique lue à la Société de Versailles, le 15 janvier 1800. Avec des additions par Jérôme de Lalande," in Montucla's *Histoire des mathématiques*, IV, 662–672; G. Sarton, "Montucla (1725–1799). His Life and Works," in *Osiris*, **1** (1936), 519–567, with a portrait, the title page of each of his works, two previously unpublished letters, and further bibliographical information; and Kurt Vogel, "L'historiographie mathématique avant Montucla," in *Actes du XIᵉ Congrès international d'histoire des sciences*. III, 179–184.

KURT VOGEL

MOORE, ELIAKIM HASTINGS (*b.* Marietta, Ohio, 26 January 1862; *d.* Chicago, Illinois, 30 December 1932)

Moore was prominent among the small circle of men who greatly influenced the rapid development of American mathematics at the turn of the twentieth century. The son of David Hastings Moore, a Methodist minister, and Julia Sophia Carpenter, he had an impressive preparation for his future career. While still in high school he served one summer as an assistant to Ormond Stone, the director of the Cincinnati Observatory, who aroused his interest in mathematics. He later attended Yale University, from which he received the A.B. in 1883 as class valedictorian and the Ph.D. in 1885. The mathematician Hubert Anson Newton, his guiding spirit at Yale, then financed a year's study abroad for him at the universities of Göttingen and Berlin. He spent the summer of 1885 in Göttingen, where he studied the German language; and the winter of 1885–1886 in Berlin, where Kronecker and Weierstrass were lecturing. The work of Kronecker impressed him, as did the rigorous methods of Weierstrass and Klein, who was then at Leipzig.

In 1886 Moore returned to the United States to begin his career in mathematics. He accepted an instructorship at the academy of Northwestern University for 1886–1887. During the next two years he was a tutor at Yale. In 1889 he returned to Northwestern as an assistant professor and in 1891 was promoted to associate professor. When the University of Chicago first opened in the autumn of 1892, Moore was appointed professor and acting head of the mathematics department. In 1896, after successfully organizing the new department, he became its permanent chairman, a post he held until his partial retirement in 1931. Shortly before assuming his post at Chicago, he married a childhood playmate, Martha Morris Young, on 21 June 1892, in Columbus, Ohio. They had two sons, David and Eliakim.

During his career Moore became a leader at the University of Chicago and in mathematical associations. He helped shape the character of the university and gave it great distinction. With his faculty colleagues Oskar Bolza and Heinrich Maschke, he modified the methods of undergraduate instruction in mathematics. Casting aside textbooks, he stressed fundamentals and their graphical interpretations in his "laboratory courses." Although a gentle man, he sometimes displayed impatience as he strove for excellence in his classes. He became a teacher of teachers. Among his supervised Ph.D.'s were L. E. Dickson, O. Veblen, and G. D. Birkhoff.

Moore also advanced his profession outside the

classroom. In 1894 he helped transform the New York Mathematical Society into the American Mathematical Society, of which he was vice-president from 1898 to 1900 and president from 1900 to 1902. A founder of the society's *Transactions* in 1899, he was chief editor until 1907. He served on the editorial boards of the *Rendiconti del Circolo matematico di Palermo* (1908–1932), the University of Chicago Science Series (chairman, 1914–1929), and the *Proceedings of the National Academy of Sciences* (1915–1920). With his encouragement in, 1916 H. E. Slaught saw through the formation of the Mathematical Association of America. In 1921 Moore was president of the American Association for the Advancement of Science.

Rigor and generalization characterized the mathematical research of Moore. His research fell principally into the areas of (1) geometry; (2) algebra, groups, and number theory; (3) the theory of functions; and (4) integral equations and general analysis. Among these he emphasized the second and fourth areas. In geometry he examined the postulational foundations of Hilbert, as well as the earlier works of Pasch and Peano. He skillfully analyzed the independence of the axioms of Hilbert and formulated a system of axioms for n-dimensional geometry, using points only as undefined elements instead of the points, lines, and planes of Hilbert in the three-dimensional case. During his investigation of the theory of abstract groups, he stated and proved for the first time the important theorem that every finite field is a Galois field (1893). He also discovered that every finite group G of linear transformations on n variables has a Hermitian invariant (1896–1898). His probe of the theory of functions produced a clarified treatment of transcendentally transcendental functions and a proof of Goursat's extension of the Cauchy integral theorem for a function $f(z)$ without the assumption of the continuity of the derivative $f'(z)$.

His work in the area of integral equations and general analysis sparkled most. He brought to culmination the study of improper definite integrals before the appearance of the more effective integration theories of Borel and Lebesgue. He diligently advanced general analysis, which for him meant the development of a theory of classes of functions on a general range. The contributions of Cantor, Russell, and Zermelo underlay his research here. While inventing a mathematical notation for his analytical system, he urged Florian Cajori to prepare his two-volume *History of Mathematical Notations* (1928–1929). Throughout his work in general analysis, Moore stressed fundamentals, as he sought to strengthen the foundations of mathematics. His research set a trend for precision

in American mathematical literature at a time when vagueness and uncertainty were common.

Honors were bestowed upon Moore for his distinguished contributions to mathematics and education. The University of Göttingen awarded him an honorary Ph.D. in 1899, and the University of Wisconsin an LL.D. in 1904. Yale, Clark, Toronto, Kansas, and Northwestern subsequently granted him honorary doctorates in science or mathematics. In 1929 the University of Chicago established the Eliakim Hastings Moore distinguished service professorship, while he was still an active member of the faculty. Besides belonging to American, English, German, and Italian mathematical societies, he was a member of the American Academy of Arts and Sciences, the American Philosophical Society, and the National Academy of Sciences.

BIBLIOGRAPHY

I. ORIGINAL WORKS. Moore wrote *Introduction to a Form of General Analysis* (New Haven, 1910); and *General Analysis*, published posthumously in *Memoirs of American Philosophical Society*, 1 (1935).

His articles include "Extensions of Certain Theorems of Clifford and Cayley in the Geometry of n Dimensions," in *Transactions of the Connecticut Academy of Arts and Sciences*, 7 (1885), 1–18; "Note Concerning a Fundamental Theorem of Elliptic Functions, As Treated in Halphen's Traité," 1, 39–41, in *Rendiconti del Circolo matematico di Palermo*, 4 (1890), 186–194; "A Doubly-Infinite System of Simple Groups," in *Bulletin of the New York Mathematical Society*, 3 (1893), 73–78; "A Doubly-Infinite System of Simple Groups," in *Mathematical Papers Read at the International Mathematical Congress in Chicago 1893* (New York, 1896), 208–242; "Concerning Transcendentally Transcendental Functions," in *Mathematische Annalen*, 48 (1897), 49–74; "On Certain Crinkly Curves," in *Transactions of the American Mathematical Society*, 1 (1900), 72–90; "A Simple Proof of the Fundamental Cauchy-Goursat Theorem," *ibid.*, 499–506; "The Undergraduate Curriculum," in *Bulletin of the American Mathematical Society*, 7 (1900), 14–24; "Concerning Harnack's Theory of Improper Definite Integrals," in *Transactions of the American Mathematical Society*, 2 (1901), 296–330; and "On the Theory of Improper Definite Integrals," *ibid.*, 459–475.

Subsequent articles are "Concerning Du Bois-Reymond's Two Relative Integrability Theorems," in *Annals of Mathematics*, 2nd ser., 2 (1901), 153–158; "A Definition of Abstract Groups," in *Transactions of the American Mathematical Society*, 3 (1902), 485–492; "On the Foundations of Mathematics," in *Bulletin of the American Mathematical Society*, 9 (1903), 402–424; also in *Science*, 2nd ser., 17 (1903), 401–416, his retiring address as president of the American Mathematical Society; "The Subgroups of the Generalized Finite Modular Group," in *Decennial Publications of the University of Chicago* (1903), 141–190; "On a Form of General Analysis with Application to Linear Differential and Integral Equations," in *Atti del IV Congresso internazionale dei matematici* (Rome, 6–11 Apr. 1908), II (1909), 98–114; "The Role of Postulational Methods in Mathematics" (address at Clark University, 20th Anniversary), in *Bulletin of the American Mathematical Society*, **16** (1909), 41; "On the Foundations of the Theory of Linear Integral Equations," *ibid.*, **18** (1912), 334–362; "On the Fundamental Functional Operation of a General Theory of Linear Integral Equations," in *Proceedings of the Fifth International Congress of Mathematicians* (Cambridge, 1912), I (1913), 230–255; "Definition of Limit in General Integral Analysis," in *Proceedings of the National Academy of Sciences of the United States of America*, **1** (1915), 628–632; "On Power Series in General Analysis," in *Mathematische Annalen*, **86** (1922), 30–39; and "A General Theory of Limits," in *American Journal of Mathematics*, **44** (1922), 102–121, written with H. L. Smith.

II. SECONDARY LITERATURE. Articles on Moore are G. A. Bliss, "Eliakim Hastings Moore," in *Bulletin of the American Mathematical Society*, **39** (1933), 831–838; and "The Scientific Work of Eliakim Hastings Moore," *ibid.*, **40** (1934), 501–514, with bibliography of Moore's publications; and G. A. Bliss and L. E. Dickson, "Eliakim Hastings Moore (1862–1932)," in *Biographical Memoirs. National Academy of Sciences*, **17** (1937), 83–102.

RONALD S. CALINGER

MOORE, ROBERT LEE (*b*. Dallas, Texas, 14 November 1882; *d*. Austin, Texas, 4 October 1974)

Moore was the fifth of the six children of Charles Jonathan and Louisa Ann (Moore) Moore. His father had moved to the southern United States from Connecticut to fight on the side of the South during the Civil War and eventually settled in Dallas, where he established a hardware and feed store. Moore attended a private school in Dallas and the University of Texas (now the University of Texas at Austin), where he spent most of his professional life. In 1910 he married Margaret MacLelland Key of Brenham, Texas; they had no children.

According to the registrar's records, while Moore was at the University of Texas (1898–1902), he did very well in mathematics courses under George Bruce Halsted and Leonard Eugene Dickson. He obtained both the B.S. and the M.A. in 1901. He continued at the university as a fellow for the year 1901–1902. In one of his classes Halsted posed a problem that resulted in Moore's proving that one of the axioms in David Hilbert's *Grundlagen der Geometrie* (1899) was not independent of the other axioms. This was brought to the attention of Eliakim Hastings Moore (no direct relation), the leading professor of mathematics at the University of Chicago, who was able to provide R. L. Moore with a scholarship for graduate work at Chicago beginning in 1903. R. L. Moore was taking courses under Halsted in 1902, but when the university regents refused, over Halsted's protests, to renew Moore's teaching fellowship, Moore went to teach for a year (1902–1903) at a high school in Marshall, Texas. Halsted was himself fired by the regents in December 1902 for reasons that remain unclear.

In 1905 Moore received his doctoral degree at Chicago with a dissertation entitled "Sets of Metrical Hypotheses for Geometry" and supervised by Oswald Veblen. After Chicago, Moore held teaching positions at the University of Tennessee (1905–1906), Princeton University (1906–1908), Northwestern University (1908–1911), and the University of Pennsylvania (1911–1920). In 1914 he became an associate editor of *Transactions of the American Mathematical Society* and continued in this position to 1927. In 1920 Moore returned to the University of Texas as associate professor of mathematics and three years later was appointed professor.

By 1920 Moore had published seventeen papers making use of the axiomatic procedures then being developed by mathematicians under the influence principally of Veblen, E. H. Moore, and others at Chicago. He had, however, his own distinctive approach and took little interest in such topics as the logical status of the Axiom of Choice, a problem in the foundations of mathematics that interested many mathematicians during most of Moore's career. He seemed more interested in using axiomatics as a tool in developing a unique approach within set-theoretic topology or, as he termed it, point-set topology.

The first edition of Moore's only book, *Foundations of Point Set Theory* (1932), represented the culmination of the major part of his research to date. It also formed the basis of his subsequent work, which was expressed more through his teaching and his students than through publications: fifty of his total of sixty-eight publications appeared before 1932, and forty-one of his fifty doctoral students were awarded their degrees in the period 1932 to 1969. A revised edition of his book (1962) incorporated many of the results of his students and others in the field during the previous thirty years.

In his book Moore gradually reveals a collection of axioms and develops at each stage the consequences of the axioms admitted thus far. For example, chapter 2 is entitled "Consequences of Axioms 0, 1 and 2''; Euclidean space of any finite dimension and Hilbert space are examples that satisfy these axioms. By chapter 4, axioms 3, 4, and 5 have been added and, as Moore states in his preface, from these six axioms "it is possible to prove a very considerable portion of the well known topological propositions of the plane." The fruitfulness of Moore's axioms lies in the fact that, however close they may appear to determine the Euclidean plane, a space satisfying them need not be metric and indeed may depart rather wildly from Euclidean space.

Though his courses followed his book in subject and axiomatic style, Moore told his graduate students not to read it or any other mathematically relevant literature, and he strongly discouraged any mathematical communication between students outside of class. He regarded his classes as research sessions in which students learned by presenting their work at the blackboard and by critically evaluating others' presentations. Moore presented possible definitions, axioms, and theorems, and the ground rules for the class, but otherwise took the role of a researcher himself. His technique has been much analyzed and imitated because, though its basic idea may not be original with him, in his hands it resulted in what is regarded by many mathematicians outside the Moore school as the most distinguished group of mathematicians in the United States to have been taught by the same person.

Most of Moore's students became research mathematicians and professors at universities and used some version of his teaching method. Some continued to make use of his axiom system in the study of abstract spaces and the structure of continua (F. Burton Jones, for example) or in the related area of set-theoretic topology (Mary E. Estill Rudin). Others entered related branches, such as algebraic topology (Raymond L. Wilder), analytic topology (Gordon T. Whyburn), and topology of manifolds (R. H. Bing).

The University of Texas regulations in 1953 allowed Moore to continue to teach beyond the usual retirement age of seventy, and he taught until he was eighty-six. Although willing to continue, he was then retired. His last official contact with the university occurred in 1973, when he sent his appreciation to the regents for naming the new building housing the departments of mathematics, physics, and astronomy after him.

Moore's career spanned the period of rapid growth in American mathematics that began at the turn of the century. He contributed a branch of topology and created an influential method of teaching math-

ematics. His honors included election to the National Academy of Sciences (1931); visiting lecturer of the American Mathematical Society, the first American to be so honored (1931–1932); and the presidency of the American Mathematical Society (1937–1938).

BIBLIOGRAPHY

I. ORIGINAL WORKS. Moore's principal work, *Foundations of Point Set Theory*, appeared as volume 13 of the American Mathematical Society Colloquium Publications. The first edition (New York, 1932) was brought up to date in many details in a revised edition (Providence, R.I., 1962) that included a much more extensive bibliography. It was reprinted with corrections in 1970. A complete bibliography of Moore's articles can be found in Raymond L. Wilder's biographical article (see below).

The R. L. Moore Collection in the Archives of American Mathematics, University Archives, University of Texas at Austin, contains Moore's correspondence, personal papers, library, and other items from his home.

II. SECONDARY LITERATURE. General biographical articles on Moore include R. E. Greenwood, "In Memoriam—Robert Lee Moore," in *Documents and Minutes of the General Faculty* (Austin, Tex., 1974–1975), 11653–11665, and "The Kinship of E. H. Moore and R. L. Moore," in *Historia Mathematica*, **4** (1977), 153–155; and Raymond L. Wilder, "Robert Lee Moore, 1882–1974," in *Bulletin of the American Mathematical Society*, **82** (1976), 417–427, which includes a bibliography of Moore's publications. D. Reginald Traylor, William Bane, and Madeline Jones, *Creative Teaching. Heritage of R. L. Moore* (Houston, 1972) includes the names and publications of Moore's doctoral students and of each successive generation of their students; it is reviewed by P. R. Halmos in *Historia Mathematica*, **1** (1974), 188–192. Moore's work is treated in Raymond L. Wilder, "The Mathematical Work of R. L. Moore: Its Background, Nature and Influence," in *Archive for History of Exact Sciences*, **26** (1982), 73–97.

Studies of Moore's teaching method include F. Burton Jones, "The Moore Method," in *American Mathematical Monthly*, **84** (1977), 273–278; Lucille E. Whyburn, "Student-Oriented Teaching—The Moore Method," *ibid.*, **77** (1970), 351–359; and the fifty-five-minute motion picture *Challenge in the Classroom: The Method of R. L. Moore*, produced by the Mathematical Association of America in 1965.

ALBERT C. LEWIS

MORDELL, LOUIS JOEL (*b.* Philadelphia, Pennsylvania, 28 January 1888; *d.* Cambridge, England, 12 March 1972)

Mordell was the third child of Phineas Mordell, who later became a noted Hebrew scholar, and of Annie Feller Mordell. Both were poor Jewish immigrants from Lithuania. At a young age he went to England, where he spent the rest of his life, and became a British subject in 1929. In May 1916 he married Mabel Elizabeth Cambridge; they had a daughter and a son.

At the age of fourteen, when he entered Central High School in Philadelphia, Mordell was already fascinated with mathematics learned from used books he had bought for five or ten cents at a well-known Philadelphia bookstore. Many of the examples in these books were taken from Cambridge scholarship or tripos papers, a fact that gave Mordell the desire to attend Cambridge. Having demonstrated his mathematical abilities by completing the four-year high school mathematics course in two years and earning a very high grade on a test administered by a friend of his father's, he scraped together the fare to Cambridge. In 1907 he placed first on the scholarship examination and received a scholarship to St. John's College. He took part I of the mathematical tripos in 1909 and was third wrangler (after P. J. Daniell and E. H. Neville). On completing the tripos he began research in the theory of numbers, in which there was then little interest in England; he regarded himself as self-taught in the subject.

Mordell's work was a systematic study of the integral solutions (x,y) of the Diophantine equation

$$y^2 = x^3 + k. \tag{1}$$

This equation has a long history, going back to Pierre de Fermat (1601–1665) for some values of k, but Mordell decided the solubility for many new values of k and in some cases gave complete solutions. He also showed that the determination of the solutions was equivalent to solving the set of equations $f(u,v) = 1$, where f runs through representatives of the equivalence classes of integral cubic forms of discriminant $-4k$. This won him a Smith's Prize, but he failed to obtain a college fellowship. He went on to show that the determination of the integral solutions (x,y) of an equation

$$y^2 = ax^3 + bx^2 + cx + d \tag{2}$$

is equivalent to determining the solutions of $f(u, v) = 1$, where f now runs through representatives of a class of quartic forms with given invariants. Axel Thue had already shown that equations of the type $f(u, v) = 1$ have only finitely many solutions, which implies that this is also the case for (1) and (2); but Mordell learned of Thue's work only later, and at the time believed that some equations (1) or (2) could have infinitely many integral solutions.

From 1913 to 1920 Mordell was a lecturer at Birkbeck College, London. His main interest was in modular forms, and he made two important advances, both anticipating approaches that remain central in the theory. One of these concerned the tau function, introduced by Srinivasa Ramanujan, who had conjectured that it has the property of multiplicativity. This Mordell proved. The central argument (the Hecke operator) was rediscovered by Erich Hecke in 1937. The tau function is the set of coefficients of a certain modular form, and Hecke showed that Mordell's theorem is a special case of a general and important phenomenon. Mordell's other advance was to systematize the theory of the representation of integers as the sum of a fixed number n of squares of integers. Many special results were known. Mordell showed how to deduce those results and to obtain new ones by using the finite dimensionality of the space of modular forms of a given type. In the hands of Hecke and others, this idea was exploited with great effect in the study of representation by positive definite quadratic forms in general.

During the period from 1920 to 1922, when he was lecturer at Manchester College of Technology, Mordell worked out the result for which he is most widely known, his "finite basis theorem." Henri Poincaré had shown that the determination of all the rational points on a given curve of genus 1 defined over the rationals is equivalent, once one rational point has been given, to the determination of the rational points on a curve

$$y^2 = 4x^3 - g_2x - g_3, \tag{3}$$

where g_2, g_3 are given rational numbers (depending on the given curve). The rational points on (3) have a natural structure as an abelian group, and Poincaré conjectured that this group is finitely generated. In the course of an investigation with another aim, Mordell found a proof of this conjecture. The curve (3) is an abelian variety of dimension 1. The finite basis theorem was extended by André Weil to abelian varieties of any dimension and to any algebraic number field as ground field, and there are further generalizations. The theorem plays a key role in many aspects of Diophantine analysis. Mordell, however, played no part in these later developments.

Toward the end of the paper just discussed, Mordell conjectures that there are only finitely many rational points on any curve of genus greater than unity. This acquired notoriety as "Mordell's conjecture" and was proved by Gerd Faltings in 1983.

In 1922 Mordell moved to the University of Manchester, where from 1923 to 1945 he was Fielden professor of pure mathematics and head of the mathematics department; in 1924 he was elected to the Royal Society—while still an American citizen. There was already a fine tradition of mathematics at Manchester, and during Mordell's tenure it became a leading center. He gave great attention both to teaching and to research and built up a strong team that attracted many visitors. He was extremely active in assisting refugees from continental tyrannies, and for some of them he found temporary or even permanent positions. Mordell's own research ranged widely within the theory of numbers. One problem (suggested by Harold Davenport) was the estimation of trigonometric sums and of the number of points on curves and other varieties defined over finite fields. Mordell devised an averaging argument that gave stronger results than those already known. The results were largely superseded by the Riemann hypothesis for function fields of Hasse and Weil, but Mordell's argument suggested to Ivan Vinogradov his technique for estimating more general sums. In the late 1930's, with Harold Davenport and Kurt Mahler (both then at Manchester), Mordell initiated a period of great advances in the geometry of numbers.

In 1945 Mordell succeeded Godfrey Harold Hardy as Sadleirian professor of pure mathematics at Cambridge, and became a fellow of St. John's. He rapidly built up a strong research school. After his retirement in 1953 he continued to live in Cambridge but traveled widely. He retained his passionate interest in mathematics and did much to foster that interest in others, particularly beginners. He published many papers; perhaps none were of the first rank, but some nevertheless display an extraordinary virtuosity with comparatively elementary techniques. Mordell was a problem solver, not a system builder. Even when his work revealed a system waiting to be built (as, for example, with modular forms or the finite basis theorem) he turned to other work after solving the problem of interest to him.

Mordell enjoyed robust health throughout his life. After a very brief period of ill health, he slipped into unconsciousness and died five days later.

BIBLIOGRAPHY

I. ORIGINAL WORKS. Mordell gives an entertaining account of his early career in "Reminiscences of an Octogenarian Mathematician," in *American Mathematical Monthly*, **78** (1971), 952–961.

Mordell wrote only one book: *Diophantine Equations* (London, 1969). Significant papers include "The Diophantine Equation $y^2 - k = x^3$," in *Proceedings of the London Mathematical Society*, 2nd ser., **13** (1913), 60–80; "Indeterminate Equations of the Third and Fourth Degrees," in *Quarterly Journal of Pure and Applied Mathematics*, **45** (1914), 170–186; "On Mr. Ramanujan's Empirical Expansion of Modular Functions," in *Proceedings of the Cambridge Philosophical Society*, **19** (1917), 117–124; "On the Representation of a Number as a Sum of an Odd Number of Squares," in *Transactions of the Cambridge Philosophical Society*, **22** (1919), 361–372; "On the Rational Solutions of the Indeterminate Equations of the 3rd and 4th Degrees," in *Proceedings of the Cambridge Philosophical Society*, **21** (1922), 179–192; "A Theorem of Khintchine on Linear Diophantine Approximation," in *Journal of the London Mathematical Society*, **12** (1937), 166–167; "On Numbers Represented by Binary Cubics," in *Proceedings of the London Mathematical Society*, 2nd ser., **48** (1943), 198–228; and "Observations on the Minimum of a Positive Quadratic Form in Eight Variables," in *Journal of the London Mathematical Society*, **19** (1944), 3–6.

II. SECONDARY LITERATURE. There is an account of Mordell's life and work by John W. S. Cassels in *Biographical Memoirs of Fellows of the Royal Society*, **19** (1973), 493–520, with a complete bibliography. A slightly different version of this account is in *Bulletin of the London Mathematical Society*, **6** (1974), 69–96, also with a complete list of his publications. A short biographical memoir by Harold Davenport is in *Acta arithmetica*, **9** (1964), 1–22, with a bibliography and a portrait.

JOHN W. S. CASSELS

MORLAND, SAMUEL (*b*. Sulhamstead Bannister, Berkshire, England, 1625; *d*. Hammersmith, Middlesex [now London], England, 30 December 1695)

Morland was the son of Thomas Morland, rector of Sulhamstead Bannister, from which village Samuel Morland took his title when he was created baronet. He was educated at Winchester College from 1639 and at Magdalene College, Cambridge, from 1644. Elected a fellow of the college on 30 November 1649, he continued his studies of mathematics there until 1653.

From 1653 to the Restoration in 1660, Morland was deeply involved in politics. He was a supporter and associate of Oliver Cromwell, who employed him on two foreign embassies, to Sweden in 1653 and to the duke of Savoy in 1655, with the object of persuading him to grant amnesty to the Waldenses. Morland was finally successful and in 1658 he published a history of the Waldensian church.

Close association with the intrigues of Cromwell and John Thurloe and, in particular, knowledge of a plot to murder Charles II and his brother disgusted Morland with the Commonwealth cause; and he began working as an agent to promote the restoration of the monarchy. Despite serious charges brought against him, he was granted a full pardon by Charles II in 1660, knighted, and later in the same year was created a baronet. He was also appointed gentleman of the privy chamber, but he did not receive the financial help he had hoped for. From 1660 he devoted himself to experimental work with occasional support from the king, who named him "Master of Mechanicks" in 1681.

Morland was married five times and was survived by only one son, Samuel, who became the second and last baronet of the family. Morland became blind three years before his death and retired to Hammersmith, where he died on 30 December 1695.

Morland's studies of mathematics and his inventiveness led him to make two "arithmetick instruments," or hand calculators, with gear wheels operated by a stylus, for pedagogic use. His perpetual almanac was a concise form of pocket calendar, adapted for use on coin-sized disks, sundials and other instruments, and snuffboxes. A speaking trumpet, described in his treatise on the subject as a "*tuba stentoro-phonica*," was another of his inventions; with it he estimated that a conversation could be carried on at a distance of three-quarters of a mile. It has recently been established that Morland also invented the balance barometer and the diagonal barometer.

Morland's most important work was in the field of hydrostatics. There was much interest in the mid-seventeenth century in mechanical methods of raising water. Morland invented an apparatus using an airtight cistern from which air was expelled by a charge of gunpowder, the water below rising to fill the vacuum thus produced. The *London Gazette* for 30 July 1681 describes how at Windsor Castle, "Sir Samuel Morland, with the strength of eight men, forced the water (mingled with a Vessel of Red Wine to make it more visible) in a continuous stream, at the rate of above sixty Barrels an hour, from the Engine below at the Parkpale, up to the top of the Castle, and from thence into the Air above sixty Foot high."

Morland's efforts to raise water at Versailles led to the publication of *Élévation des eaux* in 1685, but in the manuscript version in the British Museum, written in 1683, there is an account of the use of steam power to raise water. Although he did not develop the steam engine, his experiment is one of the first to show the practical possibilities of steam power.

BIBLIOGRAPHY

I. ORIGINAL WORKS. A list of Samuel Morland's published works is given in app. 2 to the biography by H. W. Dickinson cited below. The main scientific works are *Tuba stentoro-phonica, an Instrument of Excellent use as Well at sea as at Land; Invented, and Variously Experimented, in the year 1670* . . . (London, 1671); *The Description and Use of two Arithmetick Instruments. Together With a Short Treatise Explaining and Demonstrating the Ordinary Operations of Arithmetick. As Likewise A Perpetual Almanack, and Several Useful tables* (London, 1673); *Élévation des eaux par toute sorte de machines réduite à la mesure, au poids, à la balance par le moyen d'un nouveau piston & Corps de pompe d'un nouveau mouvement cyclo-elliptique* . . . (Paris, 1685); *The Poor Man's Dyal With an Instrument to Set It. Made Applicable to Any Place in England, Scotland, Ireland, &c.* (London, 1689); and *Hydrostaticks: or Instructions Concerning Water-works, Collected out of the Papers of Sir Samuel Morland. Containing the Method Which he Made use of in This Curious art,* Joseph Morland, ed. (London, 1697). There is MS material at the British Museum, Lambeth Palace Library, and Cambridge University Library, all noted by Dickinson. Examples of Morland's calculating machines are at the Science Museum, London; Museum of the History of Science, Oxford; and the Museo di Storia della Scienza, Florence; a speaking trumpet is at Trinity College, Cambridge.

II. SECONDARY LITERATURE. See J. O. Halliwell, *A Brief Account of the Life, Writings, and Inventions of Sir Samuel Morland* (Cambridge, 1838); W. E. Knowles Middleton, "Sir Samuel Morland's Barometers," in *Archives internationales d'histoire des sciences*, **5** (1962), 343–351. H. W. Dickinson, *Sir Samuel Morland, Diplomat and Inventor 1625–1695* (Cambridge, 1970), published eighteen years after the author's death by the Newcomen Society, includes an iconography and a bibliography; and D. J. Bryden, "A Didactic Introduction to Arithmetic, Sir Charles Cotterell's 'Instrument for Arithmeticke' of 1667," in *History of Education*, **2** (1973), 5–18.

G. L'E. TURNER

MOSTOWSKI, ANDRZEJ (*b*. Lvov, Poland, 1 November 1913; *d*. Vancouver, Canada, 22 August 1975)

Mostowski belonged to the first generation of mathematical logicians who investigated foundational questions from a purely mathematical (rather than a philosophical) viewpoint and who also transformed axiomatic set theory into a branch of logic. For three decades after World War II he was the leader of mathematical logic in Poland. A man of considerable talent, energy, and charm, he was known for his personal and scientific generosity. Philosophically, he was a realist concerning the real numbers and, after Cohen's 1963 independence results, a formalist concerning set theory.

His father, Stanislaw Mostowski, an assistant in the department of physical chemistry at the University of Lvov, joined the army in 1914 and died a year after his son was born. Mostowski's mother, Zofia Mostowska, whose maiden name was Kramstyk, worked in a bank. During the winter of 1914 the family went to Zakopane for a vacation; World War I forced them to stay until 1920, when they moved to Warsaw. There, from 1923 to 1931, Mostowski attended the Stefan Batory Gymnasium. A good student, he was interested in both mathematics and physics. When he was sixteen, he fell seriously ill, and this later kept him from serving in the army.

In 1931 Mostowski entered the University of Warsaw, where he was attracted to logic, set theory, and the foundations of mathematics. His teachers in these subjects were eminent researchers—Kuratowski, Leśniewski, Lukasiewicz, Sierpiński, and the two who influenced him most: Lindenbaum and, above all, Tarski.

After Mostowski received a master's degree in 1936 and wrote his doctoral dissertation, he went abroad to study. During the summer semester of 1937, at the University of Vienna, he attended Gödel's course on constructible sets, where the relative consistency of the axiom of choice was first established. In Zurich, convinced that he needed a practical skill in order to find a job in Poland (where positions in mathematics were scarce), Mostowski studied statistics in order to become an actuary. Bored with that subject, he enjoyed lectures by Polya and by Hermann Weyl as well as a seminar by Bernays. He did research on recursion theory and on the axiom of choice.

In 1938 Mostowski returned to Warsaw, where, in February 1939, he defended his doctoral dissertation, showing that various definitions of finiteness are not provably equivalent in logic without the axiom of choice. Tarski, who was then a *Privatdozent*, directed the dissertation, but the official supervisor was Kuratowski. Unable to find a position at the University of Warsaw, Mostowski worked at the National Meteorological Institute.

A year after the Nazis invaded Poland in September 1939, Mostowski became an accountant in a small plant that manufactured roofing and remained there until 1944. From 1942 to 1944 he also taught analytic geometry and Galois theory at the Underground University of Warsaw. One of the students there was Maria Matuszewska, whom he married in September 1944; they had a daughter and two sons, one of whom became a mathematician. Sierpiński, a colleague at the Underground University, remarked in 1945 that Mostowski was very close to being habilitated there in July 1944. Then came

the Warsaw uprising of August 1944, when the Nazis devastated the city. Afterward, as he was about to be sent to a concentration camp, some Polish nurses helped Mostowski to escape, spiriting him through the German lines to a hospital.

Many of Mostowski's wartime results—on the hierarchy of projective sets, on arithmetically definable sets of natural numbers, and on consequences of the axiom of constructibility in descriptive set theory—were lost when his apartment was destroyed during the uprising. He had to choose whether to flee with a thick notebook containing those results or with bread. He chose bread.

Later Mostowski was able to reconstruct just a fraction of his discoveries, such as the decidability of the theory of well-ordering (a result obtained in 1941 but only announced, jointly with Tarski, in 1949 and only published in 1978).

In January 1945 the unemployed Mostowski tried to make a living by giving private lessons, then had to pawn his few possessions. For a few months shortly after the war he held a position as a research fellow at the Silesian Polytechnic (temporarily housed in Cracow). Then he taught briefly at the Jagellonian University in Cracow, where his *Habilitationsschrift* was approved in 1945. From January to September 1946 he was an acting professor at Lodz University.

Nevertheless, Mostowski's career was to be in Warsaw. In 1946 he returned to the University of Warsaw as an acting professor, becoming an extraordinary professor the following year and ordinary (full) professor in 1951. He occupied the chair of philosophy of mathematics, then the chair of algebra, and finally the chair of foundations of mathematics. In 1952 he served as dean of the Faculty of Mathematics and Physics. From 1948 to 1968 he was also head of the division of the foundations of mathematics at the National Institute of Mathematics (which became the Mathematics Institute of the Polish Academy of Sciences). From 1968 until his death he headed the section on the foundations of mathematics at the University of Warsaw.

When he returned to Warsaw in 1946, Mostowski was the only logician there left from the vigorous group that before the war had included Leśniewski, Lukasiewicz, and Tarski. Although Mostowski had little previous experience as an organizer and disliked administrative duties, he threw himself into rebuilding Warsaw as a major center for mathematical logic. In this effort he was quite successful. He also considered it important to strengthen algebra as an adjunct to logic. In this spirit he wrote for a Polish audience a number of textbooks in algebra, logic, and set theory. As early as 1946 he attracted excellent graduate students, the first of whom (Andrzej Grze-gorczyk and Helena Rasiowa) received doctorates in 1950. Among his students were also Henry Hiz, Antoni Janiczak, and Andrzej Ehrenfeucht. After 1965 the number of his students increased and he conducted a large seminar on the foundations of mathematics.

A variety of honors came to Mostowski, beginning with a Polish state prize in 1952 (and another in 1966). In 1956 he was elected an associate member of the Polish Academy of Sciences and became a full member seven years later. In 1972 he received a Jurzykowski Foundation prize and also became president of the division of logic, methodology, and philosophy of science of the International Union for the History and Philosophy of Science. Internationally he was highly respected by his fellow logicians.

Mostowski did much editorial work, serving on the editorial boards of *Fundamenta Mathematicae* and *Journal of Symbolic Logic*, as well as *Annals of Mathematical Logic*, which he helped to found. Moreover, he coedited the series for mathematics, physics, and astronomy of the *Bulletin* of the Polish Academy of Sciences. Beginning in 1966, he also served as an editor of the series "Studies in Logic and the Foundations of Mathematics" published by North-Holland.

Mostowski traveled abroad repeatedly, spending the academic years 1948–1949 at the Institute for Advanced Study in Princeton, 1958–1959 at the University of California at Berkeley, and 1969–1970 at All Souls College, Oxford. In addition, he participated in many congresses and conferences in Europe and America. After spending the summer of 1975 at Berkeley and Stanford, he was on his way to a conference in Ontario when he stopped at Simon Fraser University in Vancouver to deliver a lecture. There he died suddenly.

Mostowski's earliest publications prior to World War II, on Boolean algebras and on Fraenkel-Mostowski (FM) models for set theory, illustrate two major themes of his work: algebra applied to logic, and the semantics of set theory. His early research on recursion theory and undecidability, a third theme, did not appear in print until after the war.

His work on FM models was stimulated in 1935 when Lindenbaum posed the problem of how to formulate Fraenkel's independence results on the axiom of choice in a logically unobjectionable way. Lindenbaum and Mostowski did so, developing the theory of FM models and carefully distinguishing the object language and the metalanguage in the

manner of Tarski. In 1939 Mostowski published a rigorous proof that the axiom of choice cannot be deduced from the ordering principle; Fraenkel's earlier argument had not been adequate. He went beyond Fraenkel by showing that Tarski's five notions of finiteness were nonequivalent, both in the theory of types and in Bernays-Gödel set theory with urelements. In 1948 Mostowski proved that the principle of dependent choices does not imply the axiom of choice. This result used an uncountable set of urelements, while all earlier independence results relied on a countable set. Mostowski's *Habilitationsschrift* (1945) established necessary and sufficient conditions for the axiom of choice restricted to families of m-element sets to imply the axiom for n-element sets. His isomorphism theorem (1949) on transitive models was fundamental to later research on models of set theory. Finally, during the 1970's he worked on Kelley-Morse set theory and its models.

During World War II, Mostowski began investigating recursion theory and undecidability. He developed the analytical hierarchy of sets of integers, as Kleene did independently. In 1939 Mostowski, working with Tarski, reduced Gödel's incompleteness theorems to a form that depended only on finitely many first-order arithmetic axioms, thus enabling many theories to be proved undecidable. They prepared their results for publication a decade later with R. M. Robinson. At that time Mostowski also developed an algebraic method for proving non-deducibility results in intuitionistic logic. In 1959 he introduced β-models for second-order arithmetic (models that make well-orderings absolute). He showed that some ω-models are not β-models and was one of those to establish the existence of a minimal β-model.

Much of Mostowski's postwar work in logic concerned extensions of first-order logic. Thus, in a 1957 paper he introduced the notion of generalized quantifiers and, in particular, quantifiers such as "there exist uncountably many." He showed that many logics with generalized quantifiers do not have a recursively enumerable set of valid sentences and posed the completeness problem for the remaining such logics: Does there exist a recursively enumerable set of axioms and rules of inference such that a sentence is provable if and only if it is valid? In the same paper he also established that in any logic with a generalized quantifier not definable from "for all" and "there exists," the Löwenheim-Skolem-Tarski theorem fails; this result helped lead to Lindstrom's characterization of first-order logic in terms of the Löwenheim-Skolem theorem and the compactness theorem. With Grzegorczyk and Ryll-Nardzewski, Mostowski extended Gödel's incompleteness results to second-order arithmetic supplemented by the ω-rule. In 1961, solving a problem of Tarski's, he showed that the theory of real numbers cannot be axiomatized in weak second-order logic. Finally, in 1962 he proved that the completeness problem has a positive solution for some very general kinds of many-valued first-order logic.

Several of Mostowski's papers from the 1950's involve model theory. In 1952 he studied the conditions under which the truth of a sentence is preserved by a finite direct product of models, thereby stimulating more general work by Vaught and by Feferman. Three years later he exhibited a first-order theory (a form of set theory) with no recursively enumerable models. But Mostowski's most important model-theoretic research, done jointly with Ehrenfeucht (1956), introduced the notion of indiscernible elements and of models generated by such elements, giving conditions under which a theory has a model with many such elements. These ideas proved very fruitful in model theory and set theory.

BIBLIOGRAPHY

I. ORIGINAL WORKS. A bibliography of Mostowski's works is in *Foundational Studies: Selected Works*, Kazimierz Kuratowski *et al.*, eds., 2 vols. (Amsterdam, 1979), containing about half of his published and unpublished works (translated into English when originally in another language, since Mostowski published in English, French, German, and Polish). His monograph *Thirty Years of Foundational Studies* (New York, 1966) remains the best historical introduction to logic during the seminal years 1930 to 1964.

II. SECONDARY LITERATURE. The best biography is Stanislaw Krajewski and Marian Srebrny, in *Wiadomości matematyczne*, **22** (1979), 53–64. *Foundational Studies* contains a short biography by Wiktor Marek as well as essays on Mostowski's contributions to recursion theory (by Andrzej Grzegorczyk), model theory (by Leszek Pacholski), logical calculi (by Cecylia Rauszer), second-order arithmetic (by Pawel Zbierski), and set theory (by Wojciech Guzicki and Wiktor Marek). A biography by Helena Rasiowa appears in Robin O. Gandy and J. M. E. Hyland, eds., *Logic Colloquium 76* (Amsterdam, 1977), 139–144. See also Wiktor Marek *et al.*, eds., *Set Theory and Hierarchy Theory: A Memorial Tribute to Andrzej Mostowski*, Springer Lecture Notes, no. 537 (Berlin, 1976), for a brief biography, bibliography, and an unpublished paper. Fragmentary autobiographical reminiscences are

in John N. Crossley, ed., *Algebra and Logic*, Springer Lecture Notes, no. 450 (Berlin, 1975), 7–47.

GREGORY H. MOORE

MOUFANG, RUTH (*b*. Darmstadt, Germany, 10 January 1905; *d*. Frankfurt, Germany, 26 November 1977)

Ruth Moufang was the younger daughter of Dr. Eduard Moufang, an industrial chemist, and his wife, Else Fecht Moufang. Her interest in mathematics was first stimulated at the Realgymnasium in Bad Kreuznach, which she attended from 1921 to 1924. From 1925 to 1930 she studied mathematics at the University of Frankfurt. In 1929 she took her teacher's examination, and in October 1931 she received her Ph.D. with a dissertation on projective geometry supervised by Max Dehn. She held a fellowship in Rome during 1931 and 1932, and the following academic year a teaching assignment at the University of Königsberg.

Moufang then returned to Frankfurt, where she held teaching assignments from 1934 to 1936. During this period she continued working on the geometry of the projective plane, and in 1936 she completed her habilitation thesis to qualify as a university lecturer. By this time, however, the Nazi government had made a distinction between the habilitation and the *venia legendi* (which conferred the right to teach). On 9 February 1937 Moufang became the third woman in Germany to receive the habilitation in mathematics. A month later, however, the Ministry of Education informed her that she could not receive a *Dozentur*. A *Dozent* had to qualify as a leader of an almost exclusively male student body, argued the ministry, and "in the future the preconditions for the fruitful activity of a female *Dozent* are lacking."

With the help of a friend, Moufang found employment as an industrial mathematician at the Krupp research laboratories in Essen; she worked there from November 1937 to August 1946, during which time she authored and coauthored several papers, most of them on applied elasticity theory. In 1946 Moufang was asked to return to the University of Frankfurt, where she was given the *venia legendi*. There she held a lecturer's position until her appointment as associate professor in December 1947; she became full professor in February 1957. In the years after the war she published almost nothing, although she was a successful teacher.

Moufang's work from 1931 to 1937 was the main

starting point for a new specialty in mathematics, the study of projective planes, in which geometrical and algebraical structures are closely interrelated. At the turn of the century David Hilbert had shown the existence of non-Desarguian planes. With her dissertation of 1931 Moufang started the systemic study of such planes. Her adviser, Max Dehn, had posed the problem of surveying the interdependence of closure theorems like Desargues's in planes. Such theorems state the closure of a geometric configuration if certain incidences of points and lines are given. In the case of a plane generated by four points, Moufang showed that all closure theorems can be derived from one special case of Desargues's theorem in which the vertices of one of the perspective triangles lie on the sides of the other.

In 1932 Moufang studied the plane generated by five points and showed the equivalence of the above theorem, which she called D_9, with the theorem of the complete quadrilateral. The latter can be used in coordinatization to deduce all algebraic laws for a field except associativity. This is a special case of what is now called a "Moufang plane." In two further papers (1933, 1934) she took up the concept of an alternative division ring (introduced by Max Zorn in 1930), an algebraic structure in which all laws for a field hold except the associative law, for which a weaker "alternation law" is valid. Moufang proved the fundamental theorem for Moufang planes: that if D_9 or, equivalently, the theorem of the complete quadrilateral holds in a projective plane, then and only then can it be coordinatized by an alternative division ring (of characteristic not 2). The main theorem in this field was then proved by Skornjakov (1950) and by Bruck and Kleinfeld (1951): that any alternative division ring of characteristic other than 2 is either associative or a Cayley-Dickson algebra over its center. In 1934 Moufang also studied the multiplicative structure of alternative division rings, which led to what today is called a "Moufang loop."

BIBLIOGRAPHY

I. Original Works. Important papers are "Zur Struktur der projektiven Geometrie der Ebene," in *Mathematische Annalen*, **105** (1931), 536–601; "Die Schnittpunktsätze des projektiven speziellen Fünfecksnetzes in ihrer Abhängigkeit voneinander," *ibid.*, **106** (1932), 755–795; "Alternativkörper und der Satz vom vollständigen Vierseit (D_9)," in *Abhandlungen aus dem Mathematischen Seminar der Hamburgischen Universität*, **9** (1933), 207–222; and "Zur Struktur von Alternativkörpern," in *Mathematische Annalen*, **110** (1934), 416–430.

II. Secondary Literature. A brief biography and description of Moufang's work, including a list of publications (incomplete in applied mathematics), is in Bhama Srinivasan, "Ruth Moufang 1905–1977," in *Mathematical Intelligencer*, **6**, no. 2 (1984), 51–55.

H. Mehrtens

MOULTON, FOREST RAY (*b.* Osceola County, Michigan, 29 April 1872; *d.* Wilmette, Illinois, 7 December 1952)

Forest Ray Moulton was the eldest of eight children born to Belah and Mary Smith Moulton. He was named Forest Ray because his poetic mother thought him a "perfect ray of light and happiness in that dense forest." He received his early education in a typical frontier school and at home. At the age of sixteen he taught in this same school, where one of the students was his brother Harold, who was later to become the first head of the Brookings Institute. At the age of eighteen he enrolled in Albion College, where he received his B.A. in 1894. Moulton received his Ph.D. in astronomy, *summa cum laude*, from the University of Chicago (1899). He also received honorary degrees from Albion College (1922), Drake University (1939), and the Case School of Applied Science (1940).

Moulton had a variety of careers. His academic life began at the University of Chicago with his appointment, while a graduate student, in 1896 as an assistant in astronomy, and it continued through his appointment as professor in 1912 until retirement in 1926. From 1927 to 1936 he was a director of the Utilities Power and Light Corporation of Chicago. He was also a trustee of the Exposition Committee of Chicago's Century of Progress from 1920 to 1936, and its director of concessions from 1931 to 1933. From 1936 to 1940 he was executive secretary of the American Association for the Advancement of Science. During his tenure in this position, he edited more than twenty symposium volumes.

In 1898, while still a graduate student at Chicago, Moulton was invited by Thomas Crowder Chamberlin, then chairman of the geology department, to participate in an investigation of the earth's origin. Chamberlin's investigations on glacial movements had raised doubts that were relevant to the then existing theories. Kant had originally proposed his nebular hypothesis in 1755. Half a century later, and with no knowledge of Kant's theory, Laplace developed a similar theory. He suggested that the earth had originated in a vast mass of blazing gas, which had been thrown off by the sun and had liquefied into a molten sphere. According to this theory the earth was steadily cooling off from its original molten state. After the primordial sun, which was five and a half billion miles in diameter, had cast away the planets, it reached its present diameter and a rotational velocity of 270 miles per second. When Moulton imagined that all planets were returned to the sun, his calculations indicated that the sun would not have enough momentum to hurl off any rings of matter. Chamberlin and his group investigated everything that was written on the origin of the solar system. The most promising prospect was offered by that of nebular "knots," revealed in photographs of spiral nebulae, which could have served as collecting centers.

On 28 May 1900 there was an eclipse of the sun. Chamberlin and Moulton meticulously studied the photographs that illustrated the sun's eruptive nature. Their observation of great clouds of gaseous matter flaring out and away from the sun's surface led to the planetesimal hypothesis proposed in 1904. They proposed that the nebula quickly cooled and solidified, creating small chunks of matter, the planetesimals. Although today neither the Laplace-Kant nor the Moulton-Chamberlin hypothesis stands by itself, both provide a basis for current theories.

During World War I Moulton was assigned to do ballistics research at Fort Sill. Here he is said to have effectively doubled the range of artillery. His work was the forerunner of the efforts in World War II to get improved ballistics tables faster and more accurately, which was one of the links giving impetus to contemporary high speed electronic computing equipment.

In 1920, Moulton, one of the founders of the Society for Visual Education, gave the first radio address broadcast from the University of Chicago. As one of the pioneers of educational broadcasting, Moulton was heard weekly in Chicago from 1934 to 1936, and in Washington from 1938 to 1940.

Moulton was a fellow of the American Academy of Arts and Sciences, the American Physical Society, and the Royal Astronomical Society; President of Sigma Xi, and Honorary Foreign Associate of the British Association for the Advancement of Science. He was also an active member of many other professional societies.

In 1897 Moulton married Estelle Gillete. They had four children and were divorced in 1938. In 1939 he married Alicia Pratt of Winnetka, Illinois. They were divorced in 1951.

BIBLIOGRAPHY

I. ORIGINAL WORKS. No complete bibliog. of Moulton's publications has been published. His major bks. include

An Introduction to Celestial Mechanics (London–New York, 1902, 1914, 1935); *Descriptive Astronomy* (Chicago, 1912, 1921, 1923); *Periodic Orbits* (Washington, 1920); *Differential Equations* (New York, 1930), written with D. Buchanan, T. Buck, F. Griffin, W. Longley, and W. MacMillan; and *New Methods in Exterior Ballistics* (Chicago, 1926). The last work is the beginning of a contemporary mathematical approach to the science of ballistics. For interesting and opposing reviews of this work see J. E. Rowe, *Bulletin of the American Mathematical Society*, **34** (1928), 229–332, and L. S. Dederick, *ibid.*, 667.

The first twenty vols. of the *Carnegie Institution of Washington Yearbooks* (1902–1921) provide a clear picture of the work of Moulton and Chamberlin on the planetesimal hypothesis. *Yearbook*, no. 2 (1903), 261–270, contains a report by T. C. Chamberlin, entitled "Fundamental Problems of Geology," in which he describes the progress of the investigators and collaborators, and their roles and status to date. *Yearbook*, no. 3 (1904), 255–256, contains a letter from Moulton to Chamberlin describing different hypotheses and their applications, pertinent observational data, and the laws derived from the data. Other vols. of the *Yearbook* and their relevant p. nos. are no. 1, 25–43; no. 3, 195–258; no. 4, 171–190; no. 5, 166–172; no. 6, 195; no. 7, 204–205; no. 8, 28–52, 224–225; no. 9, 48–222; no. 10, 45, 222–225; no. 11, 13–44, 264–266; no. 12, 52, 292, 297; no. 13, 45–46, 356–357, 376; no. 14, 36–37, 289, 368; no. 15, 358–362; no. 16, 307–319; no. 17, 297; no. 18, 39, 343–345, 349–351; no. 19, 21, 366–382, 386; and no. 20, 412–425. See also "The Development of the Planetesimal Hypothesis," in *Science*, n.s. **30** (1909), 642–645, written with T. C. Chamberlin; "An Attempt to Test the Nebular Hypothesis by an Appeal to the Laws of Dynamics," in *Astrophysical Journal*, **11** (1900), 103; and "Evolution of the Solar System," *ibid.*, **22** (1905), 166.

One of Moulton's more important papers from the standpoint of current research is "The Straight Line Solutions of the Problem of n Bodies," in *Annals of Mathematics*, **12** (1910–1911), 1–17. In this paper the number of straight line solutions is found for n arbitrary masses. This is the generalization of the problem solved by Lagrange for three bodies. Moulton also attacks what is a sort of converse of this problem by determining, when possible, n masses such that if they are placed at n arbitrarily collinear points, they will, under proper initial projection, always remain in a straight line. This paper was originally presented to the Chicago Section of the American Mathematical Society on 28 December 1900 (see *Bulletin of the American Mathematical Society*, **7** [1900–1901], 249–250).

II. SECONDARY LITERATURE. The anonymous "The Washington Moultons, Forest Ray, '94, and Harold Glenn, 1907," in *Io Triumphe* (March, 1947) (Albion College Alumni Magazine), is an excellent art. with portraits of both Forest and Harold. This art. also contains a photograph of the seven Moulton brothers and their sister on the occasion of the awarding of an M.A. to Mary Moulton by Wayne University in 1945. Other biographical arts. appear in *Current Biography* (1946), 421–423; *The National Cyclopaedia of American Biography*, XLIII (1946), 314–

315; and A. J. Carlson, "Forest Ray Moulton: 1872–1952," in *Science*, **117** (1953), 545–546.

HENRY S. TROPP

MOUTARD, THÉODORE FLORENTIN (*b.* Soultz, Haut-Rhin, France, 27 July 1827; *d.* Paris, France, 13 March 1901)

Moutard was educated at the École Polytechnique from 1844 to 1846. Like many of his fellow students and alumni, he was both an engineer and a geometer. He was graduated from the École des Mines in 1849 and entered the engineering corps. He was discharged in 1852, because as a republican he refused to take the required loyalty oath after the coup d'état by Napoleon III. He was reinstated in 1870. The majority of his mathematical publications date from these years. In 1875 Moutard was appointed professor of mechanics at the École des Mines, but he retained his army rank and was named *ingénieur en chef* in 1878 and *inspecteur général* in 1886. He retired with the latter rank in 1897 but retained his position at the École des Mines. From 1883 he also served as an outside examiner at the École Polytechnique. He was one of the collaborators on *La grande encyclopédie*.

Moutard's mathematical work was primarily in the theory of algebraic surfaces, particularly anallagmatic surfaces, differential geometry, and partial differential equations. His broadest work was a memoir on elliptic functions, which was published as an appendix in Victor Poncelet's *Applications d'analyse et de géométrie*.

BIBLIOGRAPHY

I. ORIGINAL WORKS. The works by Moutard in Victor Poncelet, *Applications d'analyse et de géométrie*, 2 vols. (Paris, 1862–1864), are "Rapprochements divers entre les principales méthodes de la géométrie pure et celles de l'analyse algébrique" (I, 509–535); the work on elliptic functions, "Recherches analytiques sur les polygons simultanément inscrits et circonscrits à deux coniques" (I, 535–560), and a short note "Addition au IVᵉ cahier" (II, 363–364), on the principle of continuity. A bibliography of Moutard's papers in various journals can be found in Poggendorff, IV, 1037.

II. SECONDARY LITERATURE. An account of Moutard's life is in *La grande encyclopédie*, XXIV, 504. His work is also mentioned in Michel Chasles, *Rapport sur les progrès de la géométrie* (Paris, 1870).

ELAINE KOPPELMAN

MOUTON, GABRIEL (*b.* Lyons, France, 1618; *d.* Lyons, 28 September 1694)

Mouton became *vicaire perpétuel* of St. Paul's Church in Lyons in 1646, after taking holy orders and obtaining a doctorate in theology. He spent his whole life in his native city, fulfilling his clerical responsibilities and untroubled by any extraordinary events. During his leisure time he studied mathematics and astronomy and rapidly acquired a certain renown in the city. Jean Picard, who also was an *abbé*, held Mouton in high esteem and always visited him when in Lyons to work on the determination of the city's geographic position.

The book that made Mouton famous, *Observationes diametrorum solis et lunae apparentium* (1670), was the fruit of his astronomical observations and certain computational procedures he had developed. Lalande later stated: "This volume contains interesting memoirs on interpolations and on the project of a universal standard of measurement based on the pendulum."

Mouton was a pioneer in research on natural and practicable units of measurement. He had been struck by the difficulties and disagreements resulting from the great number of units of length, for example, which varied from province to province and from country to country. First he studied how the length of a pendulum with a frequency of one beat per second varies with latitude. He then proposed to deduce from these variations the length of the terrestrial meridian, a fraction of which was to be taken as the universal unit of length. Mouton selected the minute of the degree, which he called the *mille*. The divisions and subdivisions of this principal unit, all in decimal fractions, were called *centuria, decuria, virga, virgula, decima, centesima,* and *millesima*—or alternatively, in the same order, *stadium, funiculus, virga, virgula, digitus, granum,* and *punctum*.

The *virgula geometrica* (geometric foot), for example, was 1/600,000 of the degree of meridian. In order to be able to determine the true length of this foot at any time, Mouton counted the number of oscillations of a simple pendulum of the same length over a span of thirty minutes and found it to be 3,959.2. These ideas were espoused by Picard shortly after the book appeared and a little later, in 1673, by Huygens. They were also favorably received by members of the Royal Society.

Although Mouton's proposals were seriously considered in theoretical terms in his own time, they led to no immediate practical results. Contemporary measuring procedures were too unsatisfactory to assure their valid and definitive application. It was not until 1790 that projects like Mouton's were taken up again. At a session of the Academy of Sciences on

14 April of that year, M. J. Brisson proposed that a new system be based on a natural standard. The Academy preferred to press for a geodesic survey, however, and decided to adopt one ten-millionth of the quadrant of the meridian of Paris as the standard for the meter.

In the *Observationes diametrorum* Mouton presented a very practical computational device for completing ordered tables of numbers when their law of formation is known. He used successive numerical differences, an idea previously employed by Briggs to establish his logarithmic tables.

When Leibniz went to London in January 1673, he took with him his *Dissertatio de arte combinatoria.* He summarized its contents to John Pell and, in particular, explained what he called "différences génératrices." Pell remarked that he had read something very similar in Mouton's book, which had appeared three years earlier. Leibniz had learned, during his stay in Paris, that the book was in preparation but did not know that it had been published. While visiting Oldenburg, Leibniz found Mouton's book and observed that Pell had been right; but he was able to prove that his own, more theoretical and general ideas and results had been reached independently of Mouton's.

A skillful calculator, Mouton produced ten-place tables of logarithmic sines and tangents for the first four degrees, with intervals of one second. He also determined, with astonishing accuracy, the apparent diameter of the sun at its apogee. A skilled experimentalist, he constructed an astronomical pendulum remarkable for its precision and the variety of its movements. It was long preserved at Lyons but was ultimately lost.

BIBLIOGRAPHY

I. ORIGINAL WORKS. Mouton's major work is *Observationes diametrorum solis et lunae apparentium, meridianarumque aliquot altitudinum, cum tabula declinationum solis; Dissertatio de dierum naturalium inaequalitate,* . . . (Lyons, 1670).

His trigonometric tables, which remained in MS, are now in the library of the Academy of Sciences. Esprit Pézénas, director of the observatory at Avignon, consulted this MS and used Mouton's method in preparing the new ed. of William Gardiner's *Tables of Logarithms* (to seven decimals) (Avignon, 1770).

II. SECONDARY LITERATURE. See the following (listed chronologically): J. B. Delambre, *Base du système métrique décimal ou mesure de l'arc de méridien compris entre les parallèles de Dunkerque et Barcelone, exécutée en 1792 et années suivantes par MM. Méchain et Delambre,* I (Paris, 1806), 11; *Biographie universelle ancienne et moderne,*

XXIX (Paris, 1861), 485; Rudolf Wolf, *Geschichte der Astronomie* (Munich, 1877), 623; and Moritz Cantor, *Vorlesungen über Geschichte der Mathematik,* III (Leipzig, 1901), 76–77, 310, 389, and IV (Leipzig, 1908), 362, 440.

PIERRE SPEZIALI

MUḤYI 'L-DĪN AL-MAGHRIBĪ (Muḥyi 'l-Milla wa 'l-Dīn Yaḥyā ibn Muḥammad ibn Abi 'l-Shukr al-Maghribī al-Andalusī) (*fl.* Syria, and later Marāgha, *ca.* 1260–1265)

Al-Maghribī was a Hispano-Muslim mathematician and astronomer, whose time and place of birth and death cannot be determined. Little is known about his life except that he was born in the Islamic West and flourished for a time in Syria and later in Marāgha, where he joined the astronomers of the Marāgha directed by Naṣīr al-Dīn al-Ṭūsī. He made observations in 1264–1265. It has been said that he was a guest of Hūlāgū Khān (Īl-khān of Persia, 1256–1265) and met Abu 'l Faraj (Bar Hebraeus, 1226–1286).

Suter and Brockelmann ascribe quite a long list of writings to al-Maghribī.

Trigonometry

1. *Kitāb shakl al-qaṭṭāʿ* ("Book on the Theorem of Menelaus").

2. *Mā yanfariʿu ʿan shakl al-qaṭṭāʿ* ("Consequences Deduced From *shakl al-qaṭṭāʿ*").

3. *Risala fī kayfiyyat istikhrāj al-juyūb al-wāqiʿu fī 'l-dāʾira* ("Treatise on the Calculation of Sines").

Astronomy

4. *Khulāṣat al-Majisṭī* ("Essence of the *Almagest*"). It contains a new determination of the obliquity of the ecliptic made at Marāgha in 1264, 23; 30° (the real value in 1250 was 23; 32, 19°).

5. *Maqāla fī istikhrāj taʿdīl al-nahār wa saʿat al-mashriq wa 'l-dāʾir min al-falak* ("Treatise on Finding the Meridian, Ortive Amplitude, and Revolution of the Sphere").

6. *Muqaddamāt tataʿallaqu bī-ḥarakāt al-kawākib* ("Premises on the Motions of the Stars").

7. *Tasṭīḥ al-asṭurlāb* ("The Flattening of the Astrolabe").

Editions of the Greek classics; they are called recensions (sing. *taḥrīr*).

8. Euclid's *Elements.*

9. Apollonius' *Conics.*

10. Theodosius' *Spherics.*

11. Menelaus' *Spherics.*

He also wrote more than six books on astrology and a memoir on chronology.

Al-Maghribī's writings on trigonometry contain original developments. For example, two proofs are given of the sine theory for right-angled spherical triangles, and one of them is different from those given by Nāṣir al-Dīn al-Ṭūsī; this theorem is generalized for other triangles. He also worked in several other branches of trigonometry.

Ptolemy (A.D 150) used an ingenious method of interpolation in the calculation of chord 1°. This is of course approximately equivalent to chord 1°. The same method was used for sines in Islam. To find the exact value, one must solve a cubic equation. This was done later by the Persian astronomer al-Kāshī (d. 1429/1430). Al-Maghribī, and before him Abu 'l-Wafā' (940–997/998), tried to find the value of the sine of one-third of an arc. For that purpose Abu 'l-Wafā' laid down a preliminary theorem that the differences of sines of arcs having the same origin and equal differences become smaller as the arcs become larger.

Using this preliminary theorem, al-Maghribī calculated sin 1° in the following way (see Fig. 1):

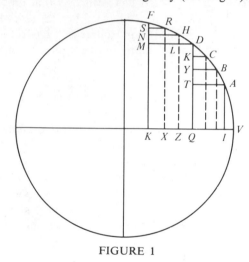

FIGURE 1

$VF = 1; 7, 30°$ and $\sin VF = FK = 1; 10, 40, 12, 34^p$.

$AV = 0; 45°$ and $\sin AV = AI = 0; 44, 8, 21, 8, 38^p$.

The arc AF is divided into six equal parts and each part $= 0; 3, 45°$; therefore,

arc DV + arc $DH = 1°$ and $\sin HV(=1°) = HZ$.

The perpendiculars AT, BY, and CK divide DT into three unequal parts: $TY > YK > DK$; $TD/3 > HL$; $DQ + TD/3 (=1; 2, 49, 43, 36, 9^p) > HZ(=\sin 1°)$. FM is divided into three unequal parts: $MN > NS > SF$; $DQ + FM/3 (=1; 2, 49, 42, 50, 40, 40^p) < NK = HZ(=\sin 1°)$. Then he found sin 1° $=1; 2, 49, 43, 24, 55^p$.

Al-Maghribī calculated sin 1° by using another method of interpolation based on the ratio of arcs greater than the ratios of sines. He found sin 1° $= 1; 2,$

49, 42, 17, 15, 12^p and said that the difference between two values of sines found by using different methods is 0; 0, 0, 0, 56^p, which is correct to four places.

Using these methods, al-Maghribī calculated the ratio of the circumference to its diameter (that is, π).

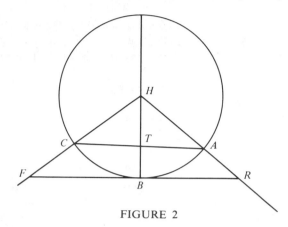

FIGURE 2

$$AC(=2AT) < \text{arc } ABC < RF$$
$$\sin AB(=3/4°) = AT = 0; 47, 7, 21, 7, 37^p$$
$$\Delta RFH \sim \Delta AHC, \qquad RF/AC = BH/TH.$$
$$RF = 1; 34, 15, 11, 19, 25^p$$
$$\text{arc } ABC = \frac{AC + RF}{2} = 1; 34, 14, 16, 47, 19, 30^p.$$

The circumference = 240. Arc $AB = 6; 16, 59, 47, 18^p$, the diameter being 2^p. The diameter being 1^p, the circumference = 3; 8, 29, 53, 34, 39^p < $3R + 1/7$, since $1/7 = 0; 8, 34, 17, 8, 34, 17^p$.

Al-Maghribī compared the latter and Archimedes' value, $3R + 1/7 <$ the circumference $< 3R + 10/71$, found by computing the lengths of inscribed and circumscribed regular polygons of ninety-six sides. Half of the difference between 10/71 and 10/70 is equal to 0; 8, 30, 40^p.

Al-Maghribī determined two mean proportionals between two lines, that is, the duplication of the cube (the problem of Delos). In antiquity many solutions were produced for this problem. It was thought that in terms of solving this problem the mathematicians of Islam stood strangely apart from those of antiquity; but recently many examples have been discovered, thus altering this opinion. The following example of al-Maghribī's is of interest in this respect. He finds two values (see Fig. 3):

AB and BC are given and $AB > BC$, and $AB \perp BC$. AC are joined. Triangle ABC is circumscribed by a circle. The perpendicular DH is drawn so that DC must pass through point R.

$$HR = AB, \quad RH/DH = BA/DH$$
$$AH = BR, \quad RH/HD = DH/HA, \text{ since angle } D = 90°$$
$$BA/DH = DH/HA$$

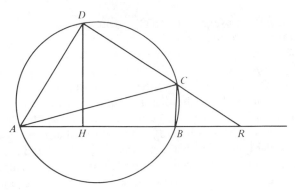

FIGURE 3

But

$$RH/DH = RB(=HA)/BC$$
$$BA/DH = DH/HA = HA/BC.$$

BIBLIOGRAPHY

The following works should be consulted: A. Aaboe, "Al-Kāshī's Iteration Method for Determination of sin 1°," in *Scripta mathematica*, **20** (1954), 24–29; and *Episodes From the Early History of Mathematics* (New Haven, 1964), 120; C. Brockelmann, *Geschichte der arabischen Literatur*, I (Leiden, 1943), 626, and supp. I (Leiden, 1937), 868–869; P. Brunet and A. Mieli, *Histoire des sciences d'antiquité* (Paris, 1935), 333–415; H. Bürger and K. Kohl, "Zur Geschichte des Transversalenzatzes," in *Abhandlungen zur Geschichte der Naturwissenschaften und der Medizin*, no. 7 (1924), 55–57, 67, 70, 71, 73–75, 89; Carra de Vaux, "Remaniement des sphériques de Théodose par Iahia ibn Muhammed ibn Abī Schukr Almaghrabī Alandalusī," in *Journal asiatique*, **17** (1891), 287–295; T. Heath, *A History of Greek Mathematics*, I (Oxford, 1921), 244–270; P. Luckey, "Der Lehrbrief über Kreis Umfang (ar-Risāla al-Muḥītīya) von Čamšid b. Mas'ūd al-Kāšī," in *Abhandlungen der Deutschen Akademie der Wissenschaften zu Berlin*, Math.-naturwiss. Kl., no. 5 (1950); and G. Sarton, *Introduction to the History of Science*, II, pt. 2 (Baltimore, 1931), 1015–1017.

H. Suter, *Die Mathematiker und Astronomen der Araber und ihre Werke* (Leipzig, 1900), 155; S. Tekeli, "Taqī al-Din's Work on Extracting the Chord 2° and sin 1°," in *Araştirma*, **3** (1965), 123–131; and "The Works on the Duplication of the Cube in the Islamic World," *ibid.*, **4** (1966), 87–105; F. Woepcke, "Sur une mesure de la circonférence du cercle due aux astronomes arabes et fondée sur un calcul d'Aboul Wafā," in *Journal asiatique*, **15** (1860), 281–320; and S. Zeki, *Asari bakiye*, I (Istanbul, 1913), 106–120.

S. TEKELI

MUNĪŚVARA VIŚVARŪPA

MUNĪŚVARA VIŚVARŪPA (*b.* Benares, India, 17 March 1603)

The member of a noted family of astronomers who originated at Dadhigrāma on the Payoṣṇī River in Vidarbha with Cintāmaṇi, a Brahmana of the Devarātragotra, in the middle of the fifteenth century, and continued with successive generations represented by Rāma (who was patronized by a king of Vidarbha), Trimalla, and Ballāla, Munīśvara was a grandson of Ballāla, born after the latter had moved the family to Benares. Ballāla had had five sons: Rāma, who wrote a commentary on the *Sudhārasasāraṇī* of Ananta (*fl.* 1525); Kṛṣṇa (*fl.* 1600–1625); Govinda, whose son Nārāyaṇa wrote commentaries on the *Grahalāghava* of Gaṇeśa (*b.* 1507) and, in 1678, on the *Jātakapaddhati* of Keśava (*fl.* 1496); Raṅganātha, who finished his commentary on the *Sūryasiddhānta*, the *Gūḍhārthaprakāśa*, in 1603; and Mahādeva. Munīśvara was the son of Raṅganātha and the pupil of Kṛṣṇa, who traces his *guruparamparā*, or lineage of teachers, back through Viṣṇu (*fl. ca.* 1575–1600) and Nṛsiṁha (*b.* 1548) to the great Gaṇeśa himself.

Although thus tracing his intellectual genealogy back to the school of Gaṇeśa and Keśava (see essay in Supplement), Munīśvara followed his uncle's example of studying the works of Bhāskara II (*b.* 1115); as Kṛṣṇa had written a commentary, the *Bījāṅkura*, on Bhāskara's *Bījagaṇita*, Munīśvara continued the task by commenting on the *Līlāvatī* in the *Nisṛṣṭārthadūtī* and on the two parts of the *Siddhāntaśiromaṇi* in the immense *Marīcī*, begun in 1635 and finished in 1638.

In the 1640's and 1650's Munīśvara's family entered into a scientific controversy with another Benares family of astronomers whose intellectual genealogy was traced back to Gaṇeśa. This second family had originated in Golagrāma in Mahārāṣṭra at about the same time that Cintāmaṇi appeared in Dadhigrāma; its representatives contemporary with Munīśvara were the three brothers Divākara (*b.* 1606), Kamalākara (*fl.* 1658), and Raṅganātha. They generally favored the *Saurapakṣa* (see essay in Supplement). And, in this connection, it should be noted that Munīśvara's greatest work, the *Siddhāntasārvabhauma*, which was completed in 1646 and on which he wrote a commentary, the *Āśayaprakāśinī*, in 1650, is fundamentally *Saura* in character; there is, however, a strong admixture of material from the *Brāhmapakṣa* (see essay in Supplement), reflecting his intense study of Bhāskara II's *Siddhāntaśiromaṇi* and of the *Siddhāntasundara* of Jñānarāja (*fl.* 1503). He also demonstrates some knowledge of Islamic astronomy, although much less acceptance of it than is shown by Kamalākara. It is around their respective attitudes toward Islamic astronomy that the controversy between the two families principally turned. Despite his negative attitude, however, the author of the

Siddhāntasārvabhauma seems to have enjoyed the patronage of Shāh Jahān (reigned 1628–1658).

Muniśvara also composed a *Pāṭīsāra* on mathematics, of which the earliest manuscript, still in Benares, was copied in 1654.

BIBLIOGRAPHY

I. ORIGINAL WORKS. Only one of Muniśvara's works has been published in full. Of the *Marīci* the part relating to the *Golādhyāya* was edited by Dattātreya Āpṭe as Ānandāśrama Sanskrit Series 122, 2 vols. (Poona, 1943–1952). Of the part relating to the *Gaṇitādhyāya*, the first chapter only was edited by Muralīdhara Jhā (Benares, 1917) and the rest by Kedāradatta Jośī in vols. II and III of his ed. of the *Grahagaṇitādhyāya* (Benares, 1964). Muralīdhara Ṭhakkura edited 2 vols. containing the first two chs. and a part of the third of the *Siddhāntasārvabhauma* with the *Āśayaprakāśinī* as Saraswati Bhavana Texts 41 (Benares, 1932–1935); no more has appeared.

II. SECONDARY LITERATURE. There are notices on Muniśvara in S. Dvivedin, *Gaṇakataraṅgiṇī* (Benares, 1933), repr. from *The Pandit*, n.s. **14** (1892), 91–94; Ś. B. Dīkṣita, *Bhāratīya Jyotiḥśāstra* (Poona, 1896, 1931), 286–287; and M. M. Patkar in *Poona Orientalist*, **3** (1938), 170–171.

DAVID PINGREE

MYDORGE, CLAUDE (*b.* Paris, France, 1585; *d.* Paris, July 1647)

Mydorge belonged to one of France's richest and most illustrious families. His father, Jean Mydorge, *seigneur* of Maillarde, was *conseiller* at the Parlement of Paris and judge of the Grande Chambre; his mother's maiden name was Lamoignon. He decided to pursue a legal career and was, first, *conseiller* at the Châtelet, then treasurer of the *généralité* of Amiens. In 1613 he married the sister of M. de la Haye, the French ambassador at Constantinople. His duties as treasurer left him sufficient time to devote himself to his passion, mathematics.

About 1625 Mydorge met Descartes and became one of his most faithful friends. In 1627, to aid Descartes in his search for an explanation of vision, Mydorge had parabolic, hyperbolic, oval, and elliptic lenses made for him. He also determined and drew their shapes with great precision. He subsequently had many lenses and burning glasses made. It was said that altogether he spent more than 100,000 écus for this purpose.

After a thorough study of Descartes's *Dioptrique*, Mydorge at first criticized the book on various points but later completely adopted his friend's theories.

Fermat, however, in 1638, wrote to Mersenne to refute the *Dioptrique*. On 1 March 1638 (see *Oeuvres de Descartes*, C. Adam and P. Tannery, eds., II, *Correspondance*, 15–23) Descartes sent a long letter to Mydorge—he knew that the latter had openly taken his side in the dispute—in which he provided him with the seven documents relating to the case and asked him to be judge and intermediary. He also asked Mydorge to make a copy of the letter and send the original to Fermat's friends Étienne Pascal and Roberval. (It should be noted that Fermat's correspondence indicates that Pascal and Roberval were in no way his friends.) Through the good offices of Mydorge and Mersenne, Descartes and Fermat were reconciled.

Mydorge was held in high regard by other famous contemporaries; for instance, on 2 March 1633 Peiresc wrote from Aix to Gassendi, who was then at Digne: "If you have any special observations by M. Mydorge, you would do me a great favor by communicating them to me" (see Galileo Galilei, *Opere* [Edizione nazionale], XVIII [Florence, 1966], 430).

Mydorge's work in geometry was directed to the study of conic sections. In 1631 he published a two-volume work on the subject, which was enlarged to four volumes in 1639. The four volumes were reprinted several times under the title *De sectionibus conicis*. A further portion of the work, in manuscript, is lost. It seems that two English friends of the Mydorge family, William Cavendish, duke of Newcastle, and Thomas Wriothesley, earl of Southampton, took it to England, where apparently it disappeared.

In his study of conic sections Mydorge continued the work of Apollonius, whose methods of proof he refined and simplified. Among the ways of describing an ellipse, for example, two from volume II may be cited. According to the first definition, an ellipse is the geometric locus of a point of a straight line the extremities of which move along two fixed straight lines. (This definition had already been demonstrated by Stevin, who attributed it to Ubaldi; actually, it goes back to antiquity, as Proclus indicates in his commentaries on Euclid.) According to the second definition, the ellipse can be deduced from a circle by extending all its ordinates in a constant relationship. In the same book Mydorge asserts that if from a given point in the plane of a conic section radii to the points of the curve are drawn and extended in a given relationship, then their extremities will be on a new conic section similar to the first. This statement constitutes the beginnings of an extremely fruitful method of deforming figures; it was successfully used by La Hire and Newton, and later by Poncelet and, especially, by Chasles, who named it *déformation homographique*.

Mydorge posed and solved the following problem in volume III: "On a given cone place a given conic section"—a problem that Apollonius had solved only for a right cone. Mydorge was also interested in geometric methods used in approximate construction, such as that of the regular heptagon. Another problem that Mydorge solved by approximation—although he did not clearly indicate his method—was that of transforming a square into an equivalent regular polygon possessing an arbitrary number of sides.

Mydorge's works on conic sections contain hundreds of problems published for the first time, as well as a multitude of ingenious and original methods that later geometers frequently used, usually without citing their source. The collection of Mydorge's manuscripts held by the Académie des Sciences contains more than 1,000 geometric problems. Finally, it should be noted that the term "parameter" of a conic section was introduced by Mydorge.

A friend of Descartes and an eminent geometer, Mydorge was also well versed in optics. He possessed a lively curiosity and was open to all the new ideas of his age. Like Fermat, he belonged to that elite group of seventeenth-century scientists who pursued science as amateurs but nevertheless made contributions of the greatest importance to one or more fields of knowledge.

BIBLIOGRAPHY

I. ORIGINAL WORKS. Mydorge's first major writing, *Examen du livre des Récréations mathématiques* (Paris, 1630; repr. 1643), with notes by D. Henrion, is a commentary on *Récréations mathématiques* (Pont-à-Mousson, 1624), published under the pseudonym H. Van Etten (actually Leurechon).

The second was *Prodromi catoptricorum et dioptricorum, sive conicorum operis . . . libri duo* (Paris, 1631), enlarged to *Conicorum operis . . . libri quattuor* (Paris, 1639, 1641, 1660), also issued as *De sectionibus conicis, libri quattuor* (Paris, 1644), which Mersenne inserted in his *Universae geometriae, mixtaeque mathematicae synopsis . . .* (Paris, 1644).

A selection of the geometry problems preserved in Paris was published by C. Henry in *Bullettino di bibliografia e di storia delle scienze matematiche e fisiche*, **14** and **16**. Mydorge's son assembled three short treatises from his father's MSS—*De la lumière*, *De l'ombre*, and *De la sciotérique*—but all trace of them has been lost.

II. SECONDARY LITERATURE. See the following, listed chronologically: C. G. Jöcher, *Allgemeines Gelehrten-Lexicon*, III (Leipzig, 1751), 787; *Biographie universelle*, XXIX (Paris, 1860), 666; *La grande encyclopédie*, XXIV (Paris, 1899), 657; M. Chasles, *Aperçu historique sur l'origine et le développement des méthodes en géométrie* (Paris, 1889), 88–89; and M. Cantor, *Vorlesungen über Geschichte der Mathematik*, II (Leipzig, 1913), 673–674, 768–769.

PIERRE SPEZIALI

MYLON, CLAUDE (*b*. Paris, France, *ca.* 1618; *d*. Paris, *ca.* 1660)

Mylon's place in the history of science derives from the service he provided in facilitating communication among more learned men in the decade from 1650 to 1660. He was the third son of Benoist Mylon, counselor to Louis XIII and Controller-General of Finance; he himself was admitted to the bar as an advocate before Parlement in 1641, even though he lacked two years of being twenty-five, the legal age of majority.

As early as 1645 Mylon had become concerned with mathematics, making written notes of new Cartesian mathematical problems. He was also in contact with Mersenne, Debeaune, and Roberval, and when Schooten passed through Paris he was able to transmit a considerable amount of new information to him. Mylon also served as secretary to the "Académie Parisienne," a continuation of the Mersenne group, under the direction of F. le Pailleur, which in 1654 received Pascal's famous "Adresse." Mylon achieved a certain importance when the death of Pailleur, in November 1654, left the papers of the society at his disposal; it was thus he who told Schooten (who told Huygens) of Fermat's and Pascal's problems and solutions concerning games of chance. He also forwarded to Holland Fermat's and Frenicle's problems in number theory. In 1655 Huygens, who was making his first trip to France, visited Mylon; the following year he suggested the "commerce scientifique" that provides the chief documentation of Mylon's career.

Mylon maintained a number of rather delicate relationships with other mathematicians. He had access to Pascal in his retirement (although to a lesser degree than did Carcavi), and while his affection for Conrart threatened his friendship with Roberval, the latter continued to make use of him as an intermediary. He was less happy in his two attempts at personal achievement: in 1658 he hazarded his own solution to the quadrature of the cubic curves known as the "perles de M. Sluse" and in January 1659, in the wake of the debate provoked by Pascal, he proposed to prove Wren's solution of the length of the cycloid. These efforts stand as a monument to his inadequacies as a mathematician, and it is with them that all mention of Mylon by Huygens stops. No publication by him is known.

BIBLIOGRAPHY

On Mylon and his work, see J.-B. du Hamel, *Astronomia physica*, . . . *Accessere P. Petiti observationes*. . . . (Paris, 1660), 12, which includes an account of Pierre Petit's pamphlet on the observation made by Mylon and Roberval of the solar eclipse of 8 Apr. 1652.

See also C. Adam and P. Tannery, eds., *Oeuvres de Descartes*, IV (Paris, 1901), 232, 397, which deals with the problem of the "trois bâtons" and Roberval's "Aristarchus."

See L. Brunschvicg, P. Boutroux, and F. Gazier, eds., *Oeuvres de Blaise Pascal*, IX (Paris, 1914), 151–156; the letter referred to here (Mylon to Pascal, 27 Dec. 1658) is at the Bibliothèque Nationale, Paris, Res. V 859, with a demonstration by Mylon of "the equality of the cycloid and its partner."

There are numerous references to Mylon in Huygens' correspondence, as well as letters from him, in *Oeuvres complètes de Christiaan Huygens*, 22 vols. (The Hague, 1888–1950); see esp. I, 517, for Roberval's demonstration on the surface of spherical triangles; II, 8–25, for Frenicle's results on compatible numbers; "Propositio Domini Wren Angli. Demonstrata a Claudio Mylon die 26 Januarii 1659," II, 335; and "La quadrature des perles de M. Sluse par Claude Mylon. En juin 1658," II, 337. Mylon's role in the problem of games of chance is discussed in "Avertissement," XIV, 4–9. See also *The Correspondence of H. Oldenburg*, I (London, 1965), 225.

PIERRE COSTABEL

NAIMARK, MARK ARONOVICH (*b.* Odessa, Russia, 5 December 1909; *d.* Moscow, U.S.S.R., 30 December 1978)

Naimark was the son of Aron Iakovlevich Naimark, a professional artist, and of Zefir Moiseevna Naimark. He showed his mathematical talents at an early age; and from 1924 to 1928, studying independently, he completed a university course in mathematical analysis. In 1929 he enrolled at the Odessa Institute of National Education, and four years later was admitted to graduate study (*aspirantura*) at Odessa State University, under the direction of Mark G. Krein. On 1 June 1932 he married Larisa Petrovna Shcherbakova; they had two sons.

Naimark defended his candidate's thesis (roughly corresponding to the U.S. doctoral dissertation) in 1936. Two years later he moved to Moscow. In 1941 he received the doctorate (often called the "big" doctorate) from the Steklov Mathematical Institute and was immediately appointed professor at the Seismological Institute of the U.S.S.R. Academy of Sciences. When the Soviet Union entered World War II, Naimark embarked upon military work, spending eighteen months in Tashkent with the evacuated Seismological Institute. He worked at a number of institutes, including the Institute of Chemical Physics and the U.S.S.R. Academy for the Arms Industry, after returning to Moscow when the war was over. In 1954 Naimark became a professor at the Moscow Physical-Technical Institute, and in 1962 he was appointed professor at the Steklov Mathematical Institute, a post he held until his death.

Naimark's life was governed by total dedication to science that led to a large scientific output. Nevertheless, he found time to read Western writers in their original languages and to follow developments in the fine arts. He was a skillful painter and knew a great deal about music.

During his early career Naimark carried a heavy load of classroom teaching. In later years he taught only graduate courses and guided the research of his many students. In the 1960's he traveled widely; in 1967 he made a lecture tour through Canada that did much to further contacts between Soviet and Western mathematicians. During his last ten years Naimark suffered from heart disease but bore his affliction with grace and humor. When too ill to sit up, he dictated mathematics to his wife.

Naimark's first mathematical writings were joint papers with Krein, mostly on the separation of roots of algebraic equations. After his arrival in Moscow, he was at the forefront of functional analysis and group representations, two fields that were in a state of rapid ferment in the Soviet Union and elsewhere. (He is, in fact, justly considered one of the founders of functional analysis and group representations.) His most famous early contribution was the elaboration of the classical Gelfand-Naimark theorem (1943), which showed that norm-closed self-adjoint algebras of operators in Hilbert space can be described by a few simple axioms that in the commutative case serve to characterize the algebras of all continuous complex-valued functions on compacta. Also in 1943 he published his generalization to locally compact abelian groups of John von Neumann's spectral theorem. In 1950 Izrail M. Gelfand and Naimark published their important treatise on irreducible unitary representations of the classical matrix groups. In this work they explicitly obtained a large number of these representations—enough, in fact, for Plancherel's theorem for these groups. Their results strongly influenced J. Michael G. Fell's work on group representations done in the 1950's and 1960's, and opened the way for Harish-Chandra's definitive work on Plancherel's theorem, done from about 1953 to about 1970. (But the irreducible unitary representations have not yet been obtained explicitly.)

Naimark also made fundamental contributions to the theory of non-self-adjoint operators in Hilbert spaces, to the theory of Banach algebras with involution, and to the theory of representations of groups and algebras in inner product spaces bearing an indefinite metric. His scientific oeuvre consists of 123 research papers and 5 books.

Naimark's books are models of lucidity, completeness, and scholarship. His *Normirovannye koltsa* (Normed rings, 1956) has gone through three editions and has been translated into German, French, and English. His *Lineinye differentsialnye operatory* (Linear differential operators, 1954) also has gone through several editions and translations. His last work, written with A. I. Shtern while he was gravely ill, is *Teoriya predstavlenii grupp* (Theory of group representations, 1976). This book, which also appeared in French and English, is both a textbook and a vade mecum on the theory of Lie groups and their finite-dimensional representations.

BIBLIOGRAPHY

I. ORIGINAL WORKS. Naimark's works are listed in *Uspekhi matematicheskikh nauk*, **15**, no. 2 (1960), 233–236; *Matematika v SSSR, 1958–1967*, II (1970), 949–950; and *Uspekhi matematicheskikh nauk*, **35**, no. 4 (1980), 139–140. His most important works include "On the Imbedding of Normed Rings into the Ring of Operators in Hilbert Space," in *Matematicheskii sbornik (Recueil mathématique)*, n.s. **12**, no. 54 (1943), 197–219, written with Izrail Gelfand (his name is misspelled as Neumark); "Polozhitelno-opredelennye operatornye funktsii na kommutativnoi gruppe" (Positive definitive operator functions on a commutative group), in *Izvestiia Akademii nauk SSSR, seriia matematicheskaia*, **7** (1943), 237–244; *Unitarnye predstavleniya klassicheskikh grupp* (Unitary representations of classical groups), in *Trudy Matematicheskogo instituta imeni V. A. Steklova*, **36** (1950), 1–288, written with Gelfand; *Lineinye differentsialnye operatory* (Moscow, 1952), trans. by E. R. Dawson and edited by W. N. Everitt as *Linear Differential Operators*, 2 vols. (New York, 1967–1968); *Normirovannye koltsa* (Moscow, 1956), trans. by Leo F. Boron as *Normed Rings* (Groningen, 1959; rev. ed., 1970); and *Teoriya predstavlenii grupp* (Moscow, 1975), trans. by Elizabeth Hewitt and edited by Edwin Hewitt as *Theory of Group Representations* (New York, 1982), written with A. I. Shtern.

II. SECONDARY LITERATURE. An obituary by Izrail M. Gelfand and others appeared in *Uspekhi matematicheskikh nauk*, **35**, no. 4 (1980), 135–139. English trans. in *Russian Mathematical Surveys*, **35**, no. 4 (1980), 157–164. See also the article in honor of Naimark's fiftieth birthday in *Uspekhi matematicheskikh nauk*, **15**, no. 2 (1960), 231–236. English trans. by W. F. Lunnon in *Russian Mathematical Surveys*, **15**, no. 2 (1960), 169–174.

EDWIN HEWITT

NAIRNE, EDWARD (*b.* Sandwich [?], England, 1726; *d.* London, England, 1 September 1806)

Nairne achieved an international reputation as one of the foremost makers of mathematical, optical, and philosophical instruments of the eighteenth century. He became free of the Spectaclemakers Company in 1748 and established his business in London at 20 Cornhill, not far from the shop of Matthew Loft, to whom he had been apprenticed in 1741. Nairne took Thomas Blunt, his own former apprentice, into partnership in 1774, and the firm, which in 1791 was moved to 22 Cornhill, continued as Nairne and Blunt until the latter's death in 1822.

In 1771 Nairne contributed to the *Philosophical Transactions of the Royal Society* the first of many papers on experiments in optics, pneumatics, and, most notably, electricity. He was elected a fellow of the Royal Society in 1776.

In 1772 Nairne invented an improved form of electrostatic machine using a cylindrical glass vessel as the generator. Its quick acceptance in England and on the Continent did much to enhance his reputation. The regular production from Nairne's shop included microscopes, telescopes, navigating and surveying instruments, electrical machines, vacuum pumps, and measuring equipment required by the new philosophical laboratories.

Franklin seems to have had a long acquaintance with Nairne and his work. In 1758 Nairne made a set of artificial magnets for him, and the swelling and shrinking of the mahogany case led to a later correspondence between them on a possible design for a hygrometer. After the Harvard College fire of 1764, Nairne was one of the makers commissioned, on Franklin's recommendation, to replace the lost instruments.

Nairne also reported on his experiments on the specific gravity and freezing point of seawater, desiccation by means of a vacuum, and the adaptation of the mercury barometer for use at sea.

BIBLIOGRAPHY

I. ORIGINAL WORKS. Nairne's papers published in the *Philosophical Transactions of the Royal Society* include "Description of a New Constructed Equatorial Telescope," **61** (1771), 223–225; "Water From Sea Ice," **66** (1776),

249–256; "Experiments With the Air-pump," **67** (1777), 614–648; and "Experiments on Electricity," **68** (1778), 823–860. Other works are *Description of a Pocket Microscope* (n.p., 1771); *Directions for Using the Electrical Machine as Made and Sold by E. Nairne* (London, 1773); *Directions for the Use of the Octant* (n.d.).

Many of Nairne's instruments survive and some may be seen in the collections of the Adler Planetarium, Chicago; Conservatoire National des Arts et Métiers, Paris; Harvard University; the museums of the history of science at Oxford and Florence; National Maritime Museum, Greenwich; Naval Museum, Madrid; Science Museum, London; and the Smithsonian Institution, Washington.

II. SECONDARY LITERATURE. See Maria Luisa Bonelli, *Catalogo degli strumenti dei Museo di storia della scienza* (Florence, 1954), 92, 131, 194, 200, 208, 210, 251–252, 254, 256; I. Bernard Cohen, *Some Early Tools of American Science* (Cambridge, Mass., 1950), 166, 169; Maurice Daumas, *Les instruments scientifiques au XVII et XVIII siècles* (Paris, 1953), 316–317; Nicholas Goodison, *English Barometers, 1680–1860* (New York, 1968), 52–53, 123, 168–170, 257; W. E. Knowles Middleton, *The History of the Barometer* (Baltimore, 1964), 163; Leslie Stephen and Sidney Lee, eds., *Dictionary of National Biography*, XIV, 25–26; E. G. R. Taylor, *The Mathematical Practitioners of Hanoverian England* (London, 1966), 50, 53, 62–63, 66, 214; Carl Van Doren, ed., *Benjamin Franklin's Autobiographical Writings* (New York, 1945), 490–494; and David P. Wheatland, *The Apparatus of Science at Harvard, 1765–1800* (Cambridge, Mass., 1968), 22–23, 79, 155–161.

RODERICK S. WEBSTER

NAPIER, JOHN (*b*. Edinburgh, Scotland, 1550; *d*. Edinburgh, 4 April 1617)

The eighth laird of Merchiston, John Napier was the son of Sir Archibald Napier by his first wife, Janet Bothwell, daughter of an Edinburgh burgess. At the age of thirteen he went to St. Salvator's College, St. Andrews, where he lodged with John Rutherford, the college principal. Little is known of his life at this time save that he gained some impetus toward theological studies during the brief period at St. Andrews. His mother's brother, Adam Bothwell, bishop of Orkney, recommended that he continue his studies abroad and it seems likely that he did so, although no explicit evidence exists as to his domicile, or the nature of his studies. At all events, by 1571 he had returned to Scotland and, in 1572, he married Elizabeth, daughter of Sir James Stirling, and took up residence in a castle at Gartnes (completed in 1574). On the death of his father in 1608, he moved to Merchiston Castle, near Edinburgh, where he lived for the rest of his life. In 1579 his wife died and he

subsequently married Agnes Chisholm of Cromlix, Perthshire. There were two children by the first marriage, a son, Archibald, who in 1627 was raised to the peerage by the title of Lord Napier, and a daughter, Joanne. By the second marriage there were ten children; the best known of these is the second son, Robert, his father's literary executor.

Napier lived the full and energetic life of a sixteenth-century Scottish landowner, participating vigorously in local and national affairs. He embraced with great fervor the opinions of the Protestant party, and the political activities of his papist father-in-law, Sir James Chisholm, involved him in continuous embarrassment. There were quarrels with his half brothers over the inheritance and disputes with tenants and neighboring landlords over land tenure and rights. In all these matters, Napier seems to have shown himself forthright and determined in the pursuit of his aims, but nonetheless just and reasonable in his demands and willing to accept a fair settlement. As a landowner, Napier gave more than the usual attention to agriculture and to the improvement of his crops and his cattle. He seems to have experimented with the use of manures and to have discovered the value of common salt for this purpose, a monopoly for this mode of tillage being granted to his eldest son, Archibald, in 1698. A monopoly was granted to Napier also for the invention of a hydraulic screw and revolving axle to keep the level of water down in coal pits (1597). In 1599 Sir John Skene mentioned that he had consulted Napier, "a gentleman of singular judgement and learning, especially in mathematic sciences," with reference to the proper methods to be used in measuring lands.

In sixteenth-century Scotland, intellectual interest centered on religion, theology, and politics rather than on science and mathematics and Napier's first literary work arose out of the fears entertained in Scotland of an invasion by Philip II of Spain. *A Plaine Discovery of the Whole Revelation of Saint John* occupied him for about five years before its publication in 1593. In this tract Napier urged the Scottish king, James VI (the future James I of England), to see that "justice be done against the enemies of Gods church" and implored him to "purge his house, family and court of all Papists, Atheists and Newtrals." Through this publication, Napier gained a considerable reputation as a scholar and theologian and it was translated into Dutch, French, and German, going through several editions in each language. It is possible that, in later life, his authority as a divine saved him from persecution as a warlock, for there are many stories told suggesting that, locally, he was suspected of being in league with the powers of darkness. Not content with opposing popery by the pen, Napier also invented various engines of war for the defense of his faith and his country. In a document preserved in the Bacon Collection at Lambeth Palace, Napier outlines four inventions, two varieties of burning mirrors for setting fire to enemy ships at a distance, a piece of artillery for destroying everything round the arc of a circle, and an armored chariot so constructed that its occupants could fire in all directions. It is not known whether any of these machines were ever constructed.

Although documentary evidence exists to substantiate the active part Napier played in public affairs in this tumultuous age, it is more difficult to trace the development of his mathematical work, which seems to have begun in early life and persisted, through solitary and indefatigable labors, to the very end, when he made contact with Henry Briggs. Some material was, apparently, assembled soon after his first marriage in 1572 and may have been prompted by knowledge he had gleaned during his travels abroad. This treatise, dealing mainly with arithmetic and algebra, survived in manuscript form and was transcribed, after Napier's death, by his son Robert for the benefit of Briggs. It was published in 1839 by a descendant, Mark Napier, who gave to it the title *De arte logistica*. From this work, it appears that Napier had investigated imaginary roots of equations, a subject he refers to as a great algebraic secret.

There is evidence that Napier began to work on logarithms about 1590; the work culminated in the publication of two Latin treatises, known respectively as the *Descriptio* (1614) and the *Constructio* (1619). The *Descriptio* bears evidence of having been written all at one time and contains, besides the tables, a brief general account of their nature and use. An English translation of this work was made by Edward Wright but was published only after Wright's death by his son, Samuel Wright (1616). Napier approved the translation, both in substance and in form. The *Constructio* was brought out by Robert Napier, after the death of his father, and consists of material which Napier had written many years before. The object of the *Constructio* was to explain fully the way in which the tables had been calculated and the reasoning on which they were based. In the *Constructio* the phrase "artificial numbers" is used instead of "logarithms," the word "logarithm" being apparently of later invention. Napier offered no explanation for the choice but Briggs, in the *Arithmetica logarithmica* (1624), explains that the name came from their inventor because they exhibit numbers which preserve always the same ratio to one another.

Although it is as the inventor of logarithms that Napier is known in the history of mathematics, the two works mentioned above contain other material of lesser importance but nonetheless noteworthy. In the course of illustrating the use and application of logarithms Napier made frequent use of trigonometric theorems and the contribution he made to the development and systematization of spherical trigonometry has been rated highly. Napier's rules (called the Napier analogies) for the right-angled spherical triangle were published in the *Descriptio* (Bk. II, Ch. 4). He expressed them in logarithmic form and exhibited their character in relation to the star pentagon with five right angles. Another achievement was the effective use he made of decimal notation (which he had learnt of from Stevin) in conjunction with the decimal point. Although he was not the first to use a decimal separatrix in this way, the publicity that he gave to it and to the new notation helped to establish its use as standard practice. In 1617 Napier's intense concern for the practicalities of computation led him to publish another book, the *Rabdologiae*, which contains a number of elementary calculating devices, including the rods known as "Napier's bones." These rods, which in essence constitute a mechanical multiplication table, had a considerable vogue for many years after his death. Each rod is engraved with a table of multiples of a particular digit, the tens and units being separated by an oblique stroke. To obtain the product 267×8, the rods 2, 6, 7 are assembled and the result is read off from the entries in the eighth row; thus gives 2,136. Book II is a practical treatment of mensuration formulas. Book III, the method of the promptuary, deals with a more complicated system of multiplication by engraved rods and strips, which has been called the first attempt at the invention of a calculating machine. The concluding section deals with a mechanical method of multiplication that was based on an "areal abacus" consisting of a checkerboard with counters, in which numbers were expressed in the binary scale.

Until recently the historical background of the invention of logarithms has remained something of an enigma. At the Napier tercentenary celebrations, Lord Moulton referred to Napier's invention as a "bolt from the blue" and suggested that nothing had led up to it, foreshadowed it, or heralded its arrival. Notwithstanding, Joost Bürgi, a maker of watches and astronomical instruments, had turned his attention to the problem about the same time and developed a system of logarithms entirely independently. Many Continental historians have accorded him priority in the actual invention, although he certainly did not have it in the publication of his *Arithmetische und geometrische Progress-Tabulen* (1620).

After the revival of learning in western Europe some of the first advances made were in trigonometry, which was developed as an independent field of study, largely in the interests of astronomy but also for surveying, mapmaking, and navigation. Much time was spent in calculating extensive tables of sines and tangents. Trigonometric tables were appearing in all parts of Europe, and stress was laid on the development of formulas, analogous to

$$\sin A \sin B = \tfrac{1}{2}(\cos \overline{A - B} - \cos \overline{A + B}),$$

which could, by converting the product of sines into sums and differences, reduce the computational difficulties. This conversion process was known as prosthaphaeresis. Formulas generated in this way were much used in astronomical calculations and were linked with the names of Longomontanus and Wittich, who both worked as assistants to Tycho Brahe. It is said that word of these developments came to Napier through a fellow countryman, John Craig, who accompanied James VI to Norway in 1590 to meet his bride, Anne of Denmark. The party landed near Tycho Brahe's observatory at Hven and was entertained by the astronomer. Although the construction of Napier's logarithms clearly owes nothing to prosthaphaeresis, the aim—that of substituting addition and subtraction for multiplication and division in trigonometrical calculations—was the same, and if Napier was already working on the problem, he may well have been stimulated to further efforts by the information he received through Craig. There is evidence in a letter written by Kepler in 1624 that he had received an intimation of Napier's work as early as 1594. This information presumably came through Tycho Brahe and Craig.

Napier's own account of his purpose in undertaking the work is printed in the author's preface to the *Descriptio* and is reprinted with slight modification in Wright's translation. Napier says that there is nothing more troublesome to mathematical practice than the "multiplications, divisions, square and cubical extractions of great numbers" and that these operations involve a tedious expenditure of time, as well as being subject to "slippery errors." By means of the tables all these operations could be replaced by simple addition and subtraction.

As presented, Napier's canon is specifically associated with trigonometric usage, in the sense that it gives logarithms of natural sines (from the tables of Erasmus Reinhold). The sine of an arc was not, at that time, given as a ratio but as the length of the semichord of a circle of given radius, subtending a specified angle at the center. In tabulating such sines, it was customary to choose a large number for the

radius of the circle (or whole sine); Napier's choice of 10^7 gave him seven significant figures before introducing fractions.

The theory of arithmetic and geometric progressions, which played a central role in Napier's constructions, was of course available from ancient times (Napier quotes Euclid). The correspondence between the terms of an arithmetic and a geometric progression had been explored in detail by many sixteenth-century mathematicians; and Stifel in *Arithmetica integra* (1544) had enunciated clearly the basic laws—but without the index notation—corresponding to

$$a^m a^n = a^{m+n}, \qquad (a^m)^n = a^{mn}.$$

But, in all this work, only the relation between discrete sets of numbers was implied. In Napier's geometric model the correspondence between the terms of an arithmetic and a geometric progression was founded on the idea of continuously moving points and involved concepts of time, motion, and instantaneous speed. Although such notions had played a prominent part in the discussions of the fourteenth-century philosophers of the Merton school (most notably Swineshead in his *Liber calculationum*), there is nothing to suggest that any of this work directly influenced Napier.

Most historical accounts of Napier's logarithms have suffered considerably through translation into modern symbolism. Napier himself used virtually no notation, and his explanatory detail is almost wholly verbal. Without any of the tools of modern analysis for handling continuous functions, his propositions inevitably remained on an intuitive basis. He had, nonetheless, a remarkably clear idea of a functional relation between two continuous variables.

Briefly, two points move along parallel straight lines, the first moving arithmetically through equal distances in equal times and the second moving geometrically toward a fixed point, cutting off proportional parts of the whole line and then of subsequent remainders, also in equal times.

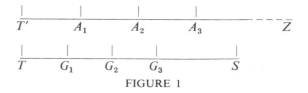

FIGURE 1

If the first point moves through the spaces $T'A_1$, A_1A_2, A_2A_3, $\cdots$, in equal times, then

$$T'A_1 = A_1A_2 = A_2A_3 = \cdots.$$

If the second point moves toward a fixed point S and is at T, G_1, G_2, G_3, $\cdots$, when the first point is at T', A_1, A_2, A_3, $\cdots$, then the spaces TG_1, G_1G_2, G_2G_3, $\cdots$, are also covered in equal times. But since the second point moves geometrically,

$$TG_1/TS = G_1G_2/G_1S = G_2G_3/G_2S = \cdots.$$

It follows that the velocity of the second point is everywhere proportional to its distance from S.

The definition of the logarithm follows: Two points start from T' and T respectively, at the same instant and with the same velocities, the first point moving uniformly and the second point moving so that its velocity is everywhere proportional to its distance from S; if the points reach L and G respectively, at the same instant, the number that measures the line $T'L$ is defined as the logarithm of GS (GS is the sine and TS, the whole sine, or radius).

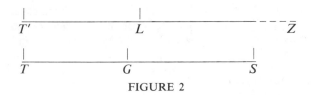

FIGURE 2

From the definition, it follows that the logarithm of the whole sine (10^7) is 0 and that the logarithm of n, where $n > 10^7$, is less than 0. In modern notation, if $T'L = y$, $y_0 = 0$, $GS = x$, $TS = x_0 = r = 10^7$, $dx/dt = -kx$, $dy/dt = kr$, $dy/dx = -r/x$, $\log_e(x/r) = -y/r$, or $\log_{1/e}(x/r) = y/r$. It remained to apply this structure in the calculation of the canon. Without any machinery for handling continuous functions it was necessary for Napier to calculate bounds, between which the logarithm must lie. His entire method depends upon these bounds, together with the corresponding bounds for the difference of the logarithms of two sines.

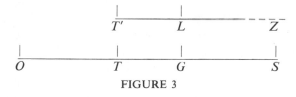

FIGURE 3

If the point O lies on ST produced such that $OS/TS = TS/SG$, then the spaces OT and TG are covered in equal times. But, since $OS > TS > GS$, the velocity at $O >$ the velocity at $T >$ the velocity at G. It follows that $OT > T'L > TG$, and $OS - TS > \log SG > TS - GS$. If $TS = r$, $GS = x$, we have

$$\frac{r - x}{x} > \frac{\log x}{r} > \frac{r - x}{r};$$

the corresponding bounds for the difference between two logarithms are given by

$$\frac{x_1 - x_2}{x_2} > \frac{\log x_2 - \log x_1}{r} > \frac{x_1 - x_2}{x_1}.$$

Napier then calculates in a series of tables the values of

$$10^7 \left(1 - \frac{1}{10^7}\right)^n, \qquad n = 0, 1, 2, 3, \cdots, 100;$$

$$10^7 \left(1 - \frac{1}{10^5}\right)^n, \qquad n = 0, 1, 2, \cdots, 50;$$

and finally,

$$10^7 \left(1 - \frac{5}{10^4}\right)^n \left(1 - \frac{1}{10^2}\right)^m, \quad n = 0, 1, 2, \cdots, 20;$$

$$m = 0, 1, 2, \cdots, 68.$$

The terms in each progression were obtained by successive subtraction, the last figure in the first table giving the starting point for the second. The final figure in the last table gave a value very little less than $10^7/2$, so that Napier had available a very large number of geometric means distributed over the interval 10^7, $10^7/2$. Using his inequalities, he was able to derive bounds for the logarithms of these numbers and, by taking an arithmetic mean between the bounds, to obtain an accuracy of seven significant figures. By interpolation, he tabulated the values of the logarithms of the sines (and tangents) of angles, taken at one-minute intervals, extending the tables to cover angles between 0 and 90 degrees.

Napier did not think in terms of a base, in the modern sense of the word, although since $\left(1 - \frac{1}{10^7}\right)^{10^7}$ is very nearly $\lim_{n\to\infty} \left(1 - \frac{1}{n}\right)^n$, it is clear that we have virtually a system of logarithms to base $1/e$. In Napier's system, the familiar rules for the logarithms of products, quotients, and exponents did not hold because of the choice of the whole sine (10^7), rather than 1, as the logarithm whose number was zero. Napier's tables were also awkward to use in working with ordinary numbers, rather than sines or tangents.

The calculation of the canon was a tremendous task and occupied Napier personally for over twenty years. Although not entirely free from error the calculations were essentially sound and formed the basis for all subsequent logarithm tables for nearly a century. The publication in 1614 received immediate recognition. Henry Briggs, then Gresham professor of geometry in the City of London, was enthusiastic and visited Napier at Merchiston in the summers of 1615 and 1616. During discussions that took place there the idea emerged of changing the system so that 0 should become the logarithm of unity and 10^{10} that of the whole sine. Briggs in the preface to *Arithmetica logarithmica* (1624) clearly attributes this suggestion to Napier and apparently believed that Napier had become convinced of the desirability of making this change, even before the publication of the *Descriptio*. Because of failing health, however, Napier did not have the energy to embark on this task, and it was left to Briggs to recalculate the tables, adapting them to use with a decimal base. The first 1,000 logarithms of the new canon were published after Napier's death by Briggs, without place or date (but at London before 6 December 1617), as *Logarithmorum chilias prima*. The earliest publication of Napier's logarithms on the Continent was in 1618, when Benjamin Ursinus included an excerpt from the canon, shortened by two places, in his *Cursus mathematici practici*. Through this work Kepler became aware of the importance of Napier's discovery and expressed his enthusiasm in a letter to Napier dated 28 July 1619, printed in the dedication of his *Ephemerides* (1620).

In matters of priority in the invention of logarithms the only serious claims have been made on behalf of Joost Bürgi. Many German historians have accorded him priority in the actual invention on the grounds that his tables had been computed about 1600, although they were not published until 1620. Since Napier's own work extended over a long period of time, both must be accorded full credit as independent inventors. The tables were quite differently conceived, and neither author owed anything to the other. Napier enjoyed the right of priority in publication.

BIBLIOGRAPHY

I. ORIGINAL WORKS. Napier's works are *A Plaine Discovery of the Whole Revelation of Saint John* (Edinburgh, 1593); *Mirifici logarithmorum canonis descriptio, ejusque usus, . . .* (Edinburgh, 1614); *Rabdologiae, seu numerationis per virgulas libri duo* (Edinburgh, 1617); *Mirifici logarithmorum canonis constructio; et eorum ad naturales ipsorum numeros habitudines* (Edinburgh, 1619); *De arte logistica*, Mark Napier, ed. (Edinburgh, 1839); *A Description of the Admirable Table of Logarithmes: . . .*, translated by Edward Wright, published by Samuel Wright (London, 1616). *The Construction of the Wonderful Canon of Logarithms* (Edinburgh, 1889), W. R. Macdonald's trans. of the *Constructio*, contains an excellent catalog of all the editions of Napier's works and their translations into French, Dutch, Italian, and German. Details are also included of the location of these works at that date. Further details and descriptions are included in R. A. Sampson, ed., "Bibliography of Books Exhibited at the Napier Tercentenary Celebrations, July 1914," in C. G. Knott, ed., *Napier Tercentenary Memorial Volume* (London, 1915).

II. SECONDARY LITERATURE. Such information as is available about Napier's life and work has been fairly well documented by his descendants. Mark Napier, *Memoirs of John Napier of Merchiston; His Lineage, Life and Times* (Edinburgh, 1834), based on careful research of the private papers of the Napier family, is the source of most modern accounts. The tercentenary of the publication of the *Descriptio* was celebrated by an international congress, organized by the Royal Society of Edinburgh. The papers communicated to this congress were published in the *Napier Tercentenary Memorial Volume* (see above) and supply much detail on the historical background to Napier's work. E. M. Horsburgh, ed., *Modern Instruments and Methods of Calculation: A Handbook of the Napier Tercentenary Exhibition* (London, 1914), is also useful. Of the various reconstructions of Napier's work, Lord Moulton's, in the *Tercentenary Memorial Volume*, pp. 1–24, is the most imaginative; E. W. Hobson, *John Napier and the Invention of Logarithms* (Cambridge, 1914), is the most useful.

Still valuable on the early history of logarithms are J. W. L. Glaisher's articles, "Logarithms," in *Encyclopaedia Britannica*, 11th ed. (1910), XVI, 868–877; and "On Early Tables of Logarithms and Early History of Logarithms," in *Quarterly Journal of Pure and Applied Mathematics*, **48** (1920), 151–192. Florian Cajori, "History of the Exponential and Logarithmic Concepts," in *American Mathematical Monthly*, **20** (1913), 5–14, 35–47, 75–84, 107–117, 148–151, 173–182, 205–210, is also useful. A more recent discussion of the development of the concept of logarithm is that of D. T. Whiteside, "Patterns of Mathematical Thought in the Later Seventeenth Century," in *Archive for History of Exact Sciences*, **1** (1961), 214–231.

MARGARET E. BARON

NĀRĀYAŅA (*fl.* India, 1356)

Nārāyaṇa, the son of Nṛsiṃha (or Narasiṃha), was one of the most renowned Indian mathematicians of the medieval period. His *Gaṇitakaumudī*, on arithmetic and geometry, was composed in 1356; in it he refers to his *Bījagaṇitāvataṃsa*, on algebra (see Supplement). The *Karmapradīpikā*, a commentary on the *Līlāvatī* of Bhāskara II (*b.* 1115), is found in several south Indian libraries attributed to Nārāyaṇa; but the author, a follower of Āryabhaṭa I (*b.* 476), may be the Kerala astronomer and mathematician Mādhava of Saṅgamagrāma (*ca.* 1340–1425).

The *Gaṇitakaumudī* consists of rules *(sūtras)* and examples *(udāharaṇas)*, which in the only edition, the two-volume one of P. Dvivedi (Benares, 1936–1942), are given separate numberings that do not coincide with the division of the work into chapters *(vyavahāras)*. In fact, the edition is based on a single manuscript which was evidently corrupt and perhaps incomplete. We do not really know in detail the contents of the *Gaṇitakaumudī*. The *Bījagaṇitāvataṃsa* is preserved in a unique and incomplete manuscript at Benares; only the first part has been edited, by K. S. Shukla as a supplement to *Ṛtam* (**1**, pt. 2 [1969–1970]).

BIBLIOGRAPHY

Various rules from the *Gaṇitakaumudī* are discussed by B. Datta and A. N. Singh, *History of Hindu Mathematics*, 2 vols. (Lahore, 1935–1938), *passim;* and the section of that work devoted to magic squares is analyzed by S. Cammann, "Islamic and Indian Magic Squares," in *History of Religions*, **8** (1968–1969), 181–209, 271–299, esp. 274 ff. The algebra of the *Bijagaṇitāvataṃsa* has been commented on by B. Datta, "Nārāyaṇa's Method for Finding Approximate Value of a Surd," in *Bulletin of the Calcutta Mathematical Society*, **23** (1931), 187–194. See also R. Garver, "Concerning Two Square-Root Methods," *ibid.*, **23** (1932), 99–102; and "The Algebra of Nārāyaṇa," in *Isis*, **19** (1933), 472–485.

DAVID PINGREE

AL-NASAWĪ, ABU 'L-ḤASAN, ʿALĪ IBN AḤMAD
(*fl.* Baghdad, 1029–1044)

Arabic biographers do not mention al-Nasawī, who has been known to the scholarly world since 1863, when F. Woepcke made a brief study of his *al-Muqniʿ fi 'l-Ḥisāb al-Hindī* (Leiden, MS 1021). The introduction to this text shows that al-Nasawī wrote, in Persian, a book on Indian arithmetic for presentation to Magd al-Dawla, the Buwayhid ruler in Khurasan who was dethroned in 1029 or 1030. The book was presented to Sharaf al-Mulūk, vizier of Jalāl al-Dawla, ruler in Baghdad. The vizier ordered al-Nasawī to write in Arabic in order to be more precise and concise, and the result was *al-Muqniʿ*. Al-Nasawī seems to have settled in Baghdad; another book by him, *Tajrīd Uqlīdis* (Salar-Jang, MS 3142) was dedicated in highly flattering words to al-Murtadā (965–1044), an influential Shīʿite leader in Baghdad. Nothing else can be said about his life except that al-Nasawī refers to Nasā, in Khurasan, where he probably was born.

Al-Nasawī has been considered a forerunner in the use of the decimal concept because he used the rules $\sqrt{n} = \sqrt{nk^2}/k$ and $\sqrt[3]{n} = \sqrt[3]{nk^3}/k$, where k is taken as a power of 10. If k is taken as 10 or 100, the root is found correct to one or two decimal places. There is now reason to believe that al-Nasawī cannot be credited with priority in this respect. The two rules were known to earlier writers on Hindu-Arabic arithmetic. The first appeared in the *Paṭīgaṇita* of

Śrīdhārācārya (750–850). Like others, al-Nasawī rather mechanically converted the decimal part of the root thus obtained to the sexagesimal scale and suggested taking k as a power of sixty, without showing signs of understanding the decimal value of the fraction. Their concern was simply to transform the fractional part of the root to minutes, seconds, and thirds. Only al-Uqlīdisī (tenth century), the discoverer of decimal fractions, retained some roots in the decimal form.

In *al-Muqniʿ*, al-Nasawī presents Indian arithmetic of integers and common fractions and applies its schemes to the sexagesimal scale. In the introduction he criticizes earlier works as too brief or too long. He states that Kūshyār ibn Labbān (*ca.* 971–1029) had written an arithmetic for astronomers, and Abū Ḥanīfa al-Dīnawarī (*d.* 895) had written one for businessmen; but Kūshyār's proved to be rather like a business arithmetic and Abū Ḥanīfa's more like a book for astronomers. Kūshyār's work, *Uṣūl Ḥisāb al-Hind*, which is extant, shows that al-Nasawī's remark was unfair. He adopted Kūshyār's schemes on integers and, like him, failed to understand the principle of "borrowing" in subtraction. To subtract 4,859 from 53,536, the Indian scheme goes as follows:

Arrange the two numbers as 53536
    4859.

Subtract 4 from the digit above it; since 3 is less than 4, borrow 1 from 5, to turn 3 into 13, and subtract. And so on. Both Kūshyār and al-Nasawī would subtract 4 from 53, obtain 49, subtract 8 from 95, and so on. Only finger-reckoners agree with them in this.

In discussing subtraction of fractional quantities, al-Nasawī enunciated the rule $(n_1 + f_1) - (n_2 + f_2) = (n_1 - n_2) + (f_1 - f_2)$, where n_1 and n_2 are integers and f_1 and f_2 are fractions. He did not notice the case when $f_2 > f_1$ and the principle of "borrowing" should be used.

Al-Nasawī gave Kūshyār's method of extracting the cube root and, like him, used the approximation $\sqrt[3]{n} = p + \dfrac{r}{3p^2 + 1}$, where p^3 is the greatest cube in n and $r = n - p^3$. Arabic works of about the same period used the better rule

$$\sqrt[3]{n} = p + \frac{r}{3p^2 + 3p + 1}.$$

Later works called $3p^2 + 3p + 1$ the conventional denominator.

Al-Muqniʿ differs from Kūshyār's *Uṣūl* in that it explains the Indian system of common fractions, expresses the sexagesimal scale in Indian numerals, and applies the Indian schemes of operation to numbers expressed in this scale. But al-Nasawī could claim no priority for these features, since others, such as al-Uqlīdisī, had already done the same thing.

Three other works by al-Nasawī, all geometrical, are extant. One of them is *al-Ishbāʿ*, in which he discusses the theorem of Menelaus. One is a corrected version of Archimedes' *Lemmata* as translated into Arabic by Thābit ibn Qurra, which was later revised by Naṣīr al-Dīn al-Ṭūsī. The last is *Tajrīd Uqlīdis* ("An Abstract From Euclid"). In the introduction, al-Nasawī points out that Euclid's *Elements* is necessary for one who wants to study geometry for its own sake, but his *Tajrīd* is written to serve two purposes: it will be enough for those who want to learn geometry in order to be able to understand Ptolemy's *Almagest*, and it will serve as an introduction to Euclid's *Elements*. A comparison of the *Tajrīd* with the *Elements*, however, shows that al-Nasawī's work is a copy of books I–VI, on plane geometry and geometrical algebra, and book XI, on solid geometry, with some constructions omitted and some proofs altered.

BIBLIOGRAPHY

I. ORIGINAL WORKS. Al-Nasawī's writings include "On the Construction of a Circle That Bears a Given Ratio to Another Given Circle, and on the Construction of All Rectilinear Figures and the Way in Which Artisans Use Them," cited by al-Ṭūsī in *Maʾkhūdhāt Arshimīdis*, no. 10 of his *Rasāʾil*, II (Hyderabad-Deccan, 1940); *al-Ishbāʿ*, trans. by E. Wiedemann in his *Studien zur Astronomie der Araber* (Erlangen, 1926), 80–85—see also H. Burger and K. Kohl, *Geschichte des Transversalensätze* (Erlangen, 1924), 53–55; *Kitāb al-lāmiʿ fī amthilat al-Zīj al-jāmiʿ* ("Illustrative Examples of the Twenty-Five Chapters of the *Zīj al-jāmiʿ* of Kūshyār"), in Ḥājjī Khalīfa, *Kashf* (Istanbul, 1941), col. 970; and *Risāla fī maʿrifat al-taqwīm waʾl-asṭurlāb* ("A Treatise on Chronology and the Astrolabe"), Columbia University Library, MS Or. 45, op. 7.

II. SECONDARY LITERATURE. See H. Suter, "Über des Rechenbuch des Ali ben Ahmed el-Nasawi," in *Bibliotheca mathematica*, 2nd ser., **7** (1906), 113–119; and F. Woepcke, "Mémoires sur la propagation des chiffres indiens," in *Journal asiatique*, 6th ser., **1** (1863), 492 ff.

See also Kūshyār ibn Labbān, *Uṣūl Ḥisāb al-Hind*, in M. Levey and M. Petruck, *Principles of Hindu Reckoning* (Madison, Wis., 1965), 55–83.

A. S. SAIDAN

AL-NAYRĪZĪ, ABUʾL-ʿABBĀS AL-FAḌL IBN ḤĀTIM (*fl.* Baghdad, *ca.* 897; *d. ca.* 922)

As his name indicates, al-Nayrīzī's origins were in Nayrīz, a small town southeast of Shīrāz, Fārs, Iran. For at least part of his active life he lived in Baghdad, where he probably served the ʿAbbāsid caliph al-Muʿtaḍid (892–902), for whom he wrote an extant treatise on meteorological phenomena (*Risāla fī aḥdāth al-jaww*) and a surviving work on instruments for determining the distances of objects.

The tenth-century bibliographer Ibn al-Nadīm refers to al-Nayrīzī as a distinguished astronomer; Ibn al-Qifṭī (*d.* 1248) states that he excelled in geometry and astronomy; and the Egyptian astronomer Ibn Yūnus (*d.* 1009) takes exception to some of al-Nayrīzī's astronomical views but shows respect for him as an accomplished geometer.

Of the eight titles attributed to al-Nayrīzī by Ibn al-Nadīm and Ibn al-Qifṭī, two are commentaries on Ptolemy's *Almagest* and *Tetrabiblos* and two are astronomical handbooks (*zījes*). Ibn al-Qifṭī indicates that the larger handbook (*Kitāb al-zīj al-kabīr*) was based on the *Sindhind*. None of these works has survived, but the commentary on the *Almagest* and one (or both?) of the handbooks were known to al-Bīrūnī. Ibn Yūnus cites, critically, a certain *zīj* in which, he states, al-Nayrīzī adopted the mean motion of the sun as determined in the *Mumtaḥan zīj*, which was prepared under the direction of Yaḥyā ibn Abī Manṣūr in the time of al-Maʾmūn (813–833). Ibn Yūnus wonders at al-Nayrīzī's adoption of this "erroneous" determination without further examination and, continuing his criticism of the "excellent geometer," refers further to oversights and errors, particularly in connection with the theory of Mercury, the eclipse of the moon, and parallax.

Al-Nayrīzī has been known mainly as the author of a commentary on Euclid's *Elements* that was based on the second of two Arabic translations of Euclid's text, both of which were prepared by al-Ḥajjāj ibn Yūsuf ibn Maṭar (see *Dictionary of Scientific Biography*, IV, 438–439). The commentary survives in a unique Arabic manuscript at Leiden (bks. I–VI) and in a Latin version (bks. I–X), made in the twelfth century by Gerard of Cremona. (The Arabic manuscript lacks the comments on definitions 1–23 of book I, but these are preserved in the Latin translation.) In the course of his own comments al-Nayrīzī quotes extensively from two commentaries on the *Elements* by Hero of Alexandria and Simplicius, neither of which has survived in the original Greek.

The first of these must have covered at least the first eight books (Hero's last comment cited by al-Nayrīzī deals with Euclid VIII.27), whereas the second, entitled "A Commentary on the Premises [*ṣadr, muṣādara, muṣādarāt*] of Euclid's *Elements*," was concerned solely with the definitions, postulates, and axioms at the beginning of book I of the *Elements.*

Simplicius' *Commentary,* almost entirely reproduced by al-Nayrīzī, played a significant part in arousing the interest of Islamic mathematicians in methodological problems. It further quotes verbatim a full proof of Euclid's postulate 5, the parallels postulate, by "the philosopher Aghānīs." The proof, which is based on the definition of parallel lines as equidistant lines and which makes use of the "Eudoxus-Archimedes" axiom, has left its mark on many subsequent attempts to prove the postulate, particularly in Islam.

Aghānīs is no longer identified with Geminus, as Heiberg and others once thought because of a similarity between their views on parallels. He almost certainly lived in the same period as Simplicius; and Simplicius' reference to him in the *Commentary* as "our associate [or colleague] Aghānīs," or, simply, "our Aghānīs" (*Aghānīsu, ṣāḥibunā,* rendered by Gerard as *socius noster Aganis*) strongly suggests that the two philosophers belonged to the same school. There is an anonymous fifteenth-century Arabic manuscript that aims to prove Euclid's parallels postulate and refers in this connection to Simplicius and Aghānīs, but spells the latter's name "Aghānyūs," thus supplying a vowel that can only be conjectured in the form "Aghānīs." Given that the Arabic "gh" undoubtedly stood for the letter γ, "Aghānyūs" may very easily have been a mistranscription of the recognizable Greek name "Agapius." Reading "Aghānyūs" for "Aghābyūs" (Arabic has no "p") may well have resulted from misplacing a single diacritical point, thereby transforming the "b" (that is, "p") into an "n." This hypothesis is the more plausible since we know that diacritical points were often omitted in Arabic manuscripts. It therefore seems reasonable to assume that Aghānīs-Aghānyūs was no other than the Athenian philosopher Agapius, a pupil of Proclus and Marinus who lectured on the philosophy of Plato and Aristotle about A.D. 511 and whose versatility was praised by Simplicius' teacher, Damascius. Agapius' name, place, date, affiliation, and interests agree remarkably with the reference in Simplicius' *Commentary.*

In his commentary on the *Elements,* al-Nayrīzī followed a conception of ratio and proportion that had previously been adopted by al-Māhānī (see *Dictionary of Scientific Biography,* IX, 21–22). Al-Nayrīzī's treatise "On the Direction of the *qibla*" (*Risāla fī samt al-qibla*) shows that he knew and utilized the equivalent of the tangent function. But in this, too, he is now known to have been preceded, for example, by Ḥabash (see *Dictionary of Scientific Biography,* V, 612).

Again, his unpublished treatise "On the Demonstration of the Well-Known Postulate of Euclid" (Paris, Bibliothèque Nationale, arabe 2467, fols. 89r–90r)

clearly depends on Aghānīs. In it al-Nayrīzī argues that, because equality is "naturally prior" to inequality, it follows that straight lines that maintain the same distance between them are prior to those that do not, since the former are the standard for estimating the latter. From this reasoning he concludes the existence of equidistant lines, accepting as a "primary proposition" that equidistant lines do not meet, however extended. His proof consists of four propositions, of which the first three state that: (1) the distance (that is, shortest line) between any two equidistant lines is perpendicular to both lines; (2) if a straight line drawn across two straight lines is perpendicular to both of them, then the two lines are equidistant; and (3) a line falling on two equidistant lines makes the interior angles on one side together equal to two right angles. These three propositions correspond to Aghānīs's propositions 1–3, while the fourth is the same as Euclid's postulate 5: If a straight line falling on two straight lines makes the interior angles on one side together less than two right angles, then the two lines will meet on that side. The proof closely follows Aghānīs.

Al-Nayrīzī, however, claims originality for the theorems that he proves in the extant but unpublished treatise for al-Mu'taḍid—"On the Knowledge of Instruments by Means of Which We May Know the Distances of Objects Raised in the Air or Set Up on the Ground and the Depths of Valleys and Wells, and the Widths of Rivers." Al-Bīrūnī also states that al-Nayrīzī, in his commentary on the *Almagest,* was the only writer known to him who had provided a method for computing "a date for a certain time, the known parts of which are various *species* that do not belong to one and the same *genus.* There is, *e.g.,* a day the date of which within a Greek, Arabic, or Persian month is known; but the name of this month is unknown, whilst you know the name of another month that corresponds with it. Further, you know an era, to which, however, these two months do *not* belong, or such an era, of which the name of the month in question is not known" (*Chronology,* p. 139).

Al-Nayrīzī's work on the construction and use of the spherical astrolabe (*Fī 'l-asṭurlāb al-kurī*), in four *maqālas,* is considered the most complete treatment of the subject in Arabic.

BIBLIOGRAPHY

I. ORIGINAL WORKS. The Arabic text of al-Nayrīzī's commentary on the *Elements* (bks. I–VI and a few lines from bk. VII) was published as *Codex Leidensis* 399, I. *Euclidis Elementa ex interpretatione al-Hadschdschadschii cum commentariis al-Narizii*, R. O. Besthorn and J. L. Heiberg, eds. (Copenhagen, 1893–1932). This ed. is in three pts., each comprising two fascicules, of which pt. III, fasc. II (bks. V–VI), is edited by G. Junge, J. Raeder and W. Thomson. Gerard of Cremona's Latin trans. is *Anaritii in decem libros priores Elementorum Euclidis commentarii . . . in codice Cracoviensi 569 servata*, Maximilianus Curtze, ed. (Leipzig, 1899), in Euclid's *Opera omnia*, J. L. Heiberg and H. Menge, eds., supp. (Suter mentions the probable existence of another MS of Gerard's trans. in "Nachträge," p. 164).

A German trans. and discussion of al–Nayrīzī's treatise on the direction of the *qibla* (*Risāla fī samt al-qibla*) is C. Schoy, "Abhandlung von al-Faḍl b. Ḥātim an Nairîzî: Über die Rechtung der Qibla," in *Sitzungsberichte der Bayerischen Akademie der Wissenschaften zu München*, Mathematisch-physikalische Klasse (1922), 55–68.

A short "chapter" (perhaps drawn from a longer work by al Nayrizi) on the hemispherical sundial was published as *Faṣl fī takhṭiṭ al-sāʿāt al-zamāniyya fī kull qubba aw fī qubba tustaʿmal lahā* ("On Drawing the Lines of Temporal [that is, unequal] Hours in Any Hemisphere or in a Hemisphere Used for That Purpose"); see *al-Rasāʾil al-mutafarriqa fī ʾl-hayʾa l ʾl-mutaqaddimīn wa-muʿāṣiri ʾl-Bīrūnī* (Hyderabad, 1947).

II. SECONDARY LITERATURE. MSS of al-Nayrīzī's works are in C. Brockelmann, *Geschichte der arabischen Literatur*, supp. vol. I (Leiden, 1937), 386–387; 2nd ed., I, (Leiden, 1943), 245; H. Suter, "Die Mathematiker und Astronomen der Araber und ihre Werke," in *Abhandlungen zur Geschichte der mathematischen Wissenschaften mit Einschluss ihrer Anwendungen*, **10** (1900), no. 88, 45; and "Nachträge und Berichtigungen zu 'Die Mathematiker . . . ,'" *ibid.*, **14** (1902), 164; and H. P. J. Renaud, "Additions et corrections à Suter 'Die Mathematiker . . . ,'" in *Isis*, **18** (1932), 171.

The little information that we have of al-Nayrīzī's activities and a list of his works are in Ibn al-Nadīm, *al-Fihrist*, G. Flügel, ed., I (Leipzig, 1871), 265, 268, 279; and Ibn al-Qifṭī, *Taʾrikh al-ḥukamāʾ*, J. Lippert, ed. (Leipzig, 1930), 64, 97, 98, 254.

For the references to al-Nayrīzī's *zij* in Ibn Yūnus' Ḥākimite *zij*, see *Notices et extraits des manuscrits de la Bibliothèque nationale . . .*, VII (Paris, 1803), 61, 65, 69, 71, 73, 121, 161, 165. Al-Bīrūnī refers to al-Nayrīzī in *Rasāʾil*, 2 (Hyderabad, 1948), 39, 51, and in *The Chronology of Ancient Nations*, C. E. Sachau, trans. (London, 1879), 139. See also E. S. Kennedy, "A Survey of Islamic Astronomical Tables," in *Transactions of the American Philosophical Society*, n.s. **46**, pt. 2 (1956), nos. 46, 63, 75.

For a description of the contents and character of Hero's commentary on the *Elements* as preserved by al-Nayrīzī, see T. L. Heath, *The Thirteen Books of Euclid's Elements*, 2nd ed. (Cambridge–New York, 1956), 21–24.

Simplicius' commentary on the *Elements*, including a proof of Euclid's parallels postulate that seems to have been omitted from the text quoted by al-Nayrīzī, is dis-cussed by A. I. Sabra in "Simplicius's Proof of Euclid's Parallels Postulate," in *Journal of the Warburg and Courtauld Institutes*, **32** (1969), 1–24.

For a detailed description of al-Nayrīzī's work on the spherical astrolabe, see Hugo Seemann and T. Mittelberger, "Das kugelförmige Astrolab nach den Mitteilungen von Alfonso X. von Kastilien und den vorhandenen arabischen Quellen," in *Abhandlungen zur Geschichte der Naturwissenschaften und der Medizin*, **8** (1925), 32–40.

For a discussion of al-Nayrīzī's concept of ratio, see E. B. Plooij, *Euclid's Conception of Ratio and His Definition of Proportional Magnitudes as Criticized by Arabian Commentators* (Rotterdam, 1950), 51–52, 61; and J. E. Murdoch, "The Medieval Language of Proportions," in A. C. Crombie, ed., *Scientific Change* (London, 1963), 237–271, esp. 240–242, 253–255.

The identity of Aghānīs is discussed in Paul Tannery, "Le philosophe Aganis est-il identique à Géminus?" in *Bibliotheca mathematica*, 3rd ser., **2** (1901), 9–11, reprinted in *Mémoires scientifiques*, III (Toulouse–Paris, 1915), 37–41; Sir Thomas Heath, *A History of Greek Mathematics*, II (Oxford, 1921), 224; *The Thirteen Books of Euclid's Elements*, I (Cambridge–New York, 1956), 27–28; A. I. Sabra, "Thābit ibn Qurra on Euclid's Parallels Postulate," in *Journal of the Warburg and Courtauld Institutes*, **31** (1968), 13. The information on Agapius is summarized in Pauly-Wissowa, *Real-Encyclopädie der classischen Altertumswissenschaft*, 1st ser., I (Stuttgart, 1894), 735.

See also the notice on al-Nayrīzī in Sarton's *Introduction*, I (Baltimore, 1927), 598–599.

A. I. SABRA

NEANDER, MICHAEL (*b.* Joachimsthal, Bohemia, 3 April 1529; *d.* Jena, Germany, 23 October 1581)

The assessment of Neander and his work is complicated by confusion with another Michael Neander (1525–1595), who came from Sorau and was a school principal in Ilfeld. The achievements of each have been credited to the other, and to date no library has correctly cataloged their respective writings. Neander from Joachimsthal, like his namesake, studied at the Protestant university in Wittenberg, where he earned his baccalaureate degree in 1549 and his master's degree in 1550; he was eighth among fifty candidates. Beginning in 1551, he taught mathematics and Greek at the Hohe Schule in Jena. In 1558, when this school became a new Protestant university, Neander obtained the doctor of medicine degree with a work on baths, *De thermis*. In 1560 he advanced from professor at the faculty of arts to the more lucrative position of professor of medicine at Jena, which post he held until his death.

Neander's scholarly reputation was based on textbooks written primarily for students at the faculty of arts. He considered the writings of the ancients, especially Galen, absolutely authoritative. In the introduction to his *Methodorum in omni genere artium . . .* (1556), he based his exposition on Galen's opinion that the best kind of demonstration is mathematical. Neander distinguished the analytic and synthetic methods and introduced proof by contradiction as a third independent possibility.

In opposition to his contemporary Petrus Ramus, Neander contended that, even from a pedagogical point of view, Euclid's *Elements* contained the essence of a satisfactory synthetic demonstration. Neander's account of the metrology of the Greeks and Romans seems to have served for a time as a sort of reference work. His *Elementa sphaericae doctrinae* (1561), which includes an appendix on calendrical computation, endorsed Melanchthon's rejection of the Copernican view of the universe. The *Elementa* influenced one of Neander's colleagues at Jena, Victorinus Strigelius, whose *Epitome doctrinae de primo motu* (1564) also placed the earth at rest in the center of the universe.

Although Neander typified the close connection between mathematics and medicine frequently seen in the sixteenth century, this link appears only indirectly in his writings.

BIBLIOGRAPHY

I. ORIGINAL WORKS. Neander's major works are Σύνοψις *mensurarum et ponderum, ponderationisque mensurabilium secundum Romanos, Athenienses . . . Accesserunt etiam quae apud Galenum hactenus extabant de ponderum et mensurarum ratione* (Basel, 1555); *Methodorum in omni genere artium brevis et succincta* ὑφήγησις (Basel, 1556); *Gnomologia graecolatina, hoc est . . . Sententiae . . . ex magno anthologio Joannis Stobaei excerptae . . . Accessit praeterea* Ὄνειρος *vel'* Ἀλεκτρυών, *id est somnium vel Gallus, dialogus Luciani . . . graece et latine . . .* (Basel, 1557); and *Elementa sphaericae doctrinae, seu de primo motu: in usum studiosae iuventutis methodicé et perspicué conscripta. Accessit praecipua computi astronomici materia, ubi temporis pleraeque differentiae explicantur* (Basel, 1561).

Biographisches Lexikon hervorragender Ärzte, IV (Berlin-Vienna, 1932), 331–332, lists a work entitled *De thermis* (Jena, 1558), but the author has been unable to verify this title in any library.

II. SECONDARY LITERATURE. Works on Neander and his work (in chronological order) are Heinrich Pantaleon, *Prosopographiae heroum atque illustrium virorum totius Germaniae* (Basel, 1566), 553; also in *Teutscher Nation Heldenbuch . . .* (Basel, 1578), 515; Paul Freher, *Theatrum virorum eruditione clarorum* (Nuremberg, 1688), 1279; Johann Caspar Zeumer, *Vitae professorum theologiae omnium Jenensium* (Jena, 1711), 14; *Hamburgische vermischte Bibliothek*, pt. 1 (Hamburg, 1743), 695–701; Christian Gottlieb Jöcher, ed., *Allgemeines Gelehrten-Lexicon*, III (Leipzig, 1751), 840; Johannes Günther, *Lebensskizzen der Professoren der Universität Jena von 1558 bis 1858* (Jena, 1858); *Allgemeine deutsche Biographie*, XXIII (Leipzig, 1886), 340; and Otto Knopf, *Die Astronomie an der Universität Jena von der Gründung der Universität im Jahre 1558 bis zur Entpflichtung des Verfassers im Jahre 1927* (Jena, 1937), 1–6.

IVO SCHNEIDER

NEKRASOV, ALEKSANDR IVANOVICH (*b.* Moscow, Russia, 9 December 1883; *d.* Moscow, 21 May 1957)

Nekrasov graduated from the Fifth Moscow Gymnasium in 1901 with a gold medal and entered the mathematical section of the Faculty of Physics and Mathematics at Moscow University. In 1906 he graduated with a first-class diploma and received a gold medal for "Teoria sputnikov Yupitera" ("Theory of the Satellites of Jupiter"). Nekrasov remained at the university to prepare for a professorship. At the same time he taught in several secondary schools in Moscow. In 1909–1911 Nekrasov passed his master's examinations in two specialties, astronomy and mechanics. In 1912 he became assistant professor in the department of astronomy and geodesy of the Faculty of Physics and Mathematics at the university, and in 1913 he was appointed to the same post in the department of applied mathematics (theoretical mechanics) of the same faculty. From 1917 until his death Nekrasov taught and conducted research at Moscow University, the Higher Technical School, the Central Aerohydrodynamics Institute, the Sergo Orjonikidze Aviation Institute, and the Institute of Mechanics of the Academy of Sciences of the U.S.S.R.

In 1922 Nekrasov was awarded the N. E. Zhukovsky Prize for "O volnakh ustanovivshegosya vida na poverkhnosti tyazheloy zhidkosti" ("On Smooth-Form Waves on the Surface of a Heavy Liquid"). For his distinguished scientific services he was elected corresponding member of the Academy of Sciences of the U.S.S.R. in 1932 and an active member in 1946. He was awarded the title Honored Worker in Science and Technology in 1947 for his services in the development of aviation technology. Nekrasov was a brilliant representative of the trend in the development of precise mathematical methods in hydromechanics and aeromechanics that is associated with Zhukovsky and S. A. Chaplygin. He published basic works on the theory of waves, the theory of whirlpools, the theory of jet streams, and gas dynamics.

Nekrasov's *Tochnaya teoria voln ustanovivshegosya vida na poverkhnosti tyazheloy zhidkosti* ("A Precise Theory of Smooth-Form Waves on the Surface of a Heavy Liquid"), on classical problems of hydromechanics, was awarded the State Prize of the U.S.S.R. in 1951. In an extensive monograph on aerodynamics, *Teoria kryla v nestatsionarnom potoke* ("Theory of the Wing in a Nonstationary Current"; 1947), he presented a systematic and detailed account of all the basic scientific works dealing with the theory of the unsmooth motion of a wing in the air without allowing for its compressibility. He not only systematized material published earlier but also analyzed and compared it, in a number of cases providing a new mathematical treatment of the subject. Other important works in aerodynamics are *Primenenie teorii integralnykh uravneny k opredeleniyu kriticheskoy skorosti flattera kryla samoleta* ("Application of the Theory of Integral Equations to the Determination of the Critical Velocity of the Flutter of an Airplane Wing"; 1947) and *Obtekanie profilya Zhukovskogo pri nalichii na profile istochnika i stoka* ("Flow on a Zhukovsky Cross Section in the Presence of a Cross Section of the Source and Outflow"). Besides his work on aerohydrodynamics Nekrasov published an excellent two-volume textbook on theoretical vector mechanics (1945–1946).

Nekrasov's works also enriched mathematics. Among his contributions are the first fruitful investigations of nonlinear integral equations with symmetrical nuclei, the books *O nelineynikh integralnykh uravneniakh s postoyannymi predelami* ("On Nonlinear Integral Equations With Constant Limits"; 1922) and *Ob odnom klasse lineynykh integro-differentsialnykh uravneny* ("On One Class of Linear Integral-Differential Equations"; 1934), and many investigations in an important area of aerohydrodynamics. The extremely varied mathematical apparatus that he used contains many original details developed by Nekrasov himself.

Nekrasov translated ir.to Russian É. Goursat's *Cours d'analyse mathématique* as *Kurs matematicheskogo analiza*. To a substantial degree this project made possible Nekrasov's assimilation of the mathematical methods that he later applied so skillfully to the solution of concrete problems in aerodynamics.

A fully worthy disciple of and successor to Zhukovsky, Nekrasov enriched Soviet science with his scientific works and, through his work in education, aided the development of many scientists and engineers.

BIBLIOGRAPHY

Many of Nekrasov's writings are in his *Sobranie sochineny* ("Collected Works"), 2 vols. (Moscow, 1961–1962).

Secondary literature includes *Aleksandr Ivanovich Nekrasov* (Moscow–Leningrad, 1950); and Y. I. Sekerzh-Zenkovich, "Aleksandr Ivanovich Nekrasov," in *Uspekhi matematicheskikh nauk*, **15**, no. 1 (1960).

A. T. Grigorian

NETTO, EUGEN (*b.* Halle, Germany, 30 June 1848; *d.* Giessen, Germany, 13 May 1919)

Netto was the grandson of a Protestant clergyman and the son of an official of the "Franckeschen Stiftungen," Heinrich Netto, and his wife, Sophie Neumann. He attended elementary school in Halle and at the age of ten entered the Gymnasium in Berlin. There he was a pupil of Karl Heinrich Schellbach, who had been Eisenstein's teacher; this famous educator aroused his interest in mathematics. In 1866, following his graduation from the Gymnasium, Netto enrolled at the University of Berlin, where he was influenced mainly by Kronecker, Kummer, and Weierstrass. In 1870 he graduated with honors from Berlin with the dissertation *De transformatione aequationis $y^n = R(x)$, designante $R(x)$ functionem integram rationalem variabilis x, in aequationem $\eta^2 = R_1(\xi)$* (Weierstrass was chief referee). After teaching at a Gymnasium in Berlin, he became an associate professor at the University of Strasbourg in 1879.

In 1882, on Weierstrass' recommendation, Netto was appointed associate professor at the University of Berlin. Besides the introductory lectures for first-semester students, he gave those on higher algebra, the calculus of variations, Fourier series, and theoretical mechanics; he also lectured on synthetic geometry. His textbook *Substitutionentheorie und ihre Anwendung auf die Algebra* (Berlin, 1882) is a milestone in the development of abstract group theory. In it two historical roots of abstract group theory are united—the theory of permutation groups and that of implicit group-theoretical thinking in number theory. Even though Netto did not yet include transformation groups in his concept of groups, he nevertheless clearly recognized the far-reaching importance of the theory of composition in a group and its significance for future developments.

In 1888 Netto became professor at the University of Giessen, where he remained until his retirement in 1913. He contributed to the dissemination of group theory in further papers; and in *Lehrbuch der Combinatorik* (Leipzig, 1901; 2nd ed., enlarged by T. Skolem and Viggo Brun, 1927) he skillfully gathered the scattered literature in this area. His *Die Determinanten* (Leipzig, 1910) was translated into Russian in 1911. Netto was a clever, persuasive, and witty teacher who demonstrated his educational abilities and productivity through additional textbooks and other publications on algebra.

BIBLIOGRAPHY

Netto's works are listed in Poggendorff, III, 962; IV, 1064; and V, 897–898.

On Netto or his work see Wilhelm Lorey, "Die Mathematiker an der Universität Giessen vom Beginn des 19. Jahrhunderts bis 1914," in *Nachrichten der Giessener Hochschulgesellschaft*, **11** (1937), 54–97; Egon Ullrich, "Die Naturwissenschaftliche Fakultät," in *Ludwigs-Universität–Justus-Liebig-Hochschule. 1607–1957. Festschrift zur 350-Jahrfeier* (Giessen, 1957), 267–287; Hans Wussing, "Zum historischen Verhältnis von Intension und Extension des Begriffes Gruppe im Herausbildungsprozess des abstrakten Gruppenbegriffes," in *NTM—Schriftenreihe für Geschichte der Naturwissenschaften, Technik und Medizin*, **4** (1967), 23–34; and Kurt-R. Biermann, "Die Mathematik und ihre Dozenten an der Berliner Universität 1810–1920" (Berlin, 1973).

KURT-R. BIERMANN

NEUBERG, JOSEPH (*b.* Luxembourg City, Luxembourg, 30 October 1840; *d.* Liège, Belgium, 22 March 1926)

Neuberg was one of the founders of the modern geometry of the triangle. The considerable body of his work is scattered among a large number of articles for journals; in it the influence of A. Möbius is clear. In general, his contribution to mathematics lies in the discovery of new details, rather than in any large contribution to the development of his subject.

Neuberg was educated at the Athénée de Luxembourg, and later at the Normal School of Sciences, which was then a part of the Faculty of Sciences of the University of Ghent. From 1884 to 1910 he was a professor at the University of Liège. He was a naturalized citizen of Belgium and was a member of the sciences section (which he headed in 1911) of the Belgian Royal Academy. From 1874 to 1880 Neuberg, with Catalán and Mansion, published the *Nouvelle correspondance mathématique*; subsequently he collaborated with Mansion in publishing *Mathesis*.

BIBLIOGRAPHY

A portrait of Neuberg and a notice with a complete bibliography of his work by A. Mineur may be found in *Annuaire de l'Académie royale de Belgique*, **98** (1932), 135–192; see also L. Godeaux, in *Biographie nationale publiée par l'Académie royale de Belgique*, XXX (1958), cols. 635–637; and in *Liber Memorialis. L'Université de Liège de 1867 à 1935*, II (Liège, 1936), 162–175.

J. PELSENEER

NEUMANN, CARL GOTTFRIED (*b.* Königsberg, Prussia [now Kaliningrad, R.S.F.S.R.], 7 May 1832; *d.* Leipzig, Germany, 27 March 1925)

Neumann's father, Franz Ernst Neumann, was professor of physics and mineralogy at Königsberg; his mother, Luise Florentine Hagen, was a sister-in-law of the astronomer F. W. Bessel. Neumann received his primary and secondary education in Königsberg, attended the university, and formed particularly close friendships with the analyst F. J. Richelot and the geometer L. O. Hesse. After passing the examination for secondary school teaching he obtained his doctorate in 1855; in 1858 he qualified for lecturing in mathematics at Halle, where he became *Privatdozent* and, in 1863, assistant professor. In the latter year he was called to Basel, and in 1865 to Tübingen. From the autumn of 1868 until his retirement in 1911 he was at the University of Leipzig. In 1864 he married Hermine Mathilde Elise Kloss; she died in 1875.

Neumann, who led a quiet life, was a successful university teacher and a productive researcher. More than two generations of future Gymnasium teachers received their basic mathematical education from him. As a researcher he was especially prominent in the field of potential theory. His investigations into boundary value problems resulted in pioneering achievements; in 1870 he began to develop the method of the arithmetical mean for their solution. He also coined the term "logarithmic potential." The second boundary value problem of potential theory still bears his name; a generalization of it was later provided by H. Poincaré.

Neumann was a member of the Berlin Academy, and the Societies of Göttingen, Munich, and Leipzig. He performed a valuable service in founding and editing the important German mathematics periodical *Mathematische Annalen*.

BIBLIOGRAPHY

I. ORIGINAL WORKS. Neumann's writings include *Vorlesungen über Riemanns Theorie der Abelschen Integrale* (Leipzig, 1865); *Untersuchungen über das logarithmische und Newtonsche Potential* (Leipzig, 1877); and *Über die nach Kreis-, Kugel- und Zylinderfunktionen fortschreitenden Entwicklungen* (Leipzig, 1881).

II. SECONDARY LITERATURE. See H. Liebmann, "Zur Erinnerung an Carl Neumann," in *Jahresberichte der Deutschen Mathematikervereinigung*, **36** (1927), 175–178; and H. Salié, "Carl Neumann," in *Bedeutende Gelehrte in Leipzig*, II, G. Harig, ed. (Leipzig, 1965), 13–23.

H. WUSSING

NEUMANN, FRANZ ERNST (*b.* Joachimsthal, Germany [now Jachymov, Czechoslovakia], 11 September 1798; *d.* Königsberg, Germany [now Kaliningrad, R.S.F.S.R.], 23 May 1895)

Neumann extended the Dulong-Petit law—that the specific heats of the elements vary inversely as their atomic weights—to include compounds having similar chemical constitutions. His work in optics contributed to the establishment of the dynamical theory of light, and he formulated mathematically the laws of induction of electric currents. He also aided in developing the theory of spherical harmonics. Neumann was a highly influential teacher; many of his students became outstanding scientists, and he inaugurated the mathematical science seminar at German universities.

Neumann's mother was a divorced countess whose family prevented her marrying his father, a farmer who later became an estate agent, because he was not of noble birth. Neumann was therefore raised by his paternal grandparents. He attended the Berlin Gymnasium, where he displayed an early talent for mathematics. His education was interrupted in 1814, when he became a volunteer in the Prussian army to fight against Napoleon. He was seriously wounded on 16 June 1815 at the battle of Ligny, the prelude to Waterloo. After recovering in a Düsseldorf hospital, he rejoined his company and was mustered out of the army in February 1816.

Because his father had lost all of his resources in a fire, Neumann pursued his education under severe financial difficulties. He completed his studies at the Gymnasium and in 1817 entered the University of Berlin, studying theology in accordance with his father's wishes. In April 1818 he left Berlin for Jena, where he began his scientific studies and was particularly attracted to mineralogy. In 1819 Neumann returned to Berlin to study mineralogy and crystallography under Christian S. Weiss, who became his close friend as well as his mentor. Weiss made the financial arrangements for Neumann to take a three-month geological field trip in Silesia during the summer of 1820, and Neumann was planning other trips for 1822 and 1823 when his father died. Thereafter Neumann and his mother became very close; his concern for her health and financial independence caused him to leave the university during 1822–1823 and manage her farm. Nevertheless, in 1823 he published his first work, *Beiträge zur Kristallonomie*, which was highly regarded in Germany; and on Weiss's recommendation he was appointed curator of the mineral cabinet at the University of Berlin in November 1823.

Neumann received the doctorate at Berlin in November 1825; and in May 1826, together with Jacobi and Dove, he became a *Privatdozent* at the University of Königsberg. Dove and Neumann were destined to assume the physics and mineralogy courses, respectively, of Karl G. Hagen, who had been teaching botany, zoology, mineralogy, chemistry, and physics. In 1828 Neumann was advanced to the rank of lecturer, and in 1829 he was named professor of mineralogy and physics. He married Hagen's daughter, Luise Florentine, in 1830; they had five children before her death in 1838. He married Wilhelmina Hagen, her first cousin, in 1843.

Neumann's early scientific works, published between 1823 and 1830, concerned crystallography; in these he introduced the method of spherical projection and extended Weiss's work on the law of zones (law of rational intercepts). At Königsberg, however, he was influenced by Bessel, Dove, and Jacobi; and he began to concentrate on mathematical physics. His first two important papers were published in Poggendorff's *Annalen der Physik und Chemie* (**23** [1831], 1–39 and 40–53); the first was entitled "Untersuchung über die specifische Wärme der Mineralien" and the second "Bestimmung der specifischen Wärme des Wassers in der Nähe des Siedpunktes gegen Wasser von niedriger Temperatur." In the first article Neumann investigated the specific heats of minerals and extended the Dulong-Petit law to include compound substances having similar chemical constitutions. He arrived at what has been termed Neumann's law, that the molecular heat of a compound is equal to the sum of the atomic heats of its constituents. In the second paper Neumann considered the specific heat of water. In earlier investigations physicists had noticed that when equal quantities of hot and cold water are mixed the temperature of the mixture is lower than the arithmetic mean of the temperatures of the original quantities. This result was generally interpreted as being due to a progressive decrease in the specific heat of water from the point of fusion to that of vaporization, a conclusion that appears to be validated by a number of experiments. Neumann disclosed errors in these experiments and concluded instead that the specific heat of water increases as its temperature increases. He failed to determine, however, that an increase occurs over only a portion of the temperature range from fusion to vaporization.

In 1832 Neumann published another important paper, again in Poggendorff's *Annalen*, "Theorie der doppelten Strahlenbrechung abgeleitet aus der Gleichungen der Mechanik." Many physicists and mathematicians of the period were concerned with determining the conditions under which waves are propagated in ordinary elastic bodies so that they might develop a model which could serve as the optical medium; that is, they wished to evolve an elastic-solid theory of the ether in order to promote the undulatory theory of light. In his article Neumann reported obtaining a wave surface identical with that determined earlier by Augustin Cauchy, and he succeeded in deducing laws of double refraction agreeing with those of Fresnel except in the case of biaxial crystals.

Neumann encountered difficulty in explaining the passage of light from one medium to another. He attempted to overcome this obstacle in an article entitled "Theoretische Untersuchungen der Gesetze, nach welchen das Licht an der Grenze zweier vollkommen durchsichtigen Medien reflectirt und gebrochen wird," published in *Abhandlungen der Preussischen Akademie der Wissenschaften*, mathematische Klasse ([1835], 1–160). In this paper Neumann raised the question of the mathematical expression of the conditions which must hold at the surface separating the two crystalline media, and he adopted the view that the density of the ether must be identical in all media.

Neumann and his contemporary Wilhelm Weber were the founders of the electrodynamic school in Germany, which later included, among others, Riemann, Betti, Carl Neumann, and Lorenz. The investigations and analyses of this group were guided by the assumption, held originally by Ampère, that electromagnetic phenomena resulted from direct action at a distance rather than through the mediation of a field. Neumann's major contributions were contained in two papers published in 1845 and 1848, in which he established mathematically the laws of induction of electric currents. The papers, transmitted to the Berlin Academy, were entitled "Allgemeine Gesetze der inducirten elektrischen Ströme" and "Über ein allgemeines Princip der mathematischen Theorie inducirter elektrischer Ströme."

As a starting point Neumann took the proposition, formulated in 1834 by F. E. Lenz after Faraday's discovery of induction, that the current induced in a conductor moving in the vicinity of a galvanic current or a magnet will flow in the direction that tends to oppose the motion. In his mathematical analysis Neumann arrived at the formula $E \cdot Ds = -\epsilon v \, C \cdot Ds$, where Ds is an element of the moving conductor, $E \cdot Ds$ is the elementary induced electromotive force, v is the velocity of the motion, $C \cdot Ds$ is the component of the inducing current, and ϵ is a constant coefficient. With this formula Neumann was able to calculate the induced current in numerous particular instances. At present a common formulation is $E = -\, dN/dt$, where E is the electromotive force generated in the circuit through which the number of magnetic lines of force is changing at the rate of dN/dt.

Continuing his analysis Neumann noticed a way in which the treatment of currents induced in closed circuits moving in what is now termed a magnetic field might be generalized. He saw that the induced current depends only on the alteration, caused by the motion, in the value of a particular function. Considering Ampère's equations for a closed circuit, Neumann arrived at what is known as the mutual potential of two circuits, that is, the amount of mechanical work that must be performed against the electromagnetic forces in order to separate the two circuits to an infinite distance apart, when the current strengths are maintained unchanged. In modern notation the potential function, Vii', is written:

$$Vii' = -ii' \iint \frac{\mathbf{ds} \cdot \mathbf{ds'}}{r},$$

$\mathbf{ds} \cdot \mathbf{ds'}$ is the scalar product of the two vectors $\mathbf{ds}$ and $\mathbf{ds'}$, and r their distance apart. If a fixed element $\mathbf{ds'}$ is taken and integrated with respect to $\mathbf{ds}$, the vector potential of the first circuit at the point occupied by $\mathbf{ds}$ is obtained. Maxwell arrived at the concept of vector potentials by another method and interpreted them as analytical measures of Faraday's electrotonic state.

According to his contemporaries, only a small portion of Neumann's original scientific work was published. But he was an extremely effective teacher, and he made known many of his discoveries in heat, optics, electrodynamics, and capillarity during his lectures, thinking that priority of discovery extended equally to lectures and publications. Thus he made numerous contributions to the theory of heat without receiving credit; on occasion he thought about raising questions concerning priority but never did.

In 1833, with Jacobi, Neumann inaugurated the German *mathematisch-physikalische* seminar, employing such sessions to supplement his lectures and to introduce his students to research methodology. Gustav Kirchhoff attended these seminars from 1843 to 1846; his first papers on the distribution of electrical conductors, and H. Weld's development of the photometer and polarimeter, were among the direct results of Neumann's seminars. Neumann pleaded continually for the construction of a physics laboratory at Königsberg, but his hopes were thwarted during his tenure as professor; a physics institute was not completed at Königsberg until 1885. In 1847, however, the inheritance from the estate of the parents of his second wife enabled Neumann to build a physics laboratory next to his home, the facilities of which he shared with his students. He retired as professor in 1873, although he continued his seminar for the next three years. He maintained his good health by making frequent walking tours throughout Germany and Austria, and he was still climbing mountains at the age of eighty.

Throughout his life Neumann was an ardent Prussian patriot. He aided in keeping peace in Königsberg during the uprisings of 1848. He pleaded continually for the unification of Germany under the leadership of Prussia, and in the early 1860's he made numerous political speeches supporting Bismarck and the war against Austria. At the fiftieth anniversary of his doctorate in 1876, he was congratulated by the crown prince, later Wilhelm II; and he received honors from Bismarck in 1892 as a veteran of the campaign of 1815. Neumann was a corresponding member of every major European academy of science; he received the Copley Medal of the Royal Society in 1887.

BIBLIOGRAPHY

I. ORIGINAL WORKS. Three of Neumann's most important works were published in Ostwalds Klassiker der Exakten Wissenschaften: *Die mathematischen Gesetze der inducirten elektrischen Ströme*, no. 10 (Leipzig, 1889); *Über ein allgemeines Princip der mathematischen Theorie inducirter elektrischer Ströme*, no. 36 (Leipzig, 1892); and *Theorie der doppelten Strahlenbrechung*, no. 76 (Leipzig, 1896). Other books are *Beiträge zur Kristallonomie* (Berlin–Posen, 1823); *Über den Einfluss der Krystallflächen bei der Reflexion des Lichtes und über die Intensität des gewöhnlichen und ungewöhnlichen Strahls* (Berlin, 1837); and *Beiträge zur Theorie der Kugelfunktionen* (Leipzig, 1878). Some of his lectures were published in *Vorlesung über mathematischen Physik gehalten an der Universität Königsberg von Franz Neumann*, Carl Neumann, C. Pape, Carl Vondermühll, and E. Dorn, eds., 5 vols. (Leipzig, 1881–1887). His collected works were published as *Franz Neumanns Gesammelte Werke*, 3 vols. (Leipzig, 1906–1928).

II. SECONDARY LITERATURE. See C. Voit, "Nekrolog auf Franz Ernst Neumann," in *Sitzungsberichte der Akademie München*, **26** (1896), 338–343; Luise Neumann, *Franz Neumann: Erinnerungsblätter* (Tübingen–Leipzig, 1904); W. Voigt, "Gedächtnissrede auf Franz Neumann," in *Franz Neumanns Gesammelte Werke*, I (Leipzig, 1906), 1–19; and Paul Volkmann, *Franz Neumann . . . den Andenken an dem Altmeister der mathematischen Physik gewidmete Blätter* (Leipzig, 1896).

See also James Clerk Maxwell, *A Treatise on Electricity and Magnetism*, 3rd ed. (Oxford, 1891), art. 542; and Sir Edmund Whittaker, *A History of the Theories of Aether and Electricity*, I (London, 1951), 137–138, 166–167, 198–200.

JOHN G. BURKE

NEVANLINNA, ROLF HERMAN (*b.* Joensuu, Finland, 22 October 1895; *d.* Helsinki, Finland, 28 May 1980)

Nevanlinna came from a Swedish-speaking Finnish family. His father, Otto Wilhelm Nevanlinna, was a noted mathematician and teacher; his mother was Margarete Romberg Nevanlinna. Rolf was the second of their four children.

Nevanlinna could already read and write when he entered primary school. Apparently he was so advanced over his classmates that he grew bored and left school for a year and a half. In 1904 the family moved to Helsinki, where school was more challenging and he learned German and French, starting the development of his superb gift for languages. Perhaps his best teacher was his father, who taught him mathematics and physics in secondary school.

When Nevanlinna graduated from secondary school in 1913, his chief interests were classics and mathematics. Between graduation and enrolling at university, he read the *Introduction to Higher Analysis* of Ernst Lindelöf, a cousin of his father and the outstanding scientist at Helsinki University. It kindled in him the enthusiasm for analysis that led to his life's work.

On 4 June 1919, after receiving the doctorate, Nevanlinna married his cousin Mary Elise Selin; they had four children. In 1918 he had been exempted from conscription for Mannerheim's war of liberation because of his low weight of 110 pounds, and instead served as a clerk.

In 1945, while helping to organize a chamber music society, Nevanlinna met Sinikka Kallio-Visapää, an author and translator (particularly of the works of Thomas Mann). His marriage was dissolved, and he and Sinikka were married in 1958. They had one daughter.

In 1919 Nevanlinna became a schoolteacher, since there were no jobs in the Finnish universities, and for a time joined the Salama Insurance Company, for which his brother Frithiof worked, while continuing to teach eighteen classes a week. He became a docent at the University of Helsinki in 1922 and professor in 1926.

During the 1920's Nevanlinna developed the theory of value distribution that bears his name. It is concerned with the distribution of roots of equations $f(z) = a$, or a-values. Here $f(z)$ is a function of the complex variable z, which is everywhere either differentiable or takes the value infinity so that $1/f(z)$ is differentiable. Such functions are called meromorphic. In 1880 Charles Émile Picard had proved that a-values exist except for at most two values of a. For instance, $f(z) = e^z$ is never 0 or infinite, and so has no 0 values or ∞ values.

Nevanlinna turned this quantitative statement into a theory of unprecedented precision. He introduced a characteristic function $T(r, f)$, which refers to the behavior of f in a circle $|z| \leq r$. For any a, Nevanlinna's first fundamental theorem states that as $r \to \infty$,

$$N(r, a) + m(r, a) = T(r) + \text{a bounded term},$$

where $N(r, a)$ measures the number of a-values in $|z| < r$ and $m(r, a)$ measures the closeness of $f(z)$ to a on $|z| = r$. The second fundamental theorem says that for any q values a_1 to a_q,

$$m(r, a_1) + m(r, a_2) + \cdots + m(r, a_v) < 2T(r) + S(r),$$

where $S(r)$ is in general small compared with $T(r)$. In particular $N(r, a)$ is never much larger than $T(r)$ and is much smaller than $\frac{1}{3}T(r)$ for at most two values of a. Nevanlinna's original result was for $q = 3$. The extension to general q was suggested by J. E. Littlewood and E. F. Collingwood in 1924.

The characteristic function $T(r)$ has allowed a much closer study of analytic functions, and it has also been useful in the study of many other situations. An analysis of multiple roots of equations $f(z) = a$ and of linear combinations of meromorphic functions with few zeros and poles has proved very fruitful.

Another concept that has been very valuable is Nevanlinna's invention of harmonic measure in 1935. The theory of harmonic measure, originally published in a series of papers, was also presented in two books, *Le théorème de Picard-Borel et la théorie des fonctions méromorphes* (1929) and *Eindeutige analytische Funktionen* (1936). Although Nevanlinna continued to write books and papers throughout his life, his reputation rests on these two works. The German book in particular contains many important concepts derived from such authors as Lars Ahlfors, Élie Cartan, and O. Frostman, as well as the Nevanlinna theory proper.

Nevanlinna traveled extensively after the age of thirty and was warmly received by mathematicians in many countries. He was visiting professor at Göttingen in 1936 and 1937 and guest professor at the Eidgenössische Technische Hochschule in Zurich from 1946 to 1973. He was rector of Helsinki University from 1941 to 1945 and president of the International Mathematical Union from 1959 to 1962. In 1948 he became one of the twelve members of the newly established Finnish Academy. He held honorary doctorates from eight universities and was an honorary or foreign member of more than a dozen scientific societies, including the Institut de France.

BIBLIOGRAPHY

I. ORIGINAL WORKS. Important works by Nevanlinna include *Le théorème de Picard-Borel et la théorie des fonctions méromorphes* (Paris, 1929); *Eindeutige analytische Funktionen* (Berlin, 1936; 2nd ed., 1953), translated by Phillip Emig as *Analytic Functions* (New York, 1970); and *Absolute Analysis*, Phillip Emig, trans. (Berlin and New York, 1973), written with Frithiof Nevanlinna.

II. SECONDARY LITERATURE. Walter K. Hayman, "Rolf Nevanlinna," in *Bulletin of the London Mathematical Society*, **14** (1982), 419–436, has a list of Nevanlinna's published books and papers.

WALTER K. HAYMAN

NEWTON, HUBERT ANSON (*b.* Sherburne, New York, 19 March 1830; *d.* New Haven, Connecticut, 12 August 1896)

Hubert was one of eleven children of William and Lois Butler Newton, both of whom were descendants of the first Puritan settlers in New England. After attending public schools in Sherburne, Newton entered Yale at age sixteen. He was an outstanding student; he won election to the Phi Beta Kappa Society and first prize for the solution of mathematics problems.

Following his graduation in 1850, Newton studied mathematics for two and a half years at his home and in New Haven. He became tutor at Yale in 1853, and almost immediately thereafter, on the death of A. D. Stanley, he was asked to chair the mathematics department. Two years later Newton was elected professor and at age twenty-five was one of the youngest persons ever to have reached that rank at Yale.

The professorship included a year's leave of absence, which he took at the Sorbonne with the geometer Chasles. That experience clearly influenced Newton, who subsequently published several important papers on mathematics.

Even though mathematics constituted his education and vocation, his principal efforts began to shift to astronomy and meteorology. His interest in those subjects was sparked by the spectacular meteor shower of 13 November 1833. Although Newton was too young to remember it, others in New Haven, like Edward C. Herrick, Alexander C. Twining, and Denison Olmsted (his undergraduate teacher in astronomy), had written about the event and had checked the records of earlier showers. Thus by 1860 rudimentary data on meteors existed and tentative hypotheses about their orbits were being proffered.

Newton's first papers on the subject (1860–1862) dealt primarily with the orbits and velocities of fireballs. In 1861 the Connecticut Academy of Arts and Sciences established a committee to obtain systematic sightings from diverse observers of the meteor showers of August and November. As one of the leaders of that group, Newton soon accumulated vast amounts of information.

From a careful study of all extant records of the shower of November 1861 Newton in 1864 published his important finding that the shower had occurred thirteen times since A.D. 902, in a cycle of 33.25 years. He reasoned that the phenomenon was caused by a swarm of meteoroids orbiting the sun and concluded that the number of revolutions they must make in one year would be $2 \pm 1/33.25$ or $1 \pm 1/33.25$ or $1/33.25$. These frequencies correspond to periods of 180.0, 185.4, 354.6, and 375.5 days and 33.25 years. Using these five values, the position of the radiant point, and the knowledge that the meteoroids' heliocentric motion is retrograde, Newton calculated five possible orbits.

He noted that the real orbit could be distinguished from the others by calculating the secular motion of the node that was due to planetary perturbations for each of the hypothetical orbits. J. C. Adams, who undertook those calculations, found that the four short periods were not compatible with the observations; the period of 33.25 years, however, corresponds to an elliptical orbit, which extends past Uranus and is subject to perturbations by Uranus and Saturn. Since Adams' determination of the effect of perturbations agreed with Newton's data for the Leonids, these meteoroids were proved to be in such an orbit with a period of 33.25 years.

The Leonids' dramatic reappearance in 1866 spurred meteoroid research and added credence to Newton's calculations; moreover, the reappearance led to the positive identification of the swarm with a comet. By 1865 Newton in the United States and Schiaparelli in Italy had independently concluded that the mean velocities of meteoroids are nearly parabolic and resemble those of comets. When it was found in 1866 that a comet and the Leonids had virtually identical orbits, their relationship was firmly established.

From about 1863 to 1866 Newton amassed and published extensive statistics from observations of sporadic meteors. From this information, he derived the paths and the numbers of meteors, plus the spatial density of meteoroids near the earth's orbit and their velocity about the sun.

Newton's next major contribution to meteor studies came in the mid-1870's when he compared the statistical distribution of known cometary orbits with the hypothetical distributions that would result from two currently leading theories for the origin of the solar system—those of Kant and Laplace. According to Kant, comets formed as part of the primeval solar nebula, while according to Laplace they originated independently from the solar system. Newton found that the distribution of comets' aphelia and inclinations agrees better with the latter theory, although he noted that the problem was unsettled.

These calculations included considerations of the effect of large planetary perturbations on the distribution of cometary orbits; such studies culminated in 1891 in his most famous paper on perturbations. During the 1870's and 1880's Newton accumulated statistical data that indicated that long period comets could be captured by Jupiter, shortening their periods.

Newton devoted the last decade of his research to Biela's comet and meteor shower, to fireballs, and to meteorites. At his death he was probably the foremost American pioneer in the study of meteors.

Besides his scientific research, Newton was active

in teaching and educational reform, especially about the metric system. He was a founder of the American Metrological Society, and he persuaded many manufacturers of scientific instruments and publishers of school arithmetic texts to adopt the system.

In 1868 the University of Michigan awarded Newton an honorary LL.D. After joining the American Association for the Advancement of Science in 1850, he served as the vice-president of its Section A in 1875, and as president of the Association in 1885. He was a president of the Connecticut Academy of Arts and Sciences, a member of the American Philosophical Society, and one of the original members of the National Academy of Sciences. In 1888 the National Academy awarded him its J. Lawrence Smith Gold Medal in recognition of his research on meteoroids. At his death he was the vice-president of the American Mathematical Society and an associate editor of the *American Journal of Science*.

Aside from societies in the United States, he was elected in 1860 corresponding member of the British Association for the Advancement of Science, in 1872 associate of the Royal Astronomical Society of London, in 1886 foreign honorary fellow of the Royal Philosophical Society of Edinburgh, and in 1892 foreign member of the Royal Society of London.

Newton's association with Yale and New Haven was long and rich. He directed the Yale mathematics department and also the observatory, which he helped organize in 1882, and he helped build the extensive collection of meteorites in the Peabody Museum. He also provided considerable assistance to poor students who wanted to attend Yale. For a time he was the only Democrat on the Yale faculty and became alderman in the strongly Republican first ward of New Haven.

BIBLIOGRAPHY

I. ORIGINAL WORKS. Newton published approximately seventy papers, an extensive bibliography of which is included in the memoir by Gibbs that is cited below. Newton's most significant writings included the following: "Explanation of the Motion of the Gyroscope," in *American Journal of Science*, 24 (1857), 253–254; "On the Geometrical Construction of Certain Curves by Points," in *Mathematics Monthly*, 3 (1861), 235–244, 268–279; "On November Star-Showers," in *American Journal of Science*, 37 (1864), 377–389; 38 (1864), 53–61; "On Shooting Stars," in *Memoirs of the National Academy of Sciences*, 1 (1866), 291–312; *The Metric System of Weights and Measures* (Washington, 1868); "On the Transcendental Curves Whose Equation Is sin y sin $my = a$ sin x sin $nx + b$," in *Transactions of the Connecticut Academy of Arts and*

Sciences, 3 (1875), 97–107, written with A. W. Phillips; "On the Origin of Comets," in *American Journal of Science*, 16 (1878), 165–179; "The Story of Biela's Comet," *ibid.*, 31 (1886), 81–94; and "On the Capture of Comets by Planets, Especially Their Capture by Jupiter," in *Memoirs of the National Academy of Sciences*, 6 (1891), 7–23.

II. SECONDARY LITERATURE. An article on meteors that gives a critique of Newton's work is M. Faye, in *Comptes rendus hebdomadaires des séances de l'Académie des sciences*, 64 (1867), 550. Biographical sketches, which were written about the time of Newton's becoming president of the American Association for the Advancement of Science, are in *Science*, 6 (1885), 161–162; in *Popular Science Monthly*, 27 (1885), 840–843; and in James Grant Wilson and John Fisk, eds., *Appleton's Cyclopedia of American Biography*, IV (New York, 1888), 506–507.

Obituaries on Newton are William L. Elkin, in *Astronomische Nachrichten*, 141 (1896), 407; unsigned writers, in *Popular Astronomy*, 4 (1896), 236–240; in *Monthly Notices of the Royal Astronomical Society*, 57 (1897), 227–231; and in *New York Times* (13 Aug. 1896), 5. Biographical articles that were written after his death were J. Willard Gibbs, in *Biographical Memoirs. National Academy of Sciences*, 4 (1902), 99–124, which includes a bibliography; Anson Phelps Stokes, in *Memorials of Eminent Yale Men* (New Haven, 1914), 48–54; and David Eugene Smith, in Dumas Malone, ed., *Dictionary of American Biography*, XIII (New York, 1934), 470–471.

RICHARD BERENDZEN

NEWTON, ISAAC (*b.* Woolsthorpe, England, 25 December 1642; *d.* London, England, 20 March 1727)

Isaac Newton was born a posthumous child, his father having been buried the preceding 6 October. Newton was descended from yeomen on both sides: there is no record of any notable ancestor. He was born prematurely, and there was considerable concern for his survival. He later said that he could have fitted into a quart mug at birth. He grew up in his father's house, which still stands in the hamlet of Woolsthorpe, near Grantham in Lincolnshire.

Newton's mother, Hannah (née Ayscough), remarried, and left her three-year-old son in the care of his aged maternal grandmother. His stepfather, the Reverend Barnabas Smith, died in 1653; and Newton's mother returned to Woolsthorpe with her three younger children, a son and two daughters. Their surviving children, Newton's four nephews and four nieces, were his heirs. One niece, Catherine, kept house for Newton in the London years and married John Conduitt, who succeeded Newton as master of the Mint.

Newton's personality was no doubt influenced by his never having known his father. That he was, moreover, resentful of his mother's second marriage and jealous of her second husband may be documented by at least one entry in a youthful catalogue of sins, written in shorthand in 1662, which records "Threatning my father and mother Smith to burne them and the house over them."[1]

In his youth Newton was interested in mechanical contrivances. He is reported to have constructed a model of a mill (powered by a mouse), clocks, "lanthorns," and fiery kites, which he sent aloft to the fright of his neighbors, being inspired by John Bate's *Mysteries of Nature and Art*.[2] He scratched diagrams and an architectural drawing (now revealed and preserved) on the walls and window edges of the Woolsthorpe house, and made many other drawings of birds, animals, men, ships, and plants. His early education was in the dame schools at Skillington and Stoke, beginning perhaps when he was five. He then attended the King's School in Grantham, but his mother withdrew him from school upon her return to Woolsthorpe, intending to make him a farmer. He was, however, uninterested in farm chores, and absent-minded and lackadaisical. With the encouragement of John Stokes, master of the Grantham school, and William Ayscough, Newton's uncle and rector of Burton Coggles, it was therefore decided to prepare the youth for the university. He was admitted a member of Trinity College, Cambridge, on 5 June 1661 as a subsizar, and became scholar in 1664 and Bachelor of Arts in 1665.

Among the books that Newton studied while an undergraduate was Kepler's "optics" (presumably the *Dioptrice*, reprinted in London in 1653). He also began Euclid, which he reportedly found "trifling," throwing it aside for Schooten's second Latin edition of Descartes's *Géométrie*.[3] Somewhat later, on the occasion of his election as scholar, Newton was reportedly found deficient in Euclid when examined by Barrow.[4] He read Descartes's *Géométrie* in a borrowed copy of the Latin version (Amsterdam, 1659–1661) with commentary by Frans van Schooten, in which there were also letters and tracts by de Beaune, Hudde, Heuraet, de Witt, and Schooten himself. Other books that he studied at this time included Oughtred's *Clavis*, Wallis' *Arithmetica infinitorum*, Walter Charleton's compendium of Epicurus and Gassendi, Digby's *Two Essays*, Descartes's *Principia philosophiae* (as well as the Latin edition of his letters), Galileo's *Dialogo* (in Salusbury's English version)—but not, apparently, the *Discorsi*—Magirus' compendium of Scholastic philosophy, Wing and Streete on astronomy, and some writings of Henry

More (himself a native of Grantham), with whom Newton became acquainted in Cambridge. Somewhat later, Newton read and annotated Sprat's *History of the Royal Society*, the early *Philosophical Transactions*, and Hooke's *Micrographia*.

Notebooks that survive from Newton's years at Trinity include an early one[5] containing notes in Greek on Aristotle's *Organon* and *Ethics*, with a supplement based on the commentaries by Daniel Stahl, Eustachius, and Gerard Vossius. This, together with his reading of Magirus and others, gives evidence of Newton's grounding in Scholastic rhetoric and syllogistic logic. His own reading in the moderns was organized into a collection of "Questiones quaedam philosophicae,"[6] which further indicate that he had also read Charleton and Digby. He was familiar with the works of Glanville and Boyle, and no doubt studied Gassendi's epitome of Copernican astronomy, which was then published together with Galileo's *Sidereus nuncius* and Kepler's *Dioptrice*.[7]

Little is known of Newton's friends during his college days other than his roommate and onetime amanuensis Wickins. The rooms he occupied are not known for certain; and we have no knowledge as to the subject of his thesis for the B.A., or where he stood academically among the group who were graduated with him. He himself did record what were no doubt unusual events in his undergraduate career: "Lost at cards twice" and "At the Taverne twice."

For eighteen months, after June 1665, Newton is supposed to have been in Lincolnshire, while the University was closed because of the plague. During this time he laid the foundations of his work in mathematics, optics, and astronomy or celestial mechanics. It was formerly believed that all of these discoveries were made while Newton remained in seclusion at Woolsthorpe, with only an occasional excursion into nearby Boothby. During these "two plague years of 1665 & 1666," Newton later said, "I was in the prime of my age for invention & minded Mathematicks & Philosophy more then at any time since." In fact, however, Newton was back in Cambridge on at least one visit between March and June 1666.[8] He appears to have written out his mathematical discoveries at Trinity, where he had access to the college and University libraries, and then to have returned to Lincolnshire to revise and polish these results. It is possible that even the prism experiments on refraction and dispersion were made in his rooms at Trinity, rather than in the country, although while at Woolsthorpe he may have made pendulum experiments to determine the gravitational pull of the earth. The episode of the falling of the apple, which Newton himself said "occasioned" the "notion of gravitation," must have occurred at either Boothby or Woolsthorpe.[9]

Lucasian Professor. On 1 October 1667, some two years after his graduation, Newton was elected minor fellow of Trinity, and on 16 March 1668 he was admitted major fellow. He was created M.A. on 7 July 1668 and on 29 October 1669, at the age of twenty-six, he was appointed Lucasian professor. He succeeded Isaac Barrow, first incumbent of the chair, and it is generally believed that Barrow resigned his professorship so that Newton might have it.[10]

University statutes required that the Lucasian professor give at least one lecture a week in every term. He was then ordered to put in finished form his ten (or more) annual lectures for deposit in the University Library. During Newton's tenure of the professorship, he accordingly deposited manuscripts of his lectures on optics (1670–1672), arithmetic and algebra (1673–1683), most of book I of the *Principia* (1684–1685), and "The System of the World" (1687). There is, however, no record of what lectures, if any, he gave in 1686, or from 1688 until he removed to London early in 1696. In the 1670's Newton attempted unsuccessfully to publish his annotations on Kinckhuysen's algebra and his own treatise on fluxions. In 1672 he did succeed in publishing an improved or corrected edition of Varenius' *Geographia generalis*, apparently intended for the use of his students.

During the years in which Newton was writing the *Principia*, according to Humphrey Newton's recollection,[11] "he seldom left his chamber except at term time, when he read in the schools as being Lucasianus Professor, where so few went to hear him, and fewer that understood him, that ofttimes he did in a manner, for want of hearers, read to the walls." When he lectured he "usually staid about half an hour; when he had no auditors, he commonly returned in a 4th part of that time or less." He occasionally received foreigners "with a great deal of freedom, candour, and respect." He "ate sparingly," and often "forgot to eat at all," rarely dining "in the hall. except on some public days," when he was apt to appear "with shoes down at heels, stockings untied, surplice on, and his head scarcely combed." He "seldom went to the chapel," but very often "went to St Mary's church, especially in the forenoon."[12]

From time to time Newton went to London, where he attended meetings of the Royal Society (of which he had been a fellow since 1672). He contributed £40 toward the building of the new college library (1676), as well as giving it various books. He corresponded, both directly and indirectly (often through Henry Oldenburg as intermediary), with scientists in England and on the Continent, including Boyle, Collins, Flamsteed, David Gregory, Halley, Hooke, Huygens, Leibniz, and Wallis. He was often busy with chemical experiments, both before and after writing the *Principia*, and in the mid-1670's he contemplated a publication on optics.[13] During the 1690's, Newton was further engaged in revising the *Principia* for a second edition; he then contemplated introducing into book III some selections from Lucretius and references to an ancient tradition of wisdom. A major research at this time was the effect of solar perturbations on the motions of the moon. He also worked on mathematical problems more or less continually throughout these years.

Among the students with whom Newton had friendly relations, the most significant for his life and career was Charles Montague, a fellow-commoner of Trinity and grandson of the Earl of Manchester; he "was one of the small band of students who assisted Newton in forming the Philosophical Society of Cambridge"[14] (the attempt to create this society was unsuccessful). Newton was also on familiar terms with Henry More, Edward Paget (whom he recommended for a post in mathematics at Christ's Hospital), Francis Aston, John Ellis (later master of Caius), and J. F. Vigani, first professor of chemistry at Cambridge, who is said to have eventually been banished from Newton's presence for having told him "a loose story about a nun." Newton was active in defending the rights of the university when the Catholic monarch James II tried to mandate the admission of the Benedictine monk Alban Francis. In 1689, he was elected by the university constituency to serve as Member of the Convention Parliament.

While in London as M.P., Newton renewed contact with Montague and with the Royal Society, and met Huygens and others, including Locke, with whom he thereafter corresponded on theological and biblical questions. Richard Bentley sought Newton's advice and assistance in preparing the inaugural Boyle Lectures (or sermons), entitled "The Confutation of Atheism" and based in part on the Newtonian system of the world.

Newton also came to know two other scientists, each of whom wanted to prepare a second edition of the *Principia*. One was David Gregory, a professor at Edinburgh, whom Newton helped to obtain a chair at Oxford, and who recorded his conversations with Newton while Newton was revising the *Principia* in the 1690's. The other was a refugee from Switzerland, Nicolas Fatio de Duillier, advocate of a mechanical explanation of gravitation which was at one time viewed kindly by Newton. Fatio soon became perhaps the most intimate of any of Newton's friends. In the early autumn of 1693, Newton apparently suffered a severe attack of depression and made fantastic accusations against Locke and Pepys and was said to have lost his reason.[15]

In the post-*Principia* years of the 1690's, Newton apparently became bored with Cambridge and his scientific professorship. He hoped to get a post that would take him elsewhere. An attempt to make him master of the Charterhouse "did not appeal to him"[16] but eventually Montague (whose star had risen with the Whigs' return to power in Parliament) was successful in obtaining for Newton (in March 1696) the post of warden of the mint. Newton appointed William Whiston as his deputy in the professorship. He did not resign officially until 10 December 1701, shortly after his second election as M.P. for the university.[17]

Mathematics. Any summary of Newton's contributions to mathematics must take account not only of his fundamental work in the calculus and other aspects of analysis—including infinite series (and most notably the general binomial expansion)—but also his activity in algebra and number theory, classical and analytic geometry, finite differences, the classification of curves, methods of computation and approximation, and even probability.

For three centuries, many of Newton's writings on mathematics have lain buried, chiefly in the Portsmouth Collection of his manuscripts. The major parts are now being published and scholars will shortly be able to trace the evolution of Newton's mathematics in detail.[18] It will be possible here only to indicate highlights, while maintaining a distinction among four levels of dissemination of his work: (1) writings printed in his lifetime, (2) writings circulated in manuscript, (3) writings hinted at or summarized in correspondence, and (4) writings that were published only much later. In his own day and afterward, Newton influenced mathematics "following his own wish," by "his creation of the fluxional calculus and the theory of infinite series," the "two strands of mathematical technique which he bound inseparably together in his 'analytick' method."[19] The following account therefore emphasizes these two topics.

Newton appears to have had no contact with higher mathematics until 1664 when—at the age of twenty-one—his dormant mathematical genius was awakened by Schooten's "Miscellanies" and his edition of Descartes's *Géométrie*, and by Wallis' *Arithmetica infinitorum* (and possibly others of his works). Schooten's edition introduced him to the mathematical contributions of Heuraet, de Witt, Hudde, De Beaune,

and others; Newton also read in Viète, Oughtred, and Huygens. He had further compensated for his early neglect of Euclid by careful study of both the *Elements* and *Data* in Barrow's edition.

In recent years[20] scholars have come to recognize Descartes and Wallis as the two "great formative influences" on Newton in the two major areas of his mathematical achievement: the calculus, and analytic geometry and algebra. Newton's own copy of the *Géométrie* has lately turned up in the Trinity College Library; and his marginal comments are now seen to be something quite different from the general devaluation of Descartes's book previously supposed. Rather than the all-inclusive "Error. Error. Non est geom." reported by Conduitt and Brewster, Newton merely indicated an "Error" here and there, while the occasional marginal entry "non geom." was used to note such things as that the Cartesian classification of curves is not really geometry so much as it is algebra. Other of Newton's youthful annotations document what he learned from Wallis, chiefly the method of "indivisibles."[21]

In addition to studying the works cited, Newton encountered the concepts and methods of Fermat and James Gregory. Although Newton was apparently present when Barrow "read his Lectures about motion," and noted[22] that they "might put me upon taking these things into consideration," Barrow's influence on Newton's mathematical thought was probably not of such importance as is often supposed.

A major first step in Newton's creative mathematical life was his discovery of the general binomial theorem, or expansion of $(a + b)^n$, concerning which he wrote, "In the beginning of the year 1665 I found the Method of approximating series & the Rule for reducing any dignity [power] of any Binomial into such a series. . . ."[23] He further stated that:

> In the winter between the years 1664 & 1665 upon reading Dr Wallis's *Arithmetica Infinitorum* & trying to interpole his progressions for squaring the circle [that is, finding the area or evaluating $_0\int^1 (1 - x^2)^{\frac{1}{2}} dx$], I found out another infinite series for squaring the circle & then another infinite series for squaring the Hyperbola. . . .[24]

On 13 June 1676, Newton sent Oldenburg the "Epistola prior" for transmission to Leibniz. In this communication he wrote that fractions "are reduced to infinite series by division; and radical quantities by extraction of roots," the latter

. . . much shortened by this theorem,

$$\overline{P + PQ}^{\frac{m}{n}} = P^{\frac{m}{n}} + \frac{m}{n} AQ + \frac{m-n}{2n} BQ$$

$$+ \frac{m-2n}{3n} CQ + \frac{m-3n}{4n} DQ + \cdots \&c.$$

where $P + PQ$ signifies the quantity whose root or even any power, or the root of a power, is to be found; P signifies the first term of that quantity, Q the remaining terms divided by the first, and m/n the numerical index of the power of $P + PQ$, whether that power is integral or (so to speak) fractional, whether positive or negative.[25]

A sample given by Newton is the expansion

$$\sqrt{(c^2 + x^2)} \quad \text{or} \quad (c^2 + x^2)^{\frac{1}{2}} = c + \frac{x^2}{2c} - \frac{x^4}{8c^3}$$

$$+ \frac{x^6}{16c^5} - \frac{5x^8}{128c^7} + \frac{7x^{10}}{256c^9} + \text{etc.}$$

where

$$P = c^2, \quad Q = x^2/c^2, \quad m = 1, \quad n = 2, \quad \text{and}$$

$$A = P^{\frac{m}{n}} = (c^2)^{\frac{1}{2}} = c, \quad B = (m/n) AQ = x^2/2c,$$

$$C = \frac{m-n}{2n} BQ = -x^4/8c^3,$$

and so on.

Other examples include

$$(y^3 - a^2 y)^{-\frac{1}{3}}$$

$$(c^5 + c^4 x - x^5)^{\frac{1}{5}},$$

$$(d + e)^{-\frac{3}{5}}.$$

What is perhaps the most important general statement made by Newton in this letter is that in dealing with infinite series all operations are carried out "in the symbols just as they are commonly carried out in decimal numbers."

Wallis had obtained the quadratures of certain curves (that is, the areas under the curves), by a technique of indivisibles yielding $_0\int^1 (1 - x^2)^n \, dx$ for certain positive integral values of n (0, 1, 2, 3); in attempting to find the quadrature of a circle of unit radius, he had sought to evaluate the integral $_0\int^1 (1 - x^2)^{\frac{1}{2}} \, dx$ by interpolation. He showed that

$$\frac{4}{\pi} = \frac{1}{_0\int^1 (1 - x^2)^{\frac{1}{2}} \, dx} = \frac{3 \cdot 3 \cdot 5 \cdot 5 \cdot 7 \cdot 7 \cdots}{2 \cdot 4 \cdot 4 \cdot 6 \cdot 6 \cdot 8 \cdots}.$$

Newton read Wallis and was stimulated to go considerably further, freeing the upper bound and then deriving the infinite series expressing the area of a quadrant of a circle of radius x:

$$x - \frac{\frac{1}{2}x^3}{3} - \frac{\frac{1}{8}x^5}{5} - \frac{\frac{1}{16}x^7}{7} - \frac{\frac{5}{128}x^9}{9} - \cdots.$$

In so freeing the upper bound, he was led to recognize that the terms, identified by their powers of x, displayed the binomial coefficients. Thus, the factors $\frac{1}{2}$, $\frac{1}{8}$, $\frac{1}{16}$, $\frac{5}{128}$, ... stand out plainly as $\binom{q}{1}$, $\binom{q}{2}$, $\binom{q}{3}$, $\binom{q}{4}$, ..., in the special case $q = \frac{1}{2}$ in the generalization

$$\int_0^x (1 - x^2)^q \, dx = X - \binom{q}{1} \cdot \frac{1}{3} X^3 + \binom{q}{2} \cdot \frac{1}{5} X^5$$

$$- \binom{q}{3} \cdot \frac{1}{7} X^7 + \frac{q}{5} \cdot \frac{1}{9} X^9 + \cdots,$$

where

$$\binom{q}{n} = \frac{q(q-1) \cdots (q - n + 1)}{n!}.$$

In this way, according to D. T. Whiteside, Newton could begin with the indefinite integral and, "by differentiation in a Wallisian manner," proceed to a straightforward derivation of the "series-expansion of the binomial $(1 - x^p)^q$ ... virtually in its modern form," with "$| x^p |$ implicitly less than unity for convergence." As a check on the validity of this general series expansion, he "compared its particular expansions with the results of algebraic division and square-root extraction $(q = \frac{1}{2})$." This work, which was done in the winter of 1664–1665, was later presented in modified form at the beginning of Newton's *De analysi*.

He correctly summarized the stages of development of his method in the "Epistola posterior" of 24 October 1676, which—as before—he wrote for Oldenburg to transmit to Leibniz:

> At the beginning of my mathematical studies, when I had met with the works of our celebrated Wallis, on considering the series, by the intercalation of which he himself exhibits the area of the circle and the hyperbola, the fact that in the series of curves whose common base or axis is x and the ordinates
>
> $$(1-x^2)^{\frac{0}{2}}, (1-x^2)^{\frac{1}{2}}, (1-x^2)^{\frac{2}{2}}, (1-x^2)^{\frac{3}{2}}, (1-x^2)^{\frac{4}{2}}, (1-x^2)^{\frac{5}{2}},$$
>
> etc., if the areas of every other of them, namely
>
> $$x, \; x-\tfrac{1}{3}x^3, \; x-\tfrac{2}{3}x^3+\tfrac{1}{5}x^5, \; x-\tfrac{3}{3}x^3+\tfrac{3}{5}x^5-\tfrac{1}{7}x^7, \quad \text{etc.}$$
>
> could be interpolated, we would have the areas of the intermediate ones, of which the first $(1 - x^2)^{\frac{1}{2}}$ is the circle. . . .[26]

The importance of changing Wallis' fixed upper boundary to a free variable x has been called "the crux of Newton's breakthrough," since the "various powers of x order the numerical coefficients and reveal for the first time the binomial character of the sequence."[27]

In about 1665, Newton found the power series (that is, actually determined the sequence of the coefficients) for

$$\sin^{-1} x = x + \tfrac{1}{6}x^3 + \tfrac{3}{40}x^5 + \cdots,$$

and—most important of all—the logarithmic series. He also squared the hyperbola $y(1 + x) = 1$, by tabulating

$$\int_0^x (1 + t)^r \, dt$$

for $r = 0, 1, 2, \cdots$ in powers of x and then interpolating

$$\int_0^x (1 + t)^{-1} \, dt.[28]$$

From his table, he found the square of the hyperbola in the series

$$x - \frac{x^2}{2} + \frac{x^3}{3} - \frac{x^4}{4} + \frac{x^5}{5} - \frac{x^6}{6} + \frac{x^7}{7}$$
$$- \frac{x^8}{8} + \frac{x^9}{9} - \frac{x^{10}}{10} + \cdots,$$

which is the series for the natural logarithm of $1 + x$. Newton wrote that having "found the method of infinite series," in the winter of 1664–1665, "in summer 1665 being forced from Cambridge by the Plague I computed the area of the Hyperbola at Boothby . . . to two & fifty figures by the same method."[29]

At about the same time Newton devised "a completely general differentiation procedure founded on the concept of an indefinitely small and ultimately vanishing element o of a variable, say, x." He first used the notation of a "little zero" in September 1664, in notes based on Descartes's *Géométrie*, then extended it to various kinds of mathematical investigations. From the derivative of an algebraic function $f(x)$ conceived ("essentially") as

$$\operatorname*{Lim.}_{o \to \text{zero}} \frac{1}{0} [f(x + 0) - f(x)]$$

he developed general rules of differentiation.

The next year, in Lincolnshire and separated from books, Newton developed a new theoretical basis for his techniques of the calculus. Whiteside has summarized this stage as follows:

[Newton rejected] as his foundation the concept of the indefinitely small, discrete increment in favor of that of the "fluxion" of a variable, a finite instantaneous speed defined with respect to an independent, conventional dimension of time and on the geometrical model of the line-segment: in modern language, the fluxion of the variable x with regard to independent time-variable t is the "speed" dx/dt.[30]

Prior to 1691, when he introduced the more familiar dot notation ($\dot{x}$ for dx/dt, $\dot{y}$ for dy/dt, $\dot{z}$ for dz/dt; then $\ddot{x}$ for d^2x/dt^2, $\ddot{y}$ for d^2y/dt^2, $\ddot{z}$ for d^2z/dt^2), Newton generally used the letters p, q, r for the first derivatives (Leibnizian dx/dt, dy/dt, dz/dt) of variable quantities x, y, z, with respect to some independent variable t. In this scheme, the "little zero" o was "an arbitrary increment of time,"[31] and op, oq, or were the corresponding "moments," or increments of the variables x, y, z (later these would, of course, become $o\dot{x}$, $o\dot{y}$, $o\dot{z}$).[32] Hence, in the limit ($o \to$ zero), in the modern Leibnizian terminology

$$q/p = dy/dx \qquad r/p = dz/dx,$$

where "we may think of the increment o as absorbed into the limit ratios." When, as was often done for the sake of simplicity, x itself was taken for the independent time variable, since $x = t$, then $p = \dot{x} = dx/dx = 1$, $q = dy/dx$, and $r = dz/dx$.

In May 1665, Newton invented a "true partial-derivative symbolism," and he "widely used the notation $\ddot{p}$ and $\dot{p}$ for the respective homogenized derivatives $x(dp/dx)$ and $x^2(d^2p/dx^2)$," in particular to express the total derivative of the function

$$\sum_i (p_i y^i) = 0$$

before "breaking through . . . to the first recorded use of a true partial-derivative symbolism." Armed with this tool, he constructed "the five first and second order partial derivatives of a two-valued function" and composed the fluxional tract of October 1666.[33] Extracts were published by James Wilson in 1761, although the work as a whole remained in manuscript until recently.[34] Whiteside epitomizes Newton's work during this period as follows:

In two short years (summer 1664–October 1666) Newton the mathematician was born, and in a sense the rest of his creative life was largely the working out, in calculus as in his mathematical thought in general, of the mass of burgeoning ideas which sprouted in his mind on the threshold of intellectual maturity. There followed two mathematically dull years.[35]

From 1664 to 1669, Newton advanced to "more general considerations," namely that the derivatives and integrals of functions might themselves be expressed as expansions in infinite series, specifically power series. But he had no general method for determining the "limits of convergence of individual series," nor had he found any "valid tests for such convergence."[36] Then, in mid-1669, he came upon Nicolaus Mercator's *Logarithmotechnica*, published in September 1668, of which "Mr Collins a few months after sent a copy . . . to Dr Barrow," as Newton later recorded.[37] Barrow, according to Newton, "replied that the Method of Series was invented & made general by me about two years before the publication of" the *Logarithmotechnica* and "at the same time," July 1669, Barrow sent back to Collins Newton's tract *De analysi.*

We may easily imagine Newton's concern for his priority on reading Mercator's book, for here he found in print "for all the world to read . . . his [own] reduction of $\log(1 + a)$ to an infinite series by continued division of $1 + a$ into 1 and successive integration of the quotient term by term."[38] Mercator had presented, among other numerical examples, that of $\log(1.1)$ calculated to forty-four decimal places, and he had no doubt calculated other logarithms over which Newton had spent untold hours. Newton might privately have been satisfied that Mercator's exposition was "cumbrous and inadequate" when compared to his own, but he must have been immeasurably anxious lest Mercator generalize a particular case (if indeed he had not already done so) and come upon Newton's discovery of "the extraction of roots in such series and indeed upon his cherished binomial expansion."[39] To make matters worse, Newton may have heard the depressing news (as Collins wrote to James Gregory, on 2 February 1668/1669) that "the Lord Brouncker asserts he can turne the square roote into an infinite Series."

To protect his priority, Newton hastily set to work to write up the results of his early researches into the properties of the binomial expansion and his methods for resolving "affected" equations, revising and amplifying his results in the course of composition. He submitted the tract, *De analysi per aequationes infinitas*, to Barrow, who sent it, as previously mentioned, to Collins.

Collins communicated Newton's results to James Gregory, Sluse, Bertet, Borelli, Vernon, and Strode, among others.[40] Newton was at that time unwilling to commit the tract to print; a year later, he incorporated its main parts into another manuscript, the *Methodus fluxionum et serierum infinitarum.* The original Latin text of the tract was not printed until long afterward.[41] Among those who saw the manuscript of *De analysi* was Leibniz, while on his second visit to London in October 1676; he read Collins' copy, and transcribed portions. Whiteside concurs with "the previously expressed opinions of the two eminent Leibniz scholars, Gerhardt and Hofmann," that Leibniz did not then "annex for his own purposes the fluxional method briefly exposed there," but "was interested only in Newton's series expansions."[42]

The *Methodus fluxionum* provides a better display of Newton's methods for the fluxional calculus in its generality than does the *De analysi*. In the preface to his English version of the *Methodus fluxionum*, John Colson wrote:

> The chief Principle, upon which the Method of Fluxions is here built, is this very simple one, taken from the Rational Mechanicks; which is, That Mathematical Quantity, particularly Extension, may be conceived as generated by continued local Motion; and that all Quantities whatever, at least by analogy and accommodation, may be conceived as generated after a like manner. Consequently there must be comparative Velocities of increase and decrease, during such generations, whose Relations are fixt and determinable, and may therefore (problematically) be proposed to be found.[43]

Among the problems solved are the differentiation of any algebraic function $f(x)$; the "method of quadratures," or the integration of such a function by the inverse process; and, more generally, the "inverse method of tangents," or the solution of a first-order differential equation.

As an example, the "moments" $\dot{x}o$ and $\dot{y}o$ are "the infinitely little accessions of the flowing quantities [variables] x and y": that is, their increase in "infinitely small portions of time." Hence, after "any infinitely small interval of time" (designated by o), x and y become $x + \dot{x}o$ and $y + \dot{y}o$. If one substitutes these for x and y in any given equation, for instance

$$x^3 - ax^2 + axy - y^3 = 0,$$

"there will arise"

$$x^3 + 3\dot{x}ox^2 + 3\dot{x}^2oox + \dot{x}^3o^3$$
$$- ax^2 - 2a\dot{x}ox - a\dot{x}^2oo$$
$$+ axy + a\dot{x}oy + a\dot{y}ox + a\dot{x}\dot{y}oo$$
$$- y^3 - 3\dot{y}oy^2 - 3\dot{y}^2ooy - \dot{y}^3o^3 = 0.$$

The terms $x^3 - ax^2 + axy - y^3$ (of which "by supposition" the sum $= 0$) may be cast out; the remaining terms are divided by o, to get

$$3\dot{x}x^2 + 3\dot{x}^2ox + \dot{x}^3oo - 2ax\dot{x} - a\dot{x}^2o + a\dot{x}y$$
$$+ a\dot{y}x + a\dot{x}\dot{y}o - 3\dot{y}y^2 - 3\dot{y}^2oy - \dot{y}^3oo = 0.$$

"But whereas o is suppos'd to be infinitely little, that it may represent the moments of quantities, consequently the terms that are multiplied by it will be nothing in respect of the rest."[44] These terms are therefore "rejected," and there remains

$$3x^2\dot{x} - 2a\dot{x}x + a\dot{x}y + a\dot{y}x - 3\dot{y}y^2 = 0.$$

It is then easy to group by $\dot{x}$ and $\dot{y}$ to get

$$\dot{x}(3x^2 - 2ax + ay) + \dot{y}(ax - 3y^2) = 0$$

or

$$\frac{\dot{y}}{\dot{x}} = -\frac{3x^2 - 2ax + ay}{ax - 3y^2},$$

which is the same result as finding dy/dx after differentiating

$$x^3 - ax^2 + axy - y^3 = 0.[45]$$

Problem II then reverses the process, with

$$3\dot{x}x^2 - 2a\dot{x}x + a\dot{x}y + a\dot{y}x - 3\dot{y}y^2 = 0$$

being given. Newton then integrates term by term to get $x^3 - ax^2 + axy - y^3 = 0$, the validity of which he may then test by differentiation.

In an example given, o is an "infinitely small quantity" representing an increment in "time," whereas, in the earlier *De analysi, o* was an increment x (although again infinitely small). In the manuscript, as Whiteside points out, Newton canceled "the less precise equivalent 'indefinitè' (indefinitely)" in favor of "infinitely."[46] Certainly the most significant feature is Newton's general and detailed treatment of "the converse operations of differentiation and integration (in Newton's terminology, constructing the 'fluxions' of given 'fluent' quantities, and vice versa)," and "the novelty of Newton's . . . reformulation of the calculus of continuous increase."[47]

Other illustrations given by Newton of his method are determining maxima and minima and drawing tangents to curves at any point. In dealing with maxima and minima, as applied to the foregoing equation, Newton invoked the rule (Problem III):

When a quantity is the greatest or the least that it can be, at that moment it neither flows backwards nor forwards: for if it flows forwards or increases it was less, and will presently be greater than it is; and on the contrary if it flows backwards or decreases, then it was greater, and will presently be less than it is.

In an example Newton sought the "greatest value of x" in the equation

$$x^3 - ax^2 + axy - y^3 = 0.$$

Having already found "the relation of the fluxions of x and y," he set $\dot{x} = o$. Thus, $\dot{y}(ax - 3y^2) = 0$, or $3y^2 = ax$, gives the desired result since this relation may be used to "exterminate either x or y out of the primary equation; and by the resulting equation you may determine the other, and then both of them by $-3y^2 + ax = 0$." Newton showed how "that famous Rule of *Huddenius*" may be derived from his own general method, but he did not refer to Fermat's earlier method of maxima and minima. Newton also found the greatest value of y in the equation

$$x^3 - ay^2 + \frac{by^3}{a + y} - xx\sqrt{ay + xx} = 0$$

and then indicated that his method led to the solution of a number of specified maximum-minimum problems.

Newton's shift from a "loosely justified conceptual model of the 'velocity' of a 'moveing body' . . ." to the postulation of "a basic, uniformly 'fluent' variable of 'time' as a measure of the 'fluxions' (instantaneous 'speeds' of flow) of a set of dependent variables which continuously alter their magnitude" may have been due, in part, to Barrow.[48] This concept of a uniformly flowing time long remained a favorite of Newton's; it was to appear again in the *Principia*, in the scholium following the definitions, as "mathematical time" (which "of itself, and from its own nature, flows equably without relation to anything external"), and in lemma 2, book II (see below), in which he introduced quantities "variable and indetermined, and increasing or decreasing, as it were, by a continual motion or flux." He later explained his position in a draft review of the *Commercium epistolicum* (1712),

I consider time as flowing or increasing by continual flux & other quantities as increasing continually in time & from the fluxion of time I give the name of fluxions to the velocitys with which all other quantities increase. Also from the moments of time I give the name of moments to the parts of any other quantities generated in moments of time. I expose time by any quantity flowing uniformly & represent its fluxion by an unit, & the fluxions of other quantities I represent by any other fit symbols & the fluxions of their fluxions by other fit symbols & the fluxions of those fluxions by others, & their moments generated by those fluxions I represent by the symbols of the fluxions drawn into the letter o & its powers o^2, o^3, &c: vizt their first moments by their first fluxions drawn into the letter o, their second moments by their second fluxions into o^2, & so on. And when I am investigating a truth or the solution of a Probleme I use all sorts of approximations & neglect to write down the letter o, but when I am demonstrating a Proposition I always write down the letter *o* & proceed exactly by the rules of Geometry without admitting any approximations. And I found the method not upon summs & differences, but upon the solution of this probleme: *By knowing the Quantities generated in time to find their fluxions.* And this is done by finding not prima momenta but primas momentorum nascentium rationes.

In an addendum (published only in 1969) to the 1671 *Methodus fluxionum,*[49] Newton developed an alternative geometrical theory of "first and last" ratios of lines and curves. This was later partially subsumed into the 1687 edition of the *Principia,* section 1, book I, and in the introduction to the *Tractatus de quadratura curvarum* (published by Newton in 1704 as one of the two mathematical appendixes to the *Opticks*). Newton had intended to issue a version of his *De quadratura* with the *Principia* on several occasions, both before and after the 1713 second edition, because, as he once wrote, "by the help of this method of Quadratures I found the Demonstration of Kepler's Propositions that the Planets revolve in Ellipses describing . . . areas proportional to the times," and again, "By the inverse Method of fluxions I found in the year 1677 the demonstration of Kepler's Astronomical Proposition. . . ."[50]

Newton began *De quadratura* with the statement that he did not use infinitesimals, "in this Place," considering "mathematical Quantities . . . not as consisting of very small Parts; but as describ'd by a continued Motion."[51] Thus lines are generated "not by the Apposition of Parts, but by the continued Motion of Points," areas by the motion of lines, solids by the motion of surfaces, angles by the rotation of the sides, and "Portions of Time by a continual Flux." Recognizing that there are different rates of increase and decrease, he called the "Velocities of the Motions or Increments *Fluxions,*" and the generated Quantities *Fluents,*" adding that "Fluxions are very nearly as the Augments of the Fluents generated in equal but very small Particles of Time, and, to speak accurately, they are in the *first Ratio* of the nascent Augments; but they may be expounded in any Lines which are proportional to them."

As an example, consider that (as in Fig. 1) areas *ABC, ABDG* are described by the uniform motion of the ordinates *BC, BD* moving along the base in the direction *AB.* Suppose *BC* to advance to any new position *bc,* complete the parallelogram *BCEb,* draw the straight line *VTH* "touching the Curve in *C,* and meeting the two lines *bc* and *BA* [produced] in *T* and *V.*" The "augments" generated will be: *Bb,* by *AB;* *Ec,* by *BC;* and *Cc,* by "the Curve Line *ACc.*" Hence, "the Sides of the Triangle *CET* are in the *first Ratio*

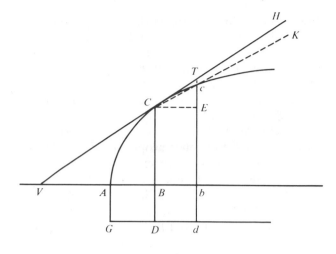

FIGURE 1

of these Augments considered as nascent." The "Fluxions of *AB, BC* and *AC*" are therefore "as the Sides *CE, ET* and *CT* of that Triangle *CET*" and "may be expounded" by those sides, or by the sides of the triangle *VBC,* which is similar to the triangle *CET.*

Contrariwise, one can "take the Fluxions in the *ultimate Ratio* of the evanescent Parts." Draw the straight line *Cc;* produce it to *K.* Now let *bc* return to its original position *BC;* when "*C* and *c* coalesce," the line *CK* will coincide with the tangent *CH;* then, "the evanescent Triangle *CEc* in its ultimate Form will become similar to the Triangle *CET,* and its evanescent Sides *CE, Ec,* and *Cc* will be *ultimately* among themselves as the sides *CE, ET* and *CT* of the other Triangle *CET,* are, and therefore the Fluxions of the Lines *AB, BC* and *AC* are in this same Ratio."

Newton concluded with an admonition that for the line *CK* not to be "distant from the Tangent *CH* by a small Distance," it is necessary that the points *C* and *c* not be separated "by any small Distance." If the points *C* and *c* do not "coalesce and exactly coincide," the lines *CK* and *CH* will not coincide, and "the ultimate Ratios in the Lines *CE, Ec,* and *Cc*" cannot be found. In short, "The very smallest Errors in mathematical Matters are not to be neglected."[52]

This same topic appears in the mathematical introduction (section 1, book I) to the *Principia,* in which Newton stated a set of lemmas on limits of geometrical ratios, making a distinction between the limit of a ratio and the ratio of limits (for example, as $x \to 0$, lim. $x^n/x \to 0$; but lim. x^n/lim. $x \to 0/0$, which is indeterminate).

The connection of fluxions with infinite series was first publicly stated in a scholium to proposition 11 of *De quadratura,* which Newton added for the 1704 printing, "We said formerly that there were first, second, third, fourth, &c. Fluxions of flowing Quantities. These Fluxions are as the Terms of an infinite converging series." As an example, he considered z^n to "be the flowing Quantity" and "by flowing" to become $(z + o)^n$; he then demonstrated that the successive terms of the expansion are the successive fluxions: "The first Term of this Series z^n will be that flowing Quantity; the second will be the first Increment or Difference, to which consider'd as nascent, its first Fluxion is proportional . . . and so on *in infinitum*." This clearly exemplifies the theorem formally stated by Brook Taylor in 1715; Newton himself explicitly derived it in an unpublished first version of *De quadratura* in 1691.[53] It should be noted that Newton here showed himself to be aware of the importance of convergence as a necessary condition for expansion in an infinite series.

In describing his method of quadrature by "first and last ratios," Newton said:

> Now to institute an Analysis after this manner in finite Quantities and investigate the *prime* or *ultimate* Ratios of these finite Quantities when in their nascent or evanescent State, is consonant to the Geometry of the Ancients: and I was willing [that is, desirous] to show that, in the Method of Fluxions, there is no necessity of introducing Figures infinitely small into Geometry.[54]

Newton's statement on the geometry of the ancients is typical of his lifelong philosophy. In mathematics and in mathematical physics, he believed that the results of analysis—the way in which things were discovered—should ideally be presented synthetically, in the form of a demonstration. Thus, in his review of the *Commercium epistolicum* (published anonymously), he wrote of the methods he had developed in *De quadratura* and other works as follows:

> By the help of the new *Analysis* Mr. *Newton* found out most of the Propositions in his *Principia Philosophiae*: but because the Ancients for making things certain admitted nothing into Geometry before it was demonstrated synthetically, he demonstrated the Propositions synthetically, that the Systeme of the Heavens might be founded upon good Geometry. And this makes it now difficult for unskilful Men to see the Analysis by which those Propositions were found out.[55]

As to analysis itself, David Gregory recorded that Newton once said "Algebra is the Analysis of the Bunglers in Mathematicks."[56] No doubt! Newton did, nevertheless, devote his main professorial lectures of 1673–1683 to algebra,[57] and these lectures were printed a number of times both during his lifetime and after.[58] This algebraical work includes, among other things, what H. W. Turnbull has described as a general method (given without proof) for discovering "the rational factors, if any, of a polynomial in one unknown and with integral coefficients"; he adds that the "most remarkable passage in the book" is Newton's rule for discovering the imaginary roots of such a polynomial.[59] (There is also developed a set of formulas for "the sums of the powers of the roots of a polynomial equation.")[60]

Newton's preference for geometric methods over purely analytical ones is further evident in his statement that "Equations are Expressions of Arithmetical Computation and properly have no place in Geometry." But such assertions must not be read out of context, as if they were pronouncements about algebra in general, since Newton was actually discussing various points of view or standards concerning what was proper to geometry. He included the positions of Pappus and Archimedes on whether to admit into geometry the conchoid for the problem of trisection and those of the "new generation of geometers" who "welcome" into geometry many curves, conics among them.[61]

Newton's concern was with the limits to be set in geometry, and in particular he took up the question of the legitimacy of the conic sections in solid geometry (that is, as solid constructions) as opposed to their illegitimacy in plane geometry (since they cannot be generated in a plane by a purely geometric construction). He wished to divorce synthetic geometric considerations from their "analytic" algebraic counterparts. Synthesis would make the ellipse the simplest of conic sections other than the circle; analysis would award this place to the parabola. "Simplicity in figures," he wrote, "is dependent on the simplicity of their genesis and conception, and it is not its equation but its description (whether geometrical or mechanical) by which a figure is generated and rendered easy to conceive."[62]

The "written record of [Newton's] first researches in the interlocking structures of Cartesian coordinate geometry and infinitesimal analysis"[63] shows him to have been establishing "the foundations of his mature work in mathematics" and reveals "for the first time the true magnitude of his genius."[64] And in fact Newton did contribute significantly to analytic geometry. In his 1671 *Methodis fluxionum*, he devoted "Prob. 4: To draw tangents to curves" to a study of the different ways in which tangents may be drawn "according to the various relationships of curves to straight lines," that is, according to the "modes" or coordinate systems in which the curve is specified.[65]

Newton proceeded "by considering the ratios of

limit-increments of the co-ordinate variables (which are those of their fluxions)."[66] His "Mode 3" consists of using what are now known as standard bipolar coordinates, which Newton applied to Cartesian ovals as follows: Let x, y be the distances from a pair of fixed points (two "poles"); the equation $a \pm (e/d)x - y = 0$ for Descartes's "second-order ovals" will then yield the fluxional relation $\pm(e/d)\dot{x} - \dot{y} = 0$ (in dot notation) or $\pm em/d - n = 0$ (in the notation of the original manuscript, in which m, n are used for the fluxions $\dot{x}$, $\dot{y}$ of x, y). When $d = e$, "the curve turns out to be a conic." In "Mode 7," Newton introduced polar coordinates for the construction of spirals; "the equation of an Archimedean spiral" in these coordinates becomes $(a/b)x = y$, where y is the radius vector (now usually designated r or ρ) and x the angle (ϑ or ϕ).

Newton constructed equations for the transformation of coordinates (as, for example, from polar to Cartesian), and found formulas in both polar and rectangular coordinates for the curvature of a variety of curves, including conics and spirals. On the basis of these results Boyer has quite properly referred to Newton as "an originator of polar coordinates."[67]

Further geometrical results may be found in *Enumeratio linearum tertii ordinis*, first written in 1667 or 1668, and then redone and published, together with *De quadratura*, as an appendix to the *Opticks* (1704).[68] Newton devoted the bulk of the tract to classifying cubic curves into seventy-two "*Classes, Genders, or Orders*, according to the Number of the Dimensions of an Equation, expressing the relation between the *Ordinates* and the *Abscissae*; or which is much at one [that is, the same thing], according to the Number of Points in which they may be cut by a Right Line."

In a brief fifth section, Newton dealt with "The Generation of Curves by Shadows," or the theory of projections, by which he considered the shadows produced "by a luminous point" as projections "on an infinite plane." He showed that the "shadows" (or projections) of conic sections are themselves conic sections, while "those of curves of the second genus will always be curves of the second genus; those of the third genus will always be curves of the third genus; and so on *ad infinitum*." Furthermore, "in the same manner as the circle, projecting its shadow, generates all the conic sections, so the five divergent parabolae, by their shadows, generate all the other curves of the second genus." As C. R. M. Talbot observed, this presentation is "substantially the same as that which is discussed at greater length in the twenty-second lemma [book III, section 5] of the *Principia*, in which it is proposed to 'transmute' any rectilinear or curvilinear figure into another of the same analytical order by means of the method of projections."[69]

The work ends with a brief supplement on "The Organical Description of Curves," leading to the "Description of the Conick-Section by Five Given Points" and including the clear statement, "*The Use of Curves in Geometry is, that by their Intersections Problems may be solved*" (with an example of an equation of the ninth degree). Newton in this tract laid "the foundation for the study of Higher Plane Curves, bringing out the importance of asymptotes, nodes, cusps," according to Turnbull, while Boyer has asserted that it "is the earliest instance of a work devoted solely to graphs of higher plane curves in algebra," and has called attention to the systematic use of two axes and the lack of "hesitation about negative coordinates."[70]

Newton's major mathematical activity had come to a halt by 1696, when he left Cambridge for London. The *Principia*, composed in the 1680's, marked the last great exertion of his mathematical genius, although in the early 1690's he worked on porisms and began a "Liber geometriae," never completed, of which David Gregory gave a good description of the planned whole.[71] For the most part, Newton spent the rest of his mathematical life revising earlier works.

Newton's other chief mathematical activity during the London years lay in furthering his own position against Leibniz in the dispute over priority and originality in the invention of the calculus. But he did respond elegantly to a pair of challenge problems set by Johann [I] Bernoulli in June 1696. The first of these problems was "mechanico-geometrical," to find the curve of swiftest descent. Newton's answer was brief: the "brachistochrone" is a cycloid. The second problem was to find a curve with the following property, "that the two segments [of a right line drawn from a given point through the curve], being raised to any given power, and taken together, may make everywhere the same sum."[72]

Newton's analytic solution of the curve of least descent is of particular interest as an early example of what became the calculus of variations. Newton had long been concerned with such problems, and in the *Principia* had included (without proof) his findings concerning the solid of least resistance. When David Gregory asked him how he had found such a solid, Newton sent him an analytic demonstration (using dotted fluxions), of which a version was published as an appendix to the second volume of Motte's English translation of the *Principia*.[73]

Optics. The study of Newton's work in optics has to date generally been limited to his published letters relating to light and color (in *Philosophical Transactions*, beginning in February 1672), his invention of

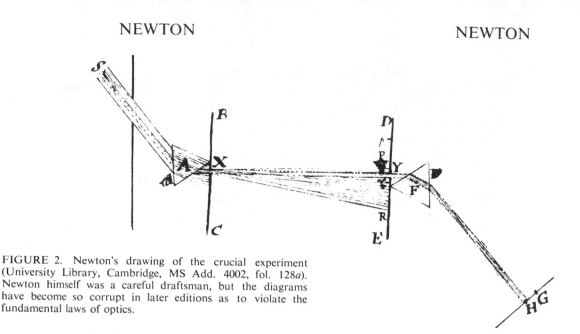

FIGURE 2. Newton's drawing of the crucial experiment (University Library, Cambridge, MS Add. 4002, fol. 128a). Newton himself was a careful draftsman, but the diagrams have become so corrupt in later editions as to violate the fundamental laws of optics.

a reflecting telescope and "sextant," and his published *Opticks* of 1704 and later editions (in Latin and English). There has never been an adequate edition or a full translation of the *Lectiones opticae.* Nor, indeed, have Newton's optical manuscripts as yet been thoroughly studied.[74]

Newton's optical work first came to the attention of the Royal Society when a telescope made by him was exhibited there. Newton was elected a fellow shortly thereafter, on 11 January 1672, and responded by offering the Society an account of the discovery that had led him to his invention. It was, he proudly alleged, "the oddest if not the most considerable detection yet made in the operations of nature": the analysis of dispersion and the composition of white light.

In the published account Newton related that in 1666 ("at which time I applyed myself to the grinding of Optick glasses of other figures than *Spherical*") he procured a triangular glass prism, "to try therewith the celebrated *Phaenomena of Colours.*" Light from a tiny hole in a shutter passed through the prism; the multicolored image—to Newton's purported surprise —was of "an *oblong* form," whereas "according to the received laws of Refraction, I expected [it] should have been *circular.*" To account for this unexpected appearance, Newton looked into a number of possibilities, among them that "the Rays, after their trajection through the Prisme did not move in curve lines," and was thereby led to the famous "experimentum crucis."[75] In this experiment Newton used two prisms: the first was employed to produce a spectrum on an opaque board (*BC*) into which a small hole had been drilled; a beam of light could thus pass through the hole to

a second board (*DE*) with a similar aperture; in this way a narrow beam of light of a single color would be directed to a second prism, and the beam emerging from the second prism would project an image on another board (Fig. 2). Thus, all light reaching the final board had been twice subjected to prismatic dispersion. By rotating the first prism "to and fro slowly about its Axis," Newton allowed different portions of the dispersed light to reach the second prism.

Newton found that the second prism did not produce any further dispersion of the "homogeneal" light (that is, of light of about the same color); he therefore concluded that "Light it self is a *Heterogeneous mixture of differently refrangible Rays*"; and asserted an exact correspondence between color and "degree of Refrangibility" (the least refrangible rays being "disposed to exhibit a *Red* colour," while those of greatest refrangibility are a deep violet). Hence, colors "are not *Qualifications* of Light, derived from Refractions, or Reflections of natural Bodies," as commonly believed, but "*Original* and *connate* properties*," differing in the different sorts of rays.[76]

The same experiment led Newton to two further conclusions, both of real consequence. First, he gave up any hope of "the perfection of Telescopes" based on combinations of lenses and turned to the principle of the reflector; second, he held it to be no longer a subject of dispute "whether Light be a Body." Observing, however, that it "is not so easie" to determine specifically "what Light is," he concluded, "I shall not mingle conjectures with certainties."[77]

Newton's letter was, as promised, read at the Royal Society on 6 February 1672. A week later Hooke delivered a report in which he criticized Newton for asserting a conclusion that did not seem to Hooke to follow necessarily from the experiments described, which—in any event—Hooke thought too few. Hooke had his own theory which, he claimed, could equally well explain Newton's experimental results.

In the controversy that followed with Hooke, Huygens, and others, Newton quickly discovered that he had not produced a convincing demonstration of the validity and significance of the conclusions he had drawn from his experiments. The objection was made that Newton had not explored the possibility that theories of color other than the one he had proposed might explain the phenomena. He was further criticized for having favored a corporeal hypothesis of light, and it was even said that his experimental results could not be reproduced.

In reply, Newton attacked the arguments about the "hypothesis" that he was said to have advanced about the nature of light, since he did not consider this issue to be fundamental to his interpretation of the "experimentum crucis." As he explained in reply to Pardies[78] he was not proposing "an hypothesis," but rather "properties of light" which could easily "be proved" and which, had he not held them to be true, he would "rather have . . . rejected as vain and empty speculation, than acknowledged even as an hypothesis." Hooke, however, persisted in the argument. Newton was led to state that he had deliberately declined all hypotheses so as "to speak of *Light* in *general* terms, considering it abstractly, as something or other propagated every way in straight lines from luminous bodies, without determining what that Thing is." But Newton's original communication did assert, "These things being so, it can be no longer disputed, whether there be colours in the dark, nor . . . perhaps, whether Light be a Body." In response to his critics, he emphasized his use of the word "perhaps" as evidence that he was not committed to one or another hypothesis on the nature of light itself.[79]

One consequence of the debate, which was carried on over a period of four years in the pages of the *Philosophical Transactions* and at meetings of the Royal Society, was that Newton wrote out a lengthy "Hypothesis Explaining the Properties of Light Discoursed of in my Several Papers,"[80] in which he supposed that light "is something or other capable of exciting vibrations in the aether," assuming that "there is an aetherial medium much of the same constitution with air, but far rarer, subtler, and more strongly elastic." He suggested the possibility that "muscles are contracted and dilated to cause animal motion," by the action of an "aethereal animal spirit," then went on to offer ether vibration as an explanation of refraction and reflection, of transparency and opacity, of the production of colors, and of diffraction phenomena (including Newton's rings). Even "the gravitating attraction of the earth," he supposed, might "be caused by the continual condensation of some other such like aethereal spirit," which need not be "the main body of phlegmatic aether, but . . . something very thinly and subtilly diffused through it."[81]

The "Hypothesis" was one of two enclosures that Newton sent to Oldenburg, in his capacity of secretary of the Royal Society, together with a letter dated 7 December 1675. The other was a "Discourse of Observations," in which Newton set out "such observations as conduce to further discoveries for completing his theory of light and colours, especially as to the constitution of natural bodies, on which their colours or transparency depend." It also contained Newton's account of his discovery of the "rings" produced by light passing through a thin wedge or layer of air between two pieces of glass. He had based his experiments on earlier ones of a similar kind that had been recorded by Hooke in his *Micrographia* (observation 9). In particular Hooke had described the phenomena occurring when the "lamina," or space between the two glasses, was "*double concave*, that is, thinner in the middle then at the edge"; he had observed "various coloured rings or lines, with differing consecutions or orders of Colours."

When Newton's "Discourse" was read at the Royal Society on 20 January 1676, it contained a paragraph (proposition 3) in which Newton referred to Hooke and the *Micrographia*, "in which book he hath also largely discoursed of this . . . and delivered many other excellent things concerning the colours of thin plates, and other natural bodies, which I have not scrupled to make use of so far as they were for my purpose."[82] In recasting the "Discourse" as parts 1, 2, and 3 of book II of the *Opticks*, however, Newton omitted this statement. It may be assumed that he had carried these experiments so much further than Hooke, introducing careful measurements and quantitative analysis, that he believed them to be his own. Hooke, on the other hand, understandably thought that he deserved more credit for his own contributions —including hypothesis-based explanations—than Newton was willing to allow him.[83] Newton ended the resulting correspondence on a conciliatory note when he wrote in a letter of 5 February 1676, "What Des-Cartes did was a good step. You have added much in several ways, and especially in taking the colours of thin plates into philosophical consideration. If I have seen further it is by standing on the shoulders of Giants."[84]

The opening of Newton's original letter on optics suggests that he began his prism experiments in 1666, presumably in his rooms in Trinity, but was interrupted by the plague at Cambridge, returning to this topic only two years later. Thus the famous eighteen months supposedly spent in Lincolnshire would mark a hiatus in his optical researches, rather than being the period in which he made his major discoveries concerning light and color. As noted earlier, the many pages of optical material in Newton's manuscripts[85] and notebooks have not yet been sufficiently analyzed to provide a precise record of the development of his experiments, concepts, and theories.

The lectures on optics that Newton gave on the assumption of the Lucasian chair likewise remain only incompletely studied. These exist as two complete, but very different, treatises, each with carefully drawn figures. One was deposited in the University Library, as required by the statutes of his professorship, and was almost certainly written out by his roommate, John Wickins,[86] while the other is in Newton's own hand and remained in his possession.[87] These two versions differ notably in their textual content, and also in their division into "lectures," allegedly given on specified dates. A Latin and an English version, both based on the deposited manuscript although differing in textual detail and completeness, were published after Newton's death. The English version, called *Optical Lectures*, was published in 1728, a year before the Latin. The second part of Newton's Latin text was not translated, since, according to the preface, it was "imperfect" and "has since been published in the *Opticks* by Sir Isaac himself with great improvements." The preface further states that the final two sections of this part are composed "in a manner purely Geometrical," and as such they differ markedly from the *Opticks*. The opening lecture (or section 1) pays tribute to Barrow and mentions telescopes, before getting down to the hard business of Newton's discovery "that . . . Rays [of light] in respect to the Quantity of Refraction differ from one another." To show the reader that he had not set forth "Fables instead of Truth," Newton at once gave "the Reasons and Experiments on which these things are founded." This account, unlike the later letter in the *Philosophical Transactions*, is not autobiographical; nor does it proceed by definitions, axioms, and propositions (proved "by Experiment"), as does the still later *Opticks*.[88]

R. S. Westfall has discussed the two versions of the later of the *Lectiones opticae*, which were first published in 1729;[89] he suggests that Newton eliminated from the *Lectiones* those "parts not immediately relevant to the central concern, the experimental demonstration of his theory of colors." Mathematical portions of the *Lectiones* have been analyzed by

D. T. Whiteside, in Newton's *Mathematical Papers*, while J. A. Lohne and Zev Bechler have made major studies of Newton's manuscripts on optics. The formation of Newton's optical concepts and theories has been ably presented by A. I. Sabra; an edition of the *Opticks* is presently being prepared by Henry Guerlac.

Lohne finds great difficulty in repeating Newton's "experimentum crucis,"[90] but more important, he has traced the influence of Descartes, Hooke, and Boyle on Newton's work in optics.[91] He has further found that Newton used a prism in optical experiments much earlier than hitherto suspected—certainly before 1666, and probably before 1665—and has shown that very early in his optical research Newton was explaining his experiments by "the corpuscular hypothesis." In "Questiones philosophicae," Newton wrote: "Blue rays are reflected more than red rays, because they are slower. Each colour is caused by uniformly moving globuli. The uniform motion which gives the sensation of one colour is different from the motion which gives the sensation of any other colour."[92]

Accordingly, Lohne shows how difficult it is to accept the historical narrative proposed by Newton at the beginning of the letter read to the Royal Society on 8 February 1672 and published in the *Philosophical Transactions*. He asks why Newton should have been surprised to find the spectrum oblong, since his "note-books represent the sunbeam as a stream of slower and faster globules occasioning different refrangibility of the different colours?" Newton must, according to Lohne, have "found it opportune to let his theory of colours appear as a Baconian induction from experiments, although it primarily was deduced from speculations." Sabra, in his analysis of Newton's narrative, concludes that not even "the 'fortunate Newton' could have been fortunate enough to have achieved this result in such a smooth manner." Thus one of the most famous examples of the scientific method in operation now seems to have been devised as a sort of scenario by which Newton attempted to convey the impression of a logical train of discovery based on deductions from experiment. The historical record, however, shows that Newton's great leap forward was actually a consequence of implications drawn from profound scientific speculation and insight.[93]

In any event, Newton himself did not publish the *Lectiones opticae*, nor did he produce his planned annotated edition of at least some (and maybe all) of his letters on light and color published in the *Philosophical Transactions*.[94] He completed his English *Opticks*, however, and after repeated requests that he do so, allowed it to be printed in 1704, although he withheld his name, save on the title page of one known copy. It has often been alleged that Newton released the *Opticks* for publication only after Hooke —the last of the original objectors to his theory of light and colors—had died. David Gregory, however, recorded another reason for the publication of the *Opticks* in 1704: Newton, Gregory wrote, had been "provoked" by the appearance, in 1703, of George Cheyne's *Fluxionum methoda inversa* "to publish his [own tract on] Quadratures, and with it, his Light & Colours, &c."[95]

In the *Opticks*, Newton presented his main discoveries and theories concerning light and color in logical order, beginning with eight definitions and eight axioms.[96] Definition 1 of book I reads: "By the Rays of Light I understand its least Parts, and those as well Successive in the same Lines, as Contemporary in several Lines." Eight propositions follow, the first stating that "Lights which differ in Colour, differ also in Degrees of Refrangibility." In appended experiments Newton discussed the appearance of a paper colored half red and half blue when viewed through a prism and showed that a given lens produces red and blue images, respectively, at different distances. The second proposition incorporates a variety of prism experiments as proof that "The Light of the Sun consists of Rays differently refrangible."

The figure given with experiment 10 of this series illustrates "two Prisms tied together in the form of a Parallelopiped" (Fig. 3). Under specified conditions, sunlight entering a darkened room through a small hole *F* in the shutter would not be refracted by the parallelopiped and would emerge parallel to the incident beam *FM*, from which it would pass by refraction through a third prism *IKH*, which would by refraction "cast the usual Colours of the Prism upon the opposite Wall." Turning the parallelopiped about its axis, Newton found that the rays producing the several colors were successively "taken out of the transmitted Light" by "total Reflexion"; first "the Rays which in the third Prism had suffered the greatest Refraction and painted [the wall] with violet and blew were . . . taken out of the transmitted Light, the rest remaining," then the rays producing green, yellow, orange, and red were "taken out" as the parallelopiped was rotated yet further. Newton thus experimentally confirmed the "experimentum crucis," showing that the light emerging from the two prisms "is compounded of Rays differently Refrangible, seeing [that] the more Refrangible Rays may be taken out while the less Refrangible remain." The arrangement of prisms is the basis of the important discovery reported in book II, part 1, observation 1.

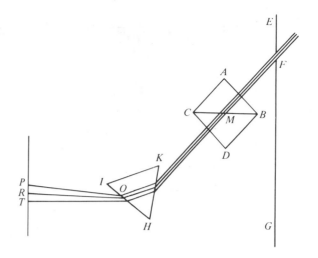

FIGURE 3

In proposition 6 Newton showed that, contrary to the opinions of previous writers, the sine law actually holds for each single color. The first part of book I ends with Newton's remarks on the impossibility of improving telescopes by the use of color-corrected lenses and his discussion of his consequent invention of the reflecting telescope (Fig. 4).

In the second part of book I, Newton dealt with colors produced by reflection and refraction (or transmission), and with the appearance of colored objects in relation to the color of the light illuminating them. He discussed colored pigments and their mixture and geometrically constructed a color wheel, drawing an analogy between the primary colors in a compound color and the "seven Musical Tones or Intervals of the eight Sounds, *Sol, la, fa, sol, la, mi, fa, sol.* . . ."[97]

Proposition 9, "Prob. IV. By the discovered Properties of Light to explain the Colours of the Rain-bow," is devoted to the theory of the rainbow. Descartes had developed a geometrical theory, but had used a single index of refraction (250:187) in his computation of the path of light through each raindrop.[98] Newton's discovery of the difference in refrangibility of the different colors composing white light, and their separation or dispersion as a consequence of refraction, on the other hand, permitted him to compute the radii of the bows for the separate colors. He used 108:81 as the index of refraction for red and 109:81 for violet, and further took into consideration that the light of the sun does not proceed from a single point. He determined the widths of the primary and secondary bows to be 2°15′ and 3°40′, respectively, and gave a formula for computing the radii of bows of any order *n* (and hence for orders of the rainbow greater than 2) for any given index of

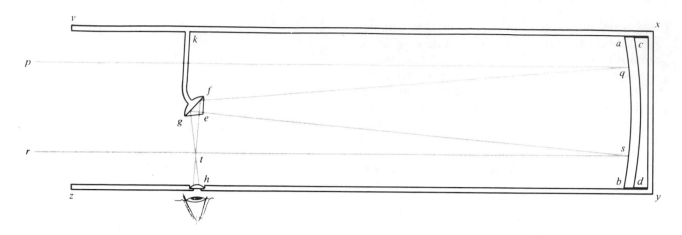

FIGURE 4. Newton's method "To shorten Telescopes": *efg* represents the prism, *abcd* the speculum, and *h* the lens.

refraction.[99] Significant as Newton's achievement was, however, he gave only what can be considered a "first approximation to the solution of the problem," since a full explanation, particularly of the supernumerary or spurious bows, must require the general principle of interference and the "rigorous application of the wave theory."

Book II, which constitutes approximately one third of the *Opticks*, is devoted largely to what would later be called interference effects, growing out of the topics Newton first published in his 1675 letter to the Royal Society. Newton's discoveries in this regard would seem to have had their origin in the first experiment that he describes (book II, part 1, observation 1); he had, he reported, compressed "two Prisms hard together that their sides (which by chance were a very little convex) might somewhere touch one another" (as in the figure provided for experiment 10 of book I, part 1). He found "the place in which they touched" to be "absolutely transparent," as if there had been one "continued piece of Glass," even though there was total reflection from the rest of the surface; but "it appeared like a black or dark spot, by reason that little or no sensible light was reflected from thence, as from other places." When "looked through," it seemed like "a hole in that Air which was formed into a thin Plate, by being compress'd between the Glasses." Newton also found that this transparent spot "would become much broader than otherwise" when he pressed the two prisms "very hard together."

Rotating the two prisms around their common axis (observation 2) produced "many slender Arcs of Colours" which, the prisms being rotated further,

"were compleated into Circles or Rings." In observation 4 Newton wrote that

> To observe more nicely the order of the Colours . . . I took two Object-glasses, the one a Plano-convex for a fourteen Foot Telescope, and the other a large double Convex for one of about fifty Foot; and upon this, laying the other with its plane side downwards, I pressed them slowly together, to make the Colours successively emerge in the middle of the Circles, and then slowly lifted the upper Glass from the lower to make them successively vanish again in the same place.

It was thus evident that there was a direct correlation between particular colors of rings and the thickness of the layer of the entrapped air. In this way, as Mach observed, "Newton acquired a complete insight into the whole phenomenon, and at the same time the possibility of determining the thickness of the air gap from the known radius of curvature of the glass."[100]

Newton varied the experiment by using different lenses, and by wetting them, so that the gap or layer was composed of water rather than air. He also studied the rings that were produced by light of a single color, separated out of a prismatic spectrum; he found that in a darkened room the rings from a single color extended to the very edge of the lens. Furthermore, as he noted in observation 13, "the Circles which the red Light made" were "manifestly bigger than those which were made by the blue and violet"; he found it "very pleasant to see them gradually swell or contract accordingly as the Colour of the Light was changed."

He concluded that the rings visible in white light represented a superimposition of the rings of the several colors, and that the alternation of light and dark rings for each color must indicate a succession of regions of reflection and transmission of light, produced by the thin layer of air between the two glasses. He set down the latter conclusion in observation 15: "And from thence the origin of these Rings is manifest; namely that the Air between the Glasses, according to its various thickness, is disposed in some places to reflect, and in others to transmit the Light of any one Colour (as you may see represented . . .) and in the same place to reflect that of one Colour where it transmits that of another" (Fig. 5).

Book II, part 2, of the *Opticks* has a nomogram in which Newton summarized his measures and computations and demonstrated the agreement of his analysis of the ring phenomenon with his earlier conclusions drawn from his prism experiments— "that whiteness is a dissimilar mixture of all Colours, and that Light is a mixture of Rays endued with all those Colours." The experiments of book II further confirmed Newton's earlier findings "that every Ray have its proper and constant degree of Refrangibility connate with it, according to which its refraction is ever justly and regularly perform'd," from which he argued that "it follows, that the colorifick Dispositions of Rays are also connate with them, and immutable." The colors of the physical universe are thus derived "only from the various Mixtures or Separations of

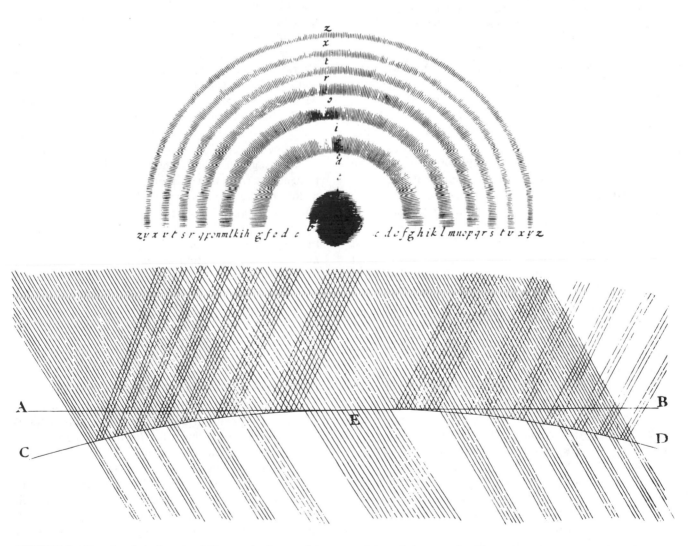

FIGURE 5. Two drawings from book II, part 1, plate 1 of the 1704 edition of the *Opticks*, illustrating Newton's studies of what are now called Newton's rings.

Rays, by virtue of their different Refrangibility or Reflexibility"; the study of color thus becomes "a Speculation as truly mathematical as any other part of Opticks."[101]

In part 3 of book II, Newton analyzed "the permanent Colours of natural Bodies, and the Analogy between them and the Colours of thin transparent Plates." He concluded that the smallest possible subdivisions of matter must be transparent, and their dimensions optically determinable. A table accompanying proposition 10 gives the refractive powers of a variety of substances "in respect of . . . Densities." Proposition 12 contains Newton's conception of "fits":

> Every Ray of Light in its passage through any refracting Surface is put into a certain transient Constitution or State, which in the progress of the Ray returns at equal Intervals, and disposes the Ray at every return to be easily transmitted through the next refracting Surface, and between the returns to be easily reflected by it.

The succeeding definition is more specific: "The returns of the disposition of any Ray to be reflected I will call its *Fits of easy Reflection*, and those of its disposition to be transmitted its *Fits of easy Transmission*, and the space it passes between every return and the next return, the *Interval of its Fits*."

The "fits" of easy reflection and of easy refraction could thus be described as a numerical sequence; if reflection occurs at distances 0, 2, 4, 6, 8, $\cdots$, from some central point, then refraction (or transmission) must occur at distances 1, 3, 5, 7, 9, $\cdots$. Newton did not attempt to explain this periodicity, stating that "I do not here enquire" into the question of "what kind of action or disposition this is." He declined to speculate "whether it consists in a circulating or a vibrating motion of the Ray, or of the Medium, or something else," contenting himself "with the bare Discovery, that the Rays of Light are by some cause or other alternately disposed to be reflected or refracted for many vicissitudes."

Newton thus integrated the periodicity of light into his theoretical work (it had played only a marginal part in Hooke's theory). His work was, moreover, based upon extraordinarily accurate measurements— so much so that when Thomas Young devised an explanation of Newton's rings based on the revived wave theory of light and the new principle of interference, he used Newton's own data to compute the wavelengths and wave numbers of the principal colors in the visible spectrum and attained results that are in close agreement with those generally accepted today.

In part 4 of book II, Newton addressed himself to "the Reflexions and Colours of thick transparent polish'd Plates." This book ends with an analysis of halos around the sun and moon and the computation of their size, based on the assumption that they are produced by clouds of water or by hail. This led him to the series of eleven observations that begin the third and final book, "concerning the Inflexions of the Rays of Light, and the Colours made thereby," in which Newton took up the class of optical phenomena previously studied by Grimaldi,[102] in which "fringes" are produced at the edges of the shadows of objects illuminated by light "let into a dark Room through a very small hole." Newton discussed such fringes surrounding the projected shadows of a hair, the edge of a knife, and a narrow slit.

Newton concluded the first edition of the *Opticks* (1704) with a set of sixteen queries, introduced "in order to a further search to be made by others." He had at one time hoped he might carry the investigations further, but was "interrupted," and wrote that he could not "now think of taking these things into farther Consideration." In the eighteenth century and after, these queries were considered the most important feature of the *Opticks*—particularly the later ones, which were added in two stages, in the Latin *Optice* of 1706 and in the second English edition of 1717–1718.

The original sixteen queries at once go beyond mere experiments on diffraction phenomena. In query 1, Newton suggested that bodies act on light at a distance to bend the rays; and in queries 2 and 3, he attempted to link differences in refrangibility with differences in "flexibility" and the bending that may produce color fringes. In query 4, he inquired into a single principle that, by "acting variously in various Circumstances," may produce reflection, refraction, and inflection, suggesting that the bending (in reflection and refraction) begins before the rays "arrive at the Bodies." Query 5 concerns the mutual interaction of bodies and light, the heat of bodies being said to consist of having "their parts [put] into a vibrating motion"; while in query 6 Newton proposed a reason why black bodies "conceive heat more easily from Light than those of other Colours." He then discussed the action between light and "sulphureous" bodies, the causes of heat in friction, percussion, putrefaction, and so forth, and defined fire (in query 9) and flame (in query 10), discussing various chemical operations. In query 11, he extended his speculations on heat and vapors to sun and stars. The last four queries (12 to 16) of the original set deal with vision, associated with "Vibrations" (excited by "the Rays of Light") which cause sight by "being propagated along the solid Fibres of the optick Nerves into the Brain." In query 13 specific wavelengths are associated with each of several colors. In query 15 Newton discussed binocular vision, along with other aspects of seeing, while in query 16 he took up the phenomenon of persistence of vision.

Newton has been much criticized for believing dispersion to be independent of the material of the prism and for positing a constant relation between deviation and dispersion in all refractive substances. He thus dismissed the possibility of correcting for chromatic aberration in lenses, and directed attention from refraction to reflecting telescopes.[103]

Newton is often considered to be the chief advocate of the corpuscular or emission theory of light. Lohne has shown that Newton originally did believe in a simple corpuscular theory, an aspect of Newton's science also forcibly brought out by Sabra. Challenged by Hooke, Newton proposed a hypothesis of ether waves associated with (or caused by) these corpuscles, one of the strongest arguments for waves probably being his own discovery of periodicity in "Newton's rings." Unlike either Hooke or Huygens, who is usually held to be the founder of the wave theory but who denied periodicity to waves of light, Newton postulated periodicity as a fundamental property of waves of (or associated with) light, at the same time that he suggested that a particular wavelength characterizes the light producing each color. Indeed, in the queries, he even suggested that vision might be the result of the propagation of waves in the optic nerves. But despite this dual theory, Newton always preferred the corpuscle concept, whereby he might easily explain both rectilinear propagation and polarization, or "sides." The corpuscle concept lent itself further to an analysis by forces (as in section 14 of book I of the *Principia*), thus establishing a universal analogy between the action of gross bodies (of the atoms or corpuscles composing such bodies), and of light. These latter topics are discussed below in connection with the later queries of the *Opticks*.

Dynamics, Astronomy, and the Birth of the "Principia." Newton recorded his early thoughts on motion in various student notebooks and documents.[104] While still an undergraduate, he would certainly have studied the Aristotelian (or neo-Aristotelian) theory of motion and he is known to have read Magirus' *Physiologiae peripateticae libri sex*; his notes include a "Cap:4. De Motu" (wherein "Motus" is said to be the Aristotelian ἐντελέχεια). Extracts from Magirus occur in a notebook begun by Newton in 1661;[105] it is a repository of jottings from his student years on a variety of physical and nonphysical topics. In it Newton recorded, among other extracts, Kepler's third law, "that the mean distances of the primary Planets from the Sunne are in

sesquialter proportion to the periods of their revolutions in time."[106] This and other astronomical material, including a method of finding planetary positions by approximation, comes from Thomas Streete's *Astronomia Carolina*.

Here, too, Newton set down a note on Horrox' observations, and an expression of concern about the vacuum and the gravity of bodies; he recorded, from "Galilaeus," that "an iron ball" falls freely through "100 braces Florentine or cubits [or 49.01 ells, perhaps 66 yards] in 5″ of an hower." Notes of a later date—on matter, motion, gravity, and levity—give evidence of Newton's having read Charleton (on Gassendi), Digby (on Galileo), Descartes, and Henry More.

In addition to acquiring this miscellany of information, making tables of various kinds of observations, and supplementing his reading in Streete by Wing (and, probably, by Galileo's *Sidereus nuncius* and Gassendi's epitome of Copernican astronomy), Newton was developing his own revisions of the principles of motion. Here the major influence on his thought was Descartes (especially the *Principia philosophiae* and the Latin edition of the correspondence, both of which Newton cited in early writings), and Galileo (whose *Dialogue* he knew in the Salusbury version, and whose ideas he would have encountered in works by Henry More, by Charleton and Wallis, and in Digby's *Two Essays*).

An entry in Newton's Waste Book,[107] dated 20 January 1664, shows a quantitative approach to problems of inelastic collision. It was not long before Newton went beyond Descartes's law of conservation, correcting it by algebraically taking into account direction of motion rather than numerical products of size and speed of bodies. In a series of axioms he declared a principle of inertia (in "Axiomes" 1 and 2); he then asserted a relation between "force" and change of motion; and he gave a set of rules for elastic collision.[108] In "Axiome" 22, he had begun to approach the idea of centrifugal force by considering the pressure exerted by a sphere rolling around the inside surface of a cylinder. On the first page of the Waste Book, Newton had quantitated the centrifugal force by conceiving of a body moving along a square inscribed in a circle, and then adding up the shocks at each "reflection." As the number of sides were increased, the body in the limiting case would be "reflected by the sides of an equilateral circumscribed polygon of an infinite number of sides (i.e. by the circle it selfe)." Herivel has pointed out the near equivalence of such results to the early proof mentioned by Newton at the end of the scholium to proposition 4, book I, of the

Principia. Evidently Newton learned the law of centrifugal force almost a decade before Huygens, who published a similar result in 1673. One early passage of the Waste Book also contains an entry on Newton's theory of conical pendulums.[109]

According to Newton himself, the "notion of gravitation" came to his mind "as he sat in a contemplative mood," and "was occasioned by the fall of an apple."[110] He postulated that, since the moon is sixty times as far away from the center of the earth as the apple, by an inverse-square relation it would accordingly have an acceleration of free fall $1/(60)^2 = 1/3600$ that of the apple. This "moon test" proved the inverse-square law of force which Newton said he "deduced" from combining "Kepler's Rule of the periodical times of the Planets being in a sesquialterate proportion of their distances from the Centers of the Orbs"—that is, by Kepler's third law, that $R^3/T^2 = $ constant, combined with the law of central (centrifugal) force. Clearly if $F \propto V^2/R$ for a force F acting on a body moving with speed V in a circle of radius R (with period T), it follows simply and at once that

$$F \propto V^2/R = 4\pi^2 R^2/T^2 R = 4\pi^2/R^2 \times (R^3/T^2).$$

Since R^3/T^2 is a constant, $F \propto 1/R^2$.

An account by Whiston states that Newton took an incorrect value for the radius of the earth and so got a poor agreement between theory and observation, "which made Sir *Isaac* suspect that this Power was partly that of Gravity, and partly that of *Cartesius*'s Vortices," whereupon "he threw aside the Paper of his Calculation, and went to other Studies." Pemberton's narration is in agreement as to the poor value taken for the radius of the earth, but omits the reference to Cartesian vortices. Newton himself said (later) only that he made the two calculations and "found them [to] answer pretty nearly."[111] In other words, he calculated the falling of the moon and the falling of a terrestrial object, and found the two to be (only) approximately equal.

A whole tradition has grown up (originated by Adams and Glaisher, and most fully expounded by Cajori)[112] that Newton was put off not so much by taking a poor value for the radius of the earth as by his inability then to prove that a sphere made up of uniform concentric shells acts gravitationally on an external point mass as if all its mass were concentrated at its center (proposition 71, book I, book III, of the *Principia*). No firm evidence has ever been found that would support Cajori's conclusion that the lack of this theorem was responsible for the supposed twenty-year delay in Newton's announcement of his "discovery" of the inverse-square law of gravitation. Nor is there evidence that Newton ever attempted to compute the attraction of a sphere until summer 1685, when he was actually writing the *Principia.*

An existing document does suggest that Newton may have made just such calculations as Whiston and Pemberton described, calculations in which Newton appears to have used a figure for the radius of the Earth that he found in Salusbury's version of Galileo's *Dialogue,* 3,500 Italian miles *(milliaria),* in which one mile equals 5,000, rather than 5,280, feet.[113] Here, some time before 1669, Newton stated, to quote him in translation, "Finally, among the primary planets, since the cubes of their distances from the Sun are reciprocally as the squared numbers of their periods in a given time, their endeavours of recess from the Sun will be reciprocally as the squares of their distances from the Sun," and he then gave numerical examples from each of the six primary planets. A. R. Hall has shown that this manuscript is the paper referred to by Newton in his letter to Halley of 20 June 1686, defending his claim to priority of discovery of the inverse-square law against Hooke's claims. It would have been this paper, too, that David Gregory saw and described in 1694, when Newton let him glance over a manuscript earlier than "the year 1669."

This document, however important it may be in enabling us to define Newton's values for the size of the earth, does not contain an actual calculation of the moon test, nor does it refer anywhere to other than centrifugal "endeavours" from the sun. But it does show that when Newton wrote it he had not found firm and convincing grounds on which to assert what Whiteside has called a perfect "balance between (apparent) planetary centrifugal force and that of solar gravity."[114]

By the end of the 1660's Newton had studied the Cartesian principles of motion and had taken a critical stand with regard to them. His comments occur in an essay of the 1670's or late 1660's, beginning "De gravitatione et aequipondio fluidorum,"[115] in which he discussed extensively Descartes's *Principia* and also referred to a letter that formed part of the correspondence with Mersenne. Newton further set up a series of definitions and axioms, then ventured "to dispose of his [Descartes's] fictions." A large part of the essay deals with space and extension; for example, Newton criticized Descartes's view "that extension is not infinite but rather indefinite." In this essay Newton also defined force ("the causal principle of motion and rest"), conatus (or "endeavour"), impetus, inertia, and gravity. Then, in the traditional manner, he reckoned "the quantity of these powers" in "a double way: that is, according to intension or extension." He defined bodies, in the later medieval language of the intension and remission of forms, as "denser when their inertia is more intense, and rarer when it is more remiss."

In a final set of "Propositions on Non-Elastic Fluids" (in which there are two axioms and two propositions), axiom 2, "Bodies in contact press each other equally," suggests that the eventual third law of motion (*Principia*, axiom 3: "To every action is always opposed an equal and opposite reaction") may have arisen in application to fluids as well as to the impact of bodies. The latter topic occurs in another early manuscript, "The Lawes of Motion," written about 1666 and almost certainly antedating the essay on Descartes and his *Principia*.[116] Here Newton developed some rules for the impact of "bodyes which are absolutely hard," and then tempered them for application to "bodyes here amongst us," characterized by "a relenting softnesse & springynesse," which "makes their contact be for some time in more points than one."

Newton's attention to the problems of elastic and inelastic impact is manifest throughout his early writings on dynamics. In the *Principia* it is demonstrated by the emphasis he there gave the concept of force as an "impulse," and by a second law of motion (Lex II, in all editions of the *Principia*) in which he set forth the proportionality of such an impulse (acting instantaneously) to the change in momentum it produces.[117] In the scholium to the laws of motion Newton further discussed elastic and inelastic impact, referring to papers of the late 1660's by Wallis, Wren, and Huygens. He meanwhile developed his concept of a continuously acting force as the limit of a series of impulses occurring at briefer and briefer intervals *in infinitum*.[118]

Indeed, it was not until 1679, or some time between 1680 and 1684, following an exchange with Hooke, that Newton achieved his mature grasp of dynamical principles, recognizing the significance of Kepler's area law, which he had apparently just encountered. Only during the years 1684–1686, when, stimulated by Halley, he wrote out the various versions of the tract *De motu* and its successors and went on to compose the *Principia*, did Newton achieve full command of his insight into mathematical dynamics and celestial mechanics. At that time he clarified the distinction between mass and weight, and saw how these two quantities were related under a variety of circumstances.

Newton's exchange with Hooke occurred when the latter, newly appointed secretary of the Royal Society, wrote to Newton to suggest a private philosophical correspondence. In particular, Hooke asked Newton for his "objections against any hypothesis or opinion of mine," particularly "that of compounding the celestiall motions of the planetts of a direct motion by the tangent & an attractive motion towards the centrall body. . . ." Newton received the letter in November, some months after the death of his mother, and evidently did not wish to take up the problem. He introduced, instead, "a fancy of my own about discovering the Earth's diurnal motion, a spiral path that a freely falling body would follow as it supposedly fell to Earth, moved through the Earth's surface into the interior without material resistance, and eventually spiralled to (or very near to) the Earth's centre, after a few revolutions."[119]

Hooke responded that such a path would not be a spiral. He said that, according to "my theory of circular motion," in the absence of resistance, the body would not move in a spiral but in "a kind [of] Elleptueid," and its path would "resemble an Ellipse." This conclusion was based, said Hooke, on "my Theory of Circular Motions [being] compounded by a Direct [that is, tangential] motion and an attractive one to a Centre." Newton could not ignore this direct contradiction of his own expressed opinion. Accordingly, on 13 December 1679, he wrote Hooke that "I agree with you that . . . if its gravity be supposed uniform [the body would] not descend in a spiral to the very centre but circulate with an alternate descent & ascent." The cause was "its *vis centrifuga* & gravity alternately overballancing one another." This conception was very like Borelli's, and Newton imagined that "the body will not describe an Ellipsoeid," but a quite different figure. Newton here refused to accept the notion of an ellipse produced by gravitation decreasing as some power of the distance—although he had long before proved that for circular motion a combination of Kepler's third law and the rule for centrifugal force would yield a law of centrifugal force in the inverse square of the distance. There is no record of whether his reluctance was due to the poor agreement of the earlier moon test or to some other cause.

Fortunately for the advancement of science, Hooke kept pressing Newton. In a letter of 6 January 1680 he wrote ". . . But my supposition is that the Attraction always is in a duplicate proportion to the Distance from the Centre Reciprocall, and Consequently that the Velocity will be in a subduplicate proportion to the Attraction, and Consequently as Kepler Supposes Reciprocall to the Distance." We shall see below that this statement, often cited to support Hooke's claim to priority over Newton in the discovery of the inverse-square law, actually shows that Hooke was not a very good mathematician. As Newton proved, the force law here proposed contradicts the alleged velocity relation.

Hooke also claimed that this conception "doth very Intelligibly and truly make out all the Appearances of the Heavens," and that "the finding out the proprietys of a Curve made by two principles will be of great Concerne to Mankind, because the Invention of the Longitude by the Heavens is a necessary Consequence of it." After a few days, Hooke went on to challenge Newton directly:

> . . . It now remains to know the proprietys of a curve Line (not circular nor concentricall) made by a centrall attractive power which makes the velocitys of Descent from the tangent Line or equall straight motion at all Distances in a Duplicate proportion to the Distances Reciprocally taken. I doubt not but that by your excellent method you will easily find out what that Curve must be, and its proprietys, and suggest a physicall Reason of this proportion.[120]

Newton did not reply, but he later recorded his next steps:

> I found now that whatsoever was the law of the forces which kept the Planets in their Orbs, the areas described by a Radius drawn from them to the Sun would be proportional to the times in which they were described. And . . . that their Orbs would be such Ellipses as Kepler had described [when] the forces which kept them in their Orbs about the Sun were as the squares of their . . . distances from the Sun reciprocally.[121]

Newton's account seems to be reliable; the proof he devised must have been that written out by him later in his "De motu corporum in gyrum."[122]

Newton's solution is based on his method of limits, and on the use of infinitesimals.[123] He considered the motion along an ellipse from one point to another during an indefinitely small interval of time, and evaluated the deflection from the tangent during that interval, assuming the deflection to be proportional to the inverse square of the distance from a focus. As one of the two points on the ellipse approaches the other, Newton found that the area law supplies the essential condition in the limit.[124] In short, Newton showed that if the area law holds, then the elliptical shape of an orbit implies that any force directed to a focus must vary inversely as the square of the distance.

But it was also incumbent upon Newton to show the significance of the area law itself; he therefore proved that the area law is a necessary and sufficient condition that the force on a moving body be directed to a center. Thus, for the first time, the true significance of Kepler's first two laws of planetary

motion was revealed: that the area condition was equivalent to the action of a central force, and that the occurrence of the ellipse under this condition demonstrates that the force is as the inverse square of the distance. Newton further showed the law of areas to be only another aspect of the law of inertia, since in linear inertial motion, in the absence of external forces, equal areas are swept out in equal times by a line from the moving body directed toward any point not on the line of motion.[125]

Newton was thus quite correct in comparing Hooke's claim and Kepler's, as he wrote to Halley on 20 June 1686:

> But grant I received it [the hypothesis of the inverse-square relation] afterwards [that is, after he had come upon it by himself, and independently of Hooke] from Mr Hook, yet have I as great a right to it as to the Ellipsis. For as Kepler knew the Orb to be not circular but oval & guest it to be Elliptical, so Mr Hook without knowing what I have found out since his letters to me, can know no more but that the proportion was duplicate *quam proximè* at great distances from the center, & only guest it to be so accurately & guest amiss in extending that proportion down to the very center, whereas Kepler guest right at the Ellipsis. And so Mr Hook found less of the Proportion than Kepler of the Ellipsis.[126]

What Newton "found out" after his correspondence with Hooke in 1679 was the proof that a homogeneous sphere (or a sphere composed of homogeneous spherical shells) will gravitate as if all its mass were concentrated at its geometric center.

Newton refrained from pointing out that Hooke's lack of mathematical ability prevented him (and many of those who have supported his claim) from seeing that the "approximate" law of speed ($v \propto 1/r$) is

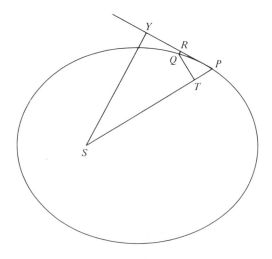

FIGURE 6

inconsistent with the true area law and does not accord with a force law of the form $f \propto 1/r^2$. Newton proved (Fig. 6: *Principia*, book I, proposition 16), that the speed at any point in an elliptical orbit is inversely proportional to the perpendicular dropped from the sun (focus) to the tangent drawn to the ellipse at that point, rather than being inversely proportional to the simple distance as Hooke and others had supposed; these two quantities being, of course, the same at the apsides. In the second edition of the *Principia* (1713) Newton shifted the corollaries to propositions 1 and 2, introducing a new set of corollaries to proposition 1, with the result that a prominent place was given to the true speed law.

Newton therefore deserves sole credit for recognizing the significance of the area law, a matter of some importance between 1679 and 1684. Following the exchange with Hooke in the earlier year, however, Newton did not at once go on to complete his work in celestial mechanics, although he did become interested in comets, corresponding with Flamsteed about their motion. He was converted from a belief in the straight-line motion of comets to a belief in parabolic paths, and thereafter attributed the motions of comets (in conic sections) to the action of the inverse-square law of the gravitation of the sun. He was particularly concerned with the comet of 1680, and in book III of the *Principia* devoted much space to its path.

In 1684, Halley visited Newton to ask about the path a planet would follow under the action of an inverse-square force: Wren, Hooke, and he had all been unsuccessful in satisfactorily resolving the matter, although Hooke had asserted (vainly) that he could do it. When Newton said to Hooke that he himself had "calculated" the result and that it was "an Ellipsis," Halley pressed him "for his calculation," but Newton could not find it among his papers and had to send it to Halley at a later date, in November. Halley then went back to Cambridge, where he saw "a curious treatise, *De Motu*." He obtained Newton's promise to send it "to the [Royal] Society to be entered upon their Register,"[127] and Newton, thus encouraged, wrote out a *De motu corporum*, of which the first section largely corresponds to book I of the *Principia* (together with an earnest of what was to become book II), while the second represents a popular account of what was later presented in book III.

Texts of both parts were deposited in the University Library, as if they were Newton's professorial lectures for 1684, 1685, and 1687; the second was published posthumously in both Latin and English, with the introduction of a new and misleading title of *De mundi*

systemate, or *The System of the World*. (This misnomer has ever since caused the second part of *De motu* to be confused with book III of the *Principia*, which is subtitled "De mundi systemate.")

Newton composed the *Principia* in a surprisingly short time.[128] The manuscript of book I was presented on 28 April 1686 to the Royal Society, which ordered it to be printed, although in the event Halley paid the costs and saw the work through the press. Halley's job was not an easy one; when Hooke demanded credit in print for his share in the inverse-square law, Newton demurred and even threatened to suppress book III. Halley fortunately dissuaded Newton from so mutilating his great treatise.

On 1 March 1687 Newton wrote to Halley that book II had been sent to him "by the Coach." The following 5 April Halley reported to Newton that he had received book III, "the last part of your divine Treatise." The printing was completed on 5 July 1687. The first edition included a short preface by Newton and an introductory ode to Newton by Halley—but book III ended abruptly, in the midst of a discussion of comets. Newton had originally drafted a "Conclusio" dealing with general aspects of natural philosophy and the theory of matter,[129] but he suppressed it. The famous conclusion, the "Scholium Generale," was first published some twenty-six years later, in 1713, in the second edition.

The development of Newton's views on comets may be traced through his correspondence with Flamsteed[130] and with Halley, and by comparing the first and second editions of the *Principia*. From Flamsteed he obtained information not only on comets, but also on the distances and periods of the satellites of Jupiter (which data appear in the beginning of book III of the *Principia* as a primary instance of Kepler's third law), and on the possible influence of Jupiter on the motion of Saturn. When Newton at first believed the great comet observed November 1680– March 1681 to be a pair of comets moving (as Kepler proposed) in straight lines, although in opposite directions, it was Flamsteed who convinced him that there was only one, observed coming and going, and that it must have turned about the sun.[131] Newton worked out a parabolic path for the comet of 1680 that was consistent with the observations of Flamsteed and others, the details of which occupy a great part of book III of the *Principia*. Such a parabolic path had been shown in book I to result from the inverse-square law under certain initial conditions, differing from those producing ellipses and hyperbolas.

In 1695, Halley postulated that the path of the comet of 1680 was an elongated ellipse—a path not very distinguishable from a parabola in the region of the sun, but significantly different in that the ellipse implies periodic returns of the comet—and worked out the details with Newton. In the second and third editions of the *Principia*, Newton gave tables for both the parabolic and elliptical orbits; he asserted unequivocally that Halley had found "a remarkable comet" appearing every seventy-five years or so, and added that Halley had "computed the motions of the comet in this elliptic orbit." Nevertheless, Newton himself remained primarily concerned with parabolic orbits. In the conclusion to the example following proposition 41 (on the comet of 1680), Newton said that "comets are a sort of planets revolved in very eccentric orbits about the sun." Even so, the proposition itself states (in all editions): "From three given observations to determine the orbit of a comet moving in a parabola."

Mathematics in the "Principia." The *Philosophiae naturalis principia mathematica* is, as its title suggests, an exposition of a natural philosophy conceived in terms of new principles based on Newton's own innovations in mathematics. It is too often described as a treatise in the style of Greek geometry, since on superficial examination it appears to have been written in a synthetic geometrical style.[132] But a close examination shows that this external Euclidean form masks the true and novel mathematical character of Newton's treatise, which was recognized even in his own day. (L'Hospital, for example—to Newton's delight—observed in the preface to his 1696 *Analyse des infiniment petits*, the first textbook on the infinitesimal calculus, that Newton's "excellent Livre intitulé *Philosophiae Naturalis principia Mathematica* . . . est presque tout de ce calcul.") Indeed, the most superficial reading of the *Principia* must show that, proposition by proposition and lemma by lemma, Newton usually proceeded by establishing geometrical conditions and their corresponding ratios and then at once introducing some carefully defined limiting process. This manner of proof or "invention," in marked distinction to the style of the classical Greek geometers, is based on a set of general principles of limits, or of prime and ultimate ratios, posited by Newton so as to deal with nascent or evanescent quantities or ratios of such quantities.

The doctrine of limits occurs in the *Principia* in a set of eleven lemmas that constitute section 1 of book I. These lemmas justify Newton in dealing with areas as limits of sums of inscribed or circumscribed rectangles (whose breadth → 0, or whose number → ∞), and in assuming the equality, in the limit, of arc, chord, and tangent (lemma 7), based on the proportionality of "homologous sides of similar figures, whether curvilinear or rectilinear" (lemma 5),

whose "areas are as the squares of the homologous sides." Newton's mathematical principles are founded on a concept of limit disclosed at the very beginning of lemma 1, "Quantities, and the ratios of quantities, which in any finite time converge continually to equality, and before the end of that time approach nearer to each other than by any given difference, become ultimately equal."

Newton further devoted the concluding scholium of section 1 to his concept of limit, and his method of taking limits, stating the guiding principle thus: "These lemmas are premised to avoid the tediousness of deducing involved demonstrations *ad absurdum*, according to the method of the ancient geometers." While he could have produced shorter ("more contracted") demonstrations by the "method of indivisibles," he judged the "hypothesis of indivisibles "to be "somewhat harsh" and not geometrical:

I chose rather to reduce the demonstrations of the following propositions to the first and last sums and ratios of nascent and evanescent quantities, that is, to the limits of those sums and ratios; and so to premise, as short as I could, the demonstrations of those limits. For hereby the same thing is performed as by the method of indivisibles; and now those principles being demonstrated, we may use them with greater safety. Therefore if hereafter I should happen to consider quantities as made up of particles, or should use little curved lines for right ones, I would not be understood to mean indivisibles, but evanescent divisible quantities; not the sums and ratios of determinate parts, but always the limits of sums and ratios; and that the force of such demonstrations always depends on the method laid down in the foregoing Lemmas.

Newton was aware that his principles were open to criticism on the ground "that there is no ultimate proportion of evanescent quantities; because the proportion, before the quantities have vanished, is not the ultimate, and when they are vanished, is none"; and he anticipated any possible unfavorable reaction by insisting that "the ultimate ratio of evanescent quantities" is to be understood to mean "the ratio of the quantities not before they vanish, nor afterwards, but [that] with which they vanish." In a "like manner, the first ratio of nascent quantities is that with which they begin to be," and "the first or last sum is that with which they begin and cease to be (or to be augmented or diminished)." Comparing such ratios and sums to velocities (for "it may be alleged, that a body arriving at a certain place, and there stopping, has no ultimate velocity; because the velocity, before the body comes to the place, is not its ultimate velocity; when it has arrived, there is none"), he imagined the existence of "a limit which the velocity at the end of the motion may attain, but not exceed," which limit is "the ultimate velocity," or "that velocity with which the body arrives at its last place, and with which the motion ceases." By analogy, he argued, "there is the like limit in all quantities and proportions that begin and cease to be," and "such limits are certain and definite." Hence, "to determine the same is a problem strictly geometrical," and thus may be used legitimately "in determining and demonstrating any other thing that is also geometrical."

In short, Newton wished to make a clear distinction between the ratios of ultimate quantities and "those ultimate ratios with which quantities vanish," the latter being "limits towards which the ratios of quantities decreasing without limit do always converge. . . ." He pointed out that this distinction may be seen most clearly in the case in which two quantities become infinitely great; then their "ultimate ratio" may be "given, namely, the ratio of equality," even though "it does not from thence follow, that the ultimate or greatest quantities themselves, whose ratio that is, will be given."

Section 1 of book I is unambiguous in its statement that the treatise to follow is based on theorems of which the truth and demonstration almost always depend on the taking of limits. Of course, the occasional analytical intrusions in book I and the explicit use of the fluxional method in book II (notably in section 2) show the mathematical character of the book as a whole, as does the occasional but characteristic introduction of the methods of expansion in infinite series. A careful reading of almost any proof in book I will, moreover, demonstrate the truly limital or infinitesimal character of the work as a whole. But nowhere in the *Principia* (or in any other generally accessible manuscript) did Newton write any of the equations of dynamics as fluxions, as Maclaurin did later on. This continuous form is effectively that published by Varignon in the *Mémoires* of the Paris Academy in 1700; Newton's second law was written as a differential equation in J. Hermann's *Phoronomia* (1716).

The similarity of section 1, book I, to the introductory portion of the later *De quadratura* should not be taken to mean that in the *Principia* Newton developed his principles of natural philosophy on the basis of first and last ratios exclusively, since in the *Principia* Newton presented not one, but rather three modes of presentation of his fluxional or infinitesimal calculus. A second approach to the calculus occurs in section 2, book II, notably in lemma 2, in which Newton introduced the concept and method of moments. This represents the first printed statement (in the first edition of 1687) by Newton himself of

his new mathematics, apart from its application to physics (with which the opening discussion of limits in section 1, book I is concerned). In a scholium to lemma 2, Newton wrote that this lemma contains the "foundation" of "a general method," one

> . . . which extends itself, without any troublesome calculation, not only to the drawing of tangents to any curve lines . . ., but also to the resolving other abstruser kinds of problems about the crookedness, areas, lengths, centres of gravity of curves, &c.; nor is it . . . limited to equations which are free from surd quantities. This method I have interwoven with that other of working in equations, by reducing them to infinite series.

He added that the "last words relate to a treatise I composed on that subject in the year 1671,"[133] and that the paragraph quoted above came from a letter he had written to Collins on 10 December 1672, describing "a method of tangents."

The lemma itself reads: "The moment of any *genitum* is equal to the mome. 's of each of the generating sides multiplied by the indices of the powers of those sides, and by their coefficients continually."[134] It may be illustrated by Newton's first example: Let AB be a rectangle with sides A, B, diminished by $\frac{1}{2}a$, $\frac{1}{2}b$, respectively. The diminished area is $(A - \frac{1}{2}a)(B - \frac{1}{2}b) = AB - \frac{1}{2}aB - \frac{1}{2}bA + \frac{1}{4}ab$. Now, by a "continual flux," let the sides be augmented by $\frac{1}{2}a$, $\frac{1}{2}b$, respectively; the area ("rectangle") will then become $(A + \frac{1}{2}a)(B + \frac{1}{2}b) = AB + \frac{1}{2}aB + \frac{1}{2}bA + \frac{1}{4}ab$ (Fig. 7). Subtract one from the other, "and there will

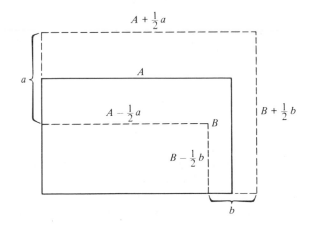

FIGURE 7

remain the excess $aB + bA$." Newton concluded, "Therefore with the whole increments a and b of the sides, the increment $aB + bA$ of the rectangle is generated." Here a and b are the moments of A and B, respectively, and Newton has shown that the moment of AB, corresponding to the moments a and b of A and B, respectively, is $aB + bA$. And, for the special case of $A = B$, the moment of A^2 is determined as $2aA$.

In order to extend the result from "area" to "content" or ("bulk"), from AB to ABC, Newton set $AB = G$ and then used the prior result for AB twice, once for AB, and again for GC, so as to get the moment of ABC to be $cAB + bCA + aBC$; whence, by setting $A = B = C$, the moment of A^3 is determined as $3aA^2$. And, in general, the moment of A^n is shown to be naA^{n-1} for n as a positive integer.

The result is readily extended to negative integral powers and even to all products $A^m B^n$, "whether the indices m and n of the powers be whole numbers or fractions, affirmative or negative." Whiteside has pointed out that by using the decrements $\frac{1}{2}a$, $\frac{1}{2}b$ and the increments $\frac{1}{2}a$, $\frac{1}{2}b$, rather than the increments a, b, "Newton . . . deluded himself into believing" he had "contrived an approach which avoids the comparatively messy appeal to the limit-value of $(A + a)/(B + b) - AB$ as the increments a, b vanish." The result is what is now seen as a "celebrated *non-sequitur*."[135]

In discussing lemma 2, Newton defined moments as the "momentary increments or decrements" of "variable and indetermined" quantities, which might be "products, quotients, roots, rectangles, squares, cubes, square and cubic sides, and the like." He called these "quantities" *genitae*, because he conceived them to be "generated or produced in arithmetic by the multiplication, division, or extraction of the root of any terms whatsoever; in geometry by the finding of contents and sides, or of the extremes and means of proportionals." So much is clear. But Newton warned his readers not "to look upon finite particles as such [moments]," for finite particles "are not moments, but the very quantities generated by the moments. We are to conceive them as the just nascent principles of finite magnitudes." And, in fact, it is not "the magnitude of the moments, but their first proportion [which is to be regarded] as nascent."

Boyer has called attention to the difficulty of conceiving "the limit of a ratio in determining the moment of AB."[136] The moment of AB is not really a product of two independent variables A and B, implying a problem in partial differentiation, but rather a product of two functions of the single independent variable time. Newton himself said, "It will be the same thing, if, instead of moments, we use either the velocities of the increments and decrements (which may also be called the motions, mutations, and fluxions of quantities), or any finite quantities proportional to those velocities."

Newton thus shifted the conceptual base of his procedure from infinitely small quantities or moments —which are not finite, and clearly not zero—to the "first proportion," or ratio of moments (rather than "the magnitude of the moments") "as nascent." This nascent ratio is generally not infinitesimal but finite, and Newton thus suggested that the ratio of finite quantities may be substituted for the ratio of infinitesimals, with the same result, using in fact the velocities of the increments or decrements instead of the moments, or "any finite quantities proportional to those velocities," which are also the "fluxions of the quantities." Boyer summarized this succinctly:

> Newton thus offered in the *Principia* three modes of interpretation of the new analysis: that in terms of infinitesimals (used in his *De analysi . . .*); that in terms of prime and ultimate ratios or limits (given particularly in *De quadratura*, and the view which he seems to have considered most rigorous); and that in terms of fluxions (given in his *Methodus fluxionum*, and one which appears to have appealed most strongly to his imagination).[137]

From the point of view of mathematics, proposition 10, book II, may particularly attract our attention. Here Newton boldly displayed his methods of using the terms of a converging series to solve problems and his method of second differences. Expansions are given with respect to "the indefinite quantity o," but there are no references to (nor uses of) moments, as in the preceding lemma 2, and, of course, there is no use made of dotted or "pricked" letters.

The proposition is of particular interest for at least two reasons. First, its proof and exposition (or exemplification) are highly analytic and not geometric (or synthetic), as are most proofs in the *Principia*. Second, an error in the first edition and in the original printed pages of the second edition was discovered by Johann [I] Bernoulli and called to Newton's attention by Nikolaus [I] Bernoulli, who visited England in September or October 1712. As a result, Newton had Cotes reprint a whole signature and an additional leaf of the already printed text of the second edition; these pages thus appear as cancels in every copy of this edition of the *Principia* that has been recorded. The corrected proposition, analyzed by Whiteside, illustrates "the power of Newton's infinitesimal techniques in the *Principia*," and may thus confute the opinion that "Newton did not (at least in principle, and in his own algorithm) know how 'to formulate and resolve problems through the integration of differential equations.' "[138]

From at least 1712 onward, Newton attempted to impose upon the *Principia* a mode of composition that could lend support to his position in the priority dispute with Leibniz: he wished to demonstrate that he had actually composed the *Principia* by analysis and had rewritten the work synthetically. He affirmed this claim, in and after 1713, in several manuscript versions of prefaces to planned new editions of the *Principia* (both with or without *De quadratura* as a supplement). It is indeed plausible to argue that much of the *Principia* was based upon an infinitesimal analysis, veiled by the traditional form of Greek synthetic geometry, but the question remains whether Newton drew upon working papers in which (in extreme form) he gave solutions in dotted fluxions to problems that he later presented geometrically. But, additionally, there is no evidence that Newton used an analytic method of ordinary fluxional form to discover the propositions he presented synthetically.

All evidence indicates that Newton had actually found the propositions in the *Principia* in essentially the way in which he there presented them to his readers. He did, however, use algebraic methods to determine the solid of least resistance. But in this case, he did not make the discovery by analysis and then recast it as an example of synthesis; he simply stated his result without proof.[139]

It has already been mentioned that Newton did make explicit use of the infinitesimal calculus in section 2, book II, of the *Principia*, and that in that work he often employed his favored method of infinite series.[140] But this claim is very different indeed from such a statement of Newton's as: ". . . At length in 1685 and part of 1686 by the aid of this method and the help of the book on Quadratures I wrote the first two books of the mathematical Principles of Philosophy. And therefore I have subjoined a Book on Quadratures to the Book of Principles."[141] This "method" refers to fluxions, or the method of differential calculus. But it is true, as mentioned earlier, that Newton stated in the *Principia* that certain theorems depended upon the "quadrature" (or integration) of "certain curves"; he did need, for this purpose, the inverse method of fluxions, or the integral calculus. And proposition 41 of book I is, moreover, an obvious exercise in the calculus.

Newton himself never did bring out an edition of the *Principia* together with a version of *De quadratura*.[142] In the review that he published of the *Commercium epistolicum*,[143] Newton did announce in print, although anonymously, that he had "found out most of the Propositions in his *Principia*" by using "the new *Analysis*," and had then reworked the material and had "demonstrated the Propositions synthetically." (This claim cannot, however, be substantiated by documentary evidence.)

Apart from questions of the priority of Newton's

method, the *Principia* contains some problems of notable mathematical interest. Sections 4 and 5 of book I deal with conic sections, and section 6 with Kepler's problem; Newton here introduced the method of solution by successive iteration. Lemma 5 of book III treats of a locus through a given number of points, an example of Newton's widely used method of interpolating a function. Proposition 71, book I, contains Newton's important solution to a major problem of integration, the attraction of a sphere, called by Turnbull "the crown of all." Newton's proof that two spheres will mutually attract each other as if the whole of their masses were concentrated at their respective centers is posited on the condition that, however the mass or density may vary within each sphere as a function of that radius, the density at any given radius is everywhere the same (or is constant throughout any concentric shell).

The "Principia": General Plan. Newton's masterwork was worked up and put into its final form in an incredibly short time. His strategy was to develop the subject of general dynamics from a mathematical point of view in book I, then to apply his most important results to solving astronomical and physical problems in book III. Book II, introduced at some point between Newton's first conception of the treatise and the completion of the printer's manuscript, is almost independent, and appears extraneous.

Book I opens with a series of definitions and axioms, followed by a set of mathematical principles and procedural rules for the use of limits; book III begins with general precepts concerning empirical science and a presentation of the phenomenological bases of celestial mechanics, based on observation.

It is clear to any careful reader that Newton was, in book I, developing mathematical principles of motion chiefly so that he might apply them to the physical conditions of experiment and observation in book III, on the system of the world. Newton maintained that even though he had, in book I, used such apparently physical concepts as "force" and "attraction," he did so in a purely mathematical sense. In fact, in book I (as in book II), he tended to follow his inspiration to whatever aspect of any topic might prove of mathematical interest, often going far beyond any possible physical application. Only in an occasional scholium in books I and II did he raise the question of whether the mathematical propositions might indeed be properly applied to the physical circumstances that the use of such words as "force" and "attraction" would seem to imply.

Newton's method of composition led to a certain amount of repetition, since many topics are discussed twice—in book I, with mathematical proofs, to illustrate the general principles of the motions of bodies, then again in book III, in application to the motions of planets and their satellites or of comets. While this mode of presentation makes the *Principia* more difficult for the reader, it does have the decided advantage of separating the Newtonian principles as they apply to the physical universe from the details of the mathematics from which they derive.

As an example of this separation, proposition 1 of book III states that the satellites of Jupiter are "continually drawn off from rectilinear motions, and are retained in their proper orbits" by forces that "tend to Jupiter's centre" and that these forces vary inversely as the square of their distances from that center. The proof given in this proposition is short and direct; the centripetal force itself follows from "Phen. I [of book III], and Prop. II or III, Book I." The phenomenon cited is a statement, based upon "astronomical observations," that a radius drawn from the center of Jupiter to any satellite sweeps out areas "proportional to the times of descriptions"; propositions 2 and 3 of book I prove by mathematics that under these circumstances the force about which such areas are described must be centripetal and proportional to the times. The inverse-square property of this force is derived from the second part of the phenomenon, which states that the distances from Jupiter's center are as the $\frac{3}{2}$th power of their periods of revolution, and from corollary 6 to proposition 4 of book I, in which it is proved that centripetal force in uniform circular motion must be as the inverse square of the distance from the center.

Newton's practice of introducing a particular instance repeatedly, with what may seem to be only minor variations, may render the *Principia* difficult for the modern reader. But the main hurdle for any would-be student of the treatise lies elsewhere, in the essential mathematical difficulty of the main subject matter, celestial mechanics, however presented. A further obstacle is that Newton's mathematical vocabulary became archaic soon after the *Principia* was published, as dynamics in general and celestial mechanics in particular came to be written in the language of differentials and integrals still used today. The reader is thus required almost to translate for himself Newton's geometrical-limit mode of proof and statement into the characters of the analytic algorithms of the calculus. Even so, dynamics was taught directly from the *Principia* at Cambridge until well into the twentieth century.

In his "Mathematical Principles" Whiteside describes the *Principia* as "slipshod, its level of verbal fluency none too high, its arguments unnecessarily diffuse and repetitive, and its content on occasion markedly irrelevant to its professed theme: the theory of bodies moving under impressed forces." This view is somewhat extreme. Nevertheless, the work might have been easier to read today had Newton chosen to rely to a greater extent on general algorithms.

The *Principia* is often described as if it were a "synthesis," notably of Kepler's three laws of planetary motion and Galileo's laws of falling bodies and projectile motion; but in fact it denies the validity of both these sets of basic laws unless they be modified. For instance, Newton showed for the first time the dynamical significance of Kepler's so-called laws of planetary motion; but in so doing he proved that in the form originally stated by Kepler they apply exactly only to the highly artificial condition of a point mass moving about a mathematical center of force, unaffected by any other stationary or moving masses. In the real universe, these laws or planetary "hypotheses" are true only to the limits of ordinary observation, which may very well have been the reason that Newton called them "Hypotheses" in the first edition. Later, in the second and third editions, he referred to these relations as "Phaenomena," by which it may be assumed that he now meant that they were not simply true as stated (that is, not strictly deducible from the definitions and axioms), but were rather valid only to the limit of (or within the limits of) observation, or were phenomenologically true. In other words, these statements were to be regarded as not necessarily true, but only contingently (phenomenologically) so.

In the *Principia*, Newton proved that Kepler's planetary hypotheses must be modified by at least two factors: (1) the mutual attraction of each of any pair of bodies, and (2) the perturbation of a moving body by any and all neighboring bodies. He also showed that the rate of free fall of bodies is not constant, as Galileo had supposed, but varies with distance from the center of the earth and with latitude along the surface of the earth.[144] In a scholium at the end of section 2, book I, Newton further pointed out that it is only in a limiting case, not really achieved on earth, that projectiles (even *in vacuo*) move in Galilean parabolic trajectories, as Galileo himself knew full well. Thus, as Karl Popper has pointed out, although "Newton's dynamics achieved a unification of Galileo's terrestrial and Kepler's celestial physics," it appears that "from a logical point of view, Newton's theory, strictly speaking, contradicts both Galileo's and Kepler's."[145]

The "Principia": Definitions and Axioms. The *Principia* opens with two preliminary presentations: the "Definitions" and the "Axioms, or Laws of

Motion." The first two entities defined are "quantity of matter," or "mass," and "quantity of motion." The former is said to be the measure of matter proportional to bulk and density conjunctively. "Mass" is, in addition, given as being generally known by its weight, to which it is proportional at any given place, as shown by Newton's experiments with pendulums, of which the results are more exact than Galileo's for freely falling bodies. Newton's "quantity of motion" is the entity now known as momentum; it is said to be measured by the velocity and mass of a body, conjunctively.

Definition 3 introduces *vis insita* (probably best translated as "inherent force"), a concept of which the actual definition and explanation are both so difficult to understand that much scholarly debate has been expended on them.[146] Newton wrote that the *vis insita* may be known by "a most significant name, *vis inertiae*." But this "force" is not like the "impressed forces" of definition 4, which change the state of rest or uniform rectilinear motion of a body; the *vis inertiae* merely maintains any new state acquired by a body, and it may cause a body to "resist" any change in state.[147]

Newton then defined "centripetal force" (*vis centripeta*), a concept he had invented and named to complement the *vis centrifuga* of Christiaan Huygens.[148] In definitions 6 through 8, Newton gave three "measures" of centripetal force, of which the most important for the purposes of the *Principia* is that one "proportional to the velocity which it generates in a given time" (for point masses, unit masses, or for comparing equal masses). There follows the famous scholium on space and time, in which Newton opted for concepts of absolute space and absolute time, although recognizing that both are usually reckoned by "sensible measures"; time, especially, is usually "relative, apparent, and common." Newton's belief in absolute space led him to hold that absolute motion is sensible or detectable, notably in rotation, although contemporaries as different in their outlooks as Huygens and Berkeley demurred from this view.

The "Axioms" or "Laws of Motion" are three in number: the law of inertia, a form of what is today known as the second law, and finally the law that "To every action there is always opposed an equal and opposite reaction." There is much puzzlement over the second law, which Newton stated as a proportionality between "change in motion" (in momentum) and "the motive force impressed" (a change "made in the direction . . ., in which that force is impressed"); he did not specify "per unit time" or "in some given time." The second law thus seems clearly to be stated for

an impulse, but throughout the *Principia* (and, in a special case, in the antecedent definition 8), Newton used the law for continuous forces, including gravitation, taking account of time. For Newton, in fact, the concepts of impulse and continuous force were infinitesimally equivalent, and represented conditions of action "altogether and at once" or "by degrees and successively."[149] There are thus two conditions of "force" in the second law; accordingly, this Newtonian law may be written in the two forms $f \propto d(mv)$ and $f \propto d(mv)/dt$, in which both concepts of force are taken account of by means of two different constants of proportionality. The two forms of the law can be considered equivalent through Newton's concept of a uniformly flowing time, which makes dt a kind of secondary constant, which can arbitrarily be absorbed in the constant of proportionality.

There may be some doubt as to whether or not Newton himself was unclear in his own mind about these matters. His use of such expressions as "vis impressa" shows an abiding influence of older physics, while his continued reference to a "vis" or a "force" needed to maintain bodies in a state of motion raises the question of whether such usage is one of a number of possibly misleading "artifacts left behind in the historical development of his [Newton's] dynamics."[150] It must be remembered, of course, that throughout the seventeenth and much of the eighteenth century the word "force" could be used in a number of ways. Most notably, it served to indicate the concept now called "momentum," although it could also even mean energy. In Newton's time there were no categories of strict formalistic logic that required a unitary one-to-one correspondence between names and concepts, and neither Newton nor his contemporaries (or, for that matter, his successors) were always precise in making such distinctions.

The careful reader of books I–III should not be confused by such language, however, nor by the preliminary intrusion of such concepts. Even the idea of force as a measure of motion or of change of motion (or of change *per se*, or rate of change) is not troublesome in practice, once Newton's own formulation is accepted and the infinitesimal level of his discourse (which is not always explicitly stated) understood. In short, Newton's dynamical and mathematical elaboration of the three books of the *Principia* is free of the errors and ambiguities implicit in his less successful attempt to give a logically simple and coherent set of definitions and axioms for dynamics. (It is even possible that the definitions and axioms may represent an independent later exercise, since there are, for example, varying sets of definitions and axioms for the same system of dynamics.) One of the most important consequences of Newton's analysis is that it must be one and the same law of force that operates in the centrally directed acceleration of the planetary bodies (toward the sun) and of satellites (toward planets), and that controls the linear downward acceleration of freely falling bodies. This force of universal gravitation is also shown to be the cause of the tides, through the action of the sun and the moon on the seas.

Book I of the "Principia." Book I of the *Principia* contains the first of the two parts of *De motu corporum*. It is a mathematical treatment of motion under the action of impressed forces in free spaces—that is, spaces devoid of resistance. (Although Newton discussed elastic and inelastic impact in the scholium to the laws, he did not reintroduce this topic in book I.) For the most part, the subject of Newton's inquiries is the motion of unit or point masses, usually having some initial inertial motion and being acted upon by a centripetal force. Newton thus tended to use the change in velocity produced in a given time (the "accelerative measure") of such forces, rather than the change in momentum produced in a given time (their "motive" measure).[151] He generally compared the effects of different forces or conditions of force on one and the same body, rather than on different bodies, preferring to consider a mass point or unit mass to computing actual magnitudes. Eventually, however, when the properties and actions of force had been displayed by an investigation of their "accelerative" and "motive" measures, Newton was able to approach the problem of their "absolute" measure. Later in the book he considered the attraction of spherical shells and spheres and of nonsymmetrical bodies.

Sections 2 and 3 are devoted to aspects of motion according to Kepler's laws. In proposition 1 Newton proceeded by four stages. He first showed that in a purely uniform linear (or purely inertial) motion, a radius vector drawn from the moving body to any point not in the line of motion sweeps out equal areas in equal times. The reason for this is clearly shown in

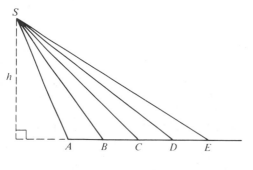

FIGURE 8

Figure 8, in which in equal times the body will move through the equal distances AB, BC, CD, DE, $\cdots$. If a radius vector is drawn from a point PS, then triangles ABS, BCS, CDS, DES, $\cdots$ have equal bases and a common altitude h, and their areas are equal. In the second stage, Newton assumed the moving object to receive an impulsive force when it reaches point B. A component of motion toward S is thereby added to its motion toward C; its actual path is thus along the diagonal Bc of a parallelogram (Figure 9).

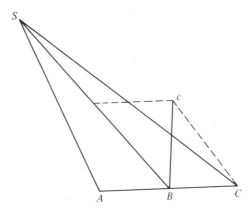

FIGURE 9

Newton then showed by simple geometry that the area of the triangle SBc is the same as the area of the triangle SBC, so that area is still conserved. He repeated the procedure in the third stage, with the body receiving a new impetus toward S at point C, and so on. In this way, the path is converted from a straight line into a series of joined line segments, traversed in equal intervals of time, which determine triangles of equal areas, with S as a common vertex.

In Newton's final development of the problem, the number of triangles is increased "and their breadth diminished *in infinitum*"; in the limit the "ultimate perimeter" will be a curve, the centripetal force "will act continually," and "any described areas" will be proportional to the times. Newton thus showed that inertial motion of and by itself implies an area-conservation law, and that if a centripetal force is directed to "an immovable centre" when a body has such inertial motion initially, area is still conserved as determined by a radius vector drawn from the moving body to the immovable center of force. (A critical examination of Newton's proof reveals the use of second-order infinitesimals.)[152] The most significant aspect of this proposition (and its converse, proposition 2) may be its demonstration of the hitherto wholly unsuspected logical connection, in the case of planetary motion, between Descartes's law of inertia and Kepler's law of areas (generalized to hold for an arbitrary central orbit).

Combining proposition 1 and proposition 2, Newton showed the physical significance of the law of areas as a necessary and sufficient condition for a central force (supposing that such forces exist; the "reality" of accelerative and motive forces of attraction is discussed in book III). In proposition 3, Newton dealt with the case of a body moving around a moving, rather than a stationary, center. Proposition 4 is concerned with uniform circular motion, in which the forces (F, f) are shown not only to be directed to the centers of the circles, but also to be to each other "as the squares of the arcs $[S, s]$ described in equal times divided respectively by the radii $[R, r]$ of the circles" $(F : f = S/R^2 : s/r^2)$. A series of corollaries demonstrate that $F : f = V^2/R : v^2 r = R/T^2 : r/t^2$, where V, v are the tangential velocities, and so on; and that, universally, T being the period of revolution, if $T \propto R^n$, $V \propto 1/R^{n-1}$, then $F \propto 1/R^{2n-1}$, and conversely. A special case of the last condition (corollary 6) is $T \propto R^{3/2}$, yielding $F \propto 1/R^2$, a condition (according to a scholium) obtaining "in the celestial bodies," as Wren, Hooke, and Halley "have severally observed." Newton further referred to Huygens' derivation, in *De horologio oscillatorio*, of the magnitude of "the centrifugal force of revolving bodies" and introduced his own independent method for determining the centrifugal force in uniform circular motion. In proposition 6 he went on to a general concept of instantaneous measure of a force, for a body revolving in any curve about a fixed center of force. He then applied this measure, developed as a limit in several forms, in a number of major examples, among them proposition 11.

The last propositions of section 2 were altered in successive editions. In them Newton discussed the laws of force related to motion in a given circle and equiangular (logarithmic) spiral. In proposition 10 Newton took up elliptical motion in which the force tends toward the center of the ellipse. A necessary and sufficient cause of this motion is that "the force is as the distance." Hence if the center is "removed to an infinite distance," the ellipse "degenerates into a parabola," and the force will be constant, yielding "Galileo's theorem" concerning projectile motion.

Section 3 of book I opens with proposition 11, "If a body revolves in an ellipse; it is required to find the law of the centripetal force tending to the focus of the ellipse." The law is: "the centripetal force is inversely . . . as the square of the distance." Propositions 12 and 13 show that a hyperbolic and a parabolic orbit imply the same law of force to a focus. It is obvious that the converse condition, that the centripetal force varies inversely as the square of the distance, does not by itself specify which conic section will constitute the orbit. Proposition 15 demonstrates that in ellipses "the periodic times are as the 3/2th power of their greater axes" (Kepler's third law). Hence the periodic times in all ellipses with equal major axes are equal to one another, and equal to the periodic time in a circle of which the diameter is equal to the greater axis of each ellipse. In proposition 17, Newton supposed a centripetal force "inversely proportional to the squares of the distances" and exhibited the conditions for an orbit in the shape of an ellipse, parabola, or hyperbola. Sections 4 and 5, on conic sections, are purely mathematical.

In section 6, Newton discussed Kepler's problem, introducing methods of approximation to find the future position of a body on an ellipse, according to the law of areas; it is here that one finds the method of successive iteration. In section 7, Newton found the rectilinear distance through which a body falls freely in any given time under the action of a "centripetal force . . . inversely proportional to the square of the distance . . . from the centre." Having found the times of descent of such a body, he then applied his results to the problem of parabolic motion and the motion of "a body projected upwards or downwards," under conditions in which "the centripetal force is proportional to the . . . distance." Eventually, in proposition 39, Newton postulated "a centripetal force of any kind" and found both the velocity at any point to which any body may ascend or descend in a straight line and the time it would take the body to get there. In this proposition, as in many in section 8, he added the condition of "granting the quadratures of curvilinear figures," referring to his then unpublished methods of integration (printed for the first time in the *De quadratura* of 1704).

In section 8, Newton often assumed such quadrature. In proposition 41 he postulated "a centripetal force of any kind"; that is, as he added in proposition 42, he supposed "the centripetal force to vary in its recess from the center according to some law, which anyone may imagine at pleasure, but [which] at equal distances from the centre [is taken] to be everywhere the same." Under these general conditions, Newton determined both "the curves in which bodies will move" and "the times of their motions in the curves found." In other words, Newton presented to his readers a truly general resolution of the inverse problem of finding the orbit from a given law of force. He extended this problem into a dynamics far beyond that commonly associated with the *Principia*. In the ancillary proposition 40, for example, Newton (again under the most general conditions of force) had sought the velocity at a point on an orbit, finding a result that is the equivalent of an integral, which (in E. J. Aiton's words) in "modern terms . . . expresses the invariance of the sum of the kinetic and gravitational potential energies in an orbit."[153]

In section 11, Newton reached a level of mathematical analysis of celestial motions that fully distinguishes the *Principia* from any of its predecessors. Until this point, he there explained, he had been "treating of the attractions of bodies towards an immovable centre; though very probably there is no such thing existent in nature." He then outlined a plan to deal with nature herself, although in a "purely mathematical" way, "laying aside all physical considerations"—such as the nature of the gravitating force. "Attractions" are to be treated here as originating in bodies and acting toward other bodies; in a two-body system, therefore, "neither the attracted nor the attracting body is truly at rest, but both . . . being as it were mutually attracted, revolve about a common centre of gravity." In general, for any system of bodies that mutually attract one another, "their common centre of gravity will either be at rest, or move uniformly" in a straight line. Under these conditions, both members of a pair of mutually attractive bodies will describe "similar figures about their common centre of gravity, and about each other mutually" (proposition 57).

By studying such systems, rather than a single body attracted toward a point-center of force, Newton proved that Kepler's laws (or "planetary hypotheses") cannot be true within this context, and hence need modification when applied to the real system of the world. Thus, in proposition 59, Newton stated that Kepler's third law should not be written $T_1{}^2 : T_2{}^2 = a_1{}^3 : a_2{}^3$, as Kepler, Hooke, and everybody else had supposed, but must be modified.

A corollary that may be drawn from the proposition is that the law might be written as $(M + m_1)T_1{}^2 : (M + m_2)T_2{}^2 = a_1{}^3 : a_2{}^3$, where m_1, m_2 are any two planetary masses and M is the mass of the sun. (Newton's expression of this new relation may be reduced at once to the more familiar form in which we use this law today.) Clearly, it follows from Newton's analysis and formulation that Kepler's own third law may safely be used as an approximation in most astronomical calculations only because m_1, m_2 are very small in relation to M. Newton's modification of Kepler's third law fails to take account of any possible interplanetary perturbations. The chief

function of proposition 59 thus appears to be not to reach the utmost generalization of that law, but rather to reach a result that will be useful in the problems that follow, most notably proposition 60 (on the orbits described when each of two bodies attracts the other with a force proportional to the square of the distance, each body "revolving about the common centre of gravity").

From proposition 59 onward, Newton almost at once advanced to various motions of mutually attractive bodies "let fall from given places" (in proposition 62), "going off from given places in given directions with given velocities" (proposition 63), or even when the attractive forces "increase in a simple ratio of their [that is, the bodies'] distances from the centres" (proposition 64). This led him to examine Kepler's first two laws for real "bodies," those "whose forces decrease as the square of their distances from their centres." Newton demonstrated in proposition 65 that in general it is not "possible that bodies attracting each other according to the law supposed in this proposition should move exactly in ellipses," because of interplanetary perturbations, and discussed cases in astronomy in which "the orbits will not much differ from ellipses." He added that the areas described will be only "very nearly proportional to the times."

Proposition 66 presents the restricted three-body problem, developed in a series of twenty-two corollaries. Here Newton attempted to apply the law of mutual gravitational attraction to a body like the sun to determine how it might perturb the motion of a moonlike body around an earthlike body. Newton examined the motion in longitude and in latitude, the annual equation, the evection, the change of the inclination of the orbit of the body resembling the moon, and the motion on the line of apsides. He considered the tides and explained, in corollary 22, that the internal "constitution of the globe" (of the earth) can be known "from the motion of the nodes." He further demonstrated that the shape of the globe can be derived from the precession constant (precession being caused, in the case of the earth, by the pull of the moon on the equatorial bulge of the spinning earth). He thus established, for the first time, a physical theory, elaborated in mathematical expression, from which some of the "inequalities" of the motion of the moon could be deduced; and he added some hitherto unknown "inequalities" that he had found. Previous to Newton's work, the study of the irregularities in the motion of the moon had been posited on the elaboration of geometric models, in an attempt to make predicted positions agree with actual observations.[154]

Section 12 of book I contains Newton's results on the attractions of spheres, or of spherical shells. He dealt first with homogeneous, then nonhomogeneous spheres, the latter being composed of uniform and concentric spherical shells so that the density is the same at any single given distance from the center. In proposition 71 he proved that a "corpuscle" situated outside such a nonhomogeneous sphere is "attracted towards the centre of the sphere with a force inversely proportional to the square of its distance from the centre." In proposition 75, he reached the general conclusion that any two such spheres will gravitationally attract one another as if their masses were concentrated at their respective centers—or, in other words, that the distance required for the inverse-square law is measured from their centers. A series of elegant and purely mathematical theorems follow, including one designed to find the force with which a corpuscle placed inside a sphere may be "attracted toward any segment of that sphere whatsoever." In section 13, Newton, with a brilliant display of mathematics (which he did not fully reveal for the benefit of the reader) discussed the "attractive forces" of nonspherical solids of revolution, concluding with a solution in the form of an infinite series for the attraction of a body "towards a given plane."[155]

Book I concludes with section 14, on the "motion of very small bodies" acted on by "centripetal forces tending to the several parts of any very great body." Here Newton used the concept of "centripetal forces" that act under very special conditions to produce motions of corpuscles that simulate the phenomena of light—including reflection and refraction (according to the laws of Snell and Descartes), the inflection of light (as discovered by Grimaldi), and even the action of lenses. In a scholium, Newton noted that these "attractions bear a great resemblance to the reflections and refractions of light," and so

> ... because of the analogy there is between the propagation of the rays of light and the motion of bodies, I thought it not amiss to add the following Propositions for optical uses; not at all considering the nature of the rays of light, or inquiring whether they are bodies or not; but only determining the curves of [the paths of] bodies which are extremely like the curves of the rays.

A similar viewpoint with respect to mathematical analyses (or models and analogies) and physical phenomena is generally sustained throughout books I and II of the *Principia*.

Newton's general plan in book I may thus be seen as one in which he began with the simplest conditions and added complexities step by step. In sections 2 and 3, for example, he dealt with a mass-point moving under the action of a centripetal force directed toward a stationary or moving point, by which the dynamical significance of each of Kepler's three laws of planetary motion is demonstrated. In section 6, Newton developed methods to compute Keplerian motion (along an ellipse, according to the law of areas), which leads to "regular ascent and descent" of bodies when the force is not uniform (as in Galilean free fall) but varies, primarily as the inverse square of the distance, as in Keplerian orbital motion. In section 8 Newton considered the general case of "orbits in which bodies will revolve, being acted upon by any sort of centripetal force." From stationary orbits he went on, in section 9, to "movable orbits; and the motion of the apsides" and to a mathematical treatment of two (and then three) mutually attractive bodies. In section 10 he dealt with motion along surfaces of bodies acted upon by centripetal force; in section 12, the problems of bodies that are not mere points or point-masses and the question of the "attractive forces of spherical bodies"; and in section 13, "the attractive forces of bodies that are not spherical."

Book II of the "Principia." Book II, on the motion of bodies in resisting mediums, is very different from book I. It was an afterthought to the original treatise, which was conceived as consisting of only two books, of which one underwent more or less serious modifications to become book I as it exists today, while the other, a more popular version of the "system of the world," was wholly transformed so as to become what is now book III. At first the question of motion in resisting mediums had been relegated to some theorems at the end of the original book I; Newton had also dealt with this topic in a somewhat similar manner at the end of his earlier tract *De motu*. The latter parts of the published book II were added only at the final redaction of the *Principia*.

Book II is perhaps of greater mathematical than physical interest. To the extent that Newton proceeded by setting up a sequence of mathematical conditions and then exploring their consequences, book II resembles book I. But there is a world of difference between the style of the two books. In book I Newton made it plain that the gravitational force exists in the universe, varying inversely as the square of the distance, and that this force accordingly merits our particular attention. In book II, however, the reader is never certain as to which of the many conditions of resistance that Newton considers may actually occur in nature.[156]

Book II enabled Newton to display his mathematical ingenuity and some of his new discoveries. Occasionally, as in the static model that he proposed to explain the elasticity and compressibility of gases according to Boyle's law, he could explore what he believed might be actual physical reality. But he nonetheless reminded his readers (as in the scholium at the end of section 1) that the condition of resistance that he was discussing was "more a mathematical hypothesis than a physical one." Even in his final argument against Cartesian vortices (section 9), he admitted the implausibility of the proposed hypothesis that "the resistance . . . is, other things being equal, proportional to the velocity." Although a scholium to proposition 52 states that "it is in truth probable that the resistance is in a less ratio than that of the velocity," Newton in fact never explored the consequences of this probable assumption in detail. Such a procedure is in marked contrast to book I, in which Newton examined a variety of conditions of attractive and centripetal forces, but so concentrated on the inverse-square force as to leave the reader in no doubt that this is the chief force acting (insofar as weight is concerned) on the sun, the planets, the satellites, the seas, and all terrestrial objects.

Book II differs further from book I in having a separate section devoted to each of the imagined conditions of resistance. In section 1, resistance to the motions of bodies is said to be as "the ratio of the velocity"; in section 2, it is as "the square of their velocities"; and in section 3, it is given as "partly in the ratio of the velocities and partly as the square of the same ratio." Then, in section 4, Newton introduced the orbital "motion of bodies in resisting mediums," under the mathematical condition that "the density of a medium" may vary inversely as the distance from "an immovable centre"; the "centripetal force" is said in proposition 15 to be as the square of the said density, but is thereafter arbitrary. In a very short scholium, Newton added that these conditions of varying density apply only to the motions of very small bodies. He supposed the resistance of a medium, "other things being equal," to be proportional to its "density."

In section 5, Newton went on to discuss some general principles of hydrostatics, including properties of the density and compression of fluids. Historically, the most significant proposition of section 5 is proposition 23, in which Newton supposed "a fluid [to] be composed of particles fleeing from each other," and then showed that Boyle's law ("the density" of a gas varying directly as "the compression") is a necessary and a sufficient condition for the centrifugal forces to "be inversely proportional to distances of their [that is, the particles'] centers."

Then, in the scholium to this proposition, Newton generalized the results, showing that for the com-

pressing forces to "be as the cube roots of the power E^{n+2}," where E is "the density of the compressed fluid," it is both a necessary and sufficient condition that the centrifugal forces be "inversely as any power D^n of the distance [between particles]." He made it explicit that the "centrifugal forces" of particles must "terminate in those particles that are next [to] them, or are diffused not much farther," and drew upon the example of magnetic bodies. Having set such a model, however, Newton concluded that it would be "a physical question" as to "whether elastic fluids [gases] do really consist of particles so repelling each other," and stated that he had limited himself to demonstrating "mathematically the property of fluids consisting of particles of this kind, that hence philosophers may take occasion to discuss that question."[157]

Section 6 introduces the "motion and resistance of pendulous bodies." The opening proposition (24) relates the quantity of matter in the bob to its weight, the length of the pendulum, and the time of oscillation in a vacuum. Because, as corollary 5 states, "in general, the quantity of matter in the pendulous body is directly as the weight and the square of the time, and inversely as the length of the pendulum," a method is at hand for using pendulum experiments to compare directly "the quantity of matter" in bodies, and to prove that the mass of bodies is proportional "to their weight." Newton added that he had tested this proposition experimentally, then further stated, in corollary 7, that the same experiment may be used for "comparing the weights of the same body in different places, to know the variation of its gravity."[158] This is the first clear recognition that "mass" determines both weight (the amount of gravitational action) and inertia (the measure of resistance to acceleration)—the two properties of which the "equivalence" can, in classical physics, be determined only by experiment.

In section 6 Newton also considered the motion of pendulums in resisting mediums, especially oscillations in a cycloid, and gave methods for finding "the resistance of mediums by pendulums oscillating therein." An account of such experiments makes up the "General Scholium" with which section 6 concludes.[159] Among them is an experiment Newton described from memory, designed to confute "the opinion of some that there is a certain aethereal medium, extremely rare and subtile, which freely pervades the pores of all bodies."

Section 7 introduces the "motion of fluids," and "the resistance made to projected bodies," and section 8 deals with wave motion. Proposition 42 asserts that "All motion propagated through a fluid diverges from a rectilinear progress into the unmoved spaces"; while proposition 50 gives a method of finding "the distances of the pulses," or the wavelength. In a scholium, Newton stated that the previous propositions "respect the motions of light and sound" and asserted that "since light is propagated in right lines, it is certain that it cannot consist in action alone (by Prop. XLI and XLII)"; there can be no doubt that sounds are "nothing else but pulses of the air" which "arise from tremulous bodies." This section concludes with various mathematical theorems concerning the velocity of waves or pulses, and their relation to the "density and elastic force of a medium."

In section 9, Newton showed that in wave motion a disturbance moves forward, but the parts (particles) of the medium in which the disturbance occurs only vibrate about a fixed position; he thereby established the relation between wavelength, frequency, and velocity of undulations. Proposition 47 (proposition 48 in the first edition) analyzes undulatory motion in a fluid; Newton disclosed that the parts (or particles) of an undulating fluid have the same oscillation as the bob of a simple pendulum. Proposition 48 (proposition 47 in the first edition) exhibits the proportionality of the velocity of waves to the square root of the elastic force divided by the density of an elastic fluid (one whose pressure is proportional to the density). The final scholium (much rewritten for the second edition) shows that Newton's propositions yield a velocity of sound in air of 979 feet per second, whereas experiment gives a value of 1,142 feet per second under the same conditions. Newton offered an ingenious explanation (including the supposition, in the interest of simplicity, that air particles might be rigid spheres separated from one another by a distance of some nine times their diameter), but it remained for Laplace to resolve the problem in 1816.[160]

Section 9, the last of book II, is on vortices, or "the circular motion of fluids." In all editions of the *Principia*, this section begins with a clearly labeled "hypothesis" concerning the "resistance arising from the want of lubricity in the parts of a fluid . . . other things being equal, [being] proportional to the velocity with which the parts of the fluid are separated from one another." Newton used this hypothesis as the basis for investigating the physics of vortices and their mathematical properties, culminating in a lengthy proposition 52 and eleven corollaries, followed by a scholium in which he said that he has attempted "to investigate the properties of vortices" so that he might find out "whether the celestial phenomena can be explained by them." The chief "phenomenon" with which Newton was here concerned is Kepler's third (or harmonic) law for the motion of the satellites

of Jupiter about that planet, and for the primary "planets that revolve about the Sun"—although Newton did not refer to Kepler by name. He found "the periodic times of the parts of the vortex" to be "as the squares of their distances." Hence, he concluded, "Let philosophers then see how that phenomenon of the 3/2th power can be accounted for by vortices."

Newton ended book II with proposition 53, also on vortices, and a scholium, in which he showed that "it is manifest that the planets are not carried round in corporeal vortices." He was there dealing with Kepler's second or area law (although again without naming Kepler), in application to elliptic orbits. He concluded "that the hypothesis of vortices is utterly irreconcilable with astronomical phenomena, and rather serves to perplex than to explain the heavenly motions." Newton himself noted that his demonstration was based on "an hypothesis," proposed "for the sake of demonstration . . . at the beginning of this Section," but went on to add that "it is in truth probable that the resistance is in a less ratio than that of the velocity." Hence "the periodic times of the parts of the vortex will be in a greater ratio than the square of the distances from its centre." But it must be noted that it is in fact probable that the resistance would be in a greater "ratio than that of the velocity," not a lesser, since almost all fluids give rise to a resistance proportional to the square (or higher powers) of the velocity.[161]

Book III, "The System of the World." In the Newtonian system of the world, the motions of planets and their satellites, the motions of comets, and the phenomena of tides are all comprehended under a single mode of explanation. Newton stated that the force that causes the observed celestial motions and the tides and the force that causes weight are one and the same; for this reason he gave the name "gravity" to the centripetal force of universal attraction. In book III he showed that the earth must be an oblate spheroid, and he computed the magnitude of the equatorial bulge in relation to the pull of the moon so as to produce the long-known constant of precession; he also gave an explanation of variation in weight (as shown by the change in the period of a seconds pendulum) as a function of latitude on such a rotating non-spherical earth. But above all, in book III Newton stated the law of universal gravitation. He showed that planetary motion must be subject to interplanetary perturbation —most apparent in the most massive planets, Jupiter and Saturn, when they are in near conjunction—and he explored the perturbing action of the sun on the motion of the moon.

Book III opens with a preface in which Newton

stated that in books I and II he had set forth principles of mathematical philosophy, which he would now apply to the system of the world. The preface refers to an earlier, more popular version,[162] of which Newton had recast the substance "into the form of Propositions (in the mathematical way)."

A set of four "rules of reasoning in [natural] philosophy" follows the preface. Rule 1 is to admit no more causes than are "true and sufficient to explain" phenomena, while rule 2 is to "assign the same causes" insofar as possible to "the same natural effects." In the first edition, rules 1 and 2 were called "hypotheses," and they were followed by hypothesis 3, on the possibility of the transformation of every body "into a body of any other kind," in the course of which it "can take on successively all the intermediate grades of qualities." This "hypothesis" was deleted by the time of the second edition.[163]

A second group of the original "hypotheses" (5 through 9) were transformed into "phenomena" 1 and 3 through 6. The first states (with phenomenological evidence) the area law and Kepler's third law for the system of Jupiter's satellites (again Kepler is not named as the discoverer of the law). Phenomenon 2, which was introduced in the second edition, does the same for the satellites of Saturn (just discovered as the *Principia* was being written, and not mentioned in the first edition, where reference is made only to the first [Huygenian] satellite discovered). Phenomena 3 through 6 (originally hypotheses 6 through 9) assert, within the limits of observation: the validity of the Copernican system (phenomenon 3); the third law of Kepler for the five primary planets and the earth— here for the first time in the *Principia* mentioning Kepler by name and thus providing the only reference to him in relation to the laws or hypotheses of planetary motion (phenomenon 4); the area law for the "primary planets," although without significant evidence (phenomenon 5); and the area law for the moon, again with only weak evidence and coupled with the statement that the law does not apply exactly since "the motion of the moon is a little disturbed by the action of the sun" (phenomenon 6).

It has been mentioned that Newton probably called these statements "phenomena" because he knew that they are valid only to the limits of observation. In this sense, Newton had originally conceived Kepler's laws as planetary "hypotheses," as he had also done for the phenomena and laws of planetary satellites.[164]

The first six propositions given in book III display deductions from these "phenomena," using the mathematical results that Newton had set out in book I. Thus, in proposition 1, the forces "by which the circumjovial planets are continually drawn off from rectilinear motions, and retained in their proper orbits" are shown (on the basis of the area law discussed in propositions 2 and 3, book I, and in phenomenon 1) to be directed toward Jupiter's center. On the basis of Kepler's third law (and corollary 6, proposition 4, book I) these forces must vary inversely as the square of the distance; propositions 2 and 3 deal similarly with the primary planets and our moon.

By proposition 5, Newton was able to conclude (in corollary 1) that there "is . . . a power of gravity tending to all the planets" and that the planets "gravitate" toward their satellites, and the sun "towards all the primary planets." This "force of gravity" varies (corollary 2) as the inverse square of the distance; corollary 3 states that "all the planets do mutually gravitate towards one another." Hence, "near their conjunction," Jupiter and Saturn, since their masses are so great, "sensibly disturb each other's motions," while the sun "disturbs" the motion of the moon and together both sun and moon "disturb our sea, as we shall hereafter explain."

In a scholium, Newton said that the force keeping celestial bodies in their orbits "has been hitherto called centripetal force"; since it is now "plain" that it is "a gravitating force" he will "hereafter call it gravity." In proposition 6 he asserted that "all bodies gravitate towards every planet"; while at equal distances from the center of any planet "the weight" of any body toward that planet is proportional to its "quantity of matter." He provided experimental proof, using a pair of eleven-foot pendulums, each weighted with a round wooden box (for equal air resistance), into the center of which he placed seriatim equal weights of wood and gold, having experimented as well with silver, lead, glass, sand, common salt, water, and wheat. According to proposition 24, corollaries 1 and 6, book II, any variation in the ratio of mass to weight would have appeared as a variation in the period; Newton reported that through these experiments he could have discovered a difference as small as less than one part in a thousand in this ratio, had there been any.[165]

Newton was thus led to the law of universal gravitation, proposition 7: "That there is a power of gravity tending to all bodies, proportional to the several quantities of matter which they contain." He had shown this power to vary inversely as the square of the distance; it is by this law that bodies (according to the third law of motion) act mutually upon one another.

From these general results, Newton turned to practical problems of astronomy. Proposition 8 deals with gravitating spheres and the relative masses and densities of the planets (the numerical calculations in this proposition were much altered for the second edition). In proposition 9, Newton estimated the force of gravity within a planet and, in proposition 10, demonstrated the long-term stability of the solar system. A general "Hypothesis I" (in the second and third editions; "Hypothesis IV" in the first) holds the "centre of the system of the world" to be "immovable," which center is given as the center of gravity of the solar system in proposition 11; the sun is in constant motion, but never "recedes" far from that center of gravity (proposition 12).

It is often asserted that Newton attained his results by neglecting the interplanetary attractions, and dealing exclusively with the mutual gravitational attractions of the planets and our sun. But this is not the case, since the most fully explored example of perturbation in the *Principia* is indeed that of the sun-earth-moon system. Thus Newton determined (proposition 25) the "forces with which the sun disturbs the motions of the moon," and (proposition 26) the action of those forces in producing an inequality ("horary increment") of the area described by the moon (although "in a circular orbit").

The stated intention of proposition 29 is to "find the variation of the moon," the inequality thus being sought being due "partly to the elliptic figure of the Moon's orbit, partly to the inequality of the moments of the area which the Moon by a radius drawn to the Earth describes." (Newton dealt with this topic more fully in the second edition.) Then Newton studied the "horary motion of the nodes of the moon," first (proposition 30) "in a circular orbit," and then (proposition 31) "in an elliptic orbit." In proposition 32, he found "the mean motion of the nodes," and, in proposition 33, their "true motion." (In the third edition, following proposition 33, Newton inserted two propositions and a scholium on the motion of the nodes, written by John Machin.) Propositions 34 and 35, on the inclination of the orbit of the moon to the ecliptic plane, are followed by a scholium, considerably expanded and rewritten for the second edition, in which Newton discussed yet other "inequalities" in the motion of the moon and developed the practical aspects of computing the elements of that body's motion and position.

Propositions 36 and 37 deal at length and in a quantitative fashion with the tide-producing forces of the sun and of the moon, yielding, in proposition 38, an explanation of the spheroidal shape of the moon and the reason that (librations apart) the same face of it is always visible. A series of three lemmas introduces the subject of precession and a fourth lemma (transformed into hypothesis 2 in the second

and third editions) treats the precession of a ring. Proposition 39 represents an outstanding example of the high level of mathematical natural science that Newton reached in the *Principia*. In it he showed the manner in which the shape of the earth, in relation to the pull of the moon, acts on its axis of rotation so as to produce the observed precession, a presentation that he augmented and improved for the second edition. Newton here employed the result he had previously obtained (in propositions 20 and 21, book III) concerning the shape of the earth, and joined it to both the facts and theory of precession and yet another aspect of the perturbing force of the moon on the motion of the earth. He thus inaugurated a major aspect of celestial mechanics, the study of a three-body system.

Lemma 4, book III initiates a section on comets, proving that comets are "higher" than the moon, move through the solar system, and (corollary 1) shine by reflecting sunlight; their motion shows (corollary 3) that "the celestial spaces are void of resistance." Comets move in conic sections (proposition 40) having the sun as a focus, according to the law of areas. Those comets that return move in elliptic orbits (corollary 1) and follow Kepler's third law, but (corollary 2) "their orbits will be so near to parabolas, that parabolas may be used for them without sensible error."

Almost immediately following publication of the *Principia*, Halley, in a letter of 5 July 1687, urged Newton to go on with his work on lunar theory.[166] Newton later remarked that his head so ached from studying this problem that it often "kept him awake" and "he would think of it no more." But he also said that if he lived long enough for Halley to complete enough additional observations, he "would have another stroke at the moon." In the 1690's Newton had depended on Flamsteed for observations of the moon, promising Flamsteed (in a letter of 16 February 1695) not to communicate any of his observations, "much less publish them, without your consent." But Newton and Flamsteed disagreed on the value of theory, which Newton held to be useful as "a demonstration" of the "exactness" of observations, while Flamsteed believed that "theories do not command observations; but are to be tried by them," since "theories are . . . only probable" (even "when they agree with exact and indubitable observations"). At about this same time Newton was drawing up a set of propositions on the motion of the moon for a proposed new edition of the *Principia*, for which he requested from Flamsteed such planetary observations "as tend to [be useful for] perfecting the theory of the planets," to serve Newton in the preparation of a second edition of his book.

Revision of the "Opticks" (the Later Queries); Chemistry and Theory of Matter. Newton's *Opticks*, published in 1704, concluded with a Third Book, consisting of eleven "Observations" and sixteen queries, occupying a bare five pages of print. A Latin translation, undertaken at Newton's behest by Samuel Clarke, appeared in 1706, and included as its most notable feature the expansion of the original sixteen queries into twenty-three. The new queries 17 through 23 correspond to the final queries 25–31 of the later editions. In a series of "Errata, Corrigenda, & Addenda," at the beginning of the Latin volume, lengthy additions are provided to be inserted at the end of query 8 and of query 11; there is also a short insertion for query 14.

In a second English edition (London, 1717) the number of queries was increased to thirty-one. The queries appearing for the first time are numbered 17 to 24, and they have no counterparts in the 1706 Latin version. Newton's own copy of the 1717 English edition, in the Babson Institute Library, contains a number of emendations and corrections in Newton's hand, some of which were incorporated into the third edition (London 1721), as was a postscript to the end of the last sentence, referring to Noah and his sons.

The queries new to the 1717 edition cover a wide range of topics. Query 17 introduces the possibility that waves or vibrations may be excited in the eye by light and that vibrations of this sort may occur in the medium in which light travels. Query 18 suggests that radiant heat may be transmitted by vibrations of a medium subtler than air that pervades all bodies and expands by its elastic force throughout the heavenly spaces—the same medium by which light is put into "fits" of "easy" reflection and refraction, thus producing "Newton's rings." In queries 19 and 20, variations in the density of this medium are given as the possible cause of refraction and of the "inflection" (diffraction) of light rays. Query 21 would have the medium be rarer within celestial bodies than in empty celestial spaces, which may "impel Bodies from the denser parts of the Medium towards the rarer"; its elasticity may be estimated by the ratio of the speed of light to the speed of sound. Although he referred in this query to the mutually repulsive "particles" of ether as being "exceedingly smaller than those of Air, or even those of Light," Newton confessed that he does "not know what this *Aether* is."

In query 22, the resistance of the ether is said to be inconsiderable; the exhalations emitted by "electrick" bodies and magnetic "effluvia" are offered as other instances of such rareness. The subject of vision is introduced in query 23. Here vision is again said to be chiefly the effect of vibrations of the medium, propagated through the "optick Nerves"; an analogy is made to hearing and the other senses. Animal motion (query 24) is considered as a result of vibrations in the medium propagated from the brain through the nerves to the muscles.

Queries 25 to 31 are the English recasting of queries 17 to 23 of the Latin edition. Query 25 contains a discussion of double refraction in calcite (Iceland spar) and a geometrical construction of both the ordinary ray and (fallaciously) the extraordinary ray; query 26 concludes that double refraction may be caused by the two "sides" of rays of light. Then, in query 27, Newton attacked as erroneous all hypotheses explaining optical phenomena by new modifications of rays, since such phenomena depend upon original unalterable properties.

Query 28 questions "all Hypotheses" in which light is supposed to be a "Pression or Motion, propagated through a fluid Medium." Newton showed that Huygens' wave theory of double refraction would fail to account for the heating of bodies and the rectilinear propagation of light. Those who would fill "the Heavens with fluid Mediums" come under attack, while Newton praised the ancient philosophers who "made a *Vacuum*, and Atoms, and the Gravity of Atoms, the first Principles of their Philosophy." He added that "the main Business of natural Philosophy is to argue from Phaenomena without feigning Hypotheses"; we are to "deduce Causes from Effects, till we come to the very first Cause, which certainly is not mechanical," since nature exhibits design and purpose.

In query 29, Newton suggested that rays of light are composed of "very small Bodies emitted from shining Substances," since rays could not have a permanent virtue in two of their sides (as demonstrated by the double refraction of Iceland spar) unless they be bodies. This query also contains Newton's famous theory that rays of light could be put into "Fits of easy Reflexion and easy Transmission" if they were "small Bodies which by their attractive Powers, or some other Force, stir up Vibrations in what they act upon." These vibrations would move more swiftly than the rays themselves, would "overtake them successively," and by agitating them "so as by turns to increase and decrease their Velocities" would put them into those "fits."[167] Newton further argued that if light were to consist of waves in an ethereal medium, then in order to have the fits of easy reflection and easy transmission, a second ether would be required, in which there would be waves (of higher velocity) to put the waves of the first ether into the necessary fits. He had, however, already argued in query 28 that it would be inconceivable for two ethers to be "diffused through all

Space, one of which acts upon the other, and by consequence is re-acted upon, without retarding, shattering, dispersing and compounding one another's Motions."

In query 30, Newton discussed the convertibility of gross bodies and light, with examples showing that nature delights in transmutations. In illustration, he cited Boyle's assertion that frequent distillations had turned water into earth. In query 31, he discussed questions ranging from the forces that hold particles of matter together to the impact of bodies on one another; also causes of motion, fermentation, the circulation of the blood and animal heat, putrefaction, the force of inertia, and occult qualities. He stated a general philosophy and concluded with the pious hope that the perfection of natural philosophy will enlarge the "Bounds of Moral Philosophy."

Newton's queries, particularly the later ones, thus go far beyond any simple questions of physical or geometrical optics. In them he even proposed tentative explanations of phenomena, although explanations that are perhaps not as fully worked out, or as fully supported by experimental evidence, as he might have wished. (Some queries even propose what is, by Newton's own definition, a hypothesis.) In each case, Newton's own position is made clear; and especially in the queries added in the Latin version of 1706 (and presented again in the English version of 1717/1718), his supporting evidence is apt to be a short essay.

One notable development of the later queries is the emphasis on an "Aethereal Medium" as an explanation for phenomena. In his first papers on optics, in the 1670's, Newton had combined his cherished conception of corpuscular or globular light with the possibly Cartesian notion of a space-filling ether, elastic and varying in density. Although Newton had introduced this ether to permit wave phenomena to exist as concomitants of the rays of light, he also suggested other possible functions for it—including causing sensation and animal motion, transmitting radiant heat, and even causing gravitation. His speculations on the ether were incorporated in the "Hypothesis" that he sent to the Royal Society (read at their meetings in 1675 and 1676) and in a letter to Boyle of 28 February 1679.[168]

In the second English edition of the Opticks (1717/1718) Newton made additions which "embodied arguments for the existence of an elastic, tenuous, aetherial medium." The new queries in the Latin version of 1706 did not deal with an ether, however, and by the time of the Principia, Newton may have "rejected the Cartesian dense aether" as well as "his own youthful aetherial speculations."[169]

Newton thus did not propose a new version of the ether until possibly the 1710's; he then suggested, in the general scholium at the conclusion of the second edition of the Principia (1713), that a most subtle "spiritus" ("which pervades and lies hid in all gross bodies") might produce just such effects as his earlier ether (or the later ethereal medium of queries 18 through 24). In the general scholium of the Principia, however, Newton omitted gravitation from the list of effects that the "spiritus" may produce. There is evidence that Newton conceived of this "spiritus" as electrical, and may well have been a precursor of the ether or ethereal medium of the 1717/1718 queries.[170] In a manuscript intended for the revised second English edition of the Opticks,[171] Newton wrote the heading, "The Third Book of Opticks. Part II. Observations concerning the Medium through which Light passes, & the Agent which emits it," a title that would thus seem to link the ethereal medium with the emission of electrical effluvia. It would further appear that Newton used both the earlier and later concepts of the ether to explain, however hypothetically, results he had already obtained; and that the concept of the ether was never the basis for significant new experiments or theoretical results. In a general scholium to book II, Newton described from memory an experiment that he had performed which seemed to him to prove the nonexistence of an ether; since Newton's original notes have never been found, this experiment, which was presumably an important element in the decline of his belief in an ether, cannot be dated.

The later queries also develop a concept of matter, further expounded by Newton in his often reprinted De natura acidorum (of which there appear to have been several versions in circulation).[172] Newton here, as a true disciple of Boyle, began with the traditional "mechanical philosophy" but added "the assumption that particles move mainly under the influence of what he at first called sociability and later called attraction."[173] Although Newton also considered a principle of repulsion, especially in gases, in discussing chemical reactions he seems to have preferred to use a concept of "sociability" (as, for example, to explain how substances dissolve).

He was equally concerned with the "aggregation" of particles (in queries 28 and 31 as well as at the end of De natura acidorum) and even suggested a means of "differentiating between reaction and transmutation."[174] Another major concern was the way in which aqua regia dissolves gold but not silver, while aqua fortis dissolves silver but not gold,[175] a phenomenon Newton explained by a combination of the attraction of particles and the relation between the size of the acid particles and the "pores" between the particles of metal. He did not, however, have a sound operational definition of acid, but referred to acids theoretically, in *De natura acidorum*, as those substances "endued with a great Attractive Force; in which Force their Activity consists." He maintained this definition in query 31, in which he further called attention to the way in which metals may replace one another in acid solutions and even "went so far as to list the six common metals in the order in which they would displace one another from a solution of aqua fortis (strong nitric acid)."[176]

Alchemy, Prophecy, and Theology. Chronology and History. Newton is often alleged to have been a mystic. That he was highly interested in alchemy has been embarrassing to many students of his life and work, while others delight in finding traces of hermeticism in the father of the "age of reason." The entries in the *Catalogue of the Portsmouth Collection* give no idea of the extent of the documents in Newton's hand dealing with alchemy; these were listed in the catalogue, but not then presented to Cambridge University. Such information became generally available only when the alchemical writings were dispersed in 1936, in the Sotheby sale. The catalogue of that sale gives the only full printed guide to these materials, and estimates their bulk at some 650,000 words, almost all in Newton's hand.

A major problem in assessing Newton's alchemical "writings" is that they are not, for the most part, original compositions, nor even critical essays on his readings (in the sense that the early "De gravitatione et aequipondio fluidorum" is an essay based on his reading in Descartes's *Principia*). It would be necessary to know the whole corpus of the alchemical literature to be able to declare that any paper in Newton's hand is an original composition, rather than a series of extracts or summaries.[177]

In a famous letter to Oldenburg (26 April 1676), Newton offered an explanation of Boyle's presentations of the "incalescence" of gold and mercury (*Philosophical Transactions*, **9**, no. 122 [1675], 515–533), and presented an explanation based on the size of the particles of matter and their mechanical action. Newton particularly commended Boyle for having concealed some major steps, since here was possibly "an inlet into something more noble, and not to be communicated without immense dammage to the world if there be any verity in the Hermetick writers." He also gave some cautionary advice about alchemists, even referring to a "true Hermetic Philosopher, whose judgment (if there be any such)" might be of interest and highly regarded, "there being other things beside the transmutation of metals (if those pretenders

bragg not) which none but they understand." The apparently positive declarations in Newton's letter thus conflict with the doubts expressed in the two parenthetical expressions.

Newton's studies of prophecy may possibly provide a key to the method of his alchemical studies. His major work on the subject is *Observations upon the Prophecies of Daniel, and the Apocalypse of St. John* (London, 1733). Here Newton was concerned with "a figurative language" used by the prophets, which he sought to decipher. Newton's text is a historical exegesis, unmarked by any mystical short-circuiting of the rational process or direct communication from the godhead. He assumed an "analogy between the world natural, and an empire or kingdom considered as a world politic," and concluded, for example, that Daniel's prophecy of an "image composed of four metals" and a stone that broke "the four metals into pieces" referred to the four nations successively ruling the earth ("*viz.* the peoples of Babylonia, the Persians, the Greeks, and the Romans"). The four nations are represented again in the "four beasts."

"The folly of interpreters," Newton wrote, has been "to foretell times and things by this Prophecy, as if God designed to make them Prophets." This is, however, far from God's intent, for God meant the prophecies "not to gratify men's curiosities by enabling them to foreknow things" but rather to stand as witnesses to His providence when "after they were fulfilled, they might be interpreted by events." Surely, Newton added, "the event of things predicted many ages before, will then be a convincing argument that the world is governed by providence." (It may be noted that this book also provided Newton with occasion to refer to his favorite themes of "the corruption of scripture" and the "corruption of Christianity.")

The catalogue of the Sotheby sale states that Newton's manuscript remains include some 1,300,000 words on biblical and theological subjects. These are not particularly relevant to his scientific work and— for the most part—might have been written by any ordinary divinity student of that period, save for the extent to which they show Newton's convinced anti-Trinitarian monotheism or Unitarian Arianism. (His tract *Two Notable Corruptions of Scripture*, for example, uses historical analysis to attack Trinitarian doctrine.) "It is the temper of the hot and superstitious part of mankind in matters of religion," Newton wrote, "ever to be fond of mysteries, and for that reason to like best what they understand least."[178]

Typical of Newton's theological exercises is his "Queries regarding the word *homoousios*." The first query asks "Whether Christ sent his apostles to preach metaphysics to the unlearned common people, and to their wives and children?" Other queries in this set are also historical; in the seventh Newton marshaled his historico-philological acumen in the matter of the Latin rendering *unius substantiae*, which he considered to have been imposed on the Western churches instead of *consubstantialis* by "Hosius (or whoever translated that [Nicene] Creed into Latin)." Another manuscript entitled "Paradoxical Questions" turns out to be less a theological inquiry than a carefully reasoned proof of what Lord Keynes called "the dishonesty and falsification of records for which St Athanasius [and his followers] were responsible." In it Newton cited, as an example, the spreading of the story that Arius died in a house of prostitution.

In a Keynes manuscript (in King's College, Cambridge), "The First Book Concerning the Language of the Prophets," Newton explained his method:

> He that would understand a book written in a strange language must first learn the language. . . . Such a language was that wherein the Prophets wrote, and the want of sufficient skill in that language is the reason why they are so little understood. John . . ., Daniel . . ., Isaiah . . . all write in one and the same mystical language . . . [which] so far as I can find, was as certain and definite in its signification as is the vulgar language of any nation. . . .

Having established this basic premise, Newton went on: "It is only through want of skill therein that Interpreters so frequently turn the Prophetic types and phrases to signify whatever their fancies and hypotheses lead them to." Then, in a manner reminiscent of the rules at the beginning of book III of the *Principia*, he added:

> The rule I have followed has been to compare the several mystical places of scripture where the same prophetic phrase or type is used, and to fix such a signification to that phrase as agrees best with all the places: . . . and when I had found the necessary significations, to reject all others as the offspring of luxuriant fancy, for no more significations are to be admitted for true ones than can be proved.

Newton's alchemical manuscripts show that he sometimes used a similar method, drawing up comparative tables of symbols and of symbolic names used by alchemists, no doubt in the conviction that a key to their common language might be found thereby. His careful discrimination among the alchemical writers may be seen in two manuscripts in the Keynes Collection, one a three-page classified list of alchemical writers and the other a two-page

selection of "authores optimi," by whom Newton perhaps meant authorities who described processes that might be repeated and verified. The Babson Collection of Newtoniana contains a two-page autograph manuscript listing 113 writers on alchemy arranged by nationalities and another seven-page manuscript of "chemical authors and their writings" in which Newton commented on the more important ones. At least two other such bibliographical works by Newton are known. An "Index Chemicus," an elaborate subject index to the literature of alchemy with page references to a number of different works (described as containing more than 20,000 words on 113 pages), is one of at least five such indexes, all in autograph manuscripts.[179]

It must be emphasized that Newton's study of alchemy was not a wholly rational pursuit, guided by a strict code of linguistic and historical investigative procedures. To so consider it would be to put it on the same plane as his chronological inquiries.[180] The chronological studies are, to a considerable degree, the result of the application of sound principles of astronomical dating to poor historical evidence—for which his *Chronology of Ancient Kingdoms Amended* was quite properly criticized by the French antiquarians of his day—while his alchemical works show that he drew upon esoterical and even mystical authors, far beyond the confines of an ordinary rational science.

It is difficult to determine whether to consider Newton's alchemy as an irrational vagary of an otherwise rational mind, or whether to give his hermeticism a significant role as a developmental force in his rational science. It is tempting, furthermore, to link his concern for alchemy with his belief in a secret tradition of ancient learning. He believed that he had traced this *prisca sapientia* to the ancient Greeks (notably Pythagoras) and to the Chaldean philosophers or magicians; he concluded that these ancients had known even the inverse-square law of gravitation. Cohen, McGuire, and Rattansi have shown that in the 1690's, when Newton was preparing a revised edition of the *Principia*, he thought of including references to such an ancient tradition in a series of new scholia for the propositions at the beginning of book III of the *Principia*, along with a considerable selection of verses from Lucretius' *De natura rerum*. All of this was to be an addendum to an already created *Principia*, which Newton was revising for a new edition.

There is not a shred of real evidence, however, that Newton ever had such concerns primarily in mind in those earlier years when he was writing the *Principia* or initially developing the principles of dynamics and of mathematics on which the *Principia* was ultimately to be based. In Newton's record of alchemical experiments (University Library, Cambridge, MS Add. 3975), the experiments dated 23 May [1684] are immediately followed by an entry dated 26 April 1686. The former ends in the middle of a page, and the latter starts on the very next line; there is no lacuna, and no possibility that a page—which chronologically might concern experiments made while the *Principia* was being written—might be missing from the notebook.[181]

The overtones of alchemy are on occasion discernible in Newton's purely scientific writings. In query 30 of the *Opticks* (first published in the Latin version, then in the second English edition), Newton said that "Nature . . . seems delighted with Transmutations," although he was not referring specifically to changing metals from one to another. (It must be remembered in fact that "transmutation" would not necessarily hold an exclusively chemical or alchemical meaning for Newton; it might, rather, signify not only transformations in general, but also particular transformations of a purely mathematical sort, as in lemma 22 of book I of the *Principia*.) This is a far cry, indeed, from Newton's extracts from the mystical Count Michael Maier and kindred authors. P. M. Rattansi particularly calls attention to the alchemist's "universal spirit," and observes: "It is difficult to understand how, without a conviction of deep and hidden truths concealed in alchemy, Newton should have attached much significance to such ideas."[182]

Notable instances of the conflation of alchemical inspiration and science occur in Newton's letter to Boyle (1679) and in the hypothesis he presented to explain those properties of light of which he wrote in his papers in the *Philosophical Transactions*. While it is not difficult to discover alchemical images in Newton's presentation, and to find even specific alchemical doctrines in undisguised form and language, the problem of evaluating the influence of alchemy on Newton's true science is only thereby compounded, since there is no firm indication of the role of such speculations in the development of Newton's physical science. The result is, at best, one mystery explained by another, like the alchemist's confusing doctrine of *ignotum per ignotius*. Rattansi further suggests that alchemy may have served as a guiding principle in the formulation of Newton's views on fermentation and the nourishment of the vegetation of the earth by fluids attracted from the tails of comets. He would even have us believe that alchemical influences may have influenced "the revival of aetherical notions in the last period of Newton's life."[183] This may be so; but what, if any, creative effect such "aetherical notions" then had on Newton's thought would seem to be a matter of pure hypothesis.

Scholars do not agree whether Newton's association with some "Hermetic tradition" may have been a creative force in his science, or whether it is legitimate to separate his alleged hermeticism from his positive science. Apart from the level of general inspiration, it must be concluded that, excluding some aspects of the theory of matter and chemistry, notably fermentation, and possibly the ether hypotheses, the real creative influence of alchemy or hermeticism on Newton's mathematics and his work in optics, dynamics, and astronomy (save for the role of the tails of comets in the economy of nature) must today be evaluated in terms of the Scottish verdict, "not proven." Investigations of this topic may provide valuable insights into the whole man, Newton, and into the complexities of his scientific inspiration. His concern for alchemy and theology should not be cast aside as irrelevant aberrations of senility or the product of a mental breakdown. Yet it remains a fact beyond dispute that such early manuscripts as the Waste Book—in which Newton worked out and recorded his purely scientific discoveries and innovations—are free from the tinges of alchemy and hermeticism.

The London Years: the Mint, the Royal Society, Quarrels with Flamsteed and with Leibniz. On 19 March 1696, Newton received a letter from Charles Montagu informing him that he had been appointed warden of the mint. He set up William Whiston as his deputy in the Lucasian professorship, to receive "the full profits of the place." On 10 December 1701 he resigned his professorship, and soon afterward his fellowship. He was designated an *associé étranger* of the Paris Académie des Sciences in February 1699, chosen a member of the Council of the Royal Society on the following 30 November, and on 30 November 1703 was made president of the Royal Society, an office he held until his death. He was elected M.P. for Cambridge University, for the second time, on 26 November 1701, Parliament being prorogued on 25 May 1702. Queen Anne knighted Newton at Trinity College on 16 April 1705; on the following 17 May he was defeated in his third contest for the university's seat in Parliament.

At the mint, Newton applied his knowledge of chemistry and of laboratory technique to assaying, but he apparently did not introduce any innovations in the art of coinage. His role was administrative and his duties were largely the supervision of the recoinage and (curious to contemplate) the capture, interrogation, and prosecution of counterfeiters. Newton used the patronage of the mint to benefit fellow scientists. Halley entered the service in 1696 as comptroller of the Chester mint, and in 1707 David

Gregory was appointed (at a fee of £250) as general supervisor of the conversion of the Scottish coinage to British.

Newton ruled over the Royal Society with an iron hand. When Whiston was proposed as a fellow in 1720, Newton said that if Whiston were chosen, he "would not be president." At Newton's urging, the council brought the society from the verge of bankruptcy to solvency by obtaining regular contributions from fellows. When a dispute arose between Woodward and Sloane, Newton had Woodward ejected from the council. Of Newton's chairmanship of meetings, Stukeley reported, "Everything was transacted with great attention and solemnity and dignity," for "his presence created a natural awe in the assembly"; there was never a sign of "levity or indecorum." As England's foremost scientist, president of the Royal Society, and civil servant, Newton appeared before Parliament in Spring 1714, to give advice about a prize for a method of finding longitude.

When Newton moved from Cambridge to London in the 1690's to take up the wardenship of the mint, he continued to work on the motion of the moon. He became impatient for Flamsteed's latest observations and they soon had a falling-out, no doubt aggravated by the strong enmity which had grown up between Halley and Flamsteed. Newton fanned the flames by the growing arrogance of his letters: "I want not your calculations but your observations only." And when in 1699 Flamsteed let it be known that Newton was working to perfect lunar theory, Newton sent Flamsteed a letter insisting that on this occasion he not "be brought upon the stage," since "I do not love to be printed upon every occasion much less to be dunned & teezed by foreigners about Mathematical things or to be thought by our own people to be trifling away my time about them when I should be about the King's business." Newton and Halley published Flamsteed's observations in an unauthorized printing in 1712, probably in the conviction that his work had been supported by the government and was therefore public property. Flamsteed had the bitter joy of burning most of the spurious edition; and he then started printing his own *Historia coelestis Brittanica*.

A more intense quarrel arose with Leibniz. This took two forms: a disagreement over philosophy or theology in relation to science (carried out through Samuel Clarke as intermediary), and an attempt on Newton's part to prove that Leibniz had no claim to originality in the calculus. The initial charge of plagiarism against Leibniz came from Fatio de Duillier, but before long Keill and other Newtonians were involved and Leibniz began to rally his own supporters. Newton held that not only had Leibniz stolen the calculus from him, but that he had also composed three tracts for publication in the *Acta eruditorum* claiming some of the main truths of the *Principia* as independent discoveries, with the sole original addition of some mistakes. Today it appears that Newton was wrong; no doubt Leibniz had (as he said) seen the "epitome" or lengthy review of the *Principia* in the *Acta eruditorum* of June 1688, and not the book, when (to use his own words) "Newton's work stimulated me" to write out some earlier thoughts on "the causes of the motions of the heavenly bodies" as well as on the "resistance of a medium" and motion in a medium.[184] Newton stated, however, that even if Leibniz "had not seen the book itself, he ought nevertheless to have seen it before he published his own thoughts concerning these matters."[185]

That Newton should have connived at declaring Leibniz a plagiarist gives witness to his intense possessiveness concerning his discoveries or inventions; hence his consequent feeling of violation or robbery when Leibniz seemed to be publishing them. Newton was also aware that Leibniz must have seen one or more of his manuscript tracts then in circulation; and Leibniz had actually done so on one of his visits, when, however, he copied out some material on series expansions, not on fluxions.[186]

No one today seriously questions Leibniz' originality and true mathematical genius, nor his independence— to the degree that any two creative mathematicians living in the same world of mathematical thought can be independent—in the formulation of the calculus. Moreover, the algorithm in general use nowadays is the Leibnizian rather than the Newtonian. But by any normal standards, the behavior of both men was astonishing. When Leibniz appealed to the Royal Society for a fair hearing, Newton appointed a committee of good Newtonians. It has only recently become known that Newton himself wrote the committee's report, the famous *Commercium epistolicum*,[187] which he presented as if it were a set of impartial findings in his own favor.

Newton was not, however, content to stop there; following publication of the report there appeared an anonymous review, or summary, of it in the *Philosophical Transactions*. This, too, was Newton's work. When the *Commercium epistolicum* was reprinted, this review was included, in Latin translation, as a kind of introduction, together with an anonymous new preface "To the Reader," which was also written by Newton. This episode must be an incomparable display of thoroughness in destroying an enemy, and Whiston reported that he had heard directly that Newton had "once pleasantly" said to Samuel Clarke that "He had broke Leibnitz's Heart with his Reply to him."

Newton's later London years were marked by creative scientific efforts. During this time he published the *Opticks*, with the two mathematical tracts, and added new queries for its later editions. He also produced, with Roger Cotes's aid, a second edition of the *Principia*, including the noteworthy general scholium, and, with assistance from Henry Pemberton, a third edition. In the last, however, Newton altered the scholium to lemma 2, book II, to prevent its being read as if Leibniz were entitled to a share of credit for the calculus—although Leibniz had been dead for nearly twelve years.

Newton died on Monday, 20 March 1727,[188] at the age of eighty-five, having been ill with gout and inflamed lungs for some time. He was buried in Westminster Abbey.

Newton's Philosophy: The Rules of Philosophizing, the General Scholium, the Queries of the "Opticks." Like others of his day, Newton believed that the study of natural philosophy would provide evidence for the existence of God the Creator in the regularities of the solar system. In the general scholium at the end of book III of the *Principia*, he said "it is not to be conceived that mere mechanical causes could give birth to so many regular motions," then concluded his discussion with observations about God, "to discourse of whom from phenomena does certainly belong to Natural Philosophy" ("Experimental Philosophy" in the second edition). He then went on to point out that he had "explained the phenomena of the heavens and of our sea, by the power of Gravity" but had not yet "assigned the cause of this power," alleging that "it is enough that Gravity does really exist, and act according to the laws which we have explained" and that its action "abundantly serves to account for all the motions of the celestial bodies, and of our sea." The reader was thus to accept the facts of the *Principia*, even though Newton had not "been able to discover the cause of those properties of gravity from phenomena." Newton here stated his philosophy, "Hypotheses non fingo."[189]

Clearly, Newton was referring here only to "feigning" a hypothesis about the cause of gravitation, and never intended that his statement should be applied on all levels of scientific discourse, or to all meanings of the word "hypothesis." Indeed, in each of the three editions of the *Principia*, there is a "hypothesis" stated in book II. In the second and third editions there are a "Hypothesis I" and a "Hypothesis II" in book III. The "phaenomena" at the beginning of book III, in the second and third editions, were largely the "hypotheses" of the first

edition. It may be that Newton used these two designations to imply that these particular statements concerning planetary motions are not mathematically true (as he proved), but could be only approximately "true," on the level of (or to the limits of) phenomena.

Newton believed that his science was based upon a philosophy of induction. In the third edition of the *Principia*, he introduced rule 4, so that "the argument of induction may not be evaded by hypotheses." Here he said that one may look upon the results of "general induction from phenomena as accurately or very nearly true," even though many contrary hypotheses might be imagined, until such time as the inductive result may "either be made more accurate or liable to exceptions" by new phenomena. In rule 3, in the second and third editions, he stated his philosophical basis for establishing general properties of matter by means of phenomena.

Newton's philosophical ideas are even more fully developed in query 31, the final query of the later editions of the *Opticks*, in which he argued for both the philosophy of induction and the method of analysis and composition (or synthesis). In both mathematics and natural philosophy, he said, the "Investigation of difficult Things by the method of Analysis, ought ever to precede the Method of Composition." Such "Analysis consists in making Experiments and Observations, and in drawing general Conclusions from them by Induction, and admitting of no Objections against the Conclusions, but such as are taken from Experiments, or other certain Truths."

In both the *Principia* and the *Opticks*, Newton tried to maintain a distinction among his speculations, his experimental results (and the inductions based upon them), and his mathematical derivations from certain assumed conditions. In the *Principia* in particular, he was always careful to separate any mathematical hypotheses or assumed conditions from those results that were "derived" in some way from experiments and observations. Often, too, when he suggested, as in various scholiums, the applicability of mathematical or hypothetical conditions to physical nature, he stated that he had not proved whether his result really so applies. His treatment of the motion of small corpuscles, in book I, section 14, and his static model of a gas composed of mutually repulsive particles, in book II, proposition 23, exemplify Newton's use of mathematical models of physical reality for which he lacked experimental evidence sufficient for an unequivocal statement.

Perhaps the best expression of Newton's general philosophy of nature occurs in a letter to Cotes (28 March 1713), written during the preparation of the second edition of the *Principia*, in which he referred to the laws of motion as "the first Principles or Axiomes" and said that they "are deduced from Phaenomena & made general by Induction"; this "is the highest evidence that a Proposition can have in this philosophy." Declaring that "the mutual & mutually equal attraction of bodies is a branch of the third Law of motion," Newton pointed out to Cotes "how this branch is deduced from Phaenomena," referring him to the "end of the Corollaries of the Laws of Motion." Shortly thereafter, in a manuscript bearing upon the Leibniz controversy, he wrote, "To make an exception upon a mere Hypothesis is to feign an exception. It is to reject the argument from Induction, & turn Philosophy into a heap of Hypotheses, which are no other than a chimerical Romance."[190] That is a statement with which few would disagree.

NOTES

1. See R. S. Westfall, "Short-writing and the State of Newton's Conscience, 1662," in *Notes and Records. Royal Society of London*, **18** (1963), 10–16. L. T. More, in *Isaac Newton* (New York, 1934), p. 16, drew attention to the necessary "mental suffering" of a boy of Newton's physical weakness, living in a lonely "farmhouse situated in a countryside only slowly recovering from the terrors of a protracted and bitter civil war," with "no protection from the frights of his imagination except that of his grandmother and such unreliable labourers as could be hired."

   F. E. Manuel, in *A Portrait of Isaac Newton* (Cambridge, Mass., 1968), has subjected Newton's life to a kind of psychoanalytic scrutiny. He draws the conclusion (pp. 54–59) that the "scrupulosity, punitiveness, austerity, discipline, industriousness, and fear associated with a repressive morality" were apparent in Newton's character at an early age, and finds that notebooks bear witness to "the fear, anxiety, distrust, sadness, withdrawal, self-belittlement, and generally depressive state of the young Newton."

   For an examination of Manuel's portrait of Newton, see J. E. McGuire, "Newton and the Demonic Furies: Some Current Problems and Approaches in the History of Science," in *History of Science*, **11** (1973), 36–46; see also the review in *Times Literary Supplement* (1 June 1973), 615–616, with letters by Manuel (8 June 1973), 644–645; D. T. Whiteside (15 June 1973), 692, and (6 July 1973), 779; and G. S. Rousseau (29 June 1973), 749.

2. See E. N. da C. Andrade, "Newton's Early Notebook," in *Nature*, **135** (1935), 360; and G. L. Huxley, "Two Newtonian Studies: I. Newton's Boyhood Interests," in *Harvard Library Bulletin*, **13** (1959), 348–354, in which Andrade has first called attention to the importance of Bate's collection, an argument amplified by Huxley.

3. Newton apparently came to realize that he had been hasty in discarding Euclid, since Pemberton later heard him "even censure himself for not following them [that is, 'the ancients' in their 'taste, and form of demonstration'] yet more closely than he did; and speak with regret of his mistake at the beginning of his mathematical studies, in applying himself to the works of Des Cartes and other algebraic writers, before he had considered the elements of Euclide with that attention, which so excellent a writer deserves" (*View of Sir Isaac Newton's Philosophy* [London, 1728], preface).

4. Newton's college tutor was not (and indeed by statute could not have been) the Lucasian professor, Barrow, but was Benjamin Pulleyn.

5. University Library, Cambridge, MS Add. 3996, discussed by A. R. Hall in "Sir Isaac Newton's Notebook, 1661–1665," in *Cambridge Historical Journal*, **9** (1948), 239–250.

6. *Ibid.*; also partially analyzed by R. S. Westfall, in "The Foundations of Newton's Philosophy of Nature," in *British Journal for the History of Science*, **1** (1962), 171–182. Westfall has attempted a reconstruction of Newton's philosophy of nature, and his growing allegiance to the "mechanical philosophy," in ch. 7 of his *Force in Newton's Physics* (London, 1971).

7. On Newton's entrance into the domains of mathematics higher than arithmetic, see the account by A. De Moivre (in the Newton MSS presented by the late J. H. Schaffner to the University of Chicago) and the recollections of Newton assembled by John Conduitt, now mainly in the Keynes Collection, King's College, Cambridge.

8. See D. T. Whiteside, "Newton's Marvellous Year. 1666 and All That," in *Notes and Records. Royal Society of London*, **21** (1966), 37–38.

9. See A. H. White, ed., William Stukeley, *Memoirs of Sir Isaac Newton's Life* (London, 1936). Written in 1752, this records a conversation with Newton about his discovery of universal gravitation (the apple story), pp. 19–20.

10. In November 1669 John Collins wrote to James Gregory that "Mr Barrow hath resigned his Lecturers place to one Mr Newton of Cambridge" (in the Royal Society ed. of Newton's *Correspondence*, 1, 15). Newton himself may have been referring to Barrow in an autobiographical note (*ca.* 1716) that stated, "Upon account of my progress in these matters he procured for me a fellowship . . . in the year 1667 & the Mathematick Professorship two years later"—see University Library, Cambridge, MS Add. 3968, §41, fol. 117, and I. B. Cohen, *Introduction to Newton's Principia*, supp. III, p. 303, n. 14.

11. Among the biographical memoirs assembled by Conduitt (Keynes Collection, King's College, Cambridge). Humphrey Newton's memoir is in L. T. More, *Isaac Newton*, pp. 246, 381, and 389.

12. According to J. Edleston (p. xlv in his ed. of *Correspondence of Sir Isaac Newton and Professor Cotes . . .*; see also pp. xlix–l), in 1675 (or March 1674, OS), "Newton obtained a Royal Patent allowing the Professor to remain Fellow of a College without being obliged to go into orders." See also L. T. More, *Isaac Newton*, p. 169.

13. This work might have been an early version of the *Lectiones opticae*, his professorial lectures of 1670–1672; or perhaps an annotated version of his letters and communications to Oldenburg, which were read at the Royal Society and published in major part in its *Philosophical Transactions* from 1672 onward.

14. Quoted in L. T. More, *Isaac Newton*, p. 217.

15. It has been erroneously thought that Newton's "breakdown" may in part have been caused by the death of his mother. But her death occurred in 1679, and she was buried on 4 June. "Her will was proved 11 June 1679 by Isaac Newton, the executor, who was the residuary legatee"; see *Correspondence*, II, 303. n. 2. David Brewster, in *Memoirs . . .*, II, 123, suggested that Newton's "ailment may have arisen from the disappointment he experienced in the application of his friends for a permanent situation for him." On these events and on contemporary discussion and gossip about Newton's state of mind, see L. T. More, *Isaac Newton*, pp. 387–388, and F. E. Manuel, *A Portrait of Isaac Newton*, pp. 220–223. Newton himself, in a letter to Locke of 5 October 1693, blamed his "distemper" and insomnia on "sleeping too often by my fire."

16. L. T. More, *Isaac Newton*, p. 368.

17. See J. Edleston, ed., *Correspondence . . . Newton and . . . Cotes*, pp. xxxvi, esp. n. 142.

18. *Mathematical Papers of Isaac Newton*, D. T. Whiteside, ed., in progress, to be completed in 8 vols. (Cambridge, 1967–   ); these will contain edited versions of Newton's mathematical writings with translations and explanatory notes, as well as introductions and commentaries that constitute a guide to Newton's mathematics and scientific life, and to the main currents in the mathematics of the seventeenth century. Five volumes have been published (1973).

19. See D. T. Whiteside, "Newton's Discovery of the General Binomial Theorem," in *Mathematical Gazette*, **45** (1961), 175.

20. Especially because of Whiteside's researches.

21. Whiteside, ed., *Mathematical Papers*, I, 1–142. Whiteside concludes: "By and large Newton took his arithmetical symbolisms from Oughtred and his algebraical from Descartes, and onto them . . . he grafted new modifications of his own" (I, 11).

22. *Ca.* 1714; see University Library, Cambridge, MS Add. 3968, fol. 21. On this often debated point, see D. T. Whiteside, "Isaac Newton: Birth of a Mathematician," in *Notes and Records. Royal Society of London*, **19** (1964), n. 25; but compare n. 48, below.

23. University Library, Cambridge, MS Add. 3968. 41, fol. 85. This sentence occurs in a passage canceled by Newton.

24. *Ibid.*, fol. 72. This accords with De Moivre's later statement (in the Newton manuscripts recently bequeathed the University of Chicago by J. H. Schaffner) that after reading Wallis' book, Newton "on the occasion of a certain interpolation for the quadrature of the circle, found that admirable theorem for raising a Binomial to a power given."

25. Translated from the Latin in the Royal Society ed. of the *Correspondence*, II, 20 ff. and 32 ff.; see the comments by Whiteside in *Mathematical Papers*, IV, 666 ff. In the second term, A stands for $P^{m/n}$ (the first term), while in the third term B stands for $(m/n) AQ$ (the second term), and so on. This letter and its sequel came into Wallis' hands and he twice published summaries of them, the second time with Newton's own emendations and grudging approval. Newton listed some results of series expansion—coupled with quadratures as needed—for $z = r \sin^{-1} [x/r]$ and the inverse $x = r \sin[z/r]$; the versed sine $r(1 - \cos[z/r])$; and $x = e^{z/b} - 1$, the inverse of $z = b \log(1 + x)$, the Mercator series (see Whiteside, ed., *Mathematical Papers*, IV, 668).

26. Translated from the Latin in the Royal Society ed. of the *Correspondence*, II, 110 ff., 130 ff.; see the comments by Whiteside in *Mathematical Papers*, IV, 672 ff.

27. See Whiteside, *Mathematical Papers*, I, 106.

28. *Ibid.*, I, 112 and n. 81.

29. The Boothby referred to may be presumed to be Boothby Pagnell (about three miles northeast of Woolsthorpe), whose rector, H. Babington, was senior fellow of Trinity and had a good library. See further Whiteside, *Mathematical Papers*, I, 8, n. 21; and n. 8, above.

30. *The Mathematical Works of Isaac Newton*, I, x.

31. *Ibid.*, I, xi.

32. Here the "little zero" o is not, as formerly, the "indefinitely small" increment in the variable t, which "ultimately vanishes." In the *Principia*, bk. II, sec. 2, Newton used an alternative system of notation in which a, b, c, $\cdots$ are the "moments of any quantities A, B, C, &c.," increasing by a continual flux or "the velocities of the mutations which are proportional" to those moments, that is, their fluxions.

33. See Whiteside, *Mathematical Works*, I, x.

34. See A. R. and M. B. Hall, eds., *Unpublished Scientific Papers of Isaac Newton* (Cambridge, 1962).

35. *Mathematical Works*, I, xi.

36. *Ibid.*, xii.

37. University Library, Cambridge, MS Add. 3968.41, fol. 86, v.

38. Whiteside, *Mathematical Papers*, II, 166.

39. *Ibid.*, 166–167.

40. *Ibid.*, I, 11, n. 27. where Whiteside lists those "known to have seen substantial portions of Newton's mathematical papers during his lifetime" as including Collins, John Craig, Fatio de Duillier, Raphson, Halley, De Moivre, David Gregory, and William Jones, "but not, significantly, John Wallis," who did, however, see the "Epistola prior" and "Epistola posterior" (see n. 25, above); and II, 168. Isaac Barrow "probably saw only the *De analysi*."

41. The *Methodus fluxionum* also contained an amplified version of the tract of October 1666; it was published in English in 1736, translated by John Colson, but was not properly printed in its original Latin until 1779, when Horsley brought out *Analysis per quantitatum series, fluxiones, ac differentias*, incorporating William Jones's transcript, which he collated with an autograph manuscript by Newton. Various MS copies of the *Methodus fluxionum* had, however, been in circulation many years before 1693, when David Gregory wrote out an abridged version. Buffon translated it into French (1740) and Castillon used Colson's English version as the basis of a retranslation into Latin (*Opuscula mathematica*, I, 295 ff.). In all these versions, Newton's equivalent notation was transcribed into dotted letters. Horsley (*Opera*, I) entitled his version *Artis analyticae specimina vel geometria analytica*. The full text was first printed by Whiteside in *Mathematical Papers*, vol. III.

42. *Mathematical Papers*, II, 170.

43. P. xi; and see n. 41, above.

44. The reader may observe the confusion inherent in using both "indefinitely small portions of time" and "infinitely little" in relation to o; the use of index notation for powers (x^3, x^2, o^2) together with the doubling of letters (oo) in the same equation occurs in the original. These quotations are from the anonymous English version of 1737, reproduced in facsimile in Whiteside, ed., *Mathematical Works*. See n. 46.

45. In this example, I have (following the tradition of more than two centuries) introduced $\dot{x}$ and $\dot{y}$ where Newton in his MS used m and n. In his notation, too, r stood for the later $\dot{z}$.

46. *Mathematical Papers*, III, 80, n. 96. In the anonymous English version of 1737, as in Colson's translation of 1736, the word "indefinitely" appears; Castillon followed these (see n. 41). Horsley first introduced "*infinité*."

47. *Ibid.*, pp. 16–17.

48. See Whiteside, *ibid.*, p. 17; on Barrow's influence, see further pp. 71–74, notes 81, 82, 84.

49. *Ibid.*, pp. 328–352. On p. 329, n. 1, Whiteside agrees with a brief note by Alexander Witting (1911), in which the "source of the celebrated 'fluxional' Lemma II of the second Book of Newton's *Principia*" was accurately found in the first theorem of this addendum; see also p. 331, n. 11, and p. 334, n. 16.

50. On this topic, see the collection of statements by Newton assembled in supp. I to I. B. Cohen, *Introduction to Newton's Principia*.

51. This and the following quotations of the *De quadratura* are from John Stewart's translation of 1745.

52. As C. B. Boyer points out, in *Concepts of the Calculus*, p. 201, Newton was thus showing that one should not reach the conclusion "by simply neglecting infinitely small terms, but by finding the ultimate ratio as these terms become evanescent." Newton unfortunately compounded the confusion, however, by not wholly abjuring infinitesimals thereafter; in bk. II, lemma 2, of the *Principia* he warned the reader that his "moments" were not finite

quantities. In the eighteenth century, many English mathematicians, according to Boyer, "began to associate fluxions with the infinitely small differentials of Leibniz."

53. University Library, Cambridge, MS Add. 3960, fol. 177. Newton, however, was not the first mathematician to anticipate the Taylor series.

54. Introduction to *De quadratura*, in John Stewart, trans., *Two Treatises of the Quadrature of Curves, and Analysis by Equations of an Infinite Number of Terms* . . . (London, 1745), p. 4.

55. *Philosophical Transactions*, no. 342 (1715), 206.

56. Attributed to Newton, May 1708, in W. G. Hiscock, ed., *David Gregory, Isaac Newton and Their Circle* (Oxford, 1937), p. 42.

57. Henry Pemberton recorded, in his preface to his *View of . . . Newton's Philosophy* (London, 1728), that "I have often heard him censure the handling [of] geometrical subjects by algebraic calculations; and his book of Algebra he called by the name of Universal Arithmetic, in opposition to the injudicious title of Geometry, which Des Cartes had given to the treatise wherein he shews, how the geometer may assist his invention by such kind of computations."

58. There were five Latin eds. between 1707 and 1761, of which one was supervised by Newton, and three English eds. between 1720 and 1769.

59. For details, see Turnbull, *The Mathematical Discoveries of Newton*, pp. 49-50.

60. See C. B. Boyer, *History of Mathematics*, p. 450.

61. *Arithmetica universalis*, English ed. (London, 1728), p. 247; see Whiteside, *Mathematical Papers*, V, 428–429, 470–471.

62. *Arithmetica universalis*, in Whiteside's translation, *Mathematical Papers*, V, 477.

63. Published by Whiteside, *Mathematical Papers*, I, pp. 145 ff.

64. See especially *ibid.*, pp. 298 ff., pt. 2, sec. 5, "The Calculus Becomes an Algorithm."

65. *Ibid.*, III, pp. 120 ff.

66. *Ibid.*

67. In "Newton as an Originator of Polar Coördinates," in *American Mathematical Monthly*, **56** (1949), 73–78.

68. Made available in English translation (perhaps supervised by Newton himself) in John Harris, *Lexicon technicum*, vol. II (London, 1710); reprinted in facsimile (New York, 1966). The essay entitled "Curves" is reprinted in Whiteside, *Mathematical Papers*, II.

69. C. R. M. Talbot, ed. and trans., *Enumeration of Lines of the Third Order* (London, 1860), p. 72.

70. On other aspects of Newton's mathematics see Whiteside, *Mathematical Papers*, specifically III, 50–52, on the development of infinite series; II, 218–232, on an iterative procedure for finding approximate solutions to equations; and I, 519, and V, 360, on "Newton's identities" for finding the sums of the powers of the roots in any polynomial equation. See, additionally, for Newton's contributions in porisms, solid loci, number theory, trigonometry, and interpolation, among other topics, Whiteside, *Mathematical Papers*, *passim*, and Turnbull, *Mathematical Discoveries*.

71. See Whiteside, *Mathematical Works*, I, XV, and Boyer, *History of Mathematics*, p. 448. Drafts of the "Liber geometria" are University Library, Cambridge, MS Add. 3963 *passim* and MS Add. 4004, fols. 129–159. Gregory's comprehensive statement of Newton's plans as of summer 1694 is in Edinburgh University Library, David Gregory MS C42; an English version in Newton's *Correspondence*, III, 384–386, is not entirely satisfactory.

72. Newton's laconic statement of his solution, published anonymously in *Philosophical Transactions*, no. 224 (1697), p. 384, elicited from Bernoulli the reply "Ex ungue, Leonem" (the claw was sufficient to reveal the lion); see *Histoire des ouvrages des savans* (1697), 454–455.

73. See I. B. Cohen, "Isaac Newton, John Craig, and the Design of Ships," in *Boston Studies for the Philosophy of Science* (in press).

74. Even the variants in the eds. of the *Optiɩk* have never been fully documented in print (although Horsley's ed. gives such information for the Queries), nor have the differences between the Latin and English versions been fully analyzed. Zev Bechler is in the process of publishing four studies based on a perceptive and extensive examination of Newton's optical MSS. Henry Guerlac is presently engaged in preparing a new ed. of the *Opticks* itself.

75. The expression "experimentum crucis" is often attributed to Bacon, but Newton in fact encountered it in Hooke's account of his optical experiments as given in *Micrographia* (observation 9), where Hooke referred to an experiment that "will prove such a one as our *thrice excellent Verulam* [that is, Francis Bacon] calls *Experimentum crucis*." While many investigators before Newton— Dietrich von Freiberg, Marci, Descartes, and Grimaldi among them—had observed the oval dispersion of a circular beam of light passing through a prism, they all tended to assign the cause of the phenomenon to the consideration that the light source was not a point, but a physical object, so that light from opposite limbs of the sun would differ in angle of inclination by as much as half a degree. Newton's measurements led him from this initial supposition to the conclusion that the effect—a spectrum some five times longer than its width—was too great for the given cause, and therefore the prism must refract some rays to a considerable degree more than others.

76. This account of the experiment is greatly simplified, as was Newton's own account, presented in his letter to Oldenburg and published in *Philosophical Transactions*. See J. A. Lohne, "Experimentum Crucis," in *Notes and Records. Royal Society of London*, **23** (1968), 169-199; Lohne has traced the variations introduced into both the later diagrams and descriptions of the experiment. Newton's doctrine of the separation of white light into its component colors, each corresponding to a unique and fixed index of refraction, had been anticipated by Johannes Marcus Marci de Kronland in his *Thaumantias, liber de arcu coelesti* (Prague, 1648). An important analysis of Newton's experiment is in A. I. Sabra, *Theories of Light*.

77. See R. S. Westfall, "The Development of Newton's Theory of Color," in *Isis*, **53** (1962), 339–358; and A. R. Hall, "Newton's Notebook," pp. 245–250.

78. Dated 13 April 1672, in *Philosophical Transactions*, no. 84.

79. See R. S. Westfall, "Newton's Reply to Hooke and the Theory of Colors," in *Isis*, **54** (1963), 82–96; an edited text of the "Hypothesis" is in *Correspondence*, I, 362–386.

80. Published in Birch's *History of the Royal Society* and in I. B. Cohen, ed., *Newton's Papers and Letters*.

81. R. S. Westfall has further sketched Newton's changing views in relation to corpuscles and the ether, and, in "Isaac Newton's Coloured Circles Twixt Two Contiguous Glasses," in *Archive for History of Exact Sciences*, **2** (1965), 190, has concluded that "When Newton composed the *Opticks*, he had ceased to believe in an aether; the pulses of earlier years became 'fits of easy reflection and transmission,' offered as observed phenomena without explanation." Westfall discusses Newton's abandonment of the ether in "Uneasily Fitful Reflections on Fits of Easy Transmission [and of Easy Reflection]," in Robert Palter, ed., *The Annus Mirabilis of Sir Isaac Newton 1666–1966*, pp. 88–104; he emphasizes the pendulum experiment that Newton reported from memory in the *Principia* (bk. II, scholium at the end of sec. 7, in the first ed., or of sec. 6, in the 2nd and 3rd eds.). Henry Guerlac has discussed Newton's return to a modified concept of the ether in a series of studies (see Bibliography, sec. 8).

82. Birch, *History of the Royal Society*, III, 299; the early text of the "Discourse" is III, 247–305, but Newton had

already published it, with major revisions, as book II of the *Opticks*. Both the "Hypothesis" and the "Discourse" are reprinted in Newton's *Papers and Letters*, 177–235. Newton's original notes on Hooke's *Micrographia* have been published by A. R. and M. B. Hall, *Unpublished Scientific Papers of Isaac Newton*, 400 ff., especially sec. 48, in which he refers to "coloured rings" of "8 or 9 such circuits" in this "order (white perhaps in the midst) blew, purple, scarlet, yellow, greene, blew. . . ."

83. Newton's notes on Hooke were first published by Geoffrey Keynes in *Bibliography of Robert Hooke* (Oxford, 1960), pp. 97–108. Hooke claimed in particular that Newton's "Hypothesis" was largely taken from the *Micrographia*; see Newton's letters to Oldenburg, 21 December 1675 and 10 January 1676, in *Correspondence*, I, 404 ff. Hooke then wrote to Newton in a more kindly vein on 20 January 1676, provoking Newton's famous reply.

84. In this presentation, attention has been directed only to certain gross differences that exist between the texts of Newton's "Discourse of Observations" of 1675 and bk. II of the *Opticks*. The elaboration of Newton's view may be traced through certain notebooks and an early essay "On Colours" to his optical lectures and communications to the Royal Society. In particular, R. S. Westfall has explored certain relations between the essay and the later *Opticks*. See also his discussion on Newton's experiments cited in n. 81, above.

85. Chiefly in University Library, Cambridge, MS Add. 3970; but see n. 76.

86. University Library, Cambridge, MS Dd. 9.67.

87. Now part of the Portsmouth Collection, University Library, Cambridge, MS Add. 4002. This MS has been reproduced in facsimile, with an introduction by Whiteside, as *The Unpublished First Version of Isaac Newton's Cambridge Lectures on Optics* (Cambridge, 1973).

88. The development of the *Opticks* can be traced to some degree through a study of Newton's correspondence, notebooks, and optical MSS, chiefly University Library, Cambridge, MS Add. 3970, of which the first 233 pages contain the autograph MS used for printing the 1704 ed., although the final query 16 is lacking. An early draft, without the preliminary definitions and axioms, begins on fol. 304; the first version of prop. 1, book I, here reads, "The light of one natural body is more refrangible than that of another." There are many drafts and versions of the later queries, and a number of miscellaneous items, including the explanation of animal motion and sensation by the action of an "electric" and "elastic" spirit and the attribution of an "electric force" to all living bodies. A draft of a proposed "fourth Book" contains, on fol. 336, a "Conclusion" altered to "Hypoth. 1. The particles of bodies have certain spheres of activity with which they attract or shun one another . . ."; in a subsequent version, a form of this is inserted between props. 16 and 17, while a later prop. 18 is converted into "Hypoth. 2," which is followed shortly by hypotheses 3 to 5. It may thus be seen that Newton did not, in the 1690's, fully disdain speculative hypotheses. On fol. 409 there begins a tract, written before the *Opticks*, entitled "Fundamentum Opticae," which is similar to the *Opticks* in form and content. The three major notebooks in which Newton entered notes on his optical reading and his early thoughts and experiments on light, color, vision, the rainbow, and astronomical refraction are MSS Add. 3975, 3996, and 4000.

89. In "Newton's Reply to Hooke and the Theory of Colors," in *Isis*, **54** (1963), 82–96; an analysis of the two versions of Newton's lectures on optics is given in I. B. Cohen, *Introduction to Newton's 'Principia,'* supp. III.

90. See "Experimentum Crucis," in *Notes and Records. Royal Society of London*, **23** (1968), 169–199.

91. See, notably, "Isaac Newton: The Rise of a Scientist 1661–1671," in *Notes and Records. Royal Society of London*, **20** (1965), 125–139.

92. University Library, Cambridge, MS Add. 3996.

93. See Sabra, *Theories of Light*; also Westfall, "The Development of Newton's Theory of Color," in *Isis*, **53** (1962), 339–358. A major source for the development of Newton's optical concepts is, of course, the series of articles by Lohne, esp. those cited in nn. 90 and 91.

94. The surviving pages of this abortive ed. are reproduced in I. B. Cohen, "Versions of Isaac Newton's First Published Paper, With Remarks on the Question of Whether Newton Planned to Publish an Edition of His Early Papers on Light and Color," in *Archives internationales d'histoire des sciences*, **11** (1958), 357–375, 8 plates. See also A. R. Hall, "Newton's First Book," in *Archives internationales d'histoire des sciences*, **13** (1960), 39–61.

95. In W. C. Hiscock, ed., *David Gregory*, p. 15. The preface to the first ed. of the *Opticks* is signed "I.N."

96. See the "Analytical Table of Contents" prepared by Duane H. D. Roller for the Dover ed. of the *Opticks* (New York, 1952) for the contents of the entire work.

97. *Opticks*, book I, part 2, proposition 6. Newton's first statement of a musical analogy to color occurs in his "Hypothesis" of 1675; for an analysis of Newton's musical theory, see *Correspondence*, I, 388, n. 14, which includes a significant contribution by J. E. Bullard.

98. As Boyer has pointed out, "In the Cartesian geometrical theory [of the rainbow] it matters little what light is, or how it is transmitted, so long as propagation is rectilinear and the laws of reflection and refraction are satisfied"; see *The Rainbow from Myth to Mathematics* (New York, 1959), ch. 9.

99. Although Newton had worked out the formula at the time of his optical lectures of 1669-1671, he published no statement of it until the *Opticks*. In the meantime Halley and Johann [I] Bernoulli had reached this formula independently and had published it; see Boyer, *The Rainbow*, pp. 247 ff. In the *Opticks*, Newton offered the formula without proof, observing merely that "The Truth of all this Mathematicians will easily examine." His analysis is, however, given in detail in the *Lectiones opticae*, part 1, section 4, propositions 35 and 36, as a note informs the reader of the 1730 ed. of the *Opticks*.

For a detailed analysis of the topic, see Whiteside, *Mathematical Papers*, III, 500–509.

100. Ernst Mach, *The Principles of Physical Optics*, John S. Anderson and A. F. A. Young, trans. (London, 1926), 139.

101. This final sentence of book II, part 2, is a variant of a sentiment expressed a few paragraphs earlier: "Now as all these things follow from properties of Light by a mathematical way of reasoning, so the truth of them may be manifested by Experiments."

102. The word "diffraction" appears to have been introduced into optical discourse by Grimaldi, in his *Physico-mathesis de lumine, coloribus, et iride* (Bologna, 1665), in which the opening proposition reads: "Lumen propagatur seu diffunditur non solùm Directè, Refractè, ac Reflexè, sed etiam alio quodam Quarto modo, DIFFRACTÈ." Although Newton mentioned Grimaldi by name (calling him "Grimaldo") and referred to his experiments, he did not use the term "diffraction," but rather "inflexion," a usage the more curious in that it had been introduced into optics by none other than Hooke (*Micrographia*, "Obs. LVIII. Of a new Property in the Air and several other transparent Mediums nam'd Inflection . . ."). Newton may thus have been making a public acknowledgment of his debt to Hooke; see n. 83.

103. Newton's alleged denial of the possibility of correcting chromatic aberration has been greatly misunderstood. See the analysis of Newton's essay "Of Refractions" in Whiteside, *Mathematical Papers*, I, 549–550 and 559–576,

esp. the notes on the theory of compound lenses, pp. 575–576, and notes 60 and 61. This topic has also been studied by Zev Bechler; see " 'A Less Agreeable Matter'—Newton and Achromatic Refraction" (in press).

104. Many of these are available in two collections: A. R. and M. B. Hall, eds., *Unpublished Scientific Papers;* and John Herivel, *The Background to Newton's Principia.* See also the Royal Society's ed. of the *Correspondence.*

105. University Library, Cambridge, MS Add. 3996, first analyzed by A. R. Hall in 1948.

106. *Ibid.,* fol. 29. See also R. S. Westfall, *Force in Newton's Physics.* Newton's entry concerning the third law was first published by Whiteside in 1964; see n. 114.

107. University Library, Cambridge, MS Add. 4004; Herivel also gives the dynamical portions, with commentaries.

108. Def. 4; see Herivel, *Background,* p. 137.

109. *Ibid.,* p. 141.

110. See William Stukeley, *Memoirs of Sir Isaac Newton's Life,* p. 20; see also Douglas McKie and G. R. de Beer, "Newton's Apple," in *Notes and Records. Royal Society of London,* 9 (1952), 46–54, 333–335.

111. Various nearly contemporary accounts are given by W. W. Rouse Ball, *An Essay on Newton's "Principia,"* ch. 1.

112. See F. Cajori, "Newton's Twenty Years' Delay in Announcing the Law of Gravitation," in F. E. Brasch, ed., *Sir Isaac Newton,* pp. 127–188.

113. This document, a tract on "circular motion," University Library, Cambridge, MS Add. 3958.5, fol. 87, was in major part published for the first time by A. R. Hall in 1957. It has since been republished, with translation, in *Correspondence,* I, 297–300, and by Herivel in *Background,* pp. 192 ff.

114. In "Newton's Early Thoughts on Planetary Motion: A Fresh Look," in *British Journal for the History of Science,* 2 (1964), 120, n. 13.

115. In A. R. and M. B. Hall, *Unpublished Papers,* pp. 89 ff.

116. University Library, Cambridge, MS Add. 3958, fols. 81–83; also in Turnbull, *Correspondence,* III, 60–64.

117. Newton's concept of force has been traced, in its historical context, by Westfall, *Force in Newton's Physics;* see also Herivel, *Background,* and see I. B. Cohen, "Newton's Second Law and the Concept of Force in the *Principia,*" in R. Palter, ed., *Annus Mirabilis,* pp. 143–185.

118. In the scholium to the Laws of Motion, Newton mentioned that Wren, Wallis, and Huygens at "about the same time" communicated their "discoveries to the Royal Society"; they agreed "exactly among themselves" as to "the rules of the congress and reflexion of hard bodies."

119. Almost all discussions of Newton's spiral are based on a poor version of Newton's diagram; see J. A. Lohne, "The Increasing Corruption of Newton's Diagrams," in *History of Science,* 6 (1967), 69–89, esp. pp. 72–76.

120. Whiteside, "Newton's Early Thoughts," p. 135, has paraphrased Hooke's challenge as "Does the central force which, directed to a focus, deflects a body uniformly travelling in a straight line into an elliptical path vary as the inverse-square of its instantaneous distance from that focus?"

121. University Library, Cambridge, MS Add. 3968.41, fol. 85r, first printed in *Catalogue of the Portsmouth Collection,* p. xviii; it is in fact part of a draft of a letter to Des Maizeaux, written in summer 1718, when Des Maizeaux was composing his *Recueil.* In a famous MS memorandum (University Library, Cambridge, MS Add. 3968, fol. 101), Newton recalled the occasion of his correspondence with Hooke concerning his use of Kepler's area law in relation to elliptic orbits; see I. B. Cohen, *Introduction to Newton's Principia,* supp. I, sec. 2.

122. University Library, Cambridge, MS Add. 3965.7, fols. 55r–62(bis)r; printed versions appear in A. R. and M. B. Hall, *Unpublished Papers*; J. Herivel, *Background*; and W. W. Rouse Ball, *Essay.*

123. See Whiteside, "Newton's Early Thoughts," pp. 135–136; and see I. B. Cohen, "Newton's Second Law and the Concept of Force in the *Principia,*" in R. Palter, ed., *Annus Mirabilis,* pp. 143–185.

124. Analysis shows that great care is necessary in dealing with the limit process in even the simplest of Newton's examples, as in his early derivation of the Huygenian rule for centrifugal force (in the Waste Book, and referred to in the scholium to prop. 4, bk. I, in the *Principia*), or in the proof (props. 1–2, bk. I) that the law of areas is a necessary and sufficient condition for a central force. Whiteside has analyzed these and other propositions in "Newtonian Dynamics," pp. 109–111, and "Mathematical Principles," pp. 11 ff., and has shown the logical pitfalls that await the credulous reader, most notably the implied use by Newton of infinitesimals of an order higher than one (chiefly those of the second, and occasionally those of the third, order).

125. See the *Principia,* props. 1–3, bk. I, and the various versions of *De motu* printed by A. R. and M. B. Hall, J. Herivel, and W. W. Rouse Ball.

126. In *Correspondence,* II, 436–437. This letter unambiguously shows that Newton did not have the solution to the problem of the attraction of a sphere until considerably later than 1679, and declaredly not "until last summer [1685]."

127. There is considerable uncertainty about what "curious treatise, *De Motu*" Halley saw; see I. B. Cohen, *Introduction,* ch. 3, sec. 2.

128. *Ibid.,* secc. 6.

129. First published by A. R. and M. B. Hall, *Unpublished Papers.*

130. Newton at first corresponded with Flamsteed indirectly, beginning in December 1680, through the agency of James Crompton.

131. In 1681, Newton still thought that the "comets" seen in November and December 1680 were "two different ones" (Newton to Crompton for Flamsteed, 28 February 1681, in *Correspondence,* II, 342); in a letter to Flamsteed of 16 April 1681 (*ibid.,* p. 364), Newton restated his doubts that "the Comets of November & December [were] but one." In a letter of 5 January 1685 (*ibid.,* p. 408), Flamsteed hazarded a "guess" at Newton's "designe": to define the curve that the comet of 1680 "described in the aether" from a general "Theory of motion," while on 19 September 1685 (*ibid.,* p. 419), Newton at last admitted to Flamsteed that "it seems very probable that those of November & December were the same comet." Flamsteed noted in the margin of the last letter that Newton "would not grant it before," adding, "see his letter of 1681." In the *Arithmetica universalis* of 1707, Newton, in problem 52, explored the "uniform rectilinear motion" of a comet, "supposing the 'Copernican hypothesis' "; see Whiteside, *Mathematical Papers,* V, 299, n. 400, and esp. pp. 524 ff.

132. As far as actual Greek geometry goes, Newton barely makes use of Archimedes, Apollonius, or even Pappus (mentioned in passing in the preface to the 1st ed. of the *Principia*); see Whiteside, "Mathematical Principles," p. 7.

133. This is the tract "De methodis serierum et fluxionum," printed with translation in Whiteside, ed., *Mathematical Papers,* III, 32 ff.

134. Motte has standardized the use of the neuter *genitum* in his English translation, although Newton actually wrote: "Momentum Genitae aequatur . . .," and then said "Genitam voco quantitatem omnem quae . . .," where *quantitas genita* (or "generated quantity") is, of course, feminine.

135. Whiteside, *Mathematical Papers,* IV, 523, note 6.

136. *Concepts,* p. 200.

137. *Ibid.;* on Newton's use of infinitesimals in the *Principia,* see also A. De Morgan, "On the Early History of Infinitesimals in England," in *Philosophical Magazine,* 4 (1852), 321–330, in which he notes especially some changes in

Newton's usage from the 1687 to the 1713 eds. See further F. Cajori, *A History of the Conceptions of Limits*, pp. 2–32.

138. Whiteside, "Mathematical Principles," pp. 20 ff.

139. Newton's method, contained in University Library, Cambridge, MS Add. 3965.10, fols. 107v and 134v, will be published for the first time in Whiteside, *Mathematical Papers*, VI.

140. Halley refers to this specifically in the first paragraph of his review of the *Principia*, in *Philosophical Transactions of the Royal Society*, no. 186 (1687), p. 291.

141. Translated from University Library, Cambridge, MS Add. 3968, fol. 112.

142. *De quadratura* was printed, together with the other tracts in the collection published by W. Jones in 1711, as a supp. to the second reprint of the 2nd ed. of the *Principia* (1723).

143. In *Philosophical Transactions of the Royal Society* (1715), p. 206.

144. Newton was aware that a shift in latitude causes a variation in rotational speed, since $v = 2r/T \times \cos\varphi$, where v is the linear tangential speed at latitude φ; r, T being the average values of the radius of the earth and the period of rotation. The distance from the center of the earth is also affected by latitude, since the earth is an oblate spheroid. These two factors appear in the variation with latitude in the length of a seconds pendulum.

145. "The Aim of Science," in *Ratio*, **1** (1957), 24–35; repr. in Karl Popper, *Objective Knowledge* (Oxford, 1972), 191–205.

146. See, for example, R. S. Westfall, *Force in Newton's Physics*. See also Alan Gabbey, "Force and Inertia in 17th-century Dynamics," in *Studies in History and Philosophy of Science*, **2** (1971), 1–67; Gabbey contests Westfall's point of view concerning the *vis insita*, in *Science*, **176** (1972), 157–159.

147. This would no longer even be called a force; some present translations, among them F. Cajori's version of Motte, anachronistically render Newton's *vis inertiae* as simple "inertia."

148. University Library, Cambridge, MS Add. 3968, fol. 415; published in A. Koyré and I. B. Cohen, "Newton and the Leibniz-Clarke Correspondence," in *Archives internationales d'histoire des sciences*, **15** (1962), 122–123.

149. See I. B. Cohen, "Newton's Second Law and the Concept of Force in the *Principia*," in R. Palter, ed., *Annus Mirabilis*, pp. 143–185.

150. R. S. Westfall, *Force*, p. 490. It is with this point of view in particular that Gabbey takes issue; see n. 146. See further E. J. Aiton, "The Concept of Force," in A. C. Crombie and M. A. Hoskin, eds., *History of Science*, X (Cambridge, 1971), 88–102.

151. In prop. 7, bk. III (referring to prop. 69, bk. I, and its corollaries), Newton argued from "accelerative" measures of forces to "absolute" forces, in specific cases of attraction.

152. See D. T. Whiteside, in *History of Science*, V (Cambridge, 1966), 110.

153. E. J. Aiton, "The Inverse Problem of Central Forces," in *Annals of Science*, **20** (1964), 82.

154. This position of the *Principia* was greatly altered between the 1st and 2nd eds.; Newton's intermediate results were summarized in a set of procedural rules for making up lunar tables and were published in a Latin version in David Gregory's treatise on astronomy (1702). Several separate English versions were later published; these are reprinted in facsimile in I. B. Cohen, *Newton's Theory of the Moon* (London, 1974).

155. W. W. Rouse Ball gives a useful paraphrase in *Essay*, p. 92.

156. See the analyses by Clifford Truesdell, listed in the bibliography to this article.

157. In his review of the *Principia*, in *Philosophical Transactions* (1687), p. 295, Halley referred specifically to this proposition, "which being rather a Physical than Mathematical Inquiry, our Author forbears to discuss."

158. This problem had gained prominence through the independent discovery by Halley and Richer that the length of a pendulum clock must be adjusted for changes in latitude.

159. This "General Scholium" should not be confused with the general scholium that ends the *Principia*. It was revised and expanded for the 2nd ed., where it appears at the end of sec. 6; in the 1st ed. it appears at the end of sec. 7.

160. In *Mécanique céleste*, V, bk. XII, ch. 3, sec. 7. Newton failed to take into account the changes in elasticity due to the "heat of compression and cold of rarefaction"; Laplace corrected Newton's formula $(v = k\sqrt{p/d})$, replacing it with his own $(v = k\sqrt{1.41\,p/d}$, where p is the air pressure and d the density of the air).

Laplace, who had first published his own results in 1816, later said that Newton's studies on the velocity of sound in the atmosphere were the most important application yet made of the equations of motion in elastic fluids: "sa théorie, quoique imparfaite, est un monument de son génie" (*Méchanique céleste*, V, bk. XII, ch. 1, pp. 95–96). Lord Rayleigh pointed out that Newton's investigations "established that the velocity of sound should be independent of the amplitude of the vibration, and also of the pitch."

161. The confutation of Descartes's vortex theory was thought by men of Newton's century to be one of the major aims of bk. II. Huygens, for one, accepted Newton's conclusion that the Cartesian vortices must be cast out of physics, and wrote to Leibniz to find out whether he would be able to continue to believe in them after reading the *Principia*. In "my view," Huygens wrote, "these vortices are superfluous if one accepts the system of Mr. Newton."

162. On the earlier tract in relation to bk. III of the *Principia*, see the preface to the repr. (London, 1969) and I. B. Cohen, *Introduction*, supp. VI.

163. At one time, according to a manuscript note, Newton was unequivocal that hypothesis 3 expressed the belief of Aristotle, Descartes, and unspecified "others." It was originally followed by a hypothesis 4, which in the 2nd and 3rd eds. was moved to a later part of bk. III. For details, see I. B. Cohen, "Hypotheses in Newton's Philosophy," in *Physis*, **8** (1966), 163–184.

164. See *De motu* in A. R. and M. B. Hall, *Unpublished Papers*, and J. Herivel, *Background*.

165. Newton apparently never made the experiment of comparing mass and weight of different quantities of the same material.

166. There has been little research on the general subject of Newton's lunar theory; even the methods he used to obtain the results given in a short scholium to prop. 35, bk. I, in the 1st ed., are not known. W. W. Rouse Ball, in *Essay*, p. 109, discusses Newton's formula for "the mean hourly motion of the moon's apogee," and says, "The investigation on this point is not entirely satisfactory, and from the alterations made in the MS. Newton evidently felt doubts about the correctness of the coefficient $\frac{11}{2}$ which occurs in this formula. From this, however, he deduces quite correctly that the mean annual motion of the apogee resulting would amount to $38°51'51''$, whereas the annual motion" is known to be $40°41'30''$. His discussion is based upon the statement, presumably by J. C. Adams, in the preface to the *Catalogue of the Portsmouth Collection* (Cambridge, 1888), pp. xii–xiii. Newton's MSS on the motion of the moon—chiefly University Library, Cambridge, MS Add. 3966—are one of the major unanalyzed collections of his work. For further documents concerning this topic, and a scholarly analysis by A. R. Hall of some aspects of Newton's researches on the motion of the moon, see *Correspondence*, V (in press), and I. B. Cohen, intro. to a facsimile repr. of Newton's pamphlet on the motion of the moon (London, in press).

167. Although Newton had suspected the association of color with wavelength of vibration as early as his "Hypothesis" of 1675, he did not go on from his experiments on rings, which suggested a periodicity in optical phenomena, to a true wave theory—no doubt because, as A. I. Sabra has suggested, his a priori "conception of the rays as discrete entities or corpuscles" effectively "prevented him from envisaging the possibility of an undulatory interpretation in which the ray, as something distinguished from the waves, would be redundant" (*Theories of Light*, p. 341).

168. Both printed in facsimile in I. B. Cohen, ed., *Isaac Newton's Papers and Letters on Natural Philosophy*. They were published and studied in the eighteenth century and had a significant influence on the development of the concept of electric fluid (or fluids) and caloric. This topic is explored in some detail in I. B. Cohen, *Franklin and Newton* (Philadelphia, 1956; Cambridge, 1966; rev. ed. in press), esp. chs. 6 and 7.

169. Henry Guerlac has studied the development of the queries themselves, and in particular the decline of Newton's use of the ether until its reappearance in a new form in the queries of the 2nd English ed. He has also noted that the concept of the ether is conspicuously absent from the Latin ed. of 1706. See especially his "Newton's Optical Aether," in *Notes and Records. Royal Society of London*, **22** (1967), 45–57. See, further, Joan L. Hawes, "Newton's Revival of the Aether Hypothesis . . .," *ibid.*, **23** (1968), 200–212.

170. A. R. and M. B. Hall have found evidence that Newton thought of this "spiritus" as electrical in nature; see *Unpublished Papers*, pp. 231 ff., 348 ff. Guerlac has shown that Newton was fascinated by Hauksbee's electrical experiments and by certain experiments of Desaguliers; see bibliography for this series of articles.

171. University Library, Cambridge, MS Add. 3970, sec. 9, fols. 623 ff.

172. These works, especially queries 28 and 31, have been studied in conjunction with Newton's MSS (particularly his notebooks) by A. R. and M. B. Hall, D. McKie, J. R. Partington, R. Kargon, J. E. McGuire, A. Thackray, and others, in their elucidations of a Newtonian doctrine of chemistry or theory of matter. *De natura acidorum* has been printed from an autograph MS, with notes by Pitcairne and transcripts by David Gregory, in *Correspondence*, III, 205–214. The first printing, in both Latin and English, is reproduced in I. B. Cohen, ed., *Newton's Papers and Letters*, pp. 255–258.

173. According to M. B. Hall, "Newton's Chemical Papers," in *Newton's Papers and Letters*, p. 244.

174. *Ibid.*, p. 245.

175. Discussed by T. S. Kuhn, "Newton's '31st Query' and the Degradation of Gold," in *Isis*, **42** (1951), 296–298.

176. M. B. Hall, "Newton's Chemical Papers," p. 245; she continues that there we may find a "forerunner of the tables of affinity" developed in the eighteenth century, by means of which "chemists tried to predict the course of a reaction."

177. In "Newton's Chemical Experiments," in *Archives internationales d'histoire des sciences*, **11** (1958), 113–152— a study of Newton's chemical notes and papers—A. R. and M. B. Hall have tried to show that Newton's primary concern in these matters was the chemistry of metals, and that the writings of alchemists were a major source of information on every aspect of metals. Humphrey Newton wrote up a confusing account of Newton's alchemical experiments, in which he said that Newton's guide was the *De re metallica* of Agricola; this work, however, is largely free of alchemical overtones and concentrates on mining and metallurgy.

178. R. S. Westfall, in *Science and Religion in Seventeenth-Century England*, ch. 8, draws upon such expressions by Newton to prove that "Newton was a religious rationalist who remained blind to the mystic's spiritual communion with the divine."

179. These MSS are described in the Sotheby sale catalog and by F. Sherwood Taylor, in "An Alchemical Work of Sir Isaac Newton," in *Ambix*, **5** (1956), 59–84.

180. These have been the subject of a considerable study by Frank E. Manuel, *Isaac Newton, Historian* (Cambridge, Mass., 1964).

181. Newton's interest in alchemy mirrors all the bewildering aspects of that subject, ranging from the manipulative chemistry of metals, mineral acids, and salts, to esoteric and symbolic (often sexual) illustrations and mysticism of a religious or philosophical kind. His interest in alchemy persisted through his days at the mint, although there is no indication that he at that time still seriously believed that pure metallic gold might be produced from baser metals— if, indeed, he had ever so believed. The extent of his notes on his reading indicate the seriousness of Newton's interest in the general subject, but it is impossible to ascertain to what degree, if any, his alchemical concerns may have influenced his science, beyond his vague and general commitment to "transmutations" as a mode for the operations of nature. But even this belief would not imply a commitment to the entire hermetic tradition, and it is not necessary to seek a unity of the diverse interests and intellectual concerns in a mind as complex as Newton's.

182. P. M. Rattansi, "Newton's Alchemical Studies," in Allen Debus, ed., *Science, Medicine and Society in the Renaissance*, II (New York, 1972), 174.

183. The first suggestion that Newton's concept of the ether might be linked to his alchemical concerns was made by Taylor; see n. 179, above.

184. Leibniz, *Tentamen* . . . ("An Essay on the Cause of the Motions of the Heavenly Bodies"), in *Acta eruditorum* (Feb. 1689), 82–96, English trans. by E. J. Collins. Leibniz' marked copy of the 1st ed. of the *Principia*, presumably the one sent to him by Fatio de Duillier at Newton's direction, is now in the possession of E. A. Fellmann of Basel, who has discussed Leibniz' annotations in "Die Marginalnoten von Leibniz in Newtons Principia Mathematica 1687," in *Humanismus und Technik*, **2** (1972), 110–129; Fellmann's critical ed., G. W. Leibniz, *Marginalia in Newtoni Principia Mathematica 1687* (Paris, 1973), includes facsimiles of the annotated pages.

185. Translated from some MS comments on Leibniz' essay, first printed in Edleston, *Correspondence*, pp. 307–314.

186. Leibniz' excepts from Newton's *De analysi*, made in 1676 from a transcript by John Collins, have been published from the Hannover MS by Whiteside, in *Mathematical Papers*, II, 248–258. Whiteside thus demonstrates that Leibniz was "clearly interested only in its algebraic portions: fluxional sections are ignored."

187. Several MS versions in his hand survive in University Library, Cambridge, MS Add. 3968.

188. At this period the year in England officially began on Lady Day, 25 March. Hence Newton died on 20 March 1726 old style, or in 1726/7 (to use the form then current for dates in January, February, and the first part of March).

189. In the 2-vol. ed. of the *Principia* with variant readings edited by A. Koyré, I. B. Cohen, and Anne Whitman; Koyré has shown that in the English *Opticks* Newton used the word "feign" in relation to hypotheses, in the sense of "fingo" in the slogan, a usage confirmed by example in Newton's MSS. Motte renders the phrase as "I frame no hypotheses." Newton himself in MSS used both "feign" and "frame" in relation to hypotheses in this regard; see I. B. Cohen, "The First English Version of Newton's *Hypotheses non fingo*," in *Isis*, **53** (1962), 379–388.

190. University Library, Cambridge, MS Add. 3968, fol. 437.

BIBLIOGRAPHY

This bibliography is divided into four major sections. The last, by A. P. Youschkevitch, is concerned with Soviet studies on Newton and is independent of the text.

ORIGINAL WORKS (numbered I–IV): Newton's major writings, together with collected works and editions, bibliographies, manuscript collections, and catalogues.

SECONDARY LITERATURE (numbered V–VI): including general works and specific writings about Newton and his life.

SOURCES (numbered 1–11): the chief works used in the preparation of this biography; the subdivisions of this section are correlated to the subdivisions of the biography itself.

SOVIET LITERATURE: a special section devoted to Newtonian scholarship in the Soviet Union.

The first three sections of the bibliography contain a number of cross-references; a parenthetical number refers the reader to the section of the bibliography in which a complete citation may be found.

ORIGINAL WORKS

I. MAJOR WORKS. Newton's first publications were on optics and appeared in the *Philosophical Transactions of the Royal Society* (1672–1676); repr. in facs., with intro. by T. S. Kuhn, in I. B. Cohen, ed., *Isaac Newton's Papers & Letters on Natural Philosophy* (Cambridge, Mass., 1958; 2nd ed., in press). His *Opticks* (London, 1704; enl. versions in Latin [London, 1706], and in English [London, 1717 or 1718]) contained two supps.: his *Enumeratio linearum tertii ordinis* and *Tractatus de quadratura curvarum*, his first published works in pure mathematics. The 1704 ed. has been repr. in facs. (Brussels, 1966) and (optical part only) in type (London, 1931); also repr. with an analytical table of contents prepared by D. H. D. Roller (New York, 1952). French trans. are by P. Coste (Amsterdam, 1720; rev. ed. 1722; facs. repr., with intro. by M. Solovine, Paris, 1955); a German ed. is W. Abendroth, 2 vols. (Leipzig, 1898); and a Rumanian trans. is Victor Marian (Bucharest, 1970). A new ed. is currently being prepared by Henry Guerlac.

The *Philosophiae naturalis principia mathematica* (London, 1687; rev. eds., Cambridge, 1713 [repr. Amsterdam, 1714, 1723], and London, 1726) is available in an ed. with variant readings (based on the three printed eds., the MS for the 1st ed. and Newton's annotations in his own copies of the 1st and 2nd eds.) prepared by A. Koyré, I. B. Cohen, and Anne Whitman: *Isaac Newton's Philosophiae naturalis principia mathematica, the Third Edition (1726) With Variant Readings*, 2 vols. (Cambridge, Mass.–Cambridge, England, 1972). Translations and excerpts have appeared in Dutch, English, French, German, Italian, Japanese, Rumanian, Russian, and Swedish, and are listed in app. VIII, vol. II, of the Koyré, Cohen, and Whitman ed., together with an account of reprs. of the whole treatise. The 1st ed. has been printed twice in facs. (London, 1954[?]; Brussels, 1965).

William Jones published Newton's *De analysi* in his ed.

of *Analysis per quantitatum series, fluxiones, ac differentias* . . . (London, 1711), repr. in the Royal Society's *Commercium epistolicum D. Johannis Collins, et aliorum de analysi promota* . . . (London, 1712–1713; enl. version, 1722; "variorum" ed. by J.-B. Biot and F. Lefort, Paris, 1856), and as an appendix to the 1723 Amsterdam printing of the *Principia*. Newton's *Arithmetica universalis* was published from the MS of Newton's lectures by W. Whiston (Cambridge, 1707); an amended ed. followed, supervised by Newton himself (London, 1722). For bibliographical notes on these and some other mathematical writings (and indications of other eds. and translations), see the introductions by D. T. Whiteside to the facs. repr. of *The Mathematical Works of Isaac Newton*, 2 vols. (New York–London, 1964–1967). Newton's *Arithmetica universalis* was translated into Russian with notes and commentaries by A. P. Youschkevitch (Moscow, 1948); English eds. were published in London in 1720, 1728, and 1769.

After Newton's death the early version of what became bk. III of the *Principia* was published in English as *A Treatise of the System of the World* (London, 1728; rev. London, 1731, facs. repr., with intro. by I. B. Cohen, London, 1969) and in Latin as *De mundi systemate liber* (London, 1728). An Italian trans. is by Marcella Renzoni (Turin, 1959; 1969). The first part of the *Lectiones opticae* was translated and published as *Optical Lectures* (London, 1728) before the full Latin ed. was printed (1729); both are imperfect and incomplete. The only modern ed. is in Russian, *Lektsii po optike* (Leningrad, 1946), with commentary by S. I. Vavilov.

For Newton's nonscientific works (theology, biblical studies, chronology), and for other scientific writings, see the various sections below.

II. COLLECTED WORKS OR EDITIONS. The only attempt ever made to produce a general ed. of Newton was S. Horsley, *Isaaci Newtoni opera quae exstant omnia*, 5 vols. (London, 1779–1785; photo repr. Stuttgart–Bad Cannstatt, 1964), which barely takes account of Newton's available MS writings but has the virtue of including (vol. I) the published mathematical tracts; (vols. II–III) the *Principia* and *De mundi systemate, Theoria lunae*, and *Lectiones opticae*; (vol. IV) letters from the *Philosophical Transactions* on light and color, the letter to Boyle on the ether, *De problematis Bernoullianis*, the letters to Bentley, and the *Commercium epistolicum*; (vol. V) the *Chronology*, the *Prophecies*, and the *Corruptions of Scripture*. An earlier and more modest collection was the 3-vol. *Opuscula mathematica, philosophica, et philologica*, Giovanni Francesco Salvemini (known as Johann Castillon), ed. (Lausanne–Geneva, 1744); it contains only works then in print.

A major collection of letters and documents, edited in the most exemplary manner, is Edleston (1); Rigaud's *Essay* (5) is also valuable. S. P. Rigaud's *Correspondence of Scientific Men of the Seventeenth Century* . . . *in the collection of* . . . *the Earl of Macclesfield*, 2 vols. (Oxford, 1841; rev., with table of contents and index, 1862) is of special importance because the Macclesfield collection is not at present open to scholars.

Four vols. of the Royal Society's ed. of Newton's *Correspondence* (Cambridge, 1959–   ) have (as of 1974) been published, vols. I–III edited by H. W. Turnbull, vol. IV by J. F. Scott; A. R. Hall has been appointed editor of the succeeding volumes. The *Correspondence* is not limited to letters but contains scientific documents of primary importance. A recent major collection is A. R. and M. B. Hall, eds., *Unpublished Scientific Papers of Isaac Newton, a Selection From the Portsmouth Collection in the University Library, Cambridge* (Cambridge, 1964). Other presentations of MSS are given in the ed. of the *Principia* with variant readings (1972, cited above), Herivel's *Background* (5), and in D. T. Whiteside's ed. of Newton's *Mathematical Papers* (3).

III. BIBLIOGRAPHIES. There are three bibliographies of Newton's writings, none complete or free of major error. One is George J. Gray, *A Bibliography of the Works of Sir Isaac Newton, Together With a List of Books Illustrating His Works*, 2nd ed., rev. and enl. (Cambridge, 1907; repr. London, 1966); H. Zeitlinger, "A Newton Bibliography," pp. 148–170 of the volume ed. by W. J. Greenstreet (VI); and *A Descriptive Catalogue of the Grace K. Babson Collection of the Works of Sir Isaac Newton . . .* (New York, 1950), plus *A Supplement . . .* compiled by Henry P. Macomber (Babson Park, Mass., 1955), which lists some secondary materials from journals as well as books.

IV. MANUSCRIPT COLLECTIONS AND CATALOGUES. The Portsmouth Collection (University Library, Cambridge) was roughly catalogued by a syndicate consisting of H. R. Luard, G. G. Stokes, J. C. Adams, and G. D. Liveing, who produced *A Catalogue of the Portsmouth Collection of Books and Papers Written by or Belonging to Sir Isaac Newton . . .* (Cambridge, 1888); the bare descriptions do not always identify the major MSS or give the catalogue numbers (*e.g.*, the Waste Book, U.L.C. MS Add. 4004, the major repository of Newton's early work in dynamics and in mathematics, appears as "A common-place book, written originally by B. Smith, D.D., with calculations by Newton written in the blank spaces. This contains Newton's first idea of Fluxions"). There is no adequate catalogue or printed guide to the Newton MSS in the libraries of Trinity College (Cambridge), the Royal Society of London, or the British Museum. The Keynes Collection (in the library of King's College, Cambridge) is almost entirely based on the Sotheby sale and is inventoried in the form of a marked copy of the sale catalogue, available in the library; see A. N. L. Munby, "The Keynes Collection of the Works of Sir Isaac Newton at King's College, Cambridge," in *Notes and Records. Royal Society of London*, **10** (1952), 40–50. The "scientific portion" of the Portsmouth Collection was given to Cambridge University in the 1870's; the remainder was dispersed at public auction in 1936. See Sotheby's *Catalogue of the Newton Papers, Sold by Order of the Viscount Lymington, to Whom They Have Descended From Catherine Conduitt, Viscountess Lymington, Great-niece of Sir Isaac Newton* (London, 1936). No catalogue has ever been made available of the Macclesfield Collection (rich in Newton MSS), based originally on the papers of John Collins and William Jones,

for which see S. P. Rigaud's 2-vol. *Correspondence . . .* (I). Further information concerning MS sources is given in Whiteside, *Mathematical Papers*, I, xxiv–xxxiii (3).

Many books from Newton's library are in the Trinity College Library (Cambridge); others are in public and private collections all over the world. R. de Villamil, *Newton: The Man* (London, 1931[?]; repr., with intro. by I. B. Cohen, New York, 1972), contains a catalogue (imperfect and incomplete) of books in Newton's library at the time of his death; an inventory with present locations of Newton's books is greatly to be desired. See P. E. Spargo, "Newton's Library," in *Endeavour*, **31** (1972), 29–33, with short but valuable list of references. See also *Library of Sir Isaac Newton. Presentation by the Pilgrim Trust to Trinity College Cambridge 30 October 1943* (Cambridge, 1944), described on pp. 5–7 of *Thirteenth Annual Report of the Pilgrim Trust* (Harlech, 1943).

SECONDARY LITERATURE

V. GUIDES TO THE SECONDARY LITERATURE. For guides to the literature concerning Newton, see . . . *Catalogue . . . Babson Collection . . .* (III); and scholarly eds., such as *Mathematical Papers* (3), *Principia* (I), and *Correspondence* (II). A most valuable year-by-year list of articles and books has been prepared and published by Clelia Pighetti: "Cinquant'anni di studi newtoniani (1908–1959)," in *Rivista critica di storia della filosofia*, **20** (1960), 181–203, 295–318. See also Magda Whitrow, ed., *ISIS Cumulative Bibliography . . . 1913–65*, II (London, 1971), 221–232. Two fairly recent surveys of the literature are I. B. Cohen, "Newton in the Light of Recent Scholarship," in *Isis*, **51** (1960), 489–514; and D. T. Whiteside, "The Expanding World of Newtonian Research," in *History of Science*, **1** (1962), 16–29.

VI. GENERAL WORKS. Biographies (*e.g.*, by Stukeley, Brewster, More, Manuel) are listed below (1). Some major interpretative works and collections of studies on Newton are Ferd. Rosenberger, *Isaac Newton und seine physikalischen Principien* (Leipzig, 1895); Léon Bloch, *La philosophie de Newton* (Paris, 1908); S. I. Vavilov, *Isaak Nyuton; nauchnaya biografia i stati*, 3rd ed. (Moscow, 1961), German trans. by Josef Grün as *Isaac Newton* (Vienna, 1948), 2nd ed., rev., German trans. by Franz Boncourt (Berlin, 1951); Alexandre Koyré, *Newtonian Studies* (London–Cambridge, Mass., 1965) which, posthumously published, contains a number of errors—a more correct version is the French trans., *Études newtoniennes* (Paris, 1968), with an *avertissement* by Yvon Belaval; and Alberto Pala, *Isaac Newton, scienza e filosofia* (Turin, 1969).

Major collections of Newtonian studies include W. J. Greenstreet, ed., *Isaac Newton 1642–1727* (London, 1927); F. E. Brasch, ed., *Sir Isaac Newton 1727–1927* (Baltimore, 1928); S. I. Vavilov, ed., *Isaak Nyuton 1643*[n.s.]–*1727*, a symposium in Russian (Moscow–Leningrad, 1943); Royal Society, *Newton Tercentenary Celebrations, 15–19 July 1946* (Cambridge, 1947); and Robert Palter, ed., *The Annus Mirabilis of Sir Isaac Newton 1666–1966* (Cambridge, Mass., 1970), based on an earlier version in *The Texas Quarterly*, **10**, no. 3 (autumn 1967).

On Newton's reputation and influence (notably in the eighteenth century), see Hélène Metzger, *Newton, Stahl, Boerhaave et la doctrine chimique* (Paris, 1930), and *Attraction universelle et religion naturelle chez quelques commentateurs anglais de Newton* (Paris, 1938); Pierre Brunet, *L'introduction des théories de Newton en France au XVIIIe siècle*, I, *Avant 1738* (Paris, 1931); Marjorie Hope Nicolson, *Newton Demands the Muse, Newton's Opticks and the Eighteenth Century Poets* (Princeton, 1946); I. B. Cohen, *Franklin and Newton, an Inquiry Into Speculative Newtonian Experimental Science . . .* (Philadelphia, 1956; Cambridge, Mass., 1966; rev. repr. 1974); Henry Guerlac, "Where the Statue Stood: Divergent Loyalties to Newton in the Eighteenth Century," in Earl R. Wasserman, ed., *Aspects of the Eighteenth Century* (Baltimore, 1965), pp. 317–334; R. E. Schofield, *Mechanism and Materialism, British Natural Philosophy in an Age of Reason* (Princeton, 1970); Paolo Casini, *L'universo-macchina, origini della filosofia newtoniana* (Bari, 1969); and Arnold Thackray, *Atoms and Powers, an Essay in Newtonian Matter-Theory and the Development of Chemistry* (Cambridge, Mass., 1970). Still of value today are three major eighteenth-century expositions of the Newtonian natural philosophy, by Henry Pemberton, Voltaire, and Colin Maclaurin.

Whoever studies any of Newton's mathematical or scientific writings would be well advised to consult J. A. Lohne, "The Increasing Corruption of Newton's Diagrams," in *History of Science*, 6 (1967), 69–89.

Newton's MSS comprise some 20–25 million words; most of them have never been studied fully, and some are currently "lost," having been dispersed at the Sotheby sale in 1936. Among the areas in which there is a great need for editing of MSS and research are Newton's studies of lunar motions (chiefly U.L.C. MS Add. 3966); his work in optics (chiefly U.L.C. MS Add. 3970; plus other MSS such as notebooks, etc.); and the technical innovations he proposed for the *Principia* in the 1690's (chiefly U.L.C. MS Add. 3965); see (4), (7). It would be further valuable to have full annotated editions of his early notebooks and of some major alchemical notes and writings.

Some recent Newtonian publications include Valentin Boss, *Newton and Russia, the Early Influence 1698–1796* (Cambridge, Mass., 1972); Klaus-Dietwardt Buchholtz, *Isaac Newton als Theologe* (Wittenburg, 1965); Mary S. Churchill, "The Seven Chapters With Explanatory Notes," in *Chymia*, 12 (1967), 27–57, the first publication of one of Newton's complete alchemical MS; J. E. Hofmann, "Neue Newtoniana," in *Studia Leibnitiana*, 2 (1970), 140–145, a review of recent literature; D. Kubrin, "Newton and the Cyclical Cosmos," in *Journal of the History of Ideas*, 28 (1967), 325–346; J. E. McGuire, "The Origin of Newton's Doctrine of Essential Qualities," in *Centaurus*, 12 (1968), 233–260; and L. Trengrove, "Newton's Theological Views," in *Annals of Science*, 22 (1966), 277–294.

SOURCES

1. *Early Life and Education.* The major biographies of Newton are David Brewster, *Memoirs of the Life, Writings,*

and Discoveries of Isaac Newton, 2 vols. (Edinburgh, 1855; 2nd ed., 1860; repr. New York, 1965), the best biography of Newton, despite its stuffiness; for a corrective, see Augustus De Morgan, *Essays on the Life and Work of Newton* (Chicago–London, 1914); Louis Trenchard More, *Isaac Newton* (New York–London, 1934; repr. New York, 1962); and Frank E. Manuel, *A Portrait of Isaac Newton* (Cambridge, Mass., 1968). Of the greatest value is the "synoptical view" of Newton's life, pp. xxi–lxxxi, with supplementary documents, in J. Edleston, ed., *Correspondence of Sir Isaac Newton and Professor Cotes . . .* (London, 1850; repr. London, 1969). Supplementary information concerning Newton's youthful studies is given in D. T. Whiteside, "Isaac Newton: Birth of a Mathematician," in *Notes and Records. Royal Society of London*, 19 (1964), 53–62, and "Newton's Marvellous Year: 1666 and All That," *ibid.*, 21 (1966), 32–41.

John Conduitt assembled recollections of Newton by Humphrey Newton, William Stukeley, William Derham, A. De Moivre, and others, which are now mainly in the Keynes Collection, King's College, Cambridge. Many of these documents have been printed in Edmund Turnor, *Collections for the History of the Town and Soke of Grantham* (London, 1806). William Stukeley's *Memoirs of Sir Isaac Newton's Life* (1752) was edited by A. Hastings White (London, 1936).

On Newton's family and origins, see C. W. Foster, "Sir Isaac Newton's Family," in *Reports and Papers of the Architectural Societies of the County of Lincoln, County of York, Archdeaconries of Northampton and Oakham, and County of Leicester*, 39 (1928–1929), 1–62. Newton's early notebooks are in Cambridge in the University Library, the Fitzwilliam Museum, and Trinity College Library; and in New York City in the Morgan Library. For the latter, see David Eugene Smith, "Two Unpublished Documents of Sir Isaac Newton," in W. J. Greenstreet, ed., *Isaac Newton 1642–1727* (London, 1927), pp. 16 ff. Also, E. N. da C. Andrade, "Newton's Early Notebook," in *Nature*, 135 (1935), 360; George L. Huxley: "Two Newtonian Studies: I. Newton's Boyhood Interests," in *Harvard Library Bulletin*, 13 (1959), 348–354; and A. R. Hall, "Sir Isaac Newton's Notebook, 1661–1665," in *Cambridge Historical Journal*, 9 (1948), 239–250. Elsewhere, Andrade has shown that Newton did not write the poem, attributed to him, concerning Charles II, a conclusion supported by William Stukeley's 1752 *Memoirs of Sir Isaac Newton's Life*, A. Hastings White, ed. (London, 1936).

On Newton's early diagrams and his sundial, see Charles Turnor, "An Account of the Newtonian Dial Presented to the Royal Society," in *Proceedings of the Royal Society*, 5 (1851), 513 (13 June 1844); and H. W. Robinson, "Note on Some Recently Discovered Geometrical Drawings in the Stonework of Woolsthorpe Manor House," in *Notes and Records. Royal Society of London*, 5 (1947), 35–36. For Newton's catalogue of "sins," see R. S. Westfall, "Short-writing and the State of Newton's Conscience, 1662," in *Notes and Records. Royal Society of London*, 18 (1963), 10–16.

On Newton's early reading, see R. S. Westfall, "The

Foundations of Newton's Philosophy of Nature," *British Journal for the History of Science*, **1** (1962), 171–182, which is repr. in somewhat amplified form in his *Force in Newton's Physics*. On Newton's reading, see further I. B. Cohen, *Introduction to Newton's Principia* (7) and vol. I of Whiteside's ed. of Newton's *Mathematical Papers* (3). And, of course, a major source of biographical information is the Royal Society's edition of Newton's *Correspondence* (II).

2. *Lucasian Professor*. For the major sources concerning this period of Newton's life, see (1) above, notably Brewster, Cohen (*Introduction*), Edleston, Manuel, More, Whiteside (*Mathematical Papers*), and *Correspondence*.

Edleston (pp. xci–xcviii) gives a "Table of Newton's Lectures as Lucasian Professor," with the dates and corresponding pages of the deposited MSS and the published ed. for the lectures on optics (U.L.C. MS Dd. 9.67, deposited 1674; printed London, 1729); lectures on arithmetic and algebra (U.L.C. MS Dd. 9.68; first published by Whiston, Cambridge, 1707); lectures *De motu corporum* (U.L.C. MS Dd. 9.46), corresponding *grosso modo* to bk. I of the *Principia* through prop. 54; and finally *De motu corporum liber secundus* (U.L.C. MS Dd. 9.67); of which a more complete version was printed as *De mundi systemate liber* (London, 1728)—see below.

Except for the last two, the deposited lectures are final copies, complete with numbered illustrations, as if ready for the press or for any reader who might have access to these MSS. The *Lectiones opticae* exist in two MS versions, an earlier one, which Newton kept (U.L.C. MS Add. 4002, in Newton's hand), having a division by dates quite different from that of the deposited lectures; this has been printed in facs., with an intro. by D. T. Whiteside as *The Unpublished First Version of Isaac Newton's Cambridge Lectures on Optics 1670–1672* (Cambridge, 1973). See I. B. Cohen, *Introduction*, supp. III, "Newton's Professorial Lectures," esp. pp. 303–306.

The deposited MS *De motu corporum* consists of leaves corresponding to different states of composition of bk. I of the *Principia*; the second state (in the hand of Humphrey Newton, with additions and emendations by Isaac Newton) is all but the equivalent of the corresponding part of the MS of the *Principia* sent to the printer, but the earlier state is notably different and more primitive. See I. B. Cohen, *Introduction*, supp. IV, pp. 310–321.

Edleston did not list the deposited copy of the lectures for 1687, a fair copy of only the first portion of *De motu corporum liber secundus* (corresponding to the first 27 sections, roughly half of Newton's own copy of the whole work, U.L.C. MS Add. 3990); he referred to a copy of the deposited lectures made by Cotes (Trinity College Library, MS R.19.39), in which the remainder of the text was added from a copy of the whole MS belonging to Charles Morgan. See I. B. Cohen, *Introduction*, supp. III, pp. 306–308, and supp. VI, pp. 327–335. This MS, an early version of what was to be rewritten as *Liber tertius: De mundi systemate* of the *Principia*, was published in English (London, 1728) and in Latin (London, 1728); see I. B. Cohen, "Newton's *System of the World*," in *Physis*,

11 (1969), 152–166; and intro. to repr. of the English *System of the World* (London, 1969).

The statutes of the Lucasian professorship (dated 19 Dec. 1663) are printed in the appendix to William Whiston's *An Account of . . . [His] Prosecution at, and Banishment From, the University of Cambridge* (London, 1718) and are printed again by D. T. Whiteside in Newton's *Mathematical Papers*, III, xx–xxvii.

It is often supposed, probably mistakenly, that Newton actually read the lectures that he deposited, or that the deposited lectures are evidence of the state of his knowledge or his formulation of a given subject at the time of giving a particular lecture, because the deposited MSS may be divided into dated lectures; but the statutes required that the lectures be rewritten after they had been read.

The MSS of Humphrey Newton's memoranda are in the Keynes Collection, King's College, Cambridge (K. MS 135) and are printed in David Brewster, *Memoirs*, II, 91–98, and again in L. T. More, *Isaac Newton*, pp. 246–251.

The evidence for Newton's plan to publish an ed. of his early optical papers, including the letters in the *Philosophical Transactions*, is in a set of printed pages (possibly printed proofs) forming part of such an annotated printing of these letters, discovered by D. J. de S. Price. See I. B. Cohen, "Versions of Isaac Newton's First Published Paper With Remarks on . . . an Edition of His Early Papers on Light and Color," in *Archives internationales d'histoire des sciences*, **11** (1958), 357–375; D. J. de S. Price, "Newton in a Church Tower: The Discovery of an Unknown Book by Isaac Newton," in *Yale University Library Gazette*, **34** (1960), 124–126; A. R. Hall, "Newton's First Book," in *Archives internationales d'histoire des sciences*, **13** (1960), 39–61. On 5 Mar. 1677, Collins wrote to Newton that David Loggan "informs me that he hath drawn your effigies in order to [produce] a sculpture thereof to be prefixed to a book of Light [&] Colours [&] Dioptricks which you intend to publish."

The most recent and detailed analysis of the Newton-Fatio relationship is given in Frank E. Manuel, *A Portrait of Isaac Newton*, ch. 9, "The Ape of Newton: Fatio de Duillier," and ch. 10, "The Black Year 1693." For factual details, see Newton, *Correspondence*, III. The late Charles A. Domson completed a doctoral dissertation, "Nicolas Fatio de Duillier and the Prophets of London: An Essay in the Historical Interaction of Natural Philosophy and Millennial Belief in the Age of Newton" (Yale, 1972).

Newton's gifts to the Trinity College Library are listed in an old MS catalogue of the library; see I. B. Cohen: "Newton's Attribution of the First Two Laws of Motion to Galileo," in *Atti del Symposium internazionale di storia, metodologia, logica e filosofia della scienza: "Galileo nella storia e nella filosofia della scienza"* (Florence, 1967), pp. xxii–xlii, esp. pp. xxvii–xxviii and n. 22.

3. *Mathematics*. The primary work for the study of Newton's mathematics is the ed. (to be completed in 8 vols.) by D. T. Whiteside: *Mathematical Papers of Isaac Newton* (Cambridge, 1967–   ). Whiteside has also provided a valuable pair of introductions to a facs. repr. of early translations of a number of Newton's tracts, *The Mathe-*

matical Works of Isaac Newton, 2 vols. (New York–London, 1964–1967); these introductions give an admirable and concise summary of the development of Newton's mathematical thought and contain bibliographical notes on the printings and translations of the tracts reprinted, embracing *De analysi*; *De quadratura*; *Methodus fluxionum et serierum infinitarum*; *Arithmetica universalis* (based on his professorial lectures, deposited in the University Library); *Enumeratio linearum tertii ordinis*; and *Methodus differentialis* ("Newton's Interpolation Formulas"). Attention may also be directed to several other of Whiteside's publications: "Isaac Newton: Birth of a Mathematician," in *Notes and Records. Royal Society of London*, **19** (1964), 53–62; "Newton's Marvellous Year: 1666 and All That," *ibid.*, **21** (1966), 32–41; "Newton's Discovery of the General Binomial Theorem," in *Mathematical Gazette*, **45** (1961), 175–180. (See other articles of his cited in (6), (7), (8) below.)

Further information concerning the eds. and translations of Newton's mathematical writings may be gleaned from the bibliographies (Gray, Zeitlinger, Babson) cited above (III). Various Newtonian tracts appeared in Johann Castillon's *Opuscula . . .* (II), I, supplemented by a two-volume ed. (Amsterdam, 1761) of *Arithmetica universalis*. The naturalist Buffon translated the *Methodus fluxionum . . .* (Paris, 1740), and James Wilson replied to Buffon's preface in an appendix to vol. II (1761) of his own ed. of Benjamin Robins' *Mathematical Tracts*; these two works give a real insight into "what an interested student could then know of Newton's private thoughts." See also Pierre Brunet, "La notion d'infini mathématique chez Buffon," in *Archeion*, **13** (1931), 24–39; and Lesley Hanks, *Buffon avant l'"Histoire naturelle"* (Paris, 1966), pt. 2, ch. 4 and app. 4. Horsley's ed. of Newton's *Opera* (II) contains some of Newton's mathematical tracts. A modern version of the *Arithmetica universalis*, with extended notes and commentary, has been published by A. P. Youschkevitch (Moscow, 1948). A. Rupert Hall and Marie Boas Hall have published Newton's October 1666 tract, "to resolve problems by motion" (U.L.C. MS Add. 3458, fols. 49–63) in their *Unpublished Scientific Papers* (II); see also H. W. Turnbull, "The Discovery of the Infinitesimal Calculus," in *Nature*, **167** (1951), 1048–1050.

Newton's *Correspondence* (II) contains letters and other documents relating to mathematics, with valuable annotations by H. W. Turnbull and J. F. Scott. See, further, Turnbull's *The Mathematical Discoveries of Newton* (London–Glasgow, 1945), produced before he started to edit the *Correspondence* and thus presenting a view not wholly borne out by later research. Carl B. Boyer has dealt with Newton in *Concepts of the Calculus* (New York, 1939; repr. 1949, 1959), ch. 5; "Newton as an Originator of Polar Coordinates," in *American Mathematical Monthly*, **56** (1949), 73–78; *History of Analytic Geometry* (New York, 1956), ch. 7; and *A History of Mathematics* (New York, 1968), ch. 19.

Other secondary works are W. W. Rouse Ball, *A Short Account of the History of Mathematics*, 4th ed. (London, 1908), ch. 16—even more useful is his *A History of the Study of Mathematics at Cambridge* (Cambridge, 1889), chs. 4–6; J. F. Scott, *A History of Mathematics* (London, 1958), chs. 10, 11; and Margaret E. Baron, *The Origins of the Infinitesimal Calculus* (Oxford–London–New York, 1969).

Some specialized studies of value are D. T. Whiteside, "Patterns of Mathematical Thought in the Later Seventeenth Century," in *Archive for History of Exact Sciences*, **1** (1961), 179–388; W. W. Rouse Ball, "On Newton's Classification of Cubic Curves," in *Proceedings of the London Mathematical Society*, **22** (1891), 104–143, summarized in *Bibliotheca mathematica*, n.s. **5** (1891), 35–40; Florian Cajori, "Fourier's Improvement of the Newton-Raphson Method of Approximation Anticipated by Mourraille," in *Bibliotheca mathematica*, **11** (1910–1911), 132–137; "Historical Note on the Newton-Raphson Method of Approximation," in *American Mathematical Monthly*, **18** (1911), 29–32; and *A History of the Conceptions of Limits and Fluxions in Great Britain From Newton to Woodhouse* (Chicago–London, 1919); W. J. Greenstreet, ed., *Isaac Newton 1642–1727* (London, 1927), including D. C. Fraser, "Newton and Interpolation"; A. R. Forsyth, "Newton's Problem of the Solid of Least Resistance"; J. J. Milne, "Newton's Contribution to the Geometry of Conics"; H. Hilton, "Newton on Plane Cubic Curves"; and J. M. Child, "Newton and the Art of Discovery"; Duncan C. Fraser, *Newton's Interpolation Formulas* (London, 1927), repr. from *Journal of the Institute of Actuaries*, **51** (1918–1919), 77–106, 211–232, and **58** (1927), 53–95; C. R. M. Talbot, *Sir Isaac Newton's Enumeration of Lines of the Third Order, Generation of Curves by Shadows, Organic Description of Curves, and Construction of Equations by Curves*, trans. from the Latin, with notes and examples (London, 1860); Florence N. David, "Mr. Newton, Mr. Pepys and Dyse," in *Annals of Science*, **13** (1957), 137–147, on dice-throwing and probability; Jean Pelseneer, "Une lettre inédite de Newton à Pepys (23 décembre 1693)," in *Osiris*, **1** (1936), 497–499, on probabilities; J. M. Keynes, "A Mathematical Analysis by Newton of a Problem in College Administration," in *Isis*, **49** (1958), 174–176; Maximilian Miller, "Newton, Aufzahlung der Linien dritter Ordnung," in *Wissenschaftliche Zeitschrift der Hochschule für Verkehrswesen, Dresden*, **1**, no. 1 (1953), 5–32; "Newtons Differenzmethode," *ibid.*, **2**, no. 1 (1954), 1–13; and "Über die Analysis mit Hilfe unendlicher Reihen," *ibid.*, no. 2 (1954), 1–16; Oskar Bolza, "Bemerkungen zu Newtons Beweis seines Satzes über den Rotationskörper kleinsten Widerstandes," in *Bibliotheca mathematica*, 3rd ser., **13** (1912–1913), 146–149.

Other works relating to Newton's mathematics are cited in (6) and (for the quarrel with Leibniz over priority in the calculus) (10).

4. *Optics.* The eds. of the *Opticks* and *Lectiones opticae* are mentioned above (I); the two MS versions of the latter are U.L.C. MS Add. 4002, MS Dd.9.67. An annotated copy of the 1st ed. of the *Opticks*, used by the printer for the composition of the 2nd ed. still exists (U.L.C. MS Adv.b.39.3—formerly MS Add. 4001). For information Cohen, *Introduction to Newton's Principia* (7), p. 34;

and R. S. Westfall, "Newton's Reply," pp. 83–84—extracts are printed with commentary in D. T. Whiteside's ed. of Newton's *Mathematical Papers* (3). At one time Newton began to write a *Fundamentum opticae*, the text of which is readily reconstructible from the MSS and which is a necessary tool for a complete analysis of bk. I of the *Opticks*, into which its contents were later incorporated; for pagination, see *Mathematical Papers* (3), III, 552. This work is barely known to Newton scholars. Most of Newton's optical MSS are assembled in the University Library, Cambridge, as MS Add. 3970, but other MS writings appear in the Waste Book, correspondence, and various notebooks.

Among the older literature, F. Rosenberger's book (VI) may still be studied with profit, and there is much to be learned from Joseph Priestley's 18th-century presentation of the development and current state of concepts and theories of light and vision. See also Ernst Mach, *The Principles of Physical Optics: An Historical and Philosophical Treatment*, trans. by John S. Anderson and A. F. A. Young (London, 1926; repr. New York, 1953); and Vasco Ronchi, *The Nature of Light: An Historical Survey*, trans. by V. Barocas (Cambridge, Mass., 1970)—also 2 eds. in Italian and a French translation by Juliette Taton.

Newton's MSS have been used in A. R. Hall, "Newton's Notebook" (1), pp. 239–250; and in J. A. Lohne, "Newton's 'Proof' of the Sine Law," in *Archive for History of Exact Sciences*, 1 (1961), 389–405; "Isaac Newton: The Rise of a Scientist 1661–1671," in *Notes and Records. Royal Society of London*, 20 (1965), 125–139; and "Experimentum crucis," *ibid.*, 23 (1968), 169–199. See also J. A. Lohne and Bernhard Sticker, *Newtons Theorie der Prismenfarben, mit Übersetzung und Erläuterung der Abhandlung von 1672* (Munich, 1969); and R. S. Westfall, "The Development of Newton's Theory of Color," in *Isis*, 53 (1962), 339–358; "Newton and his Critics on the Nature of Colors," in *Archives internationales d'histoire des sciences*, 15 (1962), 47–58; "Newton's Reply to Hooke and the Theory of Colors," in *Isis*, 54 (1963), 82–96; "Isaac Newton's Coloured Circles Twixt Two Contiguous Glasses," in *Archive for History of Exact Sciences*, 2 (1965), 181–196; and "Uneasily Fitful Reflections on Fits of Easy Transmission [and of easy reflection]," in Robert Palter, ed., *The Annus Mirabilis* (VI), pp. 88–104.

Newton's optical papers (from the *Philosophical Transactions* and T. Birch's *History of the Royal Society*) are repr. in facs. in *Newton's Papers and Letters* (I), with an intro. by T. S. Kuhn. See also I. B. Cohen, "I prismi del Newton e i prismi dell'Algarotti," in *Atti della Fondazione "Giorgio Ronchi"* (Florence), 12 (1957), 1–11; Vasco Ronchi, "I 'prismi del Newton' del Museo Civico di Treviso," *ibid.*, 12–28; and N. R. Hanson, "Waves, Particles, and Newton's 'Fits,'" in *Journal of the History of Ideas*, 21 (1960), 370–391. On Newton's work on color, see George Biernson, "Why did Newton see Indigo in the Spectrum?," in *American Journal of Physics*, 40 (1972), 526–533; and Torger Holtzmark, "Newton's *Experimentum Crucis* Reconsidered," *ibid.*, 38 (1970), 1229–1235.

An able account of Newton's work in optics, set against the background of his century, is A. I. Sabra, *Theories of Light From Descartes to Newton* (London, 1967), ch. 9–13. An important series of studies, based on extensive examination of the MSS, are Zev Bechler, "Newton's 1672 Optical Controversies: A Study in the Grammar of Scientific Dissent," in Y. Elkana, ed., *Some Aspects of the Interaction Between Science and Philosophy* (New York, in press); "Newton's Search for a Mechanistic Model of Color Dispersion: A Suggested Interpretation," in *Archive for History of Exact Sciences*, 11 (1973), 1–37; and an analysis of Newton's work on chromatic aberration in lenses (in press). On the last topic, see also D. T. Whiteside, *Mathematical Papers*, III, pt. 3, esp. pp. 442–443, 512–513 (n. 61), 533 (n. 13), and 555–556 (nn. 5–6).

5. *Dynamics, Astronomy, and the Birth of the "Principia."* The primary documents for the study of Newton's dynamics have been assembled by A. R. and M. B. Hall (II) and by J. Herivel, *The Background to Newton's Principia* (Oxford, 1965); other major documents are printed (with historical and critical essays) in the Royal Society's ed. of Newton's *Correspondence* (II); S. P. Rigaud, *Historical Essay on the First Publication of Sir Isaac Newton's Principia* (Oxford, 1838; repr., with intro. by I. B. Cohen, New York, 1972); W. W. Rouse Ball, *An Essay on Newton's Principia* (London, 1893; repr. with intro. by I. B. Cohen, New York, 1972); and I. B. Cohen, *Introduction* (7).

The development of Newton's concepts of dynamics is discussed by Herivel (in *Background*, and in a series of articles summarized in that work), in Rouse Ball's *Essay*, I. B. Cohen's *Introduction*, and in R. S. Westfall's *Force in Newton's Physics* (London–New York, 1971). On the concept of inertia and the laws of motion, see I. B. Cohen, *Transformations of Scientific Ideas: Variations on Newtonian Themes in the History of Science*, the Wiles Lectures (Cambridge, in press), ch. 2; and "Newton's Second Law and the Concept of Force in the *Principia*," in R. Palter ed., *Annus mirabilis* (VI), pp. 143–185; Alan Gabbey, "Force and Inertia in Seventeenth-Century Dynamics," in *Studies in History and Philosophy of Science*, 2 (1971), 1–68; E. J. Aiton, *The Vortex Theory of Planetary Motions* (London–New York, 1972); and A. R. Hall, "Newton on the Calculation of Central Forces," in *Annals of Science*, 13 (1957), 62–71. Newton's encounter with Hooke in 1679 and his progress from the Ward-Bullialdus approximation to the area law are studied in J. A. Lohne, "Hooke Versus Newton, an Analysis of the Documents in the Case of Free Fall and Planetary Motion," in *Centaurus*, 7 (1960), 6–52; D. T. Whiteside, "Newton's Early Thoughts on Planetary Motion: A Fresh Look," in *British Journal for the History of Science*, 2 (1964), 117–137, "Newtonian Dynamics," in *History of Science*, 5 (1966), 104–117, and "Before the *Principia*: The Maturing of Newton's Thoughts on Dynamical Astronomy, 1664–84," in *Journal for the History of Astronomy*, 1 (1970), 5–19; A. Koyré, "An Unpublished Letter of Robert Hooke to Isaac Newton," in *Isis*, 43 (1952), 312–337, repr. in Koyré's *Newtonian Studies* (VI); and R. S. Westfall, "Hooke and the Law of Universal Gravitation," in *British Journal for the History of Science*, **3** (1967), 245–261. "The Background and Early Development of Newton's Theory of Comets" is the title of a Ph.D. thesis by James Alan Ruffner (Indiana Univ., May 1966).

6. *Mathematics in the Principia*. The references for this section will be few, since works dealing with Newton's preparation for the *Principia* are listed under (5), and additional sources for the *Principia* itself are given under (7). See, further, Yasukatsu Maeyama, *Hypothesen zur Planetentheorie des 17. Jahrhunderts* (Frankfurt, 1971), and Curtis A. Wilson, "From Kepler's Laws, So-called, to Universal Gravitation: Empirical Factors," in *Archive for History of Exact Sciences*, **6** (1970), 89–170.

Two scholarly studies may especially commend our attention: H. W. Turnbull, *Mathematical Discoveries* (3), of which chs. 7 and 12 deal specifically with the *Principia*; D. T. Whiteside, "The Mathematical Principles Underlying Newton's *Principia Mathematica*," in *Journal for the History of Astronomy*, **1** (1970), 116–138, of which a version with less annotation was published in pamphlet form by the University of Glasgow (1970). See also C. B. Boyer, *Concepts of Calculus* and *History* (3), and J. F. Scott, *History* (3), ch. 11. Valuable documents and commentaries also appear in the Royal Society's ed. of Newton's *Correspondence*, J. Herivel's *Background* (5) and various articles, and D. T. Whiteside, *Mathematical Papers* (3). Especially valuable are three commentaries: J. M. F. Wright, *A Commentary on Newton's Principia*, 2 vols. (London, 1833; repr., with intro. by I. B. Cohen, New York, 1972); Henry Lord Brougham and E. J. Routh, *Analytical View of Sir Isaac Newton's Principia* (London, 1855; repr., with intro. by I. B. Cohen, New York, 1972); and Percival Frost, *Newton's Principia, First Book, Sections I., II., III., With Notes and Illustrations* (Cambridge, 1854; 5th ed., London–New York, 1900). On a post-*Principia* MS on dynamics, using fluxions, see W. W. Rouse Ball, "A Newtonian Fragment Relating to Centripetal Forces," in *Proceedings of the London Mathematical Society*, **23** (1892), 226–231; A. R. and M. B. Hall, *Unpublished Papers* (II), pp. 65–68; and commentary by D. T. Whiteside, in *History of Science*, **2** (1963), 129, n. 4.

7. *The Principia*. Many of the major sources for studying the *Principia* have already been given, in (5), (6), including works by A. R. Hall and M. B. Hall, J. Herivel, R. S. Westfall, and D. T. Whiteside. Information on the writing of the *Principia* and the evolution of the text is given in I. B. Cohen, *Introduction to Newton's Principia* (Cambridge, 1971) and the 2-vol. ed. of the *Principia* with variant readings, ed. by A. Koyré, I. B. Cohen, and Anne Whitman (I). Some additional works are R. S. Westfall, "Newton and Absolute Space," in *Archives internationales d'histoire des sciences*, **17** (1964), 121–132; Clifford Truesdell, "A Program Toward Rediscovering the Rational Mechanics of the Age of Reason," in *Archive for History of Exact Sciences*, **1** (1960), 3–36, and "Reactions of Late Baroque Mechanics to Success, Conjecture, Error, and Failure in Newton's *Principia*," in Robert Palter, ed., *The Annus Mirabilis* (VI), pp. 192–232—both articles by

Truesdell are repr. in his *Essays in the History of Mechanics* (New York–Berlin, 1968); E. J. Aiton, "The Inverse Problem of Central Forces," in *Annals of Science*, **20** (1964), 81–99; J. A. Lohne, "The Increasing Corruption" (VI), esp. "5. The Planetary Ellipse of the *Principia*"; and Thomas L. Hankins, "The Reception of Newton's Second Law of Motion in the Eighteenth Century," in *Archives internationales d'histoire des sciences*, **20** (1967), 43–65. Highly recommended is L. Rosenfeld, "Newton and the Law of Gravitation," in *Archive for History of Exact Sciences*, **2** (1965), 365–386: see also E. J. Aiton, "Newton's Aether-Stream Hypothesis and the Inverse-Square Law of Gravitation," in *Annals of Science*, **25** (1969), 255–260; and L. Rosenfeld, "Newton's Views on Aether and Gravitation," in *Archive for History of Exact Sciences*, **6** (1969), 29–37.

I. B. Cohen has discussed some further aspects of *Principia* questions in the Wiles Lectures (5) and a study of "Newton's Second Law" (5); and in "Isaac Newton's *Principia*, the Scriptures and the Divine Providence", in S. Morgenbesser, P. Suppes, and M. White, eds., *Essays in Honor of Ernest Nagel* (New York, 1969), pp. 523–548, esp. pp. 537 ff.; and "New Light on the Form of Definitions I–II–VI–VIII," where Newton's concept of "measure" is explored. On the incompatibility of Newton's dynamics and Galileo's and Kepler's laws, see Karl R. Popper, "The Aim of Science," in *Ratio*, **1** (1957), 24–35; and I. B. Cohen, "Newton's Theories vs. Kepler's Theory," in Y. Elkana, ed., *Some Aspects of the Interaction Between Science and Philosophy* (New York, in press).

8. *Revision of the Opticks (The Later Queries); Chemistry, and Theory of Matter*. The doctrine of the later queries has been studied by F. Rosenberger, *Newton und seine physikalischen Principien* (VI), and by Philip E. B. Jourdain, in a series of articles entitled "Newton's Hypothesis of Ether and of Gravitation. . . ," in *The Monist*, **25** (1915), 79–106, 233–254, 418–440; and by I. B. Cohen in *Franklin and Newton* (VI).

In addition to his studies of the queries, Henry Guerlac has analyzed Newton's philosophy of matter, suggesting an influence of Hauksbee's electrical experiments on the formation of Newton's later concept of ether. See his *Newton et Epicure* (Paris, 1963); "Francis Hauksbee: Expérimentateur au profit de Newton," in *Archives internationales d'histoire des sciences*, **17** (1963), 113–128; "Sir Isaac and the Ingenious Mr. Hauksbee," in *Mélanges Alexandre Koyré: L'aventure de la science* (Paris, 1964), pp. 228–253; and "Newton's Optical Aether," in *Notes and Records. Royal Society of London*, **22** (1967), 45–57. See also Joan L. Hawes, "Newton and the 'Electrical Attraction Unexcited,' " in *Annals of Science*, **24** (1968), 121–130; "Newton's Revival of the Aether Hypothesis and the Explanation of Gravitational Attraction," in *Notes and Records. Royal Society of London*, **23** (1968), 200–212; and the studies by Bechler listed above (4).

The electrical character of Newton's concept of "spiritus" in the final paragraph of the General Scholium has been disclosed by A. R. and M. B. Hall, in *Unpublished Papers* (II). On Newton's theory of matter, see Marie Boas [Hall],

"Newton's Chemical Papers," in *Newton's Papers and Letters* (I), pp. 241–248; and A. R. Hall and M. B. Hall, "Newton's Chemical Experiments," in *Archives internationales d'histoire des sciences*, **11** (1958), 113–152; "Newton's Mechanical Principles," in *Journal of the History of Ideas*, **20** (1959), 167–178; "Newton's Theory of Matter," in *Isis*, **51** (1960), 131–144; and "Newton and the Theory of Matter," in Robert Palter, ed., *The Annus Mirabilis* (VI), pp. 54–68.

On Newton's chemistry and theory of matter, see additionally R. Kargon, *Atomism in England From Hariot to Newton* (Oxford, 1966); A. Koyré, "Les Queries de l'Optique," in *Archives internationales d'histoire des sciences*, **13** (1960), 15–29; T. S. Kuhn, "Newton's 31st Query and the Degradation of Gold," in *Isis*, **42** (1951), 296–298, with discussion *ibid.*, **43** (1952), 123–124; J. E. McGuire, "Body and Void . . .," in *Archive for History of Exact Sciences*, **3** (1966), 206–248; "Transmutation and Immutability," in *Ambix*, **14** (1967), 69–95; and other papers; D. McKie, "Some Notes on Newton's Chemical Philosophy," in *Philosophical Magazine*, **33** (1942), 847–870; and J. R. Partington, *A History of Chemistry*, II (London, 1961), 468–477, 482–485.

For Newton's theories of chemistry and matter, and their influence, see the books by Hélène Metzger (VI), R. E. Schofield (VI), and A. Thackray (VI).

Geoffroy's summary ("extrait") of the *Opticks*, presented at meetings of the Paris Academy of Sciences, is discussed in I. B. Cohen, "Isaac Newton, Hans Sloane, and the Académie Royale des Sciences," in *Mélanges Alexandre Koyré*, I, *L'aventure de la science* (Paris, 1964), 61–116; on the general agreement by Newtonians that the queries were not so much asking questions as stating answers to such questions (and on the rhetorical form of the queries), see I. B. Cohen, *Franklin and Newton* (VI), ch. 6.

9. *Alchemy, Theology, and Prophecy. Chronology and History.* Newton published no essays or books on alchemy. His *Chronology of Ancient Kingdoms Amended* (London, 1728) also appeared in an abridged version (London, 1728). His major study of prophecy is *Observations Upon the Prophecies of Daniel, and the Apocalypse of St. John* (London, 1733). A selection of *Theological Manuscripts* was edited by H. McLachlan (Liverpool, 1950).

For details concerning Newton's theological MSS, and MSS relating to chronology, see secs. VII–¹ II of the catalogue of the Sotheby sale of the Newton papers (IV); for other eds. of the *Chronology* and the *Observations*, see the Gray bibliography and the catalogue of the Babson Collection (III). There is no analysis of Newton's theological writings based on a thorough analysis of the MSS; see R. S. Westfall, *Science and Religion in Seventeenth-Century England* (New Haven, 1958), ch. 8; F. E. Manuel, *The Eighteenth Century Confronts the Gods* (Cambridge, 1959), ch. 3; and George S. Brett, "Newton's Place in the History of Religious Thought," in F. E. Brasch, ed., *Sir Isaac Newton* (VI), pp. 259–273. For Newton's chronological and allied studies, see F. E. Manuel, *Isaac Newton, Historian* (Cambridge, 1963).

On alchemy, the catalogue of the Sotheby sale is most illuminating. Important MSS and annotated alchemical books are to be found in the Keynes Collection (King's College, Cambridge) and in the Burndy Library and the University of Wisconsin, M.I.T., and the Babson Institute. A major scholarly study of Newton's alchemy and hermeticism, based on an extensive study of Newton's MSS, is P. M. Rattansi, "Newton's Alchemical Studies," in Allen G. Debus, ed., *Science, Medicine and Society in the Renaissance: Essays to Honor Walter Pagel*, II (New York, 1972), 167–182; see also R. S. Westfall, "Newton and the Hermetic Tradition," *ibid.*, pp. 183–198.

On Newton and the tradition of the ancients, and the intended inclusion in the *Principia* of references to an ancient tradition of wisdom, see I. B. Cohen, " 'Quantum in se est': Newton's Concept of Inertia in Relation to Descartes and Lucretius," in *Notes and Records. Royal Society of London*, **19** (1964), 131–155; and esp. J. E. McGuire and P. M. Rattansi, "Newton and the 'Pipes of Pan'," *ibid.*, **21** (1966), 108–143; also J. E. McGuire, "Transmutation and Immutability," in *Ambix*, **14** (1967), 69–95. On alchemy, see R. J. Forbes, "Was Newton an Alchemist?," in *Chymia*, **2** (1949), 27–36; F. Sherwood Taylor, "An Alchemical Work of Sir Isaac Newton," in *Ambix*, **5** (1956), 59–84; E. D. Geoghegan, "Some Indications of Newton's Attitude Towards Alchemy," *ibid.*, **6** (1957), 102–106; and A. R. and M. B. Hall, "Newton's Chemical Experiments," in *Archives internationales d'histoire des sciences*, **11** (1958), 113–152.

A salutary point of view is expressed by Mary Hesse, "Hermeticism and Historiography: An Apology for the Internal History of Science," in Roger H. Stuewer, ed., *Historical and Philosophical Perspectives of Science*, vol. V of Minnesota Studies in the Philosophy of Science (Minneapolis, 1970), 134–162. But see also P. M. Rattansi, "Some Evaluations of Reason in Sixteenth- and Seventeenth-Century Natural Philosophy," in Mikuláš Teich and Robert Young, eds., *Changing Perspectives in the History of Science, Essays in Honour of Joseph Needham* (London, 1973), pp. 148–166.

10. *The London Years: the Mint, the Royal Society, Quarrels With Flamsteed and With Leibniz.* On Newton's life in London and the affairs of the mint, see the biographies by More and Brewster (1), supplemented by Manuel's *Portrait* (1). Of special interest are Augustus De Morgan, *Newton: His Friend: and His Niece* (London, 1885); and Sir John Craig, *Newton at the Mint* (Cambridge, 1946). On the quarrel with Flamsteed, see Francis Baily, *An Account of the Rev^d. John Flamsteed* (London, 1835; supp., 1837; repr. London, 1966); the above-mentioned biographies of Newton; and Newton's *Correspondence* (II). On the controversy with Leibniz, see the *Commercium epistolicum* (I). Newton's MSS on this controversy (U.L.C. MS Add. 3968) have never been fully analyzed; but see Augustus De Morgan, "On the Additions Made to the Second Edition of the *Commercium epistolicum*," in *Philosophical Magazine*, 3rd ser., **32** (1848), 446–456; and "On the Authorship of the Account of the *Commercium epistolicum*, Published in the *Philosophical Transactions*," *ibid.*, 4th ser., **3** (1852), 440–444. The most recent ed. of

The *Leibniz-Clarke Correspondence* was edited by H. G. Alexander (Manchester, 1956).

11. *Newton's Philosophy: The Rules of Philosophizing, the General Scholium, the Queries of the Opticks.* Among the many books and articles on Newton's philosophy, those of Rosenberger, Bloch, and Koyré (VI) are highly recommended. On the evolution of the General Scholium, see A. R. and M. B. Hall, *Unpublished Papers* (II), pt. IV, intro. and sec. 8; and I. B. Cohen, *Transformations of Scientific Ideas* (the Wiles Lectures, in press) (5) and "Hypotheses in Newton's Philosophy," in *Physis*, **8** (1966), 163–184.

The other studies of Newton's philosophy are far too numerous to list here; authors include Gerd Buchdahl, Ernst Cassirer, A. C. Crombie, N. R. Hanson, Ernst Mach, Jürgen Mittelstrass, John Herman Randall, Jr., Dudley Shapere, Howard Stein, and E. W. Strong.

I. B. COHEN

SOVIET LITERATURE ON NEWTON

A profound and manifold study of Newton's life and work began in Russia at the beginning of the twentieth century; for earlier works see the article by T. P. Kravets, cited below.

The foundation of Soviet studies on Newton was laid by A. N. Krylov, who in 1915–1916 published the complete *Principia* in Russian, with more than 200 notes and supplements of a historical, philological, and mathematical nature. More than a third of the volume is devoted to supplements that present a complete, modern analytic exposition of various theorems and proofs of the original text, the clear understanding of which is often too difficult for the modern reader: "Matematicheskie nachala naturalnoy estestvennoy filosofii" ("The Mathematical Principles of Natural Philosophy"), in *Izvestiya Nikolaevskoi morskoi akademii*, **4–5** (1915–1916); 2nd ed. in *Sobranie trudov akademika A. N. Krylova* ("Collected Works of Academician A. N. Krylov"), VII (Moscow–Leningrad, 1936). Krylov devoted special attention to certain of Newton's methods and demonstrated that after suitable modification and development they could still be of use. Works on this subject include "Besedy o sposobakh opredelenia orbit komet i planet po malomu chislu nabludenii" ("Discourse on Methods of Determining Planetary and Cometary Orbits Based on a Limited Number of Observations"), *ibid.*, VI, 1–149; a series of papers, *ibid.*, V, 227–298; and "Nyutonova teoria astronomicheskoy refraktsii" ("Newton's Theory of Astronomical Refraction"), *ibid.*, V, 151–225; see also his "On a Theorem of Sir Isaac Newton," in *Monthly Notices of the Royal Astronomical Society*, **84** (1924), 392–395. On Krylov's work, see A. T. Grigorian, "Les études Newtoniennes de A. N. Krylov," in I. B. Cohen and R. Taton, eds., *Mélanges Alexandre Koyré*, II (Paris, 1964), 198–207.

A Russian translation of Newton's *Observations on the Prophecies . . . of Daniel and the Apocalypse of St. John* was published simultaneously with the first Russian edition of *Principia* as *Zamechania na knigu Prorok Daniil i*

Apokalipsis sv. Ioanna (Petrograd, 1916); the translator's name is not given.

An elaborately annotated translation of Newton's works on optics is S. I. Vavilov, ed., *Optika ili traktat ob otrazheniakh, prelomleniakh, izgibaniakh i tsvetakh sveta* ("Optics"; Moscow–Leningrad, 1927; 2nd ed., Moscow, 1954). Vavilov also published Russian translations of two of Newton's essays, "Novaya teoria sveta i tsvetov" ("A New Theory of Light and Colors") and "Odna gipotesa, obyasnyayushchaya svoystva sveta, izlozhennaya v neskolkikh moikh statyakh" ("A Hypothesis Explaining the Properties of Light Presented in Several of My Papers"), in *Uspekhi fizicheskikh nauk*, **2** (1927), 121–163; and *Lektsii po optike* ("Lectiones opticae"; Leningrad, 1946). Vavilov was the first to study thoroughly the significance of the last work in the development of physics.

Newton's mathematical works published by Castillon in vol. I of *Opuscula mathematica* (1744) were translated by D. D. Mordukhay-Boltovskoy as *Matematicheskie raboty* ("Mathematical Works"; Moscow–Leningrad, 1937); the editor's 336 notes constitute nearly a third of the volume. *Arithmetica universalis* was translated by A. P. Youschkevitch with commentary as *Vseobshchaya arifmetika ili kniga ob arifmeticheskikh sintese i analise* (Moscow, 1948).

Many works dedicated to various aspects of Newton's scientific activity and to his role in the development of science were included in the tercentenary volumes *Isaak Nyuton. 1643–1727. Sbornik statey k trekhsotletiyu so dnya rozhdenia*, S. I. Vavilov, ed. (Moscow–Leningrad, 1943); and *Moskovsky universitet—pamyati Nyutona—sbornik statey* (Moscow, 1946). These works are cited below as *Symposium I* and *Symposium II*, respectively.

Z. A. Zeitlin, in *Nauka i gipotesa* ("Science and Hypothesis"; Moscow–Leningrad, 1926), studied the problem of Newton's methodology, particularly the roles of Bentley and Cotes in preparing the 2nd ed. of the *Principia*, and emphasized that both scientists had falsified Newtonian methods; the majority of other authors did not share his viewpoint. In "Efir, svet i veshchestvo v fisike Nyutona" ("Ether, Light, and Matter in Newton's Physics"), in *Symposium I*, 33–52, S. I. Vavilov traced the evolution of Newton's views on the hypothesis of the ether, the theory of light, and the structure of matter. Vavilov also dealt with Newton's methods and the role of hypothesis in ch. 10 of his biography *Isaak Nyuton* (Moscow–Leningrad, 1943; 2nd ed., rev. and enl., 1945; 3rd ed., 1961). The 3rd ed. of this work appeared in vol. III of Vavilov's *Sobranie sochinenii* ("Selected Works"; Moscow, 1956), which contains all of Vavilov's papers on Newton. The biography also appeared in German trans. (Vienna, 1948; Berlin, 1951).

B. M. Hessen in *Sotsialno-ekonomicheskie korni mekhaniki Nyutona* ("The Socioeconomic Roots of Newton's Mechanics"), presented to the Second International Congress of the History of Science and Technology held in London in 1931 (Moscow–Leningrad, 1933), attempted to analyze the origin and development of Newton's work in Marxist terms. Hessen examined the *Principia* in the light of contemporary economic and technological problems and in the context of the political, philosophical, and religious views which reflected the social conflict occurring during the period of revolution in England. His essay appeared in English as *Science at the Crossroads* (London, 1931), which is reprinted in facsimile with a foreword by Joseph Needham and an introduction by P. G. Werskey (London, 1971) and with a foreword by Robert S. Cohen (New York, 1971).

In his report on Newton's atomism, "Newton on the Atomic Theory," in Royal Society, *Newton Tercentenary Celebrations: 15–19 July, 1946* (Cambridge, 1947), Vavilov compared Newtonian chemical ideas with the development of chemistry in the nineteenth and twentieth centuries and, in particular, with the work of Mendeleev. The latter topic was also discussed in T. I. Raynov, "Nyuton i russkoe estestvoznanie" ("Newton and Russian Natural Science"), in *Symposium I,* 329–344, which also examined Lomonosov's attitude toward Newton. See also P. S. Kudriavtsev, "Lomonosov i Nyuton," in *Trudy Instituta istorii estestvoznaniya i tekhniki. Akademiya nauk SSSR,* **5** (1955), 33–51. On Newton's role in the development of chemistry see also N. I. Flerov, "Vlianie Nyutona na razvitie khimii" ("Newton's Influence on the Development of Chemistry"), in *Symposium II,* 101–106.

For detailed comments on some important problems of the *Principia,* see L. N. Sretensky, "Nyutonova teoria prilivov i figury zemli" ("Newton's Theory of Tides and of the Figure of the Earth"), in *Symposium I,* 211–234; and A. D. Dubyago, "Komety i ikh znachenie v obshchey sisteme Nyutonovykh Nachal ("Comets and Their Significance in the General System of Newton's *Principia*"), *ibid.,* 235–263. N. I. Idelson dealt with the history of the theory of lunar motion and presented a detailed study of the St. Petersburg competition of 1751, through which the theory of universal gravitation received lasting recognition, in "Zakon vsemirnogo tyagotenia i teoria dvizhenia luny" ("The Law of Universal Gravitation and the Theory of Lunar Motion"), *ibid.,* 161–210. See also Idelson's paper "Volter i Nyuton," in *Volter 1694–1778. Stati i materialy* (Moscow–Leningrad, 1948), 215–241; and A. D. Lyublinskaya's paper on the discussions between the Newtonians and the Cartesians, "K voprosu o vlianii Nyutona na frantsuzkuyu nauku" ("On the Problem of Newton's Influence on French Science"), in *Symposium I,* 361–391. On Newton's physics, see V. G. Fridman, "Ob uchenii Nyutona o masse" ("Newton's Doctrine of Mass"), in *Uspekhi fizicheskikh nauk,* **61,** no. 3 (1957), 451–460.

On Newton's optics, apart from the fundamental studies of Krylov and Vavilov, see G. G. Slyusarev, "Raboty Nyutona po geometricheskoy optike" ("Newton's Works in Geometrical Optics"), in *Symposium I,* 127–141; I. A. Khvostikov, "Nyuton i razvitie uchenia o refraktsii sveta v zemnoy atmosfere" ("Newton and the Development of Studies of the Refraction of Light in the Earth's Atmosphere"), *ibid.,* 142–160; and L. I. Mandelshtam, "Opticheskie raboty Nyutona" ("Newton's Works in Optics"), in *Uspekhi fizicheskikh nauk,* **28,** no. 1 (1946), 103–129.

P. S. Kudriavtsev treated Newtonian mechanics and physics in his *Istoria fiziki* ("History of Physics"), 2nd ed. (Moscow, 1956), I, 200–258; and also published a biography, *Isaak Nyuton* (Moscow, 1943; 2nd ed., 1955). The basic ideas of Newton's mechanics are described in A. T. Grigorian and I. B. Pogrebyssky, eds., *Istoria mekhaniki s drevneyshikh vremen do kontsa 18 veka* ("The History of Mechanics from Antiquity to the End of the 18th Century"; Moscow, 1971).

Many works on Newton as mathematician were devoted to an analysis of his views on the foundations of infinitesimal calculus and, in particular, of his conceptions of the limiting process and of moment. S. Gouriev dealt with this question in "Kratkoe izlozhenie razlichnykh sposobov izyasnyat differentsialnoe ischislenie" ("A Brief Account of Various Methods of Explaining the Differential Calculus"), in *Umozritelnye issledovanie SPb. Akademii nauk,* **4** (1815), 159–212. Gouriev's conception was subsequently reinterpreted—occasionally with disagreement—in the commentaries of Krylov and Mordukhay-Boltovskoy (see above); and in the papers of S. A. Yanovskaya related to the publication of the mathematical MSS of Karl Marx, "O matematicheskikh rukopisyakh Marksa" ("On Marx's Mathematical Manuscripts"), in *Marksism i estestvoznanie* (Moscow, 1933), 136–180. See also K. Marx, *Matematicheskie rukopisi* ("Mathematical Manuscripts"; Moscow, 1968), 573–576; S. A. Bogomolov, *Aktualnaya beskonechnost* ("Actual Infinity"; Leningrad–Moscow, 1934); N. N. Luzin, "Nyutonova teoria predelov" ("Newton's Theory of Limits"), in *Symposium I,* 53–74; S. Y. Luric, "Predshestvenniki Nyutona v filosofii beskonechno malykh" ("Newton's Predecessors in the Philosophy of Infinitesimal Calculus"), *ibid.,* 75–98; A. N. Kolmogorov, "Nyuton i sovremennoe matematicheskoe myshlenie" ("Newton and Modern Mathematical Thought"), *ibid.,* II, 27–42; and F. D. Kramar, "Voprosy obosnovania analisa v trudakh Vallisa i Nyutona" ("The Problems of the Foundation of the Calculus in the Works of Wallis and Newton"), in *Istoriko-matematicheskie issledovaniya,* **3** (1950), 486–508.

K. A. Rybnikov studied the role of infinite series as a universal algorithm in Newton's method of fluxions in "O roli algoritmov v istorii obosnovania matematicheskogo analisa" ("On the Role of Algorithms in the History of the Origin of the Calculus"), in *Trudy Instituta istorii estestvoznaniya i tekhniki. Akademiya nauk SSSR,* **17** (1957), 267–299. The history of Newton's parallelogram and its applications was discussed in N. G. Chebotaryov, "Mnogougolnik Nyutona i ego rol v sovremennom razvitii matematiki" ("Newton's Polygon and his Role in the Modern Development of Mathematics"), in *Symposium I,* 99–126. I. G. Bashmakova examined the research of Newton and Waring on the problem of reducibility of algebraic equations in "Ob odnom voprose teorii algebraicheskikh uravneny v trudakh I. Nyutona i E. Varinga" ("On a Problem of the Theory of Algebraic Equations in the Works of I. Newton and E. Waring"), in *Istoriko-matematicheskie issledovaniya,* **12** (1959), 431–456. Newton's use of asymptotic series was discussed in M. V.

Chirikov, "Iz istorii asimptoticheskikh ryadov" ("On the History of Asymptotic Series"), *ibid.*, **13** (1960), 441–472. On Newton's calculations equivalent to the use of multiple integrals, see V. I. Antropova, "O geometricheskom metode 'Matematicheskikh nachal naturalnoy filosofii' I. Nyutona" ("On the Geometrical Method in Newton's *Philosophiae naturalis mathematica principia*"), *ibid.*, **17** (1966), 208–228; and "O roli Isaaka Nyutona v razvitii teorii potentsiala" ("On Isaac Newton's Role in the Development of Potential Theory"), in *Uchenye zapiski Tulskogo gosudarstvennogo pedagogicheskogo instituta, Mat. kafedr,* **3** (1970), 3–56. N. I. Glagolev described Newton's geometrical ideas in "Nyuton kak geometr" ("Newton as Geometer"), in *Symposium II*, 71–80; and his mathematical discoveries were summarized in vols. II and III of A. P. Youschkevitch, ed., *Istoria matematiki s drevneyshikh vremen do nachala XIX stoletia* ("A History of Mathematics From Antiquity to the Beginning of the Nineteenth Century"; Moscow, 1970–1972).

See also two papers on Newton as historian of antiquity: S. Y. Lurie, "Nyuton—istorik drevnosti" ("Newton—Historian of Antiquity"), in *Symposium I*, 271–311; and E. C. Skrzhinskaya, "Kembridgsky universitet i Nyuton" ("Cambridge University and Newton"), *ibid.*, 392–421.

On Soviet studies of Newton, see T. P. Kravets, "Nyuton i izuchenie ego trudov v Rossii" ("Newton and the Study of His Works in Russia"), *ibid.*, 312–328; A. P. Youschkevitch, "Sovetskaya yubileynaya literatura o Nyutone" ("Soviet Jubilee Literature on Newton"), in *Trudy Instituta istorii estestvoznaniya. Akademiya nauk SSSR,* **1**, 440–455; and *Istoria estestvoznaniya. Bibliografichesky ukazatel. Literatura, opublikovannaya v SSSR (1917–1948)* ("History of Natural Science. Bibliography. Literature Published in the U.S.S.R. 1917–1948"; Moscow–Leningrad, 1949).

A. P. YOUSCHKEVITCH